June 17–21, 2013
Pittsburgh, PA, USA

I0131886

**Association for
Computing Machinery**

Advancing Computing as a Science & Profession

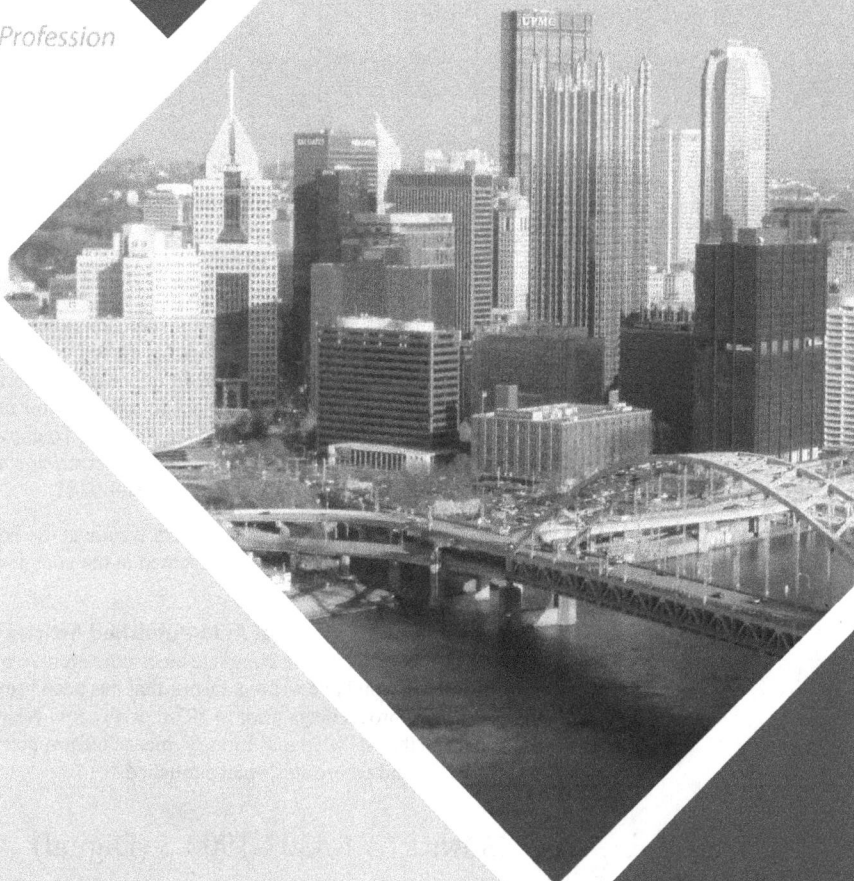

SIGMETRICS'13

Proceedings of the 2013 ACM SIGMETRICS
**International Conference on Measurement
and Modeling of Computer Systems**

Sponsored by:
ACM SIGMETRICS

Supported by:
**Akamia, Facebook, Google, Hewlett Packard, IBM,
Intel, Microsoft Research, NetApp, NSF, VMWare,
and Carnegie Mellon University**

**Association for
Computing Machinery**

Advancing Computing as a Science & Profession

The Association for Computing Machinery
2 Penn Plaza, Suite 701
New York, New York 10121-0701

Notice to Past Authors of ACM-Published Articles
ACM intends to create a complete electronic archive of all articles and/or other material previously published by ACM. If you have written a work that has been previously published by ACM in any journal or conference proceedings prior to 1978, or any SIG Newsletter at any time, and you do NOT want this work to appear in the ACM Digital Library, please inform permissions@acm.org, stating the title of the work, the author(s), and where and when published.

ISBN: 978-1-4503-1900-3 (Digital)

ISBN: 978-1-4503-2287-4 (Print)

Additional copies may be ordered prepaid from:

ACM Order Department
PO Box 30777
New York, NY 10087-0777, USA

Phone: 1-800-342-6626 (USA and Canada)
+1-212-626-0500 (Global)
Fax: +1-212-944-1318
E-mail: acmhelp@acm.org
Hours of Operation: 8:30 am – 4:30 pm ET

Printed in the USA

Message from the General Chair

It is my pleasure to welcome you to the 2013 SIGMETRICS Conference on Measurement and Modeling of Computer Systems. SIGMETRICS is the premier forum for the presentation of research on performance evaluation of computer systems. As computer systems become larger and more complex, the need for developing new performance evaluation techniques and applying these is greater than ever. SIGMETRICS brings together 200 professionals from academic and industrial backgrounds to discuss the development and application of state-of-the-art analytic, simulation, and measurement-based performance evaluation techniques.

This year SIGMETRICS is hosted by Carnegie Mellon University's School of Computer Science. The conference has grown to span 5 days, where the first and last day are devoted to tutorials and workshops. This year we have three tutorials, in the areas of distributed storage, database performance and heavy-tailed distributions. We also have 4 very timely workshops, including the first Big Data Analytics workshop and the first Joint Workshop on Pricing and Incentives in Networks and Systems, as well as workshops which have become SIGMETRICS regulars, like the GreenMetrics workshop, now in its 5th year, and the MAMA workshop, in its 15th year. The middle 3 days of the conference will include the presentation of 26 full papers and 28 posters, including a broad mix of performance evaluation techniques and applications. This year we will also have an Industrial Research Fair, expanding on the jobs fair idea introduced in recent years.

A team of people have joined together to bring you this conference. At the top of my list, I would like to thank the TPC Chairs, Jim Xu and John Douceur. They poured their heart and souls into planning the technical program and finding new ways to ensure the best possible selection of papers. First, they initiated a rebuttal process to allow authors to respond to reviews, reducing errors in the review process. Second, they orchestrated an entirely new method of ranking papers, based not on average scores but rather on each reviewer's total ordering of his/her set of papers. It has been pure joy working with and learning from Jim and John! I am also very grateful to Nancy Conway and Nicole Stenger, who together worked as Local Arrangement Chairs for the conference, and were tireless in their planning and organization of events. Cathy Xia, our workshop chair, was also the originator of the Big Data Analytics workshop. She worked hard to find fantastic chairs for each workshop and took charge of any problems that came up. Similarly Eno Thereska handled all the selection and management of tutorials, doing a great job of mixing theory and practice. Patrick Loiseau, our registration chair, was extremely efficient in setting up the regonline program and handling registration bugs. Likewise Ton Dieker was very expedient in managing all the publication materials. Thanks also to Alma Riska for her help in keeping our budget balanced. Many thanks to Urtzi Ayesta who managed the student travel grants and student activities and to the publicity chairs, Marc Lelarge and Jia Wang, for advertising the conference. Finally, I am extremely grateful to Anshul Gandhi, our Webmaster, who responded to every request for a website update within minutes, even while conducting a very busy job search.

We had an unusually high number of corporate supporters this year, underscoring the importance of performance evaluation in the computer industry today. Thanks for the generous support of Intel, Microsoft Research, Facebook, Akamai, Google, NetApp, IBM, VMWare, HP Labs, and Carnegie Mellon University. Thanks also to the NSF for funding our Student Travel Grants, which are very valuable in expanding the size of the SIGMETRICS community. Finally, I would like to thank ACM, in particular April Mosqus, for providing all the infrastructure to make the conference run.

I hope that you will have a great time at the conference. In addition to attending all the talks, posters, keynotes, and other events, we've left lots of time for socializing and enjoying the city of Pittsburgh. Looking forward to many interesting discussions on future directions for performance evaluation!

Mor Harchol-Balter
SIGMETRICS 2013 General Chair
Carnegie Mellon University, Pittsburgh, PA

Program Chairs' Welcome

Welcome to SIGMETRICS 2013. SIGMETRICS is the flagship conference of the ACM special interest group for the computer systems performance evaluation community. This year marks the fortieth anniversary since SIGMETRICS (under its prior name, SIGME) held the First National SIGME Symposium on Measurement and Evaluation in 1973. The past four decades have seen enormous changes in the field of computer science, but the importance of measurement, modeling, and performance evaluation remains as critical as ever.

This year's conference includes papers on topics that have been a mainstay since the founding of our SIG, including queuing, scheduling, resource allocation, and performance measurement. Application areas that have emerged in recent years, such as multicore systems, cellular networks, and energy optimization, continue to be represented in our program. Papers on solid-state storage have seen a significant uptick this year, and we have papers on some topics that are new to SIGMETRICS, including crowdsourcing and RFID systems. Interestingly, the program also shows a drop-off in topics that were hot just a brief while ago, such as social networks, BitTorrent, swarms, peer-to-peer, and MapReduce.

We received 196 submissions to this year's conference, of which 26 appear in the program as full papers, which is a highly competitive acceptance ratio below 14%. An additional 28 submissions appear in the abbreviated form of poster presentations with brief summaries in the proceedings.

As in some prior years, we performed reviews in two rounds. In the first round, each paper was assigned to four reviewers. In the second round, additional reviews were assigned to papers with fewer than three completed reviews and papers with highly divergent review opinions and fewer than two high-confidence reviews.

We experimented with two changes to the review process this year. The first change to the review process was the addition of a rebuttal phase between the first and second review rounds, to give authors an opportunity to respond to questions raised in first-round reviews. To impede the addition of new substantive material in the rebuttals, and instead reserve rebuttals for merely highlighting information already contained in the submission, we strictly limited each rebuttal to 500 characters. It is not easy to gauge the effectiveness of the rebuttal process: There were many occasions during the PC meeting when reviewers commented on items in authors' rebuttals, which suggests that the rebuttals provided additional information; however, reviewers mostly found that their opinions were unchanged by what they read in the rebuttals.

The second change to the review process was the use of rankings rather than ratings. Instead of rating their assigned papers with accept/reject recommendations, each PC member was asked to produce a list of assigned papers ordered by the reviewer's assessment of each paper's overall quality. Our intent was to eliminate the bias that is inherent in accept/reject recommendations because each reviewer has only a narrow view of the conference's submissions. Reviewers' individual rankings were combined into a global ranking using an algorithm similar to PageRank, and the top 60 papers were discussed at the PC meeting. During the PC meeting, whenever a paper was accepted, we identified any paper with global rank below 60 that at least one reviewer had ranked substantially higher than the accepted paper. The reviewer was given the option to add this other paper to the discussion list. About a dozen such additional papers were discussed, although none were accepted as full papers.

We are pleased to present three awards to two of this year's papers. The SIGMETRICS Best Paper Award honors the overall best paper in each year's conference, and the Kenneth C. Sevcik Outstanding Student Paper Award honors an outstanding paper whose primary author is a student. This year, both awards are presented to an outstanding student paper that is also the overall best paper in the conference: "Queueing System Topologies with Limited Flexibility," by John N. Tsitsiklis and Kuang Xu. We are inaugurating a new award this year, the SIGMETRICS Best Practical Paper Award, to honor the best paper from among those whose research has the most direct practical applicability. This award is presented to "Practical Conflict Graphs for Dynamic Spectrum Distribution," by Xia Zhou, Zengbin Zhang, Gang Wang, Xiaoxiao Yu, Ben Y. Zhao, and Haitao Zheng.

It was no mean feat to winnow a set of nearly two hundred submissions down to a set of appropriate size for a three-day conference. We offer tremendous thanks to the 56 members of the program committee and the 32 external reviewers who collectively performed this daunting task. We are grateful for the support of the SIGMETRICS board during the lengthy process of selecting this year's conference program.

There are many conference organizers whose efforts have been critical to pulling this event together, but as program chairs, we are most directly indebted to three of them: Our webmaster, Anshul Gandhi, was outstandingly responsive to every online update we requested. Our publications chair, Ton Dieker, completely offloaded the end game from us, which was a wonderful relief after the long slog leading up to the PC meeting. And most notably, it has been truly delightful to work with Mor Harchol-Balter, the most diligent, organized, and energetic general chair we could imagine.

It has been our honor to serve as this year's program co-chairs. We look forward to an engaging, interactive, and productive conference.

John Douceur
SIGMETRICS'13 Program Co-chair
Microsoft Research, USA

Jun (Jim) Xu
SIGMETRICS'13 Program Co-chair
Georgia Tech, USA

Table of Contents

Session 9: Optimizing Paths down a Tree or a Network

Session Chair: Florin Ciucu *(TU Berlin)*

Poster Session

Tutorials

Author Index

SIGMETRICS 2013 Conference Organization

General Chair: Mor Harchol-Balter *(Carnegie Mellon University, USA)*

Program Chairs: John Douceur *(Microsoft Research, USA)*
Jun Xu *(Georgia Institute of Technology, USA)*

Publicity Chairs: Jia Wang *(AT&T Labs, USA)*
Marc Lelarge *(INRIA, France)*

Workshop Chair: Cathy Xia *(The Ohio State University, USA)*

Tutorials Chair: Eno Thereska *(Microsoft Research, United Kingdom)*

Finance Chair: Alma Riska *(EMC Corporation, USA)*

Publications Chair: Ton Dieker *(Georgia Institute of Technology, USA)*

Registration Chair: Patrick Loiseau *(EURECOM, France)*

Student Activities Chair: Urtzi Ayesta *(LAAS-CNRS, France)*

Local Arrangements Chair: Nancy Conway *(Carnegie Mellon University, USA)*

Webmaster: Anshul Gandhi *(Carnegie Mellon University, USA)*

Program Committee: Tarek Abdelzaher *(University of Illinois at Urbana-Champaign, USA)*
Aditya Akella *(University of Wisconsin at Madison, USA)*
Urtzi Ayesta *(LAAS-CNRS, France)*
Sem Borst *(Bell Labs, USA, and TU/e, The Netherlands, and
     CWI, The Netherlands)*
Niklas Carlsson *(Linköping University, Sweden)*
Giuliano Casale *(Imperial College London, United Kingdom)*
Lucy Cherkasova *(HP Labs, USA)*
Florin Ciucu *(TU Berlin/Deutsche Telekom Laboratories, Germany)*
Ton Dieker *(Georgia Institute of Technology, USA)*
Do Young Eun *(North Carolina State University, USA)*
Zihui Ge *(AT&T Labs, USA)*
Garth Gibson *(Carnegie Mellon University, USA)*
Leana Golubchik *(University of Southern California, USA)*
Ajay Gulati *(VMware, USA)*
Varun Gupta *(University of Chicago, USA)*
Charlie Hu *(Purdue University, USA)*
Canturk Isci *(IBM T. J. Watson Research Center, USA)*

Program Committee (continued):

Alain Jean-Marie *(INRIA, France)*
Mike Kozuch *(Intel Research, USA)*
Marc Lelarge *(INRIA, France)*
Baochun Li *(University of Toronto, Canada)*
Bill Lin *(University of California San Diego, USA)*
Alex Liu *(Michigan State University, USA)*
John Lui *(Chinese University of Hong Kong, Hong Kong)*
Qin Lv *(University of Colorado at Boulder, USA)*
Richard Ma *(National University of Singapore, Singapore)*
Ishai Menache *(Microsoft Research, USA)*
Arif Merchant *(Google, USA)*
Vishal Misra *(Columbia University, USA)*
Jason Nieh *(Columbia University, USA)*
Ana Radovanovic *(Google, USA)*
Rhonda Righter *(UC Berkeley, USA)*
Alma Riska *(EMC Corporation, USA)*
Philippe Robert *(INRIA, France)*
Dan Rubenstein *(Columbia University, USA)*
Sujay Sanghavi *(University of Texas at Austin, USA)*
Saswati Sarkar *(University of Pennsylvania, USA)*
Karsten Schwan *(Georgia Institute of Technology, USA)*
Jiri Schindler *(NetApp, USA)*
Evgenia Smirni *(College of William and Mary, USA)*
Thrasyvoulos Spyropoulos *(EURECOM, France)*
Christopher Stewart *(The Ohio State University, USA)*
Y. C. Tay *(National University of Singapore, Singapore)*
Don Towsley *(University of Massachusetts, USA)*
Bhuvan Urgaonkar *(Pennsylvania State University, USA)*
Darryl Veitch *(University of Melbourne, Australia)*
Milan Vojnovic *(Microsoft Research, United Kingdom)*
Jia Wang *(AT&T Labs, USA)*
Tom Wenisch *(University of Michigan, USA)*
Adam Wierman *(California Institute of Technology, USA)*
Carey Williamson *(University of Calgary, Canada)*
Cathy Xia *(The Ohio State University, USA)*
Li Zhang *(IBM T. J. Watson Research Center, USA)*
Zhi-Li Zhang *(University of Minnesota, USA)*
Gil Zussman *(Columbia University, USA)*
Bert Zwart *(VU University Amsterdam and CWI, The Netherlands)*

Additional reviewers:

Vijay Kumar Adhikari
Zhifeng Bao
Berk Birand
Yingying Chen
Rohan Gandhi
David K. George
Daniel Gmach
Maria Gorlatova
James Hanson
David Hay
Yu Jin
Abhilash Jindal
Jon Lenchner
Yanhua Li
Jia Liu
Lei Lu

Yingdong Lu
Jelena Marasevic
Robert Margolies
Xiaoqiao Meng
Gyan Ranjan
Mostafa Rezazad
Wolfgang Richter
Saleh Soltan
Sahil Suneja
Jian Tan
Cheng Wang
Di Wang
Feng Yan
Huai Ying
Lei Ying
Jingbo Zhou

SIGMETRICS 2013 Sponsor & Supporters

Sponsor:

Supporters:

Google™

 facebook

IBM

 (intel®)

Microsoft Research

 NetApp

 NSF

vmware®

Carnegie Mellon University

Designing Large-scale Nudge Engines

Balaji Prabhakar
Departments of Electrical Engineering and Computer Science
Stanford University
Stanford, CA
balaji@stanford.edu

ABSTRACT

In many of the challenges faced by the modern world, from overcrowded transportation systems to overstretched health-care systems, large benefits for society come about from small changes by very many individuals. We survey the problems and the cost they impose on society, and describe a framework for designing "nudge engines"—algorithms, incentives and technology for influencing human behavior. We present a model for analyzing their effectiveness and results from transportation pilots conducted in Bangalore, at Stanford and in Singapore, and a wellness program for the employees of Accenture-USA.

Categories and Subject Descriptors

H.4 [**Information Systems Applications**]: Miscellaneous

Keywords

Sensing Engines, Cloud Services, Behavioral Economics, Big Data, Societal Neworks, Mathematical Models

1. INTRODUCTION

The global percentage of the urban population increased from a mere 13 percent in 1900 to 29 percent in 1950, and surpassed 50 percent around 2008. This phenomenon, called "Urbanization", has been a key catalyst for economic growth and raising living standards around the globe. Millions of people move to cities every month for employment opportunities and to improve their quality of life. However, investments in urban infrastructure have largely lagged behind the needs created by the exploding pace of population inflows into cities. Traffic congestion, water shortages and lack of sanitation are facts of life for many urban dwellers. Physical inactivity and high-calorie processed food diet, the hallmark characteristics of urban living, are causing chronic diseases.

Several of the challenges faced by those operating societal networks such as transportation systems, energy grids or water distribution systems can be addressed when many individuals make small changes. The stakes for society as a whole are great, but often the stakes per person are too small for people to change their behavior. For example, in 2010, road congestion caused urban Americans to spend 4.8 billion more hours on the road and purchase an extra 1.9 billion gallons of gasoline, which translated to approximately US \$101 billion of economic losses.[1] However, from a commuter's perspective, it is a question of enduring the inconvenience of crowded roads and a 10-15% saving in fuel costs by shifting to off-peak times. Against this backdrop, how can we encourage individuals to do the right thing?

The Stanford Center for Societal Networks has been running a series of projects to study the effect of incentives on nudging people to change their behavior. These projects employ platforms built using cloud, mobile and big data technology for sensing and nudging behavior. The key findings are (i) monetary rewards have several advantages over charges in terms of implementation and effectiveness — carrots are better than sticks, (ii) when the stakes are small, a random reward is more appealing than a deterministic reward of the same expected value — a fact underlying lottery systems, (iii) games make odds of winning transparent and are a fun and engaging way of conducting lotteries, (iv) data mining enables personalized recommendations and makes efficient use of monetary resources, and (v) social influence (friends influencing one another's behaviors) is a powerful motivator of change. These findings are illustrated through empiricial evidence from the projects and analyzed using a mathematical model.

2. BIOGRAPHY

Balaji Prabhakar is Professor of Electrical Engineering and Computer Science at Stanford University. His research interests are in computer networks; notably, in designing algorithms for the Internet and for Data Centers. Recently, he has been interested in Societal Networks: networks vital for society's functioning. He has been involved in developing and deploying incentive mechanisms to move commuters to off-peak times so that congestion, fuel and pollution costs are reduced.

He is an IEEE Fellow, a Terman Fellow at Stanford University, and a Fellow of the Alfred P. Sloan Foundation. He has received the CAREER award from the U.S. National Science Foundation, an IBM Faculty Development Award, the Erlang Prize from the INFORMS Applied Probability Society, the Rollo Davidson Prize from the University of Cambridge, and delivered the Lunteren Lectures. He is a co-recipient of several best paper awards. He serves on the Advisory Board of the Future Urban Mobility Initiative of the World Economic Forum.

---

[1]See David Schrank, Tim Lomax and Bill Eisele, "2011 Urban Mobility Report", Texas Transportation Institute, September 2011, p.1.

Challenges in Cloud Scale Data Centers

David A. Maltz
Microsoft, Redmond, WA, USA

ABSTRACT

Data centers are fascinating places, where the massive scale required to deliver on-line services like web search and cloud hosting turns minor issues into major challenges that must be addressed in the design of the physical infrastructure and the software platform. In this talk, I'll briefly overview the kinds of applications that run in mega-data centers and the workloads they place on the infrastructure. I'll then describe a number of challenges seen in Microsoft's data centers, with the goals of posing questions more than describing solutions and explaining how economic factors, technology issues, and software design interact when creating low-latency, low-cost, high availability services.

Categories and Subject Descriptors

C.2.1 [**Network**]: Architecture

Keywords

Cloud data centers, costs, network challenges

1. SUMMARY

Data centers are best thought of as factories, storing and processing information to produce value. Like factories, the costs in capital and ongoing expense can be huge, and so a first order concern in designing them is to ensure their costs are less than the value they produce. Since at least 2008 [2] and continuing till today, the costs of a data center are dominated by the costs of the servers, which presents both a challenge and an opportunity to the networks that connect the servers: the design of the network must be subservient to by the demands of the servers, but spending more on the network is easily justified if it improves return on investment for the servers.

As factories producing value, data centers must provide an Service Level Agreement (SLA) that describes the behavior that services can expect from their infrastructure in terms of availability, latency, cost, and throughput. However, actually defining metrics that capture SLA in a meaningful fashion is difficult. Further complicating the concept of SLA is that each server in a data center often traffics in multiple types of data simultaneously, for example, both latency-sensitive traffic like user queries or transactions [1], and throughput-sensitive traffic like data-mining or data-set replication [3, 4]. These traffic types cause conflicting demands at every layer of the stack, from network buffers to kernel interrupt behavior to disk I/O.

Experience has shown that the true measure of a data center design is not its performance when everything is going well, as is its performance in response to failure. Given the large size of cloud-scale data centers, device failure is a normal occurrence [5], and mechanisms to cope with failure are of critical importance.

2. REFERENCES

[1] M. Alizadeh, A. Greenberg, D. A. Maltz, J. Padhye, P. Patel, B. Prabhakar, S. Sengupta, and M. Sridharan. Data center TCP (DCTCP). In *SIGCOMM*, 2010.

[2] A. Greenberg, J. Hamilton, D. A. Maltz, and P. Patel. The cost of a cloud: Research problems in data center networks. In *ACM SIGCOMM Computer Communication Review*, 2008.

[3] A. Greenberg, N. Jain, S. Kandula, C. Kim, P. Lahiri, D. Maltz, P. Patel, , and S. Sengupta. Vl2: A scalable and flexible data center network. In *SIGCOMM*, 2009.

[4] S. Kandula, S. Sengupta, A. Greenberg, P. Patel, and R. Chaiken. The nature of datacenter traffic: Measurements and analysis. In *IMC*, 2009.

[5] X. Wu, D. Turner, C.-C. Chen, D. A. Maltz, X. Yang, L. Yuan, and M. Zhang. Netpilot: automating datacenter network failure mitigation. In *SIGCOMM*, 2012.

3. BIOGRAPHY

Dr. David A. Maltz leads the network portion of the Autopilot team, which won Microsoft's 2013 Technology Achievement Award[1] for advances in cloud-scale data centers. Prior to joining Autopilot, he worked in industry research and academia. He was also a founder of startup companies in network traffic management and wireless networking. He works on a broad array of projects that strive to improve the usability, performance, and cost of cloud computing. In 2010, he received the ACM Software System Award as part of the GroupLens team that did pioneering work in Collaborative Filtering and platforms for large-scale data analysis to support on-line services.

---

[1]http://www.microsoft.com/about/technicalrecognition/Autopilot.aspx

Practical Conflict Graphs for Dynamic Spectrum Distribution

Xia Zhou, Zengbin Zhang, Gang Wang, Xiaoxiao Yu§, Ben Y. Zhao and Haitao Zheng
Department of Computer Science, U. C. Santa Barbara, USA
§Tsinghua University, Beijing, P. R. China
{xiazhou, zengbin, gangw, ravenben, htzheng}@cs.ucsb.edu, yuxiaox@gmail.com

ABSTRACT

Most spectrum distribution proposals today develop their allocation algorithms that use conflict graphs to capture interference relationships. The use of conflict graphs, however, is often questioned by the wireless community because of two issues. First, building conflict graphs requires significant overhead and hence generally does not scale to outdoor networks, and second, the resulting conflict graphs do not capture accumulative interference.

In this paper, we use large-scale measurement data as ground truth to understand just how severe these issues are in practice, and whether they can be overcome. We build "practical" conflict graphs using *measurement-calibrated propagation models*, which remove the need for exhaustive signal measurements by interpolating signal strengths using calibrated models. These propagation models are imperfect, and we study the impact of their errors by tracing the impact on multiple steps in the process, from calibrating propagation models to predicting signal strength and building conflict graphs. At each step, we analyze the introduction, propagation and final impact of errors, by comparing each intermediate result to its ground truth counterpart generated from measurements. Our work produces several findings. Calibrated propagation models generate *location-dependent* prediction errors, ultimately producing conservative conflict graphs. While these "estimated conflict graphs" lose some spectrum utilization, their conservative nature improves reliability by reducing the impact of accumulative interference. Finally, we propose a graph augmentation technique that addresses any remaining accumulative interference, the last missing piece in a practical spectrum distribution system using measurement-calibrated conflict graphs.

Categories and Subject Descriptors

C.2.3 [**Network Operations**]: Network Management

Keywords

Dynamic spectrum access; conflict graphs; interference

1. INTRODUCTION

Current reforms in radio spectrum management promise to spur rapid growth of wireless technologies, by using on-demand spectrum auctions and secondary markets [3, 50]. In an ideal scenario, these markets not only maximize profit for spectrum owners, but also allows spectrum users, *e.g.* small cell providers, to purchase spectrum on-the-fly and receive exclusive usage of allocated spectrum without the hassle of sharing.

Achieving this goal requires two tightly-coupled components: *an accurate model of interference patterns* among current spectrum users, and *an allocation algorithm* that uses this interference model to distribute spectrum efficiently. For spectrum, this means maximizing utilization by parallelizing non-interfering transmissions whenever possible.

The majority of prior works have chosen to develop allocation algorithms under an abstract interference model called "conflict graphs" [20]. As the name suggests, a conflict graph is a simple graphical representation of the interference condition between any two spectrum users[1]. This simple interference structure greatly simplifies spectrum allocation design, leading to a series of highly efficient allocation algorithms with bounded performance and polynomial complexity [10, 13, 22, 32, 38, 43, 50]. In contrast, alternative physical interference models are highly complex, and have been shown in existing studies to produce unbounded performance loss when used to build allocation algorithms [9, 47].

As popular as they are, the practical value of conflict graphs is often questioned by the wireless community for two key reasons. *First,* building an accurate conflict graph for a specific physical area is very challenging. Given the complex nature of RF propagation, it requires detailed measurements covering all combinations of sender/receiver locations. This type of per-link signal measurement is feasible for indoor WLANs [5, 6, 26, 33, 39, 43, 45], but impractical for the outdoor networks targeted by spectrum markets. As a substitute, most current proposals build artificial conflict graphs using a simple distance-based criterion [7, 10, 48] or from signal strength values generated from simple RF propagation models with rule of thumb parameters [18, 32]. While these simplifications ease the process of designing and evaluating allocation algorithms, empirical studies have shown that they produce incorrect interference results that lead to poor performance [27, 34].

---

[1]For a specific frequency band, if two users can operate concurrently without visible performance degradation, then they do not conflict. Otherwise they conflict and are connected with an edge (of the specific band) [35].

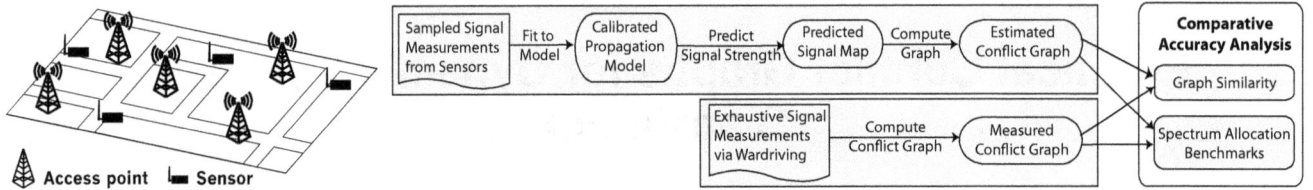

Figure 1: Our high level methodology. We build *estimated conflict graphs* by collecting limited signal measurements at a small number of randomly deployed sensors to calibrate a propagation model, and using the results to predict signal strength values and construct the conflict graph. We examine the accuracy of estimated conflict graphs by comparing them against *measured conflict graphs* built from exhaustive signal measurements, using graph similarity and spectrum allocation benchmarks.

Second, because conflict graphs only define interference conditions between any two spectrum users, they cannot capture the impact of interference accumulated from multiple concurrent transmitters in the same frequency band. Prior work [30] has shown that such "mismatch" leads to unpredicted and harmful interference at allocated users, breaking the exclusive usage guarantee offered by the spectrum market. Without guarantees that their transmissions would operate without interference, users would have little incentive to purchase from the spectrum market.

In this paper, we use a data-driven approach to gain a better understanding of the severity of these two issues. We use measurements as ground truth to quantify the severity of errors produced by building conflict graphs without exhaustive signal measurements, and to determine if these errors impact users in the form of poor spectrum allocations. We also seek to identify solutions to minimize these errors, and in doing so, addressing the community's main concerns and promoting the continued use of conflict graphs in practice.

In our study, we build conflict graphs using *measurement-calibrated propagation models*. Instead of performing exhaustive measurements, this approach performs measurements on only a subset of locations. These results are used to calibrate a propagation model, which is used to make signal strength predictions for all locations in the area. These predictions are used in lieu of exhaustive measurements to build the conflict graph. This approach has two advantages. First, prior works have shown that measurement-calibrated propagation models are much more accurate than those built with rule-of-thumb parameters [19, 29, 31, 42]. Second, because measurements can be performed by sensors or even trusted network subscribers, this approach incurs low overhead, and can offer continuous measurements in real-time. This allows conflict graphs to adapt to constantly changing network environments and users. We recognize, however, that calibrated propagation models are imperfect, and will introduce errors in the predicted signal strength maps [14, 23, 36, 40]. So we must understand whether these errors carry through to become errors in conflict graphs, and if they impact the efficacy of spectrum allocations for users. Our high level methodology is as follows:

- Use a relatively small number of signal measurements to calibrate RF propagation models;
- Use models to build predicted signal strength maps, and use those to produce "estimated conflict graphs";
- Compare estimated conflict graph to "measured conflict graph" built from exhaustive signal measurements, in the form of missing or extraneous edges between the two;

- Evaluate end-to-end impact by running spectrum allocation on both conflict graphs and comparing them while considering the impact of accumulative interference.

To the best of our knowledge, our work is the first empirical study on the practical usability of conflict graph for dynamic spectrum distribution. Our work differs from existing works on constructing conflict graphs. First, focusing on outdoor environments, our work differs from prior work [5, 6, 26, 33, 39, 43, 45] that build indoor conflict graphs using exhaustive signal measurements. Second, our work targets dynamic spectrum markets where users requesting spectrum are located at unplanned places and the resulting conflict graph can be of arbitrary shape. This is fundamentally different from cellular networks [19, 29, 46] which optimize the placement (and transmit power) of base stations to produce conflict graphs of specific shapes.

Our measurement study leads to four key findings:

- Calibrated propagation models generate location-dependent signal prediction errors. They are more likely to underpredict signal strength at short distances, and overpredict them for long distance links. We consistently observe this pattern across multiple measurement datasets.
- These prediction errors lead to conservative conflict graphs that rarely miss actual conflict edges, but commonly introduce extraneous conflict edges.
- This leads to conservative spectrum allocations with utilization loss compared to measured conflict graphs. These extra edges, on the other hand, play a critical role in reducing the impact of accumulative interference, thus achieving more reliable links than allocations using only measured conflict graphs.
- A simple graph augmentation technique can effectively eliminate the artifact of accumulative interference from both conflict graphs, boosting the reliability of spectrum allocation to more than 96%. Once augmented, estimated conflict graphs also achieve utilization that is more than 85% of the ideal allocation.

2. METHODOLOGY

Using real data, we seek to understand key issues when using conflict graphs for dynamic spectrum distribution. We consider conflict graphs built from measurement-calibrated propagation models because they are practical, requiring little measurement overhead, and much more accurate than those built with rule-of-thumb parameters.

Our approach, shown in Figure 1, consists of four steps: 1) collecting real signal maps via measurements, and using them as ground truth; 2) using sampled subsets to calibrate propagation models, and predicting network-wide signal maps; 3) building conflict graphs from both measured and predicted signal maps, and 4) quantifying the accuracy of estimated conflict graphs using measured graphs as ground truth, via both graph similarity and spectrum allocation benchmarks. By examining both efficiency and reliability of the allocation, we examine the impact of accumulative interference. Next, we briefly describe our assumptions and present each step in detail.

Assumptions. The basis of our study comes from wardriving measurements of outdoor municipal WiFi networks. We assume that each spectrum user seeks to obtain one of the WiFi channels each with the same propagation properties. We use WiFi band as an example of distributing spectrum among outdoor networks, and also because this is the only outdoor network with known base station locations. Our work can easily be extended to other frequency bands by adjusting the propagation model to account for carrier frequency differences [12, 41]. We leave this to a future work.

2.1 Collecting Signal Maps

Our study uses wardriving measurements of outdoor municipal WiFi networks at three different cities, one of which was collected by our own group. Each dataset consists of beacon RSS values of WiFi access points (AP) measured in a large outdoor area of size $3\text{-}7km^2$, along with the location of each measurement and the locations of all APs. We average multiple RSS readings per location to derive a map of average signal strengths for each participating AP. Table 1 summarizes the datasets.

GoogleWiFi. Collected by our research group in April 2010, this dataset covers a $7km^2$ residential area of the Google WiFi network in Mountain View, California. Figure 2 shows the measurement locations (as blue dots) and the APs (as red triangles). We used three co-located laptops equipped with customized WiFi cards[2] with higher receive sensitivity than normal cards. Thus this dataset records detailed signal strength values of 78 APs at 11,447 distinct locations (with an average $5m$ separation between nearby locations). More importantly, each location has signal strength values of 6+ APs in average, 2-3 times more than the other two datasets.

MetroFi. This dataset [2] consists of RSS values in a $7km^2$ area of an 802.11x municipal network in Portland, Oregon. It was collected by a research group from University of Colorado in 2007. The dataset covers 30,991 distinct measured locations of 70 APs with known GPS locations. The average number of APs heard per location is only 2.3.

TFA. Collected by researchers from Rice University, this measurement data covers 22 APs in a $3km^2$ area of the TFA network in Houston, Texas [4]. It includes measurements from 27,855 locations.

To use these datasets in our study, we treat each AP as the transmitter of a spectrum market user, and any measured location in its coverage area as the receiver positions of the market user. While our measurements are on WiFi

---

[2]We use WiFi cards from Wifly-City System Inc. Equipped with a 7dBi external omni antenna and a dual amplifier, they double the sensing range of standard WiFi cards. Following FCC rules, we only use the RX path of the card to receive beacons, with its TX path always turned off.

Table 1: Summary of the datasets used in our study

Dataset	Area size (km^2)	# of APs w/ GPS info	# of measured locations	Avg. # of APs heard per location
GoogleWiFi	7	78	11,447	6.2
MetroFi	7	70	30,991	2.3
TFA	3	22	27,855	2.7

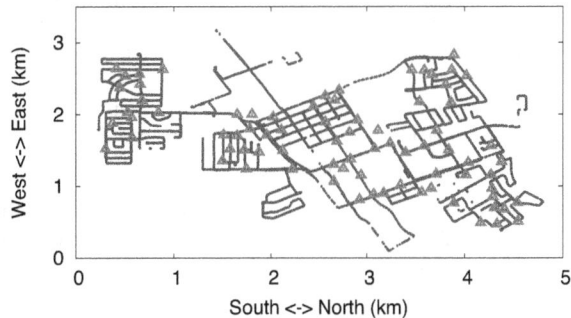

Figure 2: Measured area in the GoogleWiFi dataset. Red triangles are the APs detected and blue dots are measured locations on the streets.

networks, both the measured signal maps and the resulting conflict graphs are independent of specific MAC protocols used. This is important, since it matches the exclusive usage scenario, where a spectrum market user is free to use any MAC protocol in its authorized spectrum range.

2.2 Calibrating Propagation Models

To generate "estimated conflict graphs," we use samples of our measurements to calibrate existing propagation models. We select several well-known models designed specifically for urban street environments that match our datasets, including the simple uniform path loss model, and complex models that support specific environmental features like streets and building structures. We now describe our high-level approach to model calibration and signal map prediction. We leave the detailed discussion on each model and their calibration procedure to Section 3.

We begin by choosing sub-samples from the exhaustive measurement data. Since the search for optimal sampling methods is still an open problem [49], we randomly sample our data, and vary the density of the sample data between 1.4 and 100 samples per km^2. We then use the Minimum Mean Squared Error (MMSE) fitting method to determine the best-fit parameters for each propagation model. Once the parameters have been calibrated for a given model, we then interpolate the signal values at other locations to build the complete signal strength map.

2.3 Constructing Conflict Graphs

We now have two signal strength maps, one from our exhaustive signal strength measurement data, and one interpolated from our calibrated signal propagation model. We use them respectively to build a *measured conflict graph*, *i.e.* ground truth, and an *estimated conflict graph*. These conflict graphs represent the interference patterns of spectrum market users, where each spectrum market user maps to a stationary transmitter, *i.e.* an AP in our signal maps, and its coverage region corresponds to locations for its receivers.

The resulting conflict graph consists of a set of nodes, each mapping to a spectrum market user, and a set of edges, each representing a conflict between two nodes. To determine if two users conflict, we place their transmitters on the same spectrum channel and examine whether they both receive "exclusive spectrum usage." A market user receives exclusive spectrum usage if γ-percentile of its qualified transmissions have signal to noise and interference ratio (SINR) above β [22]. Along with coverage area and transmit power, γ and β are operating parameters configured by spectrum market users in their spectrum purchase requests.

Consider two nodes i and j. Let $\text{SINR}_u^{i,j}$ represent the SINR value at location u in node i's coverage area: $\text{SINR}_u^{i,j} = \frac{S_u^i}{I_u^j + N_0}$, $u \in U_i$, where S_u^i is the received signal strength at u from i's transmitter, I_u^j is the interference strength from j's transmitter, N_0 is the thermal noise, and U_i is the coverage area of i. We sort locations within each node's coverage area by their SINR, and determine conflict conditions using the bottom $(1 - \gamma)$-percentile value. That is, node i and j conflict if and only if for either of the two coverage areas, the percentage of locations with $\text{SINR} \geq \beta$ is less than γ:

$$p_{ij} = \min(q_j^i, q_i^j) < \gamma , \qquad (1)$$

where $q_i^j = \frac{|\{u|u \in U_i, SINR_u^{i,j} \geq \beta\}|}{|U_i|}$. Here $(1 - \gamma)$ represents the percentage of coverage holes a spectrum user is willing to tolerate to maximize capacity [1]. When $\gamma = 1$, eq. (1) reduces to the minimal SINR-based criterion [9, 47, 48].

Configuring Coverage Area and β. For simplicity, we assume each market user's coverage area includes all measurement locations whose $\text{SNR} \geq \beta$. If a single location falls into the coverage area of multiple users, we assume that it is associated with the user that maximizes its signal strength. We set β=10dB, which is the minimum SNR required to decode beacons in GoogleWiFi measurements. This allows us to use all measurement locations in our graph analysis. We have also experimented other β values (8–20dB). Since they lead to the same trend, we omit the results for brevity.

2.4 Evaluating Graph Accuracy

Finally, we examine the accuracy of the estimated conflict graphs and the artifact of accumulative interference not captured by these graphs. To do so, we compare the estimated (measurement-calibrated) conflict graph against the measured conflict graph built directly from measurements. Our analysis uses both graph similarity metrics and spectrum allocation benchmarks.

For graph similarity, we perform edge-based comparison of the two conflict maps, using the measured conflict graph as ground truth. This produces a set of "extraneous edges" and "missing edges" that capture the differences between the estimated graph and the measured graph. We analyze the patterns of extraneous and missing edges, and explain their appearance based on errors in signal map prediction.

To understand the impact of graph edge errors on spectrum users, we feed each type of conflict graphs to two well-known spectrum allocation benchmarks and compare the allocation results. These end-to-end tests provide answers to two questions: will the edge errors lead to significant loss in spectrum efficiency and reliability, and will the "uncaptured" accumulative interference also lead to significant loss?

In the following, we present detailed results of each of our analysis steps. We begin by examining the accuracy of signal map prediction using calibrated propagation models (Section 3). Then we build and compare measured and estimated conflict graphs in terms of graph similarity (Section 4) and spectrum allocation performance (Section 5).

3. SIGNAL PREDICTION ACCURACY

To examine the concern on the accuracy of measurement-calibrated conflict graphs, we begin with understanding the types of errors introduced when we use incomplete measurements to calibrate propagation models and predict signal strength values. More specifically, are there patterns in prediction errors likely to manifest later as errors in conflict graphs. Our goal is to answer the question: *how accurate are signal strength predictions made by measurement-calibrated propagation models, and does receiver location play a role in prediction accuracy?* We take several representative propagation models, calibrate them using controlled samples of our measurement data, and evaluate their signal strength predictions for locations missing from the sample, using the full dataset as ground truth.

3.1 Propagation Models and Calibration

We choose four representative propagation models for our work, because they capture urban street environments that best match our datasets. They range from the simplest uniform pathloss model to sophisticated models that incorporate features like streets and changes in terrain.

Uniform Pathloss Model (Uniform) [14]. The simplest and most-used model, this captures signal attenuation over distance using a single pathloss exponent. Calibration is straightforward: use Minimum Mean Square Error (MMSE) to determine the best-fit pathloss exponent.

Two-Ray Model (Two-Ray) [14]. This model uses two pathloss exponents to capture the dual slope feature of signal propagation in urban environments, *i.e.* signal attenuates faster after a certain distance. It offers higher accuracy than the uniform pathloss model in urban street environments [16]. To calibrate this model, we partition the sample measurements into two sets using a distance threshold, and for each set we use a separate MMSE fitting to determine the best-fit pathloss exponent. We also optimize the partition to minimize the overall MMSE.

Terrain-based Model (Terrain) [42]. This model leverages terrain information to capture the non-uniformity of radio propagation caused by different terrains. It divides the transmitter's coverage area into sectors, and applies a terrain-specific shadowing factor in each sector. We follow the procedure in [42] to calibrate this model. Since we do not have terrain information (street, buildings, *etc.*) for the MetroFi and TFA datasets, we only provide results for our GoogleWiFi dataset.

Street Model (Street) [15]. This model targets urban microcell networks, and assumes that signals are constrained to propagate along the streets along line-of-sight, with minor reflection and/or diffraction to cross streets. To calibrate this model, we categorize signal propagation into three types based on the number of reflections it encounters. These include those without any reflection, *i.e.* line-of-sight, those with one reflection, and those with multiple reflections. We divide measurement samples into these categories and train

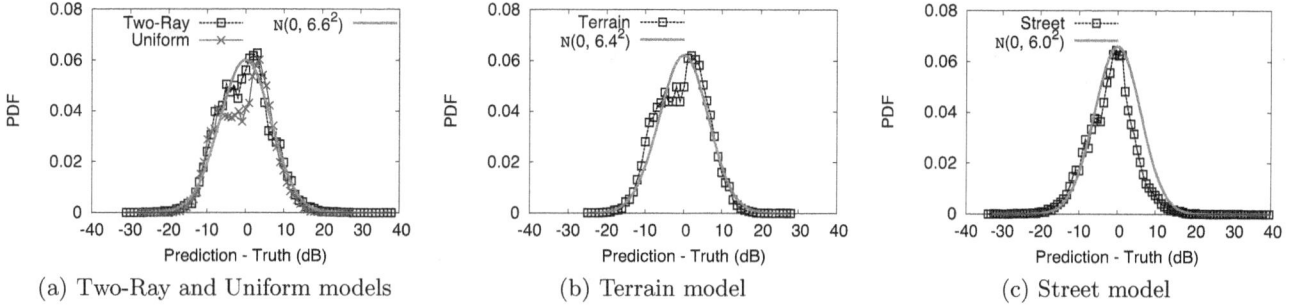

(a) Two-Ray and Uniform models   (b) Terrain model   (c) Street model

Figure 3: Probability density distributions of prediction errors using four calibrated propagation models. The reference zero-mean Gaussian curves are also displayed for each calibrated model. Prediction errors approximately follow zero-mean Gaussian distributions with standard deviation in [6, 6.6].

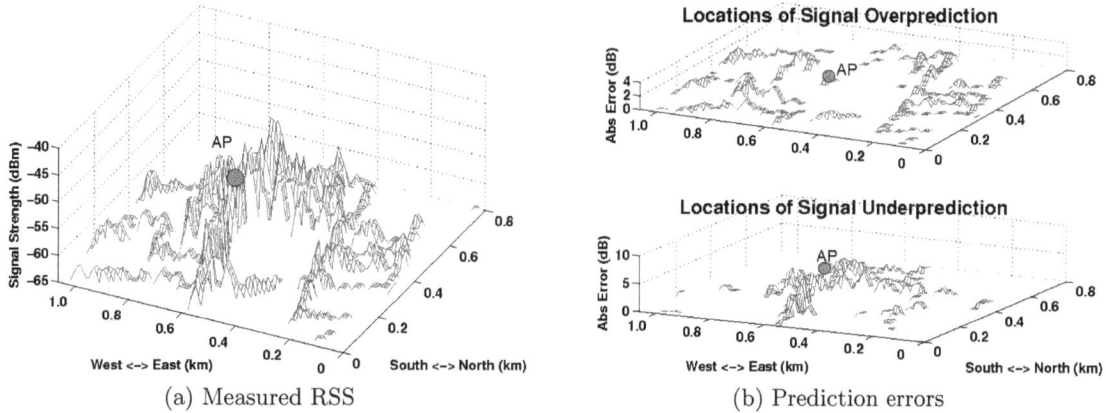

(a) Measured RSS   (b) Prediction errors

Figure 4: (a) Spatial distribution of measured signal strength values. Signal strength generally follows the power law, but varies significantly over space. Measurements could not be performed in areas with buildings or obstacles, and they show up as blank areas in plots. (b) Areas of signal overprediction and underprediction and absolute error values. Predictions use the Street model. Locations close to the AP tend to be underpredicted while those further away tend to be overpredicted.

the parameters for each propagation type separately. Like Terrain, this model requires street information, and thus can only be calibrated using the GoogleWiFi dataset.

3.2 Signal Prediction Results

We quantify signal prediction errors as the difference between the predicted signal strength (in dBm) and the measured signal strength (in dBm). We observe prediction errors that range from -30dB (under-prediction) to 30dB (over-prediction). We make three key observations.

Observation 1: Impact of Sampling. To calibrate our models, we randomly select sub-samples from the exhaustive measurement data. We vary the density of these samples from 1.4 to 100 samples per km^2, or 10 to 700 total samples for an area of size $7km^2$. For all four models, we observe that increasing density beyond 34 samples per km^2 (239 total samples) leads to negligible gain in performance. Thus we use this sampling density for all our later tests. We also observe that calibration often yields surprising results, *e.g.* we find that the calibrated pathloss exponent for the Uniform model varies between 1.15 and 2.20 for our three datasets, while typical rule of thumb suggests 2 or 3.

Table 2: Standard deviation of prediction error

Dataset	Standard deviation			
	Uniform	Two-Ray	Terrain	Street
GoogleWiFi	6.6	6.6	6.4	6.0
MetroFi	8.4	8.1	N/A	N/A
TFA	7.6	7.4	N/A	N/A

Observation 2: Impact of Models. We observe that prediction errors are visible, but they do not vary significantly across models (the street model performs slightly better). This matches prior work [14, 23, 36, 40]. Specifically, prediction error varies across locations, and can be approximated by a zero-mean Gaussian distribution. Figure 3 shows the probability density function (PDF) of the prediction errors and its Gaussian approximation using the GoogleWiFi dataset. The same trend holds for MetroFi and TFA, and we omit those results for brevity. Table 2 lists the standard deviation of the prediction error under each model and dataset.

Observation 3: Impact of Receiver Location. When examining the correlation between prediction error and location, we observe that *all four propagation models tend to un-*

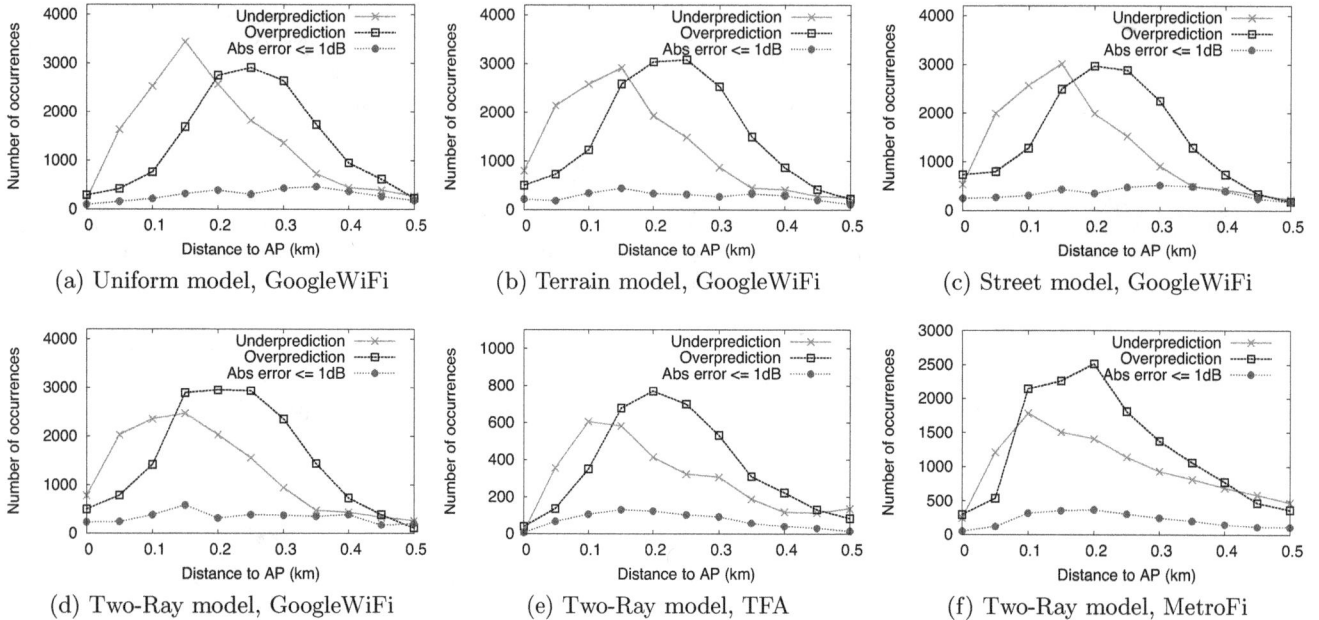

Figure 5: As the distance to AP increases, the main prediction error gradually switches from underprediction to overprediction. Here each data point summarizes the prediction errors within a distance interval of 0.05km. We show results with distances < 0.55km because the number of data points above this range is insufficient to demonstrate any trends.

derpredict signal strength in area near the transmitter, and overpredict signal strength in areas far from the transmitter.

We illustrate this pattern graphically in Figure 4 by plotting the measured signal strength distribution of a randomly selected AP, and the levels of signal overprediction and underprediction at different locations. We define signal overprediction (under-prediction) to be when the predicted signal strength is larger (smaller) than the actual value by more than 1dB. This result shows a strong correlation between locations (in terms of their distance to the AP) and the type of expected error.

A closer look shows that this effect is consistent across all four propagation models and all three datasets. In Figure 5, we sort each AP's measurement locations by their distances to the AP, and group them into buckets of 0.05km. For each interval, we calculate the occurrence of locations with accurate signal prediction (absolute error ≤ 1dB) and those with overprediction and underprediction. We observe that the trend is consistent across all settings.

One possible explanation is that these propagation models still cannot fully capture how RF signals in urban street environments experience faster attenuation after traveling a certain distance [16, 17, 14]. Although both the Terrain and Street models seek to capture the impact of non-uniform signal propagation, they still use the single-slope pathloss model, and cannot fully reflect the dual slope feature of signal propagation. Thus the dual slope effect is more evident on these models. The Two-Ray model considers this feature, but is limited by the use of a uniform breakpoint distance that does not exist in practice [17]. Thus we still observe some errors for this model.

Summary of Findings. Our accuracy analysis shows that propagation models, even after careful calibration, in-

troduce visible but location-dependent errors in signal map prediction. This naturally leads to the question: how will the signal prediction errors translate into errors in estimated conflict graphs? We explore this question next.

4. CONFLICT GRAPH ACCURACY

Having analyzed the errors introduced by predictions from calibrated signal propagation models, we now examine the actual accuracy of the "estimated conflict graphs" produced using these results. More specifically, we ask the question: *what is the impact of imperfect signal strength predictions on the accuracy of their resulting conflict graphs?* As before, we use our measurement data as ground truth to produce "measured conflict graphs," and use them to gauge the accuracy of "estimated conflict graphs."

Here, we use similarity between the conflict graphs as a measure of the accuracy of estimated conflict graphs. Since both types of conflict graphs share the same vertices, graph similarity in this context reduces to a measure of overlap in the set of edges between graphs. In addition, our analysis is limited to the GoogleWiFi dataset, because lower receiver sensitivity in the other datasets resulted in extremely sparse conflict graphs with less than 20 edges. For each estimated conflict graph, we use 50 random sampling sets to produce 50 graph instances. Since these graphs across different samples are highly similar (≤ 3 edge difference), we only show average results here for brevity.

4.1 Graph Similarity Results

We compare each estimated conflict graph against the measured conflict graph, and classify each edge in the estimated graph as correct, extraneous, or missing:

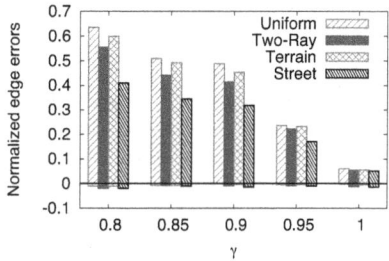

(a) Model-estimated conflict graphs

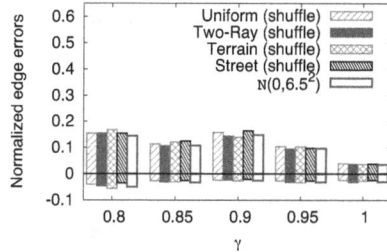

(b) Modified estimated conflict graphs

Figure 7: (a) Edge errors in the estimated conflict graph, normalized by the number of edges in the measured conflict graph. Negative (positive) bars denote the normalized count of missing (extraneous) edges. (b) Edge errors in the "modified" estimated conflict graph by removing the location dependency of the prediction errors. The amount of extraneous edges reduces significantly.

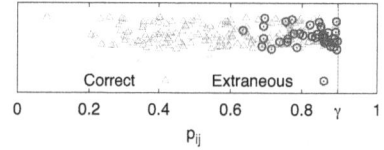

Figure 8: The values of p_{ij} for both correct and extraneous edges in the estimated conflict graph, using the Street model and $\gamma = 0.9$. We denote the two kinds of edges with different markers, and spread them out vertically using random Y values.

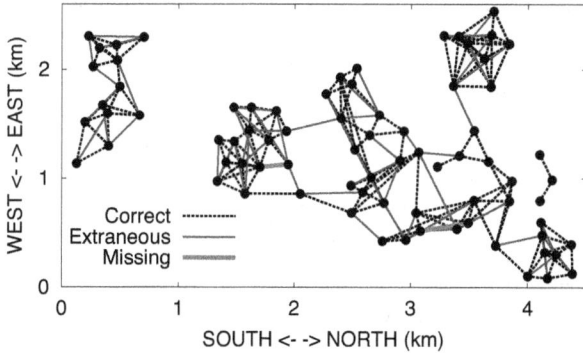

Figure 6: Accuracy of an estimated conflict graph.

- *Correct edges*: edges found in both estimated and measured conflict graphs.

- *Extraneous edges*: edges in the estimated conflict graph but not in the measured conflict graph; these edge errors make the estimated conflict graph more conservative, reducing spectrum utilization.

- *Missing edges*: edges in the measured conflict graph but missing in the estimated conflict graph; these errors are more harmful than extraneous edges, because they reduce the reliability of the estimated conflict graph and lead to harmful interference when conflicting nodes are assigned to the same channel.

Figure 6 shows a sample of estimated conflict graph generated using the Street model. Distances between nodes are shown to scale. Compared to the measured conflict graph with 162 edges, the estimated graph misses only 2 edges (thick red lines) and introduces 51 extraneous edges (blue lines). While slightly conservative, the estimated conflict graph is able to capture most of the edges.

We then compute the *normalized edge errors* as the number of extraneous and missing edges normalized by the total number of edges in the measured conflict graph. Figure 7(a) shows the normalized edge errors as the value of γ varies. We display normalized extraneous edges as positive values and the normalized missing edges as negative values. The

results show that the majority of edge errors are extraneous edges. Missing edges account for less than 2% of the edges of the measured graph. This pattern holds across different propagation models and for different values of γ.

Comparing across propagation models, we see that the choice of propagation models has only minor impact on the accuracy of the estimated conflict graph. The Uniform model is the most conservative and generates a slightly higher ratio of extraneous edges, and the Street model provides the best overall performance. This is likely because of the higher accuracy achieved by the Street model, which treats the reflected paths as the main components in non-line-of-sight (NLOS) scenarios. As a result, it is more accurate for urban street environments such as Mountain View, and leads to less edge errors in estimated graphs.

Figure 7(a) also shows that the normalized occurrence of extraneous edges decreases as γ increases. This is because increasing γ lowers the bar for two nodes to conflict with each other, thus producing more[3] edges in the measured conflict graph, and shrinking the pool of potential extraneous edges for the estimated graph. Thus the ratio of extraneous edges decreases from 40-60% ($\gamma = 0.8$) to 5-8% ($\gamma = 1$).

4.2 Why Do Extraneous Edges Dominate?

The fact that extraneous edges dominate the errors can be attributed to two factors. The first is the location-dependent pattern of signal prediction errors described in Section 3. It causes under-prediction of signal strength and over-prediction of interference strength. Hence the majority (70+%) of pairwise SINR values are underpredicted, leading to many extraneous edges.

To verify this hypothesis, we build a new set of *modified* estimated conflict graphs using the same model-predicted signal maps, but make the prediction error randomly distributed across locations. We use two methods to remove the location dependency. The first method gathers the prediction errors of the model-generated signal maps, shuffles them randomly across different measurement locations, and adds them back to the measured signal map. The second method produces a synthetic pattern of prediction errors from a zero-mean Gaussian distribution with standard de-

---

[3]As γ grows from 0.8 to 1, the edge counts of the measured conflict graphs are 104, 132, 162, 243, 446, respectively.

viation of 6.5, and adds them to the measured signal map. Figure 7(b) shows that normalized edge errors in these modified estimated graphs have much fewer extraneous edges than their unmodified counterparts, only 5–15% vs. 5–60%. This confirms our hypothesis.

The second factor contributing to more extraneous edge errors is the fact that missing edge errors occur under more stringent conditions, *i.e.* it takes more signal errors to remove an edge than to add an edge. To erroneously remove an edge between i and j, both predicted ratios of conflict-free locations (q_i^j and q_j^i, defined by Eq. (1)) must exceed γ. In contrast, erroneously adding an edge between i and j only requires one of these two estimates to fall below γ. This factor explains why extraneous edges still outrun missing edges even after removing the location-dependency in the prediction errors (Figure 7(b)).

We note that these extraneous edges are not due to possible under-measurement of interference in our dataset, *i.e.* some weak interference signals may not be captured by our measurement receivers. This is because when computing SINR values used to build estimated graphs, we ignore interferers whose signals are not captured by the dataset.

Can We Identify Extraneous Edges? Since extraneous edges make up most of our observed edge errors, it is tempting to try to identify those edges in the estimated conflict graph and correct them. After carefully examining our traces, we found no distinctive characteristics that distinguish extraneous edges from correct edges. For example, Figure 8 plots the value of p_{ij} (defined by Eq. (1)) for each node pair i and j, calculated from the predicted signal strength distribution. We use different markers to separate the correct and extraneous edges. We see that there is no clear distinction between the two sets.

4.3 Summary of Findings

Our graph accuracy analysis reveals two key findings:

Estimated conflict graphs are conservative. The large majority of errors are extraneous edges; estimated graphs rarely miss edges (<2%).

Location-dependent signal prediction errors are the main cause of extraneous edges. The location-dependent error pattern in signal prediction triggers under-prediction of more than 70+% of SINR values, and is the main cause of extraneous edge errors.

5. IMPACT ON SPECTRUM ALLOCATION

After examining the accuracy of estimated conflict graphs at graph level, we now quantify the end-to-end impact of such graph errors on spectrum market users. Also, given the lack of representation of accumulative interference in conflict graphs, we aim to understand how such artifact affects the quality of the allocated spectrum. For this, we distribute spectrum using both measured and estimated conflict graphs, and evaluate end-to-end performance in terms of the efficiency of spectrum utilization and link reliability of allocated spectrum.

5.1 Spectrum Allocation Benchmarks

To translate conflict graphs into actual spectrum allocations, we use two representative allocation algorithms. Both seek to efficiently distribute a given spectrum range across the market users, while ensuring that no conflicting users receive the same spectrum band.

- *Single channel allocation (SCA)* seeks to allocate equal amount of continuous spectrum frequencies to each spectrum market user. This problem reduces to the well-known graph-coloring problem, which uses the minimal number of channels to ensure that each market user receives one channel and does not conflict with another [38]. The fewer the number of channels required, the greater the bandwidth assigned to each channel.
- *Multi-channel allocation (MCA)* divides the spectrum range into a large number of channels. Each market user can receive multiple channels even if they are not continuously aligned in frequency [10]. MCA distributes the channels across market users to maximize a predefined system utility, *e.g.* proportional fairness [10].

We evaluate the resulting spectrum allocation based on:

- *Spectrum efficiency*: the average amount of spectrum received per market user, normalized by the available spectrum. We calculate it by counting the number of channels the market user receives and the frequency bandwidth of each channel.
- *Spectrum reliability*: whether each market user actually receives exclusive spectrum usage. A market user has received exclusive usage if on each assigned channel, the percentage of receivers whose actual SINRs exceed β is no less than γ. This is to evaluate the actual outcome of spectrum usage in terms of end-user coverage. For our purposes, we use *network-level spectrum reliability*, which is defined as the percentage of market users receiving exclusive spectrum usage.

Given a spectrum allocation, we use our full dataset to calculate the actual SINR observed at each market user's receiver locations. The actual SINRs of each user include interference accumulated from *all* other market users operating on the same channel, which captures the true performance perceived by any allocated market user. While it is well known that the lack of coverage on accumulative interference will affect spectrum allocations under conflict graphs, our goal is to understand the severity of such degradation, and seek solutions to effectively suppress them.

5.2 Spectrum Allocation Results

Spectrum Efficiency. Figure 9 compares the spectrum efficiency of using the measured and estimated conflict graphs in allocating spectrum. Because extraneous conflict edges will prevent some non-conflicting users from reusing spectrum, spectrum efficiency using estimated graphs is lower than that of the measured graph. The efficiency loss, however, never exceeds 30%, even for cases where estimated graphs introduce 40%–60% extra edges (those with $\gamma = 0.8$). The loss of efficiency also reduces as γ increases, because the amount of extraneous edges reduces significantly. As before, the Street model outperforms the other models modestly because of its higher accuracy in signal prediction, which leads to less edge errors in the resulted conflict graph.

Spectrum Reliability. Using the actual SINR as the metric, we now examine the link reliability of the allocated spectrum. As expected, we see from Figure 10 that the reliability is not 100% for both allocation algorithms. Unless $\gamma = 1$, the measured conflict graph makes 10–50% of market

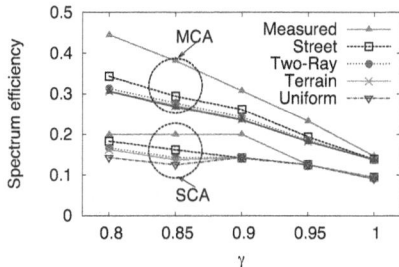

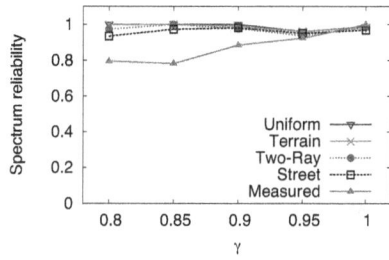

(a) SCA

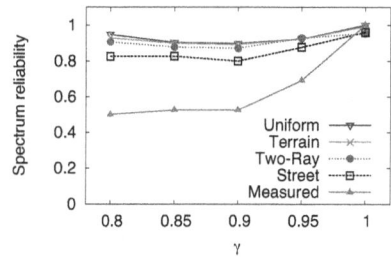

(b) MCA

Figure 9: Spectrum efficiency using measured and estimated conflict graphs to distribute spectrum. The use of estimated conflict graphs leads to spectrum efficiency loss, which is bounded by 30% and becomes negligible as γ approaches 1.

Figure 10: Spectrum reliability when using measured and estimated conflict graphs to distribute spectrum. The reliability is between 80%-98% for the estimated graph and drops to 50% for the measured conflict graph. This indicates that the impact of accumulative interference is noticeable and it is not captured by these conflict graphs.

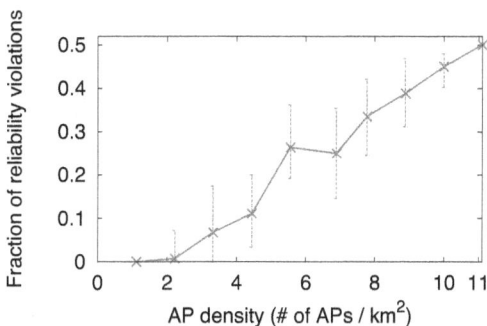

Figure 11: Reliability violations increase with the AP density. $\gamma = 0.9$, using measured conflict graphs. For the GoogleWiFi dataset, the AP density is 11 APs per km^2.

users unsatisfactory. In comparison, the estimated graphs actually lead to more reliable spectrum usage for market users because of having extraneous edges. In this regard, the extraneous-edge errors help ensure spectrum reliability.

The results demonstrate that accumulative interference does cause noticeable impact on the spectrum usage. Because interference experienced by a receiver is the accumulative sum of signals from transmitters operating on the same frequency band, the higher the spectrum reuse in the neighborhood, the higher the level of accumulative interference. When using the measured conflict graph, the spectrum reuse level is very high, *e.g.* 30 market users per channel for $\gamma = 0.8$. Therefore the effect of accumulative interference is significant. As γ increases, the reuse level decreases, and so does the effect of accumulative interference. For estimated conflict graphs, their conservative allocation from extraneous conflict edges reduces spectrum reuse, and thus the level of accumulative interference. This effect also motivates us to further examine the conditions under which accumulative interference would be a prevalent effect.

How Prevalent Is Accumulative Interference? In contrast to our results, prior work on a 32-node network reports that accumulative interference has negligible effect on wireless transmissions [11]. This begs the question: under what conditions will accumulative interference matter? To answer this, we first examine the spatial locations of the

market users with reliability violations in our GoogleWiFi dataset. We see that most of them are clustered in the center of the physical area with high market user density. This indicates that node density is a large contributing factor.

To examine the impact of node density, we build a set of new market configurations by sampling the APs in GoogleWiFi dataset uniformly, while keeping each AP's coverage area unchanged. For each new configuration, we build a conflict graph from the exhaustive signal measurements, and examine its reliability using the MCA allocation. Figure 11 shows the percentage of market users with reliability violations, which grows with the AP density. For the current GoogleWiFi network, the average density is 11 APs per km^2, which is common for municipal wireless networks. Thus we conclude that accumulative interference does matter in many current and future wireless deployments. We must address such artifact in order to use conflict graphs in practice.

6. GRAPH AUGMENTATION

The spectrum reliability violations we found for both measured and estimated conflict graphs are clearly undesirable for the practical deployment of spectrum markets. In this section, we seek for solutions to eliminate the artifact of accumulative interference for both conflict graphs. This ensures exclusive spectrum usage with reasonable level of reliability, addressing the key concerns on conflict graphs and promoting their practical usage.

6.1 Challenges

To reduce the impact of accumulative interference, one intuitive method is to augment the existing conflict graphs by adding more edges and making them more conservative. This essentially reduces the number of users who get allocated with the same spectrum channel, thus the amount of accumulative interference. However, adding more edges inevitably leads to loss in spectrum efficiency. Hence the key challenge is to minimize the number of edge additions while eliminating the artifact of accumulative interference.

To show the level of difficulty in this task, let us begin with two straw-man solutions. The first solution is to randomly add edges to unconnected node pairs (referred to as *Random*). A smarter alternative is to first sort unconnected node pairs by the physical distance between their transmit-

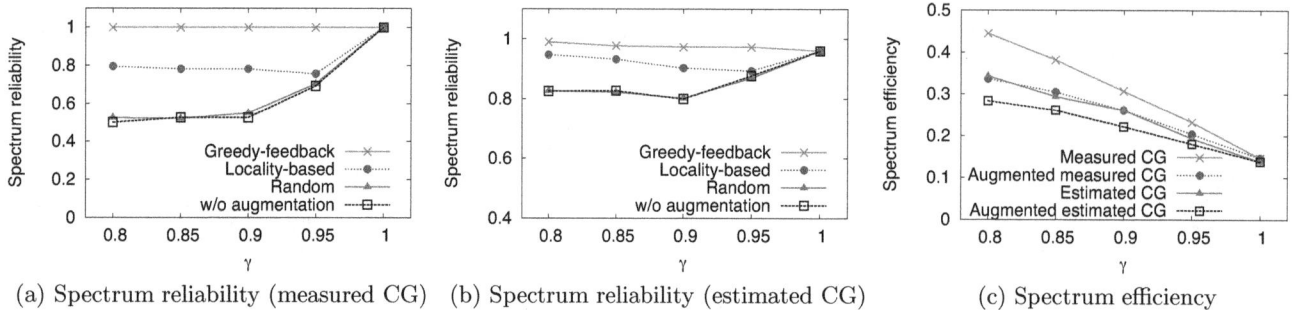

(a) Spectrum reliability (measured CG) (b) Spectrum reliability (estimated CG) (c) Spectrum efficiency

Figure 12: The performance of graph augmentation. The estimated graphs are generated from the Street model. (a)-(b) Spectrum reliability results before and after graph augmentation, using different augmentation algorithms (Greedy-Feedback, Locality-based, and Random). Greedy-Feedback is highly effective, and outperforms the other two. (c) Spectrum efficiency before and after graph augmentation via Greedy-Feedback. The improvement in reliability is at the cost of slightly degraded spectrum efficiency. The gap between measured and estimated graphs reduces to less than 15% after augmentation.

ters, and only add edges to the top-K closest node pairs. We refer to this approach as *Locality-based augmentation*. While simple, these two solutions face two drawbacks: 1) each added edge might not effectively reduce accumulative interference; and 2) it is difficult to determine the correct number of edges to add.

6.2 Greedy-Feedback Graph Augmentation

We overcome the above challenge by proposing a greedy algorithm to gradually and intelligently add edges. This algorithm stops adding edges when the (estimated) reliability reaches 100%, assuming wireless interference is the only source of reliability loss. Because the level of accumulative interference depends on the spectrum allocation algorithm, we integrate graph augmentation with spectrum allocation.

More specifically, the augmentation procedure works as follows. After allocating spectrum using the current conflict graph, we examine the reliability performance of each node, and identify the node i with the lowest reliability and its worst channel m. Next, we find node j, who is currently allocated with channel m, and whose removal will lead to the largest reliability improvement at i. We then add an edge between node i and j, and repeat the above process until all nodes have met the reliability requirement γ.

We use this approach to augment both measured and estimated conflict graphs. The only difference is that when augmenting a measured graph, we compute reliability using the real signal strength map. In contrast, we augment estimated graphs by estimating reliability from the predicted signal strength map.

6.3 Evaluation Results

We evaluate the effectiveness of our augmentation algorithm by comparing spectrum reliability and efficiency before and after augmentation. Our evaluation uses the MCA allocation since it suffers more accumulative interference.

Effectiveness of Graph Augmentation. In Figure 12(a)-(b), we first compare the three augmentation techniques in terms of spectrum reliability. For a fair comparison, we apply Random and Locality-based augmentation to add the same number of edges as that of Greedy-Feedback.

Greedy-Feedback graph augmentation is highly effective and significantly outperforms the other two techniques. It

completely removes the impact of accumulative interference on the measured conflict graph, and boosts the reliability of the estimated graphs to 96+%. The reliability of estimated graphs is not always 100%, because the augmentation algorithm relies on reliability predictions from signal strength estimates. In contrast, Random graph augmentation leads to no visible improvement on reliability while Locality-based augmentation is half way between Random and Greedy-Feedback.

By adding edges, graph augmentation does lead to lower spectrum efficiency. From Figure 12(c), we see that by using Greedy-Feedback, we get relative efficiency loss between 0–25% for the measured graph and 0–15% for the estimated graphs. The loss for the estimated graphs is lower because it adds less number of edges. We see that the proposed graph augmentation is effective against accumulative interference.

We also observe that graph augmentation has no effect when $\gamma = 1$. This is because both types of conflict graphs already contain a large number of edges (440+). The resulting spectrum allocation has very limited reuse across users, and the impact of accumulative interference is negligible.

Accuracy of Augmented Conflict Graphs. Applying graph augmentation to our measured conflict graph produces an *ideal* conflict graph, one that captures real conflicts and the impact of accumulative interference. We now look at how close the augmented, estimated conflict graph is relative to this ideal graph. Figure 13(a) plots the normalized edge errors of the estimated graphs after graph augmentation. The ratios of extraneous edges reduce from 5%–60% (Figure 7(a)) to 5%–40%, while the ratios of missing edges remain similar. This is because the augmentation on the measured graph adds more edges, and some of these edges already appear in the estimated graph.

Finally, we look at the spectrum efficiency and reliability of the estimated graph after augmentation, and see that both have improved relative to the ideal graph. Figure 13(b)-(c) show that the use of estimated conflict graphs achieves nearly 100% spectrum reliability and only leads to at most 21% loss in spectrum efficiency. Overall, we see that the Street model is the most efficient ($\leq 15\%$ efficiency loss, 96+% reliability) among the four propagation models.

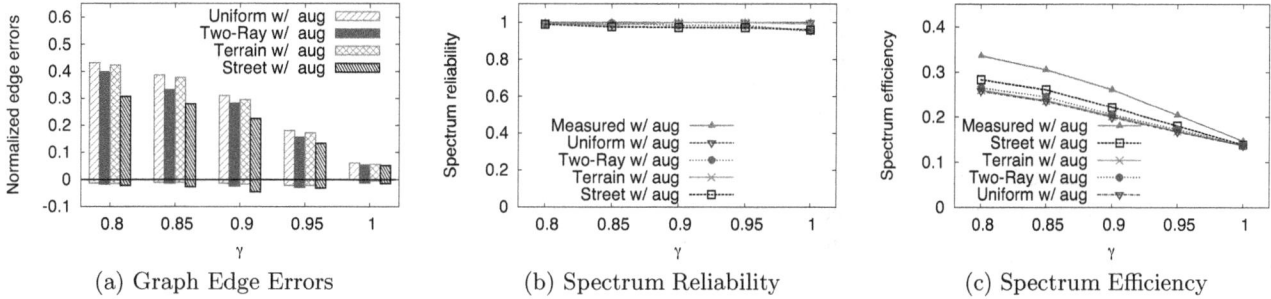

| (a) Graph Edge Errors | (b) Spectrum Reliability | (c) Spectrum Efficiency |

Figure 13: Accuracy of augmented estimated conflict graphs using the four propagation models, compared to the ideal conflict graph. (a) The edge errors reduce considerably with graph augmentation. (b) The reliability of using estimated graphs in spectrum allocation increases to 96+%. (c) The efficiency loss of using estimated graphs reduces to no more than 21%.

Key Findings.   We summarize the key results on graph augmentation as the following two findings:

- **Graph augmentation is effective against accumulative interference.** Proper graph augmentation effectively boosts spectrum reliability to 96-100%, while maintaining spectrum efficiency.

- **Augmentation improves the accuracy of estimated conflict graphs.** Augmentation reduces the difference between measured and estimated conflict graphs. Using estimated graphs in spectrum allocation results in only 15% or less loss in spectrum efficiency.

7. DISCUSSION

We discuss possible extensions of our methodology beyond the scenarios covered by our study.

Temporal Signal Variations.   Our work focuses on the long-term impact of interference by considering the average signal values. To understand the impact of temporal signal variations, we can adapt the conflict graphs based on periodical sensor measurements. For applications that must consider fast signal fading, the conflict edge can be determined using the outage SINR, the bottom x% of SINR observed within a certain time period. Examining the accuracy of such conflict graphs is an interesting future study.

Incorporating MAC Protocols.   Our analysis does not consider the impact of MAC protocols because in the exclusive usage scenario, a spectrum market user can use any MAC protocol [3, 50]. However, for scenarios where all the users adopt the same MAC protocol, one can integrate a traffic-driven model [25, 43] into the conflict graph.

8. RELATED WORK

Conflict Graphs and Interference Models.   We divide existing works into two categories based on the type of conflict graphs they use. The first category uses per-link signal measurements to capture interference conditions among individual links, using either active measurements [5, 6, 26, 33, 34, 37, 39, 43], or passive measurements [8, 21, 28, 45]. These link-based conflict graphs are for indoor WiFi networks where transmission links are known a priori. They are impractical for outdoor networks with mobile users that spectrum markets target.

The second category of works builds coverage-based conflict graphs based on propagation models, either with rule-of-thumb parameters [18, 32, 48], or calibrated by on-site measurements [24]. However, no one has used real-world measurements to evaluate the conflict graph accuracy. Our work is the first measurement study on this problem. We use both graph and spectrum allocation analysis to understand the feasibility of building accurate coverage-based conflict graphs for dynamic spectrum distribution.

Aside from conflict graphs, recent work examines the accuracy of general interference models for small-scale networks using per-link measurements [27]. Our work was inspired by this work, yet focuses on large-scale outdoor networks where per-link measurement is infeasible. We use conflict graphs as interference models because they are widely used by spectrum allocation solutions. Our methodology can be extended to other interference models such as SINR [9, 47].

Measurement-calibrated Propagation Models.   Measurement studies show that RF propagation models with rule-of-thumb parameters introduce large errors in signal strength estimation [14, 23, 36]. When calibrated using on-site measurements, however, these propagation models offer higher accuracy, and have been used in cell planning [19, 29], interference management [40] and coverage prediction [31, 42]. Our work complements these prior works, and is also inspired by prior work on measurement-calibrated models for social network graphs [44].

9. CONCLUSION

Using large-scale signal measurements, we examined the severity of two key concerns on using conflict graphs for dynamic spectrum distribution. We focused on conflict graphs built from measurement-calibrated propagation models, and studied their accuracy and the end-to-end impact on spectrum allocation. We found that the resulting "estimated conflict graphs" are conservative compared to precise conflict graphs built from exhaustive signal measurements. Yet surprisingly, these extraneous edges improve link reliability by alleviating the impact of accumulative interference, an artifact not captured by conflict graphs. We proposed a graph augmentation technique to suppress the impact of accumulative interference. With this new technique, estimated conflict graphs can produce spectrum allocations that provide near-perfect link reliability, with spectrum efficiency less than 15% away from the ideal allocation. We believe that for the WiFi frequencies studied by this paper, (and their nearby frequencies), our proposed techniques address existing concerns on conflict graphs, and provide a scalable and accurate end-to-end solution for spectrum allocation.

10. ACKNOWLEDGMENTS

We thank the anonymous reviewers for their helpful feedback, and Lei Yang for his help with the measurements. This work was supported in part by NSF grants CNS-0905667 and CNS-0915699.

11. REFERENCES

[1] Coverage or capacity? best use of 802.11n. Trapeze Networks Whitepaper.

[2] MetroFi. http://crawdad.cs.dartmouth.edu/pdx/metrofi/2007/coverage.

[3] Secondary markets in radio spectrum. http://www.fcc.gov/events/secondary-markets-radio-spectrum.

[4] TFA. http://tfa.rice.edu/measurements/.

[5] AHMED, N., ISMAIL, U., AND KESHAV, S. Online estimation of RF interference. In Proc. of CoNEXT (2008).

[6] AHMED, N., AND KESHAV, S. SMARTA: a self-managing architecture for thin access points. In Proc. of CoNEXT (2006).

[7] ALICHERRY, M., BHATIA, R., AND LI, L. E. Joint channel assignment and routing for throughput optimization in multi-radio wireless mesh networks. In Proc. of MobiCom (2005).

[8] CAI, K., ET AL. Non-intrusive, dynamic interference detection for 802.11 networks. In Proc. of IMC (2009).

[9] CAO, L., ET AL. Optimus: SINR-Driven Spectrum Distribution via Constraint Transformation. In Proc. of DySPAN (2010).

[10] CAO, L., AND ZHENG, H. Distributed spectrum allocation via local bargaining. In Proc. of SECON (2005).

[11] DAS, S. M., ET AL. Characterizing multi-way interference in wireless mesh networks. In Proc. of WiNTECH (2006).

[12] DEB, S., SRINIVASAN, V., AND MAHESHWARI, R. Dynamic spectrum access in DTV whitespaces: design rules, architecture and algorithms. In Proc. of MobiCom (2009).

[13] GANDHI, S., BURAGOHAIN, C., CAO, L., ZHENG, H., AND SURI, S. A general framework for wireless spectrum auctions. In Proc. of DySPAN (2007).

[14] GOLDSMITH, A. Wireless communications. Cambridge Univ Pr.

[15] GOLDSMITH, A., AND GREENSTEIN, L. A measurement-based model for predicting coverage areas of urban microcells. IEEE JSAC 11, 7 (1993).

[16] GREEN, E. Radio link design for microcellular systems. British Telecom technology journal 8, 1 (1990), 85–96.

[17] GREEN, E., AND HATA, M. Microcellular propagation measurements in an urban environment. In Proc. of PIMRC (1991).

[18] HAAS, Z., WINTERS, J., AND JOHNSON, D. Simulation study of the capacity bounds in cellular systems. In PIMRC/WCN (1994).

[19] HURLEY, S. Planning effective cellular mobile radio networks. IEEE TVT 51, 2 (2002), 243–253.

[20] JAIN, K., PADHYE, J., PADMANABHAN, V. N., AND QIU, L. Impact of interference on multi-hop wireless network performance. In Proc. of MobiCom (2003).

[21] JANG, K.-Y., ET AL. Passive on-line in-band interference inference in centralized WLANs. In Tech. Rep. 916, USC (2010).

[22] KATZELA, I., AND NAGHSHINEH, M. Channel assignment schemes for cellular mobile telecommunication systems: a comprehensive survey. Personal Communications, IEEE 3, 3 (1996), 10 –31.

[23] KOTZ, D., ET AL. Experimental evaluation of wireless simulation assumptions. In Proc. of MSWiM (2004).

[24] KUURNE, A. Mobile measurement based frequency planning in GSM networks. MS thesis, Helsinki University of Technology (2001).

[25] LI, Y., ET AL. Predictable performance optimization for wireless networks. In Proc. of SIGCOMM (2008).

[26] LIU, X., ET AL. DIRC: Increasing indoor wireless capacity using directional antennas. In Proc. of SIGCOMM (2009).

[27] MAHESHWARI, R., JAIN, S., AND DAS, S. R. A measurement study of interference modeling and scheduling in low-power wireless networks. In Proc. of SenSys (2008).

[28] MANWEILER, J., ET AL. Order matters: Interference-aware transmission reordering in wireless networks. In Proc. of MobiCom (2009).

[29] MISHRA, A. Fundamentals of cellular network planning and optimisation. Wiley Online Library, 2004.

[30] MOSCIBRODA, T., WATTENHOFER, R., AND WEBER, Y. Protocol design beyond graph-based models. In Proc. of HotNets (2006).

[31] MURTY, R., ET AL. SenseLess: A database-driven white spaces network. In Proc. of DySPAN (2011).

[32] NECKER, M. C. Towards frequency reuse 1 cellular FDM/TDM systems. In Proc. of MSWiM (2006).

[33] NICULESCU, D. Interference map for 802.11 networks. In Proc. of IMC (2007).

[34] PADHYE, J., ET AL. Estimation of link interference in static multi-hop wireless networks. In Proc. of IMC (2005).

[35] PENG, C., ZHENG, H., AND ZHAO, B. Y. Utilization and fairness in spectrum assignment for opportunistic spectrum access. MONET 11, 4 (2006), 555–576.

[36] PHILLIPS, C., SICKER, D., AND GRUNWALD, D. Bounding the error of path loss models. In Proc. of DySPAN (2011).

[37] QIU, L., ET AL. A general model of wireless interference. In Proc. of MobiCom (2007).

[38] RAMANATHAN, S. A unified framework and algorithm for channel assignment in wireless networks. Wirel. Netw. 5, 2 (1999), 81–94.

[39] RAYANCHU, S., ET AL. FLUID: improving throughputs in enterprise wireless LANs through flexible channelization. In Proc. of MobiCom (2011).

[40] REIS, C., ET AL. Measurement-based models of delivery and interference in static wireless networks. In Proc. of SIGCOMM (2006).

[41] RIBACK, M., ET AL. Carrier frequency effects on path loss. In Proc. of VTC (2006).

[42] ROBINSON, J., SWAMINATHAN, R., AND KNIGHTLY, E. W. Assessment of urban-scale wireless networks with a small number of measurements. In Proc. of MobiCom (2008).

[43] ROZNER, E., ET AL. Traffic-aware channel assignment in enterprise wireless networks. In Proc. of ICNP (2007).

[44] SALA, A., CAO, L., WILSON, C., ZABLIT, R., ZHENG, H., AND ZHAO, B. Y. Measurement-calibrated graph models for social network experiments. In Proc. of WWW (2010).

[45] SHRIVASTAVA, V., ET AL. PIE in the sky: Online passive interference estimation for enterprise WLANs. In Proc. of NSDI (2011).

[46] SONG, L., AND SHEN, J. Evolved cellular network planning and optimization for UMTS and LTE. CRC Press, 2010.

[47] SUBRAMANIAN, P., ET AL. Near-optimal dynamic spectrum allocation in cellular networks. In Proc. of DySPAN (2008).

[48] YANG, L., CAO, L., AND ZHENG, H. Physical interference driven dynamic spectrum management. In Proc. of DySPAN (2008).

[49] YOUNIS, M., AND AKKAYA, K. Strategies and techniques for node placement in wireless sensor networks: A survey. Ad Hoc Networks 6, 4 (2008), 621 – 655.

[50] ZHOU, X., GANDHI, S., SURI, S., AND ZHENG, H. eBay in the sky: Strategy-proof wireless spectrum auctions. In Proc. of MobiCom (2008).

A First Look at Cellular Network Performance during Crowded Events

M. Zubair Shafiq[†], Lusheng Ji[‡], Alex X. Liu[†], Jeffrey Pang[‡], Shobha Venkataraman[‡], Jia Wang[‡]
[†]Department of Computer Science and Engineering, Michigan State University, East Lansing, MI, USA
[‡]AT&T Labs – Research, Florham Park, NJ, USA
{shafiqmu,alexliu}@cse.msu.edu, {lji,jeffpang,shvenk,jiawang}@research.att.com

ABSTRACT

During crowded events, cellular networks face voice and data traffic volumes that are often orders of magnitude higher than what they face during routine days. Despite the use of portable base stations for temporarily increasing communication capacity and free Wi-Fi access points for offloading Internet traffic from cellular base stations, crowded events still present significant challenges for cellular network operators looking to reduce dropped call events and improve Internet speeds. For effective cellular network design, management, and optimization, it is crucial to understand how cellular network performance degrades during crowded events, what causes this degradation, and how practical mitigation schemes would perform in real-life crowded events. This paper makes a first step towards this end by characterizing the operational performance of a tier-1 cellular network in the United States during two high-profile crowded events in 2012. We illustrate how the changes in population distribution, user behavior, and application workload during crowded events result in significant voice and data performance degradation, including more than two orders of magnitude increase in connection failures. Our findings suggest two mechanisms that can improve performance without resorting to costly infrastructure changes: radio resource allocation tuning and opportunistic connection sharing. Using trace-driven simulations, we show that more aggressive release of radio resources via 1-2 seconds shorter RRC timeouts as compared to routine days helps to achieve better tradeoff between wasted radio resources, energy consumption, and delay during crowded events; and opportunistic connection sharing can reduce connection failures by 95% when employed by a small number of devices in each cell sector.

Categories and Subject Descriptors

C.2.3 [**Computer System Organization**]: Computer Communication Networks—*Network Operations*

Keywords

Cellular Network; Crowded Events; Performance

1. INTRODUCTION

Crowded events, such as football games, public demonstrations, and political protests, put an extremely high demand for communication capacity on cellular networks around the duration of the events [5]. Cellular networks are facing unprecedent challenges in dealing with such spiky demand. First, cellular network utilization has already been rapidly approaching its full capacity throughout the world due to the increasing prevalence of cellular devices such as smartphones, tablets, and Machine-to-Machine (M2M) devices. Even in the United States, cellular network usage is at an all-time high even under normal operating conditions and projections show that traffic volume will further increase by 26 times by 2015 as compared to 2010 [3, 4]. Second, the spiky demand caused by crowded events is often extremely high because there maybe a large number (often tens of thousands) of users gathered in a small region (such as a football stadium) that is covered by only a small number of cell towers. Even worse, people tend to use their cellular devices more than usual during the events to either talk with their friends or access the Internet (such as uploading a photo to Facebook or a video clip to YouTube during a football game). Third, it is critical for cellular networks to cope with such high demand during crowded events because poor performance will affect a large number of people and cause widespread user dissatisfaction. Although cellular network operators have deployed remediation solutions, such as portable base stations called Cells on Wheels (COWs) for temporarily increasing communication capacity and free Wi-Fi access points for offloading Internet traffic from cellular base stations, crowded events still remain a major challenge for cellular network operators.

To the best of our knowledge, this paper presents the first thorough investigation of cellular network performance during crowded events. Based on the real-world voice and data traces that we collected from a tier-1 cellular network in the United States during two high-profile crowded events in 2012, we aim to answer the following three key questions.

• **How does cellular network performance degrade during crowded events as compared to routine days?** To answer this question, we characterize cellular network performance during both the pre- and post-connection phases, which helps us to understand user experience before and after acquiring radio resources. For pre-connection phase, we find that pre-connection failures dramatically increase during the crowded events by 100-5000 times as compared to their average on routine days. These failures occur because when too many users attempt to acquire radio resources at the same time, they exhaust the limited bandwidth of the signaling channel resulting in connection timeouts and failures. We find that this resource exhaustion occurs not only at the event venue, but also as far as 10 miles around the event as users arrive and depart. Moreover, some failures, such as dropped and blocked voice calls, are most likely to occur in bursts just before, after, and during event intermissions. For post-connection phase, we find that voice network performance in terms of dropped and blocked calls degrades during crowded events by 7-30 times, and data network performance in terms of packet loss ratio and round trip time (RTT) degrades during crowded events by 1.5-7 times, compared to their average on routine days.

• **What causes the performance degradation?**
To answer this question, we analyze user traffic patterns in terms of both aggregate network load and user-level session characteristics. For aggregate network load, we find that uplink traffic volume increases by 4-8 times, and both downlink traffic volume and the number of users increase by 3 times, during the crowded events as compared to their average on routine days. We conclude that the large number of users trying to access radio resources at the same time is a major cause of the observed excessive pre-connection failures. For user-level session characteristics, we find that the average byte volume per session decreases by 0.5 times during the events even though the average session length increases. Our investigation suggests that this change in workload is due to a change in application usage during these events, such as the increased use of online social networks. We conclude that lower byte volume per session, despite an increase in average session length, is a major cause of the waste of radio resources in the post-connection phase.

• **How would practical mitigation schemes perform in real-life?**
To answer this question, we investigate two practical mitigation schemes that do not require making significant changes to the cellular infrastructure: radio resource allocation tuning and opportunistic connection sharing. Radio resource allocation tuning addresses the issue of inefficient radio resource allocation in the post-connection phase by adjusting cellular network resource allocation parameters. Cellular networks allocate resources to each user using a Radio Resource Control (RRC) state machine, which is synchronously maintained by the network and devices. Different states of the RRC state machine correspond to different amount of radio resources allocated by the network and energy consumption by cellular devices. Since a large number of users contend for limited radio resources during crowded events, we show that more aggressive release of radio resources via 1-2 seconds shorter RRC timeouts helps to achieve a better tradeoff between wasted radio resources, energy consumption, and delay during crowded events. Note that cellular network operators often know the time and location of large crowded events beforehand; thus, it is practical for them to adjust cellular network parameters before events and restore them after events. Opportunistic connection sharing addresses increased pre-connection failures by aggregating traffic from multiple devices into a single cellular connection. That is, by having some devices share their cellular connection with nearby devices over their Wi-Fi or Bluetooth interface (i.e., "tethering"), opportunistic connection sharing should reduce the number of overall cellular connec-

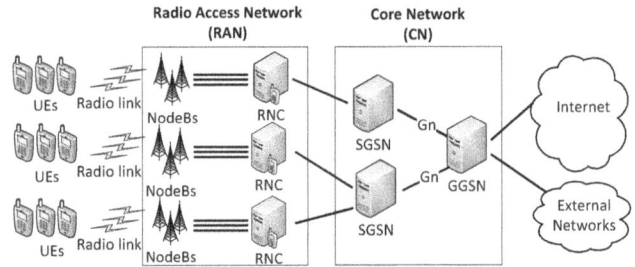

Figure 1: Cellular network architecture

tion requests, thereby reducing request congestion and connection failures. Using trace-driven simulations, we show that connection sharing can reduce connection failures by more than 95% when employed by a small number of devices in each cell sector. Although much work has been done on opportunistic connection sharing to address issues such as mobility, energy use, and incentives [1, 11, 17], no prior work has demonstrated the significant benefit that such connection sharing can achieve based on real-life cellular network data.

The rest of this paper is organized as follows. In Section 2, we present details of the data collection process. Section 3 presents the characterization of performance issues during the crowded events and Section 4 presents various aspects of user traffic patterns to study the underlying causes of performance issues. We conduct trace-driven simulations to evaluate radio network parameter tuning and opportunistic connection sharing in Section 5. Section 6 reviews related work and the paper is concluded in Section 7.

2. DATA SET

2.1 Background

A typical cellular network, shown in Figure 1, can be visualized as consisting of two major components: Radio Access Network (RAN) and Core Network (CN). RAN consists of NodeBs and Radio Network Controllers (RNCs). Each NodeB has multiple antennas, where each antenna corresponds to a different cell sector. CN consists of Serving GPRS Support Nodes (SGSNs) facing the user and Gateway GPRS Support Nodes (GGSNs) facing the Internet and other external networks. A user via user equipment (UE) connects to one or more cell sectors in the RAN. The traffic generated by a UE is sent to the corresponding NodeB by cell sectors. Each RNC controls and exchanges traffic with multiple NodeBs, each of which serves many users in its coverage area. RNCs manage control signaling such as Radio Access Bearer (RAB) assignments, transmission scheduling, and handovers. RNCs send traffic from NodeBs to SGSNs, which then send it to GGSNs. GGSNs eventually send traffic to external networks, such as the Internet.

RAN dynamically allocates resources to a UE. Specifically, every UE negotiates allocation of radio resources with the RAN based on a wide range of factors, such as available radio resources and signal strength [7]. Every UE follows the RRC protocol for dynamic acquisition and dropping of radio resources. The RRC state machine of each user is synchronously maintained by the UE and network. Different states in the RRC state machine correspond to different amounts of allocated radio resources by the network and en-

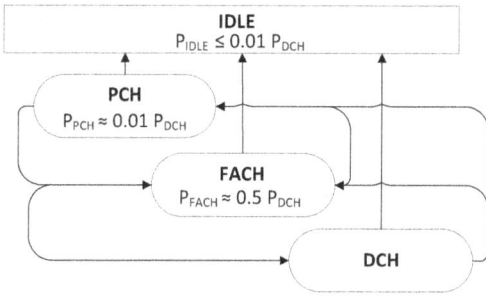

Figure 2: RRC protocol state transitions

ergy consumption by UEs. Figure 2 shows all RRC protocol state transitions. According to RRC protocol, a UE transitions to Dedicated Channel (DCH) state or Forward Access Channel (FACH) state for uplink or downlink data transfer. RAN assigns a dedicated or shared channel for DCH and FACH states, respectively. If a UE does not have any data to transfer, it transitions to Paging Channel (PCH) state before the transition to IDLE state. Generally, state promotions are controlled by data buffer size thresholds and state demotions are controlled by inactivity timeouts. Furthermore, the energy consumption by a UE is roughly inversely proportional to the amount of allocated radio resources. The energy consumption by a UE is maximum in DCH state, which is about halved when it transitions to FACH state, and is reduced to less than 1/100th in PCH and IDLE states [20].

2.2 Data Collection

The data set used in this study contains anonymized logs collected from RAN and CN of a tier-1 cellular network in the United States serving over 100 million customers. Our data set consists of two separate collections, each covering a metropolitan area during a high-profile event in 2012. The collections include information from hundreds of thousands of users and thousands of cell locations over multiple days including the event days. The first event, referred to as Event A hereafter, is a sporting event that consists of two segments of activities separated by an intermission. The second event, referred to as Event B hereafter, is a conference event that consists of multiple segments of activities separated by intermissions of varying lengths. In terms of publicly available attendance statistics, event A is roughly twice the size of event B. The activity segments in both events are illustrated by gray bars in all timeseries figures presented in this paper. Furthermore, it is noteworthy that free Wi-Fi service was provided to all users during both of the events to offload as much cellular network traffic as possible. However, we do not have measurements on the network traffic that was offloaded to these Wi-Fi services; thus, we acknowledge that our results may be biased by this offloading.

The anonymized logs collected at an RNC in RAN contain throughput and RRC protocol request/response information. Using RRC requests from UEs and responses from the RNC, the RAB status of all UEs can be monitored. The anonymized logs collected from the CN contain TCP header information of IP flows carried in PDP context tunnels. They are collected from the Gn interfaces between SGSNs and GGSNs in the core network. They contain timestamp, per-flow traffic volume, content publisher, RTT computed during TCP handshake [13], and estimated packet loss ratio

for each TCP flow aggregated in 5 minute bins. All device and user identifiers (*e.g.*, IMSI, IMEI) are anonymized to protect privacy without affecting the usefulness of our analysis. The data set does not permit the reversal of the anonymization or re-identification of users. We note that logs collected at RNCs encompass both voice and data traffic, whereas logs collected from the CN contain only data traffic information.

Next, we characterize performance issues during the aforementioned two high-profile events in Section 3. To study the underlying causes of the identified performance issues, we then correlate network performance with various aspects of user traffic patterns in Section 4. Throughout, we present results of the event day in relation to a routine day for baseline comparison. We normalize the actual measurement values by their mean values on the routine day (unless stated otherwise); our results thus effectively represent how the event differs from routine conditions. We omit absolute numbers from some non-normalized plots due to proprietary reasons.

3. CHARACTERIZING PERFORMANCE ISSUES

Generally speaking, a user's experience about network performance can be divided into two phases. The *pre-connection phase* is characterized by the UE attempting to establish a connection with the cellular network, or in other words establishing a RAB. In this phase, the user waits for connection establishment, while not being able to exchange traffic at this time. The *post-connection phase* starts after a RAB is assigned. In this phase, user experience is related to more traditional voice call performance metrics such as call drop and block rate or end-to-end TCP performance metrics, such as delay and packet loss. Below, we separately discuss both pre- and post-connection network performance experienced by users during both events.

3.1 Pre-connection Network Performance

Users may experience difficulty in establishing RABs in the pre-connection phase due to a wide variety of reasons. Every time a request to allocate more radio resources is denied by the RNC, a RRC failure and its underlying reason is logged by our measurement apparatus. In our analysis, we study the logs of various types of RRC failures that are collected at the RNC. Each type of RRC failure corresponds to a specific problem in the cellular network operation. The 3 most common types of failures observed in our data set are the following.

1. *Radio link setup failures* occur when a user's request to setup a radio link is not served due to poor RF channel quality, which is often caused by increased interference.

2. *Radio link addition failures* occur when a user's request to add a radio link to an existing radio connection for soft handovers is denied.

3. *Too many serving cell users* indicates blocking for new users which results when all available RABs are occupied by existing users.

Figure 3 plots the timeseries of the most common types of RRC failures on the event and routine days for both events. We observe that RRC failures increase sharply on the event days, whereas they are negligible (and steady) on the routine days for both events. For both events, RRC failures

(a) Event A

(b) Event B

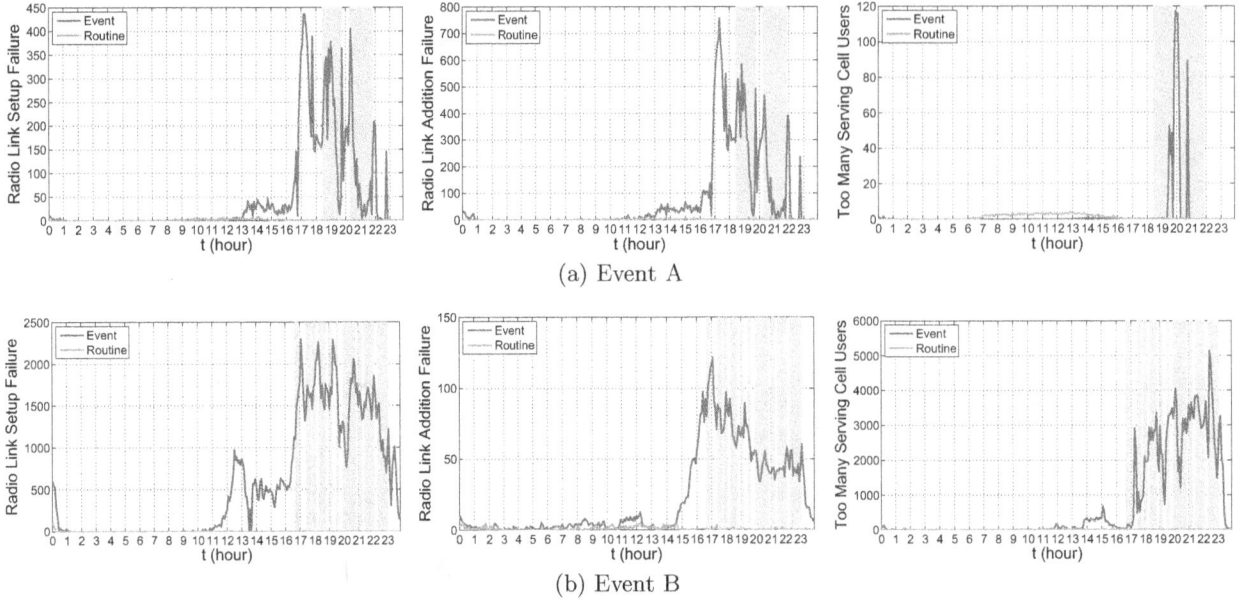

Figure 3: (Normalized) Timeseries of common types of RRC failures

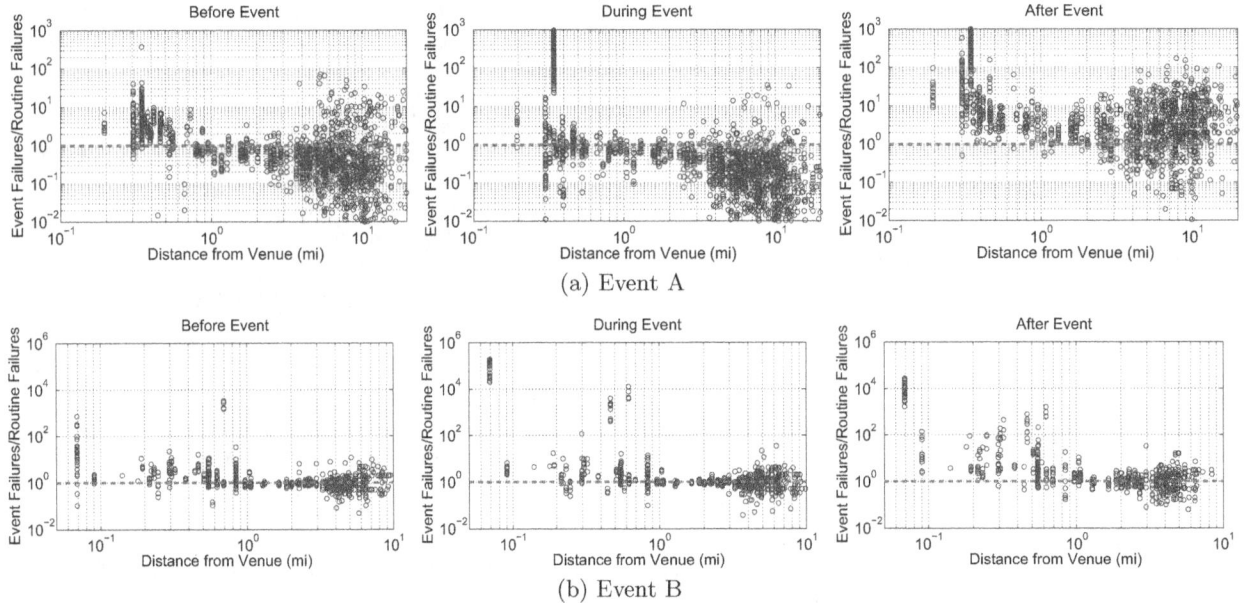

(a) Event A

(b) Event B

Figure 4: RRC failure ratios plotted as a function of distance to the venue and for time intervals before, during, and after the event

start occurring around noon and generally reach their peak either just before or during the event. Specifically, *radio link addition failures* peak at more than 700x their average on the routine day for event A and *too many serving cell users* peak at more than 5000x their average on the routine day for event B.

The nature of RRC failures for both events indicates that their potential root cause is high network load and congestion due to a large number of competing users at cell sector level. Therefore, we next analyze RRC failures at cell sector level before, during, and after the events as a function of distance from the venue. Figure 4 shows the scatter plots between the distance of cell sectors from the venue (in miles) and the ratio of the number of RRC failures on the event

day to that on the routine day. The horizontal dashed line at $y = 1$ is a reference for the data points where RRC failures on the event and routine days are equal. So the data points above the reference line represent cell sectors that have more RRC failures on the event day than the routine day. Likewise, the data points below the reference line represent cell sectors that have less RRC failures on the event day than the routine day. Both x- and y-axes are converted to logarithmic scale for the sake of clarity. Note that there are many cell sectors equidistant from the venue, especially those cell sectors that are close to the venue. These cell sectors are mounted at the same cell tower but face different directions, and have different tilt angles and frequencies.

(a) Event A

(b) Event B

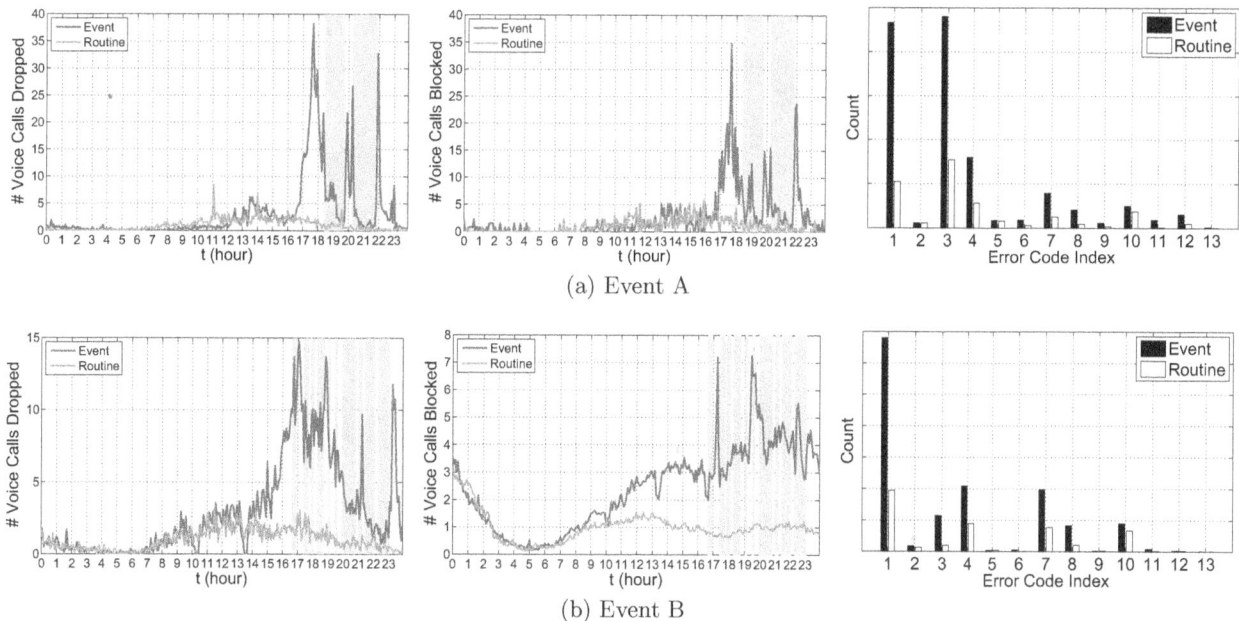

Figure 5: (Normalized) Voice performance measurements

Overall, we observe that cell sectors closer to the venue have 2-3 orders of magnitude more RRC failures on the event day than the routine day. The RRC failure ratios progressively decrease as the distance of cell sectors to the venue increases. For both events, we observe interesting dynamics across the scatter plots for time intervals before, during, and after the event. For event A, we observe that the failure ratios generally increase by 2-3 orders of magnitude for cell sectors less than half a mile from the venue throughout the event day. In contrast, for the cell sectors that are far from the venue, their failure ratios drop during the event and jump by 1-2 orders of magnitude after the event finishes. The aforementioned observations can be linked to the sporting nature of event A, where people swarm the venue before and during the event, creating a void in surrounding areas. The post-event jump in the failure ratio is likely correlated with most people leaving the venue and using their devices to share their experience with others via voice calls or social network posts (we show later in this section that the observed user activity supports this hypothesis). We observe similar trends for event B as well; however, the post-event jump in the failure ratio is clearly visible only for cells within 1 mile of the venue. For these reasons, while characterizing user network traffic in the next section, we focus our attention on the cell sectors that are within 1 mile radius of the venues for both events.

Summary: Pre-connection failures (especially those pertaining radio link addition and indicating too many serving cell users) peak by a factor of 700 (for event A) and 5000 (for event B) relative to their average on the routine days. These failures increase by 2-3 orders of magnitude in cell sectors very close to the venues before and during the events, but only increase in cell sectors further away after the venues.

3.2 Post-connection Network Performance

As discussed in Section 2, during the RAB setup phase, the RNC verifies that the needed radio resource for the request actually exists before it assigns a RAB. In other words,

Table 1: Description of voice call error codes

Index	Category	Description
1	Unspecified	All cases which do not map to the ones described below
2	Radio Connection Supervision	Radio Link Control (RLC) unrecoverable
3	Radio Connection Supervision	Maximum number of RLC retransmissions
4	Radio Connection Supervision	Expiry of timer
5	Radio Connection Supervision	Radio link failure indication
6	Operations & Management	Cell lock indication
7	Soft Handover	No active set addition update
8	Soft Handover	No active set deletion update
9	Soft Handover	No active set replacement update
10	Soft Handover	Cell not in the neighbor set
11	Soft Handover	High speed-downlink shared channel cell change failure
12	Inter-Frequency Handover	Inter-frequency handover failure
13	Channel Switching	Transition to DCH state not completed

if a device has successfully acquired a RAB for communication, its performance should theoretically remain acceptable per operator's configuration even if the overall network demand level exceeds network capacity. This is because excessive demand requests will get blocked off by the RNC from acquiring any RAB. However, network conditions can quickly change even for UEs that have already acquired a RAB because of factors such as interference, mobility, *etc.* Such dynamic network conditions can force UEs to request a change in current RAB status, initiating a series of RRC failures which could in turn result in degraded voice and data performance. Below, we separately discuss voice and data performance.

3.2.1 Voice Performance

To quantify voice performance, we study voice call drop and block rates for both events in Figure 5. Similar to our observations about pre-connection network performance, the

(a) Event A

(b) Event B

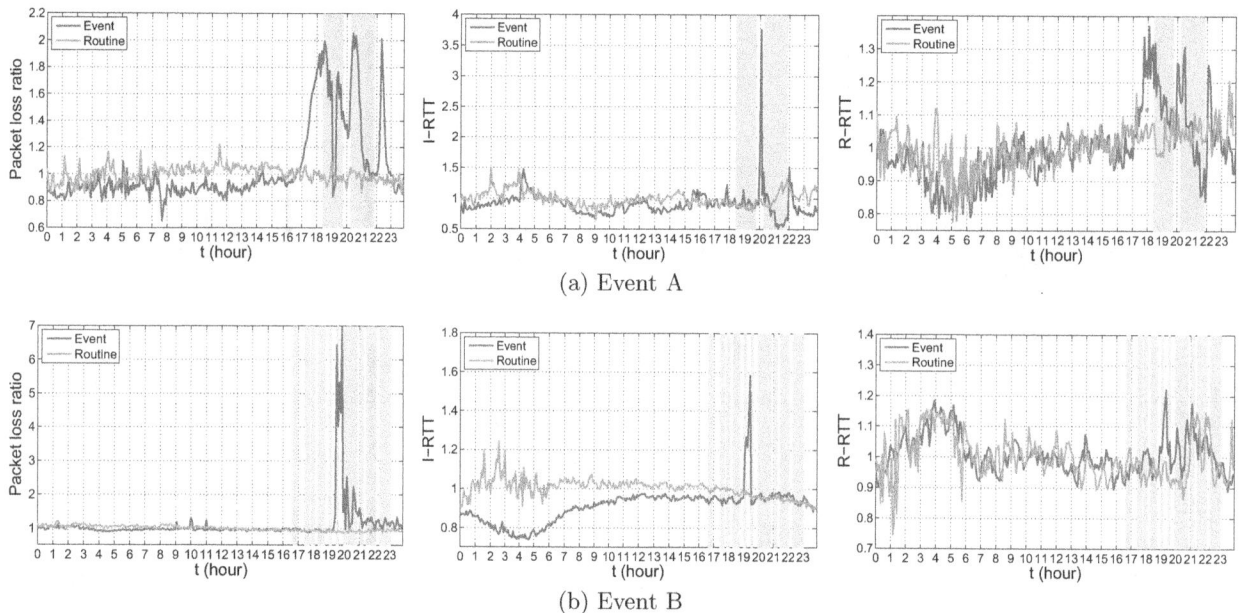

Figure 6: (Normalized) Data performance measurements

number of voice call drops and blocks increase substantially on the event days as compared to the routine days for both events. Specifically, we observe peak increases of more than 30x and 7x relative to their average on the routine days for events A and B, respectively. It is noteworthy that voice call drop and block rates peak just before the start of the events, during the intermissions, and at the end of the events. This observation is consistent with our expectation that users are less likely to make voice calls during event activities and more likely to make voice calls either before the start of events, after the end of events, or during intermissions between event activities. To further investigate the root causes of voice call blocks and drops, we also plot the histogram of their error codes in Figure 5. The error code descriptions in Table 1 indicate that the two most common categories of error codes for both events are related to radio connection supervision and soft handovers, which in turn point to interference and mobility as the root cause.

3.2.2 Data Performance

To quantify data performance, we study two key end-to-end TCP performance metrics: packet loss ratio and RTT for both events.[1] Packet loss ratio quantifies network reliability. We only have packet loss ratio measurements for TCP flows, which constitute approximately 95% of all flows in our data set. RTT quantifies network delay and is defined as the duration of time taken by a packet to reach the server from the UE plus the duration of time taken by a packet to reach the UE from the server. It is important to note that RTT measurements are biased by differences in the paths between different UEs and the external servers they communicate with. Similar to packet loss ratio measurements, we only have RTT measurements for TCP flows.

---

[1]Because end-to-end TCP performance also involves additional parameters such as back-haul bandwidth and even remote server load, we leave a more detailed investigation of TCP performance to future work.

RTT measurements for TCP flows are estimated by SYN, SYN-ACK, and ACK packets in the TCP handshake. In a cellular network, RTT essentially consists of two components: radio network RTT and Internet RTT. Radio network RTT (R-RTT) is the time duration between the SYN-ACK packet from server passing the Gn interface and the ACK packet from the UE passing the Gn interface. Internet RTT (I-RTT) is the time duration between the SYN packet from the UE passing the Gn interface and the SYN-ACK packet from the server passing the Gn interface. Thus, RTT = R-RTT + I-RTT.

Figure 6 shows the timeseries plots of packet loss ratio, Internet RTT, and radio network RTT for both events. Packet loss ratio peaks at 2x and 7x relative to its average on the routine days for events A and B, respectively. We observe different trends for radio network RTT and Internet RTT for both events. There is only a minor increase in radio network RTT on the event days. Internet RTT increases during the intermissions for both events; however, this increase indicates congestion at remote servers caused by increased event-driven traffic. Overall, data performance results indicate that users experience data connection performance issues to varying extents during the two events.

Summary: Post-connection performance degradation is observed for both voice and data network during the events. Specifically, voice call failures (dropped calls and call blocks) increase by a factor of as much as 30 (for event A) and 7 (for event B). Moreover, packet loss ratio increases by a factor of 2 (for event A) and 7 (for event B); while the RTT increases by a factor of 3.5 (for event A) and 1.5 (for event B). While these indicate a degradation in performance experienced by users already connected to the network, this is substantially smaller than the pre-connection failures discussed in Section 3.1. Overall, pre- and post-connection network performance results highlight that limited radio resources are the major bottleneck during crowded events.

(a) Event A

(b) Event B

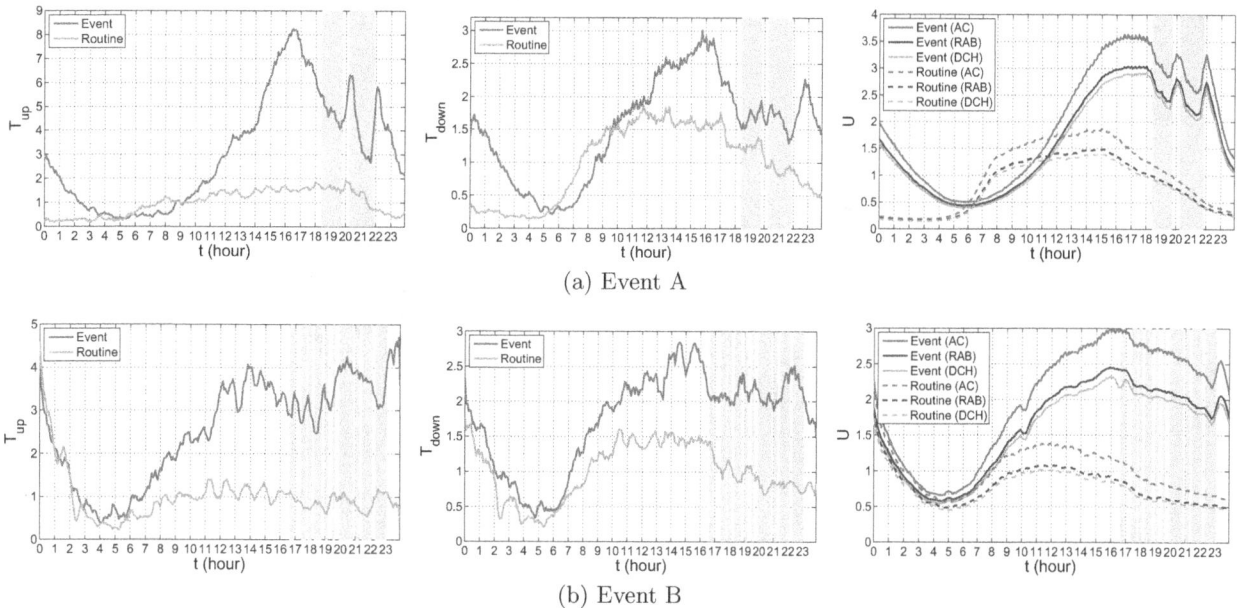

Figure 7: (Normalized) Network load measurements

4. UNDERSTANDING PERFORMANCE ISSUES

Next, we characterize user network traffic to identify patterns that correlate with the observed pre- and post-connection performance degradation during the events. Using the insights obtained from this characterization, we aim to identify network optimization opportunities that can potentially improve end-user experience in crowded locations. We characterize network traffic in terms of both aggregate network load and user-level session characteristics.

4.1 Aggregate Network Load

We quantify aggregate network load in terms of the following two metrics: throughput and user counters. Throughput or bit-rate is sampled for all UEs at the RNC every couple of seconds. Based on the direction of traffic, we can split the throughput into *uplink throughput* (T_{up}) and *downlink throughput* (T_{down}). Figure 7 plots the timeseries of uplink and downlink throughput on the event and routine days for both events. For the routine days, both uplink and downlink throughput peak around the noon time and decline steadily afterwards, reaching the bottom during late night and early morning. We observe a different trend for uplink throughput on the event days. For instance, the peak uplink throughput on the event day is more than 8x and 4x the average throughput on the routine day for events A and B, respectively. We also observe that the uplink throughput peaks and event activities are approximately aligned. For instance, uplink throughput sharply increases at the start and end of the second segment for event A. Similar, though less pronounced, patterns are also observable for event B. In contrast to the uplink throughput, increases in the downlink throughput timeseries are steadier for both events.

To further analyze traffic volume characteristics, we plot the traffic flow count histograms for top content publishers in Figure 8. We focus on flows rather than bytes to avoid bias towards high volume applications, such as video streaming. We observe that flow counts of social networking content publishers more than double on the event day as compared

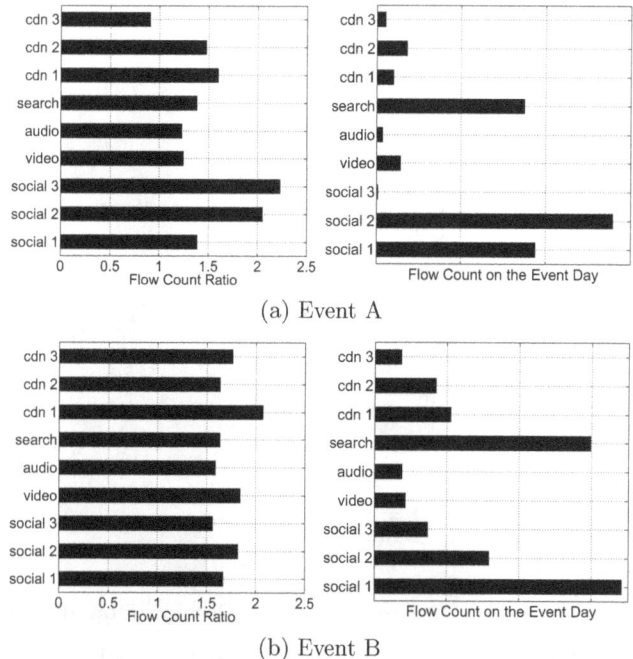

(a) Event A

(b) Event B

Figure 8: Flow count histograms for top content publishers in our data set

to the routine day for event A. Likewise, social networking content accounts for most flows on the event day for event B. Our further investigation (not shown here) revealed that social networking content is at least 2x more upstream heavy as compared to other content types, which explains the increase in uplink throughput during both events.

We also analyze user counters for the event and routine days for both events. Users are classified into the following overlapping categories based on their RRC states: *admission control* (AC), *radio access bearer* (RAB), and *dedicated channel* (DCH). AC category includes the users who have completed the admission control procedure. RAB category includes the users who have been assigned a RAB after ad-

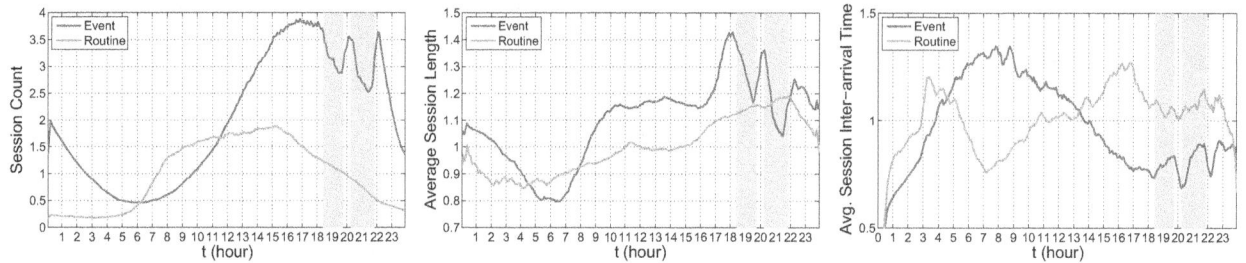

(a) Event A

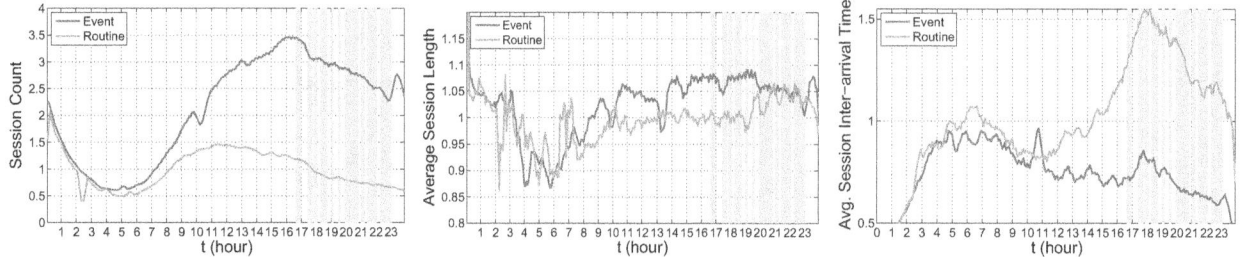

(b) Event B

Figure 9: (Normalized) Session Count, Average Length, Average Inter-arrival Time

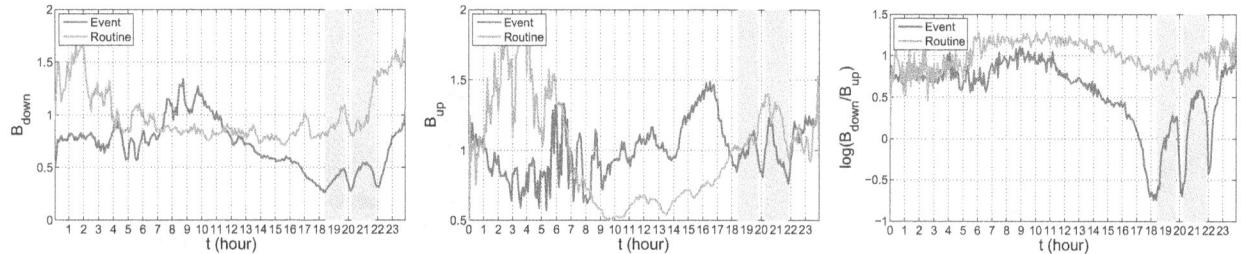

(a) Event A

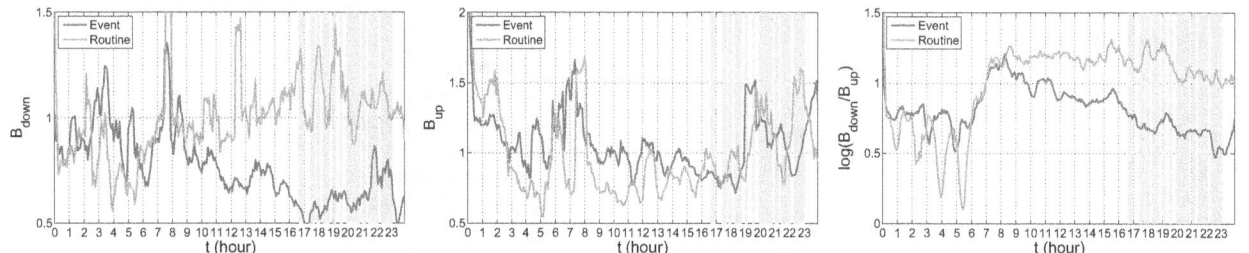

(b) Event B

Figure 10: (Normalized) Per-Session Downlink Bytes (B_{down}), Uplink Bytes (B_{up}), Ratio ($B_{down}/(B_{up})$

mission control. Such users are typically in either FACH or DCH state. Finally, DCH category only includes the users who are in DCH state. Let U denote the number of users, also let U_{AC}, U_{RAB}, and U_{DCH} denote the number of users in the aforementioned categories. As a general rule, $U_{AC} \geq U_{RAB} \geq U_{DCH}$. Figure 7 plots the timeseries of number of users in AC, RAB, and DCH categories. These timeseries show a trend similar to the throughput measurements. All user counters have higher values on the events days as compared to the respective routine days for both events. Specifically, the number of users with admission control peaks at more than 3x during the events as compared to its average on the routine days.

Summary: Both aggregate uplink and downlink throughput increase during the event days; uplink throughput increases by a factor of as much as 8 and 4 (for events A and

B respectively), while downlink throughput increases by a factor of 3 (for both events). Moreover, there is a substantial increase in the traffic volume of social networking content during the events, which is relatively more upstream heavy. Likewise, number of users with admission control increase by a factor of 3 for both event days. Overall, our aggregate network load characterization shows that increased user activity during the events, specifically in terms of uplink throughput and user counters, is correlated with increased pre-connection failures. To reduce the impact of increased network load during crowded events, we will investigate the effectiveness of opportunistic connection sharing in Section 5.2.

4.2 User-level Sessions

We now analyze characteristics of user-level traffic sessions for both events. A session consists of consecutive time

(a) Event A

(b) Event B

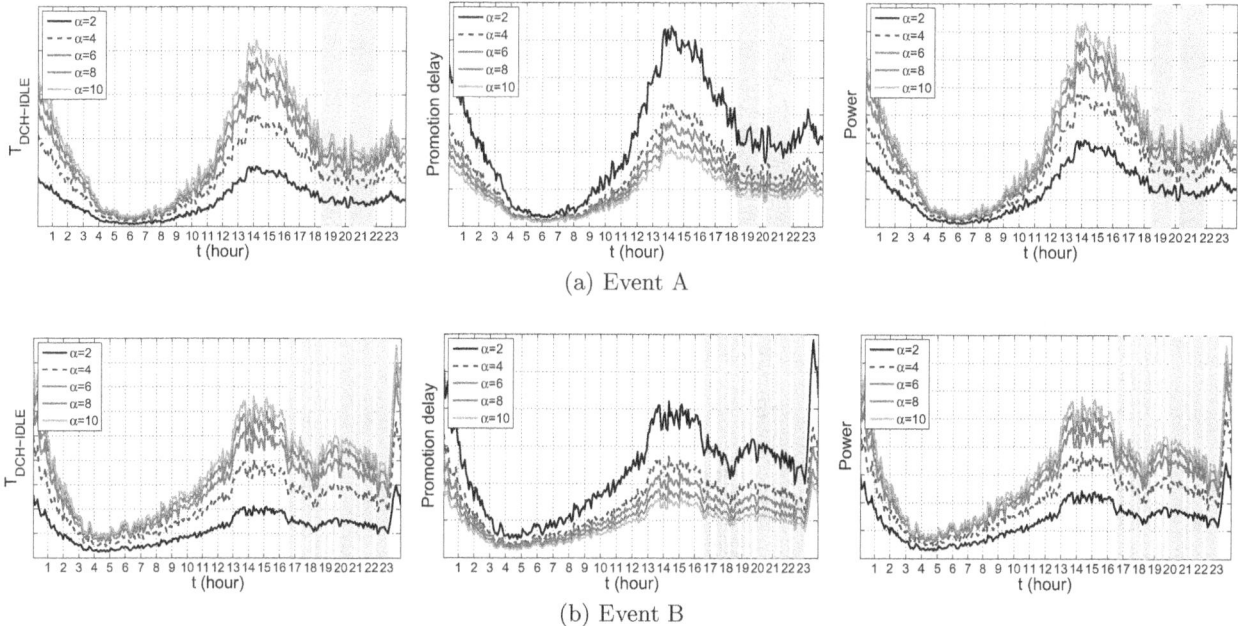

Figure 11: Experimental results for radio network parameter tuning

intervals with uplink or downlink byte transfer and its end is marked by an inactivity timeout of τ seconds. The results presented in this section are computed for $\tau = 5$ seconds. Changing the value of τ does not qualitatively affect the analysis results. Figure 9 shows the timeseries of session count, average session length, and average session inter-arrival time for both events. Session count follows a similar trend to the earlier aggregate network load metrics – at peak, there is more than 3.5x increase relative to the average on the routine days for both events. Furthermore, we observe an increase in average session length on the event days as compared to the routine days, e.g., there is more than 1.4x increase for event A. On the contrary, average session inter-arrival time decreases sharply on the event days as compared to the routine days – this indicates that users are initiating sessions much more frequently during the events. To further investigate the nature of changing session patterns, we plot the timeseries of average downlink bytes per session (B_{down}), average uplink bytes per session (B_{up}), and the average ratio of downlink bytes to uplink bytes per session in Figure 10. We observe that average downlink bytes per session sharply decreases up to 0.5x during the event days; whereas, average uplink bytes per session exhibits a mixed trend. The ratio (B_{down}/B_{up}) also sharply decreases during the events, which is due to the increased traffic volume of upstream-heavy social networking content.

Summary: User sessions are on average longer during both events (by a factor of as much as 1.4) – as well as more numerous and more frequently initiated. However, users exchange only as much as half the bytes per session on average. This change in workload is due to a change in the application usage during these events, such as greater proportion of social networking flows observed earlier. These trends point to potential waste of radio resources by UEs, which can be mitigated by tuning radio network parameters. Towards this end, we will investigate the effectiveness of varying RRC timeouts in Section 5.1.

5. EVALUATING MITIGATION SCHEMES

In this section, we evaluate two proposals to mitigate cellular network performance degradation during crowded events.

5.1 Radio Network Parameter Tuning

We first investigate whether tuning radio network parameters can result in more efficient radio resource usage during crowded events. As mentioned in Section 2, UEs acquire and release radio resources by transitioning to different RRC states. A UE is promoted to a higher energy state depending on buffer occupancy and it is demoted to a lower energy state depending on timeouts. Here, we study how RRC timeouts can be tuned for more efficient radio resource utilization, without explicit feedback from individual UEs. Recall from Figures 9 and 10 that average bytes per session decreases during the events, despite the increase in average session length. This observation highlights potential waste of radio resources and UE energy consumption in crowded locations. Therefore, a natural suggestion would be to reduce RRC timeouts to mitigate the radio resource wastage. However, reducing RRC timeouts can result in more frequent state promotions, which can introduce state promotion delays resulting in degraded user experience [14, 20]. Hence, there is a tradeoff between performance and resource efficiency.

5.1.1 Simulation Setup

We conduct trace-driven simulations to quantitatively study the tradeoffs involved in changing RRC timeouts. We simulate the RRC state machine of every user using the RNC logs while focusing on the DCH state, which has the highest allocated radio resources and energy consumption among all RRC states. Specifically, we study DCH→FACH RRC timeout parameter, which is denoted by α hereafter. As mentioned earlier, changing RRC timeouts introduces tradeoffs among radio resource wastage, user experience, and UE energy consumption. We use the following three performance metrics to quantify these factors. (1) The DCH state idle occupation time, denoted by $T_{\text{DCH-IDLE}}$, quantifies the radio resources wasted by UEs in DCH state. (2) The promotion delay quantifies the additional delay caused when UEs transition to DCH state from FACH state. (3) The power consumption quantifies the total energy consumed by UEs during DCH state occupation and in FACH to DCH transitions. We use the following simulation parameters in our experiments (inferred by Qian *et al.* in [20]): (1) FACH→DCH promotion radio power = 700mW, (2) DCH state power = 800mW, (3) FACH→DCH promotion delay = 2 sec, and (4) RLC buffer threshold = 500 bytes.

5.1.2 Results and Discussions

Similar to the evaluation of opportunistic connection sharing, we evaluate radio network parameter tuning for a subset of cell sectors that are within 1 mile radius of the venues. We conduct trace-driven simulations of individual users' RRC state machines on this subset for both event and routine days. Figure 11 shows the timeseries plots of the aforementioned three performance metrics for varying α values. We observe that the DCH state idle occupation time and UE energy consumption increase for larger α values. On the other hand, promotion delay decreases for larger α values. These observations indicate that decreasing the RRC timeout values reduces the waste of scarce DCH channels and UE energy consumption. However, this benefit is achieved at the cost of increased promotion delay that may degrade user experience, especially for applications that are not delay-tolerant.

To systematically study the tradeoffs between these performance metrics on the event days and compare them to routine days, we plot them as a function of α. Figure 12 plots the max-normalized average of the performance metrics as a function of α for the event and routine days. In theory, we want to select a value of α which simultaneously minimizes the values of all performance metrics. In this case, the crossover points (highlighted by black circles in Figure 12) and their corresponding α values represent suitable performance tradeoff. We find that these crossover points shift to smaller α values – by 1-2 seconds – on the event days as compared to the routine days. In practice, however, α is typically set to achieve a target delay or resource overhead. In this case, as observable from Figure 12, we can tune α to smaller values to achieve the same targets and achieve strictly better performance during crowded events.

5.2 Opportunistic Connection Sharing

We now evaluate a simple opportunistic connection sharing scheme to reduce the network load at individual cell sectors for eradicating RRC failures observed in Section 3.1. The basic idea is that users can share their connection to NodeBs with other users to reduce the overall network load in terms of occupied radio channels. In this scheme, a selected set of UEs act as Wi-Fi hotspots for other UEs in their vicinity. Therefore, other UEs, instead of wastefully establishing separate connections, can connect to NodeBs via the UEs acting as Wi-Fi hotspots. Using this approach, we aim to reduce the number of UEs that are directly connected to NodeBs to free up channels, although the overall throughput carried by the network remains the same.

5.2.1 Simulation Setup

To evaluate the potential benefit of the opportunistic connection sharing scheme, we conduct cell sector level trace-driven simulations. With respect to the mobility of the users,

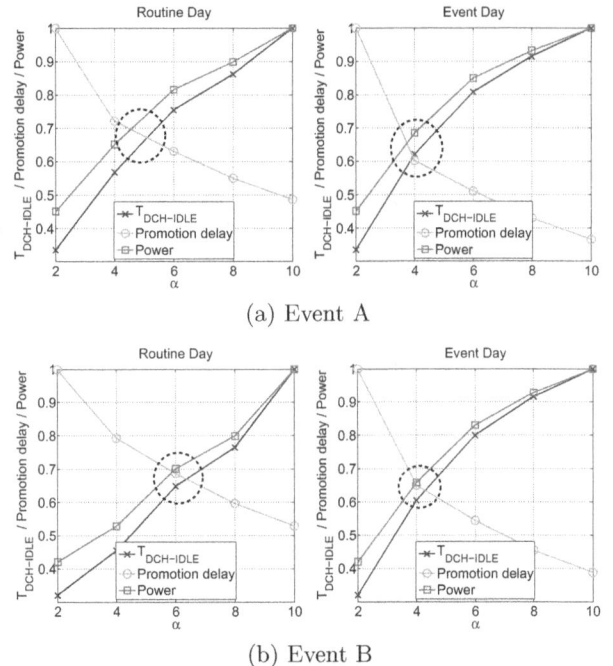

(a) Event A

(b) Event B

Figure 12: Tradeoff between performance metrics for varying RRC timeout (α) values. Y-axis is max-normalized for each metric. α values corresponding to black circles achieve better performance tradeoff.

we assume that the users are static within 1 minute time bins. This is a reasonable assumption for crowded events in stadiums, auditoriums, and conference rooms. We do not have fine-grained location information of users in our data set; therefore, we have to simulate the locations of users. In this paper, we aim to generate the locations of users in a grid-like scenario – similar to how people are typically seated in stadiums and conferences. Towards this end, we use Complete Spatial Randomness (CSR) point generation model with hard-core inhibition [9]. CSR with hard-core inhibition does not allow neighbors within a pre-defined radius around the randomly generated points, resulting in a grid-like setting. The points in the realizations denote the locations of users in our simulations. In our simulations, Wi-Fi hotspots are selected randomly because we do not have access to other relevant information, such as battery life and signal strength, that may be used to optimize this selection. Once a UE connects to a Wi-Fi hotspot, it is disconnected after 1 minute of inactivity. The locations of inactive users are updated using the above CSR model. In our simulations, the cell sectors are set to have $2,250,000$ ft^2 coverage area, the inhibition radius is set to 2 ft, the Wi-Fi range of users is simulated as $\mathcal{N} \sim (200$ ft, 20 ft$)$, and the upper limit on the number of simultaneous connections for each Wi-Fi hotspot is set to 5. The cell sector coverage area is in typical range for crowded urban locations, the inhibition radius is set to be reasonably large, and the Wi-Fi range and the maximum number of simultaneous connections are conservatively set. We assess the benefit of the connection sharing scheme in terms of the following metrics: the number of users in DCH state (U_{DCH}) and the number of RRC failures.

5.2.2 Results and Discussions

Since we are primarily interested in deploying this scheme in congested locations, we focus our evaluations on a subset

(a) Event A

(b) Event B

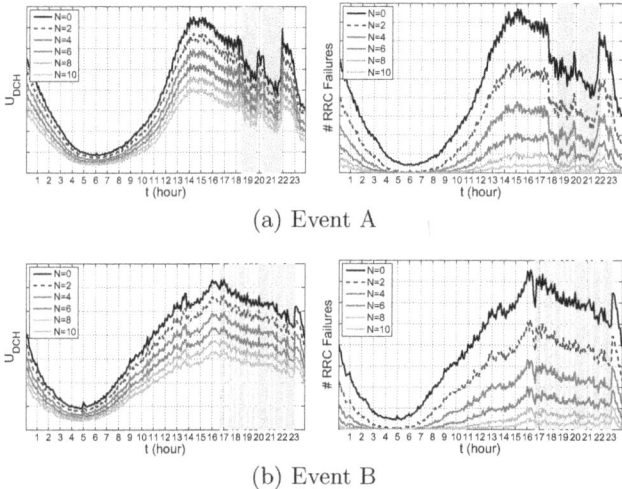

Figure 13: Experimental results for opportunistic connection sharing

of cell sectors in our data set that are within 1 mile radius of the venues. We evaluate the opportunistic connection sharing scheme using trace-driven simulations on this subset on the event days. The results plotted in Figure 13 are the average of 1000 independent simulation runs. We plot the time-series of the number of occupied DCH channels (U_{DCH}) for varying number of Wi-Fi hotspots per cell sector (denoted by N). As expected, we observe that U_{DCH} values become smaller for larger values of N, freeing up DCH channels that are now available for UEs unable to transition to the DCH state due to RRC failures. We also plot the number of RRC failures for varying values of N in Figure 13. Again, as expected, we observe that RRC failures decrease for increasing values of N. Consequently, based on instantaneous load conditions, the cellular network can dynamically vary the required number of users acting as Wi-Fi hotspots to minimize RRC failures. We note that this connection sharing scheme successfully eradicates more than 95% RRC failures for both events when $N = 10$. This substantial reduction in the number of RRC failures in congested cell sectors will likely result in improved performance for users.

5.2.3 Practical Issues

Below, we discuss some practical issues of opportunistic connection sharing.

• *Wi-Fi Hotspot Selection*: The selection of Wi-Fi hotspots can be mediated by the cellular network based on a variety of factors, such as battery life and signal strength. UEs acting as Wi-Fi hotspots may experience high energy drain and may run out of battery power. To address this issue, the role of Wi-Fi hotspot can be periodically rotated among the user pool by the cellular network. The cellular network should prefer UEs with better signal strength because UEs consume significantly more energy and suffer reduced effective bit rate when the signal strength is poor [22]. On the other hand, the UEs that are unable to get RAB assignments can discover Wi-Fi hotspots in their range using the standard Wi-Fi discovery methods. In case of multiple options, UEs should prefer hotspots with better signal strength.

• *Initial Connection Delay*: After a device connects to a Wi-Fi hotspot, similar to RRC protocol, it disconnects after a pre-defined inactivity timer expires. However, the value of this timer should be set much higher than the correspond-

ing RRC timers so that the device does not have to incur initial delay, which is up to several seconds, for every data transfer. In our simulations, the inactivity timer was set to be 1 minute.

• *Out of Range*: A device has to request RAB assignment when it moves out of a hotspot's Wi-Fi range. If it is unable to get a RAB due to congestion then the RNC can dynamically assign more Wi-Fi hotspots in the cell sector to provide connectivity to more users.

• *Radio Technologies*: Opportunistic connection sharing is only usable when a majority of devices in the cellular network have built-in Wi-Fi capability. In our simulations, we assume that all devices have Wi-Fi capability. In case Wi-Fi is not available, other technologies such as Bluetooth can also be used. Bluetooth has lower power consumption, smaller radio range, and supports less data rate as compared to Wi-Fi. Consequently, it can be used as a low power alternative for small transmissions such as tweets.

• *Wi-Fi-Cellular Handovers*: Working extensions to the Wi-Fi standard already address the issue of smooth handovers between Wi-Fi and cellular networks, including 3GPP Access Network Discovery and Selection Function (ANDSF), Hotspot 2.0 initiative [18], and other techniques [2].

• *Voice Traffic Offloading*: In this opportunistic connection sharing scheme, voice traffic can be tunneled via the Wi-Fi connection using the well-known Voice over Wi-Fi solutions, such as Wi-Fi certified Voice-Enterprise [6].

• *Incentives*: Cellular network operators may provide billing based incentives to users for participating in this opportunistic connection sharing scheme.

5.3 Limitations

Below, we briefly mention two limitations of our trace-driven simulation evaluations. First, our simulation based evaluations cannot account for changes in traffic workload resulting from different network conditions due to our proposed mitigation schemes. Second, they also cannot account for low-level dependencies between performance metrics and network load. For example, some types of RRC failures are impacted by interference, which in turn is a function of network load. Addressing these limitations requires experiments on operational cellular networks, which are beyond the scope of this work. However, despite these limitations, we believe that the sheer magnitude of the improvements observed in our simulations indicates that the mitigation schemes discussed in this paper would accrue some benefit in practice.

6. RELATED WORK

We divide related work into the following categories.

Cellular Performance Characterization: The areas of cellular performance characterization have recently received much attention by the research community. For example, small-scale studies have characterized application performance [12,26] and fairness [7]. Large-scale studies have characterized throughput and airtime [19], smartphone traffic [25], M2M device traffic [24], smartphone app traffic [23,27], and heavy users [10]. In contrast to these studies, we believe that we are the first to analyze cellular performance changes specifically during crowded events.

Radio Network Parameter Tuning: Prior work on radio network parameter tuning study the impact of RRC timers on network performance and smartphone energy consumption. Most prior work is based on user-end measurements performed using a few cellular devices. For instance, Liu *et al.* characterized performance in a 1xEV-DO network using measurements obtained from two laptops equipped with Sierra Wireless data cards [16]. Balasubramanian *et al.* proposed a UE based approach, called TailEnder, to alter traffic patterns based on the prior knowledge of RRC state machine [8]. Some studies are based on theoretical analysis and simulation. For instance, Liers *et al.* proposed a scheme to adaptively tune RRC timeout parameters based on the demand and load situation, and validated it using simulations [15]. Yeh *et al.* proposed a scheme to tune RRC timeout parameters using analytical models based on available radio resources, energy consumption, quality of service, and processing overheads of the radio access network [28]. Qian *et al.* conducted trace-driven RRC state machine simulations using network-end measurements to investigate the optimality of RRC timeout parameters [20]. Furthermore, they proposed an application-aware tail optimization protocol to simultaneously optimize radio and energy resources [21]. Similar to the prior work by Qian *et al.* [20,21], our analysis of radio network parameter tuning is based on trace-driven RRC state machine simulations. However, we focus on network-end tuning of RRC timeouts without any cooperation from UEs.

Opportunistic Connection Sharing: We build on existing work on opportunistic traffic offloading [11, 17]. Luo *et al.* proposed a unified architecture, where mobile clients use both 3G cellular link and Wi-Fi based peer-to-peer links for routing packets via peer-to-peer links to the appropriate destinations [17]. Han *et al.* proposed content-specific opportunistic communication scheme to offload cellular traffic via Wi-Fi or Bluetooth [11]. However, neither of these proposals were evaluated using real-world traces, and both approaches require architectural changes to network protocols and hardware. Our work complements these proposals by showing that their simplest and most practical instantiation — a simple one-hop connection sharing scheme that does not require architectural changes — can be very effective in real-life crowded events. To the best of our knowledge, this paper is the first to evaluate practical connection sharing techniques on real-world traces.

7. CONCLUSION

This paper presents the first performance characterization of an operational cellular network during crowded events. We make three key contributions in this study based on the real-world voice and data traces that we collected from a tier-1 cellular network in the United States during two high-profile crowded events in 2012. First, we measured how cellular network performance degrades during crowded events as compared to routine days. Second, we analyzed what causes the observed performance degradation. Third, we evaluated how practical mitigation schemes for the observed performance degradation would perform in real-life crowded events using trace-driven simulations. Our findings from this study are crucial for cellular design, management, and optimization during crowded events.

8. REFERENCES

[1] Architecture enhancements for non-3GPP accesses. http://www.3gpp.org/ftp/Specs/html-info/23402.htm.
[2] Offload service. http://www.devicescape.com/offload-service.
[3] Wireless networks are near capacity. http://www.pcworld.com/businesscenter/article/235964/survey_wireless_networks_are_near_capacity.html.
[4] Cisco Visual Networking Index: Global Mobile Data Traffic Forecast Update, 2010-2015. Cisco White Paper, February, 2011.
[5] Actix Press Release. http://www.actix.com/sites/www.actix.com/files/Actix_Hotspots_Study_Findings.pdf, June 2012.
[6] Wi-Fi CERTIFIED Voice-Enterprise, Delivering Wi-Fi voice to the enterprise. White Paper, May 2012.
[7] V. Aggarwal, R. Jana, K. Ramakrishnan, J. Pang, and N. Shankaranarayanan. Characterizing fairness for 3G wireless networks. In *IEEE LANMAN*, 2011.
[8] N. Balasubramanian, A. Balasubramanian, and A. Venkataramani. Energy consumption in mobile phones: A measurement study and implications for network applications. In *ACM IMC*, 2009.
[9] R. S. Bivand, E. J. Pebesma, and V. Gomez-Rubio. *Applied Spatial Data Analysis with R.* Springer, 2008.
[10] A. Botta, A. Pescape, G. Ventre, E. Biersack, and S. Rugel. Performance footprints of heavy-users in 3G networks via empirical measurement. In *International Symposium on Modeling and Optimization in Mobile, Ad Hoc and Wireless Networks (WiOpt)*, 2010.
[11] B. Han, P. Hui, V. S. A. Kumar, M. V. Marath, G. Pei, and A. Srinivasan. Cellular traffic offloading through opportunistic communications: A case study. In *ACM MobiCom Workshop on Challenged Networks*, 2011.
[12] J. Huang, Q. Xu, B. Tiwana, Z. M. Mao, M. Zhang, and V. Bahl. Anatomizing application performance differences on smartphones. In *ACM MobiSys*, 2010.
[13] H. Jiang and C. Dovrolis. Passive estimation of TCP round-trip times. *SIGCOMM CCR*, 32(3), 2002.
[14] P. P. C. Lee, T. Bu, and T. Woo. On the detection of signaling DoS attacks on 3G wireless networks. In *IEEE Infocom*, 2007.
[15] F. Liers and A. Mitschele-Thiel. UMTS data capacity improvements employing dynamic rrc timeouts. In *16th IEEE International Symposium on Personal, Indoor and Mobile Radio Communications (PIMRC)*, 2005.
[16] X. Liu, A. Sridharan, S. Machiraju, M. Seshadri, and H. Zang. Experiences in a 3G network: Interplay between the wireless channel and applications. In *ACM MobiCom*, 2008.
[17] H. Luo, R. Ramjeey, P. Sinhaz, L. E. Liy, and S. Lu. UCAN: A unified cellular and adhoc network architecture. In *ACM MobiCom*, 2003.
[18] B. Orlandi and F. Scahill. Wi-Fi Roaming – Building on ANDSF and Hotspot 2.0. Technical report, Alcatel-Lucent and BT, 2012.
[19] U. Paul, A. P. Subramanian, M. M. Buddhikot, and S. R. Das. Understanding traffic dynamics in cellular data networks. In *IEEE Infocom*, 2011.
[20] F. Qian, Z. Wang, A. Gerber, Z. M. Mao, S. Sen, and O. Spatscheck. Characterizing radio resource allocation for 3G networks. In *ACM IMC*, 2010.
[21] F. Qian, Z. Wang, A. Gerber, Z. M. Mao, S. Sen, and O. Spatscheck. TOP: Tail optimization protocol for cellular radio resource allocation. In *IEEE ICNP*, 2010.
[22] A. Schulman, V. Navda, R. Ramjee, N. Spring, P. Deshpande, C. Grunewald, K. Jain, and V. N. Padmanabhan. Bartendr: A practical approach to energy-aware cellular data scheduling. In *ACM MobiCom*, 2010.
[23] M. Z. Shafiq, L. Ji, A. X. Liu, J. Pang, and J. Wang. Characterizing geospatial dynamics of application usage in a 3G cellular data network. In *IEEE INFOCOM*, 2012.
[24] M. Z. Shafiq, L. Ji, A. X. Liu, J. Pang, and J. Wang. A first look at cellular machine-to-machine traffic - large scale measurement and characterization. In *ACM SIGMETRICS/Performance*, 2012.
[25] M. Z. Shafiq, L. Ji, A. X. Liu, and J. Wang. Characterizing and modeling Internet traffic dynamics of cellular devices. In *ACM SIGMETRICS*, 2011.
[26] M. P. Wittie, B. Stone-Gross, K. Almeroth, and E. Belding. MIST: Cellular data network measurement for mobile applications. In *IEEE BROADNETS*, 2007.
[27] Q. Xu, A. Gerber, Z. M. Mao, J. Pang, and S. Venkataraman. Identifying diverse usage behaviors of smartphone apps. In *ACM IMC*, 2011.
[28] J.-H. Yeh, J.-C. Chen, and C.-C. Lee. Comparative analysis of energy saving techniques in 3GPP and 3GPP2 systems. *IEEE Transactions on Vehicular Technology*, 58(1):432–438, January, 2009.

Characterizing and Modeling the Impact of Wireless Signal Strength on Smartphone Battery Drain

Ning Ding
Purdue University

Daniel Wagner
University of Cambridge

Xiaomeng Chen
Purdue University

Y. Charlie Hu
Purdue University

Andrew Rice
University of Cambridge

ABSTRACT

Despite the tremendous market penetration of smartphones, their utility has been and will remain severely limited by their battery life. A major source of smartphone battery drain is accessing the Internet over cellular or WiFi connection when running various apps and services. Despite much anecdotal evidence of smartphone users experiencing quicker battery drain in poor signal strength, there has been limited understanding of how often smartphone users experience poor signal strength and the quantitative impact of poor signal strength on the phone battery drain. The answers to such questions are essential for diagnosing and improving cellular network services and smartphone battery life and help to build more accurate online power models for smartphones, which are building blocks for energy profiling and optimization of smartphone apps.

In this paper, we conduct the first measurement and modeling study of the impact of wireless signal strength on smartphone energy consumption. Our study makes four contributions. First, through analyzing traces collected on 3785 smartphones for at least one month, we show that poor signal strength of both 3G and WiFi is routinely experienced by smartphone users, both spatially and temporally. Second, we quantify the extra energy consumption on data transfer induced by poor wireless signal strength. Third, we develop a new power model for WiFi and 3G that incorporates the signal strength factor and significantly improves the modeling accuracy over the previous state of the art. Finally, we perform what-if analysis to quantify the potential energy savings from opportunistically delaying network traffic by exploring the dynamics of signal strength experienced by users.

Categories and Subject Descriptors

C.4 [**Computer System Organization**]: Performance of Systems—*Modeling techniques*; C.2.3 [**Computer System Organization**]: Computer Communication Networks—*Network Operations*

General Terms

Experimentation, Measurement

Keywords

Signal strength, smartphone, energy, battery drain, power model

1. INTRODUCTION

The smartphone market has been growing at a phenomenal rate. A recent study [3] finds that out of the world's 4 billion mobile phones, over one billion are smartphones, and projects that by the year 2014, there will be more smartphone users surfing the Web than desktop users. Despite such an incredible adoption rate of smartphones, the user experience has been, and will remain, severely limited by the phone battery life. As such, understanding and optimizing the energy consumption of apps running on mobile devices is of significant importance.

A major source of smartphone energy consumption is accessing the Internet via 3G or WiFi [4, 20, 18] when running various interactive apps and background services. The energy consumed by the wireless interfaces is perceived as a necessity – after all, a smartphone provides the user with a ubiquitous portal to the Internet. Ideally, accessing the Internet should consume an amount of energy commensurate with the amount of traffic being transported and the (peak) throughput supported by the wireless technology used.

In practice, the wireless channel can be noisy and a fundamental law governs wireless networking performance: wireless channel capacity is upper-bounded by the signal-to-noise ratio (SNR), which measures the ratio of the level of a desired signal to the level of background noise, as dictated by the Shannon-Hartley theorem. In other words, poor signal strength can significantly affect the achievable network performance. How to achieve the upper-bound channel capacity under a given SNR is at the very center of of wireless communication research.

In this paper, we contend that poor wireless signal strength not only affects network performance, but also –in the context of energy-constrained mobile devices perhaps more importantly – can significantly inflate the actual energy consumption by the wireless interface to be much higher than under good signal strength, while transferring the same amount of network traffic. The more obvious impact on energy drain is that reduced signal strength triggers rate adaptation at the PHY layer to lower the data rate which elongates packet transmission and hence increases power consumption by the radio. There are also several additional, less obvious, impact factors. Weak signal strength can result in retransmissions, *e.g.*, in the link layer in 3G and at the MAC layer in WiFi, and even at the transport layer, all of which lead to extra radio power consumption. Retransmissions at the transport layer (*e.g.*, TCP) can further increase the number of times and hence the total duration the wireless interface stays in the tail power state [4, 19, 20], wasting "tail" energy. Further, poor signal strength can cause disassociation and reassociation with the access point which incur extra energy drain.

Despite the above intuitive understanding of the energy impact of poor signal strength and much anecdotal evidence that smartphone users frequently have experienced quicker battery drain when the wireless signal strength is poor, we have a rather limited understanding of (1) how often smartphone users experience poor signal strength, and (2) the quantitative impact of poor signal strength on the phone battery drain. The answers to such questions are essential to assessing cellular network service qualities, and diagnosing and reducing their negative impact on smartphone battery life. Further, answering question (2) above enables us to develop an online power model for smartphones that is more accurate than previous work [19], by explicitly capturing the potentially significant impact of signal strength. Accurate online power models for smartphones form building blocks for energy profiling and optimization of smartphone apps [18], and the new signal-strength-aware power model enables what-if analysis of techniques that explore signal strength dynamics to reduce the energy drain of wireless interfaces, *e.g.,* by delaying and aggregating network traffic for latency insensitive apps and services.

In this paper, we conduct to our knowledge the first measurement and modeling study of the impact of wireless signal strength on smartphone energy consumption. Our study makes four specific contributions and findings.

- We collected a cellular and WiFi signal strength and traffic volume trace from 3785 smartphones, geographically distributed over 145 countries, each trace covering at least a one-month period with an average of 4.2 months. Our trace analysis shows that (1) WiFi and 3G are dominant wireless technology choices among users, (2) individual users are experiencing significant signal variations in daily life and during active phone usage, (3) on average 43% and 21% of their foreground data are transferred during poor 3G and WiFi signal strength, respectively, (4) 19% of 3G transfer and 4% of WiFi transfer can be classified as background data and thus can be potentially deferred to times with better signal strength, and (5) the signal variations are correlated with popular user locations to some extent which also manifests itself in a correlation with time of day.

- We then conducted controlled experiments to quantify the extra energy consumption for data transfers that is induced by poor wireless signal strength and its breakdown to different factors including rate adaptation, power control, link layer retransmissions and TCP retransmissions. Our measurements refined packet-driven power models for WiFi and 3G to be signal-strength-aware and hence much more accurate than before. Our energy impact analysis shows that for WiFi the lower bit rate and MAC layer retransmission when the Received Signal Strength Indicator (RSSI) drops from -50dBm to -90dBm cost 810.5% more energy for a typical mobile download of 100KB with 30ms server RTT; for 3G the increased energy on data transfer and RRC state demotion when the RSSI drops from -85dBm to -105dBm dominates the extra energy consumption, resulting in 52.0% more energy for the same 100KB download with 30ms server RTT.

- We further derived a new system-call-driven power model for WiFi and 3G that improves the state of the art [19] by incorporating the impact of signal strength and RTT. Our evaluation shows that the new model drastically improves the modeling accuracy over the prior art. Specifically, under poor signal strength, the new model reduces the energy estimation error from 61.0% to 5.4% for WiFi, and from 52.1% to 7.2% for 3G.

- We present a case study showing how our new system-call-

driven power model can be used to perform what-if analysis of the effectiveness of energy optimization techniques that explore signal strength dynamics. Specifically, our analysis shows that for three selected subsets of users who experienced predominantly good, fair, and poor signal strength, opportunistically delaying background network traffic till the signal strength becomes better, can reduce the total energy consumption of data communication by up to 23.7% and 21.5% under WiFi and 3G, respectively.

The rest of the paper is organized as follows. §2 briefly reviews the impact of signal strength on the network layers in 3G and WiFi. §3 presents the trace analysis. §4 gives the context for the remaining impact analysis, power modeling, and what-if analysis. §5 presents our controlled measurement study of the energy impact of signal strength on WiFi and 3G. §6 presents our new power model which incorporates the signal strength and RTT factors, and §7 presents a case study of using the power model to perform what-if analysis. We discuss related work in §8 and conclude in §9.

2. BACKGROUND

In this section, we first review the basics about the multiple power states of 3G and WiFi. We then examine the impact of signal strength on the extra energy consumption at various network layers.

2.1 Power States and Transitions

A wireless device like a 3G or WiFi radio can be in several operating modes, known as *power states* for that device, each draining a different amount of power. Each device has an idle base state which is the power state where that particular device consumes least power. A device can further have one or more levels of productive power states, depending on the workload. Finally, both 3G and WiFi radios exhibit a tail power phenomenon where the radio stays in a high power state after active usage and continues to consume energy in anticipation of more communication [4, 20, 19], before eventually returning to the base power state.

In a 3G network, the power state of a user equipment (UE) is determined by the Radio Network Controller (RNC) via the Radio Resource Control (RRC) protocol. The power states of the 3G device we measured on an HTC Nexus One phone are shown in Figure 1(a): (1) *IDLE:* A UE is in the IDLE state when it does not send or receive any data; the 3G radio draws nearly zero power. (2) *FACH:* At low transfer rate, the UE establishes the connection and enters the FACH state which does not have a dedicated channel. The 3G radio consumes moderate power in the FACH state. (3) *DCH:* At high transfer rate, the UE enters the DCH state, which usually has its dedicated data channel but also consumes high power. (4) The transitions from IDLE to FACH and from FACH to DCH – known as promotions – take a certain amount of time and consume a certain amount of power. (5) Similarly, the transitions from DCH to FACH and from FACH to IDLE have specific timeouts and incur tail power costs. In particular, in T-Mobile network 3G stays in DCH and FACH after active usage for 3.6s and 3.3s, respectively, before switching to the next lower power state.

The power states and transitions for WiFi are simpler, as shown in Figure 1(b). In WiFi, the tail power state is a result of 802.11 Dynamic Power Saving Mode (PSM) [5]; after transmitting/receiving, the device will stay in the high power state for a pre-defined duration (called PSM timeout) before going into PSM.

The above power state behavior of 3G and WiFi suggests that the total energy drain of 3G/WiFi in carrying out a fixed amount of traffic equals the sum of the energy consumed while in productive power states and while in the tail state, which is determined by the

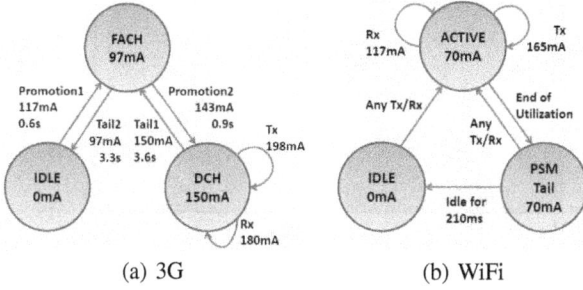

(a) 3G   (b) WiFi

Figure 1: 3G and WiFi power state machine for HTC Nexus One phone. All parameters are for under good signal strength.

total duration they stay in these states, $T_{productive}$, T_{tail}:

$$E_{total} = P_{productive} * T_{productive} + P_{tail} * T_{tail}$$

The total time spent in a productive state is affected by the data rate and retransmissions. The total time spent in the tail state depends on the total number of times the device enters the tail state and the duration of each episode.

2.2 Energy Impact of Weak Signal Strength

Weak wireless signal strength can result in smartphone apps consuming significantly more energy than under good signal strength. In particular, weak signal strength can increase the total time spent in productive and tail power states, $T_{productive}$, T_{tail}, as well as transmit power, $P_{productive}$, when sending and receiving data by affecting the behavior of almost all layers of the network stack.

Rate adaption. Rate adaptation is a dynamic, continuous link adaptation process where the modulation, coding and other signal and protocol parameters of the wireless communication are adapted to match the dynamically changing channel conditions, in order to reduce bit error rates and improve the effective rate of transmission. In general, weak signal strength leads to reduced data rate, which effectively elongates per-packet transmission time and thereby the total time the device stays in the productive state, $T_{productive}$.

WiFi switches between multiple modulation types and data rates in the PHY layer. A large number of autorate schemes have been proposed, including link-layer approaches [13, 14, 25] and physical-layer approaches [10, 22]. 3G blurs the notion of PHY and MAC and rate adaptation forms part of the tightly integrated link adaptation. In the 3G link layer, poor signal strength therefore not only leads to reduced data rate, which directly elongates the transmission time of a packet, but also increases the retransmissions of transport block sets of information bits within a packet, which indirectly elongate the transmission time.

Power control. Another form of link adaptation that could be triggered by signal strength variation is transmission power control, which performs intelligent selection of transmitting power to achieve good link data rate, network capacity, and/or geographic coverage. Increased transmission power can increase the SNR and hence reduce the bit error rates at the receiver, or allow transmission at a higher data rate using rate adaptation. However, it can also increase the power consumption of the transmitting radio, e.g., of a mobile device, and increase the interference to other users in the same frequency band.

WiFi MAC Retransmission. Poor signal strength can lead to dropped packets and retransmissions at the WiFi MAC layer. Packet loss is discovered when a sender does not receive the ACK frame within a fixed time interval and the MAC retransmits the same packet up

Table 1: Trace statistics.

Devices > 1 month trace (3/6/9/12 months)	3785 (1728/835/463/232)
Aggregate trace duration	1334 years
Median trace duration	82 days
Countries of origin	145
Mobile operators	896
Unique phone types	487
Rate of mobile RSSI reading	when signal changes, effective: 1/min
Rate of network usage reading	every 5 minutes

to a fixed number of retries. Clearly retransmitting the same packet multiple times increases the energy consumption per packet.

TCP Retransmission. When the signal strength is extremely weak, retransmissions at the link layer may not guarantee eventual packet delivery. When this happens, it triggers packet retransmission and potentially reduces the sending rate from congestion control at the TCP layer which again leads to extra energy consumption.

Re-Association and Handoffs. Weak wireless signal strength due to the mobility of smartphone users, e.g., during driving while connected to 3G, or walking on a campus covered with WiFi, can result in disassociations and reassociation with the wireless network (3G tower or WiFi AP), as well as handoffs between 3G and 2G [17], which consume significant amount of extra energy. We note that this can happen even if the user is not actively interacting with the smartphone and no app requires network access.

Tail Energy. Conceptually, the tail power state phenomenon is independent of the signal strength. However, for TCP flows, since the radio is in the tail state in between consecutive TCP windows, retransmissions due to packet loss can increase the number of times the radio enters the tail state and hence the total tail state duration.

Wait Energy. All of the above categories of extra energy consumption due to weak signal strength incur on the wireless device itself. Weak signal strength can further have a secondary effect that wastes energy on other components of a smartphone. In particular, the delay induced by the slower transfers from lower data rate or retransmissions can cause other phone components such as CPU and screen to stay awake longer while waiting for the network transfer to complete. This secondary effect is app usage dependent and we leave quantifying it as future work.

3. TRACE ANALYSIS

In this section, we present a trace analysis of the signal strength experienced by 3785 smartphone users from 145 countries.

3.1 Trace Collection

We developed a free Android app that users can install on their smartphone to contribute data anonymously. We collected information from 3785 volunteers worldwide. Each user trace ranges from 1 month to 19 months in length, with an average of 4.2 months (median 84 days). The collected data include cellular and WiFi signal strength, operator name, bytes transferred, coarse (network-based) location, screen on/off state and battery level. The detailed characteristics of the trace are shown in Table 1.

The very first observation we make is that the vast majority of the users spend most of the time using 3G cellular networks and WiFi. In particular, we find that over 80% (60%) of the 3785 users spent at least 44% (63%) of the time using 3G (UMTS or HSPA) networks or WiFi. We therefore focus on these two wireless technologies in the rest of the paper. For clarity, we only plot the distribution of various statistics for a stratified sample of 100 users drawn from

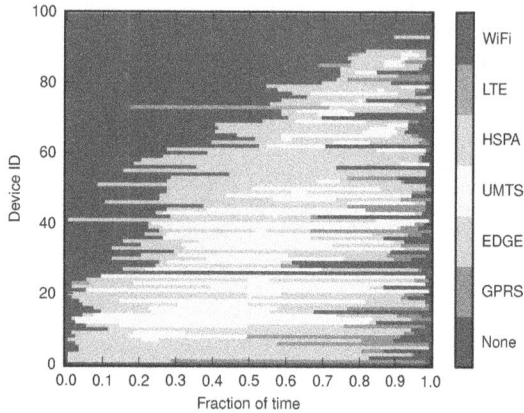

Figure 2: Wireless technologies over time.

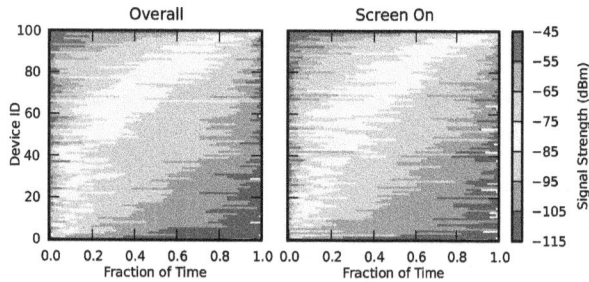

Figure 3: Overall 3G signal strength (left) and while screen was on (right) as observed by 100 sampled devices.

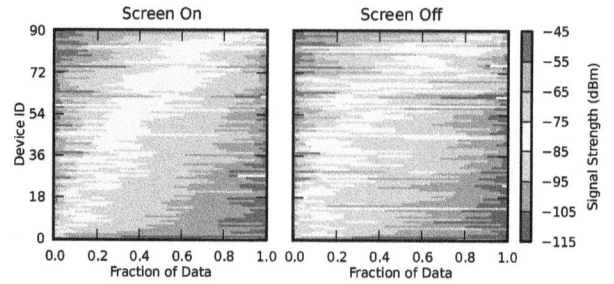

Figure 4: Data transferred over 3G with a given signal strength. Devices without mobile data traffic were excluded.

the whole dataset of 3785 users—incorporating the data from all users does not alter the visual characteristics. Figure 2 shows the fraction of time (*i.e.*, non-cumulative, as in the other figures of this type) spent in different wireless technologies for the stratified sample of 100 users. Each horizontal row (y-axis) corresponds to a single user, and each unique color segment shows the faction of time (along the x-axis) for which the primary data communication mechanism was a particular technology. For example, the 20th row contains a dark green segment of width 0.1, indicating this particular user made use of some WiFi network 10% of the time.

3.2 3G Signal Strength

We make three key observations from analyzing the 3G signal strength experienced by 3785 users.

Observation 1: *3G signal strength over the entire trace varies considerably across users and over time.* Figure 3 (left) shows the fraction of the total trace collection time of different signal levels experienced by the 100 sampled users. The figure for all 3785 users has the same visual characteristics. Research by the UK communications regulator Ofcom considers a good signal to have a power of -91.7 dBm or higher (shown in colors from orange to green in Figure 3).[1] By this definition, the 3785 users in our dataset saw a poor signal on average 47% of the time, and over 80% (60%) of them experienced signal strength weaker than -91.7 dBm for over 13% (31%) of the time.

Observation 2: *Signal strength also varies considerably during active usage across users and over time.* Clearly, periods of poor signal strength are only relevant to users if they notice the effects of

bad signal strength. These effects will be most pronounced when the user is actively using the phone. We define periods of active usage as periods when the device's screen is turned on. Figure 3 (right) shows the distribution of signal levels experienced during active usage remains almost identical to that for the entire tracing period in Figure 3 (left). In particular, across our dataset of 3785 users we observe poor signal, *i.e.*, below -91.7 dBm, during 47% of active usage time, and over 80% (60%) of users experienced poor signal strength for over 15% (32%) of their active usage time.

Observation 3: *Users transfer significant amounts of data during poor signal strength periods.* Periods of poor signal strength matter most to users if significant amounts of data are transferred during those periods. We therefore investigate the amount of data transferred over mobile networks by the individual devices and further distinguish between foreground and background network traffic. Since there is no explicit indication of traffic class from the OS, we approximately partition data into foreground and background classes as follows. We assume that data transmitted while the screen is off are solely non-interactive background data, whereas data transmitted while the screen is on are primarily foreground data. This is an underestimate of the amount of background data which could happen while the screen is on. For the 3785 users, this approach labels on average 19% of the total bytes transferred on 3G as background data.

Signal strength is collected upon change through notifications from the OS. As it may change in the middle of a 5-minute network usage polling interval, we assume that the network usage is uniform across each interval. This allows us to calculate the number of bytes transmitted by each wireless device at different signal levels. We find that by this definition, the 3785 users performed on average 43% of their foreground data transfers during poor signal strength of below -91.7 dBm, with over 80% (60%) of the 3785 users seeing over 11% (26%) of their foreground data transfer during such poor signal strength periods.

The figures for background data transfers are identical to the above numbers for foreground data transfers. Background data transfers during poor signal strength in the user's daily cycle can potentially be deferred until a strong signal is available, while we assume foreground transfers to be time-critical. In §7, we show how to use our new WiFi and 3G power model to estimate the energy reduction from deferring background data.

Finally, Figure 4 shows that the fraction of data transferred for the 100 sampled devices during different signal conditions are largely similar during screen on and screen off, suggesting the network behavior of users is in general not affected by poor signal conditions.

3.3 WiFi Signal Strength

We next analyze the WiFi signal conditions experienced by our 3785 users. For WiFi, we consider -80 dBm and below *poor signal*

---

[1] http://stakeholders.ofcom.org.uk/ market-data-research/other/telecoms-research/ mobile-not-spots/ Appendix 1

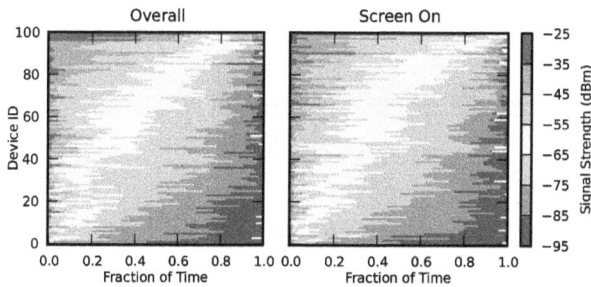

Figure 5: Overall WiFi signal strength (left) and while screen was on (right) as observed by 100 sampled devices.

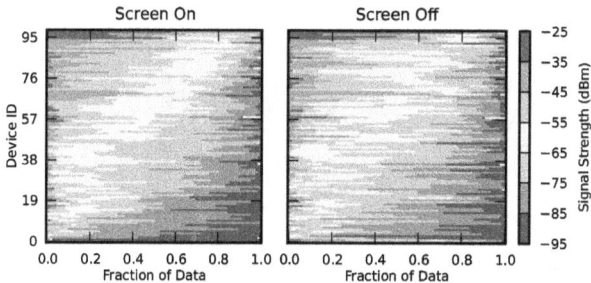

Figure 6: Data transferred over WiFi with a given signal strength. Devices without WiFi data traffic were excluded.

strength, which can significantly affect data transfer time and energy drain, as shown in §5. We find the same three key observations made for 3G above hold true for WiFi as well. In particular, (1) the 3785 users on average experienced poor WiFi signal, *i.e.*, below -80 dBm, 25% of the time, and over 80% (60%) of them experienced poor WiFi signal strength over 5% (13%) of the time; (2) during active device usage on WiFi, the 3785 users saw poor signal on average 23% of the time, and over 80% (60%) of them experienced poor signal condition over 5% (13%) of the time; (3) foreground data traffic on WiFi is much more prevalent, with the 3785 users transferring on average 96% of their total WiFi data volume during active device usage. On average 21% of these data transfers occurred during poor WiFi signal strength, with over 80% (60%) of the 3785 users transferring over 2% (8%) of their foreground data during poor signal strength.

Figure 5 and Figure 6 plot the WiFi signal strength experienced and fraction of data transfers during different WiFi signal conditions, respectively, for the 100 sampled devices. We observe they look largely similar to the previous same figures for 3G.

We also find that significantly more data usage occurs over WiFi than over 3G. In fact, the ratio of data downloaded to uploaded changes from 6:1 when using cellular networks to around 20:1 on WiFi. One explanation for this could be that users consume different types of content on WiFi, such as streaming audio and video or downloading larger files. Indeed many market applications which perform background data transfer offer an option to limit this activity to WiFi networks only. However, this is probably motivated more by cost implications than energy usage.

3.4 Insights for Poor Signal Strength

The most likely explanation for the prevalence of poor signal strength experienced by a significant fraction of users is the compound effect of geographic variation in cellular network coverage and the fact that a user principally stays in a few locations throughout a day. Figure 7 gives supporting evidence by analyzing three selected users from the dataset in detail under 3G. The figure for

WiFi looks similar and is omitted due to page limit. We see that the distribution of signal strength at the top three most popular locations for each user has a considerably tighter distribution than their overall distribution of signal strength. As a consequence, we expect that a user's daily routine will also give rise to a correlation between signal strength and time of day. This is confirmed by the circular plots in Figure 7. These daily cycles in signal strength suggest that all three users can benefit from a system that delays background data usage to exploit periods of improved signal strength.

4. OVERVIEW OF IMPACT ANALYSIS AND POWER MODELING

The motivation for quantifying the impact of wireless signal strength on device energy drain is to develop more accurate power models which will enable accurate energy profiling of mobile apps and ultimately help to optimize the energy efficiency of mobile apps.

Power models for mobile devices in general and wireless components such as WiFi, 3G and 4G radios have gone through three generations. The first generation of power models on smartphones (*e.g.*, [24, 26]) are based on the fundamental yet intuitive assumption that the (actual) utilization of a hardware component (*e.g.*, NIC) corresponds to a certain power state and the change of utilization is what triggers the power state change of that component. Consequently, these designs all use the notion of utilization of a hardware component as the "trigger" in modeling power states and state transitions. Such models do not take into account non-utilization-based power behavior of modern wireless components such as the promotion and tail power behavior of 3G and 4G, and thus can incur high modeling error.

The second generation of power models capture the non-utilization-based power behavior, in particular, non-utilization power states and transitions, using power state machines. In essence, such power state machines reverse-engineer the built-in state machine of the wireless radio, *e.g.*, the RRC state machine in 3G, and annotate each state or transition with power draw and duration. These include [4, 15, 20, 16] for WiFi and 3G and most recently [11] for a commercial LTE network. However, such models suffer two drawbacks. First, they use packet-level trace, *e.g.*, collected using TCP-Dump, as the triggers to drive the power state machine (*e.g.*, [20]), which are fairly heavy weight. Second, they cannot map the power activities of the wireless component back to the program entities in the app source such as subroutines and threads, which is essential for energy profiling.

In [19], the authors propose a third-generation power model which overcomes the above two drawbacks. The new power model uses system calls issued from apps as triggers in a system-call-driven finite state machine which captures both utilization and non-utilization based power behavior of smartphone components including wireless devices. The new model thus does not require packet-level traces, and allows direct mapping of power activities to program entities, making fine-grained energy profiling of apps a straightforward task [18].

However, none of above models takes into account the signal strength factor, and hence will incur high modeling error in the presence of poor signal strength which we have shown to be very common. Concurrent to our work, [16] extends the 3G RRC power state machine in [20] to incorporate the impact of signal strength on DCH and FACH and their tails, but not on promotion transitions.

Given the above context, we proceed with our measurement and modeling study in three steps. First, we perform controlled experiments to quantify the impact of poor WiFi and 3G signal strength on the device energy drain, and in doing so effectively refine the

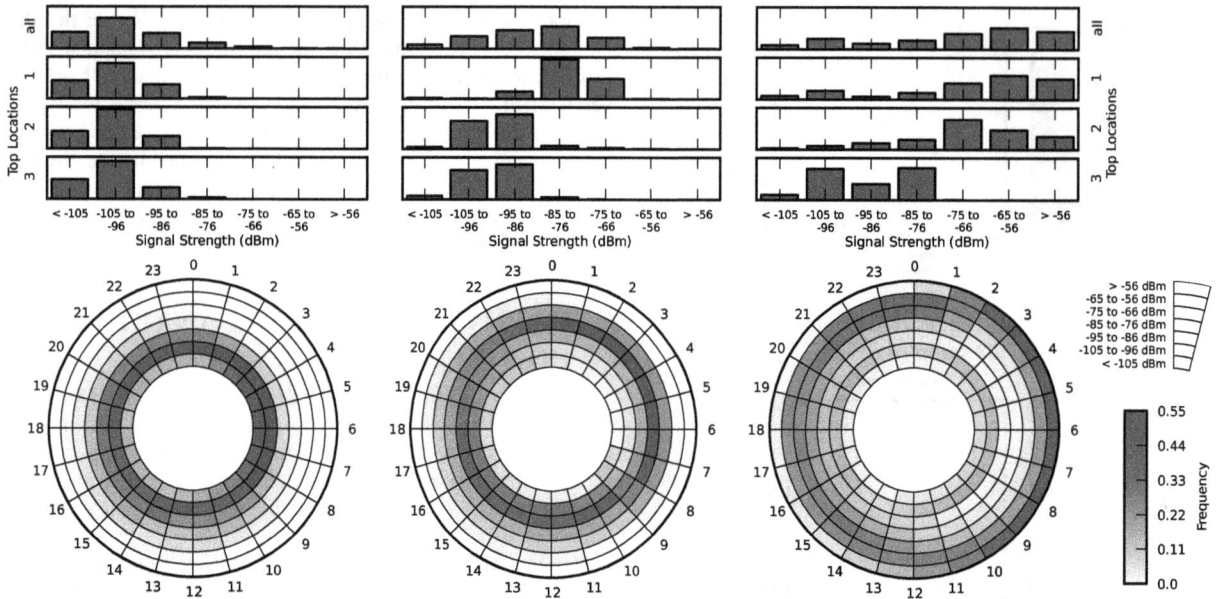

Figure 7: 3G RSSI per hour of the day for three devices experiencing predominantly bad, average and good signal (left to right).

Table 2: Mobile handsets used throughout the paper.

Handset	OS (kernel)	Cellular
HTC Nexus One	Android 2.3.4 (Linux 2.6.37)	T-Mobile 3G
Motorola Atrix 4G	Android 2.3.7 (Linux 2.6.32)	AT&T 3G
Sony Xperia S	Android 4.0.4 (Linux 3.0.8)	AT&T 3G

second-generation packet-driven power models to be signal-strength-aware and hence much more accurate (§5). For WiFi our analysis goes deeper than previous packet-level power modeling as we also quantify the impact on MAC retransmission and PHY rate adaptation. Second, we develop a refined third-generation, system-call-driven power model that takes into account signal strength (§6). Finally, we show how our new, signal-strength-aware system-call-driven power model enables what-if analysis of the effectiveness of energy optimization techniques that explore signal strength dynamics (§7).

5. CONTROLLED EXPERIMENTS

In this section, we present controlled experiments to quantify the impact of signal strength on the energy consumption of the WiFi and 3G devices and refine packet-driven power models.

5.1 Methodology

5.1.1 Devices and Tools

Table 2 lists the three smartphones used in our measurement study. The WiFi is provided by a Netgear WGR614v9 802.11 b/g wireless router. To measure the energy consumption, we use a Monsoon Power Monitor [2], which supplies power to the phone and samples the power draw every 0.2ms. During the measurement, we close all other apps and only run our benchmarks. Since our benchmark simply performs socket sending/receiving, the energy consumption of other phone components is close to 0 and the power draw measured by the powermeter is primarily the energy cost of WiFi or 3G NIC. Unless otherwise stated, we keep the phone's screen on during the experiment, and subtract the display energy from the total energy consumption.

We focus on data download since our trace presented in §3.3 shows real life download volumes to far exceed upload volumes over both 3G and WiFi; results for upload were omitted due to page limit. The phone downloads data from a local server, which is connected to the wireless router via 100Mbps LAN. Since the RTT between the WiFi AP and the server (*server RTT* for short) is less than 1ms, we use the Linux traffic control API `tc` to emulate different RTTs when accessing the Internet. Similarly, for 3G, the server RTT is to emulate the Internet delay between GGSN and the server, *i.e.,* excluding the time for the packets to travel through the UMTS Terrestrial Radio Access Network (UTRAN), which is typically in the order of tens to hundreds of milliseconds [12].

The data download is implemented using a simple client/server program written in C and running on the phone and the server. The client opens a TCP socket, sends a request, receives data, and closes the socket. The data downloads are separated by 1s and 30s, for WiFi and 3G, respectively, to make sure that each transfer starts from the IDLE state of the interface. We conducted the measurement at late night, so that there is minimum interference in WiFi and the cellular network is lightly loaded.

5.1.2 Data Transfer

We set the base case data download size to 100KB, which is in the same order of typical transfer sizes in mobile web browsing. We set the default server RTT to 30ms, which is representative of typical Internet RTTs. We also vary the flow size and server RTT and study how they affect the impact of signal strength on energy consumption. For each configuration, we repeat the download 50 times; results presented below are averaged over the 50 trials.

5.1.3 WiFi Analysis

We control the WiFi signal strength by adjusting the distance between the phone and the AP, and record the signal strength by logging the RSSI in the `WifiStateTracker` and `WifiStateMachine` classes in the Android framework. To capture frame retransmissions, and to read the data rate of frames from the radiotap header, we set up two laptops right next to the phone and the AP in the monitor mode using the Airmon-ng tool in Aircrack-ng suite [1], to eavesdrop WiFi link layer frames sent out by the phone and the AP, including DATA and ACK frames, control frames and beacons.

Energy breakdown. We break down the total energy of the WiFi NIC measured by the powermeter into six splits to quantify the impact on different network layers: (1) *Unique Tx:* Energy spent in the transmission of unique TCP ACK frames. (2) *Unique Rx:* Energy spent in the receiving of unique DATA frames. (3) *ReTx:* Energy spent in retransmitting TCP ACK frames. (4) *ReRx:* Energy spent in receiving retransmitted DATA frames. (5) *Idle:* Energy spent while waiting for frames from the AP, *i.e.*, in between frames or TCP windows. Its power equals the WiFi PSM tail power. (6) *PSM Tail:* Energy spent in the final WiFi tail power state, *i.e.*, after the flow completes while waiting for the PSM timeout to expire. The default PSM timeout on all three handsets is 210ms.

With the power profile from the powermeter and the eavesdropped link layer packet trace from the laptops, the above energy breakdown can be accomplished as follows.

First, we synchronize the time between the power profile and the monitor mode network traffic trace, by aligning the start of the first frame transmission with the start of the first WiFi power spike. Next, we categorize each frame sent or received by the phone WiFi NIC in the trace as either unique Tx/Rx or ReTx/ReRx, following their definitions above. Note ReTx/ReRx frames include both MAC and TCP retransmissions.

We next calculate the duration of each frame transmission by dividing the frame size by its transfer rate, which is indicated in the 802.11 radiotap header. For every sent ACK or received DATA frames eavesdropped by the laptop, since the timestamp indicates the time when the frame is finished transmitting, we backtrack the start of the transmission by subtracting the duration from the timestamp of the frame, and account the energy during the transmission interval between the start and finish time as the Tx/Rx energy. The energy drain between frame transmissions is counted as idle energy.

Finally, the energy drains belonging to each category are summed together and give the six-way split of the total energy drain.

Refining packet-driven power models. Since the packet-driven models use the packet time in the packet trace to determine the state transition time, inferring the refined packet-driven power models to incorporate signal strength boils down to inferring the power draw of each state under different signal conditions. In particular, for WiFi, with the synchronized power profile and link layer packet trace, we derive the Tx/Rx power under different signal strength by calculating the average power draw of WiFi NIC during a burst of packet sending/receiving.

5.1.4 3G Analysis

We adjust the 3G signal strength by changing the location of the phone, and record the signal strength by logging the RSSI in the `GsmServiceStateTracker` class in the Android framework. We observe that during experiment the signal strength variation is within 2dBm at good and fair signal strength locations, and within 3dBm at poor signal strength locations.

Energy breakdown. Unlike WiFi, there is no easy way to eavesdrop link layer packet transmissions in 3G. We instead resort to TCPDump to capture the packet trace. As such, we cannot observe the block set retransmissions or changing data rate in each packet transmission. The compound effect of the two factors makes it difficult to infer either one based on the observed transmission time of a packet, and hence we cannot separate the link layer retransmission from unique Tx/Rx as in the WiFi case.

To break down the energy, we first synchronize the time between the packet trace, which is timestamped by the phone, and the power profile, by inserting controlled power events (*e.g.*, a CPU spike) and

recording its time on the phone. We then play the packet trace to infer the 3G state transitions by leveraging the prior knowledge of the 3G state machines, following the methodology studied in-depth in [21, 20]. The energy drain during the duration of each 3G state is counted as the energy for the state. The energy drain of DCH during data transfer is further divided into data transmission energy and idle energy, based on whether the phone is sending/receiving packets or waiting for packets from the server.

Following this methodology, we break down the energy into following categories: (1) *Promotion1:* Energy spent in the first promotion phase, *i.e.*, IDLE to FACH in T-Mobile network and IDLE to DCH in AT&T network. (2) *Promotion2:* Energy spent in the second promotion phase, *i.e.*, FACH to DCH in both T-Mobile and AT&T network. (3) *Data transmission:* Energy spent in receiving DATA and transmitting ACK packets. This entails the impact of link layer rate adaptation and retransmissions. (4) *Tail1:* Energy spent in the first 3G tail state, *i.e.*, tail of DCH state. (5) *Tail2:* Energy spent in the second 3G tail state, *i.e.*, tail of FACH state. (6) *Idle:* Energy spent while waiting in DCH for packets from the server, *i.e.*, in between TCP windows. The duration is primarily determined by the end-to-end RTT.

Refining packet-driven power models. With the above energy breakdown, we then calculate the average power draw for each 3G state under each signal strength to derive the signal-strength-aware power model for 3G. Note for both new WiFi and 3G models, we only present parameters at discrete RSSI values, and hence in using the models, we use linear interpolation to estimate the parameters for RSSIs that are between the discrete points.

5.2 WiFi Results

5.2.1 Data Transfer Energy Breakdown: Base Case

Due to page limit, we only show the measurement result for the Nexus One phone. Figure 8(a) plots the time and energy consumption to download 100KB data with 30ms server RTT. [2] While the flow time only changes mildly from -50dBm to -80dBm, we see a 142.2% increase at -85dBm, followed by a dramatic increase of 1345.5% at -90dBm, compared to -50dBm. Similarly, the energy cost of downloading increases by 113.3%, 810.5% at -85dBm and -90dBm, respectively.

To understand the reason for the flow time and energy inflation, we break down the energy consumption in Figure 8(b). We make the following observations.

First, from -50dBm to -80dBm, most energy drain is from idle energy and PSM tail energy, while at -85dBm and -90dBm the idle energy dominates the total energy consumption. The reason is that for transfers of 100KB at good or medium signal strength, *i.e.*, above -80dBm, the active NIC transmitting/receiving time is generally in the order of tens of milliseconds, much shorter than the aggregate idle time and PSM tail time, which are in the order of hundreds of milliseconds. When the signal strength further drops, the average idle interval between frames increases significantly, from 0.28ms at -50dBm to 0.84ms at -85dBm and 5.47ms at -90dBm, leading to drastically increased idle energy.

Second, both unique Tx/Rx energy and retransmission energy increase significantly under poor signal strength. The total energy

---

[2]For simplicity, we represent power draw using the current drawn by the phone in milliAmperes. The actual power consumed would be the current drawn multiplied by 3.7V, the standard battery voltage supply. Similarly, energy is reported in μAh (micro Ampere Hours), and the actual energy would be the μAh value multiplied by 3.7V. These metrics are used since smartphone batteries are rated using these metrics and hence is easy to correlate.

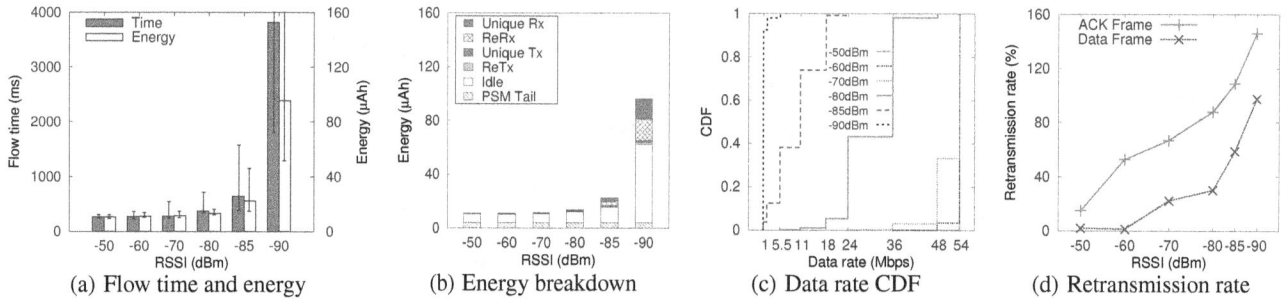

(a) Flow time and energy   (b) Energy breakdown   (c) Data rate CDF   (d) Retransmission rate

Figure 8: WiFi experiment: 100KB download with 30ms server RTT.

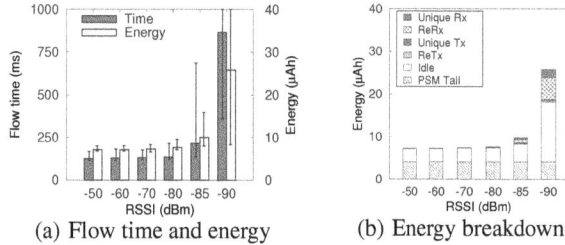

(a) Flow time and energy   (b) Energy breakdown

Figure 9: Time, energy and energy breakdown for downloading 10KB with 30ms server RTT under WiFi.

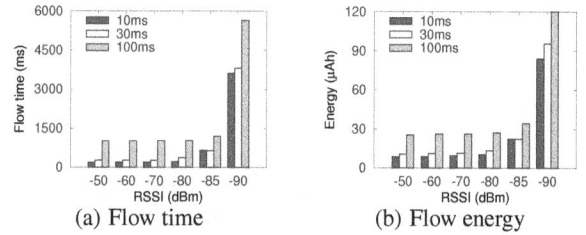

(a) Flow time   (b) Flow energy

Figure 10: Time and energy for downloading 100KB with different server RTT under WiFi.

spent on data transfer, including unique Tx/Rx and ReTx/ReRx, increases from $0.60\mu Ah$ at -50dBm to $6.79\mu Ah$ at -85dBm, and further to $33.95\mu Ah$ at -90dBm. To understand the reason, we plot the frame data rate CDF in Figure 8(c). We observe that from -50dBm to -70dBm, most frames are transmitted at 54.0Mbps, which is the highest rate supported by 802.11g. When signal strength drops below -70dBm, frames are transmitted at much lower rates due to rate adaptation. For example, at -85dBm 74.0% of the frames are transmitted at rates equal to or lower than 11.0Mbps, while at -90dBm a majority of frames (92.6%) are transmitted at the lowest rate 1.0Mbps. Figure 8(d) plots the retransmission rate of DATA frames from the AP and of TCP ACK frames from the phone. The DATA frame retransmission rate has a sharp increase from 1.3% at -60dBm to 58.7% at -85dBm, and 97.7% at -90dBm, while the retransmission rate of ACK frames increases almost linearly from 14.9% at -50dBm to 146.0% at -90dBm.

Scanning. When the signal strength is below -80dBm, we observe the phone occasionally performs active scanning by exchanging Probe Request and Probe Response frames with the AP. Normally such a process takes from 40ms to 100ms. However, at poor signal conditions, both the Probe frames and their ACKs may get lost and it takes up to 1s to complete the scanning, with tens of retransmissions, consuming significant amount of energy on the phone.

5.2.2   Impact of Size

We next study the relative impact of signal strength on different transfer sizes. Figure 9 shows the flow time, energy consumption and energy breakdown for downloading 10KB using WiFi with 30ms server RTT. Similarly as in the 100KB download, the transfer time and energy consumption remain roughly the same as signal strength varies from -50dBm to -80dBm, but increase significantly by 70.7% and 40.8% at -85dBm, and by 586.1% and 263.4% at -90dBm. Compared to 100KB transfer, the transfer time and energy inflation due to poor signal strength is much less since the effect of lower data rate and higher retransmission rate are more pronounced in larger transfers.

Table 3: Signal-strength-aware WiFi power model. The unit of RSSI is dBm and the unit of Tx/Rx/Tail current is mA.

RSSI	Nexus		Atrix		Xperia	
	Rx	Tx	Rx	Tx	Rx	Tx
-50	117	165	115	175	120	251
-60	120	191	115	178	133	270
-70	125	251	139	197	133	308
-80	116	203	120	245	120	267
-85	104	207	118	242	118	256
-90	89	207	83	237	115	253

PSM Tail	Nexus	Atrix	Xperia
	70	68	50

5.2.3   Impact of RTT

We next study the relative impact of signal strength under different server RTTs. Figure 10 shows the time and energy consumption to download 100KB with different server RTTs. We observe that as the RTT increases from 30ms to 100ms, the flow time increases by 287.1% and 48.1% under -50dBm and -90dBm, respectively, and the energy drain increases by 144.8% and 26.6% under -50dBm and -90dBm, respectively. This suggests that RTT has a significant impact on the flow time and energy in WiFi downloading, at both good and bad signal strength. A large RTT leads to longer idle time between TCP windows, and hence more idle energy. The smaller increase ratio at -90dBm compared to -50dBm is because under -90dBm the idle interval between frames, due to heavy packet loss, dominates the flow time and energy consumption.

5.2.4   New Power Model

Table 3 shows the new signal-strength-aware packet-driven WiFi power model for the three handsets. The PSM tail power remains constant under different signal strength. We observe that for all three handsets, the average Tx and Rx power reach their peak at -70dBm (except the Tx power for Atrix). This is due to the compound effect of power control, rate adaptation and frame loss: as the RSSI drops, while the radio transmitting power tends to increase, the data rate decreases and more frame loss occurs, which leads to longer idle interval between frames, hence lower average power.

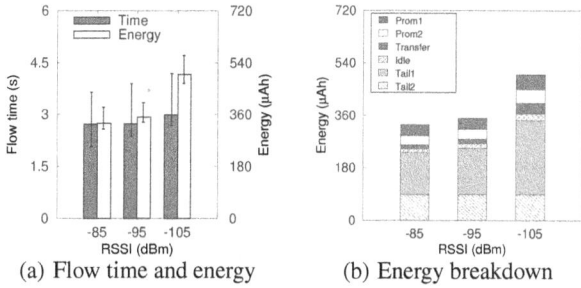

(a) Flow time and energy   (b) Energy breakdown

Figure 11: Time, energy and energy breakdown for downloading 100KB with 30ms server RTT under 3G.

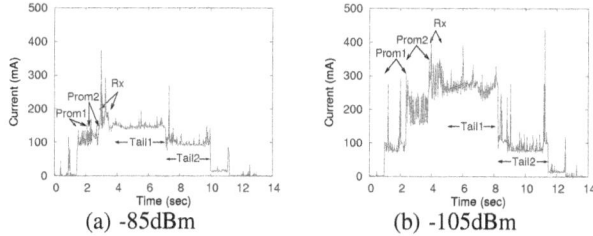

(a) -85dBm   (b) -105dBm

Figure 12: 3G power snapshots for downloading 100KB with 30ms server RTT under different signal strength.

These three factors interplay and lead to the non-monotonic correlation between the signal strength and the average Tx/Rx power.

Another interesting observation is that, while in general Nexus One is the most power efficient in Tx/Rx among the three handsets, it has the highest PSM tail power; and Xperia S is the opposite.

5.3 3G Results

5.3.1 Data Transfer Energy Breakdown: Base Case

As with the WiFi experiment, we use 100KB download with 30ms server RTT as the base case and only show the result for the Nexus One phone due to page limit. Figure 11(a) plots the flow time and energy consumption for the base case. We see that from -85dBm to -95dBm, the flow time remains similar and the energy consumption increases mildly by 6.6%; while at -105dBm, the flow time increases by 7.3% and the energy consumption dramatically increases by 52.0%, compared to -85dBm.

To gain insight into the increase, we again break down the total energy, as shown in Figure 11(b). An immediate observation is that, most of the energy increase comes from increased data transfer and tail1 (DCH tail) energy. The powermeter output snapshots in Figure 12 confirm the significant power draw increase of the above two states.

5.3.2 Impact of Size

Figure 13 plots the flow time, energy consumption and energy breakdown for 10KB downloads under different signal strength. Compared to 100KB downloads, 10KB downloads on average only consume 6.3%, 5.8%, 8.0% less energy under good, medium and bad signal strength, respectively, as the promotion and tail energy dominate the total energy consumption under all signal strength.

5.3.3 Impact of RTT

Figure 14 plots the time and energy consumption to download 100KB with different server RTTs, under different signal conditions. We observe that the impact of server RTT on flow time and energy consumption is less significant in 3G compared to that in

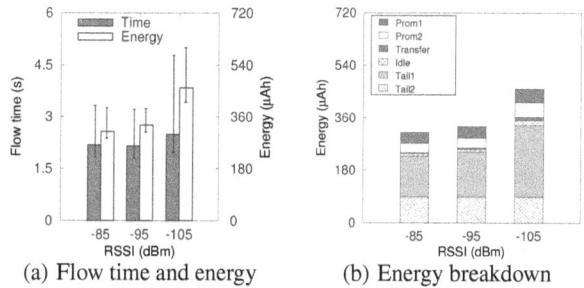

(a) Flow time and energy   (b) Energy breakdown

Figure 13: Time, energy and energy breakdown for downloading 10KB with 30ms server RTT under 3G.

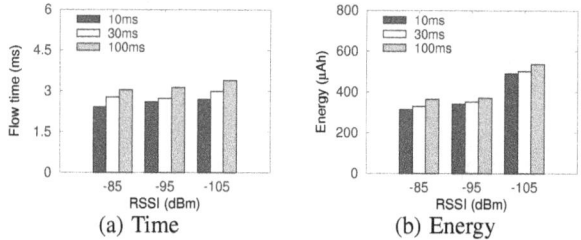

(a) Time   (b) Energy

Figure 14: Time and energy for downloading 100KB with different server RTTs under 3G.

WiFi. Under -105dBm, the flow time and energy only increase by 25.9% and 9.4%, respectively, when the RTT varies from 10ms to 100ms, in contrast to 56.0% and 44.2% under WiFi at -90dBm. There are several reasons that contribute to the difference: (1) the 3G network used has a relatively large internal delay (about 100ms) which diminishes the server delay difference; (2) the promotion time in 3G, which is in the order of seconds and hence much larger than the server RTT, dominates the flow time for small and medium size downloads; and (3) the tail energy is also much higher in 3G than in WiFi, dominating the total flow energy consumption.

5.3.4 New Power Model

Table 4 shows the inferred new signal-strength-aware 3G power model for the three handsets. We see that while tail2 power stays constant across different signal strength, the power draw of all other states increases as the RSSI decreases, especially when the signal strength drops below -95dBm. In particular, compared to -85dBm, the tail1 power at -105dBm increases by 73.3%, 172.2% and 253.3%, for Nexus One, Atrix 4G and Xperia S, respectively.

5.4 Implications on App Design

We further draw implications from our new understanding of the energy impact of signal strength on how developers can optimize the energy drain of their apps. (1) App developers need to be conscious about the behavior of their apps in case of weak signal strength during the app development. For example, delaying elastic data transfers till good signal strength can potentially reduce the apps' energy consumption. A notification scheme supported in the OS or the framework that informs apps of when signal strength is good can help delay-tolerant apps (e.g., peer-to-peer file sharing) to save energy by avoiding data transfers during poor signal strength moments. (2) Tail energy must be curtailed in case of small transfers since they consume a significant fraction of the total energy, especially under poor signal strength. (3) Aggregating data transfers in an app whenever possible can significantly reduce the total energy drain of the app, and the energy savings from doing so are even more pronounced when taking signal strength into account. For example, aggregating 10 separate 10KB transfers under -90dBm into

Table 4: Signal-strength-aware 3G power model. The unit of RSSI is dBm and unit of current of states is mA.

Nexus						
RSSI	Prom1	Prom2	Rx	Tx	Tail1	Tail2
-85	117, 0.6s	143, 0.9s	180	198	150, 3.6s	97, 3.3s
-95	123, 0.6s	150, 0.9s	192	281	160, 3.6s	97, 3.3s
-105	140, 0.9s	195, 1.0s	333	390	260, 3.6s	97, 3.3s
Atrix						
RSSI	Prom1	Prom2	Rx	Tx	Tail1	Tail2
-85	171, 1.8s	178, 0.9s	217	417	151, 4.0s	114, 10.0s
-95	197, 1.8s	203, 0.9s	287	497	188, 4.0s	114, 10.0s
-105	320, 2.0s	320, 1.0s	520	530	411, 4.0s	114, 10.0s
Xperia						
RSSI	Prom1	Prom2	Rx	Tx	Tail1	Tail2
-85	120, 1.8s	120, 0.9s	155	303	120, 4.0s	80, 10.0s
-95	127, 1.8s	127, 0.9s	215	425	190, 4.0s	80, 10.0s
-105	306, 2.0s	306, 1.0s	488	512	424, 4.0s	80, 10.0s

a single 100KB transfer under -70dBm can reduce the total WiFi energy consumed by a factor of 22.

6. NEW SYSTEM-CALL POWER MODEL

In this section, we develop a new system-call-driven power model for WiFi and 3G that improves the state of the art [19] by incorporating the impact of signal strength and RTT.

6.1 Current Power Model

The system-call-driven power model [19] for WiFi and 3G essentially looks similar to those in Figures 1(b) and 1(a), except the send/receive transitions are triggered by send/receive system calls (as opposed to packet transmissions).

The system-call-driven power model is derived in two steps, using a set of micro benchmarks and a powermeter [19]. First, the power state machines for individual system calls are derived, by capturing state transitions and power draw and duration at each productive state and tail state. The duration at an active power state is derived using linear-regression on the data transfer size. Second, the power state machines for individual system calls are integrated by observing the power profile for concurrent system calls.

As mentioned in §4, the current system-call-driven model for WiFi and 3G does not take into account the signal strength, which can affect various model parameters. It also ignores the effect of RTT, which can affect the power states visited during a system call.

6.2 WiFi Model

Observations. To develop the new model, we first make several observations about the effects of signal strength and RTT on the power profile of a data transfer system call. Figure 15 shows the power draw over time in a 100KB download with 30ms server RTT under different signal strength. A TCP download involves multiple TCP windows of packets, with packets in a window typically arriving in a cluster. We refer to the power spike corresponding to each TCP window as a window spike.

First, the current model ignores server RTT, and assumes the device stay in the productive state throughput data transfer due to the system call. This is a simplification. Figure 15(a) shows for a typical 30ms server RTT, the device effectively enters the tail power state in between TCP windows. The duration it stays in the idle tail state depends on the RTT value, and hence the power model needs to explicitly take RTT into account.

Second, when the signal strength drops, we observe several changes in the power profile as shown in Figure 15(b) : (1) the frames are

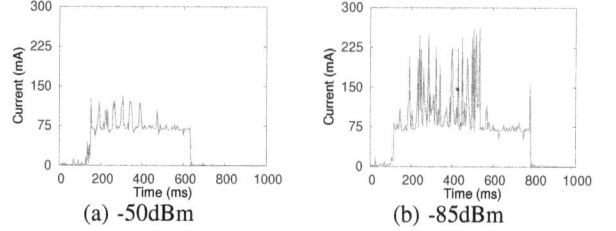

(a) -50dBm (b) -85dBm

Figure 15: WiFi power snapshots for downloading 100KB with 30ms server RTT under different signal strength.

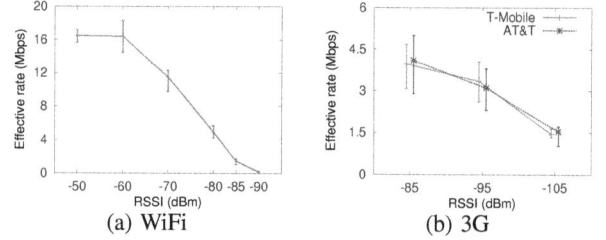

(a) WiFi (b) 3G

Figure 16: Effective receiving rates for WiFi and 3G under different signal strength.

transmitted at lower bit rates from rate adaptation, and the window spikes become wider; (2) the retransmission rate increases, and more frames are transmitted or received within each window, making each window spike even wider; (3) the power draw of spikes changes, as summarized in Table 3. In summary, poor signal strength causes TCP window spikes to have longer duration and changed power draw.

Modeling a single system call. To extend the system-call-driven power model for WiFi and 3G to take into account wireless signal strength, we need to log the signal strength and end-to-end RTT, in addition to system calls. We record the WiFi and 3G signal strength by logging the RSSIs in the `WifiStateTracker`, `WifiStateMachine` and `GsmServiceStateTracker` classes in the Android framework. The RTT of TCP connections can be retrieved from `tcp_info` struct via the `Netlink` API in Linux.

We model the power behavior of a data transfer system call in 3 steps: (1) For a transfer of size s, we first estimate the number of TCP windows and the size of each window, following the AIMD behavior. This proves to be reasonably accurate for small transfers, e.g., on the order of tens of KB, which account for the majority of the mobile traffic [8]. (2) For each TCP window w, we determine its duration t_w using linear regression on the window size, and power p_w according to Table 3, under each signal strength. (3) We then include the idle periods of staying in the PSM tail state in between the TCP windows, with the duration being the end-to-end RTT minus the window duration, as well as the final PSM tail after the last window.

The duration of a TCP window spike t_w is calculated by dividing the window size by the effective sending/receiving rate under the current signal strength. The effective rate is derived by calculating the average transfer rate of TCP windows during the training phase using micro benchmarks and the powermeter. Figure 16(a) plots the effective receiving rate for a window of 20KB measured under different signal strength. We see a sharp decrease of the effective rate from -70dBm, which captures the effect of lower bit rate and higher retransmission rate in the link layer, as shown in §5.2. The window spike power p_w is a function of signal strength and is directly measured during training phase. The values will be the same as in the packet-driven power model, i.e., in Table 3.

Table 5: Website traffic used in the validation experiments.

Website	Flow #	Total size	RTT
Amazon	10	164.1KB	28ms
Gmail	6	852.2KB	37ms
Wikipedia	9	176.4KB	91ms
Youtube	13	341.2KB	37ms

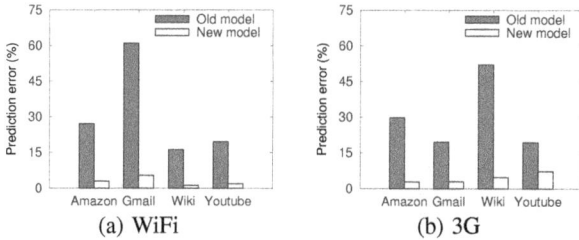

(a) WiFi   (b) 3G

Figure 17: Model validation result for Nexus One at poor signal strength locations.

Modeling multiple system calls. Once the power behavior for individual transfer is derived, we integrate them to model the power behavior for concurrent system calls. A second transfer may begin before the first transfer's power trace finishes. There are two possible scenarios: (1) If the second transfer starts when the first transfer is in final PSM tail state, then the resulting power trace can be generated by taking the maximum power of the overlapped period and keeping other periods unchanged. (2) If the second transfer starts when the first transfer has not finished all of its windows, then the window spikes of the two transfers may overlap. Whenever two window spikes overlap, the spike that starts later will be push back, till after first spike finishes. All the subsequent window spikes of that transfer will also be pushed back by the same offset.

6.3 3G Model

Extending the system-call-driven model for 3G follows the same process as for WiFi, with the following slight complication. The 3G power state machine has two productive states, and accordingly two promotion and two tail transition states. Hence in modeling a data transfer system call, we need to keep track of the transitions among those states. We infer the conditions, *e.g.,* data transfer bytes, for different transitions following the methodology in [21]. We then apply these conditions in modeling the power behavior of the consecutive windows of a transfer. Figure 16(b) plots the effective receiving rate under different signal strength for T-Mobile and AT&T 3G network.

6.4 Model Validation

We have incorporated the new model for WiFi and 3G into eprof [18] with 1K lines of code.

To validate the model, we place the phone with the powermeter in locations with different signal strength, and run benchmarks to generate network traffic, while logging the system calls, signal strength and server RTT. We then feed the logs into eprof and compare the predicted energy consumption on wireless interfaces with the energy reading from the powermeter.

Since Android apps generally consume considerable amount of energy on display, CPU and other components (*e.g.,* GPS), which complicates the energy validation, we resort to trace driven experiment to generate traffic. We first load several popular mobile websites using the Android browser and record the size and RTT of each flow, as summarized in Table 5. We then host the same contents on our local servers, emulate the RTT using `tc` and write a simple Android app to perform the downloading.

Figure 17 shows the validation result for the old model (*i.e.,* without incorporating signal strength and RTT) and the new model for Nexus One at poor signal strength locations, where the WiFi signal is below -80dBm and 3G signal is below -100dBm. We see that for WiFi, while the error rate of old model ranges from 16.1% to 61.0%, the new model prediction error stays within 5.4%. Similarly, for 3G the new model has an error rate of less than 7.2%, in contrast to 19.3% to 52.1% of the old model.

7. WHAT-IF ANALYSIS

In this section, we show how our new, signal-strength-aware system-call-driven power model enables what-if analysis for the effectiveness of energy optimization techniques that explore signal strength dynamics. In particular, we study how much energy could be saved for a subset of the users from our 3785-user trace by exploring the simple technique of delaying background network traffic to a later time when the signal strength is good.

Trace. We selected three subsets, each containing 5 user traces over a 20-day period, who experienced primarily poor, moderate, and good 3G signal conditions. Similarly we selected three subsets of user traces for WiFi. Recall the user trace contains network usage in 5-minute bins, and the signal strength upon every change.

Setup. Since the system-call-driven power model requires network system call trace as input, we synthesize a flow trace from the 5-minute bin network usage trace as follows. We first divide the traffic in each 5-minute bin into flows with an exponential flow size distribution with a mean of 4344 bytes, and assign the start time for each flow following a uniform distribution within the 5 minutes period. Then we assign end-to-end RTTs to each flow following a uniform distribution between 5ms to 100ms for WiFi [7] and 100ms to 700ms for 3G [12].

Delayed flow scheduling. Our simple signal-strength-aware flow scheduling works as follows. For each flow, we determine if it belongs to background traffic following a probability of BG_RATIO. For each background flow, if the signal strength at its start time is below RSSI_THRESHOLD and the signal strength increases to above the threshold within the following MAX_DELAY_TIME, the flow will be delayed till when the signal condition crosses the threshold. We assume signal strength can be predicted, following techniques such as [23]. The RSSI_THRESHOLD is set to -80dBm and -100dBm for WiFi and 3G, respectively.

Results. We use the new power model to calculate each user's energy consumption on data communications, with and without the delay scheduling. Figure 18 plots the energy reduction from the delay scheduling for 15 users over the 20-day period, with MAX_DELAY_TIME of 2 hours and 12 hours, respectively. We see almost linear increase in energy saving as the background traffic increases. We also observe a large variation in energy reduction across different users, ranging from 0.002% to 23.7% under WiFi and from 1.1% to 21.5% under 3G, with BG_RATIO of 40% and MAX_DELAY_TIME of 12 hours. To understand the reason, we plot the RSSI over time for three selected 3G users, who have little, moderate and a lot of energy saving (not shown due to page limit). We clearly observe that the more fluctuation the signal strength over time, the more energy saving from the delay scheduling.

8. RELATED WORK

We have already discussed related work on WiFi and 3G power modeling and how our new model differs from them in §4. To our best knowledge, our work is the first measurement study of 3G and WiFi signal strength experienced by a large number of users in

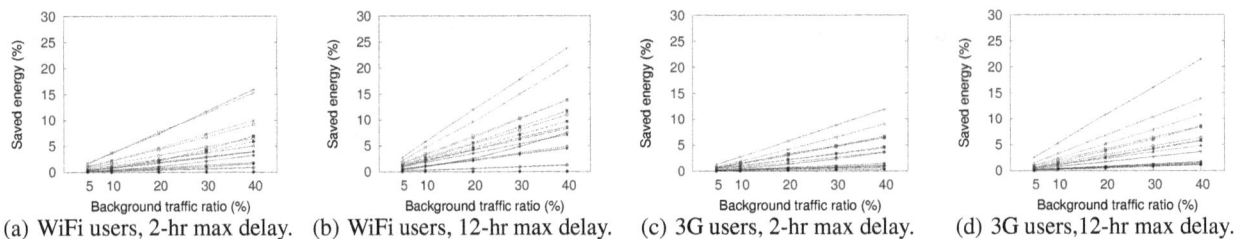

(a) WiFi users, 2-hr max delay. (b) WiFi users, 12-hr max delay. (c) 3G users, 2-hr max delay. (d) 3G users,12-hr max delay.

Figure 18: Energy reduction from delay scheduling. Each line represents a unique user.

daily life. In the following, we focus on previous work on the impact of poor signal strength on mobile device energy consumption.

Schulman *et al.* [23] observe that cellular signal varies by location, and strong signal reduces energy cost of communicating, and develop track-based signal strength prediction and energy-aware scheduling algorithms for two specific workloads by deferring or prefetching data during good signal conditions. In [9], the authors measure the power draw of WiFi-based phones to increase slightly under poor signal strength, when dynamic power control is enabled. In [6], the authors perform an in-depth study of power dissipation of smartphone components and find GSM dissipates 30% more energy when transferring at poor signal strength. Different from these work, we systematically quantify and break down the impact of poor WiFi and 3G signal strength on all relevant layers of the network stack, and for varying flow sizes and server RTTs.

9. CONCLUSION

In this paper, we have performed the first measurement study of 3G and WiFi signal strength experienced by a large number (3785) of smartphone users over 1 to 19 months of daily usage. Our analysis has shown that smartphone users are routinely experiencing significant 3G and WiFi signal variations during daily active phone usage. Further, the 3785 users we studied performed on average 43% and 21% of their foreground data transfers during poor 3G and WiFi signal strength, respectively. Our trace analysis motivates the need for diagnosing cellular network services to improve the user experience.

We further performed controlled experiments to quantify the energy impact of poor signal strength on data transfers, and drew implications on energy-efficient app design. We then developed a new system-call-driven power model that improves the accuracy over the previous state of the art by taking into account the impact of signal strength and RTT. Using our new model, we show that simply delaying of background traffic can reduce the total energy consumption of data communication by up to 23.7% and 21.5% under WiFi and 3G, respectively, assuming a maximum delay of 12 hours. Our new power model enables more accurate energy profiling for smartphone apps [18] and what-if analysis of current and future optimization techniques that explore signal strength dynamics. We plan to explore these avenues in our future work.

10. REFERENCES

[1] Aircrack-ng. http://www.aircrack-ng.org/.

[2] Monsoon power monitor. http://www.msoon.com/LabEquipment/PowerMonitor/.

[3] Smartphone statistics 2011. http://www.digitalbuzzblog.com/2011-mobile-statistics-stats-facts-marketing-infographic/.

[4] N. Balasubramanian, A. Balasubramanian, and A. Venkataramani. Energy consumption in mobile phones: a measurement study and implications for network applications. In *Proc of IMC*, 2009.

[5] I.-S. S. Board. Wireless lan medium access control (mac) and physical layer (phy) specification. *Electronics*, 1999(802.11), 1997.

[6] A. Carroll and G. Heiser. An analysis of power consumption in a smartphone. In *Proc. of USENIX ATC*, 2010.

[7] N. Ding, A. Pathak, D. Koutsonikolas, C. Shepard, Y. C. Hu, and L. Zhong. Realizing the full potential of psm using proxying. In *Proc. of IEEE INFOCOM*, 2012.

[8] H. Falaki, D. Lymberopoulos, R. Mahajan, S. Kandula, and D. Estrin. A first look at traffic on smartphones. In *Proc. of IMC*, 2010.

[9] A. Gupta and P. Mohapatra. Energy consumption and conservation in wifi based phones: A measurement-based study. In *SECON '07*, 2007.

[10] G. Holland, N. Vaidya, and V. Bahl. A rate-adaptive mac protocol for multihop wireless networks. In *Proc. of ACM MOBICOM*, 2001.

[11] J. Huang, F. Qian, A. Gerber, Z. M. Mao, S. Sen, and O. Spatscheck. A close examination of performance and power characteristics of 4g lte networks. In *Proc. of Mobisys*, 2012.

[12] J. Huang, Q. Xu, B. Tiwana, Z. M. Mao, M. Zhang, and P. Bahl. Anatomizing application performance difference on smartphones. In *Proc. of Mobisys*, 2010.

[13] A. Kamerman and L. Monteban. WaveLAN ii: A high-performance wireless LAN for the unlicensed band. In *Bell Labs Technical Journal*, 1997.

[14] M. Lacage, M. H. Manshaei, and T. Tueletti. IEEE 202.11 rate adaptation: A practical approach. In *Proc. of ACM MSWiM*, 2004.

[15] C.-Y. Li, C. Peng, S. Lu, and X. Wang. Energy-based rate adaptation for 802.11n. In *Proc. of ACM MobiCom*, 2012.

[16] R. Mittal, A. Kansal, and R. Chandra. Empowering developers to estimate app energy consumption. In *Proc. of ACM MobiCom*, 2012.

[17] A. Pathak, Y. C. Hu, and M. Zhang. Bootstrapping energy debugging for smartphones: A first look at energy bugs in mobile devices. In *Proc. of Hotnets*, 2011.

[18] A. Pathak, Y. C. Hu, and M. Zhang. Where is the energy spent inside my app? fine grained energy accounting on smartphones with eprof. In *Proc. of EuroSys*, 2012.

[19] A. Pathak, Y. C. Hu, M. Zhang, P. Bahl, and Y.-M. Wang. Fine-grained power modeling for smartphones using system-call tracing. In *Proc. of EuroSys*, 2011.

[20] F. Qian, Z. Wang, A. Gerber, Z. Mao, S. Sen, and O. Spatscheck. Profiling resource usage for mobile applications: a cross-layer approach. In *Proc. of Mobisys*, 2011.

[21] F. Qian, Z. Wang, A. Gerber, Z. M. Mao, S. Sen, and O. Spatscheck. Characterizing radio resource allocation for 3g networks. In *Proc. of IMC*, 2010.

[22] B. Sadeghi, V. Kanodia, and E. Knightly. Opportunistic media access for multirate ad hoc networks. In *Proc. of ACM MOBICOM*, 2002.

[23] A. Schulman, V. Navda, R. Ramjee, N. Spring, P. Deshpande, C. Grunewald, K. Jain, and V. N. Padmanabhan. Bartendr: a practical approach to energy-aware cellular data scheduling. In *Proc. of ACM Mobicom*, 2010.

[24] A. Shye, B. Scholbrock, and G. Memik. Into the wild: studying real user activity patterns to guide power optimizations for mobile architectures. In *MICRO*, 2009.

[25] S. Wong, H. Yang, S. Lu, and V. Bharghavan. Robust rate adaptation for 802.11 wireless networks. In *Proc. of ACM MobiCom*, 2006.

[26] L. Zhang, B. Tiwana, Z. Qian, Z. Wang, R. Dick, Z. Mao, and L. Yang. Accurate Online Power Estimation and Automatic Battery Behavior Based Power Model Generation for Smartphones. In *Proc. of CODES+ISSS*, 2010.

A Large-Scale Service System with Packing Constraints: Minimizing the Number of Occupied Servers

Alexander L. Stolyar
Bell Labs, Alcatel-Lucent
600 Mountain Ave., 2C-322
Murray Hill, NJ 07974
stolyar@research.bell-labs.com

Yuan Zhong
University of California
465 Soda Hall, MC-1776
Berkeley, CA 94720
zhyu4118@berkeley.edu

ABSTRACT

We consider a large-scale service system model proposed in [14], which is motivated by the problem of efficient placement of virtual machines to physical host machines in a network cloud, so that the total number of occupied hosts is minimized. Customers of different types arrive to a system with an infinite number of servers. A server packing *configuration* is the vector $\boldsymbol{k} = \{k_i\}$, where k_i is the number of type-i customers that the server "contains". Packing constraints are described by a fixed finite set of allowed configurations. Upon arrival, each customer is placed into a server immediately, subject to the packing constraints; the server can be idle or already serving other customers. After service completion, each customer leaves its server and the system.

It was shown in [14] that a simple real-time algorithm, called *Greedy*, is asymptotically optimal in the sense of minimizing $\sum_k X_k^{1+\alpha}$ in the stationary regime, as the customer arrival rates grow to infinity. (Here $\alpha > 0$, and X_k denotes the number of servers with configuration $\boldsymbol{k}$.) In particular, when parameter α is small, and in the asymptotic regime where customer arrival rates grow to infinity, *Greedy* solves a problem *approximating* one of minimizing $\sum_k X_k$, the number of occupied hosts. In this paper we introduce the algorithm called *Greedy with sublinear Safety Stocks (GSS)*, and show that it asymptotically solves the *exact* problem of minimizing $\sum_k X_k$. An important feature of the algorithm is that sublinear safety stocks of X_k are created automatically – when and where necessary – without having to determine *a priori* where they are required. Moreover, we also provide a tight characterization of the rate of convergence to optimality under *GSS*. The *GSS* algorithm is as simple as *Greedy*, and uses no more system state information than *Greedy* does.

Categories and Subject Descriptors

[**Network Services**]: Cloud Computing; [**Probability and Statistics**]: Markov Processes, Queueing Theory, Stochastic Processes; [**Design and Analysis of Algorithms**]: Packing and Covering Problems

General Terms

Algorithms, Performance, Theory

Keywords

Multi-dimensional Bin Packing, Infinite-Server System, Markov Chain, Safety Stocks, Fluid Scale Optimality, Local Fluid Scaling

1. INTRODUCTION

We consider a service system model [14] motivated by the problem of efficient placement of virtual machines (VMs) to physical host machines (servers) in a data center (DC) [6]. A *service policy* decides to which server each incoming VM will be placed. We are interested in service policies that minimize the total number of occupied servers in the system. It is further desirable that the policy be simple, so that placement decisions are made in real time, and depend only on the current system state, but not on system parameters.

Consider the following description of a DC. It consists of a number of servers. While servers may potentially have different characteristics, in this paper we assume that they are all the same. More specifically, let there be N different types of resources (for example, type-1 resource can be CPU, type-2 resource can be memory, etc). For each $n \in \{1, 2, \dots, N\}$, a server possesses amount $B_n > 0$ of type-n resource. I types of VMs arrive in a probabilistic fashion, and request services at the DC. Arriving VMs will be placed into the servers, occupying certain resources. More specifically, for $i \in \{1, 2, \dots, I\}$, a type-i VM requires amount $b_{i,n} > 0$ of type-n resource during service, where $n \in \{1, 2, \dots, N\}$. Once a VM completes its service, it departs the system, freeing up corresponding resources. We assume that service times of different VMs are independent.

For each $i \in \{1, 2, \dots, I\}$, let k_i be the number of type-i VMs that a server contains. Then the following *vector packing constraints* must be observed at all times. Namely, a server can contain k_i type-i VMs ($i \in \{1, 2, \dots, I\}$) simultaneously if and only if

$$\sum_i k_i b_{i,n} \leq B_n, \tag{1}$$

for each $n \in \{1, 2, \dots, N\}$. In this case, the vector $\boldsymbol{k} = (k_1, \dots, k_I)$ is called a *server configuration*.

The model considered in this paper is similar to the DC described above, but different in the following two aspects.

1. While vector packing constraints (cf. Eq. (1)) arise naturally in the context of VM placement, we make the more general assumption of so-called *monotone* packing constraints (cf. Section 2.1) in our model.

2. We consider a system with an infinite number of servers, where incoming VMs will be immediately placed into a server. For large-scale DCs, the number of servers is not a bottleneck, hence an infinite-server system reasonably approximates such DCs.

We would also like to remark that an important assumption of our model is that the service requirement of a VM is not affected by potentially other VMs occupying the same server. This is a reasonable modeling assumption for multi-core servers, for example.

There can be different performance objectives of interest. For example, we may be interested in minimizing the total energy consumption [6], or maximizing system throughput [9]. In this paper, we are interested in minimizing the total number of occupied servers. These objectives are different but related. For example, by switching off idle servers, or keeping them in stand-by mode, we can reduce energy consumption by minimizing the number of occupied servers.

In the main results of the paper, we introduce the policy called *Greedy with sublinear Safety Stocks* (GSS) and show that it asymptotically minimizes the total number of occupied servers in steady state, as the input flow rates of VMs grow to infinity. More precisely, we prove the asymptotic optimality of *GSS* for a closed version of the system model, and that of its variant, *GSS-M*, for the actual (open) system model (Theorems 6 and 7). *GSS* is a simple policy that makes placement decisions in real time, and based only on the current system state. Informally speaking, *GSS* places incoming VMs in a way that greedily minimizes a Lyapunov function, which asymptotically coincides with the total number of occupied servers. *GSS* maintains non-empty safety stocks at every server configuration k whenever X_k becomes "too small", so as to allow flexibility on VM placement. In other words, under *GSS*, there is a non-zero number of servers of every configuration, so that an incoming VM can potentially be placed into a server with any configuration. These safety stocks correspond to the discrepancy between the Lyapunov function and the total number of occupied servers, and grow "sublinearly" with the input flow rates. We also provide a characterization of the rate of convergence to optimality under *GSS*, which is tighter than the conventional fluid-scale convergence rate.

1.1 Related Works

In this section, we discuss related works, and put our results in perspective.

The most closely related work is [14], where the model considered in this paper was proposed, and a related problem was studied. In both this paper and [14], the asymptotic regime of interest is when the input flow rates grow to infinity, and the system is considered under the *fluid scaling*, i.e., when the system states are scaled down by the input flow rates. In [14], the problem of interest is minimizing $\sum_k X_k^{1+\alpha}$, where $\alpha > 0$, and X_k is the number of occupied servers with configuration k. A simple policy called *Greedy*

was introduced, which asymptotically minimizes the sum $\sum_k X_k^{1+\alpha}$, for any $\alpha > 0$, in the stationary regime. Policies *Greedy* and *GSS* differ in two important aspects. First, they try to minimize different objectives – $\sum_k X_k^{1+\alpha}$ ($\alpha > 0$) and $\sum_k X_k$, respectively. When $\alpha > 0$ is small, *Greedy* approximately solves the problem of minimizing the total number of occupied servers $\sum_k X_k$, in the asymptotic regime where the input flow rates grow to infinity, and at the fluid scale. However, if minimizing $\sum_k X_k$ is the "true" desired objective, $\alpha > 0$ need to be chosen carefully, depending on the system scale (input flow rates), which may be difficult to do. Therefore, we believe that asymptotically solving the exact problem of minimizing $\sum_k X_k$ is of substantial interest. Moreover, the policy *GSS* proposed in this paper is as simple as *Greedy*, and uses no more system state information than *Greedy* does. Second, at a technical level, to prove the asymptotic optimality of *Greedy*, [14] considered only the fluid scaling and the corresponding fluid limits. In this paper, to prove the asymptotic optimality of *GSS*, it is no longer sufficient to consider the fluid-scale system behavior alone; a *local fluid scaling* is also considered, needed to study the dynamics of safety stocks. In addition, this allows us to derive a tighter characterization of the rate of convergence to optimality under *GSS*, as opposed to the fluid-scale convergence shown in [14] for *Greedy*.

On a broader level, the model considered in this paper is related to the vast literature on classical stochastic bin packing problems. In a bin packing system, random-sized items arrive, and need to be placed into finite-sized bins. The items do not leave or move between bins, and a typical objective is to minimize the number of occupied bins. A packing problem is *one-dimensional* if sizes of the items and bins are captured by scalars, and *multi-dimensional* if they are captured by vectors. Problems with the multi-dimensional packing constraints (1) are called *vector packing*. For a good review of one-dimensional bin packing, see for example [2], and see for example [1] for a recent review of multi-dimensional packing. In bin packing *service* systems, items (customers) arrive at random times to be placed into a bin (server), and leave after a random service time. The servers can process multiple customers as long as packing constraints are observed. Customers get queued, and a typical objective of a packing algorithm is to maximize system throughput. (See for example [4] for a review of this line of work.) Our model is similar to the latter systems, except there are multiple bins (servers) – in fact, an infinite number in our case. Models of this type are more recent (see for example, [8, 9]). [8] addresses a joint routing and VM placement problem, which in particular includes packing constraints. The approach of [8] resembles Markov Chain algorithms used in combinatorial optimization. [9] considers maximizing throughput of a queueing system with a finite number of bins (servers), where VMs can wait for service. Very recently, [7] has new results on the classical one-dimensional online bin packing; it also contains heuristics and simulations for the corresponding system with item departures, which is a special case of our model.

As mentioned earlier, we consider the asymptotic regime where the input flow rates scale up to infinity. In this respect, our work is related to the (also vast) literature on queueing systems in the *many servers* regime. (See e.g. [12] for an overview. The name "many servers" reflects the fact that the average number of occupied servers scales up to infinity as well, linearly with the input flow rates.) However, packing constraints are not present in earlier works (prior to [14]) on the many servers regime, to the best of our knowledge.

The idea of maintaining sublinear safety stocks to increase system flexibility, and hence avoid "resource" starvation – the approach taken by *GSS*, the policy proposed in this paper – has also appeared in other works. For example, see [10] and the references therein for an overview. However, to the best of our knowledge, the following feature of *GSS* is novel, and has not appeared in algorithms proposed in earlier works. Namely, *GSS* creates safety stocks *automatically*, in the sense that it does not require *a priori* knowledge of the subset of configurations for which the sublinear safety stocks need to be maintained. As a result, *GSS* does not require any *a priori* knowledge of the system parameters, because the safety stocks automatically adapt to parameter changes. We remark that the policy *Greedy* proposed in [14] also creates safety stocks, but they scale linearly with the input flow rates, whereas *GSS* creates sublinear safety stocks.

Finally, an overview of some resource allocation issues that arise from VM placement in the context of cloud computing can be found in [6].

1.2 Organization

The rest of the paper is organized as follows. In Section 1.3, we introduce the notation and conventions adopted in this paper. The precise model and main results are described in Section 2. The model is introduced in Section 2.1. Here we describe two versions of the model, the closed and open system. In Section 2.2, we describe the asymptotic regime of interest. The *GSS* policy is described in Section 2.3, and the main results, Theorems 6 and 7, are stated in Section 2.4, for the closed and open system, respectively. Sections 3 and 4 are devoted to proving Theorems 6 and 7, respectively. A discussion of the results in this paper and some future directions is provided in Section 5.

1.3 Notation and Conventions

Let $\mathbb{R}$ be the set of real numbers, and let $\mathbb{R}_+$ be the set of nonnegative real numbers. Let $\mathbb{Z}$ be the set of integers, let $\mathbb{Z}_+$ be the set of nonnegative integers, and let $\mathbb{N}$ be the set of natural numbers. $\mathbb{R}^n$ denotes the real vector space of dimension n, and $\mathbb{R}_+^n$ denotes the nonnegative orthant of $\mathbb{R}^n$. $\mathbb{Z}^n$ and $\mathbb{Z}_+^n$ are similarly defined. We reserve bold letters for vectors, and plain letters for scalars and sets. For a scalar x, let $|x|$ denote its absolute value, and let $\lfloor x \rfloor$ denote the largest integer that does not exceed x. For two scalars x and y, let $x \wedge y = \min\{x, y\}$, and let $x \vee y = \max\{x, y\}$. For a vector $\boldsymbol{x} = (x_i)_{i=1}^n \in \mathbb{R}^n$, let $\|\boldsymbol{x}\|$ denote its 1-norm, i.e., $\|\boldsymbol{x}\| = \sum_{i=1}^n |x_i|$. The distance from vector $\boldsymbol{x} \in \mathbb{R}^n$ to a set $U \subset \mathbb{R}^n$ is denoted by $d(\boldsymbol{x}, U) = \inf_{\boldsymbol{u} \in U} \|\boldsymbol{x} - \boldsymbol{u}\|$. We use $\boldsymbol{e}_i$ to denote the i-th standard unit vector, with only the ith component being 1, and all other components being 0. For a set $\mathcal{N}$, let $\mathbf{1}_{\mathcal{N}}$ be the indicator function of $\mathcal{N}$. For a finite set $\mathcal{N}$, let $|\mathcal{N}|$ be its cardinality. For two sets $\mathcal{N}$ and $\mathcal{M}$, let $\mathcal{N} \backslash \mathcal{M}$ denote the set difference of $\mathcal{N}$ and $\mathcal{M}$, i.e., $\mathcal{N} \backslash \mathcal{M} = \{x \in \mathcal{N} : x \notin \mathcal{M}\}$. For a set $\mathcal{N} \subset \mathbb{R}^n$, let $\langle \mathcal{N} \rangle$ denote its convex hull, i.e., the set of all $\boldsymbol{x} \in \mathbb{R}^n$ such that there exist $\gamma_1, \ldots, \gamma_m \in \mathbb{R}_+$ and $\boldsymbol{v}_1, \ldots, \boldsymbol{v}_m \in \mathcal{N}$ with $\boldsymbol{x} = \sum_{j=1}^m \gamma_j \boldsymbol{v}_j$ and $\sum_{j=1}^m \gamma_j = 1$. Symbol $\rightarrow$ means ordinary convergence in $\mathbb{R}^n$, and $\implies$ denotes convergence in distribution of random variables taking values in $\mathbb{R}^n$,

equipped with the Borel σ-algebra. The abbreviation *w.p.1* means convergence *with probability 1*. We often write $x(\cdot)$ to mean the function (or random process) $\{x(t), \ t \geq 0\}$. We write iff as a shorthand for "if and only if", i.o for "infinitely often", LHS for "left-hand side" and RHS for "right-hand side". We also write WLOG for "without loss of generality", w.r.t for "with respect to", and u.o.c for "uniformly on compact sets".

Throughout this paper, if $x(\cdot)$ is a random process (which in most cases will be Markov), we will denote by $x(\infty)$ its random state when the process is in stationary regime; in other words, $x(\infty)$ is equal in distribution to $x(t)$ (for any t) when $x(\cdot)$ is stationary. We use the terms *steady state* and *stationary regime* interchangeably.

2. MODEL AND MAIN RESULTS

2.1 Infinite Server System with Packing Constraints

We consider the following infinite server system that evolves in continuous time. There are I types of customers, indexed by $i \in \{1, 2, \ldots, I\} \equiv \mathcal{I}$, and an infinite number of homogeneous servers. A server can potentially serve more than one customer simultaneously. We use $\boldsymbol{k} = (k_1, k_2, \ldots, k_I) \in \mathbb{Z}_+^I$, an I-dimensional vector with nonnegative integer components, to denote a *server configuration*. The general packing constraints are captured by the finite set $\bar{\mathcal{K}} \subset \mathbb{Z}_+^I$ of *feasible server configurations*. Thus, a server can simultaneously serve k_i customers of type i, $i \in \mathcal{I}$, iff $\boldsymbol{k} = (k_1, k_2, \ldots, k_I) \in \bar{\mathcal{K}}$. From now on, we drop the word "feasible", and simply call $\bar{\mathcal{K}}$ the set of server configurations.

In this paper, we assume that the set $\bar{\mathcal{K}}$ is *monotone*.

ASSUMPTION 1. $\bar{\mathcal{K}}$ *is monotone in the following sense. If* $\boldsymbol{k} \in \bar{\mathcal{K}}$, *and* $\boldsymbol{k}' \in \mathbb{Z}_+^I$ *has* $\boldsymbol{k}' \leq \boldsymbol{k}$ *component-wise, then* $\boldsymbol{k}' \in \bar{\mathcal{K}}$ *as well.*

A simple consequence of the monotonicity assumption is that $\boldsymbol{0} \in \bar{\mathcal{K}}$. We now let $\mathcal{K} = \bar{\mathcal{K}} \backslash \{\boldsymbol{0}\}$ denote the set of non-zero server configurations.

Vector Packing is Monotone. An important example of monotone packing is vector packing. Consider the vector packing constraints in (1). It is clear that if the server configuration $\boldsymbol{k} = \{k_1, \ldots, k_I\}$ satisfies (1), and if $\boldsymbol{k}' \leq \boldsymbol{k}$ component-wise, then $\boldsymbol{k}'$ also satisfies (1). On the other hand, not all monotone packing is vector packing. For example, when $I = 2$, $\bar{\mathcal{K}} = \{(0,0), (0,1), (0,2), (1,0), (2,0)\}$ is monotone, but is not described by vector packing constraints. In the sequel, we will only assume monotone packing in our model, and all our results hold under this general setting.

To exclude triviality, we also assume that for all $i \in \mathcal{I}$, $\boldsymbol{e}_i$ (the i-th standard unit vector) is an element of $\bar{\mathcal{K}}$.

As discussed in the introduction, we make the following important assumption in this paper. We assume that simultaneous services do *not* affect the service distributions of individual customers; in other words, the service time of a customer is unaffected by whether or not there are other customers served simultaneously by the same server. Let us also remark that before we consider an open system, where each arriving customer is immediately placed for service in one of the servers, and leaves the system after service completion, we will first consider a "closed" version of this open system. The reason is twofold. First, the analysis of the closed system is a stepping stone to that of the open system, and illustrates the main ideas more clearly. Second, we will see shortly that the closed system can be used to model job migration in a cloud, and is therefore of independent interest.

Denote by $X_{\boldsymbol{k}}$ the number of servers with configuration $\boldsymbol{k} \in \mathcal{K}$. The system state is then the vector $\boldsymbol{X} = \{X_{\boldsymbol{k}}, \ \boldsymbol{k} \in \mathcal{K}\}$. By convention, $X_{\boldsymbol{0}} \equiv 0$ at all times.

Closed System. Here we describe the "closed" version of the model. Let $r \in \mathbb{N}$ be given. Suppose that there are in total r customers in the system, and no exogenous arrivals. For each $i \in \mathcal{I}$, we suppose that there are $\rho_i r$ customers of type i in the system at all times. This in particular implies that $\sum_{i \in \mathcal{I}} \rho_i = 1$. It is convenient to index the system by r its total number of customers, and we use $\boldsymbol{X}^r = (X_{\boldsymbol{k}}^r, \ \boldsymbol{k} \in \mathcal{K})$ to denote a system state. The system evolves as follows. Each customer is almost always in service, except at a discrete set of time instances (which may be customer dependent), where it migrates from one server to another (possibly the same one), subject to the packing constraints imposed by $\bar{\mathcal{K}}$. For a customer, the time between consecutive migrations is called its *service requirement*. Thus, one can alternatively think of a customer as departing the system after its service requirement, and then immediately arriving to the system, to be placed into a server. For each i, we assume that the service requirements of type-i customers are i.i.d. exponential random variables with mean $1/\mu_i$, and that the service requirements are independent across different $i \in \mathcal{I}$. A (Markovian) *service policy* ("packing rule") decides to which server a customer will be placed after its service requirement, based only on the current system state $\boldsymbol{X}^r$. A service policy has to observe the packing constraints. Under any well-defined service policy, the system state at time t, $\boldsymbol{X}^r(t)$, is a continuous-time Markov chain on a finite state space. Hence, for each r, the process $\{\boldsymbol{X}^r(t), \ t \geq 0\}$ always has a stationary distribution.

Open System. In the open system, customers of type i arrive exogenously as an independent Poisson flow of rate $\lambda_i r$, where λ_i is fixed and r is a scaling parameter. Each arriving customer has to be placed for service immediately in one of the servers, subject to the packing constraints imposed by $\bar{\mathcal{K}}$. Service times of all customers are independent. Service time of a type-i customer is exponentially distributed with mean $1/\mu_i$. After a service completion, each customer leaves the system. If we denote $\rho_i = \lambda_i/\mu_i$, then in steady state, the average number of type i customers in the system is $\rho_i r$, and the average total number of customers is $\sum_i \rho_i r$. We assume, WLOG, that $\sum_i \rho_i = 1$ – this is equivalent to re-choosing the value of parameter r, if necessary. A (Markovian) *service policy* ("packing rule") in this case decides to which server an arriving customer will be placed, based only on the current system state. A service policy has to observe the packing constraints. Similar to the closed system, we let $X_{\boldsymbol{k}}^r(t)$ denote the number of servers with configuration $\boldsymbol{k}$ at time t in the rth system. However, for the policy that we will study, $\boldsymbol{X}^r(t) = (X_{\boldsymbol{k}}^r(t))_{\boldsymbol{k} \in \mathcal{K}}$ will not be a Markov process. We postpone the discussion of a complete Markovian description of the system and the existence of the associated stationary distribution to Section 2.3.2.

2.2 Asymptotic Regime

We are interested in finding a service policy that minimizes the total number of occupied servers in the stationary regime. The exact problem is intractable, so instead we consider asymptotically optimal service policies. For both the closed and open systems, the asymptotic regime of interest is when $r \to \infty$. Informally speaking, in this limit, the *fluid-scaled* system state satisfies a conservation law (cf. Eq. (4)), and the best that a policy can do is solving a linear program, subject to this conservation law. We now describe the asymptotic regime in more detail.

First, we defined the so-called *fluid scaling*. Recall that both the closed and open systems are indexed by r, and $\boldsymbol{X}^r(t)$ is the vector that denotes the numbers of servers of various configurations at time t, in the rth system. The *fluid scaled* process is $\boldsymbol{x}^r(t) = \boldsymbol{X}^r(t)/r$. For each r, in the closed system, $\boldsymbol{X}^r(\cdot)$ has a (not necessarily unique) stationary distribution, so $\boldsymbol{x}^r(\cdot)$ also has a stationary distribution. We will see shortly that in an open system, $\boldsymbol{X}^r(\cdot)$ also has a stationary distribution (see Lemma 5). Denote by $\boldsymbol{X}^r(\infty)$ and $\boldsymbol{x}^r(\infty)$ the random states of the corresponding processes in a stationary regime. (Recall the convention in Section 1.3.)

We now argue that as $r \to \infty$,

$$\sum_{\boldsymbol{k} \in \mathcal{K}} k_i x_{\boldsymbol{k}}^r(\infty) \implies \rho_i, \quad \text{for all } i. \tag{2}$$

In a closed system, for each $i \in \mathcal{I}$, there are $\rho_i r$ customers of type i in the system at all times, so on all sample paths,

$$\sum_{\boldsymbol{k} \in \mathcal{K}} k_i x_{\boldsymbol{k}}^r(t) = \rho_i, \quad \text{for all } r, t \text{ and } i.$$

This implies that the same holds for $\boldsymbol{x}^r(\infty)$. In an open system, the total number of type-i customers is $\sum_{\boldsymbol{k} \in \mathcal{K}} k_i X_{\boldsymbol{k}}^r(\infty)$, in steady state. It is easy to see that, independent from the service policy, this quantity is a Poisson random variable with mean $\rho_i r$. Thus, as $r \to \infty$, $\sum_{\boldsymbol{k} \in \mathcal{K}} k_i x_{\boldsymbol{k}}^r(\infty) \implies \rho_i$.

Now consider the following linear program (LP).

$$\text{Minimize} \quad \sum_{\boldsymbol{k} \in \mathcal{K}} x_{\boldsymbol{k}} \tag{3}$$

$$\text{subject to} \quad \sum_{\boldsymbol{k} \in \mathcal{K}} k_i x_{\boldsymbol{k}} = \rho_i, \quad \text{for all } i \in \mathcal{I}, \tag{4}$$

$$x_{\boldsymbol{k}} \geq 0, \quad \text{for all } \boldsymbol{k} \in \mathcal{K}. \tag{5}$$

Denote by $\mathcal{X}$ the set of feasible solutions to LP:

$$\mathcal{X} = \{\boldsymbol{x} \in \mathbb{R}_+^{|\mathcal{K}|} : \sum_{\boldsymbol{k} \in \mathcal{K}} k_i x_{\boldsymbol{k}} = \rho_i, i \in \mathcal{I}\}.$$

Then $\mathcal{X}$ is a compact subset of $\mathbb{R}_+^{|\mathcal{K}|}$. Let $\mathcal{X}^*$ denote the set of optimal solutions of LP, and let u^* denote its optimal value. In light of Eqs. (2) and (4), a service policy is asymptotically optimal if, roughly speaking, under this policy and for large r, $\sum_{\boldsymbol{k} \in \mathcal{K}} x_{\boldsymbol{k}}^r(\infty) \approx u^*$ with high probability (cf. Theorems 6 and 7).

The following characterization of the set $\mathcal{X}^*$ by dual variables will be useful. The proof is elementary and omitted.

LEMMA 2. $\boldsymbol{x} = (x_{\boldsymbol{k}})_{\boldsymbol{k} \in \mathcal{K}} \in \mathcal{X}^*$ iff $\boldsymbol{x}$ is a feasible solution of LP, and there exist $\eta_i \in \mathbb{R}$, $i \in \mathcal{I}$, such that

(i) $\sum_{i \in \mathcal{I}} k_i \eta_i \leq 1$ for all $\boldsymbol{k} \in \mathcal{K}$, and

(ii) if $\sum_{i \in \mathcal{I}} k_i \eta_i < 1$, then $x_{\boldsymbol{k}} = 0$.

The following lemma relates the distance between a point $\boldsymbol{x} \in \mathcal{X}$ and the optimal set $\mathcal{X}^*$ to the objective value of LP evaluated at $\boldsymbol{x}$.

LEMMA 3. *There exists a positive constant $D \geq 1$ such that for any $\boldsymbol{x} \in \mathcal{X}$,*

$$D \left(\sum_{\boldsymbol{k} \in \mathcal{K}} x_{\boldsymbol{k}} - u^* \right) \geq d\left(\boldsymbol{x}, \mathcal{X}^*\right).$$

Note that $D \geq 1$ is necessary, since for every $\boldsymbol{x} \in \mathcal{X}$, $d\left(\boldsymbol{x}, \mathcal{X}^*\right) \geq \sum_{\boldsymbol{k} \in \mathcal{K}} x_{\boldsymbol{k}} - u^*$.

PROOF. See [15]. □

2.3 Greedy with sublinear Safety Stocks (GSS)

Now we introduce the service policy, *Greedy with sublinear Safety Stocks (GSS)*, along with a variant, which we will prove to be asymptotically optimal.

2.3.1 GSS Policy in a Closed System

GSS. Let $p \in (\frac{1}{2}, 1)$. For a given r, define a weight function $w^r : \mathbb{R}_+ \to \mathbb{R}_+$ to be $w^r(X) = 1 \wedge \frac{X}{r^p}$. Let $\mathcal{M}$ denote the set of all pairs $(\boldsymbol{k}, i) \in \mathcal{K} \times \mathcal{I}$ such that $\boldsymbol{k} \in \mathcal{K}$ and $\boldsymbol{k} - \boldsymbol{e}_i \in \bar{\mathcal{K}}$. Given $\boldsymbol{X} = \{X_{\boldsymbol{k}'}, \boldsymbol{k}' \in \mathcal{K}\}$ and $(\boldsymbol{k}, i) \in \mathcal{M}$, define $\Delta^r_{(\boldsymbol{k}, i)}(\boldsymbol{X}) = w^r(X_{\boldsymbol{k}}) - w^r(X_{\boldsymbol{k} - \boldsymbol{e}_i})$. Under *GSS*, a customer of type i is placed into a server with configuration $\boldsymbol{k} - \boldsymbol{e}_i$ where $X_{\boldsymbol{k} - \boldsymbol{e}_i} > 0$ or $\boldsymbol{k} - \boldsymbol{e}_i = \boldsymbol{0}$, such that $\Delta_{(\boldsymbol{k}, i)}(\boldsymbol{X})$ is minimal. Ties are broken arbitrarily.

Note that the *GSS* policy makes decisions based only the current system state. The parameter r which it uses is nothing else but the total number of customers in the system, which is, of course, a function of the state, and which happens to be constant in the closed system.

We now provide an intuitive explanation of the policy. Let f^r be the anti-derivative of w^r, so that

$$f^r(X) = \begin{cases} \frac{X^2}{2r^p}, & \text{if } X \in [0, r^p]; \\ X - \frac{r^p}{2}, & \text{if } X > r^p. \end{cases}$$

Let $F^r(\boldsymbol{X}) = \sum_{\boldsymbol{k} \in \mathcal{K}} f^r(X_{\boldsymbol{k}})$. Then w^r and $\Delta^r_{(\boldsymbol{k}, i)}$ capture the first-order change in F^r. Suppose that the current system state is $\boldsymbol{X} = (X_{\boldsymbol{k}})_{\boldsymbol{k} \in \mathcal{K}}$. Then, placing a type-$i$ customer into a server with configuration $\boldsymbol{k} - \boldsymbol{e}_i$ only changes $X_{\boldsymbol{k} - \boldsymbol{e}_i}$ and $X_{\boldsymbol{k}}$: $X_{\boldsymbol{k} - \boldsymbol{e}_i}$ decreases by 1 (if $X_{\boldsymbol{k} - \boldsymbol{e}_i} > 0$), and $X_{\boldsymbol{k}}$ increases by 1. Thus, the first-order change in F^r is

$$\frac{d}{dX} f^r(X) \Big|_{X = X_{\boldsymbol{k}}} - \frac{d}{dX} f^r(X) \Big|_{X = X_{\boldsymbol{k} - \boldsymbol{e}_i}} = \Delta^r_{(\boldsymbol{k}, i)}(\boldsymbol{X}).$$

In this sense, *GSS* decreases F^r greedily, by placing a customer into a server that results in the largest (first-order) decrease in F^r.

The next lemma states that $F^r(\boldsymbol{X})$ only differs from $\sum_{\boldsymbol{k}} X_{\boldsymbol{k}}$ by $O(r^p)$. The proof is straightforward and omitted.

LEMMA 4. *For any $\boldsymbol{X} \in \mathbb{R}_+^{|\mathcal{K}|}$,*

$$\sum_{\boldsymbol{k} \in \mathcal{K}} X_{\boldsymbol{k}} - \frac{|\mathcal{K}| r^p}{2} \leq F^r(\boldsymbol{X}) \leq \sum_{\boldsymbol{k} \in \mathcal{K}} X_{\boldsymbol{k}}.$$

Under the fluid scaling described earlier, the difference $O(r^p)$ between $F^r(\boldsymbol{X})$ and $\sum_{\boldsymbol{k} \in \mathcal{K}} X_{\boldsymbol{k}}$ becomes negligible, as it is of order $o(r)$. Thus, for a fluid-scaled process, minimizing $F^r(\boldsymbol{X})$ (what *GSS* tries to do) is "equivalent" to minimizing $\sum_{\boldsymbol{k} \in \mathcal{K}} X_{\boldsymbol{k}}$, when r is large.

2.3.2 GSS Policy in an Open System

First, we describe the "pure" *GSS* policy.

GSS. Let $p \in (\frac{1}{2}, 1)$. For a given system state $\boldsymbol{X}$, let $Z = Z(\boldsymbol{X})$ denote the total number of customers in the system. For a system with parameter r, define a weight function $\bar{w}^r(X) = \bar{w}^r(X; Z)$ as follows: $\bar{w}^r(X) = 1 \wedge \frac{X}{Z^p}$. (Note that $\bar{w}^r(X)$ generalizes the corresponding weight function $w^r(X) = 1 \wedge \frac{X}{r^p}$ for the closed system, because in the closed system with parameter r the total number of customers is constant $Z \equiv r$.) Let $\mathcal{M}$ denote the set of all pairs $(\boldsymbol{k}, i) \in \mathcal{K} \times \mathcal{I}$ such that $\boldsymbol{k} \in \mathcal{K}$ and $\boldsymbol{k} - \boldsymbol{e}_i \in \bar{\mathcal{K}}$. Given $\boldsymbol{X} = \{X_{\boldsymbol{k}'}, \boldsymbol{k}' \in \mathcal{K}\}$ and $(\boldsymbol{k}, i) \in \mathcal{M}$, define $\bar{\Delta}^r_{(\boldsymbol{k}, i)}(\boldsymbol{X}) = \bar{w}^r(X_{\boldsymbol{k}}) - \bar{w}^r(X_{\boldsymbol{k} - \boldsymbol{e}_i})$. Under *GSS*, an arriving customer of type i is placed into a server with configuration $\boldsymbol{k} - \boldsymbol{e}_i$ where $X_{\boldsymbol{k} - \boldsymbol{e}_i} > 0$ or $\boldsymbol{k} - \boldsymbol{e}_i = \boldsymbol{0}$, such that $\bar{\Delta}_{(\boldsymbol{k}, i)}(\boldsymbol{X})$ is minimal. Ties are broken arbitrarily.

In this paper, for the open system, we will analyze not the "pure" *GSS* policy, described above, but its slight modification, called *Modified GSS (GSS-M)*.

GSS-M. Under this policy, a *token* of type i is generated immediately upon each service completion of type i, and is placed for "service" immediately according to *GSS*. The system state $\boldsymbol{X} = \{X_{\boldsymbol{k}}, \boldsymbol{k} \in \mathcal{K}\}$ account for both tokens of type i as well as actual type-i customers for all $i \in \mathcal{I}$. Each arriving type i customer first seeks to replace an existing token of type i already in "service" (chosen arbitrarily), and if there is none, it is placed for service according to *GSS*. Each token that is not replaced by an actual arriving customer before an independent exponentially distributed timeout with mean $1/\mu_0$, leaves the system. (This modification is the same as the one introduced in [14] for the *Greedy* algorithm, to obtain the *Greedy-M* policy.)

We emphasize that *GSS* and *GSS-M* do *not* require the knowledge of parameter r.

Since the system evolution under the *GSS-M* involves both actual customers and tokens, we need to define the Markov chain describing this evolution more precisely. A *complete server configuration* is defined (in the same way as in [14]) as a pair $(\boldsymbol{k}, \hat{\boldsymbol{k}})$, where vector $\boldsymbol{k} = (k_1, \ldots, k_I) \in \mathcal{K}$ gives the numbers of all customers (both actual and tokens) in a server, while vector $\hat{\boldsymbol{k}} \leq \boldsymbol{k}$, $\boldsymbol{k} \in \bar{\mathcal{K}}$, gives the numbers of actual customers only. The Markov process state at time t is the vector $\{X^r_{(\boldsymbol{k}, \hat{\boldsymbol{k}})}(t)\}$, where the index $(\boldsymbol{k}, \hat{\boldsymbol{k}})$ takes values that are all possible complete server configurations, and superscript r, as usual, indicates the system with parameter r. Note that $\boldsymbol{X}^r(t) = \{X^r_{\boldsymbol{k}}(t), \boldsymbol{k} \in \mathcal{K}\}$ can be considered as a "projection" of $\{X^r_{(\boldsymbol{k}, \hat{\boldsymbol{k}})}(t)\}$, with $X^r_{\boldsymbol{k}}(t) = \sum_{\hat{\boldsymbol{k}} : \hat{\boldsymbol{k}} \leq \boldsymbol{k}} X^r_{(\boldsymbol{k}, \hat{\boldsymbol{k}})}(t)$ for each $\boldsymbol{k} \in \mathcal{K}$. Let $\hat{Y}^r_i(t)$, $\tilde{Y}^r_i(t)$, and $Y^r_i(t) = \hat{Y}^r_i(t) + \tilde{Y}^r_i(t)$ denote the total number of actual type-i customers, the total number of type-i tokens, and the total number of all (both actual and tokens) type-i customers in the rth system, respectively. The total number of actual customers of all types is then $Z^r(t) = \sum_i \hat{Y}^r_i(t)$. The behaviors of the processes $\{(Y^r_i(t), \hat{Y}^r_i(t)), t \geq 0\}$, are independent across all i, with $\hat{Y}^r_i(\infty)$ having Poisson distribution with mean $\rho_i r$. The following fact has the same proof as Lemma 11 in [14].

LEMMA 5. *The Markov chain $\{X^r_{(\boldsymbol{k}, \hat{\boldsymbol{k}})}(t)\}$, $t \geq 0$, is irreducible and positive recurrent for each r.*

Remark. Informally, the reason (which is the same as

in [14]) for considering a modified version of *GSS* instead of pure *GSS* in an open system is as follows. Recall that in a closed system, a customer migration can be also thought of as its departure followed immediately by an arrival of the same type. As such, departures and arrivals in a closed system are perfectly "synchronized", which in particular means that in a closed system, for every departing customer, we always have the option of putting it right back into the server which it has just departed from. This means that a greedy control, pursuing minimization of a given objective function, cannot possibly increase (up to a first-order approximation) the objective function at every customer migration. In contrast, in an open system, departures and arrivals are not synchronized. Therefore, it is not immediately clear that a greedy algorithm will necessarily improve the objective. The tokens are introduced so that, informally speaking, the decisions on placements of new type-i arrivals are made somewhat "in advance", at the times of prior type-i departures. In this sense, the behavior of an open system "emulates" that of a corresponding closed system.

2.4 Main Results

THEOREM 6. *Let $p \in (\frac{1}{2}, 1)$. For each r, consider the closed system operating under* GSS *policy, in steady state. Then there exists some constant $C > 0$, not depending on r, such that*

$$\mathbb{P}\big(d(\boldsymbol{x}^r(\infty), \mathcal{X}^*) \leq Cr^{p-1}\big) \to 1$$

as $r \to \infty$. Consequently, we have fluid-scale asymptotic optimality:

$$d(\boldsymbol{x}^r(\infty), \mathcal{X}^*) \implies 0.$$

THEOREM 7. *Let $p \in (\frac{1}{2}, 1)$. For each r, consider the open system operating under* GSS-M *policy, in steady state. Then there exists some constant $C > 0$, not depending on r, such that as $r \to \infty$,*

$$\mathbb{P}\big(d(\boldsymbol{x}^r(\infty), \mathcal{X}^*) \leq Cr^{p-1}\big) \to 1, \tag{6}$$

and

$$r^{-p} \sum_i \tilde{Y}_i^r(\infty) \implies 0. \tag{7}$$

Consequently, we have fluid-scale asymptotic optimality:

$$d(\boldsymbol{x}^r(\infty), \mathcal{X}^*) \implies 0 \quad \text{and} \quad r^{-1} \sum_i \tilde{Y}_i^r(\infty) \implies 0.$$

3. CLOSED SYSTEM: ASYMPTOTIC OPTIMALITY OF GSS

We restrict our attention to closed systems and prove Theorem 6 in this section. As mentioned earlier, it is not sufficient to consider only the system states at the fluid scale, defined in Section 2.2. We also need the concept of *local fluid scaling*, introduced below. Proposition 9 – a key step in the proof of Theorem 6 – is established in Section 3.2. In Section 3.3, we construct an appropriate probability space, quantify the drift of F^r under *GSS* (cf. Propositions 14 and 15), and prove Theorem 6.

3.1 Local Fluid Scaling

Besides the fluid-scaled processes $\boldsymbol{x}^r(t)$ defined in Section 2.2, it is also convenient to consider the system dynamics at the *local fluid scale*. More precisely, for each r and t, define the corresponding *local fluid scale* process $\tilde{\boldsymbol{x}}^r(t)$ by

$$\tilde{\boldsymbol{x}}^r(t) = \frac{1}{r^p} \boldsymbol{X}^r(t).$$

In the asymptotic regime $r \to \infty$, recall that the fluid scale process $\boldsymbol{x}^r(\cdot)$ always lives in the compact set $\mathcal{X}$ (defined in Section 2.2). This is no longer true for the local fluid scale processes $\tilde{\boldsymbol{x}}^r(\cdot)$: for a fixed t, $\{\tilde{\boldsymbol{x}}^r(t)\}_r$ can be unbounded. However, at the local fluid scale, we will always consider the following weight function $\tilde{w}$, which remains bounded.

Define the local-fluid-scale weight function $\tilde{w} : \mathbb{R} \cup \{\infty\} \to \mathbb{R}_+$ to be $\tilde{w}(\tilde{x}) = 1 \wedge \tilde{x}$. By convention, $1 < \infty$, so $\tilde{w}$ is well-defined. Note that for every r, $\tilde{w}(\tilde{x}^r) = w^r(X^r)$, where $\tilde{x}^r = X^r/r^p$. For $(\boldsymbol{k}, i) \in \mathcal{M}$, we can also define the weight difference at the local fluid scale to be

$$\Delta_{(\boldsymbol{k},i)}(\tilde{\boldsymbol{x}}) = \tilde{w}(\tilde{x}_{\boldsymbol{k}}) - \tilde{w}(\tilde{x}_{\boldsymbol{k}-\boldsymbol{e}_i}).$$

Remark. In the sequel, we will always use lower case x (or $\boldsymbol{x}$) to denote quantities at the fluid scale, $\tilde{x}$ (or $\tilde{\boldsymbol{x}}$) to denote quantities at the local fluid scale, and upper case X (or $\boldsymbol{X}$) to denote quantities without scaling.

3.2 Key Proposition

For a vector $\tilde{\boldsymbol{x}} \in (\mathbb{R}_+ \cup \{\infty\})^{|\mathcal{K}|}$ with components being possibly infinite, we can define the concept of a *Simple Improving (SI) pair associated with $\tilde{\boldsymbol{x}}$*.

DEFINITION 8 (SIMPLE IMPROVING (SI) PAIR). *For $(\boldsymbol{k}, i), (\boldsymbol{k}', i) \in \mathcal{M}$, $\{(\boldsymbol{k}, i), (\boldsymbol{k}', i)\}$ is an SI pair associated with $\tilde{\boldsymbol{x}}$ if*

(a) $k_i \geq 1$, $\tilde{x}_{\boldsymbol{k}} > 0$;

(b) *either $\boldsymbol{k}' = \boldsymbol{e}_i$, or $[k_i' > 0$ and $\tilde{x}_{\boldsymbol{k}'-\boldsymbol{e}_i} > 0]$; and*

(c) $\Delta_{(\boldsymbol{k}',i)} < \Delta_{(\boldsymbol{k},i)}$.

The idea of SI pairs is as follows. Suppose that the current system state is $\boldsymbol{X}^r$, and a type-i customer just completed its service requirement at a server with configuration $\boldsymbol{k}$. Then the first-order change in F^r is $-\Delta_{(\boldsymbol{k},i)}^r(\boldsymbol{X}^r)$. Suppose that this customer is then placed into a server with configuration $\boldsymbol{k}'$, under *GSS*. Then, the total (first-order) change in F^r after this transition is $\Delta_{(\boldsymbol{k}',i)}^r(\boldsymbol{X}^r) - \Delta_{(\boldsymbol{k},i)}^r(\boldsymbol{X}^r)$, or $\Delta_{(\boldsymbol{k}',i)}(\tilde{\boldsymbol{x}}^r) - \Delta_{(\boldsymbol{k},i)}(\tilde{\boldsymbol{x}}^r)$. The existence of an SI pair ensures that we can always improve (up to first order) the current value of F^r.

Recall that for any feasible system state $\boldsymbol{X}^r$, $\boldsymbol{x}^r = \boldsymbol{X}^r/r$ denotes the fluid-scale system state, and $\tilde{\boldsymbol{x}}^r = \boldsymbol{X}^r/r^p$ denotes the associated state at the local fluid scale. The following proposition establishes that whenever $\boldsymbol{x}^r$ is sufficiently far away from optimality, an SI pair exists.

PROPOSITION 9. *Let $D > 0$ be the same as in Lemma 3. Then, there exist a positive constant ε such that the following holds. For sufficiently large r, if $d(\boldsymbol{x}^r, \mathcal{X}^*) \geq 2D|\mathcal{K}|r^{p-1}$, then there exists an SI pair $\{(\boldsymbol{k}', i), (\boldsymbol{k}, i)\}$ (possibly depending on r) associated with $\tilde{\boldsymbol{x}}^r = (\tilde{x}_{\boldsymbol{k}}^r)_{\boldsymbol{k} \in \mathcal{K}}$, and furthermore, $\tilde{x}_{\boldsymbol{k}}^r \geq \varepsilon$, $\tilde{x}_{\boldsymbol{k}'-\boldsymbol{e}_i}^r \geq \varepsilon$, and $\Delta_{(\boldsymbol{k}',i)}(\tilde{\boldsymbol{x}}^r) - \Delta_{(\boldsymbol{k},i)}(\tilde{\boldsymbol{x}}^r) \leq -\varepsilon$.*

Proposition 9 follows from the two lemmas below.

LEMMA 10. *Consider any sequence $\{\boldsymbol{x}^r\}$ and the associated states $\tilde{\boldsymbol{x}}^r$. Let $\boldsymbol{x} \in \mathcal{X}$ be a limit point of the sequence $\{\boldsymbol{x}^r\}$, so that the the subsequence $\{r_n\}$ of $\{r\}$ satisfies*

$x^{r_n} \to x$ and $\widetilde{x}^{r_n} \to \widetilde{x}$ as $n \to \infty$, with some components of $\widetilde{x}$ being possibly infinite. If there is no SI pair associated with $\widetilde{x}$, then $x \in \mathcal{X}^*$, i.e. x is an optimal solution of LP.

PROOF OF LEMMA 10. Suppose that there is no SI pair associated with $\widetilde{x}$. We will show that $x \in \mathcal{X}^*$, i.e., x is an optimal solution of the linear program LP. To this end, we will use Lemma 2. In particular, we will construct $\eta_i \geq 0$, $i \in \mathcal{I}$ such that

(i) $\sum_{i \in \mathcal{I}} k_i \eta_i \leq 1$ for all $k \in \mathcal{K}$, and

(ii) if $\sum_{i \in \mathcal{I}} k_i \eta_i < 1$, then $\widetilde{x}_k < 1$.

Note that condition (ii) here is stronger than condition (ii) in Lemma 2.

Let $\eta_i = \widetilde{w}(\widetilde{x}_{e_i})$ for all $i \in \mathcal{I}$. Then clearly $\eta_i \in [0,1]$ for all $i \in \mathcal{I}$. We first show that condition (i) holds. To this end, we prove the following stronger statement: if $k \in \mathcal{K}$ is such that $k_i \geq 1$ implies $\eta_i > 0$, then $\sum_{i \in \mathcal{I}} k_i \eta_i = \widetilde{w}(\widetilde{x}_k)$. Suppose not. Let $k \in \mathcal{K}$ be a minimal counterexample, so that

$$\sum_{i \in \mathcal{I}} k_i \eta_i \neq \widetilde{w}(\widetilde{x}_k), \tag{8}$$

and for each $i \in \mathcal{I}$, $k_i \geq 1$ implies $\eta_i > 0$. Note that $\sum_{i \in \mathcal{I}} k_i \geq 2$, since $\eta_i = \widetilde{w}(\widetilde{x}_{e_i})$ for each $i \in \mathcal{I}$, by definition. Thus, there exists $i \in \mathcal{I}$ such that $\eta_i > 0$, $k' = k - e_i \in \mathcal{K}$, and

$$\sum_{i \in \mathcal{I}} k_i' \eta_i = \widetilde{w}(\widetilde{x}_{k'}). \tag{9}$$

Subtracting Eq. (9) from Eq. (8), we get that

$$\Delta_{(k,i)} = \widetilde{w}(\widetilde{x}_k) - \widetilde{w}(\widetilde{x}_{k'}) \neq \eta_i.$$

Thus either $\Delta_{(k,i)} > \eta_i$, or $\Delta_{(k,i)} < \eta_i$. If $\Delta_{(k,i)} > \eta_i$, we verify that $\{(k,i),(e_i,i)\}$ is an SI pair associated with $\widetilde{x}$. First, conditions (b) and (c) in Definition 8 are automatically satisfied. Second, $\Delta_{(k,i)} > \eta_i > 0$. In particular, $\widetilde{x}_k > 0$. We also have $k_i \geq 1$, so condition (a) in Definition 8 is also satisfied.

If $\Delta_{(k,i)} < \eta_i$, we verify that $\{(e_i,i),(k,i)\}$ is an SI pair associated with $\widetilde{x}$. First, condition (c) in Definition 8 is automatically satisfied. Second, since $\eta_i > 0$, $\widetilde{x}_{e_i} > 0$. Thus condition (a) in Definition 8 is satisfied. Finally, $k_i \geq 1$ by assumption, so to verify condition (b), we only need to verify that $\widetilde{x}_{k-e_i} > 0$. Since $\sum_{i \in \mathcal{I}} k_i \geq 2$, $\sum_{i \in \mathcal{I}} k_i' \geq 1$. This implies that there exists $i' \in \mathcal{I}$ such that $k_{i'}' \geq 1$. Thus $k_{i'} \geq k_{i'}' \geq 1$, so $\eta_{i'} > 0$. By Eq. (9), $\widetilde{w}(\widetilde{x}_{k'}) \geq \eta_{i'} > 0$, so $\widetilde{x}_{k'} > 0$. Thus, condition (b) in Definition 8 is verified.

In either case, we have an SI pair associated with $\widetilde{x}$, contradicting the assumption that there is no SI pair associated with $\widetilde{x}$. Thus, for all $k \in \mathcal{K}$ such that $k_i \geq 1$ implies $\eta_i > 0$,

$$\sum_{i \in \mathcal{I}} k_i \eta_i = \widetilde{w}(\widetilde{x}_k).$$

For all $k \in \mathcal{K}$, we can find $k' \leq k$ such that $k' \in \mathcal{K}$, $k_i' \geq 1$ implies $\eta_i > 0$, and $\sum_{i \in \mathcal{I}} k_i \eta_i = \sum_{i \in \mathcal{I}} k_i' \eta_i$. Thus,

$$\sum_{i \in \mathcal{I}} k_i \eta_i = \sum_{i \in \mathcal{I}} k_i' \eta_i = \widetilde{w}(\widetilde{x}_{k'}) \leq 1.$$

This establishes condition (i).

We now establish condition (ii). Suppose that condition (ii) does not hold. Let $k \in \mathcal{K}$ be minimal such that

$$\widetilde{x}_k \geq 1, \quad \text{and} \quad \sum_{i \in \mathcal{I}} k_i \eta_i < 1.$$

First, note that $k \neq e_i$ for any $i \in \mathcal{I}$, because if $\eta_i < 1$, then

$$1 > \eta_i = \widetilde{w}(\widetilde{x}_{e_i}) = 1 \wedge \widetilde{x}_{e_i}.$$

Thus $\sum_{i \in \mathcal{I}} k_i \geq 2$. Second, if $\eta_i > 0$ for all $i \in \mathcal{I}$ with $k_i \geq 1$, then from the proof of condition (i), we have that

$$1 > \sum_{i \in \mathcal{I}} k_i \eta_i = \widetilde{w}(\widetilde{x}_k) = 1 \wedge \widetilde{x}_k,$$

so we have $\widetilde{x}_k < 1$, reaching a contradiction. Thus, there exists $i \in \mathcal{I}$ such that $\eta_i = 0$ and $k_i \geq 1$. Let $k' = k - e_i$. Then $k' \in \mathcal{K}$, since $\sum_{i \in \mathcal{I}} k_i' = \sum_{i \in \mathcal{I}} k_i - 1 \geq 1$. Since $\eta_i = 0$,

$$\sum_{i \in \mathcal{I}} k_i' \eta_i = \sum_{i \in \mathcal{I}} k_i \eta_i < 1.$$

By minimality of k, we must have $\widetilde{x}_{k'} < 1$. Thus, $\widetilde{w}(\widetilde{x}_{k'}) = 1 \wedge \widetilde{x}_{k'} < 1$, and $\widetilde{w}(\widetilde{x}_k) = 1 \wedge \widetilde{x}_k = 1$. This implies that

$$\Delta_{(k,i)} > 0 = \eta_i,$$

and that $\{(k,i),(e_i,i)\}$ is an SI pair associated with $\widetilde{x}$. This is a contradiction, so condition (ii) is established. $\square$

LEMMA 11. *Consider any sequence $\{x^r\}$ and associated states $\widetilde{x}^r$. Let x^{r_n}, x, $\widetilde{x}^{r_n}$ and $\widetilde{x}$ be the same as in Lemma 10. If for all sufficiently large n, $d(x^{r_n}, \mathcal{X}^*) \geq 2D|\mathcal{K}|r_n^{p-1}$, then there is an SI pair associated with $\widetilde{x}$.*

PROOF OF LEMMA 11. We prove the lemma by contradiction. Suppose that the lemma is not true, then for sufficiently large n, $d(x^{r_n}, \mathcal{X}^*) \geq 2D|\mathcal{K}|r_n^{p-1}$, and there is no SI pair associated with $\widetilde{x}$. By Lemma 10, x is an optimal solution of LP, and from the proof of Lemma 10, $\eta = (\eta_i)_{i \in \mathcal{I}}$ is an optimal dual solution of LP, where $\eta_i = \widetilde{x}_{e_i}$ for all $i \in \mathcal{I}$.

For a given r, consider the following linear program, which we call LP^r.

$$\text{Minimize} \quad \sum_{k \in \mathcal{K}} \widetilde{x}_k \tag{10}$$

$$\text{subject to} \quad \sum_{k \in \mathcal{K}} k_i \widetilde{x}_k = \rho_i r^{1-p}, \quad \text{for all } i \in \mathcal{I}, \tag{11}$$

$$\widetilde{x}_k \geq 0, \quad \text{for all } k \in \mathcal{K}. \tag{12}$$

LP^r is just a scaled version of LP, defined in Section 2.2. For each r, the feasible set of LP^r is $r^{1-p}\mathcal{X}$, its set of optimal solutions is $r^{1-p}\mathcal{X}^*$, and its optimal value is $r^{1-p}u^*$. $r^{1-p}x$ is an optimal solution of LP^r, and η is an optimal dual solution. Furthermore, by Lemma 3, for sufficiently large n,

$$\begin{aligned}
\sum_{k \in \mathcal{K}} \widetilde{x}_k^{r_n} - r^{1-p}u^* &= r^{1-p}\left(\sum_{k \in \mathcal{K}} x_k^{r_n} - u^*\right) \\
&\geq r^{1-p}d(x^{r_n}, \mathcal{X}^*)/D \\
&\geq r^{1-p} \cdot (2D|\mathcal{K}|r^{p-1})/D \geq 2|\mathcal{K}|.
\end{aligned}$$

For each n, consider the Lagrangian $L(\widetilde{x}^{r_n}, \eta)$ of LP^{r_n}, evaluated at $\widetilde{x}^{r_n}$ and η:

$$L(\widetilde{x}^{r_n}, \eta) = \sum_{k \in \mathcal{K}} \widetilde{x}_k^{r_n} + \sum_{i \in \mathcal{I}} \eta_i \left(\rho_i r_n^{1-p} - \sum_{k \in \mathcal{K}} k_i \widetilde{x}_k^{r_n}\right).$$

We calculate the Lagrangian in two ways. First, by feasibility of $\widetilde{x}^{r_n}$, $L(\widetilde{x}^{r_n}, \eta) = \sum_{k \in \mathcal{K}} \widetilde{x}_k^{r_n}$. Second, we rewrite $L(\widetilde{x}^{r_n}, \eta)$ as

$$L(\widetilde{x}^{r_n}, \eta) = r_n^{1-p}\sum_{i \in \mathcal{I}} \rho_i \eta_i + \sum_{k \in \mathcal{K}}\left(1 - \sum_{i \in \mathcal{I}} k_i \eta_i\right)\widetilde{x}_k^{r_n}.$$

The first term on the RHS equals $r_n^{1-p}u^*$, by the dual optimality of $\boldsymbol{\eta}$. For the second term on the RHS, note that in the proof of Lemma 10, we have established that for all $\boldsymbol{k} \in \mathcal{K}$, $\sum_{i\in\mathcal{I}} k_i\eta_i \le 1$, and if $\sum_{i\in\mathcal{I}} k_i\eta_i < 1$, then $\widetilde{x}_{\boldsymbol{k}} < 1$. Since $\widetilde{\boldsymbol{x}}^{r_n} \to \widetilde{\boldsymbol{x}}$, for all sufficiently large n, if $\sum_{i\in\mathcal{I}} k_i\eta_i < 1$, then $\widetilde{x}_{\boldsymbol{k}}^{r_n} \le 1$. Thus for all sufficiently large n,

$$\sum_{\boldsymbol{k}\in\mathcal{K}}\left(1 - \sum_{i\in\mathcal{I}} k_i\eta_i\right)\widetilde{x}_{\boldsymbol{k}}^{r_n} \le |\mathcal{K}|,$$

and

$$\sum_{\boldsymbol{k}\in\mathcal{K}}\widetilde{x}_{\boldsymbol{k}}^{r_n} = L(\widetilde{\boldsymbol{x}}^{r_n}, \boldsymbol{\eta}) \le r_n^{1-p}u^* + |\mathcal{K}|,$$

contradicting the fact that

$$\sum_{\boldsymbol{k}\in\mathcal{K}}\widetilde{x}_{\boldsymbol{k}}^{r_n} - r_n^{1-p}u^* \ge 2|\mathcal{K}|$$

for sufficiently large n. This establishes Lemma 11. $\square$

Proof of Proposition 9. We are now ready to prove Proposition 9. Suppose that the proposition does not hold. Then for all $\varepsilon > 0$, there exist infinitely many r and $\boldsymbol{x}^r$ such that $d(\boldsymbol{x}^r, \mathcal{X}^*) \ge 2D|\mathcal{K}|r^{p-1}$, and for all SI pairs (if any) $\{(\boldsymbol{k}', i), (\boldsymbol{k}, i)\}$ of $\widetilde{\boldsymbol{x}}^r$, either $\widetilde{x}_{\boldsymbol{k}}^r < \varepsilon$, or $\widetilde{x}_{\boldsymbol{k}'-e_i}^r < \varepsilon$, or $\Delta_{(\boldsymbol{k}',i)}(\widetilde{\boldsymbol{x}}^r) - \Delta_{(\boldsymbol{k},i)}(\widetilde{\boldsymbol{x}}^r) > -\varepsilon$. Thus, we can find a subsequence $\{r_n\}$ of $\{r\}$ and states $\boldsymbol{x}^{r_n}$ such that

1. $\boldsymbol{x}^{r_n} \to \boldsymbol{x} \in \mathcal{X}$ as $n \to \infty$,

2. $\widetilde{\boldsymbol{x}}^{r_n} \to \widetilde{\boldsymbol{x}}$ as $n \to \infty$, with some components of $\widetilde{\boldsymbol{x}}$ being possibly infinite,

3. $d(\boldsymbol{x}^{r_n}, \mathcal{X}^*) \ge 2D|\mathcal{K}|r_n^{p-1}$ for all n, and

4. for all SI pairs $\{(\boldsymbol{k}', i), (\boldsymbol{k}, i)\}$ associated with $\widetilde{\boldsymbol{x}}^{r_n}$ (if any), either $\widetilde{x}_{\boldsymbol{k}}^{r_n} < 1/n$, or $\widetilde{x}_{\boldsymbol{k}'-e_i}^{r_n} < 1/n$, or $\Delta_{(\boldsymbol{k}',i)}(\widetilde{\boldsymbol{x}}^{r_n}) - \Delta_{(\boldsymbol{k},i)}(\widetilde{\boldsymbol{x}}^{r_n}) > -1/n$.

From Property 4, we can deduce that $\widetilde{\boldsymbol{x}}$ does not have an SI pair. But by Property 3, this contradicts Lemma 11. This establishes Proposition 9. $\square$

3.3 Proof of Theorem 6

We will assume WLOG the following construction of the probability space. For each $(\boldsymbol{k}, i) \in \mathcal{M}$, consider an independent unit-rate Poisson process $\{\Pi_{(\boldsymbol{k},i)}(t),\ t \ge 0\}$. Assume that, for each r, the Markov process $\boldsymbol{X}^r(\cdot)$ is driven by this common set of Poisson processes $\Pi_{(\boldsymbol{k},i)}(\cdot)$, as follows. For each $(\boldsymbol{k}, i) \in \mathcal{M}$, let us denote by $D_{(\boldsymbol{k},i)}^r(t)$ the total number of type-i service completions from servers of configuration $\boldsymbol{k}$, in the time interval $[0, t]$. Then

$$D_{(\boldsymbol{k},i)}^r(t) = \Pi_{(\boldsymbol{k},i)}\left(\int_0^t X_{\boldsymbol{k}}^r(\xi)k_i\mu_i d\xi\right). \quad (13)$$

LEMMA 12. *Let $T > 0$ be fixed. With probability 1, the following property holds. Consider any sequence $\{t_0^r\}_r$ with $t_0^r \in [0, Tr^{2-p}]$. Then for any $\xi \in [0, 1]$, and for any $(\boldsymbol{k}, i) \in \mathcal{M}$,*

$$\frac{1}{r^{2p-1}}\left(\Pi_{(\boldsymbol{k},i)}\left(t_0^r + \xi r^{2p-1}\right) - \Pi_{(\boldsymbol{k},i)}\left(t_0^r\right)\right) \to \xi$$

as $r \to \infty$. The convergence is uniform over t_0^r, ξ, and $(\boldsymbol{k}, i)$ in the following sense. For any $\varepsilon > 0$, there exists $r(\varepsilon)$

such that for all $r \ge r(\varepsilon)$, $\xi \in [0, 1]$, $(\boldsymbol{k}, i) \in \mathcal{M}$, and $t_0^r \in [0, Tr^{2-p}]$,

$$\max_{(\boldsymbol{k},i),\xi,t_0^r}\left|\frac{1}{r^{2p-1}}\left(\Pi_{(\boldsymbol{k},i)}\left(t_0^r + \xi r^{2p-1}\right) - \Pi_{(\boldsymbol{k},i)}\left(t_0^r\right)\right) - \xi\right| < \varepsilon.$$

The proof of Lemma 12 depends on simple large-deviation type estimates for Poisson random variables. The idea is essentially the same as that of Lemma 4.3 in [11]: we partition the interval $[0, Tr^{2p-1}]$ into subintervals of length $r^{p-1/2}$, and for each of them write the probability that the average increase rate of $\Pi_{(\boldsymbol{k},i)}$ lies outside $(1-\varepsilon, 1+\varepsilon)$. These probabilities are $\exp(-\text{poly}(r))$, and we only have $\text{poly}(r)$ such subintervals (here $\text{poly}(r)$ means a polynomial in r). This is true for any $\varepsilon > 0$. We can then cover *any* subinterval of length r^{2p-1} by these subintervals of length $r^{p-1/2}$. We omit a detailed proof here.

The following corollary is a simple consequence of Lemma 12.

COROLLARY 13. *Let T be fixed. With probability 1, the following holds. For sufficiently large r,*

$$\max_{\substack{\xi\in[0,1],\\ t_0^r\in[0,Tr^{1-p}]}} d\left(\boldsymbol{X}^r(t_0^r + \xi r^{p-1}), \boldsymbol{X}^r(t_0^r)\right) \le 2\bar{\mu}|\mathcal{K}|r^p, \quad (14)$$

where $\bar{\mu} = \max_{i\in\mathcal{I}}\mu_i$, and μ_i is the service rate for type-i customers.

PROOF. Consider the probability-1 event in Lemma 12, in which we can and do replace T with $2\bar{\mu}T$. (We do this because the total "instantaneous" rate of all transitions is upper bounded by $2\bar{\mu}r$.) The rate of departure of type-i customers is $\rho_i\mu_i r \le \rho_i\bar{\mu}r$, and the total rate of customer departure is no greater than $\sum_{i\in\mathcal{I}}\rho_i\bar{\mu} = \bar{\mu}r$. Thus, for each $\boldsymbol{k} \in \mathcal{K}$, the rate of change in $X_{\boldsymbol{k}}$ is at most $\bar{\mu}r$. For an interval of length r^{p-1}, the total change in $X_{\boldsymbol{k}}$ is at most $O(r \cdot r^{p-1}) = O(r^p)$. More precisely, with probability 1, for each $\boldsymbol{k} \in \mathcal{K}$,

$$\limsup_{r\to\infty}\frac{1}{r^p}\max_{\substack{\xi\in[0,1],\\ t_0^r\in[0,Tr^{1-p}]}}\left|X_{\boldsymbol{k}}^r(t_0^r + \xi r^{p-1}) - X_{\boldsymbol{k}}^r(t_0^r)\right| \le \bar{\mu}.$$

Thus, for sufficiently large r, and for each $\boldsymbol{k} \in \mathcal{K}$,

$$\max_{\substack{\xi\in[0,1],\\ t_0^r\in[0,Tr^{1-p}]}}\left|X_{\boldsymbol{k}}^r(t_0^r + \xi r^{p-1}) - X_{\boldsymbol{k}}^r(t_0^r)\right| \le 2\bar{\mu}r^p.$$

Summing over the above expression establishes the corollary. $\square$

PROPOSITION 14. *There exist positive constants C_1 and δ such that the following holds. Let $T > 0$ be given. Then w.p.1, for all sufficiently large r, and for any interval $[t_0, t_0 + r^{p-1}] \subset [0, Tr^{1-p}]$, if $d(\boldsymbol{x}^r(t_0), \mathcal{X}^*) \ge C_1 r^{p-1}$, then*

$$F^r\left(\boldsymbol{X}^r(t_0 + r^{p-1})\right) - F^r\left(\boldsymbol{X}^r(t_0)\right) \le -\delta r^{2p-1}.$$

PROOF. The proof idea is as follows. Consider the increase in F^r at each state transition. For concreteness, suppose that the current system state is $\boldsymbol{X}^r$, and a type-i customer just completed its service requirement on a server with configuration $\boldsymbol{k}$, and is placed into a server with configuration $\boldsymbol{k}'$. Then it is a simple calculation to see that the increase in F^r is at most

$$\Delta_{(\boldsymbol{k}',i)}^r(\boldsymbol{X}^r) - \Delta_{(\boldsymbol{k},i)}^r(\boldsymbol{X}^r) + 4r^{-p}.$$

The term $\Delta^r_{(\boldsymbol{k}',i)}(\boldsymbol{X}^r) - \Delta^r_{(\boldsymbol{k},i)}(\boldsymbol{X}^r)$ captures the first-order increase in F^r, and the term $4r^{-p}$ bounds the second-order increase in F^r. We will see that over an interval of length r^{p-1}, the increase in F^r due to first-order terms is at most $-O(r^{2p-1})$, and the increase due to second-order terms is at most a constant. We now proceed to the formal proof.

From now on, we work with the probability-1 event defined in Lemma 12, under which

$$\frac{1}{r^{2p-1}}\left(\Pi_{(\boldsymbol{k},i)}\left(t_0 + \xi r^{2p-1}\right) - \Pi_{(\boldsymbol{k},i)}\left(t_0\right)\right) \to \xi$$

as $r \to \infty$, uniformly over t_0, ξ, and $(\boldsymbol{k}, i)$. Let $C_1 = 2(\bar{\mu} + D)|\mathcal{K}|$, where $\bar{\mu} = \max_{i\in\mathcal{I}} \mu_i$ and D is the same as in Lemma 3. Let $\varepsilon > 0$ be the same as in Proposition 9, and let $\delta > 0$ be such that $\delta < \frac{1}{8}\mu_i \varepsilon^2$ for all $i \in \mathcal{I}$.

Claim that for all sufficiently large r, and for any interval $[t_0, t_0 + r^{p-1}] \subset [0, Tr^{1-p}]$, if $d(\boldsymbol{x}^r(t_0), \mathcal{X}^*) \geq C_1 r^{p-1}$, then

$$F^r\left(\boldsymbol{X}^r(t_0 + r^{p-1})\right) - F^r\left(\boldsymbol{X}^r(t_0)\right) \leq -\delta r^{2p-1}.$$

Suppose the contrary. Then there exist a subsequence of $\{r\}$ (which, with an abuse of notation, we still index by r), along which we have some $[t_0^r, t_0^r + r^{p-1}] \subset [0, Tr^{1-p}]$, such that $d(\boldsymbol{x}^r(t_0^r), \mathcal{X}^*) \geq C_1 r^{p-1}$, and

$$F^r\left(\boldsymbol{X}^r(t_0^r + r^{p-1})\right) - F^r\left(\boldsymbol{X}^r(t_0^r)\right) > -\delta r^{2p-1}. \quad (15)$$

First, for sufficiently large r, and for all $\xi \in [0,1]$, there exists a SI pair $\{(\boldsymbol{k}',i),(\boldsymbol{k},i)\}$ associated with $\boldsymbol{x}^r(t_0^r+\xi r^{p-1})$ (possibly depending on r and ξ), such that

$$\widetilde{x}^r_{\boldsymbol{k}}(t_0^r + \xi r^{p-1}) \geq \varepsilon, \quad \widetilde{x}^r_{\boldsymbol{k}'-\boldsymbol{e}_i}(t_0^r + \xi r^{p-1}) \geq \varepsilon, \text{ and} \quad (16)$$

$$\Delta_{(\boldsymbol{k}',i)}(\widetilde{\boldsymbol{x}}^r(t_0^r + \xi r^{p-1})) - \Delta_{(\boldsymbol{k},i)}(\widetilde{\boldsymbol{x}}^r(t_0^r + \xi r^{p-1})) \leq -\varepsilon. \quad (17)$$

By Corollary 13, for all $\xi \in [0,1]$, $d\left(\boldsymbol{X}^r(t_0^r + \xi r^{p-1}), \boldsymbol{X}^r(t_0^r)\right) \leq 2\bar{\mu}|\mathcal{K}|r^p$. Using triangle inequality and choosing $C_1 > 2(\bar{\mu} + D)|\mathcal{K}|$, we have that for sufficiently large r, and for all $\xi \in [0,1]$,

$$d\left(\boldsymbol{x}^r(t_0^r + \xi r^{p-1}), \mathcal{X}^*\right) \geq 2D|\mathcal{K}|r^{p-1}.$$

(16) and (17) now follow from Proposition 9.

Fix a sufficiently large r so that (16) and (17) hold. We then consider the first-order change in F^r over the interval $[t_0^r, t_0^r + r^{p-1}]$ (i.e., the difference of Δ). To do this, we partition $[t_0^r, t_0^r + r^{p-1}]$ into subintervals of length $c\varepsilon r^{p-1}$, with $c > 0$ chosen small enough so that on each subinterval, there exists a *fixed* SI pair $\{(\boldsymbol{k}',i),(\boldsymbol{k},i)\}$ such that (16) and (17) hold for this SI pair, and with ε replaced by $\varepsilon/2$. We now argue that this can be done. Consider the first such subinterval, for example. By Lemma 12, for sufficiently large r, the number of state transitions over this subinterval is at most $(c\varepsilon r^{p-1}) \cdot O(r) = O(\varepsilon r^p) < \frac{1}{8}\varepsilon r^p$, by choosing a sufficiently small c. This implies that for each $\boldsymbol{k} \in \mathcal{K}$, the change in $\widetilde{x}^r_{\boldsymbol{k}}$ over this subinterval is at most $\frac{1}{8}\varepsilon$. Thus, (16) and (17) hold for an SI pair associated with $\widetilde{\boldsymbol{x}}^r(t_0^r)$, with ε replaced by $\varepsilon/2$. The same argument holds for other subintervals.

Now concentrate on the subinterval $[t_0^r, t_0^r + c\varepsilon r^{p-1}]$, and a corresponding SI pair $\{(\boldsymbol{k}',i),(\boldsymbol{k},i)\}$ associated with $\widetilde{\boldsymbol{x}}^r(t_0^r)$ for which (16) and (17) hold on this subinterval with ε replaced by $\varepsilon/2$. The number of type-i departures from servers of configuration $\boldsymbol{k}$ is at least $\mu_i \cdot \frac{\varepsilon r^p}{2} \cdot (c\varepsilon r^{p-1}) = \frac{1}{2}c\mu_i\varepsilon^2 r^{2p-1}$. At each such departure, the first-order increase (due to the difference of Δ) in F^r is at most $-\varepsilon/2$, since GSS results in

a smaller first-order increase than moving the departure to a server with configuration $\boldsymbol{k}' - \boldsymbol{e}_i$. Summing over all such increases over type-i departures gives a first-order increase in F^r which is at most

$$-\frac{\varepsilon}{2} \cdot \left(\frac{1}{2}c\mu_i\varepsilon^2 r^{2p-1}\right) \leq -2c\varepsilon\delta r^{2p-1}.$$

Exactly the same argument holds for other subintervals, so the total first-order increase in F^r is at most $-2\delta r^{2p-1}$.

Finally, consider the second-order increase in F^r. As discussed at the beginning of the proof, the second-order increase in F^r at each state transition is at most $4r^{-p}$. For sufficiently large r, the total number of state transitions over the interval $[t_0^r, t_0^r + r^{p-1}]$ is at most $r^{p-1} \cdot O(r) = O(r^p)$, and hence the total second-order increase in F^r is at most $(4r^{-p}) \cdot O(r^p) = O(1)$. Thus, for sufficiently large r,

$$F^r\left(\boldsymbol{X}^r(t_0^r+r^{p-1})\right) - F^r\left(\boldsymbol{X}^r(t_0^r)\right) \leq -2\delta r^{2p-1} + O(1) \leq -\delta r^{2p-1}.$$

This contradicts (15), and we have established the proposition. $\square$

PROPOSITION 15. *There exist positive constants C and T such that as $r \to \infty$,*

$$\mathbb{P}\left(d\left(\boldsymbol{x}^r(Tr^{1-p}), \mathcal{X}^*\right) \leq Cr^{p-1}\right) \to 1.$$

PROOF SKETCH. The proof is very intuitive. We keep track of the evolution of F^r on the interval $[0, Tr^{1-p}]$ subdivided into r^{p-1}-long subintervals. W.p.1., for all sufficiently large r, the following is true for each subinterval $[t_0, t_0 + r^{p-1}]$: F^r decreases by at least δr^{2p-1} if $d(\boldsymbol{x}^r(t_0), \mathcal{X}^*) \geq C_1 r^{p-1}$ (by Proposition 14), and it can never increase by more than $C_3 r^p$. Therefore, if we choose T large enough, then $d(\boldsymbol{x}^r(t), \mathcal{X}^*) < C_1 r^{p-1}$ at some time $t \in [0, Tr^{1-p}]$ (because otherwise F^r would become negative), and $d(\boldsymbol{x}^r(t), \mathcal{X}^*) = O(r^{p-1})$ thereafter. We refer the readers to [15] for details. $\square$

Proof of Theorem 6. Theorem 6 is now a simple consequence of Proposition 15. For each r, consider $\boldsymbol{x}^r(\cdot)$ in the stationary regime. In particular, for any $T > 0$, $\boldsymbol{x}^r(Tr^{1-p})$ has the same distribution as $\boldsymbol{x}^r(\infty)$. Therefore, by Proposition 15,

$$\mathbb{P}\left(d\left(\boldsymbol{x}^r(\infty), \mathcal{X}^*\right) \leq Cr^{p-1}\right) \to 1,$$

as $r \to \infty$. This completes the proof of Theorem 6. $\square$

4. OPEN SYSTEM: ASYMPTOTIC OPTIMALITY OF (MODIFIED) GSS

We prove Theorem 7 in this section. The proof "extends" that of Theorem 6. The main additional step is Theorem 18, which shows that in steady state, for each $i \in \mathcal{I}$, $\tilde{Y}^r_i(t)$ the number of tokens of type-i, remains $o(r^p)$ with high probability, over $O(r^{1-p})$-long intervals. As a starting point, we need the following facts.

THEOREM 16. *Consider the sequence (in r) of open systems in steady state. Consider any fixed i. There exists a positive constant c such that, uniformly on all r,*

$$\mathbb{E}\exp\{\|r^{-1/2}(\hat{Y}^r_i(\infty) - \rho_i r, \tilde{Y}^r_i(\infty))\|\} \leq c.$$

PROOF. Refer to [15]. $\square$

For our purposes, the following corollary will suffice.

49

COROLLARY 17. *Consider the sequence (in r) of open systems in steady state. Consider any fixed i. Then, for any $q > 1/2$,*

$$\|r^{-q}(\hat{Y}_i^r(\infty) - \rho_i r, \tilde{Y}_i^r(\infty))\| \Longrightarrow 0.$$

Next we show that the property of Corollary 17 holds not just at a given time, but uniformly on a $O(r^{1-q})$-long interval.

THEOREM 18. *Consider the sequence (in r) of open systems in stationary regime. Consider any fixed i. Let $q > 1/2$ and $T > 0$ be fixed. Then, as $r \to \infty$,*

$$\sup_{t \in [0, Tr^{1-q}]} \|r^{-q}(\hat{Y}_i^r(t) - \rho_i r, \tilde{Y}_i^r(t))\| \Longrightarrow 0, \quad (18)$$

and, consequently,

$$\sup_{t \in [0, Tr^{1-q}]} r^{-q}\|Z^r(t) - r\| \Longrightarrow 0. \quad (19)$$

Clearly, the statement of Theorem 18 is equivalent to the following one: *Any subsequence of $\{r\}$ contains a further subsequence along which w.p.1,*

$$\sup_{t \in [0, Tr^{1-q}]} \|r^{-q}(\hat{Y}_i^r(t) - \rho_i r, \tilde{Y}_i^r(t))\| \to 0, \quad (20)$$

and then

$$\sup_{t \in [0, Tr^{1-q}]} r^{-q}\|Z^r(t) - r\| \to 0. \quad (21)$$

In turn, to prove the latter statement it suffices to show that *there exists a construction of the underlying probability space, for which the statement holds.*

We will need some estimates, which can be obtained from a strong approximation of Poisson processes, available in, for example, [3, Chapters 1 and 2]:

PROPOSITION 19. *A unit rate Poisson process $\Pi(\cdot)$ and a standard Brownian motion $W(\cdot)$ can be constructed on a common probability space in such a way that the following holds. For some fixed positive constants C_1, C_2, C_3, such that $\forall T > 1$ and $\forall u \geq 0$*

$$\mathbb{P}\left(\sup_{0 \leq t \leq T} |\Pi(t) - t - W(t)| \geq C_1 \log T + u\right) \leq C_2 e^{-C_3 u}.$$

If in the above statement we replace T with rT, and u with $r^{1/4}$, we obtain

$$\mathbb{P}\left(\sup_{0 \leq t \leq rT} |(\Pi(t) - t) - W(t)| < C_1 \log(rT) + r^{1/4}\right)$$
$$> 1 - C_2 e^{-C_3 r^{1/4}}. \quad (22)$$

Note also that for a fixed $\delta \in (0, q - 1/2)$ and all large r,

$$\mathbb{P}\left(\sup_{0 \leq t \leq rT} |W(t)| \leq r^{1/2+\delta}\right) \geq 1 - e^{cr^{2\delta}} \quad (23)$$

for some constant $c > 0$. If events in (22) and (23) hold for all large r, then

$$\sup_{0 \leq t \leq rT} r^{-q}|\Pi(t) - t| \to 0. \quad (24)$$

To prove Theorem 18, consider the following construction of the probability space. (We want to strongly emphasize that this construction will be used only for the purpose of

proving Theorem 18. For the proof of Theorem 7, we can and will use a different probability space construction.) For each r, we divide the time interval $[0, Tr^{1-q}]$ into r^{1-q} of T-long subintervals, namely $[(m-1)T, mT]$ with $m = 1, 2, \ldots, r^{1-q}$. In each of the subintervals, and for each r, we consider independent unit rate Poisson processes $\Pi_i^{r,m}$, $\hat{\Pi}_i^{r,m}$, $\tilde{\Pi}_i^{r,m}$, driving type i exogenous arrivals, actual customer departures and token departures, respectively. More precisely, the number of type i exogenous arrivals, actual customer departures and token departures, by time t from the beginning of the m-th interval is given by

$$\Pi_i^{r,m}(\lambda_i rt), \quad \hat{\Pi}_i^{r,m}\left(\int_0^t \mu_i \hat{Y}_i^r(\xi) d\xi\right), \quad \tilde{\Pi}_i^{r,m}\left(\int_0^t \mu_0 \tilde{Y}_i^r(\xi) d\xi\right),$$

respectively. Using (22)-(24) we obtain the following property for $\Pi_i^{r,m}$ (and analogous ones for $\hat{\Pi}_i^{r,m}$ and $\tilde{\Pi}_i^{r,m}$):

$$\max_{1 \leq m \leq r^{1-q}} \max_{0 \leq t \leq rT} |\Pi_i^{r,m}(t) - t|/r^q \to 0, \quad \text{as } r \to \infty, \quad \text{w.p.1.}$$
$$(25)$$

We denote

$$g^r(t) = (\hat{y}_i^r(t), \tilde{y}_i^r(t)) = r^{-q}(\hat{Y}_i^r(t) - \rho_i r, \tilde{Y}_i^r(t)).$$

Then, we can prove the following.

LEMMA 20. *Consider fixed realizations (for each r) of driving processes, such that the properties (25) hold with q replaced by a smaller parameter $q' \in (1/2, q)$. Consider the corresponding sequence of realizations of $(g^r(t), t \geq 0)$, with bounded initial states $\|g^r(0)\| \leq \epsilon$, $\epsilon > 0$. Then, there exists a subsequence of r along which*

$$g^r(t) \to g(t), \quad u.o.c., \quad (26)$$

where $(g(t), t \geq 0)$ is Lipschitz continuous, with $\|g(0)\| \leq \epsilon$, and it satisfies conditions

$$(d/dt)\hat{y}_i(t) = -\mu_i \hat{y}_i(t), \quad (27)$$

$$(d/dt)\tilde{y}_i(t) = \begin{cases} \mu_i \hat{y}_i(t) - \mu_0 \tilde{y}_i(t), & \text{if } \tilde{y}_i(t) > 0 \\ \max\{0, \mu_i \hat{y}_i(t) - \mu_0 \tilde{y}_i(t)\}, & \text{if } \tilde{y}_i(t) = 0 \end{cases}$$
$$(28)$$

at points $t \geq 0$, where the derivatives exist (which is almost everywhere w.r.t. the Lebesgue measure). Moreover, the convergence

$$\|g(t)\| \to 0, \quad t \to \infty, \quad (29)$$

holds and is uniform w.r.t. initial states with $\|g(0)\| \leq \epsilon$, and

$$\sup_{\|g(0)\| \leq \epsilon} \max_{t \geq 0} \|g(t)\| \to 0, \quad \epsilon \to 0. \quad (30)$$

As a consequence of (30),

$$\|g(0)\| = 0 \quad \text{implies} \quad \|g(t)\| = 0, \ \forall t. \quad (31)$$

Lemma 20 is analogous to Lemma 14 in [14], except that the space scaling by r^{-q} is applied, as opposed to the fluid scaling by r^{-1}, and the number of actual customers $\hat{Y}_i^r(t)$ is centered before scaling. The proof is somewhat more involved – the main issue is that (unlike for the fluid limit) the Lipschitz property of the limit is no longer automatic, because the rates of arrivals and departures in the system are $O(r)$, while the space is only scaled down by r^q. (That is why we need to use properties (25), as opposed to simply a strong law of large numbers.) However, this issue can be resolved as in, for example, the proof of Theorem 23 in [13]. We omit a detailed proof.

Proof of Theorem 18. By Corollary 17, we can choose a subsequence of r (increasing sufficiently fast) so that

$$\|g^r(0)\| \to 0, \quad \text{w.p.1.}$$

Then, we use the construction of the probability space specified above, which guarantees that w.p.1 the properties (25) hold with q replaced by a smaller parameter $q' \in (1/2, q)$ – let us consider any element of the probability space for which the properties (25) do hold. We claim that, for this element, (20) holds. Suppose not. Then, there exists $\epsilon > 0$ and a further subsequence of r, along which $\tau^r = \min\{t \mid \|g^r(t)\| > \epsilon\} \leq Tr^{1-q}$. By Lemma 20, we can and do choose time duration $T_1 > 0$ such that any limit trajectory $g(t)$ with $\|g(0)\| \leq \epsilon$ satisfies $\|g(T_1)\| \leq \epsilon/2$. For each r, consider the trajectory of g^r on the time interval $[\tau^r - T_1, \tau^r]$. (Suppose for now that $\tau^r \geq T_1$ for all sufficiently large r.) Then we can choose a further subsequence of r along which $g^r(\tau^r - T_1 + t) \to g(t)$ uniformly for $t \in [0, T_1]$, for a limit function $g(t)$ as in Lemma 20. But, this is impossible because then $\|g^r(\tau^r)\| \to \|g(T_1)\| \leq \epsilon/2$. The case when $\tau^r < T_1$ for infinitely many r is even simpler: we choose a further subsequence along which this is true, and consider the trajectories of g^r on the fixed time interval $[0, T_1]$. In this case any limit trajectory $g(t)$ described in Lemma 20 stays at 0 in the entire interval $[0, T_1]$, because $\|g(0)\| = \lim_r \|g^r(0)\| = 0$. This means that $\|g^r(\tau^r)\| \to 0$, again a contradiction. $\square$

From this point on, we assume the following structure of the probability space. (It is different from the one used for the proof of Theorem 18, which, as we discussed, was for that proof only.) There are common (for all r) unit rate Poisson processes driving the system, defined as follows. For each $(\boldsymbol{k}, i) \in \mathcal{M}$ and $\hat{\boldsymbol{k}} \leq \boldsymbol{k}$, consider independent unit-rate Poisson process $\hat{\Pi}_{(\boldsymbol{k}, \hat{\boldsymbol{k}}), i}(t)$, $t \geq 0$, so that the number of actual type i customer departures from configuration $(\boldsymbol{k}, \hat{\boldsymbol{k}})$ in the interval $[0, t]$ is equal to $\hat{\Pi}_{(\boldsymbol{k}, \hat{\boldsymbol{k}}), i}\left(\int_0^t \mu_i \hat{k}_i X_{(\boldsymbol{k}, \hat{\boldsymbol{k}})}^r(\xi) d\xi\right)$. Similarly, consider independent unit-rate Poisson process $\left\{\tilde{\Pi}_{(\boldsymbol{k}, \hat{\boldsymbol{k}}), i}(t), \ t \geq 0\right\}$, so that the number of type i token departures from configuration $(\boldsymbol{k}, \hat{\boldsymbol{k}})$ due to their expiration, is equal to $\tilde{\Pi}_{(\boldsymbol{k}, \hat{\boldsymbol{k}}), i}\left(\int_0^t \mu_0 (k_i - \hat{k}_i) X_{(\boldsymbol{k}, \hat{\boldsymbol{k}})}^r(\xi) d\xi\right)$. Finally, for each $i \in \mathcal{I}$, let $\{\Pi_i(t), \ t \geq 0\}$ be an independent unit-rate Poisson process, such that the number of exogenous type i arrivals in $[0, t]$ is equal to $\Pi_i(\lambda_i r t)$. For a fixed parameter $T > 0$, whose value will be chosen later, each of the above Poisson processes satisfies Lemma 12, in which we can and do replace T with $2T[(\bar{\mu} \vee \mu_0) + \sum_i \lambda_i]$. (We do this because we will "work" with system sample paths such that $\sum_i \hat{Y}_i = \sum_i (\hat{Y}_i^r + \tilde{Y}_i^r) < 2r$, and for these sample paths the total "instantaneous" rate of all transitions is upper bounded by $2r[(\bar{\mu} \vee \mu_0) + \sum_i \lambda_i]$.)

Denote by $\tilde{D}_i^r(t_1, t_2)$ the number of type-i token departures (due to their expirations), and by $\hat{A}_i^{**,r}(t_1, t_2)$ the total number of exogenous type-i arrivals (of actual customers) that do *not* replace type-i tokens, all in the interval $(t_1, t_2]$. Also, denote $Y_i^r(t_1, t_2) = Y_i^r(t_2) - Y_i^r(t_1)$.

THEOREM 21. *Consider the sequence (in r) of open systems in stationary regime. Let $T > 0$ be fixed. Then, any subsequence of r contains a further subsequence such that,*

w.p.1, the following holds:

$$\tilde{D}_i^r(t_0, t_0 + r^{p-1})/[r^p r^{p-1}] \to 0, \tag{32}$$

$$\hat{A}_i^{**,r}(t_0, t_0 + r^{p-1})/[r^p r^{p-1}] \to 0, \tag{33}$$

uniformly on all intervals $[t_0, t_0 + r^{p-1}] \subset [0, Tr^{1-p}]$.

PROOF. Indeed, by Theorem 18, we can and do choose a subsequence of r along which (20)-(21) hold w.p.1. Then, (32) follows from (20), which states that the number of tokens $\tilde{Y}_i^r(t)$ is uniformly $o(r^p)$, and from the construction of the token departure processes, with the corresponding driving processes $\tilde{\Pi}_{(\boldsymbol{k}, \hat{\boldsymbol{k}}), i}$ satisfying Lemma 12. From (20) we also have the uniform convergence

$$Y_i^r(t_0, t_0 + r^{p-1})/[r^p r^{p-1}] \to 0.$$

But, this along with (32) implies uniform convergence (33) as well, because we have the conservation law

$$Y_i^r(t_0, t_0 + r^{p-1}) = \hat{A}_i^{**,r}(t_0, t_0 + r^{p-1}) - \tilde{D}_i^r(t_0, t_0 + r^{p-1}).$$

The theorem is then proved. $\square$

Proof of Theorem 7. Consider the sequence of the system processes in stationary regime. Consider a fixed $T > 0$, chosen to be sufficiently large, as in Proposition 15. Consider any subsequence of r. Then, we can and do choose a further subsequence of r along which, w.p.1, (20)-(21) hold with some $q \in (1/2, p)$ (by Theorem 18) , and the properties stated in Theorem 21 hold. As in the proof of Proposition 15, we will keep track of the evolution of the value of $F^r(\boldsymbol{X}^r(t))$. We emphasize that this is exactly the same function F^r as defined in Section 2.3 and used in the analysis of closed system, namely it has the fixed parameter r (in the system with index r), and *not* the random "parameter" Z^r. We claim that the following property holds.

Claim: *There exist positive constants $0 < C_1 < C_2$, $\delta > 0$, such that the following holds. For all sufficiently large r, uniformly on all intervals $[t_0, t_0 + r^{p-1}] \subset [0, Tr^{1-p}]$, we have (a) $F^r(\boldsymbol{X}^r(t_0)) - ru^* \geq C_1 r^p$ implies*

$$F^r(\boldsymbol{X}^r(t_0 + r^{p-1})) - F^r(\boldsymbol{X}^r(t_0)) \leq -\delta r^{2p-1},$$

and (b) $F^r(\boldsymbol{X}^r(t_0)) - ru^* \leq C_1 r^p$ implies

$$\sup_{\xi \in [0,1]} F^r(\boldsymbol{X}^r(t_0 + \xi r^{p-1})) - ru^* \leq C_2 r^p.$$

Clearly, (b) is analogous to Corollary 13 for the closed system and is proved exactly same way, with $\bar{\mu}$ in (14) replaced by $\bar{\mu} \vee \mu_0$. Statement (a) is analogous to Proposition 14 for the closed system, and we prove it below. It is also clear that the claim, along with (20)-(21), implies the theorem statement via the argument almost verbatim repeating that in the proof of Proposition 15.

It remains to prove (a). The proof is the same as that of Proposition 14, except that we have to make additional estimates accounting for: (i) token departures due to their expiration and actual customer arrivals that do not find tokens; (ii) the fact that *GSS-M* uses weight function $\bar{w}^r = \bar{w}^r(X; Z^r)$, as opposed to function $w^r = w^r(X)$ (which has constant r as a parameter, instead of the random variable Z^r). This is because, *if we would have only transitions associated with actual customer departures and actual customer arrivals replacing tokens, and the assignment decisions would be based on weight w^r as opposed to $\bar{w}^r$, then exactly the same drift estimates as those in the proof of Proposition 14 would apply.* Note that in (i) we consider exactly those transitions for which we have properties (32)-(33). Therefore, in any interval $[t_0, t_0 + r^{p-1}]$ the "worst case" possible increase in $F^r(\boldsymbol{X}^r)$ due to such transitions is $o(r^{2p-1})$. (We omit obvious epsilon/delta formalities.) Now consider (ii). Since we have the uniform bound $|Z^r(t) - r| \leq O(r^q)$, it is easy to check that $|\bar{w}^r(X) - w^r(X)| \leq O(r^{q-1})$ for any $X \geq 0$. This means that the error in the calculation of first-order contribution into the change of $F^r(\boldsymbol{X}^r)$ in any $[t_0, t_0 + r^{p-1}]$, introduced by *GSS-M* using weight $\bar{w}^r$ instead of w^r, is uniformly bounded by $O(rr^{p-1}r^{q-1}) = O(r^{p+q-1}) = o(r^{2p-1})$. (Again, we omit epsilon/delta formalities.) We see that the potential positive contribution of both (i) and (ii) into the change of objective function in any interval $[t_0, t_0 + r^{p-1}]$ is $o(r^{2p-1})$, uniformly on the choice of the interval. The estimate in (a) follows. Thus, the proof of the above claim, and of the theorem, follows. □

5. DISCUSSION

We presented the policy *Greedy with sublinear Safety Stocks (GSS)* along with a variant, which asymptotically minimize the steady-state total number of occupied servers at the fluid scale, as the input flow rates grow to infinity. A technical novelty of *GSS* is that it *automatically* creates non-zero safety stocks, *sublinear in the system "size"*, at server configurations which have zero stocks on the fluid scale. It is important to note that the algorithm does it without *a priori* knowledge of system parameters. To prove the fluid-scale optimality of *GSS*, we also need to consider a local fluid scaling, under which the sublinear safety stocks are "visible". This in turn allows us to obtain a tight asymptotic characterization of the algorithm deviation from exact optimal packing.

We can extend *GSS* to policies that asymptotically minimize the more general objective $\sum_k c_k X_k$, where $c_k > 0$ can be interpreted as the "cost" (for example, some estimated energy cost) of keeping a server in configuration k, for each $k \in \mathcal{K}$. Instead of the weight function $w^r(X_k^r)$ for each $k \in \mathcal{K}$, consider the weight function $c_k w^r(X_k^r)$, and define Δ^r as the difference between the new weight functions. We can then define *GSS* and *GSS-M* using the new Δ^r. They minimize the fluid scale quantity $\sum_k c_k x_k$ asymptotically, and similar convergence rates can be obtained. If we assume that the cost c_k is monotonically non-decreasing in k (i.e., $c_{k'} \leq c_k$ if $k' \leq k$), then all our results and proofs still hold essentially verbatim. If costs c_k are not monotone in k, most of the statements and proofs easily extend, except those of Lemmas 10 and 11, where some dual variables η_i may need to be negative. These η_i can be defined in a similar fashion as those in the proof of Lemma 6 in [14].

There are some possible directions for future research. For example, one may expect asymptotic optimality of "pure" *GSS* in an open system, which seems more difficult to establish. Proving or disproving its optimality may require better understanding of and some new insight into the system dynamics. Another direction can be the investigation of policies other (possibly simpler) than *GSS*. *GSS* is *asymptotically* optimal as the system scale increases. However, if the number $|\mathcal{K}|$ of feasible configurations is large, the system scale may need to be very large for the near optimal performance. It is then of interest to design policies (e.g., some form of best-fit) that have provably good performance properties at a wide range of system scales.

6. REFERENCES

[1] N. Bansal, A. Caprara, M. Sviridenko. A New Approximation Method for Set Covering Problems, with Applications to Multidimensional Bin Packing. *SIAM J. Comput.*, 2009, Vol.39, No.4, pp.1256-1278.

[2] J. Csirik, D. S. Johnson, C. Kenyon, J. B. Orlin, P. W. Shor, and R. R. Weber. On the Sum-of-Squares Algorithm for Bin Packing. *J.ACM*, 2006, Vol.53, pp.1-65.

[3] M. Csörgő and L. Horváth. *Weighted Approximations in Probability and Statistics*, Wiley, 1993.

[4] D. Gamarnik. Stochastic Bandwidth Packing Process: Stability Conditions via Lyapunov Function Technique. *Queueing Systems*, 2004, Vol.48, pp.339-363.

[5] D. Gamarnik and A. L. Stolyar. Multiclass Multiserver Queueing System in the Halfin–Whitt Heavy Traffic Regime: Asymptotics of the Stationary Distribution. *Queueing Systems*, 2012, Vol.71, pp.25-51.

[6] A. Gulati, A. Holler, M. Ji, G. Shanmuganathan, C. Waldspurger, and X. Zhu. VMware Distributed Resource Management: Design, Implementation and Lessons Learned. *VMware Technical Journal*, 2012, Vol.1, No.1, pp. 45-64. http://labs.vmware.com/publications/vmware-technical-journal

[7] V. Gupta and A. Radovanovic. Online Stochastic Bin Packing. Preprint, 2012.

[8] J. W. Jiang, T. Lan, S. Ha, M. Chen, and M. Chiang. Joint VM Placement and Routing for Data Center Traffic Engineering. *INFOCOM 2012*.

[9] S. T. Maguluri, R. Srikant, and L. Ying. Stochastic Models of Load Balancing and Scheduling in Cloud Computing Clusters. *INFOCOM 2012*.

[10] S. Meyn. Dynamic Safety-Stocks for Asymptotic Optimality in Stochastic Networks. *Queueing Systems*, 2005, Vol. 50, pp.255-297.

[11] S. Shakkottai and A. L. Stolyar. Scheduling for Multiple Flows Sharing a Time-Varying Channel: The Exponential Rule. *American Mathematical Society Translations*, 2002, Series 2, Vol. 207, pp. 185-202

[12] A. L. Stolyar and T. Tezcan. Shadow Routing Based Control of Flexible Multi-Server Pools in Overload. *Operations Research*, 2011, Vol.59, No.6, pp.1427-1444.

[13] A. L. Stolyar and E. Yudovina. Tightness of Invariant Distributions of a Large-Scale Flexible Service System under a Priority Discipline. *Stochstic Systems*, 2012, Vol.2, No.2, pp.381-408.

[14] A. L. Stolyar. An Infinite Server System with General Packing Constraints. Bell Labs Technical Memo, 2012. Submitted. http://arxiv.org/abs/1205.4271

[15] A. L. Stolyar and Y. Zhong. A Large-Scale Service System with Packing Constraints: Minimizing the Number of Occupied Servers. Preprint, 2012. http://arxiv.org/abs/1212.0875

Online Energy Generation Scheduling for Microgrids with Intermittent Energy Sources and Co-Generation

Lian Lu[*]
Information Engineering Dept.
The Chinese Univ. of Hong Kong

Jinlong Tu[*]
Information Engineering Dept.
The Chinese Univ. of Hong Kong

Chi-Kin Chau
Masdar Institute of Science
and Technology

Minghua Chen
Information Engineering Dept.
The Chinese Univ. of Hong Kong

Xiaojun Lin
School of Electrical and
Computer Engineering
Purdue Univ.

ABSTRACT

Microgrids represent an emerging paradigm of future electric power systems that can utilize both distributed and centralized generations. Two recent trends in microgrids are the integration of local renewable energy sources (such as wind farms) and the use of co-generation (*i.e.,* to supply both electricity and heat). However, these trends also bring unprecedented challenges to the design of intelligent control strategies for microgrids. Traditional generation scheduling paradigms rely on perfect prediction of future electricity supply and demand. They are no longer applicable to microgrids with unpredictable renewable energy supply and with co-generation (that needs to consider both electricity and heat demand). In this paper, we study online algorithms for the microgrid generation scheduling problem with intermittent renewable energy sources and co-generation, with the goal of maximizing the cost-savings with local generation. Based on the insights from the structure of the offline optimal solution, we propose a class of competitive online algorithms, called CHASE (Competitive Heuristic Algorithm for Scheduling Energy-generation), that track the offline optimal in an online fashion. Under typical settings, we show that CHASE achieves the best competitive ratio among all deterministic online algorithms, and the ratio is no larger than a small constant 3. We also extend our algorithms to intelligently leverage on *limited prediction* of the future, such as near-term demand or wind forecast. By extensive empirical evaluations using real-world traces, we show that our proposed algorithms can achieve near offline-optimal performance. In a representative scenario, CHASE leads to around 20% cost reduction with no future look-ahead, and the cost reduction increases with the future look-ahead window.

Categories and Subject Descriptors

C.4 [**PERFORMANCE OF SYSTEMS**]: Modeling techniques; Design studies; F.1.2 [**Modes of Computation**]: Online computation; I.2.8 [**Problem Solving, Control Methods, and Search**]: Scheduling

General Terms

Algorithms, Performance

Keywords

Microgrids; Online Algorithm; Energy Generation Scheduling; Combined Heat and Power Generation

1. INTRODUCTION

Microgrid is a distributed electric power system that can autonomously co-ordinate local generations and demands in a dynamic manner [23]. Illustrated in Fig. 1, modern microgrids often consist of distributed renewable energy generations (*e.g.,* wind farms) and co-generation technology (*e.g.,* supplying both electricity and heat locally). Microgrids can operate in either grid-connected mode or islanded mode. There have been worldwide deployments of pilot microgrids, such as the US, Japan, Greece and Germany [7].

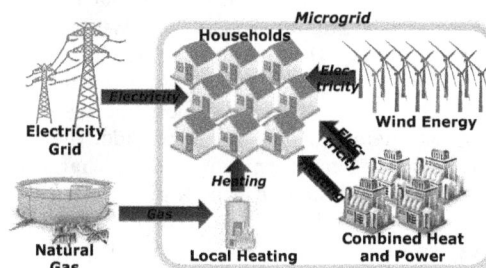

Figure 1: An illustration of a typical microgrid.

Microgrids are more robust and cost-effective than traditional approach of centralized grids. They represent an

---

[*]The first two authors are in alphabetical order.

emerging paradigm of future electric power systems [30] that address the following two critical challenges.

Power Reliability. Providing reliable and quality power is critical both socially and economically. In the US alone, while the electric power system is 99.97% reliable, each year the economic loss due to power outages is at least $150 billion [33]. However, enhancing power reliability across a large-scale power grid is very challenging [12]. With local generation, microgrids can supply energy *locally* as needed, effectively alleviating the negative effects of power outages.

Integration with Renewable Energy. The growing environmental awareness and government directives lead to the increasing penetration of renewable energy. For example, the US aims at 20% wind energy penetration by 2030 to "de-carbonize" the power system. Denmark targets at 50% wind generation by 2025. However, incorporating a significant portion of intermittent renewable energy poses great challenges to grid stability, which requires a new thinking of how the grid should operate [40]. In traditional centralized grids, the actual locations of conventional energy generation, renewable energy generation (*e.g.*, wind farms), and energy consumption are usually distant from each other. Thus, the need to coordinate conventional energy generation and consumption based on the instantaneous variations of renewable energy generation leads to challenging stability problems. In contrast, in microgrids renewable energy is generated and consumed in the *local* distributed network. Thus, the uncertainty of renewable energy is absorbed locally, minimizing its negative impact on the stability of the central transmission networks.

Furthermore, microgrids bring significant economic benefits, especially with the augmentation of combined heat and power (CHP) generation technology. In traditional grids, a substantial amount of residual energy after electricity generation is often wasted. In contrast, in microgrids this residual energy can be used to supply heat domestically. By simultaneously satisfying electricity and heat demand using CHP generators, microgrids can often be much more economical than using external electricity supply and separate heat supply [18].

However, to realize the maximum benefits of microgrids, intelligent scheduling of both local generation and demand must be established. Dynamic demand scheduling in response to supply condition, also called *demand response* [33, 11], is one of the useful approaches. But, demand response alone may be insufficient to compensate the highly volatile fluctuations of wind generation. Hence, intelligent generation scheduling, which orchestrates both local and external generations to satisfy the time-varying energy demand, is indispensable for the viability of microgrids. Such generation-side scheduling must simultaneously meet two goals. (1) To maintain grid stability, the aggregate supply from CHP generation, renewable energy generation, the centralized grid, and a separate heating system must meet the aggregate electricity and heat demand. (We do not consider the option of using energy storage in the paper, *e.g.*, to charge at low-price periods and to discharge at high-price periods. This is because for the typical size of microgrids, *e.g.*, a college campus, energy storage systems with comparable sizes are very expensive and not widely available.) (2) It is highly desirable that the microgrid can coordinate local generation and external energy procurement to minimize the overall cost of meeting the energy demand.

We note that a related generation scheduling problem has been extensively studied for the traditional grids, involving both Unit Commitment [34] and Economic Dispatch [14], which we will review in Sec. 6 as related work. In a typical power plant, the generators are often subject to several operational constraints. For example, steam turbines have a slow ramp-up speed. In order to perform generation scheduling, the utility company usually needs to forecast the demand first. Based on this forecast, the utility company then solves an offline problem to schedule different types of generation sources in order to minimize cost subject to the operational constraints.

Unfortunately, this classical strategy does not work well for the microgrids due to the following unique challenges introduced by the renewal energy sources and co-generation. The first challenge is that microgrids powered by intermittent renewable energy generations will face a significant uncertainty in energy supply. Because of its smaller scale, abrupt changes in local weather condition may have a dramatic impact that cannot be amortized as in the wider national scale. In Fig. 2a, we examine one-week traces of electricity demand for a college in San Francisco [1] and power output of a nearby wind station [4]. We observe that although the electricity demand has a relative regular pattern for prediction, the net electricity demand inherits a large degree of variability from the wind generation, casting a challenge for accurate prediction.

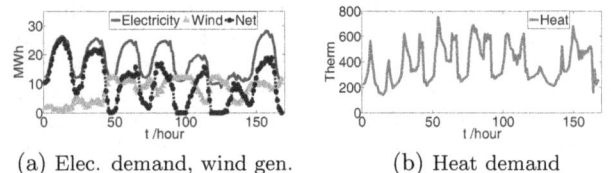

(a) Elec. demand, wind gen. (b) Heat demand

Figure 2: Electricity demand, heat demand and wind generation in a week. In (a), the net demand is computed by subtracting the wind generation from the electricity demand.

Secondly, co-generation brings a new dimension of uncertainty in scheduling decisions. Observed from Fig. 2b, the heat demand exhibits a different stochastic pattern that adds difficulty to the prediction of overall energy demand.

Due to the above additional variability, traditional energy generation scheduling based on *offline* optimization assuming *accurate* prediction of future supplies and demands cannot be applied to the microgrid scenarios. On the other hand, there are also new opportunities. In microgrids there are usually only 1-2 types of small reciprocate generators from tens of kilowatts to several megawatts. These generators are typically gas or diesel powered and can be fired up with large ramping-up/down level in the order of minutes. For example, a diesel-based engine can be powered up in 1-5 minutes and has a maximum ramp up/down rate of 40% of its capacity per minute [41]. The "fast responding" nature of these local generators opens up opportunities to increase the frequency of generator on/off scheduling that substantially changes the design space for energy generation scheduling.

Because of these unique challenges and opportunities, it remains an open question of how to design effective strategies for scheduling energy generation for microgrids.

1.1 Our Contributions

In this paper, we formulate a general problem of energy generation scheduling for microgrids. Since both the future demands and future renewable energy generation are difficult to predict, we use competitive analysis and study online algorithms that can perform provably well under arbitrarily time-varying (and even adversarial) future trajectories of demand and renewable energy generation. Towards this end, we design a class of simple and effective strategies for energy generation scheduling named CHASE (in short for Competitive Heuristic Algorithm for Scheduling Energy-generation). Compared to traditional prediction-based and offline optimization approaches, our online solution has the following salient benefits. First, CHASE gives an absolute performance guarantee without the knowledge of supply and demand behaviors. This minimizes the impact of inaccurate modeling and the need for expensive data gathering, and hence improves robustness in microgrid operations. Second, CHASE works without any assumption on gas/electricity prices and policy regulations. This provides the grid operators flexibility for operations and policy design without affecting the energy generation strategies for microgrids.

We summarize the key contributions as follows:

1. In Sec. 3.1.1, we devise an offline optimal algorithm for a generic formulation of the energy generation scheduling problem that models most microgrid scenarios with intermittent energy sources and fast-responding gas-/diesel-based CHP generators. Note that the offline problem is challenging by itself because it is a mixed integer problem and the objective function values across different slots are correlated via the startup cost. We first reveal an elegant structure of the single-generator problem and exploit it to construct the optimal offline solution. The structural insights are further generalized in Sec. 3.3 to the case with N homogeneous generators. The optimal offline solution employs a simple load-dispatching strategy where each generator separately solves a partial scheduling problem.

2. In Secs. 3.1.2-3.3, we build upon the structural insights from the offline solution to design CHASE, a deterministic online algorithm for scheduling energy generations in microgrids. We name our algorithm CHASE because it tracks the offline optimal solution in an online fashion. We show that CHASE achieves a competitive ratio of $\min(3 - 2\alpha, 1/\alpha) \leq 3$. In other words, no matter how the demand, renewable energy generation and grid price vary, the cost of CHASE without any future information is guaranteed to be no greater than $\min(3 - 2\alpha, 1/\alpha)$ times the offline optimal assuming complete future information. Here the constant $\alpha = (c_o + c_m/L)/(P_{\max} + \eta \cdot c_g) \in (0, 1]$ captures the maximum price discrepancy between using local generation and external sources to supply energy. We also prove that the above competitive ratio is the best possible for any deterministic online algorithm.

3. The above competitive ratio is attained without any future information of demand and supply. In Sec. 3.2, we then extend CHASE to intelligently leverage limited look-ahead information, such as near-term demand or wind forecast, to further improve its performance. In particular, CHASE achieves an improved competitive ratio of $\min(3 - 2 \cdot g(\alpha, \omega), 1/\alpha)$ when it can look into a future window of size ω. Here, the function $g(\alpha, \omega) \in [\alpha, 1]$ captures the benefit of looking-ahead and monotonically increases from α to 1 as ω increases. Hence,

the larger the look-ahead window, the better the performance. In Sec. 4, we also extend CHASE to the case where generators are governed by several additional operational constraints (e.g., ramping up/down rates and minimum on/off periods), and derive an upper bound for the corresponding competitive ratio.

4. In Sec. 5, by extensive evaluations using real-world traces, we show that our algorithm CHASE can achieve satisfactory empirical performance and is robust to look-ahead error. In particular, a small look-ahead window is sufficient to achieve near offline-optimal performance. Our offline (resp., online) algorithm achieves a cost reduction of 22% (resp., 17%) with CHP technology. The cost reduction is computed in comparison with the baseline cost achieved by using only the wind generation, the central grid, and a separate heating system. The substantial cost reductions show the economic benefit of microgrids in addition to its potential in improving energy reliability. Furthermore, interestingly, deploying a partial local generation capacity that provides 50% of the peak local demands can achieve 90% of the cost reduction. This provides strong motivation for microgrids to deploy at least a partial local generation capability to save costs.

Due to space limitations, all proofs are in our technical report [27].

2. PROBLEM FORMULATION

Notation	Definition
T	The total number of intervals (unit: min)
N	The total number of local generators
β	The startup cost of local generator ($)
c_m	The sunk cost per interval of running local generator ($)
c_o	The incremental operational cost per interval of running local generator to output an additional unit of power ($/Watt)
c_g	The price per unit of heat obtained externally using natural gas ($/Watt)
T_{on}	The minimum on-time of generator, once it is turned on
T_{off}	The minimum off-time of generator, once it is turned off
R_{up}	The maximum ramping-up rate (Watt/min)
R_{dw}	The maximum ramping-down rate (Watt/min)
L	The maximum power output of generator (Watt)
η	The heat recovery efficiency of co-generation
$a(t)$	The net power demand (Watt)
$h(t)$	The space heating demand (Watt)
$p(t)$	The spot price per unit of power obtained from the electricity grid ($P_{\min} \leq p(t) \leq P_{\max}$) ($/Watt)
$\sigma(t)$	The joint input at time t: $\sigma(t) \triangleq (a(t), h(t), p(t))$
$y_n(t)$	The on/off status of the i-th local generator (on as "1" and off as "0"), $1 \leq n \leq N$
$u_n(t)$	The power output level when the i-th generator is on (Watt), $1 \leq n \leq N$
$s(t)$	The heat level obtained externally by natural gas (Watt)
$v(t)$	The power level obtained from electricity grid (Watt)

Note: we use bold symbols to denote vectors, e.g., $a \triangleq (a(t))_{t=1}^T$. Brackets indicate the units.

Table 1: Key notations.

We consider a typical scenario where a microgrid orchestrates different energy generation sources to minimize cost for satisfying both local electricity and heat demands simultaneously, while meeting operational constraints of electric power system. We will formulate a microgrid cost minimization problem (**MCMP**) that incorporates intermittent energy demands, time-varying electricity prices, local generation capabilities and co-generation.

We define the notations in Table 1. We also define the acronyms for our problems and algorithms in Table 2.

Acronym	Meaning
MCMP	Microgrid Cost Minimization Problem
fMCMP	**MCMP** for fast-responding generators
fMCMP$_s$	**fMCMP** with single fast-responding generator
SP	A simplified version of **fMCMP**$_s$
CHASE$_s$	The baseline version of CHASE for **fMCMP**$_s$
CHASE$_{s+}$	CHASE for **fMCMP**$_s$
CHASE$_s^{\text{lk}(\omega)}$	The baseline version of CHASE for **fMCMP**$_s$ with look-ahead
CHASE$_{s+}^{\text{lk}(\omega)}$	CHASE for **fMCMP**$_s$ with look-ahead
CHASE$^{\text{lk}(\omega)}$	CHASE for **fMCMP** with look-ahead
CHASE$_{\text{gen}}^{\text{lk}(\omega)}$	CHASE for **MCMP** with look-ahead

Table 2: Acronyms for problems and algorithms.

2.1 Model

Intermittent Energy Demands: We consider arbitrary renewable energy supply (*e.g.*, wind farms). Let the net demand (*i.e.*, the residual electricity demand not balanced by wind generation) at time t be $a(t)$. Note that we do not rely on any specific stochastic model of $a(t)$.

External Power from Electricity Grid: The microgrid can obtain external electricity supply from the central grid for unbalanced electricity demand in an on-demand manner. We let the spot price at time t from electricity grid be $p(t)$. We assume that $P_{\min} \leq p(t) \leq P_{\max}$. Again, we do not rely on any specific stochastic model on $p(t)$.

Local Generators: The microgrid has N units of homogeneous local generators, each having an maximum power output capacity L. Based on a common generator model [21], we denote β as the startup cost of turning on a generator. Startup cost β typically involves the heating up cost (in order to produce high pressure gas or steam to drive the engine) and the time-amortized additional maintenance costs resulted from each startup (*e.g.*, fatigue and possible permanent damage resulted by stresses during startups)[1]. We denote c_m as the sunk cost of maintaining a generator in its active state per unit time, and c_o as the operational cost per unit time for an active generator to output an additional unit of energy. Furthermore, a more realistic model of generators considers advanced *operational constraints*:

1. *Minimum On/Off Periods*: If one generator has been committed (resp., uncommitted) at time t, it must remain committed (resp., uncommitted) until time $t + \mathsf{T}_{\text{on}}$ (resp., $t + \mathsf{T}_{\text{off}}$).

2. *Ramping-up/down Rates*: The incremental power output in two consecutive time intervals is limited by the ramping-up and ramping-down constraints.

Most microgrids today employ generators powered by gas turbines or diesel engines. These generators are "fast-responding" in the sense that they can be powered up in several minutes, and have small minimum on/off periods as well as large ramping-up/down rates. Meanwhile, there are also generators based on steam engine, and are "slow-responding" with non-negligible T_{on}, T_{off}, and small ramping-up/down rates.

Co-generation and Heat Demand: The local CHP generators can simultaneously generate electricity and useful heat. Let the heat recovery efficiency for co-generation be η, *i.e.*, for each unit of electricity generated, η unit of useful heat can be supplied for free. Alternatively, without co-generation, heating can be generated separately using external natural gas, which costs c_g per unit time. Thus, ηc_g is the saving due to using co-generation to supply heat, provided that there is sufficient heat demand. We assume $c_o \geq \eta \cdot c_g$. In other words, it is cheaper to generate heat by natural gas than purely by generators (if not considering the benefit of co-generation). Note that a system with no co-generation can be viewed as a special case of our model by setting $\eta = 0$. Let the heat demand at time t be $h(t)$.

To keep the problem interesting, we assume that $c_o + \frac{c_m}{L} < P_{\max} + \eta \cdot c_g$. This assumption ensures that the minimum co-generation energy cost is cheaper than the maximum external energy price. If this was not the case, it would have been optimal to always obtain power and heat externally and separately.

2.2 Problem Definition

We divide a finite time horizon into T discrete time slots, each is assumed to have a unit length without loss of generality. The microgrid operational cost in $[1, T]$ is given by

$$\text{Cost}(y, u, v, s) \triangleq \sum_{t=1}^{T} \Big\{ p(t) \cdot v(t) + c_g \cdot s(t) + \quad (1)$$

$$\sum_{n=1}^{N} \left[c_o \cdot u_n(t) + c_m \cdot y_n(t) + \beta [y_n(t) - y_n(t-1)]^+ \right] \Big\},$$

which includes the cost of grid electricity, the cost of the external gas, and the operating and switching cost of local CHP generators in the entire horizon $[1, T]$. Throughout this paper, we set the initial condition $y_n(0) = 0$, $1 \leq n \leq N$.

We formally define the **MCMP** as a mixed integer programming problem, given electricity demand a, heat demand h, and grid electricity price p as time-varying inputs:

$$\min_{y,u,v,s} \text{Cost}(y, u, v, s) \quad (2a)$$

$$\text{s.t. } 0 \leq u_n(t) \leq L \cdot y_n(t), \quad (2b)$$

$$\sum_{n=1}^{N} u_n(t) + v(t) \geq a(t), \quad (2c)$$

$$\eta \cdot \sum_{n=1}^{N} u_n(t) + s(t) \geq h(t), \quad (2d)$$

$$u_n(t) - u_n(t-1) \leq \mathsf{R}_{\text{up}}, \quad (2e)$$

$$u_n(t-1) - u_n(t) \leq \mathsf{R}_{\text{dw}}, \quad (2f)$$

$$y_n(\tau) \geq \mathbf{1}_{\{y_n(t) > y_n(t-1)\}}, t+1 \leq \tau \leq t + \mathsf{T}_{\text{on}}\text{-}1, \quad (2g)$$

$$y_n(\tau) \leq 1\text{-}\mathbf{1}_{\{y_n(t) < y_n(t-1)\}}, t+1 \leq \tau \leq t + \mathsf{T}_{\text{off}}\text{-}1, (2h)$$

$$\text{var } y_n(t) \in \{0, 1\}, u_n(t), v(t), s(t) \in \mathbb{R}_0^+, n \in [1, N], t \in [1, T],$$

where $\mathbf{1}_{\{\cdot\}}$ is the indicator function and $\mathbb{R}_0^+$ represents the set of non-negative numbers. The constraints are similar to those in the power system literature and capture the operational constraints of generators. Specifically, constraint

---

[1]It is commonly understood that power generators incur startup costs and hence the generator on/off scheduling problem is inherently a dynamic programming problem. However, the detailed data of generator startup costs are often not revealed to the public. According to [13] and the references therein, startup costs of gas generators vary from several hundreds to thousands of US dollars. Startup costs at such level are comparable to running generators at their full capacities for several hours.

(2b) captures the constraint of maximal output of the local generator. Constraints (2c)-(2d) ensure that the demands of electricity and heat can be satisfied, respectively. Constraints (2e)-(2f) capture the constraints of maximum ramping-up/down rates. Constraints (2g)-(2h) capture the minimum on/off period constraints (note that they can also be expressed in linear but hard-to-interpret forms).

3. FAST-RESPONDING GENERATOR CASE

This section considers the fast-responding generator scenario. Most CHP generators employed in microgrids are based on gas or diesel. These generators can be fired up in several minutes and have high ramping-up/down rates. Thus at the timescale of energy generation (usually tens of minutes), they can be considered as having no minimum on/off periods and ramping-up/down rate constraints. That is, $T_{on} = 0$, $T_{off} = 0$, $R_{up} = \infty$, $R_{dw} = \infty$. We remark that this model captures most microgrid scenarios today. We will extend the algorithm developed for this responsive generator scenario to the general generator scenario in Sec. 4.

To proceed, we first study a simple case where there is one unit of generator. We then extend the results to N units of homogenous generators in Sec. 3.3.

3.1 Single Generator Case

We first study a basic problem that considers a single generator. Thus, we can drop the subscript n (the index of the generator) when there is no source of confusion:

$$\textbf{fMCMP}_s : \min_{y,u,v,s} \text{Cost}(y,u,v,s) \tag{3a}$$

$$\text{s.t. } 0 \le u(t) \le L \cdot y(t), \tag{3b}$$

$$u(t) + v(t) \ge a(t), \tag{3c}$$

$$\eta \cdot u(t) + s(t) \ge h(t), \tag{3d}$$

$$\text{var } y(t) \in \{0,1\}, u(t), v(t), s(t) \in \mathbb{R}_0^+, t \in [1,T].$$

Note that even this simpler problem is challenging to solve. First, even to obtain an offline solution (assuming complete knowledge of future information), we must solve a mixed integer optimization problem. Further, the objective function values across different slots are correlated via the startup cost $\beta[y(t) - y(t-1)]^+$, and thus cannot be decomposed. Finally, to obtain an online solution we do not even know the future.

Remark: Readers familiar with online server scheduling in data centers [25, 28] may see some similarity between our problem and those in [25, 28], *i.e.*, all are dealing with the scheduling difficulty introduced by the switching cost. Despite such similarity, however, the inherent structures of these problems are significantly different. First, there is only one category of demand (*i.e.*, workload to be satisfied by the servers) in online server scheduling problems. In contrast, there are two categories of demands (*i.e.*, electricity and heat demands) in our problem. Further, because of co-generation, they can not be considered separately. Second, there is only one category of supply (*i.e.*, server service capability) in online server scheduling problem, and thus the demand must be satisfied by this single supply. However, in our problem, there are three different supplies, including local generation, electricity grid power and external heat supply. Therefore, the design space in our problem is larger and it requires us to orchestrate three different supplies, instead of single supply, to satisfy the demands.

Next, we introduce the following lemma to simplify the structure of the problem. Note that if $(y(t))_{t=1}^T$ are given, the startup cost is determined. Thus, the problem in (3a)-(3d) reduces to a linear programming and can be solved *independently in each time slot*.

LEMMA 1. *Given $(y(t))_{t=1}^T$ and the input $(\sigma(t))_{t=1}^T$, the solutions $(u(t), v(t), s(t))_{t=1}^T$ that minimize $\text{Cost}(y,u,v,s)$ are given by:*

$$u(t) = \begin{cases} 0, & \text{if } p(t) + \eta \cdot c_g \le c_o \\ \min\left\{\frac{h(t)}{\eta}, a(t), L \cdot y(t)\right\}, & \text{if } p(t) < c_o < p(t) + \eta \cdot c_g \\ \min\left\{a(t), L \cdot y(t)\right\}, & \text{if } c_o \le p(t) \end{cases} \tag{4}$$

and

$$v(t) = [a(t) - u(t)]^+, \quad s(t) = [h(t) - \eta \cdot u(t)]^+. \tag{5}$$

We note in each time slot t, the above $u(t)$, $v(t)$ and $s(t)$ are computed using only $y(t)$ and $\sigma(t)$ in the same time slot.

The result of Lemma 1 can be interpreted as follows. If the grid price is very high (*i.e.*, higher than c_o), then it is always more economical to use local generation as much as possible, without even considering heating. However, if the grid price is between c_o and $c_o - \eta \cdot c_g$, local electricity generation alone is not economical. Rather, it is the benefit of supplying heat through co-generation that makes local generation more economical. Hence, the amount of local generation must consider the heat demand $h(t)$. Finally, when the grid price is very low (*i.e.*, lower than $c_o - \eta \cdot c_g$), it is always more cost-effective not to use local generation.

As a consequence of Lemma 1, the problem **fMCMP$_s$** can be simplified to the following problem **SP**, where we only need to consider the decision of turning on ($y(t) = 1$) or off ($y(t) = 0$) the generator.

$$\textbf{SP} : \min_y \text{Cost}(y)$$

$$\text{var } y(t) \in \{0,1\}, t \in [1,T],$$

where

$$\text{Cost}(y) \triangleq \sum_{t=1}^T \left(\psi(\sigma(t), y(t)) + \beta \cdot [y(t) - y(t-1)]^+\right),$$

$\psi(\sigma(t), y(t)) \triangleq c_o u(t) + p(t)v(t) + c_g s(t) + c_m y(t)$ and $(u(t), v(t), s(t))$ are defined according to Lemma 1.

3.1.1 Offline Optimal Solution

We first study the offline setting, where the input $(\sigma(t))_{t=1}^T$ is given ahead of time. We will reveal an elegant structure of the optimal solution. Then, in Section 3.1.2 we will exploit this structure to design an efficient online algorithm.

The problem **SP** can be solved by the classical dynamic programming approach. We refer interested readers to our technical report [27] for details. However, the solution provided by dynamic programming does not seem to bring significant insights for developing online algorithms. Therefore, in what follows we study the offline optimal solution from another angle, which directly reveals its structure.

Define

$$\delta(t) \triangleq \psi(\sigma(t), 0) - \psi(\sigma(t), 1). \tag{6}$$

$\delta(t)$ can be interpreted as the one-slot cost difference between using or not using local generation. Intuitively, if

$\delta(t) > 0$ (resp. $\delta(t) < 0$), it will be desirable to turn on (resp. off) the generator. However, due to the startup cost, we should not turn on and off the generator too frequently. Instead, we should evaluate whether the *cumulative* gain or loss in the future can offset the startup cost. This intuition motivates us to define the following cumulative cost difference $\Delta(t)$. We set the initial value as $\Delta(0) = -\beta$ and define $\Delta(t)$ inductively:

$$\Delta(t) \triangleq \min\left\{0, \max\{-\beta, \Delta(t-1) + \delta(t)\}\right\}. \quad (7)$$

Note that $\Delta(t)$ is only within the range $[-\beta, 0]$. Otherwise, the minimum cap $(-\beta)$ and maximum cap (0) will apply to retain $\Delta(t)$ within $[-\beta, 0]$. An important feature of $\Delta(t)$ useful later in online algorithm design is that it can be computed given the past and current input $\sigma(\tau), 1 \leq \tau \leq t$.

Next, we construct critical segments according to $\Delta(t)$, and then classify segments by types. Each type of segments captures similar episodes of demands. As shown later in Theorem 1, it suffices to solve the cost minimization problem over every segment and combine their solutions to obtain an offline optimal solution for the overall problem **SP**.

Definition 1. We divide all time intervals in $[1, T]$ into disjoint parts called *critical segments*:

$$[1, T_1^c], [T_1^c + 1, T_2^c], [T_2^c + 1, T_3^c], ..., [T_k^c + 1, T]$$

The critical segments are characterized by a set of *critical points*: $T_1^c < T_2^c < ... < T_k^c$. We define each critical point T_i^c along with an auxiliary point $\tilde{T}_i^c$, such that the pair $(T_i^c, \tilde{T}_i^c)$ satisfies the following conditions:

- (Boundary): Either $\left(\Delta(T_i^c) = 0 \text{ and } \Delta(\tilde{T}_i^c) = -\beta\right)$ or $\left(\Delta(T_i^c) = -\beta \text{ and } \Delta(\tilde{T}_i^c) = 0\right)$.

- (Interior): $-\beta < \Delta(\tau) < 0$ for all $T_i^c < \tau < \tilde{T}_i^c$.

In other words, each pair of $(T_i^c, \tilde{T}_i^c)$ corresponds to an interval where $\Delta(t)$ goes from $-\beta$ to 0 or 0 to $-\beta$, without reaching the two extreme values inside the interval. For example, $(T_1^c, \tilde{T}_1^c)$ and $(T_2^c, \tilde{T}_2^c)$ in Fig. 3 are two such pairs, while the corresponding critical segments are (T_1^c, T_2^c) and (T_2^c, T_3^c). It is straightforward to see that all $(T_i^c, \tilde{T}_i^c)$ are uniquely defined, thus critical segments are well-defined. See Fig. 3 for an example.

Once the time horizon $[1, T]$ is divided into critical segments, we can now characterize the optimal solution.

Definition 2. We classify the *type* of a critical segment by:

- *type-start* (also call *type-0*): $[1, T_1^c]$

- *type-1*: $[T_i^c + 1, T_{i+1}^c]$, if $\Delta(T_i^c) = -\beta$ and $\Delta(T_{i+1}^c) = 0$

- *type-2*: $[T_i^c + 1, T_{i+1}^c]$, if $\Delta(T_i^c) = 0$ and $\Delta(T_{i+1}^c) = -\beta$

- *type-end* (also call *type-3*): $[T_k^c + 1, T]$

We define the cost with regard to a segment i by:

$$\text{Cost}^{\text{sg-}i}(y) \triangleq \sum_{t=T_i^c+1}^{T_{i+1}^c} \psi\big(\sigma(t), y(t)\big) + \sum_{t=T_i^c+1}^{T_{i+1}^c+1} \beta \cdot [y(t) - y(t-1)]^+$$

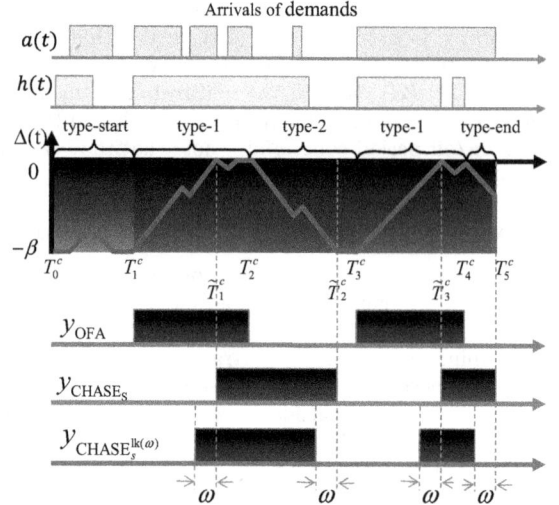

Figure 3: An example of $\Delta(t)$, y_{OFA}, y_{CHASE_s} and $y_{\text{CHASE}_s^{\text{lk}(\omega)}}$. In the top two rows, we have $a(t) \in \{0, 1\}$, $h(t) \in \{0, \eta\}$. The price $p(t)$ is chosen as a constant in $(c_o - \eta \cdot c_g, c_o)$. In the next row, we compute $\Delta(t)$ according to $a(t)$ and $h(t)$. For ease of exposition, in this example we set the parameters so that $\Delta(t)$ increases if and only if $a(t) = 1$ and $h(t) = \eta$. The solutions y_{OFA}, y_{CHASE_s} and $y_{\text{CHASE}_s^{\text{lk}(\omega)}}$ at the bottom rows are obtained accordingly to (8), Algorithms 1 and 3, respectively.

and define a subproblem for critical segment i by:

$$\mathbf{SP}^{\text{sg-}i}(y_i^l, y_i^r) : \min \text{Cost}^{\text{sg-}i}(y)$$
$$\text{s.t. } y(T_i^c) = y_i^l, \ y(T_{i+1}^c + 1) = y_i^r,$$
$$\text{var } y(t) \in \{0, 1\}, t \in [T_i^c + 1, T_{i+1}^c].$$

Note that due to the startup cost across segment boundaries, in general $\text{Cost}(y) \neq \sum \text{Cost}^{\text{sg-}i}(y)$. In other words, we should not expect that putting together the solutions to each segment will lead to an overall optimal offline solution. However, the following lemma shows an important structure property that *one optimal solution* of $\mathbf{SP}^{\text{sg-}i}(y_i^l, y_i^r)$ is independent of boundary conditions (y_i^l, y_i^r) although *the optimal value depends on boundary conditions*.

LEMMA 2. $(y_{\text{OFA}}(t))_{t=T_i^c+1}^{T_{i+1}^c}$ in (8) is an optimal solution for $\mathbf{SP}^{\text{sg-}i}(y_i^l, y_i^r)$, despite any boundary conditions (y_i^l, y_i^r).

This lemma can be intuitively explained by Fig. 3. In type-1 critical segment, $\Delta(t)$ has an increment of β, which means that setting $y(t) = 1$ over the entire segment provides at least a benefit of β, compared to keeping $y(t) = 0$. Such benefit compensates the possible startup cost β if the boundary conditions are not aligned with $y(t) = 1$. Therefore, regardless of the boundary conditions, we should set $y(t) = 1$ on type-1 critical segment. Other types of critical segments can be explained similarly.

We then use this lemma to show the following main result on the structure of the offline optimal solution.

Theorem 1. An optimal solution for **SP** is given by

$$y_{\text{OFA}}(t) \triangleq \begin{cases} 0, & \text{if } t \in [T_i^c + 1, T_{i+1}^c] \text{ is type-start/-2/-end}, \\ 1, & \text{if } t \in [T_i^c + 1, T_{i+1}^c] \text{ is type-1}. \end{cases}$$

$$(8)$$

Theorem 1 can be interpreted as follows. Consider for example a type-1 critical segment in Fig. 3 that starts from

T_1^c. Since $\Delta(t)$ increases from $-\beta$ after T_1^c, it implies that $\delta(t) > 0$, and thus we are interested in turning on the generator. The difficulty, however, is that immediately after T_1^c we do not know whether the future gain by turning on the generator will offset the startup cost. On the other hand, once $\Delta(t)$ reaches 0, it means that the cumulative gain in the interval $[T_1^c, \tilde{T}_1^c]$ will be no less than the startup cost. Hence, we can safely turn on the generator at T_1^c. Similarly, for each type-2 segment we can turn off the generator at the beginning of the segment. (We note that our offline solution turns on/off the generator at the beginning of each segment because all future information is assumed to be known.)

The optimal solution is easy to compute. More importantly, the insights help us design the online algorithms.

3.1.2 Our Proposed Online Algorithm CHASE

Denote an online algorithm for **SP** by $\mathcal{A}$. We define the competitive ratio of $\mathcal{A}$ by:

$$\mathsf{CR}(\mathcal{A}) \triangleq \max_{\sigma} \frac{\mathrm{Cost}(y_{\mathcal{A}})}{\mathrm{Cost}(y_{\mathsf{OFA}})} \qquad (9)$$

Recall the structure of optimal solution y_{OFA}: once the process is entering type-1 (resp., type-2) critical segment, we should set $y(t) = 1$ (resp., $y(t) = 0$). However, the difficulty lies in determining the beginnings of type-1 and type-2 critical segments without future information. Fortunately, as illustrated in Fig. 3, it is certain that the process is in a type-1 critical segment when $\Delta(t)$ reaches 0 for the first time after hitting $-\beta$. This observation motivates us to use the algorithm CHASE_s, which is given in Algorithm 1. If $-\beta < \Delta(t) < 0$, CHASE_s maintains $y(t) = y(t-1)$ (since we do not know whether a new segment has started yet.) However, when $\Delta = 0$ (resp. $\Delta(t) = -\beta$), we know for sure that we are inside a new type-1 (resp. type-2) segment. Hence, CHASE_s sets $y(t) = 1$ (resp. $y(t) = 0$). Intuitively, the behavior of CHASE_s is to track the offline optimal in an online manner: we change the decision only after we are certain that the offline optimal decision is changed.

Algorithm 1 $\mathsf{CHASE}_s[t, \sigma(t), y(t-1)]$

1: find $\Delta(t)$
2: **if** $\Delta(t) = -\beta$ **then**
3:    $y(t) \leftarrow 0$
4: **else if** $\Delta(t) = 0$ **then**
5:    $y(t) \leftarrow 1$
6: **else**
7:    $y(t) \leftarrow y(t-1)$
8: **end if**
9: set $u(t)$, $v(t)$, and $s(t)$ according to (4) and (5)
10: return $(y(t), u(t), v(t), s(t))$

Even though CHASE_s is a simple algorithm, it has a strong performance guarantee, as given by the following theorem.

Theorem 2. The competitive ratio of CHASE_s satisfies

$$\mathsf{CR}(\mathsf{CHASE}_s) \leq 3 - 2\alpha < 3, \qquad (10)$$

where

$$\alpha \triangleq (c_o + c_m/L)/(P_{\max} + \eta \cdot c_g) \in (0, 1] \qquad (11)$$

captures the maximum price discrepancy between using local generation and external sources to supply energy.

Remark: (i) The intuition that CHASE_s is competitive can be explained by studying its worst case input shown

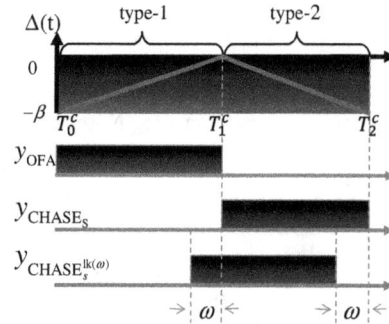

Figure 4: The worst case input of CHASE_s, and the corresponding y_{CHASE_s}, $y_{\mathsf{CHASE}_s^{\mathrm{lk}(\omega)}}$ and the offline optimal solution y_{OFA}.

in Fig. 4. The demands and prices are chosen in a way such that in interval $[T_0^c, T_1^c]$ $\Delta(t)$ increases from $-\beta$ to 0, and in interval $[T_1^c, T_2^c]$ $\Delta(t)$ decreases from 0 to $-\beta$. We see that in the worst case, y_{CHASE_s} never matches y_{OFA}. But even in this worst case, CHASE_s pays only 2β more than the offline solution y_{OFA} on $[T_0^c, T_2^c]$, while y_{OFA} pays at least a startup cost β at time T_0^c. Hence, the ratio of the online cost over the offline cost cannot be too bad. (ii) Theorem 2 says that CHASE_s is more competitive when α is large than it is small. This can be explained intuitively as follows. Large α implies small economic advantage of using local generation over external sources to supply energy. Consequently, the offline solution tends to use local generation less. It turns out CHASE_s will also use less local generation[2] and is competitive to offline solution. Meanwhile, when α is small, CHASE_s starts to use local generation. However, using local generation incurs high risk since we have to pay the startup cost to turn on the generator without knowing whether there are sufficient demands to serve in the future. Lacking future knowledge leads to a large performance discrepancy between CHASE_s and the offline optimal solution, making CHASE_s less competitive.

The result in Theorem 2 is strong in the sense that $\mathsf{CR}(\mathsf{CHASE}_s)$ is always upper-bounded by a small constant 3, regardless of system parameters. This is contrast to large parameter-dependent competitive ratios that one can achieve by using generic approach, *e.g.*, the metrical task system framework [8], to design online algorithms. Furthermore, we show that CHASE_s achieves close to the best possible competitive ratio for deterministic algorithms as follow.

Theorem 3. Let $\epsilon > 0$ be the slot length under the discrete-time setting we consider in this paper. The competitive ratio for any deterministic online algorithm $\mathcal{A}$ for **SP** is lower bounded by

$$\mathsf{CR}(\mathcal{A}) \geq \min(3 - 2\alpha - o(\epsilon), 1/\alpha), \qquad (12)$$

where $o(\epsilon)$ vanishes to zero as ϵ goes to zero and the discrete-time setting approaches the continuous-time setting.

Note that there is still a gap between the competitive ratios in (10) and (12). The difference is due to the term $1/\alpha = (P_{\max} + \eta \cdot c_g)/(c_o + c_m/L)$. This term can be interpreted as the competitive ratio of a naive strategy that always uses external power supply and separate heat supply. Intuitively, if this $1/\alpha$ term is smaller than $3 - 2\alpha$, we

---

[2] CHASE_s will turn on the local generator when $\Delta(t)$ increases to 0. The larger the α is, the slower $\Delta(t)$ increases, and the less likely CHASE_s will use the local generator.

should simply use this naive strategy. This observation motivates us to develop an improved version of CHASE$_s$, called CHASE$_{s+}$, which is presented in Algorithm 2. Corollary 1 shows that CHASE$_{s+}$ closes the above gap and achieves the asymptotic optimal competitive ratio. Note that whether or not the $1/\alpha$ term is smaller can be completely determined by the system parameters.

Algorithm 2 CHASE$_{s+}[t, \sigma(t), y(t-1)]$

1: **if** $1/\alpha \leq 3 - 2\alpha$ **then**
2:     $y(t) \leftarrow 0$, $u(t) \leftarrow 0$, $v(t) \leftarrow a(t)$, $s(t) \leftarrow h(t)$
3:     return $(y(t), u(t), v(t), s(t))$
4: **else**
5:     return CHASE$_s[t, \sigma(t), y(t-1)]$
6: **end if**

Corollary 1. CHASE$_{s+}$ achieves the asymptotic optimal competitive ratio of any deterministic online algorithm, as

$$\mathsf{CR}(\mathsf{CHASE}_{s+}) \leq \min(3 - 2\alpha, 1/\alpha). \qquad (13)$$

Remark: At the beginning of Sec. 3.1, we have discussed the structural differences of online server scheduling problems [25, 28] and ours. In what follows, we summarize the solution differences among these problems. Note that we share similar intuitions with [28], both make switching decisions when the *penalty cost* equals the switching cost. The significant difference, however, is when to reset the penalty counting. In [28], the penalty counting is reset when the demand arrives. In contrast, in our solution, we need to reset the penalty counting only when $\Delta(t)$, given in the nontrivial form in (7), touches 0 or $-\beta$. This particular way of resetting penalty counting is critical for establishing the optimality of our proposed solution. Meanwhile, to compare with [25], the approach in [25] does not explicitly count the penalty. Furthermore, the online server scheduling problem in [25] is formulated as a convex problem, while our problem is a mixed integer problem. Thus, there is no known method to apply the approach in [25] to our problem.

3.2   Look-ahead Setting

We consider the setting where the online algorithm can predict a small window ω of the immediate future. Note that $\omega = 0$ returns to the case treated in Section 3.1.2, when there is no future information at all. Consider again a type-1 segment $[T_1^c, T_2^c]$ in Fig. 3. Recall that, when there is no future information, the CHASE$_s$ algorithm will wait until $\tilde{T}_1^c$, *i.e.*, when $\Delta(t)$ reaches 0, to be certain that the offline solution must turn on the generator. Hence, the CHASE$_s$ algorithm will not turn on the generator until this time. Now assume that the online algorithm has the information about the immediate future in a time window of length ω. By the time $\tilde{T}_1^c - w$, the online algorithm has already known that $\Delta(t)$ will reach 0 at time $\tilde{T}_1^c$. Hence, the online algorithm can safely turn on the generator at time $\tilde{T}_1^c - w$. As a result, the corresponding loss of performance compared to the offline optimal solution is also reduced. Specifically, even for the worst-case input in Fig. 4, there will be some overlap (of length ω) between y_{CHASE_s} and y_{OFA} in each segment. Hence, the competitive ratio should also improve with future information. This idea leads to the online algorithm CHASE$_s^{\mathrm{lk}(\omega)}$, which is presented in Algorithm 3.

We can show the following improved competitive ratio when limited future information is available.

Algorithm 3 CHASE$_s^{\mathrm{lk}(\omega)}[t, (\sigma(\tau))_{\tau=t}^{t+w}, y(t-1)]$

1: find $(\Delta(\tau))_{\tau=t}^{t+w}$
2: set $\tau' \leftarrow \min\{\tau = t, ..., t+w \mid \Delta(\tau) = 0 \text{ or } = -\beta\}$
3: **if** $\Delta(\tau') = -\beta$ **then**
4:     $y(t) \leftarrow 0$
5: **else if** $\Delta(\tau') = 0$ **then**
6:     $y(t) \leftarrow 1$
7: **else**
8:     $y(t) \leftarrow y(t-1)$
9: **end if**
10: set $u(t)$, $v(t)$, and $s(t)$ according to (4) and (5)
11: return $(y(t), u(t), v(t), s(t))$

Theorem 4. The competitive ratio of CHASE$_s^{\mathrm{lk}(\omega)}$ satisfies

$$\mathsf{CR}\left(\mathsf{CHASE}_s^{\mathrm{lk}(\omega)}\right) \leq 3 - 2 \cdot g(\alpha, \omega), \qquad (14)$$

where $\omega \geq 0$ is the look-ahead window size, $\alpha \in (0, 1]$ is defined in (11), and

$$g(\alpha, \omega) = \alpha + \frac{(1 - \alpha)}{1 + \beta\left(Lc_o + c_m/(1-\alpha)\right)/\left(\omega(Lc_o + c_m)c_m\right)}. \qquad (15)$$

captures the benefit of looking-ahead and monotonically increases from α to 1 as ω increases. In particular, $\mathsf{CR}(\mathsf{CHASE}_s^{\mathrm{lk}(0)}) = \mathsf{CR}(\mathsf{CHASE}_s)$.

We replace CHASE$_s$ by CHASE$_s^{\mathrm{lk}(\omega)}$ in CHASE$_{s+}$ and obtain an improved algorithm for the look-ahead setting, named CHASE$_{s+}^{\mathrm{lk}(\omega)}$. Fig. 5 shows the competitive ratio of CHASE$_{s+}^{\mathrm{lk}(\omega)}$ as a function of α and ω.

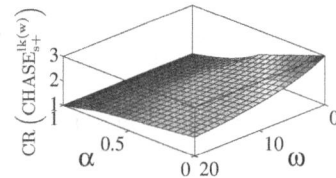

Figure 5: The competitive ratio of CHASE$_{s+}^{\mathrm{lk}(\omega)}$ as a function of α and ω.

3.3   Multiple Generator Case

Now we consider the general case with N units of homogeneous generators, each having an maximum power capacity L, startup cost β, sunk cost c_m and per unit operational cost c_o. We define a generalized version of problem:

fMCMP : $\min_{y,u,v,s} \mathrm{Cost}(y, u, v, s)$

s.t. Constraints (2b), (2c), and (2d)

var $y_n(t) \in \{0, 1\}, u_n(t), v(t), s(t) \in \mathbb{R}_0^+,$

Next, we will construct both offline and online solutions to **fMCMP** in a divide-and-conquer fashion. We will first partition the demands into sub-demands for each generator, and then optimize the local generation *separately* for each sub-demand. Note that the key is to correctly partition the demand so that the combined solution is still optimal. Our strategy below essentially slices the demand (as a function of t) into multiple layers from the bottom up (see Fig. 6). Each layer has at most L units of electricity demand and

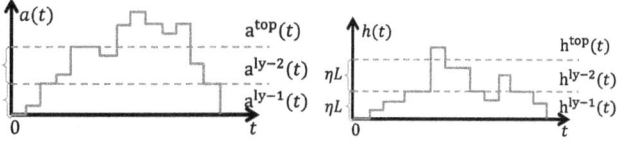

(a) An example of $(a^{\text{ly}-n})$.   (b) An example of $(h^{\text{ly}-n})$.

Figure 6: An example of $(a^{\text{ly}-n})$ and $(h^{\text{ly}-n})$. In this example, $N = 2$. We obtain 3 layers of electricity and heat demands, respectively.

$\eta \cdot L$ units of heat demand. The intuition here is that the layers at the bottom exhibit the least frequent variations of demand. Hence, by assigning each of the layers at the bottom to a dedicated generator, these generators will incur the least amount of switching, which helps to reduce the startup cost.

More specifically, given $(a(t), h(t))$, we slice them into $N + 1$ layers:

$$a^{\text{ly}-1}(t) = \min\{L, a(t)\}, \quad h^{\text{ly}-1}(t) = \min\{\eta \cdot L, h(t)\} \quad (16a)$$

$$a^{\text{ly}-n}(t) = \min\{L, a(t) - \sum_{r=1}^{n-1} a^{\text{ly}-r}(t)\}, n \in [2, N] \quad (16b)$$

$$h^{\text{ly}-n}(t) = \min\{\eta \cdot L, h(t) - \sum_{r=1}^{n-1} h^{\text{ly}-r}(t)\}, n \in [2, N] \quad (16c)$$

$$a^{\text{top}}(t) = \min\{L, a(t) - \sum_{r=1}^{N} a^{\text{ly}-r}(t)\} \quad (16d)$$

$$h^{\text{top}}(t) = \min\{\eta \cdot L, h(t) - \sum_{r=1}^{N} h^{\text{ly}-r}(t)\} \quad (16e)$$

It is easy to see that electricity demand satisfies $a^{\text{ly}-n}(t) \leq L$ and heat demand satisfies $h^{\text{ly}-n}(t) \leq \eta \cdot L$. Thus, each layer of sub-demand can be served by a single local generator if needed. Note that $(a^{\text{top}}, h^{\text{top}})$ can only be satisfied from external supplies, because they exceed the capacity of local generation.

Based on this decomposition of demand, we then decompose the **fMCMP** problem into N sub-problems **fMCMP$_s^{\text{ly}-n}$** $(1 \leq n \leq N)$, each of which is an **fMCMP$_s$** problem with input $(a^{\text{ly}-n}, h^{\text{ly}-n}, p)$. We then apply the offline and online algorithms developed earlier to solve each sub-problem **fMCMP$_s^{\text{ly}-n}$** $(1 \leq n \leq N)$ *separately*. By combining the solutions to these sub-problems, we obtain offline and online solutions to **fMCMP**. For the offline solution, the following theorem states that such a divide-and-conquer approach results in no optimality loss.

Theorem 5. Suppose (y_n, u_n, v_n, s_n) is an optimal offline solution for each **fMCMP$_s^{\text{ly}-n}$** $(1 \leq n \leq N)$. Then $((y_n^*, u_n^*)_{n=1}^{N}, v^*, s^*)$ defined as follows is an optimal offline solution for **fMCMP**:

$$y_n^*(t) = y_n(t), \quad v^*(t) = a^{\text{top}}(t) + \sum_{n=1}^{N} v_n(t)$$
$$u_n^*(t) = u_n(t), \quad s^*(t) = h^{\text{top}}(t) + \sum_{n=1}^{N} s_n(t) \quad (17)$$

For the online solution, we also apply such a divide-and-conquer approach by using (i) a central demand dispatching module that slices and dispatches demands to individual generators according to (16a)-(16e), and (ii) an online generation scheduling module sitting on each generator n $(1 \leq n \leq N)$ *independently* solving their own **fMCMP$_s^{\text{ly}-n}$** sub-problem using the online algorithm $\mathsf{CHASE}_{s+}^{\text{lk}(\omega)}$.

The overall online algorithm, named $\mathsf{CHASE}^{\text{lk}(\omega)}$, is simple to implement without the need to coordinate the control among multiple local generators. Since the offline (resp. online) cost of **fMCMP** is the sum of the offline (resp. online) costs of **fMCMP$_s^{\text{ly}-n}$** $(1 \leq n \leq N)$, it is not difficult to establish the competitive ratio of $\mathsf{CHASE}^{\text{lk}(\omega)}$ as follows.

Theorem 6. The competitive ratio of $\mathsf{CHASE}^{\text{lk}(\omega)}$ satisfies

$$\mathsf{CR}(\mathsf{CHASE}^{\text{lk}(\omega)}) \leq \min(3 - 2 \cdot g(\alpha, \omega), 1/\alpha), \quad (18)$$

where $\alpha \in (0, 1]$ is defined in (11) and $g(\alpha, \omega) \in [\alpha, 1]$ is defined in (15).

4. SLOW-RESPONDING GENERATOR CASE

We next consider the slow-responding generator case, with the generators having non-negligible constraints on the minimum on/off periods and the ramp-up/down speeds. For this slow-responding version of **MCMP**, its offline optimal solution is harder to characterize than **fMCMP** due to the additional challenges introduced by the cross-slot constraints (2e)-(2h).

In the slow-responding setting, local generators cannot be turned on and off immediately when demand changes. Rather, if a generator is turned on (resp., off) at time t, it must remain on for at least T_{on} (resp. T_{off}) time . Further, the changes of $u_n(t) - u_n(t-1)$ must be bounded by R_{up} and $-\mathsf{R}_{\text{down}}$.

A simple heuristic is to first compute solutions based on $\mathsf{CHASE}^{\text{lk}(\omega)}$, and then modify the solutions to respect the above constraints. We name this heuristic $\mathsf{CHASE}_{\text{gen}}^{\text{lk}(\omega)}$ and present it in Algorithm 4. For simplicity, Algorithm 4 is a single-generator version, which can be easily extended to the multiple-generator scenario by following the divide-and-conquer approach elaborated in Sec. 3.3.

Algorithm 4 $\mathsf{CHASE}_{\text{gen}}^{\text{lk}(\omega)}[t, (\sigma(\tau))_{\tau=1}^{t+w}, y(t-1)]$

1: $(y_s(t), u_s(t), v_s(t), s_s(t)) \leftarrow \mathsf{CHASE}_s^{\text{lk}(\omega)}[t, (\sigma(\tau))_{\tau=1}^{t+w}, y(t-1)]$
2: **if** $y(\tau_1) \leq 1 - \mathbf{1}_{\{y_s(t) > y(t-1)\}}, \forall \tau_1 \in [\max(1, t - \mathsf{T}_{\text{off}}), t-1]$
   and $y(\tau_2) \geq \mathbf{1}_{\{y_s(t) < y(t-1)\}}, \forall \tau_2 \in [\max(1, t - \mathsf{T}_{\text{on}}), t-1]$
   then
3:    $y(t) \leftarrow y_s(t)$
4: **else**
5:    $y(t) \leftarrow y(t-1)$
6: **end if**
7: **if** $u_s(t) > u(t-1)$ **then**
8:    $u(t) \leftarrow u(t-1) + \min(\mathsf{R}_{\text{up}}, u_s(t) - u(t-1))$
9: **else**
10:    $u(t) \leftarrow u(t-1) - \min(\mathsf{R}_{\text{dw}}, u(t-1) - u_s(t))$
11: **end if**
12: $v(t) \leftarrow [a(t) - u(t)]^+$
13: $s(t) \leftarrow [h(t) - \eta \cdot u(t)]^+$
14: **return** $(y(t), u(t), v(t), s(t))$

We now explain Algorithm 4 and its competitive ratio. At each time slot t, we obtain the solution of $\mathsf{CHASE}_s^{\text{lk}(\omega)}$, including $y_s(t), u_s(t), v_s(t), s_s(t)$, as a reference solution (Line 1). Then in Line 2-6, we modify the reference solution's $y_s(t)$ to our actual solution $y(t)$, to respect the constraints of minimum on/off periods. More specifically, we follow the reference solution's $y_s(t)$ (i.e., $y(t) = y_s(t)$) *if and only if* it respects the minimum on/off periods constraints (Line 2-3). Otherwise, we let our actual solution's $y(t)$ equal our previous slot's solution ($y(t) = y(t-1)$) (Line 4-5). Similarly, we modify the reference solution's $u_s(t)$ to our actual solution's $u(t)$, to respect the constraints on ramp-up/down speeds (Line 7-11). At last, in our actual solution, we use $(v(t), s(t))$ to compensate the supply and satisfy the demands (Line 12-13). In summary, our actual solution is designed to be aligned with the reference solution as much as possible. We derive an upper bound on the competitive ratio of $\mathsf{CHASE}_{\text{gen}}^{\text{lk}(\omega)}$ as follows.

Theorem 7. The competitive ratio of $\text{CHASE}_{\text{gen}}^{\text{lk}(\omega)}$ is upper bounded by $(3 - 2g(\alpha, \omega)) \cdot \max(r_1, r_2)$, where $g(\alpha, \omega)$ is defined in (15) and

$$r_1 = 1 + \max \left\{ \frac{(P_{\max} + c_g \cdot \eta - c_0)}{Lc_0 + c_m} \max\left\{0, \left(L - R_{\text{up}}\right)\right\} \right.$$

$$\left. \frac{c_o}{c_m} \max\left\{0, \left(L - R_{\text{dw}}\right)\right\} \right\},$$

and $r_2 = \dfrac{\beta + c_m \cdot T_{\text{on}}}{\beta} + \dfrac{L(P_{\max} + c_g \cdot \eta)}{\beta}(T_{\text{on}} + T_{\text{off}}).$

We note that when $T_{\text{on}} = T_{\text{off}} = 0$, $R_{\text{up}} = R_{\text{dw}} = \infty$, the above upper bound matches that of $\text{CHASE}^{\text{lk}(\omega)}$ in Theorem 6 (specifically the first term inside the min function).

5. EMPIRICAL EVALUATIONS

We evaluate the performance of our algorithms based on evaluations using real-world traces. Our objectives are three-fold: (i) evaluating the potential benefits of CHP and the ability of our algorithms to unleash such potential, (ii) corroborating the empirical performance of our online algorithms under various realistic settings, and (iii) understanding how much local generation to invest to achieve substantial economic benefit.

5.1 Parameters and Settings

Demand Trace: We obtain the demand traces from California Commercial End-Use Survey (CEUS) [1]. We focus on a college in San Francisco, which consumes about 154 GWh electricity and 5.1×10^6 therms gas per year. The traces contain hourly electricity and heat demands of the college for year 2002. The heat demands for a typical week in summer and spring are shown in Fig. 7. They display regular daily patterns in peak and off-peak hours, and typical weekday and weekend variations.

Wind Power Trace: We obtain the wind power traces from [4]. We employ power output data for the typical weeks in summer and spring with a resolution of 1 hour of an offshore wind farm right outside San Francisco with an installed capacity of 12MW. The net electricity demand, which is computed by subtracting the wind generation from electricity demand is shown in Fig. 7. The highly fluctuating and unpredictable nature of wind generation makes it difficult for the conventional prediction-based energy generation scheduling solutions to work effectively.

Electricity and Natural Gas Prices: The electricity and natural gas price data are from PG&E [5] and are shown in Table 3. Besides, the grid electricity prices for a typical week in summer and winter are shown in Fig. 7. Both the electricity demand and the price show strong diurnal properties: in the daytime, the demand and price are relatively high; at nights, both are low. This suggests the feasibility of reducing the microgrid operating cost by generating cheaper energy locally to serve the demand during the daytime when both the demand and electricity price are high.

Generator Model: We adopt generators with specifications the same as the one in [6]. The full output of a single generator is $L = 3MW$. The incremental cost per unit time to generate an additional unit of energy c_o is set to be $0.051/KWh$, which is calculated according to the natural gas price and the generator efficiency. We set the heat recovery efficiency of co-generation η to be 1.8 according to

[6]. We also set the unit-time generator running cost to be $c_m = 110\$/h$, which includes the amortized capital cost and maintenance cost according to a similar setting from [36]. We set the startup cost β equivalent to running the generator at its full capacity for about 5 hrs at its own operating cost which gives $\beta = 1400\$$. In addition, we assume for each generator $T_{\text{on}} = T_{\text{off}} = 3h$ and $R_{\text{up}} = R_{\text{dw}} = 1MW/h$, unless mentioned otherwise. For electricity demand trace we use, the peak demand is 30MW. Thus, we assume there are 10 such CHP generators so as to fully satisfy the demand.

Local Heating System: We assume an on-demand heating system with capacity sufficiently large to satisfy all the heat demand by itself and without on-off cost or ramp limit. The efficiency of a heating system is set to 0.8 according to [2], and consequently we can compute the unit heat generation cost to be $c_g = 0.0179\$/KWh$.

Cost Benchmark: We use the cost incurred by using only external electricity, heating and wind energy (without CHP generators) as a benchmark. We evaluate the cost reduction due to our algorithms.

Comparisons of Algorithms: We compare three algorithms in our simulations. (1) our online algorithm CHASE; (2) the Receding Horizon Control (RHC) algorithm; and (3) the OFFLINE optimal algorithm we introduce in Sec. 4. RHC is a heuristic algorithm commonly used in the control literature [22]. In RHC, an estimate of the near future (e.g., in a window of length w) is used to compute a tentative control trajectory that minimizes the cost over this time-window. However, only the first step of this trajectory is implemented. In the next time slot, the window of future estimates shifts forward by 1 slot. Then, another control trajectory is computed based on the new future information, and again only the first step is implemented. This process then continues. We note that because at each step RHC does not consider any adversarial future dynamics beyond the time-window w, there is no guarantee that RHC is competitive. For the OFFLINE algorithm, the inputs are system parameters (such as β, c_m and T_{on}), electricity demand, heat demand, wind power output, gas price, and grid electricity price. For online algorithms CHASE and RHC, the input is the same as the OFFLINE except that at time t, only the demands, wind power output, and prices in the past and the look-ahead window (i.e., $[1, t + w]$) are available. The output for all three algorithms is the total cost incurred during the time horizon $[1, T]$.

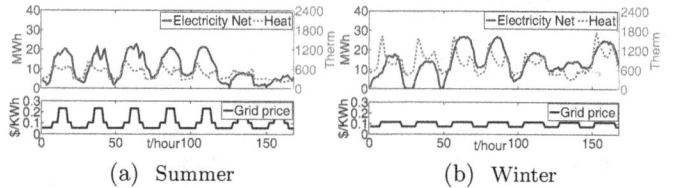

(a) Summer   (b) Winter

Figure 7: Electricity net demand and heat demand for a typical week in summer and winter. The net demand is computed by subtracting the wind generation from the electricity demand. The net electricity demand and the heat demand need to be satisfied by using the local CHP generators, the electricity grid, and the heating system.

5.2 Potential Benefits of CHP

Purpose: The experiments in this subsection aim to answer two questions. First, what is the potential savings with microgrids? Note that electricity, heat demand, wind sta-

Electricity	Summer (May-Oct.) $/kWh	Winter (Nov.-Apr.) $/kWh
On-peak	0.232	N/A
Mid-peak	0.103	0.116
Off-peak	0.056	0.072
Natural Gas	0.419$/therm	0.486$/therm

Table 3: PG&E commercial tariffs and natural gas tariffs. In the table, summer on-peak, mid-peak, and off-peak hours are weekday 12-18, weekday 8-12, and the remaining hours, respectively. Winter mid-peak and off-peak hours are weekday 8-22 and the remaining hours, respectively. The gas price is an average; monthly prices vary slightly according to PG&E.

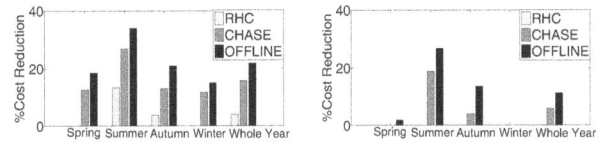

(a) Local generators with CHP (b) Local generators without CHP

Figure 8: Cost reductions for different seasons and the whole year.

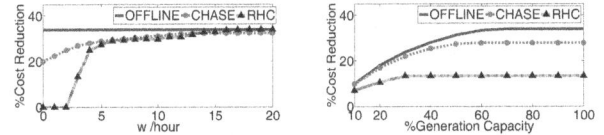

Figure 9: Cost reduction as a function of look ahead window size ω.

Figure 10: Cost reduction as a function of local generation capacity.

tion output as well as energy price all exhibit seasonal patterns. As we can see from Figs. 7a and 7b, during summer (similarly autumn) the electricity price is high, while during winter (similarly spring) the heat demand is high. It is then interesting to evaluate under what settings and inputs the savings will be higher. Second, what is the difference in cost-savings with and without the co-generation capability? In particular, we conduct two sets of experiments to evaluate the cost reductions of various algorithms. Both experiments have the same default settings, except that the first set of experiments (referred to as CHP) assumes the CHP technology in the generators is enabled, and the second set of experiments (referred to as NOCHP) assumes the CHP technology is not available, in which case the heat demand must be satisfied solely by the heating system. In all experiments, the look-ahead window size is set to be $w = 3$ hours according to power system operation and wind generation forecast practice [3]. The cost reductions of different algorithms are shown in Fig. 8a and 8b. The vertical axis is the cost reduction as compared to the cost benchmark presented in Sec. 5.1.

Observations: First, the whole-year cost reductions obtained by OFFLINE are 21.8% and 11.3% for CHP and NOCHP scenarios, respectively. This justifies the economic potential of using local generation, especially when CHP technology is enabled. Then, looking at the seasonal performance of OFFLINE, we observe that OFFLINE achieves much more cost savings during summer and autumn than during spring and winter. This is because the electricity price during summer and autumn is very high, thus we can benefit much more from using the relatively-cheaper local generation as compared to using grid energy only. Moreover, OFFLINE achieves much more cost savings when CHP is enabled than when it is not during spring and winter. This is because, during spring and winter, the electricity price is relatively low and the heat demand is high. Hence, just using local generation to supply electricity is not economical. Rather, local generation becomes more economical only if it can be used to supply both electricity and heat together (i.e., with CHP technology).

Second, CHASE performs consistently close to OFFLINE across inputs from different seasons, even though the different settings have very different characteristics of demand and supply. In contrast, the performance of RHC depends heavily on the input characteristics. For example, RHC achieves some cost reduction during summer and autumn when CHP is enabled, but achieves 0 cost reduction in all the other cases.

Ramifications: In summary, our experiments suggest that exploiting local generation can save more cost when the electricity price is high, and CHP technology is more

critical for cost reduction when heat demand is high. Regardless of the problem setting, it is important to adopt an intelligent online algorithm (like CHASE) to schedule energy generation, in order to realize the full benefit of microgrids.

5.3 Benefits of Looking-Ahead

Purpose: We compare the performances of CHASE to RHC and OFFLINE for different sizes of the look-ahead window and show the results in Fig. 9. The vertical axis is the cost reduction as compared to the cost benchmark in Sec. 5.1 and the horizontal axis is the size of lookahead window, which varies from 0 to 20 hours.

Observations: We observe that the performance of our online algorithm CHASE is already close to OFFLINE even when no or little look-ahead information is available (e.g., $w = 0, 1,$ and 2). In contrast, RHC performs poorly when the look-ahead window is small. When w is large, both CHASE and RHC perform very well and their performance are close to OFFLINE when the look-ahead window w is larger than 15 hours.

An interesting observation is that it is more important to perform intelligent energy generation scheduling when there is no or little look-ahead information available. When there are abundant look-ahead information available, both CHASE and RHC achieve good performance and it is less critical to carry out sophisticated algorithm design.

In Fig. 11a and 11b, we separately evaluate the benefit of looking-ahead under the fast-responding and slow-responding scenarios. We evaluate the empirical competitive ratio between the cost of CHASE and OFFLINE, and compare it with the theoretical competitive ratio according to our analytical results. In the fast-responding scenario (Fig. 11a), for each generator there are no minimum on/off period and ramping-up/down constraints. Namely, $T_{on} = 0$, $T_{off} = 0$, $R_{up} = \infty$, $R_{dw} = \infty$. In the slow-responding scenario (Fig. 11b), we set $T_{on} = T_{off} = 3h$ and $R_{up} = R_{dw} = 1MW/h$. In both experiments, we observe that the theoretical ratio decreases rapidly as look-ahead window size increases. Further, the empirical ratio is already close to one even when there is no look-ahead information.

5.4 Impacts of Look-ahead Error

Purpose: Previous experiments show that our algorithms have better performance if a larger time-window of accurate look-ahead input information is available. The input infor-

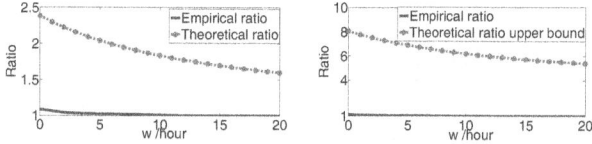

(a) Fast-responding scenario   (b) Slow-responding scenario

Figure 11: Theoretical and empirical ratios for CHASE, as functions of look-ahead window size ω. Note that the theoretical competitive ratios (or their bounds) measure the worst-case performance and are often much larger than the empirical ratios observed in practice.

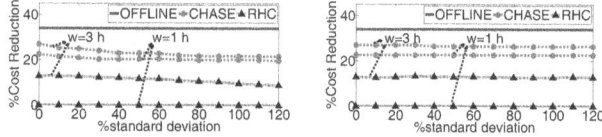

(a) Wind power forecast error   (b) Heat demand forecast error

Figure 12: Cost reduction as a function of the size prediction error (measured by the standard deviation of the prediction error as a percentage of (a)installed capacity and (b)peak heat demand).

mation in the look-ahead window includes the wind station power output, the electricity and heat demand, and the central grid electricity price. In practice, these look-ahead information can be obtained by applying sophisticated prediction techniques based on the historical data. However, there are always prediction errors. For example, while the day-ahead electricity demand can be predicted within 2-3% range, the wind power prediction in the next hours usually comes with an error range of 20-50% [20]. Therefore, it is important to evaluate the performance of the algorithms in the presence of prediction error.

Observations: To achieve this goal, we evaluate CHASE with look-ahead window size of 1 and 3 hours. According to [20], the hour-level wind-power prediction-error in terms of the percentage of the total installed capacity usually follows Gaussian distribution. Thus, in the look-ahead window, a zero-mean Gaussian prediction error is added to the amount of wind power in each time-slot. We vary the standard deviation of the Gaussian prediction error from 0 to 120% of the total installed capacity. Similarly, a zero-mean Gaussian prediction error is added to the heat demand, and its standard deviation also varies from 0 to 120% of the peak demand. We note that in practice, prediction errors are often in the range of 20-50% for 3-hour prediction [20]. Thus, by using a standard deviation up to 120%, we are essentially stress-testing our proposed algorithms. We average 20 runs for each algorithm and show the results in Figs. 12a and 12b. As we can see, both CHASE and RHC are fairly robust to the prediction error and both are more sensitive to the wind-power prediction error than to the heat-demand prediction error. Besides, the impact of the prediction error is relatively small when the look-ahead window size is small, which matches with our intuition.

5.5 Impacts of System Parameters

Purpose: Microgrids may employ different types of local generators with diverse operational constraints (such ramping up/down limits and minimum on/off times) and heat recovery efficiencies. It is then important to understand the impact on cost reduction due to these parameters. In this experiment, we study the cost reduction provided by our of-

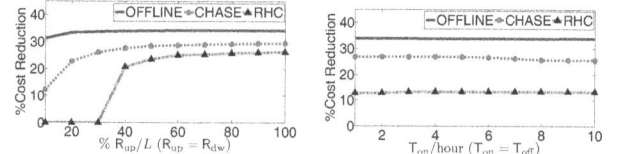

(a) cost redu. vs. R_{up} and R_{dw}(b) cost redu. vs. T_{on} and T_{off}

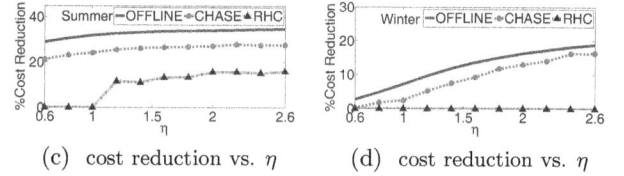

(c) cost reduction vs. η (d) cost reduction vs. η

Figure 13: Cost reduction as functions of generator parameters.

fline and online algorithms under different settings of R_{up}, R_{dw}, T_{on}, T_{off} and η.

Observations: Fig. 13a and 13b show the impact of ramp limit and minimum on/off time, respectively, on the performance of the algorithms. Note that for simplicity we always set $R_{up} = R_{dw}$ and $T_{on} = T_{off}$. As we can see in Fig. 13a, with R_{up} and R_{dw} of about 40% of the maximum capacity, CHASE obtains nearly all of the cost reduction benefits, compared with RHC which needs 70% of the maximum capacity. Meanwhile, it can be seen from Fig. 13b that T_{on} and T_{off} do not have much impact on the performance. This suggests that it is more valuable to invest in generators with fast ramping up/down capability than those with small minimum on/off periods. From Fig. 13c and 13d, we observe that generators with large η save much more cost during the winter because of the high heat demand. This suggests that in areas with large heat demand, such as Alaska and Washington, the heat recovery efficiency ratio is a critical parameter when investing CHP generators.

5.6 How Much Local Generation is Enough

Thus far, we assumed that the microgrid had the ability to supply all energy demand from local power generation in every time-slot. In practice, local generators can be quite expensive. Hence, an important question is how much investment should a microgrid operator makes (in terms of the installed local generator capacity) in order to obtain the maximum cost benefit. More specifically, we vary the number of CHP generators from 1 to 10 and plot the corresponding cost reductions of algorithms in Fig. 10. Interestingly, our results show that provisioning local generation to produce 60% of the peak demand is sufficient to obtain nearly all of the cost reduction benefits. Further, with just 50% local generation capacity we can achieve about 90% of the maximum cost reduction. The intuitive reason is that most of the time demands are significantly lower than their peaks.

6. RELATED WORK

Energy generation scheduling is a classical problem in power systems and involves two aspects, namely Unit Commitment (UC) and Economic Dispatching (ED). UC optimizes the startup and shutdown schedule of power generations to meet the forecasted demand over a short period, whereas ED allocates the system demand and spinning reserve capacity among operating units at each specific hour of operation without considering startup and shutdown of power generators.

For large power systems, UC involves scheduling of a large number gigantic power plants of several hundred if not thousands of megawatts with heterogeneous operating constraints and logistics behind each action [34]. The problem is very challenging to solve and has been shown to be NP-Complete in general[3] [16]. Sophisticated approaches proposed in the literature for solving UC include mixed integer programming [10], dynamic programming [35], and stochastic programming [37]. There have also been investigations on UC with high renewable energy penetration [38], based on over-provisioning approach. After UC determines the on/off status of generators, ED computes their output levels by solving a nonlinear optimization problem using various heuristics without altering the on/off status of generators [14]. There is also recent interest in involving CHP generators in ED to satisfy both electricity and heat demand simultaneously [17]. See comprehensive surveys on UC in [34] and on ED in [14].

However, these studies assume the demand and energy supply (or their distributions) in the entire time horizon are known *a prior*. As such, the schemes are not readily applicable to microgrid scenarios where accurate prediction of small-scale demand and wind power generation is difficult to obtain due to limited management resources and their unpredictable nature [42].

Several recent works have started to study energy generation strategies for microgrids. For example, the authors in [18] develop a linear programming based cost minimization approach for UC in microgrids. [19] considers the fuel consumption rate minimization in microgrids and advocates to build ICT infrastructure in microgrids. [24, 26] discuss the energy scheduling problems in data centers, whose models are similar with ours. The difference between these works and ours is that they assume the demand and energy supply are given beforehand, and ours does not rely on input prediction.

Online optimization and algorithm design is an established approach in optimizing the performance of various computer systems with minimum knowledge of inputs [8, 32]. Recently, it has found new applications in data centers [15, 9, 39, 25, 28, 29]. To the best of our knowledge, our work is the first to study the competitive online algorithms for energy generation in microgrids with intermittent energy sources and co-generation. The authors in [31] apply online convex optimization framework [43] to design ED algorithms for microgrids. However, the ED problem does not take into account the startup cost. In contrast, our work jointly consider UC and ED in microgrids with co-generation. Furthermore, the two works adopt different frameworks and provide online algorithms with different types of performance guarantee.

7. CONCLUSION

In this paper, we study online algorithms for the microgrid generation scheduling problem with intermittent renewable energy sources and co-generation, with the goal of maximizing the cost-savings with local generation. Based on

insights from the structure of the offline optimal solution, we propose a class of competitive online algorithms, called CHASE that track the offline optimal in an online fashion. Under typical settings, we show that CHASE achieves the best competitive ratio of all deterministic online algorithms, and the ratio is no larger than a small constant 3. We also extend our algorithms to intelligently leverage on *limited prediction* of the future, such as near-term demand or wind forecast. By extensive empirical evaluations using real-world traces, we show that our proposed algorithms can achieve near offline-optimal performance.

There are a number of interesting directions for future work. First, energy storage systems (*e.g.,* large-capacity battery) have been proposed as an alternate approach to reduce energy generation cost (during peak hours) and to integrate renewable energy sources. It would be interesting to study whether our proposed microgrid control strategies can be combined with energy storage systems to further reduce generation cost. However, current energy storage systems can be very expensive. Hence, it is critical to study whether the combined control strategy can reduce sufficient cost with limited amount of energy storage. Second, it remains an open issue whether CHASE can achieve the best competitive ratios in general cases (*e.g.,* in the slow-responding case).

8. ACKNOWLEDGMENTS

The work described in this paper was partially supported by China National 973 projects (No. 2012CB315904 and 2013CB336700), several grants from the University Grants Committee of the Hong Kong Special Administrative Region, China (Area of Excellence Project No. AoE/E-02/08 and General Research Fund Project No. 411010 and 411011), two gift grants from Microsoft and Cisco, and Masdar Institute-MIT Collaborative Research Project No. 11CAMA1. Xiaojun Lin would like to thank the Institute of Network Coding at The Chinese University of Hong Kong for the support of his sabbatical visit, during which some parts of the work were done.

9. REFERENCES

[1] California commercial end-use survey. Internet:http://capabilities.itron.com/CeusWeb/.

[2] Green energy. Internet:http://www.green-energy-uk.com/whatischp.html.

[3] The irish meteorological service online. Internet:http://www.met.ie/forecasts/.

[4] National renewable energy laboratory. Internet:http://wind.nrel.gov.

[5] Pacific gas and electric company. Internet:http://www.pge.com/nots/rates/tariffs/rateinfo.shtml.

[6] Tecogen. Internet:http://www.tecogen.com.

[7] M. Barnes, J. Kondoh, H. Asano, J. Oyarzabal, G. Ventakaramanan, R. Lasseter, N. Hatziargyriou, and T. Green. Real-world microgrids-an overview. In *Proc. IEEE SoSE*, 2007.

[8] A. Borodin and R. El-Yaniv. *Online computation and competitive analysis*. Cambridge University Press Cambridge, 1998.

[9] N. Buchbinder, N. Jain, and I. Menache. Online job-migration for reducing the electricity bill in the cloud. In *Proc. IFIP*, 2011.

---

[3]We note that **fMCMP** in (3a)-(3d) is an instance of UC, and that UC is NP-hard in general does not imply that the instance **fMCMP** is also NP-hard.

[10] M. Carrión and J. Arroyo. A computationally efficient mixed-integer linear formulation for the thermal unit commitment problem. *IEEE Trans. Power Systems*, 21(3):1371–1378, 2006.

[11] D. Chiu, C. Stewart, and B. McManus. Electric grid balancing through low-cost workload migration. In *Proc. ACM Greenmetrics*, 2012.

[12] A. Chowdhury, S. Agarwal, and D. Koval. Reliability modeling of distributed generation in conventional distribution systems planning and analysis. *IEEE Trans. Industry Applications*, 39(5):1493–1498, 2003.

[13] Joseph A Cullen. Dynamic response to environmental regulation in the electricity industry. *University of Arizona.(February 1, 2011)*, 2011.

[14] Z. Gaing. Particle swarm optimization to solving the economic dispatch considering the generator constraints. *IEEE Trans. Power Systems*, 18(3):1187–1195, 2003.

[15] A. Gandhi, V. Gupta, M. Harchol-Balter, and M. Kozuch. Optimality analysis of energy-performance trade-off for server farm management. *Performance Evaluation*, 67(11):1155–1171, 2010.

[16] X. Guan, Q. Zhai, and A. Papalexopoulos. Optimization based methods for unit commitment: Lagrangian relaxation versus general mixed integer programming. In *Proc. IEEE PES General Meeting*, 2003.

[17] T. Guo, M. Henwood, and M. van Ooijen. An algorithm for combined heat and power economic dispatch. *IEEE Trans. Power Systems*, 11(4):1778–1784, 1996.

[18] A. Hawkes and M. Leach. Modelling high level system design and unit commitment for a microgrid. *Applied energy*, 86(7):1253–1265, 2009.

[19] C. Hernandez-Aramburo, T. Green, and N. Mugniot. Fuel consumption minimization of a microgrid. *IEEE Trans. Industry Applications*, 41(3):673–681, 2005.

[20] B. Hodge and M. Milligan. Wind power forecasting error distributions over multiple timescales. In *Proc. IEEE PES General Meeting*, 2011.

[21] S. Kazarlis, A. Bakirtzis, and V. Petridis. A genetic algorithm solution to the unit commitment problem. *IEEE Trans. Power Systems*, 11(1):83–92, 1996.

[22] W. Kwon and A. Pearson. A modified quadratic cost problem and feedback stabilization of a linear system. *IEEE Trans. Automatic Control*, 22(5):838 – 842, 1977.

[23] R. Lasseter and P. Paigi. Microgrid: A conceptual solution. In *Proc. IEEE Power Electronics Specialists Conference*, 2004.

[24] K. Le, R. Bianchini, T.D. Nguyen, O. Bilgir, and M. Martonosi. Capping the brown energy consumption of internet services at low cost. In *Proc. IEEE IGCC*, 2010.

[25] M. Lin, A. Wierman, L. Andrew, and E. Thereska. Dynamic right-sizing for power-proportional data centers. In *Proc. IEEE INFOCOM*, 2011.

[26] Z. Liu, Y. Chen, C. Bash, A. Wierman, D. Gmach, Z. Wang, M. Marwah, and C. Hyser. Renewable and cooling aware workload management for sustainable data centers. In *Proc. ACM SIGMETRICS*, 2012.

[27] L. Lu, J. Tu, C. Chau, M. Chen, and X. Lin. Online energy generation scheduling for microgrids with intermittent energy sources and co-generation. Technical report, 2012. http://arxiv.org/abs/1211.4473.pdf.

[28] T. Lu and M. Chen. Simple and effective dynamic provisioning for power-proportional data centers. In *Proc. CISS*, 2012.

[29] T. Lu, M. Chen, and L. Andrew. Simple and effective dynamic provisioning for power-proportional data centers. *IEEE Trans. Parallel Distrib. Systems*, 2012.

[30] C. Marnay and R. Firestone. Microgrids: An emerging paradigm for meeting building electricity and heat requirements efficiently and with appropriate energy quality. *European Council for an Energy Efficient Economy Summer Study*, 2007.

[31] B. Narayanaswamy, V. Garg, and T. Jayram. Online optimization for the smart (micro) grid. In *Proc. ACM International Conference on Future Energy Systems*, 2012.

[32] M. Neely. Stochastic network optimization with application to communication and queueing systems. *Synthesis Lectures on Communication Networks*, 3(1):1–211, 2010.

[33] Department of Energy. The smart grid: An introduction. Internet:http://www.oe.energy.gov/SmartGridIntroduction.htm.

[34] N. Padhy. Unit commitment-a bibliographical survey. *IEEE Trans. Power Systems*, 19(2):1196–1205, 2004.

[35] W. Snyder, H. Powell, and J. Rayburn. Dynamic programming approach to unit commitment. *IEEE Trans. Power Systems*, 2(2):339–348, 1987.

[36] M. Stadler, H. Aki, R. Lai, C. Marnay, and A. Siddiqui. Distributed energy resources on-site optimization for commercial buildings with electric and thermal storage technologies. *Lawrence Berkeley National Laboratory, LBNL-293E*, 2008.

[37] S. Takriti, J. Birge, and E. Long. A stochastic model for the unit commitment problem. *IEEE Trans. Power Systems*, 11(3):1497–1508, 1996.

[38] A. Tuohy, P. Meibom, E. Denny, and M. O'Malley. Unit commitment for systems with significant wind penetration. *IEEE Trans. Power Systems*, 24(2):592–601, 2009.

[39] R. Urgaonkar, B. Urgaonkar, M. Neely, and A. Sivasubramaniam. Optimal power cost management using stored energy in data centers. In *Proc. ACM SIGMETRICS*, 2011.

[40] P. Varaiya, F. Wu, and J. Bialek. Smart operation of smart grid: Risk-limiting dispatch. *Proc. the IEEE*, 99(1):40–57, 2011.

[41] A. Vuorinen. *Planning of optimal power systems*. Ekoenergo Oy, 2007.

[42] J. Wang, M. Shahidehpour, and Z. Li. Security-constrained unit commitment with volatile wind power generation. *IEEE Trans. Power Systems*, 23(3):1319–1327, 2008.

[43] M. Zinkevich. Online convex programming and generalized infinitesimal gradient ascent. In *Proc. Int. Conf. Mach. Learn.*, 2003.

Defragmenting the Cloud Using Demand-based Resource Allocation

Ganesha
Shanmuganathan
VMware Inc
sganesh@vmware.com

Ajay Gulati
VMware Inc
agulati@vmware.com

Peter Varman
Rice University
pjv@rice.edu

ABSTRACT

Current public cloud offerings sell capacity in the form of pre-defined virtual machine (VM) configurations to their tenants. Typically this means that tenants must purchase individual VM configurations based on the peak demands of the applications, or be restricted to only scale-out applications that can share a pool of VMs. This diminishes the value proposition of moving to a public cloud as compared to server consolidation in a private virtualized datacenter, where one gets the benefits of statistical multiplexing between VMs belonging to the same or different applications. Ideally one would like to enable a cloud tenant to buy capacity in bulk and benefit from statistical multiplexing among its workloads. This requires the purchased capacity to be dynamically and transparently allocated among the tenant's VMs that may be running on different servers, even across datacenters.

In this paper, we propose two novel algorithms called BPX and DBS that are able to provide the cloud customer with the abstraction of buying bulk capacity. These algorithms dynamically allocate the bulk capacity purchased by a customer between its VMs based on their individual demands and user-set importance. Our algorithms are highly scalable and are designed to work in a large-scale distributed environment. We implemented a prototype of BPX as part of VMware's management software and showed that BPX is able to closely mimic the behavior of a centralized allocator in a distributed manner.

Categories and Subject Descriptors

C.4 [**Performance of Systems**]: Measurement techniques; C.4 [**Performance of Systems**]: Modeling techniques; D.4.7 [**Operating systems**]: Organization and Design—*Distributed systems*; K.6.2 [**Management of Computing and Information Systems**]: Installation Management—*Pricing and resource allocation*

General Terms

Algorithms, Design, Management, Measurement, Performance

Keywords

Cloud computing, Resource management, Demand-based allocation, Distributed algorithm

1. INTRODUCTION

Consider an IT department of a small company that is considering moving all of its applications to a public cloud. Currently the company is running a private cloud, where they are able to take advantage of server consolidation by using in-house virtualization and cloud management software. Several companies offer solutions in this space, such as Nebula [16], Nimbula [17], VMware vCloud Suite [27], Microsoft hyper-V [15] and others.

Within the private cloud the VMs run on a controlled physical infrastructure maintained by the IT department of the company. The private cloud is able to exploit temporal variations in the VM loads to reduce the amount of provisioned resources, by over-committing server CPU and memory. Hypervisors such as VMware ESX Server provide several techniques (like transparent page-sharing, ballooning, compression, and swap-to-SSD) to facilitate high consolidation ratios. The gains from statistical multiplexing benefit the bottom line of the company by reducing both its capital and operating expenses.

In a public cloud the physical infrastructure is distributed over multiple data centers, supporting thousands of servers and hosting VMs belonging to multiple customers (also called as tenants). The service providers typically sell VMs of different sizes, and not physical capacity, to the tenants. In this situation the benefits of workload multiplexing accrue to the cloud service provider and not directly to the tenant, as the former increases consolidation ratios without regard to specific customers.

In current public cloud offerings, tenants purchase VMs based on their configured sizes. Typically VMs are configured for peak usage, which may be significantly higher than their average loads. Consolidation allows the VMs to use each other's resources based on their run-time demands on the host. An interesting study [9] on buying capacity in terms of fixed T-shirt sizes versus doing time sharing, showed that buying per VM capacity can be twice as expensive as a time-sharing system.

One may argue that scale-out applications mitigate some of the problems since tenants can auto-scale their applica-

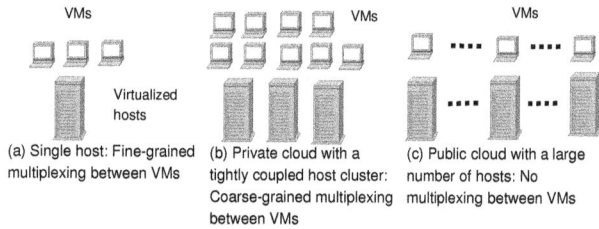

Figure 1: Hosting of VMs at different scales. As scale increases, the benefit from statistical multiplexing diminishes

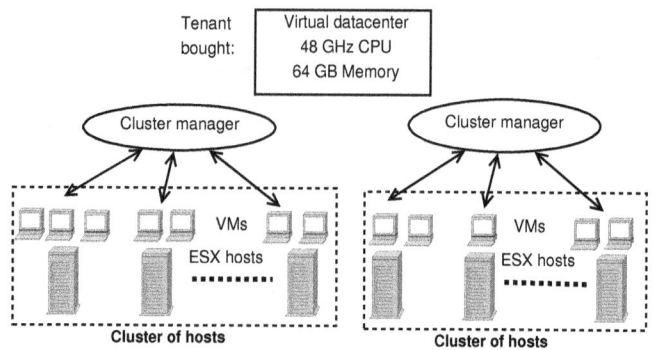

Figure 2: System overview of a datacenter and deployment model for a tenant

tions based on current demand and hourly pricing. However, there are several enterprise applications that are not designed to be scale-out and, even with scale-out applications, one still does not get the benefit of multiplexing across applications belonging to the same tenant.

As an illustration, let us assume that the company's private datacenter has 100 physical servers, each with 16 GHz compute capacity and 96 GB of RAM, for a total installed capacity of 1600 GHz of CPU and 9600 GB of RAM. By exploiting multiplexing techniques, a single server may host VMs with total virtual CPU and memory capacity that add up to 32 GHz and 192 GB respectively, providing a 2-to-1 over-commitment. Studies have noted that this ratio is typically higher for environments like virtual desktops [3, 19] and lower for enterprise workloads like Exchange and Databases.

When moving to a public cloud the company loses the advantages of over-commitment. Assuming that the customer wants to replicate the private datacenter in the public cloud, it will have to buy resources equivalent to the aggregate size of all its VMs. This comes to a total capacity of 200 physical servers, even though total demand at any instant is half of this amount. With scale-out applications, this number may be lower or fluctuate over time. However, the benefits of statistical load variations are enjoyed by the cloud service provider, who can consolidate more VMs based on their actual resource consumption instead of their configured sizes.

Figure 1 shows a comparison between three different models of running VMs: (a) on a single host, (b) on a tightly-coupled cluster of hosts in a private cloud, or (c) on a loosely-coupled ensemble of hosts in a public cloud. The models differ in the mechanisms used for resource multiplexing and the time-scales at which they operate. For example, a scheduler within the hypervisor re-allocates resources in the order of hundreds of milliseconds to few seconds, a cluster level scheduler like VMware DRS [12] does reallocation every 5 minutes.

None of the public clouds offer the capability of resource flow between the VMs of a tenant at large scale. Doing this dynamic resource flow at the scale of the public cloud is quite challenging. VMware vSphere provides a resource pool abstraction for CPU and memory resources within a small scale of up to 32 hosts using features like DRS [12] (Distributed Resource Scheduler). DRS monitors per host utilization every five minutes, and re-allocates resources among VMs based on their demand, user-set controls and host utilization values. In doing so, DRS also performs load-balancing across hosts using live migration of VMs.

In this paper we present a model for buying bulk shareable capacity in the cloud similar to that provided by a dedicated physical datacenter. The tenant can transparently multiplex this purchased capacity dynamically among its VMs. To realize this model we present two distributed resource allocation algorithms that periodically re-distribute the purchased capacity among the tenant's VMs based on their demand, and other tenant-specified controls such as reservations, limits and priority (or shares). This is a challenging problem since a tenant's VMs may be spread across an arbitrary number of physically distributed servers, and because of the need to handle tens of thousands of such customers in a public cloud. We highlight these challenges using an example in Section 2.

The distributed allocation algorithms called DBS (Distributed Binary Search) and BPX (Base + Proportional Excess) are described in Section 3. The two algorithms make different choices regarding the relative importance of VM's dynamic demands versus their static priorities, while adhering to basic allocation constraints. The allocation of DBS matches that of the centralized VMware DRS resource manager. However, unlike DRS that is centralized and limited to a small number of servers, DBS can work in a distributed environment. BPX is a fully-asynchronous distributed algorithm that avoids some thorny real-world implementation issues of DBS, thus making it more robust and scalable. Due to its better properties our experimental evaluation focused only on BPX.

We implemented BPX as a prototype in VMware's management software. Our evaluation (Section 5) demonstrates that BPX is able to dynamically allocate more of the CPU and memory resources to the high-load VMs when their demands fluctuate, as compared to a static allocation. Also BPX is able to closely match the allocations that would be made by DBS, without the implementation problems of the latter. We discuss related research in Section 6 and conclude with some directions for future work in Section 7.

2. SYSTEM OVERVIEW

We begin by looking at the physical structure of a cloud environment since it places constraints on the practicality of resource allocation mechanisms. Figure 2 shows an overview of a typical virtualized datacenter used for a public cloud environment. Tenants buy a certain amount of capacity from the cloud service provider in the form of a virtual datacenter (VDC). Tenants then deploy VMs based on the capacity available in the VDC in a self-service manner. These VMs

Buying model	Capacity Needed	Cost	Statistical multiplexing
VM's configured size	48 GHz	High	Not-needed
VM's demand	20 GHz	Low	No
Total demand with dynamic allocation	20 GHz	Low	Yes

Table 1: Comparison between various buying models in a public cloud

are deployed on top of the physically distributed infrastructure.

The physical infrastructure is divided into a large pool of compute and storage servers. The former are organized into clusters consisting of tens of servers (typically 32 or so). A public cloud may contain hundreds of such clusters to get a large-scale deployment. The VMs from a single tenant may span an arbitrary set of clusters. This architecture exists for most of the deployments based on solutions from VMware vSphere [27], Microsoft SCVMM [15] and others.

In this environment it is infeasible to simply extend currently existing resource allocation mechanisms. The state-of-the-art today includes cluster management solutions like DRS [12] that collect information about VMs from each server in the cluster, and allocate CPU and memory resources based on the demand. This clustered model has certain advantages like facilitating VM migrations between servers if the total allocation to VMs on a server exceeds its physical capacity. However, when a tenant's VMs are spread across multiple clusters, a centralized strategy becomes impractical, since it requires dynamic per VM information to be made available at a cloud-level database shared among hundreds of clusters. Not only does this require a large amount of information to be frequently exchanged between clusters, but the centralized algorithms will be CPU intensive due to the large number of VMs it needs to consider.

The problem of scalable dynamic resource flow is difficult, and we are not aware of any practical existing solution. We envision our algorithm to run at the cluster-level and allow distributed clusters to work together to provide the customer with the abstraction of buying bulk capacity. One can also run our solution at the server level, but higher-level monitoring would still be needed to balance server loads and initiate migrations from overloaded servers. Here we are assuming that CPU and memory capacity can be exchanged between VMs, if the demand is low for a certain set of VMs and higher for the rest. This is something that a hypervisor already does in a fine-grained manner using host-level CPU scheduling and memory management [28].

Example 1: We use an example to motivate the need for the bulk capacity abstraction and the desired properties of a solution. Consider a customer who wants to run eight VMs in the cloud. Four of them (called H_1, H_2, H_3 and H_4) are running a production application with high priority, while the other four VMs (called L_1, L_2, L_3 and L_4) are running an internal application of lower priority. Each high-priority VM can spike up to 8 GHz at different times, but their total workload requirements (determined by application profiling and past experience) is within 16 GHz most of the time. Similarly the low-priority VMs can peak up to 4 GHz individually, but the customer may only want to allocate a total of 4 GHz combined to all four of them.

Such usage patterns are fairly common in an IT department due to presence of a wide variety of workloads, and demand fluctuations caused by diurnal cycles. The VMs may be running in different servers on different racks, as determined by the cloud provider's software and VM placement policies. A key question is how much capacity should the customer buy from a public cloud to support such a use case? There are three possible solutions:

I. Buy configured sizes for all VMs: The customer will buy the configured size (based on peak demand) for each VM, which is 8 GHz for each of the production VMs and 4 GHz for each of the low priority VMs. In total the customer will have to buy $8 \times 4 + 4 \times 4 = 48$ GHz, of CPU resources. This solution will always meet the needs of the VMs without further intervention, but at a significantly higher cost.

II. Buy based on average VM demand: In this case, the customer will only buy the typical demand for each high priority VM, and a fixed capacity for the low priority VMs. This will be 4 GHz each for the former and 1 GHz each for the rest, for a total of 20 GHz. This solution although cost-effective, doesn't allow sharing of resources between VMs during spikes in demand.

III. Buy aggregated demand with dynamic resource allocation: In this case, the customer will still buy 20 GHz total capacity. However, the cloud resource management system will dynamically allocate this amount among VMs based on their actual demand. Customers can also distinguish between VMs by using additional VM-level resource controls, such as shares (or weights), minimum reservation, and maximum limit, which are incorporated into the allocation mechanisms. Table 1 shows the three buying models and a summary of their properties.

Another variant of solution III, is to buy aggregated demand and dynamically provision VMs based on application requirements. This approach is only suited for scale-out applications using a meta-scheduler like Mesos [13] that can coordinate scale-out application schedulers and provision VMs on their behalf. However, this requires all the applications to be designed in a scale-out manner, which is not the case for many enterprise applications. It also requires a meta-scheduler along with corresponding API changes to existing application-level schedulers.

Our solution on the other hand is completely transparent and doesn't require any changes to existing applications. Our approach can work even when there is a mixture of scale out applications with other legacy enterprise applications. Also our approach is more fine-grained in terms of moving CPU and memory capacity instead of provisioning VMs.

2.1 Allocation Requirements

We begin with a simple model where each VM i is characterized by two parameters: a *share* value $s(i)$ that reflects its priority relative to other VMs of the customer; and a *demand* value $d(i)$ that reflects the predicted demand of this VM in the immediate future. Other controls like VM reservations and limits can be added to the model quite straightforwardly, and the details are presented later in Section 4.

The demand may be based on a simple time-averaged window of actual past usage or can employ more sophisticated prediction schemes that provide margin for unexpected bursts (see Section 4). The exact prediction algorithm is an orthogonal issue to the allocation model. The share is a static parameter set by the customer at the time of VM creation, while the demand is estimated periodically by the run-time software.

The customer buys a certain aggregate amount of capacity C. The goal of the resource manager is to allocate C among the VMs in an equitable manner taking into account shares and not giving the VMs more than what they demand. An allocation scheme must satisfy certain sanity properties described below.

A. Location Obliviousness: Any two VMs with the same share value and the same demand should receive the same allocation independent of their location. Thus two identical workloads will make forward progress at the same rate, independent of the allocation algorithm or its local ecosystem.

B. Harmonious Allocation: A VM should not be allocated more than its demand if any VM has not received its demand. This requirement ensures that there is no wasted capacity, where resources are allocated to a VM that does not currently need it, while a sibling VM gets less than its current requirements.

C. Demand-Anomaly Freedom: If two VMs have the same share value then the VM with the smaller demand should not be allocated more capacity than the one with the higher demand.

D. Share-Anomaly Freedom: If two VMs have the same demand then the VM with the smaller share should not receive more allocation than the one with the larger share, unless all VMs have received their demands. This reflects the priority implied by share value and is needed if the cloud provider uses shares as part of the billing.

2.2 Allocation Policies

In this section we describe three allocation policies, one using shares alone and two that use both demands and shares. We use these to characterize and compare various allocation algorithms.

Static Allocation Policy (StAP): A simple allocation scheme is to divide C among VMs in proportion to their *share* values. The total value of the shares of all the active VMs of the tenant is tracked. The *capacity per share* (denoted by ρ) is computed by dividing C by the total number of outstanding shares. The allocation of each VM is obtained by multiplying the capacity-per-share with its share value.

Formally, let $\mathcal{A}$ denote the set of active VMs of the customer. The capacity-per-share $\rho = C / \sum_{j \in \mathcal{A}} s(j)$. The allocation of VM($i$) is $a(i) = \rho \times s(i)$. It can be seen that the above policy satisfies properties A, C and D above, but may not result in a harmonious allocation. Since the allocations are independent of demands, the policy may wastefully allocate capacity to high-share VMs with low demand, at the expense of lower-share VMs with unsatisfied demand.

Dynamic Allocation Policy (DAP): In this policy a VM's demand is an *upper bound* on the capacity allocated to it. Like in StAP, we first allocate capacity in proportion to the share values. However, if the allocation made to a VM exceeds its demand, its allocation is capped at its demand, and the unused capacity reallocated to other VMs with unsatisfied demand.

This model can be precisely formulated as a constrained resource-allocation problem using the capacity-per-share parameter ρ. Assume that the total capacity to be allocated is less than the total demand; *i.e.* $C \leq \sum_{i \in \mathcal{A}} d(i)$. We need to find ρ^* such that the allocation $a(i) = \min\{d(i), \rho^* \times s(i)\}$ and $\sum_{i \in \mathcal{A}} a(i) = C$. If the total capacity consistently exceeds the sum of demands, it indicates that the system has probably been over-provisioned. In this case, the excess can be distributed to the VMs in proportion to their shares.

The allocation can be seen to satisfy all the desired properties A through D. Notice that two VMs with the same share may receive the same allocation even if one's demand is much higher than the other. However, it would never result in a demand anomaly.

Scalable Dynamic Allocation Policy (SDAP): Like DAP, this policy also first allocates capacity on the basis of shares and caps it at the VM's demand. However, it differs in how it handles the excess capacity. SDAP allocates it to the VMs in the ratio of their unmet demands. That is, it allocates a portion of the capacity in proportion to the shares, and the remaining in proportion to unsatisfied demand. The details of this policy are described in Section 3.2. The policy satisfies all the desired allocation properties and the allocation algorithm has significant implementation advantages in a distributed environment.

We illustrate the allocation policies using four of the VMs of Example 1. Suppose the shares of H_1 and H_2 are each 400 and their demands are 1 and 8 GHz respectively. Similarly, suppose that L_1 and L_2 have shares of 100 and demands of 1 and 3 GHz respectively. Table 2 shows how the three policies will allocate a capacity of 10 GHz. StAP simply allocates it in the ratio of the shares. As can be seen, H_1 is allocated 4 GHz, which is more than its demand (1 GHz), wasting capacity that VMs H_2 and L_2 could have used.

DAP and SDAP also initially allocate capacity in the ratio of the shares. However, since they cap the allocation at the demand, H_1 and L_1 get only 1 GHz each, leaving the excess amount 3 GHz to be further allocated to H_2 and L_2. In DAP, this is assigned in the ratio of shares, resulting in additional allocations of $4/5 \times 3 = 2.4$ GHz and $1/5 \times 3 = 0.6$ GHz respectively to H_2 and L_2, which is added to their initial share-based allocation. Since these do not exceed their demands the allocation is complete. Otherwise, the process is iteratively repeated using the excess capacity generated by the newly demand-capped VMs.

In SDAP, the excess capacity of 3 GHz is allocated to H_2 and L_2 in the ratio of unmet demands, which are 4 GHz and 2 GHz respectively This results in additional allocations of 2 GHz and 1 GHz for the two VMs. One can show (see Section 3.2) that the total allocation will not exceed the demands of any of the VMs, so no additional iterations are ever needed. The allocation also satisfies all the desired properties A through D.

3. ALLOCATION ALGORITHMS

In this section we describe two distributed allocation algorithms, Distributed Binary Search (DBS) and Base plus Proportional Excess (BPX) that implement the DAP and SDAP allocation policies respectively.

3.1 Distributed Binary Search Algorithm

Recall, that the DAP policy requires one to find a value ρ^* for the capacity per share, such that $a(i) = \min\{d(i), \rho^* \times s(i)\}$ and $\sum_{i \in \mathcal{A}} a(i) = C$. For a given value of ρ, a(i) is either capped at its demand $d(i)$ or equals $\rho \times s(i)$. In the first case we say that the VM is *demand limited* for ρ. Let $\mathcal{D}_\rho$ denote the set of demand-limited VMs and $\mathcal{N}_\rho$ the remaining VMs. For a given ρ, the total allocation made to all the VMs is

VM Parameters	H_1	H_2	L_1	L_2	Total
Demand	1 GHz	8 GHz	1 GHz	3 GHz	13 GHz
Shares	400	400	100	100	1000
Allocation Policy	H_1	H_2	L_1	L_2	Wastage
StAP	4 GHz	4 GHz	1 GHz	1 GHz	yes
DAP	1 GHz	6.4 GHz	1 GHz	1.6 GHz	no
SDAP	1 GHz	6 GHz	1 GHz	2 GHz	no

Table 2: Comparison between allocation policies, when total capacity of 10 GHz is distributed among VMs

given by $\mathcal{A}(\rho) = \sum_{i \in \mathcal{D}_\rho} d(i) + \rho \sum_{i \in \mathcal{N}_\rho} s(i)$. In Lemma 1 below we show that $\mathcal{A}(\rho)$ is a monotonically non-decreasing function of ρ. This allows us to design an efficient sequential search strategy to find ρ^* in a centralized setting, and a binary-search like strategy in a distributed setting.

LEMMA 1. *If $\mathcal{N}_{\rho_1} \neq \emptyset$ then $\rho_2 > \rho_1$ implies that $\mathcal{A}(\rho_2) > \mathcal{A}(\rho_1)$.*

Proof: Consider any $j \in \mathcal{N}_{\rho_1}$. If $j \in \mathcal{N}_{\rho_2}$ then its allocation $\rho_2 \times s(j)$ is clearly greater than its allocation $\rho_1 \times s(j)$ under ρ_1. Otherwise j is demand-limited under ρ_2 and its allocation is $d(j)$; since $j \in \mathcal{N}_{\rho_1}$ its allocation under ρ_1 was less than $d(j)$. Hence for all $j \in \mathcal{N}_{\rho_1}$ the allocation under ρ_2 exceeds that under ρ_1. To complete the proof, note that if $j \in \mathcal{D}_{\rho_1}$ then j is also in $\mathcal{D}_{\rho_2}$, and its allocation remains unchanged at $d(j)$.

Define the normalized demand of VM(i) as $u_i = d(i)/s(i)$, and reindex the VMs so that the u_i are in non-decreasing order. A *centralized algorithm* searches for ρ^* by trying out successive values of $\rho = u_i$ in increasing order of u_i, till it finds a pair of successive indexes $k, k+1$, such that $\mathcal{A}(u_k) < \mathcal{C} \leq \mathcal{A}(u_{k+1})$. VMs with index $1 \cdots k$ are demand limited and will receive their demand; ρ^* is obtained by dividing the remaining capacity by the total number of shares of the non demand-limited VMs. That is $\rho^* = (\mathcal{C} - \sum_{i=1}^{k} d(i)) / \sum_{i=k+1}^{n} s(i)$. The centralized algorithm requires the sorted list of all VMs in order of normalized demands, and requires $O(n)$ iterations. Hence, it is not a good solution in a distributed environment.

A distributed algorithm to determine ρ^* based on a binary search strategy is shown in Algorithm 1. At the start of an iteration the value of ρ^* will have been narrowed to lie within an interval $[\rho_L, \rho_H]$ that is known to all VMs. Each VM chooses a probe value of ρ in the interval (for instance the mid-point), and then computes the allocation $a(i)$ based on this assumed value of ρ. These $a(i)$ are added together in a distributed manner and the sum $\mathcal{A}(\rho)$ is returned to all VMs. The sum is compared with the actual amount of capacity $\mathcal{C}$ to be allocated. If $\mathcal{C} > \mathcal{A}(\rho)$ then by Lemma 1 the value of ρ needs to be increased to make the total allocation equal to $\mathcal{C}$, and the search interval is narrowed to $[\rho, \rho_H]$; else the search interval is $[\rho_L, \rho]$.

The process continues till $|\mathcal{C} - \mathcal{A}(\rho)| < \epsilon$ where ϵ is an acceptably small margin. The algorithm will converge in $O(\log_2(\mathcal{C}/\epsilon))$ rounds. As described above, in each round the distributed value of the allocations need to be added up and the sum broadcast to all VMs. The number of rounds can be decreased by doing a multi-way search rather than a binary search, at the expense of communicating more information between the VMs in the addition phase. For instance, at each round the VMs could use $k > 1$ probe values of ρ,

---

Algorithm 1: DBS Algorithm

Input
VM settings: $\mathbf{A} = [a(1) \cdots a(n)]$, $\mathbf{D} = [d(1) \cdots d(n)]$
$\mathcal{C}$: Capacity to *allocate*.

Result: ρ^*: Desired value of ρ.
$\rho_L = 0$; $\rho_H = \mathcal{C}$; $\mathcal{A} = 0$;

repeat the following steps until $|\mathcal{C} - \mathcal{A}| < \epsilon$

foreach $i = 1, \cdots, n$ **do**
  /* Select tentative ρ and compute allocation */
  $\rho = (\rho_L + \rho_H)/2$
  $a(i) = \min\{\rho \times s(i), d(i)\}$
/* Distributed sum of a(i) */
$\mathcal{A}(\rho) = \sum_j a(j)$
foreach $i = 1, \cdots, n$ **do**
  /* Refine search interval */
  if $\mathcal{A}(\rho) < \mathcal{C}$ **then**
   | $\rho_L = \rho$
  else
   | $\rho_H = \rho$

$\rho_1, \rho_2, \cdots \rho_k$, to narrow the search interval even further in each round of communication. The allocations for each of these ρ_i values are computed and summed independently. The next search interval is $[\rho_i, \rho_{i+1}]$ where $\mathcal{A}(\rho_i) \leq \mathcal{C}$ and $\mathcal{A}(\rho_{i+1}) > \mathcal{C}$.

Although the distributed algorithm uses only a logarithmic (or fewer) number of rounds (compared to linear in the number of VMs of a sequential search strategy), it has practical drawbacks. Specifically, the communication has to be synchronous. Only after all the allocations of all the nodes have been summed for a particular search range, can the next range be chosen. Having multiple synchronous rounds is slow and vulnerable to delays and failures of the underlying VMs, hosts, and communication network.

3.2 BPX Algorithm

In this section we describe a distributed algorithm that implements the SDAP policy. The solution uses a core algorithm called **basicBPX** shown in Algorithm 2. This routine will also be the core component in the general solution that considers other VM controls like reservations and limits.

In **basicBPX** each VM(i) is characterized by two parameters: a lower bound on its allocation $\lambda(i)$ and an upper bound $\mu(i)$. The capacity $\mathcal{C}$ to be allocated is assumed to be at least the sum of the lower bounds. The routine first allocates each VM its lower bound $\lambda(i)$. It then divides the remaining capacity among the VMs in the ratio of $(\mu(i) - \lambda(i))$ denoted as $\delta(i)$. In a distributed setting two global sums need to be computed and returned to the VMs: the sum of individual $\lambda(i)$ and the sum of the individual $\delta(i)$.

Algorithm 2: basicBPX Algorithm

Input
VM settings: $\Lambda = [\lambda(1) \cdots \lambda(n)]$, $\mathbf{U} = [\mu(1) \cdots \mu(n)]$
$\mathcal{C}$: Capacity to *allocate*, $\mathcal{C} \geq \sum_{i=i}^{n} \lambda(i)$.

Result: $a(i)$: Allocation computed for VM(i).

Variables: $\mathcal{E}$, $\delta(i)$, $i = 1 \cdots n$.

foreach $i = 1, \cdots, n$ **do**
    /* First allocate each VM its lower bound */
    /* $\delta(i)$ is the unmet need of VM(i) */
    $a(i) = \lambda(i)$
    $\delta(i) = \mu(i) - \lambda(i)$
/* $\mathcal{E}$ is the remaining capacity */
$\mathcal{E} = \mathcal{C} - \sum_{i=1}^{n} \lambda(i)$
foreach $i = 1, \cdots, n$ **do**
    /* Allocate $\mathcal{E}$ in ratio of the unmet needs */
    $a(i) = a(i) + \frac{\delta(i)}{\sum_{j=1}^{n} \delta(j)} \times \mathcal{E}$

We use **basicBPX** to implement the SDAP allocation policy. We first divide the capacity among the VMs in proportion to their shares. We call this the *fair share* of the VM. VMs whose demand is less than their fair share are *demand-limited*, and their allocation is capped at their demand. The remaining VMs will be allocated additional capacity over their fair share. This will be done in the ratio of their unmet demand *i.e.* the difference between their fair share and demand.

Algorithm 3 describes the allocation algorithm formally. We call this algorithm as **shareBPX**. A VM's fair share $f(i)$ is computed by dividing the capacity $\mathcal{C}$ in proportion to the shares. Define the *entitlement* $e(i)$ to be the smaller of the demand and fair share of VM(i): $e(i) = \min\{f(i), d(i)\}$. We then invoke **basicBPX** with the vector of entitlements $\mathbf{E} = [e(1) \cdots e(n)]$ as the lower-bound and the vector of demands $\mathbf{D} = [d(1) \cdots d(n)]$ as the upper bound; **basicBPX** first gives each VM its lower bound $e(i)$, and then allocates the excess capacity $\mathcal{E} = \mathcal{C} - \sum_{1 \leq i \leq n} e(i) \geq 0$ in the ratio of their unmet demands $\delta(i) = d(i) - e(i)$. Demand-limited VMs have $e(i) = d(i)$ and hence do not receive additional allocation, while the rest receive a proportional amount of the excess capacity.

The allocation made by **shareBPX** will satisfy the properties described in Section 2. The harmonious property ensures that no VM will get more than its demand unless all the VMs do so; otherwise the algorithm would waste needed capacity. Freedom from share and demand anomalies are also satisfied. Note it is not obvious that these properties (particularly freedom from share anomaly) hold, since the allocation is made up of two parts: a share-sensitive part that allocates more capacity to VMs with higher shares and a demand-sensitive part that allocates capacity in proportion to unmet demand.

For two VMs with the same demand and unequal shares, the higher share VM will have less unmet demand compared to the lower share VM. Hence, the former will be allocated less capacity than the latter in the demand-sensitive allocation. One needs to ensure that the demand-sensitive allo-

cation does not overwhelm the share-sensitive part in this situation, to avoid share anomalies. We show this property in Lemma 5.

Algorithm 3: shareBPX: Divvy with **D, S**

foreach $i = 1, \cdots, n$ **do**
    /* Compute fair share and entitlement per VM */
    $\rho = \mathcal{C} / \sum_{j=1}^{n} s(j)$
    $f(i) = \rho \times s(i)$
    $e(i) = \min(f(i), d(i))$
Call **basicBPX**($\mathcal{C}$,**E**, **D**)

If we apply **shareBPX** to the VM example in Section 2.2, it will result in the allocations shown previously in Table 2. We end the section by formally showing that **shareBPX** satisfies the allocation properties.

Let $\mathcal{D}$ and $\mathcal{N}$ denote the set of demand-limited VMs and non-demand-limited VMs respectively. Let $\mathcal{U} = \mathcal{D} \cup \mathcal{N}$ denote the set of all VMs. We use $\sum_k$ as a shorthand to denote the sum over all $k \in \mathcal{U}$.

LEMMA 2. *The allocations of* **shareBPX** *are harmonious.*

Proof: We will prove the harmonious condition by contradiction. Assume, to the contrary, that there is a pair of VMs i, j such that $a(i) \geq d(i)$ and $a(j) < d(j)$. The allocation made to VM(i) by **shareBPX** is: $a(i) = e(i) + \delta(i)/\sum_k \delta(k) \times \mathcal{E} \geq d(i)$. Rearranging, $\delta(i)/\sum_k \delta(k) \times \mathcal{E} \geq d(i) - e(i) = \delta(i)$ or $\mathcal{E} \geq \sum_k \delta(k)$ Writing a similar inequality for $a(j)$ results in: $a(j) = e(j) + \delta(j)/\sum_k \delta(k) \times \mathcal{E} < d(j)$; *i.e.* $\mathcal{E} < \sum_k \delta(k)$. This proves the contradiction.

LEMMA 3. *The allocation made by* **shareBPX** *satisfies:*

$$a(i) = \begin{cases} d(i) & i \in \mathcal{D} \\ \alpha s(i) + \beta d(i) & otherwise \end{cases}$$

where $\alpha = \rho(1 - \beta)$, $\beta = \frac{\mathcal{E}}{\sum_k \delta(k)}$, *and* $\mathcal{E} = \mathcal{C} - \sum_k e(k)$.

Proof: The allocation to VM(i) can be written as: $a(i) = e(i) + \delta(i)/\sum_k \delta(k) \times \mathcal{E}$ where $\delta(k) = d(k) - e(k)$. For a demand-limited VM, $e(i) = d(i)$ and $\delta(i) = 0$; hence the allocation $a(i) = d(i)$. For a VM that is not demand limited, $e(i) = f(i) = s(i) \times \rho$. Hence, $a(i) = e(i) + ((d(i) - e(i))/\sum_k \delta(k)) \times \mathcal{E} = e(i) + \beta(d(i) - e(i)) = e(i)(1 - \beta) + \beta d(i) = s(i)\rho(1 - \beta) + \beta d(i)$. Hence we get: $a(i) = \alpha s(i) + \beta d(i)$.

LEMMA 4. *Allocations made by* **shareBPX** *are free of demand anomalies.*

Proof: Suppose VMs i and j have the same share, $s(i) = s(j)$. If either or both i and j are demand-limited then the result is easy to see. If neither is demand limited, then from Lemma 3, $a(i) = \alpha s(i) + \beta d(i)$ and $a(j) = \alpha s(j) + \beta d(j)$. Hence $a(i) - a(j) = \beta(d(i) - d(j))$. Since $\beta > 0$, it follows that $a(i) > a(j)$ if and only if $d(i) > d(j)$. In fact the difference in the allocations of two equal-share VMs is proportional to the difference in their demands.

LEMMA 5. *Allocations made by* **shareBPX** *are free of share anomalies if* $\mathcal{C} \leq \sum_k d(k)$.

72

Proof: If VMs i and j have the same demand, $d(i) = d(j)$. The case when neither is demand-limited needs to be shown. Using Lemma 3, we get $a(i) - a(j) = \alpha(s(i) - s(j))$. We must show that $\alpha > 0$ in the region of interest. Since $\alpha = \rho(1 - \beta)$ and $\rho > 0$ we require $\beta < 1$.

By definition, $\mathcal{C} = \sum_k f(k)$ and $\beta = \mathcal{E}/\sum_k \delta(k)$. Also we have, $\mathcal{E} = \mathcal{C} - \sum_k e(k) = \sum_k f(k) - \sum_k e(k)$. Hence, $\mathcal{E} = \sum_{k \in \mathcal{U}} f(k) - (\sum_{k \in \mathcal{N}} f(k) + \sum_{k \in \mathcal{D}} d(k)) = \sum_{k \in \mathcal{D}} (f(k) - d(k))$.

For $\beta < 1$, we require that $\mathcal{E} < \sum_{k \in \mathcal{U}} \delta(k) = \sum_{k \in \mathcal{N}} \delta(k) = \sum_{k \in \mathcal{N}} (d(k) - f(k))$. This is true if $\sum_{k \in \mathcal{D}} f(k) + \sum_{k \in \mathcal{N}} f(k) < \sum_{k \in \mathcal{D}} d(k) + \sum_{k \in \mathcal{N}} d(k)$, or $\mathcal{C} \leq \sum_{k \in \mathcal{U}} d(k)$. This is true by hypothesis.

4. BPX IMPLEMENTATION

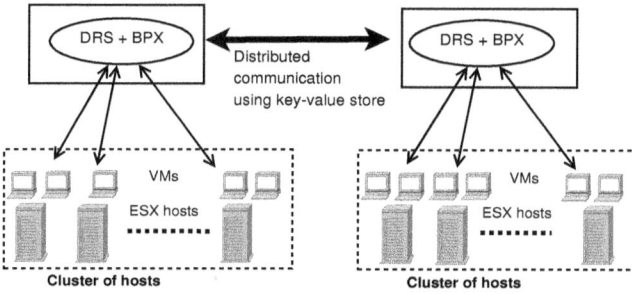

Figure 3: System architecture with clusters and an instance of DRS managing each cluster. Data is shared between different clusters using a key-value store that spans the cloud environment

In this section we present the details of implementing BPX as a prototype in our cluster management solution called DRS [12]. DRS runs as part of VMware's virtual center software that can manage hundreds of ESX servers in a virtual environment. An administrator creates a cluster of up to 32 hosts; in a cloud environment there may be tens to hundreds of clusters, each managed by an instance of DRS. Figure 3 shows an overview of the system. Figure 4 shows an example distribution of tenants across the clusters. BPX allows a tenant's VMs to be spread across multiple clusters, and each cluster can have VMs from multiple tenants.

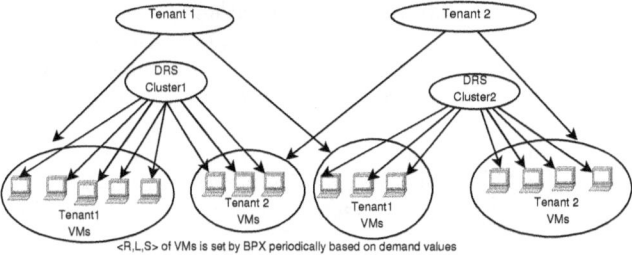

Figure 4: Tenant VMs are deployed across clusters and a cluster may host multiple tenants

DRS offers three controls for each VM: minimum *reservation* (r), maximum *limit* (l) and *shares* (s) for both CPU and memory resources. We first extend the BPX algorithm (previously described using only shares and demands) to incorporate VM reservations and limits as well. We then describe how the implementation integrates into the existing DRS infrastructure to provide a scalable resource allocation mechanism based on the BPX algorithm.

BPX has two properties that help the algorithm to scale. First it summarizes information simply by adding together VM-level statistics. Only this aggregated information is needed for allocation, minimizing the information exchanged between participating nodes, and simplifying distributed implementation. Secondly, the allocations can be computed at any granularity (VM, server, cluster). Server-level allocations can be done by aggregating the required statistics over the VMs in each server, and then using BPX to perform the allocation using these values. Similarly, one can compute allocations at the cluster level by aggregating the statistics over the VMs of a tenant across all the servers belonging to the cluster, requiring only one set of statistics to be communicated between clusters.

Periodically, (every 1 minute in our prototype), each DRS cluster publishes a set of aggregated statistics for each of its tenants to a distributed key-value store that can be accessed by all DRS clusters. Each cluster only has to publish one fixed size record (of six aggregated statistics) per tenant. This leads to a huge reduction in the overall communication, from one record per VM to one per tenant, which is a much smaller number.

The published record includes the sum of the reservations, limits, shares, demand, and two entitlement values (see Algorithm 4) for VMs of the tenant in the cluster. DRS also runs periodically (every 5 minutes in our prototype) in each cluster to compute new allocations. It reads the aggregated statistics published by the other clusters in the shared key-value store, and sums them to obtain the total aggregate values. It then uses BPX to divvy out the allocation. The VM allocations are then pushed to the corresponding ESX servers in the cluster.

4.1 BPX Divvying with R, L and S controls

We now discuss the complete resource model and its BPX implementation. The tenant purchases capacity in the form of a total tenant reservation $\mathcal{R}$ and a total tenant limit $\mathcal{L}$. $\mathcal{R}$ will be divided among the active VMs, based on their shares and demands, to increase their run-time reservations over their static values. Similarly, the tenant specifies $\mathcal{L}$ as an overall cap on resource usage by all its VMs. This will be used to place run-time limits on individual VMs, which may be more conservative than their static values depending on their importance (share) and current demand.

The extended BPX algorithm is described in Algorithm 4. $VM(i)$ has two additional static parameters $r(i)$ (reservation) and $l(i)$ (limit), in addition to share $s(i)$ and demand $d(i)$. The demand $d(i)$ is first adjusted to lie between $r(i)$ and $l(i)$. The algorithm computes capacity-per-share, fair share, and entitlement (just as in Algorithm 3) for capacity equal to both $\mathcal{R}$ and $\mathcal{L}$. These are denoted by the superscript on the variables. For allocating limit values, it also computes an additional entitlement e^* based on dividing the unallocated capacity generated by demand-limited VMs among the the non-demand limited VMs, in proportion to their shares.

Aggregate values E_1 to E_6 are computed by Algorithm 4. E_1, E_5 and E_6 are simply the sums of the reservations, de-

---

Algorithm 4: FinalBPX: Divvy with full VM model

---

foreach $i = 1, \cdots, n$ **do**

  /* Compute fair share and entitlement of R */

  $d(i) = \max(\min(l(i), d(i)), r(i))$

  $\rho^R = \mathcal{R} \ / \sum_{j=1}^{n} s(j)$

  $f^R(i) = \rho^R \times s(i)$

  $e^R(i) = \max(\min(f^R(i), d(i)), r(i))$

  /* Compute fair share and entitlement of L */ ;

  $\rho^L = \mathcal{L} \ / \sum_{j=1}^{n} s(j)$

  $f^L(i) = \rho^L \times s(i)$

  $e^L(i) = \max(\min(f^L(i), d(i)), r(i))$

  $\sigma = \sum_{j=1}^{n} \max((f^L(i) - d(i)), 0)$

  if $(f^L(i) \geq d(i))$ **then**

    | $e_i^* = e_i^L$

  else

    Let $\mathcal{N} = \{k : f^L(k) < d(k)\}$

    $e^*(i) = \min(e^L(i) + \sigma \times (s(i) / \sum_{k \in \mathcal{N}} s(k)), d(i))$

/* Find aggregates */

$E_1 = \sum_i r(i)$	$E_2 = \sum_i e^R(i)$
$E_3 = \sum_i e^L(i)$	$E_4 = \sum_i e^*(i)$
$E_5 = \sum_i d(i)$	$E_6 = \sum_i l(i)$

Let $\mathcal{C}$ denote either $\mathcal{R}$ or $\mathcal{L}$

Find the interval $[E_i, E_{i+1}]$ such that $E_i < \mathcal{C} \leq E_{i+1}$

Call **basicBPX**$(\mathcal{C}, \mathbf{E_i}, \mathbf{E_{i+1}})$

---

mands, and limits of all the VMs. E_2, E_3 and E_4 are obtained by summing the different entitlements. To divvy a capacity $\mathcal{C}$ (either $\mathcal{R}$ or $\mathcal{L}$) we find which interval $[E_i, E_{i+1}]$ in which $\mathcal{C}$ lies, and use E_i as the lower bound and E_{i+1} as the upper bound for **basicBPX**. By using these multiple aggregates E_i, BPX reduces the portion of the capacity that is allocated based on demand. This allows it to more closely approach the allocation of the DAP policy, while still maintaining its implementation advantages over the DBS algorithm. All of the allocation properties still hold with this enhancement.

4.2 Additional Implementation Issues

We address some of the issues that need to be handled in a complete implementation.

Physical Capacity Limits: Our goal is to flow resources from low-demand VMs of a tenant to its VMs with high demand. These are independent decisions made without explicit consideration of the underlying physical capacity. It is possible that the server running the VMs may not have enough capacity to handle all the new resource settings. DRS makes sure that each server can satisfy the resource requirements for the VMs running on it. If that is not the case, DRS recommends VM migrations to make sure that each server can handle these resource requirements.

In rare cases, an entire cluster can run short of resources to support the dynamic allocations. If this is a recurrent situation, the solution is to add more hardware to the cluster. Alternatively, one can migrate some VMs out of that cluster to another. In our implementation, we reduce the per VM allocation based on its share without going below

its static reservation. So a VM with high shares will loose less as compared to a VM with low shares.

Demand estimation: So far we have assumed VM demands as one of the inputs to our algorithm. In practice both CPU and memory demands are computed by the ESX hypervisor and published as a periodic statistic. A VM's CPU demand is computed as its actual CPU consumption, CPU_{used}, plus a scaled portion of CPU_{ready}, the time it was ready to execute, but queued due to contention:

$$CPU_{demand} = CPU_{used} + \frac{CPU_{run} \times CPU_{ready}}{(CPU_{run} + CPU_{sleep})} \quad (1)$$

A VM's memory demand is computed by tracking a set of randomly-selected pages in the VM guest OS physical address space, and computing how many of them are touched within a certain time interval [28]. For BPX, the above raw metrics are aggregated into a single number that represents demand for the entire divvying interval. We used 5 minute average demand in our prototype.

Shares across multiple tenants: Since multiple tenants may be sharing the same underlying cluster, share values must be comparable across tenants. In addition, the share value of a VM must scale with number of vCPUs and memory size to avoid priority inversion when the same amount of resources is spread over more CPUs or memory. We therefore chose to use certain pre-configured values like high (2000), medium (1000) and low (500) per unit of resource.

Placement of VMs across clusters and hosts: Keeping VMs of a tenant within a small number of clusters (possibly one) is preferred. This can reduce stress on the bisection bandwidth and the complexity of BPX divvying in the system. The placement algorithm we use has a preference for a cluster where the tenant already has lot of VMs, and it selects a new cluster only if some constraint cannot be satisfied or if it will cause imbalance beyond a threshold for a resource.

Similarly if VMs from the same tenant are running on the same host, they can be grouped under a resource pool and the sum of their allocated reservation and limits can be set as the resource pool control instead of using per VM controls. This optimization allows the flow of resources within the host at sub-second granularity.

5. EXPERIMENTAL EVALUATION

In this section we present results from our evaluation of the BPX algorithm using both a simulated setup and a real cluster of VMware ESX hosts and virtual machines with diverse workloads. The goal of our experiments is to show that BPX can dynamically allocate resources among a tenant's VMs similar to a centralized scheduler, although in a much more scalable manner. We also compared allocations made by BPX with a centralized allocator and a static partitioning of tenant capacity across VMs.

5.1 Simulation Setup

Our BPX prototype is implemented as part of the DRS cluster manager. We used the same DRS simulator framework that is used for internal code development, to construct a cluster with a set of simulated ESX hosts and virtual machines. The implementations of BPX and DRS in the simulator are identical to that used in a real inventory.

The simulator allows us to create VM and host profiles with diverse configurations. A VM profile includes the number of virtual CPUs (vCPUs), configured CPU (in MHz) and configured memory size (in MB), while a host profile includes the number of physical cores, CPU (MHz) per core, total memory size, idle power consumption etc. The simulator also supports arbitrary time-varying workload specifications for each VM, and generates CPU and memory demand values based on the specification.

In addition to creating a cluster, the simulator also mimics the behavior of the ESX CPU and memory schedulers and allocates resources to the VMs in a manner consistent with the behavior of ESX hosts. The simulator supports all the resource controls supported by the real ESX hosts, including reservations, limits and shares for each VM. Every 5 minutes, the simulator invokes the actual DRS code to figure out if any VM migrations are needed to meet VM demands. It also keeps track of the resource demands of each VM and the amount of resources actually provided to them. This is used to calculate our key evaluation metric that reflects how well the demand-based allocation works.

The main metric used to study the effectiveness of a resource allocation policy is the *cumulative allocated percentage metric* that is defined in Equation 2. The time t varies over the simulation interval and k varies over all VMs active at t.

$$\sum_t \sum_k \frac{(Satisfied\ demand\ for\ VM(k)\ at\ t)}{Cloud\ capacity\ at\ t} * 100 \quad (2)$$

The numerator denotes the total amount of resource allocated to all the VMs in the cluster and the denominator denotes the total capacity of the cluster for that resource. This metric is calculated separately for both CPU and memory. For CPU, the metric captures the percentage of the total number of CPU cycles in the cluster (on all the hosts) over the period of the experiment, that were usefully spent. The memory metric denotes a similar percentage. In both cases, higher values represent better allocations.

In our experiments, we used multiple clusters each managed by DRS and ran BPX across the clusters. We used BPX to allocate the overall resources bought by a tenant, among its VMs. The BPX allocation is enforced by DRS. If in some cases, the sum of VM level settings becomes higher than the host capacity for CPU or memory, DRS would move VMs between hosts to make sure that VMs are able to meet their allocation. The overhead in terms of CPU and memory for a VM migration is also captured by the simulator which penalizes the cumulative metric based on time taken for migration and depends on how actively the memory is being dirtied.

5.2 Single Tenant with Diverse Workloads

In the first experiment, we tried out the scenario mentioned in Section 2. There are 4 high-share VMs (2000 shares each) and 4 low-share VMs (500 shares each) belonging to a tenant. The high priority VMs mostly consumes less than 4 GHz and sometimes spike to 8 GHz. The low share VMs consume 1 GHz and occasionally spike to 4 GHz. These eight VMs were run across 3 clusters each with 6 hosts. Figure 5 shows the demands and utilizations of one of the high-

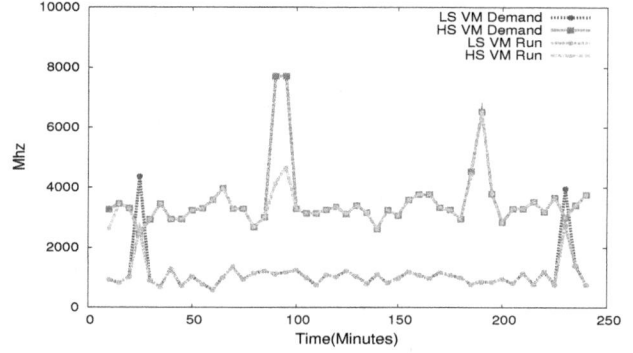

Figure 5: Demand and consumption (run) of a high-share and a low-share VM

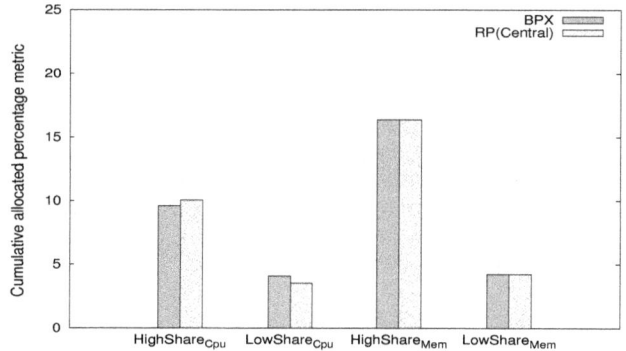

Figure 6: Cumulative BPX allocations compared with central divvy

share VMs and one of the low-share VMs. Note that the high-share VM is able to get more resources when its demand is higher, and the low-share VM is also able to get more resources during periods of low demand from other VMs. Occasionally a high share VM might demand more than what is available on the host it is running. If the increase in demand is for a very short duration, DRS cannot move the VM and hence even a high share VM might not meet its full demand. This happens around $t = 90$ minutes.

To compare with a centralized solution, we ran all 8 VMs in a single DRS cluster and measured the resources allocated to VMs by DRS. Figure 6 shows the comparison of the BPX and DRS allocations over 200 minutes. Overall the high-share VMs and low-share VMs got similar allocation under both schemes. The small difference in allocation where high-share VMs get slightly less using BPX is because the central scheduler does allocation based entirely on shares whereas BPX does part of its allocation based on shares and rest using the demand values.

5.3 Large Setup with Coordinated Workloads

In the next experiment, we evaluated how BPX performs in a larger setup with co-ordinated workload changes across a set of VMs. This is one of the adversarial workloads for BPX since the workload changes are not randomly distributed but synchronized. The setup consists of 300 VMs belonging to a single tenant distributed over 120 hosts spread across 3 clusters. The VMs had a mix of high, medium and low shares that correspond to a ratio of 4 : 2 : 1 respectively.

VMType	Scenario1	Scenario2	Shares	#VMs
HS1	High, Low	High, Low	2000	50
HS2	High, Low	Low, High	2000	50
MS1	High, Low	High, Low	1000	50
MS2	High, Low	Low, High	1000	50
LS1	High, Low	High, Low	500	50
LS2	High, Low	Low, High	500	50

Table 3: Tenant VM specifications. High load is uniformly distributed between 3 GHz and 4 GHz. Low load is less than 400 MHz.

We also divided the VMs with same share values into two sets. So we had a total of six sets denoted as HS1, HS2, MS1, MS2, LS1 and LS2. Here HS, MS and LS stand for high share, medium share and low share respectively.

We simulated a periodic workload where the workload switches between high and low intensity states every one hour. The detailed VM specifications are mentioned in Table 3. In the high intensity state, a VM's workload value is randomly chosen, uniformly between between 3 GHz and 4 GHz. In the low intensity state, the workload value is randomly chosen between 0 and 400 MHz. The tenant's purchased capacity is assumed to be 160 GHz of CPU and 160 GB of Memory. Since we are varying CPU demand, the results show the CPU allocation for VMs or the whole group.

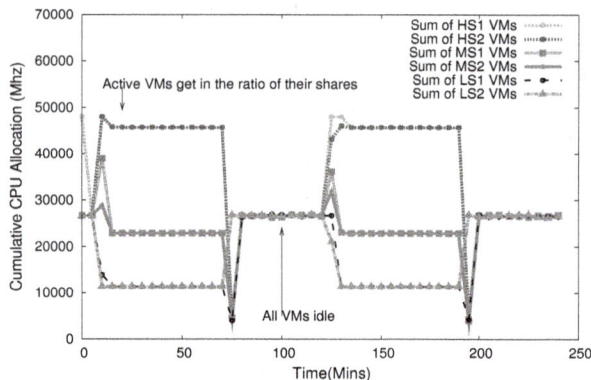

Figure 7: Active VM allocations are in the ratio of their shares (4:2:1) when they have enough demand. In low-demand phases, all VMs get similar allocation because the capacity exceeds total demand.

In the first scenario, all the VMs have a high intensity workload for one hour followed by a low intensity workload for another one hour. Figure 7 shows the overall allocation of all the 50 VMs of each type. Initially note that the allocations of VMs are in proportion to their shares. At $t = 60$ minutes, all the VMs abruptly become idle. Each cluster immediately sees its own VMs becoming idle and its allocation gets very low. It takes few minutes to get updated statistics from the other clusters. It then realizes that other VMs have also gone idle, and hence the allocation bounces back to a value that is greater than the demand. All VMs get a similar allocation due to the lack of demand.

At $t = 120$ minutes, all the VMs become active at the same time and the system allocates the resources to the VMs again in the ratio of $4 : 2 : 1$, following a short transient

where each cluster grabs a little bit more for its VMs than it should. The key takeaway here is that high share VMs are always able to get more resources when they have enough demand, and otherwise, all VMs get equal resources due to lack of demand.

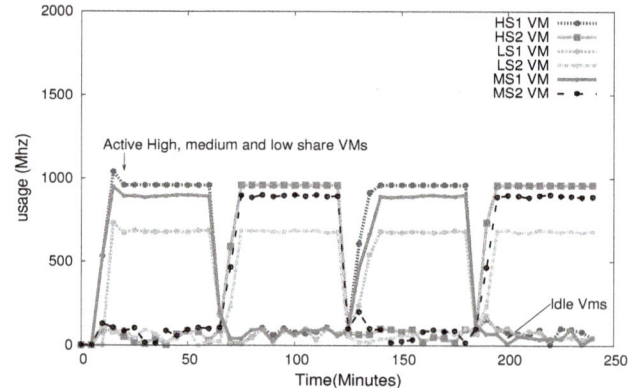

Figure 8: CPU allocation for a high-share, a medium-share and a low-share VM in each of the sets. Note that the allocations are higher based on the shares and demands of the VMs.

In the next scenario, we tried a case where some sets of VMs become idle when the others become active. HS1 with high shares, MS1 with medium shares and LS1 with low shares become active together, and HS2, MS2 and LS2 become active together. This is an interesting scenario for BPX as one set of high, medium and low-share VMs become idle giving up their share to other VMs. Figure 8 shows the allocation of one VM of each type. First, we observe that the active VMs are always able to get a larger portion of the overall allocation. Second, the excess given up by the idle VMs is divided among all the active VMs and the allocations are in the order of shares but not directly proportional to them. This is expected semantics from BPX.

Figure 9 shows the sum of the allocation made to all the 50 VMs in each set. For their cumulative allocations, the high-share VMs get more than the medium-share VMs and the medium-share VMs get more than the low-share VMs. The allocation is not exactly in the ratio of $4 : 2 : 1$ as the excess given up by the idle VMs is distributed among the active VMs based on their demand and not just shares. However, as expected high-share VMs always get more than medium-share VMs and medium-share VMs get more than low-share VMs.

5.4 Comparison with other Allocation Policies

We also compared BPX with two other implementations: (1) static partitioning between clusters with dynamic allocation within a cluster and (2) centralized allocation for all VMs. In the first scheme, the overall capacity is statically divvied among clusters based on the number of VMs and their shares in the cluster. Within a cluster, DRS then uses the centralized algorithm to dynamically allocate the per-cluster capacity every 5 minutes. This is already a very good contender since within a cluster we are doing dynamic allocation but not across clusters. We expect this to cause some wastage of the tenant's purchased capacity when one cluster has idle resources and other clusters have demands that exceed the allocation.

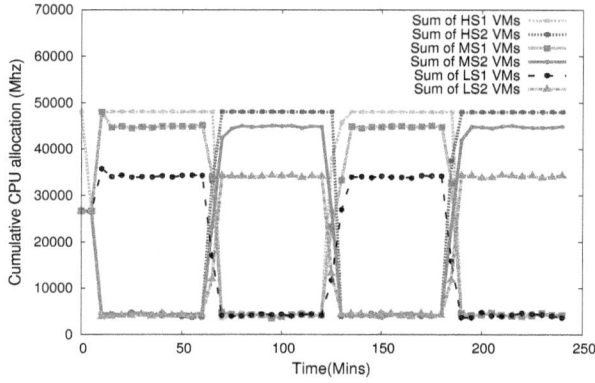

Figure 9: Cumulative CPU allocation over time for VMs in all six sets, as they becomes active and idle.

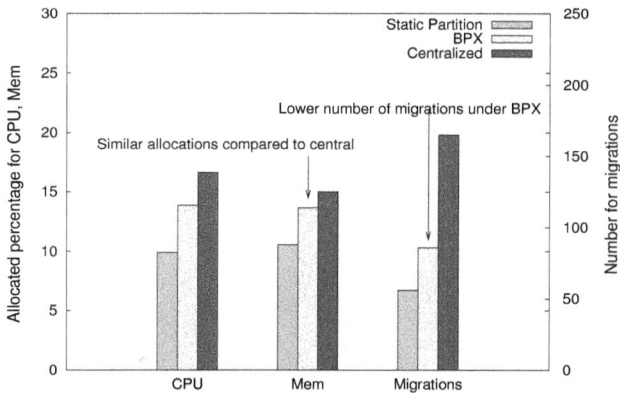

Figure 10: Comparison of BPX with static partitioning and centralized allocation mechanisms. The cumulative CPU and memory allocations of BPX are similar to the centralized scheme, but BPX is less aggressive as shown by the fewer number of migrations.

As a second scheme, we tested a centralized divvy where we collect the demands of all the 300 VMs in one location and do allocation per VM using the centralized algorithm mentioned in Section 3.2. This is equivalent to running the VMs in a single large cluster, which is how we implemented this mechanism. This solution obviously cannot scale, when we have large number of tenants or large number of VMs per tenant in a cloud environment. In all three schemes, the DRS load balancing algorithm was run in each cluster to migrate VMs within the cluster when the VM allocations exceeded the host capacity.

Figure 10 shows the comparison among various schemes in terms of CPU and memory allocation metrics and the overall number of migrations that was done by DRS. The centralized algorithm is very aggressive in terms of dynamic allocation and re-allocating resources from VMs that are idle to the active ones. This is apparent from the large number of migrations that DRS performed in the case of the centralized solution. The total allocation metric for CPU and memory is also slightly better as compared to BPX because the central divvy can redistribute resources much more quickly.

With BPX, it takes some time for the allocations to happen and this causes the cumulative allocation metric to be slightly lower as compared to the centralized solution. The partitioned allocation scheme can re-distribute resources in a cluster but it cannot re-distribute resources across clusters, and ends up wasting resources that the tenant had bought. This causes the allocation metrics to be significantly lower. This experiment shows that BPX provides a good trade-off between a non-scalable centralized solution and a demand-agnostic partitioned solution.

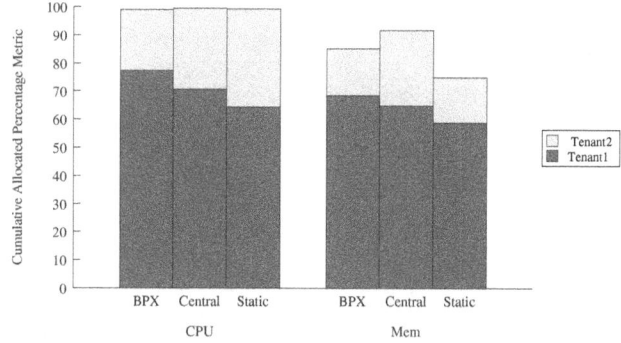

Figure 11: Comparison of BPX with static partitioning and centralized allocation mechanisms when allocating spare capacity in a cloud. Note that Tenant1 is able to get its reservation both under BPX and centralized allocation.

5.5 Allocating Spare Capacity with BPX

One of the key goals for cloud service providers is to be able to simultaneously host tenants that buy overall reservation upfront along with tenants that buy spare capacity at lower rate. To emulate this behavior we experimented with two tenants, Tenant1 and Tenant2, with the following characteristics. Tenant1 has bought 70% of the overall capacity of the cloud as reservation while Tenant2 is running VMs to consume spare capacity in a Pay-as-you-go fashion without reservation. Tenant1 denotes the cumulative capacity that is purchased at the regular price while Tenant2 denotes the cumulative availability-based capacity. Since Tenant1 has paid for reservation its VMs should be able to get up to 70% of the cloud cluster when they demand it and rest is charged based on a pay-as-you-go model. Both tenants have 600 VMs each.

All the VMs ran on a total of 120 hosts spread over three clusters. Again, we measured the cumulative payload for CPU and memory for VMs of both tenants. In order to stress the dynamic reallocation of BPX, we used VMs with periodic workloads that alternate between active and idle phases. The active and idle periods are not synchronized among the VMs. To get high cumulative payload, the allocation algorithm needs to flow resources quickly as even a small subset (25%) of Tenant1's 600 VMs can consume all the purchased reservation.

We implemented BPX along with central and static divvy schemes as described in the previous section for comparison. The central divvy scheme consisted of all 120 hosts in a single cluster, which is an ideal baseline for comparison. In case of static divvy, the reservation was statically partitioned between three clusters, which use DRS to reallocate its share of the reservation to the VMs.

Figure 11 shows the cumulative memory and CPU payload of the VMs under each scheme for both tenants. In the case of CPU, the payload is similar for all three schemes because the ESX scheduler is work conserving. So even if a VM has reservation but no demand, it is not scheduled and some other VM on the host with enough demand is able to get those reserved CPU MHz. With static divvying, the VMs belonging to the tenant without reservation (Tenant2) get more resources than they deserve. This is because the reservation cannot be reallocated across clusters to handle demand imbalance. The cumulative payload of the VMs of the tenant without reservations was more than 40% of the cloud capacity. With centralized DRS, the tenant with reservation got exactly 70% of the cloud capacity as the divvying is done synchronously. With BPX, because of the distributed nature, the VMs with reservation get a little more than what they deserve and end up with 77% of the cloud capacity.

For memory, if a VM has reservations, it is not given to other VMs even when the VM is not using it, since memory is a less fungible resource and reclamation is not instantaneous. Hence the total payload is different for the three schemes as the ESX host is not completely work conserving. In this case, if we do not flow the memory reservation to the VMs that need it, other idle VMs take up the reservation and the total payload is lower. The centralized divvying has the best payload since it can divvy instantaneously. BPX is closer to the central divvying than static partitioning and is also able to give about 70% of the reserved resources to Tenant1 VMs.

5.6 Real Deployment of Hadoop and VDI VMs

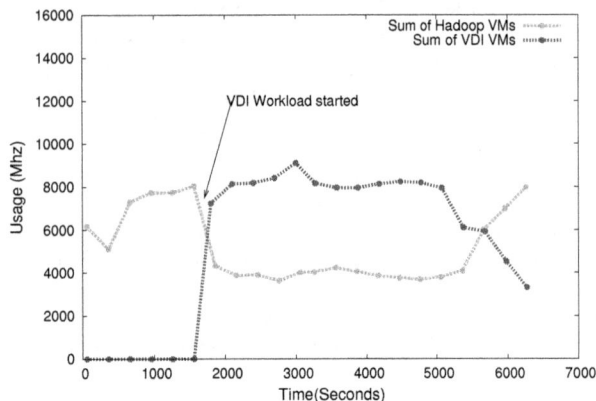

Figure 12: Sum of CPU usage of all Hadoop VMs and VDI VMs.

We also experimented with a real deployment with ESX hosts and VMs running various real workloads. We used two clusters with a total of 8 ESX hosts. The clusters were in two separate but nearby datacenters. Each cluster was managed by the DRS cluster manager software with our prototype BPX implementation. We ran a Hadoop workload in one cluster and a virtual desktop interface (VDI) workload in another cluster. We set the controls to reflect a tenant who has bought 12 GHz of CPU capacity and 12 GB of memory. Both the Hadoop workload and the VDI workload were

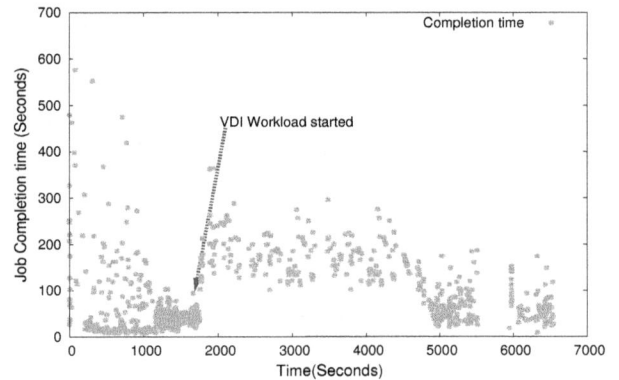

Figure 13: Hadoop job completion times over duration of the experiment.

run using this capacity. There were also other background workloads belonging to other tenants in the clusters running CPU-intensive server workloads. We mainly focus on the tenant workload under study.

The Hadoop VMs were setup using Serengeti [26] and consisted of 10 worker VMs, one Master VM and one client VM. The Hadoop workload consisted of running the teragen and terasort programs. Teragen was run with one billion rows and 800 map jobs. Terasort was followed by 800 map and 500 reduce jobs.

The VDI workload consisted of 11 VDI (desktop VMs) and was run using the ViewPlanner benchmark from VMware [3]. The workload consisted of a mix of desktop applications such as power point, zip, movie player etc. The ViewPlanner harness VMs were not part of the tenant, and hence did not consume from the 12 GHz available to the tenant. The VDI VMs were configured with high shares, as they are interactive workload while all the Hadoop VMs had low shares. The shares were in the ratio of $4 : 1$.

Initially the workload was started in the Hadoop cluster. Since the Hadoop VMs were the only VMs belonging to the tenant, they were able to use all of the purchased capacity up to their demand. The Hadoop workloads were consuming as much CPU as they needed. At $t = 1700$ seconds, the VDI workload was started, which powered on all the 11 VDI VMs in the second cluster and started the workloads inside them. Since the tenant has only 12 GHz, and all the high-share VDI VMs suddenly spiked up, the Hadoop VMs in the other cluster were throttled, which caused their CPU consumption to go down and their job completion times to go up.

The VDI workload lasted for one hour and then its VMs slowly became idle. As this happened, the Hadoop VMs were able to pick up the slack and they were given resources that were left idle by the VDI VMs. Figure 12 shows the sum of CPU usage of all the Hadoop and the VDI VMs. Each point in the graph denotes the sum of the five minute moving average of the CPU usage of the VMs of each type. Note that the overall sum is always 12 GHz. Figure 13 shows the job completion time as measured by the Hadoop. The job completion time is plotted against the time when the job started. Note that when the VDI workload was started, the job times of Hadoop increased as expected. Overall, these results show that BPX is able to allocate the overall bulk capacity purchased by a tenant among its VMs based on their demand and overall importance as denoted by shares. BPX also supports reservations and limit controls per VM, which we didn't specifically evaluate here.

6. RELATED WORK

Resource allocation and buying models in a public cloud environment is a fast evolving area. Here we focus on three broad topics: (1) capacity planning and demand prediction, (2) meeting application level SLAs and (3) dynamic resource distribution among VMs in a cloud.

Capacity planning and demand prediction are critical in deploying workloads in a cloud. Several approaches [10, 11, 34] have been proposed for demand prediction based on trace analysis, and using it for capacity estimation, and admission control. These approaches are complementary to BPX and can help a user estimate virtual capacity purchase decisions. Gmach et al. [8] proposed a global controller to create a self-managing pool of virtualized servers to satisfy time-varying service level objectives and workload demands. This is similar to DRS cluster manager software, which is quite useful but may not scale well to a large number of servers. Wang et al. [32] studied how the cloud provider should allocate resources to different pricing schemes, such as PAYG and spot auctions so as to maximize revenue, while [18], proposed a new pricing scheme for selling network bandwidth reservations. This is an orthogonal problem to the issue solved by BPX.

Urgaonkar et al. [23] proposed an analytical model based on networks of queues to predict performance of multi-tiered applications for capacity planning. Casale et al. [6] showed how to incorporate burstiness into the analytical queuing network models. These approaches provide sound foundational basis for medium term or offline capacity estimation, in contrast to our adaptive approach based on measured performance. Several studies [4, 20] have proposed approaches for performance modeling and SLA based resource allocations for multi-tier applications. Providing QoS guarantees to applications while overcommitting the servers has been studied in [25, 29]. Such application-level approaches can be used in cases where a public cloud provider allows a user to set arbitrary resource controls on its VMs.

Mesos [13] proposes a two-level approach to allocate resources to frameworks like Hadoop and MPI that may share an underlying cluster of servers. Mesos (and related solutions) rely on OS-level abstractions like resource containers [1, 2, 5], which are quite useful but not in common use in IaaS based public clouds, and are less flexible then the VM controls used here. R-Opus [7] provides an elegant framework to map application workload demands to various allocation priorities exposed by the workload manager. However both the application level QoS requirements and resource controls used by R-Opus are quite different from the ones used in public cloud environments.

The computational complexity of VM placement to improve consolidation ratios was studied in [24, 31]. In [14] a trace-based approach that takes in application level SLA's and determines which VMs are best run together on the same host was proposed to accommodate a number of concurrent workloads. In [22] a stochastic model to guide resource provisioning, and determine minimum capacity levels to meet service availability levels was proposed. In [30] a stochastic model that incorporates both diurnal variation and fast time-scale burstiness was analyzed. The authors also studied the tradeoff between capacity and QoS for future performance requirements.

In [21] resource usage patterns were analyzed using PCA techniques and shown to improve server consolidation ratios. In [33], they estimated resource requirements when workloads are moved from physical to a virtualized infrastructure.

Many of these solutions are complementary to BPX and can be used to determine the overall capacity that the tenant should buy. BPX can then handle runtime demand fluctuations by allocating the purchased capacity to the deserving VMs.

7. CONCLUSIONS AND FUTURE WORK

In this paper, we studied the problem of selling cloud resources in bulk to tenants. In our model, customers can flexibly deploy VMs based on their aggregated dynamic resource *usage* rather than their configured sizes. This provides the customer with the abstraction of having a dedicated physical infrastructure of the size of the purchased bulk capacity. Customers can therefore instantiate VMs whose total configured capacity exceeds the purchased amount. This allows them to overcommit the resources just as they could in a dedicated datacenter, and reap the benefits of statistical multiplexing.

We proposed two distributed resource allocation algorithms called DBS and BPX that dynamically allocate the purchased capacity among a tenant's VMs based on their dynamic demand, shares, reservation, and limit settings. BPX is highly scalable and robust in a distributed environment, and enjoys several desired properties of a resource allocation policy. We implemented BPX as part of VMware's management software and showed that it can re-allocate resource in the order of minutes among a set of VMs running across different hosts and racks in a datacenter.

We contend that this model will make it even more attractive for a customer to embrace a public cloud deployment, beyond simply buying VMs with fixed capacity and paying for their configured size.

Acknowledgments

We would like to thank Anne Holler, Roopak Parikh, Madhura Sharangpani and other members of resource management team at VMware for insightful comments and discussions. We greatly appreciate the help with test-bed setup from Nachiket Karmarkar and Pradeep Padala. Thanks also to the members of the ViewPlanner and Serengeti teams for their respective software. Thanks also to Naveen Nagaraj, Rajit Kambo and Jennifer Anderson for motivating us to work on these problems and supporting this work. We are also grateful to the anonymous reviewers for their insightful comments that helped in improving the overall quality of the paper.

Part of the research was performed while the third author was a Scholar-In-Residence at VMware Inc., Palo Alto, CA. Partially supported by NSF Grant 0917157.

8. REFERENCES

[1] Linux containers (LXC) overview document. http://lxc.sourceforge.net/lxc.html.

[2] Solaris Resource Management.
http://docs.sun.com/app/docs/doc/817-1592.

[3] B. Agrawal, L. Spracklen, S. Satnur, and R.Bidarkar. Vmware view 5.0 performance and best practices. 2011. http://www.vmware.com/files/pdf/view/VMware-View-Performance-Study-Best-Practices-Technical-White-Paper.pdf.

[4] D. Ardagna, M. Trubian, and L. Zhang. SLA based resource allocation policies in autonomic environments. *J. Parallel Distrib. Comput.*, 67(3):259–270, 2007.

[5] G. Banga, P. Druschel, and J. C. Mogul. Resource containers: a new facility for resource management in server systems. In *OSDI '99*.

[6] G. Casale, N. Mi, L. Cherkasova, and E. Smirni. How to parameterize models with bursty workloads. *SIGMETRICS Perform. Eval. Rev.*, 36(2):38–44, 2008.

[7] L. Cherkasova and J. A. Rolia. R-opus: A composite framework for application performability and qos in shared resource pools. In *DSN*, pages 526–535, 2006.

[8] D. Gmach, J. Rolia, and L. Cherkasova. Satisfying service level objectices in a self-managing resource pool. In *SASO*, 2009.

[9] D. Gmach, J. Rolia, and L. Cherkasova. Selling t-shirts and time shares in the cloud. In *CCGRID*, pages 539–546, 2012.

[10] D. Gmach, J. Rolia, L. Cherkasova, G. Belrose, T. Turicchi, and A. Kemper. An integrated approach to resource pool management: Policies, efficiency and quality metrics. In *DSN*, pages 326–335, 2008.

[11] D. Gmach, J. Rolia, L. Cherkasova, and A. Kemper. Capacity management and demand prediction for next generation data centers. In *ICWS*, pages 43–50, 2007.

[12] A. Gulati, A. Holler, M. Ji, G. Shanmuganathan, C. Waldspurger, and X. Zhu. VMware Distributed Resource Management: Design, Implementation, and Lessons Learned. In *VMware Technical Journal*, March 2012.

[13] B. Hindman, A. Konwinski, M. Zaharia, A. Ghodsi, A. D. Joseph, R. Katz, S. Shenker, and I. Stoica. Mesos: a platform for fine-grained resource sharing in the data center. In *Proceedings of the 8th USENIX conference on Networked systems design and implementation*, NSDI'11, 2011.

[14] X. Meng, C. Isci, J. O. Kephart, L. Zhang, E. Bouillet, and D. E. Pendarakis. Efficient resource provisioning in compute clouds via vm multiplexing. In *ICAC*, pages 11–20, 2010.

[15] Microsoft, Inc. Microsoft Hyper-V Server. 2012. http://www.microsoft.com/en-us/server-cloud/hyper-v-server/default.aspx%.

[16] Nebula, Inc. 2012. http://www.nebula.com/.

[17] Nimbula, Inc. 2012. http://www.nimbula.com/.

[18] D. Niu, C. Feng, and B. Li. Pricing cloud bandwidth reservations under demand uncertainty. In *SIGMETRICS*, pages 151–162, 2012.

[19] L. Spracklen, B. Agrawal, R.Bidarkar, and H. Sivaraman. Comprehensive user experience monitoring. March 2011. VMware Technical Journal.

[20] C. Stewart and K. Shen. Performance modeling and system management for multi-component online services. In *NSDI*, 2005.

[21] J. Tan, P. Dube, X. Meng, and L. Zhang. Exploiting resource usage patterns for better utilization prediction. In *ICDCS Workshops*, pages 14–19, 2011.

[22] Y. Tan, Y. Lu, and C. H. Xia. Provisioning for large scale cloud computing services. In *SIGMETRICS*, pages 407–408, 2012.

[23] B. Urgaonkar, G. Pacifici, P. J. Shenoy, M. Spreitzer, and A. N. Tantawi. An analytical model for multi-tier internet services and its applications. In *SIGMETRICS*, pages 291–302, 2005.

[24] B. Urgaonkar, A. L. Rosenberg, and P. J. Shenoy. Application placement on a cluster of servers. *Int. J. Found. Comput. Sci.*, 18(5), 2007.

[25] B. Urgaonkar, P. J. Shenoy, and T. Roscoe. Resource overbooking and application profiling in shared hosting platforms. In *OSDI*, 2002.

[26] VMware Big Data team. 2012. http://www.vmware.com/hadoop/serengeti.html.

[27] VMware, Inc. VMware vCloud Suite. 2012. http://www.vmware.com/products/datacenter-virtualization/vcloud-suite/o%verview.html.

[28] C. A. Waldspurger. Memory Resource Management in VMware ESX Server. In *USENIX OSDI '02*.

[29] H. Wang, K. Doshi, and P. Varman. Nested QoS: Adaptive burst decomposition for SLO guarantees in virtualized servers. *Intel Technology Journal*, 16:156–181, June 2012.

[30] K. Wang, M. Lin, F. Ciucu, A. Wierman, and C. Lin. Characterizing the impact of the workload on the value of dynamic resizing in data centers. In *SIGMETRICS*, pages 405–406, 2012.

[31] M. Wang, X. Meng, and L. Zhang. Consolidating virtual machines with dynamic bandwidth demand in data centers. In *INFOCOM*, 2011.

[32] W. Wang, B. Li, and B. Liang. Towards optimal capacity segmentation with hybrid cloud pricing. In *ICDCS*, pages 425–434, 2012.

[33] T. Wood, L. Cherkasova, K. M. Ozonat, and P. J. Shenoy. Profiling and modeling resource usage of virtualized applications. In *Middleware*, pages 366–387, 2008.

[34] Q. Zhang, L. Cherkasova, G. Mathews, W. Greene, and E. Smirni. R-capriccio: A capacity planning and anomaly detection tool for enterprise services with live workloads. In *Middleware*, 2007.

Efficient Crowdsourcing for Multi-class Labeling

David R. Karger
Massachusetts Institute of
Technology
karger@mit.edu

Sewoong Oh
University of Illinios at
Urbana-Champaign
swoh@illinois.edu

Devavrat Shah
Massachusetts Institute of
Technology
devavrat@mit.edu

ABSTRACT

Crowdsourcing systems like Amazon's Mechanical Turk have emerged as an effective large-scale human-powered platform for performing tasks in domains such as image classification, data entry, recommendation, and proofreading. Since workers are low-paid (a few cents per task) and tasks performed are monotonous, the answers obtained are noisy and hence unreliable. To obtain reliable estimates, it is essential to utilize appropriate inference algorithms (e.g. Majority voting) coupled with structured redundancy through task assignment. Our goal is to obtain the best possible trade-off between reliability and redundancy.

In this paper, we consider a general probabilistic model for noisy observations for crowd-sourcing systems and pose the problem of minimizing the total price (i.e. redundancy) that must be paid to achieve a target overall reliability. Concretely, we show that it is possible to obtain an answer to each task correctly with probability $1 - \varepsilon$ as long as the redundancy per task is $O\big((K/q)\log(K/\varepsilon)\big)$, where each task can have any of the K distinct answers equally likely, q is the *crowd-quality* parameter that is defined through a probabilistic model. Further, effectively this is the best possible redundancy-accuracy trade-off *any* system design can achieve. Such a single-parameter crisp characterization of the (order-)optimal trade-off between redundancy and reliability has various useful operational consequences. Further, we analyze the robustness of our approach in the presence of adversarial workers and provide a bound on their influence on the redundancy-accuracy trade-off.

Unlike recent prior work [13, 17, 19], our result applies to non-binary (i.e. $K > 2$) tasks. In effect, we utilize algorithms for binary tasks (with inhomogeneous error model unlike that in [13, 17, 19]) as key subroutine to obtain answers for K-ary tasks. Technically, the algorithm is based on low-rank approximation of weighted adjacency matrix for a random regular bipartite graph, weighted according to the answers provided by the workers.

Categories and Subject Descriptors

G.3 [**Probability and Statistics**]: Statistical computing; F.2 [**Analysis of Algorithms and Problem of Complexity**]: Miscellaneous

Keywords

Crowd-sourcing, Low-rank Matrices, Random Graphs

1. INTRODUCTION

In this paper, we are interested in designing crowd-sourcing systems that are efficient in the sense of achieving *reliability* at the minimal cost of *redundancy*. We will provide appropriate definitions of redundancy and reliability later in this section. More generally, this work is aimed at addressing the following scenarios.

Scenario One. Using MTurk[1] platform for obtaining count of cancerous tumor cells in each microscope image for a very large collection of images leads to answers that are noisy – a good fraction of answers are either nearly correct or arbitrary (cf. see [14]) as the workers either make honest mistakes or they are not making any effort.

Scenario Two. Clinicians collect and record medical history of patients by asking them various questions and classifying the patients' symptoms for type, severity, and duration. Such medical opinions are subject to observer errors and different clinicians may give different values due to variety of reasons (cf. see [9]) such as different wording of questions, different interpretation of the scales, etc.

Scenario Three. Scores are collected from reviewers in the reviewing process of conferences such as Sigmetrics 2013. Each paper, though may have an *innate* score, receives varying scores from different reviewers for reasons such as different reviews have different subjective interpretation of score-scale, or value the contribution of papers differently.

In all of the above scenarios, we have numerous 'multiple choice' tasks at hand and means to collect noisy answers on those tasks by either assigning the tasks using MTurk, getting medical opinions from clinicians, or asking reviewers to review papers. If we are parsimonious and collect only one opinion per task, then we have no other way than to trust that opinion which could be erroneous. To increase reliability, a common practice is to utilize redundancy – each task is assigned to multiple MTurk workers, clinicians or reviewers. Naturally, the more redundancy we introduce, the better accuracy we can hope to achieve. The goal of this paper

---

[1] http://www.mturk.com

is to get the most accurate estimates from given amount of redundancy. To this end, we develop an algorithm for deciding which tasks to assign to which workers, and estimating the answers to the tasks from noisy answers collected from those assigned workers.

Model and problem formulation. Our interest is in finding answers to the tasks, each of which has one true answer from a set of K possible choices denoted by $\mathcal{K} \equiv \{1, \ldots, K\}$. Each worker, when given a task with true answer k, provides an answer $\ell \in \mathcal{K}$ with probability $\pi_{k\ell}$; by definition $\sum_{\ell \in \mathcal{K}} \pi_{k\ell} = 1$ for all $k \in \mathcal{K}$. We call $\pi = [\pi_{k\ell}] \in [0,1]^{K \times K}$ to be the *confusion* (probability) matrix of that worker. Without loss of generality[2], let each task have correct answer equal to k with probability θ_k independently and let worker have confusion matrix π drawn from a distribution $\mathcal{D}$ on space of confusion matrices. As one example, we can define a generalization of the *spammer-hammer* model from [18], where each worker is either a 'hammer' with probability q or is a 'spammer' with probability $1 - q$. A hammer, who always gives the correct answer, has the identity confusion matrix $\pi = \mathbf{I}_{K \times K}$, where $\mathbf{I}$ is the identity matrix. A spammer, who gives answers that are independent of the true answers, has a uniform confusion matrix $\pi = (1/K)\mathbf{1}_K \cdot p^T$, where $\mathbf{1}$ is the vector of all ones, and p^T denoted the transpose of a probability vector p. For example, a spammer might always answer 'one' for any tasks, in which case $p = [1, 0, \ldots, 0]$, or give uniformly random answers, in which case $p = (1/K)[1, 1, \ldots, 1]$. We use t_i to denote the groundtruth answer to the i-th task (which we assume is drawn randomly from a distribution θ), and $\pi^{(j)}$ for the confusion matrix of the j-th worker (which we assume is drawn randomly from a distribution $\mathcal{D}$).

Given this setting, we wish to find answers to a given set of n tasks using m workers so that we are confident that answer to any particular task is correctly with probability at least $1 - \varepsilon$ for some small positive ε, and hence *reliable*. Indeed, if a given task is assigned to only one worker, the probability of making an error is given by

$$\sum_{1 \leq \ell \leq K} \theta_\ell (1 - \mathbb{E}[\pi_{\ell\ell}]),$$

where expectation in $\mathbb{E}[\pi_{\ell\ell}]$ is with respect to $\mathcal{D}$. To further reduce error down to $1 - \varepsilon$ for any ε, one might choose to assign the same task to multiple workers and then take majority of the received answers. Such an approach can lead to reduced error at the cost of increase in the *redundancy*, i.e. the average number of answers received per task. In practice, increase in redundancy typically leads to increase in the cost, e.g., payment to MTurk workers or time to finish reviews.

In general, consider the case when we have n tasks to complete and m workers available. Assigning tasks can be viewed as constructing a bipartite graph $G = (T, W, E)$ with $T = \{t_1, \ldots, t_n\}$ representing tasks, $W = \{w_1, \ldots, w_m\}$ representing workers and $E \subset T \times W$ representing task assignment: $(t_i, w_j) \in E$ if task t_i is assigned to worker w_j. In this case, the per task redundancy is $|E|/n$, that is, the average degree of task vertices in graph G. Once tasks are as-

signed according to a graph G, the workers provide answers $A = [A_{ij}] \in \{\mathcal{K} \cup \mathsf{null}\}^{n \times m}$ where $A_{ij} = \mathsf{null}$ if $(t_i, w_j) \notin E$, i.e. worker w_j is not assigned to task t_i, and it is equal to the answer provided by the worker w_j to the task t_i if $(t_i, w_j) \in E$. Once all the answers $\{A_{ij}\}_{(i,j) \in E}$ are collected, we want to estimate the true answers to the tasks. With abuse of notation, we shall use t_i to represent both node in bipartite graph G and the true answer (in $\mathcal{K}$) to the i-th task. Let $\hat{t}_i \in \mathcal{K}$ be the estimation produced. Then, the probability of error is defined as

$$P_{\mathsf{err}} = \frac{1}{n} \sum_{i=1}^{n} \mathbb{P}(t_i \neq \hat{t}_i), \tag{1}$$

where the probability is taken over all realizations of $\{t_i\}$, $\{\pi^{(j)}\}$, $\{A_{ij}\}$, and any randomness in the task assignment and inference algorithm.

The goal in designing a reliable and cost-efficient crowd-sourcing system is to obtain P_{err} smaller than given target $\varepsilon \in (0, 1/2)$ with minimal redundancy by appropriately choosing task assignment graph G and the inference algorithm to estimate $\{\hat{t}_i\}$.

Next, we define a few quantities that will be useful to describe the result precisely in the subsequent text (readers may skip these definitions till "summary of results"). For any task i and worker j, define the following probabilities

$$p_k^+ \equiv \mathbb{P}(A_{ij} > k | t_i > k) = \sum_{k < \ell \leq K} \sum_{k < \ell' \leq K} \frac{\theta_\ell \, \pi_{\ell\ell'}^{(j)}}{\theta_{>k}},$$

$$p_k^- \equiv \mathbb{P}(A_{ij} \leq k | t_i \leq k) = \sum_{1 \leq \ell \leq k} \sum_{1 \leq \ell' \leq k} \frac{\theta_\ell \, \pi_{\ell\ell'}^{(j)}}{1 - \theta_{>k}}, \tag{2}$$

where $\theta_{>k} = \sum_{k < \ell \leq K} \theta_\ell$. Also define $q_k \equiv \mathbb{E}[(p_k^+ + p_k^- - 1)^2]$ for $1 \leq k < K$ where the expectation is with respect to the distribution $\mathcal{D}$ of the confusion matrix. Define crowd-quality parameter $q = \min_{1 \leq k < K} q_k$. For example, under the *spammer-hammer* model, a hammer has $p_k^+ = p_k^- = 1$ and a spammer has $p_k^+ + p_k^- = 1$ for all k. If a randomly drawn worker is a hammer with probability $\tilde{q}$ and a spammer otherwise, we have $q_k = \tilde{q}$ for all k and $q_k = \tilde{q}$.

Define the maximum *bias* of the true answers as $|\bar{s}| = \max_{k=1}^{K-1} |\bar{s}^k|$, where $\bar{s}^k = 2\theta_{>k} - 1$ is the bias in the a priori distribution of the true answers in binary classification task "is t_i larger than k?". For uniform prior $\theta_\ell = 1/K$ and hence the maximum bias is $1 - 2/K$. We will see that in order to achieve average probability of error less than ε, we need to have redundancy that scales as $(1/(q(1 - |\bar{s}|))) \log(K/\varepsilon)$ which in the case of uniform prior scales as $(K/q) \log(K/\varepsilon)$.

Prior work. Though crowd-sourcing is a recent phenomenon, similar questions were considered by Dawid and Skene [9] in the context of *Scenario Two* described earlier. They introduced an iterative algorithm for inferring the solutions and reliability of workers, based on the expectation maximization (EM) [10]. EM is a heuristic inference algorithm that iteratively does the following: given workers' answers to the tasks, the algorithm attempts to estimate the reliability of the workers and given estimation of reliability (error probabilities) of workers, it estimates the solution of the tasks; and repeat. Due to particular simplicity of the EM algorithm, it has been widely applied in classification problems where the training data is annotated by low-cost noisy 'labelers' [16, 23]. Sheng et al. [26] have extensively studied the al-

---

[2]This is without loss of generality, as the results stated in this paper hold even if we use the empirical distribution in place of the distribution assumed for prior on tasks as well as worker confusion matrices.

gorithm's performance empirically. Now EM algorithm has various shortcomings: (i) it is a heuristic and there are no rigorous guarantees known about its correctness or overall performance; (ii) a priori it is not clear that for this particular problem EM is convergent; and (iii) the role of the task allocation is not at all understood with the EM algorithm.

More rigorous approaches towards designing task assignment graphs and inference algorithms were recently proposed starting [13, 17]. In these work, task assignment was done through random graphs (Erdos-Renyi in [13], random regular in [17]) and inference was done through low-rank approximations. They, however, assumed binary tasks (i.e. $K = 2$) and homogeneous error model (i.e. $\pi_{12} = \pi_{21}$ with $K = 2$); and resulted in sub-optimal trade-off between redundancy and error. This was further improved upon to reach order-optimal error-redundancy trade-off by means of belief propagation based iterative estimation algorithm in [19]. This algorithm uses weighted majority voting where the weights are computed by an approximate belief propagation. Our approach is similar but the weights are computed by singular value decomposition (SVD). The major difference is that SVD based approach generalizes to more general probabilistic models we study in this paper, whereas the belief propagation based approach only works for a simpler model where the underlying structure is a rank one matrix. More recently, it was shown that the resulting design and inference algorithm are optimal even with respect to adaptive system design [18]. The key limitation of all of the above, definitely very impressive, results is applicability to binary tasks with homogeneous error model.

Given graphical models such as the one studied in these prior work, one can solve the inference problem using a standard belief propagation. The main challenge in such an approach is that the inference algorithm requires the priors from which the distribution of the quality of the workers are drawn. In this paper, we do not assume any knowledge of the prior. However, it was shown through experiments on real and simulated datasets in [21] that when the prior is known, improved performance can be achieved.

It should be noted that crowdsourcing is currently extremely active research area in terms of designing actual platforms like [2, 3, 1, 4, 5], empirical results based on experiments like [16, 7, 23, 6, 28, 27] and deciding on issues like pricing such as results in [22, 15]. The main focus of this paper is rigorous treatment of crowdsourcing system design and hence we only provide a limited coverage of prior work related to general crowdsourcing. In particular, we do not address some practical questions such as embedding golden questions which you know the answers to, screening workers with accuracy thresholds, and paying only on accurate responses.

Summary of results. As the main result of this paper, we provide a crowdsourcing system design that is asymptotically order-optimal for the general noise model considered here for K-ary tasks for any $K \geq 2$. This is the first rigorous result for K-ary (even for $K = 2$) tasks with non-homogeneous error model. In a sense, it resolves the question raised by Dawid and Skene [9] in the context of medical record collection or more generally noisy computation. Formally, we show that it is possible to achieve $P_{\text{err}} \leq \varepsilon$ for any $\varepsilon \in (0, 1)$ with per task redundancy $O\left(\frac{1}{q(1-|\bar{s}|)} \log \frac{K}{\varepsilon}\right)$. The minimum bias $|\bar{s}|$ depends on the prior distribution

$(\theta_1, \ldots, \theta_K)$; for uniform prior, it is such that $1 - |\bar{s}| = 2/K$. That is, effectively, for uniform prior, our result states that redundancy requirement scales as $O\left(\frac{K}{q} \log \frac{K}{\varepsilon}\right)$. And, (using result of [17, 19]) for any system to achieve $P_{\text{err}} \leq \varepsilon$, redundancy of $\Omega\left(\frac{1}{q} \log \frac{1}{\varepsilon}\right)$ is needed. Thus, for any fixed K (i.e. treating K as a constant), with respect to $q, \varepsilon \to 0$ asymptotic, our system design is order optimal; non-asymptotically off by $(K/q) \log K$.

2. MAIN RESULT

In this section, we describe our task allocation and inference algorithm accompanied by theorems describing it's performance.

2.1 Task allocation

Given n tasks, to utilize redundancy of $\ell \times R$ per task, we shall utilize $n \times R$ workers. Specifically, we shall choose R distinct (ℓ, ℓ) random regular graph $G_1, \ldots, G_R$ for task allocation – in each of these R graphs, we, of course, use the same n tasks but use distinct n workers; thus utilizing $n \times R$ total workers. Each graph G_r, $1 \leq r \leq R$ is generated as per the scheme known as the *configuration model*, cf. [8, 24]. Intuitively, the random regular graphs are good choice because they are known to be good 'expanders' and therefore allows us to efficiently extract the true answers from noisy data matrix using low-rank approximation. We will make independent estimates of the tasks (using low-rank matrix approximations) based on each of these R datasets collected independently. For each task, we will combine these R estimates (using majority voting) to further refine our estimate and guarantee order optimal performance.

2.2 Inference algorithm

Let $A(r) = [A_{ij}(r)] \in (\{\text{null}\} \cup \mathcal{K})^{n \times n}$ be the noisy answers obtained using the r-th, random (ℓ, ℓ)-regular task allocation graph G_r, for $1 \leq r \leq R$. From these datasets on the answers $\{A(r)\}_{1 \leq r \leq R}$, we wish to obtain estimates $\{\hat{t}_i\} \in \mathcal{K}^n$ on what the true answers are for all n tasks. We shall utilize combination of low-rank matrix approximation and majority voting to obtain estimates as described below.

We first reduce the K-ary classification tasks into a series of $K - 1$ simple binary classification tasks. Using each dataset $A(r)$ for $1 \leq r \leq R$, we first produce binary estimates $\hat{t}^k(r) = [\hat{t}_i^k(r)] \in \{-1, 1\}^n$ for $1 \leq k < K$ where

$$\hat{t}_i^k(r) = \begin{cases} -1 & \text{if we believe that } t_i \leq k \text{ based on } A(r), \\ +1 & \text{if we believe that } t_i > k \text{ based on } A(r). \end{cases}$$

The low-rank matrix approximation algorithm for estimating $\hat{t}_i^k(r)$ based on $A(r)$ is explained later in this section in detail. Based on these binary estimates on each independent datasets $A(r)$, we further refine our estimates by combining our estimates using majority aggregation over the whole data $\{A(r)\}_{1 \leq r \leq R}$, to get $\hat{t}^k = [\hat{t}_i^k]$. The estimate $\hat{t}_i^k$ for the i-th task is our estimated answer to the question "is t_i larger than k?", determined through majority voting as

$$\hat{t}_i^k = \text{sign}\left(\sum_{r=1}^{R} \hat{t}_i^k(r)\right) \tag{3}$$

where $\text{sign}(x) = 1$ if $x \geq 0$ and -1 if $x < 0$. As we will show in Section 3.1, the main reason we use R independent datasets is to use concentration inequalities to get a tighter bound on the probability of error.

Focusing on a particular task i, if our estimates $\hat{t}_i^k$ are accurate for all $k \in \mathcal{K}$, then we expect them to have a single switch at the true answer $k = t_i$:

$$(\hat{t}_i^1, \ldots, \hat{t}_i^{t_i-1}, \hat{t}_i^{t_i}, \ldots, \hat{t}_i^K) = (\underbrace{+1, \ldots, +1}_{t_i-1}, \underbrace{-1 \ldots, -1}_{K-t_i+1}) ,$$

where we define $\hat{t}_i^K = -1$ for all i. This naturally defines the following rule for producing our final estimates $\hat{t} = [\hat{t}_i]$:

$$\hat{t}_i = \min \left\{ k : \hat{t}_i^k = -1 \right\}. \tag{4}$$

Other methods for aggregating the binary estimates to get a full K-ary estimates are $\hat{t}_i = (1/2)(2 + K + \sum_{k=1}^K \hat{t}_i^k)$ or finding the index that minimize the inconsistencies: $\min_k |\{a < k : \hat{t}_i^a = -1\} \cup \{a \geq k : \hat{t}_i^a = +1\}|$. However, the simple aggregation rule above is powerful enough to ensure that we achieve order-optimal performance.

Now we describe how $A(r)$ is used to produce $\hat{t}^k(r)$, for $1 \leq k < K$. Define matrices $A^k(r) = [A_{ij}^k(r)]$ for $1 \leq k < K$ where

$$A_{ij}^k(r) = \begin{cases} 0 & \text{if } A_{ij}(r) = \text{null} \\ 1 & \text{if } k < A_{ij}(r) \leq K \\ -1 & \text{if } 1 \leq A_{ij}(r) \leq k. \end{cases} \tag{5}$$

That is, entries of matrix $A^k(r)$ converts (quantizes) the answers $A(r)$ into greater than k ($+1$), less or equal to k (-1), and null (0). Define an $n \times n$ projection matrix L as

$$L \equiv \mathbf{I} - \frac{1}{n}\mathbf{1}\mathbf{1}^T , \tag{6}$$

where $\mathbf{I}$ is the identity matrix and $\mathbf{1}$ is the all-ones vector. Consider the projected matrices $B^k(r) = LA^k(r)$. Let $u^k(r)$, $v^k(r)$ be the pair of normalized (unit norm) left and right singular vectors respectively of $B^k(r)$ corresponding to the largest singular value of $B^k(r)$. Produce quantized estimates of tasks $\hat{t}^k(r) = [\hat{t}_i^k(r)]$ as

$$\hat{t}^k(r) = \begin{cases} \text{sign}(u^k(r)) & \text{if } \sum_{j:v_j^k(r) \geq 0}(v_j^k(r))^2 \geq 1/2 , \\ \text{sign}(-u^k(r)) & \text{if } \sum_{j:v_j^k(r) \geq 0}(v_j^k(r))^2 < 1/2 , \end{cases} \tag{7}$$

where $\text{sign}(\cdot)$ is a function that outputs entry-wise sign of a vector, such that $\text{sign}(x) = [\text{sign}(x_i)]$. Even when the largest singular value is unique, the left singular vector $u^k(r)$ is only determined up to a sign. To resolve this ambiguity we use the right singular vector $v^k(r)$ to determine the sign of our final estimate. We can also use other means of resolving this ambiguity up to a sign, such as asking *golden* questions with known answers, if we have them available.

We can also interpret (7) as a weighted majority voting with the right singular vector as the weights. Since $u^k(r) = A^k(r)v^k(r)$, our estimate for the i-th task is

$$\begin{aligned} \hat{t}_i^k(r) &= \text{sign}(u_i^k(r)) \\ &= \text{sign}\Big(\sum_j A_{ij}^k(r) v_j^k(r) \Big) , \end{aligned}$$

assuming we have resolved the ambiguity in sign. Effectively, we are weighting each response, $A_{ij}^k(r)$, by how reliable each worker is, $v_j^k(r)$. In proving the main results, we will show in (14) that $v_j^k(r)$ is an estimate for $(p_k^+ + p_k^- - 1)$ for the j-th worker. Intuitively, the larger $v_j^k(r)$ is the more reliable the worker j is.

2.3 Performance

Here we describe the performance of the algorithm introduced above. For this, define the maximum *bias* of the true answers as $|\bar{s}| = \max_{k=1}^{K-1} |\bar{s}^k|$, where $\bar{s}^k = 2\theta_{>k} - 1$ is the bias in the a priori distribution of the true answers in binary classification task "is t_i larger than k?". For results below to hold, we shall assume that the random variables p_k^+ and p_k^- defined in (2) satisfy $p_k^+ + p_k^- \geq 1$ for all $1 \leq k < K$ with probability one according to the the distribution $\mathcal{D}$ of the confusion matrix. However, this assumption is only necessary to ensure that we can resolve the ambiguity of the sign in deciding whether to use $u^k(r)$ or $-u^k(r)$ for our inference in (7). If we have alternative way of resolving this ambiguity, for instance embedding golden questions with known answers, then the following theorem holds for any $\mathcal{D}$.

THEOREM 2.1. *For any $\varepsilon \in (0, 1/2)$ and a choice of $\ell = \Theta\big(\frac{1}{q(1-|\bar{s}|)^3}\big)$ and $R = \Theta\big(\log(K/\varepsilon)\big)$, there exists a $N(\varepsilon, \ell, \bar{s}, q)$ that depends on $\varepsilon, \ell, \bar{s},$ and q such that for all $n \geq N(\varepsilon, \ell, \bar{s}, q)$, we have*

$$P_{\text{err}} = \frac{1}{n}\sum_{i=1}^n \mathbb{P}(\hat{t}_i \neq t_i) \leq \varepsilon,$$

where the probability is over the randomness in the choice of task allocation graph, true answers to the tasks, worker confusion matrices, and the the realization of the answers submitted by the workers.

In terms of the *redundancy* and *reliability* trade-off, the above theorem states that we need to collect $\ell R = \Theta\big(\frac{1}{q(1-|\bar{s}|)^3}\log(K/\varepsilon)\big)$ answers per task to ensure that we achieve error rate less than ε.

Dealing with $\bar{s}$. Let us discuss the dependence of the required redundancy on $\bar{s}$. When we have uniformly distributed true answers, $\theta_\ell = 1/K$ for $1 \leq \ell \leq K$, then $|1 - \bar{s}| = 2/K$ leading to the redundancy dependence scale as $O\big((K^3/q)\log(K/\varepsilon)\big)$ in Theorem 2.1. While K is treated as a constant, for moderate size of K, this is terrible dependence. It is, indeed, possible to improve this dependence on $\bar{s}$ by modifying the estimation step (7) as follows: let $\hat{u}^k(r) = u^k(r) + \frac{\bar{s}^k}{\sqrt{(1-(\bar{s}^k)^2)n}}\mathbf{1}$, then

$$\hat{t}^k(r) = \begin{cases} \text{sign}(\hat{u}^k(r)) & \text{if } \sum_{j:v_j^k(r) \geq 0}(v_j^k(r))^2 \geq 1/2 \\ \text{sign}(-\hat{u}^k(r)) & \text{if } \sum_{j:v_j^k(r) \geq 0}(v_j^k(r))^2 < 1/2 \end{cases} \tag{8}$$

The above estimation step, however, requires knowledge of $\bar{s}^k$ which is quite feasible as it's population level aggregation (i.e. knowledge of θ_ℓ, $1 \leq \ell \leq K$). With the above estimation, we get the following improved bound with change of $\ell = \Theta(1/q(1-|\bar{s}|))$ in place of $\ell = \Theta\big(1/q(1-|\bar{s}|)^3\big)$.

THEOREM 2.2. *Under the hypotheses of Theorem 2.1, for any $\varepsilon \in (0, 1/2)$ and a choice of $\ell = \Theta\big(\frac{1}{q(1-|\bar{s}|)}\big)$ and $R = \Theta\big(\log(K/\varepsilon)\big)$, there exists a $N(\varepsilon, \ell, \bar{s}, q)$ such that for all $n \geq N(\varepsilon, \ell, \bar{s}, q)$, the estimates in (8) achieve $P_{\text{err}} \leq \varepsilon$.*

When designing a task assignment, we choose how much *redundancy* we want to add per task, which is the average number of answers we are collecting per task. Let $\gamma = \ell R$ denote the redundancy per task. According to the above theorem, to achieve an average error probability less than ε, we need the redundancy per task that scales as $\gamma =$

$O((1/q(1-|\bar{s}|))\log(K/\varepsilon))$. Then, this implies that the probability of error achieved by our approach is upper bounded by $P_{\text{err}} \leq K e^{-C\gamma q(1-|\bar{s}|)}$ for a positive constant C. Figure 1 illustrates this exponential dependency of P_{err} on the redundancy γ for fixed K, q and $|\bar{s}|$. Compared to an algorithm-independent analytical lower bound, this shows that the constant C in the error exponent is very close to the optimal one, since the slop of the error probability is very close to that of the lower bound.

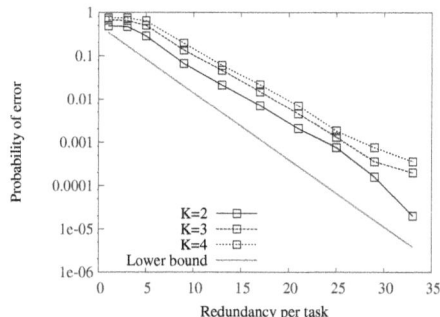

Figure 1: Average probability of error decreases exponentially as redundancy increases and is weakly dependent on the alphabet size K.

For this example, we used uniform prior of $\theta_k = 1/K$ and the spammer-hammer model described in Section 1 to generate the data with $q = q_k = 0.3$. We plot the average number of errors over 1000 tasks averaged over 50 random instances of this problem. As we increase the alphabet size, the slop of the (log) probability of error does not change. If our upper bound on P_{err} was tight, we expect the slop to scale as $(1-|\bar{s}|)$, which in this numerical example is $1/K$.

Optimality. In [17, 19], it was shown that for binary model ($K = 2$) with homogeneous noise model (i.e. $\pi_{12} = \pi_{21}$ for all π), to obtain $P_{\text{err}} \leq \varepsilon$, the per task redundancy must scale as $\Omega\left(\frac{1}{q}\log(\frac{1}{\varepsilon})\right)$. This lower-bound on redundancy requirement is independent of the choice of any task-allocation and inference algorithm. Clearly, this is a special case of our general model and hence applies to our setting. From Theorem 2.2, it follows that our algorithm is within a factor of K of optimal redundancy requirement for $K = O(1/\epsilon)$. Equivalently, in the asymptotic of $\varepsilon, q \to 0$, our algorithm is order-optimal, since the dependencies on ϵ and q are the same as the optimal budget requirement.

Running time of algorithm. The key step in our inference algorithm is obtaining rank-1 approximation of the $n \times n$ matrices $LA^k(r)$ for $1 \leq k < K$ and $1 \leq r \leq R$. In practice, n is the number of papers submitted to a conference, number of patients, or the number of images we want to label, and it is likely to be very large. Standard iterative methods, such as the power iteration or the Lanczos method can be used to compute the leading singular vector of such large matrices. These iterative methods only rely on the matrix-vector product, which can be done quite efficiently by exploiting the structure of $LA^k(r)$.

The standard power-iteration algorithm leads to identification of rank-1 approximation (i.e. left, right singular vectors) within error of δ with number of iterations $O\left(\frac{\log(n/\delta)}{\log(\sigma_1/\sigma_2)}\right)$,

where σ_1, σ_2 are the largest and second largest singular values of matrix $LA^k(r)$. In the process of establishing Theorem 2.1, we shall show that $\sigma_2/\sigma_1 = O(1/\sqrt{\ell q_k})$, and with $\ell = \Theta(1/q_k)$ this can be made as small as we want.

At each iteration of the power iteration algorithm, we compute matrix-vector multiplication of

$$x^{(t+1)} = L A^k(r)(A^k(r))^T L x^{(t)},$$

and it is known that $x^{(t)}$ eventually converges to the left singular vector of matrix $LA^k(r)$ up to a normalization. Each computation of this multiplication can be done efficiently in $O(n\ell)$ time. Since $A^k(r)$ is a sparse matrix with $n\ell$ non-zero entries, we can compute $(A^k(r))^T y$ with $O(n\ell)$ operations. Since $L = \mathbf{I} - (1/n)\mathbf{1}\mathbf{1}^T$, we can compute $Ly = y - (1/n)\mathbf{1}\mathbf{1}^T y$ in $O(n)$ operations.

Finally, we only need to compute an approximate singular vector up to a certain error. Let u be the left singular vector of $LA^k(r)$ and define $t^k = [t_i^k]$ to be the true answer for a binary classification problem:

$$t_i^k = \begin{cases} -1 & \text{if } t_i \leq k, \\ +1 & \text{if } t_i > k. \end{cases}$$

In the process of establishing Theorem 2.1, we will utilize the fact that the singular vector u is at most distance $C/\sqrt{\ell q_k}$ from the true answers that we want: $\|u - (1/\sqrt{n})t^k\| \leq C/\sqrt{\ell q_k}$. Hence, we only need an approximate singular vector up to error $\delta = C/\sqrt{\ell q_k}$ and the same result holds with this approximate singular vector. Therefore, total computation cost of computing the top left singular vector of $LA^k(r)$ scales as $O\left(n\ell \frac{\log(n\ell q_k)}{\log(\ell q_k)}\right)$ (this is assuming $\ell q_k > 1$).

Operational implications. Here we discuss a few concrete and highly attractive operational implications of crisp result we obtain in Theorem 2.1. Suppose there are M classes of worker: workers of class $m, 1 \leq m \leq M$, have confusion matrix distribution $\mathcal{D}_m$ such that the corresponding quality parameter is q_m and each of them requires payment of c_k to perform a task. Theorem 2.1 immediately suggests that we should hire the worker class m^* that maximizes q_m/c_m over $1 \leq m \leq M$.

The next variation is on the assumed knowledge of q. When designing the regular bipartite graph for task assignment, it requires selecting the degree $\ell = \Theta(1/q(1-|\bar{s}|))$. This assumes that we know a priori the value of q. One way to overcome this limitation is to do binary search for appropriate value of ℓ. This results in a cost of additional constant factor in the budget, i.e. scaling of cost per task still remains $\Theta\left((1/q(1-|\bar{s}|))\log(K/\varepsilon)\right)$. Use following iterative procedure to test the system with $q = 2^{-a}$ at iteration a, and we stop if the resulting estimates are consistent in the following sense. At iteration a, design two replicas of the system for $q = 2^{-a}$, and compare the estimates obtained by these two replicas for all n tasks. If they agree amongst $n(1 - 2\varepsilon)$ tasks, then we stop and declare that as the final answer. Or else, we increase a to $a + 1$ and repeat. Note that by our main result, it follows that if 2^{-a} is less than the actual q then the iteration must stop with high probability.

Robustness against adversarial attacks. We consider two scenarios: first case is where the malicious workers are able to choose their own confusion matrix but still give answers according to our probabilistic model, and second case is where malicious workers are able to give any answers they want. We want to see how robust our approach is when α proportion of the workers are adversarial, that is when αnR workers are adversarial among total nR workers.

Under the first scenario, it follows from Theorem 2.1 that the effect of such adversarial workers is fully captured in q_k', where now each worker with probability $1 - \alpha$ has $\pi^{(j)}$ coming from $\mathcal{D}$ and with probability α has $\pi^{(j)}$ chosen by the adversary. Then, even in the worst case, $q_k' \geq (1 - \alpha)\mathbb{E}_{\mathcal{D}}[(p_k^+ + p_k^- - 1)^2]]$. The new 'crowd quality' is now degraded to $q' \geq (1 - \alpha)q$. In terms of the redundancy necessary to achieve error rate of ε, we now need a factor of $1/(1 - \alpha)$ more redundancy to achieve the same error rate with the presence of α proportion of adversarial workers. This suggests that our approach is robust, since this is the best dependency on α one can hope for. Let M be the number of workers necessary under non-adversarial setting. If we have adversaries among the workers, and let us even assume that we can detect any adversary, even then we need $M/(1 - \alpha)$ total workers to get M non-adversarial workers. Our approach requires the same number of 'good' workers as the one that can detect all adversaries. A similar analysis, in the case of binary tasks (i.e., K=2) and homogeneous error model (i.e., $\pi_{12} = \pi_{21}$ with $K = 2$) was provided in [13].

Under the second scenario, we assume that αnR workers are adversarial as before, but those adversarial workers can submit any answers they want. In particular, this model includes the adversaries who are colluding to manipulate our crowdsourcing system. We want to prove a bound on how much the performance of our algorithm degrades as the number of such adversaries increases. The following theorem proves that our algorithm is robust, in the sense that the same guarantee is achieved with redundancy that scales in the same way as when there are no adversaries, as long as the proportion of adversaries is bounded by $\alpha = cq(1 - |\bar{s}^k|)$ for some positive constant c.

THEOREM 2.3. *Under the hypotheses of Theorem 2.1, there exists a constant c such that when the proportion of the adversarial workers is $\alpha \leq cq(1 - |\bar{s}^k|)^3$, our estimates in (7) aggregated as in (3) achieve $P_{\mathrm{err}} \leq \varepsilon$ with a choice of $\ell = \Theta\big(\frac{1}{q(1-|\bar{s}|)^3}\big)$ and $R = \Theta\big(\log(K/\varepsilon)\big)$ for $n \geq N(\varepsilon, \ell, \bar{s}, q)$. Further, if we use estimates in (8), then the same guarantee holds with $\alpha \leq cq(1 - |\bar{s}^k|)$ and $\ell = \Theta\big(\frac{1}{q(1-|\bar{s}|)}\big)$.*

3. PROOF OF MAIN RESULTS

In this section, we provide the proofs of the main results and technical lemmas.

3.1 Proof of Theorem 2.1

First we consider a single binary estimation problem on a single dataset $A(r)$ and a classification threshold $k \in \mathcal{K}$. We will show that, with choice of $\ell = \Theta(1/(q(1-|\bar{s}^k|)^3))$, we can get good estimates from each dataset $A(r)$ on each binary classification task such that the probability of making an error on each task is less than $1/4$:

$$p_e^+ \equiv \mathbb{P}(\hat{t}_i^k(r) = -1 | t_i^k = +1) \leq 1/4 \text{ , and}$$
$$p_e^- \equiv \mathbb{P}(\hat{t}_i^k(r) = +1 | t_i^k = -1) \leq 1/4 \text{ .}$$

By symmetry p_e^+ and p_e^- do not depend on r or i, but it does depend on k. However, the upper bound holds for any k and we omit the dependence on k to lighten the notations. We

can achieve a significantly improved accuracy by repeating the data collection and estimation process R times on independently chosen task assignment graph and completely different set of workers. These R estimates then can be aggregated using (3): $\hat{t}_i^k = \text{sign}\Big(\sum_{r=1}^R \hat{t}_i^k(r) \Big)$. We claim that each $\hat{t}_i^k(r)$ are independent estimates with error probability less than $1/4$. Applying Hoeffding's inequality, we have

$$
\begin{aligned}
\mathbb{P}\big(\hat{t}_i^k \neq t_i^k\big) &\leq \theta_{>k}\mathbb{P}\Big(\sum_{r=1}^R \hat{t}_i^k(r) \leq 0 \,\Big|\, t_i^k = +1 \Big) \\
&\quad + \theta_{\leq k}\mathbb{P}\Big(\sum_{r=1}^R \hat{t}_i^k(r) \geq 0 \,\Big|\, t_i^k = -1 \Big) \\
&\leq \theta_{>k}\exp\Big\{ -\frac{2(2p_e^+ - 1)^2 R^2}{4R} \Big\} \\
&\quad + \theta_{\leq k}\exp\Big\{ -\frac{2(2p_e^- - 1)^2 R^2}{4R} \Big\} \\
&\leq \exp\{-R/8\} \text{ ,}
\end{aligned}
$$

where we used the fact that $p_e^+ \leq 1/4$ and $p_e^- \leq 1/4$.

For each task i, if we did not make any errors in the $K - 1$ binary estimations, than we correctly recover the true answer to this task as per rule (4). This happens with probability at least $1 - Ke^{-R/8}$, which follows from the union bound over $k \in \mathcal{K}$. It follows that the average error probability over all n tasks is also bounded by

$$P_{\mathrm{err}} \leq Ke^{-R/8} \text{ .}$$

Setting $R = 8\log(K/\varepsilon)$, the average error probability is guaranteed to be less than ε for any $\varepsilon \in (0, 1/2)$. This finishes the proof of Theorem 2.1.

Now we are left to prove that error probabilities on a single dataset are bounded by $1/4$. Recall that $t_i^k = -1$ if $t_i \leq k$, and $+1$ if $t_i > k$. Given a single dataset $A(r)$, we 'quantize' this matrix to get $A^k(r)$ as defined in (5). Then we multiply this matrix on the left by a projection L defined in (6), and let $B^k(r) = LA^k(r)$ be the resulting matrix. We use the top left singular vector of this matrix $B^k(r)$, to get an estimate of t_i^k as defined in (7). This can be formulated as a general binary estimation problem with heterogeneous error model as follows: when $t_i^k = +1$, the 'quantized' answer of a worker is $+1$ if actual answer is greater than k. This happens with probability

$$
\begin{aligned}
&\mathbb{P}(\text{'quantized' answer} = +1 | t_i^k = +1) \\
&= \sum_{\ell > k} \mathbb{P}(\text{'actual' answer} = \ell | t_i^k = +1) \\
&= \sum_{\ell, \ell' > k} \mathbb{P}(\text{'actual' answer} = \ell, \ t_i = \ell' | t_i^k = +1) \\
&= \sum_{\ell, \ell' > k} \pi_{\ell' \ell} \frac{\theta_{\ell'}}{\theta_{>k}} \equiv p_k^+. \quad (9)
\end{aligned}
$$

Similarly, when $t_i^k = -1$,

$$
\begin{aligned}
&\mathbb{P}(\text{'quantized' answer} = -1 | t_i^k = -1) \\
&= \sum_{\ell, \ell' \leq k} \pi_{\ell' \ell} \frac{\theta_{\ell'}}{1 - \theta_{>k}} \equiv p_k^-. \quad (10)
\end{aligned}
$$

Thus, the probability of receiving correct answer for such binary tasks (i.e. $> k$ or $\leq k$) depends on whether the true answer is $+1$ (i.e. $> k$) or -1 (i.e. $\leq k$) and they are p_k^+ and

p_k^- respectively. In the prior works [13, 17, 19], the binary task model considers a setting where $p_k^+ = p_k^-$. In that sense, in this paper, we shall extend the results for binary tasks when p_k^+ need not be equal to p_k^-.

For such problem of tasks with binary answers with heterogeneous probability of correct answers, the following lemma provides an upper bound on the probability of error (technically, this is the key contribution of this work).

LEMMA 3.1. *There exists positive numerical constants C and C' such that*

$$\frac{1}{n} \sum_{i=1}^{n} \mathbb{I}\big(\hat{t}_i^k(r) \neq t_i^k \big) \leq \frac{C}{\ell q_k (1 - |\bar{s}^k|)^2} \quad (11)$$

with probability at least $1 - 2e^{-n(1-|\bar{s}^k|)^2/8} - e^{-q_k^2 n/2} - n^{-C'\sqrt{\ell}}$ where $\bar{s}^k$ and q_k are parameters defined earlier. The probability is over all the realization of the random graphs, the answers submitted by the workers, worker confusion matrices, and the true answers to the tasks.

Since $q \equiv \min_k q_k$ and $\bar{s} = \max_k |\bar{s}^k|$, with our choice of $\ell = \Omega(1/(q(1 - \bar{s})^3))$ and for n large enough (dependent on $q, |\bar{s}|$ and ε), we can guarantee that the probability of error is upper bounded by:

$$\frac{1}{n} \sum_{i=1}^{n} \mathbb{P}\big(\hat{t}_i^k(r) \neq t_i^k \big) \leq \frac{1 - |\bar{s}^k|}{8} . \quad (12)$$

By the symmetry of the problem, the probability of error for all the positive tasks are the same and the error probability for all the negative tasks are also the same. Let p_e^+ and p_e^- denote these error probability for positive and negative tasks respectively. Then p_e^+ cannot be larger than $1/4$, since even if we make no mistake on the negative tasks, there are $(1/2)(1 + \bar{s}^k)n$ positive tasks with equal probability of error. From the upper bound on average error probability in (12), we get that $p_e^+(1/2)(1 + \bar{s}^k) \leq (1 - |\bar{s}^k|)/8$. Since $1 - |\bar{s}^k| \leq 1 + \bar{s}^k$, this implies that $p_e^+ \leq 1/4$. Similarly, we can also show that $p_e^- \leq 1/4$.

3.2 Proof of lemma 3.1

A rank-1 approximation of our data matrix $B^k(r) = LA^k(r)$ can be easily computed using singular value decomposition (SVD). Let the singular value decomposition of $B^k(r)$ be

$$B^k(r) = \sum_{i=1}^{n} u^{(i)} \sigma_i (v^{(i)})^T ,$$

where $u^{(i)} \in \mathbb{R}^n$ and $v^{(i)} \in \mathbb{R}^n$ are the i-th left and right singular vectors, and $\sigma_i \in \mathbb{R}$ is the i-th singular value. Here and after, $(\cdot)^T$ denotes the transpose of a matrix or a vector. For simplicity, we use $u = u^{(1)}$ for the first left singular vector and $v = v^{(1)}$ for the first right singular vector. Singular values are typically assumed to be sorted in a nonincreasing order satisfying $\sigma_1 \geq \sigma_2 \geq \cdots \geq 0$. Then, the optimal rank-1 approximation is given by a rank-1 projector $\mathcal{P}_1(\cdot) : \mathbb{R}^{m \times n} \to \mathbb{R}^{m \times n}$ such that

$$\mathcal{P}_1(B^k(r)) = \sigma_1 uv^T , \quad (13)$$

It is a well known fact that $\mathcal{P}_1(B^k(r))$ minimizes the mean squared error. In formula,

$$\mathcal{P}_1(B^k(r)) = \arg \min_{X:rank(X) \leq 1} \sum_{i,j} (B^k(r)_{ij} - X_{ij})^2$$

Let $\pi^{(j)}$ be a $K \times K$ confusion matrix for worker $j \in \{1, \ldots, n\}$. In this section, we use p^+ to denote the n-dimensional vector such that p_j^+ is the probability that worker j makes an error on a positive task: $p_j^+ = \sum_{a>k,b\leq k} \pi_{ab}^{(j)}$. Similarly, we let $p_j^- = \sum_{a\leq k,b>k} \pi_{ab}^{(j)}$. We use $t^k = [t_i^k] \in \{-1, +1\}^n$ to denote the n-dimensional vector of true answers.

Recall that conditioned on a given vectors p^+, p^-, and a true answer vector t^k, the conditional expectation of the responses results in a matrix

$$\mathbb{E}[A^k(r)|t^k, p^+, p^-] = $$
$$\frac{\ell}{n} t^k (p^+ + p^- - \mathbf{1}_n)^T + \frac{\ell}{n} \mathbf{1}_n (p^+ + p^-)^T .$$

Since this is a sum of two rank-1 matrices, the rank of the conditional expectation is at most two. One way to recover vector t^k from this expectation is to apply a projection that eliminates the contributions from the second term, which gives

$$\mathbb{E}[LA^k(r)|t^k, p^+, p^-] = \frac{\ell}{n}(t^k - \bar{t}^k \mathbf{1}_n)(p^+ + p^- - \mathbf{1}_n)^T , \quad (14)$$

where $L = \mathbf{I} - (1/n)\mathbf{1}_n \mathbf{1}_n^T$, $\bar{t}^k = (1/n)\sum_i t_i^k$, and we used the fact that $L\mathbf{1}_n = 0$. In the following, we will prove that when $A^k(r)$ is close to its expectation $\mathbb{E}[A^k(r)]$ in an appropriate spectral distance, then the top left singular vector of $LA^k(r)$ provides us a good estimate for t^k.

Let u be the left singular vector of $LA^k(r)$ corresponding to the leading singular value. Ideally, we want to track each entry u_i for most realizations of the random matrix $A^k(r)$, which is difficult. Instead, our strategy is to upper bound the spectral radius of $L(A^k(r) - \mathbb{E}[A^k(r)|t^k, p^+, p^-])$, and use it to upper bound the Euclidean distance between the left top singular vectors of those two matrices: u and $(1/\|t^k - \bar{t}^k \mathbf{1}\|)(t^k - \bar{t}^k \mathbf{1})$. Once we have this, we can related the average number of errors to the Euclidean distance between two singular vectors using the following series of inequalities:

$$\frac{1}{n} \sum_i \mathbb{I}(t_i^k \neq \text{sign}(u_i)) \leq \frac{1}{n} \sum_i \mathbb{I}(t_i^k u_i \leq 0)$$
$$\leq \frac{1}{n} \sum_i \left(\frac{1 + |\bar{t}^k|}{1 - |\bar{t}^k|}\right) \left(\sqrt{n} u_i - \frac{t_i^k - \bar{t}^k}{\sqrt{1 - (\bar{t}^k)^2}}\right)^2$$
$$= \left(\frac{1 + |\bar{t}^k|}{1 - |\bar{t}^k|}\right) \left\| u - \frac{t^k - \bar{t}^k \mathbf{1}}{\|t^k - \bar{t}^k \mathbf{1}\|} \right\|^2 , \quad (15)$$

where we used the fact that $\|t^k - \bar{t}^k \mathbf{1}\| = \sqrt{n(1 - (\bar{t}^k)^2)}$ which follows from the definition $\bar{t}^k = (1/n)\sum_i t_i^k$.

To upper bound the Euclidean distance in (15), we apply the next lemma to two rank-1 matrices: $\mathcal{P}_1(LA^k(r))$ and $\mathbb{E}[LA^k(r)|t^k, p^+ p^-]$ where $\mathcal{P}_1(LA^k(r))$ is the best rank-1 approximation of the matrix $LA^k(r)$. This lemma states that if two rank-1 matrices are close in Frobenius norm, then the top singular vectors are also close in the Euclidean distance. For the proof of this lemma, we refer Section 3.3.

LEMMA 3.2. *For two rank-1 matrices with singular value decomposition $M = x\sigma y^T$ and $M' = x'\sigma'(y')^T$, we have*

$$\min \{ \|x + x'\| , \|x - x'\| \} \leq \frac{\sqrt{2} \|M - M'\|_F}{\max\{\sigma, \sigma'\}} ,$$

where $\|x\| = \sqrt{\sum_i x_i^2}$ denotes the Euclidean norm and $\|X\|_F = \sqrt{\sum_{i,j}(X_{ij})^2}$ denotes the Frobenius norm.

Define a random variable $\mathbf{q} = (1/n)\sum_{j=1}^n (p_j^+ + p_j^- - 1)^2$ such that $\mathbb{E}[\mathbf{q}] = q_k$. Then, the conditional expectation matrix $\mathbb{E}[LA^k(r)|t^k, p^+, p^-]$ has top singular value of

$$\frac{\ell}{n}\|t^k - \bar{t}^k \mathbf{1}\|\|p^+ + p^- - \mathbf{1}\| = \frac{\ell}{n}\sqrt{n(1-(\bar{t}^k)^2)}\sqrt{n\mathbf{q}}$$
$$= \sqrt{\ell^2 \mathbf{q}(1-(\bar{t}^k)^2)}$$

and the corresponding left and right singular vectors are $(1/\|t^k - \bar{t}^k \mathbf{1}\|)(t^k - \bar{t}^k \mathbf{1})$ and $(1/\|p^+ + p^- - \mathbf{1}\|)(p^+ + p^- - \mathbf{1})$. Before we apply the above lemma to this matrix together with $\mathcal{P}_1(LA^k(r))$, notice that we have two choices for the left singular vector. Both u and $-u$ are valid singular vectors of $\mathcal{P}_1(LA^k(r))$ and we do not know a priori which one is closer to $(t^k - \bar{t}^k \mathbf{1})$. For now, let us assume that u is the one closer to the correct solution, such that $\|u - (1/\|t^k - \bar{t}^k \mathbf{1}\|)(t^k - \bar{t}^k \mathbf{1})\| \le \|u + (1/\|t^k - \bar{t}^k \mathbf{1}\|)(t^k - \bar{t}^k \mathbf{1})\|$. Later in this section, we will explain how we can identify u with high probability of success. Then, from Lemma 3.2, we get

$$\left\| \frac{1}{\|t^k - \bar{t}^k \mathbf{1}\|}(t^k - \bar{t}^k \mathbf{1}) - u \right\| \le \qquad (16)$$

$$\sqrt{\frac{2}{\ell^2 \mathbf{q}(1-(\bar{t}^k)^2)}}\left\| \mathbb{E}[LA^k(r)|t^k, p^+, p^-] - \mathcal{P}_1(LA^k(r)) \right\|_F.$$

In the following we will prove that the Frobenius norm of the difference $\|\mathbb{E}[LA^k(r)|t^k, p^+, p^-] - \mathcal{P}_1(LA^k(r))\|_F$ is upper bounded by $C\sqrt{\ell}$ with probability at least $1 - n^{-C'\sqrt{\ell}}$ for some positive constants C and C'. Together with (16) and (15), this implies

$$\frac{1}{n}\sum_{i=1}^n \mathbb{I}(t^k)i \ne \mathrm{sign}(u_i)) \le \frac{C}{\ell\mathbf{q}(1-|\bar{t}^k|)^2}.$$

Next, we use standard concentration inequalities to relate random quantities $\mathbf{q}$ and $\bar{t}^k$ to q_k and $\bar{s}^k$. By standard concentration results, we know that

$$\mathbb{P}\big(\mathbf{q} - q_k < -q_k/2\big) \le e^{-q_k^2 n/2}.$$

Hence, with probability at least $1 - e^{-q_k^2 n/2}$, we have $\mathbf{q} \ge q/2$. Similarly, for $\bar{t}^k = (1/n)\sum_i t_i^k$, and assuming without loss of generality that $\bar{s}^k = 2\theta_{>k} - 1$ is positive,

$$\mathbb{P}\big(1 - |\bar{t}^k| < (1/2)(1-\bar{s}^k)\big) = \mathbb{P}\big(|\frac{1}{n}\sum_i t_i^k| > (1/2)(1+|\bar{s}^k|)\big)$$
$$\le 2e^{-n(1-\bar{s}^k)^2/8}.$$

Hence, it follows that with probability at least $1 - 2e^{-n(1-\bar{s}^k)^2/8} - e^{-q_k^2 n/2} - n^{-C'\sqrt{\ell}}$,

$$\frac{1}{n}\sum_{i=1}^n \mathbb{I}(t^k)i \ne \mathrm{sign}(u_i)) \le \frac{C}{\ell q_k(1-|\bar{s}^k|)^2}.$$

This proves Lemma 3.1.

Now, we are left to prove an upper bound on the Frobenius norm in (16). Notice that for any matrix X of rank-2, $\|X\|_F \le \sqrt{2}\|X\|_2$, where $\|X\|_2 \equiv \max_{\|x\|,\|y\| \le 1} x^T X y$ de-

notes the operator norm. Therefore, by triangular inequity,

$$\|\mathbb{E}[LA^k(r)|t^k, p^+, p^-] - \mathcal{P}_1(LA^k(r))\|_F$$
$$\le \sqrt{2}\|\mathbb{E}[LA^k(r)|t^k, p^+ p^-] - \mathcal{P}_1(LA^k(r))\|_2$$
$$\le \sqrt{2}\|\mathbb{E}[LA^k(r)|t^k, p^+, p^-] - LA^k(r)\|_2$$
$$+ \sqrt{2}\|LA^k(r) - \mathcal{P}_1(LA^k(r))\|_2$$
$$\le 2\sqrt{2}\|\mathbb{E}[LA^k(r)|t^k, p^+, p^-] - LA^k(r)\|_2$$
$$\le 2\sqrt{2}\|\mathbb{E}[A^k(r)|t^k, p^+, p^-] - A^k(r)\|_2, \qquad (17)$$

where in the last inequity we used the fact that $\mathcal{P}_1(LA^k(r))$ is the minimizer of $\|LA^k(r) - X\|_2$ among all matrices X of rank one, whence $\|LA^k(r) - \mathcal{P}_1(LA^k(r))\|_2 \le \|LA^k(r) - \mathbb{E}[LA^k(r)|t^k, p^+, p^-]\|_2$.

The following key technical lemma provides a bound on the operator norm of the difference between random matrix $A^k(r)$ and its (conditional) expectation. This lemma generalizes a celebrated bound on the second largest eigenvalue of d-regular random graphs by Friedman-Kahn-Szemerédi [12, 11, 20]. The proof of this lemma is provided in Section 3.4.

LEMMA 3.3. *Assume that an (ℓ, ℓ)-regular random bipartite graph G with n left and right nodes is generated according to the configuration model. $A^k(r)$ is the weighted adjacency matrix of G with random weight $A^k(r)_{ij}$ assigned to each edge $(i,j) \in E$. With probability at least $1 - n^{-\Omega(\sqrt{\ell})}$,*

$$\|A^k(r) - \mathbb{E}[A^k(r)|t^k, p^+, p^-]\|_2 \le C' A_{\max}\sqrt{\ell}, \quad (18)$$

for all realizations of t^k, p^+, and p^-, where $|A^k(r)_{ij}| \le A_{\max}$ almost surely and C' is a universal constant.

Under our model, $A_{\max} = 1$ since $A^k(r)_{ij} \in \{\pm 1\}$. We then apply this lemma to each realization of p^+ and p^- and substitute this bound in (17). Together with (16) and (15), this finishes the proof Lemma 3.1.

Now, we are left to prove that between u and $-u$, we can determine which one is closer to $(1/\|t^k - \bar{t}^k \mathbf{1}\|)(t^k - \bar{t}^k \mathbf{1})$. Given a rank-1 matrix $\mathcal{P}_1(LA^k(r))$, there are two possible pairs of left and right 'normalized' singular vectors: (u, v) and $(-u, -v)$. Let $\mathcal{P}_+(\cdot) : \mathbb{R}^n \mapsto \mathbb{R}^n$ denote the projection onto the positive orthant such that $\mathcal{P}_+(v)_i = \mathbb{I}(v_i \ge 0)v_i$. Our strategy is to choose u to be our estimate if $\|\mathcal{P}_+(v)\|^2 \ge 1/2$ (and $-u$ otherwise). We claim that with high probability the pair (u, v) chosen according to our strategy satisfies

$$\left\| \frac{1}{\|t^k - \bar{t}^k \mathbf{1}\|}(t^k - \bar{t}^k \mathbf{1}) - u \right\| \le \left\| \frac{1}{\|t^k - \bar{t}^k \mathbf{1}\|}(t^k - \bar{t}^k \mathbf{1}) + u \right\|. (19)$$

Assume that the pair (u, v) is the one satisfying the above inequality. Denote the singular vectors of $\mathbb{E}[A^k(r)|t^k, p^+, p^-]$ by $x = (1/\|t^k - \bar{t}^k \mathbf{1}\|)(t^k - \bar{t}^k \mathbf{1})$ and $y = (1/\|p^+ + p^- - \mathbf{1}_n\|)(p^+ + p^- - \mathbf{1}_n)$, and singular value $\sigma' = \|\mathbb{E}[A^k(r)|t^k, p^+, p^-]\|_2$. Let $\sigma = \|\mathcal{P}_1(A^k(r))\|_2$. Then, by triangular inequality,

$$\|y - v\| = \left\| \frac{1}{\sigma'}\mathbb{E}[A^k(r)|t^k, p^+, p^-]^T x - \frac{1}{\sigma}\mathcal{P}_1(A^k(r))^T u \right\|$$
$$\le \left\| \frac{1}{\sigma'}\mathbb{E}[A^k(r)|t^k, p^+, p^-]^T(x - u) \right\|$$
$$+ \left\| \frac{1}{\sigma'}(\mathbb{E}[A^k(r)|t^k, p^+, p^-] - \mathcal{P}_1(A^k(r)))^T u \right\|$$
$$+ \left\| \left(\frac{1}{\sigma'} - \frac{1}{\sigma}\right)\mathcal{P}_1(A^k(r))^T u \right\|$$
$$\le \frac{C_1}{\sqrt{\ell\mathbf{q}(1-(\bar{t}^k)^2)}}.$$

The first term in the second line is upper bounded by

$$\|(1/\sigma')\mathbb{E}[A^k(r)|t^k,p^+,p^-]^T(x-u)\| \leq \|x-u\|\,,$$

which is again upper bounded by $C_2/(\ell q_k(1-(\bar{t}^k)^2))^{1/2}$ using (16). The second term is upper bounded by

$$\|(1/\sigma')(\mathbb{E}[A^k(r)|t^k,p^+,p^-] - \mathcal{P}_1(A^k(r)))^T u\|$$
$$\leq (1/\sigma')\|\mathbb{E}[A^k(r)|t^k,p^+,p^-] - \mathcal{P}_1(A^k(r))\|_2\,,$$

which is again upper bounded by $C_3/(\ell q_k(1-(\bar{t}^k)^2))^{1/2}$ using (18) and $\sigma' \geq \sqrt{(1/2)\ell^2 q_k(1-(\bar{t}^k)^2)}$. The third term is upper bounded by $\|\left(\frac{1}{\sigma'} - \frac{1}{\sigma}\right)\mathcal{P}_1(A^k(r))^T u\| \leq |\sigma - \sigma'|/\sigma'$, which is again upper bounded by $C_4/(\ell q_k(1-(\bar{t}^k)^2))^{1/2}$ using the following triangular inequality:

$$\frac{1}{\sigma'}\left|\|\mathbb{E}[A^k(r)|t^k,p^+,p^-]\|_2 - \|\mathcal{P}_1(A^k(r))\|_2\right|$$
$$\leq \frac{1}{\sigma'}\|\mathbb{E}[A^k(r)|t^k,p^+,p^-] - \mathcal{P}_1(A^k(r))\|_2\,.$$

Since we assume that $p_j^+ + p_j^- \geq 1$, we have $y_j = p_j^+ + p_j^- - 1 \geq 0$ for all j. It follows that $\|y-\mathcal{P}_+(v)\| \leq \|y-v\|$ for any vector v. This implies that

$$\|\mathcal{P}_+(v)\| \geq \|y\| - \|y-\mathcal{P}_+(v)\|$$
$$\geq 1 - \|y-v\|$$
$$\geq 1 - \frac{C_1}{(\ell q(1-(\bar{t}^k)^2))^{1/2}}\,.$$

Notice that we can increase the constant C in the bound (11) of the main theorem such that we only need to restrict our attention to $(\ell q(1-(\bar{t}^k)^2))^{1/2} > 4C_1$. This proves that the pair (u,v) chosen according to our strategy satisfy (19), which is all we need in order to prove Lemma 3.1.

3.3 Proof of Lemma 3.2

A more general statement for general low-rank matrices is proved in [20, Remark 6.3]. Here we provide a proof of a special case when both matrices have rank one. For two rank-1 matrices with singular value decomposition $M = x\sigma y^T$ and $M' = x'\sigma'(y')^T$, we want to upper bound $\min\{\|x+x'\|, \|x-x'\|\}$. Define the angle between the two vectors to be $\theta = \arccos(|x^Tx'|)$ such that $\min\{\|x+x'\|, \|x-x'\|\} = 2\sin(\theta/2)$ and $\min_a \|x-ax'\| = \sin\theta$. It follows from $2\sin(\theta/2) = (1/\cos(\theta/2))\sin\theta \leq \sqrt{2}\sin\theta$ for all $\theta \in [0,(1/2)\pi]$ that

$$\min\{\|x+x'\|, \|x-x'\|\} \leq \sqrt{2}\min_a\|x-ax'\|\,.$$

Define the inner product of two vectors or matrices as $\langle A,B\rangle =$

$\mathrm{Trace}(A^T B)$. We take $a^* = (\sigma'/\sigma)y^T y'$. Then,

$$\min\{\|x+x'\|, \|x-x'\|\} \leq \sqrt{2}\|x-a^*x'\|$$
$$\leq \max_{u\in\mathbb{R}^n,\|u\|\leq 1}\sqrt{2}\langle u,x-a^*x'\rangle$$
$$\leq \max_{u\in\mathbb{R}^n,\|u\|\leq 1}\sqrt{2}\langle u,x-(\sigma'/\sigma)y^T y'x'\rangle$$
$$\leq \max_{u\in\mathbb{R}^n,\|u\|\leq 1}\sqrt{2}\langle u,(1/\sigma)(\sigma xy^T - \sigma'x'(y')^T)y\rangle$$
$$\leq \max_{u\in\mathbb{R}^n,\|u\|\leq 1}(\sqrt{2}/\sigma)\langle uy^T,\sigma xy^T - \sigma'x'(y')^T\rangle$$
$$\leq \max_{u\in\mathbb{R}^n,\|u\|\leq 1}(\sqrt{2}/\sigma)\|uy^T\|_F\|M-M'\|_F$$
$$\leq \frac{\sqrt{2}\|M-M'\|_F}{\sigma}\,.$$

By symmetry, the same inequality holds with σ' in the denominator. This proves the desired claim.

3.4 Proof of Lemma 3.3

Since the proof does not depend on the specific realizations of t^k, p^+, and p^-, we will drop the conditions on these variables in this section and write $\mathbb{E}[A^k(r)]$ for $\mathbb{E}[A^k(r)|t^k,p^+,p^-]$. Define an ℓ_2-ball $\mathcal{B}_n \equiv \{x\in\mathbb{R}^n : \|x\|\leq 1\}$ in n-dimensions. We want to show that, with high probability,

$$|x^T(A^k(r) - \mathbb{E}[A^k(r)])y| \leq C'A_{\max}\sqrt{\ell}\,, \qquad (20)$$

for all $x\in\mathcal{B}_n$ and $y\in\mathcal{B}_n$. The technical challenge is that the left-hand side of (20) is a random variable indexed by x and y each belonging to a set with infinite number of elements. Our strategy, which is inspired by [12] and is similar to the techniques used in [11, 20], is as follows:
(i) Reduce x, y belonging to a finite discrete set $\mathcal{T}_n$;
(ii) Bound the contribution of *light couples* using concentration of measure result on a random variable

$$Z \equiv \sum_{(i,j)\in\mathcal{L}} x_i A^k(r)_{ij}y_j - x^T\mathbb{E}[A^k(r)]y$$

and applying union bound over (exponentially many but finite) choices of x and y;
(iii) Bound the contribution of *heavy couples* using *discrepancy property* of the random graph G.
The definitions of *light* and *heavy couples* and *discrepancy property* is provided later in this section.
Discretization. Fix some $\Delta \in (0,1)$ and define a discretization of $\mathcal{B}_n$ as

$$\mathcal{T}_n \equiv \left\{x\in\left\{\frac{\Delta}{\sqrt{n}}\mathbb{Z}\right\}^n : \|x\|\leq 1\right\}\,.$$

Next proposition allows us to restrict our attention to discretized x and y and is proved in [12, 11].

PROPOSITION 3.4. *Let $M\in\mathbb{R}^{n\times n}$ be a matrix. If $|x^TMy| \leq B$ for all $x\in\mathcal{T}_n$ and $y\in\mathcal{T}_n$, then $|x'^TMy'| \leq (1-\Delta)^{-2}B$ for all $x'\in\mathcal{B}_n$ and $y'\in\mathcal{B}_n$.*

It is thus enough to show that the bound (20) holds with high probability for all $x,y\in\mathcal{T}_n$. A naive approach would be to apply tail bound on the random variable $\sum_{i,j} x_i(A^k(r)_{ij} - \mathbb{E}[A^k(r)_{ij}])y_j$. However, this approach fails when x or y have entries of value much larger than the typical size $O(n^{-1/2})$. Hence, we need to separate the contribution into two parts.

Define a set of *light couples* $\mathcal{L} \subseteq [n] \times [n]$ as

$$\mathcal{L} \equiv \left\{ (i,j) : |x_i y_j| \leq \frac{\sqrt{\ell}}{n} \right\},$$

and the set of heavy couples $\overline{\mathcal{L}}$ as its complement. Using this definition, we can separate the contribution from light and heavy couples.

$$\left| x^T(A^k(r) - \mathbb{E}[A^k(r)])y \right| \leq$$

$$\left| \sum_{(i,j) \in \mathcal{L}} x_i A^k(r)_{ij} y_j - x^T \mathbb{E}[A^k(r)]y \right| + \left| \sum_{(i,a) \in \overline{\mathcal{L}}} x_i A^k(r)_{ij} y_j \right|.$$

In the following, we prove that both of these contributions are upper bounded by $(C'/2)A_{\max}\sqrt{\ell}$ for all $x, y \in \mathcal{T}_n$. By Proposition 3.4, this finishes the proof of Lemma 3.3.

Bounding the contribution of light couples. Let $\mathbf{Z} = \sum_{(i,j) \in \mathcal{L}} x_i A^k(r)_{ij} y_j - x^T \mathbb{E}[A^k(r)]y$. Using the fact that $\mathbb{E}[\mathbf{Z}] = -\sum_{(i,j) \in \overline{\mathcal{L}}} x_i \mathbb{E}[A^k(r)_{ij}]y_j$, we get

$$\begin{aligned}
|\mathbb{E}[\mathbf{Z}]| &\leq \sum_{(i,j) \in \overline{\mathcal{L}}} \frac{|\mathbb{E}[A^k(r)_{ij}]|(x_i y_j)^2}{|x_i y_j|} \\
&\leq \frac{n}{\sqrt{\ell}} \max_{i,j} |\mathbb{E}[A^k(r)_{ij}]| \leq A_{\max}\sqrt{\ell}, \quad (21)
\end{aligned}$$

where, in the second inequality, we used $|x_i y_j| \geq \sqrt{\ell}/n$ for any $(i,j) \in \overline{\mathcal{L}}$, and the last inequality follows from the fact that $|\mathbb{E}[A^k(r)_{ij}]|$ is at most $(\ell/n)A_{\max}$. Together with the next lemma, this implies that when restricted to the discretized sets $\mathcal{T}_n$, the contribution of light couples is bounded by $C_5 A_{\max}\sqrt{\ell}$ with high probability.

LEMMA 3.5. *There exists numerical constants C_6 and C_7 such that, for any $x \in \mathcal{T}_n$ and $y \in \mathcal{T}_n$,*

$$\mathbb{P}\left(|\mathbf{Z} - \mathbb{E}[\mathbf{Z}]| > C_6 A_{\max}\sqrt{\ell} \right) \leq e^{-C_7 n}.$$

If the edges were selected independently, this lemma can be proved using routine tail bounds. In the case of (l,r)-regular graphs, we can use a martingale construction known as Doob's martingale process [25]. The proof follows closely the technique used in the proof of [12, Lemma 2.4], where an analogous statement is proved for unweighted non-bipartite random d-regular graphs. For the proof of this lemma, we refer to a journal version of this paper.

Cardinality of the discrete set $\mathcal{T}_n$ can be bounded using a simple volume argument: $|\mathcal{T}_n| \leq (10/\Delta)^n$ [11]. In Lemma 3.5, we can choose a large enough C_6 such that $C_7 > 2\log(10/\Delta)$. Applying union bound over all $x, y \in \mathcal{T}_n$, this proves that the contribution of light couples is bounded by $C_5 A_{\max}\sqrt{\ell}$ uniformly for all $x, y \in \mathcal{T}_n$ with probability $1 - e^{-\Omega(n)}$.

Bounding the contribution of heavy couples. Let $Q \in \{0,1\}^{m \times n}$ denote the standard (unweighted) adjacency matrix corresponding to the bipartite graph G. Then,

$$\left| \sum_{(i,j) \in \overline{\mathcal{L}}} x_i A_{ij} y_j \right| \leq A_{\max}\left(\sum_{(i,j) \in \overline{\mathcal{L}}} Q_{ij}|x_i y_j| \right). \quad (22)$$

We can upper bound the right-hand side using discrepancy property of random graphs. It is a well-known result in

graph theory that a random graph does not contain an unexpectedly dense subgraph with high probability. This discrepancy property plays an important role in the proof of structural properties such as expansion and spectrum of random graphs.

- *Bounded discrepancy.* We say that G (equivalently, the adjacency matrix Q) has bounded discrepancy property if, for any pair $L \subseteq [n]$ and $R \subseteq [n]$, (at least) one of the following is true. Here, $e(L,R) = |\{(i,j) \in E : i \in L, j \in R\}|$ denotes the number of edges between a subset L of left nodes and a subset R of right nodes, and $\mu(L,R) \equiv |L||R||E|/n^2$ denotes the average number of edges between L and R.

  (i) $e(L,R) \leq C_1 \mu(L,R)$,

  (ii) $|L|, |R|,$ and $e(L,R)$ are all at most $C_2\sqrt{\ell}$,

  (iii) $e(L,R) \log\left(\frac{e(L,R)}{\mu(L,R)} \right)$
  $$\leq C_3 \max\{|L|, |R|\} \log\left(\frac{n}{\max\{|L|, |R|\}} \right),$$

  for some constants C_1, C_2, and C_3 which only depend on m/n.

- *Bounded degree.* The graph G has degree of the left nodes bounded by ℓ and the right nodes also by ℓ.

For a random (ℓ, ℓ)-regular graph G, the bounded degree property is always satisfied. Next lemma shows that G also satisfies the discrepancy property [12, Lemma 2.5].

LEMMA 3.6. *For an (ℓ, ℓ)-regular random graph G, with probability $1 - n^{\Omega(\sqrt{\ell})}$, every pair $L \subseteq [n]$ and $R \subseteq [n]$ satisfies the bounded discrepancy property.*

Together with (22) and Lemma 3.6, the next lemma implies that the contribution of heavy couples is upper bounded by $C_4 A_{\max}\sqrt{\ell}$ with probability $1 - n^{\Omega(\sqrt{\ell})}$.

LEMMA 3.7. *If a bipartite graph G satisfies the bounded degree and bounded discrepancy properties, then there exists a positive constant C_4 such that for any $x, y \in \mathcal{T}_n$ the adjacency matrix Q satisfy*

$$\sum_{(i,j) \in \overline{\mathcal{L}}} |x_i Q_{ij} y_j| \leq C_4\sqrt{\ell}.$$

A similar statement was proved in [20, Remark 4.5] for Erdős-Renyi graph. Due to a space constraint, the proof is omitted here.

3.5 Proof of Theorem 2.2

The proof follows closely the techniques we used in proving Theorem 2.1. In fact, the only difference is in the following key technical lemma. This lemma improves the upper bound in Lemma 3.1 by a factor of $(1 - |\bar{s}^k|)^2$. Once we have this, we can use the same arguments as in Section 3.1 to get the improved bound on error probability as in Theorem 2.2.

LEMMA 3.8. *There exists positive numerical constants C and C' such that the estimates of (8) achieve*

$$\frac{1}{n}\sum_{i=1}^{n} \mathbb{I}\left(\hat{t}_i^k(r) \neq t_i^k \right) \leq \frac{C}{\ell q_k} \quad (23)$$

with probability at least $1 - 2e^{-n(1 - |\bar{s}^k|)^2/8} - e^{-q_k^2 n/2} - n^{-C'\sqrt{\ell}}$ where $\bar{s}^k$ and q_k are parameters defined earlier.

PROOF. In proving Theorem 2.1, we are using the left singular vectors of $A^k(r)$, which we denote by $u^k(r)$. Assuming for simplicity that $\sum_{j:v_j^k(r)\geq 0}(v_j^k(r))^2 \geq 1/2$, we make a decision on whether t_i^k is more likely to be a positive task or a negative task based on whether $u^k(r)_i$ is positive or negative: $\hat{t}^k(r)_i = \text{sign}(u^k(r)_i)$. Effectively, we are using a *threshold* of zero to classify the tasks using $u^k(r)_i$ as a noisy observation of that task.

If we have a good estimate of $\bar{s}^k$, we can use it to get a better threshold of $-\bar{s}^k/\sqrt{(1-(\bar{s}^k)^2)n}$. This gives a new decision rule of (8): $\hat{t}^k(r)_i = \text{sign}\big(u^k(r)_i + \frac{\bar{s}^k}{\sqrt{(1-(\bar{s}^k)^2)n}}\big)$, when $\sum_{j:v_j^k(r)\geq 0}(v_j^k(r))^2 \geq 1/2$. We can prove that with this new threshold, the bound on the number of errors improve by a factor of $(1-|\bar{s}^k|)^2$. The analysis of follows closely the proof of Lemma 3.1.

Let u be the left singular vector of $LA^k(r)$ corresponding to the leading singular value. From Section 3.2, we know that the Euclidean distance between u and $(1/\|t^k - \bar{t}^k\mathbf{1}\|)(t^k - \bar{t}^k\mathbf{1})$ is upper bounded by $\sqrt{C/(\ell q_k(1-(\bar{t}^k)^2))}$. We can use the following series of inequalities to related this bound to the average number of errors. From $\|t^k - \bar{t}^k\mathbf{1}\| = \sqrt{n(1-(\bar{t}^k)^2)}$ which follows from the definition of $\bar{t}^k = (1/n)\sum_i t_i^k$, we have

$$\frac{1}{n}\sum_i \mathbb{I}\Big(t_i^k \neq \text{sign}\big(u_i + \frac{\bar{t}^k}{\sqrt{(1-(\bar{t}^k)^2)n}}\big)\Big)$$
$$\leq \frac{1}{n}\sum_i \mathbb{I}\Big(t_i^k\big(u_i + \frac{\bar{t}^k}{\sqrt{(1-(\bar{t}^k)^2)n}}\big) \leq 0\Big)$$
$$\leq \frac{1}{n}\sum_i \big(1-(\bar{t}^k)^2\big)\Big(\sqrt{n}u_i - \frac{t_i^k - \bar{t}^k}{\sqrt{1-(\bar{t}^k)^2}}\Big)^2$$
$$= \big(1-(\bar{t}^k)^2\big)\Big\|u - \frac{t^k - \bar{t}^k\mathbf{1}}{\|t^k - \bar{t}^k\mathbf{1}\|}\Big\|^2 \leq \frac{C}{\ell q_k}.$$

$\square$

3.6 Proof of Theorem 2.3

Let us focus on a dataset $A(r)$ that is collected from n workers, αn of which are are adversarial. Since we assign tasks according to a random graph, the performance does not depend on the indices assigned to particular workers, and hence we let the first αn workers be the adversarial ones. Let $\tilde{A}^k(r) \in \{\text{null}, +1, -1\}^{n\times n}$ be the $n \times n$ matrix of 'quantized' answers when adversaries are present. Define a random matrix $A^k(r)$ to be the answers we would get on the same graph and same set of non-adversarial workers for the last $(1-\alpha)n$ workers but this time replacing all of the adversarial workers with randomly chosen non-adversarial workers with confusion matrix drawn from $\mathcal{D}$. The dataset $A^k(r)$ represent the answers we would get if there were no adversaries. We want to bound the effect of adversaries on our estimate, by bounding difference, in spectral norm, between the random matrix $\tilde{A}^k(r)$ and conditional expectation of non-adversarial answers $\mathbb{E}[A^k(r)|t^k, p_k^+, p_k^-]$. We claim that

$$\big\|\tilde{A}^k(r) - \mathbb{E}[A^k(r)|t^k, p_k^+, p_k^-]\big\|_2 \leq C(\sqrt{\ell} + \ell\sqrt{\alpha}) \quad (24)$$

Once we have this bound, we can finish our analysis following closely the proof of Theorem 2.1. Let u be the top left singular vector of the matrix $\tilde{A}^k(r)$. From Section 3.2, we

know that

$$\frac{1}{n}\sum_{i=1}^n \mathbb{I}(t_i^k \neq \text{sign}(u_i)) \leq \frac{16\big\|\tilde{A}^k(r) - \mathbb{E}[A^k(r)|t^k, p_k^+, p_k^-]\big\|_2^2}{\ell^2 q_k(1-|\bar{s}^k|)^2}$$

Substituting (24) into the above, and using the fact that $(a+b)^2 \leq 2a^2 + 2b^2$, we get

$$\frac{1}{n}\sum_{i=1}^n \mathbb{I}(t_i^k \neq \text{sign}(u_i)) \leq \frac{C(1+\alpha\ell)}{\ell q_k(1-|\bar{s}^k|)^2}.$$

Further, in a similar way as we proved Theorem 2.2, if we have a good estimate of $\bar{s}^k$, then we can find a better threshold as in (8) and improve the upper bound as

$$\frac{1}{n}\sum_{i=1}^n \mathbb{I}\Big(t_i^k \neq \text{sign}\big(u_i + \frac{\bar{t}^k}{\sqrt{(1-(\bar{t}^k)^2)n}}\big)\Big) \leq \frac{C(1+\alpha\ell)}{\ell q_k}.$$

Substituting this bound in Lemma 3.1 from Section 3.1 and following the same argument, this finishes the proof of Theorem 2.3.

Now, we are left to prove the upper bound in (24). Let $\tilde{A}_a^k(r)$ denote the answers from adversarial workers and $\tilde{A}_g^k(r)$ denote the answer from the non-adversarial workers such that $\tilde{A}^k(r) = [\,\tilde{A}_a^k(r)\ \tilde{A}_g^k(r)\,]$. Let $B = \mathbb{E}[A^k(r)|t^k, p_k^+, p_k^-]$ be the conditional expectation of non-adversarial data. We use B_0 to denote the first αn columns of B and B_1 for the last $(1-\alpha)n$ columns of B, such that $B = [\,B_0\ B_1\,]$. By the triangular inequality, we get

$$\big\|\tilde{A}^k(r) - B\big\|_2 = \big\|[\,\tilde{A}_a^k(r)\ \tilde{A}_g^k(r)\,] - [\,B_0\ B_1\,]\big\|_2$$
$$\leq \big\|\tilde{A}_g^k(r) - B_1\big\|_2 + \big\|B_0\big\|_2 + \big\|\tilde{A}_a^k(r)\big\|_2.$$

To upper bounded the first term, notice that it is a projection of a $n \times n$ matrix where the projection P sets the first αn columns to zeros: $\tilde{A}_g^k(r) - B_1 = P(\tilde{A}^k(r) - B)$. Since a projection can only decrease the spectral radius, we have $\big\|\tilde{A}_g^k(r) - B_1\big\|_2 \leq \big\|\tilde{A}^k(r) - B\big\|_2$. From Lemma 3.3 we know that this is upper bounded by $C\sqrt{\ell}$. For the second term, recall that $B_0 = (\ell/n)\mathbf{1}_n\mathbf{1}_{\alpha n}^T$. This gives $\|B_0\|_2 = \ell\sqrt{\alpha}$.

To upper bound the last term, let M_α be an $n \times \alpha n$ matrix that have the same pattern as $\tilde{A}_a^k(r)$, but all the non-zero entries are set to one. Statistically, this is the first αn columns of the adjacency matrix of a random (ℓ, ℓ)-regular graph. Since M_α is a result of taking the absolute value of the matrix $\tilde{A}_a^k(r)$, we have $\big\|\tilde{A}_a^k(r)\big\|_2 \leq \|M_\alpha\|_2$. By triangular inequality, $\|M_\alpha\|_2 \leq \big\|E[M_\alpha]\big\|_2 + \big\|M_\alpha - E[M_\alpha]\big\|_2$. The first term is bounded by $\big\|E[M_\alpha]\big\|_2 = \|B_0\|_2 = \ell\sqrt{\alpha}$. To bound the second term, we use the same technique of projection. Let M be an $n \times n$ adjacency matrix of a random (ℓ, ℓ)-regular graph such that the first αn columns are equal to M_α. Then, $\big\|A_{M_\alpha} - E[M_\alpha]\big\|_2 \leq \|M - \mathbb{E}[M]\|_2$. Friedman, Kahn, and Szemeredie [12] proved that this is upper bounded by $C\sqrt{\ell}$ with probability at least $1 - n^{-C'\ell}$. Collecting all the terms, this proves the upper bound in (24).

4. CONCLUSIONS

In this paper, we considered the question of designing crowd-sourcing platform with the aim of obtaining best trade-off between reliability and redundancy (equivalently, budget). Operationally, this boiled down to developing appropriate task allocation (worker-task assignment) and estimation of task answers from noisy responses of workers. We presented task allocation based on random regular bipartite graph and estimation algorithm based on low-rank approximation of appropriate matrices. We established that the design we have presented achieves (order-)optimal performance for the generic model of crowd-sourcing (cf. model considered by Dawid and Skene [9]).

Ours is the first rigorous result for crowd-sourcing system design for generic K-ary tasks with general noise model. The algorithms presented are entirely data-driven and hence useful for the setting even when the precise probabilistic model is not obeyed.

One limitation of the current model is that the tasks are assumed to be equally difficult. It is of great practical interest to accommodate differences in task difficulties. Our approach exploits low-rank structure inherent in the probabilistic model studied in this paper. However, more general models proposed in crowdsourcing literature lack such low-rank structures, and it is an interesting future research direction to understand the accuracy-redundancy trade-offs for more general class of models.

Acknowledgements

DK is supported in parts by a grant from the National Science Foundation. DS is supported in parts by Army Research Office under MURI Award 58153-MA-MUR.

5. REFERENCES

[1] Casting Words. http://castingwords.com.

[2] Crowd Flower. http://crowdflower.com.

[3] Crowd Spring. http://www.crowdspring.com.

[4] ESP game. http://www.espgame.org.

[5] Soylent. http://projects.csail.mit.edu/soylent/.

[6] M. S. Bernstein, J. Brandt, R. C. Miller, and D. R. Karger. Crowds in two seconds: enabling realtime crowd-powered interfaces. In *Proceedings of the 24th annual ACM symposium on User interface software and technology*, UIST '11, pages 33–42, 2011.

[7] M. S. Bernstein, G. Little, R. C. Miller, B. Hartmann, M. S. Ackerman, D. R. Karger, D. Crowell, and K. Panovich. Soylent: a word processor with a crowd inside. In *Proceedings of the 23nd annual ACM symposium on User interface software and technology*, ACM UIST, pages 313–322, New York, NY, USA, 2010.

[8] B. Bollobás. *Random Graphs*. Cambridge University Press, Jan. 2001.

[9] A. P. Dawid and A. M. Skene. Maximum likelihood estimation of observer error-rates using the em algorithm. *Journal of the Royal Statistical Society. Series C (Applied Statistics)*, 28(1):20–28, 1979.

[10] A. P. Dempster, N. M. Laird, and D. B. Rubin. Maximum likelihood from incomplete data via the em algorithm. *Journal of the Royal Statistical Society. Series B (Methodological)*, 39(1):pp. 1–38, 1977.

[11] U. Feige and E. Ofek. Spectral techniques applied to sparse random graphs. *Random Struct. Algorithms*, 27(2):251–275, 2005.

[12] J. Friedman, J. Kahn, and E. Szemerédi. On the second eigenvalue in random regular graphs. In *Proceedings of the Twenty-First Annual ACM Symposium on Theory of Computing*, pages 587–598, Seattle, Washington, USA, may 1989. ACM.

[13] A. Ghosh, S. Kale, and P. McAfee. Who moderates the moderators?: crowdsourcing abuse detection in user-generated content. In *Proceedings of the 12th ACM conference on Electronic commerce*, pages 167–176. ACM, 2011.

[14] S. Holmes. Crowd counting a crowd. March 2011, Statistics Seminar, Stanford University.

[15] P. G. Ipeirotis, F. Provost, and J. Wang. Quality management on amazon mechanical turk. In *Proceedings of the ACM SIGKDD Workshop on Human Computation*, HCOMP '10, pages 64–67. ACM, 2010.

[16] R. Jin and Z. Ghahramani. Learning with multiple labels. In *Advances in neural information processing systems*, pages 921–928, 2003.

[17] D. R. Karger, S. Oh, and D. Shah. Budget-optimal crowdsourcing using low-rank matrix approximations. In *Proc. of the Allerton Conf. on Commun., Control and Computing*, 2011.

[18] D. R. Karger, S. Oh, and D. Shah. Budget-optimal task allocation for reliable crowd sourcing systems. 2011. http://arxiv.org/abs/1110.3564.

[19] D. R. Karger, S. Oh, and D. Shah. Iterative learning for reliable crowdsourcing systems. In *Advances in neural information processing systems*, pages 1953–1961, 2011.

[20] R. H. Keshavan, A. Montanari, and S. Oh. Matrix completion from a few entries. *IEEE Trans. Inform. Theory*, 56(6):2980–2998, June 2010.

[21] Q. Liu, J. Peng, and A. Ihler. Variational inference for crowdsourcing. In *Advances in Neural Information Processing Systems 25*, pages 701–709, 2012.

[22] V. C. Raykar and S. Yu. Eliminating spammers and ranking annotators for crowdsourced labeling tasks. *J. Mach. Learn. Res.*, 13:491–518, mar 2012.

[23] V. C. Raykar, S. Yu, L. H. Zhao, G. H. Valadez, C. Florin, L. Bogoni, and L. Moy. Learning from crowds. *J. Mach. Learn. Res.*, 99:1297–1322, August 2010.

[24] T. Richardson and R. Urbanke. *Modern Coding Theory*. Cambridge University Press, march 2008.

[25] E. Shamir and J. Spencer. Sharp concentration of the chromatic number on random graphs $G_{n,p}$. *Combinatorica*, 7:121–129, 1987.

[26] V. S. Sheng, F. Provost, and P. G. Ipeirotis. Get another label? improving data quality and data mining using multiple, noisy labelers. In *Proceeding of the 14th ACM SIGKDD international conference on Knowledge discovery and data mining*, KDD '08, pages 614–622. ACM, 2008.

[27] P. Welinder, S. Branson, S. Belongie, and P. Perona. The multidimensional wisdom of crowds. In *Advances in Neural Information Processing Systems*, pages 2424–2432, 2010.

[28] J. Whitehill, P. Ruvolo, T. Wu, J. Bergsma, and J. Movellan. Whose vote should count more: Optimal integration of labels from labelers of unknown expertise. In *Advances in Neural Information Processing Systems*, volume 22, pages 2035–2043, 2009.

Root Cause Detection in a Service-Oriented Architecture

Myunghwan Kim[*]
Stanford University
Stanford, CA, USA
mykim@stanford.edu

Roshan Sumbaly
LinkedIn Corporation
Mountain View, CA, USA
rsumbaly@linkedin.com

Sam Shah
LinkedIn Corporation
Mountain View, CA, USA
samshah@linkedin.com

ABSTRACT

Large-scale websites are predominantly built as a service-oriented architecture. Here, services are specialized for a certain task, run on multiple machines, and communicate with each other to serve a user's request. An anomalous change in a metric of one service can propagate to other services during this communication, resulting in overall degradation of the request. As any such degradation is revenue impacting, maintaining correct functionality is of paramount concern: it is important to find the root cause of any anomaly as quickly as possible. This is challenging because there are numerous metrics or sensors for a given service, and a modern website is usually composed of hundreds of services running on thousands of machines in multiple data centers.

This paper introduces MonitorRank, an algorithm that can reduce the time, domain knowledge, and human effort required to find the root causes of anomalies in such service-oriented architectures. In the event of an anomaly, MonitorRank provides a ranked order list of possible root causes for monitoring teams to investigate. MonitorRank uses the historical and current time-series metrics of each sensor as its input, along with the call graph generated between sensors to build an unsupervised model for ranking. Experiments on real production outage data from LinkedIn, one of the largest online social networks, shows a 26% to 51% improvement in mean average precision in finding root causes compared to baseline and current state-of-the-art methods.

Categories and Subject Descriptors: C.4 [Performance of Systems]: Modeling Techniques; I.2.6 [Artificial Intelligence]: Learning; D.2.8 [Software Engineering]: Metrics

Keywords: call graph, monitoring, service-oriented architecture, anomaly correlation

1. INTRODUCTION

The modern web architecture consists of a collection of *services*, which are a set of software components spread across multiple machines that respond to requests and map to a specific task [25]. That is, a user request is load balanced to a front end service, which fans out requests to other services to collect and process the data to finally respond to the incoming request. The callee services of this request can also call other services, creating a call graph of requests.

For example, LinkedIn, one of the largest online social networks, has a recommendation feature called "People You May Know" that attempts to find other members to connect with on the site [20]. To show this module, several services are called: a web server wrapped as a service to receive and parse the member's request, a recommendation service that receives the member id from the web server and retrieves recommendations, and finally a profile service to collect metadata about the recommended members for decorating the web page shown to users.

In this web architecture, a service is the atomic unit of functionality. Such an architecture allows easy abstraction and modularity for implementation and reuse, as well as independent scaling of components. Modern websites consist of dozens and often hundreds of services to encompass a breadth of functionality. For example, to serve its site, LinkedIn runs over 400 services on thousands of machines in multiple data centers around the world.

Naturally, for business reasons, it is important to keep the services running continuously and reliably, and to quickly diagnose and fix anomalies. As site availability is of paramount concern due to its revenue-impacting nature, web properties have dedicated monitoring teams to inspect the overall health of these services and immediately respond to any issue [8]. To that end, these services are heavily instrumented and alert thresholds are set and aggressively monitored.

However, if an alert is triggered or an anomalous behavior is detected, it is difficult and time-consuming to find the actual root cause. First, considerable user functionality and the various types of services make the request dependencies between services complex. That is, these dependencies follow the transitive closure of the call chain, where services reside on multiple machines, can be stateless or stateful, and could call other services serially or in parallel. Due to this complexity in dependencies, a monitoring team has to maintain deep domain knowledge of almost every service and its semantics. However, it is very hard for the team to keep updating such knowledge, particularly when the site evolves quickly through rapid deployment of new features. Second, the total number of services is large and each service can generate hundreds of metrics. This means that mining and understanding the metrics for diagnosis is time-consuming. Last, even though heuristics and past knowledge are applied by the monitoring teams to narrow the search space in the event of an anomaly, evaluation can only be done in human time—which is, at a minimum, in the tens of seconds per possible root cause. For these reasons, automated tools to help narrow down the root cause in the event of an anomaly can substantially reduce the time to recovery.

This paper introduces *MonitorRank*, a novel unsupervised algorithm that predicts root causes of anomalies in a service-oriented

---

[*]Work was performed while the author was interning at LinkedIn.

SIGMETRICS'13, June 17–21, 2013, Pittsburgh, PA, USA.
Copyright 2013 ACM 978-1-4503-1900-3/13/06 ...$15.00.

architecture. It combines historical and latest service metric data to rank, in real time, potential root causes. This ranked list decreases the overall search space for the monitoring team. MonitorRank is unsupervised, eliding the need for time-consuming and cumbersome training required for learning the system.

As part of our evaluation, we analyzed anomalies such as latency increases, throughput drops, and error increases in services over the course of 3 months at LinkedIn. MonitorRank consistently outperformed the basic heuristics that were employed by LinkedIn's monitoring team and current state-of-the-art anomaly correlation algorithms [23]. In terms of mean average precision, which quantifies the goodness of root cause ranking, MonitorRank yields 26% to 51% more predictive power than any other technique we tried.

The rest of the paper is organized as follows. Section 2 provides background on service-oriented architectures and Section 3 showcases related work. In Section 4, we discuss the challenges of detecting root causes in a service-oriented architecture. We then present our approach, MonitorRank, in Section 5. Section 6 evaluates our algorithm against the current state-of-the-art techniques using labeled data from previous anomalies at LinkedIn. We close with future work in Section 7.

2. BACKGROUND

At a very high level, a website architecture consists of 3 tiers of services: the frontend, middle tier and data tier. Services act as the building blocks of the site and expose various APIs (Application programming interface) for communication. Figure 1 presents the high-level architecture of LinkedIn.

The *frontend tier*, also called the *presentation tier*, consists of services responsible for receiving requests from members and translating the requests to calls to other downstream services. In practice, most user-facing features map to only one of these frontend services. The *middle tier*, or the *application tier*, is responsible for processing the requests, making further calls to the data tier, then joining and decorating the results. The services at this tier may also communicate among themselves. For example, a service handling the social network updates for users injects suggestions from the service in charge of recommendations. Based on the APIs called, the recommendation service may provide member, jobs, or group recommendations. Finally, the *data tier* has services that maintain a thin decoration wrapper around the underlying data store, while also performing other storage strategies such as caching and replication. Other nomenclature commonly used is *backend tier*, which encompasses both the middle and data tier.

LinkedIn runs approximately 400 services, deployed on thousands of machines in multiple data centers. These services are continuously developed and deployed by many engineers. As the number of features on the site grows, the number of services also increases. Furthermore, because each service maintains various APIs, the overall number of *sensors*, meaning <service, API> tuples, is very high.

Hence, the problem of detecting the root cause of an anomaly among many sensors demands considerable human effort. The root cause finding problem requires manual scanning of sensor logs and following all possible downstream trajectories of sensors. Domain knowledge might be used for making the diagnosis faster by restricting the candidate trajectories to a small subset of sensors. However, it is difficult to keep up-to-date with information about all of these sensors if the site is rapidly evolving. In the worst case, all teams involved in developing the downstream sensors need to be involved in finding the root cause, which hurts overall productivity.

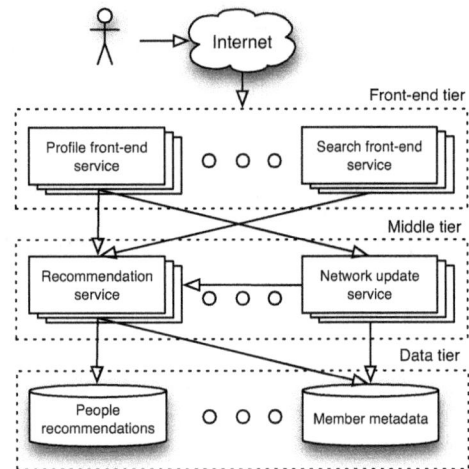

Figure 1: A generic web site architecture consisting of multiple tiers of services

3. RELATED WORK

Finding the root causes of anomalies has been extensively studied in various areas including chemical engineering [37, 38] and computer networks [27]. In computer networks, effort has been made on handling both real-time metrics/events and link information [4, 6, 16, 36]. However, the links in the computer network structure represent a reliable dependency. For instance, if a router has an anomaly, then all traffic flowing through it is affected. On the other hand, in the context of web sites, a sensor generating a lot of exceptions may not necessarily propagate this behavior to its callers. Due to this lossy nature in our use case, strong assumptions with respect to links do not hold.

In terms of large-scale system troubleshooting, many attempts have been made to develop middleware that efficiently finds the root causes of anomalies. In particular, VScope [32] and Monalytics [31] allow monitoring teams to consider the relationships between sensors for root cause finding. However, such middleware rely on manual rule-based configuration thereby requiring deep domain knowledge. In contrast, our algorithm aims to reduce human effort in troubleshooting without domain knowledge.

There has also been a great deal of focus on using machine learning techniques for finding root causes in systems. One methodology is to learn from historical data and find anomalies in the current data [1, 7, 18]. These methods employ supervised algorithms, in contrast to the unsupervised method we adopted. Another direction of work has focused on anomaly correlation with graph structure features [2, 11, 15, 23]. These algorithms make an assumption that a link between two nodes represents a strong dependency, which is not true in practice for sensor call graphs. Other techniques attempt to capture dependencies between nodes by using correlation [13]. This assumption too does not hold as there have been cases in various production logs at LinkedIn where correlation in normal state is not the same as in an anomalous state. MonitorRank finds dependencies between sensors based on pseudo-anomalies and uses the call graph in a randomized way.

Anomaly detection algorithms is also related to this work, as used by a clustering algorithm inside MonitorRank. Our proposed algorithm implements a heuristic method, but can easily be extended to more sophisticated algorithms, including subspace methods [17, 22, 35], matrix factorization [34], or streaming methods [9, 21, 28].

4. ROOT CAUSE FINDING PROBLEM

This section formally describes in detail the problem of finding the root cause sensor and its challenges.

4.1 Problem definition

Before defining the problem, we summarize the data available for diagnosis. Individual sensors emit metrics data (for example, latency, error count, and throughput) with a unique universal identifier. This identifier is generated in the first frontend service receiving the user request and then propagated down to the downstream callee services. This metrics data is collected and stored in a consolidated location so as to create the complete *call graph* by joining on the universal identifier. A call graph is a directed graph where each node represents a sensor, and an edge from node v_i to node v_j indicates that sensor v_i called sensor v_j. For simplicity, this paper assumes a single unweighted edge between two nodes even though there can be multiple calls between two sensors during a request. Also, though this paper presents results at a sensor level, that is, service and API combination, it can be extended to work at a coarser (for example, just a service) or finer (for example, a combination of <service, API, server> tuple) granularity.

Based on the described data, the formal description of the root cause finding problem is as follows. Suppose that an anomaly is observed in metric m of a frontend sensor v_{fe} at time t. Then, given the metric m of other sensors and the call graph, our goal is to identify sensors that caused the anomaly. To help with diagnosis, MonitorRank provides an ordered list of sensors to examine. In the best case, the first sensor presented in the ranked output of Monitor-Rank is the exact root cause of the anomaly after investigation. In other words, our objective is to rank sensors directly relevant to the root cause higher compared to those unrelated to it.

We restrict our focus to diagnosis after an anomaly has been reported, thereby distinguishing our work from the anomaly detection literature [3, 5, 26]. The detection of the anomaly happens through either a user report or a threshold-based alert. In both cases, MonitorRank is provided with a metric corresponding to the anomalous sensor and the approximate time range of the anomalous behavior.

4.2 Challenges

MonitorRank uses two primary pieces of data: the metric data of each sensor and the call graph between sensors. However, using just the bare-bones call graph is more challenging compared to the metric data. First, the call graph might not represent the true dependency between sensors in production. It does not account for various external factors that can influence the behavior of a service. For example, malicious bot behavior on the site can increase latency or a human error during maintenance can decrease throughput. Also, if co-located on the same hardware, two sensors may face the same problem, such as high CPU utilization, even though these sensors do not have a direct call edge between them. These examples demonstrate that similar anomalous behaviors between sensors may be independent of their relationship in the call graph.

Second, the calls between sensors are not homogeneous. A sensor can call multiple sensors in series or in parallel. Serial and parallel calls would result in different dependency type even though the schematic of the sensor calls is the same. For example, call latency for a service would be greater than the sum of its downstream calling service's latency for serial calls, but be maximum in case of parallel calls. Even the same pair of sensors can have different dependencies among the sensors. For example, the same operation of displaying recent network updates on a social network web site can generate a different call graph dependency for a user with 1000 connections than a user with just 10. The user with 1000 connections may have

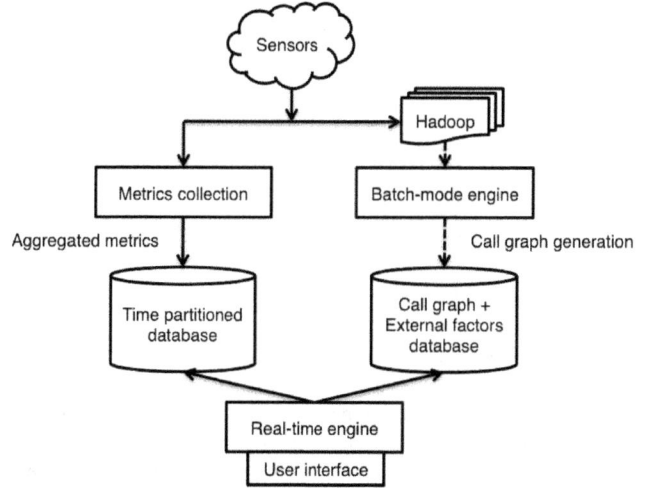

Figure 2: Sub-components required by MonitorRank. The dashed lines signify only periodic updates

a bottleneck on the update generation sensor, while for a user with just 10 connections all updates might be cached and the bottleneck would instead be the profile information fetching sensor.

Third, the dependencies between sensors are dynamic with relationships changing over time. For example, if a new algorithm is deployed to improve the running time of some API call, then the dependency between sensors, with respect to latency metric, would be different before and after a new deployment.

Due to these reasons, the call graph may not reliably represent dependencies between sensors. Therefore, the final algorithm of finding the root cause has to consider each edge of the call graph as one of the possible routes of anomaly propagation.

Our algorithm attempts to find the root cause of an anomaly as an unsupervised problem because in many cases labeled data for training may not be available. Even if the labeled data exists, we cannot guarantee the correctness of the data at any given time due to the rapidly changing underlying system.

Finally, the algorithm should display the results quickly. Because the user is provided a degraded experience during the period of diagnosis, the recovery time is of utmost importance. Hence, the algorithm is required to have subquadratic runtime, with any call graph computation being faster than $O(N^2)$, where N, the number of sensors, is typically large.

5. OUR APPROACH

To rank the sensors that are potentially contributing to the given anomaly, MonitorRank assigns a *root cause score* for each sensor. To give the score, our framework, illustrated in Figure 2, uses three sub-components: metrics collection system, a batch-mode engine, and a real-time engine. We briefly introduce each sub-component here and later explain them in detail in the following subsections.

First, the metrics collection system receives and aggregates metrics from all the sensors, and finally stores them into a time-partitioned database.

The batch-mode engine executes periodically on a snapshot of metric data to generate the call graph and extract the external factors. The output of this is stored back into another database. The external factors are extracted by a *pseudo-anomaly clustering* algorithm, described further in Section 5.2. Generation of the call graph periodically makes MonitorRank robust to rapid service evolution.

Last, when an anomaly occurs, the monitoring team interacts with the real-time engine via a user interface. The inputs provided are the frontend sensor, approximate time period of anomaly, and the metric under consideration. The first sensor causing an anomaly is easy to find in the context of web sites because of their one-to-one mapping to a user-facing feature. For example, an error reading a LinkedIn message would point to the `getMessageForMember()` API call in the *inbox frontend* service. The real-time engine then loads necessary data from the two databases and provides the ranked list of root-cause sensors. With this data, the real-time engine performs a random walk algorithm, as described in Section 5.3.

5.1 Metrics Collection

As the number of sensors grows, it becomes important to standard-ize on the metrics naming and collection so as to help the monitoring team analyze and remediate user-facing issues quickly. All APIs in LinkedIn implement a generic interface that provide standard metrics, such as latency, throughput, and error count. Introduction of new sensors results in automatic generation of new metric data. The metrics from these sensors are passed to an agent: a simple program located on all machines, which periodically pushes the metrics to a centralized broker via a publish/subscribe system called Kafka [19]. The data in Kafka is then continuously consumed by our metrics collection application, buffered and aggregated to a coarser time granularity and then stored into a time-partitioned database. This centralized metrics database serves various applications such as a real-time monitoring visualization dashboard; a simple thresh-old alerting system; or the focus of this paper, that is, a root cause finding dashboard.

5.2 Batch-mode Engine

The metrics data from Kafka is also consumed by Hadoop, a batch processing system, and stored on Hadoop's distributed file system (HDFS). A regularly scheduled Hadoop job takes as its input a snapshot of the metrics data and outputs the call graph and external factors.

Call Graph Generation

Every individual metric data point stored on Hadoop contains the unique universal identifier introduced by a frontend sensor and then passed down along the call chain. The metric data point also contains the caller and callee sensor name. A Hadoop job joins the snapshot metrics data on the universal id and then combines the individual sensor names to generate the call graph.

Pseudo-anomaly Clustering

However, the call graph does not reliably represent dependencies between sensors due to external factors as described in Section 4. When a certain external factor causes an anomaly, sensors affected by the external factor show highly correlated metric pattern in the anomaly time window.

For instance, if two sensors do not call the same API but are co-located, one sensor would be affected whenever the other shows anomalous behavior due to hardware problems. Moreover, as the location of the sensors would not rapidly change over time, this colocation effect can be captured from the historical metric data. Figure 3(a) shows an instance of the call graph from LinkedIn where sensors v_1 and v_2 were co-located. Figure 3(b) shows the correlation between v_1 and v_2 versus the correlation between v_1 and v_3, plotted for the error count metric. If v_1 and v_2 were correlated only through a common neighbor sensor v_3, without any external factors, most data points would have clustered into the ellipsoid area only. However, we also notice a different cluster, highlighted as a rectangle in Figure 3(b), where the correlation between v_1 and v_2 is highly independent of that between v_1 and v_3. This rectangular area

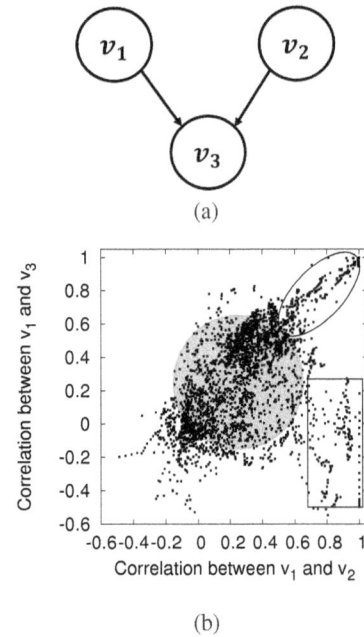

(a)

(b)

Figure 3: **Effect of external factor.** Even though a sensor v_3 is called by both v_1 and v_2 in (a), the correlation between v_1 and v_2 can be high even when the correlation between v_1 and v_3 is low in the rectangle area of (b). The rectangle area is caused by the colocation of v_1 and v_2.

is caused by the external factor, in this case due to their colocation. Using the above ideas, we propose a *pseudo-anomaly clustering* algorithm that groups sensors together based on historical metrics correlation, thereby capturing cases like the rectangle area.

Since the prerequisite to clustering is to detect anomalies, we use one of the various detection algorithms in literature on the historical metric data. The output of the detection algorithm is an anomalous frontend sensor, the corresponding metric and time range (moment). Because these detected anomalies may not necessarily capture only true reported anomalies, we refer to them as *pseudo-anomalies*. Then for every pseudo-anomaly we need to compute the similarity of the corresponding metric data against those of all the other sensors.

The measurement of relevance between the frontend sensor and the others, is defined by the *pattern similarity* between their corre-sponding metric values. If some external factor caused an anomaly in the same set of sensors, including the given seed frontend sensor, the metric patterns of those sensors should be similar with respect to the pseudo-anomaly event. Conversely, if we investigate the metric pattern similarity among sensors at pseudo-anomaly moments and find a group of sensors that usually show high pattern similarity in common, then we can assume the influence of some external factor.

Conditional clustering. To consider external factors in our algo-rithm for each frontend sensor, we need to find a group of sensors that are commonly related during our detected pseudo-anomalies. This problem is slightly different from a conventional clustering problem for the following reasons. First, the algorithm needs to solve a separate clustering problem for each frontend sensor be-cause the detected pseudo-anomaly time ranges vary depending on the seed sensor. Second, only groups that consist of sensors with high pattern similarity need to be considered. Since we can discard time ranges where the metric values for the seed sensor do not look similar to those of the other sensors, the false positive rate of the underlying detection algorithm becomes less critical. Hence, the clustering problem is conditioned on pseudo-anomaly moments of the seed sensor, as well as the pattern similarity scores of the other sensors with respect to the seed sensor.

Based on the above requirements, the clustering problem is formulated as follows. Let pseudo-anomaly time ranges (moments) be $t_1, t_2, \cdots, t_M$ for a given frontend sensor v_{fe}. For each moment t_k, we denote the pattern similarity between the frontend sensor v_{fe} and all the other sensors by $S^{(t_k)} = [S_1^{(t_k)}, S_2^{(t_k)}, \cdots, S_{|V|}^{(t_k)}]$ such that each $|S_i^{(t_k)}| \leq 1$. Without loss of generality, we set $v_1 = v_{fe}$. The objective is then to find clusters from $S^{(t_k)}$, where the number of cluster is not specified. We aim to create a sparse set of sensors per cluster, such that the pattern similarity scores within the group is very high. Also, even though we learn the clusters from the historical data, matching of a given current metric data to a cluster should be possible in real-time. Finally, assuming that external factors consistently influence the same set of sensors for a reasonable time, we only consider clusters supported by large number of samples.

Suppose that the seed frontend sensor and other sensors $n_1, \cdots, n_c$ are affected by the same external factor. Then, at pseudo-anomaly moment t when this external factor causes an anomaly,

$$S_i^{(t)} \sim \begin{cases} \mu^{(t)} + \epsilon^{(t)} & \text{for } i = n_1, n_2, \cdots n_c \\ \mathcal{N}(0, \delta^2) & \text{otherwise} \end{cases} \quad (1)$$

for a shared variance δ^2, the average relevance $\mu^{(t)}$ with respect to each pseudo-anomaly moment t, and a small error $\epsilon^{(t)}$. We also assume that $\delta < \mu^{(t)}$ to make external factors distinguishable from random effects. In other words, if sensors are affected by the same external factor, their pattern similarity scores with regard to the seed sensor will be close and high; otherwise, sensors that do not belong to a given cluster show low pattern similarity scores.

These assumptions simplify the real-world, but make sense when we revisit Figure 3(b). We ignore the cluster in the center because it represents low similarity between each sensor and the frontend one sensor (that is, mixed with random effects). The remaining two areas (rectangle and ellipsoid) agree with our assumption since sensors unrelated to a given pseudo-anomaly represent small pattern similarity scores. Also the related sensors in these areas show high similar scores between each other. In practice, this phenomenon was also observed for other combinations of sensors, thereby validating our assumption.

Algorithmic detail. Now we describe the pseudo-anomaly clustering algorithm in detail. The inputs to the clustering algorithm are (a) a seed frontend sensor v_{fe} (that is, v_1), (b) various pseudo-anomaly moments from historical data ($t_1, \cdots, t_k$), and (c) pattern similarity scores of the sensors ($S^{(t_1)}, \cdots, S^{(t_k)}$). The historical data is limited to recent few weeks thereby restricting the amount of data to handle. The pseudo-anomaly moments where the pattern similarity scores of all services represent low values are filtered out. This way false positive moments produced by the detection algorithm can be removed.

We then capture the sensors of high pattern similarity scores with respect to each of the cleaned pseudo-anomaly moments. Using the assumption in (1), we categorize sensors (except for the frontend sensor) into two groups based on the pattern-similarity scores of the sensors. While one group consists of sensors representing low pattern similarity scores (near zero), the other group contains the sensors showing high pattern similarity scores (near $\mu^{(t)}$ in (1)). We refer to the latter group as the cluster for the given pseudo-anomaly moment. Finally, we make this cluster sparse to maintain only key sensors with regard to a certain external factor.

To fulfill the above objective, we formulate the optimization problem with respect to each pseudo-anomaly moment t_k. Let x_i be the variable indicating whether the sensor v_i belongs to a cluster of the moment t_k for $i = 2, \cdots, |V|$. That is, x_i is either 0 or 1, where $x_i = 1$ means that the sensor v_i belongs to the cluster. We do not consider x_1 because we set v_1 as a given frontend seed sensor. From (1), we then minimize not only the errors $\epsilon^{(t)}$ of sensors in the cluster but also the variance of the other sensors. Further, to make a sparse cluster, we also minimize the cardinality of x as follows:

$$\min_{\mu^{(t)}, x} \frac{1}{2}||S^{(t_k)} - \mu^{(t)}x||_2^2 + \frac{\delta^2}{2}card(x) \quad (2)$$
$$\text{subject to} \quad x \in \{0, 1\}^{|V|-1}$$
$$\mu^{(t)} \geq \delta$$

where $card(x)$ means the cardinality of a vector x and $\mu^{(t)}$ indicates the average relevance of sensors in the cluster.

To reformulate this problem by L1-regularization and convex relaxation, we obtain the following convex optimization problem:

$$\min_{\mu^{(t)}, x} \frac{1}{2}||S^{(t_k)} - x||_2^2 + \frac{\delta^2}{2}|x|_1 \quad (3)$$
$$\text{subject to} \quad 0 \leq x_i \leq \mu^{(t)} \quad i = 2, \cdots, |V|$$
$$\mu^{(t)} \geq \delta.$$

Note that the minimum of the objective function value does not increase as $\mu^{(t)}$ increases. Hence, without influence on the solution of x, the variable $\mu^{(t)}$ can be dropped from the problem. This helps in simplifying the problem and the allow us to find x by Lasso [10, 29].

Once a solution (x^*) is obtained, the set of sensors $\{v_i|x_i^* > 0\}$ are referred to as an *active set* A_k with respect to pseudo-anomaly moment t_k. The active set is generated for each moment and then is run through two filtering steps. First, if the seed frontend sensor ends up with one leaf node, then we remove the corresponding active set since the high anomaly correlation in this set can be explained by propagation from the leaf-node sensor. Second, to make the number of clusters small, we filter out active sets using a support threshold value θ. The remaining active sets are then regarded as the final pseudo-anomaly clusters and are stored into the same database storing the call graph. This data is eventually used by the real-time engine while running MonitorRank.

This pseudo-anomaly clustering algorithm need not to be performed in real-time since the amount of historical data is massive. The algorithm translates into a couple of Hadoop job that are run periodically and update all the clusters in the database at once. The implementation is also inherently parallel as we can run the above jobs for each frontend sensor concurrently.

5.3 Real-time Engine

While the metrics collection pipeline and the batch-mode engine run continuously in the background, the real-time engine is responsible for serving the queries from the monitoring team. A simple user interface allows them to enter a frontend sensor, a metric, and a time period corresponding to the observed anomaly. The result is an ordered list of root-cause sensors. The interactive nature of the user interface allows the team to change their inputs continuously while getting back diagnosis guidelines in near real-time.

Pattern Similarity

One way of finding the root cause sensor in real-time is to search for sensors showing similar "patterns" in a metric to the frontend sensor where the anomaly is observed. For instance, suppose that many errors suddenly occurred in a data tier sensor due to a timeout. These errors propagate up the sensor-call path, resulting in a similar increasing pattern throughout. Generalizing this idea, if two services have similar abnormal patterns in a certain metric, we can imagine that the patterns may be caused by the same root cause. In particular, the metric data of two sensors can look similar when the same anomaly causes a change, regardless of whether the data looks similar in the normal situation.

Therefore, we use the similarity of the metric between the anomalous sensor and its corresponding downstream sensors as the key feature of MonitorRank. For each sensor v_i, computation of the metric pattern similarity score S_i, with respect to the anomalous sensor v_{fe}, is as follows:

$$S_i = \text{Sim}(m_i, m_{fe}) \qquad (4)$$

$\text{Sim}(\cdot, \cdot)$ is a fixed similarity function between two time series data (for example, correlation) and $m_i \in \mathcal{R}^T$ represents the time series metric data of sensor v_i during a time period of length T, which is provided as an input. This similarity score S_i signifies the relevance of the service v_i to the given anomaly.

Random Walk Algorithm

Although the metric pattern similarity score is useful for detecting the relevance of sensors to the given anomaly, using just this score can result in false positive root causes. This is because sensors with no relation to the anomaly may still have a very high similarity score with the anomalous sensor. For example, seasonal effects can result in nearly all sensors having a similar increase in throughput, thereby resulting in a high similarity score. As correlation does not necessarily imply causality, the similar anomalous metric pattern between two sensors cannot be the only factor to determine whether one sensor is causing an anomaly in the other. Instead, these pairs are taken as candidates and further addition of the call graph is required to rank the candidate sets better.

The call graph is incorporated using a randomized algorithm, keeping in mind that it does not reliably represent the dependencies between sensors. The basic idea of our approach is to do a random walk over the call graph depending on the similarity score. More specifically, sensors are selected in sequence by randomly picking up the next sensor among the neighbors in the call graph. The pickup probability of each neighbor is proportional to its relevance to a given anomaly, which is captured by the pattern similarity score. We then assume that more visits on a certain sensor by our random walk implies that the anomaly on that sensor can best explain the anomalies of all the other sensors. Under this assumption, the probability of visiting each sensor is regarded as the root cause score of the sensor in our algorithm. This allows us to blend the relevance of each sensor, for a given anomaly, into the call graph.

Our procedure is analogous to the *Weighted* PageRank algorithm [24, 33]. However, we do not consider sensors that look uncorrelated with a given anomaly. Therefore, MonitorRank uses the *Personalized* PageRank algorithm [14], by taking teleportation probability (preference vector) as determined by the given anomaly. The nature of the this PageRank algorithm allows teleportation to any sensor uniformly at random.

Basic setup. The random walk algorithm is defined as follows. Let the call graph be $G = <V, E>$, where each node indicates a sensor and each edge $e_{ij} \in E$ is set to 1 when sensor v_i calls sensor v_j. We assume that there is no self edge, that is, $e_{ii} \notin E$.

The other inputs to the algorithm include an anomalous frontend sensor node v_{fe} and the pattern similarity score S_i of each sensor

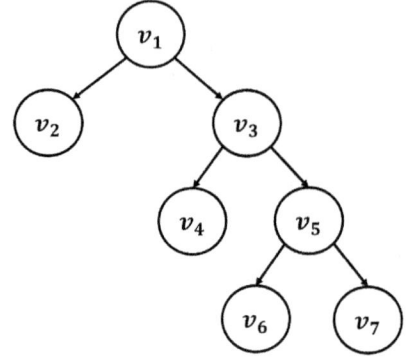

Figure 4: Natural trapping in the call graph. Due to the nature of downward sensor calls (from frontend to backend tier), when the random walker falls into the branch of v_3, the random walk cannot visit v_2 until the next teleportation even if there is no sensor related to the given anomaly in $v_4 \sim v_7$.

$v_i \in V$. Again, without loss of generality, let v_1 be v_{fe}. For convenience, the similarity score vector of all the sensors is denoted by $S = [S_1, \cdots, S_{|V|}] \in (0,1]^{|V|}$. For the random walker to visit each node v_i proportionally to its pattern similarity score S_i, the strength of each edge e_{ij} is assigned as S_j. The transition probability matrix Q of this movement is represented by:

$$Q_{ij} = \frac{A_{ij} S_j}{\sum_j A_{ij} S_j} \qquad (5)$$

for $i, j = 1, 2, \cdots, |V|$ for the binary-valued adjacency matrix A of the call graph G.

Self-edges. By definition, the random walker is enforced to move to another node even if the current node shows a higher pattern similarity score and all the neighboring nodes do not. This type of movement increases the stationary probabilities of nodes unrelated to the given anomaly.

To avoid forcibly moving to another node, a self-edge is added to every node. The random walker then stays longer on the same node if there is no neighboring node of high similarity score. A strength value of the self edge is determined by the pattern similarity score of the target node and its neighboring nodes. Specifically, for each node v_i, the strength of the corresponding self edge e_{ii} is equal to the similarity score S_i subtracted by the maximum similarity score of child nodes ($\max_{j:e_{ij} \in E} S_j$). This way the random walker is encouraged to move into the nodes of high similarity scores, but is prevented from falling into the nodes irrelevant to the given anomaly. As an exception we do not add a self-edge to the frontend node, that is, $e_{11} = 0$, as the random walker does not need to stay at v_1.

Backward-edges. When the random walker falls into nodes that look less relevant to the given anomaly, there is no way to escape out until the next teleportation. As the direction of an edge in the call graph tends to be from the frontend to the backend, the random walker is likely to be naturally trapped inside branches of the call graph. In Figure 4, suppose that an anomaly is observed at the frontend sensor v_1 and node v_2 is the only sensor relevant to the given anomaly. The resulting pattern similarity score of node v_2 with regard to the given anomaly is even higher than those for the other nodes $v_3 \sim v_7$. If the pattern similarity scores of nodes $v_3 \sim v_7$ are not negligible, the random walker can fall into the right part of descendants in Figure 4 (nodes $v_3 \sim v_7$). In this case, the random walker would stay on the nodes $v_3 \sim v_7$ until the next random teleportation occurs, no matter how irrelevant the nodes are with respect to the given anomaly.

To resolve this issue, backward edges are added so that the random walker flexibly explores nodes of high pattern similarity score. While random teleportation in the Personalized PageRank algorithm makes a random walker explore globally, the backward edges allow the random walker to explore locally. By adding these backward edges, we achieve the restriction imposed by the call graph, but with the added flexibility to explore. However, because we add backward edges by means of local teleportation, less strength is set on each backward edge than the strength of true edges ending up to the same node. For every pair of nodes v_i and v_j, such that $e_{ij} \in E$ and $e_{ji} \notin E$, while the strength of e_{ij} is equal to S_j, the strength of e_{ji} is set as ρS_i for some constant $\rho \in [0, 1)$. If the value of ρ is high, the random walker is more restricted to the paths of the call graph, that is, from upstream to downstream. Alternately, when the value of ρ is low, the random walker explores the nodes with more flexibility. If the call graph represents a true dependency graph between sensors, we would set ρ higher, and vice versa.

To incorporate both backward and self edges, we define a new real value adjacency matrix A' with the call graph G and the similarity score S as follows:

$$A'_{ij} = \begin{cases} S_j & \text{if } e_{ij} \in E \\ \rho S_i & \text{if } e_{ji} \in E, e_{ij} \notin E \\ \max(0, S_i - \max_{k:e_{jk} \in E}) & j = i > 1 \end{cases} \quad (6)$$

Using A', the new transition probability matrix P is defined as:

$$P_{ij} = \frac{A'_{ij}}{\sum_j A'_{ij}} \quad (7)$$

for $i, j = 1, 2, \cdots, |V|$.

Given an anomaly and related frontend sensor v_1, the Personalized PageRank vector (PPV) $\pi_{PPV} \in (0, 1]^{1 \times |V|}$ serves as the root cause score for each node. For a preference vector u of the random walk (personalized teleportation probability vector), the pattern-similarity score S is used for $v_2, \cdots, v_{|V|}$. That is, $u_i = S_i$ for $i = 2, 3, \cdots, |V|$. In this way, a random walker jumps more to anomaly-related sensors whenever the random teleportation occurs. Also because staying at the frontend sensor v_1 is out of focus for the random walk, the value in the preference vector corresponding to the frontend sensor v_1 is assigned as zero ($u_1 = 0$). Even though we do not make a random teleportation to the v_1, we still require this frontend sensor v_1 as a connecting node between the neighboring nodes of the v_1.

Once we determine the transition probability P and the preference vector u, PPV is obtained as follows:

$$\pi_{PPV} = \alpha \pi_{PPV} P + (1 - \alpha) u. \quad (8)$$

where α is a random teleportation probability in $[0, 1]$. Similarly for the backward edge probability constant ρ, we set the α higher when the call graph is thought of as a true dependency graph. In the extreme case that $\alpha = 0$, this random walk model is equivalent to using only the metric pattern similarity.

Why the random walk algorithm?. MonitorRank is inspired by the idea that biological organisms efficiently search for their target (for example, the source of scent) by performing a random walk, even though the sensory data from the organisms is not reliable [12, 30]. Furthermore, a random walk algorithm is also analogous to human behavior during diagnosis. When an engineer from the monitoring team has no knowledge about the system, except for the call graph, one of natural diagnosis methods is to randomly traverse sensors by following the call graph with preferentially looking at misbehaving nodes. Hence, the stationary probability by random

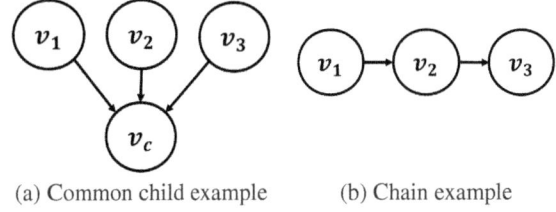

(a) Common child example   (b) Chain example

Figure 5: Graph examples that benefit from the random walk model

walk represents the behavior of multiple non-expert engineers monitoring each sensor node. A high stationary probability for a certain node implies that this node is "democratically" the most important to investigate without prior knowledge.

The PageRank algorithm tends to rank the nodes with more edges higher, as such nodes have more incoming paths. However, our approach naturally mitigates the effect of this advantage to some extend. Because we allow a self-edge for every node except for a given frontend node, a node having low connections, but showing similar anomaly patterns to the frontend sensor, can also high stationary probability by acting like a dead end.

The random walk algorithm can provide a higher score to a common child sensor node of some frontend sensors (that is, a common backend sensor called by the frontend sensors) if all of the frontend sensors have the same anomalies. For example, think of sensor v_c called by three sensors v_1, v_2, and v_3 in Figure 5(a). Then suppose that v_c causes an anomaly to propagate to all the other sensors $v_1 \sim v_3$ and the anomaly is observed on the sensor v_1. Because all the sensors show anomalies caused by the same root cause, the pattern similarity scores of the sensors with respect to the anomaly-observed sensor v_1 are similarly high, that is, $S_2 \approx S_3 \approx S_c$. The random walk algorithm lifts up the rank of the common sensor v_c, the actual root cause of the given anomaly.

Also, if the similarity function is correct in extracting only sensors relevant to a given anomaly and there exists an explicit anomaly causal path chain as visualized in Figure 5(b), we can prove that our random walk algorithm can successfully find the exact root cause.

THEOREM 1. *Suppose that a set of nodes $V' \subset V$ consists of a chain graph such that $v'_1 \to v'_2 \cdots \to v'_m$ for $m = |V'| \geq 1$. If $S_{v'} = p \leq 1$ for $v' \in V'$ and $S_v = 0$ for $v \notin V'$, then $\pi_{v'_m} > \pi_{v'_i}$ for $i = 1, 2, \cdots, m - 1$.*

PROOF. See Appendix. $\square$

Finally, by overlaying multiple transition probability matrices and preference vectors the random walk approach can handle the situation where-in anomalies are seen on multiple frontends simultaneously. We do not implement and test this scenario in this paper due to its rare occurrence in production.

External Factors

The random walk algorithm that we described so far incorporates the call graph generated by the batch-mode engine with the current metric data. On the other hand, the batch-mode engine also learns external factors not captured by the call graph. MonitorRank blends the pseudo-anomaly clusters with the random walk algorithm by finding the best-match cluster with the current metric data and giving more scores to sensors in the selected cluster.

The selection of cluster, for a given anomaly and frontend sensor, is based on Gaussian assumption, as described in (1). That is, if the current similarity score is $S = \{S_1, \cdots, S_{|V|}\}$ and the root cause of the current anomaly is the common external factor of some pseudo-anomaly cluster C, then the pattern similarity scores of sensors in C

would be higher than any sensor not in C. MonitorRank selects the best-fit cluster C^* by comparing the minimum score among sensors in each cluster to the maximum score of the others as follows:

$$C^* = \arg \max_C \frac{\min_{c \in C} S_c}{\max_{c' \notin C} S_{c'}}. \qquad (9)$$

Once the best-fit cluster C^* is selected, it is combined with the random walk algorithm. If the pattern similarity score ratio described in (9) is less than 1 or the average of pattern similarity scores of sensors in C^* is less than δ, we discard the selected cluster C^* and run the random walk algorithm as if C^* were not chosen. Otherwise, by regarding the average pattern similarity score of sensors in C^* as the pattern similarity score of the external factor corresponding to C^*, we add this average score to S_c for every sensor $c \in C^*$. In this way, we leverage the fact that engineers in the monitoring team examine the sensors related to the external factor first. After adding the average score, we run the same random walk algorithm to finally obtain the rank of sensors to examine.

Because the procedure described in (9) scans S_i once for each cluster C, it requires $O(N_C|V|)$ time for the number of clusters N_C. As $N_C \ll |V|$ in general, it takes time even less than $O(|V|^2)$. Furthermore, the random walk algorithm takes $O(|E|)$ time, which is also much faster than $O(|V|^2)$ (particularly in a sparse call graph). Therefore, overall, MonitorRank requires only $O(N_C|V| + |E|)$ time, which is feasible in real time.

6. EXPERIMENTS

In this section, we evaluate MonitorRank by using real-world metrics and anomalies at LinkedIn. Moreover, we decompose our algorithm into three subcomponents – pattern similarity, pseudo-anomaly clustering, and random walk on the call graph, and investigate the effect of each subcomponent.

6.1 Experimental Setup

Datasets and Implementation

In LinkedIn, there is a dedicated team monitoring site behavior and detecting any anomalies. When an anomaly occurs, the monitoring team first tries to resolve it by manually going through the list of sensors, and in the worst case, fall back to alerting the engineering team responsible for the anomalous sensor. Over time this team has stored these anomalies and corresponding list of ranked root causes in a central site-issue management system. This dataset is used for evaluation of MonitorRank. The following three primary metrics were used for our evaluation:

- Latency: Average of latency of the sensor call over a minute (25 examples)
- Error-count: The number of exceptions returned by the sensor call in a minute (71 examples)
- Throughput: The number of sensor requests in a minute (35 examples)

The metric data is aggregated up to a fixed coarser time granularity (1 minute) thereby providing predictable runtime for our analysis. This granularity also helps in reliably catching the change of metrics, making it resilient to issues such as out-of-sync clock times.

Note that the directions of anomaly propagation in the call graph are different depending on the metrics. An anomaly in throughput may propagate from the frontend sensor to the backend sensor, whereas an anomaly in error count or latency is likely to propagate in the opposite direction, from the backend to the frontend. Therefore, when applying our algorithm on the test sets, we use the original directed call graph (frontend → backend) for throughput, while we use the reverse direction of call graph (backend → frontend) for latency and error-count.

For our pattern similarity function, we use the sliding-window correlation. In particular, we compute the correlation of two given metrics on a time window of fixed length. By moving this window over the anomaly time range, we average the correlation values computed by each time window slot. For our experiments, we used 60 minute time window after manually trying out various candidates between $10 \sim 120$ minutes. The 60 minute time window is long enough to distinguish a sudden change in the metric from the normal variance of the metric. But the 60 minute period is also short enough to highlight the local change caused by anomalies rather than compare the long-term trend in the metric of normal state.

MonitorRank requires both historical and current metrics of sensors. For experiments, we use the time period of anomaly marked by the monitoring team. However, we found the time period of an anomaly ranging between 10 minutes and 3 hours (for example, a data center outage) in our experimental data. If the specified anomaly time period is less than the 60 minutes, we extend the anomaly time period to 60 minutes by inserting the data before the time period as much as required. For historical data, we group each metric week by week and use the data two weeks prior to the given anomaly.

Finally, with regard to an anomaly detection algorithm (for pseudo-anomalies), we apply a heuristic method that determines anomalies based on the ratio of current metric value and the maximum value in the previous time window, that is, previous 60 minutes in our case. For instance, if we set a threshold as 1.2, when the maximum value of a give metric in previous 60 minutes is 100, we label the current time period as an anomaly if the current metric value is over 120. This way can capture abrupt increases in metric values. Similarly, we can define the anomalies that show sudden decrease in metric values.

Note that we may not require the best quality of anomaly detection algorithms. Most of the detection algorithms aim to reduce the false positives as much as possible, but we are tolerant of these false positives because our objective is to cluster sensors. Furthermore, as our clustering algorithm relies on the metric pattern similarity between frontend and backend sensors, the false positive anomaly moments which are not correlated with other sensors would be naturally filtered out.

Baseline Methods

For the purpose of comparison, we introduce some baseline methods, which includes three heuristic algorithms and one algorithm using the call graph as a dependency graph. We describe each algorithm as follows:

- *Random Selection* (RS): A human without any domain knowledge will examine sensors in random order. We mimic this behavior by issuing random permutations.
- *Node Error Propensity* (NEP): Under the assumption that an anomaly on a certain sensor would produce errors on the same sensor, one can view the error count on a time window as a measure of anomaly.
- *Sudden Change* (SC): A natural way for a human to find root causes is to compare the metrics in the current and previous time windows and check any sudden change between the two time windows. For example, if there is a sudden latency increase at a certain time, then the average latency after this time should be notably higher than before. We therefore define the ratio of average metrics on both the time periods and refer to this ratio as the root cause score of each sensor.

	RS	NEP	SC	TBAC	MonitorRank	Improvement compared to (RS, NEP, SC)	Improvement compared to TBAC
Latency							
PR@1	0.120	0.160	0.560	0.840	1.000	78.6%	19.0%
PR@3	0.120	0.093	0.613	0.787	0.920	50.1%	16.9%
PR@5	0.144	0.112	0.650	0.756	0.852	31.1%	12.7%
MAP	0.143	0.206	0.559	0.497	0.754	34.9%	51.8%
Error Count							
PR@1	0.042	0.133	0.577	0.746	0.901	56.2%	20.8%
PR@3	0.049	0.493	0.653	0.552	0.850	30.2%	54.0%
PR@5	0.084	0.616	0.743	0.482	0.813	9.4%	68.7%
MAP	0.091	0.465	0.659	0.442	0.818	24.1%	85.0%
Throughput							
PR@1	0.229	0.000	0.086	0.971	1.000	336%	3.0%
PR@3	0.200	0.667	0.133	0.962	0.990	34.9%	2.9%
PR@5	0.183	0.800	0.149	0.897	0.971	21.4%	8.2%
MAP	0.210	0.634	0.210	0.714	0.779	22.9%	9.1%

Table 1: Performance of each algorithm on each test set: MonitorRank outperforms the baseline methods in every case.

- *Timing Behavior Anomaly Correlation* (TBAC): For a non-heuristic baseline method, we use the method of anomaly correlation using a dependency graph [23]. Because this algorithm works with metric correlations between sensors and the call graph, it is comparable to our experimental setting. The difference compared to our approach is that this algorithm regards the call graph as a reliable directed acyclic dependency graph (DAG).

Evaluation Metric

To compare MonitorRank to the baseline methods, we require appropriate evaluation metrics. All the algorithms provide a rank of sensors with respect to each anomaly case. We refer to the rank of each sensor v_i with respect to an anomaly a as $r_a(i)$ and define the indicator variable $R_a(i)$ to represent whether sensor i is the root cause of an anomaly a or not (that is, either 0 or 1). To quantify the performance of each algorithm on a set of anomalies A, we use the following metrics:

- *Precision at top K* (PR@K) indicates the probability that top K sensors given by each algorithm actually are the root causes of each anomaly case. It is important that the algorithm captures the final root cause at a small value of K, thereby resulting in lesser number of sensors to investigate. Here we use $K = 1, 3, 5$. More formally, it is defined as

$$\text{PR@}K = \frac{1}{|A|} \sum_{a \in A} \frac{\sum_{i:r_a(i) \leq K} R_a(i)}{\min\left(K, \sum_i R_a(i)\right)}. \quad (10)$$

- *Mean Average Precision* (MAP) quantifies the goodness of a give rank result by putting more weight on the higher rank result (where high rank sensor, which has lower $r_a(i)$, means that this sensor is more likely to be a root cause). It can be formulated as follows:

$$\text{MAP} = \frac{1}{|A|} \sum_{a \in A} \sum_{1 \leq r \leq N} \text{PR@}r \quad (11)$$

for the number of sensors N.

Note that PR@K is a measurement on each anomaly case. Hence, we compute the average of PR@K per test set (latency, error count, and throughput) to represent the overall performance of an algorithm. On the other hand, MAP quantifies the overall performance of an algorithm per test set by itself.

6.2 Performance Evaluation

First, we evaluate MonitorRank and all the baseline methods on each test set, corresponding to latency, error count, and throughput

metrics. For every anomaly case in the test sets, each algorithm gives the root cause rank of sensors. We can evaluate the given rank in terms of the evaluation metrics PR@1, PR@3, PR@5, and MAP.

Table 1 compares the performance of algorithms for each test set. In every test set and evaluation metric, MonitorRank outperforms the baseline methods by a large factor. When we consider the average MAP metric on all the test sets, the improvement over the non-heuristic baseline method (TBAC) is approximately 51.4%. If we compare to the best heuristic method (RS, NEP, and SC) on each test set, MonitorRank increases performance by 25.7% on average. Also in terms of PR@K, MonitorRank consistently represents better predictive power compared to the other methods. More specifically, MonitorRank improves 49.7% and 24.5% prediction accuracy (PR@K) on average, in comparison to the heuristic method and TBAC, respectively.

However, while TBAC method shows an unbalanced performance depending on rank (better performance at top-K than overall), MonitorRank shows the consistent performance regardless of the rank. Moreover, even at the top-K root cause results, MonitorRank outperforms TBAC, although both methods incorporate the call graph based on the metric correlation.

Finally, in terms of PR@K, the performance decreases in some cases as K increases (for example, in the case of MonitorRank in every test set). This drop might seem counter-intuitive because if we cover more services by increasing K then the probability that the root cause sensor is chosen among the K should increase as well. However, in some cases of our test set, multiple sensors are labeled as root causes for a given anomaly. When such multiple root cause sensors exist, the decreasing trend of PR@K makes sense as more selection can cause more false-positives.

6.3 Analysis of Our Approach

In this section we provide a detailed analysis of the subcomponents of the MonitorRank algorithm. Recall that our algorithm consists of three main parts: pattern similarity, a random walk on the call graph, and pseudo-anomaly clustering. We perform the same experiment as the previous section, but use the following algorithms:

- Pattern-Similarity-Only (PS) uses only the pattern similarity score without the call graph or the pseudo-anomaly clustering
- With-Random-Walk (PS+RW) runs the random walk algorithm on the call graph without pseudo-anomaly clustering
- With-Pseudo-Anomaly-Clustering (PS+PAC) uses the pseudo-anomaly clustering without using the random walk algorithm
- With-All (ALL) represents the full version of MonitorRank

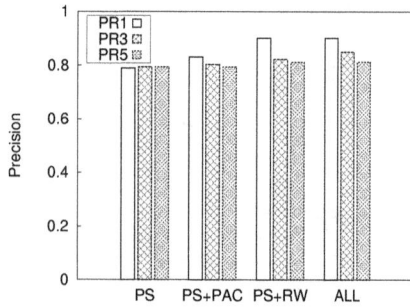

Figure 6: Effect of each subcomponent. Both the pseudo-anomaly clustering and the random walk algorithm are useful for the improvement of performance, while the effect of using the call graph is larger than the pseudo-anomaly clustering.

By running these subcomponents incrementally, we can compare the effect that each subcomponent has on the final results.

Figure 6 illustrates the effects of subcomponents by showing $PR@K$ for $K = 1, 3, 5$ on each algorithm. For the purpose of visualization, we show the average of $PR@K$ from all three test sets. We note that the pattern similarity plays an important role in the performance of MonitorRank, but using the call graph (random walk) lifts the performance by a significant factor. In particular, the With-Random-Walk (PS+RW) makes 14.2% improvement over the Pattern-Similarity-Only (PS) in $PR@1$. This improvement is achieved because the inclusion of the call graph limits candidate root cause sensors. If some sensor represents a high pattern-similarity score but its neighboring sensors do not, the random walk algorithm naturally adjusts the final root cause score to the lower value. In contrast, if sensors connected in the call graph show high pattern-similarity scores together, the root cause scores of the sensors would be properly leveraged by the random walk algorithm.

On the other hand, the pseudo-anomaly clustering seems helpful in finding the root causes of anomalies, but its effect is not as much as the random walk algorithm. When comparing the performance of With-All (ALL) and With-Random-Walk (PS+RW) in Figure 6, both algorithms (ALL and PS+RW) show similar performance in $PR@1$ and $PR@5$. However, we observe about 5% improvement (ALL over PS+RW) for $PR@3$ due to external factors being included. When an anomaly is caused by an external factor, using the call graph has no effect on finding all the sensors related to the external factor. In this case the With-Random-Walk (PS+RW) algorithm results in some false positives because of missing external factors. In contrast, the pseudo-anomaly clustering algorithm captures all the sensors relevant to the external factor and produce higher root cause scores. Thus, using With-All (ALL) ranks sensors relevant to the external factor are higher than the sensors that are regarded as false positives in With-Random-Walk (PS+RW).

Finally, we also investigate the contribution of the random walk algorithm on the call graph to capture non-explicit dependencies between sensors as described in Section 4. For this investigation, we compare the following algorithms: Pattern-Similarity-Only (PS), With-Random-Walk (PS+RW), and Timing-Behavior-Anomaly-Correlation (TBAC). TBAC assumes that the call graph is a strong dependency graph. Figure 7 compares the performance of each algorithm in terms of $MAP@5$, which is the average value of $PR@1 \sim 5$. The randomized algorithm (PS+RW) takes advantage of the call graph to find root causes better than the Pattern-Similarity-Only (PS). However, TBAC, which regards the call graph as a dependency graph, shows poorer performance, even compared to the Pattern-Similarity-Only (PS). This result is particularly inter-

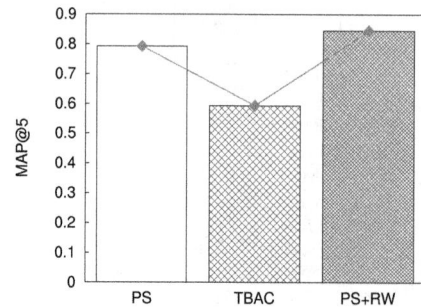

Figure 7: Effect of graph algorithm. Randomized use of the call graph improves performance, but the deterministic algorithm may degrade performance.

esting because an invalid assumption on the dependency between sensors can make the performance worse. In conclusion, when the call graph does not reliably represent a dependency graph, the randomized algorithm (PS+RW) on the call graph is helpful in finding root causes and we observe that treating the call graph as a strong dependency graph can be harmful in this context.

7. CONCLUSION

In this paper, we addressed the problem of finding the root causes for a given anomaly in a service-oriented web architecture. More specifically, when an anomaly is detected on a website's frontend sensor (that is, a service and API combination), our goal is to offer a ranked list of sensors to examine, with the higher ranked sensors more likely to be the root cause. This problem is challenging because the call graph, composed of API calls, does not reliably depict a dependency graph due to missing external factors.

To use call graph to increase the rank quality, we propose a random walk algorithm with preference given to similar looking sensors. Furthermore, to capture external factors not obtained by the call graph, we introduce a pseudo-anomaly clustering algorithm on historical data. We combine the two features by running the computationally intensive clustering algorithm offline and the random walk algorithm online, and provide quick results in the event of a user-facing outage. We evaluate our algorithm on production labeled anomaly dataset from LinkedIn and show significant improvement over baseline models.

We also found that even though the call graph does not represent a true dependency graph of sensors, it can be used to extract useful information during ranking. This extraction method is generic and can be leveraged by other applications, such as data center optimization.

References

[1] T. Ahmed, B. Oreshkin, and M. Coates. Machine Learning Approaches to Network Anomaly Detection. In *SysML*, 2007.

[2] A. Arefin, K. Nahrstedt, R. Rivas, J. Han, and Z. Huang. DIAMOND: Correlation-Based Anomaly Monitoring Daemon for DIME. In *ISM*, 2010.

[3] M. Basseville and I. V. Nikiforov. *Detection of Abrupt Changes - Theory and Application*. Prentice-Hall, 1993.

[4] A. T. Bouloutas, S. Calo, and A. Finkel. Alarm Correlation and Fault Identification in Communication Networks. *TCOM*, 42(2–4):523–533, 1994.

[5] V. Chandola, A. Banerjee, and V. Kumar. Anomaly Detection: A Survey. *CSUR*, 41(3):15:1–15:58, 2009.

[6] C. S. Chao, D. L. Yang, and A. C. Liu. An Automated Fault Diagnosis System Using Hierarchical Reasoning and Alarm Correlation. *JNSM*, 9(2):183–202, 2001.

[7] M. Chen, A. X. Zheng, J. Lloyd, M. I. Jordan, and E. Brewer. Failure Diagnosis Using Decision Trees. In *ICAC*, 2004.

[8] L. Cherkasova, K. Ozonat, N. Mi, J. Symons, and E. Smirni. Automated Anomaly Detection and Performance Modeling of Enterprise Applications. *TOCS*, 27(3):6:1–6:32, 2009.

[9] P. H. dos Santos Teixeira and R. L. Milidiú. Data stream anomaly detection through principal subspace tracking. In *SAC*, 2010.

[10] B. Efron, I. Johnstone, T. Hastie, and R. Tibshirani. The Least Angle Regression Algorithm for Solving the Lasso. *Annals of Statistics*, 32(2):407–451, 2004.

[11] J. Gao, G. Jiang, H. Chen, and J. Han. Modeling Probabilistic Measurement Correlations for Problem Determination in Large-Scale Distributed Systems. In *ICDCS*, 2009.

[12] A. M. Hein and S. A. Mckinley. Sensing and Decision-making in Random Search. *PNAS*, 109(30):12070–12074, 2012.

[13] A. Jalali and S. Sanghavi. Learning the Dependence Graph of Time Series with Latent Factors. In *ICML*, 2012.

[14] G. Jeh and J. Widom. Scaling Personalized Web Search. In *WWW*, 2003.

[15] M. Jiang, M. A. Munawar, T. Reidemeister, and P. A. S. Ward. Dependency-aware Fault Diagnosis with Metric-correlation Models in Enterprise software systems. In *CNSM*, 2010.

[16] R. Jiang, H. Fei, and J. Huan. Anomaly Localization for Network Data Streams with Graph Joint Sparse PCA. In *KDD*, 2011.

[17] I. T. Jolliffe. *Principal Component Analysis*. Springer, second edition, Oct. 2002.

[18] M. Khan, H. K. Le, H. Ahmadi, T. Abdelzaher, and J. Han. DustMiner: Troubleshooting Interactive Complexity Bugs in Sensor Networks. In *Sensys*, 2008.

[19] J. Kreps, N. Narkhede, and J. Rao. Kafka: A Distributed Messaging System for Log Processing. In *NetDB*, 2011.

[20] D. Liben-Nowell and J. Kleinberg. The link prediction problem for social networks. In *CIKM*, pages 556–559, 2003.

[21] Y. Liu, L. Zhang, and Y. Guan. A Distributed Data Streaming Algorithm for Network-wide Traffic Anomaly Detection. In *SIGMETRICS*, 2009.

[22] A. Mahimkar, Z. Ge, J. Wang, J. Yates, Y. Zhang, J. Emmons, B. Huntley, and M. Stockert. Rapid Detection of Maintenance Induced Changes in Service Performance. In *CoNEXT*, 2011.

[23] N. Marwede, M. Rohr, A. V. Hoorn, and W. Hasselbring. Automatic Failure Diagnosis Support in Distributed Large-Scale Software Systems Based on Timing Behavior Anomaly Correlation. In *CSMR*, 2009.

[24] L. Page, S. Brin, R. Motwani, and T. Winograd. The PageRank Citation Ranking: Bringing Order to the Web. Technical Report 1999-66, Stanford InfoLab, 1999.

[25] M. P. Papazoglou and W.-J. Heuvel. Service Oriented Architectures: Approaches, Technologies and Research Issues. *The VLDB Journal*, 16(3):389–415, July 2007.

[26] A. B. Sharma, L. Golubchik, and R. Govindan. Sensor Faults: Detection Methods and Prevalence in Real-World Datasets. *TOSN*, 6(3):23:1–23:39, 2010.

[27] M. Steinder and A. S. Sethi. A Survey of Fault Localization Techniques in Computer Networks. *Science of Computer Programming*, 53(2):165–194, 2004.

[28] S. C. Tan, K. M. Ting, and T. F. Liu. Fast Anomaly Detection for Streaming Data. In *IJCAI*, 2011.

[29] R. Tibshirani. Regression Shrinkage and Selection via the Lasso. *J. Royal. Stats. Soc B.*, 58(1):267–288, 1996.

[30] G. M. Viswanathan, S. V. Buldyrev, S. Havlin, M. G. E. da Luz, E. P. Raposo, and H. E. Stanley. Optimizing the Success of Random Searches. *Nature*, 401:911–914, 1999.

[31] C. Wang, K. Schwan, V. Talwar, G. Eisenhauer, L. Hu, and M. Wolf. A Flexible Architecture Integrating Monitoring and Analytics for Managing Large-Scale Data Centers. In *ICAC*, 2011.

[32] C. Wang, I. A. Rayan, G. Eisenhauer, K. Schwan, V. Talwar, M. Wolf, and C. Huneycutt. VScope: Middleware for Troubleshooting Time-Sensitive Data Center Applications. In *Middleware*, 2012.

[33] W. Xing and A. Ghorbani. Weighted PageRank Algorithm. In *CNSR*, 2004.

[34] L. Xiong, X. Chen, and J. Schneider. Direct Robust Matrix Factorization for Anomaly Detection. In *ICDM*, 2011.

[35] H. Xu, C. Caramais, and S. Sanghavi. Robust PCA via Outlier Pursuit. In *NIPS*, 2010.

[36] H. Yan, A. Flavel, Z. Ge, A. Gerber, D. Massey, C. Papadopoulos, H. Shah, and J. Yates. Argus: End-to-end Service Anomaly Detection and Localization from an ISP's Point of View. 2012.

[37] F. Yang and D. Xiao. Progress in Root Cause and Fault Propagation Analysis of Large-Scale Industrial Processes. *Journal of Control Science and Engineering*, 2012:1–10, 2012.

[38] Z.-Q. Zhang, C.-G. Wu, B.-K. Zhang, T. Xia, and A.-F. Li. SDG Multiple Fault Diagnosis by Real-time Inverse Inference. 87(2):173–189, 2005.

APPENDIX

PROOF OF THEOREM 1. Let $m^* = \arg\max_i \pi_{v'_i}$. We will then show $m^* = m$.

We first show that $\max_i \pi_{v'_i} > \min_i \pi_{v'_i}$. Suppose that $\max_i \pi_{v'_i} = \min_i \pi_{v'_i}$, which implies that $\pi_{v'_i} = \frac{1}{m}$ for all $i = 1, 2, \cdots, m$. To see the stationary state at v'_m, the following statement should hold:

$$\pi_{v'_m} = \frac{\alpha}{1+\rho}\pi_{v'_{m-1}} + (1-\alpha)\frac{1}{m}, .$$

However, it is a contradiction because $\pi_{v'_m} = \pi_{v'_{m-1}} = \frac{1}{m}$ and $\rho < 1$. Hence, $\max_i \pi_{v'_i} > \min_i \pi_{v'_i}$.

Now suppose that $2 \le m^* \le m - 1$. In other words, there exists l and r such that $v'_l \to v'_{m^*} \to v'_r$. At $v_{m'}$, we state the stationary probability as follows:

$$\pi_{v'_m} = \alpha\left(\frac{1}{1+\rho}\pi_{v'_l} + \frac{\rho}{1+\rho}\pi_{v'_r}\right) + (1-\alpha)\frac{1}{m}.$$

However, because $\max_i \pi_{v'_i} > \min_i \pi_{v'_i}$, $\pi_{v'_m} > \frac{1}{m}$. Also, by definition $\pi_{v'_m} \ge \pi_{v'_l}$ or $\pi_{v'_r}$. This means that the left-hand side is greater than the right-hand side in the above stationary probability equation, so it is contradiction. Therefore, m^* is not $2, \cdots, m-1$.

If $m^* = 1$, to see $\pi_{v'_1}$,

$$\pi_{v'_1} = \alpha\frac{\rho}{1+\rho}\pi_{v'_2} + (1-\alpha)\frac{1}{m}.$$

Similarly, because $\pi_{v'_1} \ge \pi_{v'_2}$ and $\pi_{v'_1} > \frac{1}{m}$, this is a contradiction. Therefore, $m^* = m$. □

The Design Space of Probing Algorithms for Network-Performance Measurement

Aaron D. Jaggard[*]
Rutgers University
adj@dimacs.rutgers.edu

Swara Kopparty[†]
Harvard University
skopparty@post.harvard.edu

Vijay Ramachandran[‡]
Colgate University
vijayr@cs.colgate.edu

Rebecca N. Wright[§]
Rutgers University
rebecca.wright@rutgers.edu

ABSTRACT

We present a framework for the design and analysis of probing methods to monitor network performance, an important technique for collecting measurements in tasks such as fault detection. We use this framework to study the interaction among numerous, possibly conflicting, optimization goals in the design of a probing algorithm. We present a rigorous definition of a probing-algorithm design problem that can apply broadly to network-measurement scenarios. We also present several metrics relevant to the analysis of probing algorithms, including probing frequency and network coverage, communication and computational overhead, and the amount of algorithm state required. We show inherent tradeoffs among optimization goals and give hardness results for achieving some combinations of optimization goals. We also consider the possibility of developing approximation algorithms for achieving some of the goals and describe a randomized approach as an alternative, evaluating it using our framework. Our work aids future development of low-overhead probing techniques and introduces principles from IP-based networking to theoretically grounded approaches for concurrent path-selection problems.

Categories and Subject Descriptors

C.2.3 [**Computer-Communication Networks**]: Network Operations—*Network monitoring*; C.4 [**Performance of Systems**]: Measurement techniques; F.2.3 [**Analysis of Algorithms and Problem Complexity**]: Tradeoffs among Complexity Measures

General Terms

Algorithms, Measurement

Keywords

Network-performance analysis; probing algorithms; probing metrics and complexity measures; design-space tradeoffs; hardness results; randomized probing; coupon-collector's problem

1. INTRODUCTION

Operators must monitor performance of their networks for many reasons, *e.g.*, providers may want to ensure that customers' service-level agreements (SLAs) are being fulfilled [22], or administrators of a datacenter may want to detect and diagnose abnormalities affecting latency-critical applications [20]. The measurement data used to analyze performance or to detect anomalies can be inferred from observing existing traffic, or they can be collected from analyzing the properties of test packets (or probes) injected into the network. Both types of methods have benefits and drawbacks. For example, the former, more passive, type of measurement is lower cost but restricts analysis to data that happens to be available. Probing can give more current and accurate information about the state of the network; but, realizing the benefits of probing without incurring substantial overhead involves important design decisions, because the injected test traffic can consume network resources. Thus, the design of low-overhead probing methods is an important, ongoing area of research.

However, the "correct" definition of "low-overhead" is unclear, because overhead of a probing method can be described in many ways, *e.g.*: the raw amount of additional probing traffic, the distribution of probing traffic among nodes and links in the network, the number of monitoring stations involved, the amount of state required to coordinate probing, *etc*. Optimizing any one of these measures may come at the detriment of another. More importantly, there may be tradeoffs among these overhead-minimization goals and the quality of the measurements obtained or the scope of the network that can be monitored properly. We demonstrate several such tradeoffs in this paper.

[*]Partially supported by NSF grants 0751674, 0753492, and 1101690. Work done in part while Visiting Assistant Professor of Computer Science, Colgate University. Current affiliation: Formal Methods Section (Code 5543), U.S. Naval Research Laboratory.

[†]Work done in part during the 2010 DIMACS/DIMATIA U.S./Czech International REU Program while supported by NSF grants 0753492 and 1004956.

[‡]Partially supported by NSF grant 0753061 and by the DIMACS special focus on Algorithmic Foundations of the Internet. Work done in part while visiting DIMACS, Rutgers University.

[§]Partially supported by NSF grants 0753061 and 1101690.

Our goal in this paper is neither to posit a single "correct" notion of overhead nor is it to propose a single probing method that achieves the "correct" balance among overhead and measurement quality. Instead, we seek to build on work that investigates tradeoffs in probing-method design (*e.g.*, [3,5,18]) by beginning a thorough exploration of the space of probing algorithms and the various tradeoffs inherent in that space. A good deal of research has studied how to infer performance characteristics from end-to-end measurements (the field of network tomography, *e.g.*, [8,10]), and how to use network measurements to diagnose traffic anomalies (*e.g.*, [9]). However, research that studies the design and impact of the measurement technique itself is more sparse and generally considers a small set of optimization goals at a time. In this paper, we attempt to understand the relationships among a broad set of optimization goals in a more general sense. Towards this end, we focus here on unicast probing along traffic-routable paths that is used to collect end-to-end measurements; we present, and work with, an abstraction of the probing-design problem that is general enough to capture the problem of designing a probing strategy for a variety of tasks, including anomaly detection or tomography. This allows us to investigate the tradeoffs in the design of probing techniques.

1.1 A motivating example

Probing can be used for detecting performance anomalies by recording transmission failures, slow speeds, *etc.*, as probe packets travel along paths in the network. It is unreasonable to probe all possible paths all the time; this would detect anomalies quickly, but it could unreasonably burden the network with probing traffic (and even exacerbate problems that it might be used to detect). Instead, consider a minimum set-covering approach (a variant of that used in [5]): Precompute (or approximate) a minimum-size subset of paths that includes all the links of interest, and then probe only these paths at repeated time intervals. After the precomputation phase, the probing can be decentralized with little state (because source nodes for probing packets need only keep track of the destinations of precomputed probing paths); in addition, it is guaranteed to measure every link of interest, resulting in reasonably fast anomaly detection. However, as shown by Barford *et al.* [3], this procedure can create unnecessary load on links, probing them from multiple sources in the same time interval. And, as we show in Sec. 6, because finding a minimal set of paths is NP-complete, it may be unreasonable to perform the computation (even though a $O(\log n)$-approximation exists) whenever the network topology or routing changes.

Alternately, Barford *et al.* [3] propose an algorithm that balances the tradeoff among two important goals: ensuring that each network link is probed "often enough" (parameterized by an importance value I_ℓ for each link ℓ) and ensuring that the the link load is kept low (measured by the number of concurrent probing streams transiting a link). Their experimental results show an improvement in load over the minimal set-covering technique. The algorithm selects a subset of paths to probe in each time interval based on a dynamic weight that helps track which links were probed in previous intervals; in this way, paths that contain links that have not been probed in some time (relative to their importance) will be chosen, but links will tend not to be "over-probed." More formally, initialize the dynamic weight w_ℓ of each link ℓ to be 0, and let the weight of a path be the sum of the weights of the links it comprises. Then in each timestep, for fixed parameters k and K, k paths selected randomly from the K paths of largest weight are probed. For the next timestep, link weights are updated in the following manner: the weight of every link just probed is set to 0; the weight of every

other link is updated to $w_{\ell}' = \min\left(I_\ell, w_\ell + \frac{I_\ell}{(N-1)/k}\right)$, where N is the total number of paths that can be probed.

Although this algorithm achieves a balance among the two important goals mentioned above, it comes at the expense of other algorithm properties that might be desirable; in particular, there are properties that the set-covering approach has that this algorithm does not. First, this algorithm requires some additional, constantly updated, state, because the dynamic link weights used for path selection must be adjusted at every timestep. Second, it requires some amount of centralization or communication among the nodes sending probing packets, because the number of paths selected and the updates to link weights must be coordinated; nodes cannot meet the algorithm's specification by independently deciding when to send probing packets. Third, we show that there are inputs for which this algorithm may never probe some particular links. (We give such an example in Sec. 7.1.2.)

It is not clear whether the combinations of properties achieved by these two different approaches are mutually exclusive or not. More generally, it is not clear from previous work what, if any, tradeoffs are inherent in the design of probing algorithms. This paper begins to address these types of questions by identifying algorithmic properties of interest and investigating their relationships.

1.2 Our contributions

In this paper, we rigorously develop a framework for analyzing the design space of probing algorithms. We give a formal definition of an abstraction for the probing-algorithm design problem (Sec. 3) that is general enough to capture various goals of unicast probing techniques used for end-to-end measurements. Applications of our results include the design of network-tomography or anomaly-detection algorithms. We highlight assumptions about inputs to the problem, often taken for granted in previous work, that are relevant to the difficulty of solving the problem. Our framework also includes different types of metrics (Sec. 4) that can be used to evaluate probing-path selection; these metrics correspond to realistic optimization goals and constraints that network operators may have.

We use this framework to demonstrate some inherent tradeoffs in the design space of probing algorithms (Sec. 5). Specifically, there exist networks such that algorithms that perform well with respect to some metrics will perform badly with respect to other metrics. Further, for numerous combinations of optimization goals, it is computationally intractable to find a sequence of paths that achieves that combination of goals, even approximately (Sec. 6). Finally, we consider a randomized approach (Sec. 7) as an alternative, evaluating it using the properties defined in our framework.

2. RELATED WORK

Barford *et al.* [2] were among the first to examine tradeoffs in probing-strategy design. They introduce the concept of marginal utility to probing-node selection for topology discovery. They find that adding nodes to the set of probing sources has quickly diminishing utility (*i.e.*, provides little additional topology information) beyond the second node, while adding nodes to the set of probing destinations is much more helpful. Because that work is focused on topology discovery, issues of constant monitoring overhead are not considered.

Bejerano and Rastogi [5] address the problem of low-overhead probing for anomaly detection with a two-phase approach, separately considering the number of source nodes involved in probing and the cost of probing traffic resulting from that choice. They show that the optimization problem in each phase is NP-hard but admits approximation based on well-known algorithms for Minimum Set Cover and Minimum Vertex Cover. Their work does not consider the relationship between the two phases' optimization goals, nor does it consider how minimizing overall network load (a sum over all paths chosen) might impact individual links in terms of load. (We examine versions of both of these tradeoffs in Sec. 5.) It also does not consider probing frequency (in that all chosen paths are continually used for monitoring). Further, their formulation is more specific than ours, in that its measurement strategy sends a probe from the same source node to both endpoints of a link; thus the network-coverage requirements of the selected nodes and paths differ slightly from our setting.

Nguyen *et al.* [18] present a variant of the probing-design problem with a polynomial-time solution: they consider how to design a probing strategy, by choosing the frequency at which paths are probed, that minimizes the total number of probing packets needed to detect two different types of reachability failures; by allowing different coverage requirements of probes based on the type of failure being detected, they are able to reduce their optimization problem to linear programming. Their setting is more specific than most previous work and our work because of the coverage relaxation; similar toBejerano and Rastogi [5], Nguyen *et al.* use a network-wide definition of overhead without considering per-link impacts.

As discussed above in Sec. 1.1, Barford *et al.* [3] propose an algorithm for anomaly detection that attempts to balance the frequency at which links are probed with the per-link load imposed by probes. That work does not use network-wide overhead metrics, such as the total number of paths or packets, as optimization goals. In addition to the algorithm for anomaly detection, Barford *et al.* propose a probing strategy for localization of the anomaly.

Song *et al.* [23] develop the NetQuest framework and apply it to additive performance metrics (such as delay, in contrast to nonlinear metrics such as failure). They use Bayesian experimental design to (centrally) choose the paths that would be probed in a way that would maximize the benefit to the experiment (according to a chosen metric). They also consider the problem, distinct from what we consider here, of how to best infer information about the network from a limited set of measurements.

As we do here, Breslau *et al.* [7] provide a theoretical treatment of problems relevant to network monitoring, but they focus on novel facility-location problems. Their work, like ours, includes properties of IP networks in the definition of an optimization problem requiring the choice of paths to cover network resources. For example, sets of paths are included in the problem input to account for a preselection of forwarding paths by some underlying network-routing mechanism.

There are several relevant theoretically grounded results about difficult path-selection problems. However, many of these problems do not account for routing issues. For example, the Multiple Edge Disjoint Paths problem [11] seeks a maximum-cardinality subset of given source-destination pairs such that a directed path can be assigned to each pair with no two pairs' paths sharing an edge in common. This problem is NP-hard in general. Although it resembles the problem of finding a maximum-cardinality set of non-overlapping probing paths in a network, there is an important difference: in the network-probing setting, there is often only one possible directed path to assign to any source-destination pair (*e.g.*, the IP-forwarding path from the source to the destination computed by some routing protocol). We show in Sec. 6 that, unfortunately, this restriction does not make the problem easy.

Parekh and Segev [19] describe the Path Hitting problem, which has a direct correlation to minimum covering in our setting. Assuming that each path $p \in \mathscr{D}$ is associated with a cost c_p, and saying that $p \in \mathscr{H}$ hits $p' \in \mathscr{D}$ if p and p' share at least one edge, the Path Hitting problem is: Given two sets of paths $\mathscr{D}$ and $\mathscr{H}$ in an undirected graph G, find a minimum-cost subset of $\mathscr{H}$ whose members collectively hit those of $\mathscr{D}$. The NP-complete Minimum Set Cover problem reduces to Path Hitting, and Path Hitting is a special case of Minimum Set Cover, implying the same approximation results for Path Hitting as for Set Cover. We use a similar reduction to show a hardness result for one of our probing-design problem variants (see Sec. 6).

3. FORMALIZING THE PROBLEM

The following is our definition of the abstract problem of probing-algorithm design for a network. The output corresponds to an implementation of selecting paths to probe over time. Like the problem definitions in [7]—but unlike routing-agnostic formulations, *e.g.*, the Maximum Edge Disjoint Paths problem [11], in which any set of links can be chosen to form paths between source-destination pairs—we assume that the set of possible probing paths is somehow constrained (*e.g.*, by some underlying routing system) and thus forms part of the input to the problem.

DEFINITION 3.1 (PROBING ALGORITHM). *For an undirected network* $G = (V, E)$ *and a set of paths* $\mathscr{P} \subseteq 2^E$, *define a (possibly randomized) algorithm* $f : \mathbb{N} \to 2^{\mathscr{P}}$ *that, for each discrete timestep* $t = 1, 2, \ldots$, *selects a set of paths from* $\mathscr{P}$. *We call* f *a* probing algorithm *for* $(G, \mathscr{P})$ *(or just a* probing algorithm*), and we think of* $f(t)$ *as the set of paths that will be probed at time* t.

Of course, without any additional requirements, the problem is uninteresting; thus, at various points below, we impose different additional restrictions on f and $\mathscr{P}$, occasionally requiring additional parameters as input to the design problem. Such additional requirements might also be needed to ensure that a probing algorithm is suitable for a particular application or that it achieves certain other goals that may also be desired. For example, consider the problem of designing a sequence that guarantees measurement across some of the network's links: here, we may assume that the input specifies a subset of links $F \subseteq E$ and may require that every link in F appears in at least one path in $\cup_t f(t)$. Sec. 4 presents five categories of metrics and optimization goals that we use to vary the problem definition in this way.

Specifying the set $\mathscr{P}$ as part of the input is motivated by the possibility of having a predefined subset of *probing nodes* $R \subseteq V$ that are the allowed sources and destinations of the probing messages (or *probes*). If $u \in R$ may send a probe to $v \in R$, the path that this takes may be determined by the underlying routing system; this path (but not necessarily *all* paths from u to v in G) would then be included in $\mathscr{P}$.

Some additional requirements on the structure of $\mathscr{P}$ that are of interest below (but which are not, in general, assumed to hold) are: (1) $\mathscr{P}$ contains a path between every ordered pair of distinct nodes in $R \times R$; (2) $\mathscr{P}$ contains only one path for each ordered probing-node pair (u, v) (but the path for (v, u) need not be its reverse);[1] (3) $\mathscr{P}$ corresponds to destination-based IP routing, *i.e.*, the various paths in $\mathscr{P}$ must not be inconsistent with their being parts of routing sink trees (in particular, if $\mathscr{P}$ contains multiple paths with destination $v \in R$ that also include the node $u \in V$, then all of these paths coincide between u and the destination v); (4) $\mathscr{P}$ corresponds to paths that are consistent with a *coherent* cost function [12] used

---

[1]This assumption precludes multipath routing and load balancing due to traffic engineering, but it permits our analysis to assume, with certainty, which links are covered by a given probe.

as the basis for route selection.[2] We will explicitly highlight when any of these assumptions hold and when those assumptions impact our results.

A variation of this problem (*e.g.*, similar to that considered in [5]) is one in which the probing nodes R are not predefined but must be chosen, perhaps to optimize some metric. This is a special case of the problem above: let $R = V$, let $\mathscr{P}$ contain viable probing paths between all ordered pairs of nodes, and additionally require that the union of source and destination nodes over all sets of paths output by the algorithm (*i.e.*, the target R) meets the desired constraints.

In some cases, it makes sense to perform some precomputation on the input (like the first step of the two-phase approach in [5]) to limit $\mathscr{P}$ to a selected subset of paths from the original network as a starting point for designing a probing algorithm. One useful property (that we use in some analyses below) for such a set of paths is the following.

DEFINITION 3.2 (MINIMAL SET OF PATHS). *A set of paths $\mathscr{P}$ is* minimal *with respect to a set of edges $F \subseteq E$ if every path in $\mathscr{P}$ must be probed to cover all edges in F; i.e., every $P \in \mathscr{P}$ traverses at least one link that does not appear in any of the other paths in $\mathscr{P}$.*

This is not a strong property: given any set of paths whose union covers all the edges in F, we may simply go through the paths in some arbitrary order and discard any whose edges all appear in previously seen paths. It does not guarantee that the resulting set is of *minimum* possible size; however, it lets us assume that we can always produce a minimal set and therefore decouple the problem of finding the "best" (*e.g.*, minimum-sized) minimal set from the problem of designing an algorithm to probe all the paths in a given minimal set.

4. METRICS AND OPTIMIZATION GOALS

We have five categories of metrics by which we analyze probing algorithms. Different applications may lead to a focus on different combinations of these (and perhaps other) metrics.

4.1 Number of probes or probing nodes used

This family of metrics corresponds to optimization goals that appear most often in previous work to represent low overhead or resource minimization, *e.g.*, [5, 18].

Let $X = \cup_t f(t)$ be the set of paths probed[3] by algorithm f, and let $N \subseteq R$ be the set of probing nodes used by the sequence; these are endpoints of paths in X. (Note that some previous work, *e.g.*, [2, 5], has separately categorized sources and destinations of probing paths.) Then, $|X|$ (the number of probing paths, which is the number of distinct probes needed) and $|N|$ (the number of probing nodes) serve as natural metrics for f, with the corresponding possible optimization goals: (1) require that f minimize $|X|$; and/or (2) require that f minimize $|N|$. We explore the interaction among these goals in Secs. 5 and 6.1.

4.2 Probing frequency

This family of metrics formalizes the flexibility in probing-algorithm design explored in [3, 18], *i.e.*, that dividing probes over time can reduce overhead while retaining effectiveness as long as measurements are collected "often enough." The following ways

to characterize the frequency at which links are probed attempt to make this notion precise so that we can better describe the tradeoffs between frequent and infrequent probing. Of course, it is trivial to minimize the delay between measurements if no additional restrictions are placed on the algorithm: just probe every path at every timestep. We investigate the difficulty of combining this goal with others in Sec. 6.

Probing probability: Assume there exists a parameter k that describes a length of time (in number of timesteps). We can then measure the minimum probability, over all time windows of length k (intervals of consecutive timesteps of length k), that a given link is probed by f. For a corresponding optimization goal, assume that each link $\ell \in E$ is assigned a parameter p_ℓ, and require that, for every time window of length k and for every link ℓ, f probes ℓ with probability bounded below by p_ℓ. A simpler version of this goal (especially appropriate for deterministic f) is to ensure that a subset of links is probed with some regularity (or at all), *i.e.*, there exists a subset of "links of interest" $F \subseteq E$ such that $p_\ell = 1$ for $\ell \in F$ and $p_\ell = 0$ for $\ell \notin F$. We note that certain hardness proofs below require setting $F = E$.

Probing delay: We can measure the (average, maximum, *etc.*) time between probes of a given link. For an optimization goal, assume that every link ℓ has a parameter k_ℓ; we can then require that, for all links ℓ and for all times t, the expected time it will take to next probe ℓ after t is bounded above by k_ℓ. A simpler condition on f would be to require that the expected time to probe every link is bounded (*i.e.*, finite).

4.3 Load on links

In order to better understand the tradeoffs between additional probing and other goals, we want to characterize the effect of generated probing traffic on network resources. For example, an algorithm that probes on all paths in every timestep will minimize measurement delay on all links covered but uses a lot of network traffic.

The following two metrics focus on per-link effects of probing traffic (in contrast to the more global measures in Sec. 4.1 and in [5, 18]). We can measure, for some time parameter k and for every link $\ell \in E$: (1) the (expected, maximum, *etc.*) number of times that probes traverse ℓ over all time windows of length k; (2) the probability that ℓ is probed more than once (or more than some threshold L_ℓ) in a time window of size k. Analogously, we can impose as a requirement on a probing algorithm that, given parameters k and per-link load limits L_ℓ, the expected number of times ℓ is probed in any time window of length k is at most L_ℓ.

We note that it is also trivial to minimize per-timestep link loads if no additional restrictions are placed on the algorithm: simply iterate through probing paths, probing one at each timestep. This, of course, may probe many links with low frequency; if link load must be kept at a minimum while simultaneously increasing probing frequency, the design problem becomes difficult (see Sec. 6).

4.4 Load on nodes

The probing nodes, *i.e.*, source and destination nodes for messages sent to acquire measurements, incur some computational load for having to generate and process probe traffic. Thus, we may be interested in evaluating how many requests a probing algorithm imposes on probing nodes.

More precisely, we can measure the number of probe messages for which each node $r \in R$ is a source or destination in a time window of some size k; as a design goal, we may require that an algorithm involve each node r as a probing source or destination at

---

[2]*I.e.*, each directed edge is assigned a cost—with negative-cost edges allowed as long as all directed cycles have positive cost—and the lowest-cost directed path is chosen for routing.

[3]For a randomized algorithm f, we take this to be the set of paths that f might possibly probe.

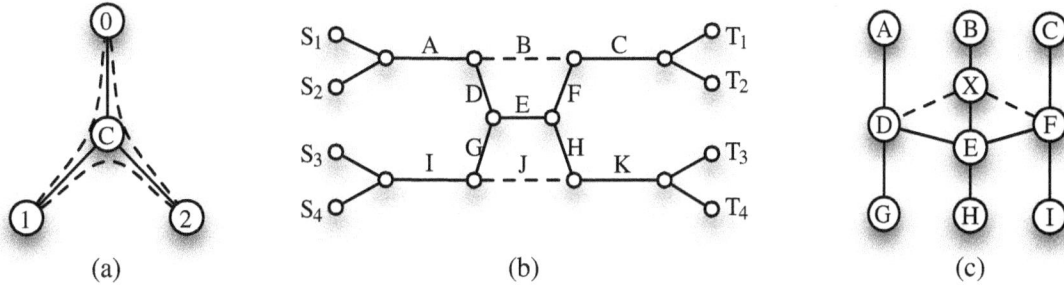

Figure 1: Example networks illustrating various tradeoffs among probing-algorithm design goals.

most n_r times in a time window of size k, given input parameters n_r (for each node r) and k. We investigate this type of goal in Sec. 6.2.

There may also be some computational load incurred by non-probing nodes while forwarding probing packets. This load may not be accurately captured by link-load metrics used in previous work; *e.g.*, in a star topology, the central node is involved in the communication of a probing packet for every link, even if it is not a probing node itself. Thus, we may want to measure the total load on non-probing nodes and perhaps try to bound it when designing an algorithm.

It is possible to transform networks so that link-load metrics may capture load on nodes: expand each node v into a pair of connected nodes (i, j) such that all paths through v now traverse i then j (and never in reverse), connecting i and j to the expanded versions of the neighbors of v in the original network; then, the number of probing packets traversing v corresponds to the number traversing the link (i, j) in the transformed network.

4.5   State complexity

Different probing algorithms may require different amounts or kinds of internal state to be implemented, as discussed in Sec. 1.1. The algorithms that we consider will typically use some combination of fixed-length values, *e.g.*, constants and counters, but they might also keep track of dynamic-length values, *e.g.*, sets of probing paths (or sequences of such sets). These might be global values, or they may be stored at each network node, stored for each network link, or stored for each probing path. We are able to obtain at least partial comparisons among different algorithms' levels of complexity and implementation difficulty by considering the amount and type of state required by their implementations.

5.   TRADEOFFS

In this section, we use three example networks (shown in Fig. 1) to illustrate tradeoffs among some of the probing-algorithm design goals discussed in Sec. 4. In particular, we demonstrate that optimization of one metric may come at the expense of another metric. Although the examples are small, toy networks, it is possible to produce networks of larger size or of more realistic topologies that have similar properties. However, even these small examples are enough to show the existence of networks on which it may be impossible to choose a probing strategy that achieves multiple optimization goals.

5.1   Probing frequency and number of probing paths used

Our first example is shown in Fig. 1(a), a star with four nodes. Here, the possible probing paths (the set $\mathscr{P}$) are all three of the paths between two degree-1 vertices, shown as dashed lines. Sup-

pose we place a link-load bound of one probing message per timestep for every link. Then, at most one path in $\mathscr{P}$ can be probed in any timestep, and it is impossible to probe every link in every timestep. However, probing any two distinct paths from this set will cover all three links in the network over two timesteps; this can be done using two different approaches. The first approach probes all three paths (at different times), *e.g.*, sending a probe from i to $i + 1$ (all indices considered modulo 3) when time $t \equiv i \mod 3$. The second approach selects any two of the paths (which necessarily have a link in common) and then alternates between which one is used to probe (*e.g.*, sending a probe from node 2 to node i when time $t \equiv i \mod 2$).

Under each of these approaches, every link in the network is probed at least once every two timesteps, and, in each timestep, some link is not probed. In the first approach, every link is uniformly not probed every third timestep; in the second approach, one link is probed every timestep while the other two are probed at alternating timesteps. Uniformity of probing frequencies across all links (which may be desirable if, *e.g.*, the different network links are of equal importance) comes at the cost of using all three possible probing paths. In the second approach, the set of paths that used for probing is smaller (size 2).

This example easily generalizes to a star on $2k + 2$ nodes (whose degree-1 nodes we label $0, 1, \ldots, 2k$). With $2k + 1$ degree-1 vertices, the algorithm can probe every link $2k$ out of every $2k + 1$ timesteps if uniformity is desired. At the opposite extreme, the algorithm may probe $1/3$ of the links in every timestep (if $2k + 1$ is also a multiple of 3) and the other $2/3$ of the links in half of the timesteps. Both of these approaches still ensure that no link is probed less frequently than every other timestep and that no link carries more than one probe per timestep.

5.2   Balancing load and frequency among various links

Our second example, shown in Fig. 1(b), illustrates the potential benefit that an increase in the link-load limit on just a single link can have with respect to the load imposed on other links, even while also requiring a particular probing frequency for links in the network.

Note that, in the diagram in Fig. 1(b) for this example network, the links, not nodes, are labeled; furthermore, assume that B and J represent groups of links (*i.e.*, paths containing many links). In this network, consider the probing paths S_1ABCT_1, $S_2ADEFCT_2$, $S_3IGEHKT_3$, and S_4IJKT_4. Suppose that links A, C, I, K all should be probed at every timestep, while the links in B, J, and the remaining links in the network need to be probed much less frequently. If link E has a link-load limit of 1 probe per timestep, then in order to probe A, C, I, K, we must probe one of B or J in every timestep, exceeding its target probing frequency and unnecessarily imposing probing load. By increasing the limit on link E to 2, the paths $ADEFC$ and $IGEHK$ can sometimes be used simultaneously instead, equalizing the burden among E, the links in B, and the links in J. Thus, allowing E to occasionally have a load of 2 can reduce the number of extra[4] probes on links over some number of timesteps.

5.3 Number of probing paths and number of probing nodes

Our third example, shown in Fig. 1(c) (ignoring for now the dashed links), shows a network for which the set of paths minimizing the number of probing paths used has a different size than the set of paths minimizing the number of probing nodes used. Let $\mathscr{P}$ contain the paths $ADG, BXEH, CFI, ADEH, CFEH, DEF$; the node-minimizing set uses all of these paths except DEF, involving nodes A, B, C, G, H, I; the path-minimizing set uses only ADG, $BXEH$, CFI, DEF requiring the use of probing nodes $A, B, C, D,$ F, G, H, I.

We note that, in this example, $\mathscr{P}$ does not contain a probing path between every pair of nodes (e.g., between A and C). We may modify this example by adding the dashed links and adding to $\mathscr{P}$ a single probing path between every pair of nodes—all paths except DEF, $ADEH$, $CFEH$ use the new dashed links through X. The node-minimizing and path-minimizing sets are the same as before; in particular, different sets minimize the number of probing nodes and the number of number of probing paths.

However, in the modified example, the paths in $\mathscr{P}$ no longer form a routing tree (i.e., the paths $CFEH$ and $IFXEH$ both have destination H and contain intermediate node F but different subpaths from F to H). We conjecture that there is a set of probing paths covering all network links that minimizes both the number of paths needed to do this and the number of probing nodes that must be used to do this, under the following assumptions: (1) the union of all probing paths covers all links in the underlying network; (2) there is a probing path between every two probing nodes; and, (3) for every probing node, the probing paths to that node form a routing tree.

6. HARDNESS AND APPROXIMATION

6.1 Minimizing number of probes/nodes used

Suppose we want to design a probing algorithm that covers a target set of links $F \subseteq E$ in the network, but does so either by using as few probing paths or by using as few probing nodes as possible. The results below demonstrate that these probing-design problems are computationally difficult.

THEOREM 6.1. *Given an instance of the probing-algorithm design problem along with a target set of links $F \subseteq E$ to probe, computing a set of probing paths of minimum size that covers F is NP-complete.*

PROOF. It is straightforward to show that the problem is in NP. To show NP-hardness, we give a reduction from Minimum Set Cover (MSC) that is a modification of the reduction from MSC to the Path Hitting problem in [19]. Begin with an instance of MSC: there is a universe of elements U and subsets of those elements $S_1, S_2, \ldots, S_n$; our goal is to choose a minimum-size collection C of

subsets such that the union of the subsets selected for C includes all the elements in U.

Create a probing network based on the MSC input as follows: Let G be a bipartite graph with vertices $x_1, \ldots, x_m$ and $y_1, \ldots, y_m$, where $m = |U|$. For each $i = 1, \ldots, m$, add an edge between x_i and y_i, and let F consist of these edges. These edges correspond to the elements of U, which we assume can be ordered $1, \ldots, m$. For each subset S_j, create an ordered list of indices $k_1, \ldots, k_{S_j}$ that correspond to the order on U. Then, for every adjacent pair of elements k_a, k_{a+1} in the ordered list, create an edge from y_{k_a} to $x_{k_{a+1}}$. Thus there is a path connecting the corresponding (x_i, y_i) edges in G for each the subsets given in the MSC problem, each of which is added to the set of probing paths $\mathscr{P}$. With this construction, a minimum-size set of probing paths selected from $\mathscr{P}$ that covers F maps directly to a minimum-size set cover. $\square$

The above argument shows that designing a probing algorithm that minimizes the number of probing paths used to cover a target set F of network links is computationally intractable. A similar argument can be used to show that minimizing the number of probing nodes is, too: In the reduction above, simply modify G so that, for any path from x_i to y_j corresponding to a subset in the MSC problem, there is an extra vertex adjacent to x_i and an extra vertex adjacent to y_j that serve as the probing source and destination nodes for that path; furthermore, these extra vertices should be unique for each subset in the MSC problem. Then, the number of probing nodes used to probe F corresponds exactly with the number of subsets that would cover U.

We note that our reduction does not construct a set of probing paths consistent with a coherent cost function. The hardness of finding minimizing sets when $\mathscr{P}$ is consistent with a coherent cost function remains an open question.

Because these probing-design problems are special cases of Minimum Set Cover, the standard MSC approximation algorithms apply to finding probe- and node-minimizing sets of probing paths (just as they do to the related Path Hitting problem [19]).

6.2 Limiting work of probing nodes

Suppose we want to limit the load of each probing node to one probe per timestep; in other words, we insist that each probing node send or receive at most one probing packet per timestep. This would mean the maximum number of paths we could probe per timestep is $\lfloor |R| / 2 \rfloor$, although achieving this upper bound might depend on the topology and other constraints. To minimize the number of timesteps needed to probe all links with this node-load constraint, we want the algorithm f to decompose the probing paths into a minimum-length sequence of sets such that no two paths in a set share a probing node. Unfortunately, this design problem is computationally intractable.

THEOREM 6.2. *Designing a probing algorithm that minimizes the number of timesteps in which all possible links are probed while limiting the probing-node load to one probe per timestep is NP-complete.*

PROOF. To simplify the proof, we use the decision version of the probing-design problem in the theorem statement, i.e., designing an algorithm in which the number of timesteps is bounded by some parameter k. The reductions between the decision and optimization versions of the problem are straightforward. It is also easy to see that the problem is in NP.

To show NP-hardness, we give a straightforward reduction from Minimum Edge Coloring (MEC), which is NP-complete [14]. Begin with any instance of MEC: the input is a graph $G = (V, E)$ and

---

[4]I.e., the sum over all links of the number of probes traversing the link minus the number of probes that are required to traverse that link based on its target frequency.

a parameter k, and we are to decide if it is possible to partition E into k disjoint sets $E_{1,\ldots,k}$ such that for each set E_i, no two edges in E_i share a common endpoint. Now, let G be the probing network; let the set R of probing nodes be equal to V, and let the set $\mathscr{P}$ of probing paths be equal to E (so that each probing path consists of a single edge between nodes in the network). Then there is a sequence of sets of probing paths of length k covering the entire network in which each probing node is a source or destination of at most one probing path in each set if and only if the original graph G is k-edge-colorable. $\square$

We note that this reduction creates an instance of the probing-design problem in which the constructed probing-path set $\mathscr{P}$ has no link overlap among paths; in particular, it is minimal.

6.3 Minimizing probing delay with a restriction on link load

As noted in Sec. 4.2, it is trivial to minimize the number of timesteps between probes along every network link if we do not consider any other metrics (simply by probing all paths at every timestep). If we additionally bound the number of probes that may traverse a link in any timestep, then it becomes interesting to ask whether it is possible to probe along all paths in a given probing-path set using at most k timesteps. (In particular, if the probing-path set is minimal, we would need to probe every path to cover all links of interest with delay at most k).

6.3.1 Basic hardness result

We will now show that answering the above question is computationally intractable. We start with the following definition:

DEFINITION 6.3 (L-STRONG k-COLORABLE HYPERGRAPH). *A hypergraph $\mathscr{H}$ is L-strongly k-colorable if there is a k-coloring of the vertices of $\mathscr{H}$ such that no edge of $\mathscr{H}$ has more than L vertices of any one color.*

The L-strong k-colorability problem for hypergraphs is computationally difficult to solve exactly and to approximate. The following theorem provides reductions, in both directions, between this problem and the probing-design problem considered in this subsection (minimizing probing delay subject to a link-load restriction). This result and the reductions in its proof are used to justify the computational intractability of exactly or approximately solving the probing-design problem.

THEOREM 6.4. *Polynomial-time reductions exist between the following two problems: (1) deciding whether a hypergraph is L-strongly k-colorable; and (2) deciding, for a given probing-design-problem input, whether all the probing paths in $\mathscr{P}$ can be probed within k timesteps without imposing a load of more than L on any link in any timestep.*

PROOF. *Reduction from (2) to (1):* Consider a probing problem consisting of a graph $G = (V, E)$ and the set $\mathscr{P}$ of probing paths. Construct a hypergraph $\mathscr{H}$ as follows: The vertices of $\mathscr{H}$ correspond (bijectively) to the elements of $\mathscr{P}$. For each edge $e \in G$, add as an edge in $\mathscr{H}$ the set of those vertices in $\mathscr{H}$ that correspond to the paths in $\mathscr{P}$ that include the edge e. Viewing the colors of vertices in $\mathscr{H}$ as assignments of elements of $\mathscr{P}$ to timesteps, the colorings of $\mathscr{H}$ with i colors in which j is the maximum number of vertices in any one edge with a single color bijectively correspond to the assignments of elements of $\mathscr{P}$ to i timesteps in which the maximum load on any edge in any timestep is j. In particular, deciding L-strong k-colorability of $\mathscr{H}$ decides whether $\mathscr{P}$ can

be probed in k timesteps without an edge load exceeding L in any timestep.

Reduction from (1) to (2): Conversely, consider a hypergraph $\mathscr{H} = (V_{\mathscr{H}}, E_{\mathscr{H}})$ and fixed values of k and L; we wish to decide whether $\mathscr{H}$ is L-strongly k colorable. Fix an ordering $\hat{e}_1, \ldots, \hat{e}_m$ of the edges of $\mathscr{H}$. Construct a network with m disjoint links $e_1, \ldots, e_m$; for the purposes of our construction, make these directed (we will ignore these directions when probing). For each vertex $v \in V_{\mathscr{H}}$ that is contained in at least one hypergraph edge, let ℓ_v be the number of hypergraph edges that contain v, and add to the network the $\ell_v + 1$ nodes s_v, t_v, and $\{x_{(v,i)}\}_{i=1}^{\ell_v - 1}$.

Add to the network $2\ell_v$ links as follows: Let the hyperedges that contain v be (in order) $\{\hat{e}_{i_j}\}_{j=1}^{\ell_v}$. Add a link from s_v to the tail of e_{i_1}, and add a link from the head of $e_{i_{\ell_v}}$ to t_v. For $j = 1, \ldots, \ell_v - 1$, add a link from the head of e_{i_j} to $x_{(v,i_j)}$ and a link from $x_{(v,i_j)}$ to the tail of $e_{i_{j+1}}$.

Once this network is constructed, let the set $\mathscr{P}$ of probing paths contain the $|V_{\mathscr{H}}|$ paths that were implicitly constructed above; the probing path corresponding to a hypergraph vertex v is the (undirected) path whose links are: the link from s_v to the tail of e_{i_1} (where i_1 is as above for this particular v), the link e_{i_1}, the link from the head of e_{i_1} to $x_{(v,i_1)}$, the link from $x_{(v,i_1)}$ to the tail of e_{i_2}, etc., until the link from the head of $e_{i_{\ell_v}}$ to t_v. Note that only one path in $\mathscr{P}$ goes through each network node $x_{(v,i)}$ and the two links incident upon it.

If we have an assignment of probing paths to timesteps $1, \ldots, t$, we may view that as a t-coloring of the vertices of the original hypergraph; vertex v is assigned the color i if and only if its corresponding probing path is probed in timestep i. If the maximum number of probing paths that traverse the network link e_j in any timestep is M, then $\hat{e}_j$ has M, but no more, vertices of one color. (If there are vertices in $\mathscr{H}$ that did not belong to any edge, these can be colored arbitrarily without affecting this. Similarly, if there are empty edges in $\mathscr{H}$, there will be some isolated links in the network; however, these are not part of any probing path.) In particular, an assignment of probing paths to k distinct timesteps such that no link ever carries more than L probes in a timestep is possible if and only if $\mathscr{H}$ was L-strongly k-colorable. Note that the resulting network was constructed with $2|E_{\mathscr{H}}| + \sum_{v \in E_{\mathscr{H}}} d(v)$ nodes (where $d(v)$ is the number of hyperedges containing v) and $|E_{\mathscr{H}}| + 2\sum_{v \in E_{\mathscr{H}}} d(v)$ links. $\square$

Because hypergraph L-strong k-colorability is NP-complete [1], Thm. 6.4 shows that minimizing probing delay subject to a link-load restriction is NP-complete as well. We note that the result applies to the general probing-design problem; it is possible that assumptions on the structure of the probing-path set $\mathscr{P}$ may admit a feasible solution.

6.3.2 Hardness of approximation

Approximating a minimum-delay sequence of probes subject to a link-load restriction is also computationally difficult. Numerous results (*e.g.* [15]) have established the hardness of approximate hypergraph coloring. For each reduction in the proof of Thm. 6.4, note that a solution of size k' in one problem corresponds to a solution of size k' in the other problem. Thus, approximation results for hypergraph coloring also carry over to the probing-design setting.

6.3.3 Link load at most one

Consider the special case of restricting the per-link probing load to one message per timestep. Given the hardness results above, one might attempt to use a greedy bin-packing approach to approximate an optimal selection of probing paths; intuitively, the idea is to "fill" a timestep with the maximum number of concurrent, disjoint probing paths possible before proceeding to the next timestep.

Unfortunately, it turns out that the component problem in this approach, *i.e.*, finding the maximum number of concurrent, disjoint probes, is also computationally intractable.

THEOREM 6.5. *Deciding whether it is possible to probe at least k paths from a given set $\mathscr{P}$ simultaneously when links can carry at most 1 probing message is NP-complete.*

PROOF. It is obvious that the probing decision problem is in NP. To show NP-hardness, we give a straightforward reduction from Independent Set. Given a graph with $|V|$ vertices and $|E|$ edges (sorted in an arbitrary order), construct a network as follows: Create $|V|$ disjoint paths, each with $3|E|$ links. Iterate through the edges of the graph ($i = 0, \ldots, |E| - 1$). For each edge i, let x and y be its endpoints in the graph, and identify the $(3 \cdot i + 2)^{\text{th}}$ edges in the paths corresponding to x and y so that these paths use the same edge in the $(3 \cdot i + 2)^{\text{th}}$ position. Thus, the paths corresponding to x and y may be probed in the same timestep if and only if x and y are not adjacent in the original graph. In particular, the graph has an independent set of size k if and only if at least k of the paths in the network constructed can be probed in the same timestep without sending more than one probe across any single link. □

7. RANDOMIZED PROBING

Our analysis thus far has dealt with deterministic approaches to probing. Because, as we have shown, it is computationally difficult even to approximate an optimal probing algorithm for certain combinations of goals, we now turn instead to randomized probing algorithms. Our focus here will not be on absolute guarantees but on identifying what we can expect (on average) from a baseline class of randomized algorithms.

From an analytic perspective, the class of randomized algorithms we consider can be guaranteed to provide finite expected delay[5] in detecting a network abnormality. Additionally, we can bound the delay more precisely with more assumptions on the probing probabilities used in the algorithm. This is in contrast to previous work (*e.g.*, [3]) that used randomized probing approaches.

However, randomized path selection makes it difficult to disentangle the causes of poor algorithm performance. The probing-design problem is different than problems considered in existing analytical work on concurrent path selection in networks (*e.g.*, [11]) because probes must follow paths determined by an underlying routing system on the network. For example, because it is reasonable to assume that we can only probe the whole paths that appear in the path set (and not their proper subpaths that do not appear in the set), we do not have link- or node-level choice over what gets probed. If we pick paths randomly, it is difficult to say if link- or node-level load is high because certain links or nodes appear on many paths, or whether a particular run of the algorithm was "unlucky" in its random choices. Thus, in order to get more insight into how these randomized algorithms perform with respect to the metrics introduced in Sec. 4, we present simulations of the performance of algorithms from this class.

7.1 Analytic results

A member of the class of randomized algorithms that we consider is described by a set of probabilities $\{g_t(P)\}_{t \geq 1, P \in \mathscr{P}}$. Here,

---

[5]Recall from Sec. 4.2 that the *probing delay* of a link is the number of timesteps between consecutive probes of that link. In the randomized setting, there may not be a fixed pattern describing when a link is probed; thus, we focus on the expected probing delay given the sequence of path-probing probabilities used by the algorithm.

t ranges over all possible timesteps, and P ranges over all probing paths; $g_t(P)$ is the probability that P is probed at time t. (From such a description, we can obtain the description of a probing algorithm in the sense of Def. 3.1.) In particular, the decisions to probe paths are made independently at each timestep, so nodes do not need to retain state. (We discuss below some possibilities for using state, the nature of which may serve as another metric.)

We now investigate the metric of expected probing delay (or expected probing frequency) under various assumptions about the sequence of path-probing probabilities used by the algorithm.

7.1.1 Lower-bounded probabilities

To begin, assume that the path-probing probabilities are strictly positive for all timesteps and for all paths in the probing-path set. We then obtain the following result.

THEOREM 7.1. *If there exists some ε such that $0 < \varepsilon < 1$ and $g_t(P) \geq \varepsilon$ for all timesteps t and for all paths P, then the expected probing delay for any path is finite (in particular, bounded above by $1/\varepsilon^2$).*

PROOF. Let $E_t(P)$ be the expected number of timesteps following timestep t until path P is probed. We may write this as:

$$E_t(P) = 1 \cdot g_{t+1}(P) + 2 \cdot (1 - g_{t+1}(P))(g_{t+2}(P)) \\ + 3(1 - g_{t+1}(P))(1 - g_{t+2}(P))(g_{t+3}(P)) + \ldots \quad (1)$$

In the above expression, we know that all the $g_t(P)$ probabilities are bounded below by ε; thus, every $1 - g_t(P)$ term is bounded above by $1 - \varepsilon$. Furthermore, because each $g_t(P)$ is a probability, we know that it is bounded above by 1. Using these bounds (and the fact that $\varepsilon < 1$), we may bound the expression in (1) as:

$$\begin{aligned} E_t(P) &\leq 1 \cdot 1 + 2 \cdot (1 - \varepsilon)(1) + 3(1 - \varepsilon)^2(1) + \ldots \\ &= \sum_{i=0}^{\infty} i \cdot (1 - \varepsilon)^{i-1} \\ &= \frac{1}{\varepsilon^2}. \end{aligned}$$

Because this calculation is independent of the starting timestep t and the choice of path P, this means that the expected delay for any path P in the network is finite and bounded above by $1/\varepsilon^2$. □

By extension, for finite networks, the above result implies that the time until all paths in the network are probed, regardless of the starting timestep, is also finite.

If we further assume that $g_t(P) = \varepsilon$ for every timestep t and every path P, then we can rewrite the expression in (1) exactly as:

$$\begin{aligned} E_t(P) &= 1 \cdot \varepsilon + 2 \cdot (1 - \varepsilon) \cdot \varepsilon + 3 \cdot (1 - \varepsilon)^2 \cdot \varepsilon + \cdots \\ &= \sum_{i=0}^{\infty} i \cdot (1 - \varepsilon)^{i-1} \cdot \varepsilon \\ &= \frac{1}{\varepsilon}. \end{aligned}$$

This means that, no matter the initial timestep t or path P, the number of expected number of timesteps to probe path P is $1/\varepsilon$. Because we know that each link in the network is covered by some path in the probing-path set, we can be confident that the expected probing delay of any link is bounded by $1/\varepsilon$.

It is important that the path-probing probabilities are nonzero; without this, as we discuss in the next section, it is possible that some links in a network might be forever ignored by the probing algorithm.

7.1.2 Example algorithm with links ignored

The randomized algorithm in [3] probes k paths selected randomly from the K paths of largest dynamic weight, where the dynamic weight of a path is the sum of the dynamic weights of constituent links. Initially, the dynamic weight w_ℓ of each link ℓ is 0. In each timestep after probing, weights are updated as follows: the weight of every link just probed is set to 0; the weight of every other link is updated to $w_\ell' = \min\left(I_\ell, w_\ell + \frac{I_\ell}{(N-1)/k}\right)$, where N is the total number of paths that can be probed and I_ℓ is a link-specific importance parameter. Here, we provide an example in which the algorithm never probes some particular links.

Let $k = K = 1$. Consider a network with three disjoint paths P_1, P_2, and P_3, and let $I_\ell = 1$ for each link ℓ in the network. Let each path P_i have length L_i (number of links), such that $L_1 < L_2 < L_3$ and $L_2 > L_1 \cdot (N-1)/k$. Suppose P_3 is probed in some timestep. All links in P_3 have their dynamic weight set to 0, making P_3 have path weight 0. The maximum dynamic weight of links in P_1 is 1, so the maximum dynamic weight for P_1 is L_1. The minimum dynamic weight for each link in P_2 is $k/(N-1)$ (in the case that P_2 was probed in the previous timestep), so the minimum path weight for P_2 is $L_2 \cdot k/(N-1)$. However, because $L_2 > L_1 \cdot (N-1)/k$, $L_2 \cdot k/(N-1) > L_1$, and as a result P_2 is guaranteed to be probed in the next timestep. Similarly, for the following timestep, since $L_3 > L_2$ and consequently $L_3 \cdot k/(N-1) > L_1$, P_3 will be probed next. Thus, once P_3 is probed, P_2 and P_3 will be alternately probed in the following time steps, and P_1 will never be probed.

7.1.3 State complexity and probing frequency

In Sec. 4.2, we considered the optimization goal of requiring that our probing algorithm, for every time window of length k and for every link ℓ, probes ℓ with probability bounded below by p_ℓ, which is a per-link parameter.

We note that achieving a probability $p_\ell = 1$ is impossible with a "purely probabilistic algorithm" of the type described above (meaning that all paths are probed with probabilities strictly less than 1). In other words, to *guarantee* that certain links are probed for every window of length k, it is not enough to leave probing completely to chance.

To address this, we can use a modification to the randomized approach such as the following: Each timestep, probe a random set of paths combined with the set of paths not probed within the last k timesteps (for some parameter k). This ensures that some "catch-up" probing occurs to account for random selection of paths that were probed in the previous k timesteps.

The downside to this workaround is that additional state is required by the probing algorithm at each node; in particular, source nodes are required to maintain the last time that each potential destination was probed. We note that, without synchronization, using this "last time probed" value may not provide an actual guarantee of timely measurements; thus, additional global coordination may be necessary to achieve stronger algorithm guarantees.

7.1.4 Restriction to one probing path per timestep

Suppose we wish to restrict the number of probing paths per timestep to 1. A randomized probing algorithm with this restriction may proceed as follows: in each timestep, choose one of the paths from the probing-path set according to some probability distribution. Such an algorithm enforces very low overhead (in terms of the metrics of link load, node load, and number of probing nodes and paths used), perhaps at the cost of expected probing delay.

To analyze the expected probing delay of such an algorithm, we relate the probing algorithm to the classic *coupon-collector's prob-*

lem [17]: There are n different coupons, each of which can be drawn with equal probability; if, every day, one coupon is drawn and then returned to the pool of coupons, in how many days will all the coupons have been drawn at least once? The answer is known to be $O(n \log n)$ days.

This result can be fashioned into a probing-frequency result. If we have n paths, and, in each timestep, probing each path is equally likely, then the coupon-collector's result states that $O(n \log n)$ timesteps are needed before every path is probed at least once.

An extension on the coupon collector's result is the case in which coupons are drawn with differing probabilities. That is, every day a coupon is drawn with replacement (as above), however, each coupon i has probability p_i of being drawn (instead of equal probabilities $1/n$ as in the original version). In the probing-algorithm context, we still assume that there are n different paths, but each path i is probed in a given timestep with probability p_i. Berenbrink and Sauerwald [6] show that the bound on the number of timesteps needed to probe every path is $O(\log \log n \cdot \sum_{i=1}^{n} i \cdot 1/p_i)$.

To find a bound on this value, let p_e be the minimum of the probabilities p_i. We use that $\sum_{i=1}^{n} i \cdot 1/p_e = 1/p_e \cdot H_n$, where H_n is the nth harmonic number. Given the asymptotics for the harmonic numbers, we have the bound that $1/p_e \cdot H_n = O(1/p_e \cdot \log n)$. Thus, the final upper bound on expected probing delay would be $O(\log \log n \cdot 1/p_e \log n)$.

7.2 Simulation results

In this section, we present empirical analysis of the basic randomized probing algorithm discussed above with an expected delay bound $1/\varepsilon$, for some path-probing probability ε ($0 < \varepsilon < 1$).

In this basic approach, we assume the existence of this global probability parameter p and, in each timestep, each path is probed with probability p. (Below, we show the effect of different values of p on the algorithm's performance metrics.) To simulate and analyze the behavior of this algorithm, we wrote a set of simulation procedures in Python 2.7; our routines use data structures and algorithms in the NetworkX [13] graph-theoretic library to represent the network and to compute a network routing (used to induce a probing-path set for a network).

The simulation inputs (each a network topology and set of probing paths) include some network topologies that are randomly generated[6] and others taken from the Internet Topology Zoo repository [16]. To compute path-set variations for each network topology, we randomly selected a subset of the network's nodes as probing nodes (potential source and destination nodes for probing traffic); we then computed shortest-path routes on the entire network and filtered out paths that did not start or end at one of the probing nodes in the selected subset. These variations were created using probing-node subsets ranging in size from 33–100% of the whole set of network nodes. In all, the simulation results that we present capture performance analysis of 6515 inputs to the basic randomized algorithm.

7.2.1 Probing delay

It is obvious that the higher the probability parameter p used to determine whether a path is probed or not in a given timestep, the more frequently network links will be probed and the shorter the amount of time between probes of that link (*i.e.*, the link's probing delay). However, because a given link may appear on any number of the potential probing paths, depending on the underlying routing system, the exact relationship between probability and link probing delay is less clear.

---

[6]We used the fast version of the Erdős-Rényi graph generator [4] implemented in NetworkX [13].

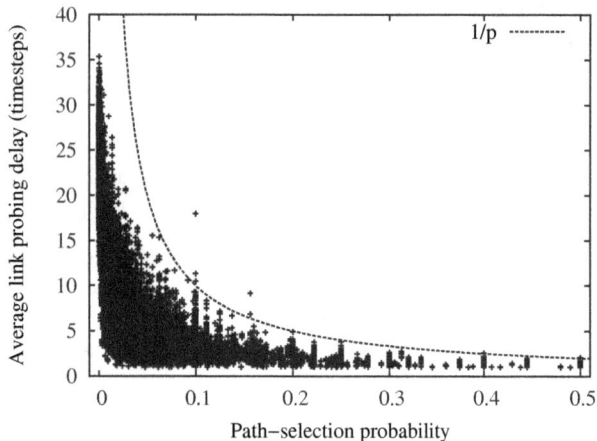

Figure 2: Relationship between the number of timesteps between probes of a link (averaged over all links) and the path-selection probability used for probing.

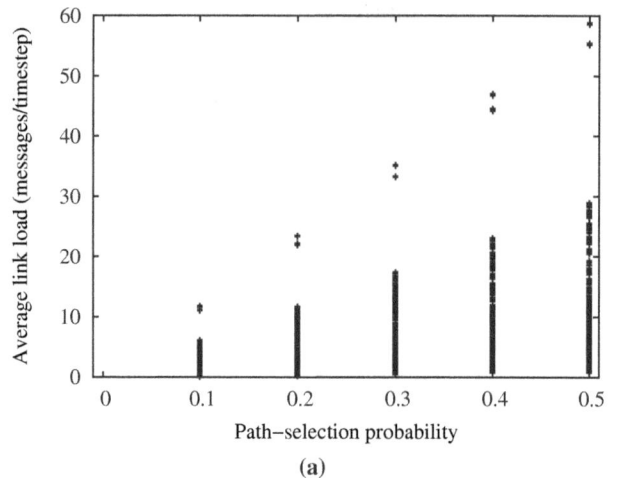

(a)

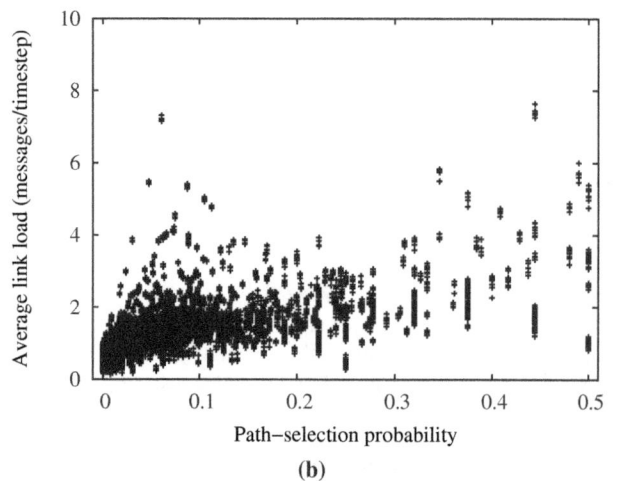

(b)

Figure 3: Relationship between the probing node on links (averaged over all links) and the path-selection probability used for probing, when the probability is chosen (a) without examining the network topology or (b) after examining the network topology.

The basic randomized approach we tested avoids maintaining state for coordinating probing-path selection across nodes in a given timestep. We ran over 40 trials for each input combination of a network and a path-set, using different path-selection probabilities across those trials (ranging from near 1% to 50%). Each trial involved running 50 timesteps of the basic randomized probing algorithm. In each timestep, each probing node independently decided to send a probe to each possible destination with the trial's assigned path-selection probability p.

Figure 2 shows the results of this simulation. The horizontal axis shows the path-selection probability p for the trials, while the vertical axis shows the average link probing delay for that trial. This delay was computed by averaging, over all links, the mean amount of time between probes of a link during that trial. Even with links appearing in multiple probing paths, the probing frequency for a link seems to be correlated with $1/p$, where p is the path-selection probability; however, as expected from the results of Sec. 7.1.1, $1/p$ does serve as a rough upper bound for probing delay.

7.2.2 Link load

Given that each path is probed or not probed independently of all the other probing decisions, it is possible that the basic randomized algorithm might probe all of the probing paths in a single timestep. While this is a worst-case scenario in terms of link load, there is still a reasonable chance that the simple approach produces unacceptably (or at least undesirably) high load on some links.

Thus, we attempt to quantify the effect of path-probing probability on link load, again realizing that the appearance of links on multiple probing paths chosen independently at random makes the connection potentially unclear. Figure 3 shows the results of analyzing link load from the simulation trials described above in Sec. 7.2.1. The horizontal axes of both plots show the path-selection probability p, while the vertical axes show the average load on links (computed by averaging, over all links, the mean load over the 50 timesteps in the trial).

Figure 3(a) shows results from simulation trials where p was chosen from the set $F = \{0.1, 0.2, 0.3, 0.4, 0.5\}$, regardless of topology. As expected, load grows with increased path-selection probability; moreover, the results suggest that it can grow to unacceptably high levels. For any given probability in F, trials showed a variety of average-load levels, mostly scattered uniformly throughout the range between 0 and $60 \cdot p$.

On the other hand, Fig. 3(b) shows the load results from simulation trials where p was set to range between two topology-dependent values: In particular, in a given network $G = (V, E)$ with a given probing-path set $\mathcal{P}$, compute for each link $e \in E$ the fraction f_e of paths in $\mathcal{P}$ that contain e; then, the selection probability p for this second set of trials ranged between $\min_{e \in E} f_e$ and $\max_{e \in E} f_e$. This set of topology-dependent probabilities produced a significant improvement in link load.

(Note that, although the horizontal axes of the two plots in Fig. 3 span the same range of values, the vertical axis of Fig. 3(b) spans a smaller range of values than that of Fig. 3(a), reflecting an improvement in link load.)

Still, the randomized approach does not compare well with probing a subset of paths produced by using the standard $O(\log n)$-approximation-factor minimum-set-cover (MSC) approximation algorithm [21]. In this algorithm, a subset of probing paths $S \subseteq \mathcal{P}$ is chosen in the following manner:

- Initialize $S = \{\}$;

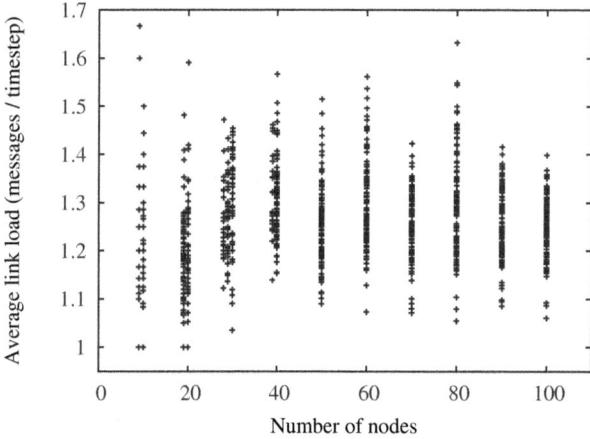

Figure 4: Relationship between average link load in a minimum set cover and the number of nodes, for trials involving the randomly generated graphs.

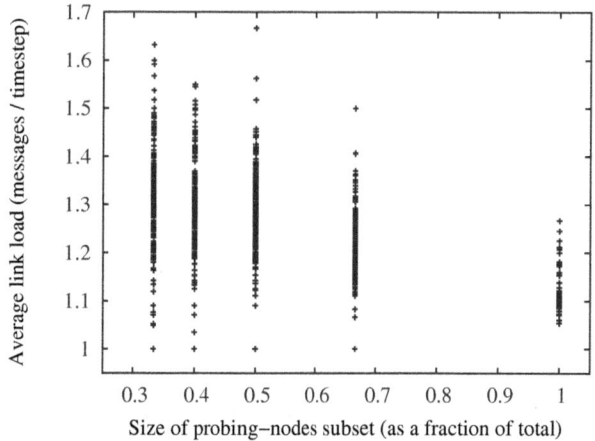

Figure 5: Relationship between average link load in a minimum set cover and the number of edges, for trials involving the randomly generated graphs.

- Iteratively pick the path $P \in \mathscr{P} - S$ that covers the most uncovered links, and add that path P to S;
- Terminate when all links are covered.

Figures 4–6 show the average link load that would be incurred by probing the entirety of the MSC set of paths S in a single timestep. (Each data point represents the average link load for one of the randomly generated inputs; recall that each input is a combination of a network topology and a probing-path set.) Doing so would give a probing delay of 1 (because every edge appears in the set cover), with an average load of no more than 1.7. The figures show that there is no strong relationship between average link load for the minimum set cover with respect to the number of nodes, number of links, or size of the probing-node subset for any of the randomly generated inputs.

Of course, the set-cover approach comes with its own downsides, as discussed before: the approximation algorithm requires iteratively selecting paths covering the most yet-uncovered edges, which can be a costly pre-computation for large networks.

The randomized approach can achieve some level of balance without the pre-computation: Simulation results point to a number of inputs where a path-selection probability of 0.2 leads to an average load of about 2 with average delay also about 2.

8. CONCLUSIONS AND FUTURE WORK

In this paper, we have introduced a formal framework for evaluating probing strategies for network-performance measurement. We have formalized metrics that capture the performance of such algorithms with respect to various desiderata. This identifies areas for improving existing approaches. We have also identified some formal tradeoffs among different desiderata and have showed that achieving certain combinations are computationally intractable (even to approximate). Our analysis includes both deterministic and randomized approaches to network probing.

The framework and results that we present here suggest numerous directions for future work, as follows:

In terms of analysis, this framework should be applied to probing algorithms that are currently in use in order to assess their strengths and weaknesses and to gain insight into their suitability for various applications. At the same time, our theoretical analysis should be

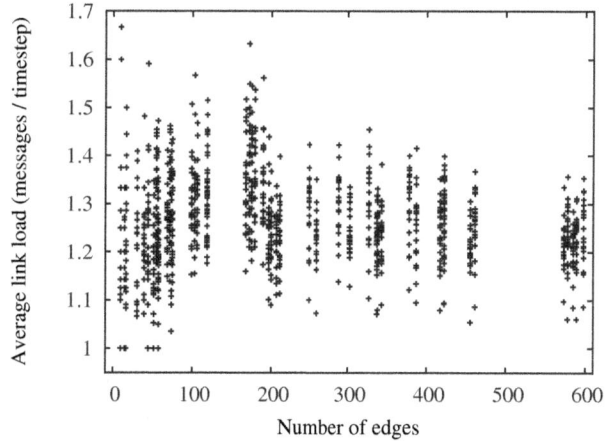

Figure 6: Relationship between average link load in a minimum set cover and the fraction of nodes chosen for the probing-node subset, for trials involving the randomly generated graphs.

extended to identify additional fundamental tradeoffs between different metrics (including three or more metrics taken together).

In terms of algorithms, as this framework is used to study existing algorithms in settings of current interest, it will identify the need for new algorithms to meet certain performance goals suggested by the metrics we identify here. Such algorithms will need to be developed. This process will also make the development of active-probing algorithms more rigorous.

The development of this framework will also promote the identification of other desiderata for probing algorithms. Those, in turn, will suggest new metrics for evaluating the performance of algorithms. Those metrics will need to be applied to existing and new algorithms; of particular interest, their relationships to other metrics (correlations and tradeoffs) will need to be evaluated.

9. ACKNOWLEDGMENTS

We thank Joel Sommers for the many valuable conversations that helped motivate and shape this paper, and we thank the referees for their helpful feedback.

10. REFERENCES

[1] G. Agnarsson and M. M. Halldórsson. Strong colorings of hypergraphs. In *Proc. Approximation and Online Algorithms (WAOA'04)*, pages 253–266, Bergen, Norway, Sept. 2004. Springer-Verlag LNCS 3351.

[2] P. Barford, A. Bestavros, J. Byers, and M. Crovella. On the marginal utility of network topology measurements. In *Proc. ACM IMW'01*, pages 5–17, Nov. 2001.

[3] P. Barford, N. Duffield, A. Ron, and J. Sommers. Network performance anomaly detection and localization. In *Proc. IEEE INFOCOM 2009*, pages 1377–1385, Apr. 2009.

[4] V. Batagelj and U. Brandes. Efficient generation of large random networks. *Phys. Rev. E*, 71(3):1–5, 2005.

[5] Y. Bejerano and R. Rastogi. Robust monitoring of link delays and faults in IP networks. *IEEE/ACM Trans. Net.*, 15(5):1092–1103, Oct. 2006.

[6] P. Berenbrink and T. Sauerwald. The weighted coupon collector's problem and applications. In *Proc. COCOON'09*, pages 449–458, July 2009.

[7] L. Breslau, I. Diakonikolas, N. G. Duffield, Y. Gu, M. Hajiaghayi, D. S. Johnson, H. J. Karloff, M. G. C. Resende, and S. Sen. Disjoint-path facility location: Theory and practice. In *Proc. SIAM ALENEX'11*, pages 60–74, Jan. 2011.

[8] M. Coates, A. Hero, R. Nowak, and B. Yu. Internet tomography. *IEEE Sig. Proc. Mag.*, 19(3):47–65, May 2002.

[9] A. Dhamdhere, R. Teixeira, C. Dovrolis, and C. Diot. NetDiagnoser: Troubleshooting network unreachabilities using end-to-end probes and routing data. In *Proc. ACM CoNEXT'07*, Dec. 2007.

[10] N. Duffield. Network tomography of binary network performance characteristics. *IEEE Trans. Inf. Theory*, 52(12):5373–5388, Dec. 2006.

[11] T. Erlebach. Approximation algorithms for edge-disjoint paths and unsplittable flow. In E. Bampis, K. Jansen, and C. Kenyon, editors, *Efficient Approximation and Online Algorithms*, pages 97–134. Springer-Verlag, 2006.

[12] T. G. Griffin, F. B. Shepherd, and G. Wilfong. The stable paths problem and interdomain routing. *IEEE/ACM Trans. Net.*, 10(2):232–243, Apr. 2002.

[13] A. A. Hagberg, D. A. Schult, and P. J. Swart. Exploring network structure, dynamics, and function using NetworkX. In *Proceedings of the 7th Python in Science Conference (SciPy2008)*, pages 11–15, Pasadena, CA USA, Aug. 2008.

[14] I. Holyer. The NP-completeness of edge-coloring. *SIAM J. Comput.*, 10(4):718–720, 1981.

[15] S. Khot. Hardness results for approximate hypergraph coloring. In *Proc. ACM STOC'02*, May 2002.

[16] S. Knight, H. X. Nguyen, N. Falkner, R. Bowden, and M. Roughan. The internet topology zoo. *IEEE JSAC*, 29(9):1765–1775, Oct. 2011.

[17] R. Motwani and P. Raghavan. *Randomized Algorithms*, Sec. 3.6.1, pages 57–59. Cambridge Univ. Press, Aug. 1995.

[18] H. X. Nguyen, R. Teixeira, P. Thiran, and C. Diot. Minimizing probing cost for detecting interface failures: Algorithms and scalability analysis. In *Proc. IEEE INFOCOM 2009*, pages 1386–1394, Apr. 2009.

[19] O. Parekh and D. Segev. Path hitting in acyclic graphs. *Algorithmica*, 52(4):466–486, Dec. 2008.

[20] P. Singh, M. Lee, S. Kumar, and R. R. Kompella. Enabling flow-level latency measurements across routers in data centers. In *Proc. USENIX Hot-ICE'11*, Mar. 2011.

[21] P. Slavík. A tight analysis of the greedy algorithm for set cover. In *Proc. ACM STOC'96*, pages 435–441, May 1996.

[22] J. Sommers, P. Barford, N. Duffield, and A. Ron. Multiobjective monitoring for SLA compliance. *IEEE/ACM Trans. Net.*, 18(2):652–665, Apr. 2010.

[23] H. H. Song, L. Qiu, and Y. Zhang. NetQuest: A flexible framework for large-scale network measurement. *IEEE/ACM Trans. Net.*, 17(1):106–119, Feb. 2009.

Delays and Mixing Times in Random-Access Networks

Niek Bouman, Sem C. Borst, Johan S.H. van Leeuwaarden[*]
Eindhoven University of Technology
Den Dolech 2, 5612 AZ Eindhoven, The Netherlands
{n.bouman, s.c.borst, j.s.h.v.leeuwaarden}@tue.nl

ABSTRACT

We explore the achievable delay performance in wireless random-access networks. While relatively simple and inherently distributed in nature, suitably designed backlog-based random-access schemes provide the striking capability to match the optimal throughput performance of centralized scheduling mechanisms. The specific type of activation rules for which throughput optimality has been established, may however yield excessive backlogs and delays.

Motivated by that issue, we examine whether the poor delay performance is inherent to the basic operation of these schemes, or caused by the specific kind of activation rules. We derive delay lower bounds for backlog-based activation rules, which offer fundamental insight in the cause of the excessive delays. For fixed activation rates we obtain lower bounds indicating that delays and mixing times can grow dramatically with the load in certain topologies as well.

Categories and Subject Descriptors

G.3 [**Probability and Statistics**]: Markov Processes

Keywords

Delay Performance; Mixing Times; Random-Access Networks; Wireless Networks

1. INTRODUCTION

Emerging wireless mesh networks typically lack any centralized access control entity, and instead vitally rely on the individual nodes to operate autonomously and to efficiently share the medium in a distributed fashion. A popular mechanism for distributed medium access control is provided by the so-called Carrier-Sense Multiple-Access (CSMA) protocol, various incarnations of which are implemented in IEEE 802.11 networks. In the CSMA protocol each node attempts to access the medium after a certain random back-off time, but nodes that sense activity of interfering nodes freeze their back-off timer until the medium is sensed idle.

While the CSMA protocol is fairly easy to understand at a local level, the interaction among interfering nodes gives rise to quite intricate behavior and complex throughput characteristics on a macroscopic scale. In recent years relatively parsimonious models have emerged that provide a useful tool in evaluating the throughput characteristics of CSMA-like networks. These models were originally developed by Boorstyn et al. [2], and further pursued in the context of IEEE 802.11 systems by Wang & Kar [28], Durvy et al. [5, 6] and Garetto et al. [8]. Although the representation of the IEEE 802.11 back-off mechanism in the above-mentioned models is less detailed than in the landmark work of Bianchi [1], they accommodate a general interference graph and thus cover a broad range of topologies. Experimental results of Liew et al. [15] demonstrate that these models, while idealized, provide throughput estimates that match remarkably well with measurements in actual IEEE 802.11 systems.

Despite their asynchronous and distributed nature, CSMA-like algorithms have been shown to offer the capability of achieving the full capacity region and thus match the optimal throughput performance of centralized scheduling mechanisms operating in slotted time, see for instance Jiang & Walrand [13], Liu et al. [16] and Tassiulas & Ephremides [26]. More specifically, any throughput vector inside the convex hull associated with the independent sets in the interference graph can be achieved through suitable back-off rates and/or transmission lengths. Based on this observation, various clever algorithms have been developed for finding the back-off rates that yield a particular target throughput vector or that optimize a certain concave throughput utility function in scenarios with saturated buffers, see for instance Jiang et al. [12, 13] and Marbach & Eryilmaz [18]. In the same spirit, several powerful approaches have been devised for adapting the transmission lengths based on backlog information, and been shown to guarantee maximum stability, see for instance Rajagopalan et al. [20], Shah & Shin [22] and Shah et al. [23].

Roughly speaking, the maximum-stability guarantees were established under the condition that the activity factors of the various nodes behave as logarithmic functions of the backlogs. Unfortunately, simulation experiments demonstrate that such activity factors can induce excessive backlogs and delays, which has triggered a strong interest in de-

[*]This work was supported by Microsoft Research through its PhD Scholarship Programme, by the European Research Council (ERC) and by the Netherlands Organisation for Scientific Research (NWO).

veloping approaches for improving the delay performance, see for instance Ghaderi & Srikant [10], Lotfinezhad & Marbach [17], Ni *et al.* [19] and Shah & Shin [21]. These results indicate that the maximum-stability guarantees are preserved for activity functions that are essentially linear for all practical values of the backlogs, although asymptotically the activity rate must grow slower than any positive power of the backlog.

In order to gain insight in the root cause for the poor delay performance, we establish in the present paper lower bounds for the average steady-state delay. To the best of our knowledge, the derivation of lower bounds for the average steady-state delay in random-access networks has received hardly any attention so far. An interesting paper by Shah *et al.* [24] showed that low-complexity schemes cannot be expected to achieve low delay in arbitrary topologies (unless P equals NP), since that would imply that certain NP-hard problems could be solved efficiently. However, the notion of delay in [24] is a transient one, and it is not exactly clear what the implications are for the average steady-state delay in specific networks, if any.

Jiang *et al.* [11, 14] derived *upper* bounds for the average steady-state delay based on mixing time results for Glauber dynamics, where the mixing time represents the amount of time required for the process to come close to its equilibrium distribution. The bounds show that for sufficiently low load the delay only grows polynomially with the number of nodes in bounded-degree interference graphs. Subramanian & Alanyali [25] presented similar upper bounds for bounded-degree interference graphs with low load based on analysis of neighbor sets and stochastic coupling arguments. While some of the conceptual notions in the present paper are similar (cliques, mixing times), we focus on *lower* rather than upper bounds, and exploit quite different techniques.

The lower bounds that we derive for backlog-based activation rules show that the rules that guarantee maximum stability yield excessive delays. We further obtain lower bounds for the delay and mixing time in case fixed back-off rates are used. In both cases, the bounds bring to light that the delay and mixing time can grow dramatically with the load of the system ρ. Specifically, we establish that the expected delay grows as $F(1/(1 - \rho))$ as $\rho \uparrow 1$, where $F(\cdot)$ is a superlinear function, implying that the growth rate may be polynomially or even exponentially faster than is typically the case at high load. The specific form and growth rate of the function $F(\cdot)$ depends on the activation rule as well as the topology of the network, as we will show for several scenarios of interest. Various partial versions of the results presented here appeared in Bouman *et al.* [3, 4].

The remainder of the paper is organized as follows. In Section 2 we present a detailed model description. Some preliminary results are derived in Section 3 and an overview of our main results is provided in Section 4. In Section 5 we derive delay lower bounds for backlog-based activation schemes. We establish generic lower bounds for the delay and mixing time in case of fixed back-off rates in Section 6. In Section 7 we apply these generic bounds to a canonical class of partite interference graphs, which includes several specific cases of interest such as grid topologies, relegating some of the proofs to Appendix A. Simulation experiments are conducted in Section 8 to support the analytical results. In Section 9, we make some concluding remarks and identify topics for further research.

2. MODEL DESCRIPTION

Network, interference graph, and traffic model. We consider a network of several nodes sharing a wireless medium according to a random-access mechanism. The network is represented by an undirected graph $G = (V, E)$ where the set of vertices $V = \{1, \ldots, N\}$ correspond to the various nodes and the set of edges $E \subseteq V \times V$ indicate which pairs of nodes interfere. Nodes that are neighbors in the interference graph are prevented from simultaneous activity, and thus the independent sets of G correspond to the feasible joint activity states of the network. A node is said to be blocked whenever the node itself or any of its neighbors is active, and unblocked otherwise. Define $\Omega \subseteq \{0, 1\}^N$ as the set of all feasible joint activity states of the network.

Packets arrive at node i as a Poisson process of rate λ_i. The packet transmission times at node i are independent and exponentially distributed with mean $1/\mu_i$. Denote by $\rho_i = \lambda_i/\mu_i$ the traffic intensity of node i.

Let $U(t) \in \Omega$ represent the joint activity state of the network at time t, with $U_i(t)$ indicating whether node i is active at time t or not. Denote by $L_i(t)$ the number of packets at node i at time t (including any packet that may be in the process of being transmitted).

Random-access mechanism. The nodes share the medium according to a random-access mechanism. When a node ends an activity period (consisting of possibly several back-to-back packet transmissions), it starts a back-off period. The back-off times of node i are independent and exponentially distributed with mean $1/\nu_i$. The back-off period of a node is suspended whenever it becomes blocked by activity of any of its neighbors, and only resumed once the node becomes unblocked again. Thus the back-off period of a node can only end when none of its neighbors are active. Now suppose a back-off period of node i ends at time t. Then the node starts a transmission with probability $\phi_i(L_i(t))$, and begins a next back-off period otherwise. When a transmission of node i ends at time t, it releases the medium and begins a back-off period with probability $\psi_i(L_i(t^+))$, or starts the next transmission otherwise. We allow for $\phi_i(0) > 0$ and $\psi_i(0) < 1$, so a node may be active even when its buffer is empty, and transmit dummy packets. A dummy transmission is terminated when a new packet arrives and the transmission of this packet is started immediately. Equivalently, node i may be thought of as activating at an exponential rate $f_i(L_i(t)) = \nu_i\phi_i(L_i(t))$, whenever it is unblocked at time t, and de-activating at rate $g_i(L_i(t)) = \mu_i\psi_i(L_i(t) - 1)$, whenever it is active at time t. For conciseness, the functions $f_i(\cdot)$ and $g_i(\cdot)$ will be referred to as activation and de-activation functions, respectively, and we define $h_i(\cdot) = f_i(\cdot)/g_i(\cdot)$ as the nominal activation function.

Network dynamics. Under the above-described backlog-based schemes, the process $\{(U(t), L(t))\}_{t \geq 0}$ evolves as a Markov process with state space $\Omega \times \mathbb{N}_0^N$. Transitions (due to arrivals) from a state (U, L) to $(U, L + e_i)$ occur at rate λ_i, transitions (due to activations) from a state (U, L) with $U_i = 0$ and $U_j = 0$ for all neighbors j of node i to $(U + e_i, L)$ occur at rate $f_i(L_i)$, transitions (due to transmission completions followed back-to-back by a subsequent transmission) from a state (U, L) with $U_i = 1$ to $(U, L - e_i\mathrm{I}_{\{L_i > 0\}})$ occur at rate $\mu_i - g_i(L_i)$, transitions (due to transmission completions followed by a back-off period) from a state (U, L) with $U_i = 1$ to $(U - e_i, L - e_i\mathrm{I}_{\{L_i > 0\}})$ occur at rate $g_i(L_i)$.

3. PRELIMINARY RESULTS

For any $u \in \Omega$, define $\pi(u) = \lim_{t \to \infty} \mathbb{P}\{U(t) = u\}$ as the steady-state probability that the activity process resides in state u. Further define $\theta_i = \sum_{u \in \Omega} \pi(u) u_i$ as the steady-state fraction of time that node i is active. Note that for fixed activation and de-activation rates, i.e., $\phi_i(\cdot) \equiv \phi_i$ and $\psi_i(\cdot) \equiv \psi$, the activity process $\{U(t)\}$ does not depend on the process $\{L(t)\}$, and in fact constitutes a reversible Markov process with a product-form stationary distribution [2],

$$\pi(u) = Z^{-1} \prod_{i=1}^{N} \sigma_i^{u_i}, \qquad u \in \Omega, \qquad (1)$$

and normalization constant

$$Z = \sum_{u \in \Omega} \prod_{i=1}^{N} \sigma_i^{u_i},$$

with $\sigma_i = \nu_i \phi_i / (\mu_i \psi_i)$ representing a nominal activity factor.

Stability. In general it is difficult to establish under what conditions the system is stable, i.e., when the process $\{(U(t), L(t))\}_{t \geq 0}$ is positive recurrent. Denoting by $\text{conv}(\cdot)$ the convex hull operator and by $\text{int}(\text{conv}(\cdot))$ its interior, it is easily seen that $(\rho_1, \ldots, \rho_N) \in \text{int}(\text{conv}(\Omega))$ is a necessary condition for stability.

In [10, 20, 22] it is shown that this condition is in fact also sufficient for activation and de-activation functions $f_i(l) = r_i(l)/(1 + r_i(l))$ and $g_i(l) = 1/(1 + r_i(l))$ with suitably chosen $r_i(\cdot)$, e.g., $r_i(l) = \log(l + 1)$. For more aggressive backlog-based activation functions, [9] shows that the necessary condition is not always sufficient though.

In the case of fixed activation and de-activation rates, a simple necessary and sufficient condition for stability is $\rho_i < \theta_i$, for all $i = 1, \ldots, N$. Furthermore, there exists a unique vector $(\sigma_1, \ldots, \sigma_N)$ that yields $(\theta_1, \ldots, \theta_N) \in \text{int}(\text{conv}(\Omega))$ [13, 27]. Hence, for any traffic intensity vector obeying the necessary stability condition, $(\rho_1, \ldots, \rho_N) \in \text{int}(\text{conv}(\Omega))$, there exists a vector $(\sigma_1, \ldots, \sigma_N)$ such that $(\rho_1, \ldots, \rho_N) < (\theta_1, \ldots, \theta_N) \in \text{int}(\text{conv}(\Omega))$, though determining the right vector $(\sigma_1, \ldots, \sigma_N)$ is non-trivial in general.

Performance lower bounds. In the remainder of the paper we derive lower bounds for the delay and will assume that the system under consideration is stable, because otherwise such lower bounds are not particularly meaningful. More specifically, we derive lower bounds for the expected aggregate stationary queue length in subsets of nodes $\mathcal{A} \subseteq V$. Note that, using Little's law, this also provides a lower bound for the expected aggregate stationary delay. That is, $\sum_{i \in \mathcal{A}} \mathbb{E}\{L_i\} \geq \alpha$ implies that $\sum_{i \in \mathcal{A}} \lambda_i \mathbb{E}\{W_i\} \geq \alpha$, with W_i a random variable representing the waiting time of an arbitrary packet at node i.

The notion of a *clique* will play a pivotal role in the derivation of the lower bounds. A clique is a subset $\mathcal{C} \subseteq V$ of vertices in the interference graph G such that the subgraph induced by $\mathcal{C}$ is complete. Note that in a clique at most one node can be active at a time. The aggregate load in a clique should therefore be less than 1 if the system is to be stable. For compactness, we use the notation $\lambda_{\mathcal{C}} = \sum_{j \in \mathcal{C}} \lambda_j$ and $\rho_{\mathcal{C}} = \sum_{j \in \mathcal{C}} \rho_j$. We say that a clique $\mathcal{C}$ is in heavy traffic when $\rho_{\mathcal{C}}$ is close to 1. Further we denote by $L_{i,\mathcal{C}}$ the number of packets at node i at an arbitrary epoch during a non-serving interval for the clique $\mathcal{C}$, i.e., a time interval during which none of the nodes in $\mathcal{C}$ is transmitting a packet.

Observe that the total number of packets in the clique $\mathcal{C}$ is bounded from below by that in a single node carrying the aggregate traffic, yielding the simple lower bound

$$\sum_{i \in \mathcal{C}} \mathbb{E}\{L_i\} \geq \frac{\lambda_{\mathcal{C}} \sum_{i \in \mathcal{C}} \lambda_i / \mu_i^2}{1 - \rho_{\mathcal{C}}} + \rho_{\mathcal{C}}. \qquad (2)$$

Thus, the total expected number of packets in any system grows at least linearly in $1/(1 - \rho)$ as ρ increases to 1, with $\rho = \max_{\mathcal{C}} \rho_{\mathcal{C}}$ the maximum traffic intensity in any clique.

Lower bounds for the activity state. The lower bound in (2) is only based on sheer load considerations and does not account for the effect of the back-off mechanism. We will derive lower bounds for backlog-based strategies and fixed-rate strategies that do capture the effect of the back-off mechanism, and turn out to be considerably tighter and exhibit superlinear growth in $1/(1 - \rho_{\mathcal{C}})$.

Stability of the system requires that the non-serving intervals for a clique in heavy traffic should be short or happen infrequently. That is, in each clique, most of the time, one of the nodes should be active, since otherwise the average rate of arriving packets would exceed the average rate of departing packets. For this to be the case, the activity factors should be big at high load. The next lemma quantifies this statement.

LEMMA 3.1. *Assume that the system is stable, then, for any clique $\mathcal{C} \subseteq V$ containing node i,*

$$\frac{\mathbb{E}\{f_i(L_{i,\mathcal{C}})\}}{\mathbb{E}\{g_i(L_i)\}} \geq \frac{\rho_i}{1 - \rho_{\mathcal{C}}}. \qquad (3)$$

PROOF. Observing that the mean number of activations at node i equals the mean number of de-activations at node i per unit of time, we obtain

$$\mathbb{E}\{f_i(L_i) \mathrm{I}_{\{U_j = 0 \text{ for all } j \in \mathcal{N}_i^+\}}\} = \rho_i \mathbb{E}\{g_i(L_i^d)\}, \qquad (4)$$

where $\mathcal{N}_i^+$ denotes the set of neighbors of node i in the graph G, along with i itself, and L_i^d denotes the number of packets waiting for transmission at node i at a departure epoch. Note that L_i^d is, in distribution, equal to L_i.

Further,

$$\mathbb{E}\{f_i(L_i) \mathrm{I}_{\{U_j = 0 \text{ for all } j \in \mathcal{N}_i^+\}}\}$$
$$\leq \mathbb{E}\{f_i(L_i) \mathrm{I}_{\{U_j = 0 \text{ for all } j \in \mathcal{C}\}}\}$$
$$= \mathbb{E}\{f_i(L_{i,\mathcal{C}})\} \mathbb{P}\{U_j = 0 \text{ for all } j \in \mathcal{C}\}. \qquad (5)$$

Since the events $\{U_j = 1\}$ are mutually exclusive for all $j \in \mathcal{C}$, it follows that

$$\mathbb{P}\{U_j = 0 \text{ for all } j \in \mathcal{C}\} = 1 - \mathbb{P}\{U_j = 1 \text{ for some } j \in \mathcal{C}\}$$
$$= 1 - \sum_{j \in \mathcal{C}} \mathbb{P}\{U_j = 1\} = 1 - \sum_{j \in \mathcal{C}} \theta_j. \qquad (6)$$

Thus, we find (3) using (4), (5), and the fact that $\rho_i \leq \theta_i$ for all $i \in V$ is a necessary condition for stability of the system. $\square$

In particular, for fixed-rate strategies it follows that

$$\sigma_i \geq \frac{\rho_i}{1 - \rho_{\mathcal{C}}}, \qquad (7)$$

which could in fact also have been established using the product-form distribution (1).

4. OVERVIEW

Lemma 3.1 shows that the activity factors in each clique should be big at high load. In the remainder of the paper we will demonstrate that this also causes the delay and mixing time to grow dramatically in heavy traffic.

Backlog-based strategies. For backlog-based strategies we examine activation functions that are such that a node becomes increasingly more aggressive when the total number of packets at that node increases in Section 5. For that natural class of activations functions, we utilize the result of Lemma 3.1 to find a lower bound of the form $h^{-1}(1/(|\mathcal{C}|(1-\rho_\mathcal{C})))$ for the aggregate number of packets in the clique $\mathcal{C}$, where $h^{-1}(\cdot)$ is the inverse function of $h(\cdot)$.

A prominent example is $f(l) = r(l)/(1+r(l))$ and $g(l) = 1/(1+r(l))$ with $r(l) = \log(l+1)$, so that $h^{-1}(l) = \exp(l) - 1$, the class of backlog-based strategies for which maximum stability is guaranteed as mentioned earlier. In this case we find that the queue length scales at least exponentially in $1/(1-\rho)$. To illustrate the performance ramifications, note that for $\rho = 0.9$, this exponential growth factor is already a factor 2000 larger than the normal growth factor at that load, while at larger loads it is even worse!

Fixed-rate strategies. In the case of fixed-rate strategies the bounds we derive revolve around two simple observations: (i) *high activation rates* cause *long mixing times*, in particular *slow transitions between dominant activity states*; (ii) *slow transitions between dominant states* imply *long starvation periods* for some nodes, and hence *huge queue lengths and delays*. In Section 6 we formalize (ii), and establish lower bounds for the expected aggregate weighted queue length and delay in terms of the expected return times of the process $\{U(t)\}$.

In order to lower bound these return times, we will build in Section 7 on insight (i) for a canonical class of partite interference graphs. That is, we examine topologies where the nodes belong to one of K different components such that nodes in the same component do not interfere with each other and every node belongs to a clique of size K (of which the other $K-1$ nodes necessarily belong to $K-1$ different components). This class of K-partite interference graphs covers a wide range of network topologies with nearest-neighbor interference, e.g., linear topologies, ring networks with an even number of nodes, two-dimensional grid networks, tori (two-dimensional grid networks with a wrap-around boundary), and *complete K-partite graphs*, where all nodes are connected except those that belong to the same component, with star topologies as a prime example.

In Theorem 7.2 we prove that, if the interference graph is a complete K-partite graph, the expected queue length grows at least as fast as $1/(1-\rho)^{M-1}$, with M the size of the largest component. To illuminate the performance repercussions, note that for $\rho = 0.9$ and $M = 5$, the growth factor is already a factor 1000 larger than the normal growth factor at that load, while at larger loads it is even worse!

Based on observations (i) and (ii) this may be heuristically explained as follows. In order for the system to be stable, each node must at least have an activation rate of the order $1/(1-\rho)$, see Lemma 3.1. In turn, the transition times between the various activity states as governed by the maximum-size component occur on a time scale of the order ν^{M-1}, when each node has a fixed activation rate ν.

In Theorem 7.8 we extend the results of Theorem 7.2 to the broader class of K-partite interference graphs and show that the expected queue length grows at least as fast as $1/(1-\rho)^{M(1-H^*)}$ as ρ approaches 1. The coefficient H^* depends on the topology and is in general hard to calculate. We however know that $\frac{1}{M} \leq H^* \leq 1$ and for some specific topologies we can explicitly determine H^*.

Besides the expected delay we also find a lower bound for the mixing time of the activity process $\{U(t)\}$. In Theorems 7.3 and 7.9 we find lower bounds for the mixing time for a complete K-partite interference graph and a general K-partite interference graph, respectively. We show that the heavy-traffic behavior of this lower bound is identical to that of the corresponding lower bound we found for the queue length in both cases.

Comparison and discussion. As described above, the fact that the activity factors need to be big at high load causes the delay to grow dramatically in heavy traffic, both for backlog-based and fixed-rate strategies. The specific arguments considerably differ however in both cases. Backlog-based strategies for which stability has been shown, involve slow, logarithmic, activation functions, which require enormous queue lengths at every node for the activity factors to be big enough, and cause the exponential delay scaling. The delays for fixed-rate strategies are caused by excessive mixing times due to a bottleneck in the network topology together with the big activity factors required for stability.

We further observe that the network topology plays a crucial role in case of a fixed-rate strategy, while it does not seem to directly matter in case of a backlog-based strategy. It is worth emphasizing that the activation rule for which maximum stability is guaranteed, however, *does* depend on the network topology. Also, the lower bounds rely on the presence of (critically-loaded) cliques, and hence the network topology does implicitly play a role in the case of backlog-based strategies as well.

For complete partite interference graphs, a comparison of the two cases shows that the expected delay for backlog-based strategies grows faster than the lower bound $1/(1-\rho)^{M-1}$ for fixed activation and de-activation rates when $h(l)$ increases slower than $l^{1/(M-1)}$. This is for example the case if $f(l) = r(l)/(1+r(l))$ and $g(l) = 1/(1+r(l))$, with $r(l) = \log(l+1)$. On the other hand, when $h(l)$ increases faster than $l^{1/(M-1)}$, the lower bound for fixed activation and de-activation rates could potentially be beaten. It is worth observing that the fluid limits for the joint queue length process exhibit *slow* mixing properties in that case. On the other hand, the maximum-stability guarantees in [20, 22, 23] seem to require *fast mixing* of the fluid limits. Hence, in arbitrary topologies there are not even any guarantees that more aggressive functions $h(l)$ provide queue stability, let alone better delay performance. In the specific case of complete partite interference graphs, however, potential instability for more aggressive functions does not seem to be a concern. Indeed, simulation results in Section 8 confirm that more aggressive backlog-based strategies can outperform fixed-rate strategies.

A natural question to ask is whether the delay lower bounds that we derive are sharp in some sense. While we do not rigorously address that question in the present paper, the simulation results suggest that the bounds are indeed asymptotically tight in a broad range of scenarios.

5. BACKLOG-BASED STRATEGIES

In this section we investigate the delay behavior of backlog-based strategies that use a concave activation function or a convex de-activation function. For compactness, we use the notation $\xi_\mathcal{C} = \sum_{j \in \mathcal{C}} \xi_j$ and $(\rho\xi)_\mathcal{C} = \sum_{j \in \mathcal{C}} \rho_j \xi_j$.

THEOREM 5.1. *Assume λ_i, ν_i, μ_i, $f_i(\cdot)$ and $g_i(\cdot)$, $i = 1, \ldots, N$, are such that the system is stable. Then, for any clique $\mathcal{C} \subseteq V$,*

(i) If $f_i(\cdot) \equiv f(\cdot)$ for $i \in \mathcal{C}$ is an increasing concave function and $g_i(\cdot) \geq \xi_i > 0$ for $i \in \mathcal{C}$, then

$$\sum_{i \in \mathcal{C}} \mathbb{E}\{L_i\} \geq \frac{\lambda_\mathcal{C} \sum_{i \in \mathcal{C}} \lambda_i/\mu_i^2}{1 - \rho_\mathcal{C}} + |\mathcal{C}|f^{-1}\Big(\frac{1}{|\mathcal{C}|}\frac{(\rho\xi)_\mathcal{C}}{1 - \rho_\mathcal{C}}\Big) + \rho_\mathcal{C}. \quad (8)$$

(ii) If $f_i(\cdot) \leq \xi_i$ for $i \in \mathcal{C}$ and $g_i(\cdot) \equiv g(\cdot)$ for $i \in \mathcal{C}$ is a decreasing convex function, then

$$\sum_{i \in \mathcal{C}} \rho_i \mathbb{E}\{L_i\} \geq \rho_\mathcal{C} g^{-1}\Big(\frac{(1 - \rho_\mathcal{C})\xi_\mathcal{C}}{\rho_\mathcal{C}}\Big). \quad (9)$$

(iii) If $f_i(\cdot) \equiv f(\cdot)$ for $i \in \mathcal{C}$ is an increasing concave function and $g_i(\cdot) \equiv g(\cdot)$ for $i \in \mathcal{C}$ is a decreasing convex function, then

$$\sum_{i \in \mathcal{C}} \mathbb{E}\{L_i\} \geq h^{-1}\Big(\frac{1}{|\mathcal{C}|}\frac{\rho_\mathcal{C}}{1 - \rho_\mathcal{C}}\Big). \quad (10)$$

PROOF. The Fuhrmann-Cooper decomposition property [7] (applied to the total number of packets in the clique $\mathcal{C}$) implies

$$\sum_{i \in \mathcal{C}} \mathbb{E}\{L_i\} = \frac{\lambda_\mathcal{C} \sum_{i \in \mathcal{C}} \lambda_i/\mu_i^2}{1 - \rho_\mathcal{C}} + \sum_{i \in \mathcal{C}} \mathbb{E}\{L_{i,\mathcal{C}}\} + \rho_\mathcal{C}. \quad (11)$$

This corroborates (2) since the second term in (11) is non-negative, but in case (i) that term might in fact be dominant as we now proceed to show. From (3) we know that, in case (i),

$$(1 - \rho_\mathcal{C}) \sum_{i \in \mathcal{C}} \mathbb{E}\{f_i(L_{i,\mathcal{C}})\} \geq (\rho\xi)_\mathcal{C}.$$

Since $f(\cdot)$ is concave, it follows from Jensen's inequality that

$$\sum_{i \in \mathcal{C}} \mathbb{E}\{f(L_{i,\mathcal{C}})\} \leq |\mathcal{C}|f\Big(\frac{1}{|\mathcal{C}|}\sum_{i \in \mathcal{C}} \mathbb{E}\{L_{i,\mathcal{C}}\}\Big). \quad (12)$$

Because $f(\cdot)$ is increasing we thus get

$$\sum_{i \in \mathcal{C}} \mathbb{E}\{L_{i,\mathcal{C}}\} \geq |\mathcal{C}|f^{-1}\Big(\frac{1}{|\mathcal{C}|}\frac{(\rho\xi)_\mathcal{C}}{1 - \rho_\mathcal{C}}\Big)$$

which completes the proof for case (i).

The proof for case (ii) proceeds along similar lines. From (3) we obtain

$$\sum_{i \in \mathcal{C}} \rho_i \mathbb{E}\{g(L_i)\} \leq (1 - \rho_\mathcal{C})\xi_\mathcal{C}.$$

Since $g(\cdot)$ is convex, it follows from Jensen's inequality that

$$\sum_{i \in \mathcal{C}} \rho_i \mathbb{E}\{g(L_i)\} \geq \rho_\mathcal{C} g\Big(\frac{1}{\rho_\mathcal{C}}\sum_{i \in \mathcal{C}} \rho_i \mathbb{E}\{L_i\}\Big). \quad (13)$$

Since $g(\cdot)$ is decreasing we thus get

$$\sum_{i \in \mathcal{C}} \rho_i \mathbb{E}\{L_i\} \geq \rho_\mathcal{C} g^{-1}\Big(\frac{(1 - \rho_\mathcal{C})\xi_\mathcal{C}}{\rho_\mathcal{C}}\Big),$$

yielding (9).

To prove case (iii), note that combining (11) and (12) gives

$$\sum_{i \in \mathcal{C}} \mathbb{E}\{f(L_{i,\mathcal{C}})\} \leq |\mathcal{C}|f\Big(\frac{1}{|\mathcal{C}|}\Big(\sum_{i \in \mathcal{C}} \mathbb{E}\{L_i\} - \frac{\lambda_\mathcal{C} \sum_{i \in \mathcal{C}} \lambda_i/\mu_i^2}{1 - \rho_\mathcal{C}} - \rho_\mathcal{C}\Big)\Big)$$

and hence, because $f(\cdot)$ is increasing,

$$\sum_{i \in \mathcal{C}} \mathbb{E}\{f(L_{i,\mathcal{C}})\} \leq |\mathcal{C}|f\Big(\sum_{i \in \mathcal{C}} \mathbb{E}\{L_i\}\Big).$$

Further, since $\rho_i \leq \rho_\mathcal{C}$ for $i \in \mathcal{C}$ and because $g(\cdot)$ is decreasing we obtain from (13) that

$$\sum_{i \in \mathcal{C}} \rho_i \mathbb{E}\{g(L_i)\} \geq \rho_\mathcal{C} g\Big(\sum_{i \in \mathcal{C}} \mathbb{E}\{L_i\}\Big).$$

From (3) we then find

$$|\mathcal{C}|f\Big(\sum_{i \in \mathcal{C}} \mathbb{E}\{L_i\}\Big)(1 - \rho_\mathcal{C}) \geq \rho_\mathcal{C} g\Big(\sum_{i \in \mathcal{C}} \mathbb{E}\{L_i\}\Big),$$

or

$$h\Big(\sum_{i \in \mathcal{C}} \mathbb{E}\{L_i\}\Big) \geq \frac{1}{|\mathcal{C}|}\frac{\rho_\mathcal{C}}{1 - \rho_\mathcal{C}}.$$

Thus as $h(\cdot) = f(\cdot)/g(\cdot)$ is increasing because $f(\cdot)$ is increasing and $g(\cdot)$ is decreasing, we get (10). □

The three cases covered in Theorem 5.1 all reveal the same effect, namely that the mean number of packets in a clique is at least of the order of $h^{-1}(1/(|\mathcal{C}|(1 - \rho_\mathcal{C})))$, where $h^{-1}(\cdot)$ is the inverse function of $h(\cdot)$. In case (ii) this effect is observed because the argument of $g^{-1}(\cdot)$ is reciprocal. Further, noting that $f(l) = \log(l+1)/(1 + \log(l+1))$ is an increasing concave function and $g(l) = 1/(1 + \log(l+1))$ is a decreasing convex function, we have

$$\sum_{i \in \mathcal{C}} \mathbb{E}\{L_i\} \geq \mathrm{Exp}\Big(\frac{1}{|\mathcal{C}|}\frac{\rho_\mathcal{C}}{1 - \rho_\mathcal{C}}\Big) - 1$$

for the class of functions for which maximum stability is guaranteed.

The results of Theorem 5.1 suggest that in order to improve the delay performance one should use more aggressive access schemes. In fact, if $h(\cdot)$ is a superlinear function, i.e., if $h(\cdot)$ grows faster than linear, we find a lower bound that is loose in heavy traffic and (2) provides a better lower bound in that case. Remember however that maximum stability is not guaranteed in this case, hence the delay performance might deteriorate if a superlinear $h(\cdot)$ is used.

6. FIXED-RATE STRATEGIES

In the previous section we derived delay bounds for backlog-based activation rules and we saw that the type of activation rules for which throughput optimality has been established yield excessive delays and backlogs. We now proceed to construct lower bounds for the expected aggregate weighted queue length and delay in the case of fixed activation and de-activation rates, i.e., we take $\phi_i(\cdot) \equiv \phi_i$ and $\psi_i(\cdot) \equiv \psi_i$.

We first introduce some useful notation. Define $Q(S)$ as the transition rate out of the subset $S \subseteq \Omega$, i.e.,

$$Q(S) = \sum_{u \in S} \sum_{u' \in \Omega \setminus S} \pi(u)q(u, u') = \sum_{u \in \Omega \setminus S} \sum_{u' \in S} \pi(u)q(u, u'),$$

with $q(u, u')$ denoting the transition rate from state u to state u' of the component $\{U(t)\}$ of the Markov process as specified in Section 2, i.e., $q(u, u + e_i) = \nu_i \phi_i$ and $q(u + e_i, u) = \mu_i \psi_i$, $u, u + e_i \in \Omega$. With minor abuse of notation, denote by $\pi(S) = \sum_{u \in S} \pi(u)$ the fraction of time that the system resides in one of the activity states in the subset S. The bottleneck ratio of the subset S is defined as

$$\Phi(S) = \frac{Q(S)}{\pi(S)}.$$

Further define for arbitrary weights $w \in \mathbb{R}_+^N$ and for any $\mathcal{A} \subseteq V$, $S \subseteq \Omega$,

$$Y(w, \mathcal{A}, S) = \max_{u \in S} \sum_{i \in \mathcal{A}} w_i \mu_i u_i,$$

and denote

$$D(w, \mathcal{A}, S) = \sum_{i \in \mathcal{A}} w_i \lambda_i - Y(w, \mathcal{A}, S).$$

The coefficient $Y(w, \mathcal{A}, S)$ represents the maximum aggregate weighted service rate of the nodes in $\mathcal{A}$ when the system resides in one of the activity states in the subset S. Noting that $\sum_{i \in \mathcal{A}} w_i \lambda_i$ is the weighted arrival rate of the nodes in $\mathcal{A}$, the coefficient $D(w, \mathcal{A}, S)$ may thus be interpreted as the minimum drift in the aggregate weighted queue length of the nodes in $\mathcal{A}$ when the system resides in one of the activity states in the subset S.

PROPOSITION 6.1. *For any* $w \in \mathbb{R}_+^N$, $\mathcal{A} \subseteq V$,

$$\sum_{i \in \mathcal{A}} w_i \mathbb{E}\{L_i\} \geq \frac{1}{2} \max_{S \subseteq \Omega} D(w, \mathcal{A}, S) \pi(S) \frac{1}{\Phi(S)}. \quad (14)$$

PROOF. Denote by T_S a random variable representing the equilibrium return time to the subset of activity states $\Omega \setminus S$ and denote by T_S^e a random variable representing the elapsed equilibrium lifetime of T_S, i.e.,

$$\mathbb{P}\{T_S^e < t\} = \frac{1}{\mathbb{E}\{T_S\}} \int_{s=0}^{t} \mathbb{P}\{T_S > s\} \mathrm{d}s. \quad (15)$$

Now observe that when the system resides in one of the activity states in S, which is the case with probability $\pi(S)$, the aggregate weighted queue length of the nodes in $\mathcal{A}$ have experienced a drift no less than $D(w, \mathcal{A}, S)$ for an expected amount of time $\mathbb{E}\{T_S^e\}$. This observation indicates that the expected aggregate weighted queue length of the nodes in $\mathcal{A}$ is bounded from below by $\pi(S) D(w, \mathcal{A}, S) \mathbb{E}\{T_S^e\}$ for any choice of S and hence,

$$\sum_{i \in \mathcal{A}} w_i \mathbb{E}\{L_i\} \geq \max_{S \subseteq \Omega} D(w, \mathcal{A}, S) \pi(S) \mathbb{E}\{T_S^e\}. \quad (16)$$

Using (15) we obtain

$$\mathbb{E}\{T_S^e\} = \frac{1}{\mathbb{E}\{T_S\}} \int_{t=0}^{\infty} \int_{s=t}^{\infty} \mathbb{P}\{T_S > s\} \mathrm{d}s \mathrm{d}t$$
$$= \frac{\mathbb{E}\{T_S^2\}}{2\mathbb{E}\{T_S\}} \geq \frac{1}{2}\mathbb{E}\{T_S\}.$$

Finally, because $Q(S)$ is the expected number of times the process enters S per unit of time and $\mathbb{E}\{T_S\}$ is the expected amount of time the process stays in S after entering, the expected fraction of the time the process resides in S, $\pi(S)$, is given by $\pi(S) = Q(S)\mathbb{E}\{T_S\}$. Thus, $\mathbb{E}\{T_S\} = \frac{1}{\Phi(S)}$, and (14) follows. $\square$

The question arises how to choose S such that the maximum and thus the tightest possible lower bound in (14) is obtained. Evidently, the more S includes states with some of the nodes in $\mathcal{A}$ active, the larger the potential aggregate weighted service rate of the nodes in $\mathcal{A}$, i.e., the larger $Y(w, \mathcal{A}, S)$, and the smaller $D(w, \mathcal{A}, S)$. In other words, we need to ensure that S excludes some of the states with nodes in $\mathcal{A}$ active. Indeed, if S includes all states with maximal subsets of the nodes in $\mathcal{A}$ active, then $Y(w, \mathcal{A}, S) = \max_{u \in \Omega} \sum_{i=1}^{N} \hat{w}_i \mu_i u_i$, with $\hat{w}_i = w_i$ if $i \in \mathcal{A}$ and $\hat{w}_i = 0$ otherwise. The fact that $(\rho_1, \ldots, \rho_N) \in \text{int}(\text{conv}(\Omega))$ then implies that $Y(w, \mathcal{A}, S) \geq \sum_{i=1}^{N} \hat{w}_i \mu_i \rho_i = \sum_{i=1}^{N} \hat{w}_i \lambda_i = \sum_{i \in \mathcal{A}} w_i \lambda_i$, so that $D(w, \mathcal{A}, S) \leq 0$, yielding an irrelevant lower bound. However, observe that the expected equilibrium return time to $\Omega \setminus S$, $\mathbb{E}\{T_S\}$, may be small when S includes very few states. Hence, to obtain the sharpest possible lower bound, it may not necessarily be optimal to exclude all the states with nodes in $\mathcal{A}$ active from S. For high values of ν, which are necessary for stability at high load as Lemma 3.1 showed, the above argument suggests that we should choose S so that it contains a state with many active nodes, while the boundary of S only contains states with few active nodes.

Define

$$\partial S = \{u \in S : \sum_{u' \notin S} q(u, u') > 0\}$$

as the 'boundary' of S and $K(S', \mathcal{A}') = \max_{u \in S'} \sum_{i \in \mathcal{A}'} u_i$. In order to get a tight lower bound in (14) we thus need to find a subset S such that $K(S, V)$ is large, $K(\partial S, V)$ is small, and $K(S, \mathcal{A})$ is small.

We will now first give an example to illustrate the use of Proposition 6.1.

Example 1. Suppose that S is such that $u + e_i \notin \Omega \setminus S$ for all $u \in \partial S$. In case $\phi_i \equiv 1$, $\psi_i \equiv 1$, $\mu_i \equiv 1$ and $\nu_i \equiv \nu \geq 1$, we then have $Q(S) \leq N\pi(\partial S)$, and thus using (1),

$$\frac{1}{\Phi(S)} = \frac{\pi(S)}{Q(S)} \geq \frac{\sum_{u \in S} \pi(u)}{N \sum_{u \in \partial S} \pi(u)} = \frac{\sum_{u \in S} \nu^{\sum_{i=1}^{N} u_i}}{N \sum_{u \in \partial S} \nu^{\sum_{i=1}^{N} u_i}}$$
$$\geq \frac{1}{N} \nu^{K(S,V) - K(\partial S, V)}.$$

We thus see that in this example we indeed need to choose S such that $K(S, V) - K(\partial S, V)$ is maximized.

Now suppose the interference graph is a symmetric complete bipartite graph. That is, the nodes in $V_1 = \{1, \ldots, N/2\}$ interfere with, and only with, the nodes in $V_2 = \{N/2 + 1, \ldots, N\}$. In this case we have $K(S, V) \leq N/2$. Further, as S is such that $u + e_i \notin \Omega \setminus S$, we have $S = \Omega$ if and only if $K(\partial S, V) = 0$. Thus, because $S = \Omega$ yields an irrelevant lower bound, we have $K(\partial S, V) \geq 1$.

Assuming that $\mathcal{A} \subseteq V_1$ it is clear that $K(S, \mathcal{A}) = 0$ if S only contains states where nodes in V_2 are active. Hence in this case we should choose $S = \{u \in \Omega : \sum_{i \in V_2} u_i \geq 1\}$, the set of activity states where at least one of the nodes in V_2 is active, as this gives $K(S, V) = N/2$, $K(\partial S, V) = 1$ and $K(S, \mathcal{A}) = 0$. We thus see that the delay grows at least as fast as $\nu^{N/2 - 1}$.

As mixing times are typically long when transitions between dominant activity states are slow, it is likely that we can construct a lower bound for the mixing time that is similar to (14). The mixing time of a process represents the amount of time required for the process to come close to its equilibrium distribution, and is formally defined as

$$t_{\mathrm{mix}}(\epsilon) = \inf\{t : d(t) \leq \epsilon\},$$

where $d(t)$ denotes the maximal distance (in total variation) between $U(t)$ and π, i.e.,

$$d(t) = \max_{U(0) \in \Omega} \frac{1}{2} \sum_{u \in \Omega} |\mathbb{P}\{U(t) = u\} - \pi(u)|.$$

As the next proposition shows, the bottleneck ratio $\Phi(\cdot)$ provides a lower bound on the mixing time of the activity process $\{U(t)\}$.

PROPOSITION 6.2. *The mixing time of $\{U(t)\}$ satisfies*

$$t_{\mathrm{mix}}(\epsilon) \geq \max_{S \subseteq \Omega} (1 - 2\epsilon - \pi(S)) \frac{1}{\Phi(S)}. \qquad (17)$$

PROOF. Zocca *et al.* [29] show that

$$t_{\mathrm{mix}}(\epsilon) \geq (1 - 2\epsilon - r) \frac{1}{\Phi_r^*},$$

with

$$\Phi_r^* = \min_{\{S \subseteq \Omega : \pi(S) \leq r\}} \Phi(S).$$

Therefore,

$$t_{\mathrm{mix}}(\epsilon) \geq \max_r \max_{\{S \subseteq \Omega : \pi(S) \leq r\}} (1 - 2\epsilon - r) \frac{1}{\Phi(S)}$$
$$= \max_r \max_{\{S \subseteq \Omega : \pi(S) = r\}} (1 - 2\epsilon - r) \frac{1}{\Phi(S)},$$

and (17) follows. $\square$

We thus found a lower bound on the mixing time that has a similar form as the bound we found in Proposition 6.1 for the aggregate weighted queue length. Note, however, that to find a tight lower bound on the mixing time, for sufficiently small ϵ, we only need $K(S, V)$ to be large and $K(\partial S, V)$ to be small.

7. PARTITE GRAPHS

In the previous section we derived generic lower bounds for the expected aggregate weighted queue length and delays in terms of the bottleneck ratio of any subset $S \subseteq \Omega$, an approach that is also used to find a lower bound for the mixing time of the activity process $\{U(t)\}$. In this section we describe how to find a subset $S \subseteq \Omega$ with the desired properties discussed in the previous section, for a broad class of K-partite interference graphs. We additionally assume that each of the nodes belongs to at least one clique of size K (of which the other $K - 1$ nodes necessarily belong to $K - 1$ different components).

We first introduce some further notation and state a few preparatory lemmas. Denote by $V_k \subseteq V$ the subset of nodes that belong to the k-th component and $M_k = |V_k|$, $k = 1, \ldots, K$. For compactness, define

$$\Upsilon_k = \prod_{i \in V_k} (1 + \sigma_i) - 1 = \sum_{I \subseteq V_k} \prod_{i \in I} \sigma_i - 1 = \sum_{\emptyset \neq I \subseteq V_k} \prod_{i \in I} \sigma_i.$$

In particular when $\sigma_i \equiv \hat{\sigma}_k$ for all $i \in V_k$, we have $\Upsilon_k = (1 + \hat{\sigma}_k)^{M_k} - 1$.

Throughout this section we assume that $\rho_i = \hat{\rho}_k$ for all $i \in V_k$, and denote $\rho = \sum_{k=1}^K \hat{\rho}_k$, and $\rho_{\min} = \min_{k=1,\ldots,K} \hat{\rho}_k$. For convenience, we also assume $\phi_i \equiv 1$, $\psi_i \equiv 1$, $\mu_i \equiv 1$, so that $\sigma_i = \nu_i$ for all $i = 1, \ldots, N$. Define $M = \max_{k=1,\ldots,K} M_k$ as the maximum component size.

7.1 Complete partite graphs

In order to gain some useful intuition, we first focus on *complete K-partite graphs*, where all nodes are connected except those that belong to the same component. In other words, the complement of the graph consists of K fully connected components. Thus, transmission activity is mutually exclusive across the various components.

In this case, the normalization constant in (1) satisfies

$$Z = 1 + \sum_{k=1}^K \sum_{\emptyset \neq I \subseteq V_k} \prod_{i \in I} \sigma_i = 1 + \sum_{k=1}^K \Upsilon_k.$$

For any $k = 1, \ldots, K$, define $S_k = \{u \in \Omega : \sum_{i \in V_k} u_i \geq 1\}$ as the set of activity states where at least one of the nodes in V_k is active. We will use these sets to find a lower bound for the delay and mixing time. As discussed in Example 1, these sets are likely to provide a tight lower bound.

LEMMA 7.1. *For any activation rate vector $(\nu_1, \ldots, \nu_N)$ such that the system is stable, for any $k = 1, \ldots, K$,*

$$Q(S_k) = Q(\Omega \setminus S_k) < M_k (1 - \sum_{l \neq k} \hat{\rho}_l) \left(\frac{1 - \rho}{\hat{\rho}_k} \right)^{M_k - 1}, \quad (18)$$

$$\hat{\rho}_k < \pi(S_k) < 1 - \sum_{l \neq k} \hat{\rho}_l, \qquad (19)$$

$$\sum_{l \neq k} \hat{\rho}_l < \pi(\Omega \setminus S_k) < 1 - \hat{\rho}_k. \qquad (20)$$

PROOF. Using (1) we obtain

$$\theta_i = Z^{-1} \sum_{u \in \Omega, u_i = 1} \prod_{j=1}^N \sigma_j^{u_j}$$
$$\geq Z^{-1} \sigma_i \prod_{l \in V_k \setminus \{i\}} (1 + \sigma_l) = Z^{-1} \frac{\sigma_i}{1 + \sigma_i} (\Upsilon_k + 1).$$

Also, from (1) we know

$$\theta_i = \sigma_i \mathbb{P}\{U_j = 0 \text{ for all } j \in \mathcal{N}_i^+\}.$$

Furthermore,

$$\mathbb{P}\{U_j = 0 \text{ for all } j \in \mathcal{N}_i^+\} \leq \mathbb{P}\{U_j = 0 \text{ for all } j \in \mathcal{C}\},$$

and hence we get

$$\theta_i \leq \sigma_i [1 - \sum_{j \in \mathcal{C}} \theta_j],$$

from (6), which may be rewritten as

$$\theta_i \leq \frac{\sigma_i}{1 + \sigma_i} [1 - \sum_{j \in \mathcal{C} \setminus \{i\}} \theta_j],$$

so that

$$\Upsilon_k \leq Z[1 - \sum_{j \in \mathcal{C} \setminus \{i\}} \theta_j] - 1,$$

and thus, using the fact that $\rho_i < \theta_i$ for all $i \in V$ is a necessary condition for stability,

$$\Upsilon_k < Z[1 - \sum_{j \in \mathcal{C} \setminus \{i\}} \rho_j] - 1. \qquad (21)$$

Next, note that $Q(\Omega \setminus S_k) = \pi(0) \sum_{i \in V_k} \sigma_i$, and similarly,

$$Q(S_k) = \pi(0) \sum_{i \in V_k} \sigma_i = \frac{1}{Z} \sum_{i \in V_k} \sigma_i.$$

Using this we get,

$$Q(S_k) \leq \frac{M_k}{Z} \max_{i \in V_k} \sigma_i = M_k \max_{i \in V_k} \frac{\frac{\sigma_i}{1+\sigma_i}(\Upsilon_k + 1)}{\frac{1}{1+\sigma_i}(\Upsilon_k + 1)}$$

$$= \frac{M_k}{Z} \max_{i \in V_k} \frac{\frac{\sigma_i}{1+\sigma_i}(\Upsilon_k + 1)}{\prod_{l \in V_k \setminus \{i\}}(1 + \sigma_l)}$$

$$< \frac{M_k(\Upsilon_k + 1)}{Z(1 + \min_{i \in V_k} \sigma_i)^{M_k - 1}}.$$

Invoking Lemma 3.1 and (21) gives (18).

Also, because $\hat{\rho}_k < \pi(S_k) = \Upsilon_k / Z$ is needed for stability, (21) gives,

$$\pi(S_k) < 1 - \sum_{l \neq k} \hat{\rho}_l - \frac{1}{Z},$$

which proves (19). Noting that $\pi(S_k) + \pi(\Omega \setminus S_k) = 1$ gives (20). $\square$

Using Lemma 7.1 we can find a lower bound for the expected aggregate weighted queue length at some subset of nodes in $\mathcal{A} \subseteq V_k$.

THEOREM 7.2. *For any activation rate vector* $(\nu_1, \ldots, \nu_N)$ *such that the system is stable and for any* $w \in \mathbb{R}_+^N$, $\mathcal{A} \subseteq V_k$,

$$\sum_{i \in \mathcal{A}} w_i \mathbb{E}\{L_i\} > \frac{1}{2M} (\rho_{\min})^{M+1} \sum_{i \in \mathcal{A}} w_i \lambda_i \left(\frac{1}{1-\rho}\right)^{M-1}.$$

For the symmetric scenario $M_k \equiv M$ *and* $\hat{\rho}_k \equiv \rho/K$ *for all* $k = 1, \ldots, K$,

$$\mathbb{E}\{L_i\} > \frac{(K-1)^2 \rho^{M+2}}{2MK^{M+1}(K - (K-1)\rho)} \left(\frac{1}{1-\rho}\right)^{M-1}.$$

PROOF. The proof relies on applying Proposition 6.1, taking S to be (i) $\Omega \setminus S_k$ and (ii) S_l, $l \neq k$. In either case, $u_i = 0$ for all $i \in \mathcal{A}$, $u \in S$, so that $Y(w, \mathcal{A}, S) = 0$, i.e.,

$$D(w, \mathcal{A}, S) = \sum_{i \in \mathcal{A}} \lambda_i w_i.$$

First consider case (i). In this case we obtain the lower bound

$$\sum_{i \in \mathcal{A}} w_i \mathbb{E}\{L_i\} > \frac{\left(\sum_{l \neq k} \hat{\rho}_l\right)^2}{2M_k} \sum_{i \in \mathcal{A}} w_i \lambda_i \left(\frac{\hat{\rho}_k}{1-\rho}\right)^{M_k - 1}$$

from Proposition 6.1 and Lemma 7.1. Taking $\mathcal{A} = V_k$ yields the second statement of the lemma for a symmetric scenario.

In order to complete the proof of the first part of the lemma, we now turn to case (ii). Using Proposition 6.1 and Lemma 7.1, we arrive at the lower bound

$$\sum_{i \in \mathcal{A}} w_i \mathbb{E}\{L_i\} > \frac{\hat{\rho}_l^2}{2M_l} \sum_{i \in \mathcal{A}} w_i \lambda_i \left(\frac{\hat{\rho}_l}{1-\rho}\right)^{M_l - 1}.$$

Combining the above two lower bounds yields the first part of the lemma. $\square$

For $M = 1$ (full interference graph), the lower bound established in Theorem 7.2 is loose, reflecting that it is not the slow transitions between the various components that cause the delays to be long in that case, but the sheer load. For $M = 2$, the lower bound could also have been obtained by treating cliques as single-resource systems and is in fact similar to (2). For $M \geq 3$, the lower bound is particularly relevant, and reflects that the slow transitions between the various components cause the delays to be exponentially larger than can be explained from sheer load considerations alone.

Lemma 7.1 also provides a lower bound for the mixing time of the activity process $\{U(t)\}$ as we will show next.

THEOREM 7.3. *For any activation rate vector* $(\nu_1, \ldots, \nu_N)$ *such that the system is stable,*

$$t_{\mathrm{mix}}(\epsilon) > ((K-1)\rho_{\min} - 2\epsilon) \frac{(\rho_{\min})^M}{M} \left(\frac{1}{1-\rho}\right)^{M-1}.$$

PROOF. Applying Proposition 6.2 for $S = S_k$ and using Lemma 7.1 gives

$$t_{\mathrm{mix}}(\epsilon) > (1 - 2\epsilon - (1 - \sum_{l \neq k} \hat{\rho}_l)) \frac{\hat{\rho}_k}{M_k(1 - \sum_{l \neq k} \hat{\rho}_l)} \left(\frac{\hat{\rho}_k}{1-\rho}\right)^{M_k - 1}$$

$$> ((K-1)\rho_{\min} - 2\epsilon) \frac{\rho_{\min}}{M_k} \left(\frac{\rho_{\min}}{1-\rho}\right)^{M_k - 1},$$

for $k = 1, \ldots, K$, and the result follows. $\square$

Note that the bound derived in Lemma 7.3 is not necessarily the best bound we can find using the results of Lemma 7.1. In fact, the bound is irrelevant if $\epsilon > (K-1)\rho_{\min}/2$. However, if $\rho_{\min} > 0$ and ϵ is small enough, we can conclude that the mixing time grows at least like $1/(1-\rho)^{M-1}$ as ρ increases to 1.

For equal activation rates, i.e., for the activation rate vector $(\nu, \ldots, \nu)$, it is shown in [29] that $t_{\mathrm{mix}}(\epsilon) \sim \nu^{M^*-1}$ as $\nu \to \infty$, with M^* the size of the second largest component, so that the heavy-traffic behavior is governed by M^* instead of M. Note however that this activation rate vector does not provide a stable system, unless $\rho_{\min} = 0$ or $M = M^*$, as follows from Lemma 7.1 and the fact that $\pi(S_k) \to 0$ as $\nu \to \infty$ for all k such that $M_k < M$. Hence the activity process mixes slower in heavy traffic if the system is stable as compared to a system with equal activation rates.

7.2 Extensions

We now return to the broader class of (not necessarily complete) K-partite graphs. Thus, transmission activity is no longer mutually exclusive across the various components. However, we make the next assumption implying that joint activity across various components is relatively inefficient. Denote by $v^{(k)} = 1_{V_k}$ the incidence vector of V_k, i.e., $v_i^{(k)} = 1$ if $i \in V_k$ and $v_i^{(k)} = 0$ otherwise, and define $\Omega^* = \{v^{(1)}, \ldots, v^{(K)}\}$.

Assumption 1. For any $u \in \Omega$,

$$H(u) = \sum_{k=1}^K \sum_{i \in V_k} \frac{u_i}{M_k} \leq 1,$$

with strict inequality for any $u \notin \Omega^*$.

Based on the above assumption, we define

$$\zeta = 1 - \max_{u \in \Omega \setminus \Omega^*} H(u) > 0.$$

An illustrative example is provided by a $2B \times 2B$ grid with nodes labeled as $\{(i,j)\}$, $i,j = 1,\ldots,2B$, and nearest-neighbor interference. The two components are $V_1 = \{(i,j) : (i + j) \bmod 2 = 1\}$ and $V_2 = \{(i,j) : (i + j) \bmod 2 = 0\}$, with $M_1 = M_2 = 2B^2$. In order for $m \geq 1$ nodes in V_1 to be active, at least $m + 1$ or $m + 3$ nodes in V_2 must be inactive (depending on whether or not we assume a wrap-around boundary). Thus $\sum_{i=1}^{2B} \sum_{j=1}^{2B} u_{(i,j)} \leq 2B^2 - 1$ (or $2B^2 - 3$) for all $u \in \Omega \setminus \Omega^*$, and $\zeta = \frac{1}{2B^2}$ (or $\frac{3}{2B^2}$).

The next lemma shows that in order for the system to be stable, joint activity across the various components can only occur a negligible fraction of the time at high load. The proof of this lemma is deferred to Appendix A.1.

LEMMA 7.4. *In order for the system to be stable, it should hold that*

$$\sum_{u \in \Omega \setminus \Omega^*} \pi(u) < \frac{1 - \rho}{\zeta},$$

and

$$\pi(v^{(k)}) > \hat{\rho}_k - \frac{1 - \rho}{\zeta}.$$

In the next lemma, whose proof can be found in Appendix A.2, we show that the fraction of time the activity process $\{U(t)\}$ spends in any component V_k relative to the traffic intensity of the nodes in that component, is almost equal for all components if ρ is large enough.

LEMMA 7.5. *Assume the system is stable and $\rho \geq \rho_\gamma = 1 - \gamma \zeta \rho_{\min}^2$, $\gamma > 0$. Then*

$$\min_{k=1,\ldots,K} \frac{1}{\hat{\rho}_k} \prod_{i \in V_k} \sigma_i \geq (1 - 3\gamma) \max_{k=1,\ldots,K} \frac{1}{\hat{\rho}_k} \prod_{i \in V_k} \sigma_i.$$

In order to state a lower bound for the expected aggregate weighted queue length at some subset of nodes $\mathcal{A} \subseteq V_k$, we now first introduce some further notation and concepts.

A sequence of states $(u^{(0)}, u^{(1)}, \ldots, u^{(l)})$, with $u^{(k)} \in \Omega$, $k = 0,\ldots,l$, is called a *path* from $u^{(0)}$ to $u^{(l)}$ if $(u^{(k)}, u^{(k+1)})$ are feasible transitions, i.e., $q(u^{(k)}, u^{(k+1)}) > 0$ for all $k = 0,\ldots,l-1$. For a given path $p = (u^{(0)}, u^{(1)}, \ldots, u^{(l)})$, denote by $m(p) = \min_{k=0,1,\ldots,l} H(u^{(k)})$ the minimum value of the function $H(\cdot)$, as defined in Assumption 1, along the path. For given states $u, v \in \Omega$, denote by $P(u,v)$ the collection of all paths from u to v. Define $M(u,v) = \max_{p \in P(u,v)} m(p)$ as the maximum of the minimum value of the function $H(\cdot)$ along any path from state u to state v, with the convention that $M(u,u) = \infty$.

For all $\mathcal{A} \subseteq V$ such that $\mathcal{A} \subseteq V_k$ for some $k \in \{1,\ldots,K\}$, denote by $\Delta(\mathcal{A})$ the set of states in which the expected drift of the aggregate weighted queue length in $\mathcal{A}$ is non-positive, i.e.,

$$\Delta(\mathcal{A}) = \{u \in \Omega : \sum_{i \in \mathcal{A}} w_i \lambda_i \leq \sum_{i \in \mathcal{A}} w_i \mu_i u_i\}.$$

Further define $\delta(\mathcal{A})$ as the minimal expected drift of the aggregate weighted queue length in $\mathcal{A}$ if the system does not reside in of one of the states in $\Delta(\mathcal{A})$, i.e.,

$$\delta(\mathcal{A}) = \sum_{i \in \mathcal{A}} w_i \lambda_i - \max_{u \in \Omega \setminus \Delta(\mathcal{A})} \sum_{i \in \mathcal{A}} w_i \mu_i u_i.$$

Note that $\delta(\mathcal{A}) > 0$ by construction. For all $l \neq k$, define $m_l(\mathcal{A}) = \max_{u \in \Delta(\mathcal{A})} M(v^{(l)}, u)$, and

$$S_l(\mathcal{A}) = \{u \in \Omega : M(v^{(l)}, u) > m_l(\mathcal{A})\}$$

as the set of states that can be reached from $v^{(l)}$ via a path p with $m(p) > m_l(\mathcal{A})$. Also, define $m_k(\mathcal{A}) = \max_{l \neq k} m_l(\mathcal{A})$, and

$$S_k(\mathcal{A}) = \{v \in \Omega : \max_{u \in \Delta(\mathcal{A})} M(u,v) > m_k(\mathcal{A})\}$$

as the set of states that can be reached from $\Delta(\mathcal{A})$ via a path p with $m(p) > m_k(\mathcal{A})$.

Finally, define $H_l(\mathcal{A}) = \max_{u \in \partial S_l(\mathcal{A})} H(u)$, $H^*(\mathcal{A}) = \min_{l=1,\ldots,K} H_l(\mathcal{A})$ and $H^*_{\min} = \min_{\mathcal{A} \subseteq V : \exists k : \mathcal{A} \subseteq V_k} H^*(\mathcal{A})$.

In the remainder of this subsection we will assume that the activation rates of nodes in the same component are equal, i.e. $\sigma_i = \hat{\sigma}_k$ if $i \in V_k$ for all $k = 1,\ldots,K$. Denote $\sigma^* = \min_{k=1,\ldots,K} \hat{\sigma}_k^{M_k}$ and $k^* = \operatorname{argmin}_{k=1,\ldots,K} \hat{\sigma}_k^{M_k}$.

Remark 1. It is not clear when there exists an activation rate vector $(\nu_1,\ldots,\nu_N)$ with $\nu_i = \nu_j$ if $i,j \in V_k$ that stabilizes the system. For symmetric topologies, e.g. ring networks with an even number of nodes or tori with an even number of nodes in both directions, it seems plausible that such an activation rate vector can stabilize the system for any $\rho < 1$. For asymmetric typologies, e.g. linear topologies and two-dimensional grid networks, this is not clear.

In the next lemma we derive an upper bound for the fraction of the time the system spends in the boundary of $S_l(\mathcal{A})$ for any $l = 1,\ldots,K$. The proof of this lemma is deferred to Appendix A.3.

LEMMA 7.6. *Assume the system is stable and $\rho \geq \rho_\gamma = 1 - \gamma \zeta \rho_{\min}^2$, $\gamma > 0$. Then*

$$\max_{u \in \partial S_l(\mathcal{A})} \prod_{j=1}^{N} \sigma_j^{u_j} \leq \left(\frac{\sigma^*}{(1 - 3\gamma)\rho_{\min}} \right)^{H_l(\mathcal{A})}.$$

We are now in the position to derive bounds for $Q(S_l(\mathcal{A}))$, $\pi(S_l(\mathcal{A}))$ and $\pi(\Omega \setminus S_l(\mathcal{A}))$ that are qualitatively similar to the bounds in Lemma 7.1.

LEMMA 7.7. *Assume $\rho \geq \rho_\gamma = 1 - \gamma \zeta \rho_{\min}^2$, $\gamma > 0$. For any activation rate vector $(\nu_1,\ldots,\nu_N)$ such that the system is stable and with $\nu_i = \nu_j$ if $i,j \in V_k$ for some k, for any $l = 1,\ldots,K$,*

$$Q(S_l(\mathcal{A})) = Q(\Omega \setminus S_l(\mathcal{A}))$$
$$< \frac{2^N}{(1 - 3\gamma)\rho_{\min}} \left(\frac{\rho_{k^*}}{1 - \rho} \right)^{M(H_l(\mathcal{A}) - 1)}, \quad (22)$$

$$(1 - \gamma)\rho_{\min} < \pi(S_l(\mathcal{A})) < 1 - (1 - \gamma)\rho_{\min}, \quad (23)$$

$$(1 - \gamma)\rho_{\min} < \pi(\Omega \setminus S_l(\mathcal{A})) < 1 - (1 - \gamma)\rho_{\min}. \quad (24)$$

PROOF. First note that $Q(S_l(\mathcal{A})) = \sum_{u \in \partial S_l(\mathcal{A})} \pi(u)$ and $Q(\Omega \setminus S_l(\mathcal{A})) = \sum_{u \in \partial S_l(\mathcal{A})} \pi(u)$. Further,

$$Q(S_l(\mathcal{A})) = \sum_{u \in \partial S_l(\mathcal{A})} \pi(u) = Z^{-1} \sum_{u \in \partial S_l(\mathcal{A})} \prod_{j=1}^{N} \sigma_j^{u_j}$$

$$\leq Z^{-1} |\partial S_l(\mathcal{A})| \max_{u \in \partial S_l(\mathcal{A})} \prod_{j=1}^{N} \sigma_j^{u_j}.$$

Noting that $Z \geq \sigma^*$ and $|\partial S_l(\mathcal{A})| \leq 2^N$ yields, using Lemma 7.6,

$$Q(S_l(\mathcal{A})) \leq \frac{2^N \left(\frac{\sigma^*}{(1-3\gamma)\rho_{\min}}\right)^{H_l(\mathcal{A})}}{\sigma^*} \leq \frac{2^N (\sigma^*)^{H_l(\mathcal{A})-1}}{(1-3\gamma)\rho_{\min}},$$

and (22) follows from Lemma 3.1.

Further, using Lemma 7.4,

$$\pi(S_l(\mathcal{A})) = \pi(S_l(\mathcal{A})) \geq \pi(v^{(l)}) > \hat{\rho}_l - \frac{1-\rho}{\zeta} \geq (1-\gamma)\rho_{\min}.$$

Now note that by definition $S_l \cap \Delta(\mathcal{A}) = \emptyset$ for $l \neq k$ and $\Delta(\mathcal{A}) \subseteq S_k$ if $\mathcal{A} \subseteq V_k$. Hence, for $l \neq k$,

$$\pi(S_l(\mathcal{A})) \leq 1 - \pi(v^{(k)}) < 1 - (1-\gamma)\rho_{\min},$$

and

$$\pi(S_k(\mathcal{A})) \leq 1 - \sum_{l \neq k} \pi(v^{(l)}) < 1 - (K-1)(1-\gamma)\rho_{\min},$$

which gives (23). Noting that $\pi(S_l(\mathcal{A})) + \pi(\Omega \setminus S_l(\mathcal{A})) = 1$ gives (24). □

Using a similar approach as in Subsection 7.1, the bounds in Lemma 7.7 can be utilized to establish a lower bound for the expected aggregate weighted queue length in some subset of nodes and for the mixing time of the activity process.

THEOREM 7.8. *Assume* $\rho \geq \rho_\gamma = 1 - \gamma\zeta\rho_{\min}^2$, $\gamma > 0$. *For any activation rate vector* $(\nu_1, \ldots, \nu_N)$, *with* $\nu_i = \nu_j$ *if* $i, j \in V_k$ *for some* k, *such that the system is stable and for any* $w \in \mathbb{R}_+^N$, $\mathcal{A} \subseteq V_k$,

$$\sum_{i \in \mathcal{A}} w_i \mathbb{E}\{L_i\} > \frac{\delta(\mathcal{A})(1-4\gamma)\rho_{\min}^{M+3}}{2^{N+1}} \left(\frac{1}{1-\rho}\right)^{M(1-H^*(\mathcal{A}))},$$

PROOF. The proof of this theorem proceeds along similar lines as the proof of Theorem 7.2 and relies on applying Proposition 6.1, taking S to be (i) $\Omega \setminus S_k(\mathcal{A})$ and (ii) $S = S_l(\mathcal{A})$, $l \neq k$. First note that by definition $S_l(\mathcal{A}) \cap \Delta(\mathcal{A}) = \emptyset$, and thus $D(w, \mathcal{A}, S_l(\mathcal{A})) \geq \delta(\mathcal{A})$, $l \neq k$. Also note that $\Delta(\mathcal{A}) \subseteq S_k(\mathcal{A})$, so that $D(w, \mathcal{A}, \Omega \setminus S_k(\mathcal{A})) \geq \delta(\mathcal{A})$.

Further, using Lemma 7.7 we obtain the lower bound

$$\sum_{i \in \mathcal{A}} w_i \mathbb{E}\{L_i\} > \frac{\delta(\mathcal{A})(1-4\gamma)\rho_{\min}^{M+3}}{2^{N+1}} \left(\frac{1}{1-\rho}\right)^{M(1-H_l(\mathcal{A}))},$$

for $l = 1, \ldots, K$, and the result follows. □

THEOREM 7.9. *Assume* $\rho \geq \rho_\gamma = 1 - \gamma\zeta\rho_{\min}^2$, $\gamma > 0$. *For any activation rate vector* $(\nu_1, \ldots, \nu_N)$ *such that the system is stable and with* $\nu_i = \nu_j$ *if* $i, j \in V_k$ *for some* k,

$$t_{\mathrm{mix}}(\epsilon) > ((1-\gamma)\rho_{\min} - 2\epsilon) \frac{(1-4\gamma)\rho_{\min}^{M+2}}{2^N} \left(\frac{1}{1-\rho}\right)^{M(1-H_{\min}^*)}.$$

PROOF. Take $\mathcal{A} \subseteq V$ such that there exists a k such that $\mathcal{A} \subseteq V_k$. Using Lemma 7.1 we then find for any $l \in \{1, \ldots, K\}$,

$$\frac{1}{\Phi(S_l(\mathcal{A}))} > \frac{(1-\gamma)\rho_{\min}(1-3\gamma)\rho_{\min}}{2^N} \left(\frac{\rho_{k^*}}{1-\rho}\right)^{M(1-H_l(\mathcal{A}))}$$

$$\geq \frac{(1-4\gamma)\rho_{\min}^{M+2}}{2^N} \left(\frac{1}{1-\rho}\right)^{M(1-H_l(\mathcal{A}))}.$$

Hence, using Proposition 6.2,

$$t_{\mathrm{mix}}(\epsilon) > ((1-\gamma)\rho_{\min} - 2\epsilon) \frac{(1-4\gamma)\rho_{\min}^{M+2}}{2^N} \left(\frac{1}{1-\rho}\right)^{M(1-H_l(\mathcal{A}))},$$

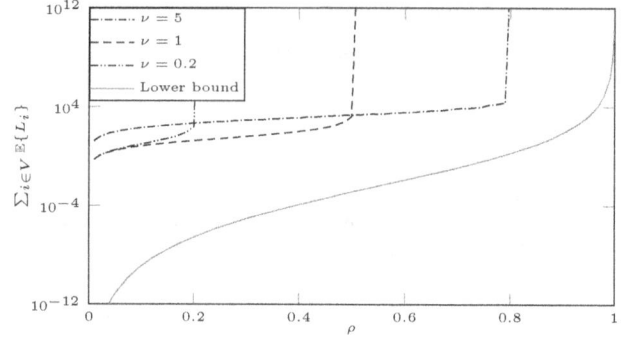

Figure 1: **Average total number of packets for several fixed activation rates.**

and the result follows by optimizing over l and $\mathcal{A}$. □

The value of the coefficient $H^*(\mathcal{A})$ depends strongly on the specific properties of the interference graph G. For a complete partite graph, the sets $S_l(\mathcal{A})$ coincide with those in the previous subsection, and we have $\partial S_l(\mathcal{A}) = \bigcup_{i \in V_l} \{e_i\}$, so that $H_l(\mathcal{A}) = 1/M_l$, and $H^*(\mathcal{A}) = 1/M$, recovering the result of Theorem 7.2. On the other hand, when the graph consists of N/K fully connected components, we have $H_l(\mathcal{A}) \equiv 1$, and the result trivializes. An interesting intermediate situation is the $2B \times 2B$ grid mentioned earlier with $M = M_1 = M_2 = 2B^2$, for which we conjecture that $H^*(\mathcal{A}) = H_1 = H_2 = 1 - 1/B$ or $1 - 1/(2B)$ if $B \geq 2$, depending on whether or not we assume a wrap-around boundary, suggesting that the mean queue lengths would grow as $1/(1-\rho)^B$ or $1/(1-\rho)^{2B}$.

8. SIMULATION EXPERIMENTS

In this section we will illustrate the theoretical results for the growth behavior of the aggregate queue length through simulation experiments. For cross comparison, we consider throughout a system that can be represented by a symmetric complete bipartite ($K = 2$) interference graph with components of size $M = 5$. Because of page limitations we do not report simulation results for other cases, but we observed qualitatively similar behavior in a broad range of scenarios.

To estimate the expected aggregate queue length for a given value of ρ, we set $t = 10^6$ and calculate the average total number of packets in the time intervals $[0, t]$ and $[t + 1, 2t]$, starting from an initially empty system. We take the average of the two values to be our estimate if the values are less than 5% apart. Otherwise we set $t = 2t$ and repeat the procedure.

Figure 1 shows the average total number of packets in the system for various fixed activation rates. Note that we used a log-lin scale. We see that the simulated curves lie well above the lower bound of Theorem 7.2 for all chosen values of ν. Note that the system is not stable for all values of ρ, e.g. for $\nu = 1$ the system is unstable if $\rho \geq 2\theta_i = \frac{32}{63}$, explaining the jumps in the simulation result. Further note that the expected time between activation of nodes in the two components is smaller for small values of ν. This explains why small values of ν tend to perform better in case ρ is small, i.e., for large values of ν the nodes in one component will often be transmitting dummy packets while

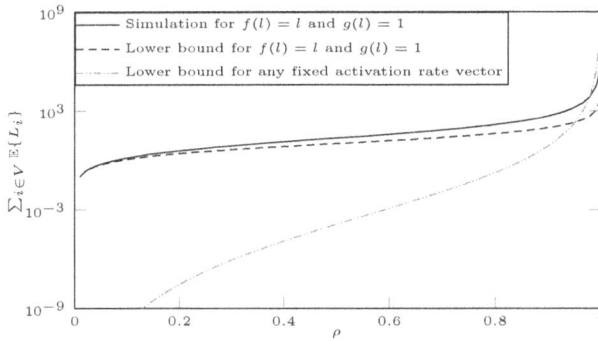

Figure 2: Average total number of packets for $f(l) = l$ and $g(l) = 1$.

the nodes in the other component do have packets waiting to be transmitted.

Figure 2 shows the average total number of packets in the system for $f(l) = l$ and $g(l) = 1$. We see that the lower bound of Theorem 5.1 is remarkably close to the simulation result for small values of ρ. For larger values of ρ the bound and simulation result are farther apart. One explanation for this lies in the approximation made in (5). For small values of ρ this approximation is relatively good while for large values of ρ this approximation is off by a factor of about 2 in this case. While this does not explain the total discrepancy in this case, it does explain all discrepancies in case the rate of increase of the activation function is slow, e.g. $f(l) = \log(l+1)$.

Finally note that the simulation result lies, for large values of ρ, below the lower bound for fixed activation rates established in Theorem 7.2. This suggests that the activation function $f_i(l) \equiv f(l) = l$ performs better in heavy traffic than $f_i(l) = \nu_i$ for any choice of the activation rate vector $(\nu_1, \ldots, \nu_N)$.

9. CONCLUSIONS

We have established lower bounds for the expected queue lengths and delays in wireless random-access networks. The bounds indicate that the delay for fixed activation rates can dramatically grow with the load in certain topologies. We further showed that the delay for backlog-based activation and de-activation strategies exceeds this lower bound when the degree of aggressiveness grows slowly as function of the backlog. An interesting issue for further research is to determine when better delay performance can be achieved when the aggressiveness grows faster as function of the backlog.

10. REFERENCES

[1] G. Bianchi. Performance analysis of the IEEE 802.11 distributed coordination function. *IEEE J. Sel. Areas Commun.*, 18(3):535–547, 2000.

[2] R. Boorstyn, A. Kershenbaum, B. Maglaris, and V. Sahin. Throughput analysis in multihop CSMA packet radio networks. *IEEE Trans. Commun.*, 35:267–274, 1987.

[3] N. Bouman, S. Borst, and J. van Leeuwaarden. Achievable delay performance in CSMA networks. In *Proc. 49th Allerton Conf.*, 2011.

[4] N. Bouman, S. Borst, J. van Leeuwaarden, and A. Proutière. Backlog-based random access in wireless networks: fluid limits and delay issues. In *Proc. ITC 23*, 2011.

[5] M. Durvy, O. Dousse, and P. Thiran. Modeling the 802.11 protocol under different capture and sensing capabilities. In *Proc. Infocom 2007 Conf.*, 2007.

[6] M. Durvy and P. Thiran. A packing approach to compare slotted and non-slotted medium access control. In *Proc. Infocom 2006 Conf.*, 2006.

[7] S. Fuhrmann and R. Cooper. Stochastic decompositions for the M/G/1 queue with generalized vacations. *Oper. Res.*, 33:1117–1129, 1985.

[8] M. Garetto, T. Salonidis, and E. Knightly. Modeling per-flow throughput and capturing starvation in CSMA multi-hop wireless networks. *IEEE/ACM Trans. Netw.*, 16(4):864–877, 2008.

[9] J. Ghaderi, S. Borst, and P. Whiting. Backlog-based random-access algorithms: fluid limits and stability issues. In *Proc. WiOpt 2012 Conf.*, 2012.

[10] J. Ghaderi and R. Srikant. On the design of efficient CSMA algorithms for wireless networks. In *Proc. CDC 2010 Conf.*, 2010.

[11] L. Jiang, M. Leconte, J. Ni, R. Srikant, and J. Walrand. Fast mixing of parallel glauber dynamics and low-delay CSMA scheduling. In *Proc. Infocom 2011 Mini-Conf.*, 2011.

[12] L. Jiang, D. Shah, J. Shin, and J. Walrand. Distributed random access algorithm: scheduling and congestion control. *IEEE Trans. Inf. Theory*, 56(12):6182–6207, 2010.

[13] L. Jiang and J. Walrand. A distributed CSMA algorithm for throughput and utility maximization in wireless networks. *IEEE/ACM Trans. Netw.*, 18(3):960–972, 2010.

[14] L. Jiang and J. Walrand. Stability and delay of distributed scheduling algorithms for networks of conflicting queues. *Queueing Syst.*, 72(1):161–187, 2012.

[15] S. Liew, C. Kai, J. Leung, and B. Wong. Back-of-the-envelope computation of throughput distributions in CSMA wireless networks. *IEEE Trans. Mob. Comp.*, 9(9):1319–1331, 2010.

[16] J. Liu, Y. Yi, A. Proutière, M. Chiang, and H. Poor. Towards utility-optimal random access without message passing. *Wireless Commun. Mob. Comput.*, 10(1):115–128, 2010.

[17] M. Lotfinezhad and P. Marbach. Throughput-optimal random access with order-optimal delay. In *Proc. Infocom 2011 Conf.*, 2011.

[18] P. Marbach and A. Eryilmaz. A backlog-based CSMA mechanism to achieve fairness and throughput-optimality in multihop wireless networks. In *Proc. Allerton 2008 Conf.*, 2008.

[19] J. Ni, B. Tan, and R. Srikant. Q-CSMA: queue length based CSMA/CA algorithms for achieving maximum throughput and low delay in wireless networks. In *Proc. Infocom 2010 Mini-Conf.*, 2010.

[20] S. Rajagopalan, D. Shah, and J. Shin. Network adiabatic theorem: an efficient randomized protocol

for contention resolution. In *Proc. ACM SIGMETRICS/Performance 2009 Conf.*, 2009.

[21] D. Shah and J. Shin. Delay-optimal queue-based CSMA. In *Proc. ACM SIGMETRICS 2010 Conf.*, 2010.

[22] D. Shah and J. Shin. Randomized scheduling algorithm for queueing networks. *Ann. Appl. Prob.*, 22:128–171, 2012.

[23] D. Shah, J. Shin, and P. Tetali. Medium access using queues. In *Proc. FOCS 2011 Conf.*, 2011.

[24] D. Shah, D. Tse, and J. Tsitsiklis. Hardness of low delay network scheduling. *IEEE Trans. Inf. Theory*, 57(12):7810–7817, 2011.

[25] V. Subramanian and M. Alanyali. Delay performance of CSMA in networks with bounded degree conflict graphs. In *Proc. ISIT 2011 Conf.*, 2011.

[26] L. Tassiulas and A. Ephremides. Stability properties of constrained queueing systems and scheduling policies for maximum throughput in multihop radio networks. *IEEE Trans. Aut. Contr.*, 37:1936–1948, 1992.

[27] P. van de Ven, A. Janssen, J. van Leeuwaarden, and S. Borst. Achieving target throughputs in random-access networks. *Perf. Eval.*, 68(11):1103–1117, 2011.

[28] X. Wang and K. Kar. Throughput modeling and fairness issues in CSMA/CA based ad-hoc networks. In *Proc. Infocom 2005 Conf.*, 2005.

[29] A. Zocca, S. Borst, and J. van Leeuwaarden. Mixing properties of CSMA networks on partite graphs. In *Proc. ValueTools 2012 Conf.*, 2012.

APPENDIX

A. PROOFS

A.1 Proof Lemma 7.4

In order for the system to be stable, we must have $\rho_i < \theta_i$ for all $i = 1, \ldots, N$. Thus,

$$\rho = \sum_{k=1}^{K} \hat{\rho}_k = \sum_{k=1}^{K} \frac{1}{M_k} \sum_{i \in V_k} \rho_i$$

$$< \sum_{k=1}^{K} \frac{1}{M_k} \sum_{i \in V_k} \sum_{u \in \Omega} \pi(u) u_i = \sum_{u \in \Omega} \pi(u) \sum_{k=1}^{K} \frac{1}{M_k} \sum_{i \in V_k} u_i$$

$$= \sum_{u \in \Omega^*} \pi(u) \sum_{k=1}^{K} \frac{1}{M_k} \sum_{i \in V_k} u_i + \sum_{u \in \Omega \setminus \Omega^*} \pi(u) \sum_{k=1}^{K} \frac{1}{M_k} \sum_{i \in V_k} u_i$$

$$\leq \sum_{u \in \Omega^*} \pi(u) + (1 - \zeta) \sum_{u \in \Omega \setminus \Omega^*} \pi(u)$$

$$= 1 - \zeta \sum_{u \in \Omega \setminus \Omega^*} \pi(u),$$

where the last inequality follows from Assumption 1. The first part of the lemma follows.

Also, for any $i \in V_k$,

$$\hat{\rho}_k = \rho_i < \sum_{u \in \Omega} \pi(u) u_i \leq \pi(v^{(k)}) + \sum_{u \in \Omega \setminus \Omega^*} \pi(u),$$

which combined with the first statement yields the second part of the lemma.

A.2 Proof Lemma 7.5

For compactness, we denote $\Pi_k = \prod_{i \in V_k} \sigma_i$ and $R_k = \Pi_k/\hat{\rho}_k$, and define $k_{\min} = \arg\min_{k=1,\ldots,K} R_k$ and $k_{\max} = \arg\max_{k=1,\ldots,K} R_k$.

Lemma 7.4 implies

$$\hat{\rho}_{k_{\min}} - \gamma \rho_{\min}^2 \leq \hat{\rho}_{k_{\min}} - (1 - \rho)/\zeta \leq \pi(v^{(k_{\min})}) = Z^{-1} \Pi_{k_{\min}}$$

$$\leq \frac{\Pi_{k_{\min}}}{\sum_{k=1}^{K} \Pi_k}$$

$$= \frac{\Pi_{k_{\min}}}{\Pi_{k_{\min}} + \Pi_{k_{\max}} + \sum_{k \neq k_{\min}, k_{\max}} \Pi_k}$$

$$\leq \frac{\Pi_{k_{\min}}}{\Pi_{k_{\min}} + \Pi_{k_{\max}} + \sum_{k \neq k_{\min}, k_{\max}} \frac{\hat{\rho}_k}{\hat{\rho}_{k_{\min}}} \Pi_{k_{\min}}},$$

yielding

$$(1 - (\hat{\rho}_{k_{\min}} + \sum_{k \neq k_{\min}, k_{\max}} \hat{\rho}_k)(1 - \frac{\gamma \rho_{\min}^2}{\hat{\rho}_{k_{\min}}})) \frac{\Pi_{k_{\min}}}{\Pi_{k_{\max}}} \geq \hat{\rho}_{k_{\min}} - \gamma \rho_{\min}^2,$$

or equivalently,

$$(1 - (\rho - \hat{\rho}_{k_{\max}})(1 - \gamma \rho_{\min}^2/\hat{\rho}_{k_{\min}})) \Pi_{k_{\min}} \geq (\hat{\rho}_{k_{\min}} - \gamma \rho_{\min}^2) \Pi_{k_{\max}}.$$

Using $\rho \geq 1 - \gamma \zeta \rho_{\min}^2$ and $\rho_{\min} \leq \hat{\rho}_{k_{\min}}$, it follows that

$$(1 - (1 - \gamma \zeta \rho_{\min}^2 - \hat{\rho}_{k_{\max}})(1 - \gamma \rho_{\min})) \Pi_{k_{\min}} \geq (1 - \gamma) \hat{\rho}_{k_{\min}} \Pi_{k_{\max}}.$$

This yields

$$(1 + 2\gamma) \hat{\rho}_{k_{\max}} \Pi_{k_{\min}} \geq (1 - \gamma) \hat{\rho}_{k_{\min}} \Pi_{k_{\max}},$$

and thus,

$$R_{k_{\min}} \geq \frac{(1 - \gamma) R_{k_{\max}}}{1 + 2\gamma} \geq (1 - 3\gamma) R_{k_{\max}}.$$

A.3 Proof Lemma 7.6

Since $\sigma_i = \hat{\sigma}_k$ for all $k = 1, \ldots, K$, we obtain

$$\max_{u \in \partial S_l(\mathcal{A})} \prod_{j=1}^{N} \sigma_j^{u_j} = \max_{u \in \partial S_l(\mathcal{A})} \prod_{k=1}^{K} \prod_{i \in V_k} \sigma_i^{u_i}$$

$$= \max_{u \in \partial S_l(\mathcal{A})} \prod_{k=1}^{K} \hat{\sigma}_k^{\sum_{i \in V_k} u_i}$$

$$= \max_{u \in \partial S_l(\mathcal{A})} \prod_{k=1}^{K} (\hat{\sigma}_k^{M_k})^{\frac{1}{M_k} \sum_{i \in V_k} u_i}.$$

Lemma 7.5 gives

$$\hat{\sigma}_k^{M_k} \leq \frac{\hat{\rho}_k}{1 - 3\gamma} \min_{l=1,\ldots,K} \frac{1}{\hat{\rho}_l} \hat{\sigma}_l^{M_l} \leq \frac{\sigma^*}{(1 - 3\gamma) \rho_{\min}},$$

and thus,

$$\max_{u \in \partial S_l(\mathcal{A})} \prod_{j=1}^{N} \sigma_j^{u_j} \leq \max_{u \in \partial S_l(\mathcal{A})} \prod_{k=1}^{K} \left(\frac{\sigma^*}{(1 - 3\gamma) \rho_{\min}} \right)^{\frac{1}{M_k} \sum_{i \in V_k} u_i}$$

$$\leq \max_{u \in \partial S_l(\mathcal{A})} \left(\frac{\sigma^*}{(1 - 3\gamma) \rho_{\min}} \right)^{\sum_{k=1}^{K} \frac{1}{M_k} \sum_{i \in V_k} u_i}$$

$$= \left(\frac{\sigma^*}{(1 - 3\gamma) \rho_{\min}} \right)^{\max_{u \in \partial S_l(\mathcal{A})} H(u)}$$

$$= \left(\frac{\sigma^*}{(1 - 3\gamma) \rho_{\min}} \right)^{H_l(\mathcal{A})}.$$

Scheduling of Users with Markovian Time-Varying Transmission Rates[*]

Fabio Cecchi[†]
University of Pisa, Italy
BCAM — Basque Center for
Applied Mathematics, Spain
cecchi@mail.dm.unipi.it

Peter Jacko[‡]
Lancaster University, UK
BCAM — Basque Center for
Applied Mathematics, Spain
p.jacko@lancaster.ac.uk

ABSTRACT

We address the problem of developing a well-performing and implementable scheduler of users with wireless connection to the base station. The main feature of such real-life systems is that the quality conditions of the user channels are time-varying, which turn into the time-varying transmission rate due to different modulation and coding schemes. We assume that this phenomenon follows a Markovian law and most of the discussion is dedicated to the case of three quality conditions of each user, for which we characterize an optimal index policy and show that threshold policies (of giving higher priority to users with higher transmission rate) are not necessarily optimal. For the general case of arbitrary number of quality conditions we design a scheduler and propose its two practical approximations, and illustrate the performance of the proposed index-based schedulers and existing alternatives in a variety of simulation scenarios.

Categories and Subject Descriptors

F.2.2 [**Analysis of Algorithms and Problem Complexity**]: Nonnumerical Algorithms and Problems—*Sequencing*

[*]The authors are grateful to U. Ayesta for many fruitful discussions and the four anonymous referees for valuable suggestions that helped to improve the presentation of the paper. This research was mostly done during the stay of F. Cecchi at BCAM during August-October 2012 funded by the BCAM Internship program. This research was partially supported by grant MTM2010-17405 (Ministerio de Ciencia e Innovación, Spain).

[†]Full addresses: Dipartimento di Matematica, University of Pisa, Largo Bruno Pontecorvo 5, 56127, Pisa, Italy; BCAM - Basque Center for Applied Mathematics, Mazarredo 14, 48009 Bilbao (Basque Country), Spain.

[‡]P. Jacko is co-funded by the LANCS Initiative. Full addresses: Department of Management Science, Lancaster University Management School, Lancaster, LA1 4YX, UK; BCAM - Basque Center for Applied Mathematics, Mazarredo 14, 48009 Bilbao (Basque Country), Spain.

and scheduling; C.2.1 [**Computer-Communication Networks**]: Network Architecture and Design—*Wireless communication*; C.4 [**Performance of Systems**]: Modeling techniques; G.3 [**Probability and Statistics**]: Queueing theory

General Terms

Theory, Algorithms, Performance

Keywords

wireless networks, opportunistic scheduling, performance evaluation, Markov decision processes, stochastic scheduling, stability

1. INTRODUCTION

This paper is motivated by the necessity of designing an appropriate scheduler for wireless systems such as Long Term Evolution (4G LTE), heterogeneous networks (HetNet) or vehicular communications systems. Such a scheduler must be capable of exploiting the base station's capacity to serve the heterogeneous demands of the users that are within the base station's power range in order to optimize the system performance and user experience. We model such a system as the multi-class queueing system with multiple preemptive servers, in which users of different classes randomly arrive and depart once their job is completed. Different classes may have different sets of accessible transmission rates associated with the finite class-dependent number of quality conditions of the channels, whose evolution is class-dependent and Markovian. Further, the classes may have heterogeneous waiting costs and mean job sizes. The model covers both the downlink and synchronized uplink wireless systems.

Several schedulers have been proposed recently for such a *flow-level* scheduling problem based on ad-hoc arguments, simulation outcomes or approximate optimization, e.g., in [17, 9, 8, 1, 3, 15]. The pioneering work was done by [17], who showed that the system capacity can be improved by opportunistically serving users whose current transmission rate is maximal. Such a scheduler, known as the *MaxRate* scheduler in the wireless networks literature is thus *naively opportunistic*: it is myopically throughput optimal (maximizing one-slot transmission rate) and simple to implement, but it ignores the possible future evolution and was shown to perform bad in the long-term. For instance, it may quickly become unstable (i.e., the number of waiting users explodes) as the load increases, while other schedulers may keep the system stable [1, 3]. It may also be extremely unfair to users whose highest accessible transmission rate is lower than the transmission rates of others. This scheduler is also known as the $c\mu$-rule in the stochastic scheduling literature, and we will adopt this name in this paper.

Gradient-based schedulers are the state-of-the-art in opportunistic scheduling, in particular the Proportionally Fair (PF) scheduler, patented [11], was proposed to be implemented in the CDMA 1xEV-DO system of 3G cellular networks [6]. PF maximizes the logarithmic throughput of the network, providing thus an improved fairness over $c\mu$-rule [18]. [9] analyzed flow-level stability of PF by approximating it by the *Relatively Best* (RB) scheduler, which gives priority to users according to their ratio of the current transmission rate to the mean transmission rate. This scheduler is thus *fairly opportunistic*: it takes the possible future evolution into account, it is not myopically throughput optimal, performs well with respect to guaranteeing a minimal throughput to the users with low accessible transmission rates, however, it is not maximally stable at flow-level [1].

The schedulers proposed in [8, 1, 3], called the *Score Based* (SB) [7], *Proportionally Best* (PB) and *Potential Improvement* (PI) [5] schedulers, respectively, belong to the family of the *best-condition* schedulers. A best-condition scheduler gives absolute priority to the users in their respective best accessible quality condition over the others, hence ignoring the transmission rate associated with such a best condition. Such a policy is thus *smartly opportunistic*: this feature still ignores the possible future evolution, but it is not myopic, and turns out to perform well in the long-term and in heavily loaded systems, for being maximally stable [4, 16]. Fairness of best-condition schedulers has not been addressed adequately yet, only [3] illustrated in one simulation scenario that PI maintained the average number of uncompleted jobs significantly more balanced than other schedulers.

It has been typically assumed in the previous work that the channel evolution is independent and identically distributed (iid). Consideration of Markovian channel evolution (rather than the iid evolution) is however important, because it is known that channels do have a memory, although the precise evolution is usually unknown or difficult to estimate (and moreover can change over time). For instance, random processes in signal processing are often modeled by the autoregressive model of order 1, which is Markovian (and not iid).

In this paper we give insights into answers to the fundamental questions about scheduling in the Markovian channels setting:

- What is the structure of an optimal policy?
- Why are there no optimality results available? (Only maximal stability has been established.)
- How do the actions taken in the non-best states influence the performance? (Maximal stability only indicates what to do in the channel condition with the highest transmission rate.)
- (When) are the maximally stable policies preferable in practice?
- How to resolve the trade-off between being naively opportunistic, smartly opportunistic, and prioritizing "short" jobs?
- Do the maximally stable policies perform well even in case of classes with heterogeneous waiting costs?

- How fair are the maximally stable policies?

We are still far from providing definite answers, but we believe that this paper can develop some intuition and point to the main issues and avenues to focus on in future research in this area.

In section 2 we formalize the system and the scheduling problem. An MDP approach is described in section 3 in order to formulate a single-user optimization problem in which a price must be paid for service. This problem is addressed in section 4, where we develop index policies and study solvability by threshold policies. We solve the problem for channel evolution over three quality conditions and partially characterize the optimal solution in general. It is important to note that threshold policies (of giving higher priority to users with higher transmission rate) are not necessarily optimal. That is, when a single wireless user is competing even with a non-time-varying user, it may be optimal to serve the wireless user in channel conditions with the highest and the lowest transmission rates, but to prefer the other user if the wireless one is in channel condition with the medium transmission rate. Based on these results, we propose a new scheduler and two practical approximations in section 5. Their performance is evaluated and contrasted with schedulers proposed in previous literature in section 6. Finally, section 7 concludes. The proofs are omitted due to lack of space.

2. PROBLEM DESCRIPTION

We consider a time-slotted system, so that we study a discrete-time job scheduling problem. The decisions are taken in time epochs/instants $t \in \mathcal{T} := \{0, 1, \dots\}$, and are applied during the time slots $t \in \mathcal{T}$ of duration τ seconds, where slot t corresponds to the interval between epochs $[t, t+1)$.

2.1 Job-Channel-User Classes

Suppose that there are K classes of users, labeled $k \in \mathcal{K} := \{1, 2, \dots, K\}$. Each user is uniquely associated with the job it requests to download and with the dedicated wireless channel.

User Arrivals.

For each class $k \in \mathcal{K}$, the number of class-k users arriving to the system, $A_k(t)$, at each time epoch $t \in \mathcal{T}$, creates an iid arrival process $\{A_k(t)\}_{t \in \mathcal{T}}$ with generic element A_k and mean $\lambda_k := \mathbb{E}_0[A_k] < \infty$, where $\mathbb{E}_0[\cdot]$ denotes the expectation conditional to information available at time epoch 0. The arrivals are assumed to be mutually independent across user classes.

Job Sizes.

The (integer-valued) job/flow size b_k of class-k user is measured in *bits* and has the geometric distribution with $\mathbb{E}[b_k] < \infty$ for classes $k \in \mathcal{K}$. This assumption is the main limitation of existing models (including this paper), but to the best of our knowledge there has not been any attempt to analytically approach the case of non-geometric job sizes in the literature.

Channel Conditions.

For each user, the quality of the channel (the *channel condition*) is changing from slot to slot, independently of all other users present in the system (including other users of the same class) and, for each class-k user, takes values in the finite set $\mathcal{N}'_k := \{1, 2, \ldots, N_k\}$. Moreover, the channel condition an arriving class-k user finds the channel in, is also independent of channel conditions of other users and the slot it arrives at, and is n with probability $q_{k,n} \geq 0$, which satisfies $\sum_{n \in \mathcal{N}'_k} q_{k,n} = 1$.

Channel Condition Transitions.

We assume that at each slot, for a class-k user, its channel condition evolves according to a distribution which may depend on k and on the channel condition in the current slot (i.e., is Markovian). Thus, for each user of class $k \in \mathcal{K}$, we can define a (time-homogeneous) Markov chain with state space $\mathcal{N}^{(k)}$.

We denote by $q_{k,n,m} := \mathbb{P}(Z_k(t+1) = m | Z_k(t) = n)$ the probability that the channel quality condition of a class-k user moves from the state n to the state m in one slot. The class k channel condition transition probability matrix is thus

$$
\mathbf{Q}_k := \quad
\begin{array}{c}
 \\
1 \\
2 \\
\vdots \\
N_k
\end{array}
\begin{array}{c}
\begin{array}{cccc}
1 & 2 & \cdots & N_k
\end{array} \\
\left(
\begin{array}{cccc}
q_{k,1,1} & q_{k,1,2} & \cdots & q_{k,1,N_k} \\
q_{k,2,1} & q_{k,2,2} & \cdots & q_{k,2,N_k} \\
\vdots & \vdots & \ddots & \vdots \\
q_{k,N_k,1} & q_{k,N_k,2} & \cdots & q_{k,N_k,N_k}
\end{array}
\right)
\end{array}
$$

where $\sum_{m \in \mathcal{N}'_k} q_{k,n,m} = 1$ for every condition $n \in \mathcal{N}'_k$. We emphasize that channel condition transitions of users are independent across users. In this paper we assume that $\mathbf{Q}_k$ is irreducible and aperiodic for every k.

Transmission Rates.

Different channel conditions correspond to different transmission rates associated with the available modulation and coding schemes (MCS). When a class-k user is in channel condition $n \in \mathcal{N}'_k$, she can receive data at transmission rate $s_{k,n}$ bits per second. Without loss of generality we assume that the higher the channel condition, the higher the transmission rate, i.e., $0 \leq s_{k,1} < s_{k,2} < \cdots < s_{k,N_k}$.

To avoid trivial cases, we assume that each class k can be served, i.e., $s_{k,N_k} > 0$. We further restrict our attention to the case in which at least one class k is time-varying, i.e., $s_{k,1} < s_{k,N_k}$.

For each class k we define $B_k := \lceil b_k / s_{k,N_k} \rceil$, the number of slots in the best quality condition (N_k) needed to complete the job. Thus, B_k is the minimum number of slots that a job of size b_k must spend in service in order to be completed. We denote by $\mathbb{E}[B_k]$ (positive integer) the mean of this random variable of class k. We further define the traffic intensity of class k as $\varrho_k := \lambda_k \mathbb{E}[B_k]$.

Waiting Costs.

For every user of class k the operator accrues a waiting cost $c_k > 0$ for every slot while it is uncompleted.

2.2 Server

At the beginning of every slot t, the server (base station) observes the actual state of all the users present in the system, and decides which (up to its capacity constraint C) of them to serve during the slot. We assume that the server is preemptive, that is at every decision epoch it is permitted to suspend the service of a user whose job is not yet concluded. Moreover, the server is allowed to be allocated to an already completed job, in this case no transmission occurs. Motivated by practical implementation, the observations of the processes defined below at epoch t always include arrivals at epoch t, while during the time interval $(t, t+1)$ only service but no new arrivals occur.

2.3 Objectives

The aim is to identify scheduling policies that perform well with respect to the following objectives (or their combination):

- minimization of the expected time-average waiting cost per user;
- minimization of the expected time-average number of uncompleted jobs per slot;
- maximization of some time-average fairness function across classes.

3. MDP APPROACH

In this section we set out to employ a Markov decision process (MDP) approach to design a well-grounded scheduling policy. Indeed, we extend the modeling framework introduced for the scheduling problem with iid channel condition evolution in [3] based on restless bandits [21]. Other scheduling policies were designed in an ad hoc way ([8, 1]), or based on solving an optimization problem under the time-scale separation assumption ([2]).

In order to employ the MDP framework, we simplify the problem: we assume a fixed population of users present in the system at the initial slot (i.e., ignore the arrivals). That is, there is a single user of each class k. On the other hand, in order to admit an analytical approach, we introduce discounting of the waiting costs, with discount factor $0 \leq \beta < 1$. The results for the undiscounted case, which corresponds to the time-average criterion, will be obtained in the limit $\beta \to 1$.

These twists are still not sufficient to solve the problem optimally. Nevertheless, this approach was shown useful for designing in the iid special case a scheduler [3] that is well-performing, maximally stable and fluid-optimal under arbitrary arrivals [4]. The approach requires to analyze a single-user problem in which one pays price ν for service. This parameter appears from the Lagrangian relaxation (omitted here) as the Lagrangian parameter.

Before defining the MDP elements, we will further need to define the departure probabilities. We denote by $\mu_{k,n}$ the probability that the job k in state n, if served, will be completed in the current slot. Since we consider jobs with geometric size, we can employ the results from [3, 15] that $\mu_{k,n} = \min\{1, 1 - (1 - 1/\mathbb{E}_0[b_k])^{\tau s_{k,n}}\}$ which can be approximated, if $\tau s_{k,n}/\mathbb{E}_0[b_k] \approx 0$ by

$$
\mu_{k,n} \approx \tau s_{k,n} / \mathbb{E}_0[b_k]. \tag{1}
$$

Note that the departure probabilities are increasing: $0 \leq \mu_{k,1} < \cdots < \mu_{k,N_k} \leq 1$.

3.1 Job-Channel-User MDP

At the beginning of every time slot, the generic user k can be allocated zero capacity of the base station or be one of the users served. We denote by $\mathcal{A}_k$ the action space relative to user k. We have that $\mathcal{A}_k := \{0, 1\}$ where the action 0 means not serving, while action 1 means serving.

Every job-channel-user k is characterized by the tuple $(\mathcal{N}_k, (\boldsymbol{W}_k^a)_{a \in \mathcal{A}}, (\boldsymbol{R}_k^a)_{a \in \mathcal{A}}, (\boldsymbol{P}_k^a)_{a \in \mathcal{A}})$, where

- $\mathcal{N}_k := \{0\} \cup \mathcal{N}_k'$ is the *state space*, the state 0 indicates that the job is completed, while the set $\mathcal{N}_k'$ represents the possible channel quality conditions;

- $\boldsymbol{W}_k^a := (W_{k,n}^a)_{n \in \mathcal{N}_k}$, where $W_{k,n}^a$ is the expected one-slot capacity consumption, or *work* required by user k at state n if action a is selected at a time epoch. Specifically, for every state $n \in \mathcal{N}_k$,

$$W_{k,n}^1 := 1, \qquad W_{k,n}^0 := 0;$$

- $\boldsymbol{R}_k^a := (R_{k,n}^a)_{n \in \mathcal{N}_k}$, where $R_{k,n}^a$ is the expected one-slot *reward* earned by user k at state n if action a is selected at a time epoch. Specifically, for every state $n \in \mathcal{N}_k'$,

$$R_{k,0}^a := 0, \quad R_{k,n}^1 := -c_k(1 - \mu_{k,n}), \quad R_{k,n}^0 := -c_k;$$

- $\boldsymbol{P}_k^a := (p_{k,n,m}^a)_{n,m \in \mathcal{N}_k}$, where $p_{k,n,m}^a$ is the probability for user k of moving from state n to state m if action a is chosen at a time epoch. These one-slot *state-transition probability matrices* are

$$\boldsymbol{P}_k^0 = \begin{pmatrix} 1 & 0 & 0 & 0 \\ 0 & q_{k,1,1} & \cdots & q_{k,1,N_k} \\ 0 & q_{k,2,1} & \cdots & q_{k,2,N_k} \\ \vdots & \vdots & \ddots & \vdots \\ 0 & q_{k,N_k,1} & \cdots & q_{k,N_k,N_k} \end{pmatrix},$$

$$\boldsymbol{P}_k^1 = \begin{pmatrix} 1 & 0 & 0 & 0 \\ \mu_{k,1} & \widetilde{\mu}_{k,1} q_{k,1,1} & \cdots & \widetilde{\mu}_{k,1} q_{k,1,N_k} \\ \mu_{k,2} & \widetilde{\mu}_{k,2} q_{k,2,1} & \cdots & \widetilde{\mu}_{k,2} q_{k,2,N_k} \\ \vdots & \vdots & \ddots & \vdots \\ \mu_{k,N_k} & \widetilde{\mu}_{k,N_k} q_{k,N_k,1} & \cdots & \widetilde{\mu}_{k,N_k} q_{k,N_k,N_k} \end{pmatrix},$$

where we have denoted by $\widetilde{\mu}_{k,n} := 1 - \mu_{k,n}$.

The dynamics of user k are thus captured by the *state process* $X_k(\cdot)$ and the *action process* $a_k(\cdot)$, which correspond to state $X_k(t) \in \mathcal{N}_k$ and action $a_k(t) \in \mathcal{A}$ at all time $t \in \mathcal{T}$. At time slot t the choice of action $a_k(t)$ for the user k in state $X_k(t)$ entails the consumption of the allocated capacity (work), the gain of the reward and the evolution of the state to $X_k(t+1) \in \mathcal{N}_k$.

3.2 Optimization Problem

We present now the optimization problem we consider. Let Π_{X_k, a_k} be the space of all randomized, history dependent and non-anticipative policies, depending on the state-process $X_k(\cdot)$ and deciding the action-process $a_k(\cdot)$.

Let $\mathbb{E}_0^\pi$ denote the expectation over the future state process $X_k(\cdot)$ and the action process $a_k(\cdot)$, conditioned on the initial state $X_k(0)$ and on the policy $\pi \in \Pi_{X_k, a_k}$. For the given discount factor β and for every value of price ν, the aim is to find a policy minimizing the expected waiting cost over an infinite horizon under the discounted criterion,

$$\max_{\pi \in \Pi_{X_k, a_k}} \sum_{t=0}^{\infty} \beta^t \, \mathbb{E}_0^\pi \left[R_{k, X_k(t)}^{a_k(t)} - \nu W_{k, X_k(t)}^{a_k(t)} \right]. \qquad (2)$$

4. INDEX-BASED SOLUTION

In this section we focus on the single-user subproblem (2) for a generic user k, and we will omit the subscript k to simplify the notation.

4.1 Index Values and Threshold Policies

Let us adapt to our scenario the definition of *index values* and *indexability*, following [14].

DEFINITION 1 (INDEXABILITY). *We say that the problem (2) is* indexable *if there exist values $\nu_n^* \in \mathbb{R} \cup \{-\infty, \infty\}$ for all $n \in \mathcal{N}$ such that*

1. *it is optimal to serve the user in state n if $\nu_n^* \geq \nu$, and*

2. *it is optimal not to serve the user in state n if $\nu_n^* \leq \nu$.*

Such values ν_n^* are called the (Whittle) index values*, and define an optimal* index policy *for the problem.*

As described in [12, 21, 19] the optimal solution can sometimes be found by means of the index policies. The index values represent, in certain way, the benefit which is obtained by serving an user in a certain state. It has been shown that for some non-trivial problems such index may not exist.

From the point of view of intuition and implementability, one is often interested in solving the problem by threshold policies.

DEFINITION 2 (SOLVABILITY BY THRESHOLD POLICIES). *We say that the problem (2) is* solvable by threshold policies *if for any value of ν, there exists a threshold state $n(\nu)$ such that*

1. *it is optimal to serve the user in state n if $n \geq n(\nu)$, and*

2. *it is optimal not to serve the user in state n if $n < n(\nu)$.*

Such policies are called threshold policies.

We can see that the indexability property is much more general than solvability by threshold policies. Indeed, if the problem is indexable and the index values are non-increasing in n, then it is solvable by threshold policies. However, an indexable problem is not be solvable by threshold policies if the index values are not non-increasing in n; then the optimal solution may look counter-intuitive.

The restless bandit problem and their index-based solution was introduced in [21], generalizing the so-called Gittins index policy that was proved optimal for the multi-armed bandit problem in [13]. [21] gave an intuitive definition of indices. An algorithm for computing index values and sufficient indexability conditions were introduced later; see [19] for a survey. The algorithm is called *Adaptive-Greedy*, shortly $\mathcal{AG}$-*algorithm*. It was also shown that if a problem is indexable then the $\mathcal{AG}$-algorithm computes the index values.

4.2 Index Values Characterization

The arguments in this section are based on the conjecture of indexability.

CONJECTURE 1. *Problem (2) is indexable.*

Establishing indexability by the currently known approaches is likely to be technically extremely tedious. However, we believe in its validity based on the computational testing we have performed on many (including random) problem instances. Also, indexability was proved and index values were characterized in two important special cases in [3, 15]. We state it below for completeness.

THEOREM 1 ([3]). *If the channel condition evolves in an iid fashion, i.e., $q_{n,m} = q_m$ for each $n \in \mathcal{N}'$, then problem (2) is indexable and the index values are*

$$\nu_n^* = \frac{c\mu_n}{1 - \beta + \beta \sum_{m=n+1}^{N} q_m(\mu_m - \mu_n)}.$$

THEOREM 2 ([15]). *If the channel evolves according to the Gilbert-Elliot model, i.e., $N = 2$, then problem (2) is indexable and the index values are*

$$\nu_2^* = \frac{c\mu_2}{1 - \beta} \qquad \nu_1^* = \frac{c\mu_1}{1 - \beta + \beta q_{1,2}^*(\mu_2 - \mu_1)},$$

where

$$q_{1,2}^* = \frac{1}{\frac{\beta(1-\mu_2)}{q_2^{SS}} + \frac{1 - \beta(1-\mu_2)}{q_{1,2}}}.$$

We now continue with characterization of the index values in our, general, model. The following theorem identifies the highest index value in closed form.

THEOREM 3. *Under Conjecture 1, the index value $\nu_N^* = \frac{c\mu_N}{1 - \beta}$ and we have that $\nu_N^* \geq \nu_n^*$ for every $n \in \mathcal{N}'$.*

This result is thus an extension to the Markovian setting of the characterization of the highest index value in the iid and 2-state special cases stated above. What we see is that the highest index value is *always* associated with the state with the highest transmission rate, N, and, rather surprisingly, it *always* has a simple expression, which grows to $+\infty$ as $\beta \to 1$.

4.3 Index Values for 3-State Channel

Now we concentrate on problem (2) in the case $N = 3$. If Conjecture 1 holds, we already know by Theorem 3 that the highest index is the one associated with state 3. There are therefore two possibilities: the index value of state 2 is greater than that of state 1 (i.e., the problem is solvable by threshold policies), or vice versa.

THEOREM 4. *Under Conjecture 1, if problem (2) with $N = 3$ is solvable by threshold policies, then*

$$\nu_2^* = \frac{c\mu_2}{q_2^*(\mu_3 - \mu_2)},$$

where

$$q_2^* := \frac{1}{\frac{1-\mu_3}{q_3^{SS}} + \frac{\mu_3}{\bar{q}_2}}, \qquad \bar{q}_2 := q_{1,3}p_1^{(2)} + q_{2,3}p_2^{(2)},$$

where the weights $p_1^{(2)} = \frac{q_{21}}{1-q_{11}+q_{21}}$ and $p_2^{(2)} = \frac{1-q_{11}}{1-q_{11}+q_{21}}$ are the elements of the steady state probability vector of the 2×2 matrix created from $\boldsymbol{Q}$ by omitting row 3 and merging column 3 with 2. If the problem is solvable by threshold policies after relabeling states 1 and 2, then these results hold as well.

We can further characterize the index value of state 1. Let us denote by

$$\begin{aligned}\alpha = {}&-q_{2,1}q_{1,2} + q_{1,1}q_{2,2} + q_{1,2}q_{3,1} - q_{1,1}q_{3,2} + q_{2,1}q_{3,2} \\ &- q_{3,1}q_{2,2} - q_{1,1} - q_{2,2} + q_{3,1} + q_{3,2} + 1,\end{aligned}$$

$$\begin{aligned}U = {}&(1 - \mu_2)(1 - \mu_3)\alpha + \mu_3(1 - \mu_2)(1 - q_{2,2} + q_{1,2}) \\ &+ \mu_2(1 - \mu_3)(1 - q_{3,3} + q_{1,3}) + \mu_2\mu_3,\end{aligned}$$

$$\begin{aligned}V = {}&(\mu_2 - \mu_1)[(q_{1,2}q_{3,1} - q_{1,1}q_{3,2} + q_{3,2})(1 - \mu_3) + q_{1,2}\mu_3] \\ &+ (\mu_3 - \mu_1)[(-q_{1,2}q_{2,1} + q_{1,1}q_{2,2} - q_{2,2} \\ &- q_{1,1} + 1)(1 - \mu_2) + q_{1,3}\mu_2].\end{aligned}$$

THEOREM 5. *If Conjecture 1 holds for problem (2) with $N = 3$ in the undiscounted case ($\beta = 1$) and it is solvable by threshold policies, then the index value of state 1 is the lowest and equals*

$$\nu_1^* = \frac{c\mu_1 U}{V}. \tag{3}$$

Unfortunately, we have not been able to write this formula in a more readable form. However, an interesting approximation can be obtained for large jobs.

THEOREM 6. *Let us fix a bound M such that $\mu_3 \leq M \leq 1$, i.e., in view of (1) the expected job size is approximately at least $\tau s_N / M$ bits. Then we have that the index value of state 1,*

$$\nu_1^* = \frac{c\left(\mu_1 + \mathcal{O}\left(M^2\right)\right)}{\sum_{m=2,3} q_m^{SS}(\mu_m - \mu_1) + \mathcal{O}\left(M^2\right)}, \tag{4}$$

and of state 2,

$$\nu_2^* = \frac{c\left(\frac{\mu_2}{q_3^{SS}} + \mathcal{O}\left(M^2\right)\right)}{\mu_3 - \mu_2}. \tag{5}$$

As a consequence, if M is small enough so that terms $\mathcal{O}(M^2)$ can be neglected, then we have the following approximation for the index value of state 1,

$$\nu_1^* \approx \frac{c\mu_1}{\sum_{m=2,3} q_m^{SS}(\mu_m - \mu_1)}, \tag{6}$$

and of state 2,

$$\nu_2^* \approx \frac{c\mu_2}{q_3^{SS}(\mu_3 - \mu_2)}. \tag{7}$$

This characterization is nothing but the index value in the iid setting (cf. Theorem 1), where the steady-state distribution is employed while the underlying Markovian channel evolution is irrelevant. The precision of this approximation is excellent for large jobs, as showed in Table 1 for condition 1. Both the absolute error and the relative error increase approximately linearly in M, i.e., decrease hyperbolically in job size.

Note that the larger the job, the smaller the parameter M, and the precision of this approximation could be interpreted as a sort of time-scale separation effect arising naturally in the solution: the *steady-state channel distribution* approximates well in which channel conditions the job will be served, whereas for shorter jobs the Markovian channel

M	Absolute Error	Relative Error	ε
1	0.3880	14.08%	$+\infty$
0.5	0.1854	7.424%	0.16667
0.3	0.1273	4.498%	0.04286
0.1	0.0399	1.571%	0.00370
0.05	0.0237	0.828%	0.00088
0.01	0.0051	0.176%	0.00003
0.001	0.0005	0.017%	0.00000

Table 1: **Mean absolute and relative errors of the approximation** (6) **in a sample of** 2000 **job-channel-user instances for each upper bound** $M \geq \mu_3$.

evolution may be more important indicating which channel condition is hit first if starting from the current condition. However, note that this phenomenon differs from the time-scale separation as often simplistically assumed in other literature, which implies that the jobs realize the *time-average throughput*, see [2].

4.4 Solvability by Threshold Policies for 3-State Channel

We have given in the previous subsection formulas for computing the index values of a 3-state channel assuming they are solvable by threshold policies in the undiscounted case $\beta = 1$. We will give now two sufficient conditions for having such property satisfied and we will observe that they are satisfied in a large number of problem instances.

THEOREM 7. *If Conjecture 1 holds for problem* (2) *with* $N = 3$ *in the undiscounted case* ($\beta = 1$), *then we have that* $q_{13} \geq q_{23}$ *implies that the index value of state* 2 *is greater than or equal to the index value of state* 1, *i.e., the problem is solvable by threshold policies.*

This fact seems quite evident, indeed $q_{13} \geq q_{23}$ means that the one-slot probability to move to any better state is surely higher if the user is in state 1 than in state 2. Moreover we observe that the hypothesis is satisfied for the iid special case, recovering again the the result of solvability by threshold policies by [3].

THEOREM 8. *Let us denote by* $\Delta := \min\{\mu_3 - \mu_2, \mu_2 - \mu_1\}$ *and* $1 > M \geq \mu_3$. *If Conjecture 1 holds for problem* (2) *with* $N = 3$ *in the undiscounted case* ($\beta = 1$), *then we have that*

$$\Delta \geq \varepsilon := \frac{M^2}{3(1-M)}$$

implies that the index value of state 2 *is greater than or equal to the index value of state* 1, *i.e., the problem is solvable by threshold policies.*

In the last column of Table 1 we show how small could be $\Delta \geq \varepsilon$ given a range of upper bounds $M \geq \mu_3$. This condition seems to be really strong if M is small, which is the condition we required to employ the approximation of ν_1^* in the previous subsection. We emphasize that this is still quite a rough sufficient condition (see the proof). Finally, we remark that the counter-intuitive case that the index value of state 1 is greater than the index value of state 2 happens with frequency of around 2.5% for $\beta = 0.999$.

Algorithm 1 Algorithmic scheme of PI* scheduler
> At every slot t,
> $C' \leftarrow$ Number of users with uncompleted jobs in their condition N_k
> **if** $C' \geq C$ **then**
>   Serve C users from among the users in their condition N_k (breaking ties randomly)
> **else**
>   Serve C' users in their condition N_k
>   Serve $C - C'$ users not in condition N_k with highest index value $\nu_{k, X_k(t)}^*$ (breaking ties randomly)
> **end if**

5. PROPOSED SCHEDULERS

Now we come back to the original multi-class problem with arrivals, as described in section 2. We set out to design feasible schedulers for the problem where it is allowed to serve up to C users in every slot. We are interested in the undiscounted case, which is essentially the case of optimization under the time-average criterion. We will do so by deploying the results obtained in the previous section. We thus define the *Markovian Potential Improvement* (PI*) scheduler, which is written algorithmically in Algorithm 1.

However, as we have seen in the previous section, the index values $\nu_{k,n}^*$ are likely not to admit a simple closed-form characterization in the general setting, except for $\nu_{k,N_k}^* = +\infty$. We nevertheless gave a closed-form solution for $N_k = 3$. Therefore, we propose two approximations for the index values, which give rise to additional two new schedulers for general N_k.

First, we define the PI$^{\mathcal{AG}}$ scheduler, which approximates $\nu_{k,n}^*$ for $n \in \mathcal{N} \setminus \{N\}$ by running the $\mathcal{AG}$-algorithm with β as close as possible to 1 while avoiding numerical instability problems. Note that this algorithm performs $\mathcal{O}(N_k^3)$ elementary operations, and requires the knowledge of the matrix $\boldsymbol{Q}_k$. On the other hand, this algorithm is likely to identify if the threshold policies are not optimal, and so these approximated index values may not necessarily be increasing in n.

Second, we define the PI^{SS} scheduler, which approximates $\nu_{k,n}^*$ for $n \in \mathcal{N} \setminus \{N\}$ by the formula

$$\frac{c_k \mu_{k,n}}{\sum_{m > n} q_{k,m}^{\mathrm{SS}} (\mu_{k,m} - \mu_{k,n})}. \tag{8}$$

This approximation is based on conjecturing generalizability of Theorem 6, which requires that $\mu_{k,N_k} \leq M$, where M is small enough so that terms bounded by M^2 can be neglected. It is easy to prove that these approximated index values are increasing in n and that their computation requires $\mathcal{O}(N_k)$ elementary operations (once the steady-state distribution is known). On the other hand, knowledge of the matrix $\boldsymbol{Q}_k$ is not required, since only the steady-state distribution is used, which may be significantly easier and more precise to estimate in practice.

We adopt the name of the potential improvement scheduler introduced in [3], since [15] for the 2-state channel and the previous section for the 3-state channel show that the index value is the ratio of the one-slot holding cost saving and the (weighted) potential improvement of the departure probability. This can be seen also as a way of optimally resolving the trade-off between opportunistic scheduling and short-jobs prioritization, but we note that yet another dimension (the Markovian evolution) comes into play and shows that it may be sometimes better to neither be opportunistic nor give priority to (myopically) shorter job. We can summarize the main features of this rule by saying that the priority is given to users which cannot improve their actual condition by much.

The PI* scheduler and both its approximations PI$^{\mathcal{AG}}$ and PI^{SS} reduce to a scheduler that is optimal if $N_k = 1$ for all k and there is a single server ($C = 1$) under arbitrary arrivals [10]. Also, they belong to the family of the best-condition schedulers, which give always priority to users currently in their best condition over users which are not, and which have important stability properties in Markovian setting as shown in [16].

THEOREM 9. *In the single server case $C = 1$, the PI* scheduler and both its approximations PI$^{\mathcal{AG}}$ and PI^{SS} are maximally stable under arbitrary arrivals.*

We believe that maximal stability is true even in the multi-server case. In fact, it is easy to argue that the stability region is upperbounded even in the case of generally distributed job sizes as follows.

THEOREM 10. *If $\varrho := \sum_{k \in \mathcal{K}} \varrho_k > C$, then there is no scheduler that stabilizes the system.*

We are, unfortunately, unable to conclude anything with respect to (asymptotic) optimality of the proposed schedulers in systems with arrivals. In the next section we evaluate the performance of PI* and compare it to existing schedulers proposed for this problem by previous literature.

6. EXPERIMENTAL STUDY

In this section we investigate the behavior of the PI* scheduler and its approximations that we have proposed. In order to be able to evaluate the performance of these policies, we present several scenarios, in which we compare them with the schedulers proposed in previous literature. These policies are all priority-based, in the sense that the users served are the ones with highest index values. We however note that these alternative schedulers are based on indices that are *not* Whittle indices, i.e., they have not been shown optimal in the single-user subproblem.

For the sake of completeness we give their definitions, especially because we have modified them to incorporate the waiting costs (originally equal to 1 for RB, PB and SB):

- the *cμ* rule, i.e. $\nu_{k,n}^{c\mu} = c_k \mu_{k,n}$;
- the **Relatively Best** rule, i.e. $\nu_{k,n}^{RB} = \dfrac{c_k \mu_{k,n}}{\sum\limits_{m=1}^{N_k} q_{k,m}^{SS} \mu_{k,m}}$;
- the **Proportionally Best** rule, i.e. $\nu_{k,n}^{PB} = \dfrac{c_k \mu_{k,n}}{\mu_{k,N_k}}$;
- the **Score Based** rule, i.e. $\nu_{k,n}^{SB} = c_k \sum_{m=1}^{n} q_{k,m}^{SS}$.

We restrict our attention to the case with at most one user served during each slot of time, i.e. $C = 1$ (if more than one user has the highest index value, we break the ties randomly), and we consider only 2 classes of users, in order to be able to easily point out the differences in the performance of the policies generated by the above scheduling rules.

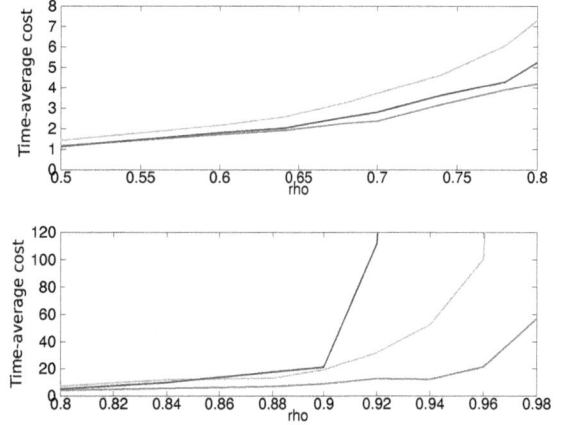

Figure 1: Scenario 1 - Time-average waiting cost of PI*,SB,PB (red), RB (green), $c\mu$ (blue) as a function of varying ϱ, computed from simulation over 330 sec.

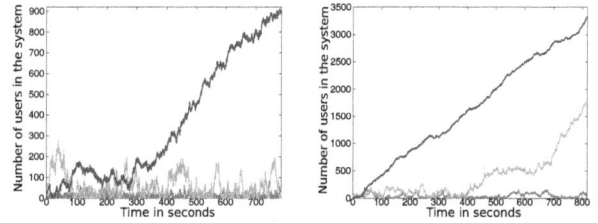

(a) $\varrho = 0.94$, over 785 sec.   (b) $\varrho = 0.98$, over 820 sec.

Figure 2: Scenario 1 - Evolution of the number of users in the system during simulation of PI*,SB,PB (red), RB (green), $c\mu$ (blue).

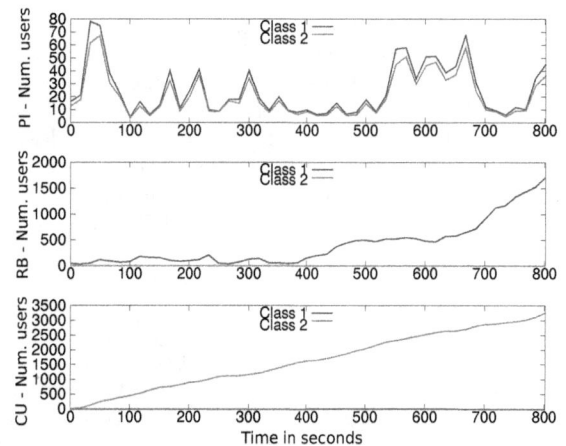

Figure 3: Scenario 1 - Number of users of class 1 (blue) and class 2 (red) for $\varrho = 0.98$, the values are averaged over intervals of 10000 slots (16.7 seconds).

Each class k is characterized by a time independent value $\lambda_k \in [0,1]$, representing the probability that during a slot a new user belonging to class k enters the system. The restriction to Bernoulli arrivals is justified by the shortness of the slot considered, which is $\epsilon = 1.67$msec.

In order to simulate scenarios as realistic as possible we consider transmission rates $s_{k,n}$ employed in LTE networks, see Table 2, which is adapted from [20]. Each class will be identified by one of the following three types of files to be downloaded, typical in a wireless data network:

- HTML web page (or e-mail) with expected job size $\mathbb{E}_0[b_k] = 0.5$Mb (64kB)
- PDF document (or image) with expected job size $\mathbb{E}_0[b_k] = 5$Mb (640kB)
- MP3 audio (or short video) with expected job size $\mathbb{E}_0[b_k] = 50$Mb (6.25MB)

For every class of users we select some channel conditions among the ones defined in Table 2, in this way, we determine the departure probabilities using the formula (1).

Moreover in every simulation we vary the value of ϱ between 0.5 and 1, but for simplicity it is always maintained that $\varrho_1 = \varrho_2$. In this way it is possible to determine the rate of arrivals of the specific class, which is given by the formula $\lambda_k = \varrho_k \mu_{k,N_k}$ for $k = 1, 2$. The channel condition possessed by a user at the moment of his arrival is supposed to be determined by an equidistributed variable among her states, i.e., $q_{k,n} = 1/N_k$.

It is interesting to point out that the condition $c_k = c$ for all k implies that SB and PB are best-condition schedulers. Such a property is guaranteed for the $c\mu$ and RB rule under the condition that respectively the values $c_k \mu_{k,N_k}$ and $\nu_{k,N_k}^{\mathrm{RB}}$ are the same for each user k. On the other hand PI* rule generates a BR policy unconditionally. The property of being a best-condition policy is important since it identifies policies that are maximally stable. The parameters for all the scenarios are summarized in Table 3.

6.1 Scenario 1

In this scenario the users are divided into two different classes, each user requires a job of expected size 0.5Mb and costs $c_1 = c_2 = 1$ for every slot of waiting. Therefore our objective is to minimize the time-average number of users (uncompleted flows) in the system. The channel condition transition matrix for the two classes is a randomly generated matrix, see Table 3. We suppose that the first class of users has the opportunity to be always served with a better transmission rate than the second class, indeed it can be seen in Table 2 and Table 3 that $s_{1,1} = 53.76$Mb/sec while $s_{2,3} = 33.6$Mb/sec.

It can be checked that in this scenario the rules PI*, SB and PB generate the same policy. Figure 1 shows the time-average waiting cost accrued by employing the different policies for varying ϱ. It appears that the behavior of all the policies until $\varrho \le 0.84$ is quite similar, even if the $c\mu$ and the PI* rules seem to slightly outperform the RB rule. The $c\mu$ rule seems to become unstable between $\varrho = 0.92$ and $\varrho = 0.94$. Indeed in Figure 2 it can be seen that the average increase of users in the system per slot is about 1.2 users per second for $\varrho = 0.94$ (note that the average number of arrivals per second is 75.8 for class 1 and 31.5 for class 2). For such a value of ϱ the other rules are still stable, it appears that RB and PI* rules cost on the average respectively about 60

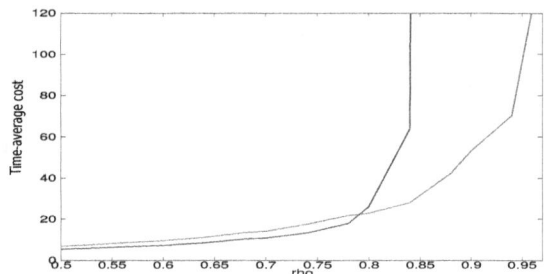

Figure 4: Scenario 2 - Time-average waiting cost of PI* (red), $c\mu$,SB,PB,RB (blue) as a function of varying ϱ, computed from simulation over 330 sec.

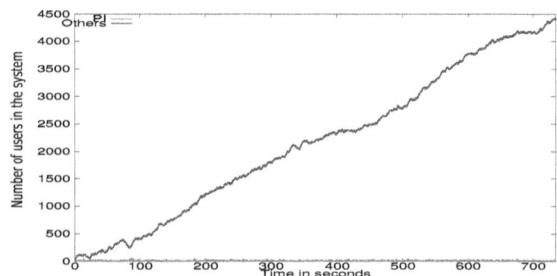

Figure 5: Scenario 2 - Evolution of the number of users in the system with $\varrho = 0.88$ during simulation of PI* (red), $c\mu$,SB,PB,RB (blue).

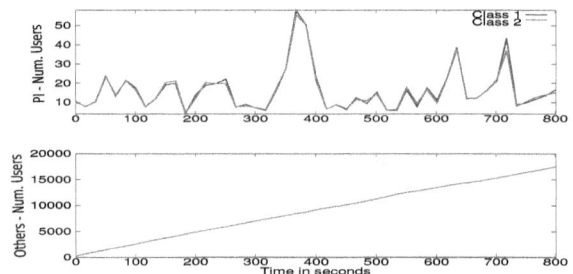

Figure 6: Scenario 2 - Number of users of class 1 (blue) and class 2 (red) for $\varrho = 0.98$, the values are averaged over intervals of 10000 slots of time (16.7 seconds).

and 10 per slot. Raising ϱ up to 0.98 (i.e., increasing the average number of arrivals per second to 79 for class 1 and 32.9 for class 2), also the RB policy becomes unstable, and the average increase in the number of users due to the employment of this policy is about 2.1 users per second. It is still better than the average increase caused by the $c\mu$ rule which is of about 4.2 users per second. However these policies are strongly outperformed by the PI* rule, indeed with $\varrho = 0.98$ this rule is still stable and time-average cost is less than 60 per slot. In Figure 3 we display the evolution of the number of users in the system per class. It can be observed that the policies considered behave in a completely different way. In fact, the PI* rule seems to be quite fair between the two classes, the $c\mu$ rule gives priority to the first class users (so that class-2 users accumulate) while on the contrary the RB favors the second one (so that class-1 users accumulate).

6.2 Scenario 2

In this scenario we would like to observe the behavior of the different rules when they have to deal with users that are totally identical, except for their "importance". Indeed the users that characterize this scenario possess the same parameters, reported in Table 3. The two classes differ from each other only in the waiting cost, in particular $c_1 = 10$ and $c_2 = 1$. Thus, classes 1 and 2 may represent business vs individual customers, or contracted vs prepaid customers, or proper vs roamed ones.

It is important to notice that in such a scenario the rules RB, SB, $c\mu$ and PB lead to the same policy, the PI* rule is the only one that differs. It can be checked that the policies different from the PI* rules give absolute priority to the users of the first class, so that a user of the second class can be served only when no users of the first class are in the system. Figure 4 displays the average cost per slot on varying ϱ, and it appears that the behavior of all the policies until $\varrho \leq 0.8$ is similar. To be more precise, the PI* seems to behave a bit worse than the others. At the same time it is possible to observe that for greater values of ϱ the situation reverses completely, indeed all the policies generated by rules different from PI* do not succeed in avoiding the accumulation of the users (of second class, see Figure 6). In Figure 5 we show the evolution of the number of users in the system during a simulation of about 12 minutes and $\varrho = 0.88$. It can be observed that the average increase of users in the system due to the employment of the rules different from PI* is about 6 users per second (out of 71 arrivals per second for each class). Meanwhile, the policy generated by the PI* rule leads to a stable system even for $\varrho = 0.98$, indeed the average cost is less than 180 per slot. In Figure 6 we show the evolution of the number of users of the different classes in the system during a simulation of around 14 minutes under $\varrho = 0.98$. We can see that the PI* rule does not care so much about the difference of importance between the two classes and keeps the number of users balanced across classes.

6.3 Scenario 3

In this scenario the users belonging to the first class require a job (PDF) of expected size ten times bigger than the second class ones (HTML), however, the users of the first class have a better-quality channel (e.g., they are closer to the base station). Moreover, the interesting thing is that the users requiring a smaller service are almost unable to reach

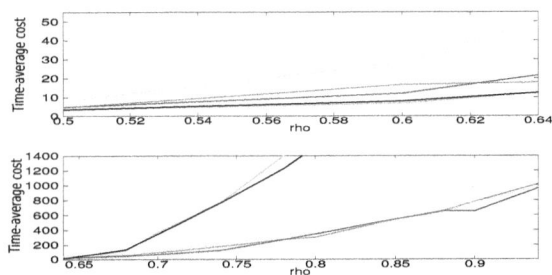

Figure 7: Scenario 3 - Time-average cost of PI* (red), PB (yellow), SB (blue), RB (green), $c\mu$ (black) as a function of varying ϱ, computed from simulation over 330 sec.

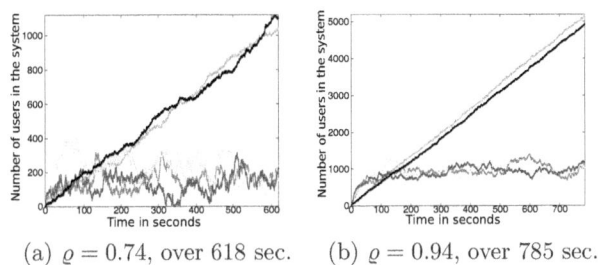

(a) $\varrho = 0.74$, over 618 sec. (b) $\varrho = 0.94$, over 785 sec.

Figure 8: Scenario 3 - Evolution of the number of users in the system during simulation of PI* (red), PB (yellow), SB (blue), RB (green), $c\mu$ (black).

their best channel condition. Particular parameters of the two classes are reported in Table 3.

In Figure 7 we report the time-average cost obtained from a 330 seconds simulation. It is possible to see that if the arrivals are quite low, say $\varrho \leq 0.64$, the rules that work better are the $c\mu$ and the RB. These policies become unstable when we increase the probability of new arrivals. Indeed, the evolution of the number of users in the system can be seen in Figure 8, where we display the cases with $\varrho = 0.74$ and $\varrho = 0.94$. The system managed by RB and $c\mu$ rule starts to accumulate users, in particular the number of users in the system increases by about 1.9 users per second already with $\varrho = 0.74$ (there are 6 and 49.7 arrivals per second in each class, respectively). Meantime the other rules maintain stability also for high values of ϱ, in Figure 8 it can be seen that they behave quite similarly even for high values of ϱ, though they are not equivalent. Moreover, notice the interesting feature that the number of users fluctuates around an equilibrium value of 1000, without growing much nor emptying the system.

6.4 Scenario 4

In this scenario the users of the first class require the completion of a very big job $b_2 = 50$Mb compared to the second class of jobs which are one hundred times smaller. The jobs required by the first class users are considered slightly more important than the other, therefore $c_1 = 3$ and $c_2 = 1$. The channel condition of the users belonging to the second

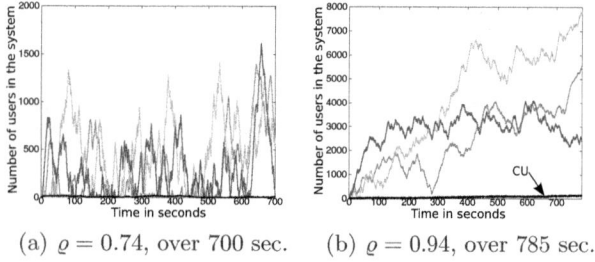

(a) $\varrho = 0.74$, over 700 sec. (b) $\varrho = 0.94$, over 785 sec.

Figure 9: Scenario 4 - Evolution of the number of user in the system during simulation of PI_* (red), SB (blue), RB, PB (green), $c\mu$ (black)

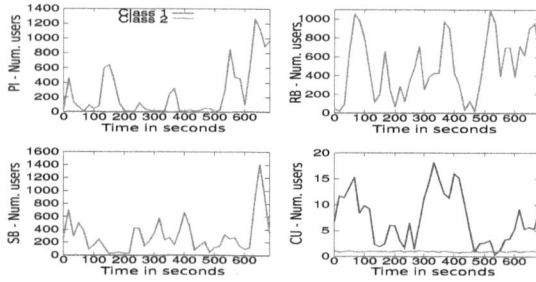

Figure 10: Scenario 4 - Number of users of class 1 (blue) and class 2 (red) for $\varrho = 0.84$, the values are averaged over intervals of 10000 slots of time (16.7 seconds).

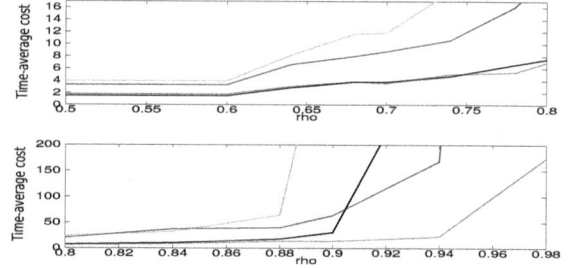

Figure 11: Scenario 5 - Time-average cost of PI* (red), SB (blue), RB,PB (green), $c\mu$ (black) as a function of varying ϱ, computed from simulation over 330 sec.

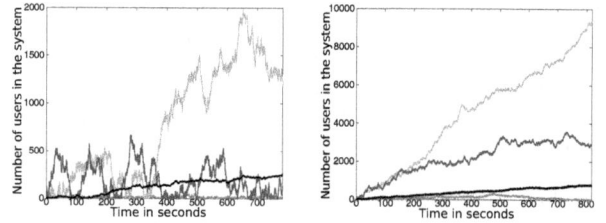

(a) $\varrho = 0.94$, over 785 sec. (b) $\varrho = 0.98$, over 820 sec.

Figure 12: Scenario 5 - Evolution of the number of users in the system during simulation of PI* (red), SB (blue), RB,PB (green), $c\mu$ (black).

class evolves in an almost iid way and their best condition is almost never reached, as can be seen in Table 3.

With these data, it can be checked that the PB and the RB rules lead to the same policy. This scenario is markedly influenced by the difference in size of the two classes, since for such a reason the departure probabilities of the two classes appear to be very unbalanced. It can be seen that as long as the rate of arrivals (and ϱ) is low, all the rules are stable. Nevertheless, there are differences: e.g., by focusing on the case with $\varrho = 0.84$ (with arrivals of 0.6 and 59.7 per second for each respective class), see Figure 9, it is evident that the $c\mu$ rule strongly outperforms the other rules. This fact can be explained by observing that the $c\mu$ rule gives priority to the second class, as it can be seen in Figure 10, and as long as there are not too many arrivals it is also able to serve the users of the other class. So, the $c\mu$ rule queues the small number of large jobs, while the other schedulers queue a big number of small jobs. It is interesting that also for $\varrho = 0.94$ case (with arrivals of 0.76 and 75.8 per second for each respective class) that leads to instability of $c\mu$ rule (see Figure 9), the average increase of users generated by the employment of this rule is only about 0.15 users per second. The other policies appear to be more stable, but it can be checked that both SB and RB are not best-condition (condition 2 of class 1 gets higher priority than condition 3 of class 2), i.e., not maximally stable. However the stability of PI* does not lead to a considerably better performance in practice, and the time-average cost of the policies PI*, RB and SB remains quite high. Such a time-average cost is

actually reached (and overcome) by the $c\mu$ rule after about 2-3 hours of service in the system.

6.5 Scenario 5

This scenario is easier to analyze than the previous one since the jobs are smaller. Still, we have that the first class of users requires the completion of a job ten times bigger than the second class, and the payment of only $c_1 = 2$. The other parameters are the same for the two classes and are reported in Table 3. It is interesting to point out the structure of the channel condition transition matrix which in this case is diagonally dominant, i.e. the users are most likely to maintain their channel condition from one slot to the following with respect to change it.

In this scenario, like in the previous one, the PB and the RB rules generate the same policy. As can be seen in Figure 11, it happens that for $\varrho \leq 0.9$ the policies generated by rules $c\mu$ and PI* outperform the other policies. Every policy considered is stable until $\varrho = 0.9$, however, the average cost per slot which arise by following the different rules is quite different, indeed it is 10, 15, 60 and 90 respectively for the rules PI*, $c\mu$, SB and RB. It is possible to see in Figure 12 that for $\varrho = 0.94$ (arrivals 7.6 and 75.8 per second) the $c\mu$ rule starts to be unstable, indeed the average increase of users is about 0.3 per second. The other policies are still stable for such ϱ even if RB queues about 1300 users per slot. This cost is reached and overcome by the $c\mu$ rule only after about 1 hour. For $\varrho = 0.98$ (arrivals 8 and 79 per second) also the policy generated by the RB rule starts to have

138

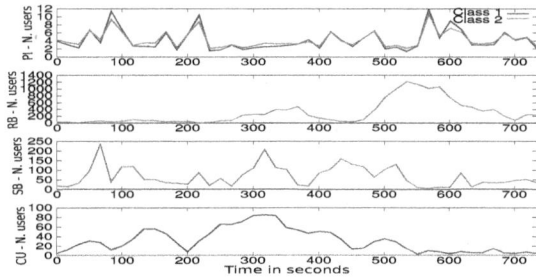

Figure 13: Scenario 5 - Number of users of class 1 (blue) and class 2 (red) for $\varrho = 0.90$, the values are averaged over intervals of 10000 slots of time (16.7 seconds).

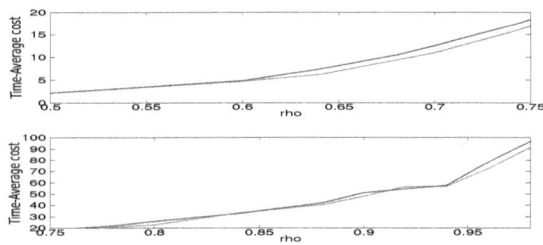

Figure 14: Scenario 6 - Time-average cost of PI$^{\mathcal{AG}}$ scheduler (red), PI*,SB,RB,PB,$c\mu$ (blue) as a function of varying ϱ, computed from simulation over 330 sec.

an unstable behavior, see Figure 12, with the employment of such a policy the number of users in the system increases by almost 12 users per slot, much worse than the 0.95 users per slot that results utilizing the $c\mu$ rule. The policies SB and PI* are still stable for such a value of ϱ even if they queue respectively around 3000 and 200 users per slot. It is really interesting to observe the way in which the different policies treat the two classes. It can be seen in Figure 13 that while the rules SB and PB favor users of the first class and the rule $c\mu$ gives priority to the second class users, the PI* maintains a balance between the two classes.

6.6 Scenario 6

In this scenario μ and $\boldsymbol{Q}$ are chosen so that the problem is not solvable by threshold policies. We create two identical classes, as can be seen in Table 3, so the system is essentially single-class. We have attempted to simulate the behavior of all the policies described above and the one induced by the indices computed through the $\mathcal{AG}$-algorithm, i.e. PI$^{\mathcal{AG}}$ scheduler rule. This scenario is quite simple and it happens that the PI^{SS}, RB, SB, PB and $c\mu$ rules lead to the same policy. Note that none of them assumes that the non-intuitive order of states (non-optimality of threshold policies) could exist. Only PI$^{\mathcal{AG}}$ captures this phenomenon.

Figure 14 displays the time-average cost that is obtained by averaging a 330 seconds simulation. As expected, PI$^{\mathcal{AG}}$ outperforms the other policies, but the differences between various policies are not significant.

7. CONCLUSION

The scheduling problem we are investigating is an elaborate problem and is far from being solved. The introduction of more general and realistic elements, like the Markovian evolution of the channel or the arbitrary number of channel conditions prohibits the possibility to furnish closed, intuitive formulas for the PI* index values. Indeed, mostly due to the Markovian property it is quite a hard job to carry out the probability of moving to a better condition, q^*, that we believe plays an important role in the computation of such index values. The problem could be considered almost solved in the 3-state case, where, if the jobs are sufficiently large, the PI^{SS} scheduler seems to work as an efficient approximation. It should be investigated if such an approximation is still effective for the general case, in particular it could be useful to identify sufficient conditions that guarantee the problem (2) to be solvable by threshold policies.

Numerical simulations suggest that PI* rule works well in a lot of different scenarios. In particular the maximal stability property assures the system to be manageable even under situations of high load. Moreover quite surprisingly even though we have not included fairness optimization in our MDP model, PI* shows to be very fair between classes, and besides it does not depend on λ (and ϱ).

On the other hand, even only the analysis of the few scenarios reported in the paper establish that in some cases it could be convenient to employ other policies instead of the PI* one. If the system is not loaded much, the $c\mu$ policy, as long as it is stable, performs often better than the other policies. It could be interesting to have knowledge of stability limit of the $c\mu$ policy in order to be able to alternately employ such a policy and the PI*.

The main theoretical limitation of this paper is the assumption of geometric job sizes. However, we believe that it is important first to understand this case, likely to be analytically the simplest, and future research should address the question of (in)sensitivity of our results to the job size distribution. Note also that the existing maximal stability results for best-condition schedulers [4, 16] also rely on the geometric job size assumption.

8. REFERENCES

[1] S. Aalto and P. Lassila. Flow-level stability and performance of channel-aware priority-based schedulers. In *Proceeding of NGI 2010 (6th EURO-NF Conference on Next Generation Internet)*, 2010.

[2] S. Aalto, A. Penttinen, P. Lassila, and P. Osti. On the optimal trade-off between SRPT and opportunistic scheduling. In *Proceedings of ACM Sigmetrics*, 2011.

[3] U. Ayesta, M. Erausquin, and P. Jacko. A modeling framework for optimizing the flow-level scheduling with time-varying channels. *Performance Evaluation*, 67:1014–1029, 2010.

[4] U. Ayesta, M. Erausquin, M. Jonckheere, and I. M. Verloop. Scheduling in a random environment: Stability and asymptotic optimality. *IEEE/ACM Transactions on Networking*, 21(1):258–271, 2013.

[5] U. Ayesta and P. Jacko. Method for selecting a transmission channel within a time division multiple access (TDMA) communications system, 2013. EU Patent.

[6] P. Bender, P. Black, M. Grob, R. Padovani,

Mod.	QPSK								16QAM				64QAM		
MCS	1	2	3	4	5	6	7	8	9	10	11	12	13	14	15
Rates	4.2	6.72	8.4	11.256	16.8	21.84	25.2	26.88	33.6	44.688	50.4	53.76	67.2	75.6	80.64

Table 2: Transmission rates in Mb/sec associated with LTE modulation and coding schemes (MCS).

	MCS	Cost	Channel Condition Transition Matrix	Expected Size
#1	$\{12,13,15\},$ $\{1,8,9\}$	(1,1)	$\left(\begin{bmatrix} 0.4 & 0.21 & 0.39 \\ 0.48 & 0.5 & 0.02 \\ 0.26 & 0.3 & 0.44 \end{bmatrix}, \begin{bmatrix} 0.34 & 0.35 & 0.31 \\ 0.27 & 0.45 & 0.28 \\ 0.45 & 0.15 & 0.4 \end{bmatrix}\right)$	(HTML,HTML)
#2	$\{8,12,15\},$ $\{8,12,15\}$	(10,1)	$\left(\begin{bmatrix} 0.38 & 0.20 & 0.42 \\ 0.43 & 0.19 & 0.38 \\ 0.48 & 0.27 & 0.25 \end{bmatrix}, \begin{bmatrix} 0.38 & 0.20 & 0.42 \\ 0.43 & 0.19 & 0.38 \\ 0.48 & 0.27 & 0.25 \end{bmatrix}\right)$	(HTML,HTML)
#3	$\{8,12,15\},$ $\{1,9,13\}$	(1,1)	$\left(\begin{bmatrix} 0.6 & 0.2 & 0.2 \\ 0.3 & 0.5 & 0.2 \\ 0.2 & 0.4 & 0.4 \end{bmatrix}, \begin{bmatrix} 0.5 & 0.499 & 0.001 \\ 0.7 & 0.299 & 0.001 \\ 0.15 & 0.849 & 0.001 \end{bmatrix}\right)$	(PDF,HTML)
#4	$\{12,13,15\},$ $\{12,13,15\}$	(3,1)	$\left(\begin{bmatrix} 0.41 & 0.31 & 0.28 \\ 0.16 & 0.5 & 0.34 \\ 0.26 & 0.34 & 0.4 \end{bmatrix}, \begin{bmatrix} 0.65 & 0.34999 & 0.00001 \\ 0.62 & 0.37999 & 0.00001 \\ 0.63 & 0.36999 & 0.00001 \end{bmatrix}\right)$	(MP3,HTML)
#5	$\{12,13,15\},$ $\{12,13,15\}$	(2,1)	$\left(\begin{bmatrix} 0.6 & 0.3 & 0.1 \\ 0.25 & 0.5 & 0.25 \\ 0.1 & 0.3 & 0.6 \end{bmatrix}, \begin{bmatrix} 0.6 & 0.3 & 0.1 \\ 0.25 & 0.5 & 0.25 \\ 0.1 & 0.3 & 0.6 \end{bmatrix}\right)$	(PDF,HTML)
#6	$\{8,9,13\},$ $\{8,9,13\}$	(1,1)	$\left(\begin{bmatrix} 0.998 & 0.0015 & 0.0005 \\ 0.002 & 0.248 & 0.75 \\ 0.01 & 0.02 & 0.97 \end{bmatrix}, \begin{bmatrix} 0.998 & 0.0015 & 0.0005 \\ 0.002 & 0.248 & 0.75 \\ 0.01 & 0.02 & 0.97 \end{bmatrix}\right)$	(HTML,HTML)

Table 3: Parameters set in the experimental study for (class 1, class 2).

N. Sindhushayana, and A. Viterbi. CDMA/HDR: a bandwidth-efficient high-speed wireless data service for nomadic users. *IEEE Communications Magazine*, 38(7):70–77, 2000.

[7] T. Bonald. Procédé de sélection de canal de transmission dans un protocole d'accès multiple à répartition dans le temps et système de communication mettant en oeuvre un tel procédé, 2004. EU Patent.

[8] T. Bonald. A score-based opportunistic scheduler for fading radio channels. In *Proceedings of European Wireless*, pages 283–292, 2004.

[9] S. Borst. User-level performance of channel-aware scheduling algorithms in wireless data networks. *IEEE/ACM Transactions on Networking*, 13(3):636–647, 2005.

[10] C. Buyukkoc, P. Varaiya, and J. Walrand. The $c\mu$ rule revisited. *Advances in Applied Probability*, 17(1):237–238, 1985.

[11] E. F. Chaponniere, P. J. Black, J. M. Holtzman, and D. N. C. Tse. Transmitter directed code division multiple access system using path diversity to equitably maximize throughput, 2002. US Patent.

[12] J. C. Gittins. Bandit processes and dynamic allocation indices. *Journal of the Royal Statistical Society, Series B*, 41(2):148–177, 1979.

[13] J. C. Gittins and D. M. Jones. A dynamic allocation index for the sequential design of experiments. In J. Gani, editor, *Progress in Statistics*, pages 241–266. North-Holland, Amsterdam, 1974.

[14] P. Jacko. Restless bandits approach to the job scheduling problem and its extensions. In A. B. Piunovskiy, editor, *Modern Trends in Controlled Stochastic Processes: Theory and Applications*, pages 248–267. Luniver Press, United Kingdom, 2010.

[15] P. Jacko. Value of information in optimal flow-level scheduling of users with Markovian time-varying channels. *Performance Evaluation*, 68(11):1022–1036, 2011.

[16] J. Kim, B. Kim, J. Kim, and Y. H. Bae. Stability of flow-level scheduling with Markovian time-varying channels. *Performance Evaluation*, 70(2):148–159, 2013.

[17] R. Knopp and P. Humblet. Information capacity and power control in single-cell multiuser communications. In *Proceedings of IEEE International Conference on Communications*, pages 331–335, 1995.

[18] H. Kushner and P. Whiting. Convergence of proportional-fair sharing algorithms under general conditions. *IEEE Transactions on Wireless Communications*, 3:1250–1259, 2004.

[19] J. Niño-Mora. Dynamic priority allocation via restless bandit marginal productivity indices. *TOP*, 15(2):161–198, 2007.

[20] S. Sesia, I. Toufik, and M. Baker. *LTE-The UMTS Long Term Evolution: From Theory to Practice*. Wiley, 2011.

[21] P. Whittle. Restless bandits: Activity allocation in a changing world. *A Celebration of Applied Probability, J. Gani (Ed.), Journal of Applied Probability*, 25A:287–298, 1988.

Lingering Issues in Distributed Scheduling

Florian Simatos, Niek Bouman, Sem Borst[*]
Eindhoven University of Technology
Den Dolech 2
5612 AZ Eindhoven, The Netherlands
{f.simatos, n.bouman, s.c.borst}@tue.nl

ABSTRACT

Recent advances have resulted in queue-based algorithms for medium access control which operate in a distributed fashion, and yet achieve the optimal throughput performance of centralized scheduling algorithms. However, fundamental performance bounds reveal that the "cautious" activation rules involved in establishing throughput optimality tend to produce extremely large delays, typically growing exponentially in $1/(1-\rho)$, with ρ the load of the system, in contrast to the usual linear growth.

Motivated by that issue, we explore to what extent more "aggressive" schemes can improve the delay performance. Our main finding is that aggressive activation rules induce a lingering effect, where individual nodes retain possession of a shared resource for excessive lengths of time even while a majority of other nodes idle. Using central limit theorem type arguments, we prove that the idleness induced by the lingering effect may cause the delays to grow with $1/(1-\rho)$ at a quadratic rate. To the best of our knowledge, these are the first mathematical results illuminating the lingering effect and quantifying the performance impact.

In addition extensive simulation experiments are conducted to illustrate and validate the various analytical results.

Categories and Subject Descriptors

G.3 [**Probability and Statistics**]: Markov Processes

General Terms

Algorithms, Performance, Theory

Keywords

Delay Performance; Distributed Scheduling Algorithms; Heavy Traffic Scaling; Wireless Networks

[*]This work was supported by Microsoft Research through its PhD Scholarship Programme and a TOP grant from NWO.

1. INTRODUCTION

As networks continue to grow in size and complexity, they increasingly rely on scheduling algorithms for efficient allocation of shared resources and arbitration between users. As a result, the design and analysis of scheduling algorithms for complex network scenarios has attracted significant attention over the last several years.

One of the centerpieces in the scheduling literature is the celebrated MaxWeight algorithm as proposed in the seminal work [18, 19]. The MaxWeight algorithm provides throughput optimality and maximum queue stability in a variety of scenarios, and has emerged as a powerful paradigm in cross-layer control and resource allocation problems [5].

While not strictly optimal in terms of delay performance, MaxWeight algorithms do achieve so-called equivalent workload minimization and offer favorable scaling characteristics in heavy traffic conditions [13, 16]. As a further key appealing feature, MaxWeight algorithms only need information on the queue lengths and instantaneous service rates, and do not rely on any explicit knowledge of the underlying system parameters.

On the downside, solving the maximum-weight problem tends to be challenging and potentially NP-hard. This is exacerbated in a network setting, where a centralized control entity may be lacking or require global state information, creating a substantial communication overhead in addition to the computational burden. This concern is especially pertinent as the maximum-weight problem needs to be solved at a high pace, commensurate with the fast time scale on which scheduling algorithms typically need to operate.

This issue has provided a strong impetus for devising algorithms that entail *lower computational complexity and communication overhead,* but retain the *maximum stability and throughput guarantees* of the MaxWeight algorithm. Various approaches in that direction were proposed in [2, 10, 14, 15, 17, 20]. An exciting breakthrough in this quest was recently achieved in the design of random back-off schemes for wireless medium access control that seem to offer the best of both worlds. These schemes operate in a *distributed fashion, requiring no centralized control entity or global state information,* and yet, remarkably, provide the *capability of achieving throughput optimality and maximum stability.* More specifically, clever algorithms have been developed for finding the back-off rates that yield any given target throughput vector in the capacity region [8, 9]. In the same spirit, powerful algorithms have been devised for adapting the back-off rates based on queue length information, and been shown to guarantee maximum stability [7, 11, 12].

While the maximum-stability guarantees for the above-mentioned algorithms have strong appeal, they do not extend to performance metrics such as expected queue lengths or delays. In fact, fundamental performance bounds [1] indicate that the "cautious" back-off functions involved in establishing maximum stability tend to produce extremely large delays, typically growing *exponentially* in $1/(1-\rho)$, with ρ the load of the system, in contrast to the usual *linear* growth. More specifically, the bounds show that the expected queue lengths grow as $\psi^{-1}(1-\rho)$ as $\rho \uparrow 1$. Here ψ^{-1} represents the inverse of the (decreasing) function ψ, specifying the probability of a node entering a back-off as a function of its current queue length. The bounds may be explained by noting that the queue lengths govern the fraction of back-off time through the function ψ. Since the fraction of back-off time cannot exceed the surplus capacity in order for the system to be stable, however, it is ultimately the amount of surplus $1-\rho$ that dictates the queue lengths through the function ψ^{-1}. We note that maximum stability has been established under the condition that the function $\psi(a)$ decays (no faster than) *inverse-logarithmically* as $a \to \infty$, i.e., $\psi(a) \sim 1/\log a$. This entails that $\psi^{-1}(s)$ grows (no slower than) *exponentially* in $1/s$ as $s \downarrow 0$, yielding the stated exponential growth of $\psi^{-1}(1-\rho)$ in $1/(1-\rho)$ as $\rho \uparrow 1$.

The above lower bounds suggest that the delay performance may be improved when the function ψ decays faster, e.g., *inverse-polynomially*: $\psi(a) \sim a^{-\beta}$, with $\beta > 0$, so that $\psi^{-1}(s) \sim s^{-1/\beta}$ as $s \downarrow 0$. The larger the value of the exponent β, the slower the growth of $\psi^{-1}(1-\rho) \sim (1-\rho)^{-1/\beta}$ as $\rho \uparrow 1$. In particular, it might seem plausible that for $\beta \geq 1$, the expected queue lengths will only exhibit the usual linear growth in $1/(1-\rho)$ as $\rho \uparrow 1$. Note that a larger value of β means that a node is more "aggressive", in the sense that it is less likely to enter a back-off and more inclined to hold on to the medium, and hence the coefficient β will be referred to as the aggressiveness parameter. It is worth observing that maximum stability for the above back-off functions is not guaranteed by existing results, which do not apply for any $\beta > 0$. In fact, for $\beta > 1$, maximum stability has been shown not to hold in certain topologies [6].

In the present paper we aim to gain fundamental insight whether a larger aggressiveness parameter can improve the delay performance. Our main finding is that for large values of β, a *lingering effect* can cause the mean stationary delay to increase in heavy traffic as $1/(1-\rho)^2$, and we focus on the simplest topology where this effect occurs. This topology, described in later sections, may seem at first sight rather restrictive in view of recent results [7, 11, 12] that apply to general topologies. We believe however that our results give insight into more general situations and discuss this in Section 7.

The remainder of the paper is organized as follows. We start in Section 2 by discussing an example that will explain the model that we consider as well as the lingering effect. In Section 3 we present a detailed model description. In Section 4 we provide an overview of the results and discuss the main performance implications. We conduct comprehensive simulation experiments to illustrate the various heavy traffic results in Section 5. In Section 6 we present a detailed asymptotic analysis and proof arguments, and we conclude in Section 7 by discussing the broader implications of our results.

2. ILLUSTRATIVE EXAMPLE

Consider a network consisting of four queues which are split into two groups, say groups 1 and 2, in such a way that if any queue of group 1 is transmitting a packet, no queue of group 2 may transmit. A group is said to be *active* if one of its queues is transmitting a packet, and a queue is said to be active if it belongs to the active group. The other group and queues are said to be *inactive*.

Active queues adhere to the following algorithm: after each transmission, each active queue flips a coin and *advertizes a release* with probability $(1+a)^{-\beta}$, with a the number of packets that this queue has to transmit and $\beta > 0$. If the two active queues advertize a release simultaneously, then active queues become inactive and vice-versa: such a time is called a *switching time*. This simple distributed algorithm gives rise to dynamics as illustrated in Figure 1, where the system is considered over three consecutive switching times t_1, t_2 and t_3. Between switching times, the backlog of active queues is drained while packets accumulate at inactive queues. The dynamics shown in Figure 1 are representative of the case $\beta > 1$ where a switch does not occur until both active queues have emptied as will be established later.

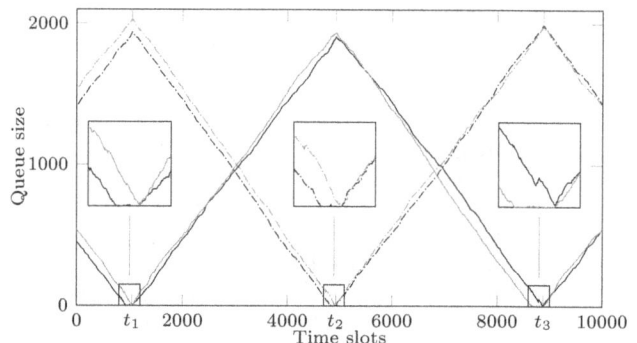

Figure 1: A typical sample path in the case $\beta > 1$. The three boxes zoom in to show the lingering effect. One queue hovers around zero while the other queue is yet to empty, resulting in an inefficient use of the resource.

Let us now give a flavor of the lingering effect. Imagine that the two active queues start with initial queue lengths of the same order, say Q. As just mentioned, queues retain the shared resource until the time T^* at which the last active queue has emptied, thus preventing other queues from activating until this time. The law of large numbers suggests that T^* is of order Q (i.e., active queues are drained linearly as in Figure 1), but the central limit theorem suggests that up to time T^*, the first active queue to have emptied, while waiting for the other queue to empty, will be empty of the order of $\sqrt{Q}$ units of time. This lingering effect is illustrated in Figure 1, which will be explained in greater detail in Section 5.

This $(1/\sqrt{Q})$-fraction of the time the shared resource is used inefficiently may at first sight seem negligible, and indeed queues seem to empty at the same time on the coarse time scale of Figure 1. However, we will actually establish that it has a significant impact in heavy traffic, causing queue lengths to grow at a rate $1/(1-\rho)^2$ as $\rho \uparrow 1$, instead of the optimal $1/(1-\rho)$.

142

3. MODEL DESCRIPTION

3.1 Informal description

Let us now give a more precise definition of our model. As mentioned in the introduction, in order to analyze the lingering effect in the simplest possible setting, we focus on a symmetric system consisting of two groups of $R \geq 2$ queues. At any given point in time, one of the groups is *active* while the other is *inactive*.

Time is slotted and inactive queues have simple dynamics, driven by independent and identically distributed numbers of packet arrivals in each slot, so that they each simply grow according to random walks with step distribution denoted by ξ. During each time slot, active queues increase by independent amounts distributed as ξ as well, but, if at least one packet is present at the start of the slot, an active queue also flushes exactly one packet.

Moreover, at the end of each time slot, each active queue tosses a coin and advertizes a *momentary release* with probability $\psi(a)$, with a the number of packets in the queue at the end of the time slot. This (momentary) release gives inactive queues an opportunity to become active: if all the active queues *simultaneously* advertize a release, then inactive queues become active and active queues become inactive. Such a time is called a *switching time*. We will assume in the sequel that $\psi(a) = (1+a)^{-\beta}$ for some parameter $\beta > 0$, called the aggressiveness parameter. In particular, $\psi(a) \to 0$ as $a \to +\infty$, and so active queues are less likely to advertize a release when they are highly loaded; this mechanism thus gives priority to highly loaded queues in a distributed fashion. There is a cost associated with advertizing a release: each time an active queue advertizes a release and is not empty, it incurs an additional increase distributed according to some random variable ζ.

The above-described model qualitatively resembles the canonical models for queue-based medium access control mechanisms. The main difference with continuous-time models in the literature is that in our model, back-off periods are infinitesimally short (hence, the releases are qualified as momentary), and the jump size ζ represents the number of packets that would have arrived during a non-zero back-off period. The key advantage of our model is that it avoids the complication of requiring back-off periods to overlap to define a switching time. Moreover, simulation experiments show that our main results extend to models with non-infinitesimal back-off periods. We did not include these simulations to comply with page limitations.

Remark. The system may be interpreted as a set of R single-server two-queue polling systems, where servers are only allowed to switch between queues in a synchronized fashion. Such models with simultaneous service of several queues and synchronized switches are natural in applications (e.g., traffic lights at intersections), but appear not to have been considered.

3.2 Parameters

The model described in the previous subsection is defined through four parameters: the number $R \geq 2$ of queues in each group, two integer-valued random variables $\xi, \zeta \in \mathbb{N} = \{0, 1, \ldots\}$ and a real number $\beta \in (0, \infty]$, which defines the $[0, 1]$-valued sequence $(\psi(a), a \geq 0)$ via $\psi(a) = (1+a)^{-\beta}$ for $a \geq 0$, to be understood for $\beta = +\infty$ as $\psi(0) = 1$ and

$\psi(a) = 0$ for $a > 0$. Note that only the asymptotic behavior of $\psi(\cdot)$ matters, and our results could easily be extended to any $\psi(\cdot)$ with $a^\beta \psi(a) \to \ell \in (0, \infty)$ as $a \to +\infty$.

We assume that ξ and ζ have finite means, respectively $\mathbb{E}\xi = \rho/2$ and $\mathbb{E}\zeta = z$, and that ξ has finite variance denoted by $v = \mathbb{E}[(\xi - \rho/2)^2]$. It will be argued that the system is stable if and only if $\rho < 1$ and so we will refer to ρ as the load of the system (note that by symmetry, each queue is active half the time, which explains the factor 2 in the definition $\rho = 2\mathbb{E}\xi$ of ρ).

3.3 Formal description

Because of the symmetry of the system, we do not need to label the queues individually, but only need to keep track of the state of active and inactive queues. We will consider the system embedded at switching times, and define $Q_r^a(k)$ and $Q_r^i(k)$ as the numbers of packets in the rth active and inactive queue, respectively, just after the kth switch occurred. We will be interested in the Markov chain $(\mathbf{Q}(k), k \geq 0)$ which we also write as $\mathbf{Q} = (\mathbf{Q}^a, \mathbf{Q}^i)$ with $\mathbf{Q}^a = (Q_r^a, r \in \mathcal{R})$, $\mathbf{Q}^i = (Q_r^i, r \in \mathcal{R})$, $\mathcal{R} = \{1, \ldots, R\}$ and we reserve in the sequel bold notation for vectors (of functions or numbers).

As informally described in Section 3.1, the dynamics of $\mathbf{Q}$ in between two switching times are governed by two R-dimensional processes $\mathbf{S} = (S_r, r \in \mathcal{R})$ and $\mathbf{A} = (A_r, r \in \mathcal{R})$: $\mathbf{S}$ gives the increments of the inactive queues, while $\mathbf{A}$ gives the state of the active queues. The dynamics are as follows:

- the $2R$ processes A_r, S_r are independent;
- for each $r \in \mathcal{R}$, $(S_r(k), k \geq 0)$ is a random walk with step distribution ξ, started at 0;
- for each $r \in \mathcal{R}$, $(A_r(k), k \geq 0)$ is a space-inhomogeneous random walk with the following dynamics: for any $a \in \mathbb{N}$ and any function $f : \mathbb{N} \to [0, \infty)$, we have

$$\mathbb{E}\left[f(A_r(1)) \mid A_r(0) = a\right]$$
$$= \mathbb{E}\left[f\left(Y(a) + \zeta \mathbb{I}_{\{Y(a) > 0, U < \psi(Y(a))\}}\right)\right], \quad (1)$$

where $Y(a) = a + \xi - \mathbb{I}_{\{a > 0\}}$ is the number of packets at the end of the time slot and U is uniformly distributed in $[0, 1]$, and U, ξ and ζ are independent.

The equation (1) describes the dynamics of an active queue and can be interpreted as follows. At each time slot, an active queue increases by ξ and, if not empty at the beginning of the time slot, flushes a packet, which brings the queue to state $Y(a)$. If $U < \psi(Y(a))$, we say that the active queue advertizes a release, which thus happens with the (conditional) probability $\psi(Y(a))$ as described in Section 3.1. If at the end of the time slot the queue is not empty and it advertizes a release, i.e., $Y(a) > 0$ and $U < \psi(Y(a))$, then the active queue also incurs an additional increase by ζ.

To define the $2R$-dimensional process $\mathbf{Q} = (\mathbf{Q}^a, \mathbf{Q}^i)$ from $\mathbf{S}$ and $\mathbf{A}$, it remains to adopt notation for the switching time, which we denote by T^*. Thus T^* is the first time at which all active queues advertize a release at the same time. Note that T^* and $\mathbf{S}$ are independent. With these definitions, the dynamics of $\mathbf{Q}$ as informally described in Section 3.1 obey the following equation: for any $\mathbf{q} = (\mathbf{q}^a, \mathbf{q}^i) \in \mathbb{N}^R \times \mathbb{N}^R$ and any function $f : \mathbb{N}^{2R} \to [0, \infty)$,

$$\mathbb{E}\left[f(\mathbf{Q}(1)) \mid \mathbf{Q}(0) = \mathbf{q}\right]$$
$$= \mathbb{E}\left[f(\mathbf{q}^i + \mathbf{S}(T^*), \mathbf{A}(T^*)) \mid \mathbf{A}(0) = \mathbf{q}^a\right]. \quad (2)$$

The special case $\beta = +\infty$ will be of particular importance. Indeed, we will show that it is representative of the system's behavior in the range $\beta > 1$. The case $\beta = +\infty$ has been studied in [3], which refer to it as the random capture algorithm. When $\beta = +\infty$, active queues only advertize a release when they are empty (in which case there is no additional term ζ), and so $\mathbf{A}(T^*) = \mathbf{0}$ and $T^* = \inf\{k \geq 0 : \mathbf{A}(k) = \mathbf{0}\}$.

3.4 Additional notation

In the remainder of the paper, and similarly as we have just done in (2), we will use the common symbol $\mathbb{E}$ to denote expectation with respect to the laws of $\mathbf{Q}$ and $(\mathbf{A}, \mathbf{S})$. Initial conditions will be denoted by a subscript, and it should always be clear from the context whether we consider initial conditions of $\mathbf{Q}$, $\mathbf{A}$ or some A_r (remember that $\mathbf{S}(0)$ is always equal to $\mathbf{0}$). For instance, (1) and (2) can be rewritten as follows:

$$\mathbb{E}_a\left[f(A_r(1))\right] = \mathbb{E}\left[f\left(Y(a) + \zeta \mathrm{I}_{\{Y(a)>0, U<\psi(Y(a))\}}\right)\right],$$

and

$$\mathbb{E}_\mathbf{q}\left[f(\mathbf{Q}(1))\right] = \mathbb{E}_{\mathbf{q}^a}\left[f(\mathbf{q}^i + \mathbf{S}(T^*), \mathbf{A}(T^*))\right].$$

The probability distributions corresponding to these various expectations are written as $\mathbb{P}_a$, $\mathbb{P}$, $\mathbb{P}_\mathbf{q}$ and $\mathbb{P}_{\mathbf{q}^a}$. We also define $\mathbb{P}_\infty$ with corresponding expectation $\mathbb{E}_\infty$ as the laws of $\mathbf{Q}$ and $(\mathbf{A}, \mathbf{S})$ started in the stationary distribution of $\mathbf{Q}$, provided $\mathbf{Q}$ is positive recurrent.

When $\beta = +\infty$, we see based on (2) that $\mathbf{Q}^i(k) = \mathbf{0}$, except maybe for $k = 0$. In particular, when $\mathbf{Q}$ is positive recurrent, $\mathbf{Q}^i(0)$ is $\mathbb{P}_\infty$-almost surely equal to $\mathbf{0}$ and (2) therefore becomes

$$\mathbb{E}_\infty\left[f(\mathbf{Q}^a(0))\right] = \mathbb{E}_\infty\left[f(\mathbf{S}(T^*))\right] \quad (\beta = +\infty). \quad (3)$$

Further, in the remainder of the paper we let

$$\tau_r = \inf\{k \geq 0 : A_r(k) = 0\}, \qquad \tau_{\max} = \max_{r \in \mathcal{R}} \tau_r,$$

and we define the $\tau_{(r)}$'s as the order statistics of the τ_r's, i.e., $\tau_{(1)} \leq \cdots \leq \tau_{(R)}$ and $\{\tau_{(r)}\} = \{\tau_r\}$. Let finally $|\cdot|$ be the L_∞ norm and $\|\cdot\|$ be the L_1 norm, i.e., if $J \geq 1$ and $\mathbf{x} \in \mathbb{R}^J$ then $|\mathbf{x}| = \max_j |x_j|$ (which is just the absolute value for $J = 1$) and $\|\mathbf{x}\| = |x_1| + \cdots + |x_J|$.

4. OVERVIEW OF MAIN RESULTS

4.1 Two regimes

As stated in the introduction, we aim to gain fundamental insight in the impact of the function $\psi(\cdot)$, through the aggressiveness parameter β, on the system performance in terms of expected queue lengths and delays. We will demonstrate, based on a combination of heuristic arguments, simulation experiments and theoretical results, that the system's behavior changes as β increases from 0 to ∞. In the small β regime, typically $\beta < 1/2$, the system is characterized by a mean-reverting effect that induces (stationary) queue lengths of the order of $1/(1-\rho)^{1/\beta}$. This regime was already hinted upon in [1], where a corresponding lower bound was rigorously proved in a general setting. In the present paper we go one step further, by providing a heuristic argument in Section 4.2, explaining why this lower bound is sharp for

small β, and corroborating this by extensive simulation results in Section 5.2. However, when β increases, this mean-reverting effect vanishes, which causes the lower bound to become loose. For $\beta > 1$, we show that the system's performance is dominated by another phenomenon, which we call a lingering effect. The investigation of this latter effect constitutes the main contribution of the paper. We provide a heuristic explanation of this effect in Section 4.3, examine it via simulation experiments in Section 5.2, and prove various theoretical results in Section 6.

4.2 Small β: a mean-reverting effect

Consider for a moment a given queue and let $\Delta(a)$ be the mean increase of this queue starting from level a. Because of symmetry, the queue will be active half the time and inactive the other half of the time, so that

$$\Delta(a) \approx \frac{1}{2}\mathbb{E}_a\left[\text{increase} \mid \text{inactive}\right] + \frac{1}{2}\mathbb{E}_a\left[\text{increase} \mid \text{active}\right].$$

From the dynamics described in Section 3.3 we may deduce for large a (approximating $Y(a) \approx a$ and neglecting the possibility of $Y(a) = 0$) that $2\Delta(a) \approx \mathbb{E}\xi + \mathbb{E}(\xi - 1 + \zeta \mathrm{I}_{\{U<\psi(a)\}})$, which leads to

$$2\Delta(a) \approx \rho - 1 + z\psi(a).$$

This last approximation points to a mean-reverting effect: the average drift is negative for $a > a^*$ and positive for $a < a^*$, where a^* is determined by the equation $\rho - 1 + z\psi(a^*) = 0$, which gives, since $\psi(a) = (1+a)^{-\beta}$, $a^* \approx 1/(1-\rho)^{1/\beta}$. Using the convexity of $\psi(\cdot)$ and Jensen's inequality, it is not difficult to convert the above back-of-the-envelope computations into a rigorous proof and show that $1/(1-\rho)^{1/\beta}$ is a lower bound for the stationary mean number of packets in the system, as established in [1] in a continuous-time setting.

However, our explanation of this lower bound through this mean-reverting effect goes one step further, and shows that this lower bound should be sharp for small values of β. Indeed, $\Delta(a)$ is the mean drift obtained by averaging over the active and inactive states. Roughly speaking, this quantity describes the drift experienced by a queue if the queue rapidly changes states, i.e., if the time needed for the queue to switch state is negligible compared to n, with n the length of the queue. Otherwise, the queue stays in the active or inactive state for a long period of time, during which it experiences (almost) constant drift, either positive or negative. This explanation bears some similarity with a random walk in a dynamic random environment, where the random walk essentially sees a constant environment if the random environment mixes rapidly.

To conclude our arguments, it remains to note that, at least intuitively, queues will switch more rapidly for smaller values of β. We will provide simulation experiments showing that the stationary mean number of packets grows as $1/(1-\rho)^{1/\beta}$ for small values of β. As β increases however, this mean-reverting effect vanishes. The main contribution of this paper is to reveal and quantify a previously unknown effect, called the lingering effect, which explains the system's behavior in this case.

4.3 Large β: the effect of lingering

As described in the introduction, when the function $\psi(\cdot)$ decays sufficiently fast, once a queue gains possession of the resource, it holds onto it, even when some or all of the other queues in the same group are empty, and it would be more efficient for the queues in the other group to receive the resource. This causes a lingering effect as illustrated in Figure 1 for a scenario with $R = 2$, $\beta = 2$. It may appear that the two queues in the same group drain around the same time (as can indeed be shown to be the case on a "fluid scale"). When we zoom in, however, we see that there is actually a time period where one of the queues is already empty, while the other one clings to the resource and prevents the two queues in the other group from activating.

Let us now provide a somewhat more technical description of this phenomenon in the case $\beta = +\infty$, where it is easiest to see thanks to the simplification of the dynamics (3). Moreover, we will argue that the case $\beta \in (1, +\infty)$ is essentially a perturbation of the case $\beta = +\infty$.

By applying (3) to $f = \|\cdot\|$, we obtain $\mathbb{E}_\infty \left(\|\mathbf{Q}^a(0)\| \right) = \mathbb{E}_\infty \left(\|\mathbf{S}(T^*)\| \right)$ and since $\|\mathbf{S}(\cdot)\|$ is a random walk with drift $R\mathbb{E}\xi$ independent of T^* and $\mathbf{A}(0) = \mathbf{Q}^a(0)$ (by definition), we obtain $\mathbb{E}_\infty \left(\|\mathbf{A}(0)\| \right) = R\mathbb{E}(\xi)\mathbb{E}_\infty \left(T^* \right)$ and so by symmetry,

$$\mathbb{E}_\infty \left(A_1(0) \right) = \mathbb{E}(\xi)\mathbb{E}_\infty \left(T^* \right). \tag{4}$$

The goal is now to relate $\mathbb{E}_\infty(T^*)$ to $\mathbb{E}_\infty(A_1(0))$. Remember that $T^* = \inf\{k : \mathbf{A}(k) = \mathbf{0}\}$ when $\beta = +\infty$. It is not difficult to show that $T^* \approx \tau_{\max}$, essentially because once all queues have hit 0, it is only a matter of constant time for all queues to be empty simultaneously (this will be justified in Lemma 6.1). Then, the central limit theorem shows that $\tau_r \approx A_r(0)/(1 - \mathbb{E}\xi) + A_r(0)^{1/2}$ (where we neglect multiplicative constants, possibly random, appearing in front of first- or second-order terms and that do not influence the order of magnitude of the final result), which leads to the approximation $\tau_{\max} \approx |\mathbf{A}(0)|/(1 - \mathbb{E}\xi) + |\mathbf{A}(0)|^{1/2}$. Since under $\mathbb{P}_\infty$ queues are symmetric, we have $|\mathbf{A}(0)| \approx A_1(0) + A_1(0)^{1/2}$ which finally leads to $T^* \approx A_1(0)/(1 - \mathbb{E}\xi) + A_1(0)^{1/2}$, i.e.,

$$\mathbb{E}_\infty \left(A_1(0) \right) \approx \frac{\mathbb{E}\xi}{1 - \mathbb{E}\xi} \mathbb{E}_\infty \left(A_1(0) \right) + \mathbb{E}_\infty \left[A_1(0)^{1/2} \right].$$

Thus upon a concentration-like result of the kind

$$\mathbb{E}_\infty [A_1(0)^{1/2}] \approx [\mathbb{E}_\infty (A_1(0))]^{1/2}$$

it is reasonable to expect

$$\left(1 - \frac{\mathbb{E}\xi}{1 - \mathbb{E}\xi} \right) \mathbb{E}_\infty \left(A_1(0) \right) \approx [\mathbb{E}_\infty (A_1(0))]^{1/2}.$$

Since $1 - \mathbb{E}(\xi)/(1 - \mathbb{E}\xi) \approx 1 - \rho$ this shows that $\mathbb{E}_\infty(A_1(0))$, and hence $\mathbb{E}_\infty(\|\mathbf{Q}(0)\|)$, should grow as $1/(1 - \rho)^2$. While admittedly crude, the above heuristic arguments provide the correct estimates, and serve as a useful guide for a rigorous proof in Section 6.1.

As reflected in the above computations, the square factor really stems from the relation $T^* \approx \tau_{(1)} + |\mathbf{A}(0)|^{1/2}$, i.e., T^* occurs somehow long after $\tau_{(1)}$, the time at which it would be optimal to switch in order to avoid inefficient use of the resource. But it is difficult to make the system switch exactly at $\tau_{(1)}$ in a distributed fashion, and here the penalty incurred is a square root. Interestingly, the penalty may seem negligible, since it is only a square root, but this small inefficiency has a significant impact in heavy traffic.

We explain in the next subsection how we formalize the analysis of this square root effect.

4.4 Main results

In this subsection we present our main results. They are discussed in the following sections based on a combination of rigorous proofs, heuristic arguments and simulation results, and we explain our contributions in more detail at the end of this subsection. Our first main result introduces the notion of *scaling exponent*, which essentially determines the polynomial growth rate of the mean number of packets in stationarity.

MAIN RESULT 1. $\mathbf{Q}$ *is positive recurrent if $\rho < 1$ and transient if $\rho > 1$. Moreover, the limit*

$$\lim_{\rho \uparrow 1} \left(\frac{\log \mathbb{E}_\infty(\|\mathbf{Q}(0)\|)}{\log(1/(1 - \rho))} \right) \stackrel{\text{def.}}{=} \alpha \tag{5}$$

exists and is called scaling exponent.

Remark. The transience of $\mathbf{Q}$ when $\rho > 1$ is easy to see. Indeed, if $L(k)$ is the number of packets at the beginning of the kth time slot, L is lower bounded by a random walk with drift $R(\rho - 1)$. Thus when $\rho > 1$, we have $L(k) \to +\infty$ as $k \to +\infty$ and since $(\|\mathbf{Q}(k)\|, k \geq 0)$ is a subsequence of $(L(k), k \geq 0)$ this proves the transience of $\mathbf{Q}$.

Stability for $\rho < 1$ is very intuitive but more challenging to establish. If the active queues are in state $\mathbf{a} = (a_r)$ with $a_r > 0$ for every r, the variation of the mean number of packets in the system over the next time slot is equal to

$$-R \left(1 - \rho - z \sum_{r=1}^{R} \psi(a_r) \right).$$

Since $\psi(a) \to 0$ as $a \to +\infty$, the drift is negative, close to $-R(1 - \rho)$, when each a_r is large enough. The problem in formalizing this argument is twofold: first, in order to prove stability, one must be able to control every possible initial configuration, not only those where every a_r is large; second, this argument considers the system on the normal time scale, whereas we are interested in the system embedded at switching times.

Our interest in the scaling exponent comes from an expected polynomial growth of $\mathbb{E}_\infty(\|\mathbf{Q}(0)\|)$ in heavy traffic. In general, we expect as $\rho \uparrow 1$ a behavior of the kind

$$\mathbb{E}_\infty \left(\|\mathbf{Q}(0)\| \right) \approx \frac{C}{(1 - \rho)^\alpha} \tag{6}$$

for some finite constant $C > 0$ (note that this would be stronger than (5)). The scaling exponent depends on the four model parameters R, ξ, ζ and β. However, we will mostly be interested in the dependence of α on β and thus write $\alpha(\beta)$ when the other three parameters are kept fixed. In fact, our results suggest that α does not depend on these other parameters, at least in the two extreme regimes we studied in detail. As explained in Section 4.3, the lingering makes $\mathbb{E}_\infty(\|\mathbf{Q}(0)\|)$ grow as $1/(1 - \rho)^2$ when $\beta > 1$, which can be formalized as follows.

MAIN RESULT 2. *If $\beta > 1$, then $\alpha(\beta) = 2$.*

It seems quite challenging to prove the existence of, and find a closed-form expression for, $\alpha(\beta)$ when $\beta \leq 1$. Nonetheless, the heuristic arguments of Section 4.2 suggest that the lower bound $\alpha(\beta) \geq 1/\beta$ of [1] is sharp as $\beta \downarrow 0$, which leads to the following result.

MAIN RESULT 3. $\beta\alpha(\beta) \to 1$ as $\beta \to 0$.

We now explain in more detail how these three results are established in the rest of the paper. The case $\beta = +\infty$ is treated rigorously: positive recurrence of $\mathbf{Q}$ when $\rho < 1$ and the result that $\alpha(\infty) = 2$ proved in Section 6.1. For $\beta > 1$, we explain in Section 6.2 why it can be seen as a perturbation of the case $\beta = +\infty$: we give some partial results toward a full proof in Sections 6.2.1 to 6.2.3, and heuristic arguments in Section 6.2.4 explaining the technical steps missing for a complete proof. These results are backed up by simulation results in Section 5. Finally, the main result 3 is discussed based on the simulation results of Section 5.2, which back up the heuristic arguments of Section 4.2.

5. SIMULATION EXPERIMENTS

In the previous section we provided an overview of the main results characterizing the heavy traffic behavior of the expected queue lengths. Before presenting detailed proof arguments in the case $\beta > 1$ in the next section, we first discuss comprehensive simulation experiments that we conducted to illustrate the stated growth behavior.

The detailed asymptotic analysis and proofs in the next section will reveal that the value of R and the precise distributions of ξ and ζ do not affect the stability of the system or the value of the scaling exponent. Throughout this section we therefore focus on the case where ξ is geometrically distributed with parameter $2/(2+\rho)$ and $\mathbb{P}(\zeta = 1) = 1$. We ran simulations using different distributions for ξ and ζ as well, including extreme cases such as distributions with infinite third moment (even infinite second moment for ζ). Because of page limitations we do not include these cases, but they yielded very similar results.

5.1 Simulations for the main result 1

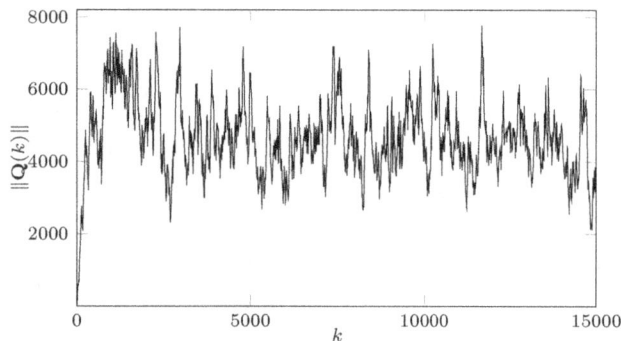

Figure 2: $\|\mathbf{Q}(k)\|$ vs. k for $R = \beta = 2$ and $\rho = 0.99$.

We now examine the case $R = \beta = 2$ in detail. Figures 2 and 3 show the evolution of $\|\mathbf{Q}(k)\|$, starting at $\mathbf{Q}(0) = \mathbf{0}$, for $\rho = 0.99$ and $\rho = 1.01$ respectively. When $\rho = 0.99$, Figure 2 shows that $\|\mathbf{Q}(k)\|$ fluctuates between 2000 and 8000 for k large enough, which strongly suggests that $\mathbf{Q}$ is positive recurrent.

When $\rho = 1.01$, Figure 3 shows that $\|\mathbf{Q}(k)\|$ increases until we stop the simulation when $1.5 \cdot 10^6$ packets are present in the system. Note that for a transient system we would expect that, when the queues are large, the total queue size grows by a constant amount on average in every time slot

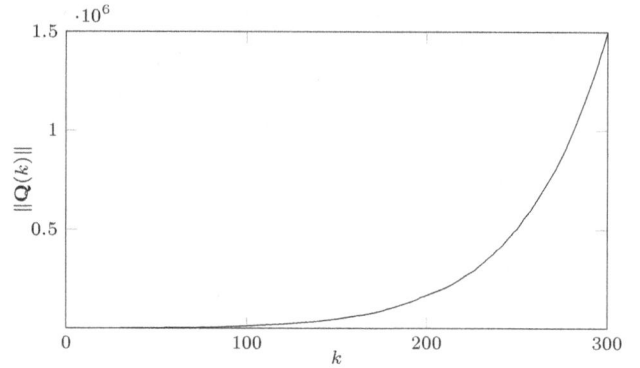

Figure 3: $\|\mathbf{Q}(k)\|$ vs. k for $R = \beta = 2$ and $\rho = 1.01$.

and that the time between two consecutive switching times increases. This explains the super-linear growth of $\|\mathbf{Q}(k)\|$ as we consider the system at switching times. In fact, the reasoning in Section 4.3 suggests that when $\|\mathbf{Q}(k)\|$ is large we have $\|\mathbf{Q}(k+1)\|/\|\mathbf{Q}(k)\| \approx \mathbb{E}\xi/(1 - \mathbb{E}\xi)$. This gives a heuristic explanation for the exponential growth (at rate $\rho/(2-\rho) > 1$) observed in Figure 3. All in all, this suggests that $\mathbf{Q}$ is transient for $\rho = 1.01$.

Observe moreover that it may in general be difficult to distinguish between positive recurrent and transient systems based on simulation results. Here however, $\mathbf{Q}$ obeys two clearly distinguishable types of behavior: stochastic fluctuations when $\rho < 1$, and almost deterministic exponential growth when $\rho > 1$.

5.2 Simulations for the main results 2 and 3

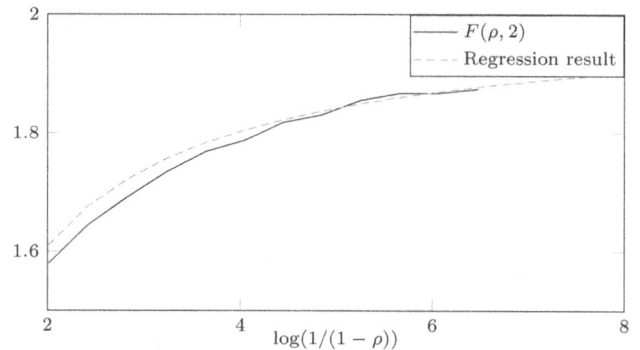

Figure 4: Approximating $\alpha(2)$ for $R = 2$.

From the results in Figure 2 we find by averaging over time $\mathbb{E}_\infty(\|\mathbf{Q}(0)\|) \approx 4700$ for $\rho = 0.99$, corresponding in view of the definition (5) of the scaling exponent to the estimate $\alpha(2) \approx \log 4700/\log 100 \approx 1.84$. To simplify the discussion define in the sequel

$$F(\rho, \beta) = \frac{\log \mathbb{E}_\infty(\|\mathbf{Q}(0)\|)}{\log(1/(1 - \rho))}, \quad \beta \in (0, \infty], \rho < 1. \quad (7)$$

Then, the scaling exponent $\alpha(\beta)$ is defined in (5) via a limiting procedure, namely $\alpha(\beta) = F(1-, \beta) = \lim_{\rho\uparrow 1} F(\rho, \beta)$. Using the results of Figure 2 to estimate $\alpha(2)$ amounts to using the approximation $F(1-, 2) \approx F(0.99, 2)$. In order to check whether this approximation is valid, we performed the same simulation for different values of ρ. In Figure 4 the value of $F(\rho,2)$ is plotted for different values of $\rho \in (0.87, 0.999)$. $F(\rho,2)$ is plotted versus $\log(1/(1-\rho))$ in order to "dilate" time around the value $\rho = 1$ that we are interested in (the quantity $\beta\alpha(\beta)$ is plotted versus $1/\beta$ in Figure 6 for the same reason), and also because it is natural to regress $F(\rho,2)$, as function of ρ, against $\log(1/(1-\rho))$ (see forthcoming discussion).

Figure 4 shows that the limit $F(1-,2)$ seems to exist, but $F(\rho,2)$ is still significantly increasing for $\rho = 0.999$. Thus $F(0.999,2)$, and in particular $F(0.99,2)$, cannot be used as an estimate of $\alpha(2)$. It is numerically difficult to run a simulation for even higher values of ρ, and so to circumvent this problem we use the simulation results displayed in Figure 4 to find the asymptotic value of $F(\rho,2)$. To do so, we use the approximation (6) to infer the form of $F(\rho,\beta)$, namely

$$F(\rho,\beta) \approx \alpha(\beta) + \frac{\log C}{\log(1/(1-\rho))}, \qquad (8)$$

which suggests, as mentioned above, to regress $F(\rho,2)$ against $a + b/x$ in the scale $x = \log(1/(1-\rho))$. We performed this regression for the curve displayed in Figure 4 and found an optimal value $a = 1.9984 \approx \alpha(2)$.

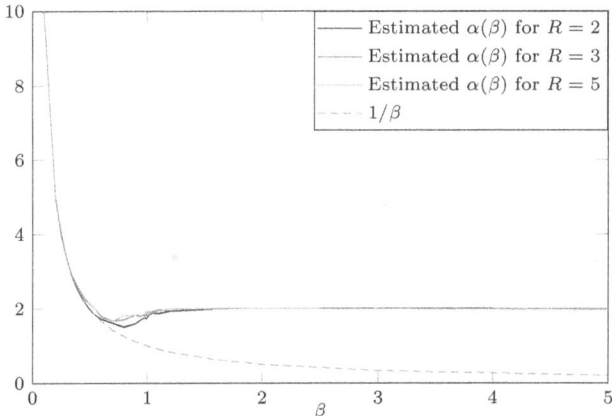

Figure 5: $\alpha(\beta)$ **vs.** β **for** $R \in \{2,3,5\}$.

Applying the same approach, we can find an estimate for $\alpha(\beta)$ for any value of β. The results for $R = 2$, 3 and 5 are given in Figure 5, and confirm that R does not seem to influence $\alpha(\beta)$. Further, the approximation $\alpha(\beta) \approx 2$ appears to be very good for any $\beta > 1.2$, namely, the estimated value of $\alpha(\beta)$ is at most 3% away from 2 for any $\beta > 1.2$ and any $R = 2,3,5$, in very good agreement with the main result 2. In Section 6.2.4 we will discuss in greater detail the case where $\beta > 1$ is close to 1.

Finally, for small values of β, we observe that $\alpha(\beta)$ is close to the lower bound $1/\beta$. To see how close $\alpha(\beta)$ is to the lower bound, we made a plot for $\beta\alpha(\beta)$ in Figure 6. We observe that $\beta\alpha(\beta) \in (0.98, 1.02)$ for any $\beta < 0.45$, which supports our claim made in the main result 3 and the heuristic argument given in Section 4.2.

6. ANALYSIS OF THE CASE $\beta \in (1,\infty]$

6.1 The case $\beta = +\infty$

We study here in detail the case $\beta = \infty$. In Section 6.2 we explain why the case $\beta > 1$ can be seen as a perturbation of

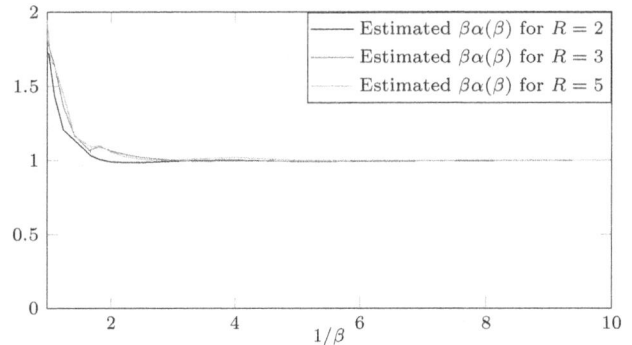

Figure 6: $\beta\alpha(\beta)$ **vs.** $1/\beta$ **for** $R \in \{2,3,5\}$.

this case. In the remainder of this subsection we assume that $\beta = \infty$, so that $\mathbf{A}(T^*) = \mathbf{0}$ and $T^* = \inf\{k \geq 0 : \mathbf{A}(k) = \mathbf{0}\}$.

6.1.1 Control of T^*

We first prove that $T^* \approx \tau_{\max}$, i.e., the time at which the R independent random walks A_r simultaneously hit 0, is close to the first time at which each process has visited 0 at least once.

LEMMA 6.1. $\sup_{\mathbf{a},\rho} \mathbb{E}_{\mathbf{a}}(T^* - \tau_{\max})$ is finite, where the supremum is taken over $\mathbf{a} \in \mathbb{N}^R$ and $\rho \leq 1$.

PROOF. By monotonicity of T^* in ρ, it is enough to show that $\sup_{\mathbf{a}} \mathbb{E}_{\mathbf{a}}(T^* - \tau_{\max})$ is finite for $\rho = 1$. So assume in the remainder of the proof $\rho = 1$: then each active queue is stable (for that we only need $\rho < 2$) and in particular, T^* is almost surely finite. Thus the strong Markov property at time $\tau_{\max} \leq T^*$ gives

$$\mathbb{E}_{\mathbf{a}}(T^* - \tau_{\max}) = \mathbb{E}_{\mathbf{a}}\left[\mathbb{E}_{\mathbf{A}(\tau_{\max})}(T^*)\right].$$

When A_r hits 0 for the first time at time τ_r, we can couple it with a stationary version $\tilde{A}_r$ of A_1 in such a way that $\tilde{A}_r(k) \geq A_r(k)$ for every $k \geq \tau_r$ (this is the usual coupling between two processes starting from different initial conditions and sharing the same stochastic primitives). By monotonicity and since queues are independent, we obtain

$$\mathbb{E}_{\mathbf{a}}(T^* - \tau_{\max}) \leq \mathbb{E}_{\varrho}(T^*),$$

where for any $r \geq 2$, we define $\varrho = (X_1,\ldots,X_R) \in \mathbb{N}^R$ with $(X_i, i \geq 1)$ i.i.d. with common distribution the stationary distribution X of A_r.

Define $\sigma(0) = 0$ and for $k \geq 1$, $\tau(k) = \tau_{\max} \circ \theta_{\sigma(k-1)}$ and $\sigma(k) = \sigma(k-1) + \tau(k)$, where θ is the shift operator. In words, $\sigma(k+1)$ is the smallest time after $\sigma(k)$ such that every queue will have visited 0 at least once after (and including) time $\sigma(k)$. Note that if $\mathbf{A}(\sigma(k)) = \mathbf{0}$ for some k, then $\sigma(k') = \sigma(k)$ for $k' \geq k$. In particular, the limit $\sigma(\infty)$ as $k \to +\infty$ exists, and is by construction equal to T^*. Since $\tau(k) = \sigma(k) - \sigma(k-1)$ this can be rewritten as $T^* = \sum_{k\geq 1}\tau(k)$.

By construction, A_r takes the value 0 at least once between $\sigma(k)$ and $\sigma(k+1)$: at this time we can couple it with a stationary version of itself that stays above it. Following this stationary process from this time until the time $\sigma(k+1)$, this gives the existence of i.i.d. random variables $(X_r(k), r \in \mathcal{R}, k \geq 0)$ with common distribution X such that $A_r(\sigma(k)) \leq X_r(k)$ for every r and k.

Considering the time needed for every queue to visit 0 at least once starting from $(X_r(k), r \in \mathcal{R})$ gives an upper bound on $\tau(k)$. Each time we do so, there is a probability $p = \mathbb{P}_\varrho(\mathbf{A}(\tau_{\max}) = \mathbf{0}) \in (0, 1)$ that we reach $\mathbf{0}$ at time $\tau_{\max}$. Thus, T^* is (stochastically) upper bounded by $\tau_1' + \cdots + \tau_G'$ with G a geometric random variable with parameter $1 - p$ and (τ_i') i.i.d., independent from G and with common distribution $\tau_{\max}$ under $\mathbb{P}_\varrho$. This implies

$$\mathbb{E}_\varrho(T^*) \leq \mathbb{E}\left(\tau_1' + \cdots + \tau_G'\right) = \frac{\mathbb{E}_\varrho(\tau_{\max})}{\mathbb{P}_\varrho(\mathbf{A}(\tau_{\max}) = \mathbf{0})}.$$

Since $\tau_{\max} \leq \tau_1 + \cdots + \tau_R$, $\mathbb{E}_{a_r}(\tau_r) = a_r/(1 - \mathbb{E}\xi)$ and X has finite mean (because ξ is assumed to have finite second moment), $\mathbb{E}_\varrho(\tau_{\max})$ is finite and so the proof is complete. $\square$

The previous lemma justifies the approximation $T^* \approx \tau_{\max}$, and to further control $\tau_{\max}$, we will use the fact that $(\tau_r, r \in \mathcal{R})$ under $\mathbb{P}_\mathbf{a}$ is equal in distribution to $(V_r(a_r), r \in \mathcal{R})$, where $(V_r, r \in \mathcal{R})$ are i.i.d. random walks started at 0 and with step distribution δ, equal in distribution to τ_1 under $\mathbb{P}_1$ (i.e., δ is the time needed for a random walk with step distribution $\xi - 1$ to go from 1 to 0). Then δ has finite mean $1/(1 - \mathbb{E}\xi)$ and also finite variance, which we denote by ν. To control the maximum of random walks, we will use the following result.

LEMMA 6.2. *If (W_r) are i.i.d. random walks started at 0 with step distribution having mean m and variance w, then for any $\mathbf{x} = (x_r) \in \mathbb{N}^R$ it holds that*

$$\mathbb{E}\left(\max_r W_r(x_r)\right) \leq m|\mathbf{x}| + R(w|\mathbf{x}|)^{1/2}.$$

PROOF. Defining $Y_r = (W_r(x_r) - mx_r)/(wx_r)^{1/2}$, we have $\max_r W_r(x_r) = \max_r(mx_r + (wx_r)^{1/2}Y_r)$ so that

$$\max_r W_r(x_r) \leq m|\mathbf{x}| + (w|\mathbf{x}|)^{1/2}\|\mathbf{Y}\|$$

which proves the result since $\mathbb{E}(\|\mathbf{Y}\|) = \sum_r \mathbb{E}(|Y_r|) \leq R$. $\square$

6.1.2 Proof of $\alpha(\infty) = 2$

Before proving the main result 2 in the case $\beta = +\infty$, we first need to prove stability and finiteness of the stationary mean.

PROPOSITION 6.3. *Assume that $\beta = +\infty$ and that $\rho < 1$. Then $\mathbf{Q}$ is positive recurrent and $\mathbb{E}_\infty(\|\mathbf{Q}(0)\|) < +\infty$.*

PROOF. Let $\Phi(\mathbf{q}) = |\mathbf{q}^a| + |\mathbf{q}^i|$: to prove Proposition 6.3, it is enough to prove that

$$\lim_{K \to +\infty} \sup_{\mathbf{q}:\Phi(\mathbf{q}) \geq K} \left(\frac{\mathbb{E}_\mathbf{q}[\Phi(\mathbf{Q}(2)) - \Phi(\mathbf{q})]}{\Phi(\mathbf{q})}\right) < 0. \quad (9)$$

Indeed, this shows that Φ is a Lyapunov function, which implies positive recurrence of $\mathbf{Q}$ using for instance the Foster-Lyapunov criterion. But it shows more than that: in the terminology of [4] it implies that Φ is a geometric Lyapunov function, and Theorem 5 in [4] shows that (9) implies that $\mathbb{E}_\infty[\Phi(\mathbf{Q}(0))]$, and in particular $\mathbb{E}_\infty(\|\mathbf{Q}(0)\|)$, is finite. Thus we only have to prove (9).

Since $|\mathbf{x} + \mathbf{y}| \leq |\mathbf{x}| + |\mathbf{y}|$, (2) implies that

$$\mathbb{E}_\mathbf{q}[\Phi(\mathbf{Q}(1))] \leq |\mathbf{q}^i| + \mathbb{E}_{\mathbf{q}^a}(|\mathbf{S}(T^*)|) + \mathbb{E}_{\mathbf{q}^a}(|\mathbf{A}(T^*)|).$$

Since $\mathbf{S}$ and T^* are independent, Lemma 6.2 gives that $\mathbb{E}_\mathbf{a}(|\mathbf{S}(T^*)|) \leq \mathbb{E}(\xi)\mathbb{E}_\mathbf{a}(T^*) + R\mathbb{E}_\mathbf{a}((vT^*)^{1/2})$ for any $\mathbf{a} \in \mathbb{N}^R$

(recall that v is the variance of ξ, assumed to be finite). Thus after rearranging the terms, we end up with the bound

$$\mathbb{E}_\mathbf{q}[\Phi(\mathbf{Q}(1)) - \Phi(\mathbf{q})] \leq -(1 - \rho)\mathbb{E}_{\mathbf{q}^a}(T^*) + \Psi(\mathbf{q}^a), \quad (10)$$

where

$$\Psi(\mathbf{a}) = \mathbb{E}_\mathbf{a}\left(|\mathbf{A}(T^*)| + (1 - \mathbb{E}\xi)T^* - |\mathbf{A}(0)| + R(vT^*)^{1/2}\right).$$

We now argue that $\Psi(\mathbf{a}) \leq c[\mathbb{E}_\mathbf{a}(T^*)]^{1/2}$ for some finite constant c independent of $\mathbf{a}$. Since we are considering the case $\beta = +\infty$, we have $|\mathbf{A}(T^*)| = 0$ and so we only have to show that $(1 - \mathbb{E}\xi)\mathbb{E}_\mathbf{a}(T^*) - |\mathbf{a}| \leq c[\mathbb{E}_\mathbf{a}(T^*)]^{1/2}$. By Lemma 6.1, we have $\mathbb{E}_\mathbf{a}(T^*) \leq \mathbb{E}_\mathbf{a}(\tau_{\max}) + c'$ for some finite constant c' independent of $\mathbf{a}$. Further, since $\tau_{\max}$ is equal in distribution to $\max_r V_r(a_r)$, Lemma 6.2 gives (recall that ν is the variance of the step distribution of the V_r's)

$$\mathbb{E}_\mathbf{a}(T^*) \leq \frac{|\mathbf{a}|}{1 - \mathbb{E}\xi} + R(\nu|\mathbf{a}|)^{1/2} + c',$$

which implies the existence of the desired constant c such that $\Psi(\mathbf{a}) \leq c[\mathbb{E}_\mathbf{a}(T^*)]^{1/2}$. Defining

$$\Gamma(\mathbf{a}) = (1 - \rho)\mathbb{E}_\mathbf{a}(T^*) - c[\mathbb{E}_\mathbf{a}(T^*)]^{1/2}, \quad (11)$$

(10) can be rewritten as $\mathbb{E}_\mathbf{q}[\Phi(\mathbf{Q}(1)) - \Phi(\mathbf{q})] \leq -\Gamma(\mathbf{q}^a)$. Using the Markov property and (2), this gives

$$\mathbb{E}_\mathbf{q}[\Phi(\mathbf{Q}(2)) - \Phi(\mathbf{q})]$$
$$\leq -\mathbb{E}_{\mathbf{q}^a}\left(\Gamma(\mathbf{q}^a) + \Gamma(\mathbf{q}^i + \mathbf{S}(T^*))\right). \quad (12)$$

When $\Phi(\mathbf{q}) = |\mathbf{q}^a| + |\mathbf{q}^i|$ is large, at least one of the $2R$ coordinates of $\mathbf{q}$ must be large. Since $\mathbb{E}_\mathbf{a}(T^*) \geq a_r/(1 - \mathbb{E}\xi)$ (as a consequence of $T^* \geq \tau_r$ and $\mathbb{E}_a(\tau_r) = a/(1 - \mathbb{E}\xi)$), it is not hard to show that

$$\lim_{K \to +\infty} \inf_{\mathbf{q}:\Phi(\mathbf{q}) \geq K} \frac{\mathbb{E}_{\mathbf{q}^a}\left(\Gamma(\mathbf{q}^a) + \Gamma(\mathbf{q}^i + \mathbf{S}(T^*))\right)}{\Phi(\mathbf{q})} > 0,$$

which completes the proof of the result. $\square$

Now that we have stability and finiteness of the stationary mean, we prove that $\alpha(\infty) = 2$. The proof will make use of the following result.

LEMMA 6.4. *If (W_j) are J i.i.d. random walks started at 0 with non-negative step distribution having mean m and variance w, then for any $\mathbf{x} = (x_j) \in \mathbb{N}^J$ it holds that,*

$$\mathbb{E}\left[\left(\max_j W_j(x_j)\right)^{1/2}\right] \geq (m|\mathbf{x}|)^{1/2} - (w/m^{3/2})|\mathbf{x}|^{-1/2}.$$

PROOF. Since $\mathbb{E}(\max_j W_j(x_j)) \geq \max_j \mathbb{E}(W_j(x_j))$ it is enough to prove the result for $J = 1$. Fix $k \geq 0$ and let $Y = (W_1(k) - mk)/(mk)^{1/2}$ and

$$f(y) = \frac{1 + y/2 - (1 + y)^{1/2}}{y^2}, \quad y \geq -1.$$

Since $\mathbb{E}Y = 0$ and $Y \geq -(km)^{1/2}$, we can rewrite after some algebra

$$\mathbb{E}(W_1(k)^{1/2}) = (km)^{1/2} - (km)^{-1/2}\mathbb{E}\left[Y^2 f((km)^{-1/2}Y)\right],$$

and since $\sup f = 1/2$ and $\mathbb{E}(Y^2) = w/m$ this gives the result. $\square$

THEOREM 6.5. *If* $\beta = +\infty$, *then*

$$0 < \liminf_{\rho \uparrow 1} \left[(1-\rho)^2 \mathbb{E}_\infty \left(\|\mathbf{Q}(0)\| \right) \right]$$
$$\leq \limsup_{\rho \uparrow 1} \left[(1-\rho)^2 \mathbb{E}_\infty \left(\|\mathbf{Q}(0)\| \right) \right] < +\infty. \quad (13)$$

In particular, $\alpha(\infty) = 2$.

PROOF. Since $\beta = +\infty$, we have

$$\mathbb{E}_\infty(\|\mathbf{Q}(0)\|) = \mathbb{E}_\infty(\|\mathbf{A}(0)\|) = R \mathbb{E}_\infty(A_1(0)).$$

Thus we only need to prove

$$\limsup_{\rho \uparrow 1} \left[(1-\rho)^2 \mathbb{E}_\infty (A_1(0)) \right] < +\infty, \quad (14)$$

which implies the lower bound in (13), and

$$\liminf_{\rho \uparrow 1} \left\{ (1-\rho) \mathbb{E}_\infty \left[A_1(0)^{1/2} \right] \right\} > 0 \quad (15)$$

which by Jensen's inequality implies the upper bound in (13).

Proof of (14). Starting from (4), using that $\mathbb{E}_a(\tau_1) = a/(1 - \mathbb{E}\xi)$, subtracting on both sides $\mathbb{E}(\xi)\mathbb{E}_\infty(\tau_1)$ (for this precise operation we need the finiteness of the stationary first moment, to avoid doing $\infty - \infty$) and dividing by $\mathbb{E}\xi$, we end up with

$$\frac{1}{\mathbb{E}\xi}\left(1 - \frac{\mathbb{E}\xi}{1 - \mathbb{E}\xi} \right) \mathbb{E}_\infty (A_1(0)) = \mathbb{E}_\infty(T^* - \tau_1).$$

Then, adding and subtracting $\tau_{\max}$ in the right hand side, and using that $\mathbb{E}\xi = \rho/2$, we obtain

$$g_\rho(1-\rho)\mathbb{E}_\infty(A_1(0)) = \mathbb{E}_\infty(\tau_{\max} - \tau_1) + \mathbb{E}_\infty(T^* - \tau_{\max}),$$

with $g_\rho = 4/(\rho(2-\rho))$. Thus in view of Lemma 6.1, to prove (14) we only have to show that

$$\limsup_{\rho \uparrow 1} \left(\frac{\mathbb{E}_\infty(\tau_{\max} - \tau_1)}{[\mathbb{E}_\infty(A_1(0))]^{1/2}} \right) < +\infty. \quad (16)$$

Applying Lemma 6.2 to $\tau_{\max}$ under $\mathbb{P}_\mathbf{a}$ (equal in distribution to $\max_r V_r(a_r)$), we obtain, denoting temporarily $\mu = 1/(1 - \mathbb{E}\xi)$, $\mathbb{E}_\mathbf{a}(\tau_{\max} - \tau_1) \leq \mu(|\mathbf{a}| - a_1) + R\nu|\mathbf{a}|^{1/2}$. Integrating over the stationary distribution of $\mathbf{Q}$ and using Jensen's inequality, we obtain

$$\mathbb{E}_\infty(\tau_{\max} - \tau_1) \leq \mu \mathbb{E}_\infty(|\mathbf{A}(0)| - A_1(0))$$
$$+ R\nu \left[\mathbb{E}_\infty(A_1(0)) \right]^{1/2}.$$

In particular, to prove (16) it is enough to show that

$$\limsup_{\rho \uparrow 1} \left(\frac{\mathbb{E}_\infty(|\mathbf{A}(0)| - A_1(0))}{[\mathbb{E}_\infty(A_1(0))]^{1/2}} \right) < +\infty. \quad (17)$$

We have already shown in the proof of Proposition 6.3 that

$$\mathbb{E}_\infty(|\mathbf{A}(0)|) = \mathbb{E}_\infty(|\mathbf{S}(T^*)|) \leq \mathbb{E}(\xi)\mathbb{E}_\infty(T^*) + Rv \left[\mathbb{E}_\infty(T^*) \right]^{1/2},$$

and since $\mathbb{E}_\infty(A_1(0)) = \mathbb{E}(\xi)\mathbb{E}_\infty(T^*)$ this gives

$$\mathbb{E}_\infty(|\mathbf{A}(0)| - A_1(0)) \leq Rv \left[\mathbb{E}_\infty(A_1(0))/\mathbb{E}\xi \right]^{1/2}.$$

This proves (17) which completes the proof of (14).

Proof of (15). We have

$$\mathbb{E}_\infty \left[(Q_1^a(0))^{1/2} \right] = \mathbb{E}_\infty \left[(S_1(T^*))^{1/2} \right] \geq \mathbb{E}_\infty \left[(S_1(\tau_{\max}))^{1/2} \right].$$

Applying Lemma 6.4 to $S_1(\tau_{\max})$ by using the independence between S_1 and $\tau_{\max}$, we obtain

$$\mathbb{E}_\infty \left[(Q_1^a(0))^{1/2} \right] \geq (\mathbb{E}\xi)^{1/2} \mathbb{E}_\infty \left[(\tau_{\max})^{1/2} \right]$$
$$- c\mathbb{E}_\infty \left[(\tau_{\max})^{-1/2} \right]$$

for some finite constant c independent of ρ. Applying again Lemma 6.4 to $\tau_{\max}$ we obtain

$$\mathbb{E}_\infty \left[(Q_1^a(0))^{1/2} \right] \geq (\mu\mathbb{E}\xi)^{1/2} \mathbb{E}_\infty (|\mathbf{Q}^a(0)|^{1/2})$$
$$- c\mathbb{E}_\infty (|\mathbf{Q}^a(0)|^{-1/2}) - c\mathbb{E}_\infty \left[(\tau_{\max})^{-1/2} \right].$$

Subtracting $(\mu\mathbb{E}\xi)^{1/2}\mathbb{E}_\infty(Q_1^a(0)^{1/2})$ on both sides we finally end up with

$$h_\rho(1-\rho)\mathbb{E}_\infty \left[(Q_1^a(0))^{1/2} \right]$$
$$\geq (\mu\mathbb{E}\xi)^{1/2} \mathbb{E}_\infty \left(|\mathbf{Q}^a(0)|^{1/2} - (Q_1^a(0))^{1/2} \right)$$
$$- c\mathbb{E}_\infty \left(|\mathbf{Q}^a(0)|^{-1/2} \right) - c\mathbb{E}_\infty \left[(\tau_{\max})^{-1/2} \right],$$

with $h_\rho = (1-(\rho/(2-\rho))^{1/2})/(1-\rho) \to 1$ as $\rho \to 1$. The two last terms of the previous lower bound vanish as $\rho \uparrow 1$. As for the first term, it is not hard based on (2) to show that the R-dimensional vector $((Q_1^a(0) + 1)^{-1/2}(Q_r^a(0) - Q_1^a(0)), r \in \mathcal{R})$ under $\mathbb{P}_\infty$ converges weakly as $\rho \uparrow 1$, from which one readily deduces thanks to the continuous mapping theorem that $|\mathbf{Q}^a(0)|^{1/2} - (Q_1^a(0))^{1/2}$ also converges weakly as $\rho \uparrow 1$ to a random variable which is not identically zero. Using Fatou's lemma, this implies that

$$\liminf_{\rho \uparrow 1} \mathbb{E}_\infty \left(|\mathbf{Q}^a(0)|^{1/2} - (Q_1^a(0))^{1/2} \right) > 0,$$

which concludes the proof. $\square$

6.2 The case $\beta > 1$

6.2.1 *Main result and a perturbation argument*

In the previous subsection, we analyzed in detail the case $\beta = \infty$ and proved $\alpha(\infty) = 2$. On the other hand, the simulation results, see Figure 5, strongly suggest that $\alpha(\beta) = 2$ for any $\beta > 1$, and the goal of this subsection is to explain this result. The key to understand the behavior of $\mathbf{Q}$ for $\beta > 1$ is Proposition 6.6.

This proposition 6.6 is only concerned with the behavior of an active queue, i.e., a queue subject to the dynamic (1). Thus in order to prove Proposition 6.6, we only need to assume $\rho < 2$, which is the stability condition for an active queue. It is easy to see that these results actually hold uniformly in $\rho \leq 1$, which is what would be needed in order to go in heavy traffic for the full model.

In the sequel, we let T_1 be the time at which A_1 advertizes a release for the first time.

PROPOSITION 6.6. *If* $\beta > 1$, *then* $(A_1(T_1), T_1 - \tau_1)$ *under* $\mathbb{P}_{a_1}$ *converges weakly as* $a_1 \to +\infty$ *to a non-degenerate random variable.*

By non-degenerate, we mean a random variable $(X, Y) \in \mathbb{N} \times \mathbb{Z}$ such that both X and Y are non-deterministic and almost surely finite (an explicit expression for the weak limit of $(A_1(T_1), T_1 - \tau_1)$ is given in Lemma 6.9). Note that from Proposition 6.6, which is concerned with the behavior of one active queue, one can easily deduce the behavior of $\mathbf{A}(T^*)$

and T^* (the proof of the following result is only sketched in order to comply with page limitations).

COROLLARY 6.7. *Assume that $\beta > 1$ and consider any sequence of initial states $\mathbf{a}_n = (a_{n,r})$ such that $\min_r a_{n,r} \to +\infty$: then $(\mathbf{A}(T^*), T^* - \tau_{\max})$ under $\mathbb{P}_{\mathbf{a}_n}$ converges weakly as $n \to +\infty$ to a non-degenerate random variable.*

PROOF (SKETCH). At time T^*, each active queue needs to have advertized a release at least once. At this time, the active queue was of order one by Proposition 6.6 and since it is stable, it remains of order one at time T^*. $\square$

In the extreme case $\beta = +\infty$ we have by definition $\mathbf{A}(T^*) = \mathbf{0}$ and (by Lemma 6.1) $T^* \approx \tau_{\max}$. By showing that both $\mathbf{A}(T^*)$ and $T^* - \tau_{\max}$ are of order one when $\beta > 1$, Corollary 6.7 therefore justifies seeing the case $\beta > 1$ as a perturbation of the case $\beta = +\infty$. In particular, treating $\mathbb{E}_\infty(\mathbf{A}(T^*))$ and $\mathbb{E}_\infty(T^* - \tau_{\max})$ as constants, the heuristic reasoning outlined in Section 4.3 goes through and again predicts a scaling exponent $\alpha(\beta) = 2$ for any $\beta > 1$. This is indeed in very good agreement with the simulation results discussed in Section 5.2 and was stated as our main result 2.

The remainder of this subsection is devoted to the proof of Proposition 6.6. The proof proceeds in two steps: in the first step we show that the proof of Proposition 6.6 reduces to proving a simpler property of some particular random walk (see (18)). In the second step we prove that this property holds when $\beta > 1$.

6.2.2 First step

Since before time T_1, the active queue A_1 does by definition not advertize any release, it is enough to prove Proposition 6.6 in the case $\zeta = 0$, which we assume in the remainder of this subsection. In particular, A_1 is a random walk with step distribution $\xi - 1$ reflected at 0. The reduction of the proof of Proposition 6.6 to proving (18) relies on the following coupling of the processes A_1 for all possible initial states $a \geq 0$.

Let V and $W^\uparrow$ be two independent processes with the following distribution. Let V be a version of A_1 under $\mathbb{P}_0$, i.e., $(V(k), k \geq 0)$ is a random walk started at 0, with step distribution $\xi - 1$ and reflected at 0.

Let $W^\uparrow$ be a random walk started at 0, with step distribution $1 - \xi$ and conditioned on never visiting 0 after time 0: since $\mathbb{E}(1 - \xi) > 0$ this conditioning is well-defined. Let moreover $\kappa(a) = \max\{k \geq 0 : W^\uparrow(k) = a\}$ be the time of the last visit to $a \in \{0, 1, \ldots, \infty\}$ (to be understood as $\kappa(a) = +\infty$ for $a = +\infty$), so that $\kappa(a)$ is almost surely finite if a is finite. Let finally $W_a^\uparrow$ be the process $W^\uparrow$ stopped at $\kappa(a)$, i.e., $W_a^\uparrow(k) = W^\uparrow(k)$ if $k \leq \kappa(a)$ and $W_a^\uparrow(k) = W^\uparrow(\kappa(a)) = a$ if $k \geq \kappa(a)$.

LEMMA 6.8. *Extend A_1 on $\mathbb{Z}$ by setting $A_1(k) = A_1(0)$ for $k \leq 0$, and let $A^+ = (A_1(\tau_1 + k), k \geq 0)$ and $A^- = (A_1(\tau_1 - k), k \geq 0)$. Then for any finite $a \geq 0$, (A^+, A^-) under $\mathbb{P}_a$ is equal in distribution to $(V, W_a^\uparrow)$.*

In particular, as $a \to +\infty$, (A^+, A^-) under $\mathbb{P}_a$ converges weakly to $(V, W^\uparrow)$.

PROOF. That A^+ is equal in distribution to V and is independent from A^- follows from the strong Markov property at time τ_1. That A^- is equal in distribution to $W_a^\uparrow$ comes from duality. The weak convergence result then follows from the fact that $\kappa(a) \to +\infty$ almost surely as $a \to +\infty$, so that $(V, W_a^\uparrow) \to (V, W^\uparrow)$ almost surely as $a \to +\infty$. $\square$

Essentially, this representation of A_1 shifts the origin of time at τ_1: A^+ looks at A_1 from time τ_1 forward in time, while A^- looks at A_1 from τ_1 backward in time. Moreover, this representation couples all the processes A_1 with different initial states on the same probability space, which yields a simple representation for the law of $(A_1(T_1), T_1 - \tau_1)$. Let in the sequel $Z = (Z(k), k \in \mathbb{Z})$ be the following process (indexed by $\mathbb{Z}$): $Z(k) = V(k)$ if $k \geq 0$ and $Z(k) = W^\uparrow(-k)$ if $k \leq 0$. The previous coupling immediately implies the following result.

LEMMA 6.9. *Let $(U_k, k \in \mathbb{Z})$ be i.i.d., uniformly distributed in $[0, 1]$, independent from Z, and for $0 \leq a \leq +\infty$ and $k \in \mathbb{Z}$ let*

$$D_{a,k} = \begin{cases} 0 & \text{if } k < -\kappa(a), \\ \mathrm{I}_{\{U_k < \psi(Z(k))\}} & \text{else,} \end{cases}$$

and $T_a^Z = \inf\{k \in \mathbb{Z} : D_{a,k} = 1\}$. Then for any finite $a \geq 0$, $(A_1(T_1), T_1 - \tau_1)$ under $\mathbb{P}_a$ is equal in distribution to $(Z(T_a^Z), T_a^Z)$ and in particular, it converges weakly as $a \to +\infty$ to $(Z(T_\infty^Z), T_\infty^Z)$ (with $Z(T_\infty^Z) = +\infty$ if $T_\infty^Z = -\infty$).

PROOF. The equality in law between $(A_1(T_1), T_1 - \tau_1)$ and $(Z(T_a^Z), T_a^Z)$ is clear from the construction, and not difficult (although a bit heavy in notation) to formalize. Moreover, T_a^Z is by construction decreasing in a and so its limit as $a \to +\infty$ exists. It is not hard to show that its limit is exactly T_∞^Z and by continuity we deduce that $Z(T_a^Z) \to Z(T_\infty^Z)$ as $a \to +\infty$, which implies the result. $\square$

Thus to prove Proposition 6.6, we only have to establish that $|T_\infty^Z|$ is (almost surely) finite. Since V is positive recurrent and starts at 0, it is clear that $\min\{k \geq 0 : D_{\infty,k} = 1\}$ is finite and so to prove that $|T_\infty^Z|$ is finite, we only have to demonstrate that $\inf\{k \leq 0 : D_{\infty,k} = 1\}$ is finite. In other words, we have to prove that $\sup\{k \geq 0 : U_{-k} < \psi(W^\uparrow(k))\}$ is finite, which informally means that $W^\uparrow$ advertizes a release only finitely many times.

So in the sequel, we consider $(U_k, k \geq 0)$ i.i.d. random variables, uniformly distributed on $[0, 1]$ and independent of $W^\uparrow$, and we define

$$N = \sum_{k \geq 0} \mathrm{I}_{\{U_k < \psi(W^\uparrow(k))\}}$$

as the number of times $W^\uparrow$ advertizes a release. The proof of Proposition 6.6 will thus be complete if we can prove that

$$\mathbb{P}(N < +\infty) = 1. \tag{18}$$

6.2.3 Second step

We now assume that $\beta > 1$ and we prove that $\mathbb{P}(N > n) \to 0$ as $n \to +\infty$, which will prove (18). By definition,

$$\mathbb{P}(N = 0) = \mathbb{P}\left(U_k > \psi(W^\uparrow(k)), k \geq 0\right),$$

and since $W^\uparrow$ and the U_k's are independent this gives

$$\mathbb{P}(N = 0) = \mathbb{E}\left[\prod_{k \geq 0} \left(1 - \psi(W^\uparrow(k))\right)\right].$$

Let $a \geq 0$: introducing $\varphi(a) = -\log(1 - \psi(a))$ and $L^\uparrow(a) =$

$\sum_{k \geq 0} I_{\{W^\uparrow(k)=a\}}$, the local time at level a, we obtain

$$\mathbb{P}(N = 0) = \mathbb{E}\left[\exp\left(-\sum_{a \geq 0} \varphi(a)L^\uparrow(a)\right)\right]. \quad (19)$$

LEMMA 6.10. *The quantity* $\sup_{a \geq 0} \mathbb{E}(L^\uparrow(a))$ *is finite. In particular,* $\mathbb{P}(N = 0) > 0$.

PROOF. Let W^- be a random walk with step distribution $\xi - 1$, started at 0 and independent from $W^\uparrow$, and for $k \in \mathbb{Z}$ define $W^*(k) = W^\uparrow(k)$ if $k \geq 0$ and $W^*(k) = W^-(-k)$ if $k \leq 0$. Thus, defining $L^*(a) = \sum_{k \in \mathbb{Z}} I_{\{W^*(k)=a\}}$ we have the obvious inequality $L^\uparrow(a) \leq L^*(a)$ and so we only have to prove that $\sup_{a \in \mathbb{Z}} \mathbb{E}(L^*(a))$ is finite.

It is clear that L^* stays the same if W^* is shifted in time, and that shifting L^* in time amounts to shifting W^* in space. Moreover, for any $w \in \mathbb{Z}$ the process $(W^*(k) + w, k \in \mathbb{Z})$ shifted at the time of last visit to 0 is equal in distribution to W^*. Combining these facts, we see that L^* is a stationary sequence and in particular, $\sup_{a \in \mathbb{Z}} \mathbb{E}(L^*(a)) = \mathbb{E}(L^*(0))$. But by the strong Markov property, it is clear that $L^*(0)$ is a geometric random variable, in particular it has finite first moment. This proves the finiteness of $\sup_a \mathbb{E}(L^\uparrow(a))$.

As for $\mathbb{P}(N > 0)$, we have

$$\mathbb{E}\left(\sum_{a \geq 0} \varphi(a)L^\uparrow(a)\right) \leq \sup_a \mathbb{E}(L^\uparrow(a)) \sum_{a \geq 0} \varphi(a),$$

and since $\varphi(a) \sim a^{-\beta}$ as $a \to +\infty$ and $\beta > 1$, the sum $\sum_a \varphi(a)$ is finite which implies, in view of the last display, that the random variable $\sum_a \varphi(a)L^\uparrow(a)$ is almost surely finite. This proves $\mathbb{P}(N = 0) > 0$ in view of (19) and concludes the proof of the lemma. $\square$

We now prove that $\mathbb{P}(N > n) \to 0$ as $n \to +\infty$. Let W be a random walk with step distribution $1 - \xi$ and $I = \inf_{k \geq 1} W(k)$. Then, $W^\uparrow$ is by definition equal in distribution to W under $\mathbb{P}_0(\cdot \mid I \geq 1)$ (where the subscript refers to the initial state of W). Let moreover B_n be the time at which W advertizes a release for the nth time, so that

$$\mathbb{P}(N = n) = b\mathbb{P}_0(B_n < +\infty, B_{n+1} = +\infty, I \geq 1),$$

with $b = 1/\mathbb{P}_0(I \geq 1)$. Writing the event $\{I \geq 1\}$ as the union between the two events $\{\inf_{1 \leq k \leq B_n} W(k) \geq 1\}$ and $\{\inf_{k > B_n} W(k) \geq 1\}$, the strong Markov property at time B_n entails

$$\mathbb{P}(N = n) = b\mathbb{E}_0\left(p(W(B_n)); B_n < +\infty, \inf_{1 \leq k \leq B_n} W(k) \geq 1\right),$$

with $p(w) = \mathbb{P}_w(N = 0, I \geq 1)$. Coupling W under $\mathbb{P}_w$ with a version of W under $\mathbb{P}_0$ that stays below it, it is easy to see that $p(w)$ is increasing in w and so

$$\mathbb{P}(N = n) \geq bp(0)\mathbb{P}_0\left(B_n < +\infty, \inf_{1 \leq k \leq B_n} W(k) \geq 1\right)$$

$$\geq bp(0)\mathbb{P}_0(B_n < +\infty, I \geq 1).$$

This last lower bound is equal to $p(0)\mathbb{P}_0(B_n < +\infty \mid I \geq 1)$ which by definition is equal to $p(0)\mathbb{P}(N > n)$. Since $p(0) = \mathbb{P}(N = 0)/b$ is > 0 by Lemma 6.10, dividing by $p(0)$ leads to

$$\mathbb{P}(N > n) \leq \frac{b\mathbb{P}(N = n)}{\mathbb{P}(N = 0)}.$$

Since $\mathbb{P}(N = n) \to 0$, this finally proves (18) and hence Proposition 6.6.

6.2.4 *More on the case* $\beta > 1$, $\beta \approx 1$

The simulation results in Section 5 show a rather fuzzy behavior of $\alpha(\beta)$ for β close to 1. Indeed, the curves shown in Figure 5 are smooth for small and large values (say, $\beta < 1/2$ and $\beta > 1.2$) but for β close to one it is difficult to obtain stable numerical results. Our goal here is to discuss potential interesting phenomena arising for $\beta > 1$ close to one.

The shape of the function $\rho \mapsto F(\rho, \beta)$ depicted in Figure 4 is typical for large values of β, say $\beta > 1.2$. In particular, this function is increasing which makes the regression of F against $1/\log(1/(1 - \rho))$, such as in (8), reasonable. However, as β gets closer to one, the shape of this function changes. For instance, Figure 7 shows simulation results for $F(\rho, 1.2)$ which are representative of $F(\rho, \beta)$ for small β, say $1 < \beta < 1.2$. Noticeably, the function $F(\rho, 1.2)$ is not monotone in ρ and so the approximation (8) cannot be valid for every ρ. Rather, we find that $F(\rho, \beta)$ decreases and then increases, and that the regression against $1/\log(1/(1 - \rho))$ is only accurate past the minimum.

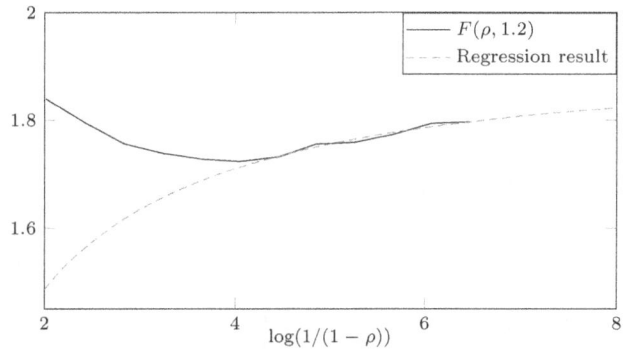

Figure 7: Approximating $\alpha(1.2)$ **for** $R = 2$.

Regressing the curve obtained in Figure 7 past the minimum leads to the approximation $\alpha(1.2) \approx 1.94$, which is still very much in line with our theoretical result $\alpha(1.2) = 2$. However, the point where the minimum of the function $\rho \mapsto F(\rho, \beta)$ is attained, shifts to the right when β gets closer to 1, leaving us with less points against which to regress. In particular, for $\beta < 1.2$ one would need to simulate the system at loads higher than 0.999 to get accurate results.

We suspect that this numerical instability is caused by heavy tails phenomena that seem to appear for $\beta < 2$. More precisely, inspecting the proofs of Proposition 6.3 and Theorem 6.5, one sees that Corollary 6.7 is not strong enough for the proofs of the case $\beta = +\infty$ to go through directly. Indeed, instead of controlling the behavior of $\mathbf{A}(T^*)$ and T^* in distribution, one needs (at least, with the proposed proof strategy) to control their mean behavior. Let us do a small computation: let T_∞^Z be the random variable introduced in Lemma 6.9, which is the weak limit of $T_1 - \tau_1$, and let $B^\uparrow$ be the first time the process $W^\uparrow$ advertizes a release. Then

$$\mathbb{E}(|T_\infty^Z|; T_\infty^Z \leq 0) = \mathbb{E}(B^\uparrow; B^\uparrow < +\infty) = \sum_{k \geq 0} k\mathbb{P}(B^\uparrow = k),$$

and, as before, we have

$$\mathbb{P}(B^\uparrow = k) = \mathbb{E}\left[\psi(W^\uparrow(k)) \prod_{i<k}(1 - \psi(W^\uparrow(i)))\right].$$

Thus for large k, we should have $\mathbb{P}(B^\uparrow = k) \approx k^{-\beta}$ which suggests that $B^\uparrow$, and in particular $|T_\infty^Z|$, has infinite mean for $\beta \leq 2$, although both random variables are almost surely finite for $\beta > 1$. It is possible to use this result to show that the (almost surely finite) weak limits of $\mathbf{A}(T^*)$ and $T^* - \tau_{\max}$ have infinite first moment. This potentially invalidates the back-of-the-envelope computations in Section 4.3, and so more care is needed. For instance, simulation experiments for $\beta = 1.2$ and $R = 2$ suggest that $\mathbb{E}_{a_1}(A_1(T^*))$ grows as $a_1^{0.4}$ as $a_1 \to +\infty$.

7. BROADER IMPLICATIONS

Motivated by the poor heavy traffic delay performance of "cautious" activation rules in queue-based schemes for distributed medium access control, we investigated more aggressive schemes. Our main contribution lies in highlighting a new effect that we called the lingering effect and in studying the performance ramifications of this effect for a special topology. In this section we explain and discuss various directions in which our framework could possibly be extended.

First of all, it would be straightforward to extend our results to the following asymmetric case: instead of having R queues in each group with identically distributed arrival processes across queues, we have two groups of R_1 and R_2 queues and the arrivals into the kth queue of group $g = 1, 2$ have distribution $\xi_{g,k}$. We chose to study a symmetric scenario for technical reasons, since then there is no need to label queues individually. In this setting, the lingering effect will occur whenever, informally speaking, the two dominant queues of at least one of the two groups have the same arrival rate. For instance, the delay will scale like $1/(1-\rho)^2$ with $\rho = \max_k \mathbb{E}(\xi_{1,k}) + \max_k \mathbb{E}(\xi_{2,k})$ if the condition $\mathbb{E}(\xi_{1,1}) = \mathbb{E}(\xi_{1,2}) \geq \max_{g,k} \mathbb{E}(\xi_{g,k})$ is satisfied.

We believe that the insights provided by the complete bipartite constraint graph carry over to more general topologies. Note that for a general topology, our model needs to be refined, since one needs then to specify more precisely how queues become active. One can for instance think of queues going into back-off, and then trying to grab the channel at some rate. We conjecture that whenever the constraint graph is not complete and thus contains an independent set of several nodes, the lingering effect can rear its head provided some algebraic condition between the arrival rates at the various queues is satisfied. It would be very interesting to be able to formulate a precise and formal conjecture reflecting this intuition, and most probably even more challenging to prove it.

8. REFERENCES

[1] N. Bouman, S. Borst, and J. van Leeuwaarden. Achievable delay performance in CSMA networks. In *Proc. Allerton Conf.*, 2011.

[2] P. Chaporkar and S. Sarkar. Stable scheduling policies for maximizing throughput in generalized constrained queueing. In *Proc. Infocom*, 2006.

[3] M. Feuillet, A. Proutiere, and P. Robert. Random capture algorithms: Fluid limits and stability. In *Proc. ITA Workshop*, 2010.

[4] D. Gamarnik and A. Zeevi. Validity of heavy traffic steady-state approximation in generalized Jackson networks. *Ann. Appl. Probab.*, 16(1):56–90, 2006.

[5] L. Georgiadis, M. Neely, and L. Tassiulas. Resource allocation and cross-layer control in wireless networks. *Found. Trends Netw.*, 1:1–144, 2006.

[6] J. Ghaderi, S. Borst, and P. Whiting. Backlog-based random-access in wireless networks: Fluid limits and instability issues. In *Proc. IEEE WiOpt Conf.*, 2012.

[7] L. Jiang, D. Shah, J. Shin, and J. Walrand. Distributed random access algorithm: scheduling and congestion control. *IEEE Trans. Inform. Theory*, 56(12):6182–6207, 2010.

[8] L. Jiang and J. Walrand. A distributed CSMA algorithm for throughput and utility maximization in wireless networks. In *Proc. Allerton Conf.*, 2008.

[9] P. Marbach and A. Eryilmaz. A backlog-based CSMA mechanism to achieve fairness and throughput-optimality in multihop wireless networks. In *Proc. Allerton Conf.*, 2008.

[10] E. Modiano, D. Shah, and G. Zussman. Maximizing throughput in wireless networks via gossiping. In *Proc. ACM SIGMETRICS/Performance Conf.*, 2006.

[11] S. Rajagopalan, D. Shah, and J. Shin. Network adiabatic theorem: An efficient randomized protocol for content resolution. In *Proc. ACM SIGMETRICS/Performance Conf.*, 2009.

[12] D. Shah and J. Shin. Randomized scheduling algorithm for queueing networks. *Ann. Appl. Probab.*, 22(1):128–171, 2012.

[13] D. Shah and D. Wischik. Switched networks with maximum weight policies: Fluid approximation and multiplicative state space collapse. *Ann. Appl. Probab.*, 22(1):70–127, 2012.

[14] G. Sharma, R. Mazumdar, and N. Shroff. On the complexity of scheduling in wireless networks. In *Proc. MobiCom*, 2006.

[15] G. Sharma, N. Shroff, and R. Mazumdar. Joint congestion control and distributed scheduling for throughput guarantees in wireless networks. In *Proc. Infocom*, 2007.

[16] A. Stolyar. Maxweight scheduling in a generalized switch: State space collapse and workload minimization in heavy traffic. *Ann. Appl. Prob.*, 14:1–53, 2004.

[17] L. Tassiulas. Linear complexity algorithms for maximum throughput in radio networks and input queued switches. In *Proc. Infocom*, 1998.

[18] L. Tassiulas and A. Ephremides. Stability properties of constrained queueing systems and scheduling policies for maximum throughput in multihop radio networks. *IEEE Trans. Aut. Contr.*, 37:1936–1948, 1992.

[19] L. Tassiulas and A. Ephremides. Dynamic server allocation to parallel queues with randomly varying connectivity. *IEEE Trans. Inf. Theory*, 39:466–478, 1993.

[20] X. Wu and R. Srikant. Scheduling efficiency of distributed greedy scheduling algorithms in wireless networks. In *Proc. Infocom*, 2006.

Exact Analysis of the M/M/k/setup Class of Markov Chains via Recursive Renewal Reward

Anshul Gandhi
School of Computer Science
Carnegie Mellon University
anshulg@cs.cmu.edu

Sherwin Doroudi
Tepper School of Business
Carnegie Mellon University
sdoroudi@andrew.cmu.edu

Mor Harchol-Balter
School of Computer Science
Carnegie Mellon University
harchol@cs.cmu.edu

Alan Scheller-Wolf
Tepper School of Business
Carnegie Mellon University
awolf@andrew.cmu.edu

ABSTRACT

The M/M/k/setup model, where there is a penalty for turning servers on, is common in data centers, call centers and manufacturing systems. Setup costs take the form of a time delay, and sometimes there is additionally a power penalty, as in the case of data centers. While the M/M/1/setup was exactly analyzed in 1964, no exact analysis exists to date for the M/M/k/setup with $k > 1$.

In this paper we provide the first exact, closed-form analysis for the M/M/k/setup and some of its important variants including systems in which idle servers delay for a period of time before turning off or can be put to sleep. Our analysis is made possible by our development of a new technique, Recursive Renewal Reward (RRR), for solving Markov chains with a repeating structure. RRR uses ideas from renewal reward theory and busy period analysis to obtain closed-form expressions for metrics of interest such as the transform of time in system and the transform of power consumed by the system. The simplicity, intuitiveness, and versatility of RRR makes it useful for analyzing Markov chains far beyond the M/M/k/setup. In general, RRR should be used to reduce the analysis of any 2-dimensional Markov chain which is infinite in at most one dimension and repeating to the problem of solving a system of polynomial equations. In the case where all transitions in the repeating portion of the Markov chain are skip-free and all up/down arrows are unidirectional, the resulting system of equations will yield a closed-form solution.

Categories and Subject Descriptors

C.4 [**Performance of Systems**]: Modeling techniques

Keywords

Queueing Theory; Performance; Resource Allocation

1. INTRODUCTION

Setup times (a.k.a. exceptional first service) are a fundamental component of computer systems and manufacturing systems, and therefore they have always played an important role in queueing theoretic analysis. In manufacturing systems it is very common for a job that finds a server idle to wait for the server to "warm up" before service is initiated. In retail and hospitals, the arrival of customers may necessitate bringing in an additional human server, which requires a setup time for the server to arrive. In computer systems, setup times are once again at the forefront of research, as they are the key issue in dynamic capacity provisioning for data centers.

In data centers, it is desirable to turn idle servers off, or reallocate the servers, to save power. This is because idle servers burn power at 60–70% of the peak rate, so leaving servers on and idle is wasteful [4]. Unfortunately, most companies are hesitant to turn off idle servers because the setup time needed to restart these servers is very costly; the typical setup times for servers is 200 seconds, while a job's service requirement is typically less than 1 second [16, 6]. Not only is the setup time prohibitive, but power is also burned at peak rate during the entire setup period, although the server is still not functional. Thus it is not at all obvious that turning off idle servers is advantageous.

Many ideas have been proposed to minimize the number of times that servers in a data center must undergo setup. One major line of research involves load prediction techniques [16, 21, 5, 12]. In the case where load is unpredictable, research has turned to looking at policies such as delayedoff, which delay turning off an idle server for some fixed amount of time, in anticipation of a new arrival [14, 11, 9]. Another line of research involves reducing setup times by developing low power sleep modes [11, 19].

Surprisingly, for all the importance of setup times, very little is known about their analysis. The M/G/1 with setup times was analyzed in 1964 by Welch [26]. The analysis of an M/M/k system with setup times, which we refer to as **M/M/k/setup**, however, has remained elusive, owing largely to the complexity of the underlying Markov chain. (Fig. 1 shows an M/M/k/setup with exponentially distributed setup times.) In 2010, various analytical approximations for the M/M/k/setup were proposed in [10]. These approximations work well provided that either load is low or the setup time is low. The M/M/∞/setup was also analyzed in [10] and found to exhibit product form. Other than the above, no progress has been made on the M/M/k/setup. Even less is known about the **M/M/k/setup/delayedoff**, where idle servers delay for a finite amount of time before turning off, or the **M/M/k/setup/sleep**, where idle servers can either be turned off (high setup time, zero power) or put to sleep (lower setup time, low power). Section 3 describes these models in greater detail. Section 2 describes related prior work, including existing methods for solving general Markov chains with a repeating structure.

This paper is the first to derive an exact, closed-form solution for the M/M/k/setup, the M/M/k/setup/delayedoff, and the M/M/k/setup/sleep. We obtain the Laplace transform of response time, the z-transform of power consumption, and other important metrics for all of the above models.

Our solution is made possible by our development of a new technique for solving Markov chains with a repeating structure – Recursive Renewal Reward (RRR). RRR is based on using renewal reward theory to obtain the metrics of interest, while utilizing certain recursion theorems about the chain. Unlike matrix-analytic methods [17], RRR does not require finding the "rate" matrix. Another feature of RRR is that it is simple enough to be taught in an elementary stochastic processes course.

In general, RRR should be able to reduce the analysis of any 2-dimensional Markov chain which is finite in one dimension, say the vertical dimension, and infinite (with repeating structure) in the other (horizontal dimension) to the problem of solving a system of polynomial equations. Further, if in the repeating portion all horizontal transitions are skip-free and all vertical transitions are unidirectional, the resulting system of equations will be at most quadratic, yielding a closed-form solution (see Section 10 and Fig. 6 for more details). We thus anticipate that RRR will prove useful to other researchers in analyzing many new problems.

2. PRIOR WORK

The few papers that have looked at the M/M/k/setup are discussed in Section 1. For the M/M/k/setup/delayedoff, only iterative matrix-analytic approaches have been used [9]. No analysis exists for M/M/k/setup/sleep. We now discuss papers that have considered repeating Markov chains and have proposed techniques for solving these. We then comment on how these techniques might or might not apply to the M/M/k/setup.

2.1 Matrix-analytic based approaches

Matrix-analytic methods are a common approach for analyzing Markov chains with repeating structure. Such approaches are typically numerical, generally involving iteration to find the rate matrix, R. These approaches do not, in general, lead to closed forms or to any intuition, but are very useful for evaluating chains under different parameters.

There are cases where it is known that the R matrix can be stated explicitly [17]. This typically involves using a combinatorial interpretation for the R matrix. As described in [17], the class of chains for which the combinatorial view is tractable is narrow. However, in [25], the authors show that the combinatorial interpretation extends to a broader class of chains. Their class does not include the M/M/k/setup, however, which is more complicated because the transition (setup) rates are not independent of the number of jobs in

system. Much research has been done on improving matrix-analytic methods to make the iteration faster. An example is [24], which develops a fast iterative procedure for finding the rate matrix for a broader class of chains than that in [25]. The authors in [24] also provide an explicit solution for the rate matrix in terms of infinite sums.

2.2 Generating function based approaches

Generating functions have also been applied to solve chains with a repeating structure. Like matrix-analytic methods these are not intuitive: Generating function approaches involve guessing the form of the solution and then solving for the coefficients of the guess, often leading to long computations. In theory, they can be used to solve very general chains (see for example [1]). We initially tried applying a generating function approach to the M/M/2/setup and found it to be incredibly complex and without intuition. This led us to seek a simpler and more intuitive approach.

2.3 M/M/k with vacations

Many papers have been written about the M/M/k system with vacations, see for example [28, 27, 23, 18]. While the Markov chain for the M/M/k with vacations looks similar to the M/M/k/setup, the dynamics of the two systems are very different. A server takes a vacation as soon as it is idle and there are no jobs in the queue. By contrast, a setup time is initiated by jobs arriving to the queue. In almost all of the papers involving vacations, the vacation model is severely restricted, allowing only a fixed group of servers to go on vacation at once. This is very different from our system in which any number of servers may be in setup at any time. The model in [18] comes closest to our model, although the authors use generating functions and assume that *all* idle servers are on vacation, rather than one server being in setup for each job in queue, which makes the transitions in their chain independent of the number of jobs.

2.4 Restricted models of M/M/k with setup

There have been a few papers [2, 3, 10] that consider a very restricted version of the M/M/k/setup, wherein at most one server can be in setup at a time. There has also been prior work [20] that considers an M/M/k system wherein a fixed subset of servers can be turned on and off based on load. The underlying Markov chains for all of these restricted systems are analytically tractable and lead to very simple closed-form expressions, since the rate at which servers turn on is always fixed. Our M/M/k/setup system is more general, allowing any number of servers to be in setup. This makes our problem much more challenging.

2.5 How our work differs from all of the above

To the best of our knowledge, we are the first to derive exact closed-form results for the M/M/k/setup problem, with $k > 1$. Our solution was made possible by our new RRR technique. RRR results in exact solutions, does not require any iteration, and does not involve infinite sums. Importantly, RRR is highly intuitive and very easy to apply. Using RRR, we go much further than the M/M/k setup, deriving exact closed-form results for important variants such as the M/M/k/setup/delayedoff and the M/M/k with multiple types of setups, neither of which has been solved analytically.

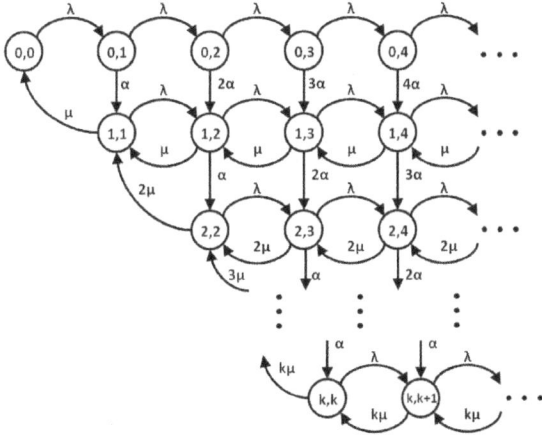

Figure 1: *M/M/k/setup Markov chain. Each state is denoted by the pair (i,j), where i is the number of on servers, and j is the number of jobs in the system. The number of servers in setup is $\min\{j-i, k-i\}$.*

3. MODEL

In our model jobs arrive according to a Poisson process with rate λ and are served at rate $\mu = \frac{1}{E[S]}$, where S denotes the job size and is exponentially distributed. For stability, we assume that $k \cdot \mu > \lambda$, where k is the number of servers in the system.

3.1 M/M/k/setup

In the M/M/k/setup system, each of the k servers is in one of three states: **off**, **on** (being used to serve a job), or **setup**. When a server is on or in setup, it consumes peak power of P_{peak} watts. When a server is off, it consumes zero power. Thus, when servers are not in use, they are immediately turned off to save power. Every arriving job that comes into the system picks an off server, if one exists, and puts it into setup mode; the job then joins the queue. We use I to denote the setup times, with $E[I] = \frac{1}{\alpha}$. Unless stated otherwise, we assume that setup times are exponentially distributed. When a job completes service at a server, say server s_1, and there are no remaining jobs left in the queue, then server s_1 is immediately turned off. However, if the queue is not empty, then server s_1 is not turned off, and the job at the head of the queue is directed to server s_1. Note that if the job at the head of the queue was already waiting on another server, say server s_2, in setup mode, the job at the head of the queue is still directed to server s_1. At this point, if there is a job in the queue that did not setup an off server on arrival (because there were no off servers), then server s_2 continues to be in setup for this job. If no such job exists in the queue, then server s_2 is turned off.

The Markov chain for the M/M/k/setup system is shown in Fig. 1. Each state is denoted by the pair (i,j), where i is the number of on servers, and j is the number of jobs in the system. Thus, the number of servers in setup is $\min\{j-i, k-i\}$. Note that the Markov chain is infinite in one dimension.

3.2 M/M/k/setup/delayedoff

The M/M/k/setup/delayedoff system is the same as the M/M/k/setup system, except that idle servers are not immediately turned off. Specifically, when a job completes service at a server, say server s_1, and there are no remaining jobs in the queue, s_1 remains waiting in the idle state

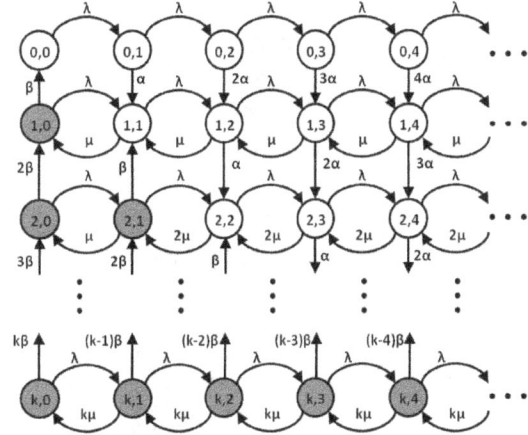

Figure 2: *M/M/k/setup/delayedoff Markov chain. Each state is denoted by the pair (i,j), where i is the number of on or idle servers, and j is the number of jobs in the system. If $i < j$, then the number of servers in setup is $\min\{j-i, k-i\}$, and there are no idle servers. If $i > j$ (gray shaded states), the number of idle servers is $(i-j)$, and there are no servers in setup. If $i = j$, no servers are idle or in setup.*

for an exponentially distributed amount of time with mean $t_{wait} = \frac{1}{\beta}$. If a new job arrives while server s_1 is waiting, the job is immediately directed to s_1, which is already on. However, if no jobs arrive during server s_1's waiting period, then server s_1 is turned off. Intuitively, a higher t_{wait} results in lower response time, since servers are on longer, but may also increase power usage, since idle servers consume significant power.

The Markov chain for the M/M/k/setup/delayedoff system is shown in Fig. 2. The chain is the same as that for M/M/k/setup, except for the new gray shaded states which represent states with idle servers. As before, each state is denoted by the pair (i,j), where i is the number of on or idle servers, and j is the number of jobs in the system. For the M/M/k/setup/delayedoff system, each server can be in one of four states: off, on (busy), idle, or setup. If $i < j$, then the number of servers in setup is $\min\{j-i, k-i\}$, and there are no idle servers. If $i > j$ (gray shaded states), the number of idle servers is $(i-j)$, and there are no servers in setup. If $i = j$, no servers are idle or in setup.

3.3 M/M/k/setup/sleep

The M/M/k/setup/sleep is motivated by servers with sleep modes [11, 19], which allow an idle server to either be turned off or put to sleep. When a server is turned off, it consumes zero power. However, turning on an off server requires an exponentially distributed setup time, with rate α. By contrast, when a server is sleeping, it consumes some non-zero power, P_{sleep} watts, which is usually much smaller than the idle power, P_{idle} watts [11, 19]. When a sleeping server is turned on, it requires an exponentially distributed setup time, with rate $\omega > \alpha$. Thus, there is a tradeoff between turning off an idle server vs putting it to sleep.

One simple idea that leverages sleep states is to designate some subset of the k servers, say the first s servers, to "sleep" when idle, whereas the remaining $(k-s)$ servers are turned off when idle. An interesting question is what is a good value of s. To answer this question we introduce the M/M/k/setup/sleep model, which is the same as the

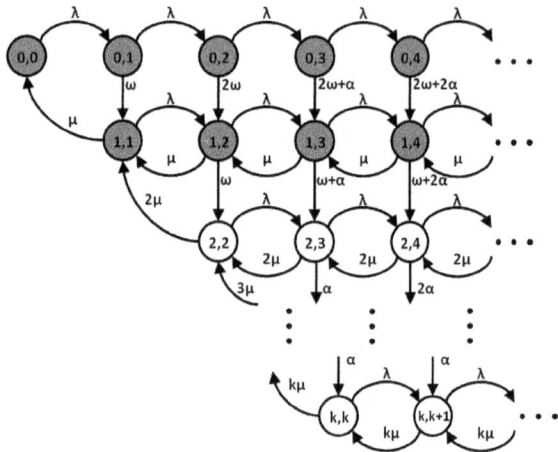

Figure 3: *M/M/k/setup/sleep Markov chain. Each state is denoted by the pair (i, j), where i is the number of on servers, and j is the number of jobs in the system. The number of servers in fast setup is s, which in this case is $s = 2$. The number of servers in setup is $\min\{j - i, k - i\}$. If $i < s$ (gray shaded states), the first $(s - i)$ servers setting up have a fast setup rate, ω, while the other servers in setup have a slow setup rate, α.*

M/M/k/setup, except that $s \leq k$ servers have a fast setup rate of ω and $(k - s)$ servers have a slow setup rate of α (see Fig. 3). As we will see later, the tradeoff between mean response time and mean power is highly sensitive to the choice of s (see Figs. 7(c) and 7(d)).

For ease of analysis, we make the following assumptions about the M/M/k/setup/sleep model: (i) In any group of servers in setup, we assume that the servers that have a fast setup rate (ω) complete setting up first. Thus, if we are in state (i, j) with $i < s$ (gray shaded states in Fig. 3), the first $(s - i)$ servers in setup will have a fast setup rate. Note that the i servers already on in state (i, j), with $i \leq s$, are those that had a fast setup rate. Thus, when we have $i \leq s$ servers busy, and a server is no longer in use, we put the server to sleep (as opposed to turning it off). (ii) If we have $i > s$ servers busy, and a server is no longer in use, we turn the server off (as opposed to putting it to sleep). This assumption allows us to save a lot of power when load goes down since off servers consume zero power. The above two assumptions are primarily for tractability of the M/M/k/setup/sleep Markov chain. In practice, ω is significantly higher than α. In this regime we simulated an M/M/k/setup/sleep system with and without the above two assumptions and found the results to be qualitatively unchanged.

4. THE RECURSIVE RENEWAL REWARD TECHNIQUE

In this section we provide a high-level description of our new Recursive Renewal Reward (RRR) technique, which yields exact, closed-form solutions for a range of Markov chains, including the M/M/k/setup (see Sections 5, 6 and 7), the M/M/k/setup/delayedoff (see Section 8) and the M/M/k/setup/sleep (see Section 9).

The RRR technique works by deriving the *expected "reward" earned per unit time in a Markov chain*, where the

reward could be any quantity of interest. In the context of our M/M/k/setup problem, the reward earned at time t, $R(t)$, could be the number of jobs in system at time t, the square of the number of jobs in system, the current power usage, the number of servers that are on, or any other reward that can be expressed as a function of the state of the Markov chain.

To analyze the average rate of earning reward, we designate a *renewal state*, say $(0, 0)$,[1] which we call the *home state*, and then consider a *renewal cycle* to be the process of moving from the home state back to the home state. By renewal-reward theory, the average rate of earning reward is the same as the mean reward earned over a renewal cycle, which we denote by $\mathcal{R}$, divided by the mean length of the renewal cycle, denoted by $\mathcal{T}$.

$$\text{Average rate of earning} = \frac{\mathcal{R}}{\mathcal{T}} = \frac{E\left[\int_{\text{cycle}} R(t) dt\right]}{E\left[\int_{\text{cycle}} 1 dt\right]}$$

For example, if the goal is to find the mean number of jobs, $E[N]$, for our chain, we simply define $R(t)$ to be the number of jobs at time t, which can be obtained from the state of the Markov chain at time t.

It turns out that the quantities $\mathcal{T}$ and $\mathcal{R}$ are very easy to compute! Consider a Markov chain, such as that in Fig. 4 or Fig. 5. The *repeating portion* of the chain is shown in gray. There are a finite number of *border states* which sit at the edge of the repeating chain and are colored black. We will see that computing $\mathcal{T}$ and $\mathcal{R}$ basically reduces to writing one equation for each border state[2]. For the case of $\mathcal{T}$, we will need the mean time to move one step left from each border state. For the case of $\mathcal{R}$, we will need the mean reward earned when moving one step left from each border state. Computing these border state quantities is made very easy via some neat recursion theorems. We demonstrate this process in the examples below. There are a few details which we will defer until after these examples. For instance, in general, it is necessary to also add equations for the non-repeating portion of the Markov chain. See Sections 7 and 10 for more details on the RRR technique.

5. M/M/1/SETUP

In this section we illustrate the RRR technique by applying it to the simple M/M/1/setup system, whose Markov chain is shown in Fig. 4. Here, the state of the system is represented as (i, j), where $i \in \{0, 1\}$ is the number of servers on and $0 \leq j < \infty$ is the number of jobs in the system. In general, i represents the *depth* (or row number) of the state, and j represents the *level* (or column number) of the state. We start by deriving $E[N]$, the mean number of jobs, and then move to more complex metrics. We choose the renewal state to be $(0, 0)$ and we define the reward earned at time t, $R(t)$, to be $N(t)$, the number of jobs in the system at time t. As explained in Section 4, all we need is $\mathcal{T}$ and $\mathcal{R}$.

---

[1]In principle any state can be chosen as the renewal state, but some states allow for an easier (or shorter) analysis.
[2]Several techniques in the literature such as matrix-analytic methods [17] and stochastic complementation [22] also deal with border states, although none of them involve renewal-reward theory.

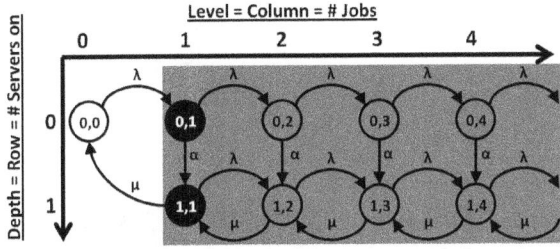

Figure 4: *M/M/1/setup Markov chain with the repeating portion highlighted in gray and the border states shaded black.*

5.1 Deriving $\mathcal{T}$ via $\mathrm{T}_{0,1}^{L}$ and $\mathrm{T}_{1,1}^{L}$

$\mathcal{T}$ is the mean time to get from our home state $(0,0)$ back to $(0,0)$. This can be viewed as $\frac{1}{\lambda}$, the mean time until we leave $(0,0)$ (which takes us to $(0,1)$) plus the mean time to get home from $(0,1)$. We make the further observation that the mean time to get home from $(0,1)$ is equal to $T_{0,1}^{L}$ (using notation from Table 1), the mean time to move left one level from $(0,1)$ (since moving left can only put us in $(0,0)$). We thus have:

$$\mathcal{T} = \frac{1}{\lambda} + T_{0,1}^{L} \tag{1}$$

We now need an equation for $T_{0,1}^{L}$ for the border state $(0,1)$, which will require looking at the other border state, $(1,1)$, as well. Starting with border state $(1,1)$, it is clear that $T_{1,1}^{L}$ is simply the mean length of an M/M/1 busy period, B_1. Thus, we have:

$$T_{1,1}^{L} = B_1 = \frac{1}{\mu - \lambda} \tag{2}$$

$T_{0,1}^{L}$ involves waiting in state $(0,1)$ for expected time $\frac{1}{\alpha+\lambda}$, before conditioning on where we transition to next. If we go to state $(1,1)$ we need an additional $T_{1,1}^{L}$. However if we go to state $(0,2)$ we need to add on the time to move one step left from $(0,2)$ (which by Fig. 4 takes us to $(1,1)$) and then an additional $T_{1,1}^{L}$. That is:

$$T_{0,1}^{L} = \frac{1}{\lambda+\alpha} + \frac{\alpha}{\lambda+\alpha} \cdot T_{1,1}^{L} + \frac{\lambda}{\lambda+\alpha}\left(T_{0,2}^{L} + T_{1,1}^{L}\right) \tag{3}$$

It is now time to invoke one of our recursion theorems, which holds for any M/M/k/setup chain:

THEOREM 1 (RECURSION THEOREM FOR MEAN TIME)
For the M/M/k/setup, the mean time to move one step left from state (i,j), $T_{i,j}^{L}$, is the same for all $j \geq k$.

Thm. 1 follows from the fact that the repeating portion of the Markov chain is identical for all states in a given row. The full proof of Thm. 1 (along with the proofs of all other theorems) is presented in Appendix A.

Using Thm. 1, we replace $T_{0,2}^{L}$ in Eq. (3) with $T_{0,1}^{L}$ to get:

$$T_{0,1}^{L} = \frac{1}{\lambda+\alpha} + \frac{\alpha}{\lambda+\alpha} \cdot T_{1,1}^{L} + \frac{\lambda}{\lambda+\alpha}\left(T_{0,1}^{L} + T_{1,1}^{L}\right) \tag{4}$$

Finally, noting that $T_{1,1}^{L} = B_1$ from Eq. (2), we have that:

$$T_{0,1}^{L} = \frac{1}{\lambda+\alpha} + \frac{\alpha}{\lambda+\alpha} \cdot B_1 + \frac{\lambda}{\lambda+\alpha}\left(T_{0,1}^{L} + B_1\right)$$

$$\implies T_{0j}^{L} = T_{0,1}^{L} = \frac{1 + (\lambda+\alpha)B_1}{\alpha} \tag{5}$$

Variable	Description
$\mathcal{T}$	Mean length of the renewal cycle
$\mathcal{R}$	Mean reward earned during a renewal cycle
$T_{i,j}^{L}$	Mean time until we first move one level left of (i,j), starting from (i,j)
$R_{i,j}^{L}$	Mean reward earned until we first move one level left of (i,j), starting from (i,j)
$p_{i\to d}^{L}$	Probability that after we first move one level left from state (i,j), we are at depth d
B_k	Mean length of an $M/M/k$ busy period

Table 1: *Variables used in our analysis of $E[N]$.*

Substituting $T_{0,1}^{L}$ from above into Eq. (1) gives us $\mathcal{T}$:

$$\mathcal{T} = \frac{\mu(\lambda+\alpha)}{\lambda\alpha(\mu-\lambda)} \tag{6}$$

5.2 Deriving $\mathcal{R}$ via $\mathrm{R}_{0,1}^{L}$ and $\mathrm{R}_{1,1}^{L}$

$\mathcal{R}$ denotes the reward earned in moving from $(0,0)$ back to $(0,0)$. Observing that we earn 0 reward in state $(0,0)$ (because there are no jobs in the system in that state), and observing that from state $(0,0)$ we can only next move to $(0,1)$, we have (using notation from Table 1):

$$\mathcal{R} = R_{0,1}^{L} \tag{7}$$

It now remains to compute the reward earned in moving one step left from $(0,1)$, which will require looking at the other border state, $(1,1)$, as well.

To do this, we invoke another recursion theorem, which again holds for any M/M/k/setup system:

THEOREM 2 (RECURSION THEOREM FOR MEAN REWARD)
For the M/M/k/setup, the mean reward earned in moving one step left from state $(i,j+1)$, $R_{i,j+1}^{L}$, satisfies $R_{i,j+1}^{L} = R_{i,j}^{L} + T_{i,j}^{L}$ for all $j \geq k$, where the reward tracks the number of jobs in the system.

Applying Thm. 2 to the Markov chain shown in Fig. 4, we have:

$$R_{1,1}^{L} = \frac{1}{\lambda+\mu} \cdot 1 + \frac{\mu}{\lambda+\mu} \cdot 0 + \frac{\lambda}{\lambda+\mu}\left(R_{1,2}^{L} + R_{1,1}^{L}\right) \tag{8}$$

$$= \frac{1}{\lambda+\mu} + \frac{\lambda}{\lambda+\mu}\left((R_{1,1}^{L} + T_{1,1}^{L}) + R_{1,1}^{L}\right)$$

$$= \frac{1}{\lambda+\mu} + \frac{\lambda}{\lambda+\mu}\left((R_{1,1}^{L} + B_1) + R_{1,1}^{L}\right)$$

(from Eq. (2))

$$\implies R_{1,1}^{L} = \frac{1 + \lambda B_1}{\mu - \lambda} \tag{9}$$

157

Variable	Description
$\dot{\mathcal{R}}$	Mean reward earned (for z-transform) during a renewal cycle
$\dot{\mathcal{E}}$	Mean reward earned (for transform of power) during a renewal cycle
$\dot{R}_{i,j}^{L}$	Mean reward earned (for z-transform) until we first move one level left of (i,j), starting from (i,j)
$\dot{E}_{i,j}^{L}$	Mean reward earned (for z-transform of power) until we first move one level left of (i,j), starting from (i,j)

Table 2: *Variables used in our transform analyses.*

Similarly, for border state $(0,1)$, we have:

$$R_{0,1}^{L} = \frac{1}{\lambda+\alpha} \cdot 1 + \frac{\alpha}{\lambda+\alpha} \cdot R_{1,1}^{L} + \frac{\lambda}{\lambda+\alpha} \left(R_{0,2}^{L} + R_{1,1}^{L} \right)$$

$$= \frac{1}{\lambda+\alpha} + \frac{\alpha}{\lambda+\alpha} \cdot R_{1,1}^{L}$$

$$+ \frac{\lambda}{\lambda+\alpha} \left(\left(R_{0,1}^{L} + T_{0,1}^{L} \right) + R_{1,1}^{L} \right) \quad \text{(from Thm. 2)}$$

$$\implies R_{0,1}^{L} = \frac{1 + \lambda T_{0,1}^{L} + (\lambda+\alpha) R_{1,1}^{L}}{\alpha}. \tag{10}$$

Substituting $R_{0,1}^{L}$ from above into Eq. (7) gives us $\mathcal{R}$:

$$\mathcal{R} = \frac{\mu(\lambda+\alpha)(\mu-\lambda+\alpha)}{\alpha^2(\mu-\lambda)^2} \tag{11}$$

5.3 Deriving E[N]

Since $E[N] = \frac{\mathcal{R}}{\mathcal{T}}$, combining Eq. (6) and Eq. (11), we get:

$$E[N] = \frac{\mathcal{R}}{\mathcal{T}} = \frac{\lambda}{\alpha} + \frac{\lambda}{\mu-\lambda} \tag{12}$$

The second term in the right hand side of Eq. (12) can be identified [15] as the mean number of jobs in an M/M/1 system (without setup). Thus, Eq. (12) is consistent with the known decomposition property for the M/M/1/setup system [26].

5.4 Deriving $\widehat{N}$(z) and $\widetilde{T}$(s)

Deriving the z-transform of the number of jobs, $\widehat{N}(z) = E[z^N]$, is just as easy as deriving $E[N]$. The only difference is that our reward function is now $R(t) = z^{N(t)}$, where $N(t)$ is again the number of jobs in the system at time t. Thus

$$\widehat{N}(z) = E[z^N] = \frac{\dot{\mathcal{R}}}{\mathcal{T}},$$

where $\dot{\mathcal{R}} = E\left[\int_{\text{cycle}} z^{N(t)} dt \right]$ and $\mathcal{T}$ is the same as before.

We will again invoke a recursion theorem which applies to any M/M/k/setup (using notation from Table 2):

THEOREM 3 (RECURSION THEOREM FOR TRANSFORM OF REWARD) *For the M/M/k/setup, $\dot{R}_{i,j+1}^{L} = z \cdot \dot{R}_{i,j}^{L}$, for all $j \geq k$, where $\dot{R}$ tracks the z-transform of the number of jobs in the system.*

Let us now express $\dot{\mathcal{R}}$ by conditioning on the first step from $(0,0)$:

$$\dot{\mathcal{R}} = \frac{1}{\lambda} + \dot{R}_{0,1}^{L} \tag{13}$$

We again need one equation per border state:

$$\dot{R}_{1,1}^{L} = \frac{1}{\lambda+\mu} \cdot z + \frac{\lambda}{\lambda+\mu} \left(z \cdot \dot{R}_{1,1}^{L} + \dot{R}_{1,1}^{L} \right)$$

$$\dot{R}_{0,1}^{L} = \frac{1}{\lambda+\alpha} \cdot z + \frac{\alpha}{\lambda+\alpha} \cdot \dot{R}_{1,1}^{L} + \frac{\lambda}{\lambda+\alpha} \left(z \cdot \dot{R}_{0,1}^{L} + \dot{R}_{1,1}^{L} \right)$$

Solving the above system and substituting $\dot{R}_{0,1}^{L}$ into Eq. (13) allows us to express $\dot{\mathcal{R}}$ in closed form. This gives us $\widehat{N}(z)$, after some algebra, as follows:

$$\widehat{N}(z) = E[z^N] = \frac{\dot{\mathcal{R}}}{\mathcal{T}} = \frac{\alpha(\mu-\lambda)}{(\mu-\lambda z)(\alpha+\lambda-\lambda z)} \tag{14}$$

To get the Laplace transform of response time, $\widetilde{T}(s)$, we use the distributional Little's Law [13] (since M/M/1/setup is a First-In-First-Out system):

$$\widetilde{T}(s) = \widehat{N}\left(1 - \frac{s}{\lambda}\right) = \frac{\alpha(\mu-\lambda)}{(s+\alpha)(\mu+s-\lambda)} \tag{15}$$

5.5 Deriving $\widehat{P}$(z)

We now derive $\widehat{P}(z)$, the z-transform of the power consumed for the M/M/1/setup. The server consumes zero power when it is off, but consumes peak power, P_{peak} watts, when it is on or in setup. This time, the reward is simply the transform of the energy consumed over the renewal cycle, $\dot{\mathcal{E}} = E\left[\int_{\text{cycle}} z^{P(t)} dt \right]$, where $P(t)$ is the power consumed at time t. We begin with the recursive theorem for $\dot{E}_{i,j}^{L}$, just like we had Thm. 3 for $\dot{R}_{i,j}^{L}$.

THEOREM 4 (RECURSION THEOREM FOR TRANSFORM OF POWER) *For the M/M/k/setup, $\dot{E}_{i,j+1}^{L} = \dot{E}_{i,j}^{L} = T_{i,j}^{L} \cdot z^{k \cdot P_{peak}}$, for all $j \geq k$.*

Thm. 4 gives us $\dot{E}_{i,j}^{L}$ in closed form, in terms of $T_{i,j}^{L}$. Following the usual renewal-reward approach, we get:

$$\widehat{P}(z) = E[z^P] = \frac{\dot{\mathcal{E}}}{\mathcal{T}} = \frac{\alpha(\mu-\lambda) + \lambda(\mu+\alpha)z^{P_{peak}}}{\mu(\lambda+\alpha)} \tag{16}$$

6. M/M/2/SETUP

The M/M/2/setup chain shown in Fig. 5 is analyzed similarly to the M/M/1/setup, except that there are now three border states, $(0,2)$, $(1,2)$, and $(2,2)$. The only complication is that when moving one level left from a given state, the resulting row is non-deterministic. For example, when moving left from $(1,3)$ in Fig. 5, we may end up in row 1 at $(1,2)$ or row 2 at $(2,2)$. We use $p_{i \to d}^{L}$ to denote the probability that once we move one level left from (i,j), we will be at depth d.[2] The following theorem proves that $p_{i \to d}^{L}$ is independent of j for all states (i,j) in the repeating portion.

THEOREM 5 (RECURSION THEOREM FOR PROBABILITY) *For the M/M/k/setup, for each $0 \leq d \leq k$ and for each $0 \leq i \leq k$, $p_{i \to d}^{L}$ is the same for all $j \geq k$.*

Thus, it suffices to compute $p_{i \to d}^{L}$ for the border states. These probabilities are used in Section 6.2.

6.1 Deriving $p_{i \to d}^{L}$

Solving for the $p_{i \to d}^{L}$ is easiest "bottom-up" (starting from the greatest depth, i). For $i = 2$, we have $p_{2 \to 2}^{L} = 1$ for all $j > 2$, since we stay at depth 2 after moving left. For $i = 1$

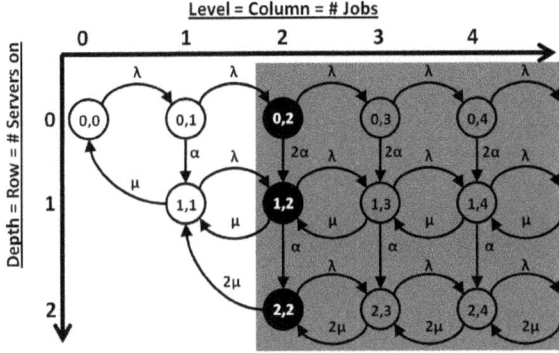

Figure 5: *M/M/2/setup Markov chain with the repeating portion highlighted in gray and the border states shaded black.*

and $i = 0$, we follow the same approach of conditioning on the first step and using recursion theorems:

$$p_{1 \to 1}^L = \frac{\mu}{\lambda + \mu + \alpha} + \frac{\lambda}{\lambda + \mu + \alpha} \left(p_{1 \to 1}^L \right)^2 \quad (17)$$

$$p_{0 \to 1}^L = \frac{2\alpha}{\lambda + 2\alpha} \left(p_{1 \to 1}^L \right) + \frac{\lambda}{\lambda + 2\alpha} \left(p_{0 \to 1}^L \right) \left(p_{1 \to 1}^L \right) \quad (18)$$

Eqs. (17) and (18) can now be solved in closed form since they are of degree at most 2. Note that $p_{1 \to 2}^L = 1 - p_{1 \to 1}^L$ and $p_{0 \to 2}^L = 1 - p_{0 \to 1}^L$.

6.2 Deriving $\widehat{N}(z)$ via $\dot{R}_{0,2}^L$, $\dot{R}_{1,2}^L$, and $\dot{R}_{2,2}$

To derive $\widehat{N}(z) = E[z^N]$, we again need to find $\dot{\mathcal{R}}$ and $\mathcal{T}$, where $\dot{\mathcal{R}} = E\left[\int_{\text{cycle}} z^{N(t)} dt\right]$, and $\mathcal{T} = E\left[\int_{\text{cycle}} 1 dt\right] = \dot{\mathcal{R}}\Big|_{z=1}$. Using $(1,1)$ as our renewal state and the same arguments as in Section 5.4, we have:

$$\dot{\mathcal{R}} = \frac{z}{\lambda + \mu} + \frac{\mu}{\lambda + \mu} \left(\frac{1}{\lambda} + \frac{z}{\lambda + \alpha} + \frac{\lambda}{\lambda + \alpha} \cdot \dot{R}_{0,2}^L \right)$$

$$+ \frac{\lambda}{\lambda + \mu} \cdot \dot{R}_{1,2}^L \quad (19)$$

It now remains to compute the reward equations for the border states: $\dot{R}_{0,2}^L$, $\dot{R}_{1,2}^L$, and $\dot{R}_{2,2}^L$.

$$\dot{R}_{2,2}^L = \frac{z^2}{\lambda + 2\mu} + \frac{\lambda}{\lambda + 2\mu} \left(z \cdot \dot{R}_{2,2}^L + \dot{R}_{2,2}^L \right) \quad (20)$$

$$\dot{R}_{1,2}^L = \frac{z^2}{\lambda + \mu + \alpha} + \frac{\alpha}{\lambda + \mu + \alpha} \cdot \dot{R}_{2,2}^L$$

$$+ \frac{\lambda}{\lambda + \mu + \alpha} \left(z \cdot \dot{R}_{1,2}^L + \left(p_{1 \to 1}^L \right) \dot{R}_{1,2}^L + \left(1 - p_{1 \to 1}^L \right) \dot{R}_{2,2}^L \right) \quad (21)$$

$$\dot{R}_{0,2}^L = \frac{z^2}{\lambda + 2\alpha} + \frac{2\alpha}{\lambda + 2\alpha} \cdot \dot{R}_{1,2}^L$$

$$+ \frac{\lambda}{\lambda + 2\alpha} \left(z \cdot \dot{R}_{0,2}^L + \left(p_{0 \to 1}^L \right) \dot{R}_{1,2}^L + \left(1 - p_{0 \to 1}^L \right) \dot{R}_{2,2}^L \right) \quad (22)$$

Solving the above system of linear equations and substituting $\dot{R}_{0,2}^L$ and $\dot{R}_{1,2}^L$ into Eq. (19) allows us to solve for $\widehat{N}(z)$

in closed form as follows:

$$\widehat{N}(z) = E[z^N] = \frac{\dot{\mathcal{R}}}{\mathcal{T}} = \frac{\dot{\mathcal{R}}}{\dot{\mathcal{R}}\big|_{z=1}}$$

$$= \frac{\lambda(\lambda + \alpha)(z + \lambda \dot{R}_{1,2}^L) + \mu(\alpha + \lambda(1 + z + \lambda \dot{R}_{0,2}^L))}{\lambda(\lambda + \alpha)(1 + \lambda T_{1j}^L) + \mu(\alpha + \lambda(2 + \lambda T_{0j}^L))} \quad (23)$$

6.3 Deriving $\widetilde{T}(s)$

For the M/M/1/setup system, we were able to derive $\widetilde{T}(s)$ directly from $\widehat{N}(z)$ via the distributional Little's Law, since the M/M/1/setup is a FIFO system. Unfortunately, the M/M/2/setup system is not FIFO, since overtaking can occur. However, we can still apply the distributional Little's Law to the queue of the M/M/2/setup since the queue *is* FIFO. The analysis of $\widehat{N_Q}(z)$ is very similar to that of $\widehat{N}(z)$ and is thus omitted:

$$\widehat{N_Q}(z) = \frac{\lambda(\lambda + \alpha)(1 + \lambda \dot{R}_{1,2}^L) + \mu(\alpha + \lambda(1 + z + \lambda \dot{R}_{0,2}^L))}{\lambda(\lambda + \alpha)(1 + \lambda T_{1j}^L) + \mu(\alpha + \lambda(2 + \lambda T_{0j}^L))} \quad (24)$$

We now apply the distributional Little's Law to get $\widetilde{T_Q}(s)$ from $\widehat{N_Q}(z)$. Finally, since $T = T_Q + S$, where $S \sim Exp(\mu)$ is the job size distribution, we have:

$$\widetilde{T}(s) = \widetilde{T_Q}(s) \cdot \frac{\mu}{s + \mu} = \widehat{N_Q}\left(1 - \frac{s}{\lambda}\right) \cdot \frac{\mu}{s + \mu}$$

$$= \frac{\mu\left(\lambda(\lambda + \alpha)(1 + \lambda \dot{R}_{1,2}^L) + \mu(\alpha - s + \lambda(2 + \lambda \dot{R}_{0,2}^L))\right)}{(s + \mu)\left(\lambda(\lambda + \alpha)(1 + \lambda T_{1j}^L) + \mu(\alpha + \lambda(2 + \lambda T_{0j}^L))\right)} \quad (25)$$

6.4 Deriving $\widehat{P}(z)$

The derivation of $\widehat{P}(z)$ is similar to that of $\widehat{N}(z)$ in Section 6.2, and is thus omitted.

$$\widehat{P}(z) = \frac{\mu(\alpha + \lambda) + \lambda(\lambda + \mu + \alpha)z^{P_{peak}}}{\mu(\alpha + \lambda) + \lambda(\lambda + \mu + \alpha) + \lambda^2(\mu T_{0j}^L + (\lambda + \alpha)T_{1j}^L)}$$

$$+ \frac{\lambda^2(\mu T_{0j}^L + (\lambda + \alpha)T_{1j}^L)z^{2P_{peak}}}{\mu(\alpha + \lambda) + \lambda(\lambda + \mu + \alpha) + \lambda^2(\mu T_{0j}^L + (\lambda + \alpha)T_{1j}^L)} \quad (26)$$

7. M/M/K/SETUP

The M/M/k/setup chain shown in Fig. 1 is analyzed similarly to M/M/2/setup. The border states for M/M/k/setup are (i, k), with $0 \le i \le k$. In the M/M/k/setup, the non-repeating portion consists of $O(k^2)$ states. For $k = 1$ and $k = 2$, we did not have to explicitly write reward equations for the non-repeating states; these were implicitly folded into other equations (see, for example, the term in parentheses in Eq. (19)). However, for arbitrarily large k, it is necessary to write reward equations for the states in the non-repeating portion. We use $R_{i,j}^H$ to denote the reward earned until we reach the home state, starting from state (i, j) in the non-repeating portion. The $R_{i,j}^H$ equations will be discussed in Section 7.3.

We illustrate the RRR technique for M/M/k/setup by deriving $\widehat{N_Q}(z)$, from which we can obtain $\widetilde{T}(s)$. For a detailed demonstration of this technique for the case of $k = 3$, see [7].

One might think that analyzing the M/M/k/setup will require solving a kth degree equation. This turns out to be false. Analyzing the M/M/k/setup via RRR only requires solving equations which are, at worst, quadratic.

We choose $(k-1, k-1)$ to be the renewal state. Using RRR, $\dot{\mathcal{R}}$ can be expressed as:

$$\dot{\mathcal{R}} = \frac{1 + (k-1)\mu \dot{R}^H_{k-2,k-2} + \lambda \dot{R}^L_{k-1,k}}{\lambda + (k-1)\mu} \quad (27)$$

We now derive the necessary $\mathbf{p^L_{i \to d}}$, $\dot{R}^L_{i,k}$, and $\dot{R}^H_{i,j}$ for computing $\dot{\mathcal{R}}$.

7.1 System of equations for $\mathbf{p^L_{i \to d}}$

The system of equations for $p^L_{i \to d}$ is as follows:[2]

$$p^L_{i \to i} = \frac{\lambda(p^L_{i \to i})^2 + i\mu}{\lambda + i\mu + (k-i)\alpha}, \quad (i < k) \quad (28)$$

$$p^L_{i \to d} = \frac{\lambda\left(\sum_{\ell=i}^{d}\left\{(p^L_{i \to \ell})(p^L_{\ell \to d})\right\}\right) + (k-i)\alpha(p^L_{i+1 \to d})}{\lambda + i\mu + (k-i)\alpha},$$
$$(i < d < k) \quad (29)$$

$$p^L_{i \to k} = 1 - \sum_{\ell=i}^{k-1} p^L_{i \to \ell}, \quad (i \leq k) \quad (30)$$

The summation in Eqs. (29) above denotes the possible intermediate depths ℓ through which we can move from initial depth i to final depth d. The above system of equations involves linear and quadratic equations (including products of two unlike variables), and can be solved *symbolically* to find $p^L_{i \to d}$ in closed form (see Appendix B).

7.2 Deriving $\dot{R}^L_{i,k}$ for the repeating portion

The system of equations for $\dot{R}^L_{i,k}$ is as follows:

$$\dot{R}^L_{0,k} = \frac{z^k + \lambda\left(z\dot{R}^L_{0,k} + \sum_{\ell=1}^{k}\left\{(p^L_{0 \to \ell})(\dot{R}^L_{\ell,k})\right\}\right) + k\alpha\dot{R}^L_{1,k}}{\lambda + k\alpha} \quad (31)$$

$$\dot{R}^L_{i,k} = \frac{z^{k-i} + \lambda\left(z\dot{R}^L_{i,k} + \sum_{\ell=i}^{k}\left\{(p^L_{i \to \ell})(\dot{R}^L_{\ell,k})\right\}\right)}{\lambda + i\mu + (k-i)\alpha}$$
$$+ \frac{(k-i)\alpha\dot{R}^L_{i+1,k}}{\lambda + i\mu + (k-i)\alpha}, \quad (0 < i < k) \quad (32)$$

$$\dot{R}^L_{k,k} = \frac{1 + \lambda(z\dot{R}^L_{k,k} + \dot{R}^L_{k,k})}{\lambda + k\mu} \quad (33)$$

In the above, we have used the fact that $\dot{R}^L_{i,k+1} = z\dot{R}^L_{i,k}$ from Thm. 3. The above system of linear equations can be easily solved to find $\dot{R}^L_{i,k}$ in closed form (see Appendix B).

7.3 Deriving $\dot{R}^H_{i,j}$ for the non-repeating portion

The system of equations for $\dot{R}^H_{i,j}$ is as follows:

$$\dot{R}^H_{0,j} = \frac{z^j + \lambda\dot{R}^H_{0,j+1} + j\alpha\dot{R}^H_{1,j}}{\lambda + j\alpha}, \quad (j < k-1) \quad (34)$$

$$\dot{R}^H_{i,j} = \frac{z^{j-i} + \lambda\dot{R}^H_{i,j+1} + i\mu\dot{R}^H_{i,j-1} + (j-i)\alpha\dot{R}^H_{i+1,j}}{\lambda + i\mu + (j-i)\alpha},$$
$$(0 < i < j < k-1) \quad (35)$$

$$\dot{R}^H_{i,i} = \frac{1 + \lambda\dot{R}^H_{i,i+1} + i\mu\dot{R}^H_{i-1,i-1}}{\lambda + i\mu}, \quad (0 < i < k-1) \quad (36)$$

$$\dot{R}^H_{i,k-1} = \frac{z^{k-1-i} + \lambda\left(\dot{R}^L_{i,k} + \sum_{\ell=i}^{k}\left\{(p^L_{i \to \ell})(\dot{R}^H_{\ell,k-1})\right\}\right)}{\lambda + i\mu + (k-1-i)\alpha}$$
$$+ \frac{i\mu\dot{R}^H_{i,k-2} + (k-1-i)\alpha\dot{R}^H_{i+1,k-1}}{\lambda + i\mu + (k-1-i)\alpha}, \quad (i < k-1) \quad (37)$$

$$\dot{R}^H_{k-1,k-1} = 0 \quad (38)$$

Eqs. (34), (35), and (36), are simply based on the rate transitions in the non-repeating portion of the Markov chain. Eqs. (37) describe the rewards earned when starting in states in the non-repeating portion of the chain that can transition to the repeating portion of the chain via the border states. When we have an arrival in one of these states, we transition to the repeating portion of the chain, and after earning some reward, return to the non-repeating portion of the chain. Finally, Eq. (38) guarantees that any transition to state $(k-1, k-1)$ will end the renewal cycle. The above system of linear equations can again be easily solved to find $\dot{R}^H_{i,j}$ in closed form (see Appendix B).

After solving for $p^L_{i \to d}$, $\dot{R}^L_{i,k}$ and $\dot{R}^H_{i,j}$, we can derive $\dot{\mathcal{R}}$, and consequently $\widehat{N_Q}(z)$, via Eq. (27). $\widetilde{T}(s)$ can then be derived by using the fact $\widetilde{T}(s) = \widetilde{T_Q}(s) \cdot \frac{\mu}{s+\mu} = \widehat{N_Q}\left(1 - \frac{s}{\lambda}\right) \cdot \frac{\mu}{s+\mu}$.

We applied the above steps to obtain a closed-form expression for $\widehat{N_Q}(z)$ for the M/M/3/setup. We refer the reader to [7] for full details.

8. M/M/K/SETUP/DELAYEDOFF

The Markov chain for M/M/k/setup/delayedoff is shown in Fig. 2. Our renewal state this time will be $(k, k-1)$; thus, $\dot{\mathcal{R}}$, the reward earned when going from $(k, k-1)$ back to $(k, k-1)$ can be expressed as:

$$\dot{\mathcal{R}} = \frac{1 + (k-1)\mu \dot{R}^H_{k,k-2} + \lambda\dot{R}^L_{k,k} + \beta\dot{R}^H_{k-1,k-1}}{\lambda + (k-1)\mu + \beta} \quad (39)$$

The analysis for M/M/k/setup/delayedoff via RRR is very similar to that of M/M/k/setup in Section 7 above. In fact, since the repeating portion for the two chains is the same, the system of equations for $p^L_{i \to d}$ and $\dot{R}^L_{i,j}$ is identical, but the non-repeating portion for the two chains is different. We now set up the system of equations for solving $\dot{R}^H_{i,j}$.

---

[2] The definition given for $p^L_{i \to d}$ applies in all cases except when $j = k$ and $d \in \{k-1, k\}$. When $j = k$, we can never end in depth k when moving one step to the left; in this case, we interpret $p^L_{i \to k}$ (or $p^L_{i \to k-1}$) as the probability that we first moved one step left *by transitioning out of a state in depth k (or $k-1$)*.

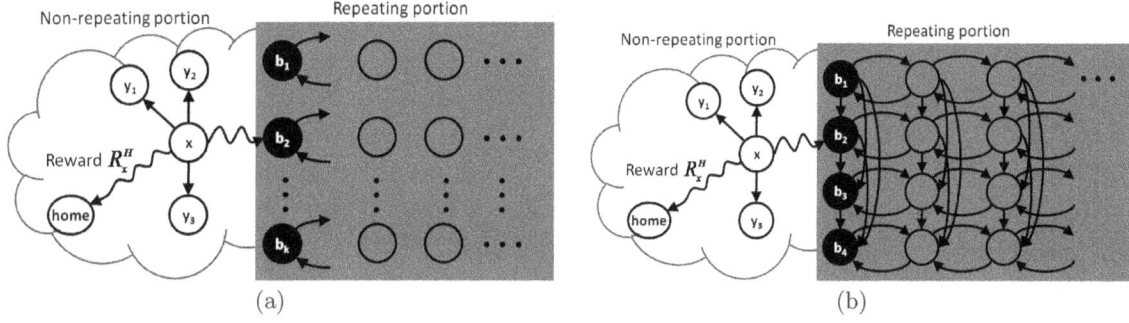

Figure 6: *Fig. 6(a) depicts the class of Markov chains that can be analyzed via RRR. The repeating portion is highlighted in gray and the border states, b_i, are shaded black. Note that y_i are the neighbors of x. Fig. 6(b) depicts the more restrictive class of Markov chain that can be analyzed in closed-form via RRR. In this class, the horizontal transitions are skip-free and the vertical transitions are unidirectional.*

8.1 Deriving $\dot{R}_{i,j}^H$ for the non-repeating portion

The system of equations for $\dot{R}_{i,j}^H$ is as follows:

$$\dot{R}_{0,j}^H = \frac{z^j + \lambda \dot{R}_{0,j+1}^H + j\alpha \dot{R}_{1,j}^H}{\lambda + j\alpha}, \quad (j < k-1) \qquad (40)$$

$$\dot{R}_{i,0}^H = \frac{1 + \lambda \dot{R}_{i,1}^H + i\beta \dot{R}_{i-1,0}^H}{\lambda + i\beta}, \quad (0 < i \le k) \qquad (41)$$

$$\dot{R}_{k,j}^H = \frac{1 + \lambda \dot{R}_{k,j+1}^H + j\mu \dot{R}_{k,j-1}^H + (k-j)\beta \dot{R}_{k-1,j}^H}{\lambda + j\mu + (k-j)\beta},$$
$$(1 \le j < k-1) \qquad (42)$$

$$\dot{R}_{i,j}^H = \frac{z^{j-i} + \lambda \dot{R}_{i,j+1}^H + i\mu \dot{R}_{i,j-1}^H + (j-i)\alpha \dot{R}_{i+1,j}^H}{\lambda + i\mu + (j-i)\alpha},$$
$$(0 < i < j < k-1) \qquad (43)$$

$$\dot{R}_{i,i}^H = \frac{1 + \lambda \dot{R}_{i,i+1}^H + i\mu \dot{R}_{i,i-1}^H}{\lambda + i\mu}, \quad (0 < i < k-1) \qquad (44)$$

$$\dot{R}_{i,j}^H = \frac{1 + \lambda \dot{R}_{i,j+1}^H + j\mu \dot{R}_{i,j-1}^H + (i-j)\beta \dot{R}_{i-1,j}^H}{\lambda + j\mu + (i-j)\alpha},$$
$$(0 < j < i < k) \qquad (45)$$

$$\dot{R}_{i,k-1}^H = \frac{z^{k-1-i} + \lambda \left(\dot{R}_{i,k}^L + \sum_{\ell=i}^{k} \left\{ (p_{i\to\ell}^L)(\dot{R}_{\ell,k-1}^H) \right\} \right)}{\lambda + i\mu + (k-1-i)\alpha}$$
$$+ \frac{i\mu \dot{R}_{i,k-2}^H + (k-1-i)\alpha \dot{R}_{i+1,k-1}^H}{\lambda + i\mu + (k-1-i)\alpha}, \quad (i \le k-1) \qquad (46)$$

$$\dot{R}_{k,k-1}^H = 0 \qquad (47)$$

The above system of linear equations can again be solved to find $\dot{R}_{i,j}^H$ in closed form. This yields $\dot{\mathcal{R}}$, and consequently $\widehat{N_Q}(z)$, via Eq. (39).

9. M/M/K/SETUP/SLEEP

The Markov chain for M/M/k/setup/sleep is shown in Fig. 3. The analysis for M/M/k/setup/sleep via RRR is again similar to that of M/M/k/setup in Section 7. The only difference is in the setup transition rate (downwards transition arrows in the Markov chain): For the M/M/k/setup, the setup rate in state (i,j) is $\alpha \cdot \min\{j-i, k-i\}$. For the M/M/k/setup/sleep, the setup rate in state (i,j) is more complicated. When $i \ge s$, the setup rate is still $\alpha \cdot \min\{j-i, k-i\}$. However, if $i < s$, the setup rate is $\omega \cdot (j-i)$ if $j \le s$ and $\omega \cdot (s-i) + \alpha \cdot \min\{j-s, k-s\}$ if $j > s$. This can be explained based on the M/M/k/setup/sleep model description in Section 3.3 and the Markov chain in Fig. 3. Based on the above setup rates, we can easily modify the M/M/k/setup sets of equations for $p_{i\to d}^L$, $\dot{R}_{i,k}^L$ and $\dot{R}_{i,j}^H$ from Sections 7.1, 7.2 and 7.3 respectively, to represent the M/M/k/setup/sleep system of equations. The equation for $\dot{\mathcal{R}}$ will change accordingly.

10. THE GENERALIZED RECURSIVE RENEWAL REWARD TECHNIQUE

The RRR technique can be applied to a very broad class of Markov chains beyond just the M/M/k/setup. In general, RRR can reduce the analysis of any 2-dimensional, irreducible Markov chain which is repeating and infinite in one dimension (as shown in Fig. 6(a)) to the problem of solving a system of polynomial equations. Further, if in the repeating portion all horizontal transitions are skip-free and all vertical transitions are unidirectional (as shown in Fig. 6(b)), the resulting system of equations will be of degree at most two, yielding a closed-form solution. In this section we explain the application of the RRR technique to general repeating Markov chains and also provide justification for the above claims regarding Figs. 6(a) and 6(b). Throughout we will assume that the reward earned at a state, (i,j), is an affine function of i and j.

In order to apply RRR, we first partition the Markov chain into a finite non-repeating portion and an infinite repeating portion as in Fig. 6(a); in principle, this partition is not unique. Then, we fix a renewal point, or home state, within the non-repeating portion. For each state, x, in the non-repeating portion of the chain, we write an equation for the mean reward, R_x^H, earned in traveling from x to the home state. Each R_x^H is a sum of the mean reward during our residence in x and a weighted linear combination of the rewards R_y^H, where y is a neighbor of x, as in Fig. 6(a). We refer to this finite set of linear equations for the R_x^Hs as (**Ia**). Since the chain is irreducible, at least one state in the non-repeating portion of the chain transitions directly to a state in the repeating portion of the chain. We refer to the states in the repeating portion that are directly accessible from the non-repeating portion as *border states*. These are shown as b_i in Fig. 6(a). We next write a set of equations for the

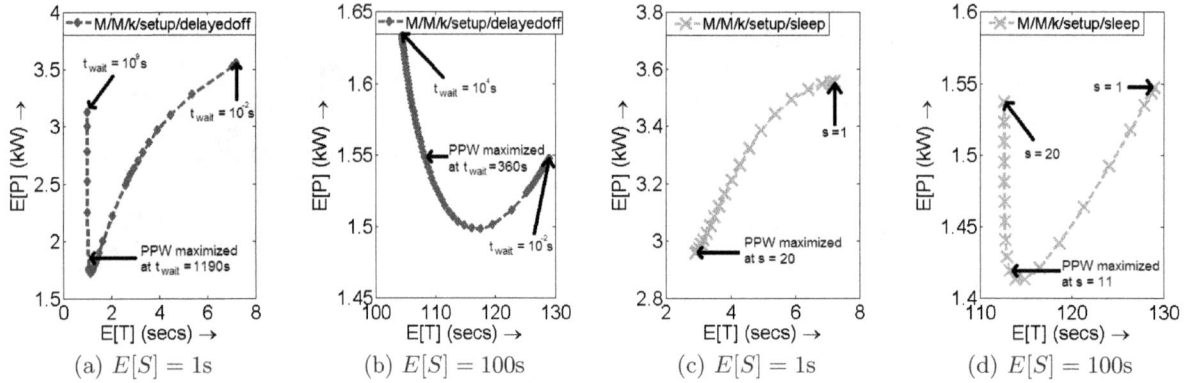

Figure 7: *E[P] versus E[T] for various values of* t_{wait} *and* s.

mean reward earned in traveling from each border state to the home state; call this set (**Ib**). Equation sets (**Ia**) and (**Ib**) together form the linear system of equations (**I**).

Within (**Ib**), the mean reward earned when returning home from each border state b consists of two parts: (i) the mean reward earned from the time we enter b until we leave the repeating portion, and (ii) the mean reward earned from when we first exit the repeating portion until returning home. Note that (ii) is simply a weighted linear combination of R_x^Hs where the weights form the probability distribution over the set of states in the non-repeating portion that we transition to (same as the $p_{i \to d}^L$s). For (i), the reward equation can be expressed as a weighted linear combination of the rewards for the neighbors of b in the repeating portion. The fact that the chain has a repeating structure allows us to express the reward from any state in the repeating portion as a linear combination of the rewards of the border states by using "recursion theorems" (similar to Thms. 2 and 3). We also need the probability distribution over the set of states we transition to when we move left (the $p_{i \to d}^L$s). At this point, to write the equations in (**Ib**), we require solving the $p_{i \to d}^L$s. We refer to the system of equations for $p_{i \to d}^L$s as (**II**).

In writing the equations for $p_{i \to d}^L$s, we again use recursion theorems (similar to Thm. 5) that exploit the repeating structure of the Markov chain. However, this time, the equations need not be linear. This is because when moving left to depth d from depth i, we might transition through various intermediate depths. Thus, $p_{i \to d}^L$ will involve several other probability terms. Unlike rewards where we sum up intermediate terms, for probability we take a product of the intermediate terms, leading to a system of higher order polynomial equations, (**II**). Note that (**II**) does not depend on (**I**), and can be solved independently. Once we get the $p_{i \to d}^L$s by solving (**II**), we substitute these back (as constants) into the set of linear equations (**Ib**). The sets of linear equations (**Ib**) and (**Ia**) can now be jointly solved using standard techniques such as symbolic matrix inversion. This yields the mean reward earned during a renewal cycle from home to home; mean time is found analogously.

In the case of Markov chains as shown in Fig. 6(b), the probability equations, (**II**), will be of degree at most two, as in Section 7.1. This is because skip-free horizontal transitions guarantee that the probability $p_{i \to d}^L$ can be expressed as a linear sum of products of only two intermediate terms of the form $p_{i \to \ell}^L \cdot p_{\ell \to d}^L$, where ℓ represents the intermediate depths that we can transition to in going from i to d (as in Section 7.1). Further, the unidirectional vertical transitions guarantee that $i \leq \ell \leq d$, which ensures that the

intermediate probability terms do not lead to higher-order dependencies between each other. Thus, the probabilities can be derived in closed-form by solving quadratic equations (including products of two unlike terms) in a particular "bottom-up" order as explained in Appendix B.

11. APPLICATIONS

In this section we use our analytical results to evaluate the performance of M/M/k, M/M/k/setup, M/M/k/setup/delayedoff and M/M/k/setup/sleep. In particular, we will be interested in the mean response time, $E[T]$, and the mean power consumption, $E[P]$, under these policies. Throughout, we assume a load of $\rho = \frac{\lambda}{k\mu} = 0.3$ (or 30% load), setup times of $\frac{1}{\alpha} = 100$s (when the server is off) and $\frac{1}{\omega} = 25$s (when the server is sleeping), and power consumption values of $P_{peak} = 200$W, $P_{idle} = 140$W, and $P_{sleep} = 14$W. These parameter values are based on empirical measurements from prior work [4, 11]. We consider job sizes with mean $E[S] = 1$s (typical web workloads [6]), $E[S] = 10$s (database queries or secured transactions), and $E[S] = 100$s (file download or upload), and system sizes ranging from $k = 5$ to $k = 100$ servers.

The M/M/k policy keeps k servers always on. Servers that are not busy serving jobs are left idle. The M/M/k/setup policy (see Section 3.1) immediately turns off idle servers to save power. However, restarting an off server requires a setup time of $\frac{1}{\alpha} = 100$s. The M/M/k/setup/delayedoff policy (see Section 3.2) is the same as the M/M/k/setup policy, except that idle servers wait for an exponentially distributed amount of time with mean $t_{wait} = \frac{1}{\beta}$ before turning off. The performance of this policy depends on the choice of the t_{wait} parameter. Finally, the M/M/k/setup/sleep policy (see Section 3.3) is the same as the M/M/k/setup policy, except that s of the k servers go to sleep as opposed to turning off, when idle. A sleeping server has a small setup time of $\frac{1}{\omega} = 25$s. The performance of this policy depends on the choice of the s parameter. Before comparing the above four policies, we first discuss how we choose the parameter value of t_{wait} for M/M/k/setup/delayedoff and s for M/M/k/setup/sleep.

11.1 Choosing optimal parameter values

The tradeoff between $E[P]$ and $E[T]$ for M/M/k/setup/delayedoff is shown in Figs. 7(a) and 7(b). Each plotted point represents an $(E[T], E[P])$ pair associated with a specific value of t_{wait}. Intuitively, as t_{wait} increases, $E[T]$ decreases since we avoid setup times. Moreover, before some threshold t_{wait}, $E[P]$ decreases as t_{wait} increases, because we avoid

(a) E[T] versus k

(b) E[P] versus k

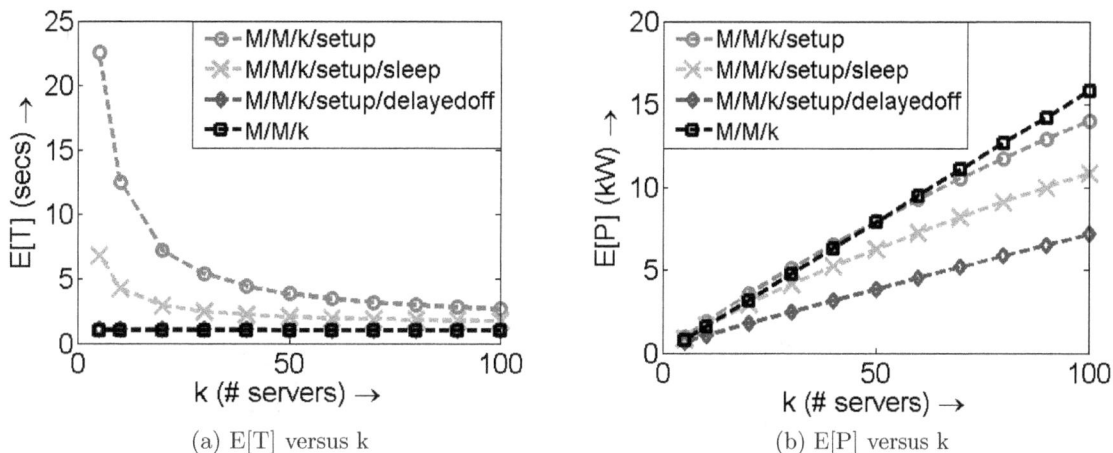

Figure 8: *Results when mean job size $E[S] = 1$.*

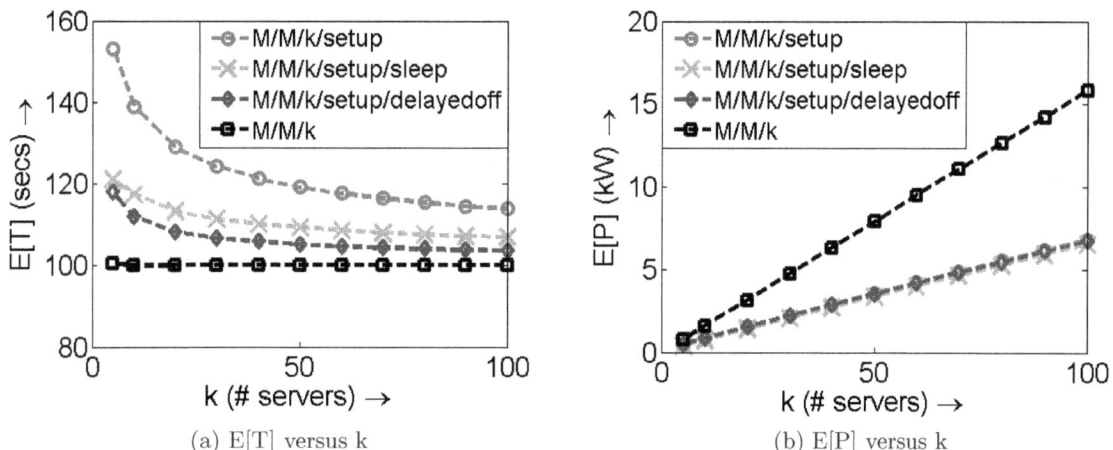

(a) E[T] versus k

(b) E[P] versus k

Figure 9: *Results when mean job size $E[S] = 100$.*

consuming power at peak rate by repeatedly putting servers in setup. However, beyond this threshold t_{wait}, $E[P]$ starts increasing on account of idle servers. Thus, as t_{wait} increases, we get the plots in Figs. 7(a) and 7(b), from right to left. We choose the t_{wait} value that optimizes (i.e., maximizes) the popular *Performance-Per-Watt* metric [11, 8], given by $PPW = (E[T] \cdot E[P])^{-1}$. These optimal values are shown in Figs. 7(a) and 7(b). We find that the optimal t_{wait} value decreases with an increase in $E[S]$.

Figs. 7(c) and 7(d) illustrate the tradeoff between $E[P]$ and $E[T]$ under M/M/k/setup/sleep for different values of s. Intuitively, as s increases, $E[T]$ decreases since we benefit from faster setup times afforded by sleeping servers. As s increases, $E[P]$ first decreases since we avoid the severe power penalty of longer setup times. But beyond a certain s, $E[P]$ increases on account of the sleeping servers. Thus, as s increases, we get the plots in Figs. 7(c) and 7(d), from right to left. Note that $E[P]$ monotonically decreases for the case of $E[S] = 1$s in Fig. 7(c). This is because $\frac{1}{\alpha} \gg E[S]$, and thus, the decrease in power consumption by avoiding power penalties of longer setup times outweighs the increase in power consumption because of P_{sleep}. We choose the s value that optimizes the PPW metric, as indicated in Figs. 7(c) and 7(d). We find that the optimal s value decreases with an increase in $E[S]$.

11.2 Comparison of all policies

Fig. 8 shows our results for $E[T]$ and $E[P]$ as a function of k for the case of $E[S] = 1$s. Comparing M/M/k (squares) and M/M/k/setup (circles), we see that M/M/k/setup has a much higher $E[T]$, and only a slightly lower $E[P]$. In fact, when k is low, $E[P]$ for M/M/k/setup is *higher* than that of M/M/k. This is because of the power penalty involved in the setup cost. Thus, **M/M/k/setup is not a good policy for small job sizes**. The M/M/k/setup/sleep (crosses) has lower $E[T]$ *and* lower $E[P]$ than the M/M/k/setup. Thus, **using sleep modes improves the M/M/k/setup policy**. Finally, we see that M/M/k/setup/delayedoff (diamonds) has $E[T]$ virtually as low as that of M/M/k, and has the lowest power consumption among all other policies. Thus, **M/M/k/setup/delayedoff is superior to all the other policies for small job sizes**. The reason for lower $E[P]$ under M/M/k/setup/delayedoff is because of t_{wait} which avoids unnecessary setups (and the associated power penalties).

Fig. 9 shows our results for the case of $E[S] = 100$s. The $E[T]$ results for this job size are qualitatively similar to the results for $E[S] = 1$s. The percentage difference between the $E[T]$ under different policies goes down as $E[S]$ goes up. This is because the setup time is not changing as $E[S]$ goes up, and thus, the queueing delay caused by setup times is not as severe for large $E[S]$. Note that the $E[T]$ under M/M/k/setup/delayedoff actually goes up as $E[S]$ goes up.

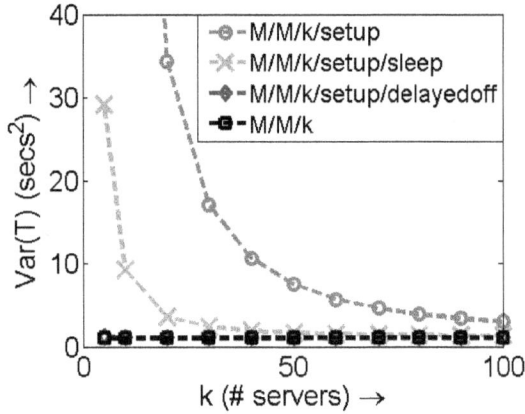

Figure 10: *Var(T) versus k for $E[S] = 1s$.*

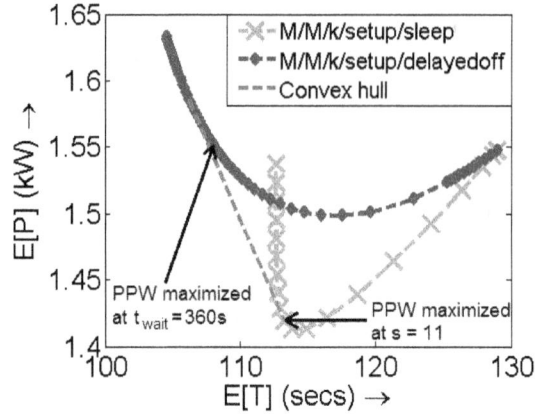

Figure 11: *E[P] versus E[T] for various values of t_{wait} and s for mean job size $E[S] = 100s$.*

This is a side-effect of the optimal t_{wait} setting which trades off lower $E[P]$ at the expense of a slightly higher $E[T]$ for bigger job sizes.

The $E[P]$ results for different job sizes indicate that $E[P]$ **under M/M/k/setup and M/M/k/setup/sleep decreases with an increase in job size, and approaches the $E[P]$ of M/M/k/setup/delayedoff**. This is because an increase in $E[S]$ necessitates an increase in the interarrival time, given fixed load, ρ. Thus, servers now spend more time in the off or sleep states, and consequently, consume less power. In fact, the M/M/k/setup/sleep has *lower* $E[P]$ as compared to M/M/k/setup/delayedoff for the case of $E[S] = 100s$. We take a closer look at these two policies in Section 11.3. Note that under M/M/k, $E[P] = k \cdot \rho \cdot P_{peak} + k \cdot (1 - \rho) \cdot P_{idle}$, which is linear in k and independent of $E[S]$.

The $E[T]$ results for these job sizes are qualitatively similar to the results for $E[S] = 1s$. The percentage difference between the $E[T]$ under different policies goes down as $E[S]$ goes up. This is because the setup time is not changing as $E[S]$ goes up, and thus, the queueing delay caused by setup times is not as severe for large $E[S]$. Note that the $E[T]$ under M/M/k/setup/delayedoff actually goes up as $E[S]$ goes up. This is a side-effect of the optimal t_{wait} setting which trades off lower $E[P]$ at the expense of a slightly higher $E[T]$ for bigger job sizes. As mentioned in Section 7, RRR also provides closed-form solutions for higher moments of response time and power. Fig. 10 shows our results for $Var(T)$, the variability in response time, for the case of $E[S] = 1s$. We see that $Var(T)$ follows the same trends as $E[T]$ in Fig. 8(a). Note that $Var(T)$ is close to 1 for M/M/k and M/M/k/setup/delayed-off. Also, $Var(T)$ converges to 1 for all policies for high k. This is because $Var(T)$ converges to $Var(S)$ (no queueing delay) in these cases, and since S is exponentially distributed with mean $E[S] = 1s$, we get $Var(T) \to Var(S) = 1s^2$.

All the results above assumed exponential setup times and exponential delay times. However, in real-world scenarios, these times would be deterministic. We use simulations to find $E[T]$ and $E[P]$ under deterministic setup times for all the above cases. We find that the relative ordering of the policies and the trends in $E[T]$ and $E[P]$ do not change significantly, despite the fact that all values become slightly higher due to the setup rates no longer being additive.

11.3 A closer look at M/M/k/setup/delayedoff versus M/M/k/setup/sleep

Fig. 11 shows the tradeoff between $E[P]$ and $E[T]$ for M/M/k/setup/delayedoff and M/M/k/setup/sleep for $E[S] = 100s$. These plots are identical to Figs. 7(b) and 7(d). We see that no policy dominates the other. If we are more concerned about reducing $E[P]$, M/M/k/setup/sleep is the better choice. However, if we are more concerned about reducing $E[T]$, M/M/k/setup/delayedoff is the better choice. Interestingly, by taking a probabilistic mixture of the two policies, we can find additional policies that are superior to the M/M/k/setup/delayedoff and the M/M/k/setup/sleep. The probabilistic mixture can be obtained by taking the convex hull of the two policies, as shown by the dashed line in Fig. 11. This suggests the potential for a policy that combines M/M/k/setup/sleep with delayedoff.

12. CONCLUSION

In this paper we develop a new analysis technique, Recursive Renewal Reward (RRR), which allows us to solve the M/M/k/setup class of Markov chains. RRR is very intuitive, easy to apply, and can be used to analyze many important Markov chains that have a repeating structure. RRR combines renewal reward theory with the development of recursion theorems for the Markov chain to yield exact, closed form results for metrics of interest such as the transform of time in system and the transform of power consumed by the system. RRR reduces the solution of the M/M/k/setup chains to solving k quadratic equations and a system of $O(k^2)$ linear equations. On an Intel Core i5-based processor machine we found RRR to be almost 5-10 times faster than the iterative matrix-analytic based methods, when using standard MATLAB implementations of both methods.

While we have only considered the M/M/k/setup, the M/M/k/setup/delayedoff, and the M/M/k/setup/sleep in this paper, we have also been able to use RRR for the derivation of exact, closed-form solutions for other important Markov chains with a repeating structure such as: (i) M/M/k/stag [10], wherein at most one server can be in setup, (ii) M/M/k/setup-threshold, wherein the servers are turned on and off based on some threshold for number of jobs in queue, (iii) M/M/k/disasters, wherein the system can empty abruptly due to disasters, and (iv) M/E$_2$/k, where the job size distribution is Erlang-2. We have also been able to apply RRR to analyze other Markov chains such as: (i)

$M_t/M/1$, where the arrival process is Poisson with a time dependent parameter, (ii) $M/H_2/k$, where the job size distribution is a 2-phase hyperexponential, and (iii) $M^x/M/k$, where there is a Poisson batch arrival process. In the above three cases, RRR reduces the analysis to solving a system of polynomial equations with degree > 2. In general, RRR should be able to reduce the analysis of any 2-dimensional Markov chain (with an affine reward function), which is finite in one dimension and infinite (with repeating structure) in the other, to solving a system of polynomial equations.

While not shown in this paper, it is possible to derive an explicit rate matrix for the M/M/k/setup, which leads to closed-form expressions for the limiting probabilities. While RRR does not utilize the rate matrix in any way, we believe that the set of Markov chains that can be solved in closed form via RRR should have an explicit rate matrix.

13. REFERENCES

[1] I. Adan and J. Resing. A class of Markov processes on a semi-infinite strip. Technical Report 99-03, Eindhoven University of Technology, Department of Mathematics and Computing Sciences, 1999.

[2] I. Adan and J. van der Wal. Combining make to order and make to stock. *OR Spektrum*, 20:73–81, 1998.

[3] J. R. Artalejo, A. Economou, and M. J. Lopez-Herrero. Analysis of a multiserver queue with setup times. *Queueing Syst. Theory Appl.*, 51(1-2):53–76, 2005.

[4] L. A. Barroso and U. Hölzle. The Case for Energy-Proportional Computing. *IEEE Computer*, 40(12):33–37, 2007.

[5] M. Castellanos, F. Casati, M.-C. Shan, and U. Dayal. iBOM: A platform for intelligent business operation management. In *Proceedings of the 21st International Conference on Data Engineering*, ICDE '05, pages 1084–1095, Tokyo, Japan, 2005.

[6] G. DeCandia, D. Hastorun, M. Jampani, G. Kakulapati, A. Lakshman, A. Pilchin, S. Sivasubramanian, P. Vosshall, and W. Vogels. Dynamo: Amazon's highly available key-value store. In *Proceedings of twenty-first ACM SIGOPS Symposium on Operating Systems Principles*, SOSP '07, pages 205–220, Stevenson, WA, 2007.

[7] A. Gandhi, S. Doroudi, M. Harchol-Balter, and A. Scheller-Wolf. Exact Analysis of the M/M/k/setup Class of Markov Chains via Recursive Renewal Reward. Technical Report CMU-CS-13-105, Carnegie Mellon University, 2013.

[8] A. Gandhi, V. Gupta, M. Harchol-Balter, and M. Kozuch. Optimality analysis of energy-performance trade-off for server farm management. *Performance Evaluation*, 67:1155–1171, 2010.

[9] A. Gandhi and M. Harchol-Balter. How Data Center Size Impacts the Effectiveness of Dynamic Power Management. *49th Annual Allerton Conference on Communication, Control, and Computing*, 2011.

[10] A. Gandhi, M. Harchol-Balter, and I. Adan. Server farms with setup costs. *Performance Evaluation*, 67:1123–1138, 2010.

[11] A. Gandhi, M. Harchol-Balter, and M. Kozuch. Are Sleep States Effective in Data Centers? *3rd IEEE International Green Computing Conference*, 2012.

[12] T. Horvath and K. Skadron. Multi-mode energy management for multi-tier server clusters. In *Proceedings of the 17th International Conference on Parallel Architectures and Compilation Techniques*, PACT '08, pages 270–279, Toronto, Canada, 2008.

[13] J. Keilson and L. Servi. A distributional form of little's law. *Operations Research Letters*, 7(5):223 – 227, 1988.

[14] J. Kim and T. S. Rosing. Power-aware resource management techniques for low-power embedded systems. In S. H. Son, I. Lee, and J. Y.-T. Leung, editors, *Handbook of Real-Time and Embedded Systems*. Taylor-Francis Group LLC, 2006.

[15] L. Kleinrock. *Queueing Systems, Volume I: Theory*. Wiley-Interscience, 1975.

[16] A. Krioukov, P. Mohan, S. Alspaugh, L. Keys, D. Culler, and R. Katz. NapSAC: Design and implementation of a power-proportional web cluster. In *Proceedings of the First ACM SIGCOMM Workshop on Green Networking*, Green Networking '10, pages 15–22, New Delhi, India, 2010.

[17] G. Latouche and V. Ramaswami. *Introduction to Matrix Analytic Methods in Stochastic Modeling*. ASA-SIAM, Philadelphia, 1999.

[18] Y. Levy and U. Yechiali. An M/M/s queue with servers' vacations. *INFOR*, 14:153–163, 1976.

[19] D. Meisner, B. T. Gold, and T. F. Wenisch. PowerNap: Eliminating server idle power. In *Proceeding of the 14th international conference on Architectural Support for Programming Languages and Operating Systems*, ASPLOS '09, pages 205–216, Washington, DC, 2009.

[20] I. Mitrani. Managing performance and power consumption in a server farm. *Annals of Operations Research*, pages 1–14, 2012.

[21] W. Qin and Q. Wang. Modeling and control design for performance management of web servers via an IPV approach. *IEEE Transactions on Control Systems Technology*, 15(2):259–275, March 2007.

[22] A. Riska and E. Smirni. M/G/1-type Markov processes: A tutorial. In *Performance Evaluation of Complex Systems: Techniques and Tools*, pages 36–63. Springer, 2002.

[23] N. Tian, Q.-L. Li, and J. Gao. Conditional stochastic decompositions in the M/M/c queue with server vacations. *Stochastic Models*, 15(2):367–377, 1999.

[24] B. Van Houdt and J. van Leeuwaarden. Triangular M/G/1-Type and Tree-Like Quasi-Birth-Death Markov Chains. *INFORMS Journal on Computing*, 23(1):165–171, 2011.

[25] J. Van Leeuwaarden and E. Winands. Quasi-birth-and-death processes with an explicit rate matrix. *Stochastic models*, 22(1):77–98, 2006.

[26] P. Welch. On a generalized M/G/1 queueing process in which the first customer of each busy period receives exceptional service. *Operations Research*, 12:736–752, 1964.

[27] X. Xu and N. Tian. The M/M/c Queue with (e, d) Setup Time. *Journal of Systems Science and Complexity*, 21:446–455, 2008.

[28] Z. G. Zhang and N. Tian. Analysis on queueing systems with synchronous vacations of partial servers. *Performance Evaluation*, 52(4):269 – 282, 2003.

APPENDIX
A.   RECURSION THEOREMS

THEOREM 1 (RECURSION THEOREM FOR MEAN TIME)
For the M/M/k/setup, the mean time to move one step left from state (i,j), $T_{i,j}^L$, is the same for all $j \geq k$.

PROOF. For any $j \geq k$, observe that when moving one step left from any state (i,j), we only visit states with level j or greater, until the final transition to level $j-1$. Hence, $T_{i,j}^L$ depends only on the structure of the "subchain" of the M/M/k/setup consisting of levels $\{j, j+1, \ldots\}$, including transition rates to level $j-1$. Now consider the subchain for each $j \geq k$; these subchains are isomorphic, by the fact that the chain is repeating from level k onward. Hence, the time to move one step left is the same regardless of the initial level $j \geq k$. $\square$

THEOREM 2 (RECURSION THEOREM FOR MEAN REWARD)
For the M/M/k/setup, the mean reward earned in moving one step left from state $(i, j+1)$, $R_{i,j+1}^L$, satisfies $R_{i,j+1}^L = R_{i,j}^L + T_{i,j}^L$ for all $j \geq k$, where the reward tracks the number of jobs in the system.

PROOF. Consider the process of moving one step left from a given state (i,j) where $j \geq k$. At the same time, consider the same process where everything is shifted over one level to the right, so that the initial state is $(i,j+1)$ At any point in time, the number of jobs seen by the second process is exactly one greater than that seen by the first process. Therefore, the total number of jobs accumulated (total reward) during the second process is $T_{i,j}^L$ greater than that of the first process, since the duration of both processes is $T_{i,j}^L$ by Theorem 1. $\square$

THEOREM 3 (RECURSION THEOREM FOR TRANSFORM OF REWARD)
For the M/M/k/setup, $\dot{R}_{i,j+1}^L = z \cdot \dot{R}_{i,j}^L$, for all $j \geq k$, where $\dot{R}$ tracks the z-transform of the number of jobs in the system.

PROOF. The proof is identical to that of Theorem 2, except that in any moment in time the second process (starting in level $(i, j+1)$) earns z times as much reward as the first process (starting at (i,j)). $\square$

THEOREM 4 (RECURSION THEOREM FOR TRANSFORM OF POWER)
For the M/M/k/setup, $\dot{E}_{i,j+1}^L = \dot{E}_{i,j}^L = T_{i,j}^L \cdot z^{k \cdot P_{peak}}$, for all $j \geq k$.

PROOF. When $j \geq k$, all k servers are either on or in setup, putting power consumption at $k \cdot P_{peak}$. So the transform of power usage is $z^{k \cdot P_{peak}}$, yielding $\dot{E}_{i,j}^L = T_{i,j}^L \cdot z^{k \cdot P_{peak}}$. It then follows immediately from Theorem 1 that $\dot{E}_{i,j+1}^L = \dot{E}_{i,j}^L$. $\square$

THEOREM 5 (RECURSION THEOREM FOR PROBABILITY)
For the M/M/k/setup, for each $0 \leq d \leq k$ and for each $0 \leq i \leq k$, $p_{i \to d}^L$ is the same for all $j \geq k$.

PROOF. Recall that $p_{i \to d}^L$ is the probability that, given that we start at depth i, we end at depth d when moving one step to the left, except when $j = k$ and $d \in \{k-1, k\}$; in these cases we interpret $p_{i \to k}^L$ (or $p_{i \to k-1}^L$) as the probabilities that we first moved one step left by *transitioning out of a state* in depth k (or $k-1$).

As with $T_{i,j}^L$, $p_{i \to d}^L$ depends only on the structure of the "subchain" consisting of levels $\{j, j+1, \ldots\}$, including transition rates to level $j-1$. Since for all $j \geq k$ the resulting subchains are isomorphic, $p_{i \to d}^L$ must be the same for all $j \geq k$. $\square$

B.   SOLUTION OF THE SYSTEM OF EQUATIONS FOR M/M/K/SETUP

The steps below illustrate how to solve the system of equations for M/M/k/setup. All of the operations in the steps below can be performed *symbolically* to obtain closed-form results.

B.1   Solving for $p_{i \to d}^L$

The system of equations for $p_{i \to d}^L$ consists of equation sets (28), (29) and (30). Eqs. (28) are k quadratic equations, each in one variable: $p_{0 \to 0}^L, p_{1 \to 1}^L, \ldots, p_{k-2 \to k-2}^L, p_{k-1 \to k-1}^L$. Thus, we can solve each equation easily using the quadratic formula. It can be easily shown that among the two roots of each equation, the greater root exceeds 1, and is thus disregarded. The lesser root can be shown to lie in the interval $[0, 1)$, making it the unique solution of interest to the quadratic equation. Note that $p_{0 \to 0}^L = 0$, as expected (we cannot move to the left when we have no servers on).

The set of equations (29) is a collection of $O(k^2)$ equations involving linear terms and products of two unlike variables. However, the structure of this system of equations reduces solving the system to solving a set of linear equations via back substitution. Consider solving this set of equations for the unknown values of $p_{i \to d}^L$ in this order:

$$p_{k-1 \to k-1}^L, p_{k-2 \to k-2}^L, p_{k-2 \to k-1}^L, \ldots, p_{0 \to 1}^L\ p_{0 \to 2}^L, \ldots, p_{0 \to k-1}^L$$

That is, solving from greatest $(k-1)$ to least (0) "original depth," but within each original depth, solving from least to greatest "target depth." Solving in this order, each equation we solve will only have one unknown, as all other variables will already have been solved for in an earlier step (including the $p_{i \to i}^L$ from Equations (28)), so these variables can be viewed as coefficients and constant terms. Once we have solved Equations (29), we can easily solve Equations (30), yielding $p_{0 \to k}^L, p_{1 \to k}^L, \ldots, p_{k-1 \to k}^L$, by taking complements. It follows that all $p_{i \to d}^L$ can be solved in closed forms that are, at worst, linear combinations of radicals (i.e., square roots).

B.2   Solving for $\dot{R}_{i,k}^L$

The system of equations for $\dot{R}_{i,k}^L$ consists of Equations (31) and (32), and Eq. (33). This system is a collection of $(k+1)$ linear equations with $(k+1)$ unknowns. Although we could solve this system using standard linear algebraic techniques, the structure of this system suggests an even simpler approach using back substitution. Solving for each $\dot{R}_{i,k}^L$ only requires knowing the $\dot{R}_{i,\ell}^L$ such that $\ell \in \{i+1, \ldots, k\}$. Eq. (33) readily gives us $\dot{R}_{k,k}^L$. Thus, we can now solve for $\dot{R}_{k-1,k}^L$, then $\dot{R}_{k-2,k}^L$, and so on. In this way, each $\dot{R}_{i,k}^L$ is found by solving a linear equation for one unknown variable.

B.3   Solving for $\dot{R}_{i,j}^H$

The system of equations for $\dot{R}_{i,j}^H$ consists of Equations (34), (35), (36) and (37), and Eq. (38). This system is a collection of $O(k^2)$ dependent linear equations with just as many unknowns. Unlike the earlier systems of equations, there is no apparent structure we can exploit, so the system can be solved via standard linear algebraic techniques such as (symbolic) matrix inversion.

Queueing System Topologies with Limited Flexibility

John N. Tsitsiklis
MIT, LIDS
Cambridge, MA 02139
jnt@mit.edu

Kuang Xu
MIT, LIDS
Cambridge, MA 02139
kuangxu@mit.edu

ABSTRACT

We study a multi-server model with n *flexible* servers and rn queues, connected through a fixed bipartite graph, where the level of flexibility is captured by the average degree, $d(n)$, of the queues. Applications in content replication in data centers, skill-based routing in call centers, and flexible supply chains are among our main motivations.

We focus on the scaling regime where the system size n tends to infinity, while the overall traffic intensity stays fixed. We show that a large capacity region (robustness) and diminishing queueing delay (performance) are jointly achievable even under very limited flexibility ($d(n) \ll n$). In particular, when $d(n) \gg \ln n$, a family of random-graph-based interconnection topologies is (with high probability) capable of stabilizing all admissible arrival rate vectors (under a bounded support assumption), while simultaneously ensuring a diminishing queueing delay, of order $\ln n/d(n)$, as $n \to \infty$. Our analysis is centered around a new class of virtual-queue-based scheduling policies that rely on dynamically constructed partial matchings on the connectivity graph. [†]

Categories and Subject Descriptors

G.3 [**Probability and Statistics**]: Queuing theory; C.2.1 [**Network Architecture and Design**]: Distributed networks

General Terms

Performance, Theory

Keywords

queueing system, flexibility, partial resource pooling, random graph, expander graph, asymptotics

[†]Research supported in part by the National Science Foundation, under grant CMMI-1234062, and an MIT-Xerox Fellowship. The authors are grateful for the feedback from the anonymous reviewers.

1. INTRODUCTION

At the heart of many modern queueing networks lies the problem of allocating processing resources (e.g., manufacturing plants, web servers, or call-center staff) to meet multiple types of demands that arrive dynamically over time (e.g., orders, data queries, or customer inquiries). It is often the case that a *fully flexible* or *completely resource-pooled* system, where every unit of processing resource is capable of serving all types of demands, delivers the best possible performance. Our inquiry is, however, motivated by the unfortunate reality that such full flexibility is often infeasible due to overwhelming implementation costs (in the case of a data center) or human skill limitations (in the case of a skill-based call center).

What are the key benefits of flexibility and resource pooling in such queueing networks? Can we harness the same benefits even when the degree of flexibility is *limited*, and how should the network be designed and operated? These are the main questions that we address in this paper. While these questions can be approached from several different angles, we will focus on the metrics of *expected queueing delay* and *capacity region*; the former is a direct reflection of *performance*, while the latter measures the system's *robustness* against *demand uncertainties*, when the arrival rates for different demand types are unknown or likely to fluctuate over time. Our main message is positive: in the regime where the system size is large, improvements in both capacity region and delay are *jointly achievable* even under very limited flexibility, given a proper choice of the interconnection topology.

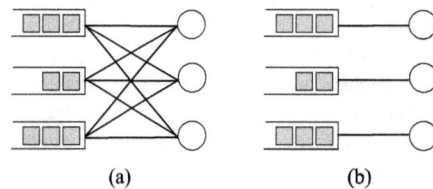

Figure 1: Extreme (in)flexibility: $d(n) = n$ **vs.** $d(n) = 1$.

Benefits of Full Flexibility. We begin by illustrating the benefits of flexibility and resource pooling using two simple examples.[1] Consider a system of n servers, each running at rate 1, and n queues, where each queue stores jobs of a particular demand type. For each $i \in \{1, \ldots, n\}$, queue i receives a Poisson arrival stream of rate $\lambda_i = \rho \in (0, 1)$, independently from all other queues. The job sizes are independent and exponentially distributed with mean 1.

---

[1]The lack of mathematical rigor in this section is intended to make the results easier to state. Formal definitions will be given in later sections.

For the remainder of this paper, we will use as a measure of flexibility the average number of servers that a demand type can receive service from, denoted by $d(n)$. Let us consider the two extreme cases: a fully flexible system, with $d(n) = n$ (Figure 1(a)), and an inflexible system, with $d(n) = 1$ (Figure 1(b)). Fixing the traffic intensity ρ, and letting the system size, n, tend to infinity, we observe the following qualitative benefits of full flexibility.

1. Diminishing Delay: Let W be the steady-state expected time in queue. In the fully flexible case and under any work-conserving scheduling policy[2], the *collection* of all jobs in the system evolves as an $M/M/n$ queue with arrival rate ρn. It is not difficult to verify that the expected total number of jobs in queue is *bounded* by a constant independent of n, and hence the expected waiting time in queue (the time from entering the queue to the initiation of service) satisfies $\mathbb{E}(W) \to 0$, as $n \to \infty$.[3] In contrast, the inflexible system is simply a collection of n *unrelated* $M/M/1$ queues, and hence the expected waiting time is $\mathbb{E}(W) = \frac{\rho}{1-\rho} > 0$, for all n. In other words, expected delay *diminishes* in a fully flexible system, as the system size increases, but stays bounded away from zero in the inflexible case.

2. Large Capacity Region: Suppose that we now allow the arrival rate λ_i to queue i to vary with i. For the fully flexible case, and treating it again as an $M/M/n$ queue, it is easy to see that the system is stable for all arrival rate vectors that satisfy $\sum_{i=1}^{n} \lambda_i < n$, whereas in the inflexible system, since all $M/M/1$ queues operate independently, we must have $\lambda_i < 1$, for all i, in order to achieve stability. Comparing the two, we see that the fully flexible system attains a much larger capacity region, and is hence more robust to uncertainties or changes in the arrival rates.

3. Joint Achievability: Finally, it is remarkable, though perhaps obvious, that a fully flexible system can achieve both benefits (diminishing delay and large capacity region) *simultaneously*, without sacrificing one for the other. In particular, for any $\rho \in (0, 1)$, the condition $\sum_{i=1}^{n} \lambda_i < \rho n$ for all n *implies* that $\mathbb{E}(W) \to 0$, as $n \to \infty$.

Preview of Main Result. Will the above benefits of flexibility continue to be present if the system is no longer fully flexible (i.e., if $d(n) \ll n$)? The main result of the paper (Theorem 1) shows that the objectives of diminishing delay and a large capacity region can still be jointly achieved, even when the amount of flexibility in the system is limited ($\ln n \ll d(n) \ll n$), as long as the arrival rates are appropriately bounded. However, when flexibility is limited, the interconnection topology and scheduling policy need to be chosen with care: our solution is based on connectivity graphs generated by the Erdős-Rényi random bipartite graph construction, combined with a new class of scheduling policies that rely on dynamically constructed partial matchings. Furthermore, the scheduling policies are completely oblivious to the exact values of λ_i, and adapt to them automatically.

1.1 Motivating Applications

We describe here some motivating applications for our model, which share a common overall architecture illustrated in Figure 2. **Content replication** is commonly used in data centers for bandwidth intensive operations such as database queries [2] or video streaming [9], by hosting the same piece of content on multiple servers. Here, a server corresponds to a physical machine in a data center, and each queue stores incoming demands for a particular piece of content (e.g., a video clip). A server j is connected to queue i if there is a copy of content i on server j, and $d(n)$ corresponds to the average number of replicas per content across the network. Similar structures also arise in **skill-based routing (SBR) in call centers**, where agents (servers) are assigned to answer calls from different categories (queues) based on their domains of expertise [15], and in **process-flexible supply chains** [3]-[8], where each plant (server) is capable of producing multiple product types (queues). In many of these applications, demand rates can be unpredictable and may change significantly over time (for instance, unexpected "spikes" in demand traffic are common in modern data centers [1]). The demand uncertainties make *robustness* an important criterion for system design. These practical concerns have been our primary motivation for studying the *trade-off* between robustness, performance, and the level of flexibility.

1.2 Related Work

Bipartite graphs serve as a natural model of the relationships between demand types and service resources. It is well known in the supply chain literature that limited flexibility, corresponding to a sparse bipartite graph, can be surprisingly effective in resource allocation even when compared to a fully flexible system [3, 4, 5, 6, 7]. The use of sparse random graphs or expanders as flexibility structures that improve robustness has recently been studied in [8] in the context of supply chains, and in [9] for content replication. Similar to the robustness results reported in this paper, these works show that expanders or random graphs can accommodate a large set of demand rate vectors. However, in contrast to our work, nearly all analytical results in this literature focus on static allocation problems, where one tries to match supply with demand in a single slot, as opposed to the queueing context, where resource allocation decisions need to be made dynamically over time.

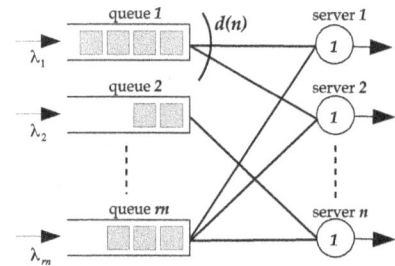

Figure 2: A processing network with rn queues and n servers.

In the queueing theory literature, the models we consider fall under the umbrella of so-called multi-class multi-server systems, where multiple queues and servers are connected through a bipartite graph. Under these (and similar) settings, complete resource pooling (full flexibility) is known to improve system performance [12, 13, 14], but much less is known when only limited flexibility is available, because systems with a non-trivial connectivity graph are very difficult to analyze, even under seemingly simple scheduling policies (e.g, first-come-first-serve) [10, 11]. Simulations in [15] show empirically that limited cross-training can be highly effective in a large call center under a skill-based routing algorithm. Using a very different set of modeling assumptions, [16] proposes a specific chaining structure with limited flexibility, which is shown to perform well under heavy traffic. Closer to the spirit of the current work is [17], which studies a partially flexible system where a fraction $p > 0$ of all processing resources are fully flexible, while the

---

[2]Under a work-conserving policy, a server is always busy whenever there is at least one job in the queues to which it is connected.

[3]The diminishing expected waiting time follows from the bounded expected total number of jobs in steady-state, Little's Law, and the fact that the total arrival rate is ρn, which goes to infinity as $n \to \infty$.

remaining fraction, $1 - p$, is dedicated to specific demand types, and shows an exponential improvement in delay scaling under heavy-traffic. However, both [16] and [17] focus on the heavy-traffic regime, which is different from the current setting where traffic intensity is assumed to be fixed while the system size tends to infinity, and provide analytical results for the special case of uniform demand rates. Furthermore, with a constant fraction of fully flexible resources, the average degree in [17] scales linearly with the system size n, whereas we are interested in the case of a much slower degree scaling. Finally, the expected delay in the architecture considered in [17] does not tend to zero as the system size increases.

At a higher level, our work is focused on the joint trade-off between robustness, delay, and the degree of flexibility in a queueing network, which is little understood in the existing literature, especially for networks with a non-trivial interconnection topology.

On the technical end, we build on several existing ideas. The techniques of batching (cf. [18, 19]) and the use of virtual queues (cf. [20, 21]) have appeared in many contexts in queueing theory, but the specific models considered in the literature bear little resemblance to ours. The study of perfect matchings on a random bipartite graph dates back to the seminal work in [22]; while it has become a rich topic in combinatorics, we will refrain from giving a thorough literature survey because only some elementary and standard properties of random graphs are used in the current paper.

Organization of the Paper. We describe the model in Section 2 along with the notation to be used throughout. The main result is stated in Section 3, with a discussion of potential improvements postponed till Section 7. Section 3.2 studies a specific flexibility structure and compares it against the architecture proposed in this paper. The rest of the paper is devoted to the proof of our main result (Theorem 1), with an overview of the proof strategy given in Section 3.3.

2. MODEL AND NOTATION

Notation. To avoid clutter, we will minimize the use of floor and ceiling notation throughout the paper (e.g., writing T_{rn} instead of $T_{\lfloor rn \rfloor}$). We will assume that all values of interest are appropriately rounded up or down to an integer, whenever doing so does not cause ambiguity or confusion. We denote by $\mathcal{G}_n$ the set of all $rn \times n$ bipartite graphs. For $g_n \in \mathcal{G}_n$, let $\deg(g_n)$ be the average degree among the rn left vertices. An $m \times n$ Erdös-Rényi random bipartite graph $G = (E, I \cup J)$,[4] where each of the mn edges is present with probability p, is referred to as an (m, n, p) random graph. We will use $\mathbb{P}_{n,p}(\cdot)$ to denote the probability measure on $\mathcal{G}_n$ induced by an (rn, n, p) random graph,

$$\mathbb{P}_{n,p}(g) = p^{|E|}(1-p)^{rn^2 - |E|}, \quad \forall g \in \mathcal{G}_n, \tag{1}$$

where $|E|$ is the cardinality of the set of edges, E. For a subset of vertices, $M \subset I \cup J$, we will denote by $g|_M$ the graph induced by g on the vertices in M. Throughout, we will use the letter K to denote a generic constant.

The following short-hand notation for asymptotic comparisons will be used; here f and g are positive functions:

1. $f(x) \lesssim g(x)$ for $f(x) = \mathcal{O}(g(x))$, and $f(x) \gtrsim g(x)$ for $f(x) = \Omega(g(x))$.

2. $f(x) \gg g(x)$ for $\liminf_{x\to\infty} \frac{f(x)}{g(x)} = \infty$, and $f(x) \ll g(x)$ for $\limsup_{x\to\infty} \frac{f(x)}{g(x)} = 0$.

3. $f(x) \sim g(x)$ for $\lim_{x\to\infty} \frac{f(x)}{g(x)} = 1$.

---

[4]Throughout, we denote by E, I, and J the set of edges and left and right vertices, respectively.

When labeling a sequence, we will use the notation $a(n)$ if the value of a has a meaningful dependence on n, or a_n if n serves merely as an index. We will use $\text{Expo}(\lambda)$ as a shorthand for the exponential distribution with parameter λ. The expression $X \stackrel{d}{=} Y$ means that X and Y have the same distribution. Whenever possible, we will use upper-case letters for random variables, and lower-case letters for deterministic values.

The Model. We consider a sequence of systems operating in *continuous time*, indexed by an integer n, where the nth system consists of n servers and rn queues, where r is a positive constant that is fixed as n varies (Figure 2). The connectivity of the system is encoded by an $rn \times n$ undirected bipartite graph $g_n = (E, I \cup J)$, where I and J represent the set of queues and servers, respectively, and E the set of edges between them.[5] A server $j \in J$ is *capable* of serving a queue $i \in I$ if and only if $(i, j) \in E$. We will denote by $\mathcal{N}(i)$ the set of servers in J connected to queue i, and similarly, by $\mathcal{N}(j)$ the set of queues in I connected to server j.

In the nth system, each queue i receives a stream of incoming jobs according to a Poisson process of rate $\lambda_{n,i}$, independent of all other streams. We will denote by $\boldsymbol{\lambda}_n$ the arrival rate vector, i.e., $\boldsymbol{\lambda}_n = (\lambda_{n,1}, \lambda_{n,2}, \ldots, \lambda_{n,rn})$. The sizes of the jobs are exponentially distributed with mean 1, independent from each other and from the arrival processes. All servers are assumed to run at a constant rate of 1. The system is assumed to be empty at time $t = 0$.

Jobs arriving at queue i can be assigned to any server $j \in \mathcal{N}(i)$ to receive service. The assignment is *binding*, in the sense that once the assignment is made, the job cannot be transferred to, or simultaneously receive service from, any other server. Moreover, service is *non-preemptive*, in the sense that once service is initiated for a job, the assigned server has to dedicate its full capacity to that job until its completion.[6] Formally, if a server j just completed the service of a previous job at time t, its available actions are: **1. Serve a new job**: Server j can choose to fetch a job from any queue in $\mathcal{N}(j)$ and immediately start service. The server will remain occupied and take no other actions until the current job is completed. **2. Remain idle**: Server j can choose to remain idle. While in the idling state, it will be allowed to initiate a service (Action 1) at any point in time.

The performance of the system is fully determined by a *scheduling policy*, π, which specifies for each server $j \in J$, when to remain idle, when to serve a new job, and from which queue in $\mathcal{N}(j)$ to fetch a job when initiating a new service.

We only allow policies that are causal, in the sense that the decision at time t depends only on the history of the system (arrivals and service completions) up to t. We allow the scheduling policy to be *centralized* (i.e., to have full control over all servers' actions), and to be based on the knowledge of the graph g_n and the past history of all queues and servers. On the other hand, a policy does *not* observe the actual sizes of jobs before they are served, and **does not know the arrival rate vector $\boldsymbol{\lambda}_n$**.

Performance metric: Let W_k be the waiting time in queue for the kth job, defined as the time from the job's arrival to a queue until

---

[5]For notational simplicity, we omit the dependence of E, I, and J on n.

[6]While we restrict ourselves to binding and non-preemptive scheduling polices in this paper, other common architectures where (a) a server can serve multiple jobs concurrently (processor sharing), (b) a job can be served by multiple servers concurrently, or (c) job sizes are revealed upon entering the system, are clearly more powerful than the current setting, and are therefore capable of implementing the scheduling policy we consider here. Hence the performance upper bounds developed in this paper also apply to these more powerful variants.

when it starts to receive service from some server. With a slight abuse of notation, we define the *expected waiting time*, $\mathbb{E}(W)$, as

$$\mathbb{E}(W) \triangleq \limsup_{k \to \infty} \mathbb{E}(W_k). \tag{2}$$

Note that $\mathbb{E}(W)$ captures the *worst-case* expected waiting time across all jobs in the long run, and is always well defined, even under scheduling policies that do not induce a steady-state distribution.

We are primarily interested in the scaling of $\mathbb{E}(W)$ in the regime where the total traffic intensity (i.e., the ratio between the total arrival rate and the total service capacity) stays fixed, while the size of the system, n, tends to infinity.

3. MAIN THEOREM

Before stating our main theorem, we first motivate a condition on the arrival rate vector, λ_n. Since we allow the arrival rates $\lambda_{n,i}$ to vary with i, and since on average each queue is connected to $d(n)$ servers, the range of fluctuations of the $\lambda_{n,i}$ with respect to i should not be too large compared to $d(n)$, or else the system would become unstable. We will therefore let the amount of *rate fluctuation* or *uncertainty* be bounded by some $u(n)$, an upper bound on $\lambda_{n,i}$ for all i. The following condition summarizes these points.

CONDITION 1. **(Rate Condition)** *We fix a constant $\rho \in (0, 1)$ (referred to as the* traffic intensity*) and a sequence $\{u(n)\}_{n \geq 1}$ of positive reals with $\inf_n u(n) > 0$. For any $n \geq 1$, the arrival rate vector λ_n satisfies:*

1. $\max_{1 \leq i \leq rn} \lambda_{n,i} \leq u(n)$.

2. $\sum_{i=1}^{rn} \lambda_{n,i} \leq \rho n$.

We denote by $\Lambda_n \subset \mathbb{R}_+^n$ the set of all arrival rate vectors that satisfy the above conditions.

We denote by $\mathbb{E}_\pi (W \mid g_n, \lambda_n)$ the expected waiting time (cf. Eq. (2)) under a scheduling policy π, a graph g_n, and an arrival rate vector λ_n. The following is the main result of the paper.

THEOREM 1. *We assume that $d(n) \gg \ln n$ and $u(n) \ll \sqrt{\frac{d(n)}{\ln n}}$, and fix $\rho \in (0, 1)$, $\gamma > 0$, and $n \geq 1$. Then, there exists a policy π_n such that for every arrival vector λ_n that satisfies Condition 1, the following hold.*

1. There exists a bipartite graph, $g_n \in \mathcal{G}_n$ (possibly depending on λ_n) such that $\deg(g_n) \leq (1 + \gamma)d(n)$, and

$$\mathbb{E}_{\pi_n} (W \mid g_n, \lambda_n) \leq \frac{K u^2(n) \ln n}{d(n)} = o(1), \tag{3}$$

where $K > 0$ is a constant independent of n, g_n and λ_n.

2. Let G_n be a random graph in $\mathcal{G}_n$, chosen at random according to the Erdös-Rényi measure $\mathbb{P}_{n, \frac{d(n)}{n}}$ (cf. Eq. (1)). Then G_n has the property in Part 1, with high probability, uniformly over all $\lambda_n \in \Lambda_n$. Formally,

$$\mathbb{P}_{n, \frac{d(n)}{n}} \left(G_n \text{ has the property in Part 1} \right) \geq 1 - \delta_n, \quad \forall \lambda_n \in \Lambda_n,$$

where $\{\delta_n\}_{n \geq 1}$ is a sequence with $\lim_{n \to \infty} \delta_n = 0$.

The reader is referred to Section 7 for a discussion on potential improvements of the result.

3.1 Remarks on Theorem 1

Note that Part 1 of the theorem is a special case of Part 2, which states that for large values of n, and for a graph chosen according to the Erdös-Rényi model, the scheduling policy will have a large probability (with respect to the random graph generation) of achieving diminishing delay, as in Eq. (3). At a higher level, Eq. (3) relates three key characteristics of the system: *delay* $\mathbb{E}(W)$, *level of robustness* $u(n)$, and *degree of flexibility* $d(n)$. Furthermore, the scheduling policy only requires knowledge of ρ, not of the arrival rate vector; this is important in practice because this vector need not be known *a priori* or may change significantly over time.

The fact that a large capacity region (as given by Condition 1) is achievable when $d \ll n$ should not be too surprising: expander graphs (such as those obtained through a random graph construction) are known to have excellent max-flow performance. The more difficult portion of the argument is to show that a diminishing delay (a temporal property) can also be achieved without significantly sacrificing the range of admissible arrival rates, through appropriately designed scheduling policies. In our proof, the achievability of a large capacity region is not shown explicitly, but comes as a by-product of the delay analysis; in fact, the scheduling policy automatically finds, over time, a feasible flow decomposition over the connectivity graph (see Section 6).

Dependence on ρ.

It is possible to incorporate the traffic intensity ρ in the leading constant in Eq. (3), to obtain a bound of the form

$$\mathbb{E}_{\pi_n} (W \mid g_n, \lambda_n) \leq \frac{K'}{1 - \rho} \cdot \frac{u^2(n) \ln n}{d(n)}, \tag{4}$$

where K' is a constant independent of ρ. This captures a trade-off between the traffic intensity and the degree of flexibility in the system. A proof of Eq. (4) is given in [26].

Adversarial Interpretation of Rate Robustness.

To better understand the power and limitations of the "rate robustness" entailed by Theorem 1, it is useful to view the system as a game between two players: an *Adversary* who chooses the rate vector λ_n, and a *Designer* who chooses the interconnection topology g_n and the scheduling policy π_n. The goal of the Designer is to achieve small average waiting time (which would also imply stability of all queues), while the goal of the Adversary is the opposite. The following definition will facilitate our discussion.

DEFINITION 1. **(Good Graphs)** *Let us fix n, $d(n)$, $u(n)$, ρ, γ, and K, as in Theorem 1. We define the set $\mathrm{Good}(\lambda_n)$ of good graphs for λ_n as the subset of $\mathcal{G}_n$ for which $\deg(g_n) \leq (1 + \gamma)d(n)$ and the inequality in Eq. (3) holds, for some policy π_n.*

We now examine the robustness implications of Theorem 1 under different *orderings of the actions* in the game, listed according to increasing levels of difficulties for the Designer.

Level 1: Adversary acts first (weak adversary). The Designer gets to pick g_n and π_n *after* observing the realization of λ_n. Note that this weak form of adversary fails to capture the rate uncertainty arising in many applications, where the arrival rates are unknown at the time when the system is designed. For this setting, it is not hard to come up with a simple deterministic construction of a good graph and a corresponding policy. Formally, the set $\mathrm{Good}(\lambda_n)$ is nonempty for every $\lambda_n \in \Lambda_n$. However, Part 1 of Theorem 1 actually makes a stronger statement. While the graph is chosen after observing λ_n, the policy is designed without knowledge of λ_n, albeit at the expense of a much more complex policy.

Level 2: Adversary and Designer act independently (intermediate adversary). Suppose that both the Adversary and the Designer make their decisions independently, *without* knowing each other's choice. This case models most practical applications, where $\boldsymbol{\lambda}_n$ is generated by some exogenous mechanism, unrelated to the design process, and is not revealed to the Designer ahead of time. Here, our randomization in the construction of the graph offers protection against the choice of the Adversary. Part 2 of the theorem can be rephrased into the statement that there exists a policy for which

$$\inf_{\boldsymbol{\lambda}_n \in \boldsymbol{\Lambda}_n} \mathbb{P}_{n, \frac{d(n)}{n}} \left(G_n \in \mathrm{Good}\left(\boldsymbol{\lambda}_n \right) \right) \to 1. \quad (5)$$

As an extension, we may consider the case where the Adversary chooses $\boldsymbol{\lambda}_n$ at random, according to some probability measure μ_n on $\boldsymbol{\Lambda}_n$, but still independently from G_n. However, this additional freedom to the Adversary does not make a difference, and it can be shown, through an easy application of Fubini's Theorem, that

$$\inf_{\mu_n} \left(\mathbb{P}_{n, \frac{d(n)}{n}} \times \mu_n \right) \left(G_n \in \mathrm{Good}\left(\boldsymbol{\lambda}_n \right) \right) \to 1, \quad (6)$$

and where $\times$ is used to denote product measure. The proof is given in [26].

Level 3: Designer acts first (strong adversary). In this case, the Adversary chooses $\boldsymbol{\lambda}_n$ *after* observing the g_n and π_n picked by the Designer. While such an adversary may be too strong for most practical applications, it is still interesting to ask whether there exist *fixed* g_n and π_n that will work well for *any* $\boldsymbol{\lambda}_n$ that satisfies Condition 1 (or even weaker conditions). We conjecture that this is the case.

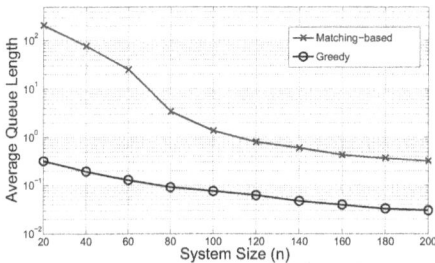

Figure 3: *Diminishing Delay.* **Simulations with $n \times n$ networks ($r = 1$), $\lambda_{n,i} = \rho = 0.95$, and $d(n) = \sqrt{n}$.**

On Practical Scheduling Policies.

The scheduling policy that we will use in the proof of Theorem 1 was mainly designed for the purpose of analytical tractability, rather than practical efficiency. For instance, simulations suggest that a seemingly naive greedy heuristic, where any free server chooses a job from a longest queue to which it is connected, can achieve a superior delay scaling (see Figure 3).[7] Unfortunately, deriving an explicit delay upper bound for the greedy policy or other similar heuristics appears to be challenging. See also the discussion in Section 7.

3.2 A Comparison with Modular Architectures

Assume for simplicity that there is an equal number of queues and servers (i.e., $r = 1$). In a *modular architecture*, the designer partitions the system into $n/d(n)$ *separate* sub-networks. Each

---

[7]The scheduling policy being simulated is a discrete-time version of the continuous-time policy analyzed in this paper.

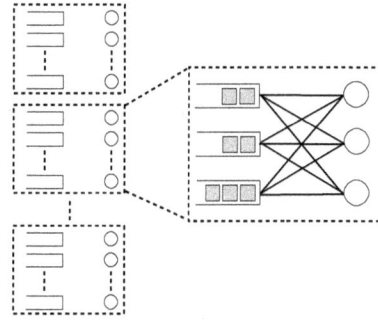

Figure 4: A modular architecture, consisting of $n/d(n)$ disconnected clusters, each of size $d(n)$. Within each cluster, all servers are connected to all queues.

sub-network consists of $d(n)$ queues and servers that are fully connected within the sub-network (Figure 4). Note that this architecture guarantees a degree of exactly $d(n)$, by construction. Assume that all queues have the same arrival rate $\rho \in (0, 1)$ and that each server uses an arbitrary work-conserving service policy. Since each sub-network is *fully connected*, it is not difficult to see that the modular architecture achieves a diminishing queueing delay as $n \to \infty$, as long as $d(n) \to \infty$. This seems even better than the random-graph-based architecture, which requires $d(n)$ to scale at least as fast as $\ln n$. However, this architecture fares much worse in terms of robustness, as we now proceed to discuss.

Since the sub-networks are completely disconnected from each other, the set of arrival rates that are admissible is severely reduced due to the requirement that the total arrival rate in *each* sub-network be less than $d(n)$, which is much more restrictive than the rate constraint given in Condition 1. Thus, the modular design may achieve a better delay scaling when the arrival rates are (almost) uniform, but at the risk of instability when the arrival rates are random or chosen adversarially, because the processing resources are not shared across different sub-networks.

3.3 Proof Overview

Sections 4 through 6 contain the proof of Theorem 1. We will provide an explicit construction of scheduling policies π_n, and then show that they achieve the delay scaling in Eq. (3). At the core of the construction is the use of *virtual queues*, whose operation is described in detail in Section 4.

The proof of Theorem 1 is completed in two steps. In Section 5, we first prove the result in the special case where all λ_i are equal to some $\lambda < 1/r$. The symmetry brought about by the uniform arrival rates will significantly simplify the notation, while almost all intuition developed here will carry over to the proof for the general case. We then show in Section 6 that, perhaps surprisingly, the original scheduling policies designed for the uniform arrival rate case can be applied directly to achieve the delay scaling in Eq. (3) for *any* $\boldsymbol{\lambda}_n$ satisfying Condition 1.

4. VIRTUAL QUEUE AND THE SCHEDULING POLICY

This section provides a detailed construction of a virtual-queue-based scheduling policy that achieves the delay scaling in Theorem 1. We begin by describing some high-level ideas behind our design.

Regularity vs. Discrepancies. Setting aside computational issues, an efficient scheduling policy is difficult to design because the future is unpredictable and random: one does not know *a pri-*

ori which part of the network will become more loaded, and hence current resource allocation decisions must take into account all possibilities of future arrivals and job sizes.

However, as the size of the system, n, becomes large, certain *regularities* in the arrival processes begin to emerge. To see this, consider the case where $r = 1$, $\lambda_{n,i} = \lambda < 1$ for all n and i, and assume that at time $t > 0$, all servers are busy serving some job. Now, during the interval $[t, t + \gamma_n)$, "roughly" $\lambda n \gamma_n$ new jobs will arrive, and $n\gamma_n$ servers will become available. For this $[t, t + \gamma_n)$ interval, denote by Γ the set of queues that received a job, and by Δ the set of roughly $n\gamma_n$ servers that became available. If γ_n is chosen so that $\lambda n \gamma_n \ll n$, these incoming jobs are likely to spread out across the queues, so that most queues receive at most one job. Assuming that this is indeed the case, we see that the connectivity graph g_n restricted to $\Gamma \cup \Delta$, denoted $g_n|_{\Gamma \cup \Delta}$, is a subgraph sampled uniformly at random among all $(\lambda n \gamma_n \times n\gamma_n)$-sized subgraphs of g_n. When $n\gamma_n$ is sufficiently large, and g_n is *well connected* (as in an Erdös-Rényi random graph with appropriate edge probability), we may expect that, with high probability, $g_n|_{\Gamma \cup \Delta}$ admits a matching (Definition 4) that includes the entire set Γ, in which case *all* $\lambda n \gamma_n$ jobs can start receiving service by the end of the interval.

Note that when n is sufficiently large, despite the randomness in the arrivals, the symmetry in the system makes delay performance at a short time scale *insensitive* to the exact locations of the arrivals. Treated collectively, the structure of the set of arrivals and available servers in a small interval becomes less random and more "regular," as $n \to \infty$. Of course, for any finite n, the presence of randomness means that *discrepancies* (events that deviate from the expected regularity) will be present. For instance, the following two types of events will occur with small, but non-negligible, probability.

1. Arrivals may be located in a poorly connected subset of g_n.
2. Arrivals may concentrate on a small number of queues.

We need to take care of these discrepancies, and show that their negative impact on performance is insignificant.

Following this line of thought, our scheduling policy aims to use most of the resources to dynamically target the *regular* portion of the traffic (via matchings on subgraphs), while ensuring that the impact of the *discrepancies* is well contained. In particular, we will create two classes of *virtual queues* to serve these two objectives:

1. A single *Matching queue* that targets *regularity* in arrival and service times, and *discrepancies* of the first type.
2. A collection of rn *Residual queues*, one for each (physical) queue, which targets the discrepancies in arrival and service times of the second type.

The queues are "virtual," as opposed to "physical," in the sense that they merely serve to conceptually simplify the description of the scheduling policy.

Good Graphs: The management of the virtual queues must comply with the underlying connectivity graph, g_n, which is fixed over time. We informally describe here some desired properties of g_n; more detailed definitions and performance implications will be given in subsequent sections, as a part of the queueing analysis. We are interested in graphs that belong to a set $\mathcal{H}_n$, defined as the intersection of the following three subsets of $\mathcal{G}_n$:

1. $\hat{\mathcal{G}}_n$ (cf. Lemma 1): For the case $r = 1$, $g_n \in \hat{\mathcal{G}}_n$ if it admits a full matching. For the more general case, a suitable generalization is provided in the context of Lemma 1. This property will be used in both Matching and Residual queues to handle *discrepancies*.

2. $\tilde{\mathcal{G}}_n$ (cf. Lemmas 5-7) We have $g_n \in \tilde{\mathcal{G}}_n$ if a randomly sampled sublinear-sized subgraph admits a full matching, with high

probability. This property will be used in the Matching queue to take advantage of *regularity*.

3. $\mathcal{L}_n$ (cf. Section 5.3) : We have $g_n \in \mathcal{L}_n$ if g_n has average degree approximately equal to $d(n)$. This property is to comply with our degree constraint.

Once the description of the policy is completed, the proof will consist of establishing the following:

(i) If $g_n \in \mathcal{H}_n$, then the claimed delay bound holds.

(ii) The probability that a random bipartite graph belongs to $\mathcal{H}_n$ tends to 1, as $n \to \infty$.

Inputs to the Scheduling Policy: Besides n and r, the scheduling policy uses the following inputs:

1. ρ, the traffic intensity as defined in Condition 1,
2. ϵ, a constant in $(0, 1 - \rho)$,
3. $b(n)$, a batch size function,
4. g_n, the interconnection topology.

4.1 Arrivals to Virtual Queues

The arrivals to the Matching and Residual queues are arranged in *batches*. Roughly speaking, a batch is a set of jobs that are treated collectively as a single entity that arrives to a virtual queue. We define a sequence of random times $\{T_B(k)\}_{k \in \mathbb{Z}_+}$, by letting $T_B(0) = 0$, and for all $k \geq 1$,

$$T_B(k) \triangleq \text{time of the } k\frac{\rho}{r}b(n)\text{th arrival to the system,}$$

where $b(n) \in \mathbb{Z}_+$ is a design parameter, and will be referred to as the *batch parameter*.[8] We will refer to the time period $(T_B(k-1), T_B(k)]$ as the *k*th **batch period**.

DEFINITION 2. (**Arrival Times to Virtual Queues**) *The time of arrival of the kth batch to all virtual queues is $T_B(k)$, and the corresponding interarrival time is $A(k) \triangleq T_B(k+1) - T_B(k)$.*

While all virtual queues share the same arrival times, the contents of their respective batches are very different. We will refer to them as the *Matching batch* and *Residual batch*, respectively.

The *k*th *Matching batch* is the set of jobs that *first* arrive to their respective queues during the *k*th batch period. Since for each queue only the first job belongs to the Matching batch, it is convenient to represent the Matching batch as the set of queues that receive at least one job during the batch period.

The *k*th batch arriving to the *i*th Residual queue is the set of all jobs, except for the first one, that arrive to queue i during the *k*th batch.

DEFINITION 3. (**Size of a Residual Batch**). *Let $H_i(k)$ be the total number of jobs arriving to queue i during the kth batch period. The size of the ith Residual batch is*

$$R_i(k) \triangleq (H_i(k) - 1)^+. \tag{7}$$

A graphical illustration of the Matching and Residual batches is given in Figure 5.

---

[8]We chose not to absorb the constant ρ/r into $b(n)$ at this point because this will allow for simpler notation in subsequent sections.

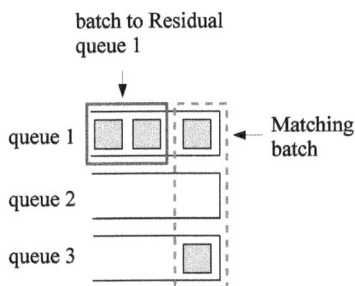

Figure 5: **An illustration of the arrivals during a single batch period.**

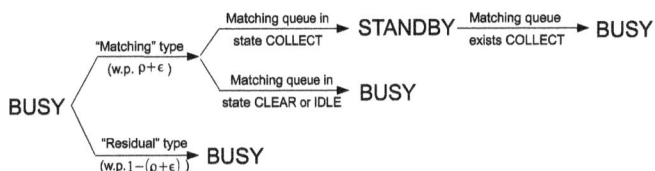

Figure 6: **State evolution of a physical server.**

4.2 State Transitions and Service Rules

This section describes how the batches will be served by the physical servers. Before getting into the details, we first describe the general ideas.

1. The sizes of Residual batches are typically quite small, and the physical servers will process them using a (non-adaptive) randomized scheduling rule.

2. For each Matching batch, we will first "collect" a number of available servers, equal to the size of the batch:
   (a) With high probability, all jobs in the Matching batch can be simultaneously processed by these servers through a matching over g_n.
   (b) With small probability, some jobs in the Matching batch are located in a poorly connected subset of g_n and cannot be matched with the available servers. In this case, all jobs in the batch will be served, one at a time, according to a *fixed* server-to-queue assignment (a "clear" phase).

To implement the above queueing dynamics, we will specify the evolution of *states* and *actions* of all physical servers and virtual queues, to be described in detail in the remainder of this section.

4.2.1 States and Actions of (Physical) Servers and Residual Queues

We first introduce the notion of an assignment function, which will be used to schedule the physical servers. An assignment function L maps each queue $i \in I$ to a server $L(i) \in J$. We say that L is an *efficient assignment function* for the connectivity graph g_n if $(i, L(i)) \in E$ for all $i \in I$, and

$$\left| L^{-1}(j) \right| \le r + 1, \tag{8}$$

for all $j \in J$. As will become clear in the sequel, our scheduling policy will use an assignment function L to ensure that every Residual queue receives at least a "minimum service rate" from some server. Let $\hat{\mathcal{G}}_n$ be the set of all $g_n \in \mathcal{G}_n$ such that g_n has an efficient assignment function. With our random graph construction, an efficient assignment function exists with high probability. The proof can be found in [26].

LEMMA 1. *Let $p(n) = d(n)/n$ and assume that $d(n) \gg \ln n$. Then,*

$$\lim_{n \to \infty} \mathbb{P}_{n,p(n)}(\hat{\mathcal{G}}_n) = 1.$$

A physical server can be, at any time, in one of two states: "BUSY" and "STANDBY;" cf. Fig. 4.2.1. The *end* of a period in the BUSY state will be referred to as an *event point*, and the time interval between two consecutive event points an *event period*. At each event

point, a new decision is to be made as to which virtual queue the server will choose to serve, during the next event period. All servers are initialized in a BUSY state, with the time until the first event point distributed as Expo (1), independently across all servers.

Recall that ϵ be a parameter in $(0, 1 - \rho)$. The state transitions defined below also involve the current state of the Matching queue, whose evolution will be given in Section 4.2.2. When a server $j \in J$ is at the kth event point:

1. With probability $\rho + \epsilon$, the kth event period is of type "matching" :
   (a) If the Matching queue is in state COLLECT, server j enters state STANDBY.
   (b) If the Matching queue is in state CLEAR, let B' be the Matching batch at the front of the Matching queue, and let $M' \subset I$ be the set of queues that still contain an unserved job from batch B'. Let $i^* = \min \{i : i \in M'\}$.

      i) If $L(i^*) = j$, then server j starts processing the job in queue i^* that belongs to B', entering state BUSY.

      ii) Else, server j goes on a vacation of length Expo (1), entering state BUSY.

   (c) If the Matching queue is in state IDLE, server j goes on a vacation of length Expo (1), entering state BUSY.

2. With probability $1 - (\rho + \epsilon)$, the kth event period is of type "residual." Let i be an index drawn uniformly at random from the set $L^{-1}(j)$.
   (a) If the ith Residual queue is non-empty, server j starts processing a job from the Residual batch that is currently at the front of the ith Residual queue, entering state BUSY.[9]
   (b) Else, server j goes on a vacation of length Expo (1), entering state BUSY.

The above procedure describes all the state transitions for a single server, except for one case: when in state STANDBY, any server can be ordered by the Matching queue to start processing a job, or initiate a vacation period. The transition out of the STANDBY state will be specified in the next subsection.

4.2.2 States and Actions of the Matching Queue

As mentioned earlier, the Matching queue is not a physical entity, but a mechanism that coordinates the actions of the physical servers. The name "Matching" reflects the fact that this virtual queue is primarily focused on using matchings to schedule batches, where a matching is defined as follows.

DEFINITION 4. **(Matching in a Bipartite Graph)** *Let $F \subset E$ be a subset of the edges of $g = (E, I \cup J)$. We say that F is a matching, if $|\{j' : (i, j') \in F\}| \le 1$, and $|\{i' : (i', j) \in F\}| \le 1$, for all $i \in I, j \in J$. A matching F is said to contain $S \subset I \cup J$ if for all $s \in S$, there exists some edge in F that is incident on s, and is said to be full if it contains I or J.*

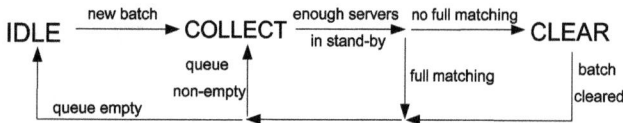

Figure 7: State evolutions of the Matching queue.

The Matching queue can be in one of three states: IDLE, COLLECT, and CLEAR. It is initialized to state IDLE.

1. If the Matching queue is in state IDLE, it remains so until the arrival of a Matching batch, upon which the Matching queue enters state COLLECT.

2. If the Matching queue is in state COLLECT, it remains so until there are exactly $(\rho/r)b(n)$ servers in state STANDBY.[10] Denote by $\Gamma \subset I$ the Matching batch currently at the front of the Matching queue, and by $\Delta \subset J$ the set of servers in STANDBY at the end of the COLLECT period. The Matching queue makes the following decisions:

   (a) If $g_n|_{\Gamma \cup \Delta}$ admits a full matching F:

   i) Let all matched servers in Δ start processing a job in the current Matching batch according to the matching F, entering state BUSY. If there are unmatched servers in Δ (which will occur if $|\Gamma| < |\Delta| = (\rho/r)b(n)$), let all unmatched servers enter state BUSY by initiating a vacation, with a length independently distributed according to Expo (1).

   ii) This completes the departure of a Matching batch from the Matching queue. If the Matching queue remains non-empty at this point, it returns to state COLLECT (to deal with the rest of the Matching batch); else, it enters state IDLE.

   (b) If $g_n|_{\Gamma \cup \Delta}$ does not admit a full matching, the Matching queue enters state CLEAR. All servers in state STANDBY enter state BUSY by initiating a vacation, with a length independently distributed according to Expo (1).

3. If the Matching queue is in state CLEAR, it remains so until all jobs in the current Matching batch have started receiving processing from one of the servers, upon which it enters state COLLECT if the Matching queue remains non-empty, or state IDLE, otherwise.

By now, we have described how the batches are formed (Section 4.1), and how each physical server operates (Section 4.2). The scheduling policy is hence fully specified, provided that the underlying connectivity graph g admits an efficient assignment function.

5. DYNAMICS OF VIRTUAL QUEUES – UNIFORM ARRIVAL RATES

We now analyze the queueing dynamics induced by the virtual-queue-based scheduling policy introduced in Section 4. In this section, we will prove Theorem 1 for the special case of uniform arrival rates, where

$$\lambda_{n,i} = \lambda < 1/r, \qquad (9)$$

$i \in I$. In particular, we have $\rho = \lambda r < 1$. Starting with this section, we will focus on a specific batch size function of the form

$$b(n) = K \frac{n \ln n}{d(n)} = K \frac{n}{y(n)}, \qquad (10)$$

---

[9]The Residual batch at the front of the Residual queue is defined to be the oldest Residual batch that contains any as yet unserved job.

[10]This particular number is equal to the total number of jobs arriving in a single batch period.

for a suitably chosen constant K, where $y(n)$ is defined by

$$y(n) = \frac{d(n)}{\ln n}. \qquad (11)$$

The specifics of the choice of K will be given later. We have assumed that $d(n) \gg \ln n$, and hence $y(n) \to \infty$ as $n \to \infty$. Note that this implies that $b(n) \ll n$. As will be seen soon, this guarantees that only a small fraction of the jobs will enter the Residual queues.

The main idea behind the delay analysis is rather simple: we will treat each virtual queue as a $GI/GI/1$ queue, and use Kingman's bound to derive an upper bound on the expected waiting time in queue. The combination of a batching policy with Kingman's bound is a fairly standard technique in queueing theory for deriving delay upper bounds (see, e.g., [19]). Our main effort will go into characterizing the various queueing primitives associated with the virtual queues (arrival rates, traffic intensity, and variances of inter-arrival and processing times), as well as in resolving the statistical dependence induced by the interactions among the physical servers. We begin by stating a simple fact on the inter-arrival-time distribution for the virtual queues. Even though in this section we assume that $r = 1$, we state the lemma for the general case.

LEMMA 2. *The inter-arrival times of batches to the virtual queues,* $\{A(k)\}_{k \geq 1}$, *are i.i.d., with* $\mathbb{E}(A(k)) = b(n)/(rn)$, *and* $\mathrm{Var}(A(k)) \lesssim b(n)/n^2$.

PROOF. By definition, $A(k)$ is equal in distribution to the time until a Poisson process with rate λrn records $\lambda b(n)$ arrivals. Therefore, $\mathbb{E}(A(k)) = (\lambda b(n))/(\lambda rn) = b(n)/(rn)$, and $\mathrm{Var}(A(k)) = \lambda b(n) \cdot \frac{1}{(\lambda rn)^2} \lesssim b(n)/n^2$. □

DEFINITION 5. **(Service Times in Virtual Queues)** *Consider the kth batch arriving at a virtual queue (Matching or Residual). Define the time of service initiation, E_k, to be when the batch first reaches the front of the queue, and the time of departure, D_k, to be when the last job in the batch starts receiving service from one of the physical servers. Let $D_k = E_k$ if the batch contains no jobs. The service time for the k batch is defined to be*

$$S(k) = D_k - E_k.$$

The interval $[E_k, D_k]$ is referred to as the service period of the kth batch.

We will denote by $S^M(k)$ and $S_j^R(k)$ the service time for the kth batch in the Matching queue and the jth Residual queue, respectively. Note that our scheduling policy (Section 4.2) induces interactions among the physical servers, and hence in general, the service times in a Residual queue are neither independent across batches or queues nor identically distributed.

5.1 Delays in Matching Queues

We first turn our attention to the service times $S^M(k)$ of the batches in the Matching queue. Based on our construction, it is not difficult to verify that the $S^M(k)$ are i.i.d. for any fixed graph, g_n. Furthermore, the value of $S^M(k)$ is equal to the length of a COLLECT period plus possibly the length of a CLEAR period, if the subgraph formed during the COLLECT period, $g_n|_{\Gamma \cup \Delta}$, fails to contain a matching that includes all queues in the current batch. We will therefore write

$$S^M(k) \overset{d}{=} S_{col} + X_{q(g_n)} \cdot S_{cle}, \qquad (12)$$

where S_{col} and S_{cle} correspond to the length of a COLLECT and CLEAR period, respectively, and X_q is a Bernoulli random variable with $\mathbb{P}(X_q = 1) = q$. The value of $q(g_n)$ is defined by

$$q(g_n) = \mathbb{P}\{g_n|_{\Gamma \cup \Delta} \text{ does not admit a full matching}\}, \quad (13)$$

where the probability is taken over the randomness in Γ and Δ, but is conditional on $G_n = g_n$.

We begin by analyzing the properties of S_{cle}. Recall from Section 4.2.1 that, when the Matching queue is in state CLEAR, the jobs in the current Matching batch are to be served in a sequential fashion (Step 1-(b)) by a designated server. In particular, letting i^* be the smallest index of the queues that contain an unserved job from the current Matching batch, then the job in queue i^*, denoted by b, will be served by server $L(i^*)$ whenever that server enters an event period of type "matching." No other unprocessed jobs in the Matching batch can be served until job b begins to receive service, and the amount of time it takes until this occurs is exponentially distributed with mean $1/(\rho + \epsilon)$, since the probability for an event period at a physical server to be of type "matching" is $(\rho + \epsilon)$ (Step 1). Since there are at most $\lambda b(n)$ jobs in a Matching batch, the length of a CLEAR period, S_{cle}, is no greater than the amount of time it takes for a Poisson process of rate $\rho + \epsilon$ to record $\lambda b(n)$ arrivals. Arguing similar to the proof of Lemma 2, we have the following lemma. Note that the distribution of S_{cle} does not depend on the structure of g_n, as long as g_n admits an efficient assignment function (cf. Lemma 1).

LEMMA 3. $\mathbb{E}(S_{cle}) = \frac{\lambda}{\rho + \epsilon} b(n)$, and $\mathbb{E}(S_{cle}^2) \lesssim b^2(n)$.

To analyze S_{col}, we argue as follows. A COLLECT period consists of the time until a first server in Δ completes service, followed by the time until one of the remaining servers completes service, etc., until we have a total of $\lambda b(n)$ service completions. Thus the length of the period is the sum of $\lambda b(n)$ independent exponential random variables with parameters $\lambda(\rho+\epsilon)n$, $\lambda(\rho+\epsilon)(n-1), \ldots, \lambda(\rho + \epsilon)(n - \lambda b(n) + 1)$. Using the fact that $b(n) \ll n$, this is essentially the same situation as in our analysis of S_{cle}, and we have the following result.

LEMMA 4. $\mathbb{E}(S_{col}) \sim (\lambda/(\rho + \epsilon)) \cdot (b(n)/n)$ and $\mathbb{E}(S_{col}^2) \lesssim b^2(n)/n^2$.

Finally, we want to focus our attention to a set $\tilde{\mathcal{G}}_n \subset \mathcal{G}_n$ of graphs that possess the following two properties.

1. The value of $\mathbb{E}(X_{q(g_n)}) = q(g_n)$ is small, for all $g_n \in \tilde{\mathcal{G}}_n$. This property will help us upper bound the service time $S^M(k)$, using Eq. (12) and the moment bounds for S_{cle} and S_{col} developed earlier.

2. The set $\tilde{\mathcal{G}}_n$ has high probability under the Erdös-Rényi random graph model.

We start with some definitions. For $m \leq n$, let $\mathcal{M}_{m,n}$ be the family of all $m \times m$ subsets of $I \cup J$, that is, $h \in \mathcal{M}_{m,n}$ if and only if $|h \cap I| = |h \cap J| = m$. Let $m(n)$ be such that $m(n) \to \infty$ as $n \to \infty$. Let $\mathbf{P}_{\mathcal{M}_{m(n),n}}$ be a probability measure on $\mathcal{M}_{m(n),n}$. Let, for each $g \in \mathcal{G}_n$,

$$l(g) = \mathbf{P}_{\mathcal{M}_{m(n),n}}\left(\{h \in \mathcal{M}_{m(n),n} : g|_h \text{ does not admit} \right.$$
$$\left. \text{a full matching}\}\right),$$

and $p(n) = d(n)/n$. We now define $\tilde{\mathcal{G}}_n$ as the set of graphs in $\mathcal{G}_n$ that satisfy

$$l(g) \leq m^2(n)(1 - p(n))^{m(n)}. \quad (14)$$

Informally, this is a set of graphs which, for the given measure $\mathbf{P}_{\mathcal{M}_{m(n),n}}$ on subgraphs, have a high probability that a random subgraph will have a full matching. Consistent with the general outline of the proof given in Section 4, we will show that a) graphs in $\tilde{\mathcal{G}}_n$ have favorable delay guarantees (Proposition 1) and b) that random graphs are highly likely to belong to $\tilde{\mathcal{G}}_n$ (Lemma 5).

LEMMA 5. (Probability of Full Matching on Random Subgraphs) With $p(n) = d(n)/n$, we have

$$\lim_{n \to \infty} \mathbb{P}_{n,p(n)}(\tilde{\mathcal{G}}_n) = 1, \quad (15)$$

Remark on Lemma 5: Eq. (15) states that graphs in $\tilde{\mathcal{G}}_n$ can be found using the Erdös-Rényi model, with high probability. This probabilistic statement is not to be confused with Eq. (14), which is a deterministic property that holds for all $g \in \tilde{\mathcal{G}}_n$. For the latter property, the randomness lies only in the sampling of subgraphs (via $\mathbf{P}_{\mathcal{M}_{m(n),n}}$). This distinction is important for our analysis, because the interconnection topology, g_n, stays fixed over time, while the random subgraph, $g_n|_{\Gamma \cup \Delta}$, is drawn independently for different batches.

Before proving Lemma 5, we state the following useful fact. The proof consists of a simple argument using Hall's marriage theorem and a union bound (cf. Lemma 2.1 in [23] for a proof of the lemma).

LEMMA 6. Let G be an (n, n, p) random bipartite graph. Then

$$\mathbb{P}_{n,p}(G \text{ does not admit a full matching}) \leq 3n(1-p)^n. \quad (16)$$

PROOF. (Lemma 5) Let H be a random element of $\mathcal{M}_{m(n),n}$, distributed according to $\mathbf{P}_{\mathcal{M}_{m(n),n}}(h)$. Let G be an $(rn, n, p(n))$ random bipartite graph over $I \cup J$, generated independently of H. Note that the distribution of G restricted to any $m(n)$-by-$m(n)$ subset of $I \cup J$ is that of an $(m(n), m(n), p(n))$ random bipartite graph. Therefore, by Lemma 6, we have

$$\mathbb{E}(l(G)) = \mathbb{P}(G|_H \text{ does not admit a full matching})$$
$$\leq 3m(n)(1 - p(n))^{m(n)}, \quad (17)$$

where $\mathbb{P}(\cdot)$ represents the distributions of both G and H. Eq. (17), combined with Markov's inequality, yields

$$\mathbb{P}_{n,p(n)}(\tilde{\mathcal{G}}_n) = 1 - \mathbb{P}\left(l(G) > m^2(n)(1 - p(n))^{m(n)}\right)$$
$$\geq 1 - \frac{\mathbb{E}(l(G))}{m^2(n)(1 - p(n))^{m(n)}} \geq 1 - \frac{3}{m(n)}, \quad (18)$$

which converges to 1 as $n \to \infty$, because $m(n) \to \infty$. $\square$

Using Lemma 5, we can now obtain an upper bound on the value of $q(g_n)$. The proof is given in [26].

LEMMA 7. Let $b(n) = Kn/y(n)$, as in Eq. (10), for some constant $K > 8/\lambda$. If $g_n \in \tilde{\mathcal{G}}_n$, then

$$q(g_n) \leq \frac{1}{y^2(n)} \cdot n^{-(\lambda K - 4)/2}.$$

We are now ready to bound the mean and variance of the service time distribution for the Matching queue, using Eq. (12) and Lemmas 3, 4, and 7. The proof is given in [26].

LEMMA 8. (Service Time Statistics for the Matching Queue) Assume that $g_n \in \tilde{\mathcal{G}}_n$, and let $b(n) = Kn/y(n)$, for some constant $K > 8/\lambda$. The service times of the Matching batches, $S^M(k)$, are i.i.d., with

$$\mathbb{E}(S^M(k)) \sim \frac{\lambda}{\rho + \epsilon} \cdot \frac{1}{y(n)}, \quad \text{and} \quad \mathrm{Var}(S^M(k)) \lesssim \frac{1}{y^2(n)}.$$

Let W_M be the steady-state **waiting time of a batch in the Matching queue**, where waiting time is defined to be the time from when the batch is formed until when all jobs in the batch have started to receive service from a physical server. The following is the main result of this subsection.

PROPOSITION 1. **(Delays in the Matching Queue)** *Assume $g_n \in \hat{\mathcal{G}}_n \cap \tilde{\mathcal{G}}_n$, where $\hat{\mathcal{G}}_n$ and $\tilde{\mathcal{G}}_n$ were defined before Lemmas 1 and 5, respectively. We have*

$$\mathbb{E}\left(W_M\right) \lesssim \frac{1}{y(n)}. \tag{19}$$

PROOF. We use Kingman's bound, which states that the expected value of the waiting time in a $GI/GI/1$ queue, W, is bounded by $\mathbb{E}\left(W\right) \leq \tilde{\lambda} \frac{\sigma_a^2 + \sigma_s^2}{2(1-\tilde{\rho})}$, where $\tilde{\lambda}$ is the arrival rate, $\tilde{\rho}$ is the traffic intensity, and σ_a^2 and σ_s^2 are the variances for the interarrival times and service times, respectively. Using Lemmas 2 and 8, the claim follows by substituting

$$\tilde{\lambda} = \frac{1}{\mathbb{E}\left(A(k)\right)} \lesssim \frac{n}{b(n)} = \frac{y(n)}{K},$$

$$\tilde{\rho} = \frac{\mathbb{E}\left(S^M(k)\right)}{\mathbb{E}\left(A(k)\right)} \leq \frac{\frac{\lambda}{\rho+\epsilon}\frac{K}{y(n)}}{\frac{K}{r y(n)}} = \frac{\rho}{\rho+\epsilon} < 1, \tag{20}$$

$$\sigma_a^2 = \operatorname{Var}\left(A(k)\right) \sim \frac{1}{\lambda}\frac{b(n)}{n^2} \lesssim \frac{1}{n y(n)},$$

$$\sigma_s^2 = \operatorname{Var}\left(S^M(k)\right) \lesssim \frac{1}{y(n)^2},$$

for all sufficiently large values of n. We obtain

$$\mathbb{E}\left(W_M\right) \lesssim y(n)\left(\frac{1}{n y(n)} + \frac{1}{y(n)^2}\right) \lesssim \frac{1}{y(n)}.$$

$\square$

5.2 Delays in a Residual Queue

The delay analysis for the Residual queues is conceptually simpler compared to that of the Matching queue, but requires more care on the technical end. The main difficulty comes from the fact that, due to the physical servers' interactions with the Matching queue, the service times in a Residual queue i, $\left\{S_i^R(k)\right\}_{k\geq 0}$, are neither identically distributed nor independent over k (Section 4.2.1). To overcome this difficulty, we will use a trick to restore the i.i.d. nature of the service times. In particular, we will create a per-sample-path coupling of the $S_i^R(k)$'s to an i.i.d. sequence $\left\{\tilde{S}_i^R(k)\right\}_{k\geq 0}$, such that $S_i^R(k) \leq \tilde{S}_i^R(k)$ for all k, almost surely. If we pretend that the $\tilde{S}_i^R(k)$'s are indeed the true service times, an upper bound on the expected waiting time can be established using Kingman's bound. We finish the argument by showing that this upper bound applies to the expected value of the original waiting time. The following proposition is the major technical result of this section.

PROPOSITION 2. *Assume $g_n \in \hat{\mathcal{G}}_n$, where $\hat{\mathcal{G}}_n$ was defined in Lemma 1. Fix any $i \in I$. Let k be the index for batches. Denote by $\left\{T_i^R(k)\right\}_{k\geq 0}$ and $\left\{S_i^R(k)\right\}_{k\geq 0}$ the sequences of interarrival and service times at the ith Residual queue, respectively, defined on a common probability space. There exists a sequence $\left\{\tilde{S}_i^R(k)\right\}_{k\geq 0}$, defined on the same probability space, that satisfies:*
1. $\mathbb{P}\left(\tilde{S}_i^R(k) \geq S_i^R(k), \forall k \in N\right) = 1$.
2. Elements of $\left\{\tilde{S}_i^R(k)\right\}$ are i.i.d. over k, and independent of $\left\{T_i^R(k)\right\}$.
3. $\mathbb{E}\left(\tilde{S}_i^R(1)\right) \lesssim \frac{b^2(n)}{n^2}$, and $\mathbb{E}\left(\tilde{S}_i^R(1)^2\right) \lesssim \frac{b^2(n)}{n^2}$.

PROOF. The proof is given in [26]. It involves an explicit coupling construction of the sequence $\left\{\tilde{S}_i^R(k)\right\}$, which is then shown to satisfy all three claims. Technicalities aside, the proof makes use of the following simple observations: **(1)** the event periods can be "prolonged" via coupling to be made independent, without qualitatively changing the scaling of the service time, $\tilde{S}_i^R(k)$, and **(2)** the first and second moments of $S_i^R(k)$ are mainly influenced by the size of the Residual batch, $R(k)$, which is small ($\lesssim \frac{b(n)}{n}$) by design. $\square$

Denote by W_i^R the steady-state **waiting times in the ith Residual queue**, where waiting time is defined to be the time from when the batch is formed till when all jobs in the batch have started to receive service. The next proposition is the main result of this subsection, which is proved using the stochastic dominance result of Proposition 2, and the same Kingman's bound as in Proposition 1. The proof is given in [26].

PROPOSITION 3. **(Delay in a Residual Queue)** *Assume $g_n \in \hat{\mathcal{G}}_n \cap \tilde{\mathcal{G}}_n$, where $\hat{\mathcal{G}}_n$ and $\tilde{\mathcal{G}}_n$ were defined before Lemmas 1 and 5, respectively. We have*[11]

$$\max_{i\in I}\mathbb{E}\left(W_i^R\right) \lesssim \frac{1}{y(n)}. \tag{21}$$

5.3 Proof of Theorem 1 Under Uniform Arrival Rates

PROOF. Let $\mathcal{H}_n' = \hat{\mathcal{G}}_n \cap \tilde{\mathcal{G}}_n$ for all $n \geq 0$, where $\hat{\mathcal{G}}_n$ and $\tilde{\mathcal{G}}_n$ were defined before Lemmas 1 and 5, respectively. Since each job is served either through the Matching queue or a Residual queue, the total queueing delay is no more than that of the waiting time in a virtual queue plus the time to form a batch ($A(k)$). Hence, letting $b(n) = Kn/y(n)$, by Lemma 2, and Propositions 1 and 3, we have

$$\mathbb{E}_\pi\left(W|g_n, \boldsymbol{\lambda}_n\right) \leq \mathbb{E}\left(A(1)\right) + \max\left\{\mathbb{E}\left(W^M\right), \mathbb{E}\left(W_1^R\right)\right\}$$
$$\leq \frac{K'}{y(n)} = K' \cdot \frac{\ln n}{d(n)}, \tag{22}$$

if $g_n \in \mathcal{H}_n'$, where K' is a constant independent of n and g_n. It is not difficult to show, by the weak law of large numbers, that there exist $\epsilon_n \downarrow 0$, such that

$$\mathbb{P}\left(1 - \epsilon_n \leq \frac{\deg\left(G_n\right)}{d(n)} \leq 1 + \epsilon_n\right) = 1, \tag{23}$$

for all n, where G_n is a $\left(rn, n, \frac{d(n)}{n}\right)$ random graph. Let $\mathcal{L}_n = \left\{g_n \in \mathcal{G}_n : \frac{\deg(g_n)}{d(n)} \in [1-\epsilon_n, 1+\epsilon_n]\right\}$, and $\mathcal{H}_n = \mathcal{H}_n' \cap \mathcal{L}_n$. By Eq. (23), and Lemmas 1 and 7, we have

$$\mathbb{P}_{n,\frac{d(n)}{n}}\left(\mathcal{H}_n\right) \geq 1 - \delta_n, \tag{24}$$

for all n, for some $\delta_n \downarrow 0$. Note that the definitions of $\hat{\mathcal{G}}_n$, $\tilde{\mathcal{G}}_n$ and $\mathcal{L}_n$ do not depend on the arrival rates $\boldsymbol{\lambda}_n$, and hence the value of δ_n also does not depend on $\boldsymbol{\lambda}_n$.

Eqs. (22) and (24) combined prove the first two claims of the theorem. Since all λ_i are equal in this case, the scheduling policy is oblivious to the arrival rates by definition. This completes the proof of Theorem 1 when $\lambda_{n,i} = \lambda < 1/r$ for all n and i. $\square$

---

[11] The expectation is defined in the sense of Eq. (2).

6. GENERAL CASE AND ARRIVAL-RATE OBLIVIOUS SCHEDULING

We now complete the proof of Theorem 1 for the general case, for λ_n satisfying Condition 1. In particular, we will show that the original virtual-queue-based scheduling policy given in Section 4.2 automatically achieves the $u^2(n) \ln n / d(n)$ delay scaling, while being fully oblivious to the values of the $\lambda_{n,i}$. We will use a definition of $\mathcal{H}_n$ identical to that in the uniform case, so that the probability of this set will still converge to 1. To avoid replicating our earlier arguments, and since the delays in each of the virtual queues are completely characterized by the statistics of arrival times and job sizes, we will examine the changes in each of these queueing primitives as we move to the general case. Throughout the section, we will analyze a system where the arrival rate vector, λ_n, satisfies Condition 1, and the scheduling rules are the same as before, with $b(n) = Kn/y(n)$.

1. Inter-arrival times of batches. The inter-arrival times to all virtual queues are equal to the time it takes to collect enough jobs to form a single batch. By the merging property of Poisson processes, the aggregate stream of arrivals to the system is a Poisson process of rate $\sum_{i \in I} \lambda_{n,i}$, with

$$\sum_{i \in I} \lambda_{n,i} \le \rho n. \tag{25}$$

We will make a further assumption, that there exists $\tilde{\rho}$, with $0 < \tilde{\rho} < \rho$, such that

$$\sum_{i \in I} \lambda_{n,i} \ge \tilde{\rho} n. \tag{26}$$

This assumption will be removed by the end of this section by a small modification to the scheduling policy. Given Eqs. (25) and (26), a result analogous to Lemma 2 holds:

$$\mathbb{E}(A(k)) = \frac{b(n)}{n}, \quad \text{and} \quad \text{Var}(A(k)) \lesssim \frac{b(n)}{n^2}. \tag{27}$$

2. Service times for Residual queues. The distributions of the times at which a server tries to fetch a job from a Residual queue can vary due to the different values of the $\lambda_{n,i}$'s. However, it is not difficult to show that the *upper bound* on the service times at the Residual queues (Proposition 2) depend only on the batch size $\frac{\ell}{r} b(n)$, and are independent of the specific values of the $\lambda_{n,i}$'s. Therefore, the only factor that may significantly change the delay distribution at the ith Residual queue is its associated Residual batch size, $R_i(k)$ (Eq. (7)). Since the arrival rates are no longer uniform, this distribution will in principle be different from the uniform setting. However, we will show that the difference is small and does not change the scaling of delay.

Denote by p_i the probability that an incoming job to the system happens to arrive at queue i. We have that

$$p_i = \frac{\lambda_{n,i}}{\sum_{i \in I} \lambda_{n,i}} \le \frac{u(n)}{\tilde{\rho} n} = \frac{1}{\frac{\tilde{\rho}}{u(n)} n}, \tag{28}$$

where $u(n)$ is the upper bound on $\lambda_{n,i}$ defined in Condition 1, and the inequality follows from the assumptions that $\lambda_{n,i} \le u(n)$ and that $\sum_{i \in I} \lambda_{n,i} \ge \tilde{\rho} n$ (Eq. (26)). Using Eq. (28), and following the same steps as in the proof of Proposition 2, one can show that

$$\max_{i \in I} \mathbb{E}(\tilde{S}_i^R(k)) \lesssim \frac{b^2(n) u^2(n)}{n^2},$$

and

$$\max_{i \in I} \text{Var}(\tilde{S}_i^R(k)) \lesssim \frac{b^2(n) u^2(n)}{n^2}.$$

We repeat the arguments in Proposition 3 by replacing, e.g., the bounds on $\text{Var}(\tilde{S}_i^R(k))$ with $\max_{i \in I} \text{Var}(\tilde{S}_i^R(k)) \lesssim \frac{b^2(n) u^2(n)}{n^2}$.

Letting $b(n) = K \frac{n \ln n}{d(n)}$, we have that, whenever $u(n) \ll \sqrt{\frac{d(n)}{\ln n}}$,

$$\max_{i \in I} \mathbb{E}(W_i^R) \lesssim \frac{n}{b(n)} \left(\frac{b(n)}{n^2} + \frac{b^2(n) u^2(n)}{n^2} \right) \lesssim \frac{b(n) u^2(n)}{n}$$

$$\lesssim \frac{\ln n}{d(n)} u^2(n). \tag{29}$$

3. Service times for the Matching queue. Surprisingly, it turns out that the bounds on the service times statistics for the Matching queue in the uniform arrival-rate case (Lemma 8) will carry over to the general setting, unchanged. Recall from Eq. (12) that the service time of a Matching batch is composed of two elements: the length of a COLLECT phase, S_{col}, and, with probability $q(g_n)$, the length of a clearing phase S_{cle}. Since the size of the Matching batch is at most $\frac{\ell}{r} b(n)$ by definition, the characterizations of S_{col} and S_{cle} given by Lemmas 3 and 4 continue to hold, with λ being replaced by $\lambda = \frac{\ell}{r}$. It remains to verify that the bound on $q(g_n)$ stays unchanged. While the $\lambda_{n,i}$'s are now different and the subgraph induced by Δ and Γ is no longer uniformly distributed, the upper bound on $q(g_n)$ given in Lemma 7 still holds, because Lemma 5 applies to arbitrary distributions of subgraphs. Therefore, the scaling in Proposition 1

$$\mathbb{E}(W^M) \lesssim \frac{1}{y(n)} = \frac{\ln n}{d(n)}, \tag{30}$$

continues to hold under non-uniform arrival rates.

Combining Eqs. (25), (29) and (30), we have, analogous to Eq. (22), that for all $n \ge 1$,

$$\mathbb{E}_\pi(W | g_n, \lambda_n) \le \mathbb{E}(A(1)) + \max \{ \mathbb{E}(W^M), \mathbb{E}(W_1^R) \}$$

$$\le \frac{K_1 \ln n}{d(n)} + \frac{K_2 u^2(n) \ln n}{d(n)} \le \frac{K u^2(n) \ln n}{d(n)}, \tag{31}$$

if $g_n \in \mathcal{H}_n$, where K_1, K_2 and K are positive constants independent of n, g_n and λ_n.

Finally, we justify the assumption made in Eq. (26), by showing that the scheduling policy could be easily modified such that Eq. (26) always holds: we simply insert to each queue an independent Poisson stream of "dummy packets" at rate δ, where δ is chosen to be any constant in $(0, \frac{1-\rho}{r})$. The dummy packets are merely place-holders: when a server begins serving a dummy packet, it simply goes on a vacation of duration Expo(1). This trivially guarantees the validity of Eq. (26), with $\tilde{\lambda} = \delta$, and since $\sum_{i \in I} \lambda_{n,i} \le \rho n$, doing so is equivalent to having a new system with ρ replaced by $\rho' = \rho + \delta r < 1$. Hence, all results continue to hold.[12] This concludes the proof of Theorem 1.

7. CONCLUSIONS AND FUTURE WORK

The main message of this paper is that the benefits of diminishing delay and large capacity region can be jointly achieved in a system where the level of processing flexibility of each server is small compared to the system size. The main result, Theorem 1, proves this using a randomly constructed interconnection topology and a virtual-queue-based scheduling policy. As a by-product, it also provides an explicit upper bound (Eq. (3)) that captures a trade-off between the delay ($\mathbb{E}(W)$), level of robustness ($u(n)$), and degree of processing flexibility ($d(n)$).

---

[12]This maneuver of inserting dummy packets is of course a mere technical device for the proof. In reality, delay and capacity would both become much less of a concern when the traffic intensity, ρ, is too small, at which point less sophisticated scheduling policies may suffice.

The scaling regime considered in this paper assumes that the traffic intensity is fixed as n increases, which fails to capture system performance in the heavy-traffic regime ($\rho \approx 1$). It would be interesting to consider a scaling regime in which ρ and n scale simultaneously (e.g., the celebrated Halfin-Whitt regime [25]), but it is unclear at this stage what exact formulations and analytical techniques are appropriate. At a higher level, it would be interesting to understand how long-term input characteristics in a queueing network (e.g., how arrival rates are drawn or evolve over time) impact its temporal performance (e.g., delay), and what role the network's intrinsic structure (e.g., flexibility) has to play here.

Theorem 1 also leaves open several promising directions for future improvements and extensions, which we discuss briefly. It is currently necessary to have that $d(n) \gg \ln n$ in order to achieve a diminishing delay. The $\ln n$ factor is essentially tight if a random-graph-based connectivity structure is to be used, because $d(n) = \Omega(\ln n)$ is necessary for an Erdös-Rényi type random graph to be connected (i.e., not have isolated queues). We suspect that the $\ln n$ factor can be reduced using a different graph generation procedure.

Fixing $u(n)$ to a constant, we observe that when $d(n) = n$ (fully connected graph), the system behaves approximately as a $M/M/n$ queue with total arrival rate $n\rho$; if ρ is held fixed, then the expected delay is known to vanish exponentially fast in n. Thus, there is a gap between this fact and the polynomial scaling of $\mathcal{O}\left(\ln n / d(n)\right)$ given in Theorem 1. We believe that this gap is due to an intrinsic inefficiency of the batching procedure used in our scheduling policy. The batching procedure provides analytical convenience by allowing us to leverage the regularity in the arrival traffic in obtaining delay upper bounds. However, the use of batching also mandates that all jobs wait for a prescribed period of time before receiving any service. This can be highly inefficient in the scaling regime that we consider, where the traffic intensity is fixed at ρ, because a $1 - \rho$ fraction of all servers (approximately) are actually idle at any moment in time. We therefore conjecture that a scheduling policy that tries to direct a job to an available server immediately upon its arrival (such as a greedy policy) can achieve a significantly better delay scaling, but the induced queueing dynamics, and the appropriate analytical techniques, may be very different from those presented in this paper.

Finally, the parameter $u(n)$ captures the level of robustness against uncertainties in the arrival rates. In terms of inducing a diminishing waiting time as $n \to \infty$, there is still a gap between the current requirement that $u(n) \ll \sqrt{d(n)/\ln n}$ and the upper bound that $u(n) = \mathcal{O}\left(d(n)\right)$ (since each queue is connected to only $d(n)$ servers on average). The $u^2(n)$ factor in the scaling of $\mathbb{E}\left(W\right)$ is due to the impact on delay by the arrival rate fluctuations in the Residual queues (cf. Eq. (29)). It is unclear what the optimal dependence of $\mathbb{E}\left(W\right)$ on $u(n)$ is. It is also possible that the condition $u(n) \ll d(n)$ alone is sufficient for achieving a diminishing delay; we conjecture that this is the case.

8. REFERENCES

[1] S. Kandula, S. Sengupta, A. Greenberg, P. Patel, R. Chaiken, "Nature of datacenter traffic: measurements and analysis," *IMC*, 2009.

[2] G. Soundararajan, C. Amza, and A. Goel, "Database replication policies for dynamic content applications," *Proc. of EuroSys*, 2006.

[3] W. Jordan and S. C. Graves, "Principles on the benefits of manufacturing process flexibility," *Management Science*, 41(4):577–594, 1995.

[4] S. Gurumurthi and S. Benjaafar, "Modeling and analysis of flexible queueing systems," *Management Science*, 49:289–328, 2003.

[5] S. M. Iravani, M. P. Van Oyen, and K. T. Sims, "Structural flexibility: A new perspective on the design of manufacturing and service operations," *Management Science*, 51(2):151–166, 2005.

[6] M. Chou, G. A. Chua, C-P. Teo, and H. Zheng, "Design for process flexibility: efficiency of the long chain and sparse structure," *Operations Research*, 58(1):43–58, 2010.

[7] D. Simchi-Levi and Y. Wei, "Understanding the performance of the long chain and sparse designs in process flexibility," submitted, 2011.

[8] M. Chou, C-P. Teo, and H. Zheng, "Process flexibility revisited: the graph expander and its applications," *Operations Research*, 59:1090–1105, 2011.

[9] M. Leconte, M. Lelarge and L. Massoulie, "Bipartite Graph Structures for Efficient Balancing of Heterogeneous Loads," *ACM Sigmetrics*, London, 2012.

[10] R. Talreja, W. Whitt, "Fluid models for overloaded multiclass many-service queueing systems with FCFS routing," *Management Sci.*, 54(8):1513-1527,2008.

[11] J. Visschers, I. Adan, and G. Weiss, "A product form solution to a system with multi-type jobs and multi-type servers," *Queueing Systems*, 70:269-298, 2012.

[12] A. Mandelbaum and M. I. Reiman, "On pooling in queueing networks," *Management Science*, 44(7):971-981, 1998.

[13] J. M. Harrison and M. J. Lopez, "Heavy traffic resource pooling in parallel-server systems," *Queueing Systems*, 33:39-368, 1999.

[14] S. L. Bell and R. J. Williams, "Dynamic scheduling of a system with two parallel servers in heavy traffic with resource pooling: asymptotic optimality of a threshold policy," *Ann. Appl. Probab.*, 11(3): 608-649, 2001.

[15] R. Wallace and W. Whitt, "A staffing algorithm for call centers with skill-based routing," *Manufacturing and Service Operations Management*, 7:276–294, 2005.

[16] A. Bassamboo, R. S. Randhawa, and J. A. Van Mieghem, "A little flexibility is all you need: on the asymptotic value of flexible capacity in parallel queuing systems," submitted, 2011.

[17] J. N. Tsitsiklis and K. Xu, "On the power of (even a little) resource pooling," *Stochastic Systems*, 2: 1–66 (electronic), 2012.

[18] M. Neely, E. Modiano and Y. Cheng, "Logarithmic delay for n×n packet switches under the crossbar constraint," *IEEE/ACM Trans. Netw.*, 15(3):657–668, 2007.

[19] J. N. Tsitsiklis and D. Shah, "Bin packing with queues," *J. Appl. Prob.*, 45(4):922–939, 2008.

[20] N. McKeown, A. Mekkittikul, V. Anantharam and J. Walrand, "Achieving 100% throughput in an input-queued switch," *IEEE Trans. on Comm.*, 47(8):1260–1267, 1999.

[21] S. Kunniyur and R. Srikant, "Analysis and design of an adaptive virtual queue," *ACM SIGCOMM*, 2001.

[22] P. Erdös and A. Rényi, "On random matrices," *Magyar Tud. Akad. Mat. Kutato Int. Kozl*, 8:455–461, 1964.

[23] S. R. Bodas, "High-performance scheduling algorithms for wireless networks," Ph.D. dissertation, University of Texas at Austin, Dec. 2010.

[24] V. F. Kolchin, B. A. Sevast'yanov, and V. P. Chistyakov, *Random Allocation*, John Wiley & Sons, 1978.

[25] S. Halfin and W. Whitt, "Heavy-traffic limits for queues with many exponential servers," *Operations Research*, 29: 567-588, 1981.

[26] J. N. Tsitsiklis and K. Xu, "Queueing system topologies with limited flexibility," *Technical Report*, http://web.mit.edu/jnt/www/Papers/c-13-SigRep.pdf.

Stochastic Modeling of Large-Scale Solid-State Storage Systems: Analysis, Design Tradeoffs and Optimization

Yongkun Li, Patrick P. C. Lee, John C. S. Lui
The Chinese University of Hong Kong
yongkunlee@gmail.com, {pclee,cslui}@cse.cuhk.edu.hk

ABSTRACT

Solid state drives (SSDs) have seen wide deployment in mobiles, desktops, and data centers due to their high I/O performance and low energy consumption. As SSDs write data out-of-place, garbage collection (GC) is required to erase and reclaim space with invalid data. However, GC poses additional writes that hinder the I/O performance, while SSD blocks can only endure a finite number of erasures. Thus, there is a performance-durability tradeoff on the design space of GC. To characterize the optimal tradeoff, this paper formulates an analytical model that explores the full optimal design space of any GC algorithm. We first present a stochastic Markov chain model that captures the I/O dynamics of large-scale SSDs, and adapt the mean-field approach to derive the asymptotic steady-state performance. We further prove the model convergence and generalize the model for all types of workload. Inspired by this model, we propose a *randomized greedy algorithm (RGA)* that can operate along the optimal tradeoff curve with a tunable parameter. Using trace-driven simulation on DiskSim with SSD add-ons, we demonstrate how RGA can be parameterized to realize the performance-durability tradeoff.

Categories and Subject Descriptors

D.4.2 [**Operating Systems**]: Storage Management—*secondary storage, garbage collection*; B.3.3 [**Memory Structures**]: Performance Analysis and Design Aids; G.3 [**Probability and Statistics**]: Markov Processes

General Terms

Performance;Theory;Algorithms

Keywords

Solid-state Drives; Garbage Collection; Wear-leveling; Cleaning Cost; Stochastic Modeling; Mean Field Analysis

1. INTRODUCTION

The increasing adoption of solid-state drives (SSDs) is revolutionizing storage architectures. Today's SSDs are mainly built on NAND flash memory, and provide several attractive features: high performance in I/O throughput, low energy consumption, and high reliability due to their shock resistance property. As the SSD price per gigabyte decreases [21], not only desktops are replacing traditional hard-disk drives (HDDs) with SSDs, but there is a growing trend of using SSDs in data centers [19, 27].

SSDs have inherently different I/O characteristics from traditional HDDs. An SSD is organized in *blocks*, each of which usually contains 64 or 128 *pages* that are typically of size 4KB each. It supports three basic operations: *read*, *write*, and *erase*. The read and write operations are performed in a unit of page, while the erase operation is performed in the block level. After a block is erased, all pages of the block become *clean*. Each write can only operate on a clean page; when a clean page is written, it becomes a *valid* page. To improve the write performance, SSDs use the *out-of-place write* approach. That is, to update data in a valid page, the new data is first written to a different clean page, and the original page containing old data is marked *invalid*. Thus, a block may contain a mix of clean pages, valid pages, and invalid pages.

The unique I/O characteristics of SSDs pose different design requirements from those in HDDs. Since each write must operate on a clean page, *garbage collection (GC)* must be employed to reclaim invalid pages. GC can be triggered, for example, when the number of clean pages drops below a predefined threshold. During GC, some blocks are chosen to be erased, and all valid pages in an erased block must first be written to a different free block prior to the erasure. Such additional writes introduce performance overhead to normal read/write operations. To maintain high performance, one design requirement of SSDs is to minimize the *cleaning cost*, such that a GC algorithm chooses blocks containing as few valid pages as possible for reclamation.

However, SSDs only allow each block to tolerate a limited number of erasures before becoming unusable. For instance, the number is typically 100K for single-level cell (SLC) SSDs and 10K for multi-level cell (MLC) SSDs [13]. With more bits being stored in a flash cell and smaller feature size of flash cells, the maximum number of erasures tolerable by each block further decreases, for example, to several thousands or even several hundreds for the latest 3-bits MLC SSDs [23]. Thus, to maintain high durability, another design requirement of SSDs is to maximize *wear-leveling* in GC, such that all blocks should have similar numbers of erasures over time so as to avoid any "hot" blocks being worn out soon.

Clearly, there is a performance-durability tradeoff in the GC design space. Specifically, a GC algorithm with a low cleaning cost may not achieve efficient wear-leveling, or vice versa. Prior work (e.g., [1]) addressed the tradeoff, but the study is mainly based on simulations. From the viewpoints of SSD practitioners, it remains an open design issue of how to choose the "best" parameters of a

GC algorithm to adapt to different tradeoff requirements for different application needs. However, understanding the performance-durability tradeoff is non-trivial, since it depends on the I/O dynamics of an SSD and the dynamics characterization becomes complicated with the increasing numbers of blocks/pages of the SSD. This motivates us to formulate a framework that can efficiently capture the optimal design space of GC algorithms and guide the choices of parameterizing a GC algorithm to fit any tradeoff requirement.

In this paper, we develop an analytical model that characterizes the I/O dynamics of an SSD and the optimal performance-durability tradeoff of a GC algorithm. Using our model as a baseline, we propose a *tunable* GC algorithm for different performance-durability tradeoff requirements. To summarize, our paper makes the following contributions:

- We formulate a stochastic Markov chain model that captures the I/O dynamics of an SSD. Since the state space of our stochastic model increases with the SSD size, we adapt the *mean field technique* [5, 38] to make the model tractable. We formally prove the convergence results under the uniform workload to enable us to analyze the steady-state performance of a GC algorithm. We also discuss how our system model can be extended for a general workload.

- We identify the optimal extremal points that correspond to the minimum cleaning cost and the maximum wear-leveling, as well as the optimal tradeoff curve of cleaning cost and wear-leveling that enables us to explore the *full* optimal design space of the GC algorithms.

- Based on our analytical model, we propose a novel GC algorithm called the *randomized greedy algorithm (RGA)* that can be tunable to operate along the optimal tradeoff curve. RGA also introduces low RAM usage and low computational cost.

- To address the practicality of our work, we conduct extensive simulations using the DiskSim simulator [8] with SSD extensions [1]. We first validate via synthetic workloads that our model efficiently characterizes the asymptotic steady-state performance. Furthermore, we consider real-world workload traces and use trace-driven simulations to study the performance tradeoff and versatility of RGA.

The rest of the paper proceeds as follows. In §2, we propose a Markov model to capture the system dynamics of an SSD and conduct the mean field analysis. We formally prove the convergence, and further extend the model for a general workload. In §3, we study the design tradeoff between cleaning cost and wear-leveling of GC algorithms. In §4, we propose RGA and analyze its performance. In §5, we validate our model via simulations. In §6, we present the trace-driven simulation results. In §7, we review related work, and finally in §8, we conclude the paper.

2. SYSTEM MODEL

We formulate a Markov chain model to characterize the I/O dynamics of an SSD under the read, write, and GC operations. We then analyze the model via the *mean field technique* when the SSD scales with the increasing number of blocks or storage capacity.

2.1 Markov Chain Model Formulation

Our model considers an SSD with N blocks of k pages each, where the typical value of k is 64 or 128 for today's commonly used SSDs. Since SSDs use the out-of-place write approach (see §1), a write to a logical page may reflect on any physical page.

Therefore, SSDs implement *address mapping* to map a logical page to a physical page. Address mapping is maintained in the software *flash translation layer (FTL)* in the SSD controller. It can be implemented in block level [43], page level [24], or hybrid form [16,33,40]. A survey of the FTL design including the address mapping mechanisms can be found in [17]. In this paper, our model abstracts out the complexity due to address mapping; specifically, we focus on the physical address space and directly characterize the I/O dynamics of physical blocks.

Recall from §1 that a page can be in one of the three states: *clean*, *valid* or *invalid*. We classify each block into a different type based on the number of valid pages containing in the block. Specifically, a block of type i contains exactly i valid pages. Since each block has k pages, a block can be of one of the $k+1$ types (i.e., from 0 to k valid pages). If a block is of type i, then we say it is in state i. Let $X_n(t)$ denote the state of block $n \in \{1, ..., N\}$ at time t. Then the state descriptor for the whole SSD is

$$\boldsymbol{X}^N(t) = (X_1(t), X_2(t), \ldots, X_N(t)), \quad (1)$$

where $X_i(t) \in \{0, 1, ..., k\}$. Thus, the state space cardinality is $(k+1)^N$. To facilitate our analysis under the large system regime (as we will show later), we transform the above state descriptor to:

$$\boldsymbol{n}^N(t) = (n_0(t), n_1(t), \ldots, n_k(t)), \quad (2)$$

where $n_i(t) \in \{0, 1, ..., N\}$ denotes the number of type i blocks in the SSD. Clearly, we have $\sum_{j=0}^{k} n_j(t) = N$, and the state space cardinality is $\binom{N+k}{k}$.

We first describe how different I/O requests affect the system dynamics of an SSD from the perspective of physical blocks. The I/O requests can be classified into four types: (1) read a page, (2) perform GC on a block, (3) program (i.e., write) new data to a page, and (4) invalidate a page. First, read requests do not change $\boldsymbol{n}^N(t)$. For GC, the SSD selects a block, writes all valid pages of that block to a clean block, and finally erases the selected block. Thus, GC requests do not change the state of $\boldsymbol{n}^N(t)$ either. On the other hand, for the program and invalidate requests, if the corresponding block is of type i, it will move from state i to state $i+1$ and to state $i-1$, respectively.

We now describe the state transition of a block in an SSD. Since the read and GC requests do not change $\boldsymbol{n}^N(t)$, we only need to model the program and invalidate requests. Suppose that the program and invalidate requests arrive as a Poisson process with rate λ. Also, suppose that the workload is *uniform*, such that all pages in the SSD will have an equal probability of being accessed (in §2.5, we extend our model for a general workload). The assumption of the uniform workload implies that (1) each block has the same probability $1/N$ of being accessed, (2) the probability of invalidating one page is proportional to the number of valid pages of the corresponding block, and (3) the probability of programming a page is proportional to the total number of invalid and clean pages of the corresponding block. Thus, if the requested block is of type i, then the probability of invalidating one page of the block is $\frac{i}{k}$, and that of programming one page in the block is $\frac{k-i}{k}$. Figure 1 illustrates the state transitions of a single block in an SSD under the program and invalidate requests. If a block is in state i, the program and invalidate requests will move it to state $i+1$ at rate $\frac{\lambda(k-i)}{Nk}$ and to state $i-1$ at rate $\frac{\lambda i}{Nk}$, respectively. Note that Figure 1 only shows the state transition of a *particular* block but not the whole SSD. Specifically, the state space cardinality of a particular block is $k+1$ as shown in Figure 1, while that of the whole SSD is $\binom{N+k}{k}$ as described by Equation (2).

To characterize the I/O dynamics of an SSD, we define the *occu-*

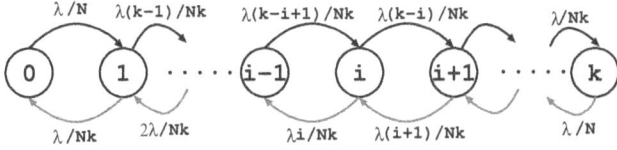

Figure 1: State transition of a block in an SSD.

pancy measure $\boldsymbol{M}^N(t)$ as the vector of fraction of type i blocks at time t. Formally, we have

$$\boldsymbol{M}^N(t) = (M_0(t), M_1(t), ..., M_k(t)),$$

where $M_i(t)$ is

$$M_i(t) = \frac{1}{N}\sum_{n=1}^{N}\mathbf{1}_{\{X_n(t)=i\}} = \frac{n_i(t)}{N}. \tag{3}$$

In other words, $M_i(t)$ is the *fraction* of type i blocks in the SSD. It is easy to see that the occupancy measure $\boldsymbol{M}^N(t)$ is a homogeneous Markov chain.

We are interested in modeling *large-scale* SSDs to understand the performance implication of any GC algorithms. By large-scale, we mean that the number of blocks N of an SSD is large. For example, for a 256GB SSD (which is available in many of today's SSD manufactures), we have $N \approx 1 \times 10^6$ and $k = 64$ for a page size of 4KB, implying a *huge* state space of $\boldsymbol{M}^N(t)$. Since $\boldsymbol{M}^N(t)$ does not possess any special structure (i.e., matrix-geometric form), analyzing it can be computationally expensive.

2.2 Mean Field Analysis

To make our Markov chain model tractable for a large-scale SSD, we employ the *mean field technique* [5, 38]. The main idea is that the stochastic process $\boldsymbol{M}^N(t)$ can be solved by a deterministic process $\boldsymbol{s}(t) = (s_0(t), s_1(t), ..., s_k(t))$ as $N \to \infty$, where $s_i(t)$ denotes the fraction of blocks of type i at time t in the deterministic process. We call $\boldsymbol{s}(t)$ the *mean field limit*. By solving the deterministic process $\boldsymbol{s}(t)$, we can obtain the occupancy measure of the stochastic process $\boldsymbol{M}^N(t)$.

We introduce the concept of *intensity* denoted by $\varepsilon(N)$. Intuitively, the probability that a block performs a state transition per time slot is in the order of $\varepsilon(N)$. Under the uniform workload, each block is accessed with the same probability $1/N$, so we have $\varepsilon(N) = 1/N$. Now, we re-scale the process $\boldsymbol{M}^N(t)$ to $\widetilde{\boldsymbol{M}}^N(t)$.

$$\widetilde{\boldsymbol{M}}^N(t\varepsilon(N)) = \boldsymbol{M}^N(t) \quad \forall t \geq 0. \tag{4}$$

For simplicity, we drop the notation t when the context is clear. We now show how the deterministic process $\boldsymbol{s}(t)$ is related to the re-scaled process $\widetilde{\boldsymbol{M}}^N(t)$. The time evolution of the deterministic process can be specified by the following set of ordinary differential equations (ODEs):

$$\frac{ds_i}{dt} = -\lambda s_i + \lambda \frac{k-i+1}{k}s_{i-1} + \lambda \frac{i+1}{k}s_{i+1}, \quad 1 \leq i \leq k-1,$$

$$\frac{ds_0}{dt} = -\lambda s_0 + \lambda \frac{1}{k}s_1, \tag{5}$$

$$\frac{ds_k}{dt} = -\lambda s_k + \lambda \frac{1}{k}s_{k-1}.$$

The idea of the above ODEs is explained as follows. For an SSD with N blocks, we express the expected change in number of blocks of type i over a small time period of length dt under

the re-scaled process $\widetilde{\boldsymbol{M}}^N(t)$. This corresponds to the expected change over the time period of length Ndt under the original process $\boldsymbol{M}^N(t)$. During this period (of length Ndt), there are $\lambda(Ndt)$ program/invalidate requests, each of which changes the state of some type i block to state $i-1$ or state $i+1$ with probability $1/N$. Since there are a total of Ns_i blocks of type i, the expected change from state i to other states is $\lambda Ndt s_i$. Using the similar arguments, the expected change in number of blocks from state $i+1$ to state i is $\lambda Ndt \frac{i+1}{k}s_{i+1}$, and that from state $i-1$ to state i is $\lambda Ndt \frac{k-i+1}{k}s_{i-1}$. Similarly, we can also specify the expected change in fraction of blocks of type 0 and type k, and we obtain the ODEs as stated in Equation (5).

2.3 Derivation of the Fixed Point

We now derive the *fixed point* of the deterministic process in Equation (5). Specifically, $\boldsymbol{s}(t)$ is said to be a fixed point if $\boldsymbol{s}(t) = \boldsymbol{\pi}$ implies $\boldsymbol{s}(t') = \boldsymbol{\pi}$ for all $t' \geq t$. In other words, the fixed point $\boldsymbol{\pi}$ describes the distribution of different types of blocks in the steady state. The necessary and sufficient condition for $\boldsymbol{\pi}$ to be a fixed point is that $\frac{d\pi_i}{dt} = 0$ for all $i \in \{0, 1, \ldots, k\}$.

Theorem 1. *Equation (5) has a unique fixed point $\boldsymbol{\pi}$ given by:*

$$\pi_i = \frac{\binom{k}{i}}{2^k}, \ 0 \leq i \leq k. \tag{6}$$

Proof: First, it is easy to check that $\boldsymbol{\pi}$ satisfies $\frac{d\pi_i}{dt} = 0$ for $0 \leq i \leq k$. Conversely, based on the condition of $\frac{d\pi_i}{dt} = 0$ for all i, we have

$$-\pi_i + \frac{k-i+1}{k}\pi_{i-1} + \frac{i+1}{k}\pi_{i+1} = 0, \quad 1 \leq i \leq k-1,$$

$$-\pi_0 + \frac{1}{k}\pi_1 = 0,$$

$$-\pi_k + \frac{1}{k}\pi_{k-1} = 0.$$

By solving these equations, we get

$$\pi_i = \binom{k}{i}\pi_k, \text{ for } 0 \leq i \leq k.$$

Since $\sum_{i=0}^{k}\pi_i = 1$, the fixed point is derived as in Equation (6). ∎

2.4 Summary

We develop a stochastic Markov chain model to characterize the I/O dynamics of a large-scale SSD system. Specifically, we solve the stochastic process with a deterministic process via the mean field technique and identify the fixed point in the steady state. We claim that the derivation is accurate when N is large, as we can formally provide that (i) the stochastic process converges to the deterministic process as $N \to \infty$ and (ii) the deterministic process specified by Equation (5) converges to the unique fixed point $\boldsymbol{\pi}$ as described in Equation (6). We refer readers to our technical report [34] for the convergence proofs.

Our model enables us to analyze the tradeoff between cleaning cost and wear-leveling of GC algorithms. As shown in §3, cleaning cost and wear-leveling can be expressed as functions of $\boldsymbol{\pi}$.

2.5 Extensions to General Workload

Our model thus far focuses on the uniform workload, i.e., all physical pages have the same probability of being accessed. For completeness, we now generalize our model to allow for the general workload, in which blocks/pages are accessed with respect to some general probability distribution. We show how we apply the mean field technique to approximate the I/O dynamics of an SSD, and we also conduct simulations using synthetic workloads to validate our approximation (see §5.1). As stated in §2.1, we focus on the program and invalidate requests, both of which can change the state of a block in the Markov chain model. We again assume that the program/invalidate requests arrive as a Poisson process with rate λ. In particular, to model the general workload, we let $p_{i,j}$ be the transition probability of a type i block being transited to state j due to one program/invalidate request. We have

$$p_{i,j} = 0, \quad \text{if } j \neq i - 1 \text{ and } j \neq i + 1,$$

$$\sum_i \sum_j p_{i,j} \left(\sum_n \mathbf{1}_{\{X_n(t)=i\}} \right) = 1,$$

where $\mathbf{1}_{\{X_n(t)=i\}}$ indicates whether block n is in state i, and thus $\sum_n \mathbf{1}_{\{X_n(t)=i\}}$ represents the number of blocks in state i. The second equation comes from the fact that each program/invalidate request can only change the state of one particular block.

In practice, $p_{i,j}$ (where $j = i - 1$ or $j = i + 1$) can be estimated via workload traces. Specifically, for each request being processed, one can count the number of blocks in state i (i.e., n_i) and the number of blocks in state i that change to state j (i.e., $n_{i,j}$). Then $p_{i,j}$ can be estimated as:

$$p_{i,j} \approx \frac{\sum_{\text{for each request}} \frac{n_{i,j}}{n_i}}{\text{total number of requests}}, \tag{7}$$

where $\frac{n_{i,j}}{n_i}$ is the probability that a block transits from state i to j in a particular request, and $p_{i,j}$ is the average over all requests.

We can derive the occupancy measure $\boldsymbol{M}^N(t)$ with a deterministic process $\boldsymbol{s}(t)$ specified by the following ODEs:

$$\frac{ds_i}{dt} = -\lambda(p_{i,i-1} + p_{i,i+1})s_i + \lambda p_{i-1,i}s_{i-1} + \lambda p_{i+1,i}s_{i+1}, 1 \leq i \leq k-1,$$

$$\frac{ds_0}{dt} = -\lambda p_{0,1}s_0 + \lambda p_{1,0}s_1,$$

$$\frac{ds_k}{dt} = -\lambda p_{k,k-1}s_k + \lambda p_{k-1,k}s_{k-1}. \tag{8}$$

We can further derive the fixed point of the deterministic process $\boldsymbol{s}(t)$ as in Theorem 2. For the convergence proof, please refer to our technical report [34].

Theorem 2. *Equation (8) has a unique fixed point $\boldsymbol{\pi}$ given by:*

$$\pi_k = \frac{1}{1 + \sum_{i=0}^{k-1} \frac{\prod_{j=k}^{i+1} p_{j,j-1}}{\prod_{j=i}^{k-1} p_{j,j+1}}},$$

$$\pi_i = \frac{\prod_{j=k}^{i+1} p_{j,j-1}}{\prod_{j=i}^{k-1} p_{j,j+1}} \pi_k, \qquad 0 \leq i \leq k-1. \tag{9}$$

Proof: The derivation is similar to that of Theorem 1. ∎

3. DESIGN SPACE OF GC ALGORITHMS

Using our developed stochastic model, we analyze how we can parameterize a GC algorithm to adapt to different performance-durability tradeoffs. In this section, we formally define two metrics, namely *cleaning cost* and *wear-leveling*, for general GC algorithms. Both metrics are defined based on the occupancy measure $\boldsymbol{\pi}$ which we derived in §2. We identify two optimal extremal points in GC algorithms. Finally, we identify the optimal tradeoff curve that explores the full optimal design space of GC algorithms.

3.1 Metrics

We now define the new parameters that are used to characterize a family of GC algorithms. When a GC algorithm is executed, it selects a block to reclaim. Let $w_i \geq 0$ (where $0 \leq i \leq k$) denote the weight of selecting a particular type i block (i.e., a block with i valid pages), such that the higher the weight w_i is, the more likely each type i block is chosen to be reclaimed. The weights are chosen with the following constraint:

$$\sum_{i=0}^k \frac{w_i}{N} \times n_i = \sum_{i=0}^k w_i \pi_i = 1. \tag{10}$$

The above constraint has the following physical meaning. The ratio w_i/N can be viewed as the probability of selecting a particular type i block for a GC operation. Since n_i is the total number of type i blocks in the system, $w_i \pi_i$ can be viewed as the probability of selecting *any* type i block for a GC operation. The summation of $w_i \pi_i$ over all i is equal to 1. Note that π_i is the occupancy measure that we derive in §2.

We now define two metrics that respectively characterize the performance and durability of a GC algorithm. The first metric is called the *cleaning cost*, denoted by $\mathcal{C}$, which is defined as the average number of valid pages contained in the block that is selected for a GC operation. This implies that the cleaning cost reflects the average number of valid pages that need to be written to another clean block during a GC operation. The cleaning cost reflects the performance of a GC algorithm, such that a high-performance GC algorithm should have a low cleaning cost. Formally, we have

$$\mathcal{C} = \sum_{i=0}^k i w_i \pi_i. \tag{11}$$

The second metric is called the *wear-leveling*, denoted by $\mathcal{W}$, which reflects how *balanced* the blocks are being erased by a GC algorithm. To improve the durability of an SSD, each block should have approximately the same number of erasures. We use the concept of the fairness index [29] to define the degree of wear-leveling $\mathcal{W}$, such that the higher $\mathcal{W}$ is, the more balanced the blocks are erased. Formally, we have

$$\mathcal{W} = \frac{(\sum_{i=0}^k \frac{w_i}{N} N\pi_i)^2}{N \sum_{i=0}^k (\frac{w_i}{N})^2 N\pi_i} = \left(\sum_{i=0}^k w_i^2 \pi_i \right)^{-1}. \tag{12}$$

Note that the rationale of Equation (12) comes from the fact that $\frac{w_i}{N}$ is the probability of selecting a *particular* type i block, and there are $N\pi_i$ type i blocks in total. For example, if all w_i's are equal to one, which implies that each block has the same probability $\frac{1}{N}$ of being selected, then the wear-leveling index $\mathcal{W}$ achieves its maximum value equal to one as $\sum_{i=0}^k \pi_i = 1$.

The set of w_i's, where $0 \leq i \leq k$, will be our selection parameters to design a GC algorithm. In the following, we show how we select w_i's for different GC algorithms subject to different tradeoffs between cleaning cost and wear-leveling. Our results are derived for a general workload subject to the system state distribution $\boldsymbol{\pi}$. Specifically, we also derive the closed-form solutions under the uniform workload as a case study.

3.2 GC Algorithm to Maximize Wear-leveling

Suppose that our goal is to find a set of weight w_i's such that a GC algorithm maximizes wear-leveling $\mathcal{W}$. We can formulate the following optimization problem:

$$\max \quad \mathcal{W} = \left(\sum_{i=0}^{k} w_i^2 \pi_i \right)^{-1} \quad (13)$$

$$s.t. \quad \sum_{i=0}^{k} w_i \pi_i = 1,$$

$$w_i \geq 0.$$

Since $\sum_{i=0}^{k} w_i^2 \pi_i - (\sum_{i=0}^{k} w_i \pi_i)^2 = \sum_{i=0}^{k} w_i^2 \pi_i - 1 \geq 0$, we always have $\mathcal{W} \leq 1$. Thus, the solution to the above optimization problem is $w_i = 1$ for all i, and the corresponding $\mathcal{W}$ is equal to 1 and achieves the maximum. The corresponding cleaning cost is $\sum_{i=0}^{k} i \pi_i$. In other words, each block has the same probability (i.e., $1/N$) of being selected for GC. Intuitively, this assignment strategy which maximizes wear-leveling is the *random algorithm*, in which each block is uniformly chosen independent of its number of valid pages.

Under the uniform workload, we can compute the closed-form solution of the cleaning cost $\mathcal{C}$ as:

$$\mathcal{C} = \sum_{i=0}^{k} i w_i \pi_i = \sum_{i=0}^{k} i \frac{\binom{k}{i}}{2^k} = \frac{k}{2}.$$

It implies that a random GC algorithm introduces an average of $k/2$ *additional page writes* under the uniform workload.

3.3 GC Algorithm to Minimize Cleaning Cost

Suppose now that our goal is to find a set of weight w_i's to minimize the cleaning cost $\mathcal{C}$, or equivalently, minimize the number of writes of valid pages during GC. The optimization formulation is:

$$\min \quad \mathcal{C} = \sum_{i=0}^{k} i w_i \pi_i \quad (14)$$

$$s.t. \quad \sum_{i=0}^{k} w_i \pi_i = 1,$$

$$w_i \geq 0.$$

Note that $\mathcal{C}$ must be non-negative. Thus, the solution to the above optimization problem is $w_0 = 1/\pi_0$ and $w_i = 0$ for all $i > 0$ (assuming that there exist some blocks of type 0), and the corresponding $\mathcal{C}$ is equal to 0 and achieves the minimum. The corresponding wear-leveling $\mathcal{W}$ is π_0. Intuitively, this assignment strategy corresponds to the *greedy algorithm*, which always chooses the block that has the minimum number of valid pages for GC.

Under the uniform workload, the closed-form solution of $\mathcal{W}$ corresponding to the minimum cost is given by:

$$\mathcal{W} = \frac{1}{w_0^2 \pi_0} = \frac{1}{2^k}.$$

The result shows that the greedy algorithm can significantly degrade wear-leveling. For today's commonly used SSDs, the typical value of k is 64 or 128. This implies that the degree of wear-leveling $\mathcal{W} \approx 0$, and the durability of the SSD suffers.

3.4 Exploring the Full Optimal Design Space

We identify two GC algorithms, namely the random and greedy algorithms, that correspond to two optimal extremal points of all GC algorithms. We now characterize the tradeoff between cleaning cost and wear-leveling, and identify the *full* optimal design space of GC algorithms. Specifically, we formulate an optimization problem: *given a cleaning cost $\mathcal{C}^*$, what is the maximum wear-leveling*

that a GC algorithm can achieve? Formally, we express the problem (with respect to w_i's) as follows:

$$\max \quad \mathcal{W} = \left(\sum_{i=0}^{k} w_i^2 \pi_i \right)^{-1} \quad (15)$$

$$s.t. \quad \sum_{i=0}^{k} w_i \pi_i = 1,$$

$$\sum_{i=0}^{k} i w_i \pi_i = \mathcal{C}^*,$$

$$w_i \geq 0.$$

Without loss of generality, we assume that $\pi_i > 0$ ($0 \leq i \leq k$). The solution of the optimization problem is stated in the following theorem.

Theorem 3. *Given a cleaning cost $\mathcal{C}^*$, the maximum wear-leveling $\mathcal{W}^*$ is given by:*

$$\mathcal{W}^* = \begin{cases} \pi_0, & \mathcal{C}^* = 0, \\ \dfrac{1}{\sum_{i=0}^{\mathcal{I}} \gamma_i^2 \pi_i}, & 0 < \mathcal{C}^* < \sum_{i=0}^{k} i \pi_i, \\ 1, & \mathcal{C}^* = \sum_{i=0}^{k} i \pi_i, \quad (16) \\ \dfrac{1}{\sum_{i=\mathcal{L}}^{k} \Gamma_i^2 \pi_i}, & \sum_{i=0}^{k} i \pi_i < \mathcal{C}^* < k, \\ \pi_k, & \mathcal{C}^* = k, \end{cases}$$

for some constants γ_i, $\mathcal{I}$, Γ_i, and $\mathcal{L}$.

Proof: The proof is in our technical report [34]. We also derive the constants $\mathcal{I}$, γ_i, $\mathcal{L}$, and Γ_i. ∎

4. RANDOMIZED GREEDY ALGORITHM

In this section, we present a *tunable* GC algorithm called the *randomized greedy algorithm* (RGA) that can operate at any given cleaning cost $\mathcal{C}^*$ and return the corresponding optimal wear-leveling $\mathcal{W}^*$; or equivalently, RGA can operate at any point along the optimal tradeoff curve of $\mathcal{C}^*$ and $\mathcal{W}^*$.

4.1 Algorithm Details

Algorithm 1 shows the pseudo-code of RGA, which operates as follows. Each time when GC is triggered, RGA *randomly* chooses d out of N blocks $b_1, b_2, \cdots, b_d$ as candidates (Step 2). Let $v(b_i)$ denote the number of valid pages of block b_i. Then RGA selects the block b^* that has the smallest number of valid pages, or the minimum $v(.)$, to reclaim (Step 3). We then invalidate block b^* and move its valid pages to another clean block (Steps 4-5). In essence, we define a *selection window* of window size d that defines a random subset of d out of N blocks to be selected. The window size d is the tunable parameter that enables us to choose between the random and greedy policies. Intuitively, the random selection of d blocks allows us to maximize wear-leveling, while the greedy selection within the selection window allows us to minimize the cleaning cost. Note that in the special cases where $d = 1$ (resp. $d \to \infty$), RGA corresponds to the random (resp. greedy) algorithm.

Algorithm 1 Randomized Greedy Algorithm (RGA)

1: **if** garbage collection is triggered **then**
2:     randomly choose d blocks $b_1, b_2, ..., b_d$;
3:     find block $b^* = \min_{v(b_i)}\{b_i : b_i \in \{b_1, b_2, ..., b_d\}\}$;
4:     write all valid pages in b^* to another clean block;
5:     erase b^*;
6: **end if**

4.2 Performance Analysis of RGA

We now derive the cleaning cost and wear-leveling of RGA. We first determine the values of weights w_i's for all i. Recall from §3.1 that $w_i\pi_i$ represents the probability of choosing any block of type i for GC. In RGA, a type i block is chosen for GC if and only if the randomly chosen d blocks all contain at least i valid pages and at least one of them contains i valid pages. Thus, the corresponding probability $w_i\pi_i$ is $(\sum_{j=i}^{k}\pi_j)^d - (\sum_{j=i+1}^{k}\pi_j)^d$. Note that this expression assumes that d blocks are chosen uniformly at random from the N blocks with replacement, while in RGA, these d blocks are chosen uniformly at random without replacement. However, we can still use it as approximation since d is much smaller than N for a large-scale SSD. Therefore, we have

$$w_i = \frac{(\sum_{j=i}^{k}\pi_j)^d - (\sum_{j=i+1}^{k}\pi_j)^d}{\pi_i}. \tag{17}$$

Based on the definitions of cleaning cost $\mathcal{C}$ in Equation (11) and wear-leveling $\mathcal{W}$ in Equation (12), we can derive $\mathcal{C}$ and $\mathcal{W}$:

$$\mathcal{C} = \sum_{i=0}^{k} i\left((\sum_{j=i}^{k}\pi_j)^d - (\sum_{j=i+1}^{k}\pi_j)^d\right), \tag{18}$$

$$\mathcal{W} = \frac{1}{\sum_{i=0}^{k}\left(\frac{(\sum_{j=i}^{k}\pi_j)^d - (\sum_{j=i+1}^{k}\pi_j)^d}{\pi_i}\right)^2 \pi_i}. \tag{19}$$

In §5, we will show the relationship between cleaning cost $\mathcal{C}$ and wear-leveling $\mathcal{W}$ based on RGA. We show that RGA almost lies on the optimal tradeoff curve of $\mathcal{C}$ and $\mathcal{W}$.

4.3 Deployment of RGA

We now highlight the practical implications when RGA is deployed. RGA is implemented in the *SSD controller* as a GC algorithm. From our evaluation (see details in §5), a small value of d (which is significantly less than the number of blocks N) suffices to make RGA lie on the optimal tradeoff curve. This allows RGA to incur low RAM usage and low computational overhead. Specifically, RGA only needs to load the meta information (e.g., number of valid pages) of d blocks into RAM for comparison. With a small value of d, RGA consumes an only small amount of RAM space. Also, RGA only needs to compare d blocks to select the block with the minimum number of valid pages for GC. The computational cost is $O(d)$ and hence very small as well. Since a practical SSD controller typically has limited RAM space and computational power, we expect that RGA addresses the practical needs and can be readily deployed.

We expect that RGA, like other GC algorithms, is only executed periodically or when the number of free blocks drops below a predefined threshold. The window size d can be tunable at different times during the lifespan of the SSD to achieve different levels of wear-leveling and cleaning cost along the optimal tradeoff curve. In particular, we emphasize that the window size d can be chosen as a *non-integer*. In this case, we can simply linearly extrapolate d between $\lfloor d \rfloor$ and $\lfloor d+1 \rfloor$. Formally, for a given non-integer value

d, when GC is triggered, RGA can set the window size as $\lfloor d \rfloor$ with probability p and set the window size as $\lfloor d+1 \rfloor$ with probability $1-p$, where p is given by:

$$d = p\lfloor d \rfloor + (1-p)\lfloor d+1 \rfloor. \tag{20}$$

Thus, we can evaluate the values of w_i's as follows:

$$w_i(d) = pw_i(\lfloor d \rfloor) + (1-p)w_i(\lfloor d+1 \rfloor),$$

based on Equation (17). The cleaning cost and wear-leveling of RGA can be computed accordingly via Equations (11) and (12) substituting $w_i(d)$. More generally, we can obtain the window size from some probability distribution with the mean value given by d. This enables us to operate at *any* point of the optimal tradeoff curve.

5. MODEL VALIDATION

We thus far formulate an analytical model that characterizes the I/O dynamics of an SSD, and further propose RGA that can be tuned to realize different performance-durability tradeoffs. In this section, we validate our theoretical results developed in prior sections. First, we validate via simulation that our system state derivations in Theorem 2 provide accurate approximation even for a general workload. Also, we validate that RGA operates along the optimal tradeoff curve characterized in Theorem 3.

5.1 Validation on Fixed-Point Derivations

Recall from §2 that we derive, via the mean field analysis, the fixed-point $\boldsymbol{\pi}$ for the system state of our model under both uniform and general workloads. We now validate the accuracy of such derivation. We use the DiskSim simulator [8] with SSD extensions [1]. We generate synthetic workloads for different read/write patterns to drive our simulations, and compare the system state obtained by each simulation with that of our model.

We feed the simulations with three different types of synthetic workloads: (1) Random, (2) Sequential, and (3) Hybrid. Specifically, Random means that the starting address of each I/O request is uniformly distributed in the logical address space. Note that its definition is (slightly) different from that of the uniform workload used in our model, as the latter directly considers the requests in the physical address space. The logical-to-physical address mapping will be determined by the simulator. Sequential means that each request starts at the address which immediately follows the last address accessed by the previous request. Hybrid assumes that there are 50% of Random requests and 50% of Sequential requests. Furthermore, for each synthetic workload, we consider both Poisson and non-Poisson arrivals. For the former, we assume that the inter-arrival time of requests follows an exponential distribution with mean 100ms; for the latter, we assume that the inter-arrival time of requests follow a normal distribution (denoted by $N(\mu, \sigma^2)$) with mean $\mu = 100$ms and standard deviation $\sigma = 10$ms.

Using simulations, we generate 10M requests for each workload and feed them to a small-scale SSD that contains 8 flash packages with 160 blocks each. We consider a small-scale SSD (i.e., with a small number of blocks) to make the SSD converge to an equilibrium state quickly with a sufficient number of requests; in §6, we consider a larger-size SSD. After running all 10M requests, we obtain the system state of the SSD for each workload from our simulation results. On the other hand, using our model, we first execute the workload and record the transition probabilities $p_{i,j}$'s based on Equation (7). We then compute the system state $\boldsymbol{\pi}$ using Theorem 2 for a general workload (which covers the uniform workload as well). We then compare the system states obtained from both the simulations and model derivations.

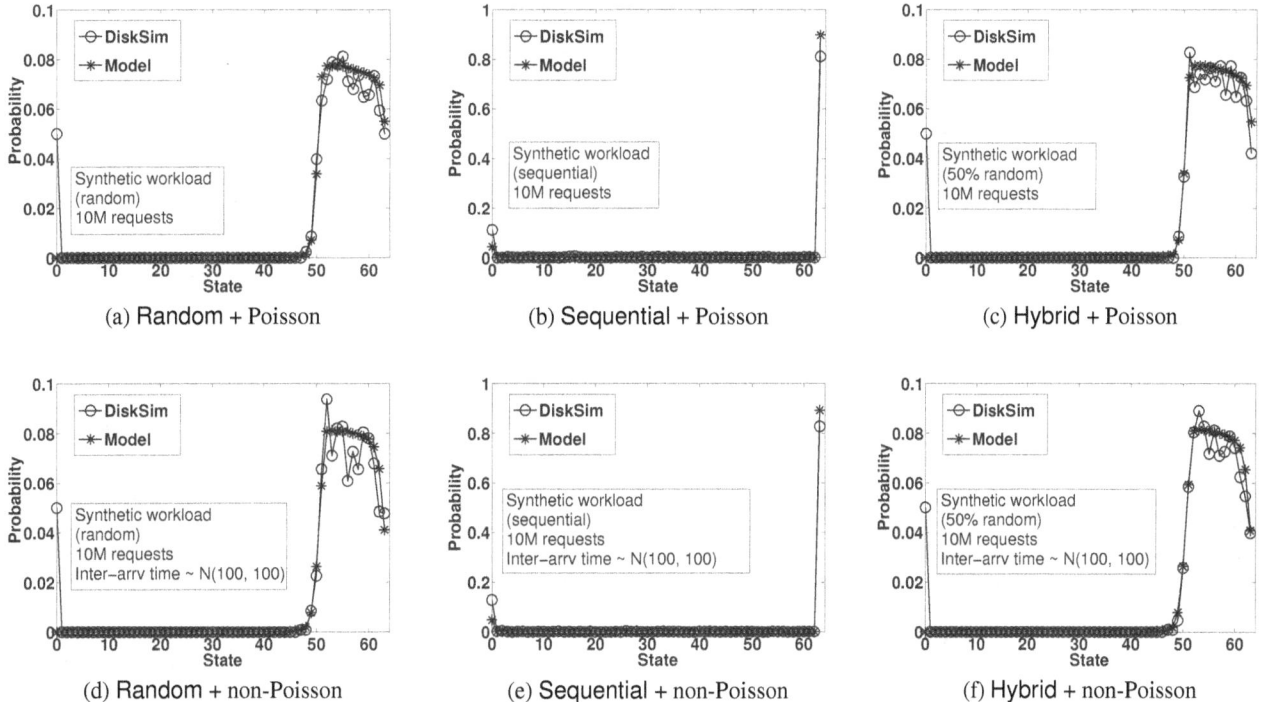

Figure 2: Model validation on the system state π. In each sub-figure, the x-axis represents the states (i.e., the number of valid pages in a block), and the y-axis indicates the state probabilities.

Figure 2 show the simulation and model results for the Random, Sequential, and Hybrid workloads, each associated with either the Poisson or non-Poisson arrivals of requests. The results show that under different synthetic workloads, our model derived from the mean field technique can still provide good approximations of the system state compared with that obtained from the simulations. Note that we also observe good approximations even for non-Poisson arrivals of requests. The results show the robustness of our model in evaluating the system state.

5.2 Validation on Operational Points of RGA

In §3, we characterize the optimal tradeoff curve between cleaning cost and wear-leveling; in §4, we present a GC algorithm called RGA that can be tuned by a parameter d to adjust the tradeoff between cleaning cost and wear-leveling. We now validate that RGA can indeed be tuned to operate on the optimal tradeoff curve.

We consider different system state distributions π to study the performance of RGA. We first consider π derived for the uniform workload (i.e., Equation (6)). We also consider three different distributions of π that are drawn from truncated normal distributions, denoted by $N(\mu, \sigma^2)$ with mean μ and standard deviation σ. Figure 3(a) illustrates the four system state distributions, where the mean and variance of each truncated normal distribution are shown in the figure.

For each system state distribution, we compute the maximum wear-leveling $\mathcal{W}^*$ for each cleaning cost $\mathcal{C}^*$ based on Theorem 3. Also, we evaluate the performance of RGA by varying the window size d from 1 to 100, and obtain the corresponding cleaning cost and wear-leveling based on Equations (18) and (19). Here, we only focus on the integer values of d.

Figure 3(b) shows the results, in which the four curves represent the optimal tradeoff curves corresponding to the four different

distributions of π, while the circles correspond to the operational points of RGA with different integer values of window size d from 1 to 100. Note that the maximum wear-leveling corresponds to RGA with window size $d = 1$ (i.e., the random algorithm). As the window size increases, the wear-leveling decreases, while the cleaning cost also decreases. We observe that RGA indeed operates along the optimal tradeoff curves with regard to different system state distributions.

It is important to note that we can realize non-integer window sizes to further fine-tune RGA along the optimal tradeoff curve (see §4.3). To validate, we consider different values of d from 1 to 2, with step size 0.05, and calculate d via linear extrapolation between 1 and 2.

Figure 3(c) shows the results for non-integer d using different system state distributions. Here, we zoom into the wear-leveling values from 0.75 to 1. Each star corresponds to the RGA with a non-integer window size obtained by Equation (20). We observe that RGA can be further fine-tuned to operate along the optimal tradeoff curves even when d is a non-integer.

6. TRACE-DRIVEN EVALUATION

In this section, we evaluate the performance of RGA under more realistic settings. Since today's SSD controllers are mainly proprietary firmware, it is non-trivial to implement GC algorithms inside a real-world SSD controller. Thus, similar to §5, we conduct our evaluation using the DiskSim simulator [8] with SSD extensions [1]. This time we focus on a large-scale SSD. We consider several real-world traces, and evaluate different metrics, including cleaning cost, I/O throughput, wear-leveling, and durability, for different GC algorithms. Note that the cleaning cost and wear-leveling

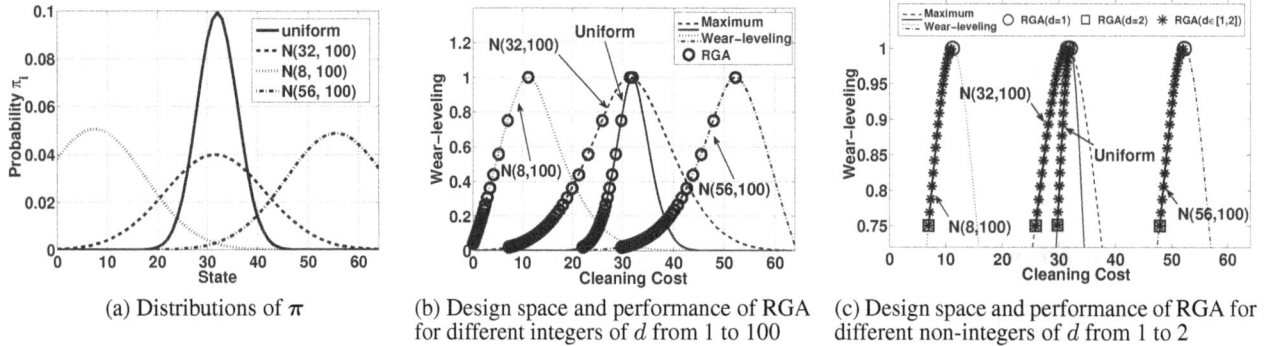

(a) Distributions of π (b) Design space and performance of RGA for different integers of d from 1 to 100   (c) Design space and performance of RGA for different non-integers of d from 1 to 2

Figure 3: Full design space and the performance of RGA.

are the metrics considered in the model, while the I/O throughput and durability are the metrics related to user experience.

Using trace-driven evaluation, our goal is to demonstrate the effectiveness of RGA in practical deployment. We compare different variants of RGA with regard to different values of window size d, as well as the random and greedy algorithms. We emphasize that we are *not* advocating a particular value of d for RGA in real deployment; instead, we show how different values of d can be tuned along the performance-durability tradeoff.

6.1 Datasets

We first describe the datasets that drive our evaluation. Since the read requests do not influence our analysis, we focus on four real-world traces that are all write-intensive:

- Financial [44]: It is an I/O trace collected from an online transaction process application running at a large financial institution. There are two financial traces in [44], namely Financial1.spc and Financial2.spc. Since Financial2.spc is read-dominant, we only use Financial1.spc in this paper.

- Webmail [46]: It is an I/O trace that describes the webmail workload of a university department mail server.

- Online [46]: It is an I/O trace that describes the coursework management workload on Moodle at a university.

- Webmail+Online [46]: It is the combination of the I/O traces of Webmail and Online.

Table 1 summarizes the statistics of the traces. The original Financial trace in [44] contains 24 application-specific units (ASUs) of a storage server (denoted by ASU0 to ASU23). We study the traces of all ASUs except ASU1, ASU3, and ASU5, whose maximum logical sector numbers go beyond the logical address space in our configured SSD (see §6.2). The remaining Financial trace contains around 4.4 million I/O requests, in which 77.82% are write requests and the remaining are read requests. Also, 1.67% of I/O requests are *sequential requests*, each of which has its starting address immediately following the last address of its prior request. The average size of each request is 5.4819KB, meaning that most requests only access one page as the size of one page is configured as 4KB in the simulation. The average inter-arrival time of two continuous requests is just around 10 ms. On the other hand, for the Webmail, Online and Webmail+Online traces obtained from [46], the write requests account for around 80% of I/O requests, and over 70% of I/O requests are sequential requests. Moreover, all requests

in those traces have size 4KB (i.e., only one page is accessed in each request), and the average inter-arrival time is much longer than that of the Financial trace. In summary, the Financial trace has the *random-write-dominant* access pattern, while the Webmail, Online, and Webmail+Online traces have the *sequential-write-dominant* access pattern.

We set the page size of an SSD as 4KB (the default value in most today's SSDs). Since the block size considered by these traces is 512 bytes, we align the I/O requests of these traces to be multiples of the 4KB page size. To enable us to evaluate different GC algorithms, we need to make the blocks in an SSD undergo a sufficient number of program-erase cycles. However, these traces may not be long enough to trigger enough block erasures. Thus, we propose to *replay* a trace; that is, in each replay cycle, we make a copy of the original trace without changing its I/O patterns, while we only change the arrival times of the requests by adding a constant value. In our simulations, we replay the traces multiple times so that each trace file contains around 50M I/O requests. Since we replay a trace, we issue the same write request to a page multiple times, and this keeps invalidating pages due to out-of-place writes. Thus, many GC operations will be triggered, and this enables us to stress-test the cleaning cost and wear-leveling metrics. We point out that this replay approach has also been used in the prior SSD work [39].

6.2 System Configuration

Table 2 summarizes the parameters that we use to configure an SSD in our evaluation. We use the default configurations from the simulator whose parameters are based on a common SLC SSD [13]. Specifically, the SSD contains 8 flash packages, each of which has its own control bus and data bus, so they can process I/O requests in parallel. Each flash package contains 8 planes containing 2048 blocks each. Each block contains 64 pages of size 4KB each. Therefore, each flash package contains 16384 physical blocks in total and the physical capacity of the SSD is 32GB. For the timing parameters, the time to read one page from the flash media to the register in the plane is $25\mu s$, and the time of programming one page from the register in the plane to the flash media is 0.2ms. For an erase operation, it takes 1.5ms to erase one block. The time of transferring one byte through the data bus line is $0.025\mu s$. Since an SSD is usually over-provisioned, we set the over-provisioning factor as 15%, which means that the advertised capacity of an SSD is only 85% of the physical capacity. Moreover, we set the threshold of triggering GC as 5%, meaning that GC will be triggered when the number of free blocks in the system is smaller than 5%.

Trace	Total # of requests	Write ratio	Sequential ratio	Avg. request size	Avg. inter-arrival time
Financial	4.4 M	0.7782	0.0167	5.4819 KB	9.9886 ms
Webmail	7.8 M	0.8186	0.7868	4 KB	222.118 ms
Online	5.7 M	0.7388	0.7373	4 KB	303.763 ms
Webmail+Online	13.5 M	0.7849	0.7597	4 KB	128.302 ms

Table 1: Workload statistics of traces.

Parameter	Value
page size	4KB
# of pages per block	64
# of blocks per package	16384
# of packages per SSD	8
SSD capacity	32 GB
read one page	0.025ms
write one page	0.2ms
erase one block	1.5ms
transfer one byte	0.000025ms
over-provisioning	15%
threshold of triggering GC	5%

Table 2: Configuration parameters.

Since flash packages are independent in processing I/O requests, GC is also triggered independently in each flash package. In the following, we only focus on a single flash package and compare the performance of different GC algorithms.

We consider two different initial states of an SSD before we start our simulations. The first one is the *empty* state, meaning that the SSD is entirely clean and no data has been stored. The second one is the *full* state, meaning the SSD is fully occupied with valid data and each logical address is always mapped to a physical page containing valid data. Thus, each write request to a (valid) page will trigger an update operation, which writes the new data to a clean page and invalidates the original page. Note that the full initial state is the default setting in the simulator. In most of our simulations (§6.3-§6.5), we use the full initial state as it can be viewed as "stress-testing" the I/O performance of an SSD. When we study the durability of SSDs (§6.6), we use the empty initial state as it can be viewed as the state of a brand-new SSD.

6.3 Cleaning Cost

We first evaluate the cleaning cost of different GC algorithms. In particular, we execute the traces with each of the GC algorithms and record the total number of GC operations and the total number of valid pages which are written back due to GC. We then derive the cleaning cost as the average number of valid pages that are written back in each GC operation.

Figure 4 shows the simulation results. In this figure, there are four groups of bars which correspond to the Financial, Webmail, Online, and Webmail+Online traces, respectively. In each group, there are seven bars which correspond to the greedy algorithm, random algorithm and RGA with different window sizes d. The vertical axis represents the cleaning cost that each GC algorithm incurs. In this simulation, the simulator starts from the full initial state. We can see that the greedy algorithm incurs the smallest cleaning cost that is almost 0, while the random algorithm has the highest cleaning cost that is close to the total number of pages in each block (i.e., k=64). The intuition is that if the greedy algorithm is used, then for every GC operation, the block containing the smallest number of valid pages is reclaimed, which means that it only needs to read out

and write back the smallest number of pages. Therefore, the cleaning cost of the greedy algorithm should be the smallest among all algorithms. Moreover, RGA provides a variable cleaning cost between the greedy and random algorithms.

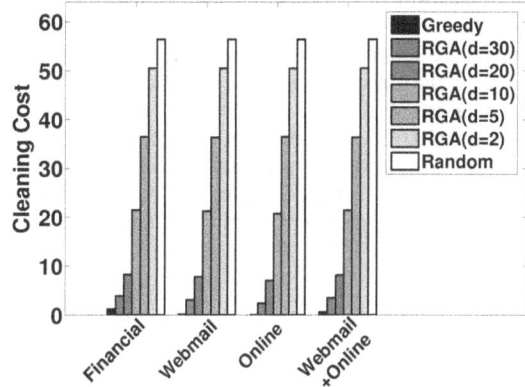

Figure 4: Cleaning cost of different GC algorithms.

6.4 Impact on I/O Throughput

We now consider the impact of different GC algorithms on the I/O throughput, using the metric Input/Output Operations Per Second (IOPS). Note that IOPS is an *indirect* indicator of the cleaning cost. Specifically, the higher the cleaning cost, the more pages needed to be moved in each GC operation. This prolongs the duration of a GC operation, and leads to smaller IOPS as an I/O request must be queued for a longer time until a GC operation is finished.

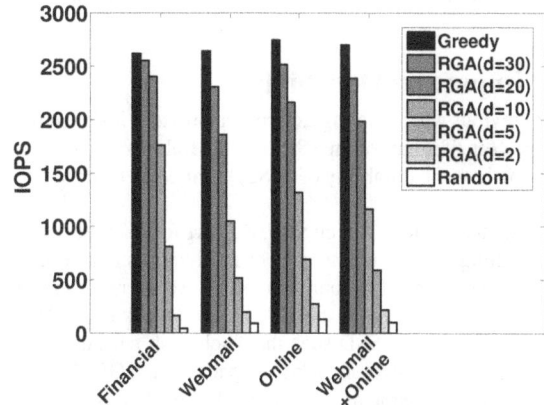

Figure 5: IOPS of different GC algorithms.

Figure 5 shows the IOPS results of different GC algorithms (note that the simulator starts from the full initial state). We can see that the greedy algorithm achieves the highest IOPS, and the random algorithm has the lowest IOPS, which is less than 5% of the IOPS achieved by the greedy algorithm. The results conform to those in Figure 4. This means that the cleaning cost, the metric that we use in our analytical model, correctly reflects the resulting I/O performance. Again, RGA can provide different I/O throughput results with different values of d.

6.5 Wear-Leveling

We now evaluate the wear-leveling of different GC algorithms. In the simulation, we execute the traces with each of the GC algorithms and record the number of times that each block has been erased. We then estimate the probability that each block is chosen for GC and derive the wear-leveling based on its definition in Equation (12).

Figure 6 shows the wear-leveling results. It is clear that the random algorithm always achieves the maximum wear-leveling, which is almost one. This implies that the random algorithm can effectively balance the numbers of erasures across all blocks. On the other hand, the greedy algorithm achieves the minimum wear-leveling which is less than 0.2 for all traces. Here, we note that in all traces, our RGA realizes different levels of wear-leveling between the random and greedy algorithms with different values of d. In particular, when $d \leq 2$, the wear-leveling of RGA is within 80% of the maximum wear-leveling of the random algorithm.

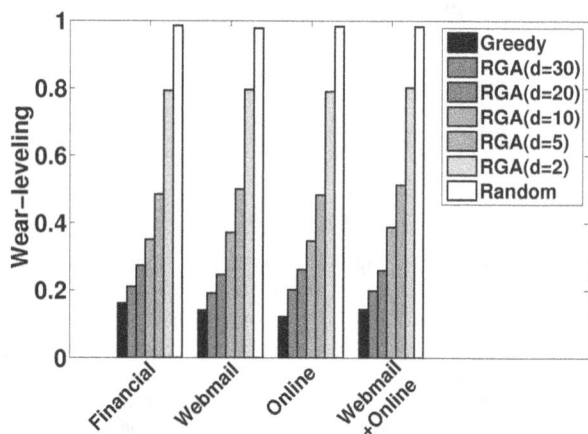

Figure 6: Wear-leveling of different GC algorithms.

6.6 Impact on Durability

The previous wear-leveling experiment provides insights into the durability (or lifetime) of an SSD. In this evaluation, we focus on examining how the durability of an SSD is affected by different GC algorithms.

To study the durability of an SSD, we have to make the SSD continue handling a sufficient number of I/O requests until it is worn out. In order to speed up our simulation, we decrease the maximum number of erasures sustainable by each block to 50. We also reduce the size of the SSD such that each flash package contains 4096 blocks, so the size of each flash package is 1GB. Other configurations are the same as we described in §6.2. Also, instead of using the real-world traces as in previous simulations, we drive the simulation with the synthetic traces that have more aggressive I/O rates so that the SSD is worn out soon. Specifically, we consider the same set of synthetic traces Random, Hybrid and Sequential as described in §5.1, but here we set the mean inter-arrival time of I/O requests to be 10ms (as opposed to 100ms in §5.1) based on Poisson arrivals.

Due to the use of bad block management [37], an SSD can allow a small percentage of bad (worn-out) blocks during its lifetime. Suppose that the SSD can allow up to $e\%$ of bad blocks for some parameter e. To derive the durability of the SSD, we first continue running each workload trace on the SSD until $e\%$ blocks are worn out, i.e., the erasure limit is reached. Then we record the length of the duration span that the SSD survives, and take it as the durability of the SSD. For comparison, we normalize the durability with respect to that of the greedy algorithm (which is expected to have the minimum durability). In this experiment, we consider the case where $e\% = 5\%$, while we also verify that similar observations are made for other values of $e\% \leq 10\%$. Also, we assume that the SSD is brand-new (i.e., the initial state is empty) and all blocks have no erasure at the beginning.

Figure 7 shows the results. We observe that the durability results of different GC algorithms are consistent with those of wear-leveling in Figure 6. We observe that the random algorithm achieves the maximum durability, and the value can be almost six times over that of the greedy algorithm (e.g., in the Sequential workload). Again, RGA provides a tunable durability between the random and greedy algorithms. When the window size $d \leq 5$, the durability of RGA can be within 68% of the maximum lifetime of the random algorithm for Random and Hybrid workloads. For the Sequential workload, the durability of RGA drops to 40% of the maximum lifetime of the random algorithm when $d = 5$. However, it is still almost 3 times higher than that of the greedy algorithm.

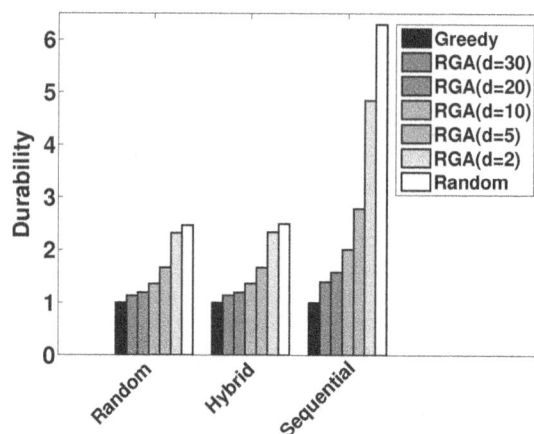

Figure 7: Durability of different GC algorithms (normalized with respect to the greedy algorithm).

6.7 Summary

From the above simulations, we see that the greedy algorithm performs the best and the random algorithm performs the worst in terms of cleaning cost and I/O throughput, while the opposite holds in terms of wear-leveling and durability. We demonstrate that our RGA provides a tradeoff spectrum between the two algorithms by tuning the window size. This simulation study not only confirms our theoretical model, but also shows that our RGA can be viewed as an effective tunable algorithm to balance between throughput performance and durability of an SSD.

7. RELATED WORK

The research on NAND-flash based SSDs has recently received a lot of attention. Many aspects of SSDs are being studied. A survey on algorithms and data structures for flash memories can be found in [22]. Kawaguchi et al. [31] propose a flash-based file system based on the log-structured file system design. Birrell et al. [6] propose new data structures to improve the write performance of SSDs, and Gupta et al. [25] suggest to exploit value locality and design content addressable SSDs so as to optimize the performance. Matthews et al. [36] use NAND-based disk caching to mitigate the I/O bottlenecks of HDDs, and Kim et al. [32] consider hybrid storage by combining SSDs and HDDs. Agrawal et al. [1] study different design tradeoffs of SSDs via a trace-driven simulator based on DiskSim [8]. Chen et al. [13] further reveal many intrinsic characteristics of SSDs via empirical measurements. Polte et al. [42] also study the performance of SSDs via experiments, and Park et al. [41] mainly focus on the energy efficiency of SSDs. Note that [1] addresses the tradeoff between cleaning cost and wear-leveling in GC, but it is mainly based on empirical evaluation.

A variety of wear-leveling techniques have been proposed, mainly from an applied perspective. Some of them are proposed in patents [2, 3, 7, 20, 26, 35, 47]. Several research papers have been proposed to maximize wear-leveling in SSDs based on *hot-cold swapping*, whose main idea is to swap the frequently-used hot data in worn blocks and the rarely-used cold data in new blocks. For example, Chiang et al. [14, 15] propose clustering methods for hot/cold data based on access patterns to maximize wear-leveling. Jung et al. [30] propose a memory-efficient design for wear-leveling by tracking only block groups, while maintaining wear-leveling performance. Authors of [10–12] also propose different strategies based on hot-cold swapping to further improve the wear-leveling performance. Our work differs from above studies in that we focus on characterizing the optimal tradeoff of GC algorithms, such that we provide flexibility for SSD practitioners to reduce wear-leveling to trade for higher cleaning performance. We also propose a tunable GC algorithm to realize the tradeoff.

From a theoretical perspective, some studies propose analytical frameworks to quantify the performance of GC algorithms. A comparative study between online and offline wear-leveling policies is presented in [4]. Hu et al. [28] propose a probabilistic model to quantify the additional writes due to GC (i.e., the cleaning cost defined in our work). They study a modified greedy GC algorithm, and implement an event-driven simulator to validate their model. Bux and Iliadis [9] propose theoretical models to analyze the greedy GC algorithm under the uniform workload, and Desnoyers [18] also analyzes the performance of LRU and greedy GC algorithms when page-level address mapping is used. Our work differs from them in the following. First, the previous work focuses on analyzing the write amplification which corresponds to the cleaning cost in our paper, but our focus is to analyze the tradeoff between cleaning cost and wear-leveling, which are both very important in designing GC algorithms, and further explore the design space of GC algorithms. Second, our analytical models are also very different. In particular, we use a Markov model to characterize the I/O dynamics of SSDs and adapt the mean field technique to approximate large-scale systems, then we develop an optimization framework to derive the optimal tradeoff curve. Finally, our model also provides a good approximation under general workload and address mapping, and it is further validated via trace-driven evaluation.

We note that an independent analytical work [45], which is published in the same conference as ours, also applies the mean-field technique to analyze different GC algorithms. Its d-choices GC algorithm has the same construction as our RGA. Our work has the following key differences. First, similar to prior analytical studies, the work [45] focuses on write amplification, while we focus on the trade-off between cleaning cost and wear leveling. Second, its analysis is limited to the uniform workload only, while we also

address the general workload. Finally, we validate our analysis via trace-driven simulations, which are not considered in the work [45].

8. CONCLUSIONS

In this paper, we propose an analytical model to characterize the performance-durability tradeoff of an SSD. We model the I/O dynamics of a large-scale SSD, and use the mean field theory to derive the asymptotic results in equilibrium. In particular, we classify the blocks of an SSD into different types according to the number of valid pages contained in each block, and our mean field results can provide effective approximation on the fraction of different types of blocks in the steady state even under the general workload. We define two metrics, namely cleaning cost and wear-leveling, to quantify the performance of GC algorithms. In particular, we theoretically characterize the optimal tradeoff curve between cleaning cost and wear-leveling, and develop an optimization framework to explore the full optimal design space of GC algorithms. Inspired from our analytical framework, we develop a tunable GC algorithm called the randomized greedy algorithm (RGA) which can efficiently balance the tradeoff between cleaning cost and wear-leveling by tuning the parameter of the window size d. We use trace-driven simulation based on DiskSim with SSD add-ons to validate our analytical model, and show the effectiveness of RGA in tuning the performance-durability tradeoff in deployment.

9. REFERENCES

[1] N. Agrawal, V. Prabhakaran, T. Wobber, J. D. Davis, M. Manasse, and R. Panigrahy. Design Tradeoffs for SSD Performance. In *Proc. of USENIX ATC*, Jun 2008.

[2] M. Assar, S. Nemazie, and P. Estakhri. Flash Memorymass Storage Architecture Incorporation Wear Leveling Technique. US patent 5,479,638, Dec 1995.

[3] A. Ban. Wear Leveling of Static Areas in Flash Memory. US patent 6732221, May 2004.

[4] A. Ben-Aroya and S. Toledo. Competitive Analysis of Flash-memory Algorithms. In *Proc. of Annual European Symposium*, Sep 2006.

[5] M. Benaïm and J.-Y. L. Boudec. A Class of Mean Field Interaction Models for Computer and Communication Systems. *Performance Evaluation*, 2008.

[6] A. Birrell, M. Isard, C. Thacker, and T. Wobber. A Design for High-performance Flash Disks. *ACM SIGOPS Oper. Syst. Rev.*, 41(2):88–93, Apr 2007.

[7] R. H. Bruce, R. H. Bruce, E. T. Cohen, and A. J. Christie. Unified Re-map and Cache-index Table with Dual Write-counters for Wear-leveling of Non-volitile Flash Ram Mass Storage. US patent 6,000,006, Dec 1999.

[8] J. S. Bucy, J. Schindler, S. W. Schlosser, and G. R. Ganger. The DiskSim Simulation Environment Version 4.0 Reference Manual. Technical Report CMUPDL-08-101, Carnegie Mellon University, May 2008.

[9] W. Bux and I. Iliadis. Performance of Greedy Garbage Collection in Flash-based Solid-state Drives. *Performance Evaluation*, November 2010.

[10] L.-P. Chang and C.-D. Du. Design and Implementation of an Efficient Wear-leveling Algorithm for Solid-state-disk Microcontrollers. *ACM Trans. Des. Autom. Electron. Syst.*, 15(1):6:1–6:36, Dec 2009.

[11] L.-P. Chang and L.-C. Huang. A Low-cost Wear-leveling Algorithm for Block-mapping Solid-state Disks. In *Proc of SIGPLAN/SIGBED Conf. on LCTES*, Apr 2011.

[12] Y.-H. Chang, J.-W. Hsieh, and T.-W. Kuo. Improving Flash Wear-Leveling by Proactively Moving Static Data. *IEEE Tran. on Computers*, 59:53–65, Jan 2010.

[13] F. Chen, D. A. Koufaty, and X. Zhang. Understanding Intrinsic Characteristics and System Implications of Flash Memory Based Solid State Drives. In *Proc. of ACM SIGMETRICS*, Jun 2009.

[14] M.-L. Chiang and R.-C. Chang. Cleaning Policies in Mobile Computers Using Flash Memory. *J. Syst. Softw.*, 48(3):213–231, Nov 1999.

[15] M.-L. Chiang, P. C. H. Lee, and R.-C. Chang. Using Data Clustering to Improve Cleaning Performance for Flash Memory. *Softw. Pract. Exper.*, 29(3):267–290, Mar 1999.

[16] T.-S. Chung, D.-J. Park, S. Park, D.-H. Lee, S.-W. Lee, and H.-J. Song. System Software For Flash Memory: A Survey. In *Proc. of Int. Conf. on Embedded and Ubiquitous Computing*, 2006.

[17] T.-S. Chung, D.-J. Park, S. Park, D.-H. Lee, S.-W. Lee, and H.-J. Song. A Survey of Flash Translation Layer. *Journal of Systems Architecture*, 55(5-6):332–343, May 2009.

[18] P. Desnoyers. Analytic Modeling of SSD Write Performance. In *Proceedings of SYSTOR*, 2012.

[19] R. Enderle. Revolution in January: EMC Brings Flash Drives into the Data Center. http://www.itbusinessedge.com/blogs/rob/?p=184, Jan 2008.

[20] P. Estakhri, M. Assar, R. Reid, Alan, and B. Iman. Method of and Architecture for Controlling System Data with Automatic Wear Leveling in a Semiconductor Non-volitile Mass Storage Memory. US patent 5,835,935, Nov 1998.

[21] D. Floyer. Flash Pricing Trends Disrupt Storage. http://wikibon.org/wiki/v/Flash_Pricing_Trends_Disrupt_Storage, May 2010.

[22] E. Gal and S. Toledo. Algorithms and Data Structures for Flash Memories. *ACM Computing Surveys*, 37(2):138–163, Jun 2005.

[23] L. M. Grupp, J. D. Davis, and S. Swanson. The Bleak Future of NAND Flash Memory. In *Proc. of USENIX FAST*, 2012.

[24] A. Gupta, Y. Kim, and B. Urgaonkar. DFTL: A Flash Translation Layer Employing Demand-based Selective Caching of Page-level Address Mappings. In *Proc. of ACM ASPLOS*, March 2009.

[25] A. Gupta, R. Pisolkar, B. Urgaonkar, and A. Sivasubramaniam. Leveraging Value Locality in Optimizing NAND Flash-based SSDs. In *Proc. of USENIX FAST*, 2011.

[26] S.-W. Han. Flash Memory Wear Leveling System and Method. US patent 6,016,275, Jan 2000.

[27] K. Hess. 2011: Year of the SSD? http://www.datacenterknowledge.com/archives/2011/02/17/2011-year-of-the-ssd/, Feb 2011.

[28] X.-Y. Hu, E. Eleftheriou, R. Haas, I. Iliadis, and R. Pletka. Write Amplification Analysis in Flash-based Solid State Drives. In *Proc. of SYSTOR*, May 2009.

[29] R. K. Jain, D.-M. W. Chiu, and W. R. Hawe. A Quantitative Measure Of Fairness And Discrimination For Resource Allocation In Shared Computer Systems. Technical report, DEC, 1984.

[30] D. Jung, Y.-H. Chae, H. Jo, J.-S. Kim, and J. Lee. A Group-based Wear-leveling Algorithm for Large-capacity Flash Memory Storage Systems. In *Proc. of Int. Conf. on Compilers, Architecture, and Synthesis for Embedded Systems*, Sep 2007.

[31] A. Kawaguchi, S. Nishioka, and H. Motoda. A Flash-memory Based File System. In *Proc. of USENIX Technical Conference*, Jan 1995.

[32] Y. Kim, A. Gupta, B. Urgaonkar, P. Berman, and A. Sivasubramaniam. HybridStore: A Cost-Efficient, High-Performance Storage System Combining SSDs and HDDs. In *Proc. of IEEE MASCOTS*, Jul 2011.

[33] S.-W. Lee, D.-J. Park, T.-S. Chung, D.-H. Lee, S. Park, and H.-J. Song. A Log Buffer-based Flash Translation Layer Using Fully-associative Sector Translation. *ACM Trans. on Embedded Computing Systems*, 6(3), Jul 2007.

[34] Y. Li, P. P. Lee, and J. C. Lui. Stochastic Modeling of Large-Scale Solid-State Storage Systems: Analysis, Design Tradeoffs and Optimization. Techinical report. arXiv:1303.4816.

[35] K. M. J. Lofgren, R. D. Norman, G. B. Thelin, and A. Gupta. Wear Leveling Techniques for Flash EEPROM Systems. US patent 6,850,443, Feb 2005.

[36] J. Matthews, S. Trika, D. Hensgen, R. Coulson, and K. Grimsrud. Intel® Turbo Memory: Nonvolatile Disk Caches in the Storage Hierarchy of Mainstream Computer Systems. *ACM Trans. on Storage*, 4(2):4:1–4:24, May 2008.

[37] Micron Technology. Bad Block Management in NAND Flash Memory. Technical Note, TN-29-59, 2011.

[38] M. Mitzenmacher. Load Balancing and Density Dependent Jump Markov Processes. In *Proc. of IEEE FOCS*, Oct. 1996.

[39] M. Murugan and D. Du. Rejuvenator: A Static Wear Leveling Algorithm for NAND Flash Memory with Minimized Overhead. In *Proc. of IEEE MSST*, May 2011.

[40] C. Park, W. Cheon, J. Kang, K. Roh, W. Cho, and J.-S. Kim. A Reconfigurable FTL (Flash Translation Layer) Architecture for NAND Flash-based Applications. *ACM Trans. Embed. Comput. Syst.*, 7(4):38:1–38:23, Aug 2008.

[41] S. Park, Y. Kim, B. Urgaonkar, J. Lee, and E. Seo. A Comprehensive Study of Energy Efficiency and Performance of Flash-based SSD. *Journal of Systems Architecture*, 57(4):354–365, April 2011.

[42] M. Polte, J. Simsa, and G. Gibson. Enabling Enterprise Solid State Disks Performance. In *1st Workshop on Integrating Solid-state Memory into the Storage Hierarchy*, March 2009.

[43] Z. Qin, Y. Wang, D. Liu, and Z. Shao. Demand-based Block-level Address Mapping in Large-scale NAND Flash Storage Systems. In *Proc. of IEEE/ACM/IFIP CODES+ISSS*, Oct 2010.

[44] Storage Performance Council. http://traces.cs.umass.edu/index.php/Storage/Storage, 2002.

[45] B. Van Houdt. A Mean Field Model for a Class of Garbage Collection Algorithms in Flash-based Solid State Drives. In *Proc. of ACM SIGMETRICS*, 2013.

[46] A. Verma, R. Koller, L. Useche, and R. Rangaswami. SRCMap: Energy Proportional Storage using Dynamic Consolidation. In *Proc. of USENIX FAST*, Feb 2010. http://sylab.cs.fiu.edu/projects/srcmap/start.

[47] S. E. Wells. Method for Wear Leveling in a Flash EEPROM Memory. US patent 5,341,339, Aug 1994.

A Mean Field Model for a Class of Garbage Collection Algorithms in Flash-based Solid State Drives

Benny Van Houdt
Department of Mathematics and Computer Science,
University of Antwerp - iMinds, Belgium
benny.vanhoudt@ua.ac.be

ABSTRACT

Garbage collection (GC) algorithms play a key role in reducing the write amplification in flash-based solid state drives, where the write amplification affects the lifespan and speed of the drive. This paper introduces a mean field model to assess the write amplification and the distribution of the number of valid pages per block for a class $\mathcal{C}$ of GC algorithms. Apart from the RANDOM GC algorithm, class $\mathcal{C}$ includes two novel GC algorithms: the d-CHOICES GC algorithm, that selects d blocks uniformly at random and erases the block containing the least number of valid pages among the d selected blocks, and the RANDOM++ GC algorithm, that repeatedly selects another block uniformly at random until it finds a block with a lower than average number of valid blocks.

Using simulation experiments we show that the proposed mean field model is highly accurate in predicting the write amplification (for drives with $N = 50000$ blocks). We further show that the d-CHOICES GC algorithm has a write amplification close to that of the GREEDY GC algorithm even for small d values, e.g., $d = 10$, and offers a more attractive trade-off between its simplicity and its performance than the WINDOWED GC algorithm introduced and analyzed in earlier studies. The RANDOM++ algorithm is shown to be less effective as it is even inferior to the FIFO algorithm when the number of pages b per block is large (e.g., for $b \geq 64$).

Categories and Subject Descriptors

D.4.2 [**Storage Management**]: Garbage collection; D.4.8 [**Performance**]: Stochastic analysis

General Terms

Performance, Algorithms

Keywords

Write amplification; flash-based solid state drives; garbage collection; mean field

1. INTRODUCTION

Data on a NAND flash-based solid state drive (SSD) is organized in blocks that each contain a fixed number of pages, where a page is the smallest writable unit. The size of a single page is typically 2 to 4 Kbyte and there can be as many as 128 pages per block. In order to write data on a page, it must first be in an *erase* state. Individual pages cannot be erased, only entire blocks can be erased. As it would be very time consuming to update pages by completely rewriting a block, out-of-place writes are performed on an SSD. Hence, when a page is updated, it is typically stored on a new location on the drive and the data on the old location is marked as *invalid*.

Ideally we only wish to perform erase operations on blocks that contain invalid pages only. However, the garbage collection (GC) algorithm, responsible for selecting the block to be erased, will often select blocks that contain some valid pages (in fact, depending on the GC algorithm blocks containing invalid pages only may not exist). This implies that these valid pages need to be rewritten elsewhere first before the block erase can take place, even though no external write operation is requested for these pages. These additional internal write operations give rise to what is known as the *write amplification*, it is the ratio of the total number of writes to the number of externally requested writes.

The write amplification not only slows down the operation of the SSD, but it also affects its lifespan. More specifically, flash memory decays and becomes unstable after a certain number of write-erase cycles (e.g., as few as 10000 in some consumer SSDs [6]), thus the higher the write amplification of an SSD the shorter its lifespan. To limit the write amplification, the total storage capacity (number of physical pages) on an SSD exceeds the user-visible capacity (number of logical pages), as this guarantees that a fraction of the pages is in the erase or invalid state. A commonly used measure for the amount of over-provisioning is the *spare factor*, defined as one minus the ratio of the user-visible to the total storage capacity.

In this paper we introduce a mean field model to assess the write amplification and the distribution of the number of valid pages per block for a class $\mathcal{C}$ of GC algorithms under uniform random writes by relying on the framework introduced in [4]. Examples of GC algorithms in the class $\mathcal{C}$ include the d-CHOICES GC algorithm, that selects d blocks uniformly at random and erases the block containing the least number of valid pages among the d selected blocks, and the RANDOM++ GC algorithm that repeatedly selects another block uniformly at random until it finds a block with a lower than average number of valid blocks.

We show that the mean field model is in perfect agreement with simulation experiments and compare the performance of the d-CHOICES and RANDOM++ GC algorithm with the GREEDY [5,7], FIFO [7,13] and WINDOWED [8] algorithm. We observe that the d-CHOICES GC algorithm can achieve a write amplification close to that of the GREEDY GC algorithm even for small d values, e.g., $d = 10$, and offers a more attractive trade-off between its simplicity and its performance than the WINDOWED GC algorithm. The RANDOM++ algorithm on the other hand is inferior to the FIFO algorithm when the number of pages b is large, e.g., for $b \geq 64$.

The flash translation layer, responsible for mapping the logical pages to physical page numbers, considered in this and the above mentioned papers is a page-level map, meaning data can be written on any page and a direct map that translates the logical to physical page numbers is maintained in memory. A block-level map reduces the memory consumption, but increases the write amplification as logical pages can still be mapped to any block, but only to one page within this block (determined by the logical page number). Consumer SSDs typically rely on some form of hybrid mapping [9], where some of the blocks are block-mapped and others are page-mapped to reduce the write amplification of random writes. When a hybrid mapping is used, *merge* operations that create new page-mapped blocks also need to be performed by the GC algorithm.

The results presented in this paper are to some extent also applicable to the garbage collection process found in log-structured file systems (LFS) [14]. In such a system the storage device is regarded as a single *log* and all data is written to the head of the log (while invalidating a possible earlier version of the data). Further, data blocks are grouped into LFS segments and the GC algorithm occasionally selects and cleans a new segment (to prevent that the system becomes full). Write amplification also occurs in this setting as valid blocks part of the selected segment are written to the head of the log first.

The d-CHOICES algorithm has been studied extensively in a balls-and-bins, hashing and load balancing setting (e.g., [2,12,15]) and was also proposed as a GC algorithm for solid-state drives in [10], a paper that is being published concurrently. The latter paper also proposes a mean field model for uniform workloads, but the system operation seems to differ significantly from ours, as the write operations do not appear to rely on a log-structure (while in our system all writes make use of the so-called write frontier, see Section 2). Further, the spare factor does not appear to be a model parameter in case of the uniform workload model in [10], while it plays a key role in our model.

The paper is structured as follows. Section 2 states the main problem, while Section 3 gives an overview of the related work. The class of GC algorithms $\mathcal{C}$ studied in this paper is introduced in Section 4 and the corresponding mean field model is presented in Section 5. Analytical and numerical results for the RANDOM, RANDOM++ and d-CHOICES GC algorithm are presented in Section 6 and 7, respectively. Conclusions are drawn and future work is discussed in Section 8.

2. PROBLEM STATEMENT

Consider a flash-based SSD consisting of N (physical) blocks that are each able to store b valid/invalid pages. At any point in time there is a special block called the *write frontier*. Pages will be written sequentially to the write frontier, until it is full. Assume that the write frontier contains $f < b$ pages at some point and a write operation takes place on a logical page that is physically stored on page k of block number n_1. This operation first writes the new content to page $f + 1$ of the write frontier and afterwards invalidates page k on block number n_1. When the write frontier is full, the GC algorithm creates a new write frontier as follows: it first selects a new block, say block number n_2, copies all the valid pages of block n_2 to the random-access memory (RAM), erases block number n_2 and copies the valid pages back from RAM to block n_2. Note, in practice one avoids the need to copy the valid pages to RAM by making use of a single *free* block [7].

If the GC algorithm copies $j < b$ valid pages, $b - j$ additional writes can be performed before the next erase operation is executed. This implies that b internal write operations took place in between two executions of the GC algorithm, while only $b - j$ external write operations were performed. In this case the *write amplification* is defined as $b/(b - j)$. In general, the write amplification is defined as

$$A = \frac{b}{b - \sum_{j=1}^{b} j p_j},$$

where p_j is the probability that the GC algorithm selects a block with j valid pages.

Denote the user-visible storage capacity as U blocks, i.e., bU pages, meaning the device *utilization* $\rho = U/N$ and the *spare factor* $S_f = 1 - U/N = 1 - \rho$. The objective of this paper is to analyze the write amplification and the distribution of the number of valid pages in a block for a class of GC algorithms under uniform random writes. Under uniform random writes there is no spacial or temporal locality and we further assume that exactly bU pages are marked as valid at all times[1]. This implies that the probability that an external write operation "updates" a page stored on a block with exactly i valid pages is proportional to i/bU times the number of blocks containing exactly i pages. Read and sequential writes operations result in a far lower write amplification, hence the performance of the GC algorithm under random writes is the most significant.

It is possible to extend the analysis presented in this paper to the hot/cold data model of Rosenblum [14]. In this model a fraction f of the complete address space corresponds to *hot* data and the remaining fraction to *cold* data. The fraction of write operations to the hot data is denoted as r. Typical case studies assume that $f \leq 0.2$ and $r \geq 0.8$, meaning more than 80% of the writes are to less than 20% of the data [7].

We do not consider the issue of wear leveling in our problem setting. Wear leveling mechanisms try to prolong the lifetime of the SSD by making sure that the number of write-erase cycles on a block does not vary too much. Some static wear leveling algorithms simply swap entire blocks (basically to move cold data to more worn out blocks), for instance by

---

[1] This is true if either the operating system or SSD does not support the ATA TRIM command (used to mark blocks as invalid when a file is deleted) and the system has been operational for a while.

swapping the least and most worn out block or by swapping the free block with a randomly selected block as in Ban's algorithm [3]. When this type of swapping is used, the distribution of the number of valid pages is not affected by the wear leveling algorithm. In fact, the results in this paper could be used to determine the additional amount of write amplification induced by Ban's wear leveling algorithm.

3. RELATED WORK

Most of the analytic studies on GC algorithms have focused on the following three algorithms:

1. The GREEDY GC algorithm selects a block that contains the least number of valid pages among all the blocks.

2. The FIFO GC algorithm selects the least-recently-written block, that is, the blocks are selected in a circular manner.

3. The WINDOWED GC algorithm makes use of a window of size $w \in \{1, \ldots, N\}$. It selects the block with the least number of valid pages among the set of the w least-recently-written blocks.

A highly accurate approximation for the write amplification of the GREEDY algorithm under uniform random writes in a system where the number of blocks N and pages per block b is large, was introduced in [11,13] and can be expressed as

$$A = \frac{1}{1 + \rho W(-e^{-1/\rho}/\rho)},$$

where $W(\cdot)$ is LambertW function (i.e., the inverse of $f(x) = xe^x$). This formula was also rediscovered in [16] and a less accurate approximation was also proposed in [1]. The above expression for A is also highly accurate for the write amplification of the FIFO algorithm [7] for large N, meaning the write amplification of the FIFO algorithm is independent of the block size b and coincides with the GREEDY algorithm if b is large. The distribution of the number of valid pages per block and the write amplification of the GREEDY algorithm for arbitrary b values (and large N) was analyzed in [5] and [7]. An analytic model for the write amplification of the WINDOWED GC algorithm was introduced in [8], but tends to result in an optimistic estimate of the write amplification [5,7]. The write amplification of the FIFO and GREEDY GC algorithm with hot/cold data was also analyzed in [7].

4. A CLASS OF GC ALGORITHMS

In this paper we introduce a mean field model to assess the write amplification and distribution of the number of valid pages in a block for a class $\mathcal{C}$ of GC algorithms defined as follows. A GC algorithm belongs to class $\mathcal{C}$ if and only if the following two conditions hold:

C1: Let m_i be the fraction of blocks containing exactly i valid pages and denote $\vec{m} = (m_0, \ldots, m_b)$, then there should exist a set of probabilities $p_j(\vec{m})$ where $p_j(\vec{m})$ reflects the probability that a block containing exactly j valid pages is selected by the GC algorithm. In other words, whether block n, for any n, is selected by the GC algorithm should only depend on the number of valid pages j on block n and the fraction of blocks m_i containing exactly i valid blocks, for $i = 0, \ldots, b$.

C2: For $j = 0, \ldots, b$, the probabilities $p_j(\vec{m})$ should be smooth in $\vec{m}$ with $\vec{m} \in \Delta = \{\vec{m} \in \mathbb{R}^{b+1} | 0 \leq m_i \leq 1, \sum_{i=0}^{b} m_i = 1, \sum_{i=1}^{b} i m_i = b\rho\}$.

The following algorithms belong to class $\mathcal{C}$, where to the best of our knowledge the RANDOM++ and d-CHOICES GC algorithm have not been proposed before as a GC algorithm:

1. The RANDOM GC algorithm simply selects a block uniformly at random, hence $p_j(\vec{m}) = m_j$. The RANDOM+ algorithm operates in the same manner, except that it repeatedly selects another block as long as the selected block contains b valid pages (as it is useless to erase a full block). We therefore have $p_j(\vec{m}) = m_j/(1 - m_b)$, which is well defined in Δ for $\rho < 1$.

2. The RANDOM++ GC algorithm repeatedly selects another block uniformly at random until it finds a block with at most $\lfloor b\rho \rfloor$ valid pages, hence

$$p_j(\vec{m}) = \frac{m_j 1[j \leq \lfloor b\rho \rfloor]}{\sum_{\ell=0}^{\lfloor b\rho \rfloor} m_\ell}, \qquad (1)$$

where $1[A] = 1$ if A is true and 0 otherwise, which is also well-defined in Δ.

3. The d-CHOICES GC algorithm selects $d \geq 2$ blocks uniformly at random and erases a block containing the least number of valid pages among the d selected blocks. As all the selected pages must contain at least j valid pages, but not $j + 1$, we have

$$p_j(\vec{m}) = \left(\sum_{\ell=j}^{b} m_\ell \right)^d - \left(\sum_{\ell=j+1}^{b} m_\ell \right)^d. \qquad (2)$$

The write amplification of the RANDOM GC algorithm is clearly equal to $1/(1-\rho)$ as a block contains $b\rho$ valid pages on average. In this paper we will provide an explicit expression for the distribution of the number of valid pages in a block under the RANDOM algorithm as N, the number of blocks, tends to infinity. The write amplification of the RANDOM+ algorithm is less obvious to analyze and we will prove that it converges to $A = \frac{b}{b - \rho(b-1)}$ as N tends to infinity. We will also provide closed form expressions for the write amplification and distribution of the number of valid pages in a block for the RANDOM++ algorithm, while for the d-CHOICES algorithm we propose a fast numerical method to determine these performance measures using a set of ODEs.

Similar to the RANDOM+(+) algorithm we can also define a d-CHOICES+(+) algorithm, however as soon as d exceeds 10 it is not very likely that the block with the least number of valid pages contains more than $\lfloor b\rho \rfloor$ valid pages; hence, the difference with the performance of the d-CHOICES algorithm is rather limited.

5. MEAN FIELD MODEL

5.1 Model definition

We define a discrete-time system by observing the system state at the time epochs just prior to the operation of the GC algorithm. Hence, in between two observations the following steps take place:

S1: The GC algorithm selects a block as the new write frontier, say block number i, and copies the j valid pages of block number i to RAM.

S2: Block number i is erased and the j valid pages are copied back from RAM to the first j pages of the new write frontier, leaving the remaining $b - j$ pages in the erase state.

S3: The pages of the next $b - j$ random writes are invalidated and written to the remaining $b - j$ pages of the write frontier.

To analyze the performance of a GC algorithm belonging to class $\mathcal{C}$, we rely on the interacting objects framework introduced in [4]. Assume the device consists of N blocks, labeled 1 to N, that can each store b (valid and invalid) pages.

Let $X_n^N(t) \in S = \{0, 1, \ldots, b\}$, for $n = 1, \ldots, N$, be the number of valid pages on block number n at time t (i.e., when the GC algorithm runs for the t-th time). Let $M^N(t)$ be the occupancy measure of $X_n^N(t)$, that is, $M^N(t) = (M_0^N(t), M_1^N(t), \ldots, M_b^N(t))$ and

$$M_i^N(t) = \frac{1}{N} \sum_{n=1}^{N} 1[X_n^N(t) = i],$$

for $i = 0, \ldots, b$. Define

$$P_{i,i'}^N(\vec{m}) = \mathbb{P}[X_n^N(t+1) = i' | X_n^N(t) = i, M^N(t) = \vec{m}],$$

for $i \neq i' \in S$, that is, it contains the probability that the number of valid pages on block number n changes from i to i' during a single transition given the occupancy measure.

Define the set $\Delta^N = \{\vec{m} \in \mathbb{R}^{b+1} | m_i N \in \{0, 1, \ldots, N\}, i \in S, \sum_{i \in S} m_i = 1, \sum_{i \in S} i m_i = b\rho\}$ and let $p_j(\vec{m})$, for $j \in S$, be the probability that the GC selects a block with j valid pages at time t provided that $M^N(t) = \vec{m}$ with $\vec{m} \in \Delta^N$. To simplify the notation we also define the binomial probabilities $B_j(n, p) = \binom{n}{j} p^j (1-p)^{n-j}$.

To determine $P_{i,i'}^N(\vec{m})$, we note that the number of valid pages of block number n only changes if the block is selected during step $S1$ or if at least one of the random write operations in during step $S3$ involves block number n. Hence, the number of valid pages of at most $b + 1$ blocks changes during a single transition. As explained below, this results in

$$P_{i,i'}^N(\vec{m}) = \frac{p_i(\vec{m})}{m_i N} B_0(b - i, i/b\rho N) 1[i' = b] +$$

$$1[i' = i - 1] \left[\sum_{j=1, j \neq b-i}^{b} p_{b-j}(\vec{m}) B_1(j, i/b\rho N) + \right.$$

$$\left. p_i(\vec{m}) \left(1 - \frac{1}{m_i N} \right) B_1(b - i, i/b\rho N) \right] + o(1/N), \quad (3)$$

for $i \neq i' \in S$ and $m_i > 0$. Note, $p_i(\vec{m})/(m_i N)$ is the probability that the GC algorithm selects block n provided that it contains i valid pages, while $i/(b\rho N)$ is the probability that block number n is involved in a random write operation provided that it contains i valid pages. In other words, the first term corresponds to the case where block n is selected by the GC algorithm, while none of the $b - i$ writes involve block n, which implies that block n contains b valid pages at time $t + 1$. The second and third term corresponds to the case where the GC algorithm does not select block

number n, while exactly one of the random write operations in step $S3$ invalidates one of the i pages of block number n and therefore decreases its number of valid pages by one. Finally, all the other cases, where either (a) block n is involved in two or more write operations or (b) where block number n is selected by the GC algorithm and is involved in at least one random write operation, are covered by the $o(1/N)$ term as they are of the form $1/N^k$ with $k \geq 2$.

When $m_i = 0$ we can define $P_{i,i'}^N(\vec{m})$ as in (3) except that the terms $\frac{p_i(\vec{m})}{m_i}$ need to be replaced by the partial derivative $\partial p_i(\vec{m})/\partial m_i$, which is properly defined as $p_j(\vec{m})$ is smooth in Δ.

Define the drift $\vec{f}^N(\vec{m})$ for $\vec{m} \in \Delta^N$ as the expected change to M^N in one transition, that is,

$$\vec{f}^N(\vec{m}) = \mathbb{E}[M^N(t+1) - M^N(t) | M^N(t) = \vec{m}]$$

$$= \sum_{i \neq i' \in S} m_i \mathbb{P}_{i,i'}^N(\vec{m})(e_{i'} - e_i), \quad (4)$$

where e_i is the $(i + 1)$-th row of the identity matrix of size $b + 1$. Let $\vec{f}^N(\vec{m}) = (f_0^N(\vec{m}), \ldots, f_b^N(\vec{m}))$, then combining (3) and (4) yields

$$f_b^N(\vec{m}) = \sum_{i=0}^{b-1} \frac{p_i(\vec{m})}{N} B_0(b - i, i/b\rho N)$$

$$- m_b \sum_{j=1}^{b} p_{b-j}(\vec{m}) B_1(j, 1/\rho N) + o(1/N), \quad (5)$$

which is also valid for $m_i = 0$. The first term corresponds to the case where $i < b$ and $i' = b$, while for the second term $i = b$ and $i' = b - 1$. For $i < b$, (3) and (4) result in

$$f_i^N(\vec{m}) = -\frac{p_i(\vec{m})}{N} B_0(b - i, i/b\rho N)$$

$$+ m_{i+1} \sum_{j=1, j \neq b-(i+1)}^{b} p_{b-j}(\vec{m}) B_1(j, (i+1)/b\rho N)$$

$$+ p_{i+1}(\vec{m}) \left(m_{i+1} - \frac{1}{N} \right) B_1(b - (i+1), (i+1)/b\rho N)$$

$$- m_i \sum_{j=1, j \neq b-i}^{b} p_{b-j}(\vec{m}) B_1(j, i/b\rho N)$$

$$- p_i(\vec{m}) \left(m_i - \frac{1}{N} \right) B_1(b - i, i/b\rho N) + o(1/N), \quad (6)$$

which is also valid for $m_i = 0$.

Next, define the intensity function $\epsilon(N) = 1/N$ and let

$$P_{i,i'}(\vec{m}) = \lim_{N \to \infty} \frac{P_{i,i'}^N(\vec{m})}{\epsilon(N)}$$

$$= \frac{p_i(\vec{m})}{m_i} 1[i' = b] + \left(\sum_{j=1}^{b} p_{b-j}(\vec{m}) j \right) \frac{i}{b\rho} 1[i' = i - 1], \quad (7)$$

for $m_i > 0$ due to (3). For $m_i = 0$ it is again sufficient to replace $\frac{p_i(\vec{m})}{m_i}$ by $\partial p_i(\vec{m})/\partial m_i$.

Similarly define $\vec{f}(\vec{m}) = (f_0(\vec{m}), \ldots, f_b(\vec{m}))$ such that for $i \in S$, $f_i(\vec{m}) = \lim_{N \to \infty} \frac{f_i^N(\vec{m})}{\epsilon(N)}$, then due to (5) and by noting that $\sum_{i=0}^{b-1} p_i(\vec{m}) = 1 - p_b(\vec{m})$, we find

$$f_b(\vec{m}) = (1 - p_b(\vec{m})) - \left(\sum_{j=1}^{b} p_{b-j}(\vec{m})j\right)\frac{bm_b}{b\rho}, \quad (8)$$

while for $i < b$, (6) yields

$$f_i(\vec{m}) = \frac{(i+1)m_{i+1} - im_i}{b\rho}\left(\sum_{j=1}^{b} p_{b-j}(\vec{m})j\right) - p_i(\vec{m}). \quad (9)$$

Finally, as in [4] define $\bar{M}^N(\tau)$ as the re-scaled process such that $\bar{M}^N(t) = M^N(\lfloor tN \rfloor)$, for $t \geq 0$. Similarly, define $\bar{X}_n^N(t)$ as the re-scaled version of $X_n^N(t)$. Further, define the deterministic process $\vec{\mu}(t) = (\mu_0(t), \ldots, \mu_b(t))$, the evolution of which is given by the following ODE:

$$\frac{d\vec{\mu}(t)}{dt} = \vec{f}(\vec{\mu}(t)), \quad (10)$$

where $\vec{f}(\vec{m}) = (f_0(\vec{m}), \ldots, f_b(\vec{m}))$ is defined by (8) and (9).

5.2 Convergence result

From the previous section, $\{(X_1^N(t), \ldots, X_N^N(t)), t \in \mathbb{N}\}$ is clearly a Markov chain on the state space Δ^N. A key feature of this Markov chain is that the state changes of X_n^N, for $n = 1, \ldots, N$, are given by the probabilities $P_{i,i'}^N(\vec{m})$, meaning the evolution of X_n^N depends on X_k^N, with $k \neq n$, only through the occupancy measure $M^N(t)$.

The mean field interaction model in [4] considers a more general class of Markov chains $\{(X_1^N(t), \ldots, X_N^N(t), R^N(t)), t \in \mathbb{N}\}$ with state space $\Delta^N \times \{1, \ldots, J\}$. $R^N(t)$ is the state of the so-called resource at time t and the evolution of X_n^N depends on the occupancy measure $M^N(t)$ and the state $R^N(t)$. Further, the model is said to use no resource if $J = 1$, meaning $R^N(t)$ is a single state Markov chain.

The convergence results presented in [4] hold if five conditions, called Conditions $H1$ to $H5$, are satisfied. Conditions $H1$ and $H4$ are related to the resource and hold trivially for $J = 1$. Condition $H2$ demands that there exists a function $\epsilon(N)$, with $\lim_{N\to\infty} \epsilon(N) = 0$, and the limits $\vec{f}(\vec{m}) = \lim_{N\to\infty} \vec{f}^N(\vec{m})/\epsilon(N)$, given by (8) and (9) in our model, are properly defined. In fact the stronger condition $H2a$, which demands that $P_{i,i'}(\vec{m}) = \lim_{N\to\infty} P_{i,i'}^N(\vec{m})/\epsilon(N)$ is well defined, holds in our case as it is given by (7).

Given that $H2a$ holds, condition $H3$ demands that the coefficient of variation of the number of objects that change their state in a single transition is bounded for large N. As at most $b + 1$ objects can change their state in a single transition condition $H3$ is satisfied. Finally, condition $H5$ demands that $\vec{f}^N(\vec{m})$, given by (5) and (6) in our model, is a smooth function of $\vec{m}$ and $1/N$. This condition is met as $\vec{f}^N(\vec{m})$ is a polynomial function of $1/N$ (this is also true for the $o(1/N)$ term) and $p_j(\vec{m})$ is smooth in Δ. The following theorem therefore follows from Corollary 1 in [4].

THEOREM 1. *If $M^N(0) \to \vec{m}$ in probability as N tends to infinity, then $\sup_{0 \leq \tau \leq T} ||\bar{M}^N(t) - \vec{\mu}(t)|| \to 0$ in probability, where $\vec{\mu}(t)$ is the unique solution of the ODE (10) with $\vec{\mu}(0) = \vec{m}$.*

In other words, for N large and finite t, we can approximate $M^N(t)$ by $\vec{\mu}(t/N)$, which is the unique solution of the ODE (10) with $\vec{\mu}(0) = M^N(0)$. As we are interested in the stationary regime of $M^N(t)$, the question remains whether the convergence extends to the stationary regime. Corollary 2 in [4] shows that it suffices to show that the ODE given by (10) has a unique fixed point that is also a global attractor.

For the RANDOM(+) GC algorithm, we provide an explicit expression for the unique fixed point of the ODE given by (10) and prove global attraction. For the RANDOM++ algorithm we have an explicit expression for the unique fixed point (but no proof of global attraction), while for the d-CHOICES algorithm, we have no closed form results for the fixed point and only a proof of a unique global attractor for $b = 2$. Instead we numerically determine a fixed point of (10) and show by means of simulation that it is highly accurate in predicting the write amplification of the d-CHOICES GC algorithm.

6. ANALYTIC RESULTS

In this section we study the set of ODEs given by (10) in more detail for some GC algorithms belonging to class $\mathcal{C}$.

6.1 The Random(+) GC algorithm

In this subsection we consider the RANDOM GC algorithm. In this particular case $p_j(\vec{m}) = m_j$ and

$$\sum_{j=1}^{b} m_{b-j}j = b - \sum_{j=0}^{b} m_{b-j}(b-j) = (1-\rho)b,$$

for $\vec{m} \in \Delta$. As a result (8) reduces to

$$f_b(\vec{m}) = (1 - m_b) - \frac{1-\rho}{\rho}bm_b, \quad (11)$$

while for $i < b$, (9) yields

$$f_i(\vec{m}) = \frac{1-\rho}{\rho}[(i+1)m_{i+1} - im_i] - m_i, \quad (12)$$

From (11) it follows that $\mu_b = \rho/(\rho + (1-\rho)b)$ for any fixed point $\vec{\mu} = (\mu_0, \ldots, \mu_b)$, while (12) implies that $\mu_i = \mu_{i+1}(1-\rho)(i+1)/(\rho + (1-\rho)i)$ holds, for $i = 0, \ldots, b-1$. Hence, we may conclude that (10) has a unique fixed point given by

$$\mu_i = \frac{\rho}{\rho + (1-\rho)i}\prod_{j=i+1}^{b}\frac{(1-\rho)j}{\rho + (1-\rho)j}, \quad (13)$$

for $i = 0, \ldots, b$. To prove global attraction of the unique fixed point $\vec{\mu}$, we note that (10) can be written as

$$\frac{d\vec{\mu}(t)}{dt} = e_b + \vec{\mu}(t)\underbrace{\begin{bmatrix} -1 & & & \\ \frac{1-\rho}{\rho} & -(1+\frac{1-\rho}{\rho}) & & \\ & \ddots & \ddots & \\ & & \frac{(1-\rho)b}{\rho} & -(1+\frac{(1-\rho)b}{\rho}) \end{bmatrix}}_{\text{matrix } Q}.$$

(14)

Hence, the unique solution $\vec{\mu}(t)$ is given by

$$\vec{\mu}(t) = e_b(-Q)^{-1}(I - e^{tQ}) + \vec{\mu}(0)e^{tQ},$$

and $\lim_{t\to\infty} \vec{\mu}(t) = e_b(-Q)^{-1} = \vec{\mu}$, for any $\vec{\mu}(0) \in \Delta$, as the diagonal entries of the bidiagonal matrix Q are negative and therefore $\lim_{t\to\infty} e^{tQ} = 0$.

THEOREM 2. *Let μ_i^N be the steady state probability that an arbitrary block contains i valid pages when the RANDOM GC algorithm is used in a system composed of N blocks of size b and spare factor S_f then*

$$\lim_{N\to\infty}\mu_i^N = \mu_i = \frac{\rho}{\rho+(1-\rho)i}\prod_{j=i+1}^{b}\frac{(1-\rho)j}{\rho+(1-\rho)j}, \quad (15)$$

for $i = 0,\ldots,b$, where $\rho = 1 - S_f$. Further, let $w_i = \sum_{k=i}^{b}\mu_k$, then $w_0 = 1$ and

$$w_i = 1 - \prod_{j=i}^{b}\frac{(1-\rho)j}{\rho+(1-\rho)j}, \quad (16)$$

for $i = 1,\ldots,b$. Finally, $\sum_{i=1}^{b}w_i = b\rho$.

PROOF. As noted in Section 5.2, the limit in (15) now follows from Corollary 2 of [4]. To establish the relationship for w_i, for $i = 1,\ldots,b$, we first note that μ_i can also be written as

$$\mu_i = \frac{\left(\prod_{j=1}^{i-1}(\rho+(1-\rho)j)\right)\rho^{1[i>0]}\left(\prod_{j=i+1}^{b}(1-\rho)j\right)}{\prod_{j=1}^{b}(\rho+(1-\rho)j)},$$

which also confirms that $\sum_{i=0}^{b}\mu_i = 1$. Hence, for $i = 1,\ldots,b$,

$$w_i = \frac{\prod_{j=i}^{b}(\rho+(1-\rho)j) - \prod_{j=i}^{b}(1-\rho)j}{\prod_{j=i}^{b}(\rho+(1-\rho)j)}.$$

Finally, using (16), we note that $\sum_{i=1}^{b}w_i = b\rho$ if and only if

$$\sum_{i=1}^{b}\left(\prod_{j=1}^{i-1}(\rho+(1-\rho)j)\right)\left(\prod_{j=i}^{b}(1-\rho)j\right) =$$
$$(1-\rho)b\prod_{j=1}^{b}(\rho+(1-\rho)j),$$

which can be proven easily by induction on b (starting with $b = 1$). □

Theorem 2 confirms that the write amplification $A = b/(b - \sum_{i=1}^{b}w_i) = 1/(1-\rho)$, as noted in Section 4. The write amplification is thus independent of the block size b and the number of blocks N when the RANDOM GC algorithm is used. The distribution of the number of valid pages within a block does however depend on both b and N. Theorem 2 provides a closed form expression for this distribution as N tends to infinity. To the best of our knowledge this concerns a new result that also enables us to determine the write amplification of the RANDOM+ algorithm.

Figure 1 depicts the distribution of the number of valid pages within a block for $b = 16$ and $\rho = 0.86$ compared to the Binomial distribution with parameters (b, ρ). The figure shows that the distribution of the number of valid pages is not close to Binomial as is sometimes assumed when analyzing GC algorithms. Thus, pages belonging to different blocks become independent for large N (due to the decoupling), but this is not the case for pages part of the same block as this would result in a Binomial distribution.

We end this section by considering the write amplification A of the RANDOM+ algorithm, which operates similar to the RANDOM GC algorithm, except that it repeatedly selects another block at random if the selected block contains b

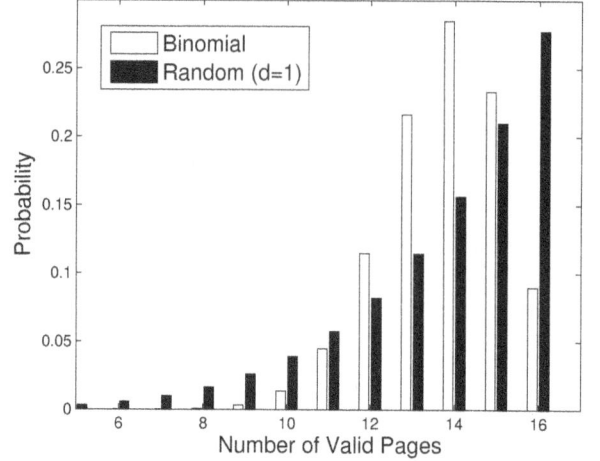

Figure 1: Distribution of the number of valid pages within a block for $S_f = (1-\rho) = 0.14$ and $b = 16$, compared to the binomial distribution with parameters (b, ρ).

valid pages. The distribution of the number of valid pages per block is clearly identical for the RANDOM and RANDOM+ algorithm (this can also be seen from (8) and (9)). The expression for the write amplification however changes from $A = b/(b - \sum_{i=0}^{b}i\mu_i) = 1/(1-\rho)$ for the RANDOM algorithm to

$$A = \frac{b}{b - \sum_{i=0}^{b-1}i\frac{\mu_i}{1-\mu_b}} = \frac{b}{b - \frac{b\rho-b\mu_b}{1-\mu_b}},$$

for the RANDOM+ algorithm, which results in the following Corollary.

COROLLARY 1. *Let A^N be the write amplification of the RANDOM+ algorithm in a system composed of N blocks of size b and spare factor $S_f = 1 - \rho$ then*

$$\lim_{N\to\infty}A^N = \frac{b}{b - \rho(b-1)}.$$

It shows that A is no longer independent of the block size b and that as b tends to infinity the RANDOM and RANDOM+ algorithm perform alike (as expected). We also note that the write amplification of the RANDOM+ algorithm is bounded above by b irrespective of the spare factor S_f. Figure 2 depicts the write amplification A of the RANDOM+ algorithm as a function of b for different values of $\rho = 1 - S_f$.

6.2 The d-Choices GC algorithm

In this subsection we consider the d-CHOICES GC algorithm with $d > 1$. Using (2) we can write

$$\sum_{j=1}^{b}p_{b-j}(\vec{m})j = b - \sum_{j=1}^{b}\left(\sum_{k=j}^{b}m_k\right)^d. \quad (17)$$

Let $\mu(t) = (\mu_0(t),\ldots,\mu_b(t))$ be the unique solution of (10) with initial condition $\mu(0)$. Define $w_i(t) = \sum_{k=i}^{b}\mu_k(t)$, for $i = 0,\ldots,b$, and $w_{b+1}(t) = 0$. Then, by means of (8) and

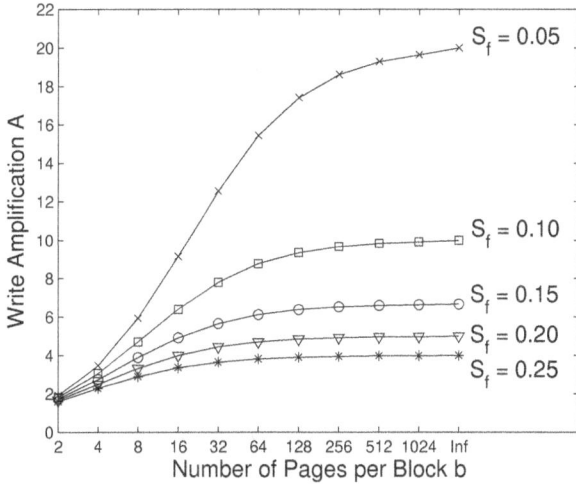

Figure 2: The write amplification A of the RANDOM+GC algorithm as a function of the block size b for different spare factors $S_f = 1 - \rho$.

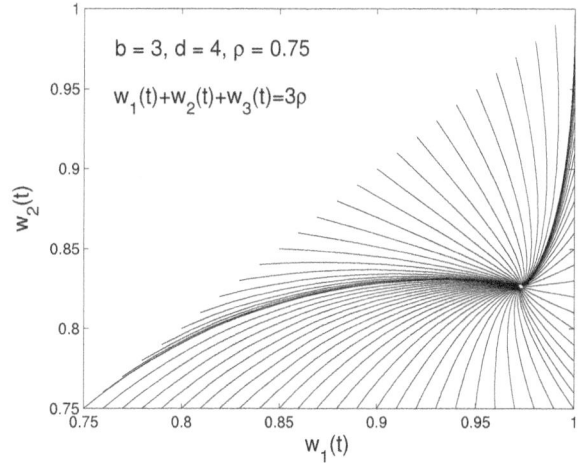

Figure 3: For $b = 3$ and $d = 4$ there is a unique global attractor in Δ for $\rho = 0.75$.

d	S_f	ODE (18)	simul. (95% conf.)
2	0.07	9.6354	9.6355 ± 0.0016
4	0.07	7.7182	7.7181 ± 0.0007
8	0.07	7.0044	7.0044 ± 0.0004
2	0.14	4.9645	4.9651 ± 0.0011
4	0.14	4.0672	4.0673 ± 0.0008
8	0.14	3.7366	3.7366 ± 0.0005
2	0.21	3.3732	3.3730 ± 0.0006
4	0.21	2.8024	2.8026 ± 0.0004
8	0.21	2.5936	2.5935 ± 0.0002

Table 1: Comparison of ODE-based results and simulation experiments for a system with $N = 50000$ blocks and $b = 64$ pages per block.

(9), we find $w_0(t) = 1$ and

$$\frac{dw_i(t)}{dt} = 1 - w_i(t)^d - \left(b - \sum_{j=1}^{b} w_j(t)^d\right) \frac{i(w_i(t) - w_{i+1}(t))}{b\rho},$$
(18)

for $i = 1, \ldots, b$.

Unless $d = 1$ (see Section 6.1), the set of equations given by (18) does not appear to have a simple closed form solution for its fixed point (for $d = b = 2$ we managed to obtain a closed form expression that already looks very involved). It is also unclear whether (10) has a global attractor in Δ, meaning we have no formal proof that the convergence to the mean field over finite time scales extends to the stationary regime for $d > 1$. When $b = 2$ the space Δ is one dimensional as $w_1(t) + w_2(t) = 2\rho$ and we can prove that a global attractor exists in Δ for any d (see Appendix A). Numerical experiments seem to suggest that a unique global attractor also exists for $b > 2$ and that the L_1-distance to the fixed point decreases along all the trajectories, as illustrated in Figure 3 for $b = 3$, $d = 4$ and $\rho = 0.75$.

To generate numerical results for the write amplification A and distribution of the number of valid pages for arbitrary b and ρ, we numerically solve the ODE given by (18) with $\mu_i(0) = \binom{b}{i}\rho^i(1-\rho)^{b-i}$ using Euler's method with a step size $h = 0.001$ until $\|w(t+h) - w(t)\|_1 < 10^{-13}$. For all the numerical experiments reported in this paper convergence occurred in a fraction of a second. Tables 1 and 2 show a perfect agreement between the simulation results and the ODE-based prediction for a system consisting of $N = 50000$ blocks[2] containing $b = 64$ and $b = 16$ pages, respectively. Depending on whether the page size is 4 or 8 Kilobyte, this results in a 12.8 or 25.6 Gigabyte system for $b = 64$. The simulation results in Tables 1 and 2 were based on 10 (for $S_f = 0.21$ and 0.14) and 50 (for $S_f = 0.07$) runs each with a length of $3tN$, where t is the smallest multiple of h such that $\|w(t+h) - w(t)\|_1 < 10^{-13}$. Initially the $b\rho N$ valid pages

were distributed randomly over the Nb available pages and the length of the warm-up period was tN. As indicated in Tables 1 and 2 in each of the experiments the width of the 95% confidence intervals was smaller than 0.1%.

Remark.

The set of ODEs given by (18) has a simple intuitive explanation. As $1 - w_i(t)^d$ is the probability that the GC algorithm selects a block with less than i valid pages, it represents the rate at which blocks with i or more pages are created. Similarly, the rate at which blocks with i pages disappear is equal to $i(w_i(t) - w_{i+1}(t))/b\rho$, the probability that one of the write operations in step $S3$ involves a block with exactly i valid pages, times $b - \sum_{j=1}^{b} w_j(t)^d$, the mean number of writes between two executions of the GC algorithm. If we let d tend to infinity in (18) we end up with the following set of ODEs:

$$\frac{dw_i(t)}{dt} = 1[w_i(t) < 1] - \left(\sum_{j=1}^{b} 1[w_j(t) < 1]\right) \frac{i(w_i(t) - w_{i+1}(t))}{b\rho}.$$
(19)

Simulating this set of ODEs produces numerical results that are in perfect agreement with the closed form results in [5] for the distribution of the number of valid pages in an ar-

---

[2]Similar results were obtained for a system consisting of $N = 5000$ blocks.

d	S_f	ODE (18)	simul. (95% conf.)
2	0.07	8.9083	8.9078 ±0.0014
4	0.07	6.6296	6.6292 ±0.0010
8	0.07	5.7766	5.7766 ±0.0009
2	0.14	4.7339	4.7345 ±0.0020
4	0.14	3.7388	3.7383 ±0.0008
8	0.14	3.3612	3.3612 ±0.0007
2	0.21	3.2639	3.2636 ±0.0009
4	0.21	2.6480	2.6482 ±0.0004
8	0.21	2.4148	2.4149 ±0.0004

Table 2: Comparison of ODE-based results and simulation experiments for a system with $N = 50000$ blocks and $b = 16$ pages per block.

bitrary block when the GREEDY GC algorithm is used. We should note that we cannot rely on the framework in [4] to verify that the above ODE is the proper limit process for the GREEDY algorithm as the right-hand side of the ODE is not smooth.

6.3 The Random++ GC algorithm

An expression for the probabilities $p_j(\vec{m})$ for the RANDOM++ algorithm is given in (1), when combined with (8) and (9), this implies that any fixed point $\vec{\mu} = (\mu_0, \ldots, \mu_b)$ must fulfill the following set of equations

$$1 = \left(\sum_{j=1}^{b} p_{b-j}(\vec{\mu})j \right) \frac{\mu_b}{\rho}, \qquad (20)$$

$$i\mu_i = (i+1)\mu_{i+1}, \qquad (21)$$

for $i = \lfloor b\rho \rfloor + 1, \ldots, b-1$ and

$$p_i(\vec{\mu}) = \frac{(i+1)\mu_{i+1} - i\mu_i}{b\rho} \left(\sum_{j=1}^{b} p_{b-j}(\vec{\mu})j \right), \qquad (22)$$

for $i = 0, \ldots, \lfloor b\rho \rfloor$. The following theorem shows that this set of equations has a unique solution in Δ.

THEOREM 3. *The set of ODEs given by (8) and (9) for the* RANDOM++ *GC algorithm, i.e., with $p_j(\vec{m})$ given by (1), has a unique fixed point in Δ given by*

$$\mu_i = \frac{(i+1)\mu_{i+1}}{i + \rho/(1 - \rho - \mu_b(bS_{\rho,b} - b + \lfloor b\rho \rfloor))}, \qquad (23)$$

for $i = 0, \ldots, \lfloor b\rho \rfloor$, with $S_{\rho,b} = \sum_{j=\lfloor b\rho \rfloor + 1}^{b} 1/j$,

$$\mu_i = b\mu_b/i, \qquad (24)$$

for $i = \lfloor b\rho \rfloor + 1, \ldots, b-1$, while

$$\mu_b = \frac{-b_\rho + \sqrt{b_\rho^2 - 4a_\rho c_\rho}}{2a_\rho},$$

with $a_\rho = b - \lfloor b\rho \rfloor - bS_{\rho,b}$, $b_\rho = \rho S_{\rho,b} + 1 - \rho$ and $c_\rho = -\rho/b$ for $\rho < 1 - 1/b$ and $\mu_b = \rho/(\rho + (1-\rho)b)$ for $\rho \geq 1 - 1/b$. Further,

$$A = \frac{b}{\sum_{j=1}^{b} p_{b-j}(\vec{\mu})j} = \frac{1}{1 - \frac{\rho - \mu_b(b - \lfloor b\rho \rfloor)}{1 - \mu_b bS_{\rho,b}}}. \qquad (25)$$

S_f	Theorem 3	simul. (95% conf.)
0.20	2.9614	2.9611 ±0.0005
0.17	3.4209	3.4209 ±0.0004
0.14	4.0663	4.0663 ±0.0005
0.11	5.0371	5.0377 ±0.0007
0.08	6.6599	6.6601 ±0.0006
0.05	9.9172	9.9166 ±0.0010

Table 3: Comparison of closed form results and simulation experiments for a system with $N = 50000$ blocks and $b = 32$ pages per block.

PROOF. We start by noting that for $\vec{\mu} \in \Delta$

$$\sum_{j=1}^{b} p_{b-j}(\vec{\mu})j = b - \sum_{j=1}^{b} p_j(\vec{\mu})j =$$

$$b - \frac{\sum_{j=1}^{\lfloor b\rho \rfloor} j\mu_j}{1 - \sum_{j > \lfloor b\rho \rfloor} \mu_j} = b - \frac{b\rho - \sum_{j > \lfloor b\rho \rfloor} j\mu_j}{1 - \sum_{j > \lfloor b\rho \rfloor} \mu_j}.$$

Due to (21), we have

$$\sum_{j > \lfloor b\rho \rfloor} j\mu_j = b\mu_b(b - \lfloor b\rho \rfloor),$$

$$\sum_{j > \lfloor b\rho \rfloor} \mu_j = b\mu_b S_{\rho,b}. \qquad (26)$$

This implies

$$\sum_{j=1}^{b} p_{b-j}(\vec{\mu})j = b \left(1 - \frac{\rho - \mu_b(b - \lfloor b\rho \rfloor)}{1 - \mu_b bS_{\rho,b}} \right),$$

which establishes (25), while (23) can now be derived from (22) and (24) is immediate from (21). The quadratic equation $f(y) = a_\rho y^2 + b_\rho y + c_\rho = 0$ for μ_b now follows from (20). Provided that the function $f(y)$ has real roots, they are both positive as $a_\rho, c_\rho \leq 0$ and $b_\rho > 0$, while $\mu_b \leq 1/(\rho S_{\rho,b})$ as $\sum_{j > \lfloor b\rho \rfloor} \mu_j \leq 1$. Further,

$$f(0) < 0, \text{ and } f(1/(\rho S_{\rho,b})) = \frac{b - \lfloor b\rho \rfloor - b\rho S_{\rho,b}}{(bS_{\rho,b})^2}.$$

Hence, $f(1/(\rho S_{\rho,b})) \geq 0$ if and only if $b - \lfloor b\rho \rfloor - b\rho S_{\rho,b} \geq 0$. This latter inequality holds as $g(\rho) = b - \lfloor b\rho \rfloor - b\rho S_{\rho,b}$ is equal to $1 - \rho$ for $\rho > 1 - 1/b$ and $g(\rho)$ increases as ρ decreases. □

Provided that the unique fixed point is a global attractor, Theorem 3 implies that the write amplification A_N in a system consisting of N blocks converges to (25) as N tends to infinity. By means of (26) we also find that the mean number of attempts needed to locate a block with at most $\lfloor b\rho \rfloor$ valid blocks can be expressed as $1/(1 - \mu_b bS_{\rho,b})$.

Table 3 compares the closed form expression for A given by Theorem 3 with simulation experiments on a system consisting of $N = 50000$ blocks and $b = 32$ pages per block. The length of a single simulation run and warm-up period was determined in a similar manner as in Section 6.2, while 10 runs were performed for $S_f > 0.1$ and 50 for $S_f < 0.1$. The results show a perfect agreement between the closed form results and simulation.

7. NUMERICAL RESULTS

In this section we present some numerical results for the d-CHOICES and RANDOM++ algorithm and compare their

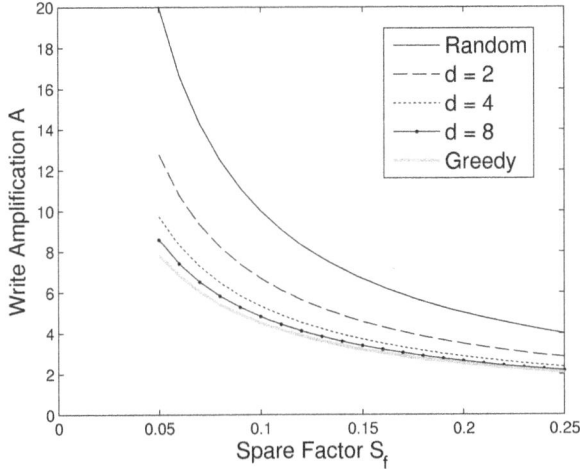

Figure 4: Write amplification A as a function of the spare factor S_f for the Random, Greedy and d-Choices algorithm for $d = 2, 4$ and 8 and $b = 32$ pages per block.

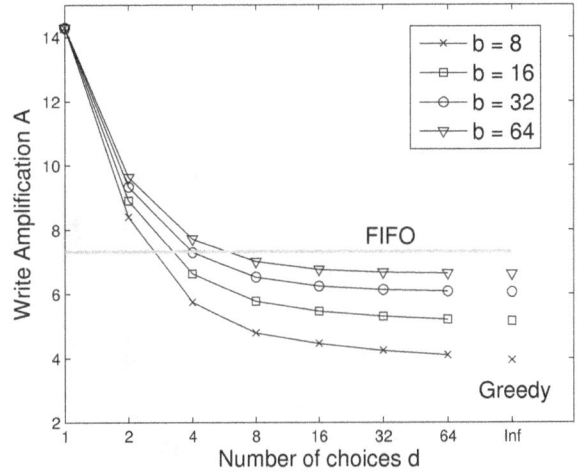

Figure 5: Write amplification A as a function of the number of choices d for the d-Choices algorithm with a spare factor $S_f = 0.07$.

performance with the Greedy, FIFO and Windowed algorithm.

7.1 The d-Choices GC algorithm

We will show that the d-Choices algorithm can approximate the write amplification of the Greedy algorithm even for small d values, e.g., $d = 10$, while maintaining the simplicity of the Random or FIFO algorithm. Further, we will show that the d-Choices algorithm is far more effective than the Windowed algorithm, that is, the d-Choices algorithm with d small, e.g., $d = 10$, has a lower the write amplification A than the Windowed algorithm with a fairly large window size, e.g., $w = 500$.

Figure 4 depicts the write amplification A as a function of the spare factor $S_f = 1 - \rho$ for the Random, Greedy and d-Choices GC algorithm for $d = 2, 4$ and 8 and $b = 32$ pages per block. The results for the write amplification (and number of valid blocks) under the Greedy GC algorithm are based on [5]. The results confirm that a small value of d suffices to approximate the write amplification A of the Greedy algorithm, especially for larger spare factors S_f. Although the Greedy algorithm has a lower write amplification A, it requires state information (essentially $b+1$ bins that contain N items in total) that needs to be updated after each write operation. The d-Choices GC algorithm maintains no state information and is only activated when a new block needs to be selected (and cleared).

In Figure 5 we also show the impact of the number of pages b per block on the write amplification A when the spare factor $S_f = 0.07$. It confirms that small d values suffice for the d-Choices algorithm to approximate the write amplification of the Greedy algorithm for different block sizes b. The FIFO algorithm, the write amplification of which does not depend on b, performs worse, especially for small b (i.e., older SSD devices) as the write amplification of the d-Choices and Greedy algorithm decreases with b (as expected).

When $b = 1$, meaning $N\rho$ blocks contain one valid page and $N(1 - \rho)$ one invalid page at all times, the d-Choices

GC algorithm has a write amplification $A = 1/(1 - \rho^d)$ as with probability $1 - \rho^d$ the selected block contains an invalid page. In fact for any $b \geq 1$, it is not hard to show that the write amplification of the d-Choices algorithm is lower bounded by $1/(1 - \rho^d)$. This can be shown by noting that the write amplification $A(t)$ at time t is equal to $b/(b - \sum_{i=1}^{b} w_i(t)^d)$ and $\sum_{i=1}^{b} w_i^d$, for $d \geq 1$, is minimized in Δ when $w_i = \rho$ for $i = 1, \ldots, b$. We can also upper bound the write amplification A by

$$\frac{b}{b - \lfloor b\rho \rfloor - (b\rho - \lfloor b\rho \rfloor)^d},$$

by noting that $\sum_{i=1}^{b} w_i^d$, for $d \geq 1$, is maximized in Δ when $w_i = 1$ for $i = 1, \ldots, k$, $w_{k+1} = b\rho - k$ and $w_i = 0$ for $i = k + 2, \ldots, b$ with $k = \lfloor b\rho \rfloor$. Note, when ρ is a multiple of $1/b$ this upper bound simplifies to $1/(1 - \rho)$, the write amplification of the Random algorithm, otherwise the upper bound is below $1/(1 - \rho)$ for $d > 1$.

The previous results indicated that the write amplification of the Greedy and d-Choices algorithm becomes similar as d increases. Figures 6 and 7 indicate that the same holds for the number of valid pages in a block on an arbitrary and a block selected by the GC algorithm, respectively, for a system with $b = 16$ pages per block and a spare factor $S_f = 0.14$. Note, for the Greedy algorithm the probability that an arbitrary block contains at most 10 valid pages is zero, while the number of valid pages on a selected block is bimodal and is always 10 or 11 in our example. Hence, at times a negligible fraction of the blocks contains exactly 10 pages and these blocks are always selected by the Greedy GC algorithm [5, 7]. For the d-Choices algorithm we observe something similar: the probability of having 10 valid pages in a block tends to zero as d increases, while the probability of selecting such a block remains significant. This can be understood by noting that even though such blocks become rare as d grows, larger d values also increase the probability that a rare block (containing the least number of valid pages) is selected by the GC algorithm.

The Windowed GC algorithm was introduced in [8] as a

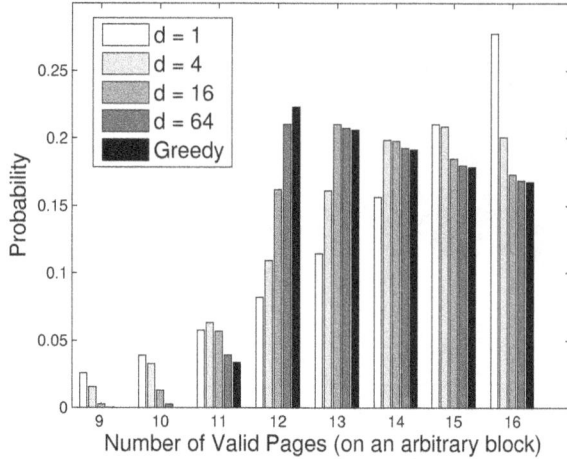

Figure 6: Distribution of the number of valid pages on an arbitrary block for the greedy and d-CHOICES algorithm with $d = 1, 4, 16$ and 64, with $S_f = 0.14$ and $b = 16$.

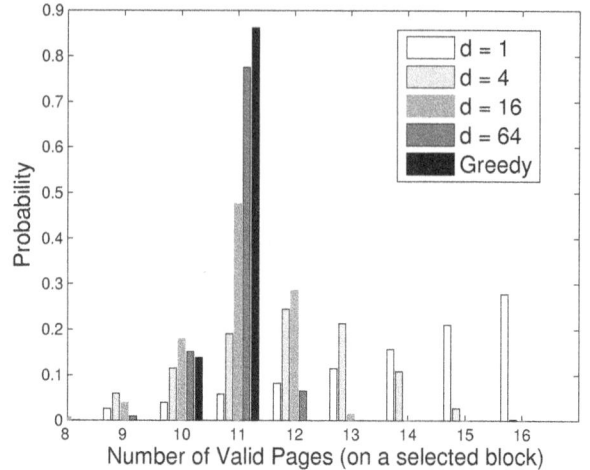

Figure 7: Distribution of the number of valid pages on a selected block for the greedy and d-CHOICES algorithm with $d = 1, 4, 16$ and 64, with $S_f = 0.14$ and $b = 16$.

trade-off between the low complexity of the FIFO algorithm and the good performance of the GREEDY algorithm. The idea is to consider only the w *oldest* blocks when searching for the block with the least number of valid pages, where setting $w = 1$ and N results in the FIFO and GREEDY GC algorithm, respectively. Larger w values reduce the write amplification, but increase the time complexity of the GC algorithm. Figure 8 shows how much the write amplification increases when the WINDOWED (with $w = 50$ and 500) or d-CHOICES (with $d = 10$ or 20) algorithm is used instead of the GREEDY algorithm in a system with $b = 64$ pages per block. Note, the curves in this figure are not smooth as the write amplification of the GREEDY algorithm is not smooth in those S_f values for which the bimodal distribution of the number of valid pages on a selected block becomes unimodal.

Figure 8 indicates that for spare factors $S_f \leq 0.2$ setting d as small as 10 suffices to beat the WINDOWED algorithm with a window size of $w = 500$, where the gain becomes more pronounced as S_f decreases. Further, setting $d = 20$ results in a write amplification that is less than 2% above the write amplification of the GREEDY algorithm, while the write amplification of the WINDOWED algorithm is still much closer to the FIFO algorithm even with a window size $w = 500$. This can be understood by remarking that blocks with a relatively high number of valid pages tend to stay within the window for a considerable amount of time. Such a drawback does not occur with the d-CHOICES algorithm as the set of d blocks is always reselected at random.

The fact that the WINDOWED GC algorithm is not very effective in reducing the write amplification for w small was also noted in [7]. The results in Figure 8 for the windowed access algorithm were obtained by simulation on a system with $N = 50000$ blocks, using 10 runs of length 10^6 each. This resulted in confidence intervals with a width below 0.1%. Note, analytical results for the WINDOWED GC algorithm were also presented in [8], but these were based on the assumption that the number of valid pages per block within the window has a binomial distribution, which tends

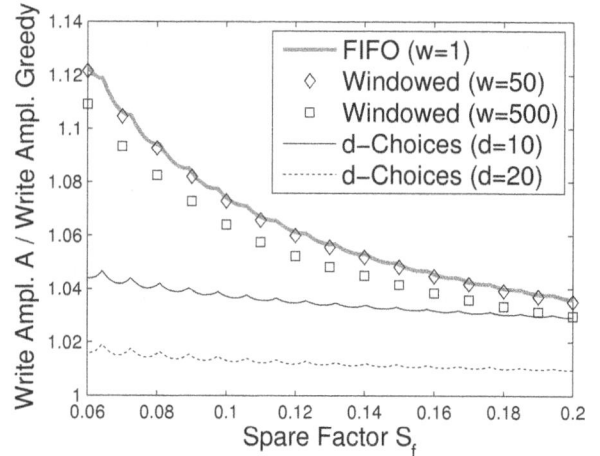

Figure 8: Relative write amplification WINDOWED versus d-CHOICES algorithm for $b = 64$ blocks per page.

to result in an optimistic estimate for the write amplification [5, 7].

7.2 The Random++ algorithm

In this section, we compare the write amplification of the RANDOM++ algorithm with the FIFO and GREEDY GC algorithm. We will show that the RANDOM++ algorithm performs worse than the FIFO algorithm when the number of pages in a block is large, e.g., $b \geq 64$, while the reverse is mostly true for small block sizes, e.g., $b \leq 16$. We will also show that the RANDOM++ algorithm typically requires less than three attempts to locate a block with at most $\lfloor b\rho \rfloor$ valid pages.

Figure 9 depicts the write amplification A of the FIFO, GREEDY and RANDOM++ GC algorithm as a function of the spare factors $S_f = 1 - \rho$ for $b = 64$ pages per block. It shows that the RANDOM++ algorithm is outperformed

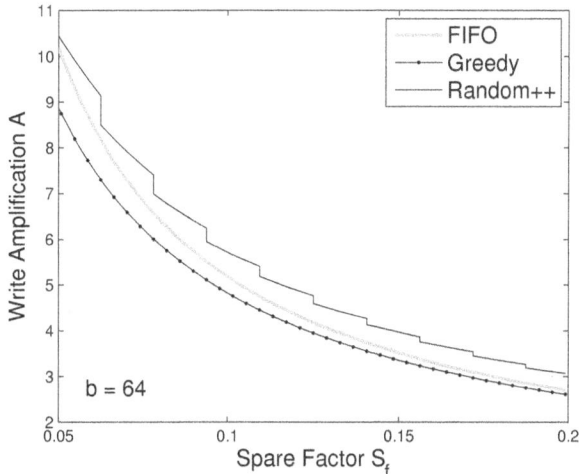

Figure 9: The write amplification A of the FIFO, GREEDY and RANDOM++ GC algorithm as a function of the spare factors $S_f = 1 - \rho$ for $b = 64$ pages per block.

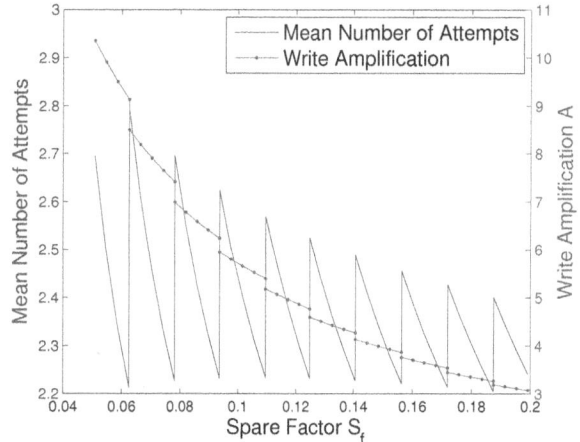

Figure 10: The write amplification A and mean number of attempts to find a block with at most $\lfloor b\rho \rfloor$ valid blocks for the RANDOM++ GC algorithm as a function of the spare factors $S_f = 1 - \rho$ for $b = 64$ pages per block.

by the FIFO algorithm for $S_f \in [0.05, 0.2]$, especially when the spare factor becomes large. We also note that the curve of the RANDOM++ algorithm contains jumps whenever the spare factor $S_f = 1 - \rho$ is a multiple of $1/b$. When S_f becomes a multiple of $1/b$ when increasing S_f, the maximum number of allowed valid pages in the block selected by the RANDOM++ algorithm decreases by one. This causes an immediate decrease in the write amplification. At the same time we can also expect a sudden rise in the mean number of attempts needed by the RANDOM++ GC algorithm to locate such a block as demonstrated in Figure 10. This figure also indicates that the mean number of attempts is between 2 and 3 for all $S_f \in [0.05, 0.2]$ for $b = 64$ pages per block.

Similar experiments, not depicted here, indicate that the RANDOM++ GC algorithm does outperform the FIFO algorithm for $S_f \in [0.05, 0.2]$ when there are only $b = 8$ pages in a block. Whether the FIFO or RANDOM++ algorithm achieves the lowest write amplification for $b = 16$ and 32 pages per block, depends in a complicated manner on the spare factor S_f (due to the jumps in the RANDOM++ curve). We end by remarking that the write amplification A of the RANDOM++ algorithm is well below that of the RANDOM algorithm, the write amplification of which equals $1/(1 - \rho)$, even for larger b values, e.g., $b = 64$.

8. CONCLUSIONS AND FUTURE WORK

In this paper we introduced a mean field model to analyze the write amplification of a class $\mathcal{C}$ of garbage collection (GC) algorithms in flash-based solid state drives under uniform random writes. Algorithms belonging to class $\mathcal{C}$ include the RANDOM(+), RANDOM++ and d-CHOICES GC algorithms, where the latter two were analyzed for the first time. Closed form results for the write amplification and the distribution of the number of valid pages in a block were obtained for the RANDOM(+) and RANDOM++ algorithm, while a fast numerical ODE-based method was proposed for the d-CHOICES algorithm. The results were shown to be highly accurate using simulation experiments.

The d-CHOICES algorithm was shown to be very effective in reducing the write amplification, while the RANDOM++ algorithm was less effective. More specifically, we showed that the d-CHOICES GC algorithm has a write amplification close to that of the GREEDY GC algorithm even for small d values, e.g., $d = 10$, and offers a more attractive trade-off than the WINDOWED GC algorithm between its simplicity and its performance.

We are currently extending the mean field model for uniform random writes introduced in this paper, to the hot/cold data model of Rosenblum [14]. Preliminary results (not shown here) indicate that the write amplification of the d-CHOICES GC algorithm gets closer to the write amplification of the GREEDY algorithm as the hot data gets hotter (i.e., as f decreases or r increases). In other words, even smaller d values suffice to get close to the performance of the GREEDY GC algorithm.

We are also planning to extend the model to study the impact of data separation techniques for hot/cold data and of the TRIM command on the write amplification. The latter will make the model also more applicable to the setting of log-structured file systems where data is often deleted.

9. REFERENCES

[1] R. Agarwal and M. Marrow. A closed-form expression for write amplification in NAND flash. In *IEEE GLOBECOM Workshops (GC Wkshps)*, pages 1846–1850, 2010.

[2] Y. Azar, A.Z. Broder, A.R. Karlin, and E. Upfal. Balanced allocations. In *SIAM Journal on Computing*, pages 593–602, 1994.

[3] A. Ban. Wear leveling of static areas in flash memory. US patent 6,732,221. Filed June 1, 2001; Issued May 4, 2004; Assigned to M-Systems., 2004.

[4] M. Benaïm and J. Le Boudec. A class of mean field interaction models for computer and communication systems. *Performance Evaluation*, 65(11-12):823–838, 2008.

[5] W. Bux and I. Iliadis. Performance of greedy garbage collection in flash-based solid-state drives. *Perform. Eval.*, 67(11):1172–1186, November 2010.

[6] F. Chen, D.A. Koufaty, and X. Zhang. Understanding intrinsic characteristics and system implications of flash memory based solid state drives. *ACM SIGMETRICS Perform. Eval. Rev.*, 37(1):181–192, 2013.

[7] P. Desnoyers. Analytic modeling of SSD write performance. In *Proceedings of International Systems and Storage Conference (SYSTOR 2012)*, 2012.

[8] X. Hu, E. Eleftheriou, R. Haas, I. Iliadis, and R. Pletka. Write amplification analysis in flash-based solid state drives. In *Proceedings of SYSTOR 2009: The Israeli Experimental Systems Conference*, SYSTOR '09, pages 10:1–10:9, New York, NY, USA, 2009.

[9] J.-U. Kang, H. Jo, J.-S. Kim, and J. Lee. A superblock-based flash translation layer for NAND flash memory. In *Proceedings of the 6th ACM & IEEE International conference on Embedded software*, EMSOFT '06, pages 161–170, New York, NY, USA, 2006.

[10] Y. Li, P.P.C. Lee, and J.C.S. Lui. Stochastic modeling of large-scale solid-state storage systems: Analysis, design tradeoffs and optimization. *ACM SIGMETRICS Perform. Eval. Rev.*, 41(1), 2013.

[11] J. Menon. A performance comparison of RAID-5 and log-structured arrays. In *Proceedings of the 4th IEEE International Symposium on High Performance Distributed Computing*, HPDC '95, pages 167–178, Washington, DC, USA, 1995.

[12] M. Mitzenmacher, A. Richa, and R. Sitaraman. The power of two random choices: a survey of techniques and results. *Handbook of Randomized Computing*, 1, 2001.

[13] J.T. Robinson. Analysis of steady-state segment storage utilizations in a log-structured file system with least-utilized segment cleaning. *SIGOPS Oper. Syst. Rev.*, 30(4):29–32, October 1996.

[14] M. Rosenblum and J. K. Ousterhout. The design and implementation of a log-structured file system. *ACM Trans. Comput. Syst.*, 10(1):26–52, February 1992.

[15] N.D. Vvedenskaya, R.L. Dobrushin, and F.I. Karpelevich. Queueing system with selection of the shortest of two queues: an asymptotic approach. *Problemy Peredachi Informatsii*, 32:15–27, 1996.

[16] L. Xiang and B. Kurkoski. An improved analytical expression for write amplification in NAND flash. In *International Conference on Computing, Networking, and Communications (ICNC)*, pages 497–501, 2012.

APPENDIX

A. UNIQUENESS FOR D > 1 AND B = 2

When $b = 2$, the space Δ is one dimensional and the evolution of $w_2(t)$ is given by

$$\frac{dw_2(t)}{dt} = 1 - w_2(t)^d - \left(2 - w_2(t)^d - (2\rho - w_2(t))^d\right)\frac{w_2(t)}{\rho},$$

due to (18) as $w_1(t) = 2\rho - w_2(t)$. Note, as $1 \geq w_1(t) \geq w_2(t) \geq 0$, $w_2(t) \in [\min(0, 2\rho - 1), \rho]$. Define $g(w) = 1 - w^d - (b - w^d - (2\rho - w)^d)w/\rho$, then $g(\min(0, 2\rho - 1)) > 0$ and $g(\rho) = -(1 - \rho^d) < 0$. Further,

$$g'(w) = -dw^{d-1} - \left(2 - w^d - (2\rho - w)^d\right)\frac{1}{\rho} + d\left(w^{d-1} - (2\rho - w)^{d-1}\right)\frac{w}{\rho},$$

meaning $g'(w) < 0$ for $w \in [\min(0, 2\rho - 1), \rho]$. Hence, there is a unique fixed point in Δ that is necessarily a global attractor.

Revisiting Widely Held SSD Expectations and Rethinking System-Level Implications

Myoungsoo Jung and Mahmut Kandemir
Department of Computer Science and Engineering
The Pennsylvania State University, University Park, PA 16802, USA
mj@cse.psu.edu and kandemir@cse.psu.edu

ABSTRACT

Storage applications leveraging Solid State Disk (SSD) technology are being widely deployed in diverse computing systems. These applications accelerate system performance by exploiting several SSD-specific characteristics. However, modern SSDs have undergone a dramatic technology and architecture shift in the past few years, which makes widely held assumptions and expectations regarding them highly questionable. The main goal of this paper is to question popular assumptions and expectations regarding SSDs through an extensive experimental analysis using 6 state-of-the-art SSDs from different vendors. Our analysis leads to several conclusions which are either not reported in prior SSD literature, or contradict to current conceptions. For example, we found that SSDs are not biased toward read-intensive workloads in terms of performance and reliability. Specifically, random read performance of SSDs is worse than their sequential and random write performance by 40% and 39% on average, and more importantly, the performance of sequential reads gets significantly worse over time. Further, we found that reads can shorten SSD lifetime more than writes, which is very unfortunate, given the fact that many existing systems/platforms already employ SSDs as read caches or in applications that are highly read intensive. We also performed a comprehensive study to understand the worst-case performance characteristics of our SSDs, and investigated the viability of recently proposed enhancements that are geared towards alleviating the worst-case performance challenges, such as TRIM commands and background-tasks. Lastly, we uncover the overheads brought by these enhancements and their limits, and discuss system-level implications.

Categories and Subject Descriptors

B.3.1 [**Hardware**]: Memory Structures—*Semiconductor Memories*; D.4.2 [**Software**]: Operating Systems—*Storage Management*; C.4 [**Computer System Organization**]: Performance of Systems

Keywords

Solid State Disk, NAND Flash, TRIM Command, Garbage Collection, Performance, Parallelism, Reliability.

1. INTRODUCTION

NAND Flash-based Solid State Disks (SSDs) have recently become immensely popular and been employed in different types of environments ranging from embedded systems to personal computers to high performance computing (HPC) systems. Moreover, various memory and storage systems have been proposed to take advantage of the performance benefits of SSDs over conventional block devices. For example, to reap the benefits of high bandwidth on writes, prior HPC studies consider SSDs as a burst buffer [32], which can absorb heavy write traffic caused by check-pointing [37]. There also exist many applications developed under the expectation that NAND flash is biased toward reads in terms of performance and reliability. Enterprise servers, for example, consider employing SSDs for applications that exhibit many random reads [33, 38, 39] or use them as read caches [28, 3, 30, 36], sitting between main memory and hard disk drive (HDD). Similarly, SSDs are also introduced as a main memory replacement, memory extension, and a part of existing virtual memory systems [13, 12, 14, 38].

While many of these SSD applications and usage scenarios are proposed and developed based on common expectations from SSDs, modern SSDs and NAND flash systems have undergone severe technology shift and architectural changes in the last couple of years. Specifically, NAND flash cells have shrunk from 5x nm to 2x nm in the past four years, and now fewer electrons are stored per floating gate. These cell-level characteristics make flash devices less reliable and introduce extra operations (e.g., multi-step I/O, verification, error correction processes) to successfully complete I/O requests, which in turn imposes longer latencies. State-of-the-art NAND flash packaging technologies employ an increased number of planes and dies within a single flash chip, a command queue, ECC engines, and faster data movement interfaces [9, 35]. These technological changes led in turn to modulations in SSD behavior and performance characteristics. In parallel, SSD internal architecture has dramatically changed; modern SSDs now employ multiple internal resources such as flash chips, I/O buses, controllers and cores in an attempt to achieve high internal parallelism. In addition, to reduce performance variations and garbage collection overheads, flash firmware employs advanced strategies such as finer-granular address mappings, DRAM buffer and background tasks. Finally, thin storage interfaces of modern SSDs define command feature sets, which provide a way to efficiently expose underlying SSD characteristics to operating systems (OS). Consequently, OS can manage SSD internal resources more efficiently by utilizing system level information.

Unfortunately, most prior works study SSD behavior and performance characteristics based on limited information, or evaluate them based on select I/O access patterns to understand SSD-level parallelism and performance implications. In our opinion, these studies do not help OS and system designers in understanding critical SSD features, and integrating SSDs into existing storage stacks and efficiently optimizing them. Further, a more problematic issue is that, even though SSD NAND flash technology has changed dramatically over the last couple of years, many research groups still employ SSDs based on assumptions that do no hold anymore.

In this paper, we conduct an extensive experimental evaluation with six state-of-the-art SSDs carefully selected by considering different types of flash fabric technologies, manufacturers, cores, chips, and over-provisioning strategies. Based on our empirical evaluations, we next perform a comprehensive data analysis and uncover critical SSD/flash characteristics, which are not reported, to the best of our knowledge, in the literature so far, and are opposite to the widely held expectations on SSDs. Our main goal is to correct common misconceptions on SSDs using new data, which greatly effect performance as well as reliability of modern SSDs, but have not been studied well in the past. We hope to motivate both academia and industry to rethink SSD system design, management and optimization based on our evaluations and data analysis. In this paper, we answer, either directly or indirectly, several questions described in the following subsections, and reveal some critical data regarding state-of-the-art SSDs, which should be, in our opinion, taken into account by both OS and SSD designers. The questions we want to address can be categorized into five groups.

1.1 Rethinking Read Performance

A well-known intrinsic characteristic of NAND flash is that their read performance is tens to hundreds times better than their write performance [34]. In addition, since SSDs have no moving parts, they are expected to provide fast random read accesses [38]. Motivated by these, many platform designers consider SSDs for the applications that contain mostly random reads.

1. Are SSDs biased toward reads at a system level? Why do random reads constitute a performance bottleneck in modern SSDs?
2. For the sequential read accesses, could SSDs support sustained performance? Is there any performance degradation on reads? How could a system achieve a sustained read performance?
3. What is the relationship between read performance and internal SSD parallelism? Can users characterize read performance by examining different I/O access patterns?

1.2 Examining Reliability on Reads

Unlike writes, reads require no erase operation or content-update on NAND flash. Consequently, many computing domains exploit SSDs as a read cache or an intermediate layer

when targeting read-intensive workloads to extend SSD lifetime and avoid heavy write penalties.

1. Do program/erase (PE) cycles of SSDs increase during read-only access periods? If it is, why do reads need a block erasure?
2. Are there performance impacts caused by internal I/O operations on reads?
3. What parameters do system-level designers need to control in order to extend SSD lifetime?

1.3 Reconsidering Write Performance

Many schemes have been proposed by prior SSD research to reduce garbage collection (GC) overheads such as over-provisioning [16], DRAM buffer [29, 20, 22], and finer-granular address mappings [19, 15, 34]. Based on this, it is expected that long GC operations can be reordered and deferred, and therefore, they do not cause severe throughput degradation at a system level.

1. How much impact do GC latencies have on system performance in practice?
2. Is there any relationship between the worst-case latency of GCs and system throughput? Could we quantify this relationship?
3. Could DRAM buffer help firmware in reducing the GC overheads? If not, why?

1.4 OS Support

TRIM commands enable OS to invalidate deleted system-level data contents, which can in turn reduce GC overheads significantly. Motivated by this, many emerging SSD platforms (e.g., flash virtual memory, file system, database) are expected to send TRIM commands to underlying SSDs as much as they can.

1. In theory, OS and users can eliminate unnecessary GC operations through TRIMs. How much of GC overheads can be eliminated using TRIM commands?
2. Does TRIM command request pattern matter?
3. Do TRIM commands themselves impose any overheads?

1.5 Characterizing Background Tasks

Since state-of-the-art SSDs employ many computational resources, they could perform SSD-internal tasks in the background. The background tasks are expected to allow SSDs to expedite foreground tasks, which in turn is expected to achieve stable and sustainable performance.

1. What types of background tasks affecting system performance exist in modern SSDs?
2. Do the background tasks of current SSDs guarantee stable and sustainable performance? If not, what is the main difficulty?

2. PRELIMINARIES

State-of-the-art SSDs are composed of multiple cores, memory modules, data buses, and storage media. In the following, we provide a quick overview of SSDs and NAND flash, basic flash firmware features, storage interfaces, and reliability issues.

2.1 SSD and NAND Flash Internals

Modern SSDs and NAND flash chips employ several components to scale their performance under a given technology.

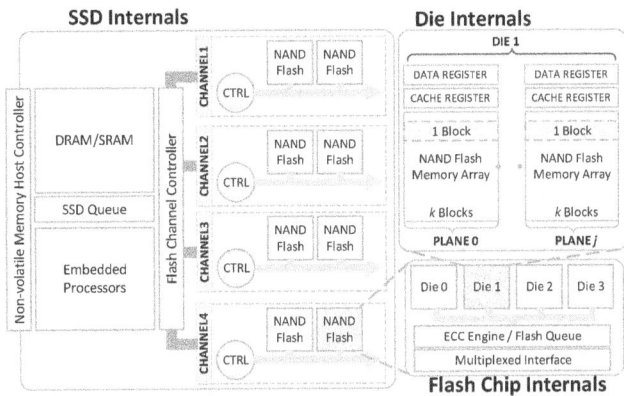

Figure 1: Modern SSD internal architecture. Note that an I/O request can be simultaneously served by many internal resources, which is one of the important characteristics of SSDs.

As shown in Figure 1, an SSD employs multiple internal resources described below.

Controllers. For physical layer (PHY) management, SSDs have two different controllers: 1) non-volatile memory host controller (NVMHC) and 2) flash channel controller (FCC). NVMHC manages the front-end PHY layer to communicate with outside through a conventional thin interface/bus. FCC, in contrast, handles the back-end PHY layer to control underlying flash packages and corresponding interfaces.

Multicore. While the controllers are responsible for handling the PHY layer, the embedded processor is dedicated to running the flash firmware, which is composed of multiple software layers. Since each layer of the firmware has a different goal and some of their functionalities can be parallelized, modern SSDs employ multiple cores (or processors) in an attempt to minimize computation overheads [23, 25].

Multiple Channels. The flash package interconnection design is very important from a parallelism angle. In general, considering hardware complexity and signal integrity, several flash packages are connected to a single data bus, referred to as *channel*, and multiple channel are used in SSDs.

Flash Package. A flash die is composed of multiple planes, and multiple dies are stacked in a single flash package, which helps one improve storage capacity and flash-level parallelism. Multiple requests can be interleaved through a limited number of CE (chip enable) and I/O pins. In addition, modern flash packages employ a queue and an ECC engine to offload system level overheads imposed by flash commands management and error code checking, respectively.

2.2 Flash Firmware

Depending on the specifics of the underlying hardware configuration, the role of flash firmware can be quite diverse. We now explain the common tasks of the firmware, which have an impact on system performance.

Parallelism. Flash firmware can strip an I/O request over multiple channels, flash packages, and dies therein, in order to improve system performance in terms of both latency and throughput [23, 25, 34, 17]. Since internal parallelism is key to boosting SSD performance, efficient parallelization of data accesses is one of the crucial tasks of the firmware.

Address Mapping. Since NAND flash allows no in-place

updates in a block, when a write arrives, flash firmware stores data in a temporal block (which is prepared in advance), and remaps the original address of the request (*virtual address*) and the actual location (*physical address*) of the corresponding data for future reads. In some cases, flash firmware can also remap the addresses in order to improve internal parallelism on writes [25, 10].

Garbage Collection. When the prepared blocks run out, flash firmware needs to reclaim physical block(s) so that it can serve an incoming update request. Since this block reclaiming task, called *garbage collection* (GC), is basically a series of extra internal operations, which include reading/writing live data from the target blocks to new block, erasing the old blocks and updating the mapping information, it can introduce long latencies and degrade performance. To reduce GC overheads as much as possible, modern SSDs employ more elaborate address mapping schemes, including some proposals that perform GC in the background.

Endurance. Flash blocks have limits in terms of the number of program (write) and erase cycles, referred to as *PE cycle*. Typically, a block that experiences higher PE cycles also experiences more errors and worse memory characteristics. Further, once a block reaches its PE cycle limit, it is not available anymore for storage. Since guaranteed PE cycles get smaller as technology shrinks, flash firmware needs to consider endurance related issues.

Wear Leveling. Since not all the information stored within the same location changes with the same frequency, it is important to keep the aging of each block as minimum and as uniform as possible. Flash firmware is also responsible for ensuring that all physical blocks are evenly used (to the maximum extent possible) and keeping the aging under a reasonable value. These tasks are collectively referred to as *wear leveling*.

Disturbance. Since a flash block is composed of multiple *NAND strings* to which the memory cells are connected in series (in groups of 64, 128, or 256), a memory operation on a specific flash cell may influence the charge contents on a different cell. This is referred to as *disturbance*, which can occur on any flash operation and lead to errors in undesignated memory cells.

2.3 Reliability Challenges on Reads

A read operation may fail because of 1) *read disturbance*, 2) *retention error* (leakage problem), and 3) *noise* (e.g., at the power rails). We now explain what SSDs do to address read failures.

ECC Recovery. To avoid failure on reads, *error-correcting codes* (ECC) are widely employed [7]. ECC can correct certain bit errors but typically introduces extra computation cycles on both reads and writes. More specifically, while the encoding takes a few cycles (on writes), the decoding requires lots of cycles. This cycle disparity between encoding and decoding imposes extra overheads on reads, which in turn degrades system performance. Since wider ECCs are required as flash technology shrinks, ECC overheads become more pronounced in modern SSDs.

Read Disturbance Management. Read disturbance can occur when reading the same target cell multiple times without any erase operation. When reading data from a specific cell, V_{read} (0 V) is applied to that cell, and all other cells are biased at V_{pass} (4~5 V), which makes them behave as pass-transistors. As a result, the cells on successive read

	Basic Test			Specific Test		
Postfix Name →	-L	-C	-Z	-A	-X	-P
Storage (GB)	120	256	256	256	240	240
DRAM (MB)	128	256	0	256	0	0
Numbers of Chips	16	16	8	8	16	16
Technology (nm)	34	25	25-32	32	25	25
Numbers of Cores	2	3	1	3	1	1
Over-provision (%)	15	7.3	14.5	9.5	14.4	14.4

Table 1: Device characteristics of SSDs used in our study.

operations can gain charge, which has similar impact on unintended writes. Since read disturbance can be corrected if the corresponding block is physically erased, it is necessary to erase the block associated with target page address causing the read disturbance. In general, to preserve data consistency, flash firmware reads all live data pages, erases the block, and writes down live pages to the erased block. Some flash firmware migrates live data to new block and remaps the address information between the old and new blocks [2]. This process, called *read block reclaiming*, introduces long latencies and degrades performance.

Runtime Bad Block Management. Even though ECC can correct certain bit errors and flash firmware keeps aging under control, endurance characteristics of flash storage get worse over time. In particular, raw bit error rate increases exponentially with PE cycles [9, 2], which leads to *uncorrectable ECC* (UECC) errors. To avoid UECC errors, flash firmware marks the blocks whose raw error rates have reached the error recovery coverage limit as "bad blocks". It then replaces each bad block with a new block by remapping addresses, in an attempt to avoid future UECC errors. Similar to read block reclaiming and GCs, this *bad block management* also degrades system performance.

2.4 Storage Interfaces, TRIM and SMART

Conventional storage interfaces hinder the scalability of modern SSDs and make efficient SSD management difficult. To help with this, high-speed interfaces such as SATA 6.0Gbps and PCI Express are employed. Further, the most recent version of SATA provides SSD-specific command feature sets, which enable underlying SSDs to expose their internal characteristics to the OS. Specifically, *TRIM*, one of these command feature sets, allows the OS to invalidate data blocks that are no longer considered in use and delete the obsolete data at a system level. TRIM commands are expected to significantly reduce GC overheads and alleviate potential write degradation in many SSD applications. *SMART* is another command feature set, which enables self-monitoring, analysis, and state-reporting. Using it, OS designers can effectively manage SSDs by retrieving internal SSD information such as PE cycles and the number of channels and physical blocks.

3. EVALUATION SETUP

Solid State Disks. Today, there exist many different SSDs on the market, with quite different performance characteristics based on the vendor and system configurations, in terms of the DRAM buffer size, the number of cores, and the number of flash chips. For our experiments, we chose six representative products shipped by five different SSD-makers. All these SSDs are manufactured between 2011 and 2012, and

their firmware are updated with the latest available version for our evaluations. Since our goal is not to perform reverse engineering or make performance comparison across these commercial products, we refer to each of them using a different postfix character, instead of giving its full name. Our SSDs and their important characteristics are listed in Table 1. Since the runtime information provided by different vendors varies a lot, in each of our evaluations, we select an appropriate subset of our SSDs and use them, and also mention the reason behind our selection. In general, SSD-L, -C, and -Z are evaluated for all basic tests, and SSD-A, -X, -P are used for more specific evaluations.

Measurement and Characterization Tools. In order to uncover hidden performance characteristics and examine widely held expectations on our SSDs, we need well-defined I/O access patterns, which can be controlled and reproduced irrespective of the underlying test platform. Consequently, we use Intel open source based storage tool, *Iometer* [18], as our default measurement and characterization tool. Iometer can generate various I/O workloads parameterized in terms of read/write ratio, sequential access/random access ratio, request sizes and the number of queue entries. However, Iometer reports performance results in terms of only average/min/max values at the end of the entire evaluation process. Therefore, for some of our evaluations that require a more microscopic view with finer resolution than what Iometer provides, we use a *modified Iometer*, which captures the latency per individual I/O requests and performance characteristics on a second-basis without any underlying software intervention. Lastly, to evaluate the PHY level latencies, especially for the TRIM command overhead characterization, we use the commercial LeCroy SATA protocol analyzer (*Sierra M6-1*) [31] and double check the protocol status with this analyzer.

Protocol Controls. To accurately evaluate different technologies employed by modern SSDs, we also need a clean evaluation chamber under our control. For example, even though an application tool can mimic system idleness to evaluate background tasks by injecting artificial idle periods, the advanced host controller interface (AHCI) driver/controller can periodically send commands like SMART to examine the underlying system, which can make SSDs continuously busy. To the best of our knowledge, there exist no public tool, which can generate a specific ATA command, check its PHY level latency, and directly handle the AHCI. This is why, for some of our investigations that require the management of ATA commands (e.g., TRIM, SMART) and the control of the AHCI, we needed an in-house driver. Therefore, we also developed an *AHCI miniport driver*, as a part of WDM (windows driver model), which can generate TRIM commands by filling target addresses for the deleted contents with different access patterns (random/sequential), handle SMART commands to check the PE cycles of the SSDs, and manually control specific power modes to examine background tasks.

Experimental System. Our experimental system is equipped with an Intel Quad Core i7 Sandy Bridge 2600 3.4 GHz processor and 4GB DDR3-1333Mhz memory. Intel Z64 chipset is employed as the I/O controller hub in southbridge, and all SSDs we tested are connected to Z64 through the SATA 6.0Gbps interface. We execute all our scenarios in Microsoft NTFS, store logs and output results into separate block devices in a full asynchronous fashion; and neither a system partition nor a file system is created on our SSD test-beds.

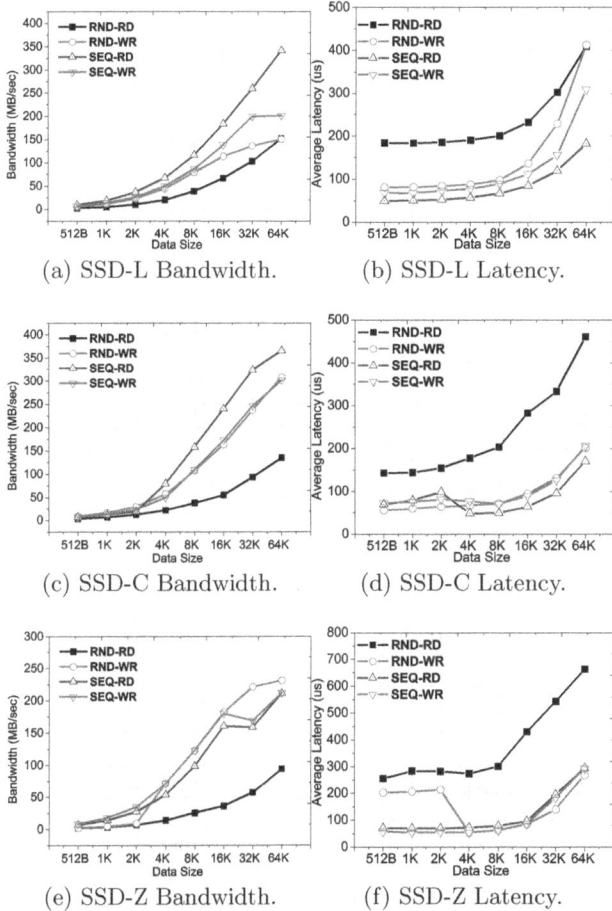

(a) SSD-L Bandwidth.

(b) SSD-L Latency.

(c) SSD-C Bandwidth.

(d) SSD-C Latency.

(e) SSD-Z Bandwidth.

(f) SSD-Z Latency.

Figure 2: Read/write performance comparison under varying data transfer sizes and access patterns. In these comparisons, *RND* and *SEQ* denote the random access pattern and sequential access pattern respectively, and *RD* and *WR* stand for read and write.

This configuration allows each SSD test-bed to be completely separated from the evaluation scenarios and tools.

4. TESTING EXPECTATIONS ON READS

The most remarkable performance characteristic shifts on modern SSDs are observed in reads, since they are vulnerable to changes in internal SSD architecture. In this section, we first examine overall performance, comparing reads with other types of operations, and then analyze the challenges on reads in terms of performance sustainability and performance dependency on internal parallelism. Lastly, we uncover reliability problems on read-intensive workloads, which is one of the most critical issues, in our opinion, for both the OS and SSD designers.

4.1 Are SSDs good for applications that exhibit mostly random reads?

To compare read performance with the performance of other types of operations, we executed different workloads composed of *sequential accesses* and *random accesses* with varying data transfer sizes (ranging from 1 sector to 128 sec-

tors) on SSD-L, -C and -Z; we observed that SSD-A exhibits similar performance characteristics to SSD-C, and SSD-P and -X achieve similar performance results to SSD-Z in this test. Performance comparison across our three SSDs is plotted in Figure 2. Specifically, Figures 2a, 2c and 2e show variance in overall bandwidth, and Figures 2b, 2d, and 2f plot variance in latency for SSD-L, -C and -Z, respectively.

Our first observation is that the *performance values with random read accesses (denoted using RND-RD) are worse than other types of access patterns and operations, including even random write accesses*, which is in *direct contrast* with the widely held expectation on read performance of SSDs in the literature. Specifically, the bandwidth values with random read accesses of SSD-L, -C, and -Z are worse than the corresponding values with random writes by 59.7%, 39.4% and 23.7%, respectively. Read latency characteristics are not much different from bandwidth; the latency values observed with random reads are worse than the latencies observed with sequential writes, random writes, and sequential reads by 41.3%, 35.2%, and 35.9%, on average, respectively.

We believe that the main reason why SSDs can experience opposite performance characteristics at a flash level (reads are much faster than writes at a memory cell level) is the lack of internal parallelism on random reads. Note that, sequential accesses can be striped over multiple channels in a round-robin fashion, and the striped sub-requests can be interleaved across multiple flash dies in each channel. In contrast, random read accesses can potentially create a scenario where multiple requests end up contending for the same internal resources (e.g., channel, package, die, plane), referred to as *resource conflicts*. A request experiencing resource conflict has to wait for the completion of the other request(s) heading to the same resources. Therefore, the resource conflict on random reads causes low parallelism and thus degrades both bandwidth and latency. Unlike reads, flash firmware can easily forward the incoming write requests to a target sitting in idle by remapping addresses, which leads to low resource conflicts and high levels of parallelism.

One potential concern on this read-write comparison would be the impact of the internal DRAM buffer. Since writes can be buffered in DRAM, if the internal DRAM does not flush the in-memory data to the flash medium, write performance would be much better than reads. However, as shown in Figures 2e and 2f, we observed that DRAM-less SSDs, namely SSD-P, -X, and -Z, exhibit very similar performance characteristics to 128MB and 256MB DRAM-equipped SSDs. Further, the amount of data written into those SSDs is over 200GB, which cannot be buffered by a small size DRAM; in fact, the DRAM capacity accounts for under 1% of the total amount of data we wrote in these experiments.

4.2 Can we achieve sustained read performance with sequential accesses?

As demonstrated in the previous section, all the SSDs tested generate their best performance on sequential read accesses. In this section, we further examine whether the sequential read performance can be sustained over time or not, which might have a significant impact on read-intensive SSD applications. For this set of experiments, we executed sequential read accesses with transfer sizes ranging from 1 to 16 sectors on two different SSD sets; "pristine" SSDs and "aged" SSDs, and measured their latencies per request with the modified Iometer. The results are presented in Figure

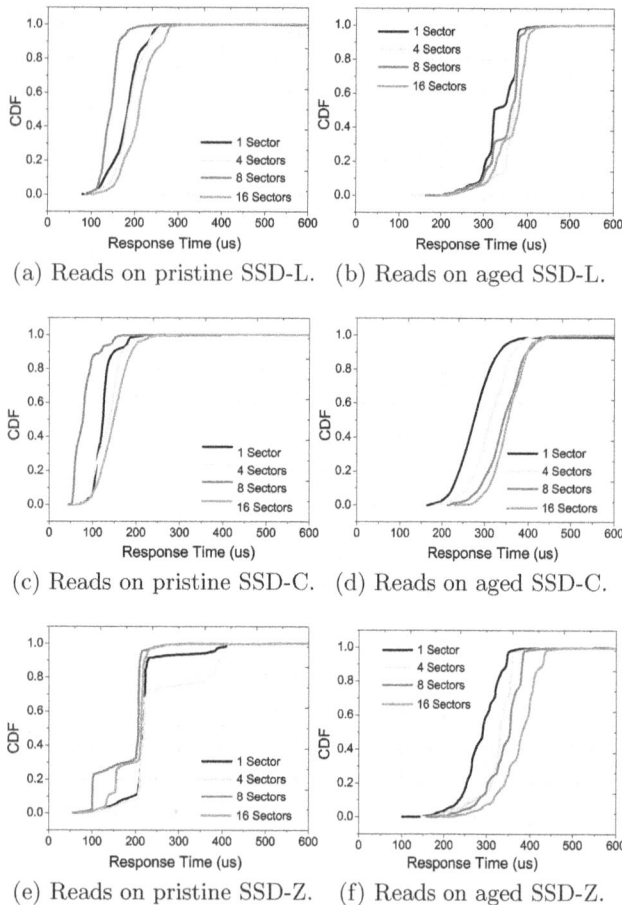

(a) Reads on pristine SSD-L. (b) Reads on aged SSD-L.

(c) Reads on pristine SSD-C. (d) Reads on aged SSD-C.

(e) Reads on pristine SSD-Z. (f) Reads on aged SSD-Z.

Figure 3: Cumulative distribution function (CDF) of latency variance in sequential reads for "pristine" SSDs and "aged" SSDs (i.e., writing data with a random access pattern to the entire storage space of SSDs). Note that all the curves presented in the CDFs are shifted from left to right as SSDs get older.

3. Specifically, Figures 3a, 3c and 3e plot cumulative distributed function (CDF) of latency for pristine SSD-L, -C and -Z, and Figures 3b, 3d and 3f plot the same for aged SSD-L, -C and -Z, respectively.

One can observe from these results that most of the read requests on all pristine SSDs are served within 300 ∼ 400 μsec. However, when SSDs get order, CDF curves shift from left to right exhibiting worse performance characteristics. The aged SSDs take over 600 μsec for serving all the I/O requests, which is two to three times worse than our pristine SSDs. One can conclude from this analysis that, *sequential read performance characteristics get worse with aging and as I/O requests are being processed*, which are unfortunately captured neither by NAND flash data sheets or nor by SSD specifications. We believe that this performance degradation on reads is mainly caused by fragmented physical data layout and reliability management overheads on reads. This read performance degradation also implies that the read behavior of an SSD cannot be easily characterized by the OS by examining only the current I/O request patterns despite recent works [6, 11] claiming that. We will provide a deeper

evaluation and more evidence on this read performance characteristic in the following sections.

4.3 What is the relationship between read performance and previous writes accesses?

In this section, we analyze read performance of SSDs by building 14 different physical layouts, in an attempt to reveal the relationship between read performance and previous writes accesses as well as internal SSD parallelism. The insight behind this evaluation is that the order of random writes can be transformed into a kind of sequential pattern by the underlying flash firmware, which may have performance impact on current writes as well as future reads. Specifically, the address remapping process allows the flash firmware to easily strip the write requests over multiple internal resources irrespective of the access pattern, which leads to high levels of parallelism as well as improved performance on random writes. However, this physical data layout construction on writes may also introduce different performance behavior for future reads. Unlike writes, for a read to occur, the data to be read should exist and it must reside in a particular location. As a result, the degree of parallelism and performance on reads depends highly on the underlying data layout, *which is constructed during the previous writes*.

To quantify this impact, we chose SSDs that have no DRAM, to minimize any potential side effects of buffering on both read and writes. We then randomly wrote data into the entire address space of the DRAM-less SSDs, SSD-P, -X and Z, with seven different data transfer sizes ranging from 4 sectors to 256 sectors. As a control group, we also wrote data into the same type of SSDs but different devices, using sequential access patterns composed of the same data transfer sizes used in the random writes. We then read the entire space of those SSDs with varying data sizes ranging from 4KB to 32KB, and measured the bandwidth and latency. The results are plotted in Figures 4 and 5.

To make our discussion easier to follow, let *RND-PDT* denote the physical data layout resulting from random writes, and *SEQ-PDT* denote the physical data layout resulting from sequential writes. In Figures 4 and 5, the dashed-lines and solid-lines indicate the read performance on RND-PDT and SEQ-PDT, respectively. One can observe that, *read performance significantly varies based on the physical data layout organization even though current I/O request access patterns are exactly the same*. More specifically, bandwidth values for all the evaluations on RND-PDT (Figure 4) are under 80 MB/s, whereas bandwidth values on SEQ-PDT reach up to 220 MB/s. As the data transfer size used during the physical data layout construction increases, the performance gains are more pronounced since this allows the flash firmware to more easily build a physical data layout by sequentially writing data back-to-back. This performance impact is also observed in our latency characterization plotted in Figure 5. While the minimum latency with RND-PDT is 210 μsec, the latency with SEQ-PDT is around 80 μsec.

Based on these evaluations, one can conclude that, since the virtual address space that the flash firmware provides on RND-PDT has been constructed during previous writes, the order of sequential read accesses on the virtual address space are jumbled. Consequently, the read accesses can suffer from multiple resource conflicts at a specific channel, chip and die, even though the access pattern itself is sequential. This in turn can degrade read performance due to low internal

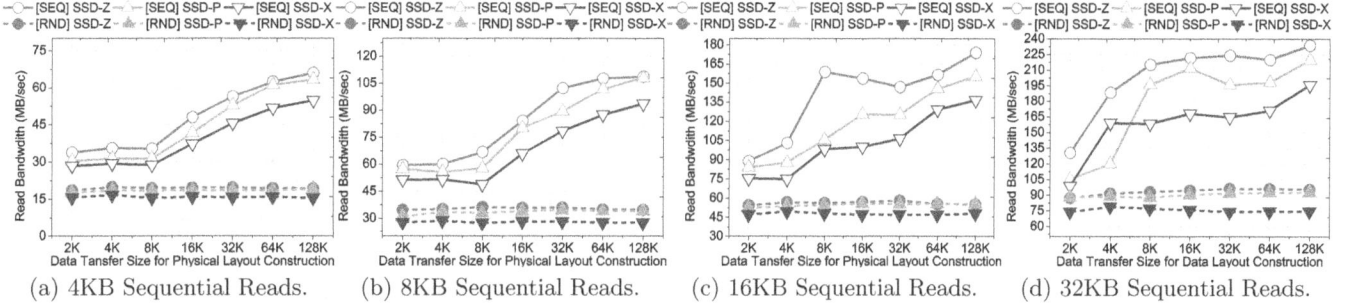

(a) 4KB Sequential Reads. (b) 8KB Sequential Reads. (c) 16KB Sequential Reads. (d) 32KB Sequential Reads.

Figure 4: Bandwidths with different physical data layouts. *SEQ* and *RND* denote sequential writes and random writes, used for the physical data (*PDT*) layout construction. Observe that throughput significantly varies based on the physical data layout, constructed by previous writes, even under same read request patterns.

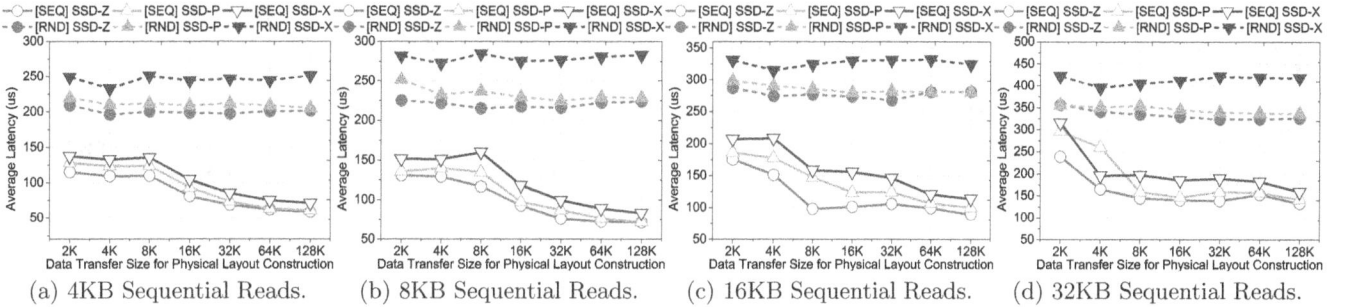

(a) 4KB Sequential Reads. (b) 8KB Sequential Reads. (c) 16KB Sequential Reads. (d) 32KB Sequential Reads.

Figure 5: Latencies with different physical data layouts. These latency comparison explains how the physical data layout is related to internal parallelism in two aspects. First, the read latency performed on RND-PDT is 2.3 times higher than that of SEQ-PDT that induces lower resource conflicts. Second, as the data movement size of reads increases, the magnitude of the latency improvement with SEQ-PDT is shorter than the improvement with RND-PDT that has many resource conflicts potential.

SSD parallelism. In contrast, sequential accesses on SEQ-PDT can be simultaneously served from multiple internal resources in different locations without any major resource conflict since there are no changes in the order of virtual addresses.

4.4 Do program/erase (PE) cycles of SSDs increase during read only operations?

To study the PE cycle characteristics on reads, we executed Iometer with two different *read-only* workloads, composed of sequential and random access patterns, about 200 rounds, each with a running time of 1 hour (total 200 hours). In each round, we sent a SMART command using our in-house AHCI minport driver and measured PE cycles by decoding return codes based on the SMART attribute table [40]. To compare the PE cycles between reads and writes, we also measured the PE cycles on write-only workloads with the same access patterns and measurement method used in the read-only workload evaluations. We observed that unfortunately all the SSDs tested provide insufficient information to understand SSD internal characteristics; in particular, all the data are normalized or provided as percentage based on their lifespan expectations, and some SSDs do not even report their PE cycles on reads. Therefore, we present the reliability evaluation results of a specific version of SSD-A, which is used in Apple MacBook Air; unlike other SSDs we tested, SSD-A provides absolute maximum/average PE cycles on both reads and writes.

Figures 6a and 6b give the variance in PE cycles on two

different SSD-A instances under sequential and random access patterns, respectively. One can see from these plots that *PE cycles increase in every evaluation round, in a direct contrast to what the current literature on systems exploiting SSDs would lead one to believe*. In sequential reads, the maximum PE cycles reach the half of PE cycles on writes, as shown in Figure 6a. Ironically, the maximum PE cycles with the random read-only workload are higher than that of writes by about 12x (Figure 6b). We believe that the reason behind this PE cycle increase on read-only workloads is the read disturbance and runtime bad block management. Since these activities require erasing block(s) and live-data migration to the target block(s), *read requests can shorten the SSD lifespan and significantly degrade overall performance*. Further, the disparity between the maximum and average PE cycles tell us another story; wear leveling strategies employed by current flash firmware mainly focus on writes, *not* on reads. While SSD-A firmware keeps reducing the gap between the maximum and average PE cycles on writes, the maximum PE cycles on reads is 247 times higher than the average PE cycles in each round, which makes certain blocks wear out faster and worsen SSD endurance characteristics.

4.5 Is there any performance impact of the reliability management on reads?

All the activities for handling read disturbance management, runtime bad block management, and ECC, referred collectively to as *reliability management on reads* (RMR), require additional I/O operations and compute cycles. These

209

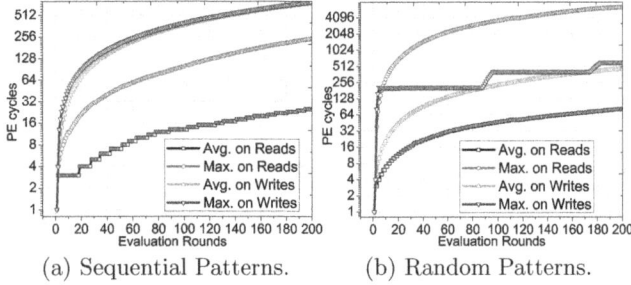

(a) Sequential Patterns. (b) Random Patterns.

Figure 6: PE-cycle comparison between reads and writes. Note that PE cycles increase under read-only workloads. Further, with random accesses, the maximum PE cycles on reads are 12 times greater than that on writes.

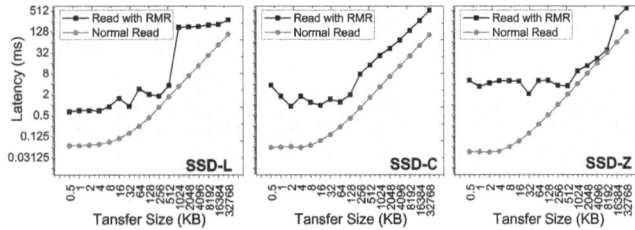

Figure 7: Latency comparison between reads with reliability management (RMR) and ordinary reads (i.e., reads without RMR). When RMR is employed, the latency is at least 5 times higher than the latency of reads without RMR.

overheads are not revealed to users, but can contribute to long latencies on normal operations. In this section, we examine the latency variation between reads *with RMR* and reads *without RMR*, which is veiled by most SSD manufactures. For our evaluation, we executed the random read-only workload, used in Section 4.4, on three devices, SSD-L, -C, and -Z, and the results are given in Figure 7.

As indicated by these plots, *the read latency with RMR is at least 5 times higher than the latency of reads without RMR*, which would be unacceptable for latency-sensitive SSD applications. Further, RMR overheads are more pronounced with small size random access patterns (1 sector ∼ 64 sectors), which is the dominant request size in many file systems. Considering 8 sector (4KB) requests as an example, while the read latencies without RMR on SSD-L, -C, and -Z are 75, 60, and 47 μsec, respectively, the increased read latencies with RMR are 685, 1787, and 4944 μsec, in the same order. Even though the latency disparity between ordinary reads and reads with RMR tends to decrease as the transfer size increases, high RMR-induced latencies with large data sizes (1MB ∼ 32MB) still seem to be problematic.

5. TESTING EXPECTATIONS ON WRITES

Modern SSD firmware and architecture are well optimized to improve write performance, but the worst-case performance on writes is still a problematic challenge. In this section, we examine the worst-case write latencies, analyze their correlation with system throughput, and investigate the impact of the internal DRAM buffer on latency. To evaluate the worst-case write latency, we prepared a set of *fully-utilized devices* by writing data (with sequential access

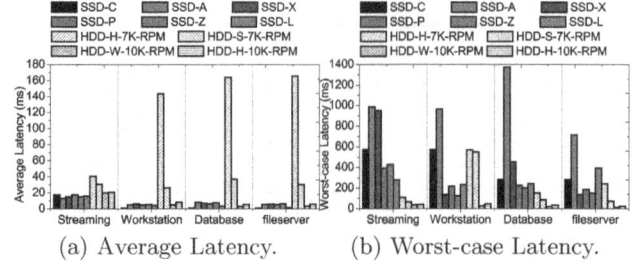

(a) Average Latency. (b) Worst-case Latency.

Figure 8: SSD and HDD latency comparison. While SSDs overall outperform HDDs, the worst-case latencies of SSDs are much higher than the worst-case latencies of HDDs.

pattern) that covers the entire storage space of SSDs. This makes SSDs reclaim block(s) for new incoming requests so that we can easily capture the worst-case latency and system throughput imposed by GCs.

5.1 How much impact does the worst-case latency have on modern SSDs?

We compare all the SSDs tested and two types of enterprise-scale HDDs (7K RPM and 10K RPM) in terms of both the average latency and the worst-case latency. To quantify the average latency, we use pristine devices, and for the worst-case latency evaluation, we employ the fully-utilized devices for SSD and HDD. We run Iometer with its enterprise open-workloads including streaming, workstation, database and fileserver applications, with the fraction of writes being 99%, 20%, 33% and 20% (of total I/Os), respectively.

Figures 8a and 8b plot the average latency and worst-case latency of our SSDs and HDDs. We see that, the average latencies of all the SSDs are better than HDDs, irrespective of the workload type used. Especially, compared to the 7K RPM HDDs, SSDs provide 2 ∼ 173 times shorter latency. However, *the worst-case latencies on fully-utilized SSDs are much worse than that of HDDs*, which is problematic for many write-intensive SSD applications. Specifically, the worst-case latencies of all the SSDs tested are 12 and 17 times worse than that of 10K RPM HDD-H and HDD-W, respectively, on an average. This is mainly because NAND flash in SSDs allows no in-place update with overwrites, which leads to GC invocations that contribute to overall latency.

5.2 What is the correlation between the worst-case latency and system throughput?

To study the correlation between GC and the worst-case latencies, we prepared two sets of fully-utilized devices, each consisting of SSD-L and -C. We then executed our modified Iometer with write-intensive workloads composed of 100% random accesses and sequential accesses for an hour on these SSDs, and measured the latency and throughput values.

Figures 9a (SSD-L) and 9c (SSD-C) plot the time series for both latency and system throughput along with GCs under the sequential access pattern. For both SSD-L and SSD-C, GCs are infrequently invoked, occasionally imposing long latencies but not impacting system throughput much. The execution in this case recovers performance immediately after the GC. In contrast, with the random write workloads, the worst-case latencies imposed by GCs significantly increase,

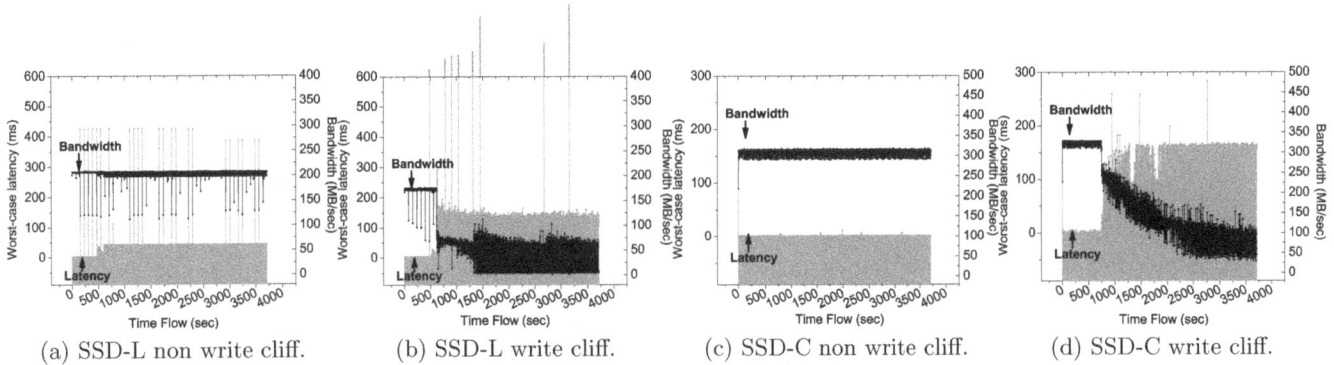

(a) SSD-L non write cliff.   (b) SSD-L write cliff.   (c) SSD-C non write cliff.   (d) SSD-C write cliff.

Figure 9: Impact of write cliff. Initially, SSDs provide reasonable performance even though GCs are invoked. However, once write cliff begins, the performance significantly degrades and is not recovered later.

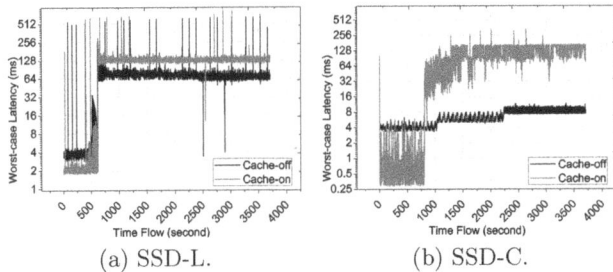

(a) SSD-L.   (b) SSD-C.

Figure 10: Worst-case latency correlation between the DRAM buffer cache and GC. The DRAM buffer provides excellent latency, but after the write cliff, it makes latencies even worse.

which in turn dramatically drop the system throughput as shown in Figures 9b and 9d. This performance characteristic caused by GCs under random write workloads is referred to as *write cliff*. Specifically, *once the write cliff begins, SSD latencies (bandwidth) become 11x (3x) worse than the normal case*. Further, *more problematic challenge of modern SSDs is that the performance degradation on the write cliff is not recovered even after many GCs are executed*. We believe that this is because the range of random access addresses is not covered by the reclaimed block(s). Consequently, block reclaims performed by GC are required for each access, which in turn leads to successive GC invocations. Even though we focused on two SSDs in this section (due to space concerns), we observed write cliffs in all the SSDs tested.

5.3 Could DRAM buffer help the firmware to reduce garbage collection overheads?

Since writes can be buffered using internal the DRAM, modern SSDs are somewhat expected to hide GC overheads. In this section, to examine the DRAM impact on GCs, we setup two fully-utilized device sets and write data with a sequential access pattern. In these experiments, one of these two sets are evaluated under the disabled (DRAM) cache (cache-off), and the other set is evaluated under the cache (cache-on). To make device status cache-off, we submit cache-disabled command, which brings the force access unit (FAU) tag of SATA 3.0 [40] for every I/O requests.

Figures 10a and 10b illustrate the time series comparison between the cache-on and cache-off status devices, SSD-L and -C, respectively. The worst-case latencies of SSD-L are hidden by the DRAM buffer before the write cliff begins.

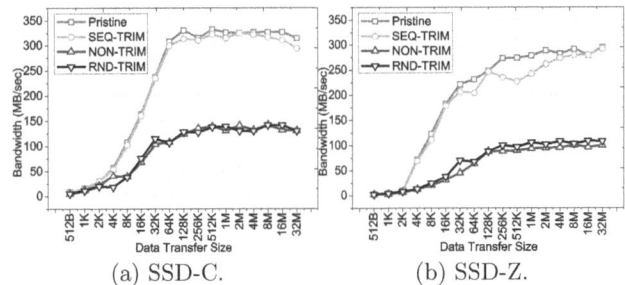

(a) SSD-C.   (b) SSD-Z.

Figure 11: Bandwidth impact of TRIM. While SEQ-TRIM (the order of target addresses is ascending) can effectively remove GCs, RND-TRIM (the order of targets is random) has no impact on GC overheads.

However, once GCs start to be invoked in a series, the latency of the cache-on SSD-L becomes two times worse than that of the cache-off SSD-L. In the case of SSD-C, the performance disparity between the cache-on and cache-off status are more pronounced. *While the DRAM buffer provides four times shorter latency compared to cache-off SSD-C before the write cliff begins, it introduces four times worse latencies when the write cliff kicks in*. Even though a system can react before the data is written into the actual flash device, the DRAM buffer needs to flush the in-memory data to the flash medium periodically. Since target addresses of the buffered data are fully random, this flushing of data introduces a large number of random accesses, which can in turn accelerate GC invocations of SSDs and introduce write cliffs.

6. TESTING EXPECTATIONS ON ADVANCED SCHEMES

In this section, we evaluate two advanced SSD schemes, TRIM OS support and background tasks, which recently received a lot of attention.

6.1 Can TRIM command reduce GC overheads?

To quantify the performance impact of TRIM commands, we first wrote data over the entire storage space of SSD-C and -Z using sequential and random access patterns, respectively. Then, at a system level, we deleted all the data written using TRIM commands, which consists of two command-composition steps. The first step is to setup the TRIM field

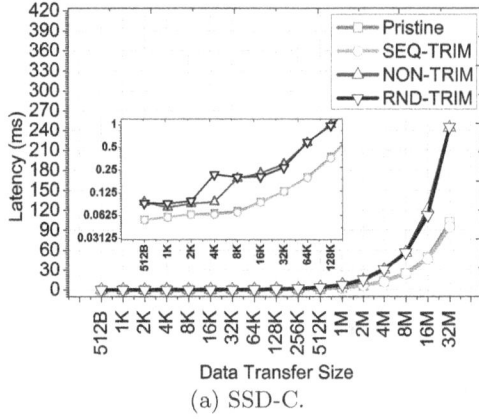

(a) SSD-C.

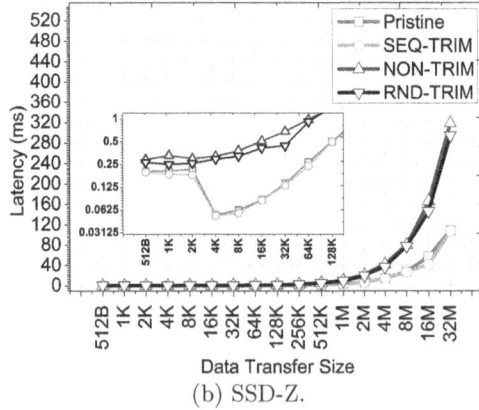

(b) SSD-Z.

Figure 12: Latency impact with TRIM. Similar to bandwidth impact, there is no latency gain with RND-TRIMs.

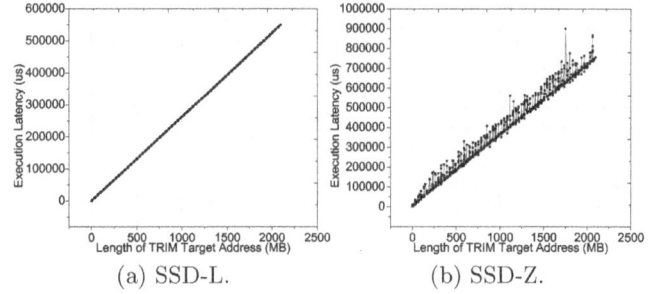

(a) SSD-L.　(b) SSD-Z.

Figure 13: E-TRIM overheads. Since E-TRIM performs block erasure on demand and do not return control to the storage system, the host can be disabled until the TRIM process finishes. The latency observed with TRIM is 3x worse than response time of 4KB writes.

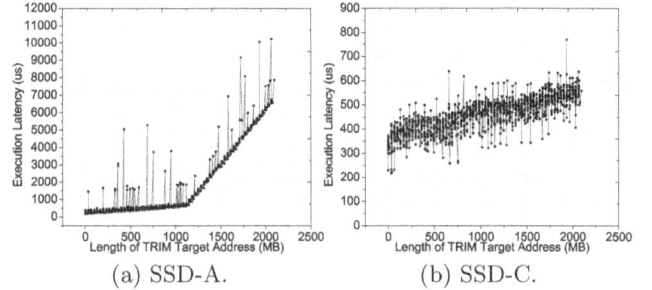

(a) SSD-A.　(b) SSD-C.

Figure 14: I-TRIM overheads. I-TRIM is more efficient in controlling the TRIM commands, but the latency overheads are still about 6 ∼ 153 times worse than a 4KB write-latency.

of the DATA-SET-MANAGEMENT command and send it to the SSD to let it know that the host wants to delete data, which is specified target addresses by following the TRIM request data (TRD) frames. Next, we need to configure the logical block address (LBA) range entries in the TRD frames and submit them to the SSD. Using multiple TRIM commands and TRD frames that cover the entire SSD address space, we wiped out all the written data in the previous step. If the order of the target LBAs in the TRD frames is ascending, we refer to the corresponding TRIM command pattern as *SEQ-TRIM*. On the other hand, if the order of the target addresses in the TRD frames form a random access pattern, which has been used for writing data in the previous step, we denote this TRIM pattern as *RND-TRIM*.

We measured performance by writing data of different sizes trimmed using SEQ-TRIM and RND-TRIM. In addition, we also evaluated the performance of our pristine-state SSDs, denoted by *Pristine*, and SSDs that have no TRIM command management, called *NON-TRIM*. The main insight from this evaluation is that, if SSDs tested handle the TRIM commands appropriately, all the written data should be successfully deleted, irrespective of which TRIM pattern is employed. As a result, the trimmed SSDs are expected to exhibit the same performance as our pristine state SSDs. As shown in Figure 11, SEQ-TRIM works very well for deleting data in both SSD-C and -Z. As expected, the bandwidth of the SSDs trimmed by SEQ-TRIM is similar to that of Pristine. In contrast, RND-TRIM shows no success in alle-

viating the GC overheads in both SSD-C and -Z. Our latency evaluation results also show similar performance characteristics. To better understand the execution-time impact of TRIM, we also studied performance at a finer-level, focusing on small data transfer sizes, ranging from 1 sectors to 256 sectors, in Figures 12a and 12b. As can be observed, the latencies of the SSDs trimmed by RND-TRIM are longer than those of the SSDs trimmed by SEQ-TRIM by about 3x on average. One can conclude from this analysis that, *SSDs do not trim all the data, and their behavior is strongly related to the TRIM command submission patterns*. In our evaluation, only SEQ-TRIM could successfully delete data, providing a similar latency to pristine SSDs.

6.2　Does a TRIM command incur any overheads?

One concern that OS designers might have is the potential overheads that can be experienced by an SSD in processing the TRIM command itself. In this section, we measure the latency incurred when processing a TRIM command, using our in-house AHCI miniport driver and the LeCroy protocol analyzer, Sierra M6-1. To do this, we wrote data varying from 512B to 2GB, which has the same address-range coverage as a TRD frame, and sent a TRIM command by filling the corresponding LBAs into the TRD frame. We then captured the time duration from the DATA-SET-MANAGEMENT command submission to the end of the response of the following TRD frames as *TRIM-latency*. Since Sierra M6-1 [31] provides a detailed protocol-level timing model for the command issue and completion, we are able to capture TRIM-latency for each TRIM process. As shown in the previous section, since SSDs do not get any benefit from RND-TRIM, in this test, we focus on measuring TRIM-latency on SEQ-TRIM.

Based on our observations and experience, we can classify existing TRIM command management strategies into two types: 1) *block erasure in real-time*, called E-TRIM, and 2) *data invalidation based on address and prompt response*, referred to as I-TRIM. As shown in Figure 13, E-TRIM requires long processing times to erase physical blocks based on the target addresses specified by TRIM. For example, to process a single TRIM command covering a storage space of 2GB, SSD-L and SSD-Z take 754 *msec* and 550 *msec*, respectively. Note that the TRIM-latency increases linearly with the amount data that LBAs in the TRD frames aim to delete due to physical block erasures.

In contrast, SSDs with I-TRIM just mark flags into a mapping table indicating that the contents are not valid anymore and return response immediately. This TRIM strategy can alleviate the time consuming activities of GCs such as the live-data lookup and relocation, even though it does not erase actual blocks. Although I-TRIM has some downsides (e.g., extra DRAM requirement, the possibility of losing in-memory TRIM data in the case of power failure), it is expected to improve SSD reliability to some extent. Specifically, 2x *nm* technology flash chips are much less reliable than larger feature size (3x~5x *nm*) flash chips, mainly because their memory array suffers considerably more from disturbance and has lower endurance characteristics. Further, the industry observed that such disturbances occur even when erasing a block and the endurance gets worse as PE cycles increase [9, 2]. Consequently, lower technology flash-equipped SSDs employ I-TRIM rather than E-TRIM in an attempt to reduce the number of block erasures as much as possible and improve reliability. From a performance perspective, the latency of I-TRIM is much shorter than the latency of E-TRIM since the former requires only a few cycles to update the underlying mapping table, as shown in Figure 14. However, I-TRIM still takes 400 μs ~10000 μs to handle individual TRIM commands. This I-TRIM latency is longer than an 8 sector write latency by 8 times ~ 153 times. We believe that this is because the flash firmware cannot maintain all the mapping information in the internal DRAM, which leads to extra I/Os on the flash medium to load/store the mapping table on demand. As a result, it takes some cycles to manage the mapping table and update the TRIM information in the appropriate entries of the table. One can conclude from this analysis that *modern SSDs require much longer latencies to trim data than normal I/Os would take*, which may put extra pressure on host systems.

6.3 What types of background tasks exist in modern SSDs?

To answer this question, we first wrote sequential data into the entire space of all our 6 SSDs to observe the background task activities. We artificially introduced idle times after writing the data right until GCs begin. In order to avoid *deceptive idle time*, which means that even though application makes the underlying storage system idle, a logical block adapter (e.g., AHCI, ATAPI) can periodically communicate with it by sending a system check command (e.g., SMART), which in turn keeps the storage system busy, we disabled the block adapter by intercepting the device-generated check commands and discarding them.We found that, among the

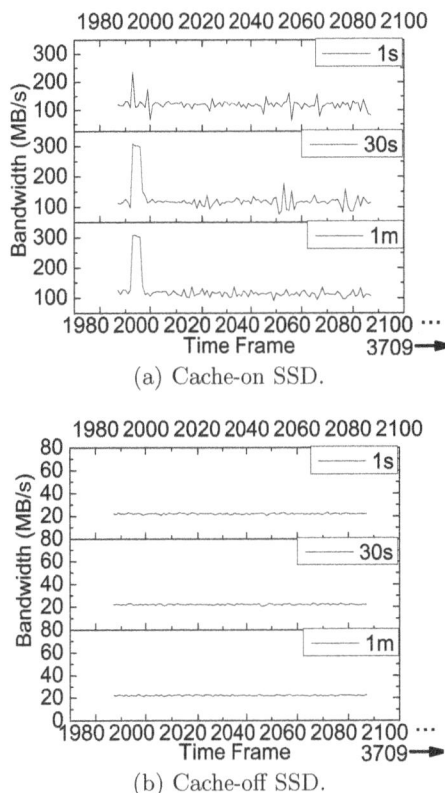

(a) Cache-on SSD.

(b) Cache-off SSD.

Figure 15: Background cache flushing (*BFLUSH*). BFLUSH writes in-memory data to the flash medium utilizing relatively short periods (30 sec) compared to the times needed by other background tasks.

6 SSDs tested, only two SSDs have background activities: SSD-C and SSD-L.

During idle periods, SSD-C flushes in-memory data into the flash medium, creating extra room, which can be used to buffer the new incoming I/O requests. This process is referred to as *background flush*, BFLUSH. *The BFLUSH writes down all in-memory structures and data within 30 seconds and improves SSD-C bandwidth by three-fold* over SSD-C without injecting any idle time, as shown in Figure 15a. To ensure that this performance benefit is coming from BFLUSH, not from any other background tasks, we also performed the same experiment on SSD-C with disabled cache. As shown in Figure 15b, we observed no performance improvement on the cache-off SSD-C, irrespective of the amount of idle time introduced.

In comparison, SSD-L performs GCs in the background, referred to as *background GC* (BGC). As shown in Figure 16a, when we introduced 30-second idle times as in the case of SSD-C, the bandwidth has been recovered to about 98% of that of the pristine state SSDs in 12 seconds. *This performance recovery property of BGC requires much longer time to provide stable performance, but it also exhibits more sustainable performance than BFLUSH*. In our evaluations, BGC needed 10 minutes to fully recover the performance loss on the write cliff. Note that, unlike BFLUSH, BGC of SSD-L can also be observed in the cache-off device. We further study the performance sustainability of these background tasks below.

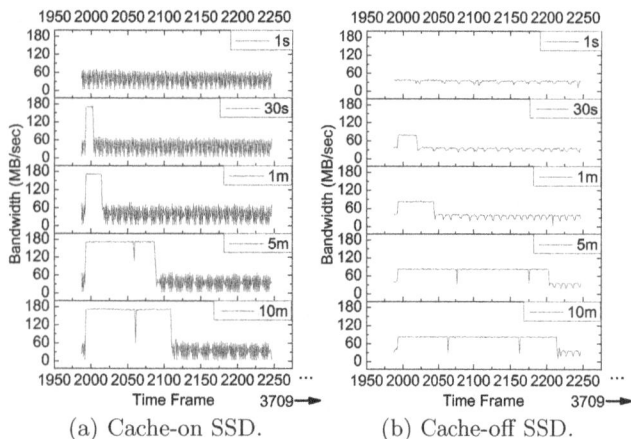

(a) Cache-on SSD. (b) Cache-off SSD.

Figure 16: Background garbage collection (*BGC*). BGC requires much longer idle times (10 minutes) compared to BFLUSH, but its recovered performance is more sustainable compared to that of BFLUSH (40 times).

6.4 Can background tasks of current SSDs guarantee sustainable performance?

Even though BFLUSH and BGC can recover their SSD performance unlike SSD-P, -X, -Z and -A that do not have any background activity, we observed that *the performance is not sustained or stable when considering the total execution time of write cliff*. Figures 15 and 16 plot performance characteristics of BFLUSH and BGC, respectively, when we inject an idle period of 1 hour. In the case of BFLUSH (Figure 17a), the recovered performance is sustained for 3 seconds, which provides stable performance for only 0.1% of the total execution time on the write cliff (1,711 seconds). As shown in Figure 17b, the performance sustainability of BGC is not much different from that of BFLUSH. Even though BGC can keep the recovered performance much longer than BFLUSH, it still sustains the recovered performance only about 120 seconds, which accounts for only 7% of the total execution time on the write cliff. We describe the difficulties behind the background tasks in the next section.

6.5 Why can't BGC help with the foreground tasks?

In public domain, there exist several benchmark results published assuming BGC, and even SSD makers indicate that they alleviate GC overheads by utilizing idle times (the vendors of 4 of our SSDs claim that they execute background tasks!). However, excluding the BFLUSH impact, we observed that SSD-L is the only device that performs BGC.

We believe that *there are three main difficulties for modern SSDs preventing them from performing BGC. 1) endurance characteristics, 2) block erasure acceleration, and 3) power consumption problem on idle state*. First, as explained in Section 6.2, lower flash technologies promise much less reliability, and endurance characteristics tend to get worse as the PE cycles increase. Considering the fact that most modern SSDs are using 2x *n*m technology now, and some of them are considering adopting 19 *n*m flash technology, it would be preferred to reduce the number of GC invocations even if they are going to be executed in the background. Second, the flash firmware has to choose victim blocks to

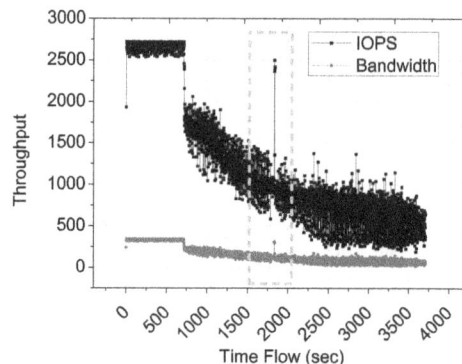

(a) SSD-C BFLUSH.

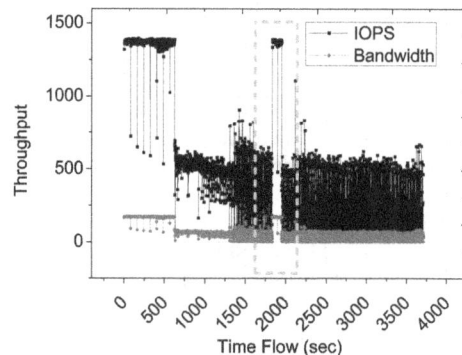

(b) SSD-L BGC.

Figure 17: Performance sustainability of the background tasks. Even though BFLUSH and BGC almost recover the performance on write cliff, they sustain the recovered performance for very short time (just a few seconds).

reclaim free pages, which are used for serving new I/O requests. If the reclaimed pages are not enough, the firmware has to perform GCs until it secures enough pages. Since each of these processes has to erase the victim blocks, many flash firmware postpone GCs as much as they can, which leads to on-demand GC rather than BGC. Lastly, BGC needs to consume power to perform GC even under the device idle state, and it is difficult to preserve data consistency in the case of power outage. Most host vendors have their own power consumption specification, which regulates the maximum bound on power usage when the device is in the idle mode. Therefore, BGC is inherently limited in page reclaiming during the idle periods. Further, while performing BGC, the firmware has to preserve data consistency by journaling meta-data for the GC in an attempt to prepare for sudden power outages. This also introduces extra I/Os at idle times.

Note that, unlike the other devices tested, SSD-L employs more reliable flash chips with 35 *n*m technology and the highest degree of over-provisioning. These two factors make the write amplification factor of SSD-L lower and thus make the device reliable [16] even though BGC introduces more block erasures. Also, SSD-L needs more power to perform BGC more than SSD-C and SSD-Z, by about 270% and 78%, respectively, in idle periods.

7. RETHINKING SSD SYSTEMS

Based on our experimental results and observations, we now provide a summary of our answers to the questions we raised at the beginning of this paper.

7.1 Reads

As against the common expectation, the random read performance of SSDs, in terms of both latency and bandwidth, is worse than the other types of operations even including writes. Further, sequential read performance is degraded over time because of two factors: 1) physical data layout changes on writes, which lead to modulations in internal parallelism, and 2) reliability management overheads on reads.

Read Request Reordering. A flash-aware I/O scheduler can transform the random order of addresses on reads to a sequential order, or schedule them by being aware of the internal parallelism, in order to avoid the poor random read performance. There are several studies in the literature that schedule write addresses [29, 20, 22]; in comparison, reordering read requests has received considerably less attention.

Read Frequency Control. Since block erasures are also involved in reads, reads may shorten the SSD lifespan. This means SSD applications need to be aware of the underlying read disturbances and runtime bad block management characteristics. Read frequency control can potentially improve SSD lifespan as well as the read performance. For example, it can remove the hot read spot regions, or reorganize file system blocks to ensure that the underlying physical blocks are accessed as evenly as possible.

De-indirection Interface. De-indirection interface [1, 41] is a promising approach to efficiently manage an SSD by removing the firmware level indirection (address remapping) [21]. Through the de-indirection interface (nameless write), a file system manages the returned physical address as a result of write, and keep updating the physical space changed by the weal-leveling scheme through a callback. In practice, a nameless write interface has to be aware of the underlying read reliability issues like read disturbances and UECC. This is because the address space can be reconstructed even on reads due to such reliability issues, which can in turn corrupt the data consistency of the file system using nameless-writes.

7.2 Writes

Modern SSDs are well optimized to hide GCs, but the throughput of writes significantly drops and the worse-case latency sharply increases when the write cliff is reached. Further, the worst-case latency of SSDs is much higher than HDDs, which implies that it needs to be paid much more attention especially in the context of latency-sensitive applications. Interestingly, the internal DRAM buffer would make the latency imposed by GCs on the write cliff much longer. This implies that the DRAM buffer management is in need of being aware of GCs in order to avoid making the worst-case latency even worse.

Background Task Scheduling. To alleviate the performance overheads on the write cliff, systems may utilize the background tasks by artificially injecting idle times. Since the recovered performance by background tasks is not sustained, the scheduler needs to periodically inject idle periods even under the I/O congestion periods [26]. In addition, considering the fact that the background tasks require long idle periods to fully recover the performance loss on the write cliff, the scheduler can inject idle times in an interleaving fashion and hide potential GC overheads over multiple SSD resources (e.g., flash array storage systems, and SSD RAID systems).

Exposing SSD Firmware API. A more promising approach to handle the background tasks would be exposing

APIs that allow a host explicitly to handle flash firmware tasks. For example, similar to the TRIM mechanism, a host can explicitly call GCs or flush data through the DATA-SET MANAGEMENT command on idle times so that the host CPU-burst time can be overlapped with the SSD internal tasks. Based on our experiments, we believe that directly handling SSD internal tasks is much better approach to handle the write cliff than implicitly scheduling the background tasks.

7.3 Advanced Schemes

The magnitude of performance gains with the TRIM commands significantly varies depending on the TRIM request pattern. While SEQ-TRIM can effectively eliminate GC overheads, RND-TRIM has no positive impact on performance. In addition, SSDs require quite long execution times to process TRIMs, which can lead to unexpected performance degradation. To address this, a file system can consider new TRIM management strategies that are aware of the TRIM-process characteristics.

TRIM Buffer and Scheduler. From the beginning of the TRIM process, the host can send TRIM commands by composing target addresses in an increasing order. Similarly, a host module can buffer TRIMs and merge the delete information under the file system in order to transform RND-TRIM to SEQ-TRIM. In addition, it is better to utilize idle times to submit TRIM commands at a system level to avoid potentiol TRIM-latency overheads. A TRIM scheduler can blend legacy I/Os with TRIMs by utilizing system idle periods, thereby hiding the long TRIM execution times.

8. RELATED WORK

A lot of prior work focused on improving SSD performance and overcoming flash-intrinsic limitations such as the erase-before-write problem. Flash translation layers (FTL) have been developed to alleviate the write performance degradation by employing different granular address mappings [8, 19, 15, 34]. In addition to FTL, various buffer management schemes [29, 20, 22] have been investigated to improve write performance. Recently, GC schedulers utilizing idle periods have been proposed to avoid heavy performance penalties on write cliff [24, 27]. There also exist several efforts on SSD architecture. For example,[10, 34, 6, 11, 5, 4] revealed internal SSD architecture in detail. In addition, [25, 17] proposed different page allocation strategies to take advantage of the internal parallelism on writes. There exists a scheduler [23] that explicitly handles I/Os by avoiding resource conflicts, thereby improving the degree of parallelism. FlashVM [38] is a flash virtual memory to reap the benefits of random read performance superiority of SSDs, and Facebook flashcache [28] is a read cache leveraging read performance superiority of SSDs to improve MySQL. [3, 30, 36] also proposed SSD cache, filling the I/O gap between main memory and disks in data centers. In general, these SSD-oriented prior studies have been performed based on common expectations. In our experiments and data analyses, we observed many unexpected performance characteristics and reliability issues, which should be addressed by both academia and industry.

9. ACKNOWLEDGEMENTS

This research is supported in part by NSF grants 1017882, 0937949, and 0833126 and DOE grant DE-SC0002156.

10. CONCLUDING REMARKS

In this paper, we examined widely held expectations and conceptions on modern SSDs using six different commercial SSDs and a series of experiments. Our experimental results revealed many previously-unreported SSD characteristics from both performance and reliability angles. We also discussed what these characteristics mean to both SSD designers and system designers. Our ongoing work includes designing and implementing system support that can take into account our newly-discovered facts on SSDs, and evaluate this support using a diverse set of workloads drawn from embedded computing, enterprise computing and high-performance computing domains.

11. REFERENCES

[1] ARPACI-DUSSEAU, A. C., ET AL. Removing the costs of indirection in flash-based ssds with namelesswrites. In *HotStorage* (2010).

[2] CAI, Y., ET AL. Flash correct-and-refresh: Retention-aware error management. In *ICCD* (2012).

[3] CANIM, M., ET AL. SSD bufferpool extensions for database systems. *VLDB* (2010).

[4] CAULFIELD, A. M., ET AL. Gordon: Using flash memory to build fast, power-efficient clusters for data-intensive applications. In *ASPLOS* (2009).

[5] CAULFIELD, A. M., ET AL. Moneta: A high-performance storage array architecture for next-generation, non-volatile memories. In *MICRO* (2010).

[6] CHEN, F., ET AL. Essential roles of exploiting internal parallelism of flash memory based solid state drives in high-speed data processing. In *HPCA* (2011).

[7] CHOI, H., ET AL. VLSI implementation of BCH error correction for multilevel cell nand flash memory. In *VLSI* (2010).

[8] CHOUDHURI, S., AND GIVARGIS, T. Deterministic service guarantees for NAND flash using partial block cleaning. In *CODES+ISSS* (2008).

[9] COOKE, J. How ClearNAND flash simplifies and enhances system designs. In *Micron White Paper* (2011).

[10] DIRIK, C., AND JACOB, B. The performance of PC solid-state disks (SSDs) as a function of bandwidth, concurrency, device architecture, and system organization. In *ISCA* (2009).

[11] FENG CHEN AND OTHERS. Understanding intrinsic characteristics and system implications of flash memory based solid state drives. In *SIGMETRICS* (2009).

[12] FUSION-IO. ioCache. In *datasheet* (2012).

[13] FUSION-IO. ioMemory. In *datasheet* (2012).

[14] FUSION-IO. ioTurbine. In *datasheet* (2012).

[15] GUPTA, A., ET AL. DFTL: A flash translation layer employing demand-based selective caching of page-level address mappings. In *ASPLOS* (2009).

[16] HU, X.-Y., ET AL. Write amplification analysis in flash-based solid state drives. In *SYSTOR* (2009).

[17] HU, Y., ET AL. Performance impact and interplay of SSD parallelism through advanced commands, allocation strategy and data granularity. In *ISC* (2011).

[18] INTEL. http://www.iometer.org/. In *Iometer User's Guide* (2003), Intel.

[19] J. KANG ET AL. A superblock-based flash translation layer for NAND flash memory. In *EMSOFT* (2006).

[20] JO, H., ET AL. FAB: flash-aware buffer management policy for portable media players.

[21] JOSEPHSON, W. K., ET AL. Dfs: A file system for virtualized flash storage. In *FAST* (2010).

[22] JUNG, M., ET AL. Memory system and data storing method thereof. *U.S. Patent 20090248987* (2009).

[23] JUNG, M., ET AL. Physically addressed queueing (PAQ): Improving parallelism in solid state disks. In *ISCA* (2012).

[24] JUNG, M., ET AL. Taking garbage collection overheads off the critical path in ssds. In *Middleware* (2012).

[25] JUNG, M., AND KANDEMIR, M. An evaluation of different page allocation strategies on high-speed SSDs. In *HotStorage* (2012).

[26] JUNG, M., AND KANDEMIR, M. Middleware - firmware cooperation for high-speed solid state drives. In *Middleware D&P* (2012).

[27] JUNG, M., AND YOO, J. Scheduling garbage collection opportunistically to reduce worst-case I/O performance in solid state disks. In *IWSSPS* (2009).

[28] KGIL, T., ROBERTS, D., AND MUDGE, T. Improving NAND flash based disk caches. In *ISCA* (2008).

[29] KIM, H., AND AHN, S. BPLRU: A buffer management scheme for improving random writes in flash storage. In *FAST* (2008).

[30] KOLTSIDAS, I., AND VIGLAS, S. The case for flash-aware multi level caching.

[31] LECROY. http://www.lecroy.com/.

[32] LIU, N., ET AL. On the role of burst buffers in leadership-class storage systems. In *MSST* (2012).

[33] LIU, Y., HUANG, J., XIE, C., AND CAO, Q. Raf: A random access first cache management to improve SSD-based disk cache. *NAS* (2010).

[34] N. AGRAWAL ET AL. Design tradeoffs for SSD performance. In *USENIX ATC* (2008).

[35] ONFI WORKING GROUP. Open nand flash interface 3.0. In *http://onfi.org/* (2012).

[36] OU, Y., ET AL. Cfdc: a flash-aware replacement policy for database buffer management. In *DAMON* (2009).

[37] OUYANG, X., ET AL. Enhancing checkpoint performance with staging I/O and SSD. In *SNAPI* (2010).

[38] SAXENA, M., ET AL. FlashVM: Virtual memory management on flash. In *USENIX ATC* (2010).

[39] SRINIVASAN, M., AND CALLAGHAN, M. Flashcache at facebook. In *Facebook White Paper* (2010).

[40] T13. *Serial ATA Specification 3.1*. 2012.

[41] ZHANG, Y., ET AL. De-indirection for flash-based ssds with namelesswrites. In *FAST* (2012).

Characterizing the Impact of Process Variation on Write Endurance Enhancing Techniques for Non-Volatile Memory Systems

Marcelo Cintra[*] and Niklas Linkewitsch
Germany Microprocessor Lab
Intel Labs Braunschweig
{marcelo.cintra|niklas.linkewitsch}@intel.com

ABSTRACT

Much attention has been given recently to a set of promising non-volatile memory technologies, such as PCM, STT-MRAM, and ReRAM. These, however, have limited endurance relative to DRAM. Potential solutions to this endurance challenge exist in the form of fine-grain wear leveling techniques and aggressive error tolerance approaches.

While the existing approaches to wear leveling and error tolerance are sound and demonstrate true potential, their studies have been limited in that i) they have not considered the interactions between wear leveling and error tolerance and ii) they have assumed a simple write endurance failure model where all cells fail uniformly. In this paper we perform a thorough study and characterize such interactions and the effects of more realistic non-uniform endurance models under various workloads, both synthetic and derived from benchmarks. This study shows that, for instance, variability in the endurance of cells significantly affects wear leveling and error tolerance mechanisms and the values of their tuning parameters. It also shows that these mechanisms interact in subtle ways, sometimes cancelling and sometimes boosting each other's impact on overall endurance of the device.

Categories and Subject Descriptors

C.4 [**Performance of Systems**]: Modeling techniques; Reliability, availability, and serviceability

General Terms

Reliability

Keywords

Non-volatile memories; wear leveling; error correction

[*]Author is on sabbatical leave from the U. of Edinburgh.

1. INTRODUCTION

With the expected power and density of DRAM technology approaching their limits, much research has been done on new memory technologies such as Phase-Change Memory (PCM), Spin-Torque Transfer Magnetoresistive Memory (STT-MRAM), and Resistive Random Access Memory (ReRAM). In addition to addressing some of the power and density issues of DRAM, such technologies also offer the benefit of being non-volatile. On the other hand, their access times are higher than those of DRAM. The main challenge, however, is that the endurance of such non-volatile memories is significantly shorter than DRAM; PCM, for instance, is expected to have endurance in the order of 10^7-10^8 writes [3, 12]. Depending on the workload's write traffic distribution, such reduced endurance may translate to an unacceptably low lifetime for the device. Approaches to dealing with this write endurance limitation include: adding a write-back cache (often made of DRAM) in front of the non-volatile main memory [10], reducing the number of writes by tracking dirty lines in a page [5, 10] and by avoiding idempotent writes at even finer granularity [1, 18, 19], allocating spare memory lines to replace damaged lines [11, 17], and applying so called wear leveling techniques [11, 15, 19]. The goal of wear leveling is to transparently spread a worload's writes more evenly across the entire physical memory space.

While some recent research have demonstrated effective wear leveling for non-volatile memories, these studies are limited in one or both of the following. *i)* They assume a write endurance failure model where all cells fail at exactly the nominal write endurance threshold. *ii)* They do not take into account the effect of error correction codes and other aggressive error handling approaches. Firstly, despite the lack of hard publicly available information on the exact failure model of these non-volatile memory cells in commercial-grade arrays, preliminary studies suggest that the first assumption is unlikely to be valid [8]. Instead, the write endurance of memory cells is likely to follow some temporal and spatial distribution, that is, some cells are likely to fail earlier than others and the endurance of neighbor cells are likely to be correlated. Second, akin to current high-end DRAM systems, one can expect non-volatile memory systems to include some degree of error correction. In fact, recent work suggests that non-volatile memory systems benefit from novel error correction mechanisms that offer higher correction capability [2, 13, 16, 17]. These studies are limited in that they either assume perfect wear leveling or wear leveling with some fixed efficiency.

In this paper, we attempt to quantify the subtle interactions among these factors, namely wear leveling, use of spares for tolerating errors, error correction, and more realistic failure models for the memory array. We perform a thorough characterization of how these interactions affect write endurance under different workloads, both synthetic and extracted from benchmarks. Our study shows that the variability in the write endurance of cells across a large array can significantly affect the expected benefits of wear leveling, spares, and error correction. This, in turn, suggests that the tuning parameters for these techniques need to be adjusted from those computed with ideal failure models in order to match the more realistic failure models. The study also shows that the effects of these endurance enhancing techniques are not always additive, but instead often either reduce each other's impact or interact in synergistic ways.

The rest of this paper is organized as follows. Section 2 provides a brief description of wear leveling and error correction approaches for non-volatile memories. Section 3 presents the various memory system models we consider. Section 4 presents the experimental setup and Section 5 presents the results of this study. Finally, Section 6 discusses related work and Section 7 concludes the paper.

2. BACKGROUND

2.1 Wear Leveling

An important parameter of memory devices is access endurance, which relates to the number of accesses that can be performed before the device can no longer reliably store information. In practice, for non-volatile memory technologies such as PCM, STT-MRAM, and ReRAM, only endurance in terms of number of write operations are of concern [9]. While some memory technologies, such as DRAM, have practically unlimited write endurance, these non-volatile memory technologies have write endurances that can be reached in practice. This limited endurance is usually dealt with in two ways: by reducing the overall number of writes to the device and by more evenly spreading the writes across the entire address space of the device. The first can be achieved by adding caches in front of the device (e.g., [10]), tracking and writing only dirty data (e.g., [5, 10]), and filtering idempotent writes (e.g., [1, 18, 19]). The second attempts to deal with the unevenness of write traffic in workloads (that is, some memory locations are written more often than others) and is achieved through wear leveling techniques.

Given the relatively low endurance of non-volatile memory devices and the high traffic to main memory, wear leveling is expected to be done at the granularity of lines and with some hardware support (e.g., [10, 11, 15, 19]). Recent schemes work by proactively moving the physical location of logical memory lines [11, 15]. By doing this frequently enough one can guarantee that bursts of heavy write traffic to some memory addresses will end up in various physical locations before any location is permanently damaged.

2.2 Error Detection/Correction

Memory devices are prone to suffer errors (or faults), which can be either transient or permanent. Some permanent faults are related to access endurance wear out (Section 2.1), but they can also be related to external events

and plain ageing. Often, intermittent transient faults occur before a permanent fault in the same location [14].

In the context of main memory, the error detection/correction mechanism of choice is ECC based on Hamming codes, which reflects the fact that DRAM devices are significantly more prone to transient than permanent faults. This, in turn, is due partly to the relatively long access endurance of DRAM and to the easiness with which the stored charge in a DRAM cell can be upset. On the other hand, the relatively low access endurance of most upcoming non-volatile memory technologies and their relative robustness to common sources of transient faults (e.g., particle strikes) suggest that permanent faults are likely to be the main source of errors in these technologies [13]. Thus, some have recently proposed replacing traditional Hamming code based ECC with other mechanisms more appropriate to handle permanent faults in addition to transient ones (e.g., [2, 13, 16, 17]). The goal is that for the same budget of error detection/correction such approaches can better deal with permanent faults and, thus, increase overall device lifetime.

3. MODELS EVALUATED

3.1 Memory Model

3.1.1 Segment Model

Following recent developments [11, 15], we consider only wear leveling approaches based on proactive line shifts instead of approaches that act based on write counts. Proactive line shifts appear better suited for wear leveling at fine granularity and under high traffic conditions, which is the case with non-volatile main memory. As pointed out in [11], such proactive approaches work best if memory is divided into segments for wear leveling purposes, as otherwise the number of writes between two consecutive shifts of a given line may become too high for the scheme to be effective. Thus, in our model we divide memory into segments containing 2^{20} lines, where each line is 64Bytes (i.e., segments of 64MBytes).

3.1.2 Spare and Segment Failure Model

In this study we consider two scenarios of how the system allocates memory resources to applications.

Spare Model I.

In this scenario the system can grant the entire memory segment to applications at any given time. We consider that the entire segment fails as soon as the first line is damaged beyond the error correction capabilities of the hardware. This is because the system has no way of identifying broken lines and can no longer guarantee correctness.

Spare Model II: Fine-Grained Remapping with ECC and Embedded Pointers (FREE-p) [17].

The FREE-p proposal [17] copes with hard failures in memory lines by first detecting them (with ECC) and then embedding in the broken line a pointer to a working line. In the original proposal in [17] the OS can freely choose pages to store remaped lines. We use a variant that allocates a certain number of memory lines per segment as spares, which are only utilized after some active line is damaged beyond the error correction capabilities. We do this in order to seamlessly integrate this error correction approach with a segment-based wear leveling approach (Section 3.4). Additionally, this allows handling of remapping entirely in the memory management unit without OS modifications. As with the original FREE-p approach, memory lines are extended with a bit to identify lines that act as pointers (e.g., broken and remaped lines) or that contain actual data. To overcome the fact that the remapped memory line contains faulty bits, the remapping pointer is replicated following a 7-modular-redundancy code to ensure its value can be retrieved. The scheme relies on a combination of ECC and verify-after-write approach to detect errors. We note that once a line is broken and turned into a remaping pointer, it will no longer be written and will suffer no further damage. Additionally, [17] proposes several enhancements to mitigate the latency costs of indirection and error correction, which we do not model as our study is not concerned with execution time performance. With this scheme, broken spares may themselves redirect to further spares, recursively, as long as there are unused spares in the segment.

3.2 Write Distribution Models

3.2.1 Statistical Models

In order to gain some insight into the interactions of wear leveling and error correction, we first consider two statistically generated traffic models (Figure 1(a)).

Statistical Traffic Model I.
This model (UT in Figure 1(a)) assumes a uniform traffic distribution over a portion of the address space of the memory segment.

Statistical Traffic Model II.
This model (NT in Figure 1(a)) assumes a normal traffic distribution over a portion of the address space of the segment.

Without loss of generality, the portions of the address space targeted by the write traffic are bundled at one end of the segment. We consider two sizes of this active portion of the address space: either 3/4 or 1/2 of the memory segment. For the normal distribution we place the peak of the distribution (the *hot spot*) at an arbitrary physical address and consider two coefficients of variance: $C_v = 0.125$, which concentrates 68.2% (i.e., one standard deviation plus and minus) of the traffic in a region of 12.5% of addresses around the hot spot; and $C_v = 0.0625$, which concentrates 68.2% of the traffic in a region of 6.25% of addresses around the hot spot. A total of 6 statistical address distribution models are evaluated.

Finally, we note that, based on published results that show virtually no effect of thermal cross-talk in non-volatile memory technologies (e.g., [9]), we assume that write traffic to one cell does not affect the endurance of its neighbor cells.

3.2.2 Benchmark Driven Models

We also consider memory traffic generated by real workloads, taken from the SPEC benchmark suite (Section 4.2). Following recent research, we assume that a memory hierarchy with non-volatile technology as main memory will contain a fairly large write-back DRAM cache before main memory [10]. This is necessary both to reduce the write traffic to non-volatile main memory and to better tolerate the

higher latency of a non-volatile device compared to DRAM. Thus, we consider only the write traffic between this DRAM cache and the non-volatile main memory, which consists of evictions from the DRAM cache, and use a simulator to generate this traffic (Section 4.3).

The actual physical targets of the applications's writes depend on the mapping of virtual addresses by the OS. This means that the absolute and relative positions of two virtual pages are not fixed and cannot be determined exactly. Moreover, multiple runs of the same application may have different virtual to physical address mappings. Some sort of approximate model is thus necessary to model long running and recurring workloads. Most research on wear leveling either ignore such virtual memory aspects or simply take the mapping given by one particular execution. We approach this difficulty by considering two mappings of virtual pages to a given memory segment of interest[1] (Figure 2).

Virtual Page Mapping to Segment Model I.
This model assumes that the virtual pages with the most write traffic to non-volatile memory happen to be mapped to the same memory segment.

Virtual Page Mapping to Segment Model II.
This model assumes that the virtual pages with the least write traffic to non-volatile memory happen to be mapped to the same memory segment.

3.3 Endurance Failure Distribution Models

The main aim of this work is to evaluate the impact of write endurance related failure distributions on memory failure and endurance enhancing techniques. Exact endurance failure distributions of commercial-grade non-volatile memory arrays are not publicly available, but preliminary evaluations of research devices exist [8, 9]. From these, one can infer that the exact write endurance of cells is likely to vary in the array due to fabrication effects. Moreover, this variation is likely to change over time and is also likely to be spatially correlated, that is, the closer the cells are physically the less independent their endurance is.

In this work we attempt to consider such variation in the write endurance of cells, and consider three failure distribution models (Figure 1(b)).

Failure Distribution Model I.
In this model (NE1 in Figure 1(b)) the variation of cell write endurance due to fabrication follows a normal distribution with average at 10^8 writes and $C_v = 0.1$. This means that 68.2% (i.e., one standard deviation plus and minus) of the cells fail after between $0.9 \cdot 10^8$ and $1.1 \cdot 10^8$ writes.

Failure Distribution Model II.
In this model (NE2 in Figure 1(b)) the variation of cell write endurance due to fabrication follows a normal distribution with average at 10^8 writes and $C_v = 0.05$. This means that 68.2% (i.e., one standard deviation plus and minus) of the cells fail after between $0.95 \cdot 10^8$ and $1.05 \cdot 10^8$ writes.

Failure Distribution Model III.
In this model (FE in Figure 1(b)) there is no variation

---

[1]With our 64MB segments (Section 3.1.1) and assuming 4KB pages, 16K pages fit into a segment.

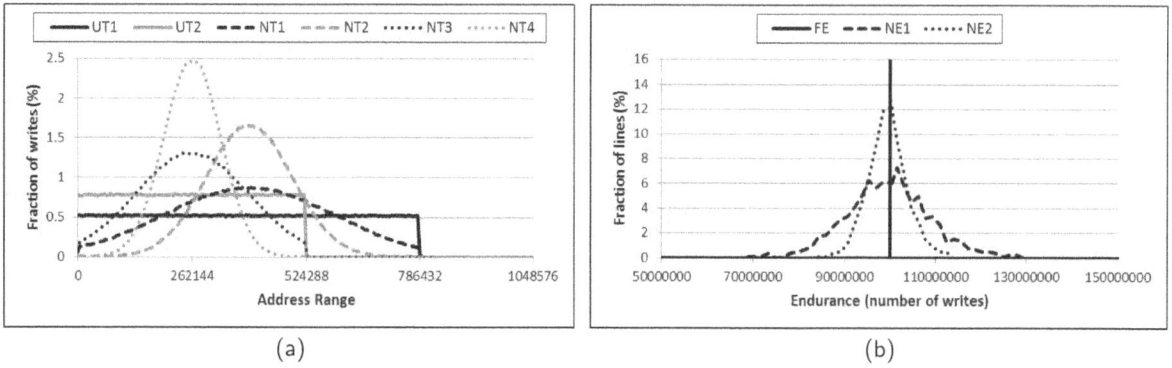

Figure 1: Statistically generated distributions: (a) Traffic (b) Endurance.

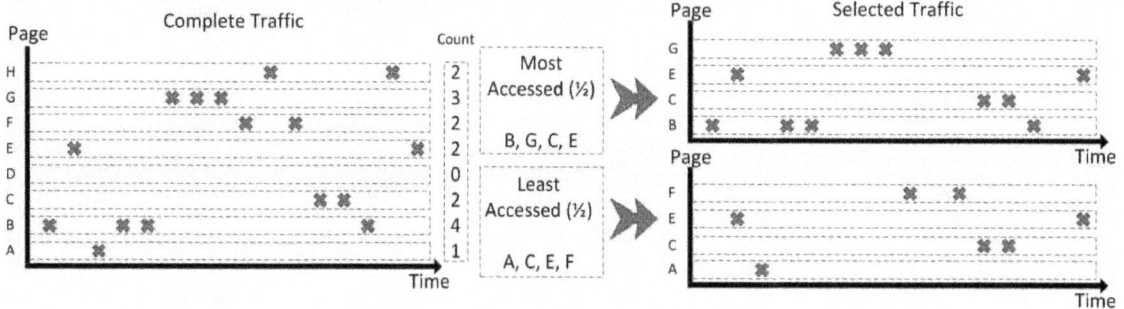

Figure 2: Benchmark traffic models.

of cell write endurance and all cells fail after exactly 10^8 writes. This is the failure model often assumed in wear leveling studies [10, 11, 15, 19].

These variances are a bit tighter than those used in [2, 13, 17], which used C_v between 0.1 and 0.3, but similar to those used in [16, 18], so that our study does not overestimate the impact of variation. The nominal endurance of 10^8 is in line with the ITRS 2011 [3] projections.

3.4 Wear Leveling Models

In this study we consider two scenarios for wear leveling.

Wear Leveling Model I.
In this scenario no wear leveling technique is used.

Wear Leveling Model II: Region Based Start-Gap (RBSG) [11].
The Start-Gap proposal [11] was the first to use a proactive approach to wear leveling. Instead of keeping track of the write count to memory locations and reactively moving data from heavily written locations to lightly written locations, data is periodically moved independent of their write counts. More specifically, at given intervals a fixed number of memory lines are chosen, their contents are exchanged, and further accesses are subsequently directed to their new locations. The expectation is that this will eventually exchange the physical location of heavily and lightly written memory locations. There are two key advantages to such approach. First, there is no need to maintain large amounts of metadata to track the write count to memory locations. Second, by employing regular shift patterns the location of moved lines can be easily identified through closed form ex-

pressions, which saves the costly (both in terms of metadata and time) indirections used in the reactive approaches.

In this paper we consider the variant Region Based Start-Gap (RBSG) [11] as our baseline wear leveling approach. The key benefit of a region based approach is that the number of writes needed to complete one shift of all lines in the region is now proportional to the region size and not the entire memory size. As discussed in [11], the number of writes to trigger a shift of one memory line (ψ) has to be:

$$\psi < \frac{W_{max}}{K} \tag{1}$$

where K is the number of lines in the region, which is 2^{20} in our case (Section 3.1.1), and W_{max} is the maximum number of writes endured by the memory cells. We compute the value of W_{max} with our failure models (Section 3.3) in two ways. First, we assign the nominal write endurance value to W_{max}, so that $W_{max} = 10^8$ and $\psi \approx 100$. This value is the same used in [11], which assumed the same region size as ours but a slightly lower fixed write endurance of $W_{max} = 3.3 \cdot 10^7$, such that we err on the conservative side of choosing a smaller and safer value of ψ. Alternatively, we assign to W_{max} a value that we have empirically determined to be more appropriate to accommodate variability in the write endurance. We have empirically found (Section 5.1.1) that variability in the write endurance leads to early failures that lead to up to an order of magnitude drop in the overall endurance. Thus, the second value we use is a conservative $\psi \approx 10$. We note that proactive moves of memory locations incur bandwidth and energy overheads as well as additional writes to the memory locations. Thus, while reduced values of ψ might be needed to guarantee that traffic is properly spread within the region, they also themselves cause a reduction in lifetime.

4. EXPERIMENTAL SETUP

4.1 Memory, Traffic and Failure Modeling

We use a custom event-driven simulator to model non-volatile main memory. For simplicity and to allow for simulations in reasonable time, a memory segment is modeled as an array of 64Byte lines, instead of individual bits. Memory lines are assumed to have independent write endurance [9] and the endurance values follow one of the distributions described in Section 3.3. Variable error correction capabilities are added to each individual line. We presently do not model any spatial correlation between write endurances of neighbor cells in a line, which is left as future work. This event-driven simulator is fed with address traces generated either with the statistical traffic distributions described in Section 3.2.1 or with traffic from real workloads as described in Section 3.2.2 (see also Section 4.3). The simulator also models both the spare scheme described in Section 3.1.2 ([17]) and the wear leveling scheme described in Section 3.4 ([11]). Table 1 summarizes the acronyms used.

Acronym	Explanation
Wear Leveling (Section 3.4)	
NWL	No wear leveling
RBSG	Region Based Start-Gap [11]
Spares (Section 3.1.2)	
NS	No spares
S	Spares with embedded pointers [17];
Error Correction	
NEC	No error correction
EC	Error correction;
Endurance (Section 3.3)	
FE	Fixed value (10^8)
NE1	Normal distribution with $\mu = 10^8$ and $C_v = 0.1$
NE2	Normal distribution with $\mu = 10^8$ and $C_v = 0.05$
Traffic	
Statistical (Section 3.2.1)	
UT1	Uniform distribution over $\frac{3}{4}$ of memory segment
UT2	Uniform distribution over $\frac{1}{2}$ of memory segment
NT1	Normal distribution with $C_v = 0.125$ over $\frac{3}{4}$ of memory segment
NT2	Normal distribution with $C_v = 0.0625$ over $\frac{3}{4}$ of memory segment
NT3	Normal distribution with $C_v = 0.125$ over $\frac{1}{2}$ of memory segment
NT4	Normal distribution with $C_v = 0.125$ over $\frac{1}{2}$ of memory segment
Benchmark driven (Section 3.2.2)	
X1	Benchmark X, most accessed pages over $\frac{3}{4}$ of memory segment
X2	Benchmark X, most accessed pages over $\frac{1}{2}$ of memory segment
X3	Benchmark X, least accessed pages over $\frac{3}{4}$ of memory segment
X4	Benchmark X, least accessed pages over $\frac{1}{2}$ of memory segment

Table 1: Summary of acronyms used to refer to the various models evaluated.

4.2 Benchmarks

We also use a representative subset of the SPEC CPU 2006 benchmarks. The benchmarks were run to completion with the reference input set. Table 2 shows the benchmarks used and some statistics related to our model, as follows. Column 2 shows the number of unique 4KB pages accessed by the benchmark. Columns 3 and 4 show the total number of writes to non-volatile main memory and the range of number of writes to individual pages. For instance, *mcf* has about 800M writes to non-volatile memory, the page with least writes had 15 writes, and the page with the most writes had about 3K writes. For benchmarks with more than 1M pages (the memory segment size) we follow the methodology in Section 3.2.2 to select the traffic targeting the memory segment. Columns 5 to 8 show the number of writes of the

resulting traffic selected with the *Most Accessed* and *Least Accessed* pages models and in each case targeting either $\frac{3}{4}$ or $\frac{1}{2}$ of the memory segment. For instance, for *mcf* with the *Most Accessed* pages over $\frac{3}{4}$ of the segment, the pages selected saw about 26M writes. These statistics help characterize how spread the traffic generated by the benchmarks are.

Bench.	Total Traffic			Selected Traffic (Writes)			
	Unique Pages	Writes	Range	Most Accessed		Least Accessed	
				Over $\frac{3}{4}$	Over $\frac{1}{2}$	Over $\frac{3}{4}$	Over $\frac{1}{2}$
mcf	429K	808M	3K–15	26M	18M	9M	4M
cactus	9K	557K	64–1	All	524K	All	371K
gems	1K	366K	20K–1	All			
xalancbmk	195	276	10–1	All			

Table 2: Characteristics of the benchmark traces.

4.3 Simulator

We use CMPsim [4], a PIN [6] based simulator, to run the benchmarks and model the memory hierarchy. The memory hierarchy model has 3 levels of cache as follows: 32KB L1 instruction and 32KB L1 data cache, 2MB unified L2 cache, and 1GB unified L3 cache, similar to that of [10]. The L1 and L2 caches are 8-way associative and the L3 cache is 2-way associative. All caches are write-back write-allocate and employ a LRU replacement policy. The output of the simulator is a trace of write-back traffic from the L3 cache to non-volatile main memory.

4.4 Metrics

Following the methodology in [11] we measure the lifetime of the memory segment (in number of writes) as the fraction achieved relative to the maximum expected lifetime (i.e., the point where all lines are expected to be broken). This metric is called *Normalized Endurance (NE)*. Thus, if every line in the segment is expected to last W_{max} and there are N lines in the segment then the maximum expected lifetime of the segment is $W_{max} \cdot N$. In this case if the segment actually breaks after W_{actual} writes then the normalized endurance is $NE = \frac{W_{actual}}{W_{max} \cdot N}$. The closest the NE value is to 1 the most effectively has the segment been used. We note that with error correction values greater than 1 are possible [2].

Our focus is on how the different failure and traffic models, as well as spares, error correction, and wear leveling, interact and affect memory endurance. We are not concerned with execution time performance and leave it to future work.

5. EXPERIMENTAL RESULTS

5.1 Statistical Traffic Distributions

5.1.1 Effects of Traffic and Failure Distributions on Baseline

We start by analyzing the effects of traffic and failure distributions on the baseline configuration with no spare lines, no error correction, and no wear leveling. Figure 3(a) shows normalized endurance for the various statistical traffic and

---

[2] The alternative is to multiply the denominator of the NE formula by the error correction capability since error correction basically extends the lifetime of each memory line. However, this would make it more difficult to directly compare NE values across configurations with different error correction capabilities.

failure distributions. The plot is organized in three groups of six bars each. In each group the first two bars correspond to uniform traffic distributions (UT) and the others correspond to normal traffic distributions (NT). The first group of bars corresponds to the fixed write endurance failure model (FE) while the others correspond to the normal write endurance failure distributions (NE). The horizontal lines on the normal failure models correspond to the resulting normalized endurance if one assumes that all lines fail at time $\mu - 6 \cdot \sigma$. This corresponds to assuming fixed write endurance failure model with a write endurance reduced by six times the standard deviation, which is a good rule-of-thumb commonly used in the industry [7].

From this figure we can make the following observations. First, comparing the results with uniform traffic distributions (UT1 and UT2) against those with normal traffic distributions (NT1 to NT4) we observe that, as expected, non-uniformity leads to reduced normalized endurance. In fact, the normalized endurances with the uniform traffics are the ones expected theoretically, namely 0.75% for UT1 and 0.50% for UT2. Furthermore, comparing the two normal traffic distributions (NT1 vs. NT2 and NT3 vs. NT4) we observe that the more concentrated the traffic (i.e., small standard deviation, NT2 and NT4) the lower the normalized endurance is. More interestingly, comparing the results with fixed write endurance (FE) against those with normal write endurance distributions (NE1 and NE2) we observe a significant drop in normalized endurance with the latter. Moreover, the more spread the write endurance (i.e., larger standard deviation – NE1) the lower the overall normalized system endurance is. This observation also holds for a uniform traffic. For instance, while a system with fixed write endurance and uniform traffic over half the physical memory space (FE-UT2) has the expected 50% normalized endurance, the comparable systems with the same traffic but normal write endurance distributions (NE1-UT2 and NE2-UT2) have only 26% and 38% normalized endurance. This highlights the fact that assuming fixed write endurance leads to very optimistic results in terms of durability of the memory. This is also the case when wear leveling is applied, as we show in Section 5.1.3, since the best outcome of wear leveling is a uniform traffic distribution.

To gain more insight, Figure 3(b) shows a breakdown at the end of simulation of all memory lines in terms of the number of writes performed to each line with respect to the nominal maximum number of writes. In other words, a breakdown of $x\%$ of memory lines in the "$0.2 < NWC < 0.4$" category means that $x\%$ of the memory lines were written to between $0.2 \cdot 10^8$ and $0.4 \cdot 10^8$ times. From this figure we see that lower normalized endurances are coupled with a large fraction of lines with few writes at the time the memory segment fails. In fact, the less spread the traffic (e.g., NT vs. UT, UT2 vs. UT1, NT2 vs. NT1, and NT4 vs. NT3) and the more spread the variability in endurance (e.g., NE vs. FE and NE1 vs. NE2) the larger the fraction of lines with few writes at the time the memory segment fails.

5.1.2 Effects of Spares and Error Correction on Baseline

We now consider the effects of adding spares to the baseline configuration. Figure 4(a) shows normalized endurance with varying number of spares. For each bar the bottom segment corresponds to the baseline (same as Figure 3(a)) and

the top segments show the added endurance provided by the spares. From this figure we can see that adding spares under the assumption of fixed write endurance (FE) leads to almost no benefits. This is in line with the results in [11] and simply reflects the fact that adding a few spare lines only brings a small boost in endurance since all lines break at the nominal endurance value. On the other hand, adding a small number of spares under the assumption of normal write endurance distributions (NE1 and NE2) leads to more significant benefits. This is because the small number of spares can "fix" the also small number of lines that break early, making the overall memory appear to last longer. This highlights again the fact that assuming fixed write endurance can lead to biased results and conclusions. Comparing the two normal write endurance models, we notice that the more spread the endurance distribution (NE1 vs. NE2) the more benefits are obtained with spares. Interestingly, the impact of the traffic distribution model does not appear to be as significant.

Comparing the results with 1K and 16K spare lines, we observe that the *relative* benefits of the latter are much smaller. This suggests that adding spare lines beyond a relatively small number is not a cost effective way to improve overall endurance. This behavior appears to be mostly independent of the failure distribution model, but there is a slightly increased benefit of more spares for failure distributions that are more spread. Overall, the boost in endurance with 16K spare lines ranges from close to null (NWL-S-FE-UT1-NEC) to 61% (NWL-S-NE1-NT2-NEC) and is 24% on average.

We now consider the effects of adding error correction to the baseline. Figure 5(a) shows normalized endurance with varying number of errors corrected. For each bar the bottom segment corresponds to the baseline (same as Figure 3(a)) and the top segments show the added endurance provided by the error correction. From this figure we can see that, as with spares, adding error correction under the assumption of fixed write endurance (FE) leads to negligible benefits. This again reflects the fact that correcting a few errors only brings a small boost in the endurance since all lines break at the nominal endurance plus the number of errors corrected. On the other hand, adding error correction under the assumption of normal write endurance distributions (NE1 and NE2) leads to significant benefits. This is because the error correction can delay the death of lines that break early, making the overall memory appear to last longer. This is especially pronounced when the traffic is uniform (UT1 and UT2) such that lines with errors are not the subject of more intense traffic than others. Comparing the results with 3 and 6 errors corrected, we observe that the *relative* benefits of the latter are much smaller. There is a slightly increased benefit of having more error correction for scenarios with more spread failure distributions.

To gain more insight, Figure 5(b) shows a few sample breakdowns at the end of simulation of all memory lines in terms of the number of errors present in each line. For readability we only show a few traffic and failure distribution cases with capability of correction of up to 6 errors. In the ideal scenario a large fraction of lines would have a high number of errors before the memory region becomes unusable. From this figure we see that, however, the fraction of lines with high error counts is relatively small. This is particularly the case under the assumptions of fixed write endurance (NWL-NS-FE-NT1-EC) or normal traffic (NWL-NS-NE1-NT1-EC). The first reflects the fact that with fixed

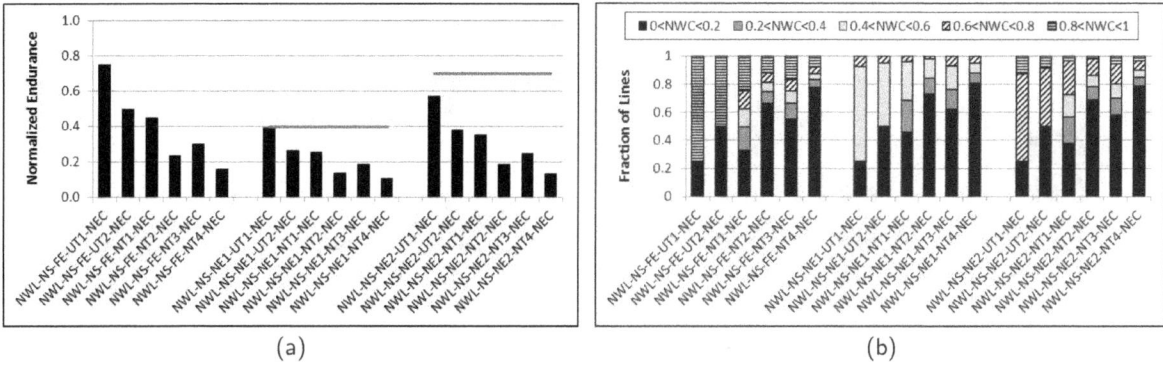

Figure 3: Effects of varying the traffic and failure distributions on the baseline configuration: (a) Normalized Endurance (b) Breakdown of write count relative to write endurance of lines.

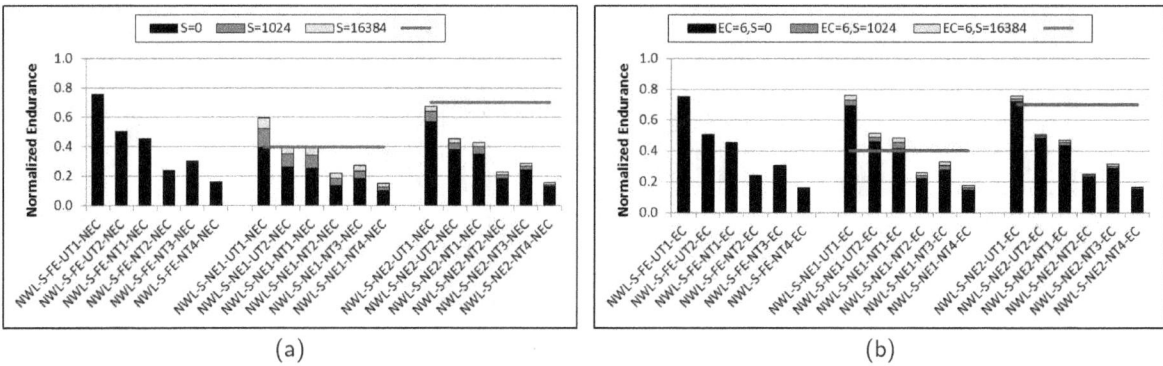

Figure 4: Effects of spares without (a) and with (b) error correction capability on the normalized endurance of the various traffic and failure distributions.

write endurance the entirety of the line breaks at the same time, rendering error correction of a portion of a line completely useless. The latter reflects the fact that with normal traffic the "hot" memory lines will accumulate errors much more quickly than the rest. Under the assumption of uniform traffic and normal write endurance (NWL-NS-NE1-UT1-EC) we see a larger fraction of lines with higher error counts, which is expected as lines suffer errors more uniformly under this traffic. Finally, we note that there is a correlation between a more spread distribution of errors over more lines and an increase in normalized endurance. Overall, the boost in endurance with the capability to correct up to 6 errors ranges from null (NWL-NS-FE-UT1-EC) to 76% (NWL-NS-NE1-UT2-EC) and is 28% on average.

Finally, we consider the effects of error correction and spares in conjunction. Figure 4(b) shows normalized endurance with varying number of spares coupled with error correction capability of 6 errors. Comparing this figure with Figures 4(a) and 5(a) we can see that combining error correction and spares can provide some additional benefits over each one alone. However, these additional benefits are somewhat incremental. Again, we can see that benefits are negligible under the assumption of fixed write endurance (FE).

5.1.3 Effects of Wear Leveling on Baseline

We start the evaluation of wear leveling on the baseline configuration with no spare lines and no error correction. Figure 6(a) shows normalized endurance with RBSG wear leveling. For each bar the bottom segment corresponds to the baseline (same as Figure 3(a)) and the top segments show the added endurance provided by RBSG with increas-

ingly aggressive values of ψ: 100 and 10 writes, as discussed in Section 3.4. From this figure we can make several interesting observations. First, adding RBSG wear leveling with the value of ψ suggested by the size of the memory region as in [11] – i.e., $\psi = 100$ – leads to negligible overall endurance benefits with the variable write endurance models (NE1 and NE2). This is because the variability in cell endurance leads to significant drops in the overall endurance, which lend the original value of ψ too large for wear leveling to be effective. On the other hand, if we assume fixed write endurance (FE) we now see some reasonable benefits from RBSG wear leveling, similar to what has been reported in [11]. These benefits vanish when the workload traffic is already more or less balanced (UT1 and UT2), because this value of ψ does not provide quick enough shifts to significantly spread the traffic over the unused part of the memory segment.

With the reduced value of $\psi = 10$ we observe that the benefits of RBSG wear leveling are now significant. RBSG wear leveling now achieves near perfect uniform spreading of the addresses, regardless of the original traffic distribution. In fact, the normalized endurance is now only a function of the failure distribution model (FE vs. NE1 vs. NE2), and for each failure model the achieved normalized endurance is nearly the same (minus the 10% overhead caused by the memory shifts) as that of a uniform input traffic over the entire memory segment (results not shown).

To gain more insight, Figure 6(b) shows, for $\psi = 10$, a breakdown similar to that of Figure 3(b). We see that RBSG wear leveling uniformly brings the vast majority of lines to the same number of writes. Furthermore, this num-

223

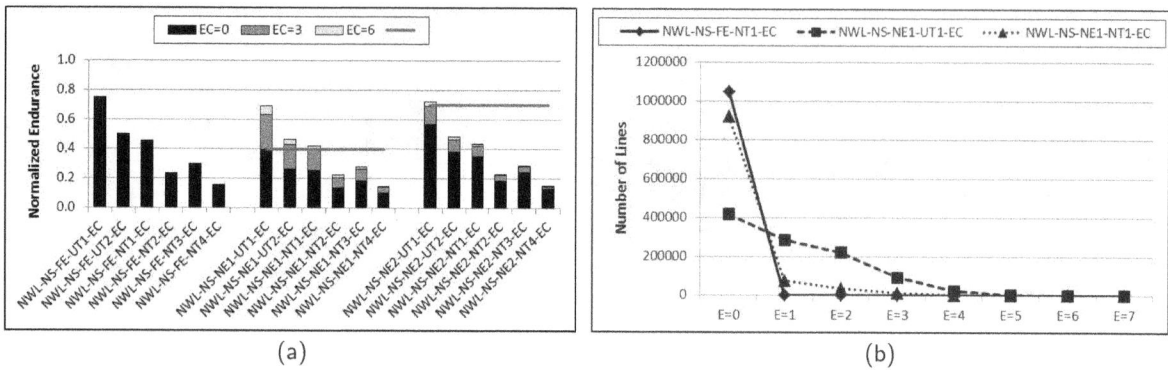

Figure 5: Effects of error correction on the various traffic and failure distributions: (a) Normalized Endurance (b) Breakdown of number of lines with the various amount of errors.

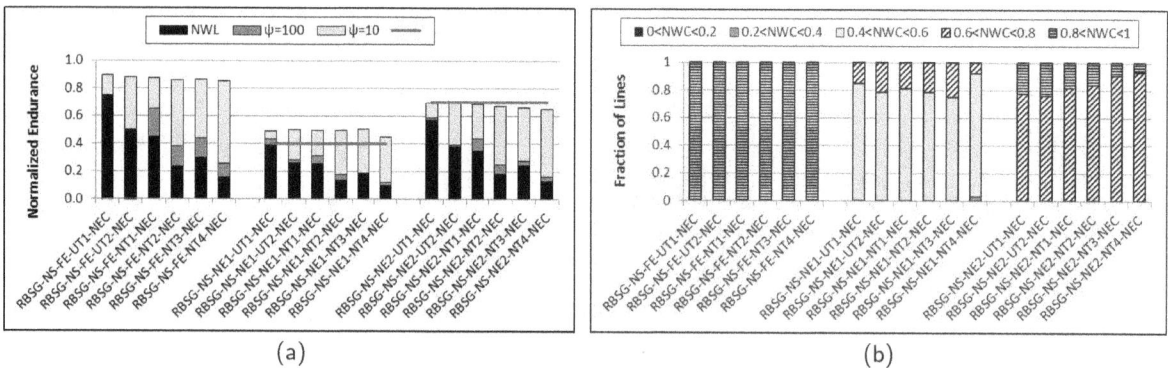

Figure 6: Effects of RBSG wear leveling on the various traffic and failure distributions: (a) Normalized Endurance (b) Breakdown of write count relative to write endurance of lines.

ber of writes received by this vast majority of lines before the first line breaks correlates exactly with the overall normalized endurance of Figure 6(a): around 0.66, 0.45, and 0.9 times the nominal maximum number of writes for NE2, NE1, and FE, respectively. Overall, the boost in endurance with $\psi = 10$ ranges from 19% (RBSG-NS-FE-UT1-NEC) to 444% (RBSG-NS-FE-NT4-NEC) and is 172% on average.

5.1.4 Combined Effects of Wear Leveling, Error Correction, and Spares

Figure 7(a) shows normalized endurance with RBSG wear leveling and varying number of spares. For each bar the bottom segment corresponds to the configuration with RBSG wear leveling with $\psi = 10$ (same as Figure 6(a)). We can see that for the normal write endurance distributions (NE1 and NE2), wear leveling and spares have mostly additive effects that boost the overall normalized endurance. This reflects the fact that once wear leveling has "flattened" the traffic distribution, the presence of a few spares can compensate for the small number of lines that break early. The resulting endurance is, as with the case of wear leveling alone, independent of the original traffic distribution. On the other hand, adding spares under the assumption of fixed write endurance (FE) leads to no benefits. In fact, we observe a small decrease of overall endurance with 16K spares caused by the fact that spares are not used in the wear leveling process. Comparing the results with 1K and 16K spare lines, we observe that, as with the case with no wear leveling, the relative benefits of the latter are smaller. Overall, the boost in endurance with 16K spare lines on top of the endurance

with wear leveling alone ranges from -2.4% (RBSG-S-FE-NT4-NEC) to 42% (RBSG-S-NE1-NT1-NEC) and is 20% on average.

Figure 8(a) shows normalized endurance with RBSG wear leveling and varying error correction capability. For each bar the bottom segment corresponds to the configuration with RBSG wear leveling with $\psi = 10$ (same as Figure 6(a)). We can see that for the normal write endurance distributions (NE1 and NE2), wear leveling and error correction have mostly additive effects. Again, once wear leveling has "flattened" the traffic distribution, the ability to correct a few errors can help "fix" the small number of lines that break early. The resulting endurance is also independent of the original traffic distribution. Adding error correction under the assumption of fixed write endurance (FE) leads to no benefits. Comparing the results with 3 and 6 errors corrected, we observe that, as with the case with no wear leveling, the relative benefits of the latter are smaller. Figure 8(b) shows a few sample breakdowns at the end of simulation of all memory lines in terms of the number of errors present in each line. Comparing this figure with Figure 5(b) we can see that wear leveling significantly increases the fraction of lines with higher error counts. As before, this effect is not present if we assume fixed write endurance (RBSG-NS-FE-NT1-EC). Overall, the boost in endurance with 6 errors corrected on top of the endurance with wear leveling alone ranges from null (RBSG-NS-FE-NT4-EC) to 87% (RBSG-NS-NE1-NT4-EC) and is 33% on average.

Finally, Figure 7(b) shows normalized endurance with RBSG wear leveling with varying number of spares coupled

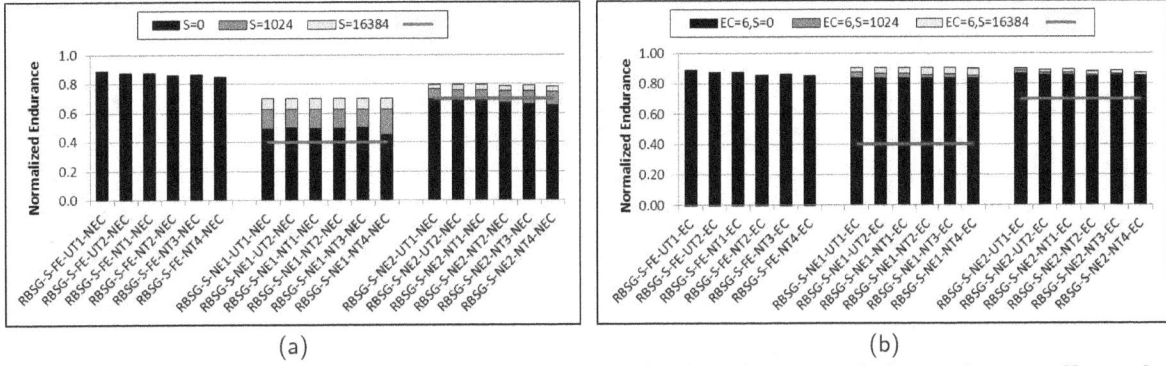

Figure 7: Effects of RBSG wear leveling on the normalized endurance of the various traffic and failure distributions: (a) With spares (b) With spares and error correction capability.

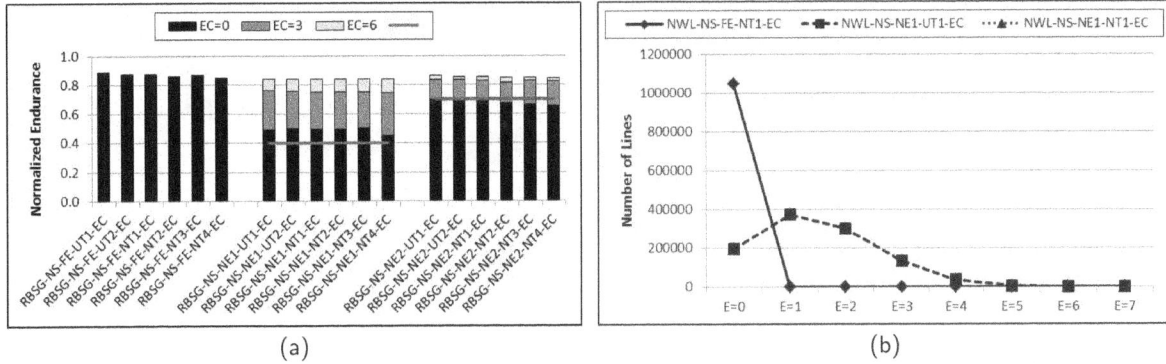

Figure 8: Effects of RBSG wear leveling on the various traffic and failure distributions with error correction capability: (a) Normalized Endurance (b) Breakdown of number of lines with the various amount of errors.

with error correction capability of 6 errors. Comparing this figure with Figures 7(a) and 8(a) we can see that combining all three endurance enhancing techniques simultaneously provides very small benefits over wear leveling combined with either spares or error correction alone.

5.1.5 Discussion

In summary, the results of the experiments with statistical traffic distributions point to the following. First, assuming fixed write endurance leads to overly *optimistic* values of normalized endurance as well as overly *pessimistic* values for the improvements from endurance enhancing techniques. In fact, the spreadness of the write endurance has a first order impact on the estimated normalized endurance. Thus, evaluation of endurance enhancing techniques should include some sensitivity analysis to this parameter. Second, with non-fixed write endurance the value chosen for the frequency of line shifts in proactive wear leveling techniques must be adjusted upwards to account for the degraded starting normalized endurance. Finally, combining wear leveling with either spares or error correction leads to valuable improvement in lifetime, but the combination of spares and error correction leads to only minor additional improvement over each technique alone.

5.2 Benchmark Driven Traffic

5.2.1 Effects of Traffic and Failure Distributions on Baseline

Figure 9 shows the normalized endurance for the benchmarks we evaluate. Compared to the synthetic traffic (Fig-

ure 3(a)), the benchmark driven traffic leads to significantly reduced normalized endurance (note the different y-axis ranges). The absolute values may be somewhat biased by the continuous re-execution in place model outlined in Section 3.2.2. Nevertheless, they do bring out the fact that real applications can generate very concentrated traffic that can damage a limited endurance memory device in a relatively short amount of time.

Comparing the results with different write endurance models we note similar trends as before. The normalized endurance with fixed write endurance (FE) is often higher than with normal write endurance (NE1 and NE2), and the more spread the write endurance (NE1 vs. NE2) the lower the overall normalized endurance is. However, both *gems* and *xalancbmk* show a similar (and very low) normalized endurance across all write endurance models. This is because the traffic generated by these benchmarks is very concentrated on a few memory lines. Comparing the results with different traffic concentration models (only on *mcf* and *cactus*), we note that, as expected, considering the traffic is concentrated on a smaller fraction ($\frac{1}{2}$ vs. $\frac{3}{4}$) of the memory segment leads to reduced normalized endurance. Interestingly, we observe little difference between the normalized endurances when we vary the traffic selection from the most accessed to the least accessed pages. This suggests that the amount of traffic is less important for bottom line endurance than the concentration/distribution of the traffic. (Note that this is true for normalized endurance, not for absolute lifetime.)

225

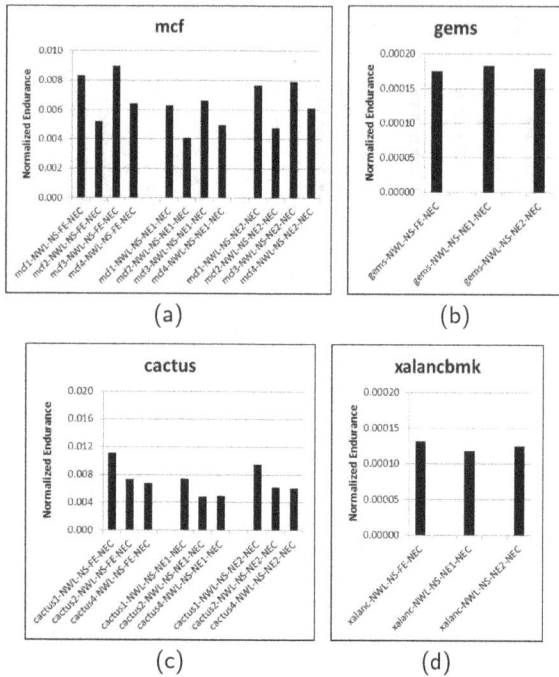

(a)   (b)

(c)   (d)

Figure 9: Effects of varying the benchmark traffic
and failure distributions on the baseline configuration.

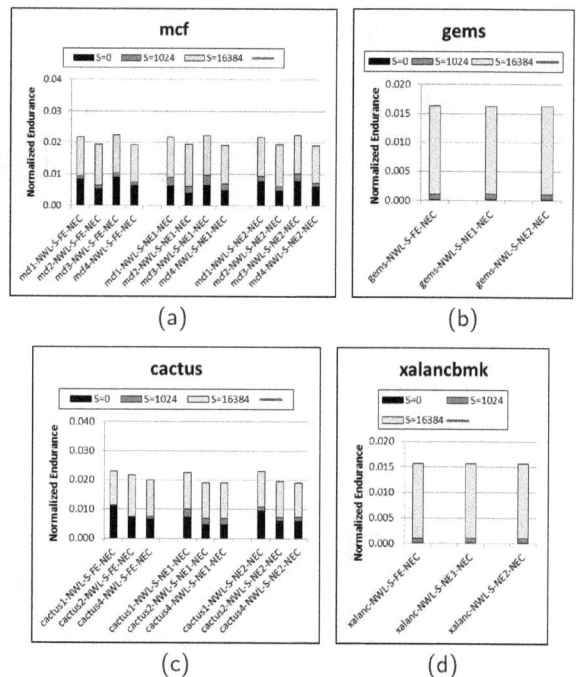

(a)   (b)

(c)   (d)

Figure 10: Effects of spares on the various benchmark traffic.

5.2.2 Effects of Spares and Error Correction on Baseline

Figure 10 shows normalized endurance for the benchmarks with varying number of spares. The bottom segments correspond to the baseline with no spares (same as Figure 9). From this figure we can see that adding spares has a much more dramatic effect on endurance for the benchmark traffic when compared to the synthetic traffic (Figure 4(a)). Unlike for the synthetic traffic, there is now a significant increase in benefit when increasing the number of spares from 1K to 16K lines. This reflects the fact that the traffic generated by the benchmarks is much more concentrated than that generated by the synthetic distributions, so that the spares can replace these relatively few hot lines when they break. Nevertheless, the resulting normalized endurance is still very low. We also note that the resulting normalized endurance seems to be only slightly dependent on the endurance model and follow the trends seen without spares.

Figure 11 shows normalized endurance for the benchmarks with varying number of errors corrected. The bottom segments correspond to the baseline with no error correction (same as Figure 9). From this figure we can see that adding error correction has a less dramatic effect on endurance for the benchmarks than adding spares (Figure 10). Nevertheless, error correction can still provide some benefits, especially for *mcf* and *cactus*, although the resulting normalized endurance is still very low. As with the synthetic traffic (Figure 5(a)), we note that adding error correction under the assumption of fixed write endurance (FE) leads to negligible benefits. Similar to the synthetic traffic, there is *relatively* less benefit from 6 versus 3 errors corrected.

5.2.3 Effects of Wear Leveling on Baseline

Figure 12 shows the normalized endurance for the bench-

marks with RBSG wear leveling. The bottom segments correspond to the baseline with no wear leveling (same as Figure 9). The effect of wear leveling is tremendous. The normalized endurances are now in the same order of magnitude as those from the synthetic traffic distributions. As with the synthetic traffic distributions, there is noticeable benefits from using the reduced value of $\psi = 10$, although its relative benefit compared to $\psi = 100$ is much reduced.

5.2.4 Combined Effects of Wear Leveling, Error Correction, and Spares

Figure 13 shows normalized endurance for the benchmarks with RBSG wear leveling and varying number of spares. The bottom segments correspond to the configuration with RBSG wear leveling with $\psi = 10$ (same as Figure 12). From this figure we can see that wear leveling and spares have mostly additive effects that boost overall normalized endurance significantly. As with the synthetic traffic distributions, comparing the results with 1K and 16K spare lines, we observe that the relative benefits of the latter are smaller.

Finally, figure 14 shows normalized endurance for the benchmarks with RBSG wear leveling and varying number of errors corrected. The bottom segments correspond to the configuration with RBSG wear leveling with $\psi = 10$ (same as Figure 12). We can see that wear leveling and error correction have mostly additive effects. Interestingly, similar to the case with synthetic traffic distributions, comparing the combination of RBSG wear leveling with error correction against that of RBSG wear leveling with spares, we notice that the former leads to noticeably better normalized endurances. There is *relatively* less benefit from 6 versus 3 errors corrected.

5.2.5 Discussion

The results with benchmark driven traffic show that these are much more concentrated than any of the synthetic

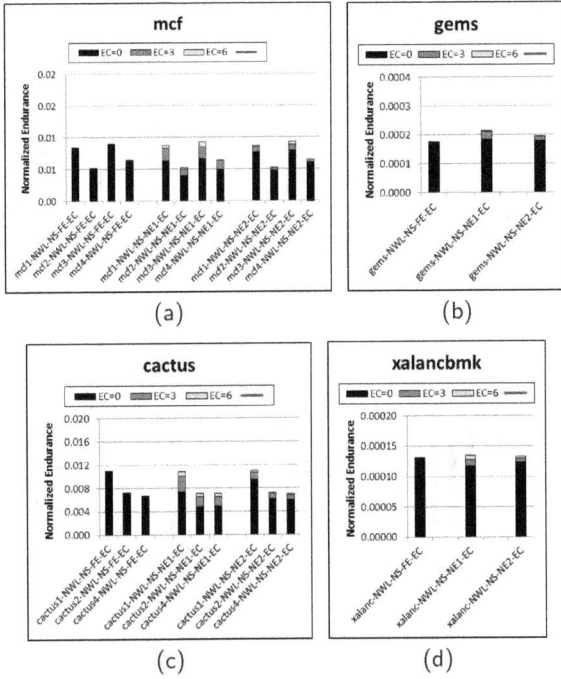

Figure 11: Effects of error correction capability on the various benchmark traffic.

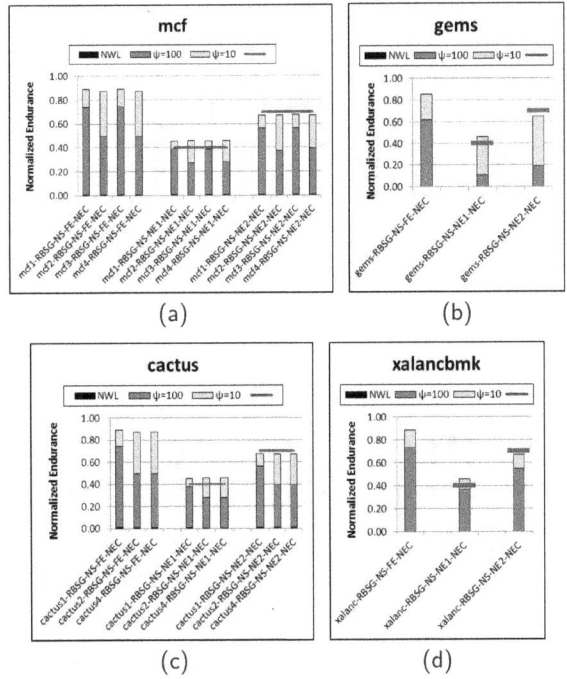

Figure 12: Effects of RBSG wear leveling on the various benchmark traffic.

benchmarks, even those with apparent high concentration (i.e., low C_v as in NT2 and NT4). This leads to *relatively* large benefits from error correction and spares, but that still achieve only minor *absolute* endurance. On the other hand, wear leveling is much more effective on the benchmark driven traffic, leading to *absolute* endurance on par with those of the synthetic traffic. Finally, the combination of wear leveling with either spares or error correction leads to valuable improvements in lifetime.

6. RELATED WORK

The endurance behavior of individual PCM cells [9, 12] and PCM arrays [8] have been studied both empirically and through simulation. The aim of these works is to establish the basic behavior of devices and point to improvements at the device or circuit level. They do not consider the interaction of endurance and architectural mechanisms, such as wear leveling and error correction.

On the other hand, various studies have investigated wear leveling [10, 11, 15, 19], error correction [2, 13, 16, 17], and write reduction [1, 5, 10, 19]. However, none considered the combined effects of wear leveling and error correction using more realistic (non-uniform) endurance failure models. For instance, [10, 11, 15] considered wear leveling, but did not consider error correction and assumed a fixed endurance limit for all cells. Similarly, [1, 5] considered write reduction, but did not consider error correction or wear leveling and assumed a fixed endurance limit, while [19] explored write reduction with wear leveling, but also did not consider error correction and assumed a fixed endurance limit. Also, [2, 13, 16, 17] considered error correction under non-uniform endurance failure models, but assumed perfect wear leveling. Finally, [18], which is arguably the closest work to ours in terms of objectives, performed a thorough evaluation of non-uniform failure models and how they affect endurance of a

PCM array. However, it assumed perfect wear leveling and no error correction.

7. CONCLUSIONS

As DRAM technology may be approaching its density and energy limits, a new class of non-volatile memory technologies – such as PCM, STT-MRAM, and ReRAM – based on resistive materials has gained much interest. These offer performance and access granularity close enough to DRAM, but present much reduced write endurance. Recently, much research has focused on extending the lifetime of such memory technologies through the use of wear leveling, write reduction, and error tolerance approaches. Such prior works, however, have not considered the interactions of these approaches and/or have not considered non-uniform write endurance failure models. In this paper, we performed a comprehensive simulation study of these approaches combined, under various workload traffic, and assuming more realistic write endurance failure models. The results show that variability in cell endurance must be taken into account when tuning the parameters of endurance enhancing techniques. They also show that combinations of such endurance enhancing techniques must be considered carefully as their effects can be, but are not necessarily, additive.

8. REFERENCES

[1] S. Cho and H. Lee. "Flip-N-Write: A Simple Deterministic Technique to Improve PRAM Write Performance, Energy and Endurance." *Intl. Symp. on Microarchitecture (MICRO),* p. 347–357, December 2009.

[2] E. Ipek, J. Condit, E. B. Nightingale, D. Burger, and T. Moscibroda. "Dynamically Replicated Memory: Building Reliable Systems from Nanoscale Resistive Memories." *Intl. Conf. on Architectural Support for Programming Languages and Operating Systems (ASPLOS),* p. 3–14, March 2010.

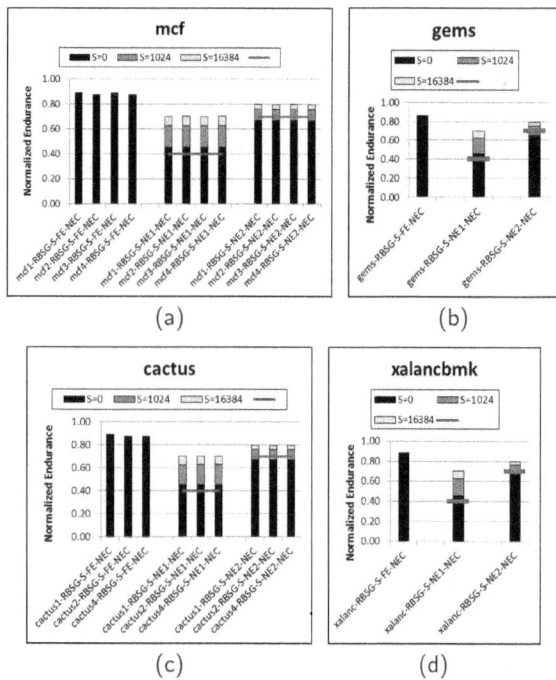

Figure 13: Effects of RBSG wear leveling with spares on the various benchmark traffic.

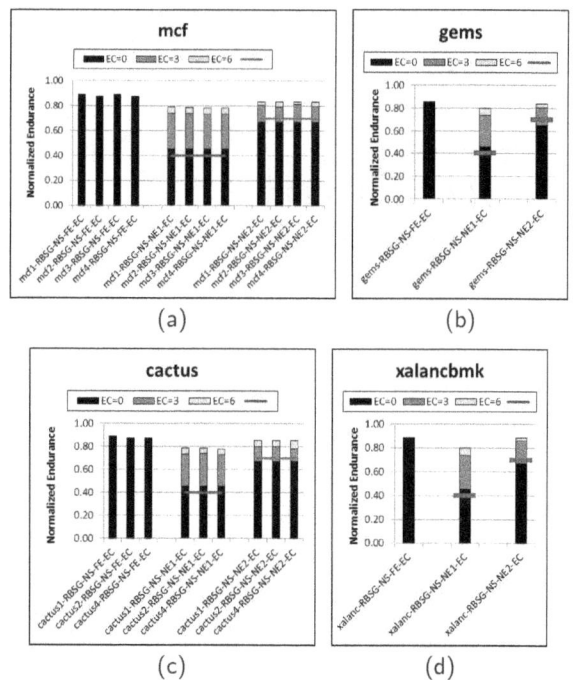

Figure 14: Effects of RBSG wear leveling with error correction capability on the various benchmark traffic.

[3] International Technology Roadmap for Semiconductors. "ITRS 2011, Emerging Research Device." http://www.itrs.net/Links/2011ITRS/Home2011.htm.

[4] A. Jaleel, R. S. Cohn, C.-K. Luk, and B. Jacob. "CMP$im: A Pin-Based On-The-Fly Multi-Core Cache Simulator." Wksp. on Modeling, Benchmarking, and Simulation (MoBS), June 2008.

[5] B. Lee, E. Ipek, O. Mutlu, and D. Burger. "Architecting Phase Change Memory as a Scalable DRAM Alternative." Intl. Symp. on Computer Architecture (ISCA), p. 2–13, June 2009.

[6] C.-K. Luk, R. Cohn, R. Muth, H. Patil, A. Klauser, G. Lowney, S. Wallace, V. J. Reddi, K. Hazelwood. "Pin: Building Customized Program Analysis Tools with Dynamic Instrumentation." Conf. on Programming Languages Design and Implementation (PLDI), p. 190–200, June 2005.

[7] D. C. Montgomery. "Statistical Quality Control: A Modern Introduction." John Wiley & Sons, 6th Edition, 2008.

[8] J. H. Oh, J. H. Park, Y. S. Lim, H. S. Lim, Y. T. Oh, J. S. Kim, J. M. Shin, J. H. Park, Y. J. Song, K. C. Ryoo, D. W. Lim, S. S. Park, J. I. Kim, J. H. Kim, J. Yu, F. Yeung, C. W. Jeong, J. H. Kong, D. H. Kang, G. H. Koh, G. T. Jeong, H. S. Jeong, and K. Kim. "Full Integration of Highly Manufacturable 512Mb PRAM based on 90nm Technology." Intl. Electron Devices Meet. (IEDM), December 2006.

[9] A. Pirovano, A. Redaelli, F. Pellizzer, F. Ottogalli, M. Tosi, D. Ielmini, and A. L. Lacaita. "Reliability Study of Phase-Change Nonvolatile Memories." IEEE Trans. on Device and Materials Reliability (TDMR), vol. 4, no. 3, September 2004.

[10] M. K. Qureshi, V. Srinivasan, and J. A. Rivers. "Scalable High Performance Main Memory System Using Phase-Change Memory Technology." Intl. Symp. on Computer Architecture (ISCA), p. 24–33, June 2009.

[11] M. K. Qureshi, J. Karidis, M. Franceschini, V. Srinivasan, L. Lastras, and B. Abali. "Enhancing Lifetime and Security of PCM-Based Main Memory with Start-Gap Wear Leveling." Intl. Symp. on Microarchitecture (MICRO), p. 14–23, December 2009.

[12] S. Raoux, G. W. Burr, M. J. Breitwisch, C. T. Rettner, Y.-C. Chen, R. M. Shelby, M. Salinga, D. Krebs, S.-H. Chen, H.-L. Lung, and C. H. Lam. "Phase-Change Random Access Memory: A Scalable Technology." IBM Journal of Research and Development, vol. 52, no. 4/5, p. 465–479, July 2008.

[13] S. Schechter, G. H. Loh, K. Strauss, and D. Burger. "Use ECP, not ECC, for Hard Failures in Resistive Memories." Intl. Symp. on Computer Architecture (ISCA), p. 141–152, June 2010.

[14] B. Schroeder, E. Pinheiro, and W.-D. Weber. "DRAM Errors in the Wild: a Large-Scale Field Study." Intl. Joint Conf. on Measurement and Modeling of Computer Systems (SIGMETRICS), p. 193–204, June 2009.

[15] N. H. Seong, D. H. Woo, and H.-H. S. Lee. "Security Refresh: Prevent Malicious Wear-out and Increase Durability for Phase-Change Memory with Dynamically Randomized Address Mapping." Intl. Symp. on Computer Architecture (ISCA), p. 383–394, June 2010.

[16] N. H. Seong, D. H. Woo, V. Srinivasan, J. A. Rivers, and H.-S. S. Lee. "SAFER: Stuck-At-Fault Error Recovery for Memories." Intl. Symp. on Microarchitecture (MICRO), p. 115–124, December 2010.

[17] D. H. Yoon, N. Muralimanohar, J. Chang, P. Ranganathan, N. Jouppi, and M. Erez. "FREE-p: Protecting Non-Volatile Memory Against Both Hard and Soft Errors." Intl. Symp. on High-Performance Computer Architecture (HPCA), p. 466–477, February 2011.

[18] W. Zhang and T. Li. "Characterizing and Mitigating the Impact of Process Variation on Phase Change based Memory Systems." Intl. Symp. on Microarchitecture (MICRO), p. 2–13, December 2009.

[19] P. Zhou, B. Zhao, J. Yang, and Y. Zhang. "A Durable and Energy Efficient Main Memory Using Phase Change Memory Technology." Intl. Symp. on Computer Architecture (ISCA), p. 14–23, June 2009.

Distributing Content Simplifies ISP Traffic Engineering

Abhigyan Sharma[†]   Arun Venkataramani[†]   Ramesh K Sitaraman[†*]
[†] University of Massachusetts Amherst   * Akamai Technologies
140 Governors Drive
Amherst MA 01003
{abhigyan,arun,ramesh}@cs.umass.edu

ABSTRACT

Several major Internet service providers today also offer content distribution services. The emergence of such "network-CDNs" (NCDNs) is driven both by market forces as well as the cost of carrying ever-increasing volumes of traffic across their backbones. An NCDN has the flexibility to determine both where content is placed and how traffic is routed within the network. However NCDNs today continue to treat traffic engineering independently from content placement and request redirection decisions. In this paper, we investigate the interplay between content distribution strategies and traffic engineering and ask whether or how an NCDN should address these concerns in a joint manner. Our experimental analysis, based on traces from a large content distribution network and real ISP topologies, shows that realistic (i.e., history-based) joint optimization strategies offer little benefit (and often significantly underperform) compared to simple and "unplanned" strategies for routing and placement such as InverseCap and LRU. We also find that the simpler strategies suffice to achieve network cost and user-perceived latencies close to those of a joint-optimal strategy with future knowledge.

Categories and Subject Descriptors

C.2.3 [**Network Operations**]: Network management; C.2.4 [**Distributed Systems**]: Distributed applications

Keywords

Traffic engineering; Content distribution; Network CDN

1. INTRODUCTION

Content delivery networks (CDNs) today provide a core service that enterprises use to deliver web content, downloads, and streaming media to a global audience of end-users. The traditional and somewhat simplified, tripartite view of content delivery involves three sets of entities as

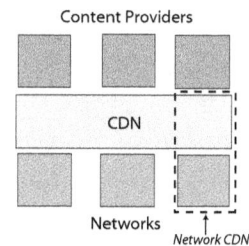

Content Providers

CDN

Networks   *Network CDN*

Figure 1: Network CDNs (NCDNs) allow a tighter integration of content delivery functionality with the ISP's network operations.

shown in Figure 1. The *content providers* (e.g., media companies, news channels, e-commerce sites, software distributors, enterprise portals, etc.) own the content and wish to provide a high-quality experience to end-users who access their content. The *networks* (e.g., telcos such as AT&T, multi-system operators such as Comcast, and ISPs) own the underlying network infrastructure and are responsible for provisioning capacity and routing traffic demand. Finally, the *CDNs* (e.g., Akamai [28], Limelight) optimize content delivery to end-users on behalf of the content providers, residing as a global, distributed overlay service [13].

Recent powerful trends are reshaping the simplified tripartite view of content delivery. A primary driver is the torrid growth of video [27, 11] and downloads traffic on the Internet. For example, a single, popular TV show with 50 million viewers, with each viewer watching an HD-quality stream of 10 Mbps, generates 500 Tbps of network traffic! The increasing migration of traditional media content to the Internet and the consequent challenges of scaling the network backbone to accommodate that traffic has necessitated the evolution of *network CDNs* (or NCDNs)[1] that vertically integrate CDN functionality such as content caching and redirection with traditional network operations [19, 26, 24, 8, 36] (refer Figure 1). Another economic driver of NCDNs is the desire of networks to further monetize the "bits" that flow on their infrastructure and to offer value-added services to their own end-user subscribers, e.g., Verizon's recent offering that delivers HBO's content to FIOS subscribers [35]. Two key trends in how networks implement NCDNs [3] are *managed CDNs* where a CDN provider (such as Akamai) deploys their own servers at the network's PoPs and operates the CDN service on behalf of the network provider [2]; and, *licensed CDNs* where the CDN provider licenses their software to the network who then deploy and operate the NCDN themselves [1, 10].

---

[1]NCDNs are also called Telco CDNs, or Carrier CDNs.

As NCDNs control both the content distribution and the network infrastructure, the costs and objectives of their interest are different both from a traditional CDN and a traditional ISP. In particular, an NCDN is in a powerful position to place content in a manner that "shapes" the traffic demand so as to optimize both network cost and user-perceived latency. Indeed, several recent works have alluded to the benefits of such joint optimization strategies in the context of cooperative or competitive interaction between ISPs and content providers [38, 14, 21, 18]. NCDNs today largely treat the content distribution layer and the traffic engineering layer separately, treating the former as an overlay over the latter. However, an NCDN is the perfect setting for fielding a joint optimization as both layers are for the first time closely alligned in terms of both the business objectives and the system architecture.

The intriguing prospect of jointly optimizing content delivery and traffic engineering raises several research questions that form the focus of this paper. How should an NCDN determine content placement, network routing, and request redirection decisions so as to optimize network cost and user-perceived latency? How much benefit do joint optimization strategies yield over simpler strategies as practiced today, and does the benefit warrant the added complexity? How do content demand patterns and placement strategies impact network cost? How do planned strategies (i.e., using knowledge of recently observed demand patterns or hints about anticipated future demands) for placement and routing compare against simpler, unplanned strategies?

Our primary contribution is to empirically analyze the above questions for realistic content demand workloads and ISP topologies. To this end, we collect content request traces from Akamai, the world's largest CDN today. We focus specifically on on-demand video and large-file downloads traffic as they are two categories that dominate overall CDN traffic and are significantly influenced by content placement strategies. Our combined traces consist of a total of 28.2 million requests from 7.79 million unique users who downloaded a total of 1455 Terabytes of content across the US over multiple days. Our main finding based on trace-driven experiments using these logs and realistic ISP topologies is that *simple, unplanned strategies for placement, routing, and redirection of NCDN content are better than sophisticated joint-optimization approaches*. Specifically,

- For NCDN traffic, simple unplanned schemes for placement and routing (such as least-recently-used and InverseCap) yield significantly lower (2.2–$17\times$) network cost and user-perceived latency than a joint-optimal scheme with knowledge of the previous day's demand[2].

- NCDN traffic demand can be "shaped" by simple placement strategies so that traffic engineering, i.e., optimizing routes with knowledge of recent traffic matrices, hardly improves network cost or user-perceived latency over unplanned routing (InverseCap).

- For NCDN traffic, unplanned placement and routing is just 1%-18% sub-optimal compared to a joint-optimal placement and routing with perfect knowledge of the next day's demand at modest storage ratios (≈ 4).

---

[2]We use the term "optimal" when placement or routing is the solution of an optimization problem, but the solution may not have the lowest cost (for reasons detailed in §5.3.1)

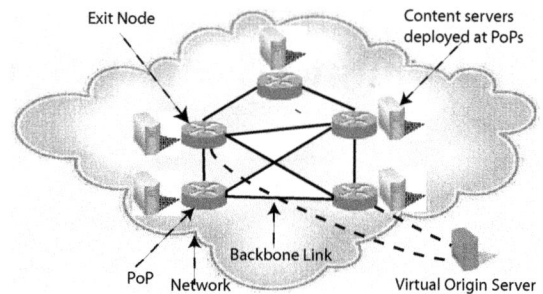

Figure 2: NCDN Architecture

- With a mix of NCDN and transit traffic, traffic engineering does lower network cost (consistent with previous studies), but the value of traffic engineering substantially diminishes as the relative volume of NCDN traffic begins to dominate that of transit traffic.

In the rest of this paper, we first overview the NCDN architecture highlighting why it changes traditional ISP and CDN concerns (§2). Next, we formalize algorithms that jointly optimize content placement and routing in an NCDN (§3). We then describe how we collected real CDN traces (§4) and evaluate our algorithms using these traces and real ISP topologies (§5). Finally, we present related work (§7) and conclusions (§8).

2. BACKGROUND AND MOTIVATION

A typical NCDN architecture, as shown in Figure 2, resembles the architecture of a global CDN but with some important differences. First, the content servers are deployed at points-of-presence (PoPs) within a single network rather than globally across the Internet as the NCDN is primarily interested in optimizing content delivery for its own customers and end-users. Second, and more importantly, content distribution and network operations are tightly alligned, so that a joint optimization of these layers is feasible. In fact, in some cases such as a Licensed CDN, a single entity may own and manage both the content servers and the underlying network. Content providers whose content is delivered by the NCDN publish their content to origin servers that they maintain external to the NCDN itself.

Each PoP is associated with a distinct set of end-users who request content such as web, video, downloads etc. An end-user's request is first routed to the content servers at the PoP to which the end-user is connected. If a content server at that PoP has the requested content in their cache, it serves that to the end-user. Otherwise, if the requested content is cached at other PoPs, the content is downloaded from a nearby PoP and served to the end-user. If the content is not cached in any PoP, it is downloaded directly from the content provider's origin servers.

2.1 Why NCDNs Change the Game

Managing content distribution as well as the underlying network makes the costs and objectives of interest to an NCDN different from that of a traditional CDN or a traditional ISP. Figure 3 (top) shows the traditional concerns of content distribution and traffic engineering as addressed by a traditional CDN and a traditional ISP respectively, while Figure 3 (bottom) shows the combined concerns that an NCDN must address. We explain these in detail below.

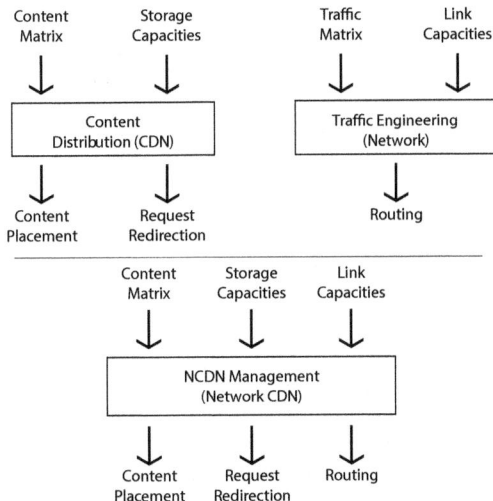

Figure 3: (Top) Traditional formulation with content distribution and traffic engineering optimized separately. (Bottom) Our new formulation of NCDN magamement as a joint optimization.

2.1.1 Content Distribution

A traditional CDN has two key decision components—*content placement* and *request redirection*—that seek to optimize the response time perceived by end-users and balance the load across its content servers. Content placement decides which objects should be cached at which nodes. An object may be stored at multiple nodes in the network or not stored in the network at all and be served from the origin server instead. Request redirection determines which server storing a replica of the object is best positioned to serve it.

Content placement schemes can either be *planned* or *unplanned*. A planned scheme calculates placement using a *content matrix* that specifies the demand for each content at each location. The content matrix is learned by monitoring a recent history of system-wide requests and possibly including hints, if any, from content providers about anticipated demand for some objects. A planned scheme uses a recent content matrix to decide on a placement periodically (e.g., daily) but does not alter its placement in between. In contrast, an unplanned scheme can continually alter its placement potentially even after every single request. A simple and widely used example of an unplanned placement scheme is LRU, where each server evicts the least-recently-used object from its cache to make room for new ones.

2.1.2 Traffic Engineering

A key component of ISP network operations is traffic engineering, which seeks to route the traffic demands through the backbone network so as to balance the load and mitigate hotspots. Traffic engineering is commonly viewed as a routing problem that takes as input a *traffic matrix*, i.e., the aggregate flow demand between every pair of PoPs observed over a recent history, and computes routes so as to minimize a network-wide cost objective. The cost seeks to capture the severity of load imbalance in the network and common objective functions include the maximum link utilization (MLU) or a convex function (so as to penalize higher utilization more) of the link utilization aggregated across all links in the network [16]. ISPs commonly achieve the computed routing either by using shortest-path routing (e.g.,

the widely deployed OSPF protocol [16]) or by explicitly establishing virtual circuits (e.g., using MPLS [15]). ISPs perform traffic engineering at most a few times each day, e.g., morning and evening each day [17].

Routing can also be classified as *planned* or *unplanned* similar in spirit to content placement. Traffic engineering schemes as explained above are implicitly planned as they optimize routing for recently observed demand. To keep the terminology simple, we also classify online traffic engineering schemes [22, 15] (that are rarely deployed today) as planned. In contrast, unplanned routing schemes are simpler and rely upon statically configured routes [7, 9], e.g., InverseCap is a static shortest-path routing scheme that sets link weights to the inverse of their capacities; this is a common default weight setting for OSPF in commercial routers [17].

2.1.3 NCDN Management

As NCDNs own and manage the infrastructure for content distribution as well as the underlying network, they are in a powerful position to control all three of placement, routing, and redirection (Figure 3). In particular, an NCDN can place content in a manner that "shapes" the traffic demands so as to jointly optimize both user-perceived latency as well as network cost.

To appreciate how placement can shape traffic, consider the simple example in Figure 4. Node C has an object in its cache that is requested by end-users at nodes A and D. Suppose that one unit of traffic needs to be routed from C to A and 0.5 units from C to D to satisfy the demand for that object. The routing that achieves the minimum MLU of 0.5 to serve the demanded object is shown in the figure. Note that the routing that achieves the MLU of 0.5 is not possible with a simple, unplanned protocol like InverseCap as that would route all the traffic demand from C to A via B, resulting in an MLU of 1. Thus, a (planned) traffic engineering scheme is necessary to achieve an MLU of 0.5.

On the other hand, NCDNs can shape the traffic demand matrix by using a judicious placement and redirection strategy. Suppose that there is some space left in the content server's cache at node B to accommodate an additional copy of the demanded object. By creating an additional copy of the object at B, the traffic demand of A can be satisfied from B and the demand of D from C achieving an MLU of 0.125. In this case, judicious content placement decreased the MLU by a factor of 4. Even more interestingly, this best MLU can be achieved using a simple routing scheme like InverseCap while also improving user-perceived latency (assuming that the latency of link BA is lower than that of the two-hop paths from C to A).

The above toy example suggests benefits to jointly optimizing placement, routing, and redirection, but raises several natural questions. How much additional benefit does such joint optimization offer compared to treating CDN and ISP concerns independently as practiced today? Is the added complexity of joint optimization strategies worth the benefit? Which of the three—placement, routing, and redirection—is the most critical to reducing network cost and user-perceived latency? How sensitive are these findings to characteristics of the content workload (e.g., video vs. download traffic)?

3. NCDN MANAGEMENT STRATEGIES

To answer the above questions, we develop an optimization model for NCDNs to decide placement, routing, and

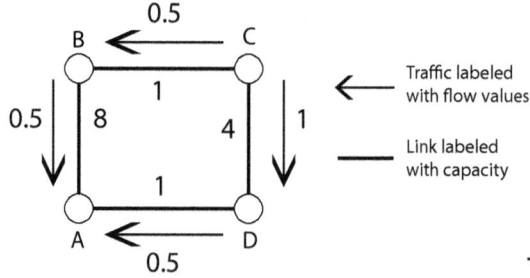

Figure 4: A simple NCDN example

Input variables and descriptions	
V	Set of nodes where each node represents a PoP
E	Set of edges where each link represents a communication link
o	Virtual origin node that hosts all the content in K
X	Set of exit nodes in V
D_i	Disk capacity at node $i \in V$ (in bytes)
C_e	Capacity of link $e \in E$ (in bits/sec)
K	the set of all content accessed by end-users
S_k	Size of content $k \in K$.
T_{ik}	Demand (in bits/sec) at node $i \in V$ for content $k \in K$

Decision variables and descriptions	
α	MLU of the network
z_k	Binary variable indicating whether one or more copies of content k is placed in the network
x_{jk}	Binary variable indicating whether content k is placed at node $j \in V \cup \{o\}$
f_{ij}	Total traffic from node j to node i
f_{ije}	Traffic from node j to node i crossing link e.
t_{ijk}	Traffic demand at node $i \in V$ for content $k \in K$ served from node $j \in V \cup \{o\}$

Table 1: List of input and decision variables for the NCDN problem formulation.

redirection so as to optimize network cost or user-perceived latency. We formulate the optimization problem as a mixed-integer program (MIP), present hardness and inapproximability results, and discuss approximation heuristics to solve MIPs for realistic problem sizes.

3.1 NCDN Model

Table 1 lists all the model parameters. An NCDN consists of a set of nodes V where each node represents a PoP in the network. The nodes are connected by a set of directed edges E that represent the backbone links in the network. The set of content requested by end-users is represented by the set K and the sizes of content are denoted by $S_k, k \in K$. The primary resource constraints are the link capacities $C_e, e \in E$, and the storage at the nodes $D_i, i \in V$. We implicitly assume that the content servers at the PoPs have adequate compute resources to serve locally stored content.

A *content matrix* (CM) specifies the demand for each content at each node. An entry in this matrix, $T_{ik}, i \in V, k \in K$, denotes the demand (in bits/second) for content k at node i. CM is assumed to be measured by the NCDN a priori over a coarse-grained interval, e.g., the previous day. The infrastructure required for this measurement is comparable to what ISPs have in place to monitor traffic matrices today.

Origin servers, owned and maintained by the NCDN's content providers, initially store all content published by content providers. We model origin servers using a single virtual origin node o external to the NCDN that can be reached via a set of exit nodes $X \subset V$ in the NCDN (Figure 2). Since we

are not concerned with traffic engineering links outside the NCDN, we model the edges (x, o), for all $x \in X$, as having infinite capacity. The virtual origin node o always maintains a copy of all the requested content. However, a request for a content is served from the virtual origin node only if no copy of the content is stored at any node $i \in V$. In this case, the request is assumed to be routed to the virtual origin via the exit node closest to the node where the request was made (in keeping with the commonly practiced *early-exit* or *hot potato* routing policy).

ISP networks carry transit traffic in addition to NCDN traffic, which can be represented as a transit traffic matrix (TTM). Each entry in the TTM contains the volume of transit traffic between two PoPs in the network.

3.2 Cost Functions

We evaluate NCDN-management strategies based on two cost functions. The first cost function is maximum link utilization (or MLU) which measures the effectiveness of traffic engineering in an NCDN. MLU is a widely used network cost function for traditional TE.

The second cost function models user-perceived latency and is defined as $\sum_{e \in E} X_e$, where X_e is the product of traffic on link e and its link latency $L(e)$. The latency of a link $L(e)$ is the sum of a fixed propagation delay and a variable utilization dependent delay. For a unit flow, link latency is defined as $L_e(u_e) = p_e(1 + f(u_e))$, where p_e is the propagation delay of edge e, u_e is its link utilization, and $f(u)$ is a piecewise-linear convex function. This cost function is similar to that used by Fortz and Thorup [16]. At small link utilizations (< 0.6), link latency is determined largely by propagation delay hence f is zero. At higher link utilizations (0.9 and above) an increase in queuing delay and delay caused by retransmissions significantly increase the effective link latency. The utilization-dependent delay is modeled as proportional to propagation delay as the impact of (TCP-like) retransmissions is more on paths with longer links. Since L_e is convex, a set of linear constraints can be written to constraint the value of X_e (as in [16]).

3.3 Optimal Strategy as MIP

We present here a joint optimization strategy for NCDN-management formulated as a MIP. This formulation takes as input a content matrix, i.e., the demand for each content at each network point-of-presence (PoP), and computes content placement, request redirection and routing that minimizes an NCDN cost function while respecting link capacity and storage constraints. The decision variables for this problem are listed in Table 1. The MIP to minimize an NCDN cost function C (either MLU or latency) is as follows:

$$\min C \qquad (1)$$

subject to

$$\sum_{j \in V} t_{ijk} + t_{iok} = T_{ik}, \quad \forall k \in K, i \in V \qquad (2)$$

$$\sum_{k \in K} t_{ijk} = f_{ij}, \quad \forall j \in V - X, i \in V \qquad (3)$$

$$\sum_{k \in K} t_{ijk} + \sum_{k \in K} \delta_{ij} t_{iok} = f_{ij}, \quad \forall j \in X, i \in V \qquad (4)$$

where δ_{ij} is 1 if j is the closest exit node to i and 0 otherwise.

Note that δ_{ij} is not a variable but a constant that is determined by the topology of the network, and hence constraint (4) is linear.

$$\sum_{p \in P(l)} f_{ijp} - \sum_{q \in Q(l)} f_{ijq} = \begin{cases} f_{ij} & \text{if } l = i, \\ -f_{ij} & \text{if } l = j, \\ 0 & \text{otherwise}, \end{cases}$$
$$\forall i, j, l \in V \quad (5)$$

where $P(l)$ and $Q(l)$ respectively denote the set of outgoing and incoming links at node l.

$$\sum_{i \in V, j \in V} f_{ije} \leq \alpha \times C_e, \quad \forall e \in E \quad (6)$$

$$\sum_{k \in K} x_{ik} S_k \leq D_i, \quad \forall i \in V \quad (7)$$

$$x_{ok} = 1, \quad \forall k \in K \quad (8)$$

$$\sum_{i \in V} x_{ik} \geq z_k, \quad \forall k \in K \quad (9)$$

$$x_{ik} \leq z_k, \quad \forall k \in K, i \in V \quad (10)$$

$$t_{ijk} \leq x_{jk} T_{ik}, \quad \forall k \in K, i \in V, j \in V \cup \{o\} \quad (11)$$

$$t_{iok} \leq T_{ik}(1 - z_k), \quad \forall k \in K \quad (12)$$

$$x_{jk}, z_k \in \{0, 1\}, \quad \forall j \in V, k \in K$$

$$f_{ije}, t_{ijk}, t_{iok} \geq 0, \quad \forall i, j \in V, e \in E, k \in K$$

The constraints have the following rationale. Constraint (2) specifies that the total traffic demand at each node for each content must be satisfied. Constraints (3) and (4) specify that the total traffic from source j to sink i is the sum over all content k of the traffic from j to i for k. Constraint (5) specifies that the volume of a flow coming in must equal that going out at each node other than the source or the sink. Constraint (6) specifies that the total flow on a link is at most α times capacity. Constraint (7) specifies that the total size of all content stored at a node must be less than its disk capacity. Constraint (8) specifies that all content is placed at the virtual origin node o. Constraints (9) and (10) specify that at least one copy of content k is placed within the network if $z_k = 1$, otherwise $z_k = 0$ and no copies of k are placed at any node. Constraint (11) specifies that the flow from a source to a sink for some content should be zero if the content is not placed at the source (i.e., when $x_{jk} = 0$), and the flow should be at most the demand if the content is placed at the source (i.e., when $x_{jk} = 1$). Constraint (12) specifies that if some content is placed within the network, the traffic from the origin for that content must be zero.

Updating the content placement itself generates traffic and impacts the link utilization in the network. For ease of exposition, we have deferred a formal description of the corresponding constraints to our tech report [32]. Finally, a simple extension to this MIP presented in the tech report [32] jointly optimizes routing given a TTM as well a CM. We have presented a CM-only formulation here as our findings (in §5) show that a joint optimization of the CM and TTM is not useful for NCDNs.

3.4 Computational Hardness

Opt-NCDN is the decision version of the NCDN problem. The proofs for these theorems are presented in Appendix A.

THEOREM 1. *Opt-NCDN is NP-Complete even in the special case where all objects have unit size, and all demands, link capacities, and storage capacities have binary values.*

COROLLARY 1. *Opt-NCDN is inapproximable to within a constant factor unless $P = NP$.*

3.5 Approximation Techniques for MIP

As solving the MIP for very large problem scenarios is computationally infeasible, we use two approximation techniques to tackle such scenarios.

The first is a two-step local search technique. In the first step, we "relax" the MIP by allowing the integral variables x_{jk} and z_k to take fractional values between 0 and 1. This converts an MIP into an LP that is more easily solvable. Note also that the optimal solution of the relaxed LP is a lower bound on the optimal solution of the MIP. However, the LP solution may contain fractional placement of some of the content with the corresponding x_{jk} variables set to fractional values between 0 and 1. However, in our experiments only about 20% of the variables in the optimal LP solution were set to fractional values between 0 or 1, and the rest took integral values of 0 or 1. In the second step, we search for a valid solution for the MIP in the local vicinity of the LP solution by substituting the values for variables that were set to 0 or 1 in the LP solution, and re-solving the MIP for the remaining variables. Since the number of integer variables in the second MIP is much smaller, it can be solved more efficiently than the original MIP.

The second approximation technique reduces the number of unique content in the optimization problem using two strategies. First, we discard the tail of unpopular content prior to optimization. The discarded portion accounts for only 1% of all requests, but reduces the number of content by 50% or more in our traces. Second, we sample 25% of the content from the trace and, in our experiments, select trace entries corresponding only to the sampled content. These approximations reduce the number of content from tens of thousands to under 5000. An MIP of this size can be solved using local search in an hour by a standard LP solver [20] for the ISP topologies in our experiments. To check for any untoward bias introduced by the sampling, we also performed a small number of experiments with the complete trace and verified that our findings remain qualitatively unchanged.

4. AKAMAI CDN TRACES

To conduct a realistic simulation of end-users accessing content on an NCDN, we collected extensive traces of video and download traffic from Akamai as described below.

Video traces. Videos are the primary source of traffic on a CDN and are growing at a rapid rate [27, 11]. Our video trace consists of actual end-users accessing on-demand videos on the Akamai network over multiple days. To make the traces as representative as possible, we chose content providers with a whole range of business models, including major television networks, news outlets, and movie portals. The videos in our traces include a range of video types from short-duration video (less than 10 mins) such as news clips to longer duration (30 min to 120 min) entertainment videos representing TV shows and movies. In all, our anonymized traces represent a nontrivial fraction of the overall traffic on Akamai's media network and accounted for a total of 27 million playbacks of over 85000 videos, 738 TBytes of traffic, served to 6.59 million unique end-users around the

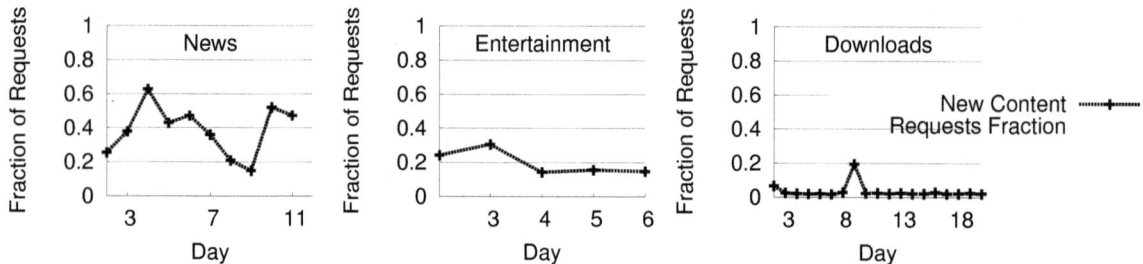

Figure 5: News and entertainment have a significant fraction of requests for new content on all days. Downloads has a small fraction of requests for new content on all days, except one.

US. Since we only had US-based network topologies with accurate link capacity information, we restricted ourselves to US-based traffic.

We collect two sets of anonymized video traces called *news trace* and *entertainment trace* respectively. The news trace was collected from a leading news outlet for an 11-day period in Sept 2011, and consists mostly of news video clips, but also includes a small fraction of news TV shows. The entertainment trace was collected for a 6 day period in January 2012, and includes a variety of videos including TV shows, clips of TV shows, movies and movie trailers from three major content providers.

The trace collection mechanism utilized a plugin embedded in the media player that is capable of reporting (anonymized) video playback information. Our traces include a single log entry for each playback and provides time of access, user id, the location of the user (unique id, city, state, country, latitude, and longitude), the url of the content, the content provider, the total length of the video (in time and bytes), the number of bytes actually downloaded, the playback duration, and the average bitrate over the playback session.

Downloads traces. Downloads of large files over HTTP is also a large large contributor of traffic in a CDN. These include software and security updates, e.g., Microsoft's Windows or Symantec's security updates, as well as music, books, movies, etc.. The large file downloads at Akamai typically use a client-side software called the download manager [28]. We collect extensive and anonymized access data reported from the download manager using Akamai's NetSession interface [4] for a large fraction of content providers for a period of a month (December 2010). Our traces represent a nontrivial fraction of the overall US-based traffic on Akamai's downloads network and accounted for a total of 1.2 million downloads, 717 TBytes of traffic, served to 0.62 million unique end-users around the US. Our traces provide a single log entry for each download and provide time of access, user id, location of the user (city, state, country, latitude, and longitude), the url identifier of the content, content provider, bytes downloaded, and file size.

Figure 5 shows the fraction of requests for new content published each day relative to the previous day for news, entertainment, and downloads traces. The news trace has up to 63% requests due to new content because the latest news clips generated each day are the most popular videos on the website. The entertainment trace also has up to 31% requests each day due to new content such as new episodes of TV shows, and the previews of upcoming TV shows. The downloads trace has only 2-3% requests due to new content on a typical day. However, on the 9th day of the trace major software updates were released, which were downloaded on the same day by a large number of users. Hence, nearly 20%

requests on that day were for new content. The fraction of requests for new content impacts the performance of planned placement strategies as we show §5.

5. EXPERIMENTAL EVALUATION

We conduct trace-driven experiments to compare different NCDN-management strategies. Our high-level goal is to identify a simple strategy that performs well for a variety of workloads. In addition, we seek to assess the relative value of optimizing content placement versus routing; the value of being planned versus being unplanned and the value of future knowledge about demand.

5.1 Trace-driven Experimental Methodology

To realistically simulate end-users accessing content on an NCDN, we combine the CDN traces (in §4) with ISP topologies as follows. We map each content request entry in the Akamai trace to the geographically closest PoP in the ISP topology in the experiment (irrespective of the real ISP that originated the request). Each PoP has a content server as shown in Figure 2, and the request is served locally, redirected to the nearest (by hop-count) PoP with a copy, or to the origin as needed.

ISP topologies. We experimented with network topology maps from two US-based ISPs. First is the actual ISP topology obtained from a large tier-1 ISP in the US (referred to as US-ISP). Second is the Abilene ISP's topology [33].

MLU computation. We compute the traffic that flow through each link periodically. To serve a requested piece of content from a PoP s to t, we update the traffic induced along all edges on the path(s) from s to t as determined by the routing protocol using the bytes-downloaded information in the trace. To compute the MLU, we partition simulation time into 5-minute intervals and compute the average utilization of each link in each 5-minute interval. We discard the values of the first day of the trace in order to warm up the caches, as we are interested in steady-state behavior. We then compute our primary metric, which is the 99-percentile MLU, as the 99th percentile of the link utilization over all links and all 5-minute time periods. We use 99-percentile instead of the maximum as the former is good proxy for the latter but with less experimental noise. Finally, for ease of visualization, we scale the 99-percentile MLU values in all graphs so that the maximum 99-percentile MLU across all schemes in each graph is equal to 1. We call this scaled MLU the *normalized MLU*. Note that only the relative ratios of the MLUs for the different schemes matter and scaling up the MLU uniformly across all schemes is equivalent to uniformly scaling down the network resources or uniformly scaling up the traffic in the CDN traces.

Latency cost computation. Our latency cost metric,

which models user-perceived latencies, is a sum of the latency on ISP backbone links and the the latency from user to its nearest PoP. Traffic served from origin incurs an additional latency from origin to the exit locations in the network. We assume origin servers to be located close to exit locations so that latency from exit locations to origin servers is a small fraction of the overall end user latency. The latency cost of a link e for a interval of a second when traffic (in bits/sec) on link e is V_e and link utilization is u_e, is calculated as $V_e \times L_e(u_e)$, where L_e is the latency function defined in §3. The aggregate latency cost of a link is calculated by summing the latency costs for all 1 sec intervals during the experiment (excluding the first day). The user-to-nearest PoP latency cost is calculated by summing the traffic (in bits) requested by a user times the propagation delay to its nearest PoP for all users.

Storage. We assume that storage is provisioned uniformly across PoPs except in §5.6 where we analyze heterogenous storage distributions. We repeat each simulation with different levels of provisioned storage. Since the appropriate amount of storage depends on the size of the working set of the content being served, we use as a metric of storage the *storage ratio*, or the ratio of total storage at all PoPs in the network to the average storage footprint of all content accessed in a day for the trace. The total storage across all nodes for a storage ratio of 1 is 228 GB, 250 GB, and 895 GB for news, entertainment and downloads respectively.

5.2 Schemes Evaluated

Each evaluated scheme has a content placement component and a routing component.

InvCap-LRU uses LRU as the cache replacement strategy and InverseCap (with ECMP) as the routing strategy. InverseCap is a static, shortest-path routing scheme where link weights are set to the inverse of the link capacity. This scheme requires no information of either the content demand or the traffic matrix. If content is available at multiple PoPs, we choose the PoP with least hop count distance while breaking ties randomly among PoPs with same hop count distance.

We added a straightforward optimization to LRU where if a user terminates the request before 10% of the video (file) is viewed (downloaded), the content is not cached (and the rest of the file is not fetched); otherwise the entire file is downloaded and cached. This optimization is used since we observe in our traces that a user watching a video very often stops watching it after watching the initial period. A similar phenomenon is observed for large file downloads, but less frequently than video.

OptR-LRU uses an unplanned placement, LRU, but it uses an planned, optimized routing that is updated every three hours. The routing is computed by solving a multicommodity flow problem identical to the traditional traffic engineering problem [16]. We assume that the NCDN measures the traffic matrix over the preceding three hours and computes routes that optimize the MLU for that matrix. The matrix incorporates the effect of the unplanned placement and the implicit assumption is that the content demand and unplanned placement result in a traffic matrix that does not change dramatically from one monitoring interval to the next—an assumption that also underlies traffic engineering as practiced by ISPs today.

OptRP computes a joint optimization of placement and

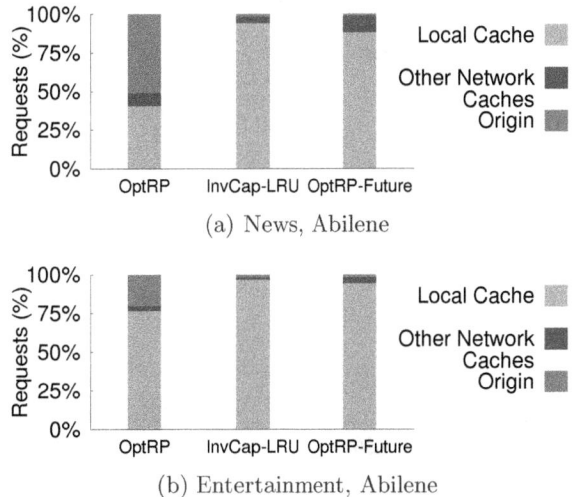

(a) News, Abilene

(b) Entertainment, Abilene

Figure 7: [Videos, Abilene] **OptRP** serves 50% and 21% of news and entertainment requests respectively from the origin. **InvCap-LRU** and **OptRP-Future** serve at most 2% from the origin.

routing once a day based on the previous day's content matrix using the MIP formulation of §3.3. **OptRP-Future** has oracular knowledge of the content matrix for the next day and uses it to calculate a joint optimization of placement, redirection and routing. OptRP and OptRP-Future are identical in all respects except that the former uses the content matrix of the past day while the latter has perfect future knowledge. These two schemes help us understand the value of future knowledge. In practice, it may be possible for an NCDN to obtain partial future knowledge placing it somewhere between the two extremes. For instance, an NCDN is likely to be informed beforehand of a major software release the next day (e.g., new version of the Windows) but may not be able to anticipate a viral video that suddenly gets "hot".

To determine the value of optimizing routing alone, we study the **InvCap-OptP-Future** scheme. This is a variant of OptRP-Future where InverseCap routing is used and content placement is optimized, rather than jointly optimizing both. This scheme is computed using the MIP formulation in §3.3 but with an additional constraint modification that ensures that InvCap routing is implemented.

We add a suffix **-L** to the names of a scheme if it is optimizing for latency cost instead of MLU, e.g. **OptRP-L**.

For all schemes that generate a new placement each day, we implement the new placement during the low-traffic period from 4 AM to 7 AM EST. This ensures that the traffic generated due to changing the content placement occurs when the links are underutilized. For these schemes, the routing is updated each day at 7 AM EST once the placement update is finished.

5.3 Comparison of Network Cost

5.3.1 Analysis of Video & Downloads Traffic

Figure 6 shows the results for the news, entertainment and downloads traces on Abilene and US-ISP. Our first observation is that a realistic planned placement and routing scheme, OptRP, performs significantly worse than a completely unplanned scheme, InvCap-LRU. OptRP has 2.2× to

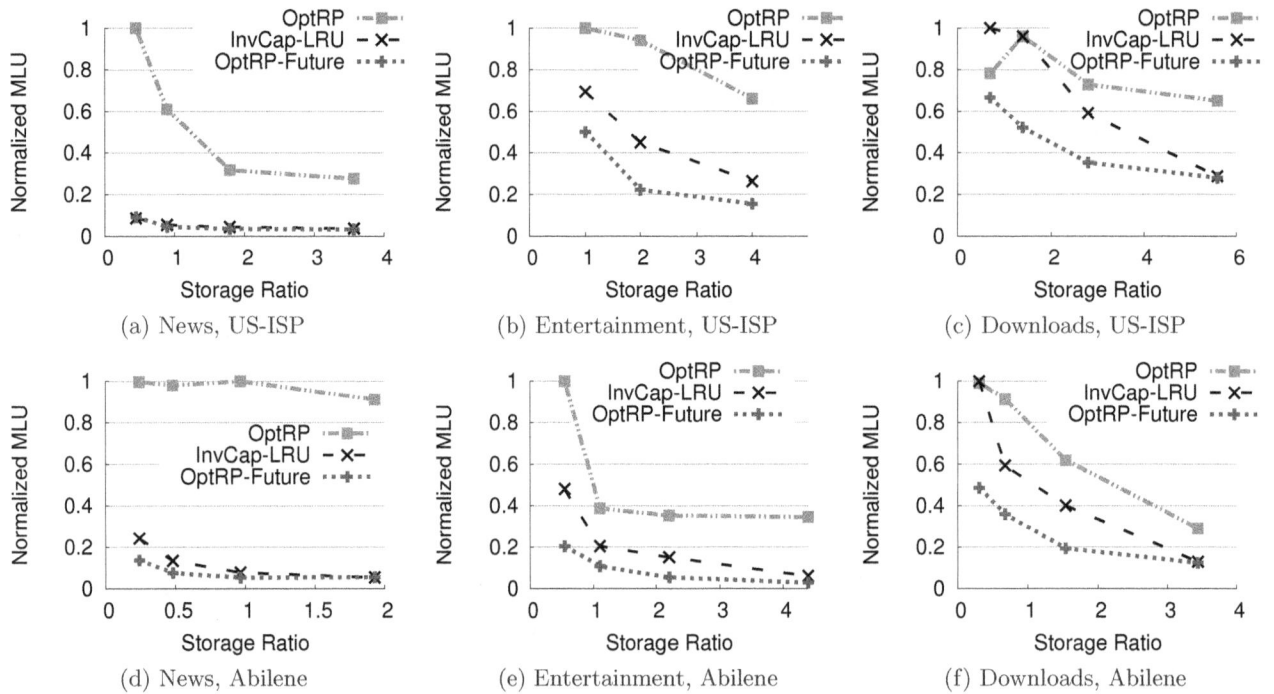

(a) News, US-ISP   (b) Entertainment, US-ISP   (c) Downloads, US-ISP

(d) News, Abilene   (e) Entertainment, Abilene   (f) Downloads, Abilene

Figure 6: Planned **OptRP** performs much worse than unplanned **InvCap-LRU**. **OptRP-Future** performs moderately better than **InvCap-LRU** primarily at small storage ratios.

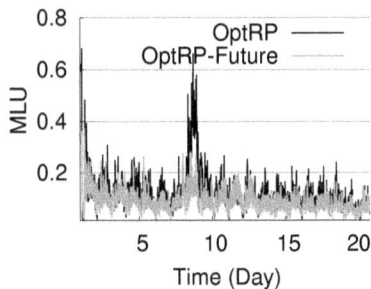

Figure 8: [Downloads, US-ISP] **OptRP** incurs a very high MLU on one "peak load" day.

17× higher MLU than InvCap-LRU even at the maximum storage ratio in each graph. OptRP has a high MLU because it optimizes routing and placement based on the previous day's content demand while a significant fraction of requests are for new content not accessed the previous day (see Figure 5). Due to new content, the incoming traffic from origin servers is significant, so the utilization of links near the exit nodes connecting to the origin servers is extremely high.

The fraction of requests served from the origin is much higher for OptRP compared to InvCap-LRU and OptRP-Future on the news and the entertainment traces. Figure 7 shows that OptRP serves 50% and 21% of requests from the origin for news and entertainment respectively. In comparison, InvCap-LRU and OptRP-Future serve less than 2% of requests from the origin. Therefore, OptRP has a much higher MLU than both InvCap-LRU and OptRP-Future on the two traces.

The downloads trace differs from other traces in that, except for one day, the traffic is quite predictable based on the previous day's history. This is reflected in the performance of OptRP that performs nearly the same as OptRP-Future on

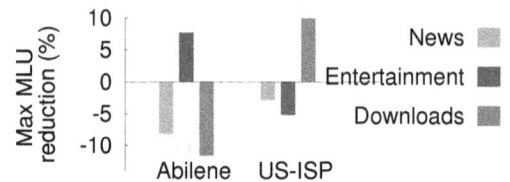

(a) MLU reduction with OptR-LRU compared to InvCap-LRU

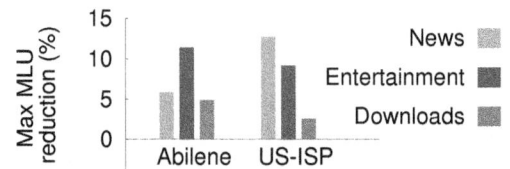

(b) MLU reduction with OptRP-Future compared to InvCap-OptP-Future

Figure 9: [All traces] Optimizing routing yields little improvement to MLU of either **InvCap-LRU** or **InvCap-OptP-Future**

all days except the ninth day of the trace (see Figure 8). The surge in MLU for OptRP on the ninth day is because nearly 20% of requests on this day is for new content consisting of highly popular software update releases (see Figure 5). The surge in MLU on this one day is mainly responsible for the poor performance of OptRP on the downloads trace.

Next, we observe that InvCap-LRU does underperform compared to OptRP-Future that has knowledge of future content demand. However, InvCap-LRU improves with respect to OptRP-Future as the storage ratio increases. The maximum difference between the two schemes is for the experiment

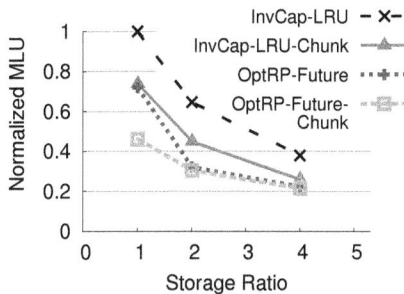

Figure 10: [Entertainment, US-ISP] Content chunking helps bridge the gap between **InvCap-LRU** and **OptRP-Future**.

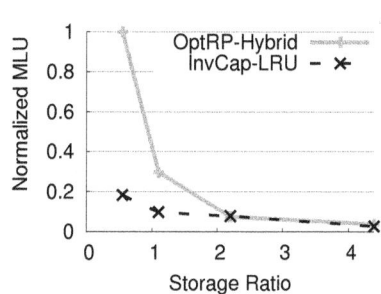

Figure 11: [Entertainment, Abilene] Hybrid placement schemes perform at best as well as **InvCap-LRU**.

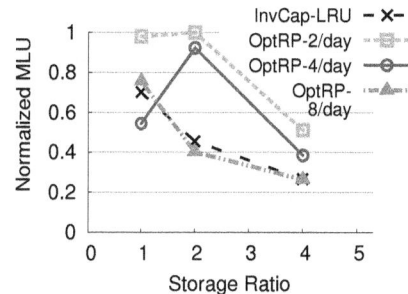

Figure 12: [Entertainment, US-ISP] **OptRP** does not outperform **InvCap-LRU** despite engineering 8 times a day.

with entertainment trace on US-ISP topology. In this case, at a storage ratio of 1, InvCap-LRU has twice the MLU of the OptRP-Future scheme; the difference reduces to 1.6× at a storage ratio of 4. This shows that when storage is scarce, planned placement with future knowledge can significantly help by using knowledge of the global demand to maximize the utility of the storage. However, if storage is plentiful, the relative advantage of OptRP-Future is smaller. An important implication of our results is that an NCDN should attempt to do planned placement only if the future demand can be accurately known or estimated. Otherwise, a simpler unplanned scheme such as LRU suffices.

How are the above conclusions impacted if InvCap-LRU were to optimize routing or OptRP-Future were to use InverseCap routing? To answer this question, we analyze the maximum reduction in MLU by using OptR-LRU over InvCap-LRU across all storage ratios in Figure 9. We similarly compare OptRP-Future and InvCap-OptP-Future. We find that OptR-LRU improves the MLU over InvCap-LRU by at most 10% across all traces suggesting that optimizing routing is of little value for an unplanned placement scheme. OptRP-Future reduces the network cost by at most 13% compared to InvCap-OptP-Future. As we consider OptRP-Future to be the "ideal" scheme with full future knowledge, these results show that the best MLU can be achieved by optimizing content placement alone; optimizing routing adds little additional value.

Why do InvCap-LRU and OptR-LRU have nearly the same network costs? While LRU does greatly reduce traffic due to a high percentage of cache hits, but this is not enough to explain why InvCap achieves nearly the same MLU as optimized routing for the residual traffic, however small. Traffic engineering gives little additional value either because traffic matrices are unpredictable and/or because the NCDN traffic matrices and ISP topologies that we consider do not give much scope for an optimized routing to reduce the MLU over InverseCap routing.

Somewhat counterintuitively, the MLU sometimes increases with a higher storage ratio for the OptRP scheme. There are three reasons that explain this. First, the optimization formulation optimizes for the content matrix assuming that the demand is uniformly spread across the entire day, however the requests may actually arrive in a bursty manner. So it may be sub-optimal compared to a scheme that is explicitly optimized for a known sequence of requests. Second, the optimization formulation optimizes the MLU for the "smoothed" matrix, but the set of objects placed by the optimal strategy with more storage may not necessarily be

a superset of the objects placed by the strategy with lesser storage at any given PoP. Third, and most importantly, the actual content matrix for the next day may differ significantly from that of the previous day. All of these reasons make the so-called "optimal" OptRP strategy suboptimal and in combination are responsible for the nonmonotonicity observed in the experiments.

5.3.2 Content Chunking

Content chunking is widely used today to improve content delivery and common protocols such as HTTP [30] and Apple HLS [5] support content chunking. This experiment analyzes the effect of content chunking on our findings. In these experiments, we split videos into chunks of 5 minute duration. The size of a video chunk depends on the video bitrate. For the downloads trace, we split content into chunks of size 50 MB.

Our results show that although chunking improves performance of both InvCap-LRU and OptRP-Future, it significantly improves the performance of InvCap-LRU relative to OptRP-Future (see Figure 10). Due to chunking, the maximum difference between the MLU of InvCap-LRU and OptRP-Future reduces from 2.5× to 1.4×. At the maximum storage ratio, InvCap-LRU is at most 18% worse compared to OptRP-Future. Our experiments on other traces and topologies (omitted for brevity) show that InvCap-LRU has at most 4% higher network cost than OptRP-Future at the maximum storage ratio. An exception is the news trace, where chunking makes a small difference as more than 95% content is of duration less than our chunk size. Hence, chunking strengthens our conclusion that InvCap-LRU achieves close to the best possible network cost for an NCDN. Even with chunking, OptRP has up to 7× higher MLU compared to InvCap-LRU (not shown in Figure 10). This is because chunking does not help OptRP's primary problem of not being able to adapt effectively to new content, so it continues to incur a high cost.

5.3.3 Alternative Planned Schemes

The experiments so far suggest that a planned scheme that engineers placement and routing once a day based on the previous day's demand performs poorly compared to an unplanned scheme, InvCap-LRU. Hence, in this section, we evaluate the performance of two alternative planned schemes.

First, we evaluate a hybrid placement scheme, which splits the storage at each node into two parts - one for a planned placement based on the previous day's content demand (80% of storage) and the other for placing the content in a unplanned LRU manner (20% of storage). We find that InvCap-

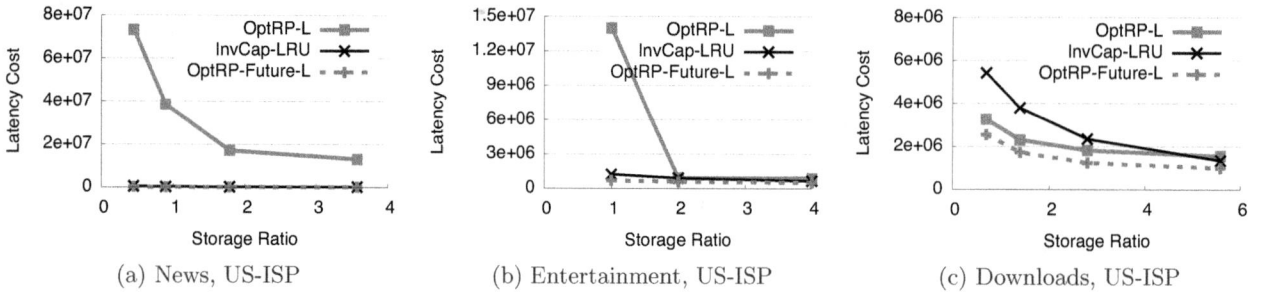

| (a) News, US-ISP | (b) Entertainment, US-ISP | (c) Downloads, US-ISP |

Figure 13: A realistic planned scheme, OptRP-L causes excessively high latency costs in some cases. InvCap-LRU achieves latency costs close to ideal planned scheme, OptRP-Future-L, at higher storage ratios.

LRU performs either as well or better than the hybrid scheme. Assigning a greater fraction of storage to unplanned placement does not change the above conclusions (graph omitted for brevity). Of course, a carefully designed hybrid scheme by definition should perform at least as well as the unplanned and planned schemes, both of which are extreme cases of a hybrid strategy. However, we were unable to design simple hybrid strategies that consistently outperformed fully unplanned placement and routing.

Next, we analyze the performance of planned schemes that engineer placement and routing multiple times each day at equal intervals - twice/day, 4 times/day, and 8 times/day. In all cases, we engineer using the content demand in the past 24 hours. As Figure 12 shows, OptRP needs to engineer 8 times/day to match the performance of the InvCap-LRU scheme. In all other cases, InvCap-LRU performs better. In fact, the experiment shown here represents the best case for OptRP. Typically, OptRP performs worse even when engineering is done 8 times/day, e.g., on the news trace, we find OptRP incurs up to 4.5× higher MLU compared to InvCap-LRU even on engineering 8 times/day.

Executing a planned placement requires considerable effort—measuring content matrix, solving a computationally intensive optimization, and moving content to new locations. Further, a planned placement needs to be executed 8 times a day (or possibly more) even to match the cost achieved by an unplanned strategy. Our position is that NCDNs are better served by opting for a much simpler unplanned strategy and provisioning more storage, in which case, an unplanned strategy already obtains a network cost close to the best a planned strategy can possibly achieve.

5.4 Comparison of Latency Cost

We compare InvCap-LRU scheme, which is a completely unplanned scheme, against OptRP-L and OptRP-Future-L, which optimize latency cost based on previous day's content matrix and based on next day's content matrix respectively.

We experiment with ISP topologies in which links are scaled down uniformly. We needed to scale down the links as our traces did not generate enough traffic to fill even 5% of the capacity of the links during the experiment; ISP networks are unlikely to operate at such small link utilizations. The network topology is scaled such that the 99-percentile MLU for results is 75% link utilization for the InvCap-LRU scheme. This ensures that network has sufficient capacity to support content demand at all storage ratios and network links are not heavily under-utilized.

We present the results of our comparison on the US-ISP topology in Figure 13. Experiments on the Abilene topol-

ogy show qualitatively similar conclusions (graph omitted for brevity). We find that on the news and entertainment traces, OptRP-L scheme results in an order of magnitude higher latency costs. OptRP-L scheme is similar to OptRP scheme except it optimizes latency instead of network cost. Like the OptRP scheme, OptRP-L is unable to predict the popularity of new content resulting in high volume of traffic from origin servers and high link utilization values. OptRP-L either exceeds link capacities or operates close to link capacity for some links which results in very high latencies.

The latency cost of InvCap-LRU relative to OptRP-Future-L improves with an increase in storage ratio. At the smallest storage ratio, InvCap-LRU has 70-110% higher latency cost than OptRP-Future-L. The difference reduces to 14-34% at the maximum storage ratio. Higher storage ratio translate to higher cache hit rates, which reduces propagation delay of transfers and lowers link utilizations. Both these factors contribute to a smaller latency cost for InvCap-LRU. This finding shows that NCDNs can achieve close to best latency costs with an unplanned scheme InvCap-LRU and provisioning moderate amounts of storage.

The performance of OptRP-L on the downloads trace is much closer to OptRP-Future-L than on the other two traces. Unlike other traces, content popularity is highly predictable on the downloads trace based on yesterday's demand, except for a day on which multiple new software releases were done. On all days except one, OptRP-L has nearly optimal latency cost and it incurs a higher latency cost on one day of the trace. As a result, OptRP-L's aggregate latency cost summed over all days is only moderately higher than that of OptRP-Future-L.

5.5 Effect of NCDN Traffic on Network Cost

This experiment, unlike previous experiments, considers a network consisting of both ISP and NCDN traffic. Our goal is to evaluate how network costs change as the fraction of NCDN traffic increases in the network. Second, we seek to examine the benefit of optimizing routing over an unplanned routing scheme, InverseCap. To this end, we compare the performance of InvCap-LRU and OptR-LRU schemes. The latter scheme optimizes routing for the combined traffic matrix due to NCDN traffic and ISP transit traffic. In order to estimate the best gains achievable with an optimized routing, we provide to the OptR-LRU scheme knowledge of future ISP traffic matrices. OptR-LRU cannot be provided the knowledge of future NCDN traffic matrices because NCDN traffic matrices can only be measured from experiment itself and we do not know them beforehand. We optimize rout-

238

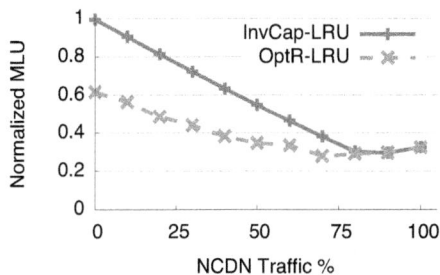

Figure 14: [News, US-ISP] Network costs at varying fractions of NCDN traffic in an ISP network.

ing once a day in this experiment. Varying the frequency of routing update did not improve OptR-LRU's performance.

We experiment with hourly transit traffic matrices spanning 7 days from the same Tier-1 ISP — US-ISP. These matrices were collected in February, 2005. Since ISP traffic volumes are much higher than NCDN traffic volumes, at first, we performed this experiment by scaling down the ISP traffic matrices, so that ISP and NCDN traffic have comparable volumes. Of the total NCDN traffic, less than 10% reaches the backbone links, rest is served locally by PoPs. For equal volumes of NCDN and ISP traffic we expected the MLU of a network with ISP traffic only to be much higher than MLU for the network with only NCDN traffic. Our experiment showed that MLU for ISP traffic and NCDN traffic are nearly the same.

We found that this was because the NCDN traffic showed highly variable link utilization even over the course of a few minutes: the maximum link utilization differed by up to 3× in the course of 15 minutes. The hourly ISP traffic matrix that we experimented with retained the same, smoothed utilization level for an hour. As a result, 99-percentile MLU's for NCDN traffic are the same as that for ISP even though its aggregate backbone traffic was much lesser.

To make the variability of NCDN traffic comparable to ISP traffic, we scaled up the volume of NCDN traffic. The scaling is done by introducing new content similar to a randomly chosen content in the original trace. Each new content is of the same size, and same video bit rate as the original content. All requests for the new content are made from the same locations, at approximately the same times (within an 1-hour window of the request of the original content), and are of the same durations as the requests for the original content. Our scaling preserves the popularity distribution of objects and the geographic and temporal distribution of requests. We scaled our trace to the maximum level so as to not exceed the memory available (8 GB) in our machine.

We present the results of our experiments on the news trace in Figure 14. We vary the fraction of NCDN to ISP traffic, and report MLUs normalized by the total volume of ISP and NCDN traffic. Our results are not independent of the scale of simulations: a larger or a smaller scaling of CDN trace may give quantitatively different conclusions. Hence, we only make qualitative conclusions from this experiment. First, we find that as the fraction of NCDN traffic increases, MLU decreases for both schemes. This is intuitive since a large fraction of NCDN traffic is served from caches located at PoPs. Second, as NCDN traffic increases optimizing routing (OptR-LRU) gives lesser benefits compared to InverseCap routing. In a network dominated by NCDN traffic, optimizing routing gives almost no benefits over InvCap-LRU. We

find these results to be consistent with our earlier experiments with NCDN traffic only.

5.6 Other Results and Implications

We summarize our main conclusions from the rest of our experiments here and refer the reader to our tech report [32] for a complete description of these experiments:

Link-utilization aware redirection: We evaluate a request redirection strategy for InvCap-LRU that periodically measures link utilizations in the network and prefers less loaded paths while redirecting requests. Our evaluation shows that such a redirection gives small benefits in terms of network cost (7% − 13%) and gives almost no benefits on latency costs. This implies that sophisticated network-aware redirection strategies may be of little value for an NCDN.

Request redirection to neighbors: If each PoP redirects requests only to its one-hop neighbor PoPs before redirecting to the origin, InvCap-LRU incurs only a moderate (6%-27%) increase in the MLU. However, if a PoP redirects to no other PoPs but redirects only to the origin, the MLU for InvCap-LRU increases significantly (25%-100%). Thus, request redirection to other PoPs helps reduce network cost, but most of this reduction can be had by redirecting only to neighboring PoPs.

Heterogenous storage: Heterogenous storage at PoPs (storage proportional to the number of requests at a PoP in a trace, and other simple heuristics) increases the MLU compared to homogenous storage for both InvCap-LRU and OptRP-Future, and makes InvCap-LRU more sub-optimal compared to OptRP-Future. This leads us to conclude that our results above with homogeneous storage are more relevant to practical settings.

Number of caches: If caches are deployed on all PoPs, MLU is significantly lower compared to scenarios when caches are deployed only at a fraction of PoPs; the total storage across PoPs is same in all scenarios. This suggests that NCDNs should deploy caches at all PoPs to minimize MLU.

OptR-LRU parameters: Whether OptR-LRU updates routing at faster timescales (every 15 minutes, or 30 minutes) or slower timescales (6 hours, or 24 hours) than the default update interval of 3 hours, its performance is nearly the same. Further, whether OptR-LRU optimizes routing using traffic matrix measured over the immediately preceding three hours (default) or using traffic matrices measured the previous day, its network cost remains nearly unchanged. This reinforces our finding that optimizing routing gives minimal improvement over InvCap-LRU.

Number of exit nodes: When the number of network exit nodes is increased to five or decreased to one, our findings in §5.3.1 remain qualitatively unchanged.

Link failures: The worst-case network cost across all single link failures for InvCap-LRU as well as OptRP-Future is approximately twice compared to their network costs during a failure-free scenario. Comparing the failure-free scenario and link failure scenarios, the relative sub-optimality of InvCap-LRU with respect to OptRP-Future remains the same at small storage ratios but reduces at higher ratios.

6. LIMITATIONS AND FUTURE WORK

Our experimental methodology suffers from some shortcomings. First, we assume that servers deployed at each PoP have enough resources to serve users requests for locally cached content. In cases when server resources are inadequate, e.g., due to flash crowds, a simple redirection strategy, e.g., redirection to the closest hop-count server used by InvCap-LRU, may result in poor user-perceived performance. In practice, NCDNs should adopt a redirection strategy that takes server load into account to handle variability of user demands. Second, we measure latency using a utility-based cost function that can be efficiently computed using flow-level simulations. An evaluation of end-user perceived metrics, e.g., TCP throughput, would be more convincing, but requires a measurement-based evaluation or a packet-level simulation. A measurement-based evaluation requires network and server infrastructure similar to an NCDN, which is beyond our resources. Even packet-level simulations become extremely time consuming at the scale of an ISP network, which we observed in an earlier work [31]. Third, the latency comparison is done for large, static objects and is not generalizable to dynamic content and small objects. We defer addressing these concerns to future work.

Another open question is whether our conclusions are generalizable for other topologies and workloads. For instance, our preliminary analysis with a synthetic workload trace (included in [32]) suggests that the InvCap-LRU scheme may not give the close to optimal costs in all scenarios. An evaluation of relative performance of schemes for general topologies and workloads would be considered in our future work.

7. RELATED WORK

Traffic engineering and content distribution have both seen an enormous body of work over more than a decade. To our knowledge, our work is the first to consider the NCDN problem, wherein a single entity seeks to address both concerns, and empirically evaluate different placement, routing, and redirection strategies.

Joint optimization: Recent work has explored the joint optimization of traffic engineering and "content distribution", where the latter term refers to the *server selection* problem. P4P (Xie et al. [38]) shows that P2P applications can improve their performance and ISPs can reduce the MLU and interdomain costs, if P2P applications adapt their behavior based on hints supplied by ISPs. Jiang et al. [21] and DiPalantino et al. [14] both study the value of joint optimization of traffic engineering and content distribution versus independent optimization of each. CaTE (Frank at al. [18]), like P4P, shows that a joint optimization can help both ISPs and content providers improve their performance. Valancius et al. [34] propose a system which helps online service providers choose the best server replica for each client considering multiple server replicas and multiple network paths to each replica. Further, they quantify the benefit of this "joint routing" approach over "content routing", i.e., choosing best replica with only a single path to each replica, and over "network routing", i.e., choosing best path to an unreplicated server among multiple paths. Xu et al. [39] study a similar problem. These works equate content distribution to server selection (or request redirection in our parlance), while the NCDN problem additionally considers content placement itself as a degree of freedom. We find that the freedom to place content is powerful enough that even unplanned placement and routing strategies suffice to achieve close to best latency and network costs for NCDNs, making joint optimization of content distribution and traffic engineering unnecessary.

Placement optimization: In the context of CDNs, many variants of content or service placement problems have been studied [29, 25, 12, 23]. A recent work is that of Applegate et al. [6], who study the content placement problem for a VoD system that seeks to minimize the aggregate network bandwidth consumed. However, they assume a *fixed routing* in the network, while one of our contributions is to assess the relative importance of optimizing routing and optimizing placement in an NCDN.

Furthermore, they find that an optimized, planned placement with a small local cache (similar to our "hybrid" strategy in §5.3.3) outperforms LRU. In contrast, our experiments suggest otherwise. There are three explanations for this disparity. First, their workload seems to be predictable even at weekly time scales, whereas the Akamai CDN traces that we use show significant daily churn. Second, their scheme has some benefit of future knowledge and is hence somewhat comparable to our OptRP-Future. For a large NCDN, obtaining knowledge about future demand may not be practical for all types of content, e.g., breakout news videos. Finally, our analysis suggests that LRU performs sub-optimally only at small storage ratios, and the difference between LRU and OptRP-Future reduces considerably at higher storage ratios (not considered in [6]).

Traffic engineering: Several classes of traffic engineering schemes such as OSPF link-weight optimization [16], MPLS flow splitting [15], optimizing routing for multiple traffic matrices [37, 40], online engineering [22, 15], and oblivious routing [7, 9], have been studied. All of these schemes assume that the demand traffic is a given to which routing must adapt. However, we find that an NCDN is in a powerful position to change the demand traffic matrix, so much so that even a naive scheme like InverseCap, i.e., no engineering at all, suffices in conjunction with a judicious placement strategy and optimizing routing further adds little value. In this respect, our findings are comparable in spirit to Sharma et al. [31]. However, they focus on the impact of location diversity, and show that even a small, fixed number of randomly placed replicas of each content suffice to blur differences between different engineering schemes with respect to a capacity metric (incomparable to MLU), but find that engineering schemes still outperform InverseCap.

8. CONCLUSIONS

We posed and studied the NCDN-mangament problem where content distribution and traffic engineering decisions can be optimized jointly by a single entity. Our trace-driven experiments using extensive access logs from the world's largest CDN and real ISP topologies resulted in the following key conclusions. First, simple unplanned schemes for routing and placement of NCDN content, such as InverseCap and LRU, outperform sophisticated, joint-optimal placement and routing schemes based on recent historic demand. Second, NCDN traffic demand can be "shaped" by effective content placement to the extent that the value of engineering routes for NCDN traffic is small. Third, we studied the value of the future knowledge of demand for placement and routing decisions. While future knowledge helps, what is perhaps surprising is that a small amount of additional storage allows simple, unplanned schemes to perform as well as planned ones with future knowledge. Finally, with a mix of NCDN and transit traffic, the benefit of traditional traffic engineering is commensurate to the fraction of traffic that is transit traffic, i.e., ISPs dominated by NCDN traffic can simply make do with static routing schemes. Overall, our findings suggest that content placement is a powerful degree of freedom that NCDNs can leverage to simplify and enhance traditional traffic engineering.

9. ACKNOWLEDGEMENTS

We sincerely thank our shepherd Richard Ma and the anonymous reviewers for their feedback. This research was supported by following grants from National Science Foundation: CNS-0845855, CNS-0917078, and CNS-1040781. We thank S. Shunmuga Krishnan, Yin Lin, and Bruce M. Maggs for their help with the Akamai trace data collection. Any opinions expressed in this work are solely those of the authors and not necessarily those of National Science Foundation or Akamai Technologies.

10. REFERENCES

[1] Akamai Licensed CDN. http://www.akamai.com/html/solutions/aura_licensed_cdn.html.
[2] Akamai Managed CDN. http://www.akamai.com/html/solutions/aura_managed_cdn.html.
[3] Akamai, AT&T strike deal for content delivery services, December 2012. http://www.marketwatch.com/story/akamai-att-strike-deal-for-cdn-services-2012-12-06.
[4] Akamai NetSession Interface. http://www.akamai.com/client.
[5] Apple. HTTP Live Streaming. http://bit.ly/MgoUED.
[6] D Applegate, A Archer, V Gopalakrishnan, S Lee, and K K Ramakrishnan. Optimal content placement for a large-scale VoD system. In Co-NEXT, 2010.
[7] D Applegate and E Cohen. Making routing robust to changing traffic demands: algorithms and evaluation. IEEE/ACM Trans. Netw., 14:1193–1206, December 2006.
[8] AT&T. Content Distribution, 2011. http://bit.ly/Lefgj2.
[9] Y Azar, E Cohen, A Fiat, H Kaplan, and H Racke. Optimal oblivious routing in polynomial time. In STOC, 2003.
[10] Edge Cast. EdgeCast Licensed CDN. http://www.edgecast.com/solutions/licensed-cdn/.
[11] Cisco. Visual Networking Index, 2011. http://bit.ly/KXDUaX.
[12] R Cohen and G Nakibly. A traffic engineering approach for placement and selection of network services. IEEE/ACM Trans. Netw., 2009.
[13] J. Dilley, B. Maggs, J. Parikh, H. Prokop, R. Sitaraman, and B. Weihl. Globally distributed content delivery. Internet Computing, IEEE, 6(5):50–58, 2002.
[14] D DiPalantino and R Johari. Traffic Engineering vs. Content Distribution: A Game Theoretic Perspective. In INFOCOM, 2009.
[15] A Elwalid, C Jin, S Low, and I Widjaja. MATE: MPLS adaptive traffic engineering. In INFOCOM, 2001.
[16] B Fortz and M Thorup. Internet traffic engineering by optimizing OSPF weights. In INFOCOM, 2000.
[17] B Fortz and M Thorup. Optimizing ospf/is-is weights in a changing world. JSAC, May 2002.
[18] B Frank, I Poese, G Smaragdakis, S Uhlig, and A Feldmann. Content-aware traffic engineering. In SIGMETRICS, 2012.
[19] HP. The edge of bandwidth growth. http://bit.ly/HwXtUO.
[20] IBM. ILOG CPLEX. http://ibm.co/KRuqhB.
[21] W Jiang, R Zhang-Shen, J Rexford, and M Chiang. Cooperative content distribution and traffic engineering in an ISP network. In SIGMETRICS, 2009.
[22] S Kandula, D Katabi, B Davie, and A Charny. Walking the tightrope: responsive yet stable traffic engineering. In SIGCOMM, 2005.
[23] Chip Killian, Michael Vrable, Alex C. Snoeren, Amin Vahdat, and Joseph Pasquale. The overlay network content distribution problem. In In Technical Report CS2005-0824, UCSD, 2005.
[24] Level3. Content Delivery Network, 2011. http://bit.ly/LvsIDm.
[25] F. Lo Presti, C. Petrioli, and C. Vicari. Distributed dynamic replica placement and request redirection in content delivery networks. In In MASCOTS, 2007.
[26] Streaming Media. Telco-CDN Whitepapers. http://bit.ly/GUDrUZ.
[27] Nielsen. Online Video Usage Up 45%. http://bit.ly/MiXiPU.
[28] E Nygren, R K Sitaraman, and J Sun. The Akamai network: a platform for high-performance internet applications. SIGOPS Oper. Syst. Rev., August 2010.
[29] Lili Qiu, V.N. Padmanabhan, and G.M. Voelker. On the placement of web server replicas. In In INFOCOM, 2001.
[30] RFC. 2616. http://www.ietf.org/rfc/rfc2616.txt.
[31] A Sharma, A Mishra, V Kumar, and A Venkataramani. Beyond MLU: An application-centric comparison of traffic engineering schemes. In INFOCOM, 2011.
[32] A Sharma, A Venkataramani, and R Sitaraman. Distributing Content Simplifies ISP Traffic Engineering. UMASS CS Technical Report. UM-CS-2012-002. https://web.cs.umass.edu/publication/docs/2012/UM-CS-2012-002.pdf.
[33] Abilene Topology. http://bit.ly/Lf8k7a.
[34] Vytautas Valancius, Bharath Ravi, Nick Feamster, and Alex C. Snoeren. Quantifying the benefits of joint content and network routing. In In SIGMETRICS, 2013.
[35] Verizon. HBO for FIOS Customers. http://bit.ly/JQ2dn8.
[36] Verizon. Velocix at Verizon, 2011. http://bit.ly/LlqGn3.
[37] H Wang, H Xie, L Qiu, Y R Yang, Y Zhang, and A Greenberg. COPE: Traffic Engineering in Dynamic Networks. In SIGCOMM, 2006.
[38] H Xie, Y R Yang, A Krishnamurthy, Y G Liu, and A Silberschatz. P4P: Provider Portal for Applications. In SIGCOMM, 2008.
[39] Hong Xu and Baochun Li. Joint request mapping and response routing for geo-distributed cloud services. In In INFOCOM, 2013.
[40] C Zhang, Y Liu, W Gong, J Kurose, R Moll, and D Towsley. On optimal routing with multiple traffic matrices. In INFOCOM, 2005.

APPENDIX

A. COMPLEXITY OF NCDN PROBLEM

Opt-NCDN is the decision version of the NCDN problem (§3). Opt-NCDN asks if the MLU of the network can be α while satisfying the constraints of the problem.

THEOREM 1 *Opt-NCDN is NP-Complete even in the special case where all objects have unit size, all demands, and link and storage capacities have binary values.*

Proof: We show a reduction from the well known SetCover problem defined as follows. **SetCover**: Let $S = \{1, 2, ..., n\}$ be a set of n elements. Let $X = \{S_1, ..., S_m\}$ where $S_i \subseteq S, 1 \le i \le m$. Let k be an integer. SetCover asks if there exists $Y = \{Y_1, ..., Y_k\}$, where $Y_k \in X$ and $Y_1 \cup ... \cup Y_k = S$. Set Y is called a set cover of size k.

The reduction from SetCover to Opt-NCDN is described using the network in Figure 15. Set $V_1 = \{1, ..., m\}$ refers to nodes in the top row. Each node $i \in V_1$ maps to the set $S_i \subset S$. Set $V_2 = \{1, ..., n\}$ refers to nodes in the bottom row excluding node s. Each node $i \in V_2$ maps to element $i \in S$. Node s is called a special node.

Directed links (i, j) exist from all nodes $i \in V_1$ to all nodes $j \in V_2$. The capacity of (i, j) is 1 unit if $i \in S_j$, otherwise capacity is zero. Node s has incoming links (i, s) from all nodes $i \in V_1$ such that the capacity of all incoming links is 1 unit. All nodes in the top row V_1 have unit storage whereas nodes in the bottom row $V_2 \cup \{s\}$ have zero storage.

The set of objects is $\{o, 1, 2, ..., (m - k)\}$ and all objects have unit size. Object o is a special object that has unit demand at nodes in set $V_2 = \{1, ..., n\}$ and zero demand at all other nodes. Objects 1, 2, .. $(m - k)$ have unit demand at special node s and zero demand at all other nodes.

CLAIM: There is a set cover of size k if and only if the above network can achieve MLU ≤ 1.

If there is a set cover of size k, then the network can achieve MLU of 1. Store the special object o at the k set cover locations in the top row and satisfy demand for o at

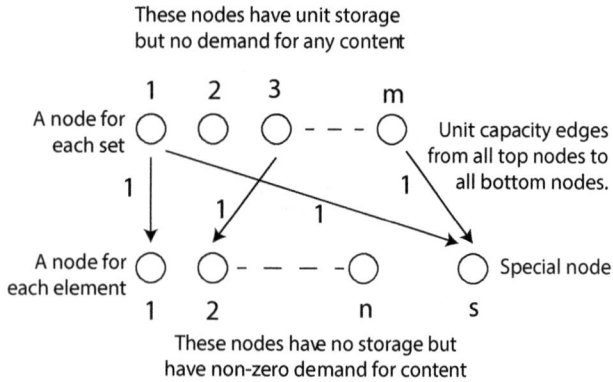

These nodes have unit storage
but no demand for any content

A node for each set

Unit capacity edges
from all top nodes to
all bottom nodes.

A node for each element

Special node

These nodes have no storage but
have non-zero demand for content

Figure 15: Reduction from SetCover to Opt-NCDN

nodes $V_2 = \{1, ..., n\}$ in the bottom row from these locations with MLU = 1. The remaining $(m - k)$ nodes in the top can be used for objects $\{1, 2, ..., (m - k)\}$ to satisfy the demand at special node s with MLU of 1.

If there is no set cover of size k, then the network must have a MLU > 1. Objects must be placed in some $(m - k)$ nodes in the node $V_1 = \{1, ..., m\}$ in the top row to satisfy the demand for special node s. Thus, at most k nodes are available for placing special object o. Since there is no set cover of size k, some bottom node $i \in V_2$ must satisfy its demand for special object o using an edge whose capacity is zero resulting in MLU $= \infty$ on that edge.

It is easy to show that Opt-NCDN $\in$ NP. Hence, Opt-NCDN is NP-Complete.

THEOREM 2 *Opt-NCDN is inapproximable within a factor β for any $\beta > 1$ unless $P = NP$.*

The proof of THEOREM 1 shows that if there is a set cover of size k, MLU = 1 and MLU $= \infty$ otherwise. Thus, if we find a solution for which MLU is finite, it implies that MLU = 1, which immediately gives a solution to the corresponding SetCover instance.

Lets assume a β-approximation ($\beta > 1$) exists for Opt-NCDN. Then, we can solve SetCover in polynomial time by mapping SetCover instance to Opt-NCDN instance, and checking if MLU $\leq \beta$ (which implies MLU = 1). As SetCover $\in$ NP-Complete, therefore, no β-approximation for Opt-NCDN exists unless P = NP.

Quantifying the Benefits of Joint Content and Network Routing

Vytautas Valancius, Bharath Ravi, Nick Feamster, and Alex C. Snoeren[†]
Georgia Tech and [†]UC San Diego

ABSTRACT

Online service providers aim to provide good performance for an increasingly diverse set of applications and services. One of the most effective ways to improve service performance is to replicate the service closer to the end users. Replication alone, however, has its limits: while operators can replicate static content, wide-scale replication of dynamic content is not always feasible or cost effective. To improve the latency of such services many operators turn to Internet traffic engineering. In this paper, we study the benefits of performing replica-to-end-user mappings in conjunction with active Internet traffic engineering. We present the design of PECAN, a system that controls both the selection of replicas ("content routing") and the routes between the clients and their associated replicas ("network routing"). We emulate a replicated service that can perform both content and network routing by deploying PECAN on a distributed testbed. In our testbed, we see that jointly performing content and network routing can reduce round-trip latency by 4.3% on average over performing content routing alone (potentially reducing service response times by tens of milliseconds or more) and that most of these gains can be realized with no more than five alternate routes at each replica.

Categories and Subject Descriptors

D.2.0 [**Computer-Communication Networks**]: General

Keywords

Wide-area routing, CDN

1. INTRODUCTION

Online service providers (OSPs) such as Facebook and Google are offering an increasingly diverse set of interactive online services ranging from social networking services to online productivity tools. Consumers expect these services to be responsive, and OSPs are continually implementing optimizations to improve their performance with significant impact to their bottom lines. Google research showed that a 500-millisecond increase in latency caused

a 20% traffic drop [8], while it was reported that a latency increase of 100 milliseconds can produce a 1% drop in revenue for Amazon [28]. Accordingly, recent years have seen many optimizations to accelerate the delivery of such services, ranging from better transport protocols [40] to browser enhancements [4, 7] to new compression and site optimization algorithms [1, 17].

One of the most common and effective ways to improve the performance of an online service is to decrease the path latency between the service and its clients by replicating the service at many geographic locations. Operators of replicated online services continually map clients to the data center that offers the best end-to-end service performance; this process is called *content routing*. Thanks to content distribution networks (*e.g.*, Akamai and Limelight), replication and content routing are prevalent for static content, but replicating full-featured Web-service logic that generates dynamic content can be difficult and costly, and, as a result, large-scale replication is not always feasible. Indeed, even the most popular Web service providers often host back-end logic at only a handful of sites. For example, Facebook serves all dynamic content from only four data centers, and Amazon serves its EC2-based properties from seven.

On the other hand, past work on detour routing [37], overlay routing [13], and multi-homing [10–12] suggests that the default wide-area Internet path between a client and any given service replica may be suboptimal: Network operators may be able to optimize the *network routing* at each replica site to improve performance. In practice, however, network operators have little visibility into the performance that a given replica would offer to a particular client or set of clients. The operations teams that perform network and content routing are often distinct, and frequently do not coordinate with one another [26]. The operators of major OSPs that we surveyed stated that their service-replica operators and network operators have only limited cooperation, and they do not attempt to reap the benefits of jointly optimizing content and network routing. Client performance suffers from this lack of coordination: operators of service replicas currently have no visibility into the performance or cost of alternate network paths between a service replica and its clients, so they optimize replica mapping based upon the current network paths that have been exposed as a result of network operators' traffic engineering optimizations. On the other hand, network operators, who do have access to alternate wide-area paths, have little insight into the application-level performance these alternate paths might provide.

To bridge this divide, we design and evaluate PECAN (Performance Enhancements with Content And Network routing), a system that performs joint content and network routing for dynamic online services. PECAN enables joint content and network routing for online services by augmenting an OSP's existing content routing framework to provide a diverse set of wide-area routes between each interactive service replica and its clients. To ensure that PECAN does not harm the performance of any existing service, it explores alternate wide-area routes using separate IP prefixes; clients can always reach the online service either via the default wide-area Internet routes or via PECAN's routes.

We measure the performance benefits that PECAN can achieve in practice by emulating an online service provider's infrastructure. We place service replicas at the Transit Portal (TP) locations [6] and clients at nodes in the PlanetLab testbed. TP allows us to emulate an OSP with a five geographically diverse, U.S.-based points-of-presence (PoPs), each of which provides access to many alternate wide-area paths to clients. There are many ways to measure performance. One metric is Web page load time, but accurately measuring page load time is challenging, as it requires instrumenting each client with browser software—a difficult task for a large-scale measurement study. Instead, we focus on network latency (i.e., round trip time), because many online service providers have identified latency as a key factor governing a user's experience [18, 34].

Using three months of data from our testbed, we find that, when compared to performing content routing alone, using *joint routing* improves performance for about 35% of clients. Moreover, over 20% benefit directly from joint content and network routing: they achieve better performance by employing an alternate route to a different replica than they would have selected if only generically optimized default routes were available. In our experiments, we find that applying content routing alone decreases service latency by 16.75% on average relative to an optimally placed non-replicated service. Joint routing delivers an additional 4.3% (or about 5 ms) average round-trip latency reduction over performing content routing alone, which may translate to at least tens of milliseconds of reduction in Web page load time [41]. Of course, the performance benefits from replication will depend on the replicas' locations, but our results show that—especially for services that are difficult to replicate widely—PECAN can offer tangible benefits. The ability of an OSP to extract these gains will vary according to the techniques employed to explore alternate network routes.

We make several contributions. First, we perform (and publicly release) millions of performance measurements over three months on a globally distributed testbed that emulates an online service provider network, to evaluate the benefits that joint content and network routing could offer to online services in practice. Although we focus on latency, we also quantify PECAN's benefits for throughput and jitter. Second, we decompose the performance results by studying how content routing and network routing alone reduce network latency on our testbed. Finally, we have developed and deployed a prototype implementation of PECAN, which we describe in Section 3.

2. STATE OF THE ART

We begin by providing an overview of both content routing and network routing as employed by online service providers today. We first describe the state of the art, as best as we can determine through discussions with network operators and online service providers. We then explain in more detail the challenges operators face in jointly performing wide-area network routing and content routing.

2.1 Content Routing

Content routing refers to the process of selecting which replica among a geographically distributed set should service a particular request. Content in the context of this work refers to both static content and interactive services. Content routing systems have been

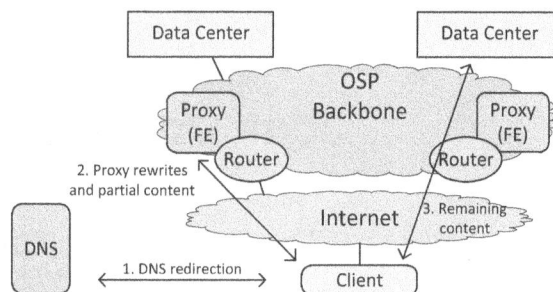

Figure 1: *Directing clients to replicas. Some services rely only on DNS; other services can use proxies for HTTP redirects and client-specific HTML rewriting.*

heavily influenced by academic research, which we overview in Section 7. Today's content routing systems deployed in practice perform three major functions: 1) collecting performance information, 2) mapping clients to replicas, and 3) directing clients to replicas according to the client-replica map.

Step 1: Collecting performance information. OSPs use many technologies to measure performance between online service replicas and their clients. Such measurements can be classified into *active*, *passive*, and *indirect*. Active measurements usually involve sending probes from replicas to clients (or *v.v.*), which provide direct information about the network performance to the client. Active measurements are problematic in at least two ways: 1) the probes might not be handled by the network in the same way the actual traffic is handled, and 2) active measurements do not scale to a large number of replicas and customers [22]. For these two reasons, OSPs typically prefer to use a combination of passive and indirect measurements.

Passive measurements record the performance of the actual online service traffic between the replica and the clients. Passive measurements scale well and can provide direct insight into the performance of a service over the network by recording information such as TCP round-trip times and packet loss. To measure performance for all <client, replica> pairs, OSPs randomly redirect a small fraction of their clients' requests to alternate replicas [38].

To map clients to replicas when no active or passive measurements are available to inform selection, OSPs often resort to indirect inference of the likely performance between replicas and clients. Commercial IP geo-location databases [29] are often augmented with historical information to estimate performance between replicas and clients. As new clients begin to use the system, the OSP can update indirectly inferred performance estimates with passive measurements.

Step 2: Mapping clients to replicas. OSPs use a variety of proprietary algorithms to map clients to replicas. Client-to-replica performance is important, but there are other inputs to the algorithms that produce these mappings as well, including service availability, servicing costs, desired load, and regulatory restrictions [45]. We focus strictly on the performance aspects of the mapping and leave potential interactions with such policy constraints to future work.

Step 3: Directing clients to replicas. OSPs use three main techniques to implement their client-to-replica mapping: 1) DNS-based redirection, 2) HTTP redirection, and 3) client-tailored HTML rewriting. DNS mapping uses DNS servers to respond to clients with IP addresses of best replicas. ("Clients" in this case most often are the DNS resolvers resolving names on behalf of the end-systems.) DNS mapping is most useful to improve the performance of initial resource requests. HTTP redirection can further redirect clients to a better replica (at a cost of initial request latency.) When the requested resource has multiple sub-components (*e.g.*, a Web page with images), the OSP can use client-tailored HTML rewriting to direct clients to retrieve sub-components from disparate replicas. Figure 1 shows an example a system which can perform content routing with both DNS-based direction and proxy-based redirection (*e.g.*, with a front end (FE) that rewrites URLs). In this study, we do not distinguish between the different ways that a network operator might perform content routing; we merely assume that an OSP can map clients to replicas in at least one of these ways.

2.2 Network Routing

Network routing refers to the process of selecting a network path that service replica will use to communicate a client. In this work we focus on the inter-domain routing where OSP has to choose wide-area paths between a service replicas at its edge PoPs and remote clients. We identify three types of approaches OSPs take to optimize wide-area routing: 1) long-term capacity planning and network build-out; 2) medium-term planning and execution of routing policy changes; and, in rare occasions, 3) deployment of off-the-shelf commercial platforms or services that enable near-real-time adjustments to inter-domain routing policies in reaction to changes in wide-area network conditions. We discuss each of these approaches below.

Long-term network planning. Large OSPs improve the performance of their interactive services by deploying their own networks and increasing the richness of their peering connections. OSPs must pick locations to build new PoPs and choose the strategy in pursuing peering, paid-peering, and provider connectivity. The variables OSPs consider include: cost of a new PoP, cost of backbone connectivity to the new PoP, the choice of peers and providers that can connect in the PoP, the customer base that will be served by the PoP, the benefit in terms of latency, throughput, or traffic cost reduction that the PoP will bring, *etc.*.

Medium-term planning and execution of routing policy changes. OSPs monitor the trends of their traffic patterns and adjust their routing policies over the existing infrastructure. Routing policy is adjusted due to changing peering and customer-provider agreements or due to shifts in traffic demand patterns. Such changes must be well thought out: changes in the egress routing policy might saturate upstream networks, while changes in ingress routing might unpredictably shift traffic loads among ingress links.

Commercial platforms and services. Avaya and Cisco offer the PathControl [36] and Performance Routing (PfR) [2] route management platforms, respectively. These platforms perform continual performance measurements to online services and adjust inter-domain routes between the services and their clients based on these performance measurements. Similarly, Internap provides route optimization services for their clients [3] by performing measurements along alternate paths and redirecting traffic between services and clients by adjusting inter-domain routing policy. These platforms and services primarily target large enterprises with multiple upstream providers. PECAN applies similar types of inter-domain route control to adjust routes between clients and replicas, and it is possible that some variant of these systems could be used to implement aspects of PECAN's network routing subsystem. Our evaluation also hints at how these services might scale to large OSPs who have have millions of clients and many replicas.

2.3 Joint Content and Network Routing

Uncoordinated content and network routing as described above exhibits the following problems. First, network operators have little

insight into application-level wide-area path performance between a service replica and all of the potential clients for that replica. As described in Section 2.1, only passive measurements can scale to collect application-level performance data to all of the OSPs clients. Second, the content routing subsystem that collects passive measurements operates only on the paths that are already selected by network operators. As a result, potential alternate paths to the clients are never explored by content routing system.

PECAN enables joint content and network routing and solves the problem described above. Joint routing in this context is the ability for content routing system to explore wide-area network path diversity to select the best path between an end-user and a service. At a high-level, PECAN operates in three steps: 1) the network routing subsystem exposes a diversity of wide-area network paths; 2) the content routing subsystem collects application-level performance over the exposed paths; and 3) each client is content-routed to the best service replica over the best path to that replica.

When designing PECAN, we assume that services are replicated at the edge of the OSP's network. This assumption holds for at least some major OSPs and their services [42]. If services are located deeper in an OSP network, the OSP would have to jointly select not only replica and wide-area paths, but intra-domain paths as well.

3. PECAN

As we discuss in Section 2, modern OSPs use sophisticated content routing systems to load balance requests between replicated data centers in an attempt to improve client performance. In this section, we describe how operators can extend their existing content routing systems to support network routing as well. In particular, we present the design of PECAN (Performance Enhancements with Content And Network routing), a system that enables seamless integration of content and network routing.

3.1 Exposing Routing Choices

The basic idea behind PECAN is to extend an OSP's current client-replica mapping infrastructure to instead map clients to <replica, route> pairs. To do so, PECAN breaks each replica into a set of virtual replicas, where each virtual replica corresponds to a different choice of routes to the replica (i.e., a single <replica, route> tuple). Figure 2 shows how PECAN allows a content routing system to tap into network route diversity. The router in the figure has a separate routing slice dedicated to each set of alternate routes (virtual replica). For example, in today's routers such a slice can be implemented using virtual routing and forwarding (VRF) instances or a host of alternative technologies.

3.1.1 Egress routes

There are a wide variety of mechanisms available to employ alternate egress routes from a given virtual replica. For example, conventional BGP multi-homing can increase route diversity; operators can use BGP's local preference setting to adjust the choice of egress routes to each client prefix. PECAN could also benefit from protocols such as Detour [37], RON [13], Platypus [35], Deflections [47], and Path Splicing [32], all of which increase an end system's choice of (and control over) egress paths. Similarly, many practitioners see industry proposals like Locator/ID Separation Protocol (LISP) [19] as a feasible improvement to BGP. LISP separates the endpoint identifier (EID) (*i.e.*, a host IP address) information from routing locator (RLOC) (*i.e.*, the information that encodes the location of the EID in the wide-area Internet.) LISP could allow an OSP to explore egress routes by selecting the entry points to a remote network as encoded with RLOCs.

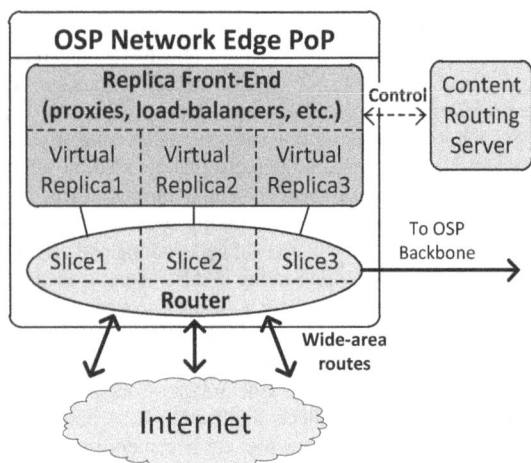

Figure 2: *Content and network routing subsystems allocate isolated resources to explore new network routes.*

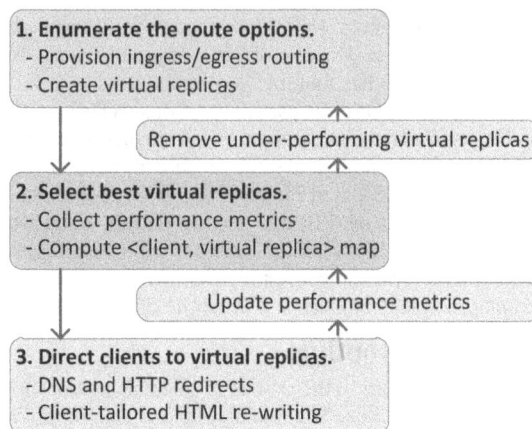

Figure 3: *Joint network and content routing selection with PECAN.*

3.1.2 Ingress routes

Affecting a virtual replica's ingress routes is more challenging since it requires changing the way other networks forward packets. The key to enabling distinct route sets for each virtual replica is to separate these routing decisions. In PECAN, an OSP allocates a distinct IP address prefix to each virtual replica. Hence, to map clients to a particular virtual replica, PECAN need only point them to an IP address within the virtual replica's prefix.

Today's Internet supports a number of ways to impact route selection, including selective prefix announcement (*i.e.*, announcing a prefix only to a subset of neighbors), prepending AS_PATH attributes, setting BGP communities or MED attributes, and BGP AS_PATH poisoning. We evaluate employing AS path poisoning in PECAN extensively in the following sections. Future technologies, such as LISP, might provide even more elegant alternatives.

Critically, by maintaining one virtual replica (address prefix) at each physical replica that always uses the default network paths, PECAN does no harm: clients can always obtain the performance provided by content routing alone if none of the joint routing options provide superior performance.

3.2 Selecting a Virtual Replica

We now describe how PECAN's virtual replicas enable the process of joint content and network routing. The joint optimization could happen in many ways; we take an iterative approach, as shown in in Figure 3. First, PECAN optimizes network routing between each client/replica pair: for each replica, PECAN identifies the network path to each client that yields the best performance, and establishes a virtual replica with that path preference. Then, for each client, PECAN selects the virtual replica that offers the best performance among the available options at each physical replica.

This process proceeds in three steps, which could be either automated or manually performed by the operators of the network and online service.

1. **Enumerate the route options.** OSP network operators must enumerate the alternate routes from each replica to clients that the system should explore. Depending on the route selection technique employed, the operator may wish to enumerate egress (*e.g.*, a choice of a next-hop neighbor) routes and ingress (*e.g.*, selective route announcement) routes separately, or jointly. Evaluating all possible alternate routes

to each client is unlikely to scale, but our evaluation (Section 6) shows considering just five virtual replicas (i.e., sets of alternate ingress routes) at each replica can realize performance improvements that are 60% of the maximum possible improvement.

2. **Select the best virtual replica for each client.** PECAN evaluates the performance of each virtual replica for each client. To evaluate a new virtual replica (route selection) for a given client and physical replica, PECAN redirects a small fraction of client requests to the virtual replicas and evaluates the performance that the client sees. PECAN gradually increases the number of clients mapped to a virtual replica to avoid overloading any network path or physical replica. Isolating test measurements from the bulk of the traffic requires a set of dedicated load-balancing proxies, as shown in Figure 2, As long as the evaluated route offers improved performance for enough clients and is reliable over the test period, PECAN maintains the virtual replica in the set of virtual replicas that can be used for joint routing.

3. **Direct clients to virtual replicas.** Once PECAN has selected the best virtual replica for each client, it implements the mapping. To implement this mapping, PECAN uses DNS load balancing to map each client to a virtual replica IP address, where the BGP prefix for that IP address corresponds to the route that the PECAN has selected for that client and replica using the previous steps. Because PECAN maps each virtual replica to its own prefix, a client always has the option of using either default content routing (*i.e.*, the route in today's CDN) or the PECAN-provided route.

4. THE CASE FOR JOINT ROUTING

We now summarize the potential gains of a joint content and network routing system; we expand on our methodology and findings in subsequent sections. We emulate an OSP setup using a globally distributed testbed that allows us to both replicate services across sites and control inbound routes to these sites. This testbed, which we describe in detail in Section 5.1, emulates an OSP with replicas in a number of geographically distinct locations with a diversity of wide-area network routes at each location.

Overview of measurements. The testbed has five replicas distributed across the United States; from each replica, we explore about 250 alternate routing choices to 174 globally distributed

Routing type	RTT	BW	Jitter
Best replica	107.35 ms	212.47 Mbps	5.95 ms
Network	4.35%	0.87%	9.32%
Content	16.75%	8.11%	11.82%
Joint	**20.44%**	**11.29%**	**17.57%**

Table 1: *Average improvement to latency (RTT), throughput (BW), and jitter. The baseline, over which improvement is measured for each technique, is the performance to the single best replica.*

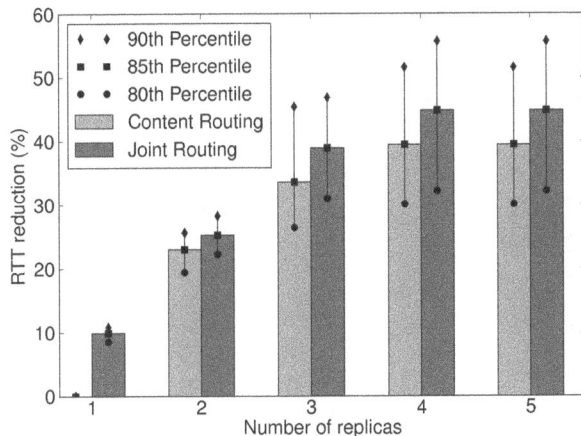

Figure 4: *Latency reduction as a function of the number of replicas; the baseline performance is the average performance to a single best replica.*

Client percentile	RTT (%)	BW (%)	Jitter (%)
Most-improved 5%	16.94	10.25	41.20
Most-improved 10%	13.43	1.42	29.24
Most-improved 20%	9.91	0.47	13.48

Table 2: *Marginal gains of joint routing over content routing. Clients in each percentile improve by at least the amount indicated.*

clients. For three months (from October to December 2011), we collected a comprehensive <client, replica, route> performance map consisting of millions of measurements. Our raw dataset available for the public to download [5]. Section 5 explains our experimental setup in more detail.

Improvement over the best replica. When OSPs roll out a new online service, it often starts at a single replica and then expands to more sites. It is interesting to know how expanding the set of replicas and/or adding joint content and network routing improves the service performance. Table 1 compares how network routing, content routing and joint routing (PECAN) each improve over a single best replica. (We formally define each metric in Section 6.)

The "network" routing row in Table 1 shows the gains if the OSP chooses to explore alternate routes only for that single best replica. Conversely, the "content" routing line shows the improvement if the OSP chooses to replicate the service to all five locations available in our testbed. Content routing provides greater performance gains than simply applying network routing for one site. Finally, the "joint" routing row shows the gains attained when the OSP chooses to both replicate the service to all five locations and perform joint content and network routing.

In practice, in addition to network-level performance, the effectiveness of both replica and network path selection depend on traffic acquisition costs, replica loads, and other variables. Unfortunately, it is hard to obtain data to model the effect of such variables. Hence, we consider only latency, throughput, and jitter. While this choice might bias our results, it similarly impacts both content routing and joint routing; thus, we can still compare the two.

Figure 4 shows that the benefits from joint routing are largely independent of the size of the replica set in our testbed: adding

more replicas to an OSP yields latency improvements for both content and joint routing. Hence—at least at the scales we study—an OSP can improve its performance using joint routing regardless of the number of replicas it currently employs. The figure shows the 80th, 85th and 90th-percentile gains over the performance of a single best replica.

Improvement over content routing. While joint routing unquestionably provides greater gains than network or content routing alone, most OSPs already deploy content routing. Hence, its practical impact is often governed by the marginal gain over content routing. Table 2 provides a breakdown of joint routing performance gains over content routing alone for various client percentiles. For example, when compared to content routing, the most-improved 10% of clients see their latency reduced by 13.43% or more, an increase of 1.42% or greater in throughput, and at least a 29.24% reduction in jitter. For online services such as search or online gaming, such latency savings are significant.

Improvement with limited route diversity. In some circumstances, it may not be practical to support all possible alternate routes to each replica. Fortunately, in our testbed, most of the improvements we observe are obtained by avoiding a few underperforming default routes. Hence, it may be possible to achieve the lion's share of the benefit with only a small set of alternate routes. In particular, for our testbed, Figure 12 (found in Section 6) shows that exploiting just five alternate routes at each replica yields 60% of the possible improvement across the hundreds of alternate routes that we consider in our evaluation.

Taken together, these results suggest that an OSP can provide tangible improvement over the state of the art by employing joint content and network routing. In the next two sections, we discuss PECAN's benefits in detail.

5. EVALUATION SETUP

This section describes our evaluation methodology. We describe the testbed infrastructure and our measurement procedures.

5.1 Infrastructure

We use PlanetLab to emulate a set of clients, from which we perform measurements to the replicas over many different sets of routes, and Transit Portal to deploy an ersatz Web service with both replica and route diversity.

5.1.1 Clients: PlanetLab

We use 174 PlanetLab nodes as our client set. From the full list of approximately 600 PlanetLab nodes, we select nodes with which we can establish sessions. We further filter the set of these "live" nodes to include only a single node per PlanetLab site. In the end, we have a client pool with 38% of the nodes in North America, 36% in Europe, 21% in Asia, and 5% in South America.

It is well known that PlanetLab nodes are not the best representation of the Internet. It is hard to quantify how much PlanetLab biases our measurements. On one hand, PlanetLab nodes are better provisioned and have better "last mile" connections to the immediate provider than their residential counterparts. On the other hand,

Service Replica	Location	# of routes (poisons)	# of measurements (RTT)		# of measurements (BW)	
			Default route	Alternate routes	Default route	Alternate routes
1	Atlanta, GA	259	292,806	1,453,137	9,535	14,679
2	Clemson, SC	253	19,401	1,442,832	14,853	22,021
3	Princeton, NJ	261	224,457	1,438,588	5,595	6,243
4	Seattle, WA	247	366,357	347,302	14,844	9,651
5	Madison, WI	247	67,473	1,389,266	7,321	14,032

Table 3: *The Transit Portal deployments that we use to emulate a replicated online service with route control. At each Transit Portal location, we host a replica of an online service; from each of these locations, we explore approximately 250 alternate routes (poisons) between each replica and the set of clients that it could reach.*

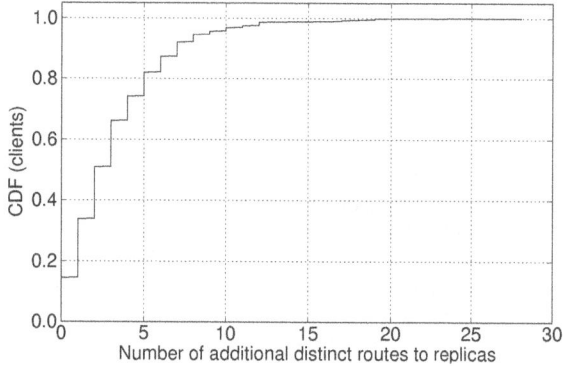

Figure 5: *Number of additional paths to replicas.*

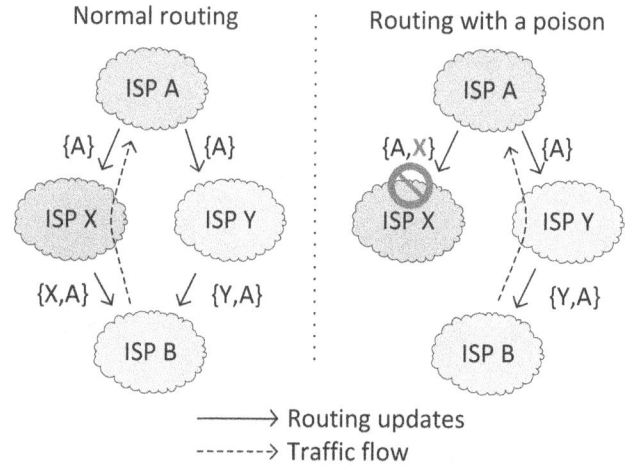

→ Routing updates
┈┈┈→ Traffic flow

Figure 6: *Obtaining alternate paths between ISP A and ISP B with poisoning. The left-hand figure shows that, by default, ISP B prefers to route traffic for ISP A through ISP X. In the figure on the right, ISP A poisons AS X, leaving the path through ISP Y as the only viable path from ISP B to ISP A.*

we focus our measurements on the performance we can gain by exploiting replica and route diversity in the network core, and not on the network edge. Our results will be more affected by how well a PlanetLab node's provider is connected to the Internet relative to an average Internet user. Most PlanetLab nodes' immediate access providers are academic institutions, whose connectivity to the Internet is often comparable to the connectivity of smaller ISPs or medium enterprises.

5.1.2 Replicas: Transit Portal

Transit Portal (TP) is a platform that enables researchers to perform experiments that require altering wide-area Internet routes [6]. There are five TP sites; each site has a functional Internet router, connecting to an upstream ISP, receiving a full Internet routing table. Each node is able to participate in BGP routing by issuing BGP updates from the IP address space and AS numbers allocated to Transit Portal. TP nodes allow multiple researchers to use these routing resources concurrently. We obtained access to the five TP sites described in Table 3, each of which acts as a replica in our testbed. In terms of Internet topology, the nodes in Atlanta and Seattle are very close to major Internet exchanges; the nodes in Clemson and Wisconsin are one AS-hop away from a Tier-1 provider, while the node in Princeton is two AS-hops away from a Tier-1 provider.

As explained below, TP sites can advertise routes using BGP AS_PATH poisoning to alter the routes that PlanetLab clients use to reach them. Using path poisoning, we discover approximately 250 different route advertisements from TP sites that result in alternate paths to at least one of the clients in our client set. Figure 5 shows a CDF of number of alternate paths per client; we find that on average, in addition to the default path, poisoning yields 3.4 paths per client to our replica set.

5.2 Experimental Procedure

We describe how we use our testbed to explore alternate routes between clients and replicas measure the performance improvements that result from these alternate routes.

5.2.1 Obtaining route diversity: poisoning

We explore wide-area route diversity by using BGP AS_PATH poisoning [16,24]. BGP AS_PATH poisoning is an unconventional technique: it finds alternate, policy-compliant wide-area ingress routes to the network that advertises the poisoned route (in our case, the replicas). Although it has a number of known drawbacks in practice, BGP AS_PATH poisoning enables us to affect wide-area route selection without requiring access to the BGP routers that control inbound and outbound traffic to our replica sites. In practice, a real OSP could control both ingress and egress routes in a variety of ways. For example, OSPs could also use BGP AS_PATH prepending, BGP community attributes, and selective advertisements; to control egress traffic, OSPs can often select among multiple neighbors to send traffic. Given the wider variety of techniques at their disposal, it is plausible that OSP operators might see even greater performance gains than our experiments suggest.

BGP AS_PATH poisoning leverages the BGP-loop prevention algorithm to explore alternate routes on the Internet. As BGP route advertisements propagate through the Internet, each router attaches its own AS number to the AS_PATH attribute. BGP's loop prevention algorithm, which is implemented on all BGP-speaking routers, says that a router must drop a BGP route update if the AS_PATH attribute of the route contains the AS number of said router. Dropping these updates prevents the router from accepting updates that the router has already received, thus preventing loops. As shown in Figure 6, an Internet Service Provider (ISP) can use BGP AS_PATH poisoning to exploit this algorithm by inserting a target ISP's AS number in the AS_PATH attribute before the update is originated. The target AS, in turn, will drop the update and its clients will likely choose alternate routes to the route originator.

We use the traceroute tool to identify the ISP networks (and their AS numbers) on the default paths from our clients to each replica. We then poison these AS numbers one by one to reveal alternate paths from clients to replicas. Not every client moves to an alternate path after we issue a poisoned update: some updates affect just a few clients, while some affect a great many. To find which clients are affected by a poison we, again, use traceroute from every client to the poisoned IP prefix. There is a possibility that a some fraction of these alternate paths are a result of network topology changes not under our control—i.e., not because of our poisoning. We repeatedly snapshot the default path between each <client, replica> pair to see how often the AS path changes to determine the "noise floor" of the Internet topology churn. We find that an average <client, replica> pair observes approximately 0.35 paths in addition to the default (un-poisoned) path during our study period. This low churn estimate gives us confidence that most of the 3.4 alternate paths that we observe (not counting the default) are due to poisoning.

5.2.2 Measuring performance improvements

There are many ways to measure network performance improvement; page load time is one of the most popular measures of OSP performance. We do not measure page load times due to the complexity of such measurements. Instead, we considered measuring median and average HTTP object download times, but find that latency is a reliable predictor for such times. (During preliminary testing we discovered that round-trip-time correlates to download time for a median-sized—400-byte [17]—object with a Pearson correlation coefficient of approximately 0.83, for both a default path as well as a poisoned path that affected 30% of the replica clients.) Hence, we measure three basic network performance primitives: latency, throughput, and jitter.

As explained in Section 3, each of our replicas advertises an un-poisoned prefix at all times. This un-poisoned prefix can always be reached to perform a measurement over the default path that rarely changes. For poisoned routes, we use the following sequence for each replica to collect a client/replica path performance map:

1. **Announce a prefix with a poisoned update.** The poison will propagate the prefix to some client networks over the alternate paths.

2. **Perform measurements to the poisoned prefix.** From every client in our client set, collect measurements to the replica using the poisoned prefix. Clients for which the poison did not affect the end-to-end path will see no improvement. Clients for which the prefix affected the end-to-end path will see either improved or reduced performance.

3. **Perform measurements to an un-poisoned prefix.** Conduct the same set of measurements over the default path (i.e., using the un-poisoned prefix) to the replica to collect a contemporaneous baseline to which we will compare our poisoned path.

As shown in Table 3, the dataset resulting from these measurements contains many more measurements of the default path than

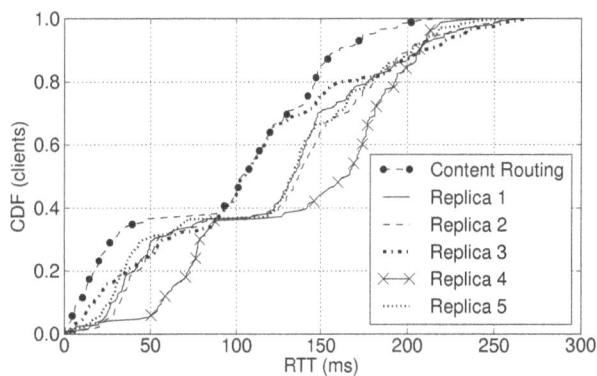

Figure 7: *Minimum latency over the default path.*

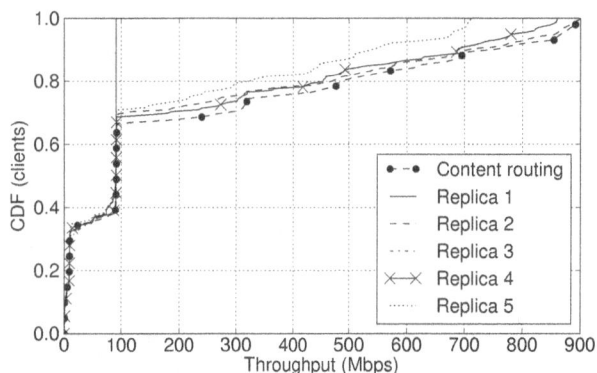

Figure 8: *Maximum throughput over the default path.*

the poisoned paths. The abundance of default path measurements allows us to establish confidence in our baseline performance measurements. We consider a poisoned path between a client and a replica to improve latency over the client's default path only if the poisoned path shows latency smaller than the minimum latency ever recorded over the default path between the client and the replica. We apply a similar litmus test for jitter measurements. For throughput, we record an improvement only if a poisoned path produced higher throughput than any throughput measurement we ever observe on a default path.

6. EVALUATION

We evaluate the benefits of joint routing with respect to latency, throughput and jitter. We also show how well joint routing performs compared to traditional content routing.

6.1 Baseline Performance

When considering the performance improvements that different routing approaches induce, we must establish a baseline to compare them against. In this section, we use two baselines for comparison: 1) a best replica baseline, and 2) a content routing baseline. Before formally defining these baseline metrics, we describe how we perform the measurements that help us establish these baselines.

Measurements of default path performance. Figure 7 shows the CDF of minimum latencies clients experience to each replica over a default path. The minimum latency for each client is obtained from a large set of measurements: On average, each client measures the default path to a replica 6,692 times. The figure shows two major groups of clients: About 40% of the clients have latencies between

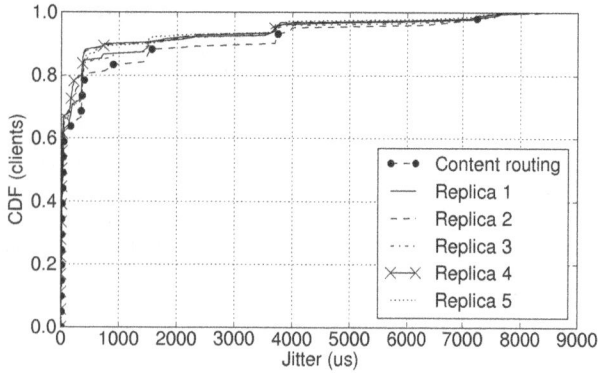

Figure 9: *Minimum jitter over the default path.*

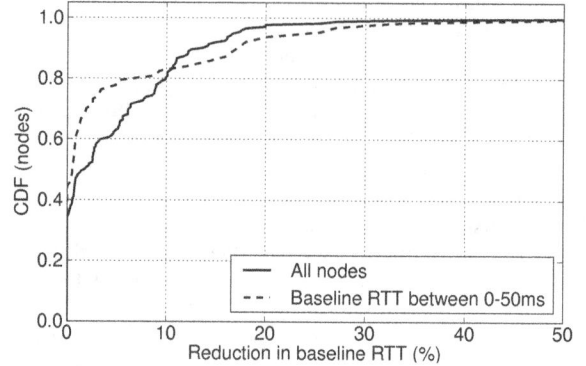

Figure 10: *Latency reduction when using joint routing.*

Replica	Latency	Throughput	Jitter
1	6.93%	7.77%	12.62%
2	1.15%	35.92%	35.92%
3	56.64%	6.77%	8.74%
4	22.54%	48.54%	18.45%
5	12.71%	0.97%	24.27%

Table 4: *Percentage of clients for which each replica is best.*

0–50 ms, and about 60% of the clients see latencies of 90 ms or larger, with just a few in between. These modalities reflect the client geographic distribution: About 38% of clients are in the U.S and Canada and see lower latencies, while the rest are overseas.

Similarly, Figures 8 and 9 show the CDFs of maximum throughput and the minimum jitter, respectively, as observed by clients to each replica. As with latencies, the maximums and minimums are computed over a set of measurements for the default path between each <client, replica> tuple. For each such tuple, we have, on average, 189 jitter and throughput measurements. Figure 8 highlights why it is difficult to measure capacity using the PlanetLab nodes as clients. The clients in the figure form three distinct groups: 1) those with 10-Mbps links, 2) those with 100-Mbps links, and 3) those with speeds above 100 Mbps. The 10-Mbps and 100-Mbps groups identify cases where the PlanetLab nodes are directly connected to a bottleneck link; in these cases the bottleneck is at the client itself and no type of routing can improve its throughput.

Best replica baseline. When a new online service is launched, it often starts with a single replica. We want to know how much the network performance improves over that single replica when the OSPs start adding more replicas and implement content routing or joint routing. We define the *best replica* for some performance metric as the replica that the largest fraction of clients would select, given that each client can select its own best replica based on that performance metric. Table 4 shows the breakdown of popularity of different replicas when each client selects a replica based on the performance of the default paths for each <client, replica> tuple. The average performance to the best replica across all clients yields the *average best replica performance*. For example, as shown previously in Table 1, the average latency that clients experience to the best replica (which, as indicated in Table 4, is replica 3 in Princeton, NJ) is 107.35 milliseconds.

Content routing baseline. PECAN extends content routing to also incorporate the benefits of network routing; to quantify the additional benefit of PECAN relative to content routing, we compare the performance of PECAN against the performance that content

routing alone provides. Recall that a content routing system maps each client to its own best replica. Formally, for a client i, the content routing latency $RTT_{content,i}$ is

$$RTT_{content,i} = \min_{j \in (1...M)} \widehat{RTT}_{ij0},$$

where M is number of replicas and $\widehat{RTT}_{ij0}$ is the minimum latency that we measured between client i and replica j over the default path (noted as path 0). Taking the average across all clients yields *average content routing performance*. In addition to showing the performance of clients to each replica, Figures 7–9 show the performance of a content routing system when each client is directed to its own best replica (labeled "content routing"). Note that the content routing system we implement uses only network performance as the basis for selecting a replica for each client; in practice, OSPs also use replica loads and costs to inform content routing decisions.

6.2 How Well Does Joint Routing Work?

We quantify the benefit that PECAN provides when compared to content routing. When PECAN is in use, we formally define client i's latency as

$$RTT_{PECAN,i} = \min_{j \in (1...M)} \min_{l \in (0...K_{ij})} \widehat{RTT}_{ijl}.$$

where M is the number of replicas, K_{ij} is the number of paths between client i and replica j, and $\widehat{RTT}_{ijl}$ is the minimum latency we recorded over the path l between client i and replica j. Recall that path $l = 0$ corresponds to the default path. With measurements of both content routing and PECAN performance, we can compute the percentage improvement as

$$100 \cdot (RTT_{content,i} - RTT_{PECAN,i})/RTT_{content,i}.$$

We use the same approach for jitter; for throughput, we take maximums instead of minimums. Below we provide a breakdown of the average performance improvements that presented in Table 1.

Latency. Joint routing delivers an additional 4.3% (or about 5-ms) round-trip latency reduction on average beyond performing content routing alone, which may translate to significant improvements in service response times [41]. Figure 10 shows the percentage improvement in latency over the content routing baseline. The solid line in the figure shows improvement for all clients, while the dashed line shows shows the latency reduction for clients that had a baseline latency of 0–50 ms. We find that 20% of our clients see a reduction in latency of at least 10%. We also observe that clients

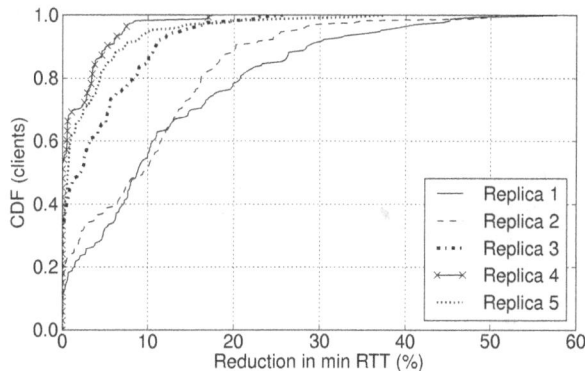

Figure 11: *Latency reduction with network routing.*

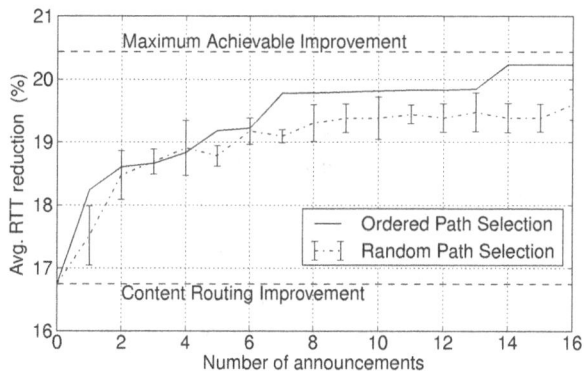

Figure 12: *Average latency reduction with increasing number of route announcements per replica.*

with baseline latencies of 0–50 ms see similar improvements, with 18% of these clients improving by 10% or more. This result is significant, since content replication can only reduce latency by placing content closer to the users. At some point, however, placing replicas close to all clients might become prohibitively expensive; in such cases, an OSP might rely on PECAN to improve routing between the closest replica and the clients nearby.

As discussed earlier, Figure 4 plots content and joint routing benefit over the best replica baseline as we increase the number of replicas. Adding replicas provides higher improvements with joint routing, but with decreasing marginal improvement at every addition. Content routing behaves similarly, albeit with a lower improvement at each step.

Throughput and Jitter. When compared to the baseline of content routing, only 5% of clients that are using PECAN experience a throughput improvement of 20% or more, while almost 90% of clients see no improvement. We attribute this limited improvement to the inability of most PlanetLab nodes, which mostly use 10-Mbps and 100-Mbps interfaces, to saturate potential Internet path bottlenecks. In case of jitter, 10% of the clients see approximately 30% less jitter, while 60% of clients see no improvement at all. As with throughput, we see that PlanetLab nodes' inability to saturate router buffers along Internet paths limits the observed jitter.

6.3 Why Does Joint Routing Work?

Joint routing improves performance over content routing alone because it provides multiple alternate network paths for each replica. As explained in Section 5, PECAN finds about 3.4 alternate paths on average for each <client, replica> tuple. Even when a client cannot improve its performance by switching replicas, network routing can often improve performance to one of the replicas. Figure 11 shows latency improvements from network routing alone for each replica. For each replica, the baseline over which we compute the latency reduction is the minimum latency over the default path to that replica. We find that 20% of the clients experience improvements of 5–20%, depending on which replica we choose to evaluate. Some replicas (*e.g.*, Replicas 1 and 2) have relatively poor default paths, so approximately 80% of clients achieve some benefit from alternate paths to these replicas.

6.4 Scalability and Stability

To be practical, PECAN must judiciously limit the number of route changes it broadcasts to the Internet; it also should limit oscillations induced by large numbers of clients changing replicas. In this section we seek to assess these requirements by analyzing two

questions: (1) How many routes must the OSP explore to achieve the benefits of joint routing? And (2) how many clients change their preferred replica after joint routing is applied?

6.4.1 Scaling route selection

OSPs that tweak egress routes can do so without affecting the Internet routing system. To explore the alternate ingress routes, however, OSPs must issue additional routing updates. All of the experiments presented so far evaluate the improvements that PECAN can provide by using approximately 250 ingress routes (achieved via poisoned BGP advertisements) at each geographic location. Over time, OSPs might be able to evaluate all of these 250 configurations, but doing so frequently may not be practical. Hence, we consider how many routes an OSP needs to explore to see improvement from joint content and network routing.

When an OSP uses a limited set of routes to feed traffic to virtual replicas, it must decide which routes to use, but selecting the optimal subset of routes for each replica is computationally intractable. To avoid exploring all possible route combinations of route advertisements from each replica, we devise a simple heuristic: for each replica, we sort, in descending order, the routes based on the average improvement they provide to all clients when compared to the performance over the default path. We then take the routes sequentially from that ordering and announce them from the replica. For example, if OSP decides to announce three of the alternate routes, it will pick three top routes from the ordered list. We compare this heuristic against selecting sets of routes at random.

Figure 12 shows how performance improves as we increase the number of announced routes. The gains in the figure are shown over the best replica baseline. The figure contains four plots: "maximum", "ordered", "random", and "content". The "maximum" line represents the maximum gain that an OSP can get with joint routing (see Table 1). The "ordered" line shows the gains as we increase number of alternate routes from 0 to 16. The routes here are picked using the heuristic described above. The "random" line shows the gains when we add additional routes at random. To generate the "random" plot, we run 10 iterations and report average and standard error values. Finally, the "content" line shows the content routing gains over the best replica (also from Table 1). In most cases, the ordered heuristic outperforms random route selection. It is also encouraging that only five additional virtual replicas per physical replica can obtain approximately 60% of the performance gains that are possible with all 250 alternate routes.

251

6.4.2 Stability of replica selection

Content providers typically take loads at each replica into account when assigning clients to replicas. With PECAN, however, clients that previously had a suboptimal replica will shift their traffic to other replicas. The OSPs must quantify such shifting and plan for it accordingly (*e.g.* by provisioning necessary capacity or by directing clients to second-best replicas).

We quantify client shift in our testbed. We find that, when optimizing for latency, 8% of clients change the choice of replica when joint routing is enabled. In other words, 92% of clients use the same replica (but perhaps over a better network path) as the one they were using when only default paths were available.

7. RELATED WORK

We first survey prior work on content routing methods; then we cover prior work on enhancing inter-domain routing; finally, we overview prior research on joint content and network routing, most of which assumes intra-domain routing context.

7.1 Content Routing

The late 1990s witnessed the first efforts in optimizing mapping of end users to content or service replicas. Bhattacharjee *et al.* [15] presented a seminal paper describing a client-to-replica mapping system. This system used IP anycast to reach a directory service (*e.g.*, DNS) which then routed the clients to the best service replica based on the client-replica performance map. Seshan *et al.* [38] invented a new way to collect a comprehensive client-replica performance map: a small fraction of clients would be directed to randomly selected replicas to estimate the performance. Andrews *et al.* [14] presented a system called Webmapper that used algorithms for performing approximate client-to-best-replica matching.

The initial step in client-to-replica mapping is usually performed using the Domain Name System (DNS). Pang *et al.* [33] evaluated the responsiveness of DNS to changes in client-to-replica mapping and found that in many cases DNS is sluggish to respond. Nonetheless, DNS is still the primary method for directing initial client requests to the best replicas. Huang *et al.* [22] introduced a DNS reflection method for client-to-replica performance map generation. Instead of usual actual client traffic, DNS reflection forces local DNS (LDNS) servers to use iterative queries to remote replicas to estimate the delay between the LDNS servers and the replicas. The LDNS performance information is then used as a proxy metric for client-to-replica performance. Most recently, Wendell *et al.* [45] describe a system called DONAR that allows DNS servers to make mapping decisions with only partial global information.

7.2 Network Routing

In the last decade there has been a lot of research on improving performance of inter-domain routing. A lot of of such research was focused on the effectiveness of multi-homing enterprise networks. Our work builds upon these efforts and extends them to include scenarios where an OSP has a choice not only of diverse network paths (network routing) but also a choice of replicas (content routing). For example, Akella *et al.* [9–12] explore the effects of multi-homing on the performance of a site that either sends or receives Internet traffic. The authors study 68 Akamai nodes in 17 cities as a testbed: A city often contains multiple nodes, each with a different upstream ISP; the authors connect to all the Akamai nodes in one city to estimate performance of each ISP in that city, effectively emulating a multi-homing setup in that city. The authors found that route optimization produces greater benefits in peak time intervals. Unfortunately, the study was limited in the

number of alternative Internet paths (only upstreams) and it did not consider joint network and content routing.

Others also study multi-homing routing but stop short of quantifying its benefits to a multi-replica configuration. Goldenberg *et al.* [20] assess the benefit of single-site multi-homing and also consider cost in the analysis. Guo *et al.* [21] analyze a commercial solution for multi-homed enterprises, which focuses on possible performance gain with two upstream ISPs. Lee *et al.* [27] explore ways to scale active measurements for multi-homed enterprises. Uhlig *et al.* [43] and Wang *et al.* [44] propose formalizing upstream ISP selection as an optimization problem. Most of the efforts mentioned above focus on the enterprise setting and do not compare content routing with network routing.

Overlay networks provide yet another way to improve inter-domain routing performance. Savage *et al.* [37] explore the benefits of an overlay routing system, Detour, that selects best performing alternative paths. In addition to a conventional routing system underneath, Detour requires an active network of overlay nodes to improve user experience. Andersen *et al.* [13] deploy and evaluate RON, a similar overlay system across diverse locations in the Internet. Commercial content distribution networks apply similar techniques for finding the best paths to pre-cached content [31].

Less conventional proposals to improve inter-domain routing include works by Yang, Xu, and Motiwala. Yang *et al.* [47] presents a system that can increase path diversity with routing deflections. End hosts in such systems can set bits that instruct routers on the path to perform deflections over better paths. Xu and Rexford [46] introduce MIRO: a system that provides increased diversity of paths choices for inter-domain routing. Motiwala *et al.* [32] present a routing algorithm for Internet routers that enables scalable exploration of Internet path diversity. Unfortunately, utilizing such systems requires changes in Internet routers and in end hosts.

7.3 Joint Routing

A sizable body of work explores joint content and network routing in the context of intra-domain routing and overlay network routing. Killian *et al.* [25] formalize a joint optimization problem to solve content placement, content routing, and network routing in an overlay network. The authors prove that computing the optimal solution is NP-complete and introduce several heuristics that perform well in realistic overlay network topologies. Jiang *et al.* [23] compare formal models of joint routing by combining the ISP's intra-domain traffic engineering problem and a content provider's server selection problem. They use concepts of cooperative game theory and simulations of their models to conclude that giving content providers some control over network routing can yield more optimal performance for both the ISP and the content provider. Yu *et al.* [48] explore the tradeoffs between using multi-path routing and deploying more replicas in an OSP network to maximize throughput between replicas and clients. Unlike our work, the authors did not explore benefits of wide-area path diversity between replicas and clients. Concurrently with our work, Sharma *et al.* [39] describe a joint optimization problem that tackles content placement, content routing, and network traffic engineering in an intra-domain routing scenario. Using real demand traces and network topologies the authors show that unplanned strategies such as IverseCap and LRU often perform better than sophisticated optimization using historical demand data.

8. LIMITATIONS AND FUTURE WORK

In this section, we discuss some limitations of our study and directions for future work. We focus in particular on how our dataset might be made more representative.

Size of the testbed. One of the most serious challenges in evaluating the performance gains that an OSPs can attain is to have a replica set that matches that of real OSPs. This equivalence entails two primary components: (1) diversity of replica locations and (2) diversity of route choice in each location. In terms of geographic diversity, our set of replicas is comparable to the set of North American Amazon EC2 data centers, although it is much smaller than the infrastructure of a large commercial OSP such as Google or Microsoft. In future work, we plan to perform similar experiments with replicas hosted across a Tier-1 ISP backbone network; we are in the process of deploying this measurement infrastructure to allow for more comprehensive studies.

Route exploration technique. Our testbed setup limits us to exploring the routing diversity at each of our replicas that BGP AS_PATH poisoning can provide. Moreover, poisoning introduces undesirable routing churn. In practice, however, OSPs have a much wider variety of techniques at their disposal for controlling both egress and ingress Internet routes as described in Section 3.1.

Client set. Another challenge in emulating real-world OSP performance is obtaining a representative client set. In our case the clients are PlanetLab nodes, which are hardly a representative set of Internet end hosts. Many of the nodes we use are housed in well-connected university campuses. It does bias our client set, but it is not clear whether performance improvements—especially latency improvements—would differ with a more representative set of clients. On one hand, PlanetLab nodes might be better connected than average Internet nodes, providing greater route diversity to and from such nodes. On the other hand, PlanetLab nodes might be better-provisioned in general than typical end hosts, and, thus, hard to improve on. Less well-connected and more remote networks might see more performance improvements from joint routing.

Measurement method. A future study might also attempt to measure or approximate the overall user experience of using a particular replica and network route, perhaps approximating user experience by page load times, as has been done in previous work on Web performance [42]. Because our clients are run from PlanetLab nodes, it is not practical to instrument a browser and record the performance from each client. A promising direction for future work would be to conduct a more comprehensive study of how systems such as PECAN can improve user-perceived performance.

PECAN deployment costs. To put the performance improvement PECAN achieves into perspective, one must measure the cost needed to build a functioning PECAN system such as the one described in Section 3. These costs depend on the ease of integration between content routing systems and inter-domain traffic engineering systems. Although existing content routing systems, such as those described in Section 2, are highly programmable, the same cannot be said about today's routers. Recent advances in software defined networking (SDN) [30] indicate that this type of programmatic integration might be less costly in the future.

9. CONCLUSION

Online service providers currently perform replica selection (content routing) and wide-area route selection (network routing) independently. We introduce PECAN (Performance Enhancements with Content And Network routing), a system that performs joint content and network routing for an OSP that wishes to improve end-to-end performance to clients. We design PECAN as an extension to the content routing systems that OSPs currently use.

We evaluate the performance of PECAN on a globally distributed testbed that emulates a modern OSP by running the replicated on-

line service on five Transit Portal (TP) sites, each offering a large choice of network paths to clients. We use 174 PlanetLab nodes as clients to estimate network performance to our replicated service. Our experiments show that PECAN reduces round trip latency by 4.3% (or nearly 5 ms) on average over simply performing content routing alone, which may translate to at least tens of milliseconds of reduction in Web page load time [41]. Finally, we find that PECAN can provide most of the potential benefit with only a few judiciously selected network paths: exploring just five sets of alternate network routes between clients and replicas in our testbed can yield 60% of the maximum possible benefit of joint routing to an online service provider. Given the increasing reliance of today's online services on even small improvements in latency, the improvements that PECAN yields over standard content routing may be warranted for certain latency-sensitive services, particularly in cases when replication itself is costly.

10. ACKNOWLEDGMENTS

This research was supported by NSF award CNS-1261357. We gratefully acknowledge our shepherd Adam Wierman and the SIG-METRICS reviewers. This work could not have been done without an army of network operators who helped us to establish and operate Transit Portal [6] testbed. We specifically want to thank Schyler Batey, Larry Billado, Michael Blodgett, Jeff Fitzwater, Scott Friedrich, Brian Parker, and Kit Patterson.

11. REFERENCES

[1] Chrome software updates: Courgette. http://dev.chromium.org/developers/design-documents/software-updates-courgette. URL retrieved April 2013.

[2] Cisco Performance Routing (PfR). http://www.cisco.com/en/US/products/ps8787/products_ios_protocol_option_home.html. URL retrieved April 2013.

[3] Internap. http://www.internap.com/. URL retrieved April 2013.

[4] node.js. http://nodejs.org. URL retrieved April 2013.

[5] PECAN measurement dataset. https://sites.google.com/site/pecanrouting/. URL retrieved April 2013.

[6] Transit Portal. http://tp.gtnoise.net. URL retrieved April 2013.

[7] V8 JavaScript engine. http://code.google.com/p/v8/. URL retrieved April 2013.

[8] Marissa Mayer at Web 2.0. http://glinden.blogspot.com/2006/11/marissa-mayer-at-web-20.html, Nov. 2006. URL retrieved April 2013.

[9] A. Akella, B. Maggs, S. Seshan, and A. Shaikh. On the performance benefits of multihoming route control. *IEEE/ACM Transactions on Networking*, 16(1), Feb. 2008.

[10] A. Akella, B. Maggs, S. Seshan, A. Shaikh, and R. Sitaraman. A measurement-based analysis of multihoming. In *Proc. ACM SIGCOMM*, Karlsruhe, Germany, Aug. 2003.

[11] A. Akella, J. Pang, B. Maggs, S. Seshan, and A. Shaikh. A comparison of overlay routing and multihoming route control. In *Proc. ACM SIGCOMM*, Portland, OR, Aug. 2004.

[12] A. Akella, S. Seshan, and A. Shaikh. Multihoming performance benefits: An experimental evaluation of practical enterprise strategies. In *Proc. USENIX Annual Technical Conference*, Boston, MA, June 2004.

[13] D. G. Andersen, H. Balakrishnan, M. F. Kaashoek, and R. Morris. Resilient Overlay Networks. In *Proc. 18th ACM Symposium on Operating Systems Principles (SOSP)*, pages 131–145, Banff, Canada, Oct. 2001.

[14] M. Andrews, B. Shepherd, A. Srinivasan, P. Winkler, and F. Zane. Clustering and server selection using passive monitoring. In *Proc. IEEE INFOCOM*, New York, NY, June 2002.

[15] S. Bhattacharjee, M. H. Ammar, E. W. Zegura, V. Shah, and Z. Fei. Application layer anycasting. In *Proc. IEEE INFOCOM*, Kobe, Japan, Apr. 1997.

[16] R. Bush, O. Maennel, M. Roughan, and S. Uhlig. Internet optometry: Assessing the broken glasses in Internet reachability. In *Proc. Internet Measurement Conference*, Chicago, Illinois, Oct. 2009.

[17] T. Callahan, M. Allman, and V. Paxson. A longitudinal view of HTTP traffic. In *Passive & Active Measurement (PAM)*, Zurich, Switzerland, Apr. 2010.

[18] J. Chu et al. *Increasing TCP's Initial Window*. Internet Engineering Task Force, Feb. 2013. `http://tools.ietf.org/pdf/draft-ietf-tcpm-initcwnd-08.pdf`. URL retrieved April 2013.

[19] D. Farinacci, V. Fuller, D. Oran, and D. Meyer. *Locator/ID Separation Protocol (LISP)*. Internet Engineering Task Force, Apr. 2008. Internet Draft (`http://tools.ietf.org/html/draft-farinacci-lisp-07`). Work in progress, expires October 2008.

[20] D. K. Goldenberg, L. Qiu, H. Xie, Y. R. Yang, and Y. Zhang. Optimizing cost and performance for multihoming. In *Proc. ACM SIGCOMM*, pages 79–92, Portland, OR, Aug. 2004.

[21] F. Guo, J. Chen, W. Li, and T. Chiueh. Experiences in building a multihoming load balancing system. In *Proc. IEEE INFOCOM*, Hong Kong, Mar. 2004.

[22] C. Huang, N. Holt, A. Wang, A. Greenberg, jin Li, and K. W. Ross. A DNS reflection method for global traffic management. In *Proc. USENIX Annual Technical Conference*, Boston, MA, June 2010.

[23] W. Jiang, R. Zhang-Shen, J. Rexford, and M. Chiang. Cooperative content distribution and traffic engineering in an ISP network. In *Proc. ACM SIGMETRICS*, Seattle, WA, June 2009.

[24] E. Katz-Bassett, C. Scott, D. R. Choffnes, I. Cunha, V. Valancius, N. Feamster, H. V. Madhyastha, T. Anderson, and A. Krishnamurthy. LIFEGUARD: practical repair of persistent route failures. In *Proc. ACM SIGCOMM*, Helsinki, Finland, Aug. 2012.

[25] C. Killian, M. Vrable, A. C. Snoeren, A. Vahdat, and J. Pasquale. Brief announcement: The overlay network content distribution problem. In *Proc. ACM PODC*, Las Vegas, NV, 2005.

[26] R. Krishnan, H. V. Madhyastha, S. Jain, S. Srinivasan, A. Krishnamurthy, T. Anderson, and J. Gao. Moving beyond end-to-end path information to optimize CDN performance. In *Proc. Internet Measurement Conference*, 2009.

[27] S. Lee, Z.-L. Zhang, and S. Nelakuditi. Exploiting as hierarchy for scalable route selection in multi-homed stub networks. In *Proc. Internet Measurement Conference*, Taormina, Italy, Oct. 2004.

[28] G. Linden. Make data useful. `https://sites.google.com/site/glinden/Home/StanfordDataMining.2006-11-28.ppt`. URL retrieved April 2013.

[29] MaxMind GeoIP Country. `http://www.maxmind.com/app/geolitecountry`. URL retrieved April 2013.

[30] N. McKeown, T. Anderson, H. Balakrishnan, G. Parulkar, L. Peterson, J. Rexford, S. Shenker, and J. Turner. OpenFlow: Enabling innovation in campus networks. *ACM Computer Communications Review*, Apr. 2008.

[31] G. Miller. Overlay routing networks (Akarouting). `http://www-math.mit.edu/~steng/18.996/lecture9.ps`. URL retrieved April 2013.

[32] M. Motiwala, M. Elmore, N. Feamster, and S. Vempala. Path Splicing. In *Proc. ACM SIGCOMM*, Seattle, WA, Aug. 2008.

[33] J. Pang, A. Akella, A. Shaikh, E. Krishnamurthy, and S. Seshan. On the responsiveness of DNS-based network control. In *Proc. Internet Measurement Conference*, Taormina, Italy, Oct. 2004.

[34] S. Radhakrishnan, Y. Cheng, J. Chu, A. Jain, and B. Raghavan. TCP fast open. In *Proc. CoNEXT*, Dec. 2011.

[35] B. Raghavan and A. C. Snoeren. A system for authenticated policy-compliant routing. In *Proc. ACM SIGCOMM*, Portland, OR, Aug. 2004.

[36] Adaptive Networking Software. `http://198.152.212.23/css/Products/P0345`. URL retrieved April 2013.

[37] S. Savage, T. Anderson, et al. Detour: A Case for Informed Internet Routing and Transport. *IEEE Micro*, 19(1):50–59, Jan. 1999.

[38] S. Seshan, M. Stemm, and R. Katz. A Network Measurement Architecture for Adaptive Applications. In *Proc. IEEE INFOCOM*, Tel-Aviv, Israel, Mar. 2000.

[39] A. Sharma, A. Venkataramani, and R. Sitaraman. Distributing content simplifies ISP traffic engineering. In *Proc. ACM SIGMETRICS*, Pittsburgh, PA, June 2013.

[40] SPDY: An experimental protocol for a faster web. `http://www.chromium.org/spdy/spdy-whitepaper`. URL retrieved April 2013.

[41] S. Sundaresan, W. de Donato, N. Feamster, R. Teixeira, S. Crawford, and A. Pescape. Broadband Internet Performance: A View from the Gateway. `http://www.ietf.org/proceedings/85/slides/slides-85-irtfopen-2.pptx`. URL retrieved April 2013.

[42] M. B. Tariq, A. Zeitoun, V. Valancius, N. Feamster, and M. Ammar. Answering "What-if" Deployment and Configuration Questions with WISE. In *Proc. ACM SIGCOMM*, Seattle, WA, Aug. 2008.

[43] S. Uhlig and O. Bonaventure. Designing bgp-based outbound traffic engineering techniques for stub ases. *ACM Computer Communications Review*, 34:89–106, Oct. 2004.

[44] H. Wang, H. Xie, L. Qiu, A. Silberschatz, and Y. Yang. Optimal ISP subscription for Internet multihoming: Algorithm design and implication analysis. In *Proc. IEEE INFOCOM*, Miami, FL, Mar. 2005.

[45] P. Wendell, J. Jiang, J. Rexford, and M. Freedman. DONAR: Decentralized server selection for cloud services. In *Proc. ACM SIGCOMM*, August/September 2010.

[46] W. Xu and J. Rexford. MIRO: Multi-path Interdomain ROuting. In *Proc. ACM SIGCOMM*, Pisa, Italy, Aug. 2006.

[47] X. Yang, D. Wetherall, and T. Anderson. Source selectable path diversity via routing deflections. In *Proc. ACM SIGCOMM*, Pisa, Italy, Aug. 2006.

[48] M. Yu, W. Jiang, H. Li, and I. Stoica. Tradeoffs in CDN designs for throughput oriented traffic. In *Proc. CoNEXT*, Dec. 2012.

High-Throughput Low-Latency Fine-Grained Disk Logging

Dilip Nijagal Simha [*]
Stony Brook University & ITRI,
NY
dnsimha@cs.stonybrook.edu

Tzi-cker Chiueh
Stony Brook University & ITRI,
Taiwan
tcc@itri.org.tw

Ganesh Karuppur
Rajagopalan
Stony Brook University, NY
ganesh.kr356@gmail.com

Pallav Bose
Stony Brook University, NY
pallavbose@gmail.com

ABSTRACT

Synchronously logging updates to persistent storage first and then asynchronously committing these updates to their rightful storage locations is a well-known and heavily used technique to improve the sustained throughput of write-intensive disk-based data processing systems, whose latency and throughput accordingly are largely determined by the latency and throughput of the underlying logging mechanism. The conventional wisdom is that logging operations are relatively straightforward to optimize because the associated disk access pattern is largely sequential. However, it turns out that to achieve both high throughput and low latency for fine-grained logging operations, whose payload size is smaller than a disk sector, is extremely challenging. This paper describes the experiences and lessons we have gained from building a disk logging system that can successfully deliver over 1.2 million 256-byte logging operations per second, with the average logging latency below 1 msec.

Categories and Subject Descriptors

D.4.2 [**Software**]: OPERATING SYSTEMS —*Storage Management*; D.4.8 [**Software**]: OPERATING SYSTEMS — *Performance*

Keywords

Logging; Hard Disk; High Throughput; Low Latency

1. INTRODUCTION

A well-known technique to enhance the throughput of write-intensive disk-based data processing systems such as on-line transaction processing (OLTP) systems is to synchronously log the incoming updates to disk and asynchronously commit them to their corresponding disk locations in a way

---

[*]All authors worked equally hard

that is optimized for the commit performance. The user-perceived response time of an update request to such systems is determined by the latency of the request's associated logging operation, because the update request is generally considered done when its logging step is completed. An ideal disk logging system is one that provides high throughput and low latency for logging operations with small payloads, e.g. 64 or 128 bytes. Small-payload logging operations are important because many applications only need to log the information associated with high-level operations, such as an update to a record in a B-tree page or a hash table bucket, and the size of this information is typically small. Low logging latency is also crucial, because it directly impacts the user-perceived response time, and because many applications are designed to be latency-bound, i.e., they cannot produce more requests unless previously submitted requests are completed.

Because logging involves append operations and thus sequential accesses, the conventional wisdom is optimizing the performance of logging operations is relatively straightforward. However, our research suggests that it is actually not at all trivial to achieve both high throughput and low latency for logging operations, especially for fine-grained ones, and has identified three key challenges. First, there is a mismatch between fine-grained logging and modern file systems. More concretely, because most modern file systems use 4KB block as the basic unit of reading and writing, logging a 64-byte or 128-byte record to a log file may require a read of the log file's last block, and a write of the same block after appending the log record to it. Second, there are multiple steps on the data path from the system call interface to the disk platter that a logging operation's payload needs to traverse, and some of these steps incur a per-operation overhead. Therefore, it is essential that consecutive logging operation requests be *properly merged* so as to effectively amortize these per-operation overheads and still rein in the average logging latency. Third, to make the best of the raw data transfer capability of modern disks, it is absolutely crucial to transform high-level logging operation requests to low-level disk access requests in such a way that the logging disks see an *un-interrupted* stream of disk write requests with consecutive target addresses. Without such careful planning and scheduling, the logging disks may end up sitting idle most of the time.

Rising to these challenges, we devise a novel disk logging system architecture called *Beluga*, which features a *floating* logging operation API that allows an application to perform a logging operation without specifying the target address of the operation's payload, and a highly streamlined disk write pipeline that aggregates logging operation requests optimally and moves aggregated operations through the pipeline in such a way that makes full use of the disk's raw data transfer capability. Empirical measurements on a fully operational 3-disk *Beluga* prototype show that it can achieve 1.2 million 256-byte logging operations per second, with each logging operation's latency kept below 1 msec. Moreover, even when logging operation requests arrive sparsely, *Beluga* is still able to achieve sub-msec logging operation latency. To the best of the authors' knowledge, this is the best disk logging performance ever reported in the literature.

Beluga is designed as a building block for constructing high-level logging and recovery subsystems, and provides the following service abstraction to its applications such as file system or DBMS: a cyclic persistent log device which is large enough (tens of gigabytes) that FIFO-based garbage collection works adequately. That is, by the time *Beluga* reaches the end of an application's log device, the log records in the beginning of the log device are no longer needed, and therefore *Beluga* could wrap around and continue logging from the beginning. In terms of functionalities, at run time, *Beluga* synchronously writes the payload of each logging operation to disk, and at recovery time, *Beluga* retrieves the active portion of a recovering application's log device and returns them to the application. However, *Beluga* cannot interpret the payloads of retrieved log records because the size and structure of each application-specific log record is completely opaque to *Beluga*. Instead, it is the application's recovery subsystem that performs such interpretation on the log records returned by *Beluga*. Similarly, a *Beluga* application needs to decide what information to log, e.g. metadata updates or checkpoint summary, and then utilizes *Beluga*'s service to log them to disk. In summary, *Beluga* writes log records to disk and reads them back at recovery time; how the log records are composed and how they should be interpreted are up to the applications using *Beluga*.

Although solid-state disk (SSD) is a promising technology for disk-intensive workloads, it is not necessarily a better fit than hard disks (HDD) for logging operations for the following reasons. First, because mainstream SSDs start to use multi-level cells, the per-cell write count limit is reduced to 10000, which may not fare well with the write-intensive nature of logging operations. Second, HDDs command a significant per-byte cost advantage over SSDs, and make it more feasible to trade space for performance by giving abundant space to each log device so as to reduce the garbage collection overhead to the minimum. Through this research, we hope to demonstrate that HDD-based disk logging is still among the most cost-competitive choice for logging applications.

2. RELATED WORK

Applications that do intensive data write operations often bottleneck on slow I/O bandwidth. A typical solution is to do delayed writing like Aries [19], which involves logging followed by an asynchronous write. The bottleneck now shifts to the logging operation and if the logging record size is small, the underlying storage has to manage high throughput with low latency even in cases of small random logging updates. Much research has been done on improving the

logging interface like the append-only logging technique [10] and we will discuss a few important works that highlight the core issues in an efficient logging system.

The idea of writing data to disk at the position where disk head happens to be can be traced back to as late as Trail [3]. Though Trail aims at the problem of minimizing seek delay and rotational latency, it's not trivial to implement it these days. It involves having accurate control over disk geometry details like rotational latency, seek latency, number of sectors in each track, zone coding, bad sectors mapping and other finer details. It's much tougher to implement this idea these days because of the advanced disk compaction techniques and more importantly disk manufacturers no longer supply the inner details of disk layout due to complicated disk management techniques and also due to competitive market. Variations of Trail include [24, 21, 8, 4] that target specific workloads using accurate disk geometry predictions. Lumb et al. [18] propose the idea of setting NCQ length to 2 and then utilize the disk seek and rotational latency to do some useful background work. *Beluga* also uses limited command queueing technique but also builds a sophisticated pipeline exploiting disk subsystem to the fullest extent. Yet another strikingly differentiating feature is in the added burden of these Trail like approaches to maintain a map of used and free blocks on disk in order to place the incoming data accurately on an unoccupied block and at the same time avoid track switch delay. *Beluga* avoids these by sweeping through the disk sequentially without leaving behind any holes in the process. As a result *Beluga* doesn't need to maintain any mapping information of the used and freed blocks.

The complexity of modern disk drives as elucidated by Gim et al. [12], an in-depth explanation of the Linux kernel storage subsystem in the book [5] gave us a good understanding of the complex sector layout schemes and the difficulties associated with the accurate estimation of the modern day hard disk geometry.

Logging disk Array [2] uses the RAID technology to handle small writes problem and NVRAM buffer to provide persistency to the cache. The buffer is flushed periodically to disk(Raid-5) when sufficient data is built up. Since RAID uses stripe size as the basic unit of data transfer to disk, NVRAM buffer is structured to hold data in multiples of the stripe size. This idea helps aggregate smaller writes and then write it at one shot to disk in units of stripe size so that no additional overhead is incurred in the transfer process. Though latency in writing to NVRAM buffer is very low(in order of microseconds), flushing NVRAM buffer to disk is not a trivial task. Though optimal size is chosen in units of stripe size, there are various other factors which determine whether the disk is utilized to the best extent. That's where this paper intends to break down the performance metrics and show how tuning certain parameters can help achieve best results. Another important factor to note is that NVRAM is a costly hardware resource which can be avoided if the inexpensive SATA disks can be carefully tuned to yield same or even better results. In many situations, writing to NVRAM can yield very slow response times [20].

LFS [22] is another major alternative developed to handle small buffer size writes. The entire file system is organized as a sequential log which converts writes from user application as append to the underlying log structure in the File System. But logging operations require persistent write to disk and hence synchronous writes are required which obviously yields a very low performance on a naive LFS. Modified techniques like [6, 13, 15, 25, 7, 17] use NVRAM or flash to make LFS handle synchronous writes efficiently. Both NVRAM and Flash are costly hardware alternatives. Further, NVRAM techniques suffer from the same drawback as explained previously. Though flash based disks provide very high throughput and very low latency, erase cycles are very slow and hence flash disks' performance goes down when its utilization factor goes up. Also, the basic block size of flash ranges from kilobytes to megabytes and is much higher than the sector size of typical magnetic hard disks. The erase operation in flash devices requires the block size to be of bigger size to get optimal results. However having a bigger block size increases the latency of smaller requests which need to be aggregated to form a bigger block size.

Flash logging [1] technique uses an array of USB flash devices to provide a fast logging infrastructure. The work proposes to use commodity USB devices as an alternative to expensive SSD based logging systems. The author discards modern day magnetic disks as ill suited for small sequential writes based on a naive logging implementation on SAS disks. *Beluga*'s evaluations convincingly show how commodity hard drives can be used to extract comparable performance as that of expensive flash based devices.

Phase Change Memory(PCM) [16] is a faster alternative to flash based disks but because of its smaller density and higher cost, it's not easy to be adopted in near future. Mohan et al. [9] propose to use PCM as the first choice for logging, since the speed of PCM is up to four orders of magnitude faster than that of flash based disks [11, 16], thereby guaranteeing very high throughputs and very low latencies.

3. VANILLA DISK LOGGING

File/Raw	Threads	Latency	Throughput
File	1	14.149	25.3
File	8	14.125	25.3
Raw	1	8.308	119.8
Raw	8	8.312	119.8

Table 1: *Latency and throughput of file-based and device-based (Raw) disk logging. The logging operation request size is 512 bytes. Throughput is measured in terms of number of logging operations per second and latency in milliseconds.*

Our first attempt was to write a user-level Linux application that synchronously appends the payload of every incoming logging operation request to a log file. As shown in Table 1, where the logging payload size is 512 bytes, the average logging latency of this disk logger is 14.1 msec, and its logging throughput on a single disk is lower than 30 logging operations per second, even with 8 threads issuing logging operation requests concurrently. A closer investigation reveals that file-based logging entails several drawbacks. First, file system caching introduces latency penalty due to extra data copying. This problem could be lessened by specifying the O_DIRECT option while opening the log file, which bypasses file system caching altogether. Second, each logging operation is embodied by a file write system call, which could trigger multiple disk I/Os because of accesses to file system metadata. Our measurement suggests that on av-

erage 5.2 disk I/Os are triggered by each file-based logging operation. Third, because the basic data read/write unit of the file systems is 4KB and caching is disabled for reasons mentioned above, a file system write operation may require a read of the disk block containing the write operation's target address range before the write if the logging operation payload is smaller than 4KB.

Our next attempt is to implement the logger as a Linux application that synchronously appends the payload of every incoming logging operation request to a raw device. This device-based logging design removes the first two problems of file-based logging by construction. The average number of disk I/Os per device-based logging operation is exactly 1. It also mitigates the third problem by using 512 bytes as its minimum data read/write unit. But, if the logging operation request size is smaller than 512 bytes, either an additional read is still needed or one disk sector is used in each logging operation. As shown in Table 1, device-based disk logging increases the logging throughput on a single disk to 120 logging operations per second when 8 threads are used. However, the average logging latency is still quite high, 8.3 msec. This high latency mainly comes from the fact that consecutive logging operations are issued synchronously. More concretely, the $N + 1$-th logging operation is issued only after the N-th logging operation is completed. This means that by the time the disk I/O for the $N + 1$-th logging operation reaches the disk, it misses its target sector and needs to wait for a full rotation, which is roughly 8.3 msec for a 7200 RPM disk drive.

Both device-based and file-based logging are based on top of Linux's block I/O layer, which abstracts the physical block I/O devices and presents a unified interface to high-level software. The block I/O layer maintains a request queue for each device to hold incoming block I/O requests destined to that device, and whenever possible merges every incoming request with some existing requests already in the queue if their target address ranges are adjacent to each other. In addition, the block I/O layer also re-orders requests in the queue to either improve the device's throughput or deliver differentiated quality of service (QoS) to different processes.

4. TOY-TRAIN DISK LOGGING

Beluga is a highly efficient disk logging system designed to address all the deficiencies observed in Section 3, and has successfully been implemented in the Linux kernel 2.6.39.1.

4.1 Conceptual Model

Our objective is to translate the raw data transfer bandwidth of modern disks into high throughput and low latency for logging operations. Towards this goal, we develop a *toy-train disk logging* technique, which constantly submits new disk write requests with consecutive target disk addresses to the logging disk so as to keep the disk fully occupied, *even in the absence of application-level logging operation requests*. This disk logging model makes it possible for the disk I/O software to have a tight grip of the disk head position without requiring intimate knowledge of the disk internals as in such previous efforts as Trail [3]. The proposed disk write pipeline is analogous to a toy train moving constantly around a closed circuit with two stations, with cargo uploaded in one station and offloaded in another. Even when no cargo is aboard, the train is still running around the circuit at full speed. In addition, this train actually never stops, because it can upload and offload cargo on the fly without slowing down. Since *Beluga* builds such a tightly controlled pipeline, it needs a dedicated logging disk without sharing it with other data workloads.

The throughput and latency performance of the proposed toy-train disk logging mechanism is excellent when the input load is dense (input logging request queue is full all the time) and sparse (input logging request queue is empty most of the time). However, when the input load is sparse, *Beluga* raises two concerns. First, *Beluga*'s constant disk writing model increases the wear of disk platters. Second, *Beluga*'s constant disk writing model increases the power consumption of logging disks. The first concern turns out to be a non-issue because of the huge capacity of modern disks. For example, given a 2-TB disk, if *Beluga* is able to write 100MB/sec, it means a given disk sector is overwritten once every 20000 (2TB/(100MB/sec)) seconds, or fewer than 5 times per day, or fewer than 2000 times per year, or fewer than 10000 times per 5 years, a disk's typical expected life time. Therefore, the level of wear induced by *Beluga* is well within the wear limit of modern hard disks.

The power consumption concern, however, is justified, because a disk's power consumption differs significantly when the disk head is idle and when it performs a read/write operation [14]. To reduce the additional power consumption when the input load is sparse, we develop a low-power version of *Beluga*, whose details are explained in Section 4.5.

4.2 Application Programming Interface

Beluga is designed to be a server's disk logging subsystem that supports logging operations from applications running on the same server. Its application programming interface (API) consists of the following three functions:

- `log_open(log_name)` takes a character string as input and returns a descriptor to a new log device, allows an application to give its log a symbolic name and associates the log's name with a log device's descriptor that later is used in logging operations.

- `log_write(device_descriptor, buffer_ptr, length)` appends the byte sequence defined by `buffer_ptr` and `length` to the end of the log device denoted by `device_descriptor`.

- `log_read(device_descriptor, buffer_ptr, length)` allows an application to read backwards from the end of the log file denoted by `device_descriptor` argument a byte sequence of size `length` to the buffer area pointed to by `buffer_ptr`.

To minimize data copying overhead for fine-grained (smaller than 512 bytes) disk logging, *Beluga* bypasses the file system and raw device access interfaces available in Linux, and uses the `ioctl` interface to implement `log_read()` and `log_write()`. More concretely, the payload of a logging or log write operation is passed directly to a *Beluga* kernel module above Linux's block I/O subsystem after entering the kernel. Upon receiving a logging operation's payload, *Beluga* prepends a *management header* to it, inserts the result into an *accumulation* queue, and later on at an appropriate moment submits the accumulated result as a single disk write request to Linux's block I/O subsystem. The per-log-record management header is application-independent and

contains the log record size, a valid bit, the associated log device descriptor and a per-device sequence ID. The valid bit holds 0 if a record is dummy or 1 if its issued from an user application. The actual contents of the log records are opaque to *Beluga*. With this arrangement, *Beluga* could combine the payloads of logging operations to different logging devices, each potentially using a *different log record size*, into a single physical disk write request and submits it to Linux's block I/O layer.

Beluga multiplexes multiple log devices, each associated with a different application, onto a physical disk, possibly in an interleaved fashion. When a server equipped with a *Beluga* disk logging subsystem fails and restarts, for each log device *Beluga* first identifies the youngest log record by performing a binary search of the underlying logging disk(s) based on the per-log-record management headers, and then waits for the applications' recovery components to read back their respective log devices for further recovery processing. *Beluga* itself does not interpret log records, and therefore is not involved in application-level recovery processing other than retrieving the requested log records.

Beluga assumes that the log device of each logging application is provisioned with sufficient storage space that the application could simply treat its log device as a cyclic FIFO buffer without applying any garbage collection mechanism. For example, a 500GB log device could hold the payloads of up to 1 billion 512-byte logging operations without overwriting any old log records, which is large enough to allow *Beluga* to simply wrap around a log device when it reaches the device's end. To accommodate applications that need longer retention period for their log records, one needs to provision atleast two disk arrays, so that while *Beluga* is logging on one disk array, one can archive logging records in the other disk array to another medium.

4.3 Streamlined Disk Write Pipeline

A major optimization goal of the *Beluga* project is to convert as much as possible a disk's raw data transfer rate into a proportionally high I/O rate, e.g., turning a byte rate of 100Mbytes/sec into an I/O rate of 100000 1KB-writes per second. The key to enable such efficient conversion is to feed the disk with write requests with consecutive start addresses in such a way that the on-disk controller constantly puts data onto the disk platters *nonstop*. Only disk drives that support command queuing could service one request after another without gap between them. Most modern SATA drives come with an efficient command queuing implementation called Native Command Queuing (NCQ) [23]. NCQ provides three optimization mechanisms. *First*, it queues disk access commands in the disk drive and makes it possible for the on-disk controller to immediately service the next command in the queue when the previous command is completed. *Second*, NCQ batches and/or schedules queued commands to reduce the number of commands that need to be serviced and the disk access overhead. *Third*, NCQ also supports interrupt coalescing, which aggregates multiple completion interrupts and signals the host once for them to reduce the total interrupt processing overhead.

The keys to maximize the logging operation rate are (a) properly batching incoming logging operation requests to balance between latency and data transport efficiency, and (b) constantly moving data to the disk platter. To embody these two ideas, we devise a four-stage pipeline to process

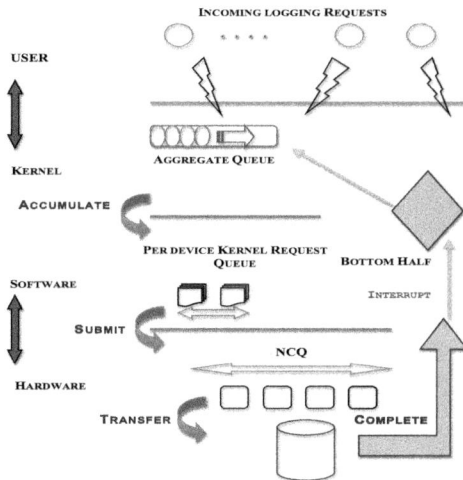

Figure 1: *The proposed four-stage disk write pipeline includes Accumulate, Submit, Transfer and Complete, and the queues involved are aggregate queue, per-device kernel request queue in the block I/O layer and on-disk NCQ queue.*

fixed-sized disk write requests, as shown in Figure 1. In the first stage (*Accumulate*), high-level logging operations are inserted in the aggregate queue and aggregated into low-level disk write requests. In the second stage (*Submit*), aggregated disk write requests are copied from the host memory to the on-disk queue managed by NCQ. In the third stage (*Transfer*), the payload of a queued disk write request is transferred to its associated location on the disk platter. In the fourth stage (*Complete*), the disk delivers a completion interrupt to the host for every completed disk write request, which in turn triggers additional processing on the host to complete each high-level logging operation associated with the completed disk write request. In this pipeline design, the on-disk controller takes care of the second half of the *Submit* stage, the *Transfer* stage and the first half of the *Complete* stage, and the rest is fully controlled by the host software. Because the on-disk controller is opaque to the host software, the cycle time of this pipeline is mainly determined by the *Transfer* stage. Of course, the time taken by the *Transfer* stage depends on the size of the disk write request's payload. So a major design issue here is to determine the optimal disk write request size so that the four stages in this pipeline are balanced, i.e., take approximately the same amount of time.

When the payload of the N-th disk write request is fully transferred to the disk platter, the on-disk controller starts the transfer of the $N + 1$-th request's payload to the disk platter, and sends a completion interrupt to the host, which arranges a DMA to move the payload of the $N + 2$-th request's payload into the disk. If the $N + 2$-th request's payload does not reach the disk in time, i.e., before the transfer of the $N+1$-request's payload is done, the on-disk controller won't be able to transfer the $N + 2$-th request's payload immediately after completing the transfer of the $N + 1$-th request's payload, thus wasting a full rotation delay. To avoid such waste, one must minimize the critical path, which includes the interrupt generation on the disk, the interrupt processing on the host and the payload DMA. To minimize the interrupt generation time, NCQ's interrupt coalescing

must be disabled. To minimize the impact of the interrupt processing time, the host software must be able to schedule the payload DMA as soon as possible after receiving the hardware interrupt. Although the raw data rate of modern PCIe bus (Gen2 or Gen3) is higher than that of the disk transfer bandwidth, the granularity of each disk write request must be sufficiently high to amortize the non-trivial fixed overhead that each PCIe bus transaction incurs. We discuss the optimal granularity or *batch size* for disk write requests in the Performance Evaluation section.

Because NCQ itself could also batch and schedule disk write requests in the on-disk queue, it could potentially increase the time taken by the *Transfer* stage by batching adjacent requests, or destroy the sequentiality of requests serviced consecutively because of its rotation delay-aware scheduling. Suppose there are five 64-KB disk write requests in the on-disk queue. It is possible that NCQ's scheduling logic may choose to service the fifth request after servicing the first request because the fifth request is closer to the first request than the second request. However, doing so seriously disrupts the pipeline. Therefore, among the three optimization mechanisms that NCQ provides, *Beluga* only wants its command queuing mechanism, and has to do away with the other two mechanisms.

4.4 Dense-Mode Logging

In the process of designing *Beluga*, we distinguish between *dense-mode logging*, in which high-level logging operations arrive at the logging subsystem at a rate equal to its maximum throughput, and *sparse-mode logging*, in which high-level logging operations arrive at the logging subsystem slower than its maximum throughput. The design goal for dense-mode logging is both high logging throughput and low logging latency, whereas the design goal for sparse-mode logging is low logging latency only.

When *Beluga* receives high-level logging operations, it queues them in its buffer area, and batches them into low-level aggregated disk write requests of optimal size, which we will explore later. Then when a completion interrupt arrives, *Beluga* dispatches an aggregated disk write request to Linux's block I/O subsystem. To prevent the merging and scheduling functionalities of Linux's block I/O subsystem from getting in the way, *Beluga* turns on the *no-merge* option and chooses the *Noop* I/O scheduler. Essentially, *Beluga* does its own buffering and batching according to the streamlined disk write pipeline design, and uses Linux's block I/O subsystem as a dumb pipe to push the aggregated disk write requests through to the disks.

To turn off the scheduling functionalities of NCQ, *Beluga* sets the NCQ queue length to 2, so that the on-disk controller does not have more than one choice at a time.

An implementation challenge for dense-mode logging is how to shorten the critical path described earlier, more specifically, how to quickly transfer the payload of the disk write request that is the next to be dispatched to the disk. The Linux kernel uses a separate kernel thread to dispatch the next disk write request and transfer its payload to the on-disk queue. This implementation introduces additional delay because after a completion interrupt arrives at the host, control goes through the interrupt handler, the OS's scheduler, the software interrupt logic, possibly other kernel threads and eventually the request-dispatching kernel thread. To remove these delays in this implementation, we attempted to modify the Linux kernel so that it dispatches the next disk write request from the aggregate queue *directly* in the context of the completion interrupt handler, thus more tightly tying a completion interrupt with the payload movement it triggers. While conceptually straightforward, it requires a non-trivial modification because in Linux, functions that could potentially block, such as `submit_bio`, are not supposed to be called from an *atomic* context, because such an execution context does not persist and thus is not supposed to block. Eventually we decided to stay with the original kernel thread-based implementation.

In *Beluga*, the target logical block address of an aggregated disk write request is determined only at the point when it is dispatched. *Late address binding* is necessary especially when multiple physical disks are used in a *Beluga* based disk logging system, where the relative timing for request completion among these disks could vary due to run-time conditions and thus is not fully deterministic. Accordingly, the target logical block address of each high-level logging operation is also determined only when its associated aggregated disk write request is dispatched.

After a disk write request is completed, *Beluga* demultiplexes this completion signal to the logging operations that compose the disk write request by invoking their corresponding post-completion request completion logic. The latency of a logging operation is the time interval between when the logging operation enters *Beluga*'s buffer and when the post-completion processing of the logging operation is finished.

To jump-start the proposed streamlined disk write pipeline, *Beluga* first issues *back to back* two disk write requests to the disk to fill up the *Transfer* and *Submit* stage, and then holds off the third disk write request until the completion interrupt of the first disk write request arrives. After that, a new aggregated disk write request is fed to the pipeline only after an existing disk write request exits the pipeline.

It is straightforward to generalize the above design to multiple logging disks, because Linux allocates a separate per-device request queue for each individual disk. However, the *Accumulate* stage is centralized and *Beluga*'s accumulation buffer is shared by the logging disks. That is, *Beluga* aggregates incoming high-level logging operations into low-level disk write requests for all logging disks, and as soon as a completion interrupt from a logging disk comes, it dispatches an aggregated disk write request to that particular logging disk. To avoid contention among logging disks, the logging disks are jump-started in a staggered fashion to prevent unwanted synchronization among them.

The optimal batch size for a disk write pipeline on a server depends on its PCIe bus and disk interface (SATA, SAS or SCSI), which affect the *Submit* stage time, and the RPM rating of the disk, which affects the *Transfer* stage time. In fact, because the *Transfer* stage time for a disk write request of a certain size may vary depending on where its target address lies on the disk surface, the optimal batch size of a disk write pipeline changes as the pipeline traverses different parts of the disk surface. More specifically, because outermost tracks (closer to track 0) have higher sector density than innermost tracks, the former's data transfer rate is higher than the latter's. Therefore, the optimal batch size is expected to increase as the target addresses of the disk write requests issued by *Beluga* increase.

In summary, for dense-mode logging, *Beluga* accumulates user-level logging operation requests, aggregates them into physical disk write requests, feeds them into a streamlined disk write pipeline, and delivers a completion response to each user-level logging operation when its payload reaches the disk. This streamlined disk write pipeline is novel because it is designed to move fixed-sized data payload in a lock-step fashion, similar to a CPU pipeline, so as to fully exploit the disk's raw data transfer capability and effectively convert its data transfer rate (Mbytes/sec) into the commensurate I/O rate (IOs/sec).

4.5 Sparse-Mode Logging

An implicit assumption underlying the design of the streamlined disk write pipeline is that there is an infinite stream of disk write requests that are waiting to fill the pipeline. This assumption is valid for dense-node logging, but does not hold for sparse-mode logging. More concretely, if a logging operation request appears after a period of inactivity, this logging operation request enters the disk write pipeline *alone* and therefore cannot benefit from any disk head position information that may be gleaned from neighboring requests, as is the case in dense-mode logging. As a consequence, the average latency of such logging operation requests may be high, because it is difficult to ensure that the target address assigned to a sparse-mode logging operation request is close to the disk head position at the time when the request is submitted.

One way to reduce the latency of sparse-mode logging operations is to constantly predict the disk head position [3], and use this prediction to derive a better target logical block address for each sparse-mode logging operation. However, as modern disks become more and more complicated, this approach becomes less and less effective, because the internal control mechanisms inside disk drives, such as NCQ, on-disk caching, interrupt coalescing, etc., tend to obscure disk head movement and thus get in the way of disk head position prediction.

In contrast, *Beluga* leverages its dense-mode logging architecture to implement sparse-mode logging. More concretely, *Beluga* constantly maintains a dummy aggregated disk write request in its buffer and dispatches this request to the disk write pipeline when it runs out of application-level logging operations. However, whenever *Beluga* occasionally receives an application-level logging operation request, it aggregates this application-level logging operation request to the dummy disk write request currently being formed. When the next disk completion interrupt comes, *Beluga* dispatches this disk write request as usual. That is, *Beluga* keeps the disk write pipeline constantly busy either with real disk write requests accumulated from application-level logging operation requests (dense-mode logging), or with dummy disk write requests (sparse-mode logging), some of which may contain high-level logging operations issued by applications.

The key advantage of this design is that it is self-adaptive to the timing variations of the disk write pipeline. That is, because the disk write pipeline is driven by events such as request completion interrupts rather than by a hardware clock, the timing experienced by each disk write request may vary. However, by keeping the disk write pipeline full with dummy write requests, all the timing variations due to firmware, software or hardware are automatically accounted for and thus removed from the implementation complexity of sparse-mode disk logging. The main drawback of this design is the additional power consumption associated with dummy disk write requests.

The original *Beluga*'s design (called *full Beluga*) continuously dispatches disk write request of size S whose target addresses are S apart, where S corresponds to the batch size. There are two possible approaches to reducing the power consumption of this design. The first approach is to submit the same sequence of disk write requests in the same way as in full *Beluga* but decrease the size of each submitted disk write request to one disk sector (512 bytes), when there are no pending logging operation requests. This way, the number of bytes written to disk could be reduced by one to two orders of magnitude when there are no pending logging operation requests. The second approach is to issue only $\frac{1}{N}$ of the disk write requests in full *Beluga*, employ the issue times and completion interrupt times of these disk write requests to estimate the issue times of the skipped $\frac{N-1}{N}$ disk write requests had they been dispatched in full *Beluga*, and use the estimated issue time for logging operation requests that arrive sparsely. This way, the number of bytes written to disk is reduced by a factor of N when there are no pending logging operation requests.

Unfortunately neither approach works as expected because some modern disks implement a *request merging* optimization: When a disk write request R arrives at a disk's NCQ queue and cannot be merged with any existing disk write request, the on-disk controller tries to merge R with some future requests by deferring servicing R for approximately 1 msec after it arrives, even if the disk head passes R's target address within this 1-msec interval. This optimization gets in the way of the above two approaches because none of the disk write requests issued in these two designs are mergeable with any existing disk write request. In addition, the on-disk controller also implements a request scheduling mechanism, which makes it difficult to predict the actual service order of disk write requests even when their target addresses are sorted.

To get around the request merging mechanism, the target address of each submitted disk write request is set at 1 msec away from the disk head position at the time when it arrives on the disk. This prevents each submitted disk write request from experiencing a full rotation delay. To get around the on-disk request scheduler, we limit the effective number of active requests in the NCQ queue to 4 and ensure that they are sufficiently far apart. Taking into account these design constraints, we come up with a low-power version of *Beluga* as follows. A sequence of *sentinel* disk write requests are dispatched to the logging disk regardless of whether applications issue any logging operation requests. When the N-th sentinel request is completed, low-power *Beluga* issues the $N+2$-th sentinel request. The distance between the target addresses of consecutive sentinel requests is D sectors, where the time it takes for the disk head to pass D sectors is at least 1 msec. Suppose the target address of a sentinel request is Sector T, then all application-issued logging operation requests that arrive between the time when the disk head passes Sector $T - M - D$ and the time when the disk head passes Sector $T - M$ are aggregated into one disk write request that is to be merged with this sentinel request. The interval marked by these two time points is the *feasible interval* associated with this sentinel request. M is an empirical safety margin in the following sense: If a new request is to be merged with an existing sentinel request without disrupting

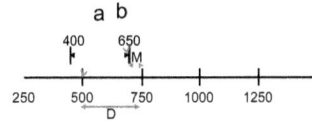

Figure 2: *An example sentinel disk write request schedule for low-power* Beluga *when the inter-sentinel-request distance is 250 sectors and the margin is 100 sectors. Logging operation requests issued by applications during an interval are aggregated into a disk write request that is merged with the corresponding sentinel request.*

the service order, the new request must arrive at the disk at least M sectors before the disk head passes the existing request's target address. The size of each sentinel request is 4KB because this is the minimum size for a request to be mergeable. This low-power *Beluga* design not only dispatches fewer disk write requests than full *Beluga*, but also keeps each request smaller than those in full *Beluga*.

Figure 2 shows an example schedule of sentinel requests in low-power *Beluga*, where D is 250 and M is 100. The target addresses of the sentinel requests are Sector 250, 500, 750, 1000, 1250, 1500, etc. The sentinel request with the target address Sector 750 is dispatched when the request with the target address Sector 250 is completed, or about 500 sectors before it is serviced. It takes more than 1 msec for the disk head to fly over 500 sectors. In addition, at most two sentinel requests are in the on-disk queue at a time. For this sentinel request (spanning Sector 750 to 757), all application-issued logging operation requests that arrive between the time when the disk head passes Sector 400 and the time when the disk head passes Sector 650 are aggregated into one disk write request whose target address is Sector 758 and submitted to the disk when the disk head passes Sector 650. If there are no application-issued logging operation requests, the number of bytes written in low-power *Beluga* is 8 sectors every 250 sectors, or roughly $\frac{1}{30}$ of that of full *Beluga*.

5. PERFORMANCE EVALUATION

We have successfully built a Linux-based *Beluga* prototype, and carried out a detailed performance evaluation of this prototype using a Dell Machine with a 1.8GHz Dual-Core processor, 2 GB Memory and three 1 TB WD Caviar Black 7200RPM SATA hard disks, and a Gen2 PCIe bus.

5.1 Methodology

A sequence of logging operation requests were fed to the *Beluga* prototype, and the average logging latency and overall logging throughput were measured. The latency of each logging operation request is the time when it enters the logging subsystem and when the logging subsystem returns a completion response for it. Throughput is defined as the total number of logging operations completed, i.e., its payload is written to disk, per second. We used an open-source tool on Linux called *blktrace* to take these measurements. *Blktrace* is a block-layer I/O tracing tool that provides detailed information on where the time is spent on the data path from the entry point to the block I/O layer until data is written to the disk and a completion interrupt is delivered.

To measure the maximum throughput of *Beluga*, we develop a kernel-level logging operation traffic generator that minimizes the overhead of creating application-level logging operation requests. The *kernel level log generator (KLG)* is installed as a loadable kernel module. Its preferred over a real-world user-level application because the logging workload from KLG is the most demanding and could best stress *Beluga*.

We modify the kernel scheduler so that immediately after the main thread of *Beluga* sets up a DMA to move logging operation payloads to the disk, it calls KLG, which generates logging operation requests according to the elapsed time since it was invoked and the input traffic load, and put them in the input queue. The *Beluga* thread then moves as many requests in the input queue to its aggregate queue as possible, whenever it has a chance to visit the input queue. Moreover, to minimize the interference between the KLG and the logging subsystem, we bind the KLG to a specific set of CPU cores, which are disjoint from those on which *Beluga* runs. The *Beluga* prototype has been stress tested with continuous input logging operations to cover all disk blocks on the log disk multiple times. However, in each experiment run, we issued 60 seconds worth of logging operations. Its also stress tested to ensure other system activities don't disturb *Beluga*'s tightly controlled pipeline. We ran several memory intensive and disk I/O intensive programs in parallel and observed that *Beluga*'s performance remained unaffected to a large extent. Different runs correspond to different combinations of batch size, logging operation request size and inter-operation interval. Although *Beluga* aggregates logging operations into disk write requests, the average logging latency is the end-to-end delay experienced by each logging operation, and the logging throughput corresponds to the number of logging operations completed per second.

5.2 Dense-Mode Logging

5.2.1 Overall Performance

The most important parameter in the proposed disk write pipeline is the *batch size*, or the granularity of the fixed-sized disk write requests that are moved through the pipeline. When the batch size is too small, the time to submit a disk write request from host memory to on-disk queue is longer than the time required to transfer it from on-disk queue to the disk platter, because of the non-trivial per-transaction overhead, and as a result, by the time the disk write request reaches the disk, the immediately previous disk write request is already done and it misses its target sector and is thus delayed by a full rotation cycle. When the batch size is too high, each logging operation request experiences a higher queuing delay in the accumulation queue, and the transfer time is also higher; consequently the average logging latency is higher. Table 2 shows the average logging latency and logging throughput for an input sequence of 10 million 256-byte logging operations under different batch size. When the batch size is 16KB, the *Submit* stage time is longer than the *Transfer* stage time, and almost every disk write request experiences a full rotation cycle time. When the transfer delay of a disk write request is increased to a full rotation delay, the aggregation delay of the logging operations in the following disk write request is also increased on average by half of the transfer delay. As a result, the average logging latency is quite high, 12.7 msec, and the logging throughput is accordingly low, 15044 operations per second, the inverse of which corresponds to the average data transfer delay.

As the batch size is increased from 16KB to 24KB and 28 KB, the probability of an aggregated disk write request experiences a full rotation delay decreases but is still non-zero. As a consequence, the average logging latency also decreases, and the logging throughput increases. When the batch size reaches 32KB and beyond, the *Submit* stage time is always smaller than the *Transfer* stage time, and *none* of the disk write requests experience a full rotation delay. The effective pipeline cycle time is the maximum of these two stage times. After the batch size grows larger than 32KB, the average logging latency is worsened, because the initial aggregation delay is higher and the pipeline cycle time is increased, which leads to longer end-to-end pipeline latency. However, the logging throughput improves with the batch size, because the fixed overhead associated with the *Submit*, *Transfer* and *Complete* stage is more efficiently amortized. Because the design goal of *Beluga* is both low logging latency and high logging throughput, the ideal batch size is the smallest batch size that enables the *Submit* stage time is smaller than the *Transfer* stage time, and the default batch size used in the current *Beluga* prototype is 32KB.

Batch Size	Latency(μsec)	Throughput(OPs/sec)
16 KB	12753	15044
24 KB	3087	108471
28 KB	2832	118157
32 KB	938	404228
40 KB	1108	428005
48 KB	1327	429665
56 KB	1536	433331
64 KB	1755	433990

Table 2: *Average latency and throughput of 256-byte logging operations on the* Beluga *prototype when the batch size is varied from 16KB to 64KB*

To examine where each logging operation spends its time in the *Beluga* prototype, we used *blktrace*, which is an analysis and instrumentation tool for Linux's block I/O layer. *Blktrace* breaks the data path from Linux's block I/O layer down into stages, and give timing measurements(in μsec) for each of them. The following are definitions of a set of terms used in our analysis:

- Aggregation Delay: the amount of time a logging operation stays in the aggregate queue.

- Q2D: Time required for an aggregated request to be inserted into and to stay in the per-device queue.

- D2C: Time between when a disk write request is issued to a disk and when it is completed, as indicated by a completion interrupt delivered to the block I/O layer.

- Q2Q: Time between two consecutive aggregate disk write requests that are inserted into the block I/O layer's request queue.

Table 3 shows the detailed breakdown of the time a logging operation spends in the disk write pipeline when the batch size is varied. Because *Beluga* aggregates logging operation requests into disk write requests, the latency experienced by a logging operation request includes the time it spends in the aggregate queue (Aggregate Delay) and the latency experienced by the disk write request to which it belongs (Q2D + D2C). D2C includes the *Submit* stage time and the *Transfer* stage time. The *Submit* stage time includes the completion interrupt processing time, which is about 100 μsec, and the data transfer time on the PCIe bus. Because *Beluga* disables the merging, sorting and the scheduling mechanisms in Linux's block I/O layer, Q2D is very small, less than 2 μsec. Q2Q corresponds to the cycle time of the disk write pipeline, and its inverse corresponds to the pipeline's throughput.

When the batch size is 16KB, D2C is 8500 μsec, which suggests that every aggregated disk write request misses its target sector when it arrives at the disk and experiences a full rotation delay, about 8.3msec for a 7200RPM disk drive, because the *Submit* stage time is higher than the disk data transfer time of 16KB, about 160 μsec. Moreover, the Aggregation Delay is 4251 μsec, which is higher than expected and is a collateral damage of the longer disk data transfer time. When the batch size is 28KB, D2C is decreased to 1786 μsec, which suggests that still a certain percentage of disk write requests miss their target sector and experience a full rotation delay, and the Aggregation Delay is decreased accordingly to 944 μsec.

When the batch size is 32KB, D2C is 523 μsec, the Aggregation Delay is 313 μsec, and none of the disk write requests experience a full rotation delay. Because Q2Q or the pipeline cycle time is 316 μsec, the throughput of this configuration is 3158 32KB disk write requests per second or 404228 256-byte logging operations per second, as shown in Table 2 . Because the *Transfer* stage time is larger than the *Submit* stage time, the *Transfer* stage time is the pipeline cycle time. Therefore, within DC2, 316 μsec is due to data transfer (Q2Q), 100 μsec is due to interrupt processing, and the remaining time (107μsec) is due to data transfer on the PCIe bus. Because there is noticeable difference between the *Transfer* stage time and the *Submit* stage time, the optimal batch size, which corresponds to the case when the *Transfer* stage time is the same as the *Submit* stage time, lies somewhere between 28KB and 32KB. Nonetheless with the batch size of 32 KB, *Beluga* delivers an average logging latency of under 1 millisecond and a logging throughput of 404K 256-byte logging operations, which exceeds 100 Mbytes/sec and is pretty close to the raw disk data transfer capability.

When the batch size is 40KB, the pipeline cycle time is increased to 373 μsec, but the throughput is also increased to 428K logging operations per second, because a 40KB aggregated disk write request contains more logging operations than that in a 32KB aggregated disk write request. Unfortunately, the average logging latency is also increased to 1108 μsec, partly because the Aggregation Delay is increased to 369 μsec.

Batch Size	Aggregation Delay (μsec	Q2D (μsec)	D2C (μsec)	Overall Latency (μsec
16 KB	4251	1.871	8500	12753
24 KB	1029	1.638	2056	3087
28 KB	943	1.625	1887	2832
32 KB	313	1.719	623	938
40 KB	369	1.829	737	1108
48 KB	442	1.688	883	1327
56 KB	512	1.904	1022	1536
64 KB	585	1.768	1168	1755

Table 3: *Detailed breakdown of the time each logging operation spends in the disk write pipeline as the batch size is varied*

Logging Operation Size	Latency (μsec)	Throughput (OPs/sec)
512 B	959	193275
256 B	938	404228
128 B	986	849461
64 B	1011	1639408

Table 4: *The average logging latency and logging throughput for a sequence of logging operations when the logging operation request size is varied from 64 bytes to 512 bytes*

Table 4 shows the impact of the log operation size on the average logging latency and throughput of *Beluga*. Smaller logging operation request size only increases the overhead of aggregating logging operation requests into disk write requests, but has no effect on the disk write pipeline. This is why the average logging latency remains largely the same when the logging operation request size is varied from 64 bytes to 512 bytes. The logging throughput, on the other hand, is inversely proportional to the logging operation request size, because the disk write pipeline's throughput also stays the same.

5.2.2 Adaptive Batch Size Selection

Starting Offset (GB)	Optimal Batch size (KBytes)	Latency (μsec)	Throughput (OPs/sec)
900	24	1183	241158
750	24	981	290390
500	28	932	356791
0	32	938	404228

Table 5: *The impact of the starting disk offset used in the logging experiment on the optimal batch size for the disk write pipeline when the logging operation request size is 256 bytes*

For results reported in previous subsections, we started each experiment run at the 0th sector of the disk. Table 5 shows the latency and throughput of 256-byte logging operations on the *Beluga* prototype when their log records are written to different parts of the disk using different batch size. As the starting disk offset of an experiment run increases, the raw data transfer rate during the experiment run lowers, the *Transfer* stage time becomes longer and thus is more likely to be larger than the *Submit* stage time, and the optimal batch size, i.e., the minimum batch size whose corresponding average logging latency is smaller than 1 msec, thus also decreases. For example, the optimal batch sizes when the starting disk offset is 0, 500GB and 750GB are 32KB, 28KB and 24KB, respectively. These batch size choices enable *Beluga* to keep the average logging latency under 1 msec. However, when the starting disk offset is 900GB, the average logging latency jumps above 1 msec regardless of the batch size, because the lower disk data transfer rate at the center of the disk sets a lower bound on the latency.

Because the optimal batch size for different parts of a modern disk is different, *Beluga* includes an adaptive batch size selection mechanism that chooses the optimal batch size according to the current disk head position. This mechanism requires the log disks to be pre-calibrated so as to extract the optimal batch size for each disk region. Figure 3 shows that *Beluga*'s adaptive batch size selection mechanism is able to keep the average logging latency below 1 msec throughout

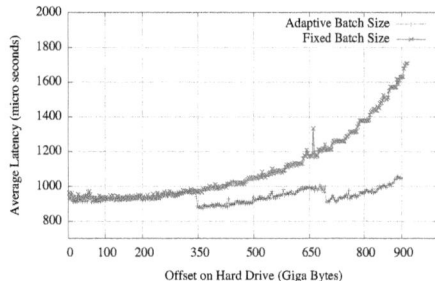

Figure 3: *The average logging latency of the* Beluga *prototype when data is written at different offsets on disk and the logging operation request size is 256 bytes*

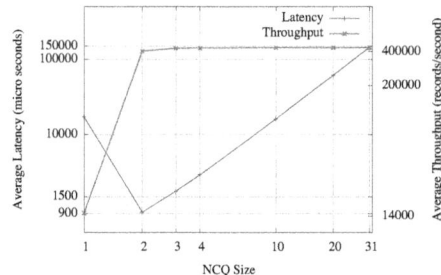

Figure 4: *The average logging latency and throughput of the* Beluga *prototype when NCQ queue length is varied and the logging operation request size is 256 bytes*

the entire disk, whereas using a fixed batch size (in this case 32KB) could lead to an increase in the average logging latency by more than 70%, when the disk heads reach the center of the disk platters.

Logging Disks	Latency (μsec)	Throughput (OPs/sec))
1	938	404228
2	934	810250
3	950	1192554

Table 6: *The average logging latency and throughput of the* Beluga *prototype when the number of disks increases from 1 to 3 and the logging operation request size is 256 bytes*

5.2.3 Sensitivity Study

The design of *Beluga* is linearly scalable with respect to the number of disks it uses, because each disk is equipped with a per-device request queue and an on-disk queue. However, all the disks in the *Beluga* system share a global aggregate queue, from which *Beluga* issues aggregated disk write requests to individual disks upon receiving completion interrupts. Until the *Beluga* system hits the write request issue rate limit, its logging throughput should scale linearly with the number of disks in it, as shown in Table 6, which also shows that the average logging latency is largely unaffected when the number of disks is increased from 1 to 3. With just three 7200 RPM SATA disks, the *Beluga* prototype is able to achieve a total logging throughput of 1.2 million 256-byte logging operations per second and keep the average logging latency under 1 msec. We believe this is the best logging performance ever reported on commodity-grade disks. The immediate bottleneck to scale up the *Beluga* prototype with even more disks is the interrupt processing overhead. Using a polling architecture rather than an interrupt-driven architecture is a possible solution to remove this bottleneck.

NCQ plays a key role in the design of the proposed streamlined disk write pipeline. However, the NCQ queue length is set to 2 by default, because we want to prevent NCQ's merging and scheduling functionalities from disrupting the carefully arranged timing for disk write payload movement. Figure 4 shows the average logging latency and throughput for 256-byte logging operations on the *Beluga* prototype when the NCQ queue size is varied. When the NCQ queue length is 1, the logging latency is very high, approximately 17msec, because there is only one disk write request in the disk at a time and it is not possible for the on-disk controller to service the next write request immediately after serving

the current write request. That is, the $N+1$-th request can be issued from the aggregate queue to the disk only after the completion interrupt for the N-th request is raised, and thus has to experience at least one full rotation delay.

When the NCQ queue length is 2, the on-disk controller could service consecutive disk write requests back to back, and the disk's raw data transfer capability is fully exploited. When the NCQ queue length is greater than 2, the on-disk controller still could service consecutive disk write requests back to back, but each disk write request's latency increases because it needs to wait longer in the NCQ queue. That is, when the NCQ queue length is 2, a disk write request is expected to be serviced soon after it arrives at the NCQ queue; however, when the NCQ queue length is 3, a disk write request is expected to wait for one full data transfer time before it is serviced. Moreover, the larger the NCQ queue length, the longer the average logging latency. As for the logging throughput, it remains the same as the NCQ queue length grows to 2 and beyond, because disk write requests are serviced one after another non-stop.

5.3 Sparse-Mode Logging

To test the effectiveness of using full *Beluga* to support sparse-mode logging, we varied the inter-logging-operation interval and measured the average logging latency, which remains virtually constant at 938 μsec, as the inter-logging-operation interval increases from 10 μsec to 0.1 second. This shows that full *Beluga* is indeed capable of servicing sparse logging operation requests with low latency.

Distance (sectors)	Average (μsec)	Re-ordering (%)
220	8395.4	18.46
230	6835.3	16.16
240	4776.9	10.36
250	2737.3	4.62
260	2033.8	2.39
270	1324.3	0.15
280	1320.3	0.004
290	1362.7	0.001
300	1411.8	0.002

Table 7: *The impact of inter-sentinel-request distance on the latency of sparse logging operation requests that are dispatched immediately after one sentinel request is completed and are merged with the next sentinel request*

Low-power *Beluga* is characterized by two configuration parameters, the target address distance (D) between consecutive sentinel requests and the safety margin (M) for merging with an existing sentinel request. We conducted a series of experiments to determine the proper value of D. In each run, we dispatched a series of sentinel requests whose target addresses are spaced by D sectors, and a sparse logging operation request immediately after every sentinel request is completed, which is to be merged with the next sentinel request. Table 7 shows the impact of D on the average latency of these sparse logging operation requests. When D is smaller than 270, the average latency is above 2 msec, and the root cause is the sentinel requests are serviced out of order when the inter-sentinel-request distance is too small. For example, when D is 220, 18.46% of the sentinel requests are serviced out of order and, together with the sparse logging operation requests that merge with them, experience a full rotation delay. The request re-ordering percentage comes down to with 1% only when D is increased to 270.

Because smaller D values lead to substantial request re-ordering, we explored the matching M value only for $D = 260$, $D = 270$, $D = 280$, $D = 290$, and $D = 300$. For each candidate D value, we tried 10 possible M values, and picked the M value that results in the minimum average latency. Given a M value, between the i-th and $i+1$-th sentinel request, we issued a sparse logging operation request at the time when the disk head passes the sector that is M sectors ahead of the target address of the $i+1$-th sentinel request, measured its latency, and computed the average of these latency measurements. When M is too large, dispatched sparse logging operation requests have to wait in the NCQ queue longer. When M is too small, dispatched sparse logging operation requests may cause re-ordering of sentinel requests already in the NCQ queue. Table 8 shows the best M value for each candidate D value. The best M value seems to be lie between 125 and 140. The *Average* column represents the average latency of sparse logging operation requests when they are dispatched to disk at the end of the feasible interval of their associated sentinel requests (Point b in Figure 2). In contrast, in Table 7 the sparse logging operation requests are dispatched to disk at the completion of the sentinel request that precedes their associated sentinel requests (Point a in Figure 2). That's why the Average numbers in these two tables are different.

Because sparse logging operation requests could arrive at any point of a feasible interval, they would experience a variable amount of waiting time before being dispatched to disk at the end of the feasible interval they fall in. The *E2E Average* column shows the end-to-end average latency of a sparse logging operation request, which includes this waiting time. As D increases, on the one hand the probability of request re-ordering and the associated latency penalty decreases, but on the other hand the size of the feasible interval and the average waiting time also increases. So the optimal D corresponds to a balanced trade-off between these two factors. In our testbed, the best-performing configuration is when the inter-sentinel-request distance (D) is 290 and the safety margin (M) is 125, and its end-to-end average latency for sparse logging operation requests is 1315.5 μsec. Although the average latency of low-power *Beluga* is even worse than the worst-case latency of full *Beluga* ((938 μsec), the number of bytes written in low-power *Beluga* when there are no application-issued logging operation requests is only 8 sectors (4KB) every 290 sectors, or a factor of $\frac{1}{36}$ smaller than full *Beluga*.

Distance (sectors)	Margin (sectors)	Average (μsec)	E2E Average (μsec)
260	140	1548	2089.7
270	125	768.2	1320.7
280	135	770.2	1353.5
290	125	711.3	1315.5
300	135	747.9	1372.9

Table 8: *The average latency for sparse logging operation requests that are dispatched at the end of the feasible interval of the sentinel requests with which they are to merge, under different inter-sentinel-request intervals and their associated margins*

Logging Operation Request Size	Latency
512 bytes	1.2 msec
2K bytes	1.34 msec
4K bytes	1.35 msec

Table 9: *The average logging latency of 1 million logging operations against an SSD-backed device when the logging operation request size is 512 bytes, 2KB and 4KB*

5.4 Comparison with SSD-based Logging

To compare the performance of the *Beluga* prototype with logging using SSDs. We measured the average latency of 1 million logging operations against an SSD-based device with the on-disk cache turned off. The SSD used in this test is a 64-Gbyte SSD based on JMicron JM612F flash controller and Samsung's SLC flash memory chips. The result, shown in Table 9, shows that the *Beluga* prototype's average logging latency is actually slightly better than that of SSD-based logging. Of course, the device-based logging implementation on SSD is not as extensively optimized. Actually we believe the streamlined disk write pipeline described in this paper is equally effective for SSDs. Nonetheless, this result demonstrates that with proper structuring and tuning, hard disk-based logging could be as performant as SSD-based logging. In fact, for MLC SSDs, which has limited write count (around 10000), a high-performance low-latency hard disk logging technique such as *Beluga* may be a useful complement to handle sequential logging workloads.

6. CONCLUSION

The disk access pattern of logging is arguably the most straightforward because it is sequential in nature, and yet, it is surprisingly difficult to achieve both high logging throughput and low logging latency, especially for fine-grained logging operations. The main reason is that modern I/O stacks and disk drives incorporate redundant request merging and scheduling functionalities that may get in each other's way. Moreover, although careful control of disk access timing is crucial in delivering high disk I/O performance, there is typically little coordination between the I/O stack and the underlying disks. As a consequence, the latency and throughput of vanilla file-based or device-based logging implementations are far away from the optimum. Incorporating our understanding of the root cause behind the observed performance problems, we devised a novel logging system architecture called *Beluga*, which features the following innovations:

- A logging API that supports fine-grained logging (i.e. logging payload size is smaller than a disk sector) with minimum metadata manipulation and data copying,

- A streamlined disk write pipeline that moves fixed-sized disk write requests at a constant rate while minimizing the pipeline cycle time, and

- A low-power sparse-mode logging scheme that achieves low logging latency without requiring disk head position prediction.

Measurements on a fully operational *Beluga* prototype that embodies all three innovations demonstrate that using three commodity disks, the *Beluga* architecture can deliver close to 1.2 million 256-byte logging operations while keeping each logging operation's end-to-end latency below 1 msec. We believe this is the best empirical disk logging performance ever reported in the open literature.

7. REFERENCES

[1] S. Chen. Flashlogging: exploiting flash devices for synchronous logging performance. In *SIGMOD '09 Proceedings of the 35th SIGMOD international conference on Management of data*, NY, USA, 2009. ACM.

[2] Y. Chen, W. W. Hsu, and H. C. Young. Logging raid an approach to fast, reliable, and low-cost disk arrays. In *Proceeding Euro-Par '00 Proceedings from the 6th International Euro-Par Conference on Parallel Processing*, pages 1302–1312, 2000.

[3] T. Chiueh. Trail: a track-based logging disk architecture for zero-overhead writes. In *Computer Design: VLSI in Computers and Processors, 1993. ICCD '93. Proceedings., 1993 IEEE International Conference on*, pages 339 – 343, 1993.

[4] T. Chiueh and L. Huang. Track-based disk logging. In *in Proceedings of International Conference on Dependable Systems and Networks*, pages 429–438, 2002.

[5] J. Corbet, A. Rubini, and G. Kroah-Hartman. *Linux Device Drivers, Third Edition*. O'Reilly Media, 2005.

[6] H. Dai, M. Neufeld, and R. Han. Elf: an efficient log-structured flash file system for micro sensor nodes. In *SenSys '04 Proceedings of the 2nd international conference on Embedded networked sensor systems*, 2004.

[7] F. Douglis, R. Caceres, M. F. Kaashoek, K. Li, B. Marsh, and J. A. Tauber. Storage alternatives for mobile computers. In *In Proceedings of the First Symposium on Operating Design and Implementation (OSDI)*, 1994.

[8] K. Elhardt and R. Bayer. A database cache for high performance and fast restart in database systems. In *ACM Transactions on Database Systems (TODS), Volume 9 Issue 4*, pages 503–525, 1984.

[9] R. Fang, H.-I. Hsiao, B. He, C. Mohan, and Y. Wang. High performance database logging using storage class memory. In *IEEE 27th International Conference on Data Engineering*, pages 1221 – 1231, Hannover, Germany, 2011. icde.

[10] R. S. Finlayson and D. R. Cheriton. Log files: An extended file service exploiting write-once storage. In *SOSP '87 Proceedings of the eleventh ACM Symposium on Operating systems principles*, NY, USA, 1987.

[11] R. Freitas and W. Wilcke. Storage-class memory: The next storage system technology. In *IBM Journal of Research and Development, Vol. 52, Issue 4*, pages 439 – 447, 2008.

[12] J. Gim and Y. Won. Extract and infer quickly: Obtaining sector geometry of modern hard disk drives. In *ACM Transactions on Storage (TOS), Volume 6 Issue 2*, NY, USA, 2010.

[13] Y. Hu and Q. Yang. Dcd - disk caching disk: A new approach for boosting i/o performance. In *Proceedings of the 23rd International Symposium on Computer Architecture*, pages 169–178, 1996.

[14] A. Hylick, R. Sohan, A. Rice, and B. Jones. An analysis of hard drive energy consumption. In *Proceedings of 16th International Symposium on Modeling, Analysis, and Simulation of Computer and Telecommunication Systems (MASCOTS 2008)*, pages 103 – 112, 2008.

[15] A. Kawaguchi, S. Nishioka, and H. Motoda. A flash-memory based file system. In *USENIX Winter*, pages 155–164, 1995.

[16] B. C. Lee, E. Ipek, O. Mutlu, and D. Burger. Architecting phase change memory as a scalable dram alternative. In *in Proceedings of ISCAï£¡09*, pages 2–13, 2009.

[17] S.-W. Lee and B. Moon. Design of flash-based dbms: An in-page logging approach. In *In Proceedings of the ACM SIGMOD*, pages 55–66, Beijing, China, 2007.

[18] C. R. Lumb, J. Schindler, and G. R. Ganger. Freeblock scheduling outside of disk firmware. In *Proceedings of the 1st USENIX conference on File and storage technologies*, FAST'02, pages 20–20, Berkeley, CA, USA, 2002. USENIX Association.

[19] C. Mohan, D. Haderle, B. Lindsay, H. Pirahesh, and P. Schwarz. Aries: a transaction recovery method supporting fine-granularity locking and partial rollbacks using write-ahead logging. *ACM Trans. Database Syst.*, 17(1):94–162, Mar. 1992.

[20] D. Narayanan, A. Donnelly, E. Thereska, S. Elnikety, and A. Rowstron. Everest: Scaling down peak loads through i/o off-loading. In *In Proceedings of OSDI*, pages 15–28, 2008.

[21] H. R. Low latency logging. http://www.bitsavers.org/pdf/xerox/parc/techReports/CSL-91-1_Low_Latency_Logging.pdf, 1991.

[22] M. Rosenblum and J. K. Ousterhout. The design and implementation of a log-structured file system. In *Journal ACM Transactions on Computer Systems (TOCS),Volume 10 Issue 1*, pages 26–52, 1992.

[23] Seagate and Intel. Serial ata native command queuing. www.seagate.com/content/pdf/whitepaper/D2c_tech_paper_intc-stx_sata_ncq.pdf, 2003.

[24] J. P. Strickland, P. P. Uhrowczik, and V. L. Watts. Ims/vs: An evolving system. In *IBM Systems Journal Volume 21*, pages 490 – 510, 1982.

[25] M. Wu and W. Zwaenepoel. envy: a non−volatile, main memory storage system. In *ASPLOS,*, pages 86–97, 1994.

On Understanding the Energy Consumption of ARM-based Multicore Servers

Bogdan Marius Tudor and Yong Meng Teo
Department of Computer Science
National University of Singapore
13 Computing Drive, 117417
{bogdan,teoym}@comp.nus.edu.sg

ABSTRACT

There is growing interest to replace traditional servers with low-power multicore systems such as ARM Cortex-A9. However, such systems are typically provisioned for mobile applications that have lower memory and I/O requirements than server application. Thus, the impact and extent of the imbalance between application and system resources in exploiting energy efficient execution of server workloads is unclear. This paper proposes a trace-driven analytical model for understanding the energy performance of server workloads on ARM Cortex-A9 multicore systems. Key to our approach is the modeling of the degrees of CPU core, memory and I/O resource overlap, and in estimating the number of cores and clock frequency that optimizes energy performance without compromising execution time. Since energy usage is the product of utilized power and execution time, the model first estimates the execution time of a program. CPU time, which accounts for both cores and memory response time, is modeled as an M/G/1 queuing system. Workload characterization of high performance computing, web hosting and financial computing applications shows that bursty memory traffic fits a Pareto distribution, and non-bursty memory traffic is exponentially distributed. Our analysis using these server workloads reveals that not all server workloads might benefit from higher number of cores or clock frequencies. Applying our model, we predict the configurations that increase energy efficiency by 10% without turning off cores, and up to one third with shutting down unutilized cores. For memory-bounded programs, we show that the limited memory bandwidth might increase both execution time and energy usage, to the point where energy cost might be higher than on a typical x64 multicore system. Lastly, we show that increasing memory and I/O bandwidth can improve both the execution time and the energy usage of server workloads on ARM Cortex-A9 systems.

Categories and Subject Descriptors

C.4 [**Computer Systems Organization**]: Performance of Systems—*Performance Attributes*; C.5.5 [**Computer System Implementation**]: Servers

Keywords

Analytical Model, Performance, Energy, Low-Power, Multicore, Servers

1. INTRODUCTION

A by-product of the smartphone revolution is the sustained improvement in performance capabilities of low-power multicore systems. In the past three years, the clock frequencies and core counts of commodity ARM processors have pronouncedly increased, to the point that their performance is within the range of traditional x64 systems. Furthermore, ARM offers comparable core counts and clock frequencies at a fraction of the energy cost of traditional multicore systems. Due to their attractive power-efficiency, price and density, many companies and research projects have started to migrate towards servers based on low-power multicores. Barcelona Supercomputing Center is developing a supercomputer based on low-power ARM Cortex-A9 systems. Nvidia, Dell and HP [2] are developing systems based on quad-core Cortex-A9 while companies such as Calxeda are developing ARM-based systems which explicitly target the server landscape [1]. In particular, these multicore systems are very attractive for datacenters, as they usher in a new generation of green computing with much lower energy budgeted for cooling or lost during core idling, than what is possible using traditional Intel/AMD x64 or Intel Atom systems.

There has always been a trade-off between power-efficiency and performance of processing systems. Many currently-available ARM Cortex-A9 systems have been configured mostly for mobile computing devices such as phones or tablets, and thus their resources are sized for the balance between cores, memory and I/O required by mobile applications. As part of this balance, they are provisioned with lower *achievable memory bandwidth* than traditional x64 server systems. For example, the memory-level parallelism in Cortex-A9 chips is limited to two outstanding memory requests [33], as compared to ten in Intel chips [34]. Because mobile apps are typically not memory-bounded, the size of the caches range between 256 kB and 1 MB in the commodity Cortex-A9 systems shipped by vendors such as Samsung, Nvidia, Texas Instruments or ST-Ericsson. In contrast, the size of the cache memory in most x64 server systems exceeds 10 MB. Furthermore, the memory subsystem in many currently available ARM Cortex-A9 chips use low power memory, with 32-bit data bus width and operating at lower clock frequencies compared with traditional memory chips. As a result of these factors, low-power computing on ARM Cortex-A9 might suffer from a larger imbalance between arithmetic and memory performance than traditional x64 systems. Considering that many types of server workloads are I/O or memory-intensive, the large gap between core and memory performance might lead to unexpected results.

Previous studies on energy efficiency in server systems have addressed the impact of the number of active versus idle systems in a cluster of servers [14, 15, 31, 38]. A well known problem in datacenter systems is low system utilization which contributes to significant energy wastage [4, 13, 15]. Additionally, the problem of selecting the optimal number of cores in a multicore system has previously been addressed from the perspective of selecting the optimal performance of area-equivalent cores that, when replicated across the entire die, offers the best system-wide throughput. Most of the previous work suggests that many cores with low individual performance (termed *wimpy cores*) may offer better system-wide throughput than the area-equivalent high performance cores (termed *brawny cores*) [12, 29], if two considerations are met. First, the workload has enough parallelism to sustain execution on many cores [17]. Second, the relative performance between wimpy to brawny nodes does not impact the overall cluster cost, programability and schedulability of the parallel tasks [18]. However, to the best of our knowledge, the problem of understanding the energy impact of the imbalance between the cores, and the memory and I/O resources has not been previously addressed. With the growth in core counts, as well as the large amount of power required just to keep the core idle, it is important to understand the extent to which the active number of cores influences the performance and power efficiency of server workloads. Furthermore, many contemporary systems have the ability to selectively power-off some of the CPU cores. However, these power states have long setup times, and thus, many users do not use them, due to the risk of not being able to power-on in time, when utilization increases. Such users would benefit from predicting exactly what is the impact of the number of cores on the performance of a particular job. If the user is satisfied that the job does not need all the available cores, it can leverage on the processor sleep states to achieve important energy savings [23].

In this paper, we propose a hybrid measurement-analytical approach to characterize the energy performance of server workloads on state-of-the-art low power multicores. Firstly, we introduce a general analytical model for predicting execution time and energy used in parallel applications, as a factor of number of active cores and core clock frequency. The key idea behind the model is to characterize the overlap between the response times of three key types of resources: processor cores, memory and network I/O resources. Using a simple queueing model, we account the overlap between CPU work cycles, CPU memory cycles and network I/O execution time, and identify the system bottleneck. Furthermore, we model the impact of changing the number of cores on each type of response time. To apply this general model, we perform a series of baseline runs of an application, during which we collect traces of the total number of cycles, total stall cycles, total last level cache misses, the time-distribution of the last level cache misses and I/O requests profile. Using a static power profile of the system and these collected metrics, we can predict the execution time and energy usage of an application for different number of cores and clock frequencies, and thus, we can select the configuration that maximizes performance without wasting energy. We validate the model against direct measurement of execution time and energy on a low-power server based on a quad-core Exynos 4412 ARM Cortex-A9 multicore processor. Validation on three types of parallel applications spanning high-performance computing, web-hosting and financial computing indicates that the relative error between predictions of our model averages 9%, with 70% of the experiments falling under 5% error.

The second contribution of our model is an analysis of execution performance and energy usage for a series of workloads covering high performance computing, web-hosting and financial applications. Firstly, using predictions of our model, we show that comparatively few types of workloads benefit from executing on large core counts. *Memcached*, a popular in-memory key-value store widely used by web giants such as Amazon, Facebook and Twitter, among

others, achieves peak performance using just two cores and slightly more than half of the maximum core frequency. Keeping more than two cores powered-on, or allowing the clock to grow to maximum frequency, does not improve the performance even under continuous demand. High performance computing applications, which require large amounts of memory bandwidth, achieve even poorer results. For example, our prediction shows that pentadiagonal matrix solver *SP* from NASA Parallel Benchmarks suite, finishes in around four hours for a grid of size 162^3. The same program finishes in under seven minutes on a dual Intel Xeon X5650 processor. Due to this large difference in execution times, *SP* with input C may consume less energy on a traditional Intel multicore than on an ARM low-power multicore. Secondly, we show that our model can predict configurations of core counts and clock frequencies that may reduce the energy incurred by one third, without significantly extending the execution time of the applications. Thirdly, we show that that server workloads can achieve better energy proportionality on low-power multicores if the performance of the memory and I/O subsystems is improved, as expected in the ARM Cortex-A15 and the upcoming 64-bit ARM Cortex-A50 families.

The rest of the paper is structured as follows. Section 2 introduces our model for energy performance. Section 3 discusses the model input parameters and the validation results against direct measurements. In Section 4, we analyze of execution performance of server workloads in low-power multicore. Related work is discussed in Section 5, and section 6 concludes the paper.

2. PROPOSED MODEL

This section describes our proposed analytical model for energy consumption. We introduce first the system assumptions and model parameters. Second, we derive our model for execution time and energy usage.

2.1 Assumptions and Model Parameters

We consider the system-wide energy used by a shared-memory parallel application. We assume the application is executing in isolation, with negligible interference from other programs or background operating system tasks. The system is composed of one low-power processor with n cores, operating at clock frequency f, where $f \in [f_{min}, f_{max}]$, based on dynamic voltage and frequency scaling. We model superscalar and out-of-order cores, where an integer operation, an floating point operation, and a memory requests can be issued during each clock cycle. The system has one memory controller connected by a memory bus, shared equally between all cores and one wired network interface. All I/O operations involve the network, thus we do not consider storage I/O. The network device is memory-mapped, and read/write operations are performed using interrupt-driven I/O using direct memory accesses (DMA) that incur negligible CPU cycles [9].

The system-wide energy used by the system is split into three categories: cores, memory and network device. During the program execution, the cores are considered to be active (i.e. in C-state 0), even when idling because of lack of workload. The cores can change frequency (i.e. change the P-state), and thus the power drawn depends on the core frequency. Furthermore, within a P-state, we consider that power drawn depends on the type of workload (i.e. integers, floating points or stalls) executed by the core. The memory is considered to have two power-states, depending if it is issuing memory requests versus just refreshing its contents. Similarly, the network device is considered active when it is sending or receiving data, and passive when idle.

The parallel applications studied are composed of t homogeneous worker threads. If the applications have threads that do not significantly participate in the work, such as threads active only during short initialization and finalization period, we do not count them in the t worker threads. We consider that the system has enough capacity to run all worker threads concurrently, $t \leq n$. We do not consider scenarios with more threads than cores, because the overhead of context switching among threads is significant on ARM systems [11, 33], and thus, such scenarios are unlikely to occur in practice. Table 1 summarizes the model parameters.

Symbol	Description
General parameters	
n	Number of cores
f	Clock frequency
Workload parameters	
c	Total cycles incurred by program
w	Work cycles executed by program
m	Stall cycles due to contention
b	Stall cycles not due to contention
r	Last level cache misses
$\bar{r}_j$	Average size of one memory burst
λ_M	Arrival rate of memory requests
$\lambda_{I/O}$	Arrival rate of I/O requests
System parameters	
s_M	Service time of one memory request
$P_{CPU,idle}$	Idle CPU power consumption
P_{WORK}	Power of CPU work cycles
P_{STALL}	Power of CPU stall cycles
$P_{M,idle}$	Memory power when idle
$P_{M,active}$	Memory power under load
$P_{I/O,idle}$	I/O power when idle
$P_{I/O,active}$	I/O power under load
Time performance	
C	CPU response time
T_M	Response time of all memory requests
I	I/O response time
I_T	I/O service time
U_{CPU}	CPU utilization
T	Execution time of a program
Energy performance	
E_{CPU}	Energy used by processor
E_M	Energy used by memory
$E_{I/O}$	Energy used by I/O device
E	Total energy of a program

Table 1: Table of Notations

2.2 Model Overview

In this section we introduce our trace-driven model for optimal core-frequency configuration that reduces execution time without wasting energy. The approach is to derive the execution time and energy used by a system while running a parallel program, as a factor of number of cores, n, and core clock frequency, f. To achieve this, first we model the impact of three key resources on the execution time of the program: cores, memory and I/O device. Next, based on the service times and the utilization of each resource, we propose a model for the energy usage of the program.

In our model, a server application consists of workloads that are serviced by three types of resources: n CPU cores, memory and I/O device. However, the response times required at these resources can overlap in time, and thus, the response time of the program cannot be established by simply adding the service and waiting time on all the resources. Modern server systems, including ones based on low-power processors, have I/O devices that can send and receive data without intervention from the CPU cores. They do so because the device is memory mapped, and all data transferred

between the device is marshalled by a special processor called a DMA controller. Therefore, I/O device response time can be overlapped with the CPU response time. Furthermore, CPU cores have deeply pipelined out-of-order executions that overlaps the execution of arithmetic operations with waiting for memory requests. Thus, in a multicore system, the arithmetic instructions executed by multiple cores in parallel are overlapped with waiting for outstanding memory requests and I/O response time on the I/O device. However, from a measurement point of view, not all active and idle times are independent. A CPU core is seen as active both during execution of arithmetic operations, and while waiting for memory requests [16]. As a result, the *CPU time* of a program effectively accounts for both memory response time and service time of arithmetic instructions. Based on the overlap between processor and

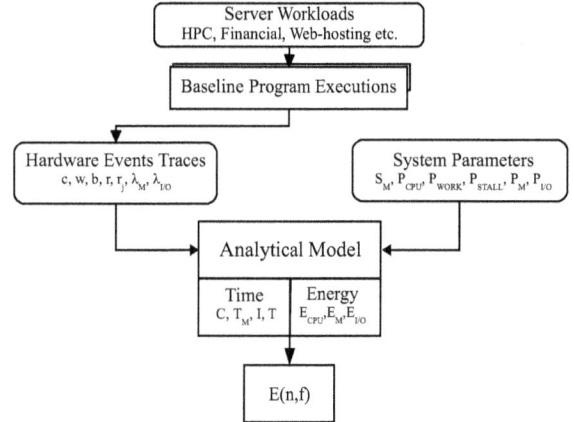

Figure 1: Approach for Applying Proposed Model

I/O resources, we define two response times in the system:

1. *CPU response time* (C) – total time during which a core is executing instructions or waiting for memory requests, for all cores;
2. *I/O response time* (I) – total time during which any core waits for the I/O device.

In this paper we target parallel server workloads that consist of multiple iterations of similar compute and I/O phases. Therefore, *either CPU response time or I/O response time dominates the execution time, and the other is completely overlapped*. First we use a bottleneck analysis technique to model the impact of CPU time and I/O time on the execution time of the entire program. Considering n cores, and that CPU time can be parallelized among these cores, while I/O time cannot be parallelized, the execution time of a program is:

$$T = max\left(\frac{C}{n}, I\right) \quad (1)$$

while the CPU utilization averaged over the entire execution of the program is:

$$U_{CPU} = \frac{C}{nT} \quad (2)$$

Figure 1 presents our trace-driven approach for applying the model to predict the energy performance of a program. We perform two baseline runs of the program, during which we collect traces the processor hardware events and I/O requests. During the first run, we execute the program on on core, alternating between the highest and lowest core frequency. Using the hardware events counters, we measure the total cycles, stall cycles, and last level cache miss profile. Using these values, we predict the CPU time as a factor of number of cores n and core clock frequency f. During a second run, we measure the I/O requests sizes and the measured inter-arrival time of the I/O requests, thus, predicting the I/O time I. Next, using a static power profile of the system and the service times for each resource, we predict the energy consumption for any configuration of number of cores and core clock frequency.

2.3 Execution Time Model

This section introduces our proposed model for deriving the CPU response time, C, and I/O response time, I.

2.3.1 CPU Response Time

The CPU time model captures the impact of the number of cores and core clock frequency on the CPU time of the program. Our model distinguishes the CPU cycles incurred due to memory contention versus clock cycles unrelated to memory contention. State-of-the art low-power processors such as ARM consist of several cores that share important off-chip resources, such as the memory bus and the main memory banks. Due to resource sharing, a well-known performance issue in multicore systems is the *memory contention among cores* [27]. When a thread suffers from memory contention among cores, each off-chip memory access takes a longer time to complete, compared to the uncontended case. When the contention is high, the thread might not have enough useful work to overlap over the memory request response time, and the thread incurs stall cycles.

Because measurement tools report CPU time as cycles, our model for CPU time uses cycles as the unit of time. Thus, all response times of core and memory requests are accounted in the CPU time based on the clock frequency and the number of cycles. If $C(n,f)$ is the CPU time of a program, and $c(n,f)$ is the total number of cycles incurred across all cores, then:

$$C(n,f) = \frac{c(n,f)}{f} \quad (3)$$

We consider the cycles incurred by a program as belonging to three categories:

- *Work cycles* (w) – the CPU cycles during which at least one integer operation, one floating point operation or one memory request is issued.

- *Stall cycles not due to memory contention* (b) – stalls caused by the latency of cache hits, pipeline bubbles or contention between the memory requests issued by the *same* core.

- *Stall cycles caused by memory contention* (m) – the stall cycles incurred because more than one core are competing for off-chip memory bandwidth.

Let $w+b$ denote the total work of the program that is independent on memory contention. In general w can be considered the parallel useful work of the program, while m as the overhead caused by memory contention. Notice that we do not consider all stall cycles as being overhead, since the focus of this model is to analyze the overhead caused by changing the number of cores on the CPU time incurred by a program. Thus, stall cycles that are independent on the memory contention among cores are treated by our model as a useful work.

Next we model the total number of cycles incurred by a program, $c(n,f)$. ARM Cortex-A9 processors have pipelined cores that execute out-of-order instructions. Thus, the core can overlap part of the time required to retrieve the data from memory, with execution of instructions for which the data is available. Because of the out-of-order execution, the CPU time incurred by a thread can be divided into a series of *instruction windows* (i.e. discrete compute time epoch). During each window, the core executes the instructions for which the operands are available, and at the same time issues memory requests for the data of the next instruction window. The next instruction window commences as soon as the data begins to arrive. If the data needs to be fetched from the main memory, the core might stall for many cycles. When several cores are issuing memory requests at the same time, the memory requests' response time

experienced by a core increases due to the service time of memory requests performed concurrently by other cores. Due to this overlap between computation and memory requests, the execution time of any compute epoch in a thread depends on two possible bottlenecks. For low core frequencies, or compute episodes with small number of main memory accesses, the core is the bottleneck and the execution time is dominated by the time required to execute the useful work $w+b$. In contrast, when the compute episode requires many main memory accesses, the execution time of the episode is dominated by the memory response time.

Let $w_j + b_j$ denote useful work cycles and m_j denote the memory contention cycles executed during one instruction window. The response time of the entire episode is:

$$c_j(n,f) = \begin{cases} w_j + b_j & \text{if core is bottleneck} \\ m_j & \text{if memory is bottleneck} \end{cases} \quad (4)$$

While the processor core is waiting for the data to be fetched from memory, it is incurring stalled cycles. Let $T_{M,j}$ be the response time for the memory requests issued by a core during instruction window j, then the stall cycles incurred by a core while waiting for the data to arrive from main memory is:

$$m_j(n,f) = T_{M,j}(n) \cdot f \quad (5)$$

The number of cycles incurred by the entire program execution is:

$$c(n,f) = \sum_j c_j(n,f) \quad (6)$$

Since the bottleneck device dominates the response time:

$$c_j(n,f) = max(w_j + b_j, f \cdot T_{M,j}) \quad (7)$$

$$c(n,f) \approx max(\sum_j w_j + b_j, f \sum_j T_{M,j}) \quad (8)$$

To infer the CPU time of a program, we model $w_j + b_j$ and $T_{M,j}(n)$.

The useful work of the program consists of cycles executing the arithmetic instructions w_j and stall cycles unrelated to memory contention b_j. For fixed-sized workloads, these values do not change when the number of cores change [37]. The useful work of the program does not depend on the number of cores. The work cycles w_j depends only on the availability of the instruction operands. If the number of cache misses does not change when changing the number of cores, then the total cycles required to execute the episode does not change. Similarly, since b_j model back-end pipeline stalls due to register contention, branch mispredictions and latency of cache hits, it does not matter how many cores split the stalls, as the total number remains constant:

$$w + b \approx \sum_j w_j + b_j \quad (9)$$

We use a queueing model to predict the response time for the memory requests $T_{M,j}(n)$, a factor of number of cores performing concurrent memory requests, n. ARM Cortex-A9 memory subsystem is a uniform memory access (UMA) architecture. All n cores equally share the bus between the memory controller and the processor. For simplicity, we consider the entire memory subsystem, consisting of a memory bus, memory controller and memory banks as a single server. The number of memory requests in the system is bounded by the memory-level parallelism of the cores, and as such, we consider the entire system a closed system model.

The memory requests that are send to the memory server are filtered by two levels of cache, and since the programs analyzed in this paper consist of server workloads, we assume that there is sufficient time between memory requests arrivals to satisfy a memory-lessness property of the memory requests inter-arrival time. However, we do not make any assumptions on the size of the memory requests, and thus, on the distribution of service times required by the memory requests. $T_{M,j}$ is composed of service time $S_{M,j}$ and waiting time $Z_{M,j}$ of the memory requests.

$$T_{M,j} = S_{M,j} + Z_{M,j} \qquad (10)$$

Let r be the total number of last level cache misses, $\bar{r}_j$ the average number of last level cache misses requested during one instruction window, and $Var(r_j)$ the variance of last level cache misses requested during one instruction window. The total number of instruction windows throughout the execution of the program is j:

$$j = \frac{r}{\bar{r}_j} \qquad (11)$$

When s_M is the service time required by one memory request, then the average and variance of the service time required by all r requests are:

$$\bar{S_{M,j}} = s_M \cdot \bar{r}$$
$$Var(S_{M,j}) = s_M^2 \cdot Var(r)$$

Let λ_M be the arrival rate of memory request from a single core. If there are n active cores that are issuing memory request, the total arrival rate of memory requests is:

$$\lambda = n \cdot \lambda_M \qquad (12)$$

The response time of the r memory requests is modeled using a M/G/1 queueing system. From Pollaczek-Khinchin formula [36]:

$$S_{M,j}(n) = \bar{r}_j s_M \qquad (13)$$

$$Z_{M,j}(n) = \bar{S_{M,j}}^2 \lambda \frac{1 + Var(S_{M,j})}{2(1 - \bar{S_{M,j}}\lambda)} \qquad (14)$$

From equations 11 to 14:

$$T_{M,j}(n) = \bar{r}s_M + \bar{r}_j^2 s_M^2 n\lambda_M \frac{1 + s_M^2 Var(r_j)}{2(1 - \bar{r}_j s_M n\lambda_M)} \qquad (15)$$

$$T_M = j \cdot T_{M,j} = rs_M \left(1 + s_M \bar{r}_j n\lambda_M \frac{1 + s_M^2 Var(r_j)}{2(1 - s_M \bar{r}_j n\lambda_M)} \right) \qquad (16)$$

Equation 16 shows that the response time of the memory requests degrades significantly with an increase in n. Furthermore, the increase in memory response time also depends on the burstiness of memory traffic. Equation 16 also describes how the workload interacts with the machine: λ_M and r depend on the workload, while s_M is a system parameter, which depends on the bandwidth of the memory system.

To apply the model, we determine the response time of one memory request as the ratio of cache line size and the effective memory bandwidth. The average memory burst size r_j is determined based on the probability profile of the burst size. In the model parameterization section, we show that server workloads fall under two categories, bursty memory traffic and non-bursty memory traffic. For bursty memory traffic we use a Pareto distribution to model $\bar{r}_j$ and $Var(r_j)$, based on inputs collected during the baseline runs. For non-bursty memory traffic, we use an exponential distribution of burst size, and reduce the M/D/1 model to an M/M/1 model. Finally, r is determined from the trace of the hardware events counters.

2.3.2 I/O Response Time

The server applications targeted involve network I/O requests operating based on a *request-reply* pattern. In general, many types of web-hosting workloads are governed by this pattern [36]. For example, a webserver receives an HTTP request on the I/O interface, forms a reply by performing some computations and then sends the reply back to the sender.

The typical mechanism employed by a program to receive data from a I/O device involves performing a system call on a network socket. To service the requests, a thread performs a system call (on Linux, typically `read` or `recvmsg`) instructing the operating system to read the content of the request from the device. If the system does not receive any data on the device, the system call blocks the calling thread until the request can be completed. When the I/O device receives the request data, the operating system copies the data to the main memory using direct memory access (DMA), and then unblocks the thread from the system call. After the reply is formed, the thread performs another system call (typically `write` or `sendmsg`) that instructs the operating system to send a reply data to the I/O device. Thus, response time of an I/O operation can be divided into:

1. I/O blocking time (I_B) – total time between the thread blocking on a read system call and the time moment when the data arrives from the sender to the I/O device, for all read system calls.

2. I/O transfer time (I_T) – total time required to transfer the data between the I/O device and the main memory.

In contrast to the read operation, the write requests do not incur blocking time until the data arrives to the destination, because this aspect of the communication protocol is controlled independently by the operating system, according to the underlying transport protocol. Figure 2 shows a typical sequence of I/O system calls and the

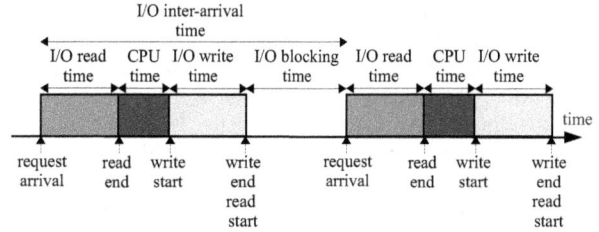

Figure 2: Overlapping of I/O Times

I/O blocking times and transfer times. I_T is the sum of the I/O read and write times. Let $\lambda_{I/O}$ be the inter-arrival time of I/O requests:

$$I_B = \frac{1}{\lambda_{I/O}} - I_T - C \qquad (17)$$

If we consider $\lambda_{I/O}$ independent of the I/O sequence response time, the blocking time and I/O transfer time of a thread can be overlapped. Thus, for a thread, the response time of the I/O incurred during the request-reply episode is:

$$I \approx max(I_T + C, \frac{1}{\lambda_{I/O}}) \qquad (18)$$

and the I/O idle time, $D_{I/O}$, is the difference between inter-arrival time and the sum of CPU time and I/O transfer time.

However, in server workloads such as *Apache* or *memcached* a thread multiplexes multiple network sockets, such that the CPU time incurred by one request-reply can overlap with the transfer time incurred by another request-reply [36]. Thus, the I/O time of a program is

$$I = max(I_T, \frac{1}{\lambda_{I/O}}) \qquad (19)$$

where I_T is determined as the ratio of transferred data to the network bandwidth, and the I/O blocking time is derived from the arrival rate of I/O requests.

2.4 Energy Model

The energy model predicts the energy used (E) used as a factor of number of cores, n and core clock frequency f. The approach is to divide the energy used based on the three types of resources: cores, memory and I/O device. The total energy of the system, E is:

$$E = E_{CPU} + E_M + E_{I/O} \qquad (20)$$

The energy used by the cores depends on how the number of active cores and the type of activity effected by the cores. Let $P_{CPU}(n, f)$ be the power drawn by the processor when n core are active and operating at frequency f. By convention we denote $P_{CPU,idle} = P_{CPU}(0, f)$. The energy consumed by the cores throughout the execution of a program is:

$$E_{CPU} = \sum_{k=0}^{\#cores} T_n P_{CPU}(n, f) \qquad (21)$$

where T_n is the total wall clock time when n cores are active. Because the workloads are fully parallelizable, the modeling of T_n can be simplified. Assuming that the program uses n threads, we split the entire execution time of the program, T, into a period during which n cores are active and periods during which no cores are active[1]:

$$\begin{aligned} E_{CPU} &= T \cdot U_{CPU} \cdot P_{CPU}(n, f) + \\ &\quad T(1 - U_{CPU})P_{CPU,idle} \end{aligned} \qquad (22)$$

The power and energy usage of the rest of the system (i.e. video, storage, peripheral devices, voltage stabilizers etc.) is considered fixed and independent of the workload, and accounted in $P_{CPU,idle}$.

The power drawn by a core depends on the type of activity effected by the core. Let $P_{WORK}(n, f)$ be the power consumed by n cores when executing work cycles, and $P_{STALL}(n, f)$ be the power consumed when executing stall cycles. Because threads are considered homogeneous, all cores execute an equal mix of instructions and the power drawn by n cores is the average of P_{WORK} and P_{STALL}, weighted with the ratio of work to stall cycles:

$$P_{CPU} = \frac{w \cdot P_{WORK} + (c - w)P_{STALL}}{c} \qquad (23)$$

Both P_{WORK} and P_{STALL} are system characteristics that depend on n and f, while w and $c(n, f)$ are workload characteristics. The energy incurred by the memory is divided into energy incurred when there are no memory requests, $E_{M,idle}$ and energy incurred when the memory is serving memory requests, $E_{M,active}$:

$$E_M = E_{M,active} + E_{M,idle} \qquad (24)$$

The total time where requests are serviced by the memory is memory service time, S_M, while the time when the memory does not service requests is $T - S_M$. Because $S_M = r \cdot s_M$:

$$\begin{aligned} E_{M,active} &= r \cdot s_M \cdot P_{M,active} \\ E_{M,idle} &= (T - r \cdot s_M)P_{M,idle} \end{aligned} \qquad (25)$$

Similarly, for the I/O requests, the time when the I/O device is busy transferring data is I_T, while the idle time is $D_{I/O} = T - I_T$:

$$\begin{aligned} E_{I/O} &= E_{I/O,active} + E_{I/O,idle} \\ E_{I/O,active} &= I_T \cdot P_{I/O,active} \\ E_{I/O,idle} &= (T - I_T) \cdot P_{I/O,idle} \end{aligned} \qquad (26)$$

The model separates the impact of the system parameters from the workload parameters. P_{WORK}, P_{STALL}, $P_{CPU,idle}$, P_M, and

---

[1] Our workloads vary less widely than online data-intensive services. For more realistic workloads this assumption results in an underestimation of the power usage, because cores become active at discrete intervals, rather than as a cohort. See Meisner et al. [32] for a detailed power characterization of such workloads.

$P_{I/O}$ are independent of workloads. Thus, they can be measured once and then used as constants in the model. In contrast, w and I_T depend only on the workload, while c, T, U_{CPU} depend both on workload and on the system, as described in the previous section.

2.5 Summary of Model

The objective of the model is to derive the energy performance of server workloads on low-power multicore systems. The model is based on the modeling the overlap of CPU cores, memory and I/O execution. Since the energy incurred is the product of power utilization and execution time, the first step is to model the execution time, based on a bottleneck analysis technique:

$$T = max\left(\frac{C}{n}, I\right) \qquad (27)$$

The model for program execution time (T) is divided into CPU response time (C) and I/O response time (I), as follows:

$$C(n, f) = max\left(\frac{w + b}{f}, T_M\right) \qquad (28)$$

$$I = max\left(I_T, \frac{1}{\lambda_{I/O}}\right) \qquad (29)$$

In modeling C, we consider two main cases. When the cores are the bottleneck, execution time is the sum of work cycles and stall cycles not due to memory contention. But when memory is the bottleneck, memory request response time is modeled using an M/G/1 queuing system and we consider two main types of memory contention. Our workload characterization shows that bursty memory traffic fits the Pareto distribution, and non-bursty memory traffic is exponentially distributed. The second step is to model the energy used by CPU, memory and the I/O device, considering the response times of these resources and the power consumption for each resource:

$$\begin{aligned} E &= T \cdot U_{CPU} \cdot \frac{w \cdot P_{WORK} + (c - w)P_{STALL}}{c} \\ &+ T(1 - U_{CPU})P_{CPU,idle} \\ &+ r \cdot s_M \cdot P_{M,active} \\ &+ (T - r \cdot s_M)P_{M,idle} \\ &+ I_T \cdot P_{I/O,active} \\ &+ (T - I_T) \cdot P_{I/O,idle} \end{aligned} \qquad (30)$$

The values of active and idle power consumption of each resource are measured during system characterization and are used as constant inputs of the model.

3. MODEL PARAMETERIZATION AND VALIDATION

In this section we present the model parameterization. We perform two baseline runs to collect the model input parameters. With these parameters, we can predict the execution time and energy consumed on any configuration of cores and clock frequency.

3.1 Workloads and System Setup

The workloads studied in this paper are representative for three types of application domain: high performance computing (HPC), web-hosting and financial computing. Table 2 shows the five programs analyzed in this paper. We chose three HPC programs from NAS Parallel Benchmark (NPB) suite that correspond to three degrees of memory contention: low (*EP*), medium (*FT*) and high (*SP*). All HPC programs are implemented in OpenMP, are highly parallel and have no I/O operations. *Memcached* is an in-memory

Domain	Program	Benchmark	Description	Problem Size	Work
HPC	EP	NPB 3.3	Monte-Carlo methods	536,870,912 pairs	Float
	FT		Fast Fourier transform	6 iterations, 256×256×128 grid	
	SP		Penta-diagonal matrices solver	1 iterations, 162^3 grid	
Web-hosting	memcached 1.4.13	memslap 0.44	In-memory key-value store	594,000 key get + 6,000 key set	Integer
Financial	blackscholes	PARSEC 2.1	European options pricing	5 million shares	Float

Table 2: Server Workloads

key-value store widely used as a caching solution for web content. We ran *memcached* on a low-power system with a cache size of 250 MB. Memcached uses pthreads as worker threads to serve requests. The request are issued by program *memslap*[2], which stores 6,000 keys in memory and performs 594,000 get operations. Memslap is run on another system (Intel Core i7), which is connected to the system under test through a 100 Mbps network interface. Memslap continously sends requests to *memcached*, with the thinking time between requests independent on the response rate of the request. *Blackscholes* is a program from the PARSEC 2.1 benchmark suite that computes a series of European options prices by solving numerically the Black-Scholes partial differential equation. *Blackscholes* uses pthreads as worker threads and has no I/O operations. The problem sizes chosen for all programs result in execution time of at least thirty seconds on all configurations of cores and clock frequency. The operating system is Linux using kernel 3.6.0. All programs are compiled using GCC with optimizations (-O2 for *memcached* and *blackscholes* and -O3 for the HPC programs). The useful work for HPC and *blackscholes* consists of NEON-VFPv3 floating point operations (without vectorization), and integer operations for *memcached*.

The low-power system used for our test is a ODROID-X with a quad-core Exynos 4412 ARM Cortex-A9 processor. The core frequencies supported are between 200 MHz and 1400 MHz, in increments of 100 MHz, the available bandwidth between cores and main memory is 800 MB/s, and the network device is a 100 Mbps Ethernet card.

PAPI version 5 is used to access the processor hardware events counters. We use strace and tcpdump to log the size and inter-arrival time of I/O requests. For measuring the power and energy consumption, we use a Yokogawa WT210 digital power meter. Figure 3 shows the setup of the system. An Intel Core i7 system is used

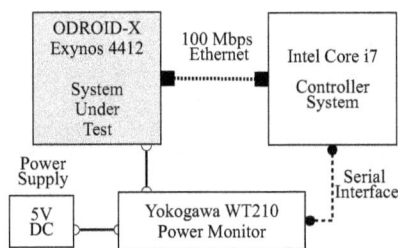

Figure 3: System Setup

as a controller, connected to the system under test using a direct 100 Mbps Ethernet link. The controller starts and stops all experiments and collects all the data. The power monitor outputs every second the average power during the last second, and total energy used.

3.2 Model Parameterization

We perform a series of measurement experiments to parameterize the input parameters of our model. The parameters are either *system characteristics* such as power consumption during different

type of activities, memory bandwidth and I/O bandwidth, or *workload characteristics* such as memory request arrival rate, memory burst size or I/O arrival time.

3.2.1 System Characteristics

To determine the system parameters used as inputs by our model, we execute a series of microbenchmarks that we have designed to determine the power consumption during different types of activities. We use three programs that each stresses one type of CPU activity: work integer cycles, work floating point cycles and stall cycles. Additionally, we collect the idle power. To determine the power drawn by memory and Ethernet device, we selectively turn on and off these components. All the power values reported in this section are obtained by averaging the results across three repetitions. Table 3 shows the static power characteristics of the system.

First we determine the total system power under idle load, when changing the core frequency. We measured total system power and processor-only power, which is obtained by discounting the power drawn by the other components. Next, we profile the processor active power when the cores execute two types of work cycles: integer operations and floating point operations. To determine this power, we use a microbenchmark designed by us that achieves close to 100% core pipeline utilization under each type of operations. The results are determined for different number of cores, under each supported clock frequency. To profile the stall cycles, we use a microbenchmark written by us that reads a large amount of data from memory, continuously attempting to miss the last level of cache. This benchmark results into more than 90% stall cycles in the cores pipeline and intense memory activity. For this microbenchmark we measure the total system power and deduct the power incurred by the memory. As shown in the table, for small core frequencies and core counts, the processor does not fully stress the memory bandwidth, and thus, the stall cycles power cannot be measured for these configurations. When applying the model, we approximate by zero the power drawn on these configurations when the cores are executing stall cycles only. The memory idle power is taken from the literature [30] and is approximated as 28 mW. We measure the active memory power by running the microbenchmark that constantly misses the cache. Under this state, the memory draws approximately 248 mW, derived after discounting the power drawn by the rest of the system. The I/O power load is determined by measuring the total power with network card under full load, under idle load and turned off. The Ethernet card draws 200 mW, irrespective of the load.

The service time for one memory request, s_M is determined as the ratio of the cache line to the available memory bandwidth. When there is no I/O operation, $s_M = 38.14$ns.

3.2.2 Workload Characterization

First we perform a baseline run of the target program, on configurations with one core, alternating between the lowest two frequencies of 200 and 300 MHz and the maximum frequencies of 1300 and 1400 MHz every ten seconds. We measure the total number of cycles incurred on all cores, stall cycles and last-level cache misses for each interval of one second spent at frequency f. By using the

---

[2]Memslap issues requests with constant size and uniform popularity, which may lead to higher CPU utilization than in actual usage of memcached. For practical traffic characteristics see Atikoglu et al. [6]

Frequency [kHz]	Idle Power [mW]		Stall cycles power [mW]				Float power [mW]				Integer power [mW]			
	System	Processor	Number of Cores				Number of Cores				Number of Cores			
			1	2	3	4	1	2	3	4	1	2	3	4
200	1,740	1,512	–	–	–	21	35	70	108	137	43	90	132	176
600	1,796	1,568	22	128	192	255	122	244	360	465	152	306	436	592
1,000	1,880	1,652	150	308	428	583	255	540	779	1,005	310	655	941	1,260
1,400	2,081	1,853	369	649	871	1,114	550	1,079	1,609	2,220	662	1,328	2,079	2,869

Table 3: Static Power Characterization

lowest two frequencies and the highest two frequencies, we obtain four data points of $C(f)$ which allows us to determine whether the program is CPU-bounded or memory-bounded. When operating at the smallest two frequencies, the program is very likely to be CPU-bounded. However, if the nature of the workload requires many off-chip requests, the program can become memory-bounded when operating at the highest two frequencies. According to equation 8, if $C(f)$ does not change significantly when f is changed, the program is CPU-bounded. However, if $C(f)$ increases with an increase in f, the program is memory bounded.

During a second run, we profile the burstiness of memory traffic by measuring the number of last level cache misses performed by one thread during each 1 millisecond interval. The run is executed on all cores, at the maximum core frequency. Additionally, during this run we profile the number of I/O operations, total data transferred over the I/O device and the inter-arrival time of I/O requests. Our analysis of the memory access rate shows that the server workloads can be classified as two types of memory traffic: bursty memory traffic or non-bursty memory traffic. Programs with bursty memory traffic exhibit a clear separation between phases of core activity versus phases of memory activity. Due to this separation, they are less likely to cause memory contention among cores. In contrast, programs which are severely memory-bounded almost always trigger memory requests, and thus, there is a more uniform utilization of the memory bandwidth. To model the size of the memory request, we use a Pareto distribution for programs with bursty memory traffic, and an exponential distribution for programs with non-bursty memory traffic.

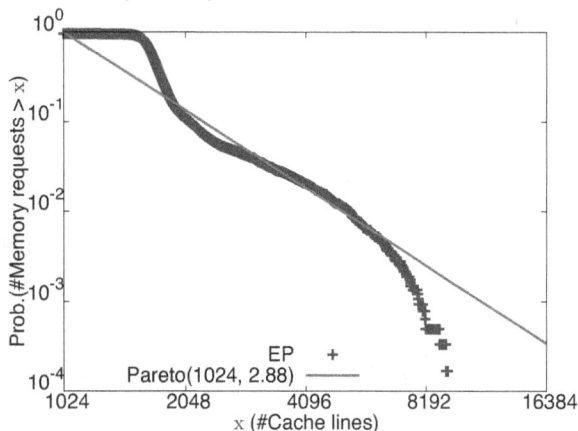

Figure 4: Bursty Memory Traffic: EP

Figure 4 shows the probability that the number of last level cache hits incurred during an interval of $1,000,000$ cycles exceeds x, for $x \in [1024, 16384]$. The probability plot, in log-log scales shows a decreasing diagonal line, which confirms the bursty nature of the memory traffic. A Pareto distribution with parameters of minimum size $x_{min} = 1024$ and hazard rate $\alpha = 2.88$ fits the measured data, with coefficient of regression $R^2 = 0.94$. Similar plots are observed for *memcached* and *blackscholes*, with slightly different α parameters. Figure 5 shows the probability distribution for the

non-bursty program SP. In constrast with EP, the number of last

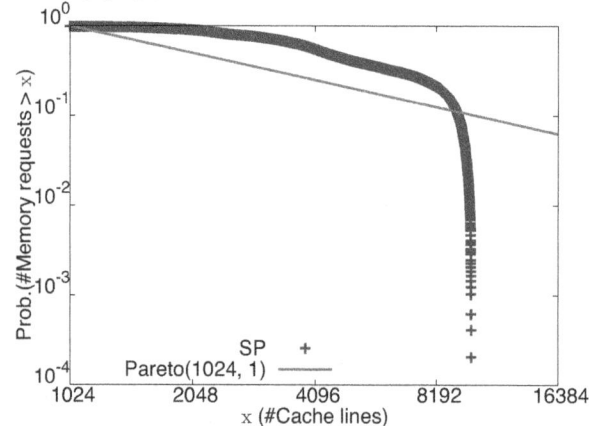

Figure 5: Non-bursty Memory Traffic: SP

level misses occurring during each $1,000,000$ cycles interval is much larger, and is not significantly bursty. The Figure also shows that even the least-bursty Pareto distribution with $x_{min} = 1024$ and $\alpha = 1$ does not fit the data. Therefore, we use an exponential distribution to model the average size of the memory request performed by programs with bursty memory traffic. HPC program *FT* has a similar behavior, but with lower memory request arrival rate.

Memcached is the only program with significant I/O operations. During each *get* requests, *memcached* reads 70 bytes and writes 1100 bytes, while a *set* request reads 1105 bytes and writes 8 bytes. The get operations are performed in batches of 24 requests. The total amount of data transferred is 700MB, while the average inter-arrival time between batches of get requests is measured at 2.5 ms. Thus, $I_T = 56$s and $I_B = 5.1$s. Because the controller and the system under test are connected using point to point network, we observe a zero packet loss rate, thus the network I/O bandwidth utilization is 100% during periods of data transfer.

Table 4 summarizes our workload characterization for the five programs. For HPC programs and *blackscholes*, we observe that

Program	Distribution	Parameters	r_M	$w + b$
EP	Pareto	$\alpha = 2.88$	1.09×10^6	1.20×10^{11}
FT	Exp.	$\lambda = 7.1 \times 10^5$	1.46×10^8	4.10×10^{10}
SP	Exp.	$\lambda = 1.7 \times 10^6$	5.11×10^8	6.16×10^{10}
memcached	Pareto	$\alpha = 2.20$	8.90×10^8	5.64×10^{10}
blackscholes	Pareto	$\alpha = 2.75$	4.43×10^7	9.20×10^{11}

Table 4: Workload Characterization

work cycles are completely dominated by executing floating point operations. Thus, when applying the power model, we use P_{WORK} values from the floating point power characterization. In contrast, for *memcached* we use P_{WORK} from the integer power characterization.

3.3 Validation

We validate the model against measurements of execution time and energy usage. First we show summary validation results for all five workloads. Due to space constraints, we focus the validation discussion on programs *memcached* and *SP*, which are the programs with largest relative error between model and measurement.

Program	Error	
	Time	**Energy**
EP	1.0%	8.7%
FT	9.3%	9.9%
SP	11.1%	11.3%
memcached	11.4%	10.7%
blackscholes	9.4%	8.2%

Table 5: Relative Error between Model and Measurement

Before the validation experiments, we applied two baseline runs for each program, during which we collect information about the useful work, memory requests and I/O requests, as described in the previous section. To validate the model, we predict the execution time $T(n, f)$ and energy $E(n, f)$ considering the number of cores n and clock frequency f fixed throughout the program execution. We compare this prediction against measurements of $T(n, f)$ and $E(n, f)$. To change the number of cores that the program is using we change the number of worker threads of the programs. For each program, we validate four cores and 13 core frequencies, giving 52 core-frequency configurations. Table 5 summarizes the relative error between measurements and predicted values, averaged over all core-frequency configurations. Overall, the error across all experiments is around 9%, and 70% of the predicted values are under 5% error.

We identify three factors that affect the accuracy of the model. The most significant source of error comes irregularities during execution. For example, *memcached* incurs more instructions on higher core frequencies, which are caused by a polling mechanism used to monitor the network sockets. This significantly increases the energy used, but does not reduce the execution time. This increase causes our model to underestimate by up to 23% the CPU cycles incurred by *memcached* on one core. The second cause for model inaccuracy is the accuracy of the system characterization parameters. In particular, the power values for active cycles, stall cycles and idleness differ by up to 20mW. This variability translates into a slight underestimate of the average power, especially for configurations with low frequencies or low core counts. Third, the measured values of execution time and energy show a variation of 3 to 11%. Figures 6 and 7 show the validation of execution time and energy used for *SP* and *memcached*.

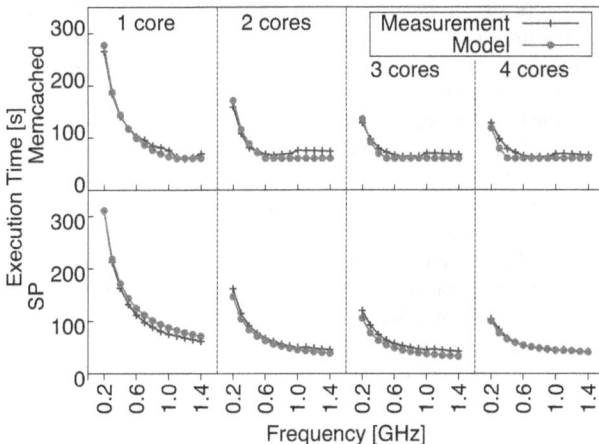

Figure 6: Execution Time Validation

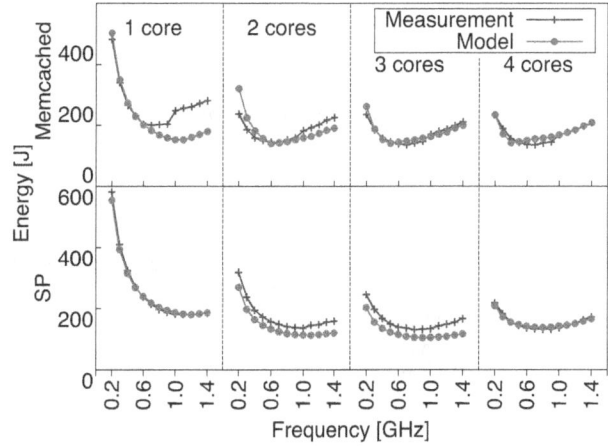

Figure 7: Energy Validation

4. ANALYSIS

We present three studies performed using our model. Firstly, we predict the configuration of number cores and clock frequency, (n, f) that achieves the minimum execution time without wasting energy, and discuss the energy savings that can be achieved. Secondly, we show that some types of workloads incur higher energy cost on low-power multicore than on traditional x64 systems. Thirdly, we show that contrary to intuition, the most energy-efficient way to balance the utilization of core, memory and I/O resources is by adding more memory and I/O resources, rather than by turning off idle cores.

4.1 Optimal Core-Frequency Configuration

We apply the model to predict the configuration of core counts and clock frequency that achieves the minimum execution time. If several configurations achieve execution times within 5% to the minimum, we chose the one with the minimum energy usage, considering that all cores are kept powered on. The results in table 6 shows that only workloads consisting entirely of arithmetic instructions make full use of all four cores. In contrast, all memory- or I/O-bounded programs achieve best performance on less than full core count and around half of maximum core frequency.

Program	Bottleneck	Configuration			
		Min. Time		**Min. Energy**	
		n	f **[GHz]**	n	f **[GHz]**
EP	Cores	4	1.4	4	1.4
FT	Memory	3	1.4	3	0.7
SP	Memory	3	1.4	3	0.9
memcached	I/O	2	0.7	2	0.7
blackscholes	Cores	4	1.4	4	1.4

Table 6: Minimum Time and Energy Configurations on Default Configuration of up to 4 Cores and 1.4 GHz

The predictions for optimal core-frequency configuration allow significant energy savings if un-necessary cores are turned off. For example, for *memcached*, by selecting the minimum time configuration we can power off two cores. Unfortunately, the operating system on our system does not allow selective power off of a subset of cores, and thus we cannot measure directly the energy savings. However, using figures from related work [23, 33], by shutting down two out of the four cores we can estimate a reduction of processor power between a conservative 25% and an optimistic 50%. With these figures, applying the configuration predicted by our model allows for a reduction in total energy savings between

13% and 31%, and without compromising the execution time performance.

4.2 Impact of Memory Bottleneck

We analyze the energy cost of low-power multicores that have limited memory bandwidth. We compare the execution of memory-bounded *SP* on low-power Cortex-A9 with traditional x64 multicore.

The x64 system used is Intel Xeon X5650 at 2.67 GHz, dual processor with 12 cores/24 hardware threads, 24 MB of L3 cache and two memory controllers, each with two memory channels. We ran program *SP* with a large input size of 400 iterations on a grid of 162^3 (input size *C* from NPB). The input results in a working set large enough to exceed the caches of both systems, but fits into 1 GB of main memory.

We apply our prediction for execution time on the low-power multicore for all core-frequency configurations, and observe that the minimum execution time exceeds 17,000 seconds. In contrast, the measured execution time on the x64 system is 330 seconds, using all cores at maximum frequency. The large gap between execution times appears because the Intel system is equipped with much larger caches, and thus, incurs 15 times less cache misses. Furthermore, the main memory bandwidth is around 8 times higher, while the bandwidth of the caches are ten times (for L1) and four times (when comparing Intel L3 to ARM L2) higher. The average power used by the Intel system (with disks turned off) is around 210W.

We extend this analysis for datacenters, factoring the additional power required for power conversion and cooling the systems. The Power Usage Effectivness (PUE) of a datacenter measures the total power required to deliver 1 Watt of IT power. From literature, we identify two PUE bounds: the lower bound is PUE=1.13, in a Google datacenter [3], while an the upper bound is 1.89 [4]. Figure 8 shows the predicted values of energy consumption on low-

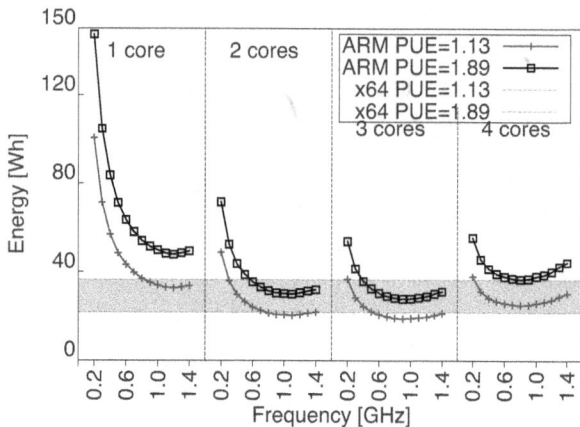

Figure 8: *SP* Energy Usage: ARM Cortex-A9 vs x64

power multicore, for all configurations of cores-frequency, compared with an execution on all x64 cores at maximum frequency, for PUE between 1.13 and 1.89. Few ARM configurations manage to achieve lower energy cost than x64, with less than 7% energy reduction, but at a cost of incurring execution time more than 50 times higher. However, the x64 execution is not energy efficient because all cores are used at maximum frequency even though the memory is the bottleneck. We conclude that memory-bounded programs can be unsuitable for low-power multicores, even if optimizing the core-frequency configuration to achieve best performance at minimum energy cost.

4.3 Energy Proportionality of Server Workloads on Low-power Multicores

Energy proportionality refers to the ability of a system to consume power proportional to their performance [7]. ARM multicores typically have good energy proportionality when used as mobile computers, due to their sleep states and low-power operation [33]. However, our previous analysis shows that resource imbalances lead to large energy wastage in server workloads. Thus, leveraging on the idea that ARM systems are highly configurable, we apply our model to understand how to improve the energy proportional executions of server workloads.

As the key to improving energy proportionality is system balance [5], we apply our model to predict the performance of program *memcached* under different hardware configurations that balance the system resources. Figure 9 shows the response times of different resources for the original hardware configuration (100Mbps Ethernet, one memory controller), when using two active cores. This number of cores is selected as it achieves the best performance at minimum energy cost. For small core frequencies, the CPU work

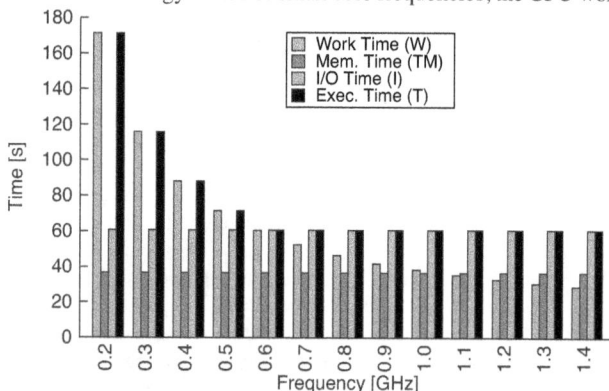

Figure 9: *Memcached* Response Times

time ($W = \frac{w+b}{f}$) is the bottleneck, but at 600MHz the CPU response time matches the I/O response time. Beyond 600MHz, the I/O bandwidth becomes the bottleneck, and the exection time does not reduce anymore.

We analyze the performance impact of replacing two system components. First, the 100Mbps Ethernet is replaced with 1GBps Ethernet, without modifying any other component. In this analysis, we consider a gigabit Ethernet adapter with a power consumption of 600mW, which is typical for a power-efficient network card. The I/O time for *memcached* is composed of transfer time $I_T = 56s$ and blocking time $T_B = 5.1s$. With a Gbit Ethernet, the total I/O time becomes $I = 10.7s$. However, because the I/O device is memory mapped, we consider that the gigabit Ethernet will utilize 125MB/s out of the 800MB/s memory bandwidth. Thus, s_M increases from 38 ns to 45ns. Applying Equation 16, T_M increases from 36.5s to 47s. Thus, the effect of moving to 1GBit Ethernet is a reduction from of execution time from $T = 61$ s to $T = 47$ s, and the system bottleneck becomes the memory. Due to the increase in I/O power by 400mW and due to the increase in stall cycles, the average power increases by approximately 500mW. Figure 10 shows that total energy decreases by switching to a Gigabit Ethernet because the decrease in execution time offsets the increase in average power. Since the new bottleneck is the memory, we consider next the impact of doubling the effective memory bandwidth (ARM Cortex-A9 systems can be configured to up to quad-memory channels, while the next generations ARM Cortex-A15 and ARM Cortex-A50 support more outstanding memory requests and can be configured to use LPDDR3). With the double memory bandwidth, the memory

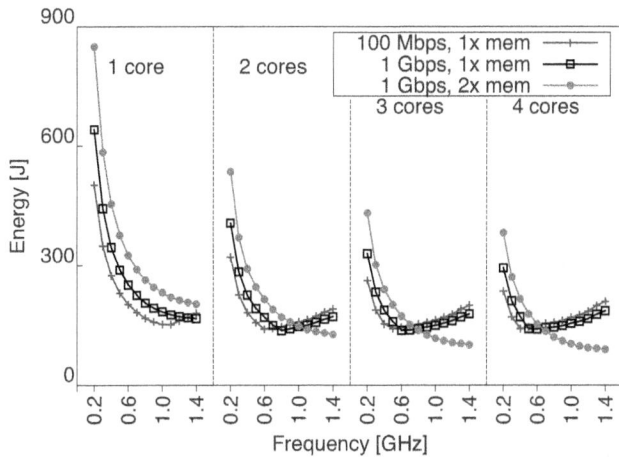

Figure 10: *Memcached* **with 1 Gbit Ethernet and Double Memory Bandwidth**

response time drops to 18.1s, and the system bottleneck becomes the core. We consider a pessimistic scenario, where power consumption is the quadruple of the original memory system (100mW idle memory power and 1W active memory power). However, the energy consumption still decreases by more than 50%, and *memcached* becomes CPU-bounded. It achieves best performance and minimum energy when using all cores at full frequency.

This analysis showed that reducing the imbalance among core, memory and I/O leads to lower energy usage. However, counter to intuition, we showed that balancing the resources by adding *more hardware resources* is the key to improving energy proportionality, even if this results in higher average power consumption. Considering that future ARM systems such as ARM Cortex-A15 and the 64-bit ARM Cortex-A50 family target much improved memory and I/O throughput, it is expected that future multicore systems based on low-power ARM multicores will deliver better energy-proportionality than current ARM Cortex-A9, even at a cost of higher power usage.

5. RELATED WORK

Previous work on understanding the performance and energy efficiency of server workloads can be broadly classified based on three criteria: (i) level of analysis (i.e. microarchitecture level, system level or cluster/datacenter level performance) (ii) workload characteristics and (iii) approach for understanding the energy usage. We discuss each category, contrasting our approach with previous research.

Level of Analysis. A large body of related work considers using voltage and frequency scaling to balance core and memory performance in single-core workloads [26, 28, 39, 40]. However, with the reduction of transistor size with each technological generation, an increasingly large component of the energy cost is caused by fixed leakage power required to keep the components powered on [23]. As such, DVFS techniques are facing diminishing returns, as they are able to reduce an increasingly small fraction of the energy cost [22]. At the other end of the spectrum, in clustered systems or datacenters, a dominant performance issue is the energy wastage due to low processor utilization. Research in this area has focused on understanding how to increase utilization by workload scheduling [15, 38] or the impact of adjusting system power [13, 19]. At multicore level, a large body of work addresses the question of how the throughput of multicore system is affected by the dichotomy of few *brawny* cores versus many *wimpy* cores, given a fixed performance-density budget [12, 17, 29]. However, these

studies do not consider the impact of off-chip resources such as main memory or I/O periferals.

Our findings are orthogonal with previous work. Because we focus on understanding the impact of memory and I/O constraints on execution perfromance, our model can predict the optimal number of cores for a workload, our model allows a better understanding of the impact of work-aggregation or different scheduling techniques in clusters of multicore servers. Furthermore, our work enables a greater reduction of energy over DVFS techniques developed for single-core systems, because it can reveal the number of unnecessary cores that can be turned off.

Workload Characteristics. The suitability of low-power systems to achieve energy-efficient executions of different type of workloads has been studied in the past for many types of systems [25, 35], including ARM [33] and Intel Atom systems [5]. Previous work on understanding the power and performance of ARM systems focused mostly on embedded [33] or mobile workloads [8], which have mostly CPU and GPU requirements. Closer to our targeted workloads is FAWN, a cluster of low-power "wimpy" AMD Geode nodes [5], designed for energy-efficient I/O intensive applications. However, FAWN nodes are single-core 500 MHz processors, thus they are severely bottlenecked by the CPU processing ability and by I/O storage bandwidth. In contrast, the multicore Cortex-A9 systems addressed by us are bottlenecked by memory or network speed. Furthermore, our analysis includes non-I/O bounded HPC programs that are more impacted by the "memory wall". Work that addresses specifically data-intesive workloads are characterized by [6] in terms of traffic characteristics and by [32] for opportunities of power savings in datacenters. Our work, although using much narrower traffic patterns, validates the conclusion that system balance is key for energy proportionality.

Modeling Approaches. Previous analytical models for predicting execution time include trace-driven analysis for predicting the speedup and speedup loss due to data-dependency [37], the impact of network communication [20] or memory contention of HPC and real-world programs in traditional multicore systems [27]. In contrast, our focus is not on performance loss, but rather on understanding energy wastage due to resource imbalance. A significant body of research has addressed analytical modeling of computer power and energy using models derived from first-order principles or linear regression [10, 21, 24, 26, 28]. Closest to our model is the approach presented by Curtis-Maury et al. [10]. They derive an empirical analytical model for predicting the impact of program concurrency and core frequency on energy usage of HPC programs in traditional multicores. Their approach is based on linear regression over measured data acquired over many training runs, but without considering the impact of resource contention. In contrast, we provide closed-form equations that explicitly model the impact of number of cores, allowing us to study directly the impact of multicore on resource imbalances. More importantly, our analysis suggests that increasing power usage can lead to energy reductions, if the added power contributes to balancing the resource utilization.We share the methodology of modeling the power usage by correlating static power characteristics with hardware events counters with [24, 26, 28]. We do not use linear correlation methods, but derive close-form equations for the power and energy consumption. Our work furthers these studies by considering the case where multiple cores execute the same workload, modeling the impact of multicore on resource contention. This increases the predictive value of our models. Furthermore we use validation against direct measurement of server workloads covering HPC, web-hosting and financial computing.

6. CONCLUSIONS

This paper proposes a trace-driven analytical model for understanding the energy usage of server workloads on low-power multicore systems. We model the effects of multicore on achieving energy-efficient executions of representative server workloads covering high performance computing, web hosting and financial computing. The key idea is the modeling of the overlap between resource demand in a program. Since the power consumed is the product of power utilization and execution time, the model first estimates the execution time of a program by considering the overlap between response times incurred by cores, memory and I/O resources. CPU time, which accounts for both cores and memory response time, is modeled as an M/G/1 queuing system. Our workload characterization shows that bursty memory traffic fits a Pareto distribution and non-bursty memory traffic can be modeled using an exponential distribution. Validation shows a relative error of 9% between model and measured execution time and energy. Applications of our model to analyze the optimal core-frequency configuration, impact of memory bottleneck and energy proportionality in multicore systems reveal a number of insights. We observe that low-power multicores may not always deliver energy-efficient executions for server workloads because large imbalances between cores, memory and I/O resources can lead to under-utilized resources and thus contribute to energy wastage. Next, resource imbalances in HPC programs may result in significantly longer execution time and higher energy cost on ARM Cortex-A9 than on a traditional x64 server. In this instance and without compromising execution time, our model predicts core frequency configurations that balance the resources with energy reduction of up to one third. Finally, we show that higher memory and I/O bandwidths can improve both execution time and energy utilization, even if it means higher power usage. Thus, it is expected that ARM Cortex-A15 and the ARM Cortex-A50 family, which target larger memory and I/O bandwidths, will deliver more energy-efficient servers than currently available ARM Cortex-A9.

Acknowledgements

We thank the anonymous reviewers and our shepherd for their constructive comments, and Lavanya Ramapantulu for helping us to uncover some aspects of the ARM Cortex-A9 processors.

7. REFERENCES

[1] *Chip maker Calxeda receives $55 million to push ARM chips into the data center*, Oct 2012. http://www.webcitation.org/6BSIjQzCM.

[2] *Dell Reaches for the Cloud With New Prototype ARM Server*, PCWorld Magazine, May 2012. http://www.webcitation.org/6BVBj0Oyz.

[3] *Google Data Center Efficiency: How We Do It*, Oct 2012. http://www.webcitation.org/6C8PjIMYd.

[4] *Uptime Institute 2012 Survey*, Oct 2012. http://uptimeinstitute.com/2012-survey-results/.

[5] D. G. Andersen et al. Fawn: a fast array of wimpy nodes. *Proc of SOSP*, pages 1–14, 2009.

[6] B. Atikoglu et al. Workload analysis of a large-scale key-value store. *Proc of SIGMETRICS/PERFORMANCE*, pages 53–64, 2012.

[7] L. A. Barroso and U. Hölzle. The case for energy-proportional computing. *Computer*, 40(12):33–37, Dec. 2007.

[8] A. Carroll and G. Heiser. An analysis of power consumption in a smartphone. *Proc of USENIX ATC*, pages 21–21, 2010.

[9] J. Corbet et al. *Linux Device Drivers, 3rd Edition*. O'Reilly Media, Inc., 2005.

[10] M. Curtis-Maury et al. Prediction models for multi-dimensional power-performance optimization on many cores. *Proc of PACT*, pages 250–259, 2008.

[11] F. M. David et al. Context Switch Overheads for Linux on ARM Platforms. *Proc. of ExpCS*, 2007.

[12] J. D. Davis et al. Maximizing cmp throughput with mediocre cores. *Proc of PACT*, pages 51–62, 2005

[13] A. Gandhi et al. Optimal power allocation in server farms. *Proc of SIGMETRICS*, pages 157–168,2009.

[14] A. Gandhi et al. Are sleep states effective in data centers? *Proc of IGCC*, pages 1–10, 2012.

[15] D. Gmach et al. Workload analysis and demand prediction of enterprise data center applications. *Proc of IISWC*, pages 171–180, 2007.

[16] J. L. Hennessy and D. A. Patterson. *Computer Architecture, Fourth Edition: A Quantitative Approach*. 2006.

[17] M. Hill and M. Marty. Amdahl's Law in the Multicore Era. *Computer*, 41(7):33–38, 2008.

[18] U. Hölzle. Brawny cores still beat wimpy cores, most of the time. *IEEE Micro*, 30(4), 2010.

[19] T. Horvath and K. Skadron. Multi-mode energy management for multi-tier server clusters. *Proc of PACT*, pages 270–279, 2008.

[20] Y. Hu et al. I/o scheduling model of virtual machine based on multi-core dynamic partitioning. *Proc of HPDC*, pages 142–154, 2010.

[21] V. Kumar and A. Fedorova. Towards better performance per watt in virtual environments on asymmetric single-isa multi-core systems. *SIGOPS Oper. Syst. Rev.*, 43(3):105–109, July 2009.

[22] E. Le Sueur and G. Heiser. Dynamic voltage and frequency scaling: The laws of diminishing returns. *Proc of HotPower*, 2010.

[23] E. Le Sueur and G. Heiser. Slow down or sleep, that is the question. *Proc of USENIX ATC*, 2011.

[24] A. W. Lewis et al. Runtime energy consumption estimation for server workloads based on chaotic time-series approximation. *ACM Trans. Archit. Code Optim.*, 9(3):15:1–15:26, Oct. 2012.

[25] K. Lim et al. Understanding and Designing New Server Architectures for Emerging Warehouse-Computing Environments. *Proc of ISCA*, pages 315–326, 2008.

[26] M. Y. Lim et al. Softpower: fine-grain power estimations using performance counters. *Proc of HPDC*, pages 308–311, 2010.

[27] F. Liu et al. Understanding How Off-chip Memory Bandwidth Partitioning in Chip Multiprocessors Affects System Performance. *Proc of HPCA*, 2010.

[28] C. W. Lively et al. Power-aware predictive models of hybrid (mpi/openmp) scientific applications on multicore systems. *Computer Science - R&D*, 27(4):245–253, 2012.

[29] P. Lotfi-Kamran et al. Scale-out Processors. *Proc of ISCA*, pages 500–511, 2012.

[30] K. Malladi et al. Towards energy-proportional datacenter memory with mobile dram. *Proc of ISCA*, pages 37–48, 2012.

[31] D. Meisner et al. PowerNap: Eliminating Server Idle Power. *Proc of ASPLOS*, pages 205–216, 2009.

[32] D. Meisner et al. Power management of online data-intensive services. *Proc of ISCA*, pages 319–330, 2011.

[33] R. Mijat. System level benchmarking analysis of the cortextm-a9 mpcore. *ARM Connected Community Technical Symposium*, 2009.

[34] D. Molka et al. Memory Performance and Cache Coherency Effects on an Intel Nehalem Multiprocessor System. *Proc of PACT*, pages 261–270, 2009.

[35] A. S. Szalay et al. Low-power Amdahl-balanced blades for data intensive computing. *SIGOPS Oper. Syst. Rev.*, 44(1):71–75, Mar. 2010.

[36] Y. C. Tay. *Analytical Performance Modeling for Computer Systems*. Synthesis Lectures on Computer Science. Morgan & Claypool Publishers, 2010.

[37] B. M. Tudor and Y. M. Teo. A practical approach for performance analysis of shared-memory programs. *Proc of IPDPS*, pages 652–663, 2011

[38] A. Verma et al. Server workload analysis for power minimization using consolidation. *Proc of USENIX ATC*, 2009.

[39] M. Weiser et al. Scheduling for reduced cpu energy. *Proc of OSDI*, 1994.

[40] A. Weissel and F. Bellosa. Process cruise control: event-driven clock scaling for dynamic power management. *Proc of CASES*, pages 238–246, 2002.

Reuse-based Online Models for Caches

Rathijit Sen
rathijit@cs.wisc.edu

David A. Wood
david@cs.wisc.edu

Department of Computer Sciences
University of Wisconsin-Madison

ABSTRACT

We develop a reuse distance/stack distance based analytical modeling framework for efficient, online prediction of cache performance for a range of cache configurations and replacement policies LRU, PLRU, RANDOM, NMRU. Our framework unifies existing cache miss rate prediction techniques such as Smith's associativity model, Poisson variants, and hardware way-counter based schemes. We also show how to adapt LRU way-counters to work when the number of sets in the cache changes. As an example application, we demonstrate how results from our models can be used to select, based on workload access characteristics, last-level cache configurations that aim to minimize energy-delay product.

Categories and Subject Descriptors

C.4 [**Performance of Systems**]: Modeling techniques ; B.3.2 [**Memory Structures**]: Cache memories

General Terms

Performance

Keywords

Cache, Stack Distance, Reuse Distance, Replacement policies, LRU, PLRU, RANDOM, NMRU

1. INTRODUCTION

Processor caches are critical components of the memory hierarchy that exploit locality to keep frequently-accessed data on chip. Caches can significantly boost performance and reduce energy usage, but their benefit is highly workload dependent. Figure 1 illustrates the miss rates for 16 multithreaded workloads over 5 different sizes of last-level cache (LLC). Some workloads (e.g., `apache`) benefit substantially from larger caches, while others (e.g., `equake`) are largely indifferent to the cache size.

In modern power and energy constrained computer systems, understanding a workload's dynamic cache behavior is

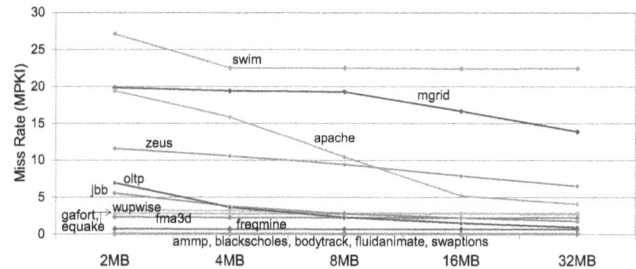

Figure 1: LLC Misses-per-thousand-instructions (MPKI) for our workloads (Section 6). There is significant miss rate variation depending on the workload and LLC size.

important for making critical resource allocation and scheduling decisions. For example, allocating excess cache capacity to a workload wastes power, as large caches dissipate significant leakage power, while allocating insufficient cache capacity hurts performance and increases main memory power. Previous research has explored placing some or all of a cache in low-power mode [4,16,18] or dynamically partitioning the cache to eliminate resource contention [35,45]. A recent Intel processor [22] can dynamically reduce its LLC's capacity to save power.

Because a workload's cache performance can vary with different execution phases, cache resource decisions must be made online and depend upon predicting the cache performance for configurations different than the current settings. For example, set-associative caches map each address to a set, each of which contains a number of ways (lines); since both sets and ways can be dynamically configured [48], we need to predict cache performance for many configurations (see Table 1). Suh, et al. [44] use hardware way-counters to predict cache miss ratios, but their technique cannot be used for configurations with a different number of sets. Gordon-Ross, et al. [20] use a hardware TCAM to track reuse distances for determining miss ratios for an 8KB L1 cache, with 12% area overhead. However, while 12% overhead may be acceptable for small L1 caches, it is prohibitively high for the multi-megabyte LLCs of modern multicore processors.

In this work we study the problem of developing efficient online techniques for predicting cache miss rates for large caches that vary in both associativity and number of sets, and have practical replacement policies such as RANDOM, NMRU, and PLRU, unlike prior work that has largely focused on LRU. Our analysis framework is inspired by two foundational works: Mattson's stack distance characteriza-

size \ assoc.	2	4	8	16	32
2MB	2^{14}	2^{13}	2^{12}	2^{11}	2^{10}
4MB	2^{15}	2^{14}	2^{13}	2^{12}	2^{11}
8MB	2^{16}	2^{15}	2^{14}	2^{13}	2^{12}
16MB	2^{17}	2^{16}	2^{15}	2^{14}	2^{13}
32MB	2^{18}	2^{17}	2^{16}	2^{15}	2^{14}

Table 1: Relation between number of sets and associativity for different cache sizes. Assuming some cache configuration is the current configuration, there are a total of 25-1=24 possible other target configurations. An inspection of the table reveals that *at most* 4 of these possible 24 configurations can have the same number of sets as the current configuration. For example, with 32MB 32-way as the current configuration, target configurations with the same number of sets (2^{14}) are: 2MB 2-way, 4MB 4-way, 8MB 8-way and 16MB-16-way. Thus, way-counters (Section 5.3) can predict for *at most* 4 of 24 possible target configurations at any time.

tion [32] (also used later as reuse distance [8,15]) and Smith's associativity model [21,40] for LRU caches.

We show how simple hardware, requiring approximately 2KB of state, can provide the dynamic information needed to drive the model. As an example application, we demonstrate that it can be used to select an LLC configuration to minimize energy-delay product (EDP). The LLC configuration can cause EDP to vary by as much as a factor of 3; using our model selects a configuration within 7% of optimal.

The major contributions of our work are:

1. We formulate an analytical framework based on generalized stochastic Binomial Matrices [43] for transforming reuse distance distributions (Sections 3, 4).

2. We formulate new miss ratio prediction models for RANDOM (Section 4.2), NMRU (Section 4.3), PLRU (Section 4.4) replacement policies.

3. We show that the traditional hardware way-counter based prediction [44] for varying associativity is a special instance of our unified framework (Section 5.3). Further, we show how way-counter data for LRU may be transformed to apply to caches with a different number of sets. (Section 5.3.2)

4. We propose a novel hardware scheme for efficient online estimation of reuse distance/stack distance distributions (Section 5.1).

5. We demonstrate one application of the model in finding the minimum EDP (energy-delay product, [19]) configuration (Section 6). The results are within 7% of the optimum.

1.1 Model overview and Paper Organization

The central theme of our predictive framework is to decouple temporal characteristics in the cache access stream from characteristics of the replacement policy. The rest of this paper is divided into five major portions:

Characterizing temporal locality: Section 2 defines reuse distributions that capture the temporal locality of address streams. Section 3 shows how to modify these to apply for a cache with a different number of sets.

Characterizing replacement policies: Section 4 introduces the notion of cache hit-functions that, when multiplied with the per-set reuse distribution, produce expected cache hit ratios. Sections 4.1.1 and 4.1.2 consider optimizations for LRU hit ratio prediction. Sections 4.2, 4.3 and 4.4 develops new prediction models for RANDOM, NMRU, PLRU respectively. Section 4.5 discusses prediction accuracy and computation overheads.

Hardware Support: Section 5.1 presents the novel, low-cost hardware for estimating reuse distributions. It also discusses two traditional hardware mechanisms – set-counters (Section 5.2) and way-counters (Section 5.3).

Example Application: Section 6 shows how our model can be used to find the minimum EDP configuration.

Epilogue: Section 7 discusses related work and Section 8 concludes the paper.

In our study, caches are characterized by the number of sets S, associativity A, and replacement policy. We assume a fixed line size of 64 bytes. Table 1 shows the relation between S, A and cache size for the configurations we study.

Our models estimate hit ratio (hit/access). This can be easily converted into other measures: miss ratio=1-hit ratio; miss rate=miss ratio*access/instruction. For evaluating prediction quality, we obtain address traces of accesses to a 32MB 32-way LLC in a simulated system (Table 2, Section 6) for our workloads (Section 6), run the traces through a standalone cache simulator (that does not model timing) and compare measured against predicted metrics.

2. MEASURES OF TEMPORAL LOCALITY

In this section we develop metrics of temporal locality in the address stream that are independent of the cache configuration. These metrics will be used for estimating the miss ratios for arbitrary cache configurations. For our study, all addresses are line addresses of cache accesses.

Consider an address trace T as a mapping of consecutive integers in increasing order, representing successive positions in the trace, to tuples (x, m) where x identifies the address and m identifies its repetition number. The first occurrence of address x in the trace is represented by $(x, 0)$. Let $t = T^{-1}$ denote the inverse function. $t(x, m)$ denotes the position of the mth occurrence of address x in the trace. We now introduce a few more definitions.

Reuse Interval: The **reuse interval** (RI) is defined only when $m > 0$ and denotes the portion of the trace enclosed between the mth and $(m-1)^{th}$ occurrence of x. Formally, $RI(x, m) =$

$$\begin{cases} \{(z, m')|t(x, m-1) < t(z, m') < t(x, m)\} & \text{if } m > 0 \\ \text{undefined} & \text{otherwise} \end{cases}$$

Unique Reuse Distance: This denotes the total number of unique addresses between two occurrences of the same address in the trace. Thus,

$$URD(x, m) = \begin{cases} \left| \{z|(z, m') \in RI(x, m)\} \right| & \text{if } m > 0 \\ \infty & \text{otherwise} \end{cases}$$

Numerically, this is 1 less than Mattson's much earlier stack distance [32].

Absolute Reuse Distance: This denotes the total number of positions between two occurrences of the same address

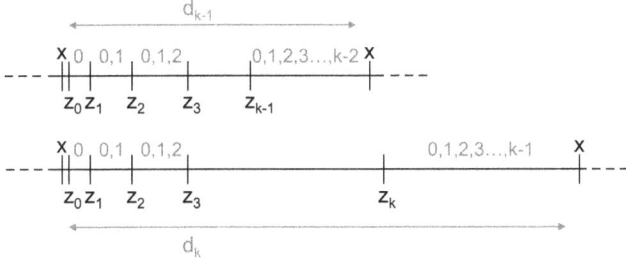

Figure 2: Schematic diagram showing relation between $d_k(t)$ and $d_{k-1}(T)$. Possible URDs for accesses in each subinterval are shown in red.

in the trace. Thus, $ARD(x,m) =$

$$\begin{cases} \left|RI(x,m)\right| = t(x,m) - t(x,m-1) - 1 & \text{if } m > 0 \\ \infty & \text{otherwise} \end{cases}$$

As an example, in the access sequence $a\ b\ b\ c\ d\ b\ a$, $URD(a,1) = 3$ and $ARD(a,1) = 5$.

2.1 Reuse Distance Distributions

Our study is concerned with average-case behavior. So instead of focusing on each individual point in T, we characterize it using probability vectors that reflect average/expected distributions.

- The **unique reuse distance distribution** of trace T is a probability distribution that we denote by row vector $r(T)$ such that the kth component, $r_k(T) = P(URD(x,m) = k), \forall (x,m) \in image(T)$. The characterization is lossy in the sense that in general, T cannot be recovered from $r(T)$ even upto permutation of entity identifiers (See Appendix A).

- The **expected absolute distance distribution** of trace T is a row vector that we denote by $d(T)$ such that the kth component, $d_k(T) = E(ARD(x,m)|URD(x,m) = k), \forall (x,m) \in image(T)$

2.2 $d(\text{T})$ Estimation

It is obvious that $ARD(x,m) \geq URD(x,m), \forall x, m$. It then follows that $d_k(T) \geq k, \forall k$ such that $r_k(T) > 0$. Also, $d_0(T) = 0$. We now show how to compute (an approximation to) $d(T)$ given $r(T)$.

Figure 2 shows a schematic of a trace and organization of URDs within a reuse interval for some address x. $z_0, z_1, ...z_k$ denote distinct addresses. This is just a conceptual tool and does not constrain the actual permutation of addresses in a particular reuse interval. The immediate next access after reference address x must be something other than x (otherwise the reuse interval would immediately terminate with $k = 0$). Between this first address z_0 and the next different address z_1, the only possible URDs of accesses must be 0. Between z_1 and z_2, the only possible URDs can be 0 and 1. Extending this reasoning till z_{k-1} and z_k we observe that $d_k(T)$ and $d_{k-1}(T)$ differ only in the last sub-sequence which consists of a run of accesses with URDs in $\{0, 1, .., k-1\}$. We approximate the length of this run with the expected number of trials to success in a geometric distribution with success probability $\sum_{i=k}^{\infty} r_i(T)$.

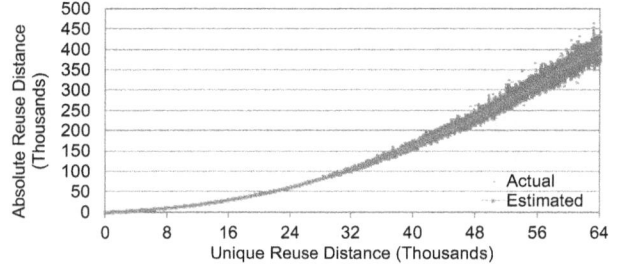

Figure 3: Actual vs estimated $d(T)$ for oltp.

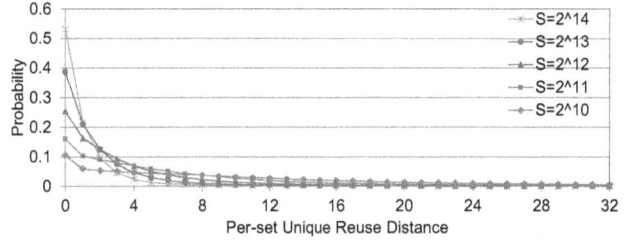

Figure 4: Effect of the number of sets (S) on per-set locality for oltp.

We thus arrive at the following recurrence:

$$\begin{aligned} d_0(T) &= 0 \\ d_k(T) &= d_{k-1}(T) + \frac{1}{\sum_{i=k}^{\infty} r_i(T)} \end{aligned} \quad (1)$$

Expanding the recurrence gives us

$$d_k(T) = \sum_{j=1}^{k} \frac{1}{\sum_{i=j}^{\infty} r_i(T)} = \sum_{j=1}^{k} \frac{1}{1 - \sum_{i=0}^{j-1} r_i(T)}$$

This is similar to known approximations for the coupon collector's problem assuming a given order of coupons [11]. We have seen good agreement in trends between observed and estimated values of $d(T)$ as illustrated in Figure 3. More accurate approximations for $d(T)$ can be considered if needed at the expense of more computation time.

3. PER-SET LOCALITY

Replacement policy decisions (determining which cache line to evict) in traditional caches happen for each individual set. This in turn influences the miss ratio. So it is essential to determine the locality in the address stream that each individual set sees on average. We refer to the temporal locality in the per-set address stream as the per-set locality.

Per-set locality is strongly influenced by the number of sets (S) in the cache. The set of *unique* addresses in the address stream is split among the sets based on the index mapping function. The address stream that any individual set sees is the subset of the original address stream consisting of *all* accesses to the addresses mapping to that set. S thus determines the degree to which the address stream is split. Decreasing S increases URDs of the per-set address streams since addresses that hitherto mapped to other sets now get mapped to the reference set, and vice versa.

Accordingly, we extend our previous notations of locality metrics to additionally include S as a parameter. Thus

$r(T, S)$ denotes the unique reuse distribution of the subsequence of T that a single set in the cache observes on average. $r(T, 1)$ is the temporal locality of the original address stream, which is also the per-set locality of a fully-associative cache ($S = 1$). Figure 4 illustrates how $r(T, S)$ changes with S for oltp. $d(T)$ is adapted to $d(T, S)$ similarly and can be estimated from $r(T, S)$ using Equation 1. For brevity of notation, we will omit specifying one or more parameters when their values are clear from the context.

As Table 1 shows, cache configurations in our study have a range of number of sets (2^{10} to 2^{18}). For efficiently predicting miss ratios it is essential to be able to determine how $r(S)$ can be transformed to $r(S')$ for $S' \neq S$. The rest of this section develops a (new) methodology for this.

3.1 $r(S')$ Estimation

For set-associative caches with $S' > 1$ we make the simplifying assumption, similar to Smith's model [21, 40], that the mapping of unique lines to cache sets are independent of each other. While this assumption does not always hold with the traditional bit selection index function, some processors use simple XOR hashing functions that increase uniformity [27]. The uniformity assumption enables both the following model and the use of uniform set-sampling techniques.

Accesses to a given set can thus be modeled as successive Bernoulli trials with the success of each trial having probability $\frac{1}{S'}$. While computing $r(S')$ from $r(1)$, we note that $r_j(S')$ is the sum of the probability of exactly j successes (j addresses mapping to the reference set) from $r_k(1), \forall k$. The generalized stochastic Binomial Matrix [43] $B(x, y)$ has the value ${}^kC_j y^j x^{k-j}$ in row k, column j, where ${}^kC_j$ denotes the jth binomial coefficient and $x + y = 1$. This is the same as the probability of exactly j successes in k Bernoulli trials with probability of each success being y. Viewing the computation of $r(S')$ from $r(1)$ through the lens of matrix multiplication, we recognize that the transformer is a generalized stochastic Binomial Matrix, $B(1 - \frac{1}{S'}, \frac{1}{S'})$. Thus,

$$r(S') = r(1) \cdot B(1 - \frac{1}{S'}, \frac{1}{S'}) \qquad (2)$$

It is straight-forward to show that the above transformation respects $\sum_{i=0}^{\infty} r_i(S') = \sum_{i=0}^{\infty} r_i(1) = 1$. Qualitatively, this transformation results in a re-distribution of mass with $r(S')$ getting compressed as S' is increased and dilated as S' is decreased (see Figure 4).

We will now show how to compute $r(S')$ from any starting cache configuration S. This shows how computations can be reused instead of always needing to start from the ground configuration ($S = 1$) and will also be useful in reasoning about way-counters (Section 5.3).

Binomial Matrices are invertible (when the second parameter is non-zero) and closed under multiplication within the same dimension [43]. Using identities $B(x, y)B(w, z) = B(x + yw, yz)$ and $B(x, y)^{-1} = B(-xy^{-1}, y^{-1})$, [43], we get

$$
\begin{aligned}
r(S') &= r(1) \cdot B(1 - \frac{1}{S'}, \frac{1}{S'}) \\
&= r(S) \cdot (B(1 - \frac{1}{S}, \frac{1}{S}))^{-1} \cdot B(1 - \frac{1}{S'}, \frac{1}{S'}) \\
&= r(S) \cdot B(1 - \frac{S}{S'}, \frac{S}{S'}) \qquad (3)
\end{aligned}
$$

Equation 3 is a general form of Equation 2. The transformer depends only on the ratio of the number of the sets

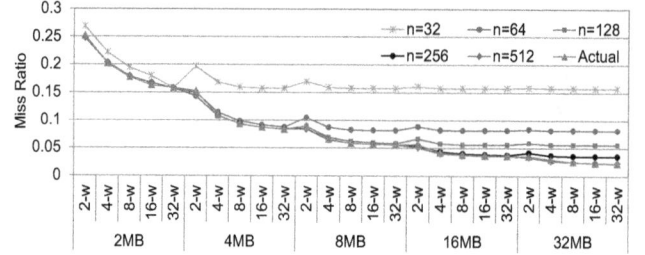

Figure 5: LRU prediction with reuse information limited to n at $r(2^{10})$ which is first computed from $r(1)$ (Equation 2).

in the current cache to that in the target cache. There are two cases to consider depending on the value of this ratio:

Case 1, $S' \geq S$: The transformation is always safe in that the computed probabilities are valid ($\in [0, 1]$) *even if $r(S)$ has not been computed binomially*. Moreover, this allows intermediate steps; for example, computing $r(2^{14})$ from $r(1)$ is equivalent to first computing $r(2^{10})$ from $r(1)$ and then computing $r(2^{14})$ from $r(2^{10})$. This provides an opportunity to *reuse intermediate computations*. So, $r(S)$ can be computed once from $r(1)$ for the smallest S (2^{10} in our study, see Table 1) and used for all other target configurations.

Case 2, $S' < S$: Since $B(1 - \frac{S}{S'}, \frac{S}{S'}) = (B(1 - \frac{S'}{S}, \frac{S'}{S}))^{-1}$, Case 2 transforms can invert Case 1 transforms provided Case 1 results have not been truncated (see below). Otherwise, the computed probabilities may not be valid ($\notin [0, 1]$).

3.2 Matrix dimension and Truncation of r

The dimension of B is determined by the maximum (per-set) URD, n, we are interested to maintain to avoid large computational costs. If r is limited to position n, $r_\infty(S)$ must be adjusted so that $r_\infty(S) = 1 - \sum_{i=0}^{n} r(S)$.

Assume $r(2^{10})$ is available, computed from $r(1)$ using Equation 2. Figure 5 shows predicted miss ratios for oltp with $r(2^{10})$ maintained for various values of n. Section 4.1 explains LRU prediction. Although the maximum associativity that we consider is 32, Figure 5 shows that n has to be much larger than that (≥ 512) for good predictions for larger caches with $S' > 2^{10}$, such as 32MB caches (see Table 1).

While $n = 512$ is good for $r(2^{10})$, the equivalent value for $r(1)$ is very large, potentially upto $512 \cdot 2^{10}$. To appreciate this, consider the $r(1)$ address stream as a merger of the 2^{10} mutually exclusive per-set address streams, each of which has reuse intervals of upto 512. Determining the long-tailed $r(1)$ distribution or using large matrices to compute $r(2^{10})$ from $r(1)$ in software is time-consuming. Section 5.1 proposes low-cost hardware support to approximately estimate $r(2^{10})$ with $n = 512$.

4. CACHE HIT FUNCTIONS

Given a target cache organization ($S', A', policy$) and a trace T, our goal is to determine a vector $\phi(r(S'), S', A', policy)$ such that the expected hit ratio for the trace is

$$h = r \cdot \phi \qquad (4)$$

The idea is to characterize workload traces by r and caches by ϕ so that the effect on hit ratio for changes in traces or cache configurations can be readily estimated.

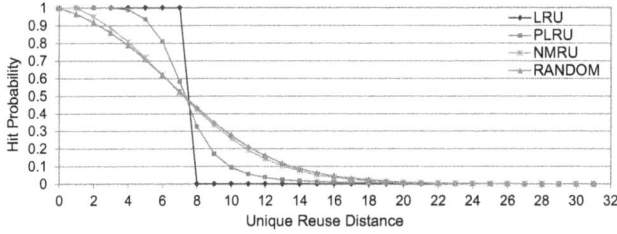

Figure 6: Representative hit ratio functions for an 8-way cache with different replacement policies but with the same trace and number of sets.

We call $\boldsymbol{\phi}$ the cache hit function. The value of the kth component, $\boldsymbol{\phi}_k$ is the conditional probability of a hit for accesses x such that $URD(x, m) = k$ where m is the repetition count for x at that point in the trace when the access happens. $\boldsymbol{\phi}_k$ monotonically decreases with k in this model. This is because non-eviction of a cache-resident address after accesses involving k other unique addresses implies non-eviction after accesses involving $k-1$ unique addresses *and* the remaining accesses. If there are no intervening accesses ($k = 0$), the access must be a hit. Accesses hitherto never seen ($k = \infty$) must miss. So,

$$\boldsymbol{\phi}_k = \begin{cases} 1 & \text{if } k = 0 \\ \leq \boldsymbol{\phi}_{k-1} & \text{if } k \geq 1 \\ 0 & \text{at } k = \infty \end{cases} \quad (5)$$

Figure 6 shows representative characteristic functions for common replacement policies. We consider the well-known, but rarely-implemented[1] LRU policy as well as the practical RANDOM, NMRU, and PLRU policies. Note that RANDOM, NMRU, PLRU have hit functions that are non-zero beyond $A'(=8$ in the figure). So, computing $\boldsymbol{r} \cdot \boldsymbol{\phi}$ upto A' is not sufficient for these replacement policies. For our evaluations, we compute the dot-product for $2A'$ terms; longer than that has diminishing returns for our workloads.

Apart from LRU, $\boldsymbol{\phi}$ is not independent of $\boldsymbol{r}$ for different replacement policies. As we shall show later, $\boldsymbol{\phi}(RANDOM)$ depends on $\boldsymbol{d}$, while $\boldsymbol{\phi}(PLRU)$ may need more information.

4.1 Estimating ϕ(LRU)

For a set-associative LRU cache with associativity A', it is well known that all accesses with addresses re-appearing with less than A' unique intervening elements must hit and all other accesses must miss. This leads us to the following characterization of the LRU hit ratio function.

$$\boldsymbol{\phi}_k(LRU) = \begin{cases} 1 & \text{if } 0 \leq k < A' \\ 0 & \text{if } k \geq A' \end{cases} \quad (6)$$

Figure 5 shows actual vs estimated ($n = 512$) miss ratios for `oltp` with LRU using Equations 3, 6 and 4. Figure 16 (Appendix F) shows more examples. As observed earlier by Hill and Smith [21], increasing A' yields diminishing returns.

4.1.1 Optimization (Smith's Model)

A naive combination of Equations 4, 6 and 3 results in $\sum_{i=0}^{A'-1}(n-i) = nA' - \frac{A'(A'-1)}{2}$ multiplications with bino-

---
[1]LRU is typically not implemented in real caches for associativity larger than 4 due to hardware complexity.

mial computations to estimate the hit ratio for a cache with S' sets and associativity A'. The number of multiplications can be reduced by observing that due to the step-function nature of $\boldsymbol{\phi}(LRU)$, some of the coefficients will sum to 1. Expanding the computation and simplifying, we get

$$h(S') = \sum_{i=0}^{A'-1} \boldsymbol{r}_i(1) + \sum_{i=A'}^{n} \boldsymbol{r}_i(1) \cdot \sum_{k=0}^{A'-1} {}^i C_k \cdot \left(\frac{1}{S'}\right)^k \cdot \left(1 - \frac{1}{S'}\right)^{(i-k)} \quad (7)$$

Equation 7 is an optimized version of Smith's associativity model [21, 40]. It requires $nA' - A'(A'-1)$ multiplications which is $\frac{A'(A'-1)}{2}$ less than the naive combination. But computing binomial terms is costly and n is usually much larger than A'.

4.1.2 Poisson approximation to Binomial

The last sum in Equation 7 is the cumulative binomial sum up to $A'-1$ with parameters i and $\frac{1}{S'}$. Cypher [13, 14] uses a Poisson approximation to binomial for reducing computational costs – when i is large and $\frac{1}{S'}$ is small, the binomial distribution can be approximated by a Poisson distribution with parameter $\lambda = \frac{i}{S'}$. This is easier to compute than with the binomial coefficients.

We can further optimize Cypher's approach by substituting the cumulative Poisson sum with piecewise linear transformations. This involves precomputing the distribution at a small number of points and storing the values which can then be used at run-time to compute the miss ratio. Values of intermediate points can be approximated using linear interpolation. This method provides good approximations with reduced computational cost but a moderate storage overhead. Appendix C shows an example approximation using ~7 precomputed points per cache configuration.

4.2 Estimating ϕ(RANDOM)

The RAND replacement algorithm [7] (also popularly called RANDOM) chooses a line (uniformly) randomly from the lines in the set for eviction on a miss.

For an A'-way set-associative cache, the probability of replacement of a given line on a miss is $\frac{1}{A'}$. Accounting for the number of misses in between successive reuses of an address is therefore needed. For expected miss rate θ, the expected number of misses for a sequence of α accesses is $\alpha \cdot \theta$. This is why $\boldsymbol{d}$ is important for RANDOM whereas LRU works independent of such information.

We make the simplifying assumption that miss occurrences (not specific addresses) are independent and hence amenable to be modeled as a Bernoulli process. While this may not be accurate, it allows us to make reasonably good predictions without tracking additional state.

Let $\boldsymbol{d}_k = \alpha$. The probability of i misses is estimated by ${}^\alpha C_i \cdot \theta^i \cdot (1-\theta)^{(\alpha-i)}$. The probability that a specific line is not replaced after i misses is $\left(1 - \frac{1}{A'}\right)^i$. We thus have

$$h(RANDOM) = \boldsymbol{r} \cdot \boldsymbol{\phi}(RANDOM)$$

$$\boldsymbol{\phi}_k(RANDOM) = \sum_{i=0}^{\alpha|\boldsymbol{d}_k=\alpha} {}^\alpha C_i \cdot \theta^i \cdot (1-\theta)^{(\alpha-i)} \cdot \left(1 - \frac{1}{A'}\right)^i$$

$$\theta = 1 - h(RANDOM) \quad (8)$$

To simplify the computation, we approximate Binomial(α, θ) by Poisson($\lambda = \alpha \cdot \theta$). Let $q = \left(1 - \frac{1}{A'}\right)$. This gives

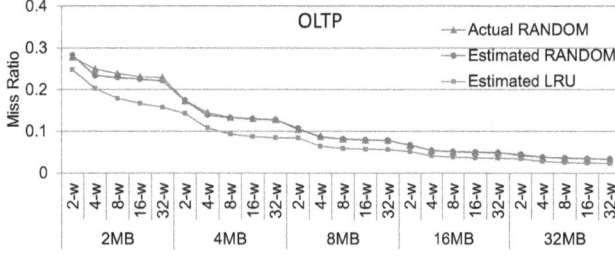

Figure 7: Actual vs estimated miss ratios for oltp with RANDOM replacement policy. LRU estimates are shown as reference. $r(2^{10})$ is first computed from $r(1)$ (Equation 2).

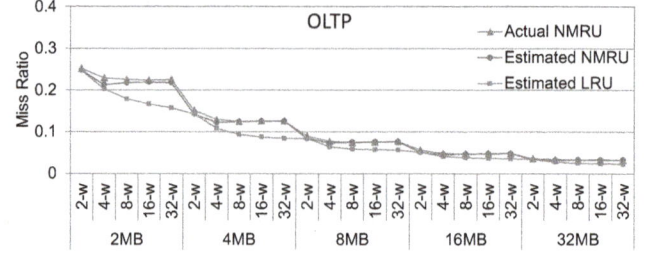

Figure 8: Actual vs estimated miss ratios for oltp with NMRU replacement policy. LRU estimates are shown as reference. $r(2^{10})$ is first computed from $r(1)$ (Equation 2).

$$
\begin{aligned}
\phi_k(RANDOM) &= \sum_{i=0}^{\alpha | d_k = \alpha} {}^\alpha C_i \cdot \theta^i \cdot (1-\theta)^{(\alpha - i)} \cdot q^i \\
&= \sum_{i=0}^{\infty} {}^\alpha C_i \cdot \theta^i \cdot (1-\theta)^{(\alpha - i)} \cdot q^i \\
&\approx \sum_{i=0}^{\infty} e^{-\lambda} \cdot \frac{\lambda^i}{i!} \cdot q^i \\
&= e^{-\lambda(1-q)} \sum_{i=0}^{\infty} e^{-\lambda q} \cdot \frac{(\lambda q)^i}{i!} \\
&= e^{\frac{-\alpha\theta}{A'}} \quad\quad (9)
\end{aligned}
$$

The system of equations in 8 can now be approximated by the following system.

$$
\begin{aligned}
h(RANDOM) &= r \cdot \phi(RANDOM) \\
\phi_k(RANDOM) &= e^{\frac{-d_k\theta}{A'}} \\
\theta &= 1 - h(RANDOM) \quad\quad (10)
\end{aligned}
$$

We solve the system of equations in 10 with the initial value $h = r_0$. d is estimated using equation 1. Usually 5 or fewer iterations suffice to reach within 1% of a fix-point. Proof of convergence is presented in Appendix D.

4.2.1 Optimization

A better approximation for $A' = 2$ can be obtained by using the fact that for the reference element not to be evicted at $URD \geq 2$, the previous element must be evicted (since the set can hold only 2 elements). The probability of the previous element to be evicted is $1 - \phi_1$. For the reference element to hit at $URD = k$, it must hit at $URD = k - 1$ and the above condition must hold. This leads us to the following approximation.

$$
\phi_k = \phi_{k-1} \cdot (1 - \phi_1), \quad k \geq 2 \quad\quad (11)
$$

This approximation is possible since the model can exactly determine the set contents for $URD >= 2$. For higher associativities, exact determination of set contents is difficult.

Figure 7 shows actual vs estimated ($n = 512$) values of miss ratios for RANDOM with the estimates computed using Equations 3, 10, 11 and 4.

4.3 Estimating ϕ(NMRU)

The NMRU (or non-MRU) replacement algorithm differentiates the most recently accessed (MRU) line from other lines in the set [41]. On a miss, a line is chosen (uniformly) randomly from among the $A' - 1$ non-MRU lines.

At $A' = 2$, $\phi(NMRU) = \phi(LRU)$. For the rest of the cases, the framework is similar to that of RANDOM except that accesses at $URD \leq 1$ are guaranteed to hit. Moreover, the replacement logic has $A' - 1$ possible choices for an eviction in case of a miss. This leads to a few simple modifications to the system of equations in 10. The modified system is shown below:

$$
\begin{aligned}
\phi_1(NMRU) &= 1 \\
h(NMRU) &= r \cdot \phi(NMRU) \\
\phi_k(NMRU) &= e^{\frac{-(d_k - d_1)\theta}{A' - 1}} \\
\theta &= 1 - h(NMRU) \quad\quad (12)
\end{aligned}
$$

Figure 8 shows actual vs estimated ($n = 512$) values of miss ratios for NMRU with the estimates computed using Equations 3, 12 and 4.

4.4 Estimating ϕ(PLRU)

Partitioned LRU [41] (also popularly called pseudo-LRU) maintains a balanced binary tree that, at each level, differentiates between the two sub-trees based on access recency. Every internal node is represented by a single bit whose value decides which of the two subtrees was accessed more recently. The cache lines are represented by the leaves of the tree. Whenever a line is accessed, the nodes on the path from the root to the leaf flip their bit values, thus pointing to the other subtree at each level. On a miss, the subtree pointed to is chosen, recursively starting from the root. The line corresponding to the leaf reached in this way is chosen for eviction. The bit-values along this path are then flipped.

In the PLRU scheme, the most recently accessed element is always known but the least recently accessed one is not. In contrast to the LRU scheme, that maintains a total access order between the lines, PLRU maintains only a partial order. Since there is no difference between partial and total orders involving 2 elements, PLRU is LRU when $A' = 2$. In contrast to LRU that guarantees exactly $A' - 1$ unique accesses before eviction, PLRU guarantees at least $log_2(A')$ (=number of tree levels) unique accesses before the reference address is evicted.

On a miss, the reference line will be evicted if and only if the immediately preceding sequence of accesses follows a particular pattern. These patterns can be described using regular expressions (see Appendix E). In contrast to RANDOM, not only the number of misses in the reuse interval, but also the pattern of accesses determines eviction probability. It is difficult to estimate $\phi(PLRU)$ by computing probabilities of the regular expressions since the distance to misses within the reuse interval as well as the ways occupied by the intervening elements are not known. Instead, we use a different approach.

First, we compute $\phi(A' = 4, PLRU)$ then compute $\phi(A' = 8, PLRU)$ by dividing traffic using a binomial distribution and applying $\phi(A' = 4, PLRU)$ on the divided traffic. We claim that an 8-way tree can be viewed as a composition of two 4-way trees with the top-node dividing traffic between the two subtrees. (See Appendix E, Figure 13 for visualization.) Similar observations hold between 8-way and 16-way trees and so on. This helps us to estimate $\phi(PLRU)$ for successively higher associativities. For ease of computation we assume that the top node divides traffic evenly between its two constituent sub-trees.

4.4.1 Base case: $A' = 4$

Since $log_2(4) = 2$, ϕ_k is 1 when $k \leq 2$. When $k \geq 4$, there are 3 elements in the tree other than the reference element, but 2 of those cannot be replaced as they have less than 2 intervening elements for themselves. The only eviction candidate other than the reference element is the 3rd element with URD 3. Thus, $\phi_k = \phi_{k-1} \cdot (1 - \phi_3)$.

The case that remains is when $k = 3$. Consider the kth element. There are two subcases here, each with probability $\frac{1}{2}$ assuming that the top node switches evenly between the two subtrees:

1. It maps to the other subtree on either being present there (hit) or being allocated there on a miss. So it cannot affect the reference element. Thus, $\phi_k = \phi_{k-1} = 1$.

2. It maps to the same subtree as the reference element. The reference element will be evicted only if the k_{th} element is not present (miss) and PLRU estimates the wrong stack. But in 4-way PLRU, there are only 3 admissible total orders of which 2 share the same last element. So the probability of a correct selection is $\frac{2}{3}$. The kth element has URD> 2. Using $h(LRU)$ as an approximation, the probability of a miss for the kth element is $\sum_{i=0}^{3} r_i - \sum_{i=0}^{2} r_i = r_3$. So the hit-probability for the reference element in this case is approximated as $\frac{2}{3} \cdot (1 - r_3)$.

Putting the two subcases together,

$$\phi_k = \begin{cases} 1 & \text{if } 0 \leq k \leq 2 \\ \frac{1}{2} + \frac{(1 - r_3)}{3} & \text{if } k = 3 \\ \phi_{k-1} \cdot (1 - \phi_3) & \text{if } k \geq 4 \end{cases} \quad (13)$$

4.4.2 Recurrence: $A' \geq 8$

Let $L = log_2(A')$ and $\psi = \phi(A'/2)$. For the first case, when $k \leq L$, ϕ_k must be 1. For $k > L$, consider the kth element. There are two subcases here:

1. It maps to the other subtree. The argument is the same as given earlier and $\phi_k = \phi_{k-1}$.

2. It maps to the same subtree as the reference element. If $k \geq \frac{A'}{2} + 2$, it is likely that there is at least one other element in the reference subtree apart from the

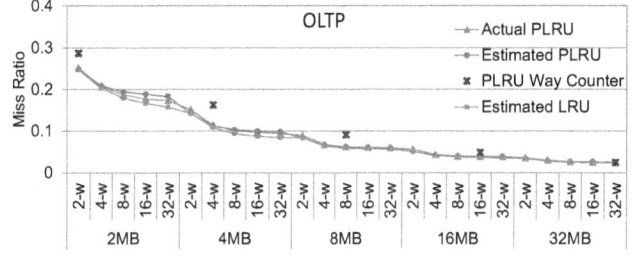

Figure 9: Actual vs estimated miss ratios for oltp with PLRU replacement policy. LRU estimates are shown as reference. $r(2^{10})$ is first computed from $r(1)$ (Equation 2). Section 5.3.1 describes PLRU Way-Counters.

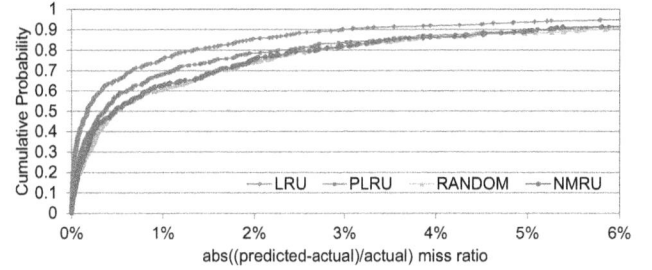

Figure 10: Relative-error density plot combined over all (16) workloads.

reference element and the kth element. So, the binomial sum starts with ψ_{2+i}. If $k \leq \frac{A'}{2} + 1$, the $\frac{A'}{2}$ other elements can all occupy the other subtree. So, the binomial sum starts with ψ_{1+i}.

Putting everything together,

$$\phi_k = \begin{cases} 1 & \text{if } 0 \leq k \leq L \\ \frac{\phi_{k-1}}{2} + \frac{1}{2} \sum_{i=0}^{k-3} {}^{k-3}C_i \left(\frac{1}{2}\right)^{(k-3)} \cdot \psi_{2+i} & \text{if } k \geq \frac{A'}{2} + 2 \\ \frac{\phi_{k-1}}{2} + \frac{1}{2} \sum_{i=0}^{k-2} {}^{k-2}C_i \left(\frac{1}{2}\right)^{(k-2)} \cdot \psi_{1+i} & \text{otherwise} \end{cases}$$

$$(14)$$

Figure 9 shows actual vs estimated ($n = 512$) values of miss ratios for PLRU with the estimates computed using Equations 3, 13, 14 and 4.

4.5 Estimation Accuracy and Compute Time

Figure 10 shows the cumulative distribution of relative errors in miss ratio prediction for all workloads. More than 90% of predictions have relative errors within 6%. Prediction for LRU is the most accurate.

A major contributor to hit ratio computation time is the determination of r. Subsection 5.1 proposes low-cost hardware to approximate $r(2^{10})$, $n = 512$ online. Assuming this is available, the average hit ratio computation time per cache configuration on a Nehalem 2.26 GHz machine were – LRU: 0.020 msec; PLRU: 0.022 msec; RANDOM, NMRU: 0.030 msec. A large fraction of this is due to computation of Equation 3 (Appendix B shows pseudocode) which takes ~ 0.080 msec, but gets amortized for caches with the same S'.

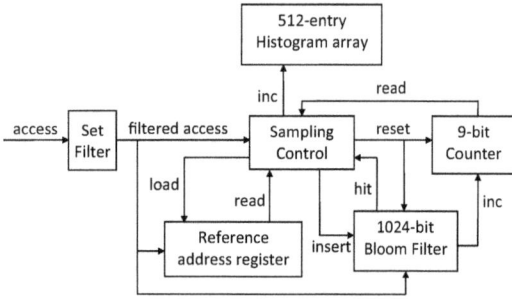

Figure 11: Schematic of new hardware support

State	Action

idle	x = rand() % 10;
	if(x) state = idle
	else state = start-sample

start-sample	ref. addr = addr state = process-sample

process-sample	if(addr == ref. addr)
	   state = end-sample-a
	else {
	   If (hit in Bloom Filter)
	      state = process-sample
	   else {
	      if (counter value == 511)
	         state = end-sample-b
	      else {
	         Increment counter
	         Insert addr into Bloom Filter
	         state = process-sample }}}

end-sample-a	Emit URD = counter value reset state = idle
end-sample-b	Emit URD = ∞ reset state = idle

Figure 12: Sampling Control for new hardware

5. HARDWARE SUPPORT

Section 3.2 discussed that to avoid expensive computation to determine $r(1)$ or compute $r(2^{10})$ from $r(1)$, we need hardware support to directly estimate $r(2^{10})$. Subsection 5.1 presents our proposed hardware technique to do this.

Subsections 5.2 and 5.3 discuss two traditional hardware mechanisms that help in cache miss ratio estimation – set-counters and way-counters.

5.1 New hardware support to estimate reuse distributions ($r(2^{10})$, n = 512)

The definition of unique reuse distance (URD) depends *only on the cardinality of the reuse interval (RI) and not on the contents of the set*. This suggests applicability of hardware signatures, such as Bloom filters [10], that can construct compact representations of sets. Whereas shadow tags store entire tag addresses, a Bloom filter uses only one bit per hash function to represent each address.

Our proposed hardware, shown in Figure 11, uses a Bloom filter (to summarize RI), a counter to determine $|RI|$, and set-sampling logic. We use a 1024-bit parallel Bloom filter [37] with two H_3 hash functions [12] and a 9-bit counter. The Bloom filter can be at most half-full (512 elements) before being reset. Larger Bloom filters can be used to reduce aliasing errors at the cost of more area/power overhead.

The hardware uses a combination of set sampling and time

sampling techniques [24–26, 33, 47]. The set sampling hardware restricts the Bloom filter to addresses matching a subset of the cache index bits. This allows to focus on addresses mapping to one set of a cache with $S = 2^{10}$, and hence track $r(2^{10})$. Once a set-sample is fixed, the hardware randomly chooses an address mapping to the set-sample as the reference address. It then estimates the length of the reuse interval to the next access with the reference address and records it in the histogram. This process is repeated. Figure 12 describes the sampling control state machine.

Assuming 4-byte counters, the size of the histogram array is $512 \times 4 = 2KB$. We model the histogram and Bloom filter arrays in CACTI [39] as direct-mapped SRAM caches (ITRS-LOP, 32nm technology) with 8-byte line sizes. The static power is ~1.2 mW and the dynamic energy per access is ~10.8 pJ leading to less than 0.03% of power overhead for the system simulated (Section 6, Table 2). CACTI numbers suggest less than 1 sq mm area overhead for the arrays.

The technique can be generalized to estimate $r(2^x)$ by sizing the Bloom filter, histogram, and set filter appropriately.

5.2 Set-Counters

Set-counters [44] use counters that track the number of accesses per set or a group of sets. However, since they can only track changes in the number of accesses per set *but not changes in per-set locality*, they would be unable to model the behavior shown in Figure 4.

5.3 Way-Counters and Shadow Tags

Way-counters [44] increment a counter associated with each logical stack position (ordered by access recency) on every cache hit. The number of hits for associativity A' is the sum of the counter values from 0 to $A' - 1$.

The above assumes $A' \leq A$ where A is the associativity of the current/predicting cache (32MB 32-way in this study). In applications such as dynamic reconfiguration situations, this is problematic since the cache may need to be sized up, not only sized down. Shadow tags [33] (or auxiliary tag directories [35]) circumvent this difficulty by maintaining a copy of the tags that is not deactivated during reconfigurations. This always maintains a stack depth to the maximum desired value and facilitates simulating the effect of hits and misses on a cache with associativity larger than that of the current cache. Qureshi, et al. [34] used dynamic set sampling to reduce storage and power costs of the shadow copy.

Way-counter values, converted to probabilities, estimate $r(S)$ upto length A. The estimation is exact for LRU caches. Their operation can be understood by deriving Equation 7 from Equation 3 instead of from Equation 2. We get

$$h(S') = \sum_{i=0}^{A'-1} r_i(S) + \sum_{i=A'}^{n} r_i(S) \cdot \sum_{k=0}^{A'-1} {}^iC_k \cdot \left(\frac{S}{S'}\right)^k \cdot \left(1 - \frac{S}{S'}\right)^{(i-k)}$$

Under the assumption $S' = S$, $h(S') = \sum_{i=0}^{A'-1} r_i(S)$ which is computationally extremely efficient.

5.3.1 Way-counters for PLRU

In PLRU, the MRU line is known with certainty but the rest of the logical ordering is not precisely known. Kedzierski, et al. [23] proposed a heuristic for approximating logical stack positions for PLRU caches to enable way-counter based prediction . Let *waynum* be the way number of the accessed line and *pathbits* denote the bit-values of the tree

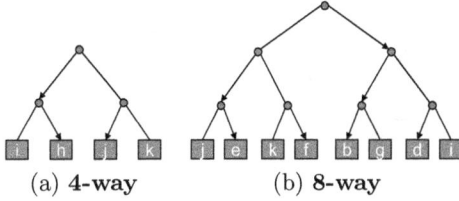

Figure 13: PLRU trees demonstrating non-inclusion. The 8-way tree does not include element **h** of the 4-way tree.

nodes along the path from the root to the leaf with root bit in MSB position. Let the function $reverse(b)$ reverse bit positions in the binary representation of b. The following heuristic is used to approximate $URD(x, m)$:

$$\hat{URD}(x, m) = A - 1 - (reverse(waynum) \oplus pathbits)$$

This approach aims to compute $\boldsymbol{r} \cdot \boldsymbol{\phi}(LRU)$ with $\boldsymbol{r}$ approximately measured using the above mechanism. However, apart from the traditional limitations of way-counters (Section 5.3), it also ignores the fact that $\boldsymbol{\phi}(PLRU) \neq \boldsymbol{\phi}(LRU)$ for $A \neq 2$. Interestingly, it fails to accurately estimate the hit ratio even for a 2-way cache where $\boldsymbol{\phi}(PLRU) = \boldsymbol{\phi}(LRU)$ *when the current configuration that does the estimation has* $A \neq 2$ (see, for example, Figure 9 where the current/predicting configuration has A=32). In contrast, our framework overcomes this by *decoupling hit ratio estimation from the organization of the current cache*.

5.3.2 Way-Counter Limitations

Way-counters (+shadow tags) have the following fundamental limitations:

Fixed number of sets: The relation $(S' = S)$ that makes way-counters efficient also implies the restriction that the number of sets must be fixed. As can be observed from Table 1, miss ratios for only 4 of 24 configurations can be predicted at any time; other predictions must be preceded by (time-consuming) re-training for the changed S'.

However, our framework reveals that Equation 5.3 may be used to transform way-counter values when $S' \geq S$ (also see discussion for Case 1 in Section 3). With reference to Table 1, maintaining shadow tags corresponding to $S = 2^{10}$ allows conversion of values for any $S' \neq S$. But, Figure 5 shows that to use way-counter values for a cache with a larger number of sets, the shadow tags and counter values must be maintained for $n(> A)$ positions.

Replacement policies with stack inclusion: Way-counters exploit the stack inclusion property [32] of LRU to predict miss ratios $\forall A' \leq A$. For replacement policies that do not guarantee stack inclusion (PLRU/RANDOM/NMRU), this is no longer true.

For example, consider the access sequence: **a b c d e d f e g h f i j i k** simultaneously to an 8-way PLRU set and a 4-way PLRU set. Figure 13 shows the two sets and associated PLRU trees after the sequence. The arrows in the figures point to the less recently used subtree. Initially, both sets were empty and the eviction bits in each tree were pointing to the "left" subtrees. At the end of the sequence, the two sets together contain 9 distinct elements (**i h j k e f b g d**) whereas a policy satisfying inclusion would have exactly 8 elements. Thus, maintaining information for 8 ways is not sufficient to accurately predict miss ratios for both a 4-way and an 8-way cache *even if* $S' = S$.

Tight coupling with replacement policy implementation: Since way-counters are tightly coupled with the implementation of replacement policies that track stack positions (e.g. LRU), they are unusable with other policies such as RANDOM that can also be predicted well using reuse information. Way-counters depend on the replacement policy mimicking stack operation, so they run into trouble when the stack is absent (PLRU/RANDOM/NMRU) (see Section 5.3.1 for a discussion on PLRU) or reconfigured ($S' \neq S$).

Shadow Tag overhead: For very large caches, tag area and power are significant. Loh, et al. [30] propose novel tag management schemes for such caches. Maintaining additional shadow tags in those systems seem difficult.

6. MINIMUM EDP CONFIGURATION

This section describes an application of our technique in finding the LLC configuration that results in the minimum full-system EDP.

Table 2 describes the 8-core CMP we use in this study. We assume an 8-banked L3 cache that is dynamically reconfigurable for a total of 25 configurations (see Table 1). The access latency is conservatively assumed to be constant for all configurations. We use 2 copies of our sampling hardware (Section 5.1), but a common histogram array. To evaluate power and performance, we perform *full-system* simulation using GEMS [31] augmented with a detailed timing and power model. We use CACTI 5.3 [39] to determine the static power and dynamic activation energy per component.

We use 7 SPEComp [6] benchmarks (`ammp`, `equake`, `fma3d`, `gafort`, `mgrid`, `swim`, `wupwise`) with "ref" inputs, 5 PARSEC [9] benchmarks (`blackscholes`, `bodytrack`, `fluidanimate`, `freqmine`, `swaptions`) with "simlarge" inputs, and 4 Wisconsin commercial workloads [2] (`apache`, `jbb`, `oltp`, `zeus`). Each workload uses 8 threads and runs for a fixed amount of work (e.g. #transactions or loop iterations [3]) that corresponds to ∼500M instructions per workload. Each simulation run starts from a mid-execution checkpoint that includes cache warmup.

Figure 14a shows, for each workload, the maximum EDP relative to the minimum EDP for that workload resulting from the different LLC configurations. The chart below the figure lists the LLC configurations that resulted in the extremum points. There exists a significant range of system EDPs, particularly for the commercial workloads; `apache` for example has max EDP more than 3.2x times the min EDP; inaccurate predictions can thus cause the system to transition to a severely suboptimal state. The chart also shows that for 11 of 16 workloads, the min EDP configuration has a cache with a different number of sets than that of the current/predicting cache.

For this experiment, the configuration using a 32MB 32-way LLC performs miss ratio and min-EDP predictions. Figure 14b shows EDP of the configuration identified as the minimum one, relative to the actual minimum EDP, using both reuse-models and PLRU way-counters for predicting LLC miss rates, assuming that the workloads were rerun with the identified configuration. This also assumes simple activity counters to track energy consumption in cores, caches, memory, and performance counters to enable online linear regression to approximate the relation between LLC misses and cycles-per-instruction.

For this evaluation, we use the average sampled reuse distance distribution obtained over all 2^{10} sets as a proxy for the

Core configuration	4-wide out-of-order, 128-entry window, 32-entry scheduler						
Functional Units	4 integer, 2 floating-point, 2 mem units						
Branch Prediction	YAGS 4K PHT 2K Exception Table, 2KB BTB, 16-entry RAS						
Disambiguation	NoSQ 1024-entry predictor, 1024-entry double-buffered SSBF						
Fetch	32-entry buffer, Min. 7 cycles fetch-dispatch time						
Inclusive	L1I Cache	private 32KB 4-way per core, 2 cycle hit latency, ITRS-HP					
	L1D Cache	private 32KB 4-way per core, 2 cycle hit latency, ITRS-HP					
	L2 Cache	private 256KB 8-way per core, 6 cycle access latency, PLRU, ITRS-LOP					
	L3 Cache	shared, configurable 2–32 MB 2–32 way, 8 banks, 14 cycle access latency, PLRU, ITRS-LOP, serial					
Coherence protocol	MESI (Modified, Exclusive, Shared, Invalid), directory						
On-Chip Interconnect	2D Mesh, 16B bidirectional links						
Number of cores	8	On-chip frequency	2132 MHz	Technology generation	32nm	Temperature	340K
Main Memory	4GB DDR3-1066, 75ns zero-load off-chip latency, 2 memory controllers, closed page, pre-stdby						

Table 2: System configuration

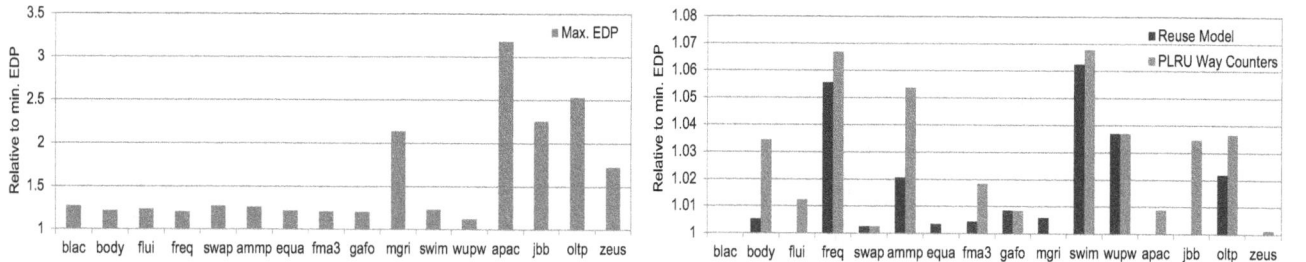

(a) Maximum EDP over 25 possible LLC configurations.　　(b) EDP of predicted minimum configurations.

workload	blac	body	flui	freq	swap	ammp	equa	fma3	gafo	mgri	swim	wupw	apac	jbb	oltp	zeus
min. config	2M-2w*	4M-8w	2M-4w	4M-8w	2M-16w	4M-8w	2M-2w*	4M-4w*	4M-4w*	32M-32w*	4M-32w	8M-32w	32M-16w	32M-8w	16M-8w	32M-8w
max. config	32M-32w*	32M-32w*	32M-32w*	32M-2w*	32M-32w*	32M-16w	32M-4w	32M-4w	32M-32w*	4M-16w	2M-32w*	32M-32w*	2M-2w*	2M-2w*	2M-2w*	2M-2w*
Reuse config	2M-2w*	2M-4w	2M-4w	2M-8w	2M-2w*	2M-8w	2M-4w	2M-8w	2M-8w	32M-16w	4M-16w	16M-16w	32M-16w	32M-8w	16M-16w*	32M-8w
Way-ctr config	2M-2w*	2M-2w*	2M-2w*	2M-2w*	2M-2w*	2M-2w*	2M-2w*	2M-2w*	2M-2w*	32M-32w*	4M-4w*	16M-16w*	32M-32w*	32M-32w*	32M-32w*	32M-32w*

Figure 14: Maximum EDP and that of model-predicted configurations, all relative to the minimum EDP for the same workload, and with PLRU replacement policy. In the above table, xM-yw denotes an x MB, y-way associative LLC. Caches with the same number of sets (2^{14}) as the current/predicting configuration (32MB 32-way) are marked with a *.

sampled distribution. A practical implementation would additionally experience inter-sample variation, but we expect it to be small for long runs. For way-counters, we assume that full shadow tags are present for comparison purposes. In practice, shadow tags would also be set-sampled [34].

Both reuse-models and way-counters predict configurations that are within 7% of the minimum, but reuse models outperform or are the same as way-counters on all except 3 workloads (`equake`, `gafort`, `mgrid`), both due to their ability to predict for a different number of sets and being generally more accurate. The chart below Figure 14b lists the configurations chosen by both models. Workloads such as `apache` require large caches whereas others such as `equake` should be allocated small caches for energy-efficient performance.

7. RELATED WORK

Characterizing cache behavior using stack distances (also known as reuse distances or gap) is well known [8, 13–15, 21, 29, 38, 40, 49]. Analyses can be viewed as being in one of 3 categories: offline, online, and mixed.

In offline algorithms, stack distances are computed offline from an address trace. Computation to determine the distribution can be reduced with efficient algorithms [5] or by approximate analysis [49]. Shi, et al. [38] perform single-pass stack simulation to project cache performance and to study

the impact of data replication for various L2 cache configurations. Online determination of the stack distance distribution cannot directly apply techniques from offline methods due to constraints on computational state and complexity.

Mixed algorithms deal with efficient online trace collection and offline processing. Tam, et al. [46] use hardware mechanisms for address sampling and post-processing software for computing stack distance distributions. Since distribution estimation and hit ratio computation is offline, it cannot react to workload changes in real time.

Online algorithms deal with all the steps of trace collection, distribution generation and hit/miss rate computation online. Agarwal, et al. [1] propose an analytical cache model that uses a binomial model and metrics for time-average of total unique number of accesses but predicting miss rates for set-associative caches is difficult. Suh, et al. [45], Qureshi, et al. [35] propose mechanisms for partitioning of shared caches (L2) among competing processes using way-counters. Suh, et al. [44] also proposes set-counters in LRU order, with each counter tracking accesses to a group of sets. We discuss set and way-counters in Sections 5.2 and 5.3 respectively. Gordon-Ross, et al. [20] use a hardware TCAM to track stack distances for LRU miss-ratio predictions.

Cypher proposes methods [13, 14] for online estimation of stack distances using hash tables. In that work, the effective distance to be tracked is reduced using filter fraction metrics which are then applied to a Poisson prediction model. However, computing filter fractions are difficult, require additional logic and could be subject to approximations depending on available hardware state. In contrast, our scheme uses set sampling that does not require complex filter logic, and Bloom filters for compact representation of sets.

The Binomial model has been successfully used to analyze cache behavior for other applications. Stone, et al. [42], Falsafi, et al. [17] use binomial probability models to model cache reload transients due to context switches based on the footprints of the competing programs and cache size. Other models, e.g. Markov models have also been used to analyze the behavior of context switch misses [28].

Reineke, et al. [36] prove relations on best and worst-case bounds of cache performance for several replacement policies. Our work, in contrast, studies average case behavior.

8. CONCLUSIONS

The central theme of this paper is an online modeling framework, new analytical models, and efficient hardware support, to predict cache performance at runtime for a range of replacement policies. It uses the concept of stack distances and transformations of probability vectors with Binomial matrices. The framework unifies previous analytical models such as Smith's associativity model, Cypher's Poisson model, and hardware techniques such as way-counters. We have discussed limitations of set and way-counters, given a method to convert way-counter values for caches with a different number of sets and shown that this requires maintaining shadow tags for more than the maximum associativity. We have also proposed a new predictor that is decoupled from the cache configuration, uses hardware signatures for compact representation of reuse intervals and can be used as an alternative to way-counters. Extending the models to other replacement policies is the focus of our ongoing work.

9. ACKNOWLEDGMENTS

This work is supported in part by the National Science Foundation (CNS-0916725, CCF-1017650, CNS-1117280, and CCF-1218323), Sandia/DOE (#MSN123960/DOE890426), and a University of Wisconsin Vilas award. The views expressed herein are not necessarily those of the NSF, Sandia or DOE. Wood has a significant financial interest in AMD. This work was inspired by Bob Cypher and improved by feedback from the anonymous reviewers and others.

10. REFERENCES

[1] A. Agarwal, J. Hennessy, and M. Horowitz. An analytical cache model. *ACM Transactions on Computer Systems*, 7(2):184–215, May 1989.

[2] A. R. Alameldeen, M. M. K. Martin, C. J. Mauer, K. E. Moore, M. Xu, D. J. Sorin, M. D. Hill, and D. A. Wood. Simulating a $2M commercial server on a $2K PC. *IEEE Computer*, 36(2):50–57, Feb. 2003.

[3] A. R. Alameldeen and D. A. Wood. IPC considered harmful for multiprocessor workloads. *IEEE Micro*, 26(4):8–17, Jul/Aug 2006.

[4] D. H. Albonesi. Selective cache ways: on-demand cache resource allocation. In *Proceedings of the 32nd Annual IEEE/ACM International Symposium on Microarchitecture*, pages 248–259, Nov. 1999.

[5] G. Almási, C. Caşcaval, and D. A. Padua. Calculating stack distances efficiently. In *Proceedings of the 2002 workshop on Memory system performance*, pages 37–43, June 2002.

[6] V. Aslot, M. Domeika, R. Eigenmann, G. Gaertner, W. Jones, and B. Parady. SPEComp: A new benchmark suite for measuring parallel computer performance. In *Workshop on OpenMP Applications and Tools*, pages 1–10, July 2001.

[7] L. A. Belady. A study of replacement algorithms for virtual-storage computer. *IBM Systems Journal*, 5(2):78–101, 1966.

[8] K. Beyls and E. D'Hollander. Reuse distance as a metric for cache behavior. In *Proceedings of the IASTED International Conference on Parallel and Distributed Computing and Systems*, pages 617–622, Aug. 2001.

[9] C. Bienia. *Benchmarking Modern Multiprocessors*. PhD thesis, Princeton University, Jan. 2011.

[10] B. H. Bloom. Space/time trade-offs in hash coding with allowable errors. *Communications of the ACM*, 13(7):422–426, July 1970.

[11] A. Boneh and M. Hofri. The coupon-collector problem revisited – a survey of engineering problems and computational methods. *Communications in Statistics. Stochastic Models*, 13(1):39–66, 1997.

[12] J. L. Carter and M. N. Wegman. Universal classes of hash functions (extended abstract). In *Proceedings of the 9th Annual ACM Symposium on Theory of Computing*, pages 106–112, May 1977.

[13] R. Cypher. Apparatus and method for determining stack distance including spatial locality of running software for estimating cache miss rates based upon contents of a hash table. *US7366871*, Apr. 2008.

[14] R. Cypher. Apparatus and method for determining stack distance of running software for estimating cache miss rates based upon contents of a hash table. *US7373480*, May 2008.

[15] C. Ding and Y. Zhong. Reuse distance analysis. Technical Report UR-CS-TR-741, University of Rochester, Feb. 2001.

[16] S. Dropsho, A. Buyuktosunoglu, R. Balasubramonian, D. H. Albonesi, S. Dwarkadas, G. Semeraro, G. Magklis, and M. L. Scott. Integrating adaptive on-chip storage structures for reduced dynamic power. In *Proceedings of the International Conference on Parallel Architectures and Compilation Techniques*, pages 141–152, Sept. 2002.

[17] B. Falsafi and D. A. Wood. Modeling cost/performance of a parallel computer simulator. *ACM Transactions on Modeling and Computer Simulation*, 7(1):104–130, Jan. 1997.

[18] K. Flautner, N. S. Kim, S. Martin, D. Blaauw, and T. Mudge. Drowsy caches: simple techniques for reducing leakage power. In *Proceedings of the 29th Annual International Symposium on Computer Architecture*, pages 148–157, May 2002.

[19] R. Gonzalez and M. Horowitz. Energy dissipation in general purpose microprocessors. In *IEEE Journal of Solid-State Circuits*, pages 1277–1284, Sept. 1996.

[20] A. Gordon-Ross, P. Viana, F. Vahid, W. Najjar, and E. Barros. A one-shot configurable-cache tuner for

improved energy and performance. In *Proceedings of the conference on Design, automation and test in Europe*, pages 755–760, Apr. 2007.

[21] M. D. Hill and A. J. Smith. Evaluating associativity in CPU caches. *IEEE Transactions on Computers*, 38(12):1612–1630, Dec. 1989.

[22] S. Jahagirdar, V. George, I. Sodhi, and R. Wells. Power management of the third generation Intel Core micro architecture formerly codenamed Ivy Bridge. In *Hot Chips 24*, Aug. 2012.

[23] K. Kedzierski, M. Moreto, F. Cazorla, and M. Valero. Adapting cache partitioning algorithms to pseudo-LRU replacement policies. In *Proceedings of the 24th IEEE International Parallel and Distributed Processing Symposium*, pages 1–12, Apr. 2010.

[24] R. E. Kessler, M. D. Hill, and D. A. Wood. A comparison of trace-sampling techniques for multi-megabyte caches. *IEEE Transactions on Computers*, 43(6):664–675, 1994.

[25] S. Laha. *Accurate low-cost methods for performance evaluation of cache memory systems*. PhD thesis, University of Illinois, Dept. of Computer Science, 1988.

[26] S. Laha, J. H. Patel, and R. K. Iyer. Accurate low-cost methods for performance evaluation of cache memory systems. *IEEE Transactions on Computers*, 37(11):1325–1336, 1988.

[27] H. Le, W. Starke, J. Fields, F. O'Connell, D. Nguyen, B. Ronchetti, W. Sauer, E. Schwarz, and M. Vaden. IBM POWER6 microarchitecture. *IBM Journal of Research and Development*, 51(6), 2007.

[28] F. Liu, F. Guo, Y. Solihin, S. Kim, and A. Eker. Characterizing and modeling the behavior of context switch misses. In *Proceedings of the International Conference on Parallel Architectures and Compilation Techniques*, pages 91–101, Oct. 2008.

[29] Y. Liu and W. Zhang. Exploiting stack distance to estimate worst-case data cache performance. In *Proceedings of the 2009 ACM Symposium on Applied Computing*, pages 1979–1983, Mar. 2009.

[30] G. H. Loh and M. D. Hill. Efficiently enabling conventional block sizes for very large die-stacked DRAM caches. In *Proceedings of the 44th Annual IEEE/ACM International Symposium on Microarchitecture*, pages 454–464, Dec. 2011.

[31] M. M. K. Martin, D. J. Sorin, B. M. Beckmann, M. R. Marty, M. Xu, A. R. Alameldeen, K. E. Moore, M. D. Hill, and D. A. Wood. Multifacet's general execution-driven multiprocessor simulator (GEMS) toolset. *Computer Architecture News*, pages 92–99, Sept. 2005.

[32] R. L. Mattson, J. Gecsei, D. R. Slutz, and I. L. Traiger. Evaluation techniques for storage hierarchies. *IBM Systems Journal*, 9(2):78–117, 1970.

[33] T. R. Puzak. *Analysis of Cache Replacement Algorithms*. PhD thesis, Dept. of Electrical and Computer Engineering, University of Massachusetts, 1985.

[34] M. K. Qureshi, D. N. Lynch, O. Mutlu, and Y. N. Patt. A case for MLP-aware cache replacement. In *Proceedings of the 33rd Annual International Symposium on Computer Architecture*, pages 167–178, June 2006.

[35] M. K. Qureshi and Y. N. Patt. Utility-based cache partitioning: A low-overhead, high-performance, runtime mechanism to partition shared caches. In *Proceedings of the 39th Annual IEEE/ACM International Symposium on Microarchitecture*, pages 423–432, Dec. 2006.

[36] J. Reineke and D. Grund. Relative competitive analysis of cache replacement policies. In *Proceedings of the 2008 ACM SIGPLAN-SIGBED conference on Languages, compilers, and tools for embedded systems*, pages 51–60, June 2008.

[37] D. Sanchez, L. Yen, M. D. Hill, and K. Sankaralingam. Implementing signatures for transactional memory. In *Proceedings of the 40th Annual IEEE/ACM International Symposium on Microarchitecture*, pages 123–133, Dec. 2007.

[38] X. Shi, F. Su, J.-K. Peir, and Z. Yang. Modeling and stack simulation of CMP cache capacity and accessibility. *IEEE Transactions on Parallel and Distributed Systems*, 20(12):1752–1763, Dec. 2009.

[39] T. Shyamkumar, N. Muralimanohar, J. H. Ahn, and N. P. Jouppi. CACTI 5.1. Technical Report HPL-2008-20, Hewlett Packard Labs, 2008.

[40] A. J. Smith. A comparative study of set associative memory mapping algorithms and their use for cache and main memory. *IEEE Transactions on Software Engineering*, SE-4(2):121–130, Mar. 1978.

[41] K. So and R. N. Rechtschaffen. Cache operations by MRU change. *IEEE Transactions on Computers*, 37(6):700–709, June 1988.

[42] H. S. Stone and D. Thibaut. Footprints in the cache. In *ACM SIGMETRICS Performance Evaluation Review*, pages 4–8, May 1986.

[43] J. E. Strum. Binomial matrices. *The Two-Year College Mathematics Journal*, 8(5):260–266, Nov. 1977.

[44] G. E. Suh, S. Devadas, and L. Rudolph. A new memory monitoring scheme for memory-aware scheduling and partitioning. In *Proceedings of the Eighth IEEE Symposium on High-Performance Computer Architecture*, Feb. 2002.

[45] G. E. Suh, L. Rudolph, and S. Devadas. Dynamic cache partitioning for CMP/SMT systems. *Journal of Supercomputing*, pages 7–26, 2004.

[46] D. K. Tam, R. Azimi, L. B. Soares, and M. Stumm. RapidMRC: approximating L2 miss rate curves on commodity systems for online optimizations. In *Proceedings of the 14th International Conference on Architectural Support for Programming Languages and Operating Systems*, pages 121–132, Mar. 2009.

[47] N. C. Thornock and J. K. Flanagan. Facilitating level three cache studies using set sampling. In *Proceedings of the 32nd conference on Winter simulation*, pages 471–479, Dec. 2000.

[48] C. Zhang, F. Vahid, and W. Najjar. A highly configurable cache architecture for embedded systems. In *Proceedings of the 30th Annual International Symposium on Computer architecture*, pages 136–146, June 2003.

[49] Y. Zhong, X. Shen, and C. Ding. Program locality analysis using reuse distance. *ACM Transactions on Programming Languages and Systems*, 31(6):1–39, Aug. 2009.

APPENDIX

A. LOSSY SUMMARIZATION

Consider two traces T_A and T_B such that they have disjoint sets of entities and different values of reuse metrics. Let T_{AB} denote a new trace formed from concatenating, in order, sequences represented by T_A and T_B. This operation is not commutative, that is, T_{AB} and T_{BA} are distinct, yet have the same values for the reuse metrics. So the reverse mapping from $\boldsymbol{r}(T)$ to T is not unique. The argument can be extended to show that any trace characterization using position-agnostic metrics must be lossy.

B. EQUATION 3 PSEUDO-CODE WITH POISSON APPROXIMATION

```
void init() {
    int i;
    for(i=0;i<9;i++)
        precomputed_exp_inc[i]=exp(-1.0/(1<<i));
    for(i=1;i<64;i++)
        precomputed_v[i]=1.0/i;
}

void compute_per_set_r(int num_set_bits, int max_assoc) {
    const double *ptr=&r_histogram[0];
    double s3=precomputed_exp_inc[num_set_bits];
    double s2=1.0;
    double base_lambda=1.0/(1<<num_set_bits);
    double lambda=0;
    int i, rd;
    for(i=0;i<512;i++) {
        double s1=s2;
        for(rd=0;rd<2*max_assoc;rd++) {
            per_set_r[num_set_bits][rd]+=ptr[i]*s1;
            s1*=lambda*precomputed_v[rd];
        }
        s2*=s3;
        lambda+=base_lambda;
    }
}
```

`compute_per_set_r` computes Equation 3, using Poisson approximation to Binomial, assuming $\boldsymbol{r}(2^{10})$ upto $n = 512$ is available. $num\_set\_bits \in [1, 9] = log_2(\frac{S'}{S})$. The computation is done for $2A'$ terms (Section 4). Time taken depends on A': 0.006 msec for $A' = 2$ to 0.080 msec for $A' = 32$. Time is measured using the `gettimeofday()` library function and does not include time taken by `init()`.

C. PIECEWISE LINEAR APPROXIMATION FOR LRU

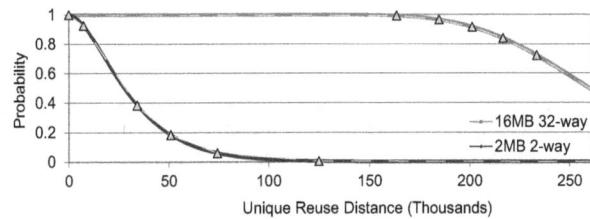

Figure 15: cumulative Poisson and piece-wise linear approximations for two cache configurations.

Figure 15 shows the cumulative Poisson transformer (Cypher's approach [13, 14]) for two very different cache organizations. The triangles and the dashed lines show the selected points for a piece-wise linear approximation that uses 7 or fewer points per transformer (with a common point $(0,1)$).

D. CONVERGENCE FOR RANDOM

First note that if a fix-point exists, the solution satisfies the general conditions of $\boldsymbol{\phi}$ (Equation 5). This is because $\boldsymbol{d}_0 = 0$ (Equation 1) and from Equation 10,

$$\frac{\boldsymbol{\phi}_k}{\boldsymbol{\phi}_{k-1}} = e^{\frac{-(\boldsymbol{d}_k - \boldsymbol{d}_{k-1})\theta}{A'}} = e^{-\left(\frac{\theta/A'}{\sum_{i=k}^{\infty} \boldsymbol{r}_i(T)}\right)}$$
$$\leq 1 \tag{15}$$

Let H denote a fix-point and h^0, h^1, h^2, ... denote successive approximations. By re-arranging the system of equations in 10 we have

$$h^{j+1} = \boldsymbol{r}_0 + \sum_{i=0}^{n} \boldsymbol{r}_i e^{\frac{\boldsymbol{d}_i(-1+h^j)}{A'}} \tag{16}$$

Since the exponential function is monotonic, H must be unique. Since $0 \leq \boldsymbol{r}_i \leq 1, \forall i, \boldsymbol{r}_0 \leq H \leq 1$.

Also, it is easy to show that $h^j \leq h^{j-1} \implies h^{j+1} \leq h^j$. Thus, successive iterations produce a chain of values $\boldsymbol{r}_0 = h^0 \leq h^1 \leq h^2 ...$.

We will now prove that $h^j \leq H, \forall j$. This is true at $j = 0$. For induction, let $h^j = H - \epsilon$ with $\epsilon \geq 0$. Then,

$$h^{j+1} = \boldsymbol{r}_0 + \sum_{i=0}^{n} \boldsymbol{r}_i e^{\frac{\boldsymbol{d}_i(-1+h^j)}{A'}}$$
$$= \boldsymbol{r}_0 + \sum_{i=0}^{n} \boldsymbol{r}_i e^{\frac{\boldsymbol{d}_i(-1+H)}{A'}} \cdot e^{-\frac{\boldsymbol{d}_i \epsilon}{A'}}$$
$$\leq \boldsymbol{r}_0 + \sum_{i=0}^{n} \boldsymbol{r}_i e^{\frac{\boldsymbol{d}_i(-1+H)}{A'}} = H \tag{17}$$

This shows a convergence chain $\boldsymbol{r}_0 = h^0 \leq h^1 \leq h^2 ... \leq H$.

E. PLRU REGULAR EXPRESSIONS

Since the PLRU tree is symmetric, we can fix any way as reference without loss of generality. Let the immediate neighbor be denoted by Q_0, the next two neighbors be collectively denoted by Q_1 and so on with the most distant group of $A/2$ neighbors denoted by $Q_{log_2(A)-1}$. To calculate the probability that the reference line will be evicted on a particular miss we need to consider the immediate past sequence of accesses to that set. A necessary and sufficient condition for the reference line to be evicted is for the suffix of the trace to have accesses that match the particular regular expression described below.

$$A = 2 \; : \; Q_0^+$$
$$A = 4 \; : \; Q_0 Q_1^+$$
$$A = 8 \; : \; Q_0(Q_1 + Q_2)^* Q_1 Q_2^+$$
$$A = 16 \; : \; Q_0(Q_1 + Q_2 + Q_3)^* Q_1(Q_2 + Q_3)^* Q_2 Q_3^+$$
$$A = 32 \; : \; Q_0(Q_1 + Q_2 + Q_3 + Q_4)^* Q_1(Q_2 + Q_3 + Q_4)^*$$
$$Q_2(Q_3 + Q_4)^* Q_3 Q_4^+$$

F. MODEL ESTIMATES

Figure 16 show actual vs estimated miss ratios for the other commercial workloads: `apache`, `jbb` and `zeus`. For these workloads, $h(LRU)$ can well-approximate $h(PLRU)$ but not $h(RANDOM)$ or $h(NMRU)$. Figure 10 (Section 4.5) shows consolidated prediction errors for all workloads.

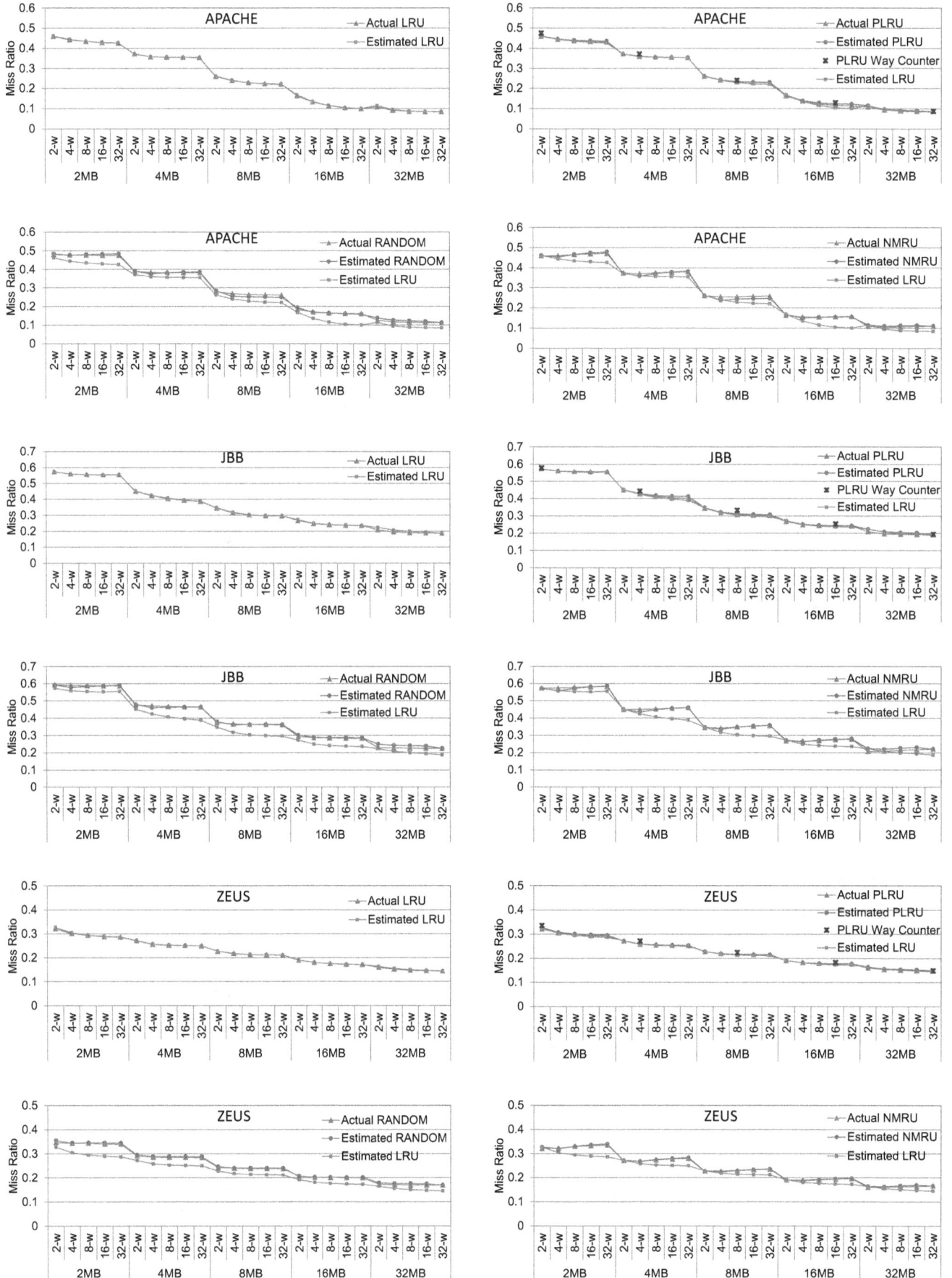

Figure 16: Actual vs estimated miss ratios for apache, jbb, zeus. $r(2^{10})$ is first computed from $r(1)$ (Equation 2). Section 5.3.1 describes PLRU Way-Counters.

Probabilistic Optimal Tree Hopping for RFID Identification

Muhammad Shahzad and Alex X. Liu
Department of Computer Science and Engineering
Michigan State University
East Lansing, Michigan, USA
{shahzadm, alexliu}@cse.msu.edu

ABSTRACT

Radio Frequency Identification (RFID) systems are widely used in various applications such as supply chain management, inventory control, and object tracking. Identifying RFID tags in a given tag population is the most fundamental operation in RFID systems. While the Tree Walking (TW) protocol has become the industrial standard for identifying RFID tags, little is known about the mathematical nature of this protocol and only some ad-hoc heuristics exist for optimizing it. In this paper, first, we analytically model the TW protocol, and then using that model, propose the Tree Hopping (TH) protocol that optimizes TW both theoretically and practically. The key novelty of TH is to formulate tag identification as an optimization problem and find the optimal solution that ensures the minimal average number of queries. With this solid theoretical underpinning, for different tag population sizes ranging from 100 to 100K tags, TH significantly outperforms the *best* prior tag identification protocols on the metrics of the total number of queries per tag, the total identification time per tag, and the average number of responses per tag by an average of 50%, 10%, and 30%, respectively, when tag IDs are uniformly distributed in the ID space, and of 26%, 37%, and 26%, respectively, when tag IDs are non-uniformly distributed.

Categories and Subject Descriptors

C.2.1 [**Computer-Communication Networks**]: Network Architecture and Design – *Wireless communication*; C.2.8 [**Mobile Computing**]: Algorithm Design and Analysis

General Terms

Algorithms, Design, Performance, Experimentation

Keywords

RFID; Tags; Identification

1. INTRODUCTION

1.1 Background and Problem Statement

As the cost of commercial RFID tags, which is as low as 5 cents per tag [21], has become negligible compared to the prices of the products to which they are attached, RFID systems are being increasingly used in various applications such as supply chain management [13], indoor localization [18], 3D positioning [27], object tracking [17], inventory control, electronic toll collection, and access control [5, 16]. For example, Walmart has started to use RFID tags to track jeans and underwear for better inventory control. An RFID system consists of tags and readers. A tag is a microchip combined with an antenna in a compact package that has limited computing power and communication range. There are two types of tags: (1) passive tags, which do not have their own power source, are powered up by harvesting the radio frequency energy from readers, and have communication ranges often less than 20 feet; (2) active tags, which come with their own power sources and have relatively longer communication ranges. A reader has a dedicated power source with significant computing power. RFID systems mostly work in a query-response fashion where a reader transmits queries to a set of tags and the tags respond with their IDs over a shared wireless medium.

This paper addresses the fundamental RFID *tag identification* problem, namely reading all IDs of a given set of tags, which is needed in almost all RFID systems. Because tags respond over a shared wireless medium, tag identification protocols are also called *collision arbitration*, *tag singulation*, or *tag anti-collision* protocols. Tag identification protocols need to be scalable as the number of tags that need to be identified could be as large as tens of thousands with the increasing adoption of RFID tags. An RFID system with a large number of tags may require multiple readers with overlapping regions. In this paper, we first focus on the *single reader* version of the tag identification problem and then extend our solution to the *multiple reader* problem.

1.2 Summary and Limitations of Prior Art

The industrial standard, EPCGlobal Class 1 Generation 2 (C1G2) RFID [9], adopted two tag identification protocols, namely framed slotted Aloha and Tree Walking (TW). In framed slotted Aloha, a reader first broadcasts a value f to the tags in its vicinity where f represents the number of time slots present in a forthcoming frame. Then each tag whose inventory bit is 0 randomly picks a time slot in the frame and replies during that slot. Each C1G2 compliant tag has

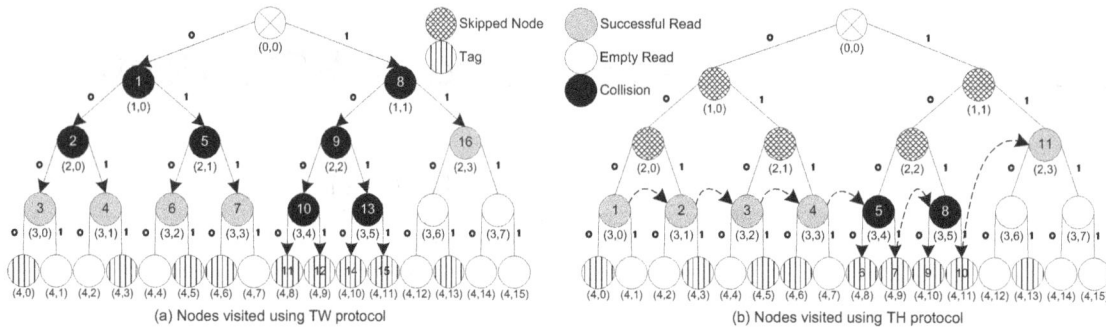

Figure 1: Identifying a population of 9 tags over ID space of 2^4 using Tree Walking and Tree Hopping

an inventory bit, which is initialized to be 0. In any slot, if exactly one tag responds, the reader successfully gets the ID of that tag and issues a command to the tag to change its inventory bit to 1. The key limitation of framed slotted Aloha is that it can not identify large tag populations due to the finite possible size of f, which is typically no more than 512 [23]. Qian *et al.* have shown that framed slotted Aloha is most efficient when f is equal to the number of tags [20]. Therefore, although theoretically any arbitrarily large tag population can be identified by indefinitely increasing the frame size, practically this is infeasible because during the entire identification process, Aloha based protocols require all tags, including those that have been identified, to stay powered up and listen to all the messages from the reader in order to maintain the value of the inventory bit. This results in high instability because any intermittent loss of power at a tag will set its inventory bit back to 0, leading the tag to contend in the subsequent frame. The instability of Aloha based protocols has formally been proven by Rosenkrantz and Towsley in [22].

TW is a fundamental multiple access protocol, which was first invented by U.S. Army for testing soldiers for syphilis during World War II [4]. TW was proposed as an RFID tag identification protocol by Law *et al.* in [12]. In TW, a reader first queries 0 and all the tags whose IDs start with 0 respond. If result of the query is a successful read (*i.e.*, exactly one tag responds) or an empty read (*i.e.*, no tag responds), the reader queries 1 and all the tags whose IDs start with 1 respond. If the result of the query is a collision, the reader generates two new query strings by appending a 0 and a 1 to the previous query string and queries the tags with these new query strings. All the tags whose IDs start with the new query string respond. This process continues until all the tags have been identified. This identification process is essentially a partial Depth First Traversal (DFT) on the complete binary tree over the tag ID space, and the actual traversal forms a binary tree where the leaf nodes represent successful or empty reads and the internal nodes represent collisions. Figure 1(a) shows the tree walking process for identifying 9 tags over a tag ID space of size 2^4. Here a `successful read` node is one that an identification protocol visits and there is exactly one tag in the subtree rooted at this node, an `empty read` node is one that an identification protocol visits and there is no tag in the subtree rooted at this node, and a `collision` node is one that an identification protocol visits and there are more than one tags in the subtree rooted at this node. The key limitation of TW based protocols is that they visit a large number of collision

nodes in the binary tree. Although several heuristics have been proposed to reduce the number of visits to collision nodes [15, 19], all these heuristics based methods are not guaranteed to minimize such futile visits. Prior Aloha-TW hybrid protocols also have this limitation.

1.3 System Model

As most commercially available tags and readers already comply with the C1G2 standard, we do not assume changes to either tags or the physical protocol that they use to communicate with readers. We assume that readers can be reprogrammed to adopt new tag identification software. For reliable tag identification, we are given the probability of successful query-response communication between the reader and a tag.

1.4 Proposed Approach

To address the fundamental limitations that lie in the heuristic nature of prior TW based protocols, we propose a new approach to tag identification called Tree Hopping (TH). The key novel idea of TH is to formulate the tag identification problem as an optimization problem and find the optimal solution that ensures the minimal expected number of queries (*i.e.*, nodes visited on the binary tree). In TH, we first quickly estimate the tag population size. Second, based on the estimated tag population size, we calculate the optimal level to start tree traversal so that the expected number of queries is minimal, *hop* directly to the left most node on that level, and then perform DFT on the subtree rooted at that node. Third, after that subtree is traversed, we re-estimate the size of remaining unidentified tag population, re-calculate the new optimal level, hop directly to the new optimal node, and perform DFT on the subtree rooted at that node. Hopping to optimal nodes in this manner skips a large number of collision nodes. This process continues until all the tags have been identified. Figure 1(b) shows the nodes traversed by TH for the same population of 9 tags as in Figure 1(a). Here a `skipped node` is one that TW visits but TH does not. We can see that TH traverses 11 nodes to identify these 9 tags. In comparison, TW traverses 16 nodes as shown in Figure 1(a). This difference scales significantly as tag population size increases.

1.4.1 Population Size Estimation

TH first uses a framed slotted Aloha based method to quickly estimate the tag population size. For this, TH requires each tag to respond to the reader with a probability q. As C1G2 compliant tags do not support this probabilistic responding, we implement this by "virtually" extending the frame size $\frac{1}{q}$ times. To estimate the tag population size, the reader announces a frame size of $\frac{1}{q}$ but terminates it after the first slot. The reader issues several single-slot frames while reducing q with a geometric distribution (*i.e.*, $q = \frac{1}{2^{i-1}}$ in the i-th frame) until the reader gets an empty slot. Suppose the empty slot occurred in the i-th frame, TH estimates the tag population size to be $1.2897 \times 2^{i-2}$ based on Flajolet and Martin's algorithm used in databases [6].

1.4.2 Finding Optimal Level

To determine the optimal level γ_{op} that TH directly hops to, we first calculate the expected number of nodes that TH will visit if it starts DFTs from nodes on any given level γ. Let b be the number of bits in each tag ID (which is 64 for C1G2 compliant tags), then, we have $1 \leq \gamma \leq b$. If γ is small, more collision nodes will be visited while if it is large, more empty read nodes will be visited. Our objective is to calculate an optimal level γ_{op} that will result in the smallest number of nodes visited. To find γ_{op}, we first derive the expression for calculating the expected number of nodes visited by TH if TH directly hops to level γ. Then we calculate the value of γ which minimizes this expression. This value of γ is the value of optimal level γ_{op}. We present the technical details of finding γ_{op} in Section 3.

1.4.3 Population Size Re-estimation

If the tags that we want to identify are uniformly distributed in the ID space $[0, 2^b - 1]$, then performing DFTs from each node on level γ_{op} will result in minimum number of nodes visited. However, in reality, the tags may not be uniformly distributed. In such cases, each time when the DFT of a subtree is finished, TH needs to re-estimate the total tag population size to find the next optimal level and the hoping destination node. TH performs the re-estimation as follows. Let z be the first tag population size estimated using the Aloha based method, x be the number of tags that have been identified, and s be the size of the tag ID space covered by the nodes visited. Naturally, $z - x$ is an estimate of the remaining tag population size; however, we cannot use this estimate to calculate the next optimal level because the remaining leftover ID space may not form a complete binary tree. Instead, based on the node density in the remaining ID space, TH extrapolates the total tag population size to be $\frac{z-x}{2^b-s} \times 2^b$ and uses it to find the next hopping destination node. Note that if tags are uniformly distributed, we have $\frac{z-x}{2^b-s} \times 2^b = z$.

1.4.4 Finding Hopping Destination

Each time after a DFT is done and the new optimal level is recalculated, TH needs to find the next node to hop to, which may not be the leftmost node on the optimal level. Consider the example shown in Figure 1(b). Assuming a uniform distribution, the optimal level to start the DFT is 3. In this paper, we use (l, p) to denote the pth node on level l. TH performs DFTs on the subtrees of nodes $(3, 0)$ to $(3, 5)$ and identifies 8 out of 9 tags. Based on the number of remaining tags after the last DFT, which is 1, the optimal level for the next hop is changed from 3 to 1. However, if TH starts the DFT from the leftmost node on level 1, which is $(1, 0)$, it will result in identifying all tags in its subtree again which is wasteful. Similarly, if TH starts the DFT from the second leftmost node on level 1, which is $(1, 1)$, it will visit the sub-

tree of $(2, 2)$, which is wasteful as all the tags in the subtree of $(2, 2)$ have already been identified. Similarly, if there had been a third leftmost node on the new optimal level and if TH starts the DFT from that third left most node, it will not visit the subtree of $(2, 3)$, resulting in tag $(4, 13)$ not being identified. To avoid both scenarios, *i.e.*, some subtrees being traversed multiple times and some subtrees with tags not being traversed, after the optimal level is recalculated, TH hops to the root of the largest subtree that can contain the next tag to be identified but does not contain any previously identified tag. The level at which this root is located can not be smaller than the new optimal level. For the example in Figure 1(b), after the subtree rooted at node $(2, 2)$ has been traversed, the recalculated optimal level is 1 and the next node that TH hops to is $(2, 3)$.

Our experimental results in Figure 2 show that when the tags are not uniformly distributed in the ID space, our technique of dynamically adjusting γ_{op} according to the leftover population size significantly reduces the total number of queries and the average number of responses per tag. The two curves "TH w re-estimation-Seq" and "TH w/o re-estimation-Seq" show the total number of queries needed, respectively, with and without the dynamic adjustment of γ_{op} for non-uniformly distributed tag IDs. For example, for 10K tags, this dynamic level adjustment reduces the total number of queries by 31.5%. Our experimental results in Figure 2 also show that when the tags are uniformly distributed in the ID space, there is no need to dynamically adjust γ_{op}. The two curves "TH w re-estimation-Uni" and "TH w/o re-estimation-Uni" show the total number of queries needed, respectively, with and without the dynamic adjustment for uniformly distributed tag IDs. These two curves are quite close because for uniformly distributed tag IDs, γ_{op} does not usually change after each DFT and thus the benefit of dynamically adjusting γ_{op} is relatively small.

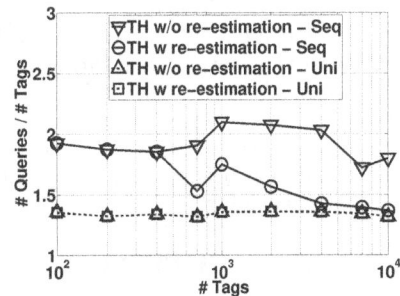

Figure 2: Impact of re-estimation

2. RELATED WORK

We review existing tag identification protocols, which can be classified as nondeterministic, deterministic, or hybrid protocols.

2.1 Nondeterministic Identification Protocols

Existing such protocols are either based on framed slotted Aloha [28] or Binary Splitting (BS) [2]. As we discussed above, Aloha based protocols only work for small tag populations. In BS [2], the identification process starts with the reader asking the tags to respond. If more than one tag responds, BS divides and subdivides the population into smaller groups until each group has only one or no tag. This process of random subdivision incurs a lot of collisions. Furthermore, BS requires the tags to perform operations that are not supported by the C1G2 standard. ABS is a BS based protocol that is designed for continuous identification of tags [14].

2.2 Deterministic Identification Protocols

There are 3 such protocols: (1) the basic TW protocol [12], (2) the Adaptive Tree Walking (ATW) protocol [24], and (3) the TW-based Smart Trend Traversal (STT) protocol [19]. ATW is an optimized version of TW that always starts DFTs from the level of $\log z$, where z is the size of tag population. This is the traditional wisdom for optimizing TW. The key limitation of ATW is that it is optimal only when all tag IDs are evenly spaced in the ID space; however, this is often not true in real-world applications. In contrast, during the identification process, our TH protocol adaptively chooses the optimal level to hop to based on distribution of IDs. STT improves TW using some ad-hoc heuristics to select prefixes for next queries based upon the type of response to previous queries. It assumes that the number of tags identified in the past k queries is the same as the number of tags that will be identified in the next k queries. This may not be true in reality.

2.3 Hybrid Identification Protocols

Hybrid protocols combine features from nondeterministic and deterministic protocols. There are two major such protocols: Multi slotted scheme with Assigned Slots (MAS) [15] and Adaptively Splitting-based Arbitration Protocol (ASAP) [20]. MAS is a TW-based protocol in which each tag that matches the reader's query picks up one of the f time slots to respond. For large populations, due to the finite practical size of $f \leq 512$, for queries corresponding to higher levels in the binary tree, the response in each of the f slots is most likely a collision, which increases the identification time. ASAP divides and subdivides the tag population until the size of each subset is below a certain threshold and then applies Aloha on each subset. For this, ASAP requires tags to be able to pick slots using a geometric distribution, which makes it incompliant with the C1G2 standard. Furthermore, subdividing the population before the actual identification is in itself very time consuming.

3. OPTIMAL TREE HOPPING

After quick population size estimation using Flajolet and Martin's algorithm [6], TH needs to find the optimal level to hop to. First, we derive an expression to calculate the expected number of queries (*i.e.*, the number of nodes that TH will visit) if it starts DFTs from the nodes on level γ, assuming that tags are uniformly distributed in the ID space. Second, as the derived expression is too complex to calculate the optimal value of γ that minimizes the expected number of queries by simply differentiating the expression with respect to γ, we present a numerical method to calculate the optimal level γ_{op}. If tags are not uniformly distributed, each time when the DFT on a node is completed, as stated in Section 1.4, TH re-estimates the total population size based on the initial estimate and the number of tags that have been identified, re-calculates the new optimal level, and finds the hopping destination node. Table 1 summarizes the symbols used in this paper.

Table 1: Notations

Symbol	Description
b	# of bits in tag ID, which is 64 for C1G2 tags
n	size of the whole ID space, which is 2^b
(l, p)	node whose top-to-down vertical level is $1 \leq l \leq b$ and left-to-right horizontal position is $0 \leq p \leq 2^b - 1$
z	estimated number of tags in the population
γ	level from which TH performs DFTs
γ_{op}	optimal level to perform DFTs
q	tag response probability used in estimation
$I(l, p)$	indicator random variable, 1 if (l, p) is visited
T	random variable for total # of nodes visited
$E[T]$	expected # of nodes visited to identify all tags in the population
$P_l \{(l, p)\}$	probability of visiting (l, p) if it is left child
$P_r \{(l, p)\}$	probability of visiting (l, p) if it is right child
m	size of ID space covered by the parent of the current node being visited
k	# of tags covered by the parent of the current node being visited
P_s, P_c, P_e	probabilities of successful read, collision, or empty read at parent of the current node
β	repetitions of query to handle unreliable channel
g	actual probability of reading a tag
u	required probability of reading a tag
V	maximum # of nodes visited to identify all tags
θ_0	# of subtrees covering no tags
θ_1	# of subtrees covering 1 tag

3.1 Average Number of Queries

Let random variable T denote the total number of nodes that TH visits to identify all tags. Note that each node visit corresponds to one reader query. We next calculate $E[T]$. Let $I(l, p)$ be an indicator random variable whose value is 1 if and only if node (l, p) is visited. Thus, T is the sum of $I(l, p)$ for all l and all p.

$$T = \sum_{l=1}^{b} \sum_{p=0}^{2^l - 1} I(l, p) \tag{1}$$

Let $P\{(l, p)\}$ be the probability that TH visits node (l, p). Thus, $E[T]$ can be expressed as follows:

$$E[T] = \sum_{l=1}^{b} \sum_{p=0}^{2^l - 1} P\{(l, p)\} \tag{2}$$

Next, we focus on expressing $P\{(l, p)\}$ using variable γ, where γ denotes the level that TH hops to. Recall that TH skips all nodes on levels from 1 to $\gamma - 1$ and performs DFT on each of the 2^γ nodes on level γ, where $1 \leq \gamma \leq b$. Note that the root node of the whole binary tree is always meaningless to visit as it corresponds to a query of length 0. Here $P\{(l, p)\}$ is calculated differently depending on whether node (l, p) is the left child of its parent or the right. Let $P_l \{(l, p)\}$ and $P_r \{(l, p)\}$ denote the probability of visiting (l, p) when (l, p) is the left and right child of its parent, respectively. If the estimated total number of tags z is zero, then $P_l \{(l, p)\} = P_r \{(l, p)\} = 0$ for all l and p. Below we assume $z > 0$. As TH skips all nodes from levels 1 to $\gamma - 1$, we have

$$P_l \{(l, p)\} = P_r \{(l, p)\} = 0 \text{ if } 1 \leq l < \gamma \tag{3}$$

As TH performs DFT from each node on level γ, it visits each node on this level. Thus, we have

$$P_l\{(l,p)\} = P_r\{(l,p)\} = 1 \ \textbf{if} \ l = \gamma \tag{4}$$

For each remaining level $\gamma < l \le b$, when (l,p) is the left child of its parent, $P_l\{(l,p)\}$ is equal to the probability that the parent of (l,p) is a collision node. When (l,p) is the right child of its parent, if the parent is a collision node and $(l,p-1)$ is an empty read node, then (l,p) will also be a collision node. Thus, instead of visiting (l,p), TH should directly hop to the left child of (l,p). Therefore, $P_r\{(l,p)\}$ is equal to the probability that the parent of (l,p) is a collision node and $(l,p-1)$ is not an empty read node.

Let k denote the number of tags *covered* by the parent of node (l,p) (*i.e.*, the number of tags that are in the subtree rooted at the parent of (l,p)). Let $m = 2^{b-l+1}$ denote the maximum number of tags that the parent of (l,p) can cover and $n = 2^b$ denote the number of tags in the whole ID space. The probability that the parent of (l,p) covers k of z tags follows a hypergeometric distribution:

$$P\{\#\text{tags} = k\} = \frac{\binom{m}{k}\binom{n-m}{z-k}}{\binom{n}{z}} \tag{5}$$

Let P_e be the probability that the parent of (l,p) is an empty read. Thus,

$$P_e = P\{\#\text{tags} = 0\} = \frac{\binom{n-m}{z}}{\binom{n}{z}} \tag{6}$$

Let P_s be the probability that the parent of (l,p) is a successful read. Thus,

$$P_s = P\{\#\text{tags} = 1\} = \frac{m\binom{n-m}{z-1}}{\binom{n}{z}} \tag{7}$$

Let P_c be the probability that the parent of (l,p) is a collision node. Thus,

$$P_c = 1 - (P_e + P_s) = 1 - \frac{\binom{n-m}{z}}{\binom{n}{z}} - \frac{m\binom{n-m}{z}}{\binom{n}{z}} \tag{8}$$

Next we calculate $P_l\{(l,p)\}$ and $P_r\{(l,p)\}$ for $\gamma < l \le b$ for the following three cases: $n - m < z - 1$, $n - m = z - 1$, and $n - m > z - 1$. Note that $n - m$ is the size of the ID space that is not covered by the parent of (l,p), and $z - k$ is the remaining number of tags that are not covered by the parent of (l,p). Thus, $z - k \le n - m$.

Case 1: $n - m < z - 1$.

In this case, $z - k \le n - m < z - 1$, which means $k \ge 2$. Thus, as the parent of (l,p) covers at least two tags, it must be a collision node, *i.e.* $P_c = 1$. Thus, if (l,p) is the left child of its parent, TH for sure visits it:

$$P_l\{(l,p)\} = 1 \tag{9}$$

If (l,p) is the right child of its parent, TH visits it if and only if node $(l,p-1)$, which is the left sibling of (l,p), is not an empty read. If $(l,p-1)$ is an empty read, as its parent is a collision node, (l,p) must also be a collision node, which means that TH will directly visit the left child of (l,p) instead of (l,p). The size of the ID space covered by $(l,p-1)$ is $\frac{m}{2}$. If $n - \frac{m}{2} \le z - 1$, then node $(l,p-1)$ covers at least one tag, which means that $(l,p-1)$ is not an empty read and TH for sure visits (l,p), *i.e.*, $P_r\{(l,p)\} = 1$. If

$n - \frac{m}{2} > z - 1$, then the probability that TH visits (l,p) is equal to the probability that $(l,p-1)$ is not an empty read, which is $1 - \binom{n-\frac{m}{2}}{z}/\binom{n}{z}$ based on Equation (6). Finally, we have

$$P_r\{(l,p)\} = \begin{cases} 1 - \dfrac{\binom{n-\frac{m}{2}}{z}}{\binom{n}{z}} & \text{if } n - \frac{m}{2} > z - 1 \\ 1 & \text{if } n - \frac{m}{2} \le z - 1 \end{cases} \tag{10}$$

Case 2: $n - m = z - 1$.

In this case, $z - k \le n - m = z - 1$, which means $k \ge 1$. As the parent of (l,p) covers $k \ge 1$ tags, the probability of the parent of (l,p) being an empty read is 0 and the probability of the parent of (l,p) being a successful read is $m\binom{n-m}{z-1}/\binom{n}{z} = m\binom{z-1}{z-1}/\binom{n}{z} = m/\binom{n}{z}$ based on Equation (7). If (l,p) is the left child of its parent, then TH visits it if and only if the parent of (l,p) is a collision node. Thus, the probability of visiting (l,p) is equal to the probability of the parent of (l,p) being a collision node, which is equal to $1 - P_e - P_s$. Thus, we have

$$P_l\{(l,p)\} = 1 - P_e - P_s = 1 - \frac{m}{\binom{n}{z}} \tag{11}$$

If (l,p) is the right child of its parent, then TH visits it if and only if both the parent of (l,p) is a collision node and $(l,p-1)$ is not an empty read. The probability that the parent of (l,p) is a collision node is $1 - m/\binom{n}{z}$ as calculated above. Given that the parent of (l,p) is a collision node, the probability that $(l,p-1)$ is an empty read is $\left(\binom{n-\frac{m}{2}}{z} - \frac{m}{2}\right)/\left(\binom{n}{z} - m\right)$.

$$P_r\{(l,p)\} = \left[1 - \frac{m}{\binom{n}{z}}\right] \cdot \left[1 - \frac{\binom{n-\frac{m}{2}}{z} - \frac{m}{2}}{\binom{n}{z} - m}\right] \tag{12}$$

Case 3. $n - m > z - 1$.

In this case, $k \ge 0$. Similar to the above calculations, based on Equations (6) and (7), we have:

$$P_l\{(l,p)\} = 1 - P_e - P_s = 1 - \frac{\binom{n-m}{z} + m\binom{n-m}{z-1}}{\binom{n}{z}} \tag{13}$$

$$P_r\{(l,p)\} = \left[1 - \frac{\binom{n-m}{z} + m\binom{n-m}{z-1}}{\binom{n}{z}}\right]$$
$$\times \left[1 - \frac{\binom{n-\frac{m}{2}}{z} - \left\{\binom{n-m}{z} + \frac{m}{2}\binom{n-m}{z-1}\right\}}{\binom{n}{z} - \left\{\binom{n-m}{z} + m\binom{n-m}{z-1}\right\}}\right] \tag{14}$$

Finally, Equations (3) through (14) completely define the probabilities $P_l\{(l,p)\}$ and $P_r\{(l,p)\}$. Note that as tags are uniformly distributed, the probability of visiting node (l,p) is independent of the horizontal position p.

The expected number of queries can now be calculated using Theorem 1.

THEOREM 1. *For a population of z tags uniformly distributed in the ID space, where each tag has an ID of b bits, if TH hops to level γ to perform DFT from each node on this level, the expected number of queries for identifying all z tags is:*

$$E[T] = 2^\gamma + \sum_{l=\gamma+1}^{b} 2^{l-1}[P_l\{(l,p)\} + P_r\{(l,p)\}] \tag{15}$$

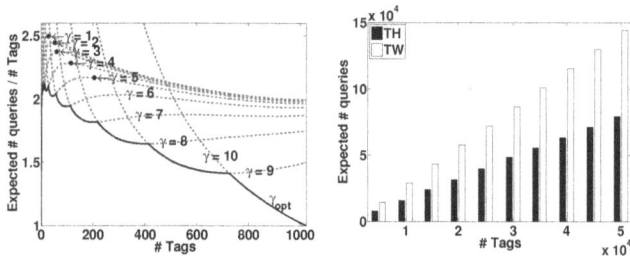

Figure 3: Norm. $E[T]$ vs. population size $\forall \gamma$

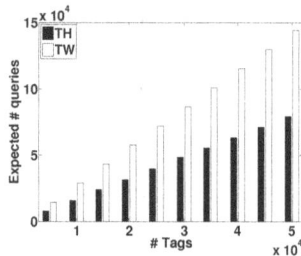

Figure 4: Expected # queries: TH vs. TW

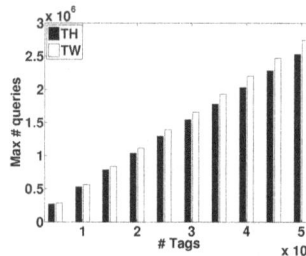

Figure 5: Maximum # queries: TH vs. TW

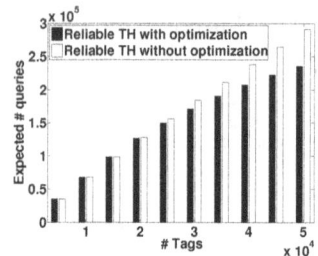

Figure 6: Expected # queries of Reliable TH

PROOF. First, on level γ, all the 2^γ nodes are visited by TH. Second, on any level l where $\gamma + 1 \le l \le b$, the probabilities of left and right nodes being visited are $P_l\{(l,p)\}$ and $P_r\{(l,p)\}$ respectively. As there are 2^{l-1} pairs of left and right nodes on level l, the expected number of nodes visited by TH on level l is $2^{l-1}[P_l\{(l,p)\} + P_r\{(l,p)\}]$. □

When $\gamma = 1$, Equation (15) is also the analytical model for calculating expected number of queries of TW protocol.

3.2 Calculating Optimal Hopping Level

Equation (15) shows that $E[T]$ is a function of γ as $n = 2^b$, $m = 2^{b-l+1}$, and b is given. For any given z, we want to find the optimal level $\gamma = \gamma_{op}$ so that $E[T]$ is minimal. The conventional approach to finding the optimal variable value that minimizes a given function is to differentiate the function with respect to that variable, equate the resulting expression to zero, and solve the equation to obtain the optimal variable value. However, it is very difficult, if not impossible, to use this approach to find the optimal level because Equation (15) for calculating $E[T]$ is too complex.

Next, we present a numerical method to find the optimal level. First, we define *normalized $E[T]$* as the ratio of $E[T]$ to tag population size. Figure 3 shows the plots of normalized $E[T]$ vs. the number of tags for different γ values ranging from 1 to b (here we used $b = 10$ for illustration). From this figure, we observe that for any tag population size, there is a unique optimal value of γ. For example, for a population of 600 tags, $\gamma_{op} = 9$. Second, we define *crossover points* as follows: *for a given ID length b, the crossover points are the tag population sizes $c_0 = 0, c_1, c_2, \cdots, c_{b+1} = 2^b$ such that for any tag population size in $[c_i, c_{i+1}]$ $(0 \le i \le b)$, $\gamma_{op} = i$.* These crossover points are essentially the x-coordinates of the intersection points of the normalized $E[T]$ curves of consecutive values of γ in Figure 3. Thus, the value of c_i can be obtained by putting $z = c_i$ and numerically solving $E[T, \gamma = i - 1] = E[T, \gamma = i]$ for c_i using the bisection method. Once c_i is calculated for each $1 \le i \le b$, γ_{op} for a given z can be obtained by simply identifying the unique interval $[c_i, c_{i+1}]$ in which z lies and then using $\gamma_{op} = i$. The solid line in Figure 3 is plotted using the values of γ_{op} obtained using the proposed strategy. As values of c_i only depend on b, it is a one time cost to calculate them. Table 2 tabulates the values of c_i obtained using this strategy for $b = 64$.

We next conduct an analytical comparison between the expected number of queries for TH and that for TW. Figure 4 shows the expected number of queries for TH, which is calculated using Equation (15) using $\gamma = \gamma_{op}$, and that for TW, which is calculated using Equation (15) using $\gamma = 1$, for 64

Table 2: All crossover points for 64-bit tag IDs

c_0	0.00E+00	c_{22}	3.84E+06	c_{44}	1.61E+13
c_1	2.00E+00	c_{23}	7.68E+06	c_{45}	3.22E+13
c_2	4.00E+00	c_{24}	1.54E+07	c_{46}	6.45E+13
c_3	7.00E+00	c_{25}	3.07E+07	c_{47}	1.29E+14
c_4	1.50E+01	c_{26}	6.12E+07	c_{48}	2.58E+14
c_5	2.90E+01	c_{27}	1.22E+08	c_{49}	5.16E+14
c_6	5.90E+01	c_{28}	2.42E+08	c_{50}	1.03E+15
c_7	1.17E+02	c_{29}	4.76E+08	c_{51}	2.06E+15
c_8	2.35E+02	c_{30}	9.22E+08	c_{52}	4.13E+15
c_9	4.69E+02	c_{31}	1.73E+09	c_{53}	8.25E+15
c_{10}	9.38E+02	c_{32}	3.04E+09	c_{54}	1.65E+16
c_{11}	1.88E+03	c_{33}	8.59E+09	c_{55}	3.30E+16
c_{12}	3.75E+03	c_{34}	1.72E+10	c_{56}	6.59E+16
c_{13}	7.51E+03	c_{35}	3.01E+10	c_{57}	1.32E+17
c_{14}	1.50E+04	c_{36}	6.44E+10	c_{58}	2.63E+17
c_{15}	3.00E+04	c_{37}	1.25E+11	c_{59}	5.24E+17
c_{16}	6.00E+04	c_{38}	2.53E+11	c_{60}	1.04E+18
c_{17}	1.20E+05	c_{39}	5.03E+11	c_{61}	2.04E+18
c_{18}	2.40E+05	c_{40}	1.01E+12	c_{62}	3.96E+18
c_{19}	4.80E+05	c_{41}	2.01E+12	c_{63}	7.42E+18
c_{20}	9.61E+05	c_{42}	4.03E+12	c_{64}	1.30E+19
c_{21}	1.92E+06	c_{43}	8.06E+12	c_{65}	1.84E+19

bit tag IDs. We observe that TH significantly outperforms TW for the expected number of queries. For example, for a population of 10K tags, the expected number of queries for TH is only 54% of that for TW. We will present detailed experimental comparison between TH and other identification protocols in Section 5.

3.3 Maximum Number of Queries

Although the primary goal of our TH protocol is to minimize the average number of queries, next, we analyze the maximum number of queries of TH and analytically show that it is still smaller than that of TW. The maximum number of queries that TH may need to identify z tags with b-bit IDs is shown in Theorem 2.

THEOREM 2. *Let V denote the number of queries that TH may need to identify a population of $z \ge 2$ tags with b-bit IDs using $\gamma = \gamma_{op}$. We have*

$$V \le z(b - \gamma_{op} + 1) - 2^{\gamma_{op}} + 2\theta_0 - \theta_1(b - \gamma_{op} - 1) \quad (16)$$

where

$$\theta_0 = 2^{\gamma_{op}} - \left\lceil \frac{z}{2^{b-\gamma_{op}}} \right\rceil$$

$$\theta_1 = \left\lceil \frac{z}{2^{b-\gamma_{op}}} \right\rceil - \left\lceil \frac{z-1}{2^{b-\gamma_{op}}} \right\rceil \left\lceil 1 - \frac{\gamma_{op}}{b} \right\rceil$$

PROOF. Let V_{TW} denote the number of queries that TW may need to identify $z \ge 2$ tags with b-bit IDs. The upper bound of V_{TW} is given as follows (proven in [12]):

298

$$V_{TW} \leq z\left(b + 1 - \log \frac{z}{2}\right) - 1 \qquad (17)$$

Because $z \geq 2$, we have $V_{TW} \leq z(b+1) - 1$.

When z tags are uniformly distributed in the ID space, TH essentially performs TW on all subtrees rooted at nodes on level γ_{op}. Let θ_0 and θ_1 denote the number of subtrees covering 0 and 1 tags, respectively. For these $\theta_0 + \theta_1$ subtrees, TH only visits the roots, which are at level γ_{op}. Let α denote the number of remaining subtrees (i.e., $\alpha = 2^{\gamma_{\mathrm{op}}} - \theta_0 - \theta_1$) and T_i denote a subtree covering $z_i \geq 2$ tags. For each subtree T_i, the maximum number of nodes that TH visits is $z_i(b - \gamma_{\mathrm{op}} + 1) - 1$. Summing all $2^{\gamma_{\mathrm{op}}}$ subtrees, we have

$$V \leq \sum_{i=0}^{\alpha-1} \left(z_i(b - \gamma_{\mathrm{op}} + 1) - 1 \right) + \theta_0 + \theta_1$$
$$= z(b - \gamma_{\mathrm{op}} + 1) - 2^{\gamma_{\mathrm{op}}} + 2\theta_0 - \theta_1(b - \gamma_{\mathrm{op}} - 1) \quad (18)$$

The right hand side (RHS) of Equation (18) is maximized when θ_0 is maximized and θ_1 is minimized, which happens when all z tag IDs are contiguous and they start from the left most leaf of a subtree at level γ_{op}. In this case, the number of subtrees with tags are $\left\lceil \frac{z}{2^{b-\gamma_{op}}} \right\rceil$ and therefore $\theta_0 = 2^{\gamma_{\mathrm{op}}} - \left\lceil \frac{z}{2^{b-\gamma_{op}}} \right\rceil$. Furthermore in this case, when $\gamma_{\mathrm{op}} \leq b-1$, there is at most one subtree at level γ_{op} that has exactly one tag i.e., $\theta_1 = \left\lceil \frac{z}{2^{b-\gamma_{op}}} \right\rceil - \left\lceil \frac{z-1}{2^{b-\gamma_{op}}} \right\rceil$; when $\gamma_{\mathrm{op}} = b$, θ_1 equals z. Combining the two cases of $\gamma_{\mathrm{op}} \leq b-1$ and $\gamma_{\mathrm{op}} = b$, we have $\theta_1 = \left\lceil \frac{z}{2^{b-\gamma_{op}}} \right\rceil - \left\lceil \frac{z-1}{2^{b-\gamma_{op}}} \right\rceil \left[1 - \frac{\gamma_{op}}{b} \right]$. $\square$

The proof above gives us the insight that *TH requires fewer queries when the tag IDs are distributed more uniformly in the ID space.* Intuitively, this makes sense because the more the tag IDs are distributed uniformly, the fewer the number of collisions encountered by TH. Experimentally, our results shown in Figures 7(a) and 7(b) in Section 5 also confirm this insight: for the same number of tags, the number of queries needed by TH when tags are uniformly distributed is less than that when tags are non-uniformly distributed.

We now conduct an analytical comparison between the maximum number of queries for TH and that for TW. Figure 5 shows the maximum number of queries for TH, which is calculated using the RHS of Equation (16), and that for TW, which is calculated using the RHS of Equation (17), for 64 bit tag IDs. We observe that TH again outperforms TW for the maximum number of queries, although slightly. For example, for a population of 10K tags, the maximum number of queries for TH is 93% of that for TW.

Algorithms 1 through 4 show the pseudocode of TH.

4. DISCUSSION

4.1 Reliable Tag Identification

So far we have assumed that the communication channel between the reader and tags is reliable, which means that each tag can receive the query from the reader and the reader can receive either the response if only one tag responds or the collision if more than one tag respond. However, this assumption often does not hold in reality because wireless communication medium is inherently unreliable. There are two existing schemes for making tag identification reliable.

Algorithm 1: IdentifyRFIDTags(b)

Input: Tag ID size b in bits
Output: IDs of all the tags IDs

1   $z_{\mathrm{init}} := \mathbf{EstimateNumberofTags}()$
2   $i_{\mathrm{ID}} := 0$
3   $s := 0$ /*counts number of leaf nodes covered*/
4   $x := 0$ /*counts number of tags identified*/
5   $z := z_{\mathrm{init}}$
6   $l := 0$
7   $p := 0$
8   **while** $s \leq 2^b$ **do**
9     $\gamma_{\mathrm{op}} := $ Calculate γ_{op} using the method of Section 3.2
10    $(l, p) := \mathbf{FindHopDest}(\gamma_{\mathrm{op}}, b, (l, p))$
11    $[\tilde{x}, \tilde{\mathrm{IDs}}] := \mathbf{TreeWalking}((l, p))$
12    $\mathrm{IDs}[i_{\mathrm{ID}} : i_{\mathrm{ID}} + |\tilde{\mathrm{IDs}}| - 1] := \tilde{\mathrm{IDs}}$
13    $i_{\mathrm{ID}} := i_{\mathrm{ID}} + |\tilde{\mathrm{IDs}}|$
14    $x := x + \tilde{x}$
15    $s := s + 2^{b-l}$
16    $z := \frac{z_{\mathrm{init}} - x}{2^b - s} \times 2^b$
17   **return** IDs

Algorithm 2: EstimateNumberofTags()

Input: None
Output: Initial estimate z_{init} of population size

1   $f := 1$
2   $i := 1$
3   $p_i := 1$
4   **repeat**
5   Provide the reader with f/p_i and a random seed R_i.
6   Run Aloha on reader and get the response.
7   **if** *slot is not empty* **then**
8     $p_{i+1} := p_i/2$
9     $i := i + 1$
10   **until** *slot is empty*
11   $z_{\mathrm{init}} := 1.2897 \times 2^{i-2}$
12   **return** z_{init}

Backes et al. proposed the scheme of letting each tag store the IDs of several other tags [1]. When the reader queries a tag, the tag transmits back its own ID as well as the IDs of other tags stored in it. When identification completes, the reader compares the set of IDs of tags that responded with

---

Algorithm 3: FindHopDest($\gamma_{\mathbf{op}}, b, (l,p)$)

Input: (1) Optimal level γ_{op}
       (2) Tag ID size b in bits
       (3) Current node location (l, p)
Output: Hop destination node location $(\tilde{l}, \tilde{p})$

1   **if** $\gamma_{op} < l$ **then**
2   **if** $p + 1 > \left(\left\lfloor \frac{p}{2^{l-\gamma_{op}}} \right\rfloor + 1 \right)(2^{l-\gamma_{op}}) - 1$ **then**
3     $\tilde{l} = \gamma_{\mathrm{op}}$
4     $\tilde{p} = \left\lfloor \frac{p}{2^{l-\gamma_{op}}} \right\rfloor$
5   **else**
6     $\tilde{l} = l$
7     $\tilde{p} = p$
8   **else if** $\gamma_{op} > l$ **then**
9    $\tilde{l} = \gamma_{\mathrm{op}}$
10   $\tilde{p} = (p+1)(2^{l-\gamma_{\mathrm{op}}}) - 1$
11   **else if** $\gamma_{op} == l$ **then**
12   $\tilde{l} = l$
13   $\tilde{p} = p$
14   $\tilde{p} = \tilde{p} + 1$
15   **return** $(\tilde{l}, \tilde{p})$

Algorithm 4: TreeWalking$((l, p))$

Input: Current node location (l, p)
Output: (1) Number of tags $\tilde{x}$ identified in the subtree whose root node is (l, p)
(2) Identifiers IDs of the tags identified in the subtree whose root node is (l, p)

```
1   l̃ := l
2   p̃ := p
3   i_ID := 0
4   x̃ := 0
5   ĨDs := [ ]
6   while p̃ < (p + 1) × 2^(l̃-l) do
7       [status, tagID] = type of response to query (l̃, p̃) /*a query
        (l̃, p̃) means l̃ bit representation of p̃*/
8       if status == collision then
9           p̃ := 2p̃
10          l̃ := l̃ + 1
11      else if status == successful then
12          x̃ := x̃ + 1
13          ĨDs[i_ID] := tagID
14          i_ID := i_ID + 1
15      q := Σ_{i=0}^{log_2 p̃} (⌊p̃/2^i⌋ - ⌊(p̃-1)/2^i⌋)
16      l̃ := l̃ - q + 1
17      p̃ := p̃/2^(q-1)
18  return [x̃, ĨDs]
```

the union of sets of IDs of other tags reported by each responding tag. If the sets are not equal, the whole process is repeated again to ensure that the missed tags are identified. This scheme has two weaknesses. First, this scheme does not comply with the C1G2 standard. Second, it assumes that the tag population remains static for the lifetime of tags as each tag is hard coded with some other tags' IDs. The second scheme is to run an identification protocol on the same population several times until probability of missing a tag falls below a threshold [7,10]. They estimate the probability of missing a tag based upon the number of tags that were identified in some runs of the protocol but not in others.

While we can use the C1G2 compliant scheme proposed in [7,10] to make TH reliable, *i.e.*, repeatedly run TH until the required reliability is achieved. We observe that in this scheme, the leaf nodes in the binary tree are queried multiple times. This is wasteful of time for the nodes that the reader successfully reads. To eliminate such waste, we propose *to query each node multiple times, instead of querying the whole binary tree multiple times.* We define the *reliability of successfully reading a tag* to be *the probability that both the tag receives the query from the reader and the reader receives the response from the tag.* For this, we calculate the maximum number of times the reader should transmit a query, which is denoted by β. Let g and u be the *given* and *required* reliability of successfully reading a tag, respectively. Thus, the probability of successfully identifying a tag is $1 - (1 - g)^\beta$. Equating it to u, we get:

$$\beta = log_{(1-g)}(1 - u) \qquad (19)$$

Our scheme of reliable tag identification works as follows: for each non-terminal node in the binary tree that TH needs to visit, TH transmits a query corresponding to that node β times; for each terminal node, TH keeps transmitting the query corresponding to that node until either that query has been transmitted β times or the reader successfully receives the tag ID.

The optimization technique of stop transmitting the query corresponding to a terminal on a successful read significantly reduces the total number of queries. Figure 6 plots the expected number of queries per tag for the reliable TH protocol with and without this optimization. For example, for a population of 50000 tags, the number of queries per tag are reduced by 24%.

4.2 Continuous Scanning

In some applications, the tag population may change over time (*i.e.*, tags leave and join the population dynamically). We adapt the continuous scanning strategy proposed by Myung *et al.* in [14]. In the first scanning of the whole tag population, TH records the queries that resulted in successful or empty reads. If the tag population does not change, by performing DFTs on the subtrees rooted at successful and empty read nodes of the previous scan, TH experiences no collision. If some new tags join the population, some of the successful read nodes of the previous scan can now turn into collision nodes and some empty read nodes can turn into successful or collision nodes. If some old tags leave the population, some successful read nodes will become empty read nodes. If any of the new empty read nodes happens to be a sibling of another empty read node, then TH discards these two nodes from the record and stores the location of their parent because the parent is also an empty read node. This strategy works well when the tag population size either remains static or increases. However, when the tag population decreases, the best choice is to re-execute TH for the subsequent scan.

4.3 Multiple Readers

An application with a large number of RFID tags requires multiple readers with overlapping regions because a single reader can not cover all tags due to the short communication range of tags (usually less than 20 feet). The use of multiple readers introduces several new types of collisions such as reader-reader collisions and reader-tag collisions. Such collisions can be handled by reader scheduling protocols such as those proposed in [3,25,26,29]. TH is compatible with all of these reader scheduling protocols.

5. PERFORMANCE COMPARISON

We implemented TH and all the 8 prior tag identification protocols in Matlab, namely the 3 nondeterministic protocols (Aloha [28], BS [2], and ABS [14]), the 3 deterministic protocols (TW [12], ATW [24], and STT [19]), and the 2 hybrid protocols (MAS [15] and ASAP [20]). As ATW starts DFTs from the level of $\log z$ which may not be a whole number, we present results for ATW by both ceiling and flooring the values of $\log z$ and representing them with ATW-c and ATW-f respectively. In terms of implementation complexity, TH and all the 8 prior protocols are implemented in the similar number of lines of code. We performed extensive testing, both manually and automatically, to ensure the correctness of each protocol implementation.

We performed the side-by-side comparison with TH, although this comparison is not completely fair for TH for two reasons. First, 3 of these 8 protocols (*i.e.*, BS, ABS, and ASAP) require modification to tags and thus do not work with standard C1G2 tags, whereas TH is fully compliant with C1G2. Second, for the framed slotted Aloha, to its best advantage, we choose the frame size to be the ideal

Table 3: Comparison with Prior C1G2 Compliant Protocols (TH/Prior Art)

		Prior Nondeterministic Protocol (=Aloha)			Prior Deterministic Protocols				Prior Hybrid Protocol (=MAS)		
		Max	Min	Mean	Best prior	Max	Min	Mean	Max	Min	Mean
Uniform	#queries/tag	0.24	0.10	0.18	ATW-f	0.51	0.50	0.50	0.39	0.38	0.39
	query time/tag	0.84	0.71	0.76	ATW-c	0.92	0.89	0.90	0.81	0.78	0.79
	#responses/tag	0.85	0.59	0.69	ATW-c	0.85	0.67	0.70	0.64	0.24	0.38
	response fairness	1.15	1.10	1.13	TW	1.12	1.07	1.11	1.12	1.07	1.10
Non-Uni	#queries/tag	0.27	0.20	0.22	ATW-f	0.75	0.68	0.74	0.47	0.18	0.33
	query time/tag	0.44	0.34	0.37	ATW-f	0.69	0.61	0.63	0.31	0.16	0.22
	#responses/tag	0.85	0.42	0.68	ATW-c	0.86	0.58	0.74	0.59	0.30	0.48
	response fairness	1.38	1.25	1.35	ATW-c	1.03	1.00	1.02	1.05	0.95	1.02

size, which is equal to the tag population size, disregarding the practical limitations on the frame sizes. We choose tag ID length to be the C1G2 standard 64 bits. We performed the comparison for both the uniform case (where the tag population is uniformly distributed in the ID space) and the non-uniform case (where the tag population is not uniformly distributed in the ID space). For the uniform case, we range tag population sizes from 100 to 100,000 to evaluate the scalability of these protocols. For the non-uniform case, we distribute tag populations in blocks where each block is a continuous sequence of tag IDs. We range block sizes from 5 to 1000. Our motivation for simulating non-uniform distribution in blocks is that in some applications, such as supply chains, tag IDs often come in such blocks when they are manufactured. For each tag population size, we run each protocol 100 times and report the mean. We compare TH with prior protocols from both reader and tag perspectives.

5.1 Reader Side Comparison

For the reader side, we compared TH with the 8 prior protocols based on the following two metrics: (1) normalized reader queries and (2) identification speed. Normalized reader queries is the ratio of the number of queries that the reader transmits to identify a tag population divided by the number of tags in the population. Similarly, identification speed is the total time that the reader takes to identify a tag population divided by the number of tags in that population.

In general, more queries implies more identification time. However, identification time is not strictly in proportion to the number of queries because different queries may take different amounts of time. According to [8] and [9], the time for a successful read t_s, an empty read t_e, and a collision t_c are $3ms$, $0.3ms$, $1.5ms$, respectively.

For each metric, in Table 3, we show the value of TH divided by that for the best prior C1G2 compliant protocol for this metric in the corresponding category of nondeterministic, deterministic, or hybrid. Note that the only prior C1G2 compliant nondeterministic tag identification protocol is the framed slotted Aloha and the only prior C1G2 compliant hybrid tag identification protocol is MAS. There are 3 prior C1G2 compliant deterministic tag identification protocols: TW, ATW, and STT. We report min, max, and mean for these ratios for tag populations ranging from 100 to 100,000.

For the two metrics defined above, the absolute performance of TH and all prior 8 tag identification protocols is shown in Figures 7(a) to 8(b), for both uniform and non-uniform distributions. Note that for non-uniform distributions, we fix the tag population size to be 5000 and range the block size from 5 to 1000.

5.1.1 Normalized Reader Queries

TH reduces the normalized reader queries of the best prior C1G2 compliant nondeterministic, deterministic, and hybrid tag identification protocols by an average of 82%, 50%, and 61%, respectively, for uniformly distributed tag populations, and by an average of 78%, 26%, and 67%, respectively, for non-uniformly distributed tag populations. Figures 7(a) and 7(b) show the normalized reader queries of all protocols for uniformly and non-uniformly distributed populations, respectively. Based on these two figures, we make the following two observations from the perspective of normalized reader queries for both uniform and non-uniform distributions. First, among all the 8 prior protocols, the traditional ATW protocol turns out to be the best. Second, the framed slotted Aloha in the C1G2 standard performs the worst even when we disregard the practical limitations on the frame sizes. Although BS is the best among the 3 prior nondeterministic tag identification protocols, it is not compliant with C1G2. Similarly, although ASAP is the best among the 2 prior hybrid tag identification protocols, it is not compliant with C1G2.

5.1.2 Identification Speed

TH improves the identification speed of the best prior C1G2 compliant nondeterministic, deterministic, and hybrid tag identification protocols by an average of 24%, 10%, and 21%, respectively, for uniformly distributed tag populations, and by an average of 63%, 37%, and 78%, respectively, for non-uniformly distributed tag populations. Figures 8(a) and 8(b) show the identification speed of all protocols for uniformly and non-uniformly distributed tag populations, respectively. Based on these two figures, we make the following two observations from the perspective of identification speed. First, among all 8 prior protocols, the traditional ATW protocol turns out to be the best for both uniform and non-uniform distributions. Second, although framed slotted Aloha is the worst in terms of normalized reader queries, its identification speed is not the worst. This is because in our experiments we allow it to use unrealistically large frame sizes, which leads to many empty slots and empty read is much faster than successful read and collision.

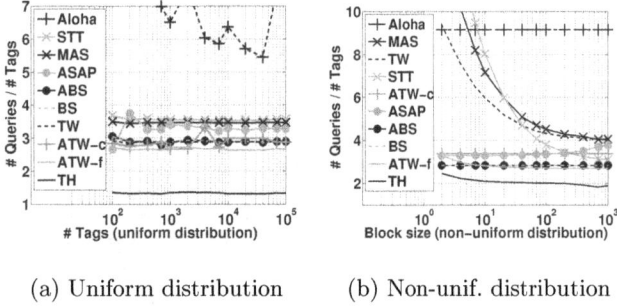

(a) Uniform distribution   (b) Non-unif. distribution

Figure 7: Normalized Queries

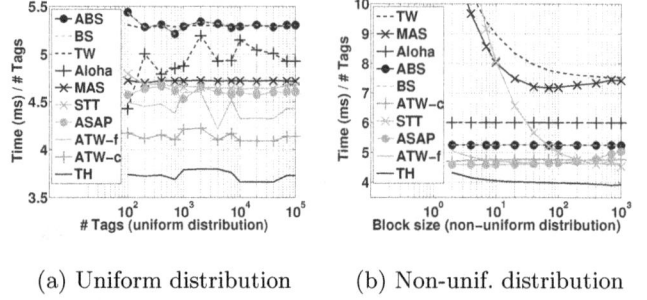

(a) Uniform distribution   (b) Non-unif. distribution

Figure 8: Identification Speed

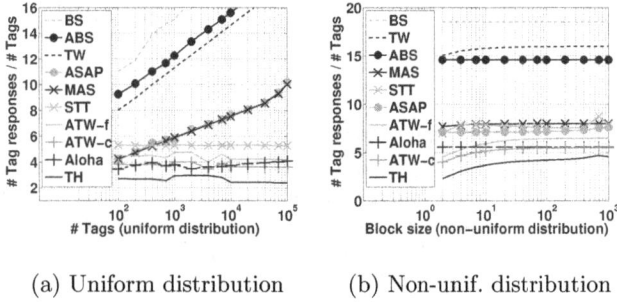

(a) Uniform distribution   (b) Non-unif. distribution

Figure 9: Normalized Responses

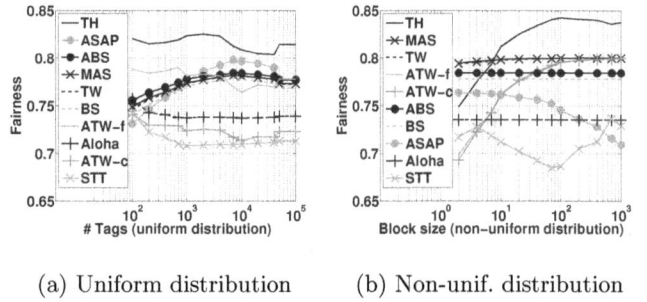

(a) Uniform distribution   (b) Non-unif. distribution

Figure 10: Response Fairness

5.2 Tag Side Comparison

On the tag side, we compare TH with the 8 prior protocols based on the following four metrics: (1) normalized tag responses, (2) response fairness, (3) normalized collisions, and (4) normalized empty reads. Normalized tag responses is the ratio of sum of responses of all tags during the identification process to the number of tags in the population. Response fairness is the Jain's fairness index given by $\frac{(\sum_{i=1}^{z} x_i)^2}{z \cdot \sum_{i=1}^{z} x_i^2}$ where x_i is the total number of responses by tag i [11]. Normalized collisions is the ratio of total number of collisions during the identification process to the number of tags in the population. Normalized empty reads is the ratio of total number of empty reads during the identification process to the number of tags in the population.

The first two metrics are important for active tags because active tags are powered by batteries. Lesser number of normalized tag responses mean lesser power consumption for active tags. Response fairness measures the variance in the number of responses per tag. Less fairness results in the depletion of the batteries of some tags more quickly compared to others. In large scale tag deployments, it is often nontrivial to identify tags with depleted batteries and replace them. Using an absolutely fair tag identification protocol, the batteries of all tags deplete at the same time and therefore all can be replaced at the same time. We use the Jain's fairness metric defined in [11]. For z tags, the fairness value is in the range $[\frac{1}{z}, 1]$. The higher this fairness value is, the more fair the protocol is. The second two metrics are important for understanding these identification protocols.

For normalized tag responses and response fairness, in Table 3, we show the value of TH divided by that for the best prior C1G2 compliant protocol in the corresponding category of nondeterministic, deterministic, or hybrid. The absolute performance of TH and all prior 8 tag identification protocols is shown in Figures 9(a) to 11(b), for both uniform and non-uniform distributions.

5.2.1 Normalized Tag Responses

TH reduces the normalized tag responses of the best prior C1G2 compliant nondeterministic, deterministic, and hybrid tag identification protocols by an average of 31%, 30%, and 62%, respectively, for uniformly distributed tag populations, and by an average of 32%, 26%, and 52%, respectively, for non-uniformly distributed tag populations. Figures 9(a) and 9(b) show the normalized tag responses of all protocols for uniformly and non-uniformly distributed tag populations, respectively. We make following 3 observations from these two figures. First, the normalized tag responses of BS, ABS, TW, MAS, and ASAP increase with increasing tag population size. Second, for non-uniformly distributed tag populations, the normalized tag responses of nondeterministic protocols is not affected by the block size because their performance is independent of tag ID distribution. In contrast, the normalized tag responses of deterministic protocols slightly increase with increasing block size. Third, among all 8 prior protocols, Aloha has the smallest number of normalized tag responses. This is because of the the unlimitedly large frame sizes that we used for Aloha. With large frame sizes, tags experience lesser collisions and thus reply fewer times.

302

5.2.2 Tag Response Fairness

TH improves the tag response fairness of the best prior C1G2 compliant nondeterministic, deterministic, and hybrid tag identification protocols by an average of 13%, 11%, and 10%, respectively, for uniformly distributed tag populations, and by an average of 35%, 2%, and 2%, respectively, for non-uniformly distributed tag populations. Figures 10(a) and 10(b) show the tag response fairness of all protocols for uniformly and non-uniformly distributed tag populations, respectively. We observe that among all 8 prior protocols, ASAP and ATW are the best for uniformly and non-uniformly distributed populations, respectively.

Figures 11(a) and 11(b) show the distribution of the number of tag responses for each protocol for uniformly and non-uniformly distributed tag populations, respectively. For any protocol, the wider the horizontal span of its distribution is, the larger the range of the number of responses per tag it has. We observe that TH has the smallest range among all protocols for the number of responses per tag.

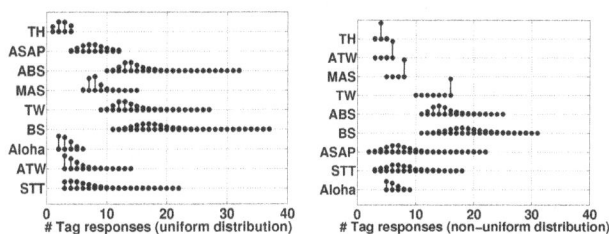

(a) Uniform distribution   (b) Non-unif. distribution

Figure 11: Distribution of tag responses

5.2.3 Normalized Collisions

TH incurs smaller number of collisions than all 8 prior protocols for uniformly and non-uniformly distributed tag populations. Figures 12(a) and 12(b) show the normalized collisions for all protocols for uniformly and non-uniformly distributed tag populations, respectively. From these figures we make following 2 observations. First, Aloha incurs the smallest number of normalized collisions among all 8 prior protocols because of the unlimitedly large frame sizes that we used for it. Second, TW mostly incurs the largest number of normalized collisions for both types of populations.

5.2.4 Normalized Empty Reads

For uniformly distributed tag populations, TH incurs a smaller number of empty reads than all 8 prior protocols. For non-uniformly distributed tag populations, for small block sizes, TH incurs smaller number of empty reads than all prior C1G2 compliant protocols; for larger block sizes, TW and MAS incur slightly lesser empty reads compared to TH. Figure 13(a) and 13(b) show the normalized empty reads of all protocols for uniformly and non-uniformly distributed tag populations, respectively. From these figures, we observe that although the two prior C1G2 compliant protocols, TW and MAS, have fewer empty reads compared to TH for large block sizes, they have much larger number of collisions compared to TH, which makes their overall identification time much larger than TH. Note that the slightly larger number

of empty reads for TH for large block sizes is immaterial because the time for an empty read is 5 times lesser than that for a collision and 10 times lesser than that for a successful read. Therefore, reducing collisions is more important than reducing empty reads.

Note that the collisions and empty reads shown in Figures 12(a) and 13(a), respectively, are consistent with the reader queries shown in Figure 7(a) as well as the identification speed shown in Figure 8(a). Similarly, the collisions and empty reads shown in Figures 12(b) and 13(b), respectively, are consistent with the reader queries shown in Figure 7(b) as well as the identification speed shown in Figure 8(b). For example, Figure 12(a) shows that TW has more collisions than Aloha, but 7(a) shows that Aloha has more queries than TW. This is because Aloha has much more empty reads than TW as shown in Figure 13(a). Although Aloha has more queries than TW, Figure 8(a) also shows that Aloha requires less identification time than TW. This is because an empty read is 5 times faster than a collision for a reader.

6. CONCLUSION

The technical novelty of this paper lies in that it represents the first effort to formulate the Tree Walking process mathematically and propose a method to minimize the expected number of queries. The significance of this paper in terms of impact lies in that the Tree Walking protocol is a fundamental multiple access protocol and has been standardized as an RFID tag identification protocol. Besides static optimality, our Tree Hopping protocol dynamically chooses a new optimal level after each subtree is traversed. We also presented methods to make our protocol reliable, to continuously scan tag populations that are dynamically changing, and to work with multiple readers with overlapping regions. Another key contribution of this paper is that we conducted a comprehensive side-by-side comparison of our protocol with eight major prior tag identification protocols that we implemented. Our experimental results show that our protocol significantly outperforms all prior tag identification protocols, even those that are not C1G2 compliant, for metrics such as the number of reader queries per tag, the identification speed, and the number of responses per tag.

7. REFERENCES

[1] M. Backes, T. R. Gross, and G. Karjoth. Tag identification system, 2008.

[2] J. I. Capetanakis. Tree algorithms for packet broadcast channels. *IEEE Transactions on Information Theory*, 25:505–515, 1979.

[3] B. Carbunar, M. K. Ramanathan, M. Koyuturk, C. Hoffmann, and A. Grama. Redundant reader elimination in RFID systems. In *Proc. IEEE Communications Society Conf. on SECON*, pages 576–580, 2005.

[4] R. Dorfman. The detection of defective members of large populations. *Annals of Mathematical Statistics*, 14:436–440, 1943.

[5] K. Finkenzeller. *RFID Handbook: Fundamentals and Applications in Contactless Smart Cards, Radio Frequency Identification and Near-Field Communication*. Wiley, 2010.

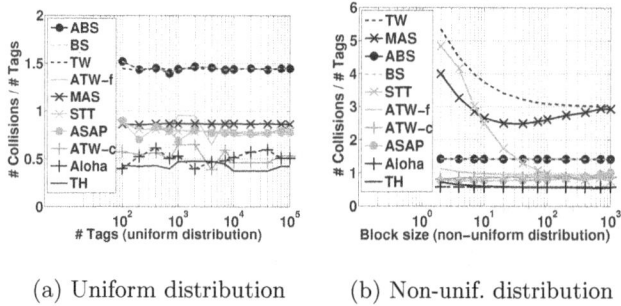

(a) Uniform distribution   (b) Non-unif. distribution

Figure 12: Normalized Collisions

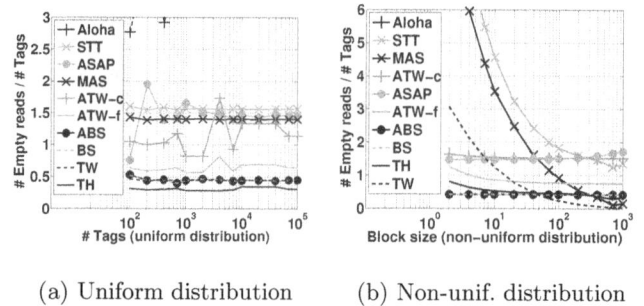

(a) Uniform distribution   (b) Non-unif. distribution

Figure 13: Normalized Empty Reads

[6] P. Flajolet and G. N. Martin. Probabilistic counting algorithms for data base applications. *Journal of Computer and System Sciences*, 31(2):182–209, 1985.

[7] K. Fyhn, , R. M. Jacobsen, P. Popovski, and T. Larsen. Fast capture – recapture approach for mitigating the problem of missing rfid tags. *IEEE Transactions on Mobile Computing*, 11(3):518–528, 2012.

[8] H. Han, B. Sheng, C. C. Tan, Q. Li, W. Mao, and S. Lu. Counting RFID tags efficiently and anonymously. In *Proc. IEEE INFOCOM*, 2010.

[9] E. Inc. *Radio-Frequency Identity Protocols Class-1 Generation-2 UHF RFID Protocol for Communications at 860 MHz–960 MHz*. EPCGlobal Inc, 1.2.0 edition, 2008.

[10] R. Jacobsen, K. F. Nielsen, P. Popovski, and T. Larsen. Reliable identification of rfid tags using multiple independent reader sessions. In *Proc. IEEE Int. Conf. on RFID*, pages 64–71, 2009.

[11] R. K. Jain, D.-M. W. Chiu, and W. R. Hawe. A quantitative measure of fairness and discrimination for resource allocation in shared computer systems. Technical report, Digital Equipment Corporation, 1984.

[12] C. Law, K. Lee, and K.-Y. Siu. Efficient memoryless protocol for tag identification. In *Proc. 4th International Workshop on Discrete Algorithms and Methods for Mobile Computing and Communications*, 2000.

[13] C. H. Lee and C.-W. Chung. Efficient storage scheme and query processing for supply chain management using RFID. In *Proc. ACM Conf. on Management of data*, pages 291–302, 2008.

[14] J. Myung and W. Lee. Adaptive splitting protocols for RFID tag collision arbitration. In *Proc. 7th ACM Int. Symposium on Mobile Ad Hoc Networking and Computing*, pages 202–213, 2006.

[15] V. Namboodiri and L. Gao. Energy-aware tag anticollision protocols for RFID systems. In *Proc. 5th IEEE Int. Conf. on Pervasive Computing and Communications*, pages 23–36, 2007.

[16] B. Nath, F. Reynolds, and R. Want. RFID technology and applications. *Proc. IEEE Pervasive Computing*, 5:22–24, 2006.

[17] A. Nemmaluri, M. D. Corner, and P. Shenoy.

Sherlock: Automatically locating objects for humans. In *Proc. Int. Conf. on Mobile Systems, Applications, and Services*, pages 187–198, 2008.

[18] L. M. Ni, Y. Liu, Y. C. Lau, and A. P. Patil. Landmarc: Indoor location sensing using active RFID. *Wireless networks*, 10:701–710, 2004.

[19] L. Pan and H. Wu. Smart trend-traversal: A low delay and energy tag arbitration protocol for large RFID systems. In *Proc. IEEE INFOCOM*, 2009.

[20] C. Qian, Y. Liu, H. Ngan, and L. M. Ni. ASAP: Scalable identification and counting for contactless RFID systems. In *Proc. 30th IEEE Int. Conf. on Distributed Computing Systems*, pages 52–61, 2010.

[21] M. Roberti. A 5-cent breakthrough. *RFID Journal*, 5(6), 2006.

[22] W. A. Rosenkrantz and D. Towsley. On the instability of slotted aloha multiaccess algorithm. *IEEE Transactions on Automatic Control*, 28(10):994–996, 1983.

[23] P. Semiconductors. *SL2 ICS11 I.Code UID Smart Label IC Functional Specification Datasheet http://www.advanide.com/datasheets/sl2ics11.pdf*, 2004.

[24] A. S. Tanenbaum. *Computer Networks*. Prentice-Hall, 2002.

[25] S. Tang, J. Yuan, X.-Y. Li, G. Chen, Y. Liu, and J. Zhao. Raspberry: A stable reader activation scheduling protocol in multi-reader RFID systems. In *Proc. IEEE Int. Conf. on Network Protocols*, pages 304–313, 2009.

[26] J. Waldrop, D. W. Engels, and S. E. Sarma. Colorwave: A MAC for RFID reader networks. In *Proc. IEEE Wireless Communications and Networking*, pages 1701–1704, 2003.

[27] C. Wang, H. Wu, and N.-F. Tzeng. RFID-based 3-D positioning schemes. In *Proc. IEEE INFOCOM*, pages 1235–1243, 2007.

[28] B. Zhen, M. Kobayashi, and M. Shimizu. Framed ALOHA for multiple RFID objects identification. *IEICE Transactions on Communications*, 88:991–999, 2005.

[29] Z. Zhou, H. Gupta, S. R. Das, and X. Zhu. Slotted scheduled tag access in multi-reader RFID systems. In *Proc. IEEE Int. Conf. on Network Protocols*, pages 61–70, 2007.

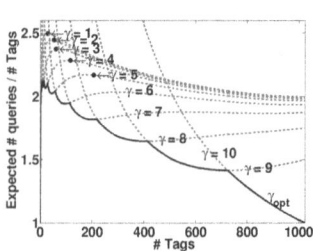

1   $\tilde{l} := l$
2   $\tilde{p} := p$
3   $i_{\text{ID}} := 0$
4   $\tilde{x} := 0$
5   $\tilde{\text{IDs}} := [\ ]$
6   **while** $\tilde{p} < (p+1) \times 2^{\tilde{l}-l}$ **do**
7     $[status, tagID]$ = type of response to query $(\tilde{l}, \tilde{p})$ /*a query
       $(\tilde{l}, \tilde{p})$ means $\tilde{l}$ bit representation of $\tilde{p}$*/
8   **if** $status ==$ collision **then**
9       $\tilde{p} := 2\tilde{p}$
10      $\tilde{l} := \tilde{l} + 1$
11   **else if** $status ==$ successful **then**
12      $\tilde{x} := \tilde{x} + 1$
13      $\tilde{\text{IDs}}[i_{\text{ID}}] := tagID$
14      $i_{\text{ID}} := i_{\text{ID}} + 1$
15    $q := \sum_{i=0}^{\log_2 \tilde{p}} \left(\lfloor \frac{\tilde{p}}{2^i} \rfloor - \lfloor \frac{\tilde{p}-1}{2^i} \rfloor \right)$
16    $\tilde{l} := \tilde{l} - q + 1$
17    $\tilde{p} := \frac{\tilde{p}}{2^{q-1}}$
18   **return** $[\tilde{x}, \tilde{\text{IDs}}]$

Multipath TCP Algorithms: Theory and Design

Qiuyu Peng
EE, California Institute of
Technology
qpeng@caltech.edu

Anwar Walid
Alcatel-Lucent Bell Labs
anwar@research.bell-labs.com

Steven H. Low
CMS & EE, California Institute
of Technology
slow@caltech.edu

ABSTRACT

Multi-path TCP (MP-TCP) has the potential to greatly improve application performance by using multiple paths transparently. We propose a fluid model for a large class of MP-TCP algorithms and identify design criteria that guarantee the existence, uniqueness, and stability of system equilibrium. We characterize algorithm parameters for TCP-friendliness and prove an inevitable tradeoff between responsiveness and friendliness. We discuss the implications of these properties on the behavior of existing algorithms and motivate a new design that generalizes existing algorithms. We use ns2 simulations to evaluate the proposed algorithm and illustrate its superior overall performance.

Categories and Subject Descriptors

C.2.1 [**Computer-Communication Networks**]: Network Architecture and Design—*Distributed networks*

Keywords

Multipath TCP, Congestion control.

1. INTRODUCTION

Traditional single-path TCP traverses one route so that only one access interface can be used by the application. This limits performance when there are multiple interfaces/routes available, e.g. most smart phones are enabled with both cellular and WiFi access, and communicating servers in data centers are connected through multiple routes. Multi-path TCP (MP-TCP) has the potential to greatly improve application performance by using multiple paths transparently. The Internet Engineering Task Force (IETF) has started the MP-TCP Working Group [3], which is chartered to develop mechanisms that enable an application to take advantage of available paths. MP-TCP is envisioned to co-exist with single-path TCP such that applications that use MP-TCP can benefit from using available capacity on multiple paths without degrading the performance of applications that use single-path TCP.

Various congestion control algorithms have been proposed as an extension of TCP NewReno for MP-TCP. A straightforward extension is to run TCP NewReno on each subpath, e.g. [5,6]. This basic extension can lead to a highly unfair

bandwidth allocation for single-path TCP users when their paths share bottleneck links with paths used by MP-TCP users. In order to resolve these unfairness issues, the Coupled [1] algorithm [4,7] is proposed and shown to be fair to single-path TCP. The underlying reason is that Coupled algorithm and TCP NewReno are associated with the same utility function. Recently in [13], it is found that Coupled algorithm can not adapt fast enough in a dynamic network environment, such that it only uses one route even if there are multiple available routes. A different algorithm is proposed in [13] (We refer to this algorithm as the Max algorithm), which is claimed to be both fair to single-path TCP and more responsive than the Coupled algorithm. However, as we show in our simulation, the Max algorithm is still unfair to single-path TCP, and the unfairness is exaggerated when the round trip time of each subpath is different.

To develop improved algorithms, certain questions need to be addressed. First, the design criteria for MP-TCP to converge to a unique equilibrium need to be identified. For single-path TCP algorithm, one can associate a strict concave utility function for each source so that the congestion control algorithm implicitly solves a network utility maximization problem [8,11]. The utility maximization interpretation provides an intuitive approach for showing the existence and uniqueness of equilibrium. For MP-TCP, it will be shown that the utility maximization interpretation fails to hold in general, necessitating the need to develop new tools for studying the equilibrium of MP-TCP algorithms. Second, the relations among different performance metrics, e.g. fairness, responsiveness and window fluctuation, need to be identified. A theoretical understanding of the design space for MP-TCP is needed so that improved algorithms can be developed. The performance metrics that we focus on are defined as follows:

- *TCP Friendliness*: MP-TCP flows can harm single-path TCP flows by taking more bandwidth when they share bottleneck links. The friendliness measure describes the degree of aggressiveness of MP-TCP flows towards single-path TCP flows.

- *Responsivness*: MP-TCP algorithms should adapt fast in dynamic network environments. Responsiveness characterizes the rate of algorithm convergence.

- *Window Fluctuation*: The congestion window fluctuates due to the additive-increase, multiplicative-decrease (AIMD) property of loss-based TCP.

In this paper, we will address the above questions and propose a new MP-TCP algorithm. The main contributions of this paper are three-fold: First, we show that there is no associated utility function for some MP-TCP algorithms, e.g. the Max algorithm. Thus the intuitive way of showing a

---

[1]This name comes from [13]

unique stable equilibrium by utility maximization interpretation fails. We consider a unified fluid model that covers a broad class of MP-TCP algorithms and prove, under mild conditions: (i) the existence and uniqueness of equilibrium, (ii) asymptotical convergence of the algorithms. Indeed, algorithms that fail to satisfy the proposed conditions, e.g. the Coupled algorithm, are likely to be unstable and may have multiple equilibria as shown in [13]. Second, we define the performance metrics of TCP friendliness, responsiveness and window fluctuation in the context of MP-TCP, and explore the algorithm design space by characterizing tradeoffs among these performance metrics. Third, based on our understanding of the design space, we propose a new MP-TCP algorithm. We evaluate the proposed algorithm and the existing algorithms using ns2 simulation, and illustrate the superior overall performance of the proposed algorithm.

We now summarize our proposed MP-TCP algorithm. Each source s has a set of routes r. Each route r maintains a congestion window w_r and can measure its round trip time τ_r. The window adaptation are as follows:

- For each ACK on route $r \in s$,

$$w_r \leftarrow w_r + \frac{x_r}{\tau_r \left(\sum x_k\right)^2} \left(\frac{1 + \alpha_r}{2}\right) \left(\frac{4 + \alpha_r}{5}\right) \qquad (1)$$

- For each packet loss on route $r \in s$,

$$w_r \leftarrow \max\left\{w_r \left(1 - \frac{1}{2}\alpha_r\right), 1\right\} \qquad (2)$$

where $x_r := w_r/\tau_r$ and $\alpha_r := \frac{\max\{x_k\}}{x_r}$.

The rest of the paper is structured as follows. In Section 2, we develop a unified model for MP-TCP and use it to model existing algorithms. In Section 3 we prove several structural properties, focusing on design criteria that guarantee the existence, uniqueness, and stability of system equilibrium, TCP-friendliness, responsiveness, and inevitable tradeoff among these properties. In section 4, we discuss the implications of these properties and design criteria on the existing algorithms. This motivates our new MP-TCP algorithm and we explain our design rationale. Finally in Section 5 we use ns2 simulation to compare the performance of the proposed algorithm with the existing algorithms. The paper is concluded in section 6.

2. MULTIPATH TCP MODEL

In this section we first propose a fluid model of MP-TCP and then use it to model existing MP-TCP algorithms in the literature. In the next section we will present some structural properties of the model and discuss their implications on the design choices made in these MP-TCP algorithms.

Unless otherwise specified, a capital letter is used to denote a matrix or a set, depending on the context. A matrix P, not necessarily symmetric, is defined as positive definite if $\mathbf{x}^T P \mathbf{x} > 0$ for any $\mathbf{x} \neq \mathbf{0}$. We emphasize that, unlike in conventional use, the definition here does not require P to be symmetric; in fact the matrices of interest in this paper are not symmetric, making the analysis difficult. Given two matrix A, B, $A \succeq B$ means $A - B$ is positive semidefinite. A boldface letter is used to denote a vector. $\|\mathbf{x}\|_n := (\sum x_i^n)^{1/n}$ defines the n norm of a vector $\mathbf{x}$. Given two vectors $\mathbf{x}, \mathbf{y} \in \mathbb{R}^n$, $\mathbf{x} \geq \mathbf{y}$ means $x_i \geq y_i$ for all components. For a vector $\mathbf{x}$, $diag\{\mathbf{x}\}$ is a diagonal matrix with entries given by $\mathbf{x}$.

2.1 Fluid model

Consider a network that consists of a set $L = \{1, \ldots, L\}$ of links with finite capacities c_l. The network is shared by a set $S = \{1, \ldots, S\}$ of sources. Available to source $s \in S$

is a fixed collection of routes r. A route r consists of a set of links l. We abuse notation and use s both to denote a source and the set of routes r available to it, depending on the context. Likewise, r is used both to denote a route and the set of links l in the route. Let $R := \{r \mid r \in s, s \in S\}$ be the collection of all routes. Let $H \in \{0, 1\}^{|L| \times |R|}$ be the routing matrix: $H_{lr} = 1$ if link l is in route r (denoted by '$l \in r$'), and 0 otherwise.

For each route $r \in R$, τ_r denotes its round trip time (RTT). For simplicity we assume τ_r are constants. Each source s maintains a congestion window $w_r(t)$ at time t for every route $r \in s$. Let $x_r(t) := w_r(t)/\tau_r$ represent the throughput on route r. Each link l maintains a congestion price $p_l(t)$ at time t. Let $q_r(t) := \sum_{l \in r} p_l(t)$ be the (approximate) aggregate price on route r. In this paper $p_l(t)$ represents the packet loss probability at link l and $q_r(t)$ represents the packet loss probability on route r.

We associate three state variables $(x_r(t), w_r(t), q_r(t))$ for each route $r \in s$. Let $\mathbf{x}_s(t) := (x_r(t), r \in s)$, $\mathbf{w}_s(t) := (w_r(t), r \in s)$, $\mathbf{q}_s(t) := (q_r(t), r \in s)$. Also let $\tau_s := (\tau_r, r \in s)$. Then $(\mathbf{x}_s(t), \mathbf{w}_s(t), \mathbf{q}_s(t))$ represents the corresponding state variables for each source $s \in S$. For each link l, let $y_l(t) := \sum_{r \in R} H_{lr} x_r(t)$ be its aggregate traffic rate.

Congestion control is a distributed algorithm that adapts $\mathbf{x}(t)$ and $\mathbf{p}(t)$ in a closed loop. Motivated by the AIMD algorithm as in TCP Reno, we model MP-TCP by

$$\dot{x}_r = k_r(\mathbf{x}_s) \left(\phi_r(\mathbf{x}_s) - \frac{1}{2}q_r\right)_{x_r}^+ \qquad r \in s \quad s \in S \qquad (3)$$

$$\dot{p}_l = \gamma_l \left(y_l - c_l\right)_{p_l}^+ \qquad l \in L, \qquad (4)$$

where $(a)_x^+ = a$ for $x > 0$ and $\max\{0, a\}$ for $x \leq 0$. We omit the time t in the expression for simplicity. Eqn. (3) models how sending rates are adapted in the congestion avoidance phase of TCP at each end system and (4) models how the congestion price is updated at each link by AQM. The MP-TCP algorithm installed at source s is specified by (K_s, Φ_s), where $K_s(\mathbf{x}_s) := (k_r(\mathbf{x}_s), r \in s)$ and $\Phi_s(\mathbf{x}_s) := (\phi_r(\mathbf{x}_s), r \in s)$. Here $K_s(\mathbf{x}_s) \geq 0$ is a positive gain that determines the dynamic property of the algorithm. $\Phi_s(\mathbf{x}_s)$ determines the equilibrium properties of the algorithm. The AQM algorithm is specified by γ_l, where $\gamma_l > 0$ is a positive gain that determines the dynamic property. This is a simplified model for the RED algorithm that assumes the loss probability is proportional to the backlog, and is used in, e.g., [7, 10, 11].

2.2 Existing MP-TCP algorithms

We first show how to relate the fluid model (3) to the window-based MP-TCP algorithms proposed in the literature. On each route r the source increases its window at the return of each ACK, and let this increment be denoted by $I_r(\mathbf{w}_s)$ where $\mathbf{w}_s$ is the vector of window sizes on different routes of source s. The source decreases the window on route r when it sees a packet loss on route r, and let this decrement by denoted by $D_r(\mathbf{w}_s)$. Let δw_r be the net change to window on route r in each round trip time. Then δw_r is roughly

$$\begin{aligned} \delta w_r &= (I_r(\mathbf{w}_s)(1 - q_r) - D_r(\mathbf{w}_s)q_r)w_r \\ &\approx (I_r(\mathbf{w}_s) - D_r(\mathbf{w}_s)q_r)w_r \end{aligned}$$

when the loss probability q_r is small. On the other hand

$$\delta w_r \approx \dot{w}_r \tau_r = \dot{x}_r \tau_r^2$$

Hence

$$\dot{x}_r = \frac{x_r}{\tau_r} \left(I_r(\mathbf{w}_s) - D_r(\mathbf{w}_s)q_r\right)$$

From (3) we have

$$\begin{cases} k_r(\mathbf{x}_s) &= \frac{2x_r}{\tau_r} D_r(\mathbf{w}_s) \\ \phi_r(\mathbf{x}_s) &= \frac{1}{2} \frac{I_r(\mathbf{w}_s)}{D_r(\mathbf{w}_s)} \end{cases} \quad (5)$$

We now present a fluid model of the existing algorithms in the literature. We will first summarize these algorithms in the form of a pseudo-code and then use (5) to derive parameters $k_r(\mathbf{x}_s)$ and $\phi_r(\mathbf{x}_s)$ of the fluid model (3).

Single-path TCP: TCP-NewReno

Single-path TCP is a special case of MP-TCP algorithm with $|s| = 1$. Hence x_s is a scalar and we identify each source with its route $r = s$. TCP-NewReno adjusts the window as follows:

- Each ACK on route r, $w_r \leftarrow w_r + 1/w_r$.
- Each loss on route r, $w_r \leftarrow w_r/2$.

From (5), this can be modeled by the fluid model (3) with

$$k_r(x_s) = x_r^2, \quad \phi_r(x_s) = \frac{1}{\tau_r^2 x_r^2}$$

We now summarize some existing MP-TCP algorithms, all of which degenerate to TCP NewReno if there is only one route per source.

EWTCP [5]

EWTCP algorithm applies TCP-NewReno like algorithm on each route independently of other routes. It adjusts the window on multiple routes as follows:

- Each ACK on route r, $w_r \leftarrow w_r + a/w_r$.
- Each loss on route r, $w_r \leftarrow w_r/2$.

From (5), this can be modeled by the fluid model (3) with

$$k_r(x_s) = x_r^2, \quad \phi_r(x_s) = \frac{a}{\tau_r^2 x_r^2}$$

where $a > 0$ is a constant.

Coupled MPTCP [4, 7]

The Coupled MPTCP algorithm adjusts the window on multiple routes in a coordinated fashion as follows:

- Each ACK on route r, $w_r \leftarrow w_r + \frac{w_r}{(\sum_{k \in s} w_k)^2}$.
- Each loss on route r, $w_r \leftarrow w_r/2$.

From (5), this can be modeled by the fluid model (3) with

$$k_r(\mathbf{x}_s) = x_r^2, \quad \phi_r(\mathbf{x}_s) = \frac{1}{(\sum_{k \in s} x_k \tau_k)^2},$$

Semicoupled MPTCP [13]

The Semi-coupled MPTCP algorithm adjusts the window on multiple routes as follows:

- Each ACK on route r, $w_r \leftarrow w_r + \frac{1}{\sum_{k \in s} w_k}$.
- Each loss on route r, $w_r \leftarrow w_r/2$.

From (5), this can be modeled by the fluid model (3) with

$$k_r(\mathbf{x}_s) = x_r^2, \quad \phi_r(\mathbf{x}_s) = \frac{1}{x_r \tau_r (\sum_{k \in s} x_k \tau_k)}$$

Max MPTCP [13]

The Max MPTCP algorithm adjusts the window on multiple routes as follows:

- Each ACK on route r, $w_r \leftarrow w_r + \min\{\frac{\max\{w_k/\tau_k^2\}}{(\sum w_k/\tau_k)^2}, \frac{1}{w_r}\}$.
- Each loss on route r, $w_r \leftarrow w_r/2$.

From (5), this can be modeled by the fluid model (3) with

$$k_r(\mathbf{x}_s) = x_r^2, \quad \phi_r(\mathbf{x}_s) = \frac{\max\{x_k/\tau_k\}}{x_r \tau_r (\sum_{k \in s} x_k)^2}$$

where we have ignored taking the minimum with the $1/w_r$ term since the performance is mainly captured by $\frac{\max\{w_k/\tau_k^2\}}{(\sum w_k/\tau_k)^2}$.

3. STRUCTURAL PROPERTIES

A point $(\mathbf{x}, \mathbf{p})$ is called an *equilibrium* of (3)–(4) if it satisfies

$$k_r(\dot{\mathbf{x}}_s) \left(\phi_r(\mathbf{x}_s) - \frac{q_r}{2} \right)_{x_r}^+ = 0$$

$$\gamma_l (y_l - c_l)_{p_l}^+ = 0$$

or equivalently, if

$$\phi_r(\mathbf{x}_s) < \frac{q_r}{2} \Rightarrow \mathbf{x}_r = 0 \text{ and } x_r > 0 \Rightarrow \phi_r(\mathbf{x}_s) = \frac{q_r}{2} \quad (6)$$

$$y_l < c_l \Rightarrow p_l = 0 \text{ and } p_l > 0 \Rightarrow y_l = c_l \quad (7)$$

In this section we identify design criteria that guarantee the existence, uniqueness, and stability of system equilibrium. We characterize algorithm parameters that determine TCP-friendliness and prove an inevitable tradeoff between responsiveness and friendliness. We discuss in the next section the implications of these structural properties on existing algorithms. All proofs are relegated to the Appendix.

3.1 Utility maximization

For single-path TCP (SP-TCP), one can associate a utility function $U_s(x_s) \in \mathbb{R} \to \mathbb{R}$ (x_s is a scalar and $|s| = 1$) with each flow s and interpret (3)–(4) as a distributed algorithm to maximize aggregate user utility [8,10,11], i.e., for SP-TCP, an $(\mathbf{x}, \mathbf{p})$ is an equilibrium if and only if $\mathbf{x}$ is optimal for

$$\text{maximize} \sum_{s \in S} U_s(x_s) \quad \text{s.t.} \quad y_l \leq c_l \quad l \in L \quad (8)$$

and $\mathbf{p}$ is optimal for the associated dual problem. Here $y_l \leq c_l$ means the aggregate traffic y_l at each link does not exceed its capacity c_l. In fact this holds for a much wider class of SP-TCP algorithms than those specified by (3)–(4) [10]. Furthermore all the main TCP algorithms proposed in the literature have strictly concave utility functions, implying a unique stable equilibrium.

The case of MP-TCP is much more delicate: whether an underlying utility function exists depends on the design choice of Φ_s and not all MP-TCP algorithms have one. Consider the multipath equivalent of (8):

$$\text{maximize} \sum_{s \in S} U_s(\mathbf{x}_s) \quad \text{s.t.} \quad y_l \leq c_l \quad l \in L, \quad (9)$$

where $\mathbf{x}_s := (x_r, r \in s)$ is the rate vector of flow s and $U_s(\mathbf{x}_s) \in \mathbb{R}^{|s|} \to \mathbb{R}$ is a concave function. Consider the condition:

C0: The Jacobians of $\Phi_s(\mathbf{x}_s)$ are symmetric for all s, i.e.,

$$\frac{\partial \Phi(\mathbf{x}_s)}{\partial \mathbf{x}_s} = \left[\frac{\partial \Phi(\mathbf{x}_s)}{\partial \mathbf{x}_s} \right]^T$$

Theorem 1. *There exists a twice continuously differentiable $U_s(\mathbf{x}_s)$ such that an equilibrium $(\mathbf{x}, \mathbf{p})$ of (3)–(4) solves (9) and its dual problem if and only if condition C0 holds.*

Condition C0 is satisfied trivially by SP-TCP. For MP-TCP, the models derived in Section 2.2 show that only EWTCP and Coupled algorithms satisfy C0 and have underlying utility functions. It therefore follows from the theory for SP-TCP that EWTCP has a unique stable equilibrium while Coupled algorithm may have multiple equilibria since its corresponding utility function is not strictly concave.

The other MP-TCP algorithms all have asymmetric Jacobian $\frac{\partial \Phi_s}{\partial \mathbf{x}_s}$. We next study the existence, unique, and stability of these MP-TCP algorithms.

3.2 Existence, uniqueness and stability of equilibrium

Given congestion prices $\mathbf{p} \geq 0$, recall that $\mathbf{q} := H^T \mathbf{p}$. Consider the following conditions:

C1: For each $s \in S$, there exists a nonnegative solution $\mathbf{x}_s := \mathbf{x}_s(\mathbf{p})$ to Eqn. (6) for any $\mathbf{p} \geq 0$. Moreover,

$$\frac{\partial y_l^s(\mathbf{p})}{\partial p_l} \leq 0, \qquad \lim_{p_l \to \infty} y_l^s(\mathbf{p}) = 0,$$

where $y_l^s(\mathbf{p}) := \sum_{r \in s} H_{lr} x_r(\mathbf{p})$, which represents the aggregate traffic at link l from source s.

C2: The Jacobian $\partial \Phi_s(\mathbf{x}_s)/\partial \mathbf{x}_s$ is negative definite and continuous for all $s \in S$.

C3: The routing matrix H has full row rank. For any $r \in R$, $\lim_{x_r \to 0} \phi_r(\mathbf{x}_s) = \infty$ and

$$\sup_{x_{-r} \in \mathbb{R}_+^{|s|-1}} \{\phi_r(\mathbf{x}_s)\} < \infty$$

if $x_r > 0$, where $x_{-r} := \{x_k \mid k \in s \setminus \{r\}\}$.

Condition C1 means that the amount of traffic through a link l from source s does not increase if the congestion price p_l on that link increases. Furthermore, the amount of traffic through that link is 0 if $p_l = \infty$. As mentioned above, the matrix $\partial \Phi_s(\mathbf{x}_s)/\partial \mathbf{x}_s$ in C2 is generally not symmetric. C2 implies that at steady state, if $\mathbf{x}_s, \mathbf{q}_s$ are perturbed by $\delta \mathbf{x}_s, \delta \mathbf{q}_s$ respectively, then $(\delta \mathbf{x}_s)^T \delta \mathbf{q}_s < 0$. When $|s| = 1$, it is equivalent to that the curvature of the utility function is negative, namely $U_s(x_s)$ is strictly concave. Condition C3 means that the rate on route r is zero if and only if it sees infinite price on that route.

The next result says that conditions C1-C3 guarantee that a multipath TCP/AQM (3)–(4) has a unique equilibrium. The proof is given in Appendix A.2.

Theorem 2. *1. Suppose C1 holds. Then (3)–(4) has at least one equilibrium.*

2. Suppose C2 and C3 hold. Then (3)–(4) has at most one equilibrium

Thus (3)–(4) has a unique equilibrium $(\mathbf{x}^*, \mathbf{p}^*)$ under C1–C3.

Conditions C1-C3 not only guarantee the existence and uniqueness of the equilibrium, they also ensure that the equilibrium is globally asymptotically stable, when the gain $k_r(\mathbf{x}_s)$ is a constant, i.e., $k_r(\mathbf{x}_s) \equiv k_r$ for all $r \in R$.

Theorem 3. *Suppose C1-C3 hold and $k_r(\mathbf{x}_s) \equiv k_r$ for all $r \in R$. Starting from any initial point $\mathbf{x}(0) \in \mathbb{R}_+^{|R|}$ and $\mathbf{p}(0) \in \mathbb{R}_+^{|L|}$, the trajectory $(\mathbf{x}(t), \mathbf{p}(t))$ generated by the MP-TCP algorithm (3)–(4) converges to the unique equilibrium $(\mathbf{x}^*, \mathbf{p}^*)$ as $t \to \infty$.*

Since we can treat the gain $k_r(\mathbf{x}_s)$ as a constant if we linearize the system (3)–(4) around the equilibrium $(\mathbf{x}^*, \mathbf{p}^*)$. Theorem 3 can also serve as a proof of $(\mathbf{x}^*, \mathbf{p}^*)$ as a local asymptotically stable equilibrium.

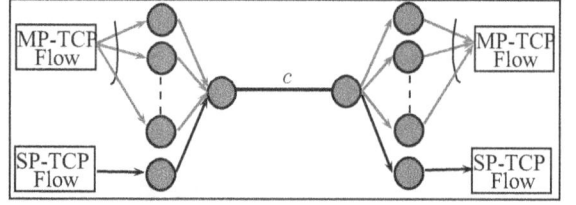

Figure 1: Test network for the definition of TCP friendliness. The link in the middle is the only bottleneck link with capacity c.

3.3 TCP Friendliness

Informally, an MP-TCP flow is said to be 'TCP friendly' if it does not dominate the available bandwidth when it shares the same network with a SP-TCP flow [3]. To define this precisely we use the test network shown in Fig. 1 where there are a fixed number of paths all traversing a single bottleneck link with capacity c. All other links have capacities strictly higher than c. The links have fixed but possibly different delays. The test network is shared by two flows, one SP-TCP and the other MP-TCP under test as shown in the figure. To compare the friendliness of two MP-TCP algorithms $M1$ and $M2$, suppose that when $M1$ shares the test network with the SP-TCP it achieves a throughput of $\|\mathbf{x}_1\|_1$ in equilibrium aggregated over the available paths. Suppose $M2$ achieves a throughput of $\|\mathbf{x}_2\|_1$ in equilibrium when it shares the test network with the SP-TCP. Then we say that $M1$ is *more friendly* than $M2$ if $\|\mathbf{x}_1\|_1 \leq \|\mathbf{x}_2\|_1$, i.e., if $M1$ receives no more bandwidth than $M2$ does when they *separately* share the test network in Figure 1 with the SP-TCP flow.

Let $D_s := \left[\frac{\partial \Phi_s(\mathbf{x}_s)}{\partial \mathbf{x}_s}\right]^{-1}$, whose existence is guaranteed by C2. Consider the following design criterion for Φ_s:

C4 : For all routes $r \in s$, $\sum_{j \in s}[D_s]_{jr} \leq 0$.

To interpret C4, note that the equilibrium condition imposes $\Phi_s(\mathbf{x}_s) = \frac{1}{2}\mathbf{q}_s$. The implicit function theorem then implies $\mathbf{1}^T \frac{\partial \mathbf{x}_s}{\partial q_r} = \sum_{j \in s} D_{jr}$ for all $r \in s$. Hence C4 says that the aggregate throughput $\mathbf{1}^T \mathbf{x}_s$ at equilibrium of a MP-TCP flow is a nonincreasing function of the price q_r on all routes $r \in s$.

The next result says that an MP-TCP algorithm is more TCP friendly if it has a smaller $\Phi_s(\mathbf{x}_s)$.

Theorem 4. *Consider two MP-TCP algorithms $M1$ with $\hat{\Phi}_s(\mathbf{x}_s)$ and $M2$ with $\tilde{\Phi}_s(\mathbf{x}_s)$. Suppose both satisfy C1–C4. Then $M1$ is more friendly than $M2$ if $\hat{\Phi}_s(\mathbf{x}_s) \leq \tilde{\Phi}_s(\mathbf{x}_s)$.*

3.4 Responsiveness

The linearized system of (3)–(4) at the equilibrium $(\mathbf{x}^*, \mathbf{p}^*)$ is defined by the Jacobian

$$J^* := \begin{bmatrix} \Lambda_k \frac{\partial \Phi}{\partial \mathbf{x}} & -\frac{1}{2}\Lambda_k H^T \\ \Lambda_\gamma H & 0 \end{bmatrix}$$

where $\Lambda_k = diag\{k_r(\mathbf{x}_s^*), r \in s\}$, $\Lambda_\gamma = diag\{\gamma_l, l \in L\}$ and $\frac{\partial \Phi}{\partial \mathbf{x}}$ is evaluated at $\mathbf{x}^*$. The stability and responsiveness (how fast does the system converges to the equilibrium locally) of the system (3)–(4) is determined by the real part of the eigenvalues of J^*. Specifically the linearized system is asymptotically stable if the real parts of all the eigenvalues of J^* are negative; moreover the more negative the real parts are the faster the linearized system converges to the equilibrium.

We are therefore interested in an upper bound on the largest (least negative) real part of the eigenvalue of J^* in terms of both K_s and $\frac{\partial \Phi_s}{\partial \mathbf{x}_s}$. Without loss of generality, assume all the links in L are active with $p_l^* > 0$. Otherwise, we can remove all the links with price $p_l^* = 0$ from our model.

Let $\lambda(J^*)$ be the set of eigenvalues of J and define the largest real part of eigenvalue:

$$\lambda_m(J^*) := \max\{\mathbf{Re}(\lambda) \mid \lambda \in \lambda(J^*)\}$$

Let $\left[\frac{\partial \Phi}{\partial \mathbf{x}}\right]^+ := \frac{1}{2}\left(\frac{\partial \Phi}{\partial \mathbf{x}} + \left[\frac{\partial \Phi}{\partial \mathbf{x}}\right]^T\right)$ and $S = \{(\mathbf{z}, \mathbf{p}) \mid \|\mathbf{z}\|_2 = \|\mathbf{p}\|_2 = 1, \mathbf{z} \in \mathbb{C}^{|R|}, \mathbf{p} \in \mathbb{C}^{|L|}\}$.

Lemma 1. *Suppose C2 holds. Then*

$$\lambda_m(J^*) \leq \overline{\lambda}_J := \max_{(\mathbf{z}, \mathbf{p}) \in S} \left\{ \frac{2\mathbf{z}^H \left[\frac{\partial \Phi}{\partial \mathbf{x}}\right]^+ \mathbf{z}}{2\mathbf{z}^H \Lambda_k^{-1} \mathbf{z} + \mathbf{p}^H \Lambda_\gamma^{-1} \mathbf{p}} \right\}$$

To understand the implication of the lemma, consider two MP-TCP algorithms $(\hat{K}_s, \hat{\Phi}_s)$ and $(\tilde{K}_s, \tilde{\Phi}_s)$. If $\hat{\Lambda}_k \geq \tilde{\Lambda}_k$ and $\frac{\partial \hat{\Phi}}{\partial \mathbf{x}} \preceq \frac{\partial \tilde{\Phi}}{\partial \mathbf{x}}$ then

$$\mathbf{z}^H \hat{\Lambda}_k^{-1} \mathbf{z} \leq \mathbf{z}^H \tilde{\Lambda}_k^{-1} \mathbf{z} \tag{10}$$

$$\mathbf{z}^H \left[\frac{\partial \hat{\Phi}}{\partial \mathbf{x}}\right]^+ \mathbf{z} \leq \mathbf{z}^H \left[\frac{\partial \tilde{\Phi}}{\partial \mathbf{x}}\right]^+ \mathbf{z} \tag{11}$$

for any $\|\mathbf{z}\|_2 = 1$ and thus $\overline{\lambda}_{\hat{J}} \leq \overline{\lambda}_{\tilde{J}}$. Note that Λ_k is a diagonal matrix consisting of $k_r(\mathbf{x}_s^*)$ for all $r \in R$ and $\partial\Phi/\partial\mathbf{x}$ is a block diagonal matrix consisting of $\partial\Phi_s/\partial\mathbf{x}_s$ for all $s \in S$. Then Eqn. (10)-(11) hold if $\hat{K}_s \geq \tilde{K}_s$ and $\frac{\partial \hat{\Phi}_s}{\partial \mathbf{x}_s} \preceq \frac{\partial \tilde{\Phi}_s}{\partial \mathbf{x}_s}$. Hence, informally Lemma 1 says that an MP-TCP algorithm with a larger $K_s(\mathbf{x}_s)$ or more negative definite $\frac{\partial \Phi}{\partial \mathbf{x}}$ is more responsive, in the sense that the real parts of the eigenvalues of the Jacobina J^* have a smaller upper bound.

Then the next result suggests an inevitable tradeoff between responsiveness and un-friendliness. Consider

C5 : For all routes $r \in s$, $\phi_r(\mathbf{x}_s) \leq (x_r \tau_r)^{-2}$.

For SP-TCP, $\phi_r(x_s) = (x_r \tau_r)^{-2}$ as shown in Section 2.2. C5 simply means that on any route $r \in s$, a MP-TCP flow is no more aggressive than a SP-TCP flow.

Theorem 5. *Consider two MP-TCP algorithms with $\hat{\Phi}_s(\mathbf{x}_s)$ and $\tilde{\Phi}_s(\mathbf{x}_s)$. Suppose both satisfy C1-C3 and C5. Then*

$$\frac{\partial \hat{\Phi}_s(\mathbf{x}_s)}{\partial \mathbf{x}_s} \preceq \frac{\partial \tilde{\Phi}_s(\mathbf{x}_s)}{\partial \mathbf{x}_s} \Rightarrow \hat{\Phi}_s(\mathbf{x}_s) \geq \tilde{\Phi}_s(\mathbf{x}_s)$$

In light of Lemma 1 and Theorem 4, Theorem 5 says that a more responsive MP-TCP design is inevitably less friendly.

4. IMPLICATION AND A NEW ALGORITHM

TCP friendliness, responsiveness and window fluctuation are crucial performance metrics of TCP algorithms. We have already studied TCP friendliness and responsiveness in section 3 under the unified fluid model (3)-(4). In this section, we will study the relation between window fluctuation, which cannot be captured in the fluid model, and the design parameters. Then we will discuss the implications of the structural properties proved in Section 3 on the behavior of existing MP-TCP algorithms. The discussions motivate a new design that generalizes and extends the existing MP-TCP algorithm. We present our design rationale and further illustrate its performance through simulations in Section 5.

4.1 Window Fluctuation

For loss based TCP algorithm, the congestion window always fluctuates due to the binary congestion signal and can

Table 1: MP-TCP Algorithms

Algorithm	C0	C1	C2-C3	C4	C5
EWTCP	Yes	Yes	Yes	Yes	Yes
Coupled	Yes	Yes	No	Yes	Yes
Semicoupled	No	Yes	Yes	Yes	Yes
Max	No	Yes	Yes	Yes	Yes
Our algorithm	No	Yes	Yes	Yes	Yes

not be avoided. It can not be captured in the fluid model (3)-(4). Therefore, the equilibrium specified by the fluid dynamics (3)-(4) represents the average realtime throughput. For TCP-NewReno, the throughput is halved in the next RTT if one packet loss is observed - we define throughput as the window size over the round trip time. Hence, the fraction of throughput reduction is $1/2$. *Window fluctuation* is a measure of how the throughput of the source fluctuates due to the binary congestion signal. In this paper, we use $\|K_s(\mathbf{x}_s)\|_1$ as a measure of the window fluctuation and smaller $\|K_s(\mathbf{x}_s)\|_1$ means smaller *window fluctuation*. A heuristic is given below that motivates this measure.

Suppose the loss probability q_r are the same for all $r \in s$. When there is one packet loss on $r \in s$, its window will decrease by $\frac{k_r(\mathbf{x}_s)\tau_r}{2x_r}$ based on Eqn. (5), which means throughput will decrease by $\frac{k_r(\mathbf{x}_s)}{2x_r}$, for each packet loss on route r. Note that the loss probability is approximately $x_r q_r$ on route r. Then each time a packet loss is detected by source s, the probability that the loss happens at route j is approximately

$$\frac{x_j q_j}{\sum_{r \in s} x_r q_r} = \frac{x_j}{\|\mathbf{x}_s\|_1},$$

provided q_r is small and the same for all routes $r \in s$. Hence, the average throughput reduction over the aggregate throughput $\|\mathbf{x}_s\|_1$ is

$$\frac{1}{\|\mathbf{x}_s\|_1} \sum_{r \in s} \frac{x_r}{\|\mathbf{x}_s\|_1} \frac{k_r(\mathbf{x}_s)}{2x_r} = \frac{\|K_s(\mathbf{x}_s)\|_1}{2\|\mathbf{x}_s\|_1^2}, \tag{12}$$

which means smaller $\|K_s(\mathbf{x}_s)\|_1$ leads to smaller throughput reduction per packet loss.

For the existing algorithms, all of them have $k_r(\mathbf{x}_s) = x_r^2$ thus their fluctuation level are the same under our metrics. Substitute $k_r(\mathbf{x}_s) = x_r^2$ into Eqn. (12), we find that it is always smaller than $1/2$. Since the the average throughput reduction is $1/2$ for TCP-NewReno by Eqn. (12), existing MP-TCP algorithms always have better window fluctuation performance than TCP NewReno. Indeed, enabling MP-TCP always improves the window fluctuation performance provided $k_r(\mathbf{x}_s) \leq x_r \|\mathbf{x}_s\|_1$. Recall that larger $K_s(\mathbf{x}_s)$ means better responsiveness performance as shown in 3.4. It means there is tradeoff between responsiveness and window fluctuation, which can be improved by using smaller $K_s(\mathbf{x}_s)$.

4.2 Implications on existing algorithms

In this subsection, we will study the equilibrium, TCP friendliness and responsiveness property of existing algorithms introduced in section 2.2. They can serve as a verification of our analysis in section 3. We have briefly summarized existing algorithms together with our algorithm, which will be proposed in the next subsection, in Table 1.

First, we will study whether there exists a unique stable equilibrium to the existing algorithms. We find that only EWTCP and Coupled algorithm satisfies C0, thus their equilibrium property can be studied in the context of utility maximization as shown in Theorem 1. However, Semicoupled and Max algorithm does not satisfy C0 and thus we indeed need to rely on Theorem 2 and 3 to study their

Table 2: Design Space

Performance	Deterministic parameter
TCP Friendliness	$\phi_r(\mathbf{x}_s) \uparrow$
Responsiveness	$k_r(\mathbf{x}_s) \uparrow,\ -\partial\Phi_s/\partial\mathbf{x}_s \uparrow$
Window Fluctuation	$\|K_s(\mathbf{x}_s)\|_1 \downarrow$

equilibrium performance by showing whether C1-C3 are satisfied. For EWTCP, it is easy to show they satisfy C1-C3. For the other existing algorithms, they can be modeled using Eqn. (13) with specified parameters.

$$\begin{cases} k_r(\mathbf{x}_s) = x_r(x_r + \eta(\|\mathbf{x}_s\|_\infty - x_r)). & \eta \geq 0 \\ \phi_r(\mathbf{x}_s) = \frac{x_r + \beta(\|\mathbf{x}_s\|_n - x_r)}{\tau_r^2 x_r \|\mathbf{x}_s\|_1^2}, & n \in \mathbb{N}_+, \beta \geq 0 \end{cases} \quad (13)$$

Max algorithm ($\beta = 1, n = \infty, \eta = 0$), Semicoupled algorithm ($\beta = 1, n = 1, \eta = 0$)[2] and Coupled algorithm ($\beta = 0, \eta = 0$) are special cases corresponding to different (β, n, η). The next theorem shows whether they satisfy C1-C3 by studying the general (13).

Theorem 6. *For any $n \in \mathbb{N}_+$, the $\phi_r(\mathbf{x}_s)$ proposed in Eqn. (13) satisfies C1 if $0 \leq \beta \leq 1$. Furthermore, it satisfies C2-C3 if $0 < \beta \leq 1$, $|s| \leq 8$ and τ_r is the same across all $r \in s$.*

Therefore, when the round trip time of each route is the same, there exits a unique stable equilibrium to Max and Semicoupled algorithm if they enable less than 8 routes. For Coupled algorithm, it does not satisfy C2-C3 and is found to have multiple equilibria in [7].

For a negative definite matrix A, it is still negative definite after some small perturbations of each entry. Therefore, Theorem 6 holds provided the RTT of each subpath does not differ much. Indeed, the round trip time of each subpath is close in reality since it is mainly determined by the distance between two hosts. In the proof of Theorem 6, the Jacobian of $\Phi_s(\mathbf{x}_s)$ becomes less negative definite when the number of routes $|s|$ increases and will finally be indefinite when $|s| > 9$. Thus smaller $|s|$ offers larger freedom of RTT heterogeneity across each route to maintain its negative definite property. However, it is a less contingent condition since each source is typically enabled 2 or 3 routes in reality.

Second, we will study the friendliness performance of existing MP-TCP algorithms. In Theorem 4, we show that algorithm with larger $\phi_r(\mathbf{x}_s)$ is less TCP friendly. For the existing MP-TCP algorithm, all of them satisfy C4 and their throughput for the network in Fig. 1 is ordered as follows:

$$\text{EWTCP}(a \geq 1)^{[3]} \geq \text{Semicoupled} \geq \text{Max} \geq \text{Coupled}$$

Since the more bandwidth the MP-TCP source occupies, the more aggressive the algorithm is. It means EWTCP is the most aggressive while Coupled algorithm is the most fair one. On the other hand, the $\phi_r(\mathbf{x}_s)$ corresponding to each algorithm in section 2.2 is ordered as follows:

$$\phi_r^{ewtcp}(\mathbf{x}_s) \geq \phi_r^{semicoupled}(\mathbf{x}_s) \geq \phi_r^{max}(\mathbf{x}_s) \geq \phi_r^{coupled}(\mathbf{x}_s)$$

for all $\mathbf{x}_s \geq 0$ if each route has the same round trip time. Thus it verifies that algorithm with larger $\phi_r(\mathbf{x}_s)$ tends to be less TCP friendly as shown in Theorem 4.

Third, we will study the responsiveness performance of existing MP-TCP algorithms. Lemma 1 informally say that an MP-TCP algorithm with a larger $K_s(\mathbf{x}_s)$ or more negative

[2]The constant in front of the variable $\mathbf{x}_s$ in the algorithms are different. But the analysis for showing whether they satisfy C1-C3 can be carried on in a similar manner.
[3]When $a < 1$, the MP-TCP source will obtain even less throughput than competing single-path TCP source sometimes.

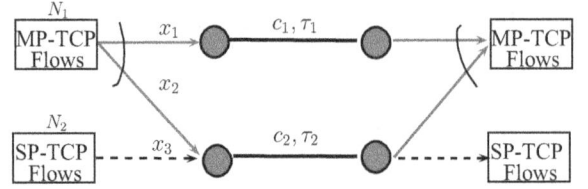

Figure 2: Network with N_1 MP-TCP flows and N_2 single-path TCP flows sharing 2 links of capacity c_1, c_2 and delay τ_1, τ_2. MP-TCP flows maintain two routes with rate x_1, x_2. Single-path TCP flows maintain one route with rate x_3.

definite $\frac{\partial\Phi_s}{\partial\mathbf{x}_s}$ is more responsive. For prior algorithms, they have the same gain function $k_r(\mathbf{x}_s) = x_r^2$ and

$$(\frac{\partial\Phi_s}{\partial\mathbf{x}_s})^{ewtcp} \preceq (\frac{\partial\Phi_s}{\partial\mathbf{x}_s})^{semicoupled} \preceq (\frac{\partial\Phi_s}{\partial\mathbf{x}_s})^{max} \preceq (\frac{\partial\Phi_s}{\partial\mathbf{x}_s})^{coupled}.$$

Out simulations in section 5 show that the responsiveness performance is the same as the above order. It means that EWTCP is the best algorithm in terms of responsiveness while Coupled algorithm, whose $\frac{\partial\Phi_s}{\partial\mathbf{x}_s}$ is merely negative semi-definite, is the worst.

4.3 A new MP-TCP design

We have discussed the relation between different performances and the corresponding parameters, which are summarized in Table 2. As discussed above the design of MP-TCP algorithms involves inevitable tradeoffs. For instance a more negative definite $\partial\Phi_s/\partial\mathbf{x}_s$ enhances responsiveness but is less friendly to SP-TCP; a higher gain $k_r(\mathbf{x}_s)$ usually improves responsiveness but is more oscillatory. Therefore it is impossible to have an algorithm that is superior for all performances.

As mentioned in section 4.1, window fluctuation is improved compared to using SP-TCP if $k_r(\mathbf{x}_s) \leq x_r\|\mathbf{x}_s\|_1$ and most current algorithms use $k_r(\mathbf{x}_s) = x_r^2$. Therefore we can sacrifice the window fluctuation performance a bit while boost up responsiveness by using a relative large $k_r(\mathbf{x}_s)$. Then it leaves us more space to improve the fairness by using small $\phi_r(\mathbf{x}_s)$. Furthermore, responsiveness is mainly affected by subpaths with small throughput while stability is mainly affected by subpaths with large throughput. We will keep $k_r(\mathbf{x}_s) = x_r^2$ nearly unchanged, which is used by default in prior algorithms, on route with large throughput but increase increase $k_r(\mathbf{x}_s)$ on route with small throughput.

Now we are left with developing a parameterized candidate, which can be tuned to reach different region in the design space. We will use the generalized algorithm of Eqn. (13) and specify the parameters (β, n, η). As discussed above, we need to choose big $k_r(\mathbf{x}_s)$ and small $\phi_r(\mathbf{x}_s)$. Note that the algorithm is computationally efficient when $n = 1$ or ∞ since there is no exponentiation. Considering these choices and the experiments in ns2, we pick $(\beta, n, \eta) = (0.2, \infty, 0.5)$. The corresponding algorithm satisfies C1-C3 based on Theorem 6 and they also satisfy C4-C5, whose proof is skipped due to space limitation. Then we can convert it into window based algorithm according to Eqn. (5), which corresponds to our algorithm at the end of section 1. Next, we will test the performance of our algorithm using ns2 simulations to confirm our analysis.

5. SIMULATION

In this section we briefly summarize our ns2 simulation results and compare the performance of our algorithm with prior algorithms. It also serves to confirm our theoretical analysis. In the simulations we set the slow start phase on each route the same as of TCP-NewReno; however, the min-

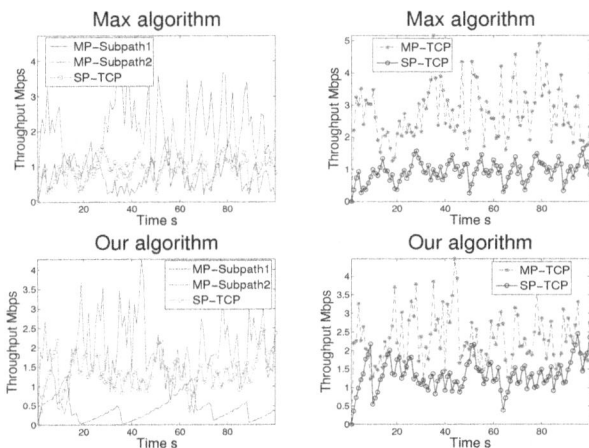

Figure 3: The throughput of MP-TCP and single-path TCP users with network topology in Fig. 2 and different RTT. The figures on the left show the throughput of each route and figures on the right show the total throughput of each source.

Table 3: Throughput of MPTCP and single-path TCP users.

	ewtcp	semi.	max	ours	coupled
MP-TCP Mbps	2.98	2.64	2.58	2.25	2.22
SP-TCP Mbps	1.01	1.32	1.35	1.61	1.67

imum *ssthresh* is set to 1 instead of 2 when there are more than 1 routes available. When the congestion avoidance phase starts, the congestion window size *cwnd* is adapted as stated in the algorithms for each subpath. We assume the advertised window *awnd* is set to be infinity.

Our simulations are divided into three parts. First, we compare the friendliness performance of our algorithm and prior algorithms. When the round trip time of each subpath is the same, we show that our algorithm is close to that of Coupled algorithm, which is the best in terms of TCP friendliness, and outperform the other prior algorithms. When the round trip time of each subpath is different, our algorithm also works well while prior algorithms, e.g. Max algorithm, is more aggressive. Second, we compare the responsiveness performance of each algorithm when there are users come and go. We show that Coupled algorithm does not work well in the dynamic environment, while our algorithm is as responsive as the other algorithms and, unlike the other algorithms, is more friendly to SP-TCP flows. Finally, we show that our algorithm achieves better window fluctuation performance than single-path TCP. Consider the experiment we have done about TCP friendliness, responsiveness and window fluctuation performance, we claim that our algorithm gives a better overall balance performance.

5.1 TCP Friendliness Performance

In this subsection, we will study the TCP friendliness performance of each algorithm using the network topology in Fig. 2. We assume all the flows are long lived and focus on the steady state throughput. For the network shown in Fig. 2, let $\tau_1 = \tau_2 = 20$ms, $c_1 = c_2 = 10$Mbps and $N_1 = N_2 = 5$. The average aggregate throughput of MP-TCP and single-path TCP users are shown in Table 3.

According to Table 3, EWTCP, Semicoupled and Max algorithm are very aggressive and severely harm the single-path TCP users, our algorithm is close to Coupled algorithm and is good in terms of TCP friendliness. Indeed, both MP-TCP and SP-TCP users should obtain 2Mbps throughput in the ideal friendly case, which means there is no traffic on the second route for all the MP-TCP users. However, since

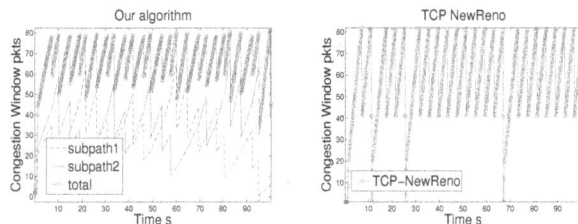

Figure 4: The window fluctuation. The figure on the left shows our algorithm and the right one is TCP-NewReno.

Table 4: Convergence Time for MP-TCP and throughput of single-path TCP

	ewtcp	semi.	max	ours	coupled
ConvergeTime s	1	2.5	4.5	4.5	54
Throughput Mbps	1.02	1.17	1.30	1.57	1.72

the minimal window size is 1 and even Coupled algorithms, which is the most fair one, also exhibit some extent of aggressiveness.

We have already shown how MP-TCP users affect the SP-TCP users for different algorithms when the round trip time of the subpath are similar. We now show that prior algorithms will be less friendly to SP-TCP when the round trip time of each subpath is different. Due to space limitation, we only show the results obtained under our algorithm and Max algorithm. Using network topology in Fig. 2 with $c_1 = c_2 = 10$Mbps, $N_1 = N_2 = 5$. But the propagation delay of the two links are different with $\tau_1 = 10$ms and $\tau_2 = 50$ms. Then the RTT for the first and second routes are roughly 20ms and 100ms. The simulation results are shown in Fig. 3. We obverse that our algorithm is quite moderate in comparison with Max algorithm.

5.2 Responsiveness Performance

In this subsection, we compare the responsiveness performance of each algorithm. Since most of the traffic in the current Internet is mice traffic, a good algorithm needs to react fast enough in this dynamic environment. We still use the network topology shown in Fig. 2 with $c_1 = c_2 = 2$Mbps, $\tau_1 = \tau_2 = 20$ms and $N_1 = N_2 = 1$. We assume that the MP-TCP flow is long lived, while the SP-TCP flow starts at 40s and end at 80s. We measure the average throughput of that single-path TCP flow from 40-80s, which reflects the aggressiveness of MP-TCP. We also measure the time for the route on the second link to recover[4] for MP-TCP users. It reflects the responsiveness performance of MP-TCP and a responsive algorithm should have small recover time. The trajectories of the throughput are shown in Fig. 5 for prior and our algorithms. The average throughput of that SP-TCP flow and the time for the MP-TCP user to recover when the single-path TCP flow leaves the network are shown in Table 4.

According to Table 4, EWTCP is the best in terms of responsiveness, and our algorithm is as responsive as the Max algorithm. It takes about 54s for the Coupled algorithm to recover, which is a serious drawback. As to the throughput, which determines friendliness property, our algorithm is still close to that of Coupled algorithm.

5.3 Window Fluctuation Performance

Finally, we consider the window fluctuation performance. We assume a toy model where there is only one link in the network. We consider two experiments. In the first

---

[4]Defined as the first time the throughput on the second route is within 90% of the average throughput after the single-path user leave.

experiment, our MP-TCP algorithm initiates two subpaths through that link, we monitor the window size of each subpath and their aggregate window size. In the second experiment, let TCP-NewReno algorithm traverse the same link and we monitor the window size. The results are shown in Fig. 4, which demonstrates that our algorithm is better than TCP-NewReno in terms of window fluctuation performance. And prior MP-TCP algorithms have similar property, that their window fluctuation performance is better than TCP NewReno, which confirms our analysis in section 4.1.

6. CONCLUSION

In this paper, we investigate the emerging problems in designing MP-TCP congestion control algorithms. We show the existence, uniqueness and stability properties of the equilibria under a unified model of MP-TCP algorithms using a new approach. Furthermore, we characterize the design space and study the tradeoffs among various performance metrics. Finally, we design a new MP-TCP algorithm and compare its performance with existing algorithms through ns2 simulation.

7. REFERENCES

[1] S. Boyd and L. Vandenberghe. Convex optimization. *Cambridge university press*, 2004.

[2] C. Cetinkaya and E. W. Knightly. Opportunistic traffic scheduling over multiple network paths. In *INFOCOM 2004.*, volume 3, pages 1928–1937. IEEE, 2004.

[3] A. Ford, C. Raiciu, M. Handley, and O. Bonaventure. Tcp extensions for multipath operation with multiple addresses. *IETF MPTCP proposal*, 2009.

[4] H. Han, S. Shakkottai, C. Hollot, R. Srikant, and D. Towsley. Overlay tcp for multi-path routing and congestion control. In *IMA Workshop on Measurements and Modeling of the Internet*, 2004.

[5] M. Honda, Y. Nishida, L. Eggert, P. Sarolahti, and H. Tokuda. Multipath congestion control for shared bottleneck. In *Proc. PFLDNeT workshop*, 2009.

[6] J. R. Iyengar, P. D. Amer, and R. Stewart. Concurrent multipath transfer using sctp multihoming over independent end-to-end paths. *Networking, IEEE/ACM Transactions on*, 14(5):951–964, 2006.

[7] F. Kelly and T. Voice. Stability of end-to-end algorithms for joint routing and rate control. *ACM SIGCOMM Computer Communication Review*, 35(2):5–12, 2005.

[8] F. P. Kelly, A. K. Maulloo, and D. K. Tan. Rate control for communication networks: shadow prices, proportional fairness and stability. *Journal of the Operational Research society*, 49(3):237–252, 1998.

[9] W. S. Lohmiller and J.-J. E. Slotine. *Contraction analysis of nonlinear systems*. PhD thesis, Massachusetts Institute of Technology, Dept. of Mechanical Engineering, 1999.

[10] S. H. Low. A duality model of tcp and queue management algorithms. *Networking, IEEE/ACM Transactions on*, 11(4):525–536, 2003.

[11] S. H. Low and D. E. Lapsley. Optimization flow control-I: basic algorithm and convergence. *IEEE/ACM Transactions on Networking (TON)*, 7(6):861–874, 1999.

[12] A. Tang, J. Wang, and S. H. Low. Is fair allocation always inefficient. In *INFOCOM 2004.*, volume 1. IEEE, 2004.

[13] D. Wischik, C. Raiciu, A. Greenhalgh, and M. Handley. Design, implementation and evaluation of congestion control for multipath tcp. In *Proceedings of the 8th USENIX conference on Networked systems design and implementation*, pages 8–8. USENIX Association, 2011.

[14] M. Zhang, J. Lai, A. Krishnamurthy, L. Peterson, and R. Wang. A transport layer approach for improving end-to-end performance and robustness using redundant paths. In *Proceedings of the annual conference on USENIX Annual Technical Conference*, pages 8–8. USENIX Association, 2004.

8. ACKNOWLEDGMENTS

This work was supported by ARO MURI through grant W911NF-08-1-0233, NSF NetSE through grant CNS 0911041, Bell Labs, Lucent-Alcatel and Wilfred Kwan.

APPENDIX

A. PROOF

Some math notations are summarized. $\mathbf{1}$ is an all one vector whose dimension is clear in the context. I is the identity matrix.

A.1 Proof of Theorem 1

The Lagrangian of (9) is:

$$
\begin{aligned}
L(\mathbf{x}, \mathbf{p}) &= \sum_{s \in S} U_s(\mathbf{x}_s) - \sum_{l \in L} p_l(y_l - c_l) \\
&= \sum_{s \in S} U_s(\mathbf{x}_s) - \sum_{l \in L} p_l(\sum_{r \in R} H_{lr} x_r - c_l) \\
&= \sum_{s \in S} \left(U_s(\mathbf{x}_s) - \sum_{r \in s} x_r q_r \right) + \sum_{l \in L} p_l c_l
\end{aligned}
$$

where $\mathbf{p} \geq \mathbf{0}$ are the dual variables and $q_r := \sum_{r \in R} H_{lr} p_l$. Then the dual problem is

$$
D(\mathbf{p}) = \sum_{s \in S} \max_{\mathbf{x}_s \geq 0} \{ B_s(\mathbf{x}_s, \mathbf{p}) \} + \sum_{l \in L} p_l c_l \quad \mathbf{p} \geq \mathbf{0}
$$

where $B_s(\mathbf{x}_s, \mathbf{p}) = U_s(\mathbf{x}_s) - \sum_{r \in s} x_r q_r$. The KKT condition implies that, at optimality, we have

$$
\frac{\partial U_s(\mathbf{x}_s)}{\partial x_r} < q_r \Rightarrow x_r = 0 \text{ and } x_r > 0 \Rightarrow \frac{\partial U_s(\mathbf{x}_s)}{\partial x_r} = q_r \quad (14)
$$

$$
y_l < c_l \Rightarrow p_l = 0 \text{ and } p_l > 0 \Rightarrow y_l = c_l \quad (15)
$$

Comparing with (6)–(7) we conclude that, if a MP-TCP algorithm defined by (3)–(4) has an underlying utility function U_s, then we must have

$$
\frac{\partial U_s(\mathbf{x}_s)}{\partial x_r} = 2\phi_r(\mathbf{x}_s) \quad r \in s, \ x_r > 0 \quad (16)
$$

Given $\phi_r(\mathbf{x}_s)$, (16) has a continuously differentiable solutions $U_s(\mathbf{x}_s)$ if and only if the Jacobian of $\Phi_s(\mathbf{x}_s)$ is symmetric, i.e., if and only if

$$
\frac{\partial \Phi(\mathbf{x}_s)}{\partial \mathbf{x}_s} = \left(\frac{\partial \Phi(\mathbf{x}_s)}{\partial \mathbf{x}_s} \right)^T
$$

A.2 Proof of Theorem 2

Proof of Part I:

For any link l, let $p_{-l} = \{ p_1, \ldots, p_{l-1}, p_{l+1}, \ldots, p_{|L|} \}$, whose component composes of all the elements in $\mathbf{p}$ except p_l. In

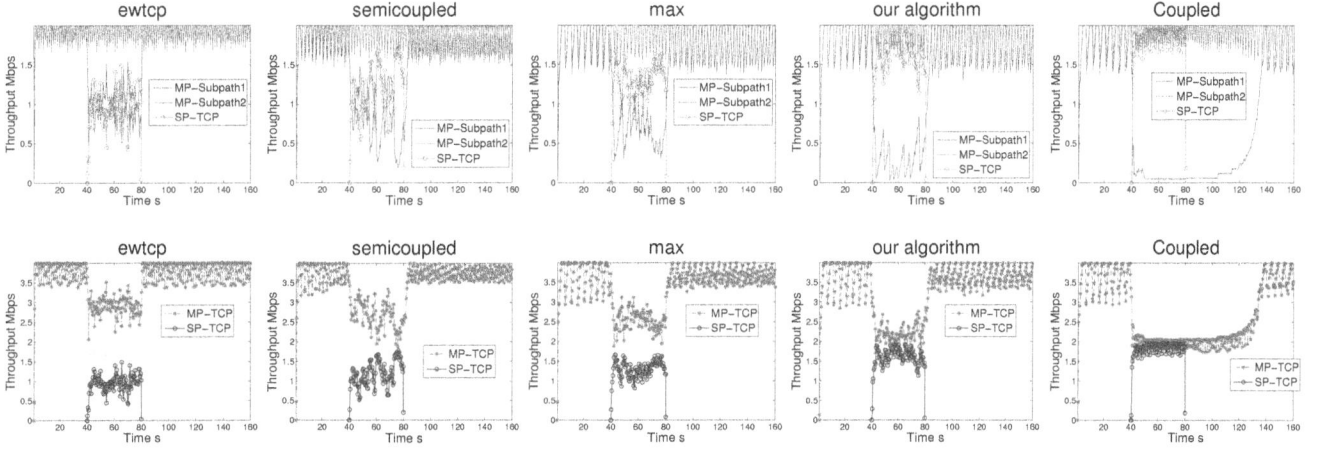

Figure 5: The dynamic behavior of MP-TCP algorithm. The topology is in Fig. 2 with long lived MP-TCP flows and short single-path TCP flows. The upper figures are the rate trajectory for each path and the lower ones are the trajectory of the total throughput for users with MP-TCP and single-path TCP algorithms.

other words, $\mathbf{p} = (p_l, p_{-l})$ for any $l \in L$. For $l \in L$, let

$$g_l(\mathbf{p}) := c_l - \sum_{r:l \in r} x_r = c_l - \sum_{s:r \in s, l \in r} y_l^s(p_l, p_{-l})$$

and $h_l(\mathbf{p}) = -g_l^2(\mathbf{p})$. According to $C1$, we have the following two facts, which will be used in the proof.

- $g_l(\mathbf{p})$ is a nondecreasing function of p_l on $\mathbb{R}_+$ since $y_l^s(\mathbf{p})$ is a nonincreasing function of p_l.

- $\lim_{p_l \to \infty} g_l(p_l, p_{-l}) = c_l$ since $\lim_{p_l \to \infty} y_l^s(\mathbf{p}) = 0$.

Next, we will show that $h_l(\mathbf{p})$ is a quasi-concave function of p_l. In other words, for any fixed p_{-l}, the set $S_a := \{p_l \mid h_l(\mathbf{p}) \geq a\}$ is a convex set. If $g_l(0, p_{-l}) \geq 0$, then

$$g_l(p_l, p_{-l}) \geq g_l(0, p_{-l}) \geq 0 \quad \forall p_l \geq 0,$$

which means $h_l(p_l, p_{-l})$ is a nonincreasing function of p_l, hence is a quasi-concave function of p_l and

$$\arg\max_{p_l} h_l(p_l, p_{-l}) = 0. \quad (17)$$

On the other hand, if $g_l(0, p_{-l}) < 0$, then there exists a $p_l^* > 0$ such that $g_l(p_l^*, p_{-l}) = 0$ since $g_l(\cdot)$ is continuous and $\lim_{p_l \to \infty} g_l(p_l, p_{-l}) = c_l > 0$. Note that $g_l(\mathbf{p})$ is a nondecreasing function of p_l, then $h_l(p_l, p_{-l})$ is nondecreasing for $p_l \in [0, p_l^*]$ and nonincreasing for $p_l \in [p_l^*, \infty)$. Hence, $h_l(p_l, p_{-l})$ is also a quasi-concave function of p_l in this case and

$$\max_{p_l} h_l(p_l, p_{-l}) = 0. \quad (18)$$

By Nash theorem, if $h_l(p_l, p_{-l})$ is a quasi-concave function of p_l for all $l \in L$ and $\mathbf{p}$ is in a bounded set, then there exists a $\mathbf{p}^* \in \mathbb{R}_+^{|L|}$ such that

$$p_l^* = \arg\max_{p_l \in \mathbb{R}_+} h_l(p_l, p_{-l}^*).$$

According to Eqn. (17) and (18), for any $l \in L$, either $p_l^* > 0$ or $g_l^*(\mathbf{p}^*) > 0$ but not both holds at any time. Therefore $\mathbf{p}^*$ satisfies Eqn. (7). Since $\mathbf{q} = R^T \mathbf{p}$, there exists a $\mathbf{x}^*$ to Eqn. (6). And we arrive at our conclusion that there exists at least one solution $(\mathbf{x}, \mathbf{p})$ which satisfies Eqn.(6) and (7).

Proof of Part II:

Lemma 2. *Assume function $F(\mathbf{x}) \in \mathbb{R}^n \to \mathbb{R}^n$ and $\partial F/\partial \mathbf{x}$ is negative definite and continuous in $\mathbb{R}^n$. Then for any $\mathbf{x}_1 \neq \mathbf{x}_2 \in \mathbb{R}^n$,*

$$(\mathbf{x}_1 - \mathbf{x}_2)^T (F(\mathbf{x}_1) - F(\mathbf{x}_2)) < 0.$$

The proof is skipped due to space limitation.

Lemma 3. *Suppose C2 and C3 hold. Then $x_r^* > 0$ at equilibrium for all $r \in R$.*

PROOF. We first show that there exists a $\bar{p} > 0$ such that $p_l^* \leq \bar{p}$ for $l \in L$. For any route $r \in s$, let

$$f_r(x_r) := \sup\{\phi_r(\mathbf{x}_s)\} \quad \text{s.t.} \quad x_{-r} \in \mathbb{R}_+^{|s|-1}.$$

Note that

$$\frac{\partial \phi_r(\mathbf{x}_s)}{\partial x_r} = \mathbf{e}_r^T \frac{\partial \Phi_s}{\partial \mathbf{x}_s} \mathbf{e}_r < 0,$$

by C2, where $\mathbf{e}_r = (\ldots, 0, 1, 0, \ldots)$ and 1 is in the r_{th} entry. Thus $\phi_r(\hat{x}_r, x_{-r}) > \phi_r(\tilde{x}_r, x_{-r})$ if $\hat{x}_r < \tilde{x}_r$ for any x_{-r}, which means $f_r(\hat{x}_r) > f_r(\tilde{x}_r)$ if $\hat{x}_r < \tilde{x}_r$. In addition $f_r(x_r) < \infty$ if $x_r > 0$ by C3. Suppose there exists a $l_1 \in L$ with bandwidth c_{l_1} such that at equilibrium $p_{l_1}^* > \bar{p}$ for any $\bar{p} > 0$. Let $N_{l_1} := \sum_{r \in R} H_{l_1 r}$ and $\bar{p} = 2 \max_{r:l \in r} \{f_r(\frac{c_{l_1}}{2N_{l_1}})\}$. Since $f_r(x_r)$ is a decreasing function of x_r and

$$f_r(x_r^*) \geq \phi_r(\mathbf{x}_s^*) = \frac{q_r^*}{2} > \frac{p_{l_1}^*}{2} \geq \frac{\bar{p}}{2} \geq f_r(\frac{c_{l_1}}{2N_{l_1}}),$$

we can obtain $x_r^* \leq \frac{c_{l_1}}{2N_{l_1}}$ for all $l_1 \in r$. However,

$$y_{l_1}^* = \sum_{r \in R} H_{lr} x_r^* \leq \frac{c_{l_1}}{2} < c_{l_1},$$

which means $p_{l_1}^* = 0$ by Eqn. (7). It contradicts $p_{l_1}^* > \bar{p}$. Thus there exists a $\bar{p}$ such that $p_l^* \leq \bar{p}$ for all $l \in L$, which means $q_r^* = \sum_{l \in r} p_l^*$ is also finite. Then if $x_r^* = 0$, we can obtain $\phi_r(0, x_{-r}^*) = \infty > q_r^*/2$, which contradicts C3. Thus, we have $x_r^* > 0$ for $r \in R$. $\square$

Suppose there exist two equilibria $(\mathbf{x}_1, \mathbf{p}_1)$ and $(\mathbf{x}_2, \mathbf{p}_2)$ to Eqn. (3-4). Let $\delta \mathbf{x} = \mathbf{x}_1 - \mathbf{x}_2$ and $\delta \mathbf{p} = \mathbf{p}_1 - \mathbf{p}_2$, then for

$s \in S$,

$$\sum_{r \in s} (x_{r1} - x_{r2}) \left(\phi_r(\mathbf{x}_{s1}) - \frac{1}{2} q_{r1} \right)$$

$$= \sum_{r \in s} \left(x_{r1} \left(\phi_r(\mathbf{x}_{s1}) - \frac{1}{2} q_{r1} \right) - x_{r2} \left(\phi_r(\mathbf{x}_{s1}) - \frac{1}{2} q_{r1} \right) \right)$$

$$= -\sum_{r \in s} \left(x_{r2} \left(\phi_r(\mathbf{x}_{s1}) - \frac{1}{2} q_{r1} \right) \right)$$

$$\geq 0 \qquad (19)$$

where the second equality holds since $x_{r1}(\phi_r(\mathbf{x}_{s1}) - q_{r1}/2) = 0$ and the last inequality holds since $\phi_r(\mathbf{x}_{s1}) - q_{r1}/2 \leq 0$ by Eqn. (6). The following inequality can be obtained by similar manner.

$$\sum_{r \in s} (x_{r1} - x_{r2}) \left(\phi_r(\mathbf{x}_{s2}) - \frac{1}{2} q_{r2} \right) \leq 0 \qquad (20)$$

Subtract Eqn. (20) from Eqn. (19), we can obtain

$$0 \leq \sum_{r \in s} \delta x_r \left(\phi_r(\mathbf{x}_{s1}) - \phi_r(\mathbf{x}_{s2}) - \frac{1}{2} \delta q_r \right)$$

$$= \sum_{r \in s} \delta x_r (\phi_r(\mathbf{x}_{s1}) - \phi_r(\mathbf{x}_{s2})) - \frac{1}{2} \delta \mathbf{x}_s^T \mathbf{q}_s$$

$$\leq -\frac{1}{2} \delta \mathbf{x}_s^T \delta \mathbf{q}_s,$$

where the last inequality follows from Lemma 2 and C2 and equality can be obtained if and only if $\delta \mathbf{x}_s = 0$. Sum the above inequality over $s \in S$,

$$0 < -\sum_{s \in S} \delta \mathbf{x}_s^T \delta \mathbf{q}_s = -\delta \mathbf{x}^T H^T \delta \mathbf{p}. \qquad (21)$$

On the other hand, for $l \in L$,

$$\delta p_l(y_{l1} - c_l) \geq 0 \text{ and } \delta p_l(y_{l2} - c_l) \leq 0$$

which is obtained using similar manner as Eqn. (19). Then we can obtain

$$\delta p_l \delta y_l \geq 0$$

Sum over the above inequality over $l \in L$, we obtain

$$\delta \mathbf{p}^T H \delta \mathbf{x} \geq 0. \qquad (22)$$

which contradicts Eqn. (21) if $\mathbf{x}_1 \neq \mathbf{x}_2$. Thus, $\mathbf{x}_1 = \mathbf{x}_2$. Next we will show $\mathbf{p}_1 = \mathbf{p}_2$. Since $x_r^* > 0$ by Lemma 3, $\phi_r(\mathbf{x}_s) = q_r/2$ according to Eqn. (6). Let $\Phi(\mathbf{x}) := (\Phi_s(\mathbf{x}_s), s \in S)$, and we can get $H^T \mathbf{p} = \mathbf{q} = 2\Phi(\mathbf{x})$. Then

$$H^T \mathbf{p}_1 = \Phi(\mathbf{x}_1) = \Phi(\mathbf{x}_2) = H^T \mathbf{p}_2,$$

which means $\mathbf{p}_1 = \mathbf{p}_2$ due to H has full row rank. Therefore there exists at most one equilibrium to Eqn. (3-4) under C2-C3.

A.3 Proof of Theorem 3

We borrow idea from contraction mapping analysis [9]. We will show that both $\dot{x}_r(t)$ and $\dot{p}_l(t)$ will be arbitrary small when t approach infinity and construct Lyapunov function based on that. Define $\delta \mathbf{x} := \mathbf{x} - \mathbf{x}^*$, $\delta \mathbf{p} := \mathbf{p} - \mathbf{p}^*$ as a perturbation of $\mathbf{x}$ and $\mathbf{p}$ around the equilibria. Let $\Lambda_k = diag\{k_r, r \in R\}$, $\Lambda_\gamma = diag\{\gamma_l, l \in L\}$. Then the Lyapunov function we develop is as follows:

$$V(\mathbf{x}, \mathbf{p}) = \delta \mathbf{x}^T \Lambda_k^{-1} \delta \mathbf{x} + \frac{1}{2} \delta \mathbf{p}^T \Lambda_\gamma^{-1} \delta \mathbf{p}. \qquad (23)$$

To show $\dot{V}(\mathbf{x}, \mathbf{p}) < 0$, we need to show both $\delta \mathbf{x}^T \Lambda_k^{-1}(\mathbf{x}) \delta \dot{\mathbf{x}}$ and $\delta \mathbf{p}^T \Lambda_\gamma^{-1} \delta \dot{\mathbf{p}}$ is smaller than 0 when $(\mathbf{x}, \mathbf{p}) \neq (\mathbf{x}^*, \mathbf{p}^*)$.

If $\delta \mathbf{x} \neq 0$, then

$$\delta \mathbf{x}^T \Lambda_k^{-1} \delta \dot{\mathbf{x}}$$

$$= \sum_{r \in R} \delta x_r \left(\phi_r(\mathbf{x}_s) - \frac{q_r}{2} \right)^+_{x_r}$$

$$\leq \sum_{r \in R} \delta x_r \left(\phi_r(\mathbf{x}_s) - \frac{q_r}{2} \right)$$

$$= \sum_{r \in R} \delta x_r \left(\phi_r(\mathbf{x}_s) - \phi_r(\mathbf{x}_s^*) - \frac{\delta q_r}{2} \right) + \sum_{r \in R} \delta x_r \left(\phi_r(\mathbf{x}_s^*) - \frac{q_r^*}{2} \right)$$

$$\leq \sum_{r \in R} \delta x_r (\phi_r(\mathbf{x}_s) - \phi_r(\mathbf{x}_s^*)) + \frac{1}{2} \sum_{r \in R} \delta x_r \delta q_r < -\frac{1}{2} \delta \mathbf{x}^T H^T \delta \mathbf{p}$$

The first inequality holds since $(\phi_r(\mathbf{x}_s) - \frac{q_r}{2})^+_{x_r} = \phi_r(\mathbf{x}_s) - \frac{q_r}{2}$ if $x_r > 0$ and $\phi_r(\mathbf{x}_s) - \frac{q_r}{2} \leq 0$, $\delta x_r = -x_r^*$ if $x_r = 0$. In the second inequality, we need

$$(x_r - x_r^*) \left(\phi_r(\mathbf{x}_s^*) - \frac{q_r^*}{2} \right) = x_r \left(\phi_r(\mathbf{x}_s^*) - \frac{q_r^*}{2} \right) \leq 0,$$

which holds since $x_r^*(\phi_r(\mathbf{x}_s^*) - \frac{q_r^*}{2}) = 0$ and $\phi_r(\mathbf{x}_s^*) - \frac{q_r^*}{2} \leq 0$ by the property of equilibrium to (3-4). The last inequality holds by Lemma 2 and C2.

On the other hand, using similar manner, we can obtain

$$\delta \mathbf{p}^T \Lambda_\gamma^{-1} \delta \dot{\mathbf{p}} = \sum_{l \in L} \delta p_l(y_l - c_l)^+_{p_l}$$

$$\leq \sum_{l \in L} \delta p_l(y_l - c_l)$$

$$\leq \sum_{l \in L} \delta p_l \delta y_l$$

$$= \delta \mathbf{p}^T H \delta \mathbf{x}$$

Therefore if $\delta \mathbf{x} \neq 0$

$$\dot{V}(\mathbf{x}, \mathbf{p}) = 2\delta \mathbf{x}^T \Lambda_k^{-1} \delta \dot{\mathbf{x}} + \delta \mathbf{p}^T \Lambda_\gamma^{-1} \delta \dot{\mathbf{p}} < 0,$$

which means $\mathbf{x}(t) \to \mathbf{x}^*$. Recall that $\dot{p}_l = \gamma_l(y_l - c_l)^+_{p_l}$, it means $\dot{p}_l \to \gamma_l(y_l^* - c_l)^+_{p_l} = 0$. By Theorem 2, there is a unique equilibrium to $(\dot{\mathbf{x}}, \dot{\mathbf{p}}) = 0$ and it means $\mathbf{p}(t) \to \mathbf{p}^*$ or $\dot{\mathbf{p}} \not\to 0$. As a result, $V(\mathbf{x}, \mathbf{p})$ is a Lyapunov function for the dynamical system (3-4).

A.4 Proof of Theorem 4

Assume the MP-TCP source runs algorithm

$$\phi_r(\mathbf{x}_s; \mu) = \mu \tilde{\phi}_r(\mathbf{x}_s) + (1 - \mu) \hat{\phi}_r(\mathbf{x}_s) \quad \mu \in [0, 1]$$

where algorithm M1 and M2 corresponds to $\mu = 0$ and 1 respectively. Let x_g and τ_g be the throughput and RTT of the TCP NewReno source in the network of Fig. 1. Denote the inverse of $\frac{\partial \Phi_s(\mathbf{x}_s, \mu)}{\partial \mathbf{x}_s}$, whose existence is ensured by C2, by $D(\mu)$ and we have $\sum_{i \in s} D_{ij}(\mu) \leq 0$ by C4. The equilibrium is defined by $F(\mathbf{x}, \mu) = 0$ where $\mathbf{x} := (\mathbf{x}_s, x_g)$ and F is given by:

$$\Phi_s(\mathbf{x}_s, \mu) - \frac{1}{\tau_g^2 x_g^2} \mathbf{1} = 0$$

$$\mathbf{1}^T \mathbf{x}_s + x_g = c,$$

where the first equation follows from

$$\frac{p^*}{2} = \frac{1}{\tau_g^2 x_g^2} = \phi_r(\mathbf{x}_s) \quad r \in s$$

314

and p^* is the congestion price at the bottleneck link. Applying implicit function theorem, we get

$$\frac{d\mathbf{x}}{d\mu} = -\left(\frac{\partial F}{\partial \mathbf{x}}\right)^{-1}\frac{\partial F}{\partial \mu}$$

$$= -\begin{bmatrix} \frac{\partial \Phi_s}{\partial \mathbf{x}_s} & \frac{2}{x_g^3}\mathbf{1} \\ \mathbf{1}^T & 1 \end{bmatrix}^{-1}\begin{bmatrix} \tilde{\Phi}_s(\mathbf{x}_s) - \hat{\Phi}_s(\mathbf{x}_s) \\ 0 \end{bmatrix},$$

where the inverse exists by condition C2. Let

$$A := \frac{\partial \Phi_s}{\partial \mathbf{x}_s} - \frac{2}{x_g^3}\mathbf{1}\mathbf{1}^T \quad \text{and} \quad d := 1 - \frac{2}{x_g^3}\sum_{i,j}D_{ij}(\mu)$$

Then

$$\begin{bmatrix} \frac{\partial \Phi_s}{\partial \mathbf{x}_s} & \frac{2}{x_p^3}\mathbf{1} \\ \mathbf{1}^T & 1 \end{bmatrix}^{-1} = \begin{bmatrix} A^{-1} & -D\mathbf{1}d \\ -d\mathbf{1}^T A^{-1} & d^{-1} \end{bmatrix}.$$

Thus

$$\mathbf{1}^T\frac{\partial \mathbf{x}_s}{\partial \mu} = -[\mathbf{1}^T 0]\left(\frac{\partial F}{\partial \mathbf{x}}\right)^{-1}\frac{\partial F}{\partial \mu}$$

$$= -\mathbf{1}^T A^{-1}(\tilde{\Phi}_s(\mathbf{x}_s) - \hat{\Phi}_s(\mathbf{x}_s)). \quad (24)$$

By matrix inverse formula,

$$A^{-1} = \left(\frac{\partial \Phi_s}{\partial \mathbf{x}_s} - \frac{2}{x_g^3}\mathbf{1}\mathbf{1}^T\right)^{-1}$$

$$= D(\mu) + \frac{1}{\frac{x_g^3}{2} - \mathbf{1}^T D(\mu)\mathbf{1}}D(\mu)\mathbf{1}\mathbf{1}^T D(\mu),$$

Substitute it into Eqn. (24), we have

$$\mathbf{1}^T A^{-1}(\hat{\Phi}_s(\mathbf{x}_s) - \tilde{\Phi}_s(\mathbf{x}_s))$$

$$= \left(1 + \frac{\mathbf{1}^T D(\mu)\mathbf{1}}{\frac{x_g^3}{2} - \mathbf{1}^T D(\mu)\mathbf{1}}\right)\mathbf{1}^T D(\mu)(\tilde{\Phi}_s(\mathbf{x}_s) - \hat{\Phi}_s(\mathbf{x}_s))$$

$$= \frac{x_g^3}{x_g^3 - 2\mathbf{1}^T D(\mu)\mathbf{1}}\sum_{r\in s}\left(\sum_{i\in s}D_{ir}(\mu)\right)(\tilde{\phi}_r(\mathbf{x}_s) - \hat{\phi}_r(\mathbf{x}_s))$$

$$\leq 0.$$

where the inequality follows from $D(\mu)$ is negative definite, $\sum_{i\in s}D_{ir}(\mu) < 0$ and $\tilde{\phi}_r(\mathbf{x}_s) - \hat{\phi}_r(\mathbf{x}_s) \geq 0$. Thus, we have $\mathbf{1}^T\frac{\partial \mathbf{x}_s}{\partial \mu} \geq 0$ for $\mu \in [0,1]$, which means M2 will gain more throughput than M1.

A.5 Proof of Theorem 5

Let $h_r(\mathbf{x}_s) := \hat{\phi}_r(\mathbf{x}_s) - \tilde{\phi}_r(\mathbf{x}_s)$ and $H(\mathbf{x}_s) := (h_r(\mathbf{x}_s), r \in s)$, whose Jacobian, $\partial H/\partial \mathbf{x}_s = \partial \hat{\Phi}_s/\partial \mathbf{x}_s - \partial \tilde{\Phi}_s/\partial \mathbf{x}_s$, is negative definite by assumption. Now we only need to show $h_r(\mathbf{x}_s) \geq 0$, namely $\hat{\phi}_r(\mathbf{x}_s) - \tilde{\phi}_r(\mathbf{x}_s) \geq 0$. By condition C5, for any x_{-r}, we have

$$\lim_{x_r\to\infty}\hat{\phi}_r(\mathbf{x}_s) \leq \lim_{x_r\to\infty}\frac{1}{x_r^2\tau_r^2} = 0$$

$$\lim_{x_r\to\infty}\hat{\phi}_k(\mathbf{x}_s) \leq \lim_{x_r\to\infty}\frac{1}{x_k^2\tau_k^2} < \infty \quad k \in s\setminus\{r\},$$

which also holds for $\tilde{\Phi}_s(\mathbf{x}_s)$. Thus,

$$\lim_{x_r\to\infty}h_r(\mathbf{x}_s) = \lim_{x_r\to\infty}(\hat{\phi}_r(\mathbf{x}_s) - \tilde{\phi}_r(\mathbf{x}_s)) = 0$$

$$\lim_{x_r\to\infty}h_k(\mathbf{x}_s) < \infty \quad k \in s\setminus\{r\},$$

By Lemma 2, for any $\mathbf{x}_s, \mathbf{z}_s \in \mathbb{R}_+^{|s|}$,

$$(\mathbf{z}_s - \mathbf{x}_s)^T(H(\mathbf{z}_s) - H(\mathbf{x}_s)) < 0,$$

which means

$$(z_r - x_r)(h_r(\mathbf{z}_s) - h_r(\mathbf{x}_s)) \quad (25)$$

$$< -\sum_{k\in s, k\neq r}(z_k - x_k)(h_k(\mathbf{z}_s) - h_k(\mathbf{x}_s))$$

Recall that $\lim_{x_r\to\infty}h_k(\mathbf{x}_s) < \infty$ for $k \neq r$, we have

$$A_r := \limsup_{z_r\to\infty}|\sum_{k\in s, k\neq r}(z_k - x_k)(h_k(\mathbf{z}_s) - h_k(\mathbf{x}_s))| \leq \infty.$$

Substitute it in Eqn. (25), we can obtain

$$\limsup_{z_r\to\infty}(h_r(\mathbf{z}_s) - h_r(\mathbf{x}_s))$$

$$\leq \limsup_{z_r\to\infty}\frac{\sum_{k\in s, k\neq r}(z_k - x_k)(h_k(\mathbf{z}_s) - h_k(\mathbf{x}_s))}{z_r - x_r}$$

$$\leq \frac{A_r}{\lim_{z_r\to\infty}(z_r - x_r)} = 0$$

Thus for any $\epsilon > 0$, we have

$$(h_r(\mathbf{z}_s) - h_r(\mathbf{x}_s)) < \epsilon \text{ and } |h_r(\mathbf{z}_s)| \leq \epsilon$$

provided z_r is large enough by condition C5. Then

$$h_r(\mathbf{x}_s) > h_r(\mathbf{z}_s) - \epsilon > -2\epsilon \quad \forall\epsilon > 0,$$

which means $h_r(\mathbf{x}_s) \geq 0$ and verifies our claim that $\hat{\phi}_r(\mathbf{x}_s) \geq \tilde{\phi}_r(\mathbf{x}_s)$.

A.6 Proof of Theorem 6

We will show the results hold for any $n \in \mathbb{N}_+$. Since $\lim_{n\to\infty}\|x\|_n = \|x\|_\infty$, the results also holds for $n = \infty$.

Proof of $\phi_r(\mathbf{x}_s)$ satisfies C1 for $\beta \geq 0$

We will first show there exists a nonnegative solution $\mathbf{x}_s(\mathbf{q}_s)$ to Eqn. (6) for any $\mathbf{q}_s \geq 0$. Since

$$\{\mathbf{q}_s \mid q_r = \sum_{l\in L}H_{lr}p_l, r \in s, \mathbf{p} \geq 0\} \subseteq \mathbb{R}_+^{|s|},$$

it implies there exists a nonnegative solution to Eqn. (6) for any $\mathbf{p} \geq 0$. For simplicity, we relabel the subpaths of source s by $s = \{1,\ldots,|s|\}$ such that $q_i\tau_i^2 \leq q_j\tau_j^2$ for $i \leq j$. Let $\mathbf{z}_s := \mathbf{x}_s/x_1$ and $C := \|\mathbf{z}_s\|_n$. Then $\phi_r(\mathbf{x}_s) = \frac{q_r}{2}$ can be expressed as

$$1 - \beta + \beta\frac{C}{z_r} = \frac{q_r\tau_r^2}{2}\|\mathbf{x}_s\|_1^2 \quad r \in s \quad (26)$$

Divide the r_{th} equation to the 1_{st} equation and note that $z_1 = 1$, we obtain

$$z_r = \frac{q_1\tau_1^2\beta C}{(q_r\tau_r^2 - q_1\tau_1^2)(1 - \beta) + q_r\tau_r^2\beta C} \quad r \in s \quad (27)$$

Note that $C = \|\mathbf{z}_s\|_n$ and substitute Eqn. (27) in it, we can obtain

$$\left(\sum_{r\in s}\left(\frac{q_1\tau_1^2\beta C}{(q_r\tau_r^2 - q_1\tau_1^2)(1 - \beta) + q_r\tau_r^2\beta C}\right)^n\right)^{\frac{1}{n}} = C$$

Let

$$\psi(C) := \left(\sum_{r\in s}\left(\frac{q_1\tau_1^2\beta C}{(q_r\tau_r^2 - q_1\tau_1^2)(1 - \beta) + q_r\tau_r^2\beta C}\right)^n\right)^{\frac{1}{n}} - C.$$

For any $C \geq 0$, we have

$$1 \leq \left(\sum_{r \in s} \left(\frac{q_1 \tau_1^2 \beta C}{(q_r \tau_r^2 - q_1 \tau_1^2)(1 - \beta) + q_r \tau_r^2 \beta C} \right)^n \right)^{\frac{1}{n}} \leq |s|^{\frac{1}{n}}$$

Thus $\psi(1) > 0$ and $\psi(\infty) < 0$. Then there exists a $\tilde{C} \geq 1$ such that $\psi(\tilde{C}) = 0$. Plug $\tilde{C}$ back in Eqn. (27), we can obtain $\mathbf{z}_s$. Note that $\mathbf{z}_s \geq 0$ because $\tilde{C} \geq 1$. Plug $\mathbf{z}_s$ into Eqn. (26), we can solve $\|\mathbf{x}_s\|_1$ and $x_1 = \|\mathbf{x}_s\|_1 / \|\mathbf{z}_s\|_1$. Finally, we can calculate $\mathbf{x}_s$ by $\mathbf{x}_s = \mathbf{z}_s x_1$.

We skip the proof of $y_l^s(\mathbf{p})$ is a nonincreasing function of p_l since it is implied by that $\partial \Phi_s(\mathbf{x}_s) / \partial \mathbf{x}_s$ is negative semidefinite, which will be proved below. And it is easy to see $y_l^s(\mathbf{p}) \to 0$ as $p_l \to \infty$ so we skip it.

Proof of $\phi_r(\mathbf{x}_s)$ satisfies C2 and C3 for $\beta > 0$ and $|s| \leq 8$

Lemma 4. *Let $\mathbf{a} \in \mathbb{R}^n$ that satisfies $\sum_{i=1}^n a_i = 1$ and $\sum_{i=1}^n a_i^2 \leq 1$. Then for any n dimensional $\mathbf{z} \neq \mathbf{0}$,*

$$f(\mathbf{z}) := \sum_{i=1}^n z_i^2 + (\sum_{i=1}^n z_i)(\sum_{i=1}^n a_i z_i) > 0$$

provided $n \leq 8$.

PROOF. Let $S_M := \{ \mathbf{z} \mid \sum_{i=1}^n z_i = M \}$ and given any M, if we can show $f(\mathbf{z}) > 0$ for $\mathbf{z} \in S_M$, we can conclude that $f(\mathbf{z}) > 0$ since $\cup_{M \in \mathbb{R}} S_M = \mathbb{R}^n$. Given any M,

$$\min_{\mathbf{z} \in S_M} f(\mathbf{z}) = \min f(\mathbf{z}) \quad \text{s.t.} \quad \sum_{i=1}^n z_i = M.$$

Its Lagrangian is given as

$$L(\mathbf{z}, \mu) = \sum_{i=1}^n z_i^2 + M(\sum_{i=1}^n a_i z_i) + \mu(\sum_{i=1}^n z_i - M),$$

where μ is the lagrangian multiplier. Let $\partial L / \partial z_i = 0$ for all $1 \leq i \leq n$ and substitute it back to $\sum_{i=1}^n z_i = M$, we can obtain $\mu = -3M/n$ and $z_i = \frac{M}{2}(\frac{3}{|s|} - a_i)$, which are the unique minimizer of $\min_{\mathbf{z} \in S_M} f(\mathbf{z})$. Then

$$\min_{\mathbf{z} \in S_M} f(\mathbf{z}) = \frac{M^2}{4} \left(\frac{9}{n} - \sum_{i=1}^n a_i^2 \right) \geq \frac{M^2}{4} \left(\frac{9}{n} - 1 \right)$$

When $M \neq 0$, $\min_{\mathbf{z} \in S_M} f(\mathbf{z}) > 0$ if $n < 9$. When $M = 0$, the minimizer is $\mathbf{z} = \mathbf{0}$ and $f(\mathbf{z}) > 0$ for $\mathbf{z} \in S_0 \setminus \{\mathbf{0}\}$. $\square$

Lemma 5. *Given a $\mathbf{x} \in \mathbb{R}_+^n$, define a vector $\mathbf{a}$ in $\mathbb{R}^n$ as follows:*

$$a_i = \frac{2x_i}{\sum_{i=1}^n x_i} - \frac{x_i^p}{\sum_{i=1}^n x_i^p} \quad 1 \leq i \leq n$$

where $p \in \mathbb{N}_+$. Then $\sum_{i=1}^n a_i = 1$ and $\sum_{i=1}^n a_i^2 \leq 1$ for any integer $p \geq 1$.

PROOF. It is straightforward to show $\sum_{i=1}^n a_i = 1$ and now we will show $\sum_{i=1}^n a_i^2 \leq 1$.

$$\sum_{i=1}^n a_i^2 = \frac{\sum_{i=1}^n x_i^{2p}}{(\sum_{i=1}^n x_i^p)^2} + \frac{4 \sum_{i=1}^n x_i^2}{(\sum_{i=1}^n x_i)^2} - \frac{4 \sum_{i=1}^n x_i^{p+1}}{(\sum_{i=1}^n x_i^p)(\sum_{i=1}^n x_i)}$$

$$\leq 1 + \frac{4 \sum_{i=1}^n x_i^2}{(\sum_{i=1}^n x_i)^2} - \frac{4 \sum_{i=1}^n x_i^{p+1}}{(\sum_{i=1}^n x_i^p)(\sum_{i=1}^n x_i)}$$

$$= 1 - 4 \frac{\sum_{n \geq i > j \geq 1} (x_i - x_j)(x_i^{p-1} - x_j^{p-1})}{(\sum_{i=1}^n x_i)^2 (\sum_{i=1}^n x_i^p)}$$

$$\leq 1$$

$\square$

Now we begin to show the Jacobian $\partial \Phi_s(\mathbf{x}_s) / \partial \mathbf{x}_s$ is negative definite if $\beta > 0$ and negative semi-definite if $\beta = 0$. Let τ be the same round trip time for each route. Let $\Lambda_s = diag\{\mathbf{x}_s\}$ and

$$\mathbf{a}_s = \left(\frac{2x_r}{\|\mathbf{x}_s\|_1} - \frac{x_r^n}{\|\mathbf{x}_s\|_n^n}, r \in s \right).$$

Then the Jacobian of Φ_s at $\mathbf{x}_s$ can be written as

$$\frac{\partial \Phi_s}{\partial \mathbf{x}_s} = -\frac{2(1-\beta)}{\tau^2 \|\mathbf{x}_s\|_1^3} \mathbf{1} \mathbf{1}^T - \beta \frac{\|\mathbf{x}_s\|_n}{\tau^2 \|\mathbf{x}_s\|_1^2} \Lambda_s^{-1} \left(I_{|s|} + \mathbf{1} \mathbf{a}_s^T \right) \Lambda_s^{-1}$$

Next, we will show $I_{|s|} + \mathbf{1} \mathbf{a}_s^T$ is positive definite. For any $\mathbf{z}_s \in \mathbb{R}^{|s|}$,

$$\mathbf{z}_s^T (I_{|s|} - \mathbf{1} \mathbf{a}_s^T) \mathbf{z}_s = \|\mathbf{z}_s\|_2^2 - (\sum_{r \in s} z_r)(\sum_{r \in s} a_r z_r). \quad (28)$$

By Lemma 5, $\|\mathbf{a}_s\|^2 \leq 1$. Hence Eqn. (28) is always greater than 0 provided $|s| \leq 8$ by Lemma 4. Hence the Jacobian is negative definite if $|s| \leq 8$. For $\beta = 0$, the Jacobian degenerates to

$$\frac{\partial \Phi_s}{\partial \mathbf{x}_s} = -\frac{2}{\tau^2 \|\mathbf{x}_s\|_1^3} \mathbf{1} \mathbf{1}^T, \quad (29)$$

which is merely negative semi-definite.

The proof that $\phi_r(\mathbf{x}_s)$ satisfies C3 for $\beta > 0$ is straightforward so we skip it.

A.7 Proof of Lemma 1

For any $\lambda_1 \in \lambda(J)$, let $(\mathbf{z}_1, \mathbf{p}_1)$ be its corresponding eigenvector such that $\|\mathbf{z}_1\|_2 = \|\mathbf{p}_1\|_2 = 1$. Then we have

$$\lambda_1 \begin{bmatrix} \mathbf{z}_1 \\ \mathbf{p}_1 \end{bmatrix} = \begin{bmatrix} \frac{1}{2} \Lambda_k & 0 \\ & \Lambda_\gamma \end{bmatrix} \begin{bmatrix} 2 \frac{\partial \Phi}{\partial \mathbf{x}} & -H^T \\ H & 0 \end{bmatrix} \begin{bmatrix} \mathbf{z}_1 \\ \mathbf{p}_1 \end{bmatrix}$$

Premultiply $diag\{2\Lambda_k^{-1}, \Lambda_\gamma^{-1}\}$ at both sides, we get

$$\lambda_1 \begin{bmatrix} 2\Lambda_k^{-1} & 0 \\ 0 & \Lambda_\gamma^{-1} \end{bmatrix} \begin{bmatrix} \mathbf{z}_1 \\ \mathbf{p}_1 \end{bmatrix} = \begin{bmatrix} 2 \frac{\partial \Phi}{\partial \mathbf{x}} & -H^T \\ H & 0 \end{bmatrix} \begin{bmatrix} \mathbf{z}_1 \\ \mathbf{p}_1 \end{bmatrix}$$

Now premultiply the conjugate of eigenvector $(\mathbf{z}_1, \mathbf{p}_1)$, we have

$$\lambda_1 = \frac{2 \mathbf{z}_1^H \frac{\partial \Phi}{\partial \mathbf{x}} \mathbf{z}_1}{2 \mathbf{z}_1^H \Lambda_k^{-1} \mathbf{z}_1 + \mathbf{p}_1^H \Lambda_\gamma^{-1} \mathbf{p}_1}$$

$$= \frac{2}{2 \mathbf{z}_1^H \Lambda_k^{-1} \mathbf{z}_1 + \mathbf{p}_1^H \Lambda_\gamma^{-1} \mathbf{p}_1} (\mathbf{Re}(\mathbf{z}_1^H \frac{\partial \Phi}{\partial \mathbf{x}} \mathbf{z}_1) + \mathbf{Im}(\mathbf{z}_1^H \frac{\partial \Phi}{\partial \mathbf{x}} \mathbf{z}_1)).$$

which means

$$\mathbf{Re}(\lambda_1) = \frac{2\mathbf{Re}(\mathbf{z}_1^H \frac{\partial \Phi}{\partial \mathbf{x}} \mathbf{z}_1)}{2 \mathbf{z}_1^H \Lambda_k^{-1} \mathbf{z}_1 + \mathbf{p}_1^H \Lambda_\gamma^{-1} \mathbf{p}_1} = \frac{2\mathbf{z}_1^H (\frac{\partial \Phi}{\partial \mathbf{x}})^+ \mathbf{z}_1}{2 \mathbf{z}_1^H \Lambda_k^{-1} \mathbf{z}_1 + \mathbf{p}_1^H \Lambda_\gamma^{-1} \mathbf{p}_1}$$

for any $\lambda_1 \in \lambda(J)$. Thus

$$\lambda_m(J) \leq \max_{(\mathbf{z}, \mathbf{p}) \in S} \left\{ \frac{2\mathbf{z}^H (\frac{\partial \Phi}{\partial \mathbf{x}})^+ \mathbf{z}}{2 \mathbf{z}^H \Lambda_k^{-1} \mathbf{z} + \mathbf{p}^H \Lambda_\gamma^{-1} \mathbf{p}} \right\}$$

Trap Array: A Unified Model for Scalability Evaluation of Geometric Routing

Guang Tan[1], Zhimeng Yin[1,2], Hongbo Jiang[2]
[1]SIAT, Chinese Academy of Sciences, Shenzhen, China
[2]Huazhong University of Science and Technology, Wuhan, China
Email: guang.tan@siat.ac.cn, zm.yin@siat.ac.cn, hongbojiang@hust.edu.cn

ABSTRACT

Scalable routing for large-scale wireless networks needs to find near shortest paths with low state on each node, preferably sub-linear with the network size. Two approaches are considered promising toward this goal: compact routing and geometric routing (geo-routing). To date the two lines of research have been largely independent, perhaps because of the distinct principles they follow. In particular, it remains unclear how they compare with each other in the worst case, despite extensive experimental results showing the superiority of one or another in particular cases. We develop a novel *Trap Array* topology model that provides a unified framework to uncover the limiting behavior of ten representative geo-routing algorithms [18, 21, 25, 24, 5, 12, 36, 27, 33, 32]. We present a series of new theoretical results, in comparison with the performance of compact routing as a baseline. In light of their pros and cons, we further design a *Compact Geometric Routing (CGR)* algorithm that attempts to leverage the benefits of both approaches. Theoretical analysis and simulations show the advantages of the topology model and the algorithm.

Categories and Subject Descriptors

C.2.2 [**Computer Systems Organization**]: Computer-Communication Networks—*Routing protocols*; D.2.8 [**Software Engineering**]: Metrics—*complexity measures, performance measures*

General Terms

Algorithms, performance

Keywords

Geometric routing, scalability

1. INTRODUCTION

Scalable routing design requires a proper tradeoff between two conflicting factors: route stretch – the ratio between

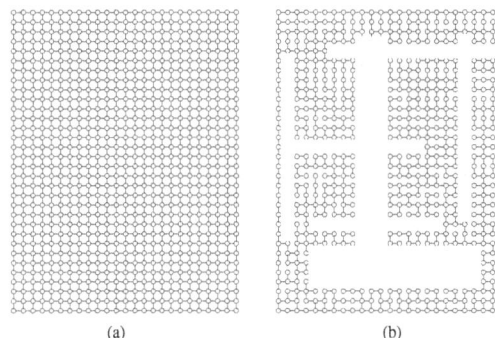

Figure 1: Two network topologies for geo-routing. (a) An ideal case where geo-routing algorithms perform optimally and provides limitless scalability. (b) An irregular topology with holes and reduced node density, where geo-routing algorithms may perform significantly worse.

the costs of generated and optimal routes, and state size – the amount of state information used by nodes for routing. The former has strong implications on connection delay, route reliability, and energy efficiency, and the latter is highly correlated with memory requirement and volume of control traffic. Early proposals for wireless routing adopt the classic approach of shortest-path routing [4], where every node maintains $O(N)$ state for an N-node network. This approach is considered unscalable for some networks where nodes have extremely limited resources [12].

A possible remedy for the scalability problem is *compact routing*. Dating back to the 1980s, the theory of compact routing explores the fundamental relationships between stretch and node state. A major outcome of this theory is a rich set of universal routing algorithms (e.g., [1, 2, 8, 10, 31]) that guarantee constant stretch (≥ 3) with sub-linear per-node state for general networks. This has generated recent interest in replacing traditional routing algorithms with the compact ones for wireless networks [26, 13, 30, 35]. For example, Mao et al.'s S4 protocol [26] is a successful adaptation of Thorup and Zwick's stretch 3 routing scheme [31] for realistic sensor networks.

In parallel to the efforts on compact routing, another line of research, namely geometric routing (or geo-routing), has considered specialized routing methods for wireless networks, by taking advantage of the nodes' geometric positions. In this approach, it is assumed that every node knows its own position, and the source of a message knows the position of the destination (through for example a distributed hash table). The algorithm forwards packets in a greedy manner by selecting next hops that are progressively closer to the destination. When the packet encounters a *local minimum* (LM) and cannot move forward, a recovery scheme is executed. The defining characteristic of geo-routing is that its performance depends on the network's geometric properties. In geometrically simple environments (e.g., Figure 1(a)), this approach produces shortest paths with state size independent of network size, offering limitless scalability. In other environments however (e.g., Figure 1(b)), it may have significantly increased stretch or state overhead.

Given the different characteristics of the two approaches, it is natural to ask: Which one is more desirable for a given network? Universal routing, either in its shortest-path or compact versions, is well understood, solidly verified, and location independent, while geo-routing may be more scalable in many situations, at the cost of being location dependent. What remains unknown is whether geo-routing is always more scalable for general network topology. Almost all geo-routing algorithms are evaluated using experiments based on a simple topology model, in which a small number of randomly placed rectangular obstacles/holes are created [18, 29, 5, 11, 12, 24, 25, 36]. However, it is not clear whether this simple model is powerful enough to expose the algorithms' limitations. The lack of a worst-case analysis thus makes a complete comparison between the two approaches difficult.

A rigorous analysis of an algorithm's limiting behavior requires establishing as tight as possible performance bounds for the algorithm. This is sometimes quite challenging: non-trivial lower bounds of stretch are known for only a few algorithms, out of the dozens published, and obtaining those bounds often requires very careful construction of network instances to stress the algorithm; see Kuhn's work [21, 22] for some excellent examples. As ingenious as they are, these constructions are on a case-by-case basis, providing little clue to the properties of other geo-routing methods.

In this paper we propose a novel *Trap Array (TA)* topology model that provides a unified framework for theoretical assessment of geo-routing algorithms. In this model, a network is composed of an array of components that attempt to 'trap' the routing process, so as to generate a high stretch. The model offers a number of features:

- Being *simple*, so that an algorithm's behavior can be easily understood and analyzed;

- Being *powerful*, in stressing an algorithm often to a level far beyond what is reported in the literature;

- Being *controllable*, by allowing a number of adjustable parameters to generate topologies of varying complexity, so that an algorithm's performance can be observed in a relatively full spectrum;

- Being *broadly applicable*, in that the model works for a variety of algorithms of distinct behaviors.

Using this model, we derive nontrivial stretch/state lower bounds[1] for ten representative geo-routing algorithms, namely

---

[1]The higher the stretch or per-node state, the worse the performance. Thus a lower bound on stretch/state suggests an upper bound on scalability.

GPSR [18], GOAFR+ [21], GDSTR [25], MDT [24], MAP [5], BVR [12], HopID [36], GEM [27], DRP [33], and CONVEX [32], with brief discussion on a few more. Most of these results are reported for the first time. The analytic results show that, somewhat surprisingly, many of the geo-routing algorithms can perform much worse than previously known, for example by producing polynomial stretch with polynomial per-node state. This *double polynomial* trade-off is obviously an undesirable outcome, compared to very basic routing algorithms which guarantee a constant bound on at least one term – for example a shortest-path/compact routing algorithm which guarantees a constant stretch, or a flooding based algorithm with constant per-node state (in which case the extended metric *transmission stretch* [12] should be considered).

Given the two approaches' advantages in different situations, we propose a new algorithm, named *Compact Geometric Routing (CGR)*, that attempts to get the best of both worlds. The key idea is simple: we organize the nodes into a two-level hierarchical structure, in which the lower level consists of clusters allowing purely greedy routing, and the higher level forms clusters based on network locality following the spirit of compact routing. We demonstrate CGR's advantages through analysis and simulation. For general graphs, our simulation shows that CGR generates average stretch below 1.07, and maximum stretch smaller than 4, for a wide range of parameter settings, where other algorithms may generate average/maximum stretch two orders of magnitudes higher. For algorithms with similar stretch performance, namely S4 and DRP, CGR uses dramatically less state, with a reduction of up to 85%.

The remainder of the paper is organized as follows: Section 2 describes related work; Section 3 establishes the TA topology model; Section 4 analyzes the performance bounds of various algorithms under the TA model; Section 5 describes the CGR algorithm, followed by simulation results in Section 6; Section 7 concludes the paper.

2. RELATED WORK

The many proposals for scalable wireless routing can be roughly divided into four (unnecessarily disjoint) categories.

Shortest-path routing. In this classical approach, a distributed form of Dijkstra's shortest path algorithm, such as Distance-Vector and Link-State [4], is used to find shortest paths. Every node stores its next hop on shortest path to every other node. For a network with N nodes, this requires $O(N)$ per-node state and $O(N^2)$ message traffic, posing a great challenge to the network's scalability. To reduce the overhead, an on-demand route discovery approach is proposed by Johnson and Maltz [17]. This algorithm uses flooding to find a route when needed, so intermediate nodes do not need to maintain up-to-date routing information. However, for applications requiring frequent route discovery, this approach incurs excessive traffic.

Near-shortest-path routing. Algorithms in this category no longer insist on shortest paths but instead try to bound the stretch with a small number, using significantly reduced per-node state. A systematic study on this problem is provided by the compact routing theory, which is primarily concerned with the fundamental stretch-state tradeoffs of general graphs. Since Peleg and Upfal's seminal work [28], numerous algorithms have been proposed to achieve different points in the tradeoff space [1, 2, 8, 10, 31]; see [14] for an overview. A few proposals have recently looked at how to translate the centralized algorithms into distributed and implementable protocols. For example, the S4 [26] protocol, based on Thorup and Zwick's stretch 3 routing scheme [31] (the TZ scheme), realizes compact routing on wireless ad hoc networks, with an emphasis on distributed control and failure resilience. Ford [13] evaluates an alternative distributed version of the TZ scheme with $\Theta(\log N)$ stretch and state. Other work (e.g., [30, 35]) has focused on different aspects of real systems such as flat names, mobility, etc.

Virtual Ring Routing (VRR) [6] maintains a logical network using techniques from DHTs. It uses roughly $O(\sqrt{N})$ per node state, but does not provide a bound on stretch for general topologies.

Hierarchical routing. Hierarchical routing (HR) attempts to reduce per-node state by recursively grouping nodes into *clusters*. An early proposal Landmark Routing (LR) [34], for example, uses a hierarchical set of landmark nodes that periodically send scoped messages for route discovery. In LR, a node only needs to hold state for their immediate neighbors and their next hop to each landmark. Other designs following a similar principle include Safari [9] and LANMAR [15]. Recently, an implementation by Iwanicki and Van Steen [16] confirms the practicality of HR in wireless sensor networks. With respect to stretch, HR suffers from the *boundary effect*, where two nodes nearby may fall in different clusters, so their route may have to go a long way through cluster heads, resulting in a large detour and hence unbounded stretch.

Geometric routing. Geo-routing algorithms mainly differ in the way local minima are dealt with. We classify the existing algorithms into four categories:

1. *Localized approach*, in which the algorithm routes off local minima with strictly local information, typically using a face routing method. The best known algorithms in this category are GFG [3], GPSR [18], and GOAFR+ [21].

2. *Abstracting approach*, in which the algorithm uses non-localized data structures to abstract the network's geometry, so as to provide guidance for the algorithm to avoid routing traps. Examples include GDSTR [25], MDT [24], and MAP [5].

3. *Embedding approach*, in which the algorithm embeds the network into a metric space. In this space, every node is assigned a set of coordinates on which geometric routing can be performed. The coordinates can be landmark-based (e.g., BVR [12], LCR [7], HopID [36]), Euclidean (e.g., NoGeo [29]), polar (e.g., GEM [27]), or hyperbolic (e.g., hyperbolic routing [20]).

4. *Partitioning approach*, in which the algorithm divides the network into relatively regular pieces where the geometry is simpler and hence greedy forwarding is efficient. The inter-piece routing is often guided by some global data structures. Examples in this category include GLIDER [11], CONVEX [32], and DRP [33].

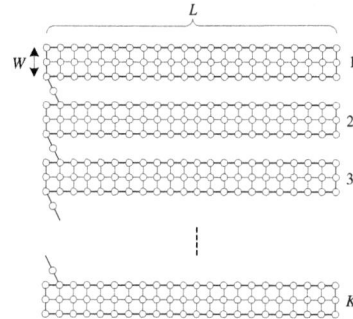

Figure 2: The basic TA model. The topology consists of K trap components each of length L and of constant width W, as well as $K-1$ bridges connecting the components.

3. THE TA TOPOLOGY MODEL

In this section we describe the structure of the TA model and the rationale behind its construction.

3.1 The model

The model assumes a multi-hop network with N nodes, each with a unique ID, on a 2D plane, forming an undirected graph G. Since we are pursuing lower bounds, we only need to concentrate on special graphs. We thus assume a unit disk graph (UDG) radio model, in which two nodes are connected if and only if their Euclidean distance is no larger than one. Furthermore, most of the nodes are placed in a grid pattern. Clearly, the lower bounds obtained under this simplified model carry over directly to general graphs.

Our goal is to characterize the algorithms' limiting behaviors, so we need a graph model that can stress the algorithms to varying extents. The main idea is to create 'traps' that lead the greedy forwarding in wrong directions repeatedly, so that a large stretch will be produced. These traps can indeed be very simple. Figure 2 shows a basic form of the model, consisting of an array of K trap components of length L each. Here the trap is simply a rectangular network of constant width W. The K components are connected by $K-1$ *bridges* of constant length.

This topology model generates what we call *trap array (TA) graphs* with several parameters: the width of a component W, the length of a trap component L, the number of trap components K, and *trap connectivity* – the way the trap components are connected. The parameter W is not critical and is chosen only for convenience of analysis; more often we will only adjust two parameters: K, which automatically determines L, and trap connectivity, which plays an important role in trapping the routing process.

The trap components are not always in a rectangular shape – they can be deformed when needed. Occasionally, some extra *helping components* such as a helping node may be used. These result in extended forms of the model.

3.2 Rationale behind the model

Node u is called a *local minimum (node) to node v* if u has no neighbor closer to v than u itself, in which case v is called u's *local minimum target*. When this is the case, we write $\mathcal{L}(u \to v) = 1$; otherwise $\mathcal{L}(u \to v) = 0$. Node u is called a *local minimum (node)* if there exists a node v such that

$\mathcal{L}(u \to v) = 1$. To quantify how frequently greedy routing fails in a network, we define the following measure:

DEFINITION 1. *The* Local Minimum Degree (LMD) *of a graph G is the number of node pairs u, v for which u is a local minimum to v, that is,*

$$\mathsf{LMD}(G) = \sum_{u,v \in V} \mathcal{L}(u \to v).$$

By definition, $0 \leq \mathsf{LMD}(G) < N^2$. The following result is easy to obtain.

LEMMA 1. *For a basic TA graph G as shown in Figure 2, $LMD(G) \in \Theta(K(K-1))$.*

When $K = 1$, the graph has no local minimum nodes, thus enables shortest-path geo-routing with constant per-node state. When K increases, G's LMD grows monotonically, until $K = \Theta(N)$ where the LMD reaches its maximum $\Theta(N^2)$, indicating that greedy routing will fail most frequently. It should be noted, however, that this does not mean an algorithm automatically produces its worst-case stretch at a maximum LMD, because generated path length does not entirely determine stretch. When local minima occur frequently, the shortest path length may also be growing, so the stretch does not necessarily change monotonically with K. Nevertheless, as our analysis and simulation will show, K (and hence LMD) can serve as a convenient 'control knob' for an algorithm's performance, which typically meets its worst case either at the ends (e.g., $O(N)$) or right in the middle (i.e., $O(\sqrt{N})$ of K's complexity range, and changes monotonically elsewhere. Thus, the TA model not only provides a framework for us to derive an algorithms' scaling properties, which may otherwise be elusive to obtain, but also offers an easily controllable tool for average case performance evaluation.

4. ALGORITHMS ANALYSIS

In this section we use the TA model to establish the stretch and state lower bounds for several algorithms. Since TA graphs are special cases of general graphs, these lower bounds naturally hold for general cases. Unnecessarily tight, these bounds will add to our understanding of the algorithms' performance in challenging cases. In the following we analyze ten algorithms picked from the four categories, namely GPSR [18], GOAFR+ [21], GDSTR [25], MDT [24], MAP [5], BVR [12], HopID [36], GEM [27], DRP [33], and CON-VEX [32]. The analysis uses two metrics:

- Hop stretch, defined for a node pair as the ratio of actually generated hop count to the minimum hop count. An algorithm's stretch for a network is the worst-case stretch for all node pairs. To take into account of the cost of flooding search during routing in some algorithms (e.g., BVR), we use an extended version of this metric, called the *transmission stretch* [12], defined for a node pair as the ratio of the number of actually transmitted packets during routing to the minimum hop count. Hereinafter we do not distinguish these two terms and simply call them *stretch*.

- State size, or simply state, measured by the number of routing table entries of individual nodes. A routing

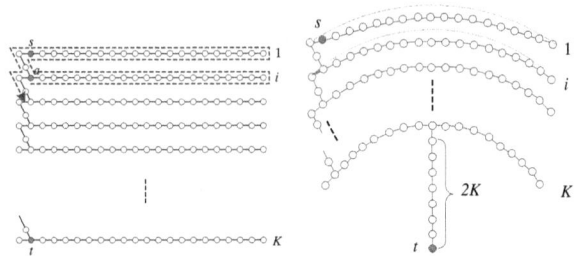

Figure 3: GPSR under the TA model. Figure 4: GOAFR+ under the TA model.

table entry mainly contains the next hop node ID, as well as some additional state information which varies from one algorithm to another. This difference however has limited effect on the scaling trend, so we use simply the number of entries to for asymptotical analysis. Our focus is on average node state, which is in line with the interest of compact routing theory, because worst-case state of a node is easy to derive (e.g., by constructing a network where there is a node with degree $\Theta(N)$).

4.1 The localized approach

GPSR uses greedy forwarding in the default mode; when encountering a local minimum, it executes a face routing algorithm on a planarized version of the original network. The face routing follows a fixed direction (e.g., following the right-hand rule), which makes it easy for the TA model to create traps.

THEOREM 2. *There exists a TA graph with $K > 1$ for which GPSR has stretch $\Omega(N)$.*

PROOF. Consider the graph in Figure 3 where a trap component is simply a linear sub-network of L nodes, and the K trap components are connected by bridges of length two. Let the second nodes of the first and last components be the source node s and target node t, respectively. Suppose that the route enters the ith bar at node a ($1 \leq i \leq K$). The algorithm will get stuck and start face routing from a. Assume the face routing uses right-hand rule (otherwise we can choose to place the bridges on the other side of the trap components), then the algorithm will follow the face path shown in blue dashed line. The length of this path has length $\Theta(i \cdot L)$; since the algorithm will traverse every component, the total path length from s to t is $\Theta(K^2 \cdot L)$. Observing that the shortest path between s and t is $\Theta(K)$, we have the stretch of the path $\Omega(K \cdot L) = \Omega(N)$. □

Kuhn et al. give an essentially equivalent lower bound with a significantly more complex construction [23]. In their result, the lower bound is expressed as $\Omega(c^2)$, where c is the minimum hop count between a node pair. Their topology contains a maze structure whose size is $\Theta(c^2)$ and can be up to $\Theta(N)$, so the lower bound $\Omega(c^2)$ is equivalent to $\Omega(N)$.

GOAFR+ is smarter than GFSR in that it tries to explore both directions of a face, so as to avoid the repeated backtracking in GPSR.

THEOREM 3. *There exists a TA graph for which GOAFR+ has stretch $\Omega(\frac{N}{N/K+K})$.*

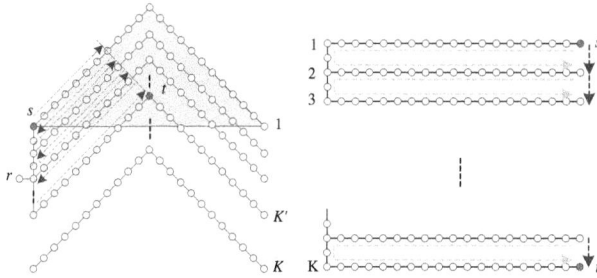

Figure 5: GDSTR under the TA model.

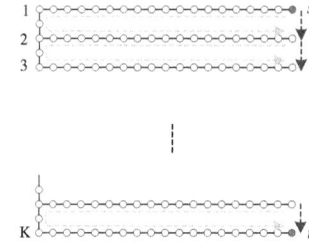

Figure 6: MDT under the TA model.

PROOF. In the construction shown in Figure 4, each trap component consists of a sequence of L nodes evenly placed on a curve. Let the nodes of the ith component be $n_{i,j}$, $1 \leq j \leq L$. The Euclidean distance between $n_{i,j}$ and t is denoted $d_{i,j}$. The nodes are arranged in such a way that $d_{i,1} > d_{i,2} > \ldots > d_{i,L/2} < d_{i,L/2+1} < \ldots < d_{i,L}$ and $d_{i,L/2} < d_{i+1,1}$. The curves can be created below the co-centric (red) arcs with spacing 2 centered at node t so that the bridges have length within a constant. (The curves are flatter than the co-centric arcs.) Pick source node $s = n_{1,2}$ and target node t as shown in the figure. The GOAFR+ route between s and t will be led to $n_{i,L/2}$ for every i. Therefore the total length of the route is $\Theta(N)$. Since the shortest path from s to t is of length $\Theta(L + K)$, the stretch is $\Omega(\frac{N}{L+K}) = \Omega(\frac{N}{N/K+K})$. □

Taking $K = \Theta(\sqrt{N})$ gives the following result.

COROLLARY 4. *There exist graphs for which GOAFR+ has stretch $\Omega(\sqrt{N})$.*

This result also agrees with Kuhn's result $\Omega(c)$ [21], where $c \in O(\sqrt{N})$. This lower bound actually applies to *any* localized geo-routing algorithms, because the greedy forwarding will have to visit at least a half of every trap component, covering a total of $\Omega(N)$ nodes. The shortest path between s and t can be $\Theta(\sqrt{N})$. Therefore the stretch lower bound is $\Omega(\sqrt{N})$.

4.2 The abstracting approach

GDSTR attempts to reduce per-node state by aggregating a group of nodes' addresses with convex hulls. The algorithm builds a *hull tree*, on which each node maintains a convex hull that contains its sub-tree nodes. By default the algorithm routes in a greedy mode; when local minima occur, it uses the convex hulls to avoid traversing sub-trees that do not contain the destination node.

THEOREM 5. *There exists a TA graph for which GDSTR has stretch $\Omega(\frac{\min(N/K,K)\cdot N}{N+K^2})$.*

PROOF. Consider the topology in Figure 5 where an additional node is created to serve as the root of the hull tree. The topology contains K trap components, each being two connected segments with angle $\pi/2$. Assume $K \in O(L)$. The target node t is on the top of the K'th component, where $K' = \min(\Theta(L), K)$. The algorithm will traverse all the yellow and shaded nodes. The total number of these nodes is $\min(\Theta(L^2), K \cdot L)$, and the shortest path between s and t is $\Theta(L + K)$. Thus the stretch is $\Omega(\frac{\min(L,K)\cdot L}{L+K}) = \Omega(\frac{\min(N/K,K)\cdot N}{N+K^2})$. □

In Theorem 5, taking $L = \Theta(\sqrt{N})$ and $K = \Theta(\sqrt{N})$ gives a stretch lower bound $O(\sqrt{N})$. GDSTR can opt to use multiple hull trees to reduce stretch. However, the construction in Figure 5 can be easily extended to handle this case by creating multiple root nodes and multiple groups of overlapping trap components, so the lower bound remains unchanged.

In its full version, GDSTR uses a mechanism called *conflicting hulls* in which a node maintains information about the set of convex hulls that intersect with its own. In Figure 5, assuming $L = \Theta(\sqrt{N})$ and $K = \Theta(\sqrt{N})$ we can verify that there are $\Theta(N)$ nodes each maintaining information about $\Theta(\sqrt{N})$ conflicting convex hulls. We thus have the following result.

COROLLARY 6. *There exist graphs for which GDSTR has stretch $\Omega(\sqrt{N})$, using $\Omega(\sqrt{N})$ average node state.*

Next we take a look at MDT. MDT is a protocol suite that maintains a multi-hop Delaunay triangulation (DT) structure over the network to guarantees data delivery. The DT structure comprises all the physical links and a set of *virtual links* that connect nodes beyond radio range with multi-hop paths.

THEOREM 7. *There exists a TA graph with $K > 1$ for which MDT has stretch $\Omega(\frac{N}{K+N/K})$, using $\Omega(N/K)$ average node state.*

PROOF. Construct a network with source node s and destination node t as shown in Figure 6. According to the requirement of DT, the end nodes of two neighboring trap components must be connected by a virtual link, which is of length $\Theta(L)$. To route from s to t, the algorithm will traverse $\Theta(K)$ such virtual links, covering $\Theta(N)$ nodes. So the stretch is $\Theta(\frac{N}{L+K}) = \Theta(\frac{N}{K+N/K})$. Also, there are $\Theta(N)$ nodes that have a virtual link of length $\Theta(N/K)$. □

In Theorem 7, taking $K = \Theta(\sqrt{N})$ gives the following result for MDT on general graphs.

COROLLARY 8. *There exist graphs for which MDT has stretch $\Omega(\sqrt{N})$ with $\Omega(\sqrt{N})$ average node state.*

Another notable algorithm that uses the abstracting approach is MAP [5]. This algorithm abstracts the network's global geometry using a medial axis based structure, which is stored at each node and serves as a guide for routing. In a TA graph of K trap components, this structure takes $\Omega(K)$ per-node state.

4.3 The embedding approach

The embedding approach assigns virtual coordinates to network nodes according to their connectivity relations, with no intention to recover the nodes' true positions. A TA graph after the embedding thus may look quite different from the original topology, making the TA graphs' 'trapping ability' less obvious. Nevertheless, we show that the connectivity pattern of the TA graphs still offers a way to test some of these algorithms.

THEOREM 9. *There exists a TA graph for which BVR has stretch $\Omega(N^{\min(2a,1)})$, assuming $\Theta(N^{1-a})(0 < a \leq 1)$ beacons.*

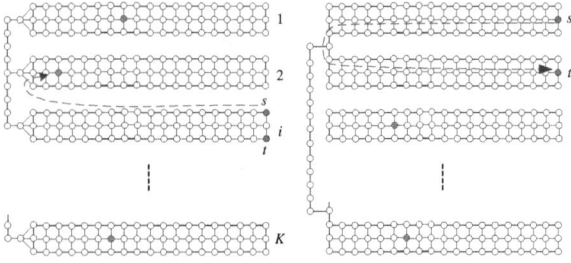

Figure 7: BVR under the TA model.

Figure 8: The TA model for HopID and GEM.

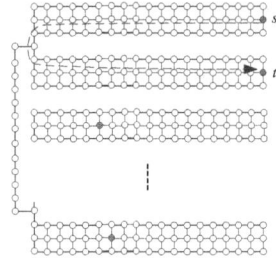

PROOF. Consider the topology shown in Figure 7. Assume the number of beacons $K' \in \Theta(N^{1-a})$. Let the width of the trap components be constant $W \geq 3$, and $K = K'+1$. By the pigeonhole principle, there exists a component, say the ith one, containing no beacon. So there are at least W nodes with exact the same coordinates. Let nodes s, t be two such nodes and that they are not neighbors, then to route from s to t, the packet needs to reach the closest beacon which is $\Omega(L)$ hops away, and then the algorithm performs scoped flooding within at least L hops. This flooding will cover $\min(N, \Omega(L^2))$ nodes, resulting in stretch $\min(N, \Omega(L^2)) = \min(N, \Omega((N/K)^2)) = \Omega(N^{\min(2a,1)})$. □

Furthermore, taking $a = 1/2$ produces a performance lower bound for BVR.

COROLLARY 10. *There exist cases where BVR has stretch $\Omega(N)$, using $\Omega(\sqrt{N})$ average node state.*

BVR's high stretch is due to *address ambiguity*, the fact that multiple nodes share the same coordinates and thus are indistinguishable in the new coordinate system. The weakly connected trap components of the TA model makes it easy to isolate the function of beacons as long as K is larger than the number of beacons. With $o(N)$ beacons for example, the TA model can set $K \in O(N)$ and generate instances where some nodes across different trap components share the same address, making the search for the destination node very expensive.

This challenge is also faced by other routing schemes using a beacon based mechanism, such as HopId [36] and LCR [7]. For HopID, we have the following result.

THEOREM 11. *There exists a TA graph for which HopID has stretch $\Omega(N^a)$, assuming $\Theta(N^{1-a})(0 < a \leq 1)$ beacons.*

PROOF. HopID deals with the address ambiguity problem with expanding ring flooding from where the greedy forwarding gets stuck. Assume HopID uses $K' \in \Theta(N^{1-a})$ beacons, then the TA model can set $K = 2(K'+1)$ in a TA graph shown in Figure 8. In this graph, the node pair s and t share the same coordinates, so flooding from s will go $\Theta(L)$ hops away in order to reach t, covering $\Theta(L^2)$ nodes. Since the shortest path between s and t has a length $\Theta(L)$, the stretch is $\Theta(L)$, or $\Omega(N^a)$. □

Setting $a = 1/2$ in Theorem 11 we obtain HopID's stretch lower bound $\Omega(\sqrt{N})$ with $\Omega(\sqrt{N})$ average node state.

The utility of the TA model also extends to the GEM algorithm [27], which routes on a polar coordinate system.

In effect, the routing scheme combines tree routing with a landmark-based localization method. The latter relies on three reference nodes, thus for a TA graph with a large enough K, the localization mechanism can be rendered useless for some trap components. This leads to the following result.

THEOREM 12. *There exists a TA graph for which GEM has stretch $\Omega(N)$, using constant average node state.*

PROOF. Consider again the example in Figure 8, where $K \geq 8$ and the top two components do not contain a reference node. We assume that the root is located on the middle of the leftmost line of nodes, and add an extra short-cut path of a constant length between s and t outside the trap components (not drawn). Following the tree routing (which omits the short-cut path), the generated path will be along the blue dashed line, which is of length $\Theta(N)$. Since the shortest path length between s and t is a constant, we have that the maximum stretch of GEM is $\Theta(N)$. □

NoGeo [29] is another well-known embedding method. Unfortunately it does not work for the TA model: it assumes a non-degenerate network boundary whereas a TA graph contains linear components. Especially, the TA model can generate a tree topology to which NoGeo has great difficulty adapting.

Finally, a graph can be embedded into a hyperbolic space [20] where greedy routing works with 100% success rate. However, it is pointed out in [20] that this approach can produce $\Theta(N)$ stretch, since hyperbolic embedding works on a spanning tree, where two nearby nodes may need to route to their common ancestor that is far away. The tree network can be easily constructed with the TA model.

4.4 The partitioning approach

In the partitioning approach, the network, often assumed to be fairly dense, is divided into relatively regular pieces where greedy routing works well. We look at a recent proposal [33] that uses a centralized planning method to minimally partition a network into LM-free components, called *greedily routing components (GRCs)* in their terminology. Each node then maintains a routing table entry for each part. In the basic TA model, an LM-free component contains at most a single trap component, so we easily have the following conclusion.

THEOREM 13. *There exists a TA graph for which DRP has average node state size $\Omega(N)$.*

PROOF. In Figure 9, the network can be decomposed to at least $\Theta(N)$ LM-free components. Since the per-node state size is linear with the number of components, we have the theorem. □

Other partitioning methods include GLIDER [11] and CONVEX [32]. The former divides the network into combinatorial Delaunay triangulation, while the latter uses convex pieces. It can be shown that neither can guarantee a constant stretch with $o(N)$ average node state.

4.5 Summary

A universal routing algorithm in its nature is independent of network topology, providing a constant vs. polynomial stretch-state tradeoff, regardless of K. This independence

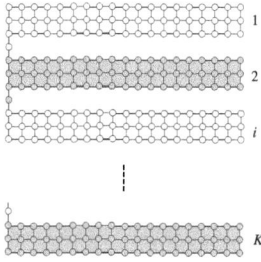

Figure 9: DRP under the TA model.

makes it robust to topological variations, but potentially miss opportunities of significant optimization, especially for a small K, where the network has a simple connectivity pattern. In contrast, geo-routing algorithms normally excel at a small K, while fall short for a large K (e.g., $O(\sqrt{N})$), to the extent of a highly undesirable double polynomial tradeoff between stretch and state. (Note that this is not always the case – for example MDT incurs the highest state overhead for $K = 2$.)

In short, universal routing and geo-routing exhibit huge gaps in performance for different network topologies, yielding no clear winner. This motivates us to leverage the benefits of the two approaches in a single design. In the next section we describe an algorithm for this goal.

5. CGR ALGORITHM

CGR works on general radio networks, without assuming a particular radio model and node distribution. It organizes the network into a two-level hierarchy by grouping nodes into clusters. At the high level, it behaves like a compact routing scheme, while at the low level, it uses geometric routing. A lower-level cluster, or *L-cluster*, is a connected sub-network that does not contain local minima for greedy routing within itself, and a higher-level cluster, or *H-cluster*, is the union of roughly $\sqrt{N'}$ nearby L-clusters, where N' is the number of L-clusters. CGR requires a node to maintain $O(\sqrt{N'})$ state on average. Figure 10 illustrates the network hierarchy.

In the following we describe CGR's main components. The hierarchical framework is similar to that of a classic HR algorithm, so we will focus on their differences and skip issues such as node dynamics already addressed in prior work (e.g., the real-system implementation in [16]).

5.1 L-Cluster Construction

In CGR, an L-cluster is actually a disk-like neighborhood network with a specified radius centered at some node, called the L-cluster's *header*. To minimize per-node state, CGR tries to minimize N', which means maximizing the size of L-clusters. To that end a header node needs to find a maximum radius R, such that its R-hop neighborhood is LM-free. To do so, the header checks the LM-freedom property of its neighborhood networks with incremental radii through centralized computation. Due to the limited computational resources, a small constant limit R_m (e.g., 3) is imposed on R. Though this limit appears very small, it can still bring a considerable gain in reducing node state. For example, suppose a network with average node degree 8 is divided into L-clusters with average radius 3, then an average L-cluster covers approximately 100 nodes, that is, $N' \approx N/100$. This

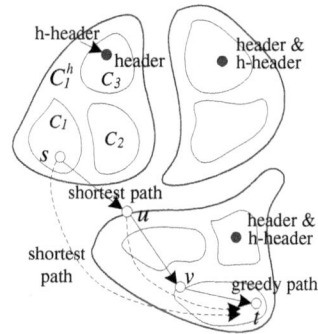

Figure 10: The two-level hierarchy of CGR. The L-clusters group nodes based on their geometric properties, and the H-clusters on network locality.

means that CGR needs only 1/10 as much per-node state as needed by the TZ/S4 compact routing scheme, which uses $O(\sqrt{N})$ per-node state.

The headers are selected in a randomized and distributed manner. Initially, each node in the network sets a timer whose length is chosen uniformly at random in $[0, T)$, where T is a system parameter. If during this period, a node is not suppressed by any other node, it declares itself a header. The new header broadcasts its status to the global network, suppressing all non-header nodes. When T is large, the above process behaves like a sequential algorithm; when T is small, headers will be selected with more parallelism. In the end of this process, every header will cover a subnetwork. Each header u then finds its R within its subnetwork, and notifies those cluster nodes of their membership associated with u. At the same time the nodes not in any cluster are released and re-start their timers specified earlier, making the header election and clustering process to continue. Eventually, every node u will be associated with a cluster C with a unique ID $ID(C)$.

5.2 Distributed L-Cluster Construction

A more aggressive, and naturally more expensive, version of L-cluster construction in CGR tries to remove the limit R_m, using a distributed *Local Minimum Freedom Checking* (LMFC) protocol to create larger L-clusters. The protocol is based on the Cross Link Deletion Protocol (CLDP) [19]. CLDP is designed to planarize a wireless network, regardless of radio irregularities. The protocol is quite simple: a probe is sent over each link to see if it is crossed by other links. A probe initially contains the coordinates of a link's endpoints, and proceeds on the graph following the right-hand rule. In a CLDP-stable network, every node has a number of adjacent faces. For example, the node labeled 'header' in Figure 11 has six adjacent faces.

Our LMFC protocol runs on a planar network generated by CLDP and sends probes along nodes' faces in a similar way, also following the right-hand rule. Assume a probe walks along some face f_i of node u, represented by a cycle of *face links* $(u, v_1), (v_1, v_2), \ldots, (v_k, u)$. The probe contains the coordinates of u and all of u's neighbors, and when traversing a face link (v_i, v_j), the protocol checks whether this link contains a point that is u's local minimum target. The following lemma explains why this routine is useful.

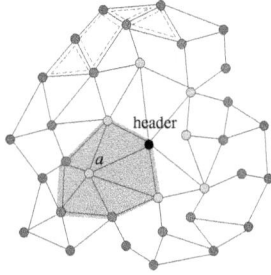

Figure 11: 1, 2, and 3-hop neighborhoods and faces.

LEMMA 14. *If node u does not have a face link containing a local minimum target, then it is not a local minimum.*

Lemma 14 provides a sufficient condition for a node to be non-local minimum. Using this method, most nodes only need to send packets around their local faces. For example, in Figure 11 the node a only need to probe the links covered by the gray area. Our simulation experiments show the involved message cost is very moderate, even without considering message aggregation, which is an obvious optimization to the basic design.

Given a header in some surrounding subnetwork, the header first floods the subnetwork, asking the nodes to start CLDP and then LMFC. The flood creates a shortest path tree, called the *command tree*, within the neighborhood. When a node's probes finish traversing all of its adjacent faces, the node reports to its flooding parent. The header collects reports from its descendants and finally decides whether the subnetwork is LM-free.

Based on the LMFC protocol, we use a simple technique to determine the maximum R in multiple rounds. For a step size parameter h (e.g., $h = 3$), the header checks the LM freedom property for neighborhood radii $h, 2h, 3h, \ldots$, until the network is no longer LM-free. Then the header chooses the latest successful R as its cluster radius.

It should be noted that CLDP and LMFC need not be executed on every node for every round. A face F with x nodes is called an *interior face*, if F is a simple polygon and the sum of its inner angles is $(x-2)\pi$ (which excludes the outer boundary face); see the blue dashed polygons in Figure 11) for some examples. A node can easily decide whether an adjacent face F is interior with the probing packet traversing F. Suppose the header starts a new round to test the r'th hop neighborhood after finishing testing the rth hop neighborhood. For $r' > r$, then all interior faces from the last round will stay idle – that is, no node will send probing packets along these faces. With this optimization, message cost will be much reduced.

5.3 H-cluster construction

An H-cluster is simply a union of several nearby L-clusters, created in a way similar to Voronoi Diagrams. In the following we describe the details.

If a node u in some L-cluster C has a neighbor u' from a different L-cluster, it is called a *boundary node* of C, and this node reports to its header following parent links; the header then remembers the first reporting node u and associates its location $loc(u)$ with the neighboring cluster. This piece of information helps to build *virtual links* between headers: a header can route to its neighboring header along two seg-

ments of paths connected by u and u', using greedy forwarding. The headers and their virtual links then form a high-level overlay network G'.

In G', a node is called an *h-node*. Two h-nodes have an h-distance of one if their corresponding L-clusters have neighboring nodes. G' continuously executes several simple routines:

1. Virtual links maintenance. The h-nodes periodically send hello messages over the virtual links to determine the status of neighbors, so as to keep a relatively up-to-date local view of G'.

2. Network size estimate. Every h-node periodically broadcasts in G' with some small and fixed probability p (e.g., $p = 0.1$); every h-node then estimate G'''s size N' by counting the heard broadcast messages and times the number by $1/p$.

3. H-headers election. The N' h-nodes elect $\sqrt{N'}$ *h-headers* in a probabilistic way following the method in [12, 26, 36], which adapts to node joins and leaves.

4. H-cluster construction based on Voronoi Diagram principle. The h-headers broadcast in G', and each h-node records its h-distance to its closest h-header, ties bing broken randomly. Every h-header u creates a group $H(u)$ comprising all the h-nodes that find u the closest among all the h-headers. For $H(u)$, the union of its members' corresponding H-clusters constitutes an H-cluster, denoted by $C^h(u)$.

The h-header will broadcast within $C^h(u)$ to notify each node of $C^h(u)$'s unique ID. By the way it collects reports from the nodes and obtains $C^h(u)$'s radius. Figure 10 gives an illustration of the two-level hierarchy. After the network finishes initialization, every node u will have an address in the form $\langle ID(C^h(u)), ID(C(u)), ID(u) \rangle$, where $ID(C^h(u))$, $ID(C(u))$ and $ID(u)$ represent the IDs of its H-cluster, L-cluster, and itself, respectively.

5.4 Boundary-synchronized broadcast

CGR borrows the technique of boundary-synchronized broadcast from [33] to realize constant stretch routing on the higher level network G'. This technique achieves the same effect as the TZ scheme offers; it is chosen over the latter because it fits better in the hierarchical structure. The main idea is to enable every node to route to every external cluster C, rather than to C's header, along a shortest path. This is realized by having all the boundary nodes of C to flood a message at (approximately) the same time, as though the flood were initiated by a single virtual node.

In CGR, the header of C performs a boundary-synchronized (or C-synchronized) broadcast as follows. It first broadcasts a message within C containing a time value $t_b = r_C \times \bar{t}$, where r_C is C's radius and $\bar{t}$ is a (possibly loose) upper bound for average transmission time between two nodes. After receiving the message, a node updates t_b with $\max(t_b - \bar{t}, 0)$ before it sends the message further away. Every boundary node of C then waits the amount of time specified by t_b before it starts broadcasting a message containing $ID(C)$. The broadcast message contains a hop counter initialized to 0. If a node outside C receives such a message for the first time, or finds that the received hop counter indicates a smaller distance to C than previously recorded, it increments the counter, takes it as its new distance to C, saves the sending node's ID, and further broadcasts the message.

The synchronization need not be perfect for the algorithm to be correct. It is mainly for the sake of minimizing message cost. When those nodes are well synchronized, then a cluster-synchronized broadcast would cost nearly the same message transmissions as caused by a traditional flood from the header.

With this primitive, every h-header u^h performs a $C^h(u^h)$-synchronized broadcast in the global network, and every header u performs a $C(u)$-synchronized broadcast within $C^h(u)$. As a result, every node u learns the next-hop node on shortest path to each C^h and the next-hop node on shortest path to each C within $C^h(u)$. The size of u's routing table is proportional to the number of H-clusters plus the number of L-clusters among $C^h(u)$.

5.5 CGR routing

Assume a source node s knows a destination node t's address. CGR works as follows:

1. If the current node (initially s) belongs to $C(t)$, then route greedily to t;

2. Else if the current node belongs to $C^h(t)$, then route to $C(t)$ along shortest path; upon reaching $C(t)$, go to 1;

3. Else, route to $C^h(t)$ along the shortest path; upon reaching $C^h(t)$, go to 2.

5.6 Steady-state performance analysis

We consider a TA graph (in any form shown in Section 4) where CGR's hierarchy is stable. For convenience of analysis we assume that the L-clusters are formed sequentially.

THEOREM 15. *For a TA graph G with K trap components (in any form shown in Section 4), CGR achieves stretch no greater than 7 with $O(\sqrt{K})$ average node state.*

PROOF. For a TA graph, CGR will produce $O(K)$ L-clusters. These give rise to $O(\sqrt{K})$ H-clusters, each comprising $O(\sqrt{K})$ L-clusters on average. Each node u in the network maintains a pointer to every H-cluster C^h and every L-cluster in $C^h(u)$, amounting to $O(\sqrt{K})$ average state.

As for stretch, consider the general case where two nodes s and t are in different H-clusters (Figure 10). Suppose that s's shortest path to $C^h(t)$ joins $C^h(t)$ at node u, and u's shortest path to $C(t)$ joins $C(t)$ at node v. Let $L^{sp}(x,y)$, $L^{cgr}(x,y)$, and $L^g(x,y)$ denote the hop counts of a shortest path, a CGR-produced path, and a greedy path, respectively. Observe that in an L-cluster in a TA graph, greedy routing always produces shortest paths, that is $L^{sp}(x,y) = L^g(x,y)$. Then we have,

$$
\begin{aligned}
L^{cgr}(s,t) &= L^{sp}(s,u) + L^{sp}(u,v) + L^g(v,t) \\
&= L^{sp}(s,u) + L^{sp}(u,v) + L^{sp}(v,t) \\
&\leq L^{sp}(s,u) + 2L^{sp}(u,v) + L^{sp}(u,t) \\
&\qquad \text{(triangle inequality)} \\
&\leq L^{sp}(s,u) + 3L^{sp}(u,t) \\
&\leq 4L^{sp}(s,u) + 3L^{sp}(s,t) \quad \text{(triangle inequality)} \\
&\leq 7L^{sp}(s,t).
\end{aligned}
$$

Thus the stretch is small than 7. □

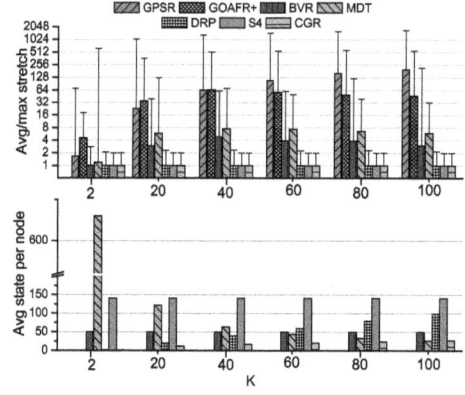

Figure 12: Performance under the TA model. Stretch is on a logarithmic scale.

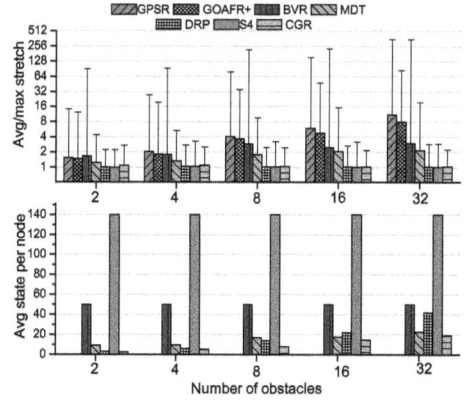

Figure 13: Performance under the obstacle model. Stretch is on a logarithmic scale.

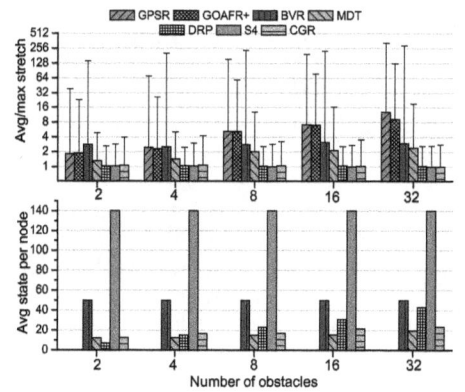

Figure 14: Performance under the obstacle+rand model. Stretch is on a logarithmic scale.

We will show by simulation that CGR's average stretch is very close to 1 for a wide range of network topologies. CGR's per node state depends on the number of L-clusters, which in turn depends the network's geometric structure; the average per-node state is upper bounded by $O(\sqrt{N})$.

6. SIMULATION

We conduct high-level simulations to study the *average* performance of various algorithms. The emphasis is on the performance impact of network geometry, a factor that has not been studied in its full depth in the past. The evaluation is concentrated on two questions:

1. How effective is the TA model in showing various algorithms' performance limits, in comparison with alternative models?

2. How does CGR compare with previous algorithms under different models?

We consider three topology models: (1) the TA model; (2) the *obstacle model*, which is widely used in previous studies [18, 29, 5, 11, 12, 24, 25, 36]. This model contains a varying number of randomly generated rectangular holes provided the network field is not disconnected (see an illustration in Figure 1). The basic obstacle mode uses the ideal UDG radio which allows us to concentrate on the influence of obstacles alone; (3) the *obstacle+rand* model, which is more realistic, using a non-uniform quasi-UDG radio model and randomized node placement.

By default CGR uses the distributed version of L-cluster construction. The network has a size 5,000 with average node degree around 8, and for all network instances we randomly pick 50,000 node pairs for calculating stretch statistics. When an algorithm involves a randomized part, such as landmark selection, we run the algorithm 100 times and report the aggregate statistics. CGR is compared against six algorithms, including GPSR, GOAFR+, MDT, BVR, DRP as representatives of the four types of geo-routing algorithms, and the S4 algorithm as a representative of universal routing. (Note that DRP uses a centralized process to partition the network.) For BVR, we select 1% of the nodes as beacons, following the default setting in its original paper.

6.1 Effectiveness of the TA model

6.1.1 Stress test ability.

Figures 12, 13, 14 present the average stretch/state of the seven algorithms under the three models. In general, *the TA model produces a 10 times wider range of stretch and a 4 times wider range of state than the obstacle models do.* For example, for MDT, the state under TA is some 28 times higher than under the obstacle model. With the TA model, it is easy to further increase K to quickly boost the stretch or state, while under the obstacle models, the network layout becomes quite complex at 32 obstacles, beyond which the performance trends start flattening due to decreased spaces for newly generated obstacles, which cause smaller disturbance to the algorithms. The large gaps in generated performance ranges indicate the TA model's power in exposing the algorithms's hidden limitations, which the traditional models are unable to show.

6.1.2 Controllability.

A close examination can show that the algorithms' average performance trends generated under the TA model agree well with the worst-case analysis in Section 4. For example, Theorem 3 gives GOAFR+'s worst-case stretch $\Omega(\frac{N}{N/K+K})$, which reaches its highest for $K = \Theta(N)$. A corresponding peak can be found from the simulation results in Figures 12, where GOAFR+'s average stretch is maximal around $70 \approx \sqrt{N}$ ($N = 5000$ in our case). A similar correspondence can be found for MDT, which finds its highest stretch at $K = \sqrt{N}$ and highest state at $K = 2$ for both worst and average cases. Moreover, under the TA model the average performance of all the algorithms changes monotonically before or after the peaks. The above results suggests that *the TA model has good controllability in tuning an algorithm's general performance.* In contrast, the obstacle models generate less deterministic trends for average performance, in addition to its serious drawback in theoretical tractability.

6.2 Performance of CGR

6.2.1 Stretch and state

Figure 12 shows the stretch results under the TA model with $W = 2$ (notice the logarithmic scale of the y-axis). It can be seen that CGR produces average stretch very close to 1 in all cases, comparable with that of S4 and DRP. In contrast, other algorithms' stretch grows steadily with K, reaching maximum at various points, before starting to decline. For example, GPSR's stretch grows almost linearly with K in the TA model, while other algorithms except DRP and S4 show an average stretch many times higher. In terms of worst-case stretch, the difference is even greater, often up to two orders of magnitudes.

Figure 12 also shows the per-node state of the algorithms (see lower half), measured by the average number of routing table entries to non-local destinations. Both GPSR and GOAFR+ do not maintain state for non-local nodes, thus their results are all zero. In all cases except for MDT with $K > 100$, CGR uses the least state, often several times lower. For MDT, it can be seen that its state is the highest when $K = 2$, where the corresponding L is the largest and MDT uses the longest virtual links.

It is also interesting to compare the state of DRP, S4, and CGR, whose stretch performance is very close to each other. The three algorithms all use address aggregation to reduce state; the difference is that DRP uses the nodes' geometrical properties, S4 uses the nodes' locality properties, while CGR uses both. As a result CGR more aggressively reduces the state and achieves much better performance.

Figures 13 show the stretch and state under the obstacle model with up to 32 obstacles. Compared to other algorithms, CGR remains advantageous with remarkable improvements. For the obstacle+rand model, Figure 14 shows the results of an example setting, where the quasi-UDG parameter $\alpha = 0.25$, the nodes are randomly distributed. In this setting, CGR is among the three algorithms whose average stretch stays close to 1. To achieve this performance CGR uses much less per-node state than the other two. CGR's per-node state is slightly higher only when compared to MDT. This is because the increased connectivity irregularity causes CGR to generate more L-clusters, thus increasing nodes' average state. On the contrary MDT is less affected by local connectivity pattern than by large obstacles.

We have also tried different α values, node density, number of obstacles, as well as a uniform random node distri-

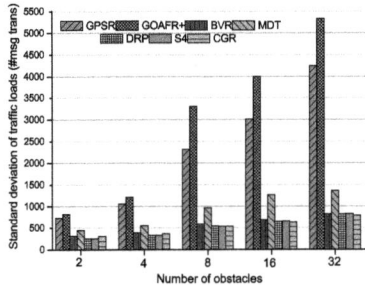

Figure 15: Standard deviation of traffic loads on nodes.

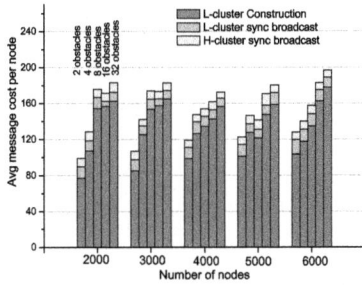

Figure 16: CGR's average message cost per node during setup.

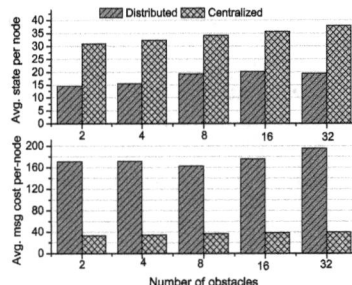

Figure 17: Centralized vs. distributed L-cluster construction in CGR.

bution, which produce similar performance trends. Generally, when the local connectivity becomes more irregular, caused by for example a larger α or a lower node density, CGR generates more L-clusters, thus increasing the state on the nodes. CGR is outperformed by only MDT on some occasions. In spite of this, CGR's per-node state is upper bounded by $O(\sqrt{N})$, which is significantly lower than MDT's $O(N)$ state in the worst case. In terms of stretch, CGR remains close to optimal when these factors change, owing to the efficient greedy forwarding within L-clusters.

6.2.2 Load balance

In this section we examine the load balancing performance of the algorithms, measured by the standard deviation of message transmissions by individual nodes. Figure 15 shows the result for the obstacle+rand topology model. It can be seen that GPSR and GOAFR+ have the worst load balancing, because they perform frequent face routing around the obstacles and thus place heavy burdens on the boundary nodes. MDT is better than these two algorithms, but is still noticeably high among the algorithms, due to its extensive use of virtual links which are also created around the obstacles. BVR uses beacons that tend to attract undue traffic, but its flooding based local minimum rescue method, which is invoked frequently in our cases, effectively spreads the traffic out, thus produces good load balancing. The remaining three algorithms, DRP, S4, and CGR have very similar performance in load balancing.

6.2.3 Setup message cost

Certainly, CGR's advantage in stretch and state comes with increased message cost, compared to for example localized algorithms such as GPSR. In this section we perform a rough estimate to see whether the cost is reasonable. CGR's setup cost is measured by the average message transmission count of a node. Our purpose here is to get a sense of the general trend, and to identify the main factors of cost. As such we focus on the message traffic incurred by the flooding operations, either scoped or network-wide. More accurate evaluation needs to consider the penalty of retransmission and the possible benefit of message aggregation (during CLDP probing), whose mixed effect will not be clear until a real system implementation is available. We leave that to future work.

Figure 16 shows a breakdown of CGR's message cost by L-

cluster construction, L-cluster-synchronized broadcast, and H-cluster-synchronized broadcast, as a function of network size and obstacle count, under the obstacle+rand topology model. We make two main observations. First, the average message cost per node ranges from 98.4 to 196.8, and tends to be higher for more obstacles. To put things in perspective, the per-node message cost ranges from 3.3% to 4.9% of the network size. Second, the majority of the message transmissions is from L-cluster construction, which involves L-cluster header election/control and CLDP probing. A closer examination shows that the latter costs more than the former. This cost can be reduced by using message aggregation, which we will explore in the future work.

6.2.4 Centralized vs. distributed L-cluster construction

The centralized version of L-cluster construction is simple to implement, but tends to generate many small L-clusters, whereas the distributed version is more traffic intensive but will generate larger L-clusters. (Both versions generate stretch very close to one.) Figure 17 depicts the per-node state and message cost for the two methods under the obstacle+rand model with a fixed network size 5000. The maximum radius R_m for the centralized L-cluster construction is set to 3. As expected, the centralized method imposes higher state on the nodes, with an increase of at least 80%. In the generated hierarchical structure, the L-clusters generated by the centralized method mostly have between 40 and 50 nodes, a size amenable to centralized processing. In terms of message cost, the centralized method is much lower than that of distributed one, due to its avoidance of message probing as required by the CLDP/LMFC protocols.

7. CONCLUSION

It is well known that geo-routing algorithms tend to perform worse with increasing irregularity of network geometry. The trend, however, has only been vaguely understood due to the lack of a proper measure for geometrical complexity, and of a topology model that embodies such a notion. We have presented the TA model that meets the need and enables us to conveniently establish performance bounds of representative geo-routing algorithms. Apart from a set of results for specific algorithms, the TA model is of interest in its own right and will hopefully lend itself to the study of other geo-routing algorithms.

We have also presented a new routing algorithm, CGR, that attempts to combine the strengths of both geometric and compact routing. Simulation experiments show its advantages over a number of previous algorithms. In the future we plan to implement the algorithm on real systems to finally bridge the gap between theory and practice.

8. ACKNOWLEDGMENTS

We thank the anonymous reviewers for their insightful comments. Guang Tan's work was supported in part by Natural Science Foundation of China (NSFC) under grant 61103243, by the Youth Innovation Promotion Association, Chinese Academy of Sciences, by the Ministry of Science and Technology 863 Key Project No. 2011AA010500, and by Shenzhen Overseas High-level Talents Innovation and Entrepreneurship Funds KQC201109050097A. Hongbo Jiang's work was supported in part by the NSFC under Grants 61073147 and 61271226, by the Fundamental Research Funds for the Central Universities under Grant 2011QN014, and by the Program for New Century Excellent Talents in University under Grant NCET-10-408.

9. REFERENCES

[1] B. Awerbuch, A. Bar-Noy, N. Linial, and D. Peleg. Improved routing strategies with succinct tables. *Journal of Algorithms.* 11(3):307–341, 1990.

[2] B. Awerbuch and D. Peleg. Routing with polynomial communication-space trade-off. *SIAM Journal on Discrete Mathematics*, 5(2):151-162, 1992.

[3] P. Bose, P. Morin, I. Stojmenovic and J. Urrutia. Routing with guaranteed delivery in ad hoc wireless networks. *Proc. of DIALM'99.*

[4] J. Broch, D. A. Maltz, D. B. Johnson, Y.-C. Hu, and J. Jetcheva. A Performance Comparison of Multi-Hop Wireless Ad Hoc Network Routing Protocols. *Proc. of MobiCom 1998.*

[5] J. Bruck, J. Gao, A. Jiang. MAP: Medial Axis Based Geometric Routing in Sensor Networks, *Proc. of MobiCom 2005.*

[6] M. Caesar, M. Castro, E. Nightingale, G. O'Shea, and A. Rowstron. Virtual ring routing: network routing inspired by DHTs. *Proc. of ACM SIGCOMM 2006.*

[7] Q. Cao and T. Abdelzaher. A scalable logical coordinates framework for routing in wireless sensor networks. *Proc. of IEEE Real-Time Systems Symposium (RTSS) 2004.*

[8] L. Cowen. Compact routing with minimum stretch. *Journal of Algorithms*, pages 170-183, 2001.

[9] S. Du, A. Khan, S. PalChaudhuri, A. Post, A. K. Saha, P. Druschel, D. B. Johnson, R. Riedi. Safari: A self-organizing, hierarchical architecture for scalable ad hoc networking. *Elsevier Ad Hoc Networks Journal*, 2007.

[10] T. Eilam, C. Gavoille, and D. Peleg. Compact routing schemes with low stretch factor. *Proc. of the ACM PODC 1998.*

[11] Q. Fang, J. Gao, L. Guibas, V. de Silva, and L. Zhang. GLIDER: Gradient landmark-based distributed routing for sensor networks. *Proc. INFOCOM 2005.*

[12] R. Fonseca, S. Ratnasamy, J. Zhao, C. T. Ee, D. Culler, S. Shenker, and I. Stoica. Beacon vector routing: Scalable point-to-point routing in wireless sensornets. *Proc. of NSDI 2005.*

[13] B. A. Ford. UIA: A Global Connectivity Architecture for Mobile Personal Devices. PhD thesis, Massachusetts Institute of Technology, September 2008.

[14] C. Gavoille. Routing in distributed networks: overview and open problems. *ACM SIGACT News – Distributed computing column*, 32(1):36-52, 2001.

[15] M. Gerla, X. Hong, and G. Pei. Landmark routing for large ad hoc wireless networks. *Proc. of Globecom*, 2000.

[16] K. Iwanicki and M. van Steen. On Hierarchical Routing in Wireless Sensor Networks. *Proc. of ACM/IEEE International Conference on Information Processing in Sensor Networks (IPSN)* 2009.

[17] D. B. Johnson and D. A. Maltz. Dynamic source routing in ad hoc wireless networks. *Mobile Computing*, edited by Tomasz Imielinski and Hank Korth, chapter 5, pages 153-181. Kluwer Academic Publishers, 1996.

[18] B. Karp and H. T. Kung. GPSR: Greedy perimeter stateless routing for wireless networks. *Proc. of MobiCom 2000.*

[19] Y-J Kim, R. Govindan, B. Karp, and S. Shenker. Geographic Routing Made Practical. *Proc. of NSDI 2005.*

[20] R. Kleinberg. Geographic Routing Using Hyperbolic Space. *Proc. of INFOCOM 2007.*

[21] F. Kuhn, R. Wattenhofer, Y. Zhang, and A. Zollinger. Geometric Ad Hoc Routing: Of Theory and Practice. *Proc. of ACM PODC*, 2003.

[22] F. Kuhn, R. Wattenhofer, and A. Zollinger. An Asymptotically Optimal Geometric Mobile Ad Hoc Routing. *Proc. of ACM DIALM-POMC 2002.*

[23] F. Kuhn, R. Wattenhofer, and A. Zollinger. Worst-Case Optimal and Average-Case Efficient Geometric Ad-Hoc Routing. *Proc. of ACM MobiHoc 2003.*

[24] S. S. Lam and C. Qian. Geographic Routing in d-dimensional Spaces with Guaranteed Delivery and Low Stretch. *Proc. Sigmetrics 2011.*

[25] B. Leong, B. Liskov, and R. Morris. Geographic Routing without Planarization. In *NSDI 2006.*

[26] Y. Mao, F. Wang, L. Qiu, S. S. Lam, and J. M. Smith. S4: Small state and small stretch routing protocol for large wireless sensor networks. In *Proc. of NSDI 2007.*

[27] J. Newsome and D. Song. Gem: Graph embedding for routing and data-centric storage in sensor networks without geographic information. In *Proc. of SenSys 2003.*

[28] D. Peleg and E. Upfal. A trade-off between space and efficiency for routing tables. *Journal of the ACM*, 36(3), 1989.

[29] A. Rao, S. Ratnasamy, C. Papadimitriou, S. Shenker, and I. Stoica. Geographic routing without location information. In *MobiCom 2003.*

[30] A. Singla, P. B. Godfrey, K. Fall, G. Iannaccone, and S. Ratnasamy. Scalable Routing on Flat Names. *Proc. of CoNext 2010.*

[31] M. Thorup and U. Zwick. Compact routing schemes. In *Proc. of ACM SPAA 2001.*

[32] G. Tan, M. Bertier and A-M. Kermarrec. Convex Partition of Sensor Networks and Its Use in Virtual Coordinate Geographic Routing. *Proc. of INFOCOM 2009.*

[33] G. Tan and A-M. Kermarrec. Greedy Geographic Routing in Large-Scale Sensor Networks: A Minimum Network Decomposition Approach. *IEEE/ACM Trans. on Networking*, 20(3): 864-877, 2012.

[34] P. F. Tsuchiya. The landmark hierarchy: a new hierarchy for routing in very large networks. *Proc. of SIGCOMM 1988.*

[35] C. Westphal and J. Kempf. A compact routing architecture for mobility. *Proc. of MobiArch*, 2008.

[36] Y. Zhao, Y. Chen, B. Li, and Q. Zhang. Hop ID: A Virtual Coordinate-Based Routing for Sparse Mobile Ad Hoc Networks. *IEEE Trans. on Mobile Computing*, 6(9), 2007.

A Tale of Two Metrics:
Simultaneous Bounds on Competitiveness and Regret

Lachlan Andrew
Swinburne University of Technology

Minghong Lin
Caltech

Adam Meyerson
Google Inc.

Siddharth Barman
Caltech

Katrina Liggett
Caltech

Alan Roytman
UCLA

Adam Wierman
Caltech

1. INTRODUCTION

We consider algorithms for "smoothed online convex optimization" (SOCO) problems, which are a hybrid between online convex optimization (OCO) and metrical task system (MTS) problems. Historically, the performance metric for OCO was regret and that for MTS was competitive ratio (CR). There are algorithms with either sublinear regret or constant CR, but no known algorithm achieves both simultaneously. We show that this is a fundamental limitation – no algorithm (deterministic or randomized) can achieve sublinear regret and a constant CR, even when the objective functions are linear and the decision space is one dimensional. However, we present an algorithm that, for the important one dimensional case, provides sublinear regret and a CR that grows arbitrarily slowly.

A SOCO problem is defined as follows. There is a convex decision/action space $F \subseteq (\mathbb{R}^+)^n$ and a sequence of cost functions $\{c^1, c^2, \dots\}$, where each $c^t : F \to \mathbb{R}^+$. At each time t, a learner/algorithm chooses an action vector $x^t \in F$ and the environment chooses a cost function c^t. The algorithm is then evaluated on the cost function and pays a *switching cost* corresponding to the difference between the actions.

The main difference between regret and CR is that the former compares the performance of an algorithm to that of the *static* optimal solution, while the latter compares with the *dynamic* optimal solution. It is desirable for an algorithm to perform well relative to both benchmarks. For example, in machine learning, the former is appropriate if the concept being learned is static, while the latter is appropriate if the concept is dynamic; if it is not known a priori whether the concept is static or dynamic, then it is important to have an algorithm that performs well in both cases.

OCO and MTS were connected in [1], which studies the special case of fixed and constant switching costs. It shows how to translate bounds on regret into bounds on the CR, and vice versa. Later, [2] used a primal-dual approach to develop an algorithm for the "α-unfair competitive ratio," a hybrid of the CR and regret defined below. The algorithm allows a tradeoff, but does not *simultaneously* perform well for regret and CR. There is also work achieving simultaneous guarantees with respect to the static and dynamic optimal solutions in other settings, e.g., [3], and there have been some attempts to use algorithmic approaches from machine learning in the context of MTSs [4, 5].

We consider several measures of cost. All are special cases of the α-*penalized cost with lookahead* i,

$$C_i^\alpha(A) = \mathbb{E}\left[\sum_{t=1}^{T} c^t(x^{t+i}) + \alpha\|x^{t+i} - x^{t+i-1}\|\right].$$

When α is omitted, it is assumed to be 1.

Within the OCO literature, the typical benchmark that is compared against is the optimal offline static action, i.e.,

$$OPT_s := \min_{x \in F} \sum_{t=1}^{T} c^t(x).$$

The *regret* of an online learning algorithm is defined as the (additive) difference between its cost and the cost of the optimal static action vector. Specifically, the regret of Algorithm A on instances $\mathfrak{C}$, $R^0(A)$, is less than $\rho(T)$ if for any sequence of cost functions $(c^1, \dots, c^T) \in \mathfrak{C}$,

$$C_0^0(A) - OPT_s \le \rho(T) \qquad (1)$$

In this traditional definition of regret, there is no switching costs or lookahead. A natural generalization is $R_i(A)$ for which $C_0^0(A)$ is replaced by $C_i^1(A)$ in (1).

Within the MTS literature, the typical benchmark that is compared against is the optimal offline (dynamic) solution:

$$OPT_d := \min_{x \in F^T} \sum_{t=1}^{T} c^t(x^t) + \|x^t - x^{t-1}\|.$$

Note that the minimal cost is the same regardless of lookahead since the cost functions are fixed.

The *competitive ratio* compares the cost of an algorithm to that of the offline optimal. The cost typically considered is $C_1(A)$, but more generally the competitive ratio with lookahead i, denoted by $CR_i(A)$, is $\rho(T)$ if for any sequence of cost functions $(c^1, \dots, c^T) \in \mathfrak{C}$

$$C_i(A) \le \rho(T)OPT_d + O(1). \qquad (2)$$

The case of $i = 1$ corresponds to the typical CR studied in the MTS literature.

There are a variety of options for bridging the use of OPT_s by regret and of OPT_d by CR. For example, Adaptive-Regret [6] is defined as the maximum regret over any interval, where the "static" optimum can differ for different intervals, and Internal regret [7] compares the online policy against a simple perturbation of that policy. The metric we use is the α-*unfair competitive ratio* [1,2,8], and we denote it with $CR_i^\alpha(A)$ in the case of i-lookahead. Formally, $CR_i^\alpha(A)$ is defined exactly the same as the competitive ratio

SIGMETRICS'13, June 17–21, 2013, Pittsburgh, PA, USA.
ACM 978-1-4503-1900-3/13/06.

except that the benchmark for comparison is

$$OPT_d^\alpha = \min_{x \in F^T} \sum_{t=1}^{T} c^t(x^t) + \alpha\|x^t - x^{t-1}\|,$$

where $\alpha \geq 1$. Specifically, $CR_i^\alpha(A)$ is $\rho(T)$ if (2) holds with OPT_d replaced by OPT_d^α. Note that OPT_d^α transitions between the dynamic optimal (when $\alpha = 1$) and the static optimal (for large enough α).

2. INCOMPATIBILITY

It is natural to seek algorithms that perform well with respect to both regret (i.e., a static benchmark) and CR (i.e., a dynamic benchmark). However, to date no algorithm has achieved this. For example, online gradient descent [9] has a regret of $O(\sqrt{T})$, or even $O(\log T)$ when the cost function has minimal curvature [10], but has infinite CR. Conversely, algorithms for general MTS problems typically have CR $O(n)$ for a decision space of size n (i.e., $O(1)$ with respect to the number of tasks T) but have linear regret, even for the special case of a one dimensional decision space with convex costs [11].

This is due to a fundamental incompatibility:

Theorem 1. *Consider an arbitrary seminorm $\|\cdot\|$ on $\mathbb{R}^n$, constants $\gamma > 0$, $\alpha > 0$ and $i \in \mathbb{N}$.*

There is a $\mathfrak{C}$ containing a single sequence of cost functions such that, for large enough T, for all deterministic and randomized algorithms A,

$$CR_{i+1}^\alpha(A) + \frac{R_i(A)}{T} \geq \gamma, \qquad (3)$$

Moreover, for any deterministic or randomized online algorithm A, there is a $\mathfrak{C}$ consisting of two cost functions such that for large enough T,

$$CR_0^\alpha(A) + \frac{R_0(A)}{T} \geq \gamma \qquad (4)$$

The incompatibility (3), which applies to the traditional notions of regret (R_0^0) and competitive ratio (CR_1^1) in the OCO and MTS communities, arises since CR_{i+1}^α and R_i require x_t to minimize c_{t-i} and c_{t-i-1} simultaneously.

The proof of (4) uses linear costs $c^t(x) = a(1-x) + b$ for $\mathbb{E}\left[x^t\right] \leq 1/2$ and $c^t(x) = ax + b$ otherwise, on decision space $[0, 1]$, where x^t is the (random) choice of the algorithm at round t. Here, a and b are fixed constants and the expectation is taken over the marginal distribution of x^t conditioned on $c_1, \ldots, c_{t-1}$, averaging out the dependence on the realizations of $x_1, \ldots, x_{t-1}$.

3. TRADEOFF

To circumvent the incompatibility in Theorem 1, we present an algorithm "Random Bias Greedy" (RBG) for one-dimensional decision spaces that is $O(1)$ (α-unfair) competitive and has ϵT regret for arbitrarily small ϵ.

The algorithm takes a norm N as its input:

Algorithm 1 (RANDOM BIAS GREEDY, RBG(N)). *Given a norm N, define $w^0(x) = N(x)$ for all x and $w^t(x) = \min_y\{w^{t-1}(y) + c^t(y) + N(x-y)\}$. Generate a random number $r \in (-1, 1)$. For each time step t, go to the state x^t which minimizes $Y^t(x^t) = w^{t-1}(x^t) + rN(x^t)$.*

Theorem 2. *For a SOCO problem in a one-dimensional normed space $\|\cdot\|$, running RBG(N) with a one-dimensional norm having $N(1) = \gamma\|1\|$ as input (where $\gamma \geq 1$) attains an α-unfair competitive ratio CR_1^α of $(1+\gamma)/\min\{\gamma, \alpha\}$ and a regret R_0 of $O(\max\{T/\gamma, \gamma\})$ with probability 1.*

To prove Theorem 2, let $c(A) := \sum_{t=1}^{T} c^t(x^{t+1})$, let $s(A) := \sum_{t=1}^{T} \|x^{t+1} - x^t\|$ and let OPT_N be the dynamic optimum under norm N with $N(1) = \gamma\|1\|$ ($\gamma \geq 1$). Theorem 2 follows from the following lemmas.

Lemma 3. *Consider a one-dimensional SOCO problem with norm $\|\cdot\|$ and an online algorithm A which, when run with norm N, satisfies $c(A(N)) \leq OPT_N + O(1)$ along with $s(A(N)) \leq \beta OPT_N + O(1)$ with $\beta = O(1)$. Fix a norm N such that $N(1) = \gamma\|1\|$ with $\gamma \geq 1$. Then $A(N)$ has α-unfair competitive ratio $CR_1^\alpha(A(N)) = (1+\beta)\max\{\frac{\gamma}{\alpha}, 1\}$ and regret $R_0(A(N)) = O(\max\{\beta T, (1+\beta)\gamma\})$ for the original SOCO problem with norm $\|\cdot\|$.*

Lemma 4. *Given a one-dimensional SOCO problem with norm $\|\cdot\|$,*

$$\mathbb{E}\left[c(RBG(N))\right] \leq OPT_N$$
$$\mathbb{E}\left[s(RBG(N))\right] \leq OPT_N/\gamma.$$

Acknowledgements

This work was supported by NSF grants CCF 0830511, and CNS 0846025, Microsoft Research, the Lee Center for Advanced Networking, and ARC grants FT0991594 and DP130101378.

4. REFERENCES

[1] A. Blum and C. Burch, "On-line learning and the metrical task system problem," *Machine Learning*, vol. 39, pp. 35–58, 2000.

[2] N. Buchbinder, S. Chen, J. Naor, and O. Shamir, "Unified algorithms for online learning and competitive analysis," in *Proc. Conf. on Learning Techniques (COLT)*, 2012.

[3] A. Blum, S. Chawla, and A. Kalai, "Static optimality and dynamic search-optimality in lists and trees," in *Proceedings of SODA*, 2002, pp. 1–8.

[4] A. Blum, C. Burch, and A. Kalai, "Finely-competitive paging," in *Proceedings of FOCS*, 1999, pp. 450–457.

[5] J. Abernethy, P. Bartlett, N. Buchbinder, and I. Stanton, "A regularization approach to metrical task systems," in *Proceedings of ALT*, 2010, pp. 270–284.

[6] E. Hazan and C. Seshadhri, "Efficient learning algorithms for changing environments," in *Proc. International Conference on Machine Learning*. ACM, 2009, pp. 393–400.

[7] A. Blum and Y. Mansour, "From external to internal regret," *Learning Theory*, pp. 1–10, 2005.

[8] A. Blum, H. Karloff, Y. Rabani, and M. Saks, "A decomposition theorem and bounds for randomized server problems," in *Proc. IEEE Symp. Foundations of Computer Science (FOCS)*, 1992.

[9] M. Zinkevich, "Online convex programming and generalized infinitesimal gradient ascent," in *Proc. Int. Conf. Machine Learning (ICML)*, T. Fawcett and N. Mishra, Eds. AAAI Press, 2003, pp. 928–936.

[10] E. Hazan, A. Agarwal, and S. Kale, "Logarithmic regret algorithms for online convex optimization," *Mach. Learn.*, vol. 69, pp. 169–192, Dec. 2007.

[11] M. Lin, A. Wierman, L. L. H. Andrew, and E. Thereska, "Dynamic right-sizing for power-proportional data centers," in *Proc. IEEE INFOCOM*, 2011.

Accelerating GPGPU Architecture Simulation

Zhibin Yu[*], Lieven Eeckhout[+], Nilanjan Goswami[#], Tao Li[#],
Lizy K. John[^], Hai Jin[&], Chengzhong Xu[*%]

[*] Shenzhen Institute of Advanced Technology, Chinese Academy of Sciences, China
[+] ELIS Department, Ghent University, Belgium
[#] Intelligent Design of Efficient Architectures Lab, University of Florida, Gainesville, FL, USA
[^] Department of Electrical and Computer Engineering, University of Texas at Austin, TX, USA
[&] Service Computing Technologies and System Lab/Cluster and Grid Computing Lab, HUST, Wuhan, China
[%] Department of Electrical and Computer Engineering, Wayne State University, MI, USA

zb.yu@siat.ac.cn, leeckhou@elis.UGent.be, nil@ufl.edu, taoli@ece.ufl.edu,
ljohn@ece.utexas.edu, jinhust@gmail.com, czxu@wayne.edu

ABSTRACT

Recently, graphics processing units (GPUs) have opened up new opportunities for speeding up general-purpose parallel applications due to their massive computational power and up to hundreds of thousands of threads enabled by programming models such as CUDA. However, due to the serial nature of existing micro-architecture simulators, these massively parallel architectures and workloads need to be simulated sequentially. As a result, simulating GPGPU architectures with typical benchmarks and input data sets is extremely time-consuming.

This paper addresses the GPGPU architecture simulation challenge by generating miniature, yet representative GPGPU kernels. We first summarize the static characteristics of an existing GPGPU kernel in a profile, and analyze its dynamic behavior using the novel concept of the divergence flow statistics graph (DFSG). We subsequently use a GPGPU kernel synthesizing framework to generate a miniature proxy of the original kernel, which can reduce simulation time significantly. The key idea is to reduce the number of simulated instructions by decreasing per-thread iteration counts of loops. Our experimental results show that our approach can accelerate GPGPU architecture simulation by a factor of 88X on average and up to 589X with an average IPC relative error of 5.6%.

Categories and Subject Descriptors

B.8 [**Hardware**]: Performance and Reliability — Simulation; C.1 [**Processor Architectures**] Single-instruction-stream, multiple-data-stream processors; C.4 [**Computer Systems Organization**] Performance of Systems — Simulation

Keywords: General Purpose Graphics Processing Unit (GPGPU), Performance, Micro-architecture Simulation

1. INTRODUCTION

In recent years, interest has grown substantially towards harnessing the explosive growth in computational power of graphics hardware to perform general-purpose tasks – referred to as GPGPU computing. GPGPU computing achieves high throughput by concurrently running massive numbers of threads enabled by general-purpose GPU programming models such as CUDA [1]. Unfortunately, existing GPGPU architecture simulators are sequential – a mismatch with the massive number of threads in the workloads and the number of parallel units in the graphics hardware – which indicates that GPGPU architecture simulation with typical benchmarks and input data sets is extremely time-consuming.

Table 1 shows the execution time of several CUDA benchmarks on a GPU device (NVIDIA GeForce 295) versus simulation time on a GPGPU performance simulator (GPGPU-Sim [2]). These measurements show that GPGPU performance simulation is approximately 9 orders of magnitude slower compared to real hardware. Given how computer architects heavily rely on simulators for exploration purposes at various stages of the design, accelerating GPGPU architectural simulation is imperative.

By characterizing existing GPGPU workloads, we find that existing CPU and GPU architectural simulation acceleration solutions cannot be readily applied to GPGPU simulation. First, the number of basic blocks and the instruction count per thread of GPGPU workloads are relatively small compared to typical CPU workloads. This implies that the prerequisites of CPU architectural simulation acceleration techniques such as sampling [3][4] do not apply. Second, the large number of branch instructions in GPGPU workloads prohibits the use of spreadsheet-based modeling techniques typically used for pure-graphics workloads based GPU performance evaluation.

We therefore propose a synthetic GPGPU workload framework that generates miniature proxies of workloads to address the GPGPU architectural simulation challenge. Experimental results show that our approach can speed up GPGPU architecture simulation by a factor of 88X on average and up to 589X, with an average IPC error of 5.6% across a broad set of GPGPU benchmarks.

2. WORKLOAD CHARACTERIZATION

To gain insight regarding how to accelerate GPGPU architectural simulation, it is important to characterize existing GPGPU workloads. We therefore developed a tool based on GPGPU-sim [2] to extract the features of GPGPU workloads at the instruction, basic block, and thread levels. We obtain three key findings. (i) The number of static basic blocks for most workloads ranges between 10 to 25 with an average of 23.4. This is relatively small compared to CPU benchmarks such as SPEC CPU (265.5 on average) and MediaBench (584.2 on average). (ii) The dynamic instruction count per thread varies from dozens to tens of

Table 1. Execution time comparison of CUDA programs on real GPU device and GPGPU architectural simulator.

benchmark	grid	CTA	GPU time(ms)	Simulation time (s)
RPES	(65535,1,1)	(64,1,1)	0.524	333641 >3.8 days
TPACF	(201,1,1)	(256,1,1)	0.054	1484125>17days
BLK	(480,1,1)	(128,1,1)	0.918	1038931>12 days
PNS	(256,1,1)	(256,1,1)	0.699	1019169>11 days

thousands, which is extremely small compared to SPEC CPU and PARSEC benchmarks. (iii) GPGPU workloads contain more irregular code compared to pure graphics programs because of higher percentages of branch instructions in GPGPU workloads.

The first two findings break the prerequisites of CPU architectural simulation acceleration techniques such as sampling and statistical simulation. Sampling techniques select snapshots from a dynamic instruction stream, implying a large number of instructions per thread. Due to the small instruction count per thread for GPGPU workloads, sampling techniques cannot be used. One possible way to use sampling is to sample a small number of threads from the large number of threads in a typical GPGPU workload to be simulated in detail but this is highly likely to alter the inter-thread interactions. Statistical simulation generates a synthetic workload with similar characteristics as the original workload while dropping basic blocks that are seldom executed. Likewise, this approach cannot be applied to GPGPU architectural simulation because of the small number of basic blocks in GPGPU workloads.

The third finding prohibits the use of spreadsheet-based modeling techniques for pure GPU performance evaluation in the GPGPU case. If the number of threads or input data sets of a GPGPU workload is reduced, the simulation results such as IPC (Instructions Per Cycle) is highly possible to be altered. Therefore, the existing architectural simulation acceleration solutions for CPUs and pure GPUs cannot be readily applied to GPGPUs.

3. GPGPU BENCHMARK SYNTHESIS

We propose GPGPU workload synthesis to accelerate GPGPU architectural simulation. As shown in Figure 1, our approach consists of three steps. In the first step, a profile is collected by capturing the threads' inherent execution characteristics by executing the GPGPU workload with a given input. Subsequently, the profile is used as input to a code generator to generate a synthetic miniature GPGPU benchmark. In the final step, the synthetic benchmark is simulated on an execution-driven architectural simulator such as GPGPU-Sim.

There are two key differences between our GPGPU synthesis and previous CPU synthesis approach. (i) We use the control flow graph of the original workload as the code skeleton for its synthetic version. (ii) We employ the same number of threads and thread layout for the original and synthetic version. Both of these features are important towards keeping similar performance between the original and synthetic code versions in terms of warp divergence, shared memory bank conflict, and memory coalescing behavior. The key idea to reduce simulation time is to decrease the iteration counts of loops. As a result, the number of simulated instructions is reduced, and faster simulation times are achieved.

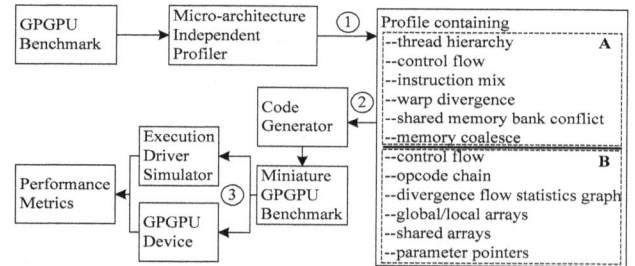

Figure 1. GPGPU benchmark synthesis framework.

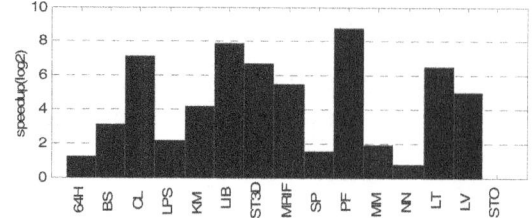

Figure 2. The speedup of micro-architecture simulation obtained by using synthesized GPGPU benchmarks

4. EVALUATION

We employ 15 benchmarks to evaluate the efficacy of our approach on the GPGPU-sim simulator. The benchmarks are taken from CUDA SDK, Rodinia, and Parboil, which are popular GPGPU benchmark suites. The GPGPU simulator is configured as a 56 SM (Streaming Multi-processor) GPGPU. Figure 2 shows the speedup of our approach. The speedup achieves 88X on average and up to 589X. The achieved speedups depend on the benchmarks' loop characteristics. For example, the iteration count of PF is large and that of STO is very small. The accuracy of our approach achieves 5.6% on average.

5. ACKNOWLEDGEMENTS

This work was supported by NSF China under grants 60973036 and 61272132.

6. REFERENCES

[1] NVIDIA CORPORATION, *CUDA Programming Guide Version 3.0*, 2010.

[2] Bakhoda. A, Yuan. G. L, Fung. W. L, Wong. H, and Aamodt. T. M. Analyzing CUDA Workloads Using a Detailed GPU Simulator. In *Proceedings of IEEE International Symposium on Performance Analysis of Systems and Software (ISPASS)*, pp. 163-174, April 2009.

[3] Wunderlich. R. E, Wenisch. T. F, Fasafi. B, and Hoe. J. C. SMARTS: Accelerating Microarchitecture Simulation via Rigorous Statistical Sampling. In *Proceedings of the 30th Annual International Symposium on Computer Architecture (ISCA)*, pp. 84-95, June 2003.

[4] Sherwood. T, Perelman. E, Hamerly. G, and Calder. B. Automatically Characterizing Large Scale Program Behavior. In *Proceedings of the 10th International Conference on Architecture Support for Programming Languages and Operating Systems (ASPLOS)*, pp. 45-57, Oct 2002.

ACE: Abstracting, Characterizing and Exploiting Peaks and Valleys in Datacenter Power Consumption

Di Wang[*], Chuangang Ren[*], Sriram Govindan[†], Anand Sivasubramaniam[*],
Bhuvan Urgaonkar[*], Aman Kansal[‡], Kushagra Vaid[†]
[*]The Pennsylvania State University, [†]Microsoft, [‡]Microsoft Research
{diw5108, cyr5126, anand, bhuvan}@cse.psu.edu, {srgovin, kansal, kvaid}@microsoft.com

ABSTRACT

Peak power management of datacenters has tremendous cost implications. While numerous mechanisms have been proposed to cap power consumption, real datacenter power consumption data is scarce. To address this gap, we collect power demands at multiple spatial and fine-grained temporal resolutions from the load of geo-distributed datacenters of Microsoft over 6 months. We conduct aggregate analysis of this data, to study its statistical properties. With workload characterization a key ingredient for systems design and evaluation, we note the importance of better abstractions for capturing power demands, in the form of peaks and valleys. We identify and characterize attributes for peaks and valleys, and important correlations across these attributes that can influence the choice and effectiveness of different power capping techniques. With the wide scope of exploitability of such characteristics for power provisioning and optimizations, we illustrate its benefits with two specific case studies.

Categories and Subject Descriptors

C.0 [**Computer Systems Organization**]: General

Keywords

Datacenters; Power Demands; Characteristics

1. INTRODUCTION

The cost, scalability and environmental concerns arising from the power consumption of datacenters has come under extensive scrutiny. While much of the prior work in the area has looked to reduce energy of computing and cooling systems, the importance of how this energy is dissipated over time (i.e. the power) has gained a lot of recent attention. Power dissipation, particularly the peak or high power draws, impact both operational (op-ex) and capital (cap-ex) expenditures. Electric utilities can charge differentially (op-ex) for peaks, especially if such high power draws coincide with high demand across the grid because of supply-demand mismatches that can lead to potential black or brown-outs. Peak power draws also determine the capacity of the power distribution and cooling infrastructure that is provisioned within the datacenter. Prior studies [1, 2] have pointed out that provisioning costs can range between $10-20 per watt, which is incurred even if that watt is not actually consumed.

To address this problem, numerous prior optimizations have been proposed. However, there is a lack of real world datacenter power consumption data to guide the design and enable thorough evaluation of these optimizations. Detailed power consumption data at different temporal scales (from seconds to months) and spatial granularities (from servers, chassis, racks, to datacenters) for datacenters serving important workloads is not easily available. This paper intends to fill this critical void by providing an in-depth analysis of measured power characteristics from the datacenter infrastructure of Microsoft corporation. Below, we present a summary of the results, with more details in our technical report [4].

2. AGGREGATE CHARACTERISTICS

In this section, we present a spatio-temporal analysis of power demand, focusing on its aggregate characteristics.

2.1 Tracing and Data Collection

We collected power measurement data from multiple geo-distributed datacenters run by Microsoft over a six month period, between July-December 2011. We specially give results here for data pertaining to 8 representative server clusters (see Table 1) in the interest of clarity. Each such cluster comprises several hundreds of servers that span multiple chassis and racks. These clusters run a variety of workloads including web-search, email, Map-Reduce jobs, and several other online cloud applications, catering to millions of users around the world. We name the 8 clusters as C_1, C_2, ..., C_8 and present the trace collection resolution and the type (soft-realtime, batch and interactive) of application that each hosts in Table 1. Apart from the IT power of the clusters, we have also collected cooling power.

Cluster Names	Data Resolution	Application Type
C_1, C_2	20 seconds	Soft-realtime, Batch
C_3, C_4, ..., C_8	120 seconds	Interactive

Table 1: **Data collection is done for a period of six months.**

2.2 Statistical Properties

Spatial Characteristics: Figure 1 shows the CDF of power consumption at multiple (spatial) levels for one of the clusters, C_1, starting from cluster-level to rack-level to chassis-level to server-level. The x-axis is normalized with respect to the sum of the maximum demand (over time) of all the servers within that cluster. At the lower levels (e.g. server), there is higher variance in power demands. However, statistical multiplexing effects of these demands, tend to smoothen the fluctuations as we go higher up the hierarchy. Thus, there is fairly good statistical multiplexing, and the likelihood of simultaneous peaks across all equipment at the same time reduces as we move higher up in the power hierarchy. These results corroborate observations made in [1], showing the rarity of peak needs at the aggregate level, further motivating the attractiveness for under-provisioning the power hierarchy (especially as we go higher up the hierarchy).

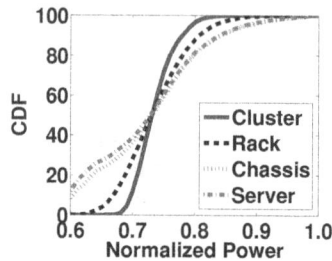

Figure 1: CDF of Power Demand at 4 different levels of C_1

Cluster Name	Hurst Parameter
C_1	0.93
C_2	0.91
C_3	0.89
C_4	0.90
C_5	0.90
C_6	0.82
C_7	0.87
C_8	0.86

Figure 2: Hurst parameter values of 8 clusters.

Temporal Characteristics: One way to understand the temporal time series of power demands is through an Autocorrelation Function (ACF) plot with different time-lags. We note that there is a fairly good time-of-day behavior that is exhibited by the power demands - lags of 24 hours (and multiples) have high correlations, and lags of 12 hours (and its odd number of multiples) are the least correlated. Furthermore, the slower than exponential decay of the ACF indicates that the demands do not follow a Poisson process, with possibility of self-similarity over time. To investigate the presence of self-similarity, we calculate the Hurst parameter, using several techniques [3], including variance, R/S method, and periodogram plots. The results are consistent across these techniques. We find a high value for the Hurst parameter, over 0.8, for all clusters (Figure 2). These quantitatively show the existence of self-similarity in the power demands.

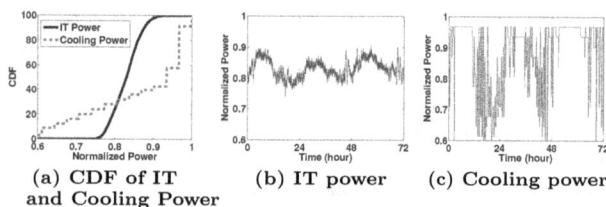

(a) CDF of IT and Cooling Power (b) IT power (c) Cooling power

Figure 3: Normalized IT and cooling power of C_1.

IT and Cooling Power: Figure 3 (a) compares the CDF of IT equipment (servers and networking devices) and cooling power consumptions both normalized with respect to their individual maximum demands for C_1. There are several interesting observations from these results: (i) Cooling power and IT power are correlated as can be seen from Figure 3 (b) and (c). The *Pearson* correlation coefficient between the two is 0.841. However, the cooling power, as is to be expected due to thermal time constants, lags 2 minutes behind the IT power to reach the maximum correlation coefficient of 0.844. As expected based on the high correlation with IT power, the cooling power also exhibits time-

of-day behavior and self-similarity. The Hurst parameter value is 0.90. (ii) The variation in cooling power is much more pronounced than that in IT power (also seen visually in Figures 3 (b) and (c)). Beyond its dependence on the IT power draw, cooling power also depends on other parameters including external temperatures, air-flow, etc. High user demand and consequently a high IT power consumption often occurs at times of the day when external temperatures are also among the highest for the day, leading to this wider fluctuation. (iii) The CDF shows that the cooling system is operating closer to its maximum actual draw, much more often than the IT systems. This is expected because cooling systems have fewer power states, resulting in more discrete modes of operation.

3. PEAKS AND VALLEYS OF POWER DEMANDS

Abstractions: We formally define peaks and valleys, their important attributes (height, width, area), and the correlations between peaks and valleys that need to be studied towards designing and understanding the potential of any peak suppression mechanism.

Characterizing Peaks and Valleys: We extensively characterize peak and valley attributes individually, and their cross-correlations. Results show that while there are an overwhelming number of small duration and small amplitude peaks, we cannot afford to ignore the few large ones that have very stringent demands. Further, while on the average, valleys do offer enough slack for load deferment or peak preparation, there are bursts of peaks which do not have sufficient valleys immediately following or preceding them. Further, there is significant potential of migrating load to exploit peaks and valleys across clusters, as long as we can restrict the number of such migrations to avoid the consequent performance penalties. These suggest aggregated optimizations of peaks and valleys.

Exploiting Characteristics: There are numerous use-cases for our characteristics, and we illustrate two specific case-studies. The first uses the characteristics to fine-tune load deferring and migration based on the kinds of peaks, in an aggregated manner. The second shows a simple approach to energy storage provisioning that only uses aggregate characteristics, rather than an extensive approach considering every possible eventuality in the entire power demand time series.

4. ACKNOWLEDGMENTS

This work was supported by NSF grants 0811670, 1152479, 1205618, 1213052, 1147388 and CAREER award 0953541.

5. REFERENCES

[1] X. Fan, W.-D. Weber, and L. A. Barroso. Power Provisioning for a Warehouse-sized Computer. In *Proceedings of ISCA*, 2007.

[2] J. Hamilton. Internet-scale Service Infrastructure Efficiency, ISCA Keynote 2009.

[3] W. E. Leland, M. S. Taqqu, W. Willinger, and D. V. Wilson. On the self-similar nature of ethernet traffic (extended version). *IEEE/ACM Trans. Netw.*, 2(1), 1994.

[4] D. Wang, C. Ren, S. Govindan, A. Sivasubramaniam, B. Urgaonkar, A. Kansal, and K. Vaid. ACE: Abstracting, Characterizing and Exploiting Peaks and Valleys in Datacenter Power Consumption. Technical Report CSE13-003, The Pennsylvania State University, 2013.

An Empirical Analysis of Intra- and Inter-Datacenter Network Failures for Geo-Distributed Services

[Extended Abstract]

Rahul Potharaju
Purdue University
rpothara@purdue.edu

Navendu Jain
Microsoft Research
navendu@microsoft.com

ABSTRACT

As cloud services continue to grow, a key requirement is delivering an 'always-on' experience to end users. Of the several factors affecting service availability, network failures in the hosting datacenters have received little attention. This paper presents a preliminary analysis of *intra-datacenter* and *inter-datacenter* network failures from a service perspective. We describe an empirical study analyzing and correlating network failure events over an year across multiple datacenters in a service provider. Our broader goal is to outline steps leveraging existing network mechanisms to improve end-to-end service availability.

Categories and Subject Descriptors

C.2.3 [**Computer-Communication Network**]: Network Operations

General Terms

Network Management, Availability, Reliability

Keywords

Data center networks, Geo-distributed services

1. INTRODUCTION

Cloud services are growing rapidly to provide a fast-response and an always-on experience to end users. Reliability is critically important for these services as failures not only hurt site availability and revenue, but also risk data loss. For example, the hurricane Sandy led to flooding of many data centers in NYC, taking down several major services such as The Huffington Post and Gawker [2]. Further, it caused failures of a large number of trans-atlantic fiber links peering from NYC significantly degrading capacity [10]. Last year, the entire US East region of Amazon became un-available due to a faulty fail-over during maintenance [1].

To increase service availability in a cost-effective manner, service providers are deploying their services across geo-distributed datacenters [5], and building their networks based on a scale-out design using inexpensive commodity hardware [7, 4]. However, as the number of devices and links in a datacenter grows, failures become the norm rather than the exception. Further, the network infrastructure also comprise long-haul links between datacenters whose failures can

lead to loss of service traffic. Unfortunately, recent studies (e.g., [9, 3]) do not analyze network failures from a cloud service perspective nor do they examine inter- datacenter network failures.

In this extended abstract, we present a preliminary study of intra- and inter-datacenter network failures from a service perspective. Our study using real-world field data focuses on understanding the failure characteristics for a network stamp of a service comprising Top-of-Rack (ToR) switches connecting servers, aggregation switches (AGGs) that aggregate traffic from ToRs, and access routers (ARs) that in-turn connect to multiple AGGs. Specifically, we present two key aspects of failure characteristics: (a) problem root causes and (b) annualized downtime. Our broader goal is to use this study to provide new insights towards improving service availability.

2. METHODOLOGY

Our methodology is based on analyzing an year's worth (July 24, 2010-11) of network event logs across thousands of devices spanning multiple datacenters. Our data covers a wide range of network data sources, including syslog and SNMP alerts, network trouble tickets, maintenance tracking and revision control system, and traffic carried by links.

There are several challenges in using these network data sources to extract failures for our study such as (i) syslog messages can be spurious with devices logging 'down' notifications even when they are operational, (ii) redundant events resulting from two devices (e.g., neighbors) sending notifications for the same event, and (iii) multiple down and up messages getting logged as different events due to a flapping event.

To address these challenges, we build on our prior work [3, 8] in analyzing network failures. We define a *failure* of a network device or link as an event that causes it to be unavailable to carry traffic. To extract meaningful failures from network logs, we apply two stages of event filtering to analyze and correlate network event data sources.

In the first stage, a *time-based filter* removes duplicate events by grouping all events with the same start and end time originating on the same interface. Further, for overlapping events on the same interface, it picks the earliest of start and end times. In the second stage, the *impact filter* identifies events impacting application performance in terms of throughput loss, number of failed connections or increased latency. Since we did not have access to application-level logs, we estimate failure impact by leveraging network traffic logs and computing the ratio of the median traffic on a

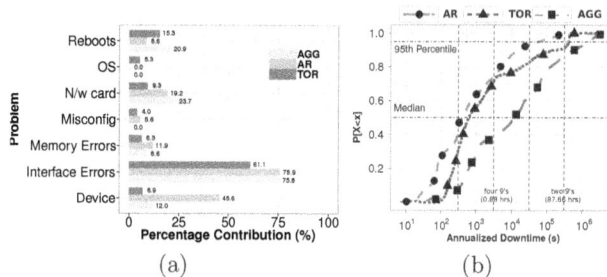

(a)   (b)

Figure 1: (a) Problems root-causes across device types, and (b) Comparing annualized downtime across ARs, ToRs and AGGs

failed device/link during a failure and its value in the recent past (e.g., preceding 8-hour window): a failure has impact if this ratio is less than one [3]. Finally, we apply NetSieve to do automated problem inference on network trouble tickets [8] for determining the problem root causes.

3. RESULTS

We study the annualized downtime and root causes of failures of network elements that significantly impact service availability.

3.1 Intra-datacenter failures

Figure 1(a) shows the histogram of the top-k problems observed obtained from network trouble tickets associated with intra- datacenter failures. Observe that many problems are due to both hardware issues and misconfigurations (e.g., ARP conflict). Interface-level errors, network card problems, and unexpected reloads were prominent amongst all three types. In addition, ToR failures were also due to OS-related problems and misconfigurations.

Next, we present the annualized downtime (see Figure 1(b)). Surprisingly, AGGs exhibited the highest downtime while ARs the lowest. ToR failures tend to be relatively infrequent compared to ARs and AGGs and hence the lower downtime. A significant contribution to ToR downtime was due to a set of older generation devices that became susceptible to end-of-life (or wear-out) problems, a phenomenon explained by the well-known bathtub curve of hardware failures.

3.2 Inter-datacenter Failures

In this section, we analyze the root causes and annualized downtime on the links connecting datacenters.

We first analyze the network trouble tickets associated with link failures. We found that link flapping (e.g., due to BGP, OSPF protocol issues and convergence) dominates problem root causes (about 35%) in inter-datacenter links. Due to optical protection configured in some areas of the network, a physical layer problem might end up triggering an optical re-route, a technique which is used to reduce the bandwidth loss by shifting existing lightpaths to new wavelengths without changing their route. However, it incurs control overhead (of about 10 seconds), and, more important, the service in the rerouted lightpaths can get disrupted [6]. Depending on the protocol timers, such an event is observed as a "link flap", yet the true underlying issues could be an optical re-route, possibly in response to a fiber cut (e.g., due to construction, hunting, shark attack).

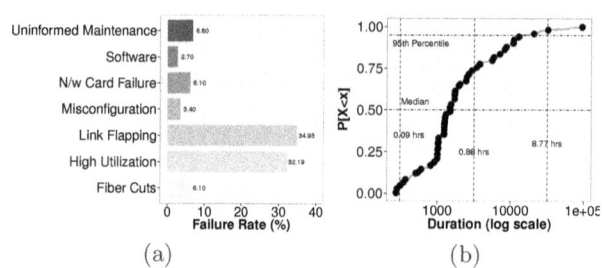

(a)   (b)

Figure 2: (a) Problem root-causes for long-haul links, and (b) Annualized downtime for long-haul links

Therefore, it is not possible in many cases to attribute the exact cause.

The second major root cause is high link utilization (about 32%). However, note that high utilization does not necessarily imply a physical circuit failure or take- down, but it may be an indicator of packet errors. Fiber cuts (ones that could be observed), configuration errors and unnotified maintenance were observed but they do not constitute a significant fraction (see Figure 2(a)).

Finally, we show the annualized downtime. We observe (see Figure 2(b)) that the average failure duration is about 1.27 hours while the median is 0.41 hours with the 95P value >3 hours, which is 2x-3x higher than the expected values.

References

[1] Amazon. Summary of the Amazon EC2 and Amazon RDS Service Disruption in the US East Region. http://goo.gl/yU1TJ, May 2011.

[2] S. G. and I. B. Websites Scramble as Hurricane Sandy Floods Data Centers. http://goo.gl/zOXDb, October 31 2012.

[3] P. Gill, N. Jain, and N. Nagappan. Understanding network failures in data centers: measurement, analysis, and implications. In *Proc. of Sigcomm*, 2011.

[4] A. Greenberg, J. Hamilton, N. Jain, S. Kandula, C. Kim, P. Lahiri, D. Maltz, P. Patel, and S. Sengupta. Vl2: a scalable and flexible data center network. *ACM Sigcomm CCR*, 2009.

[5] D. C. Knowledge. Data center global expansion trend. http://goo.gl/SOvtA, November 2012.

[6] G. Mohan and C. Murthy. Lightpath restoration in wdm optical networks. *Network, IEEE*, 14(6), 2000.

[7] R. Niranjan Mysore, A. Pamboris, N. Farrington, N. Huang, P. Miri, S. Radhakrishnan, V. Subramanya, and A. Vahdat. Portland: a scalable fault-tolerant layer 2 data center network fabric. In *Sigcomm CCR*. ACM, 2009.

[8] R. Potharaju, N. Jain, and C. Nita-Rotaru. Juggling the jigsaw: Towards automated problem inference from network trouble tickets. In *Proceedings of the 10th USENIX Conference on Networked Systems Design and Implementation*, 2013.

[9] D. Turner, K. Levchenko, A. Snoeren, and S. Savage. California fault lines: understanding the causes and impact of network failures. In *ACM Sigcomm CCR*, 2010.

[10] S. Works. Hurricane Sandy - AC2 Transatlantic Cable Cut. http://goo.gl/dywVO, October 2012.

2

Computational Analysis of Cascading Failures in Power Networks

Dorian Mazauric
Laboratoire d'Informatique Fondamentale de
Marseille
Marseille, France
dorian.mazauric@lif.univ-mrs.fr

Saleh Soltan, Gil Zussman
Electrical Engineering
Columbia University
New York, NY
{saleh,gil}@ee.columbia.edu

ABSTRACT

We focus on *cascading line failures in the transmission system of the power grid*. Recent large-scale power outages demonstrated the limitations of epidemic- and percolation-based tools in modeling the cascade evolution. Hence, based on a linearized power flow model, we obtain results regarding the various properties of a cascade. Specifically, we consider performance metrics such as the distance between failures, the length of the cascade, and the fraction of demand (load) satisfied after the cascade. We show, for example, that due to the unique properties of the model: (i) a set of initial line failures may have a smaller effect than a failure of one of the lines in the set, (ii) the distance between subsequent failures can be arbitrarily large and the cascade may be arbitrarily long, and (iii) minor changes to the network parameters may have a significant impact. Moreover, we show that finding the set of lines whose removal has the most significant impact (under different metrics) is NP-hard. Finally, for specific graphs, we develop a fast algorithm to determine if a set of line failures initiates a cascade. The results can provide insight into the design of smart grid measurement and control algorithms that can mitigate a cascade.

Categories and Subject Descriptors: C.4 [Performance of Systems]: Reliability, availability, and serviceability; G.2.2 [Discrete Mathematics]: Graph Theory–*Graph algorithms, Network problems*.

Keywords: Power Grid, Cascading Failures, Performance Metrics, Computational Complexity, Survivability.

1. CASCADING FAILURE MODEL

We adopt the linearized (or DC) *power flow model*, which is widely used as an approximation for the non-linear AC power flow model. In particular, we follow [2,3] and represent the power grid by a graph $G = (V, E)$ where V and E are the set of nodes and edges representing the buses and transmission lines, respectively. P_v is the active power supply or demand at node $v \in V$. Each node is classified either as a *supply node* ($P_v > 0$), a *demand node* ($P_v < 0$), or a *neutral node* ($P_v = 0$). We assume *pure reactive* lines, implying that each edge $\{u, v\} \in E$ is characterized by its *reactance* $x_{uv} = x_{vu}$.

Given an active power vector P, a *power flow* is a solution

Copyright is held by the author/owner(s).
SIGMETRICS'13, June 17-21, 2013, Pittsburgh, PA, USA.
ACM 978-1-4503-1900-3/13/06.

Cascading Failure Model

Input: A connected graph $G = (V, E)$ and an initial edge failures event $F_0 \subseteq E$.

Output: The length of the cascade $t \geq 0$, the sequence $(F_0, F_1, \ldots, F_t)$ of the sets of edge failures at each round, and the power flows $f_e(F_t^*) \ \forall e \in E$, at stabilization.
1: $F_0^* \leftarrow F_0$ and $i \leftarrow 0$.
2: **while** $F_i \neq \emptyset$ **do**
3:     Adjust the total demand to total supply within each connected component of $G = (V, E \setminus F_i^*)$ by decreasing the demand (supply) by the same factor at all demand (supply) nodes.
4:     Compute the new flows $f_e(F_i^*) \quad \forall e \in E$.
5:     Find the set of new edge failures F_{i+1}.
6:     $F_{i+1}^* \leftarrow F_i^* \cup F_{i+1}$ and $i \leftarrow i + 1$.
7: **return** $t = i - 1$, $(F_0, \ldots, F_t)$, and $f_e(F_t^*) \ \forall e \in E$.

(f, θ) of the following system of equations:

$$\sum_{v \in N(u)} f_{uv} = P_u, \ \forall \ u \in V \qquad (1)$$

$$\theta_u - \theta_v - x_{uv} f_{uv} = 0, \ \forall \ \{u, v\} \in E \qquad (2)$$

where $N(u)$ is the set of neighbors of node u, f_{uv} is the power flow from node u to node v, and θ_u is the phase angle of node u. Note that the edge capacities are not taken into account in determining the flows.

The *cascading failure model* described above is similar to the model used in [1,3,4]. We assume that each edge $e = \{u, v\} \in E$ has a predetermined power capacity $c_e = c_{uv} = c_{vu}$, which bounds its power flow (we define $f_e = |f_{uv}| = |f_{vu}|$) in a normal operation of the system (that is, $f_e \leq c_e$). The cascade proceeds in rounds. We denote by $F_i \subseteq E$ the set of edge failures in round i and by $F_i^* = F_{i-1}^* \cup F_i$ the set of edge failures until the end of round i ($i \geq 1$). $f_e(F)$ denotes the flows in $G \setminus F$. We assume that before the initial failure event $F_0 \subseteq E$, the power flows satisfy (1)-(2), and $f_e \leq c_e \ \forall \ e \in E$. We use a deterministic outage rule [1] assuming that edge $e \in E$ fails as soon as the flow exceeds its capacity ($f_e > c_e$). To avoid cases in which all edges of an induced path fail (due to path flow exceeding their capacities), we assume that only one edge in the path fails.

We present the metrics for evaluating the grid vulnerability following an initial failure:
Yield $(Y(G, F_0))$: The ratio between the demand supplied at stabilization and its original value. Accordingly,

$Y(G, k) = \min_{F_0 \subseteq E, |F_0| \le k} Y(G, F_0)$ is the minimum yield for any F_0 of size at most k.

Number of edge failures ($|F_+^*(G, F_0)|$): The number of edges that fail until the system stabilizes. Accordingly, $|F_+^*(G, k)| = \max_{F_0 \subseteq E, |F_0| \le k} |F_+^*(G, F_0)|$.

Number of rounds ($L(G, F_0)$): The number of cascade rounds until the system stabilizes. Accordingly, $L(G, k) = \max_{F_0 \subseteq E, |F_0| \le k} L(G, F_0)$, and $L(G) = L(G, |E|)$.

Distance between consecutive failures ($D(G, F_0)$): We define the *distance sequence* $(d_1, d_2, \ldots, d_t)$ associated with $(F_0, F_1, \ldots, F_t)$ as follows. For any i, $1 \le i \le t$, $d_i = d(F_{i-1}, F_i)$ where $d(F_{i-1}, F_i) = \min_{e \in F_{i-1}, e' \in F_i} d(e, e')$ and $d(e, e')$ is the distance between edges e and e' in G. The minimum distance between consecutive failures is $D(G, F_0) = \min_{i, 1 \le i \le t} d_i$. Accordingly, $D(G, k) = \max_{F_0 \subseteq E, |F_0| \le k} D(G, F_0)$, and $D(G) = D(G, |E|)$.

2. CASCADE PROPERTIES

The observations below demonstrate unique properties of the power flow and cascading failure models. Obs. 1 describes non-monotonicity effects of failures (i.e., a set of edge failures may have less significant impact than some of its subsets). It is shown in [1, Lemma 4.3] that a failure event F_0 may result in a lower yield than a failure event $F \supset F_0$. However, in the proof in [1], $G \backslash F$ is disconnected. Obs. 2 and 3 show that the metric values may be arbitrarily large or small even for a single edge failure event. In [1, Lemma 4.2] it was shown that cascading failures may happen within arbitrarily long distance of each other, and in [1, Lemma 4.7] it was shown that they can last arbitrarily long time. However, Obs. 3 shows that these two events can happen simultaneously. Obs. 2 and 3 are summarized in Table 1. Obs. 4 and 5 show that small changes of the parameters may have a large effect on the metric values.

OBSERVATION 1 (NON-MONOTONICITY). *There exists a graph* $G = (V, E)$, *an initial failure* $F_0 = \{e\}$, $e \in E$, *and* $F_0' \supset F_0$, *such that* $(V, E \backslash F_0')$ *is a connected graph,* $Y(G, F_0) = 0$ *and* $Y(G, F_0') = 1$.

OBSERVATION 2 (ROUNDS, FAILURES, AND YIELD). *For any* $m \ge 2$, *there exists a graph* $G = (V, E)$ *with* $|E| \ge m$, *such that* $L(G, 1) = |E| - 1$, $|F_+^*(G, 1)| = |E|$, *and* $Y(G, 1) = 0$.

OBSERVATION 3 (ROUNDS AND DISTANCE). *For any* l, $d \ge 1$, *there exists a graph* $G = (V, E)$ *such that* $L(G, 1) \ge l$ *and for any* i, $1 \le i \le l$, $d_i \ge d$. *As a result* $D(G, 1) \ge d$.

Define graphs $G_\pm^c$ and $G_\pm^x$ as modified versions of the graph $G = (V, E)$ with a small difference in the parameter of a particular edge $e \in E$ (in $G_\pm^c$, $c_e^\pm = c_e \pm \varepsilon$; and in $G_\pm^x$, $x_e^\pm = x_e \pm \varepsilon$).

OBSERVATION 4 (PARAMETERS DECREASE). *For any* $\varepsilon > 0$ *and any* $m \ge 2$, *there exists a graph* $G = (V, E)$ *with* $|E| \ge m$, *an edge* $e \in E$, *and an initial failure* $F_0 \subseteq E$ *with* $|F_0| = 1$, *such that:*
$L(G, F_0) = 0$, $|F_+^*(G, F_0)| = |F_0| = 1$, $Y(G, F_0) = 1$; *but*
(a) $L(G_-^c, F_0) = |F_+^*(G_-^c, F_0)| - 1 = |E| - 1$, $Y(G_-^c, F_0) = 0$,
(b) $L(G_-^x, F_0) = |F_+^*(G_-^x, F_0)| - 1 = |E| - 1$, $Y(G_-^x, F_0) = 0$.

OBSERVATION 5 (CAPACITY INCREASE). *There exists a graph* $G = (V, E)$, *an edge* $e \in E$, *and an initial failure* $F_0 \subseteq E$ *with* $|F_0| = 1$, *such that:*
$L(G, F_0) = 1$, $|F_+^*(G, F_0)| = |F_0| + 1 = 2$, $Y(G, F_0) = 1/3$; *but* $L(G_+^c, F_0) = 1$, $|F_+^*(G_+^c, F_0)| = 3$, $Y(G_+^c, F_0) = 0$.

Table 1: Worst case values of the metrics for cascades caused by a single edge failure.

Metric		Worst case	
Yield	$Y(G, 1)$	0	Obs. 2
Number of edge failures	$|F_+^*(G, 1)|$	$|E|$	Obs. 2
Number of rounds	$L(G, 1)$	$|E| - 1$	Obs. 2
Distance between failures	$D(G, 1)$	$O(|E|)$	Obs. 3

3. HARDNESS RESULTS

The following lemmas show that finding an initial set of failures F_0 that minimizes the *yield*, maximizes the *number of rounds*, or maximizes the *distance between consecutive failures* are all hard problems.

LEMMA 1. *Given a graph* G, *a real number* y, $0 \le y \le 1$, *and an integer* $k \ge 1$, *the problem of deciding if* $Y(G, k) \le y$ *is NP-complete.*

LEMMA 2. *Given a graph* G *and an integer* $t \ge 1$, *the problem of deciding if* $L(G) \ge t$ *is NP-complete.*

LEMMA 3. *Given a graph* G, *the problem of computing* $D(G)$ *is not in APX.*

4. ALGORITHMS

Inspired by circuit theory methods, we introduce the (r, h)-decomposition of the *single supply–single demand* graph G. It consists of replacing the network between arbitrary pairs of nodes by edges with equivalent reactance values such that the flow between the supply and demand nodes is preserved. We show below that using the pre-computed (r, h)-decomposition of the graph, it is possible to compute and recompute the flows with low complexity. When r and h are relatively small, this allows checking if a cascade has been initiated in a more efficient method than the classical one (which requires $O(|V|^3)$ time [5]).

LEMMA 4. *Given a constant integer* $r \ge 1$, *the problem of deciding if* $G = (V, E)$ *admits an* (r, h)-*decomposition for some* $h > 0$, *can be solved in* $O((|V||E|)^2)$ *time.*

LEMMA 5. *Given an* (r, h)-*decomposition of a given graph* $G = (V, E)$, *and* F_0 *of any size,* $f_e(F_0)$ $\forall e \in E$, *can be computed in* $O(r^3|E|)$ *time.*

LEMMA 6. *Given an* (r, h)-*decomposition of a given graph* $G = (V, E)$, *and* F_0 *of any size, deciding if* F_0 *initiates a cascade can be done in* $O(r^3 h |F_0|)$ *time.*

5. ACKNOWLEDGMENTS

This work was supported by NSF grant CNS-1018379 and DTRA grants HDTRA1-09-1-0057 and HDTRA1-13-1-0021.

6. REFERENCES

[1] A. Bernstein, D. Bienstock, D. Hay, M. Uzunoglu, and G. Zussman. Power grid vulnerability to geographically correlated failures - analysis and control implications. Technical Report CU-EE-2011-05-06, Columbia University, Nov. 2011.

[2] D. Bienstock. Optimal control of cascading power grid failures. *Proc. IEEE CDC-ECC*, Dec. 2011.

[3] D. Bienstock and A. Verma. The $N - k$ problem in power grids: New models, formulations, and numerical experiments. *SIAM J. Optimiz.*, 20(5):2352–2380, 2010.

[4] I. Dobson, B. Carreras, V. Lynch, and D. Newman. Complex systems analysis of series of blackouts: cascading failure, critical points, and self-organization. *Chaos*, 17(2):026103, 2007.

[5] G. H. Golub and C. F. Van Loan. *Matrix Computations*. Johns Hopkins Studies in Mathematical Sciences, 4th edition, 2012.

Data Center Asset Tracking Using a Mobile Robot

John Nelson
IBM CIO Office
Southbury, CT
jcnelson@us.ibm.com

Jonathan Connell, Canturk Isci and
Jonathan Lenchner
IBM T.J. Watson Research Center
Yorktown Heights, NY
jconnell@us.ibm.com,
canturk@us.ibm.com,
lenchner@us.ibm.com

ABSTRACT

Management and monitoring of data centers is a growing field of interest, with much current research, and the emergence of a variety of commercial products aiming to improve performance, resource utilization and energy efficiency of the computing infrastructure. Despite the large body of work on optimizing data center operations, few studies actually focus on discovering and tracking the physical layout of assets in these centers. Such asset tracking is a prerequisite to faithfully performing administration and any form of optimization that relies on physical layout characteristics.

In this work, we describe an approach to completely automated asset tracking in data centers, employing a vision-based mobile robot in conjunction with an ability to manipulate the indicator LEDs in blade centers and storage arrays. Unlike previous large-scale asset-tracking methods, our approach does not require the tagging of assets (e.g., with RFID tags or barcodes), thus saving considerable expense and human labor. The approach is validated through a series of experiments in a production industrial data center.

Categories and Subject Descriptors

I.2.9 [Robotics]: Commercial robots and applications

Keywords

Data center; asset tracking; robot

1. APPROACH

Our approach to autonomic data center asset tracking leverages a vision-based mobile robot for determining the data center layout, and the racks positioned within this layout. Previous studies have shown that a simple, low-cost robotic solution can be used to provide at least a coarse mapping of data centers, which, further, can be coupled with thermal monitoring and energy management capabilities [2, 3]. While such a robot can identify physical obstacles, and hence candidate rack locations within a discovered data center, the location of individual servers or storage modules cannot be readily discovered with such an approach. To bridge this gap in the robot's understanding of the data center layout, we leverage asset identification functionality that is built into a range of enterprise IT systems. In particular, our prototype implementation utilizes BladeCenters and BladeCenter Management Modules (BCMMs), which provide a rich and easy to use set of location capabilities via locator LEDs

[1]. Running a mobile robot in coordination with the BCMM software, we can configure each BCMM to emit a special location LED signature, or a series of LED states over time, which can then be processed by the vision processing subsystem of the mobile robot. The management module can in-effect spell out precisely what assets it contains using a binary LED pattern. The information thus obtained can then be used to enter the location into an asset management system and to keep such asset data up-to-date in an autonomous fashion, without necessitating any end user involvement.

The main advantages of our proposed, and prototyped approach are, first, we provide a very cost-effective way of tracking assets that requires little administration; second, it is much more accurate and reliable than manual asset tracking; and third, unlike some of the solutions that rely on additional tags to be placed on the IT assets, our solution operates without any such prerequisites on the asset side, aside from the asset's ability to emit locator lights.

2. EXPERIMENTS

Encoding unique identification numbers such as the serial numbers of IT equipment using existing locator lights can be approached from several directions. Of the available methods, the most time-wise efficient, was to encode each blade center using a unique binary number known to the message sender, i.e., the application resident on the blade center management modules, where a given blade server LED represents a single bit. A single blade center can house at most 14 blade servers, and thus a blade center fully populated with operable blade servers, can represent an arbitrary 14 bit number. In some cases blade centers may be populated with double-wide blade servers, reducing the number of operable bits per message to as little as 7, and in either the single-wide or double-wide cases, it may be that not all blade slots are populated, even further reducing the expressive content of potential messages.

Most racks contain perforated doors to accommodate high volume air flow to and through the equipment housed in the racks. These perforations, conveniently, also allow for the transmission of light in a way that can be observed by the robot (or for that matter, by a human being). Using the BCMM software resident on these blade centers, the indicator LEDs of the individual blade servers can be set to an on or off position.

Through a series of experiments on three blade centers, we investigated the ability of the robot to identify the intended encodings associated with these LEDs, and thereby identify the blade centers and resident blade servers at a given location in the data center. For all experiments the robot was equipped with a forward-facing Logitech C905 camera which we rotate by 90° from its standard orientation to maximize the vertical

Figure 1: Our robot equipped with four forward-pointing cameras in addition to its downward-pointing camera, used for navigation, on the left, and the results of stitching images from the four cameras, on the right. The view is of a rack with rack door removed.

field of view. In addition, in the various experiments, atop the Logitech C905 lens, we added one of two inexpensive snap-on wide angle attachment lenses to expand the robot's field of view even further. Experiments were conducted only on the bottom three blade center chassis locations. To discover blade centers and blade servers at additional rack positions one would have to mount additional forward-facing cameras. The forward-facing camera of these experiments is in addition to the existing downward-facing camera the robot uses for its basic tile-by-tile navigation. Details of the robot's basic vision-guided navigation can be found in [3, 2].

2.1 Detecting and Counting Lights

The first experiment designed was to test the viability of encoding static ID numbers using each of the available bits. The experiments were universally successful but pointed to the fact that just two chasses were sufficiently clear in the image with a wide-angle or fisheye lens to faithfully discover all available lights. Thus the final robot would have to be equipped with several cameras. Figure 1 shows such a robot.

2.2 Framing and Reading Signatures

Our approach to framing and reading chassis signatures was to first set all of the lights on, so that the robot could determine the bits available to it. After processing the locations of the available bits, the actual message could then be sent. Figure 2 shows an initial binary image with all the LEDs of a blade center turned on. This image, in conjunction with the analogous image with all LEDs turned off, allows the robot to ascertain which LEDs are available for encoding.

In some cases a message may take multiple "words," but since the robot can process images in milliseconds, even the blade centers with few available bits can process their entire signature with negligible overhead. Note that both the sender (the asset management software in conjunction with the BCMMs) and the receiver of the message (the robot) know the number of available bits by virtue of the initial framing exercise. Only BCMMs with available bits matching those found by the robot will broadcast, and further, under the assumption that the serial numbers are of uniform length, all messages will be of the same length and, hence, the same number of "words" and so the sequential transmission of these words can by readily time synchronized.

The second experiment involved first allowing the robot to identify the set of available bits by alternately setting all available indicator LEDs to the "off" position, and then to the "on" position, before performing the actual encoding. 15 trials were

Figure 2: A two-bit (black and white) image of one of the blade centers used in our experiments with all available LEDs turned on – one of two views used by the robot to determine the number of bits available for encoding. Blades 1 – 6, 8, and 11 – 14 are available.

performed with each blade center utilizing distinct encodings. Again the encodings were hand generated with an attempt to balance the utilization of each bit, and all tests were successful.

2.3 Acceptable Robot Positioning

Up until this point in our experimental protocol, the robot had been manually placed and oriented towards the front of each rack, producing very promising results. The question we therefore turned to was examining the degree of accuracy the robot required in terms of centering in front of the rack in order for visual identification of the LED states to succeed. The next experiment established the region of confidence for accurately reading a blade center's encoding, a region we ultimately referred to as the "critical teardrop" because of its roughly teardrop shape.

2.4 Ability to Achieve a Position

After identifying the "critical teardrop," i.e. getting a precise picture of where the robot must be in order to accurately read the binary encodings, a final experiment was designed to discover how accurately the robot could reach a requisite coordinate and orientation, again with successful results achieved.

3. CONCLUSION

We present a simple, automated and low-cost approach for asset tracking in data centers using blade center indicator LEDs as asset signatures. Our approach uses a vision-guided robot and leverages existing data center management capabilities to eliminate the need for prior processing, tagging of assets, additional hardware, or manual inspection. Our experimental evaluations underline the feasibility and accuracy of our method.

4. REFERENCES
[1] IBM Corporation. IBM BladeCenter advanced Management Module: Command-Line Interface Reference Guide. http://publib.boulder.ibm.com/infocenter/bladectr/ documentation/topic/com.ibm.bladecenter.advmgtmod.doc/ kp1aupdf.pdf, 2009. [Online; accessed 31-October-2012].
[2] J. Lenchner, C. Isci, J. Kephart, C. Mansley, J. Connell, and S. McIntosh. Towards data center self-diagnosis using a mobile robot. *Proceedings of the 8th International Conference on Autonomic Computing (ICAC)*, pages 81–90, 2011.
[3] C. Mansley, J. Connell, C. Isci, J. Lenchner, J. O. Kephart, S. McIntosh, and M. Schappert. Robotic mapping and monitoring of data centers. *IEEE International Conference on Robotics and Automation (ICRA)*, 2011.

Data Center Demand Response: Avoiding the Coincident Peak via Workload Shifting and Local Generation

Zhenhua Liu
California Institute of
Technology
Pasadena, CA, USA
zliu2@caltech.edu

Adam Wierman
California Institute of
Technology
Pasadena, CA, USA
adamw@caltech.edu

Yuan Chen
HP Labs
Palo Alto, CA, USA
yuan.chen@hp.com

Benjamin Razon
California Institute of
Technology
Pasadena, CA, USA
ben@caltech.edu

Niangjun Chen
California Institute of
Technology
Pasadena, CA, USA
ncchen@caltech.edu

ABSTRACT

Demand response is a crucial aspect of the future smart grid. It has the potential to provide significant peak demand reduction and to ease the incorporation of renewable energy into the grid. Data centers' participation in demand response is becoming increasingly important given the high and increasing energy consumption and the flexibility in demand management in data centers compared to conventional industrial facilities. In this extended abstract we briefly describe recent work in [1] on two demand response schemes to reduce a data center's peak loads and energy expenditure: workload shifting and the use of local power generations. In [1], we conduct a detailed characterization study of coincident peak data over two decades from Fort Collins Utilities, Colorado and then develop two algorithms for data centers by combining workload scheduling and local power generation to avoid the coincident peak and reduce the energy expenditure. The first algorithm optimizes the expected cost and the second one provides a good worst-case guarantee for any coincident peak pattern. We evaluate these algorithms via numerical simulations based on real world traces from production systems. The results show that using workload shifting in combination with local generation can provide significant cost savings (up to 40% in the Fort Collins Utilities' case) compared to either alone.

Categories and Subject Descriptors

C.0 [**Computer Systems Organization**]: General

Keywords

Demand response, coincident peak pricing, data center, workload shifting, online algorithm

1. INTRODUCTION

Demand response (DR) programs seek to provide incentives to induce dynamic demand management of customers' electricity load in response to power supply conditions, for example, reducing their power consumption in response to a peak load warning signal or request from the utility. The National Institute of Standards and Technology (NIST) and the Department of Energy (DoE) have both identified demand response as one of the priority areas for the future smart grid [2, 3]. In particular, the National Assessment of

Demand Response Potential report has identified that demand response has the potential to reduce up to 20% of the total peak electricity demand across the country [4]. Further, demand response has the potential to significantly ease the adoption of renewable energy into the grid.

Data centers represent a particularly promising industry for the adoption of demand response programs. First, data center energy consumption is large and increasing rapidly. In 2011, data centers consumed approximately 1.5% of all electricity worldwide, which was about 56% higher than the preceding five years [5, 6, 7]. Second, data centers are highly automated and monitored, and so there is the potential for a high-degree of responsiveness. Third, many workloads in data centers are delay tolerant, which enables significant flexibility for optimizing power demand. Finally, local power generation, e.g., traditional backup generators and newer renewable power installations, can help shape the power demand from the grid. In particular, local power generation combined with workload management has a significant potential to shed the peak load and reduce energy costs.

Despite wide recognition of the potential in data centers, the current reality is that industry data centers seemingly perform little, if any, demand response [5, 6]. One popular demand response programs available is Coincident Peak Pricing (CPP), which is required for medium and large industrial consumers in many regions. These programs work by charging a very high price for usage during the coincident peak hour, which is the hour when the most electricity is requested from the utility's wholesale electric supplier. This rate is often over 200 times higher than the base rate, so it is common for the coincident peak charges to account for over 23% of a customer's electric bill according to Fort Collins Utilities. Hence, from the perspective of a consumer, it is critical to control and reduce usage during the peak hour. Although it is impossible to accurately predict exactly when the peak hour will occur, many utilities identify potential peak hours and send warning signals to customers.

Coincident peak pricing is not a new phenomenon. In fact, it has been used for large industrial consumers for decades. However, it is rare for large industrial consumers to have the responsiveness that data centers can provide. Unfortunately, data centers today either do not respond to coincident peak warnings or simply respond by turning on their backup power generators. Using backup power generation seems appealing since it can be automated easily, it does not impact operations, and it provides demand response for the utility company. However, the traditional backup generators at data centers can be very "dirty" – in some cases even

SIGMETRICS'13, June 17-21, 2013, Pittsburgh, PA, USA.
ACM 978-1-4503-1900-3/13/06.

(a) Time of the day

(b) Days of the week

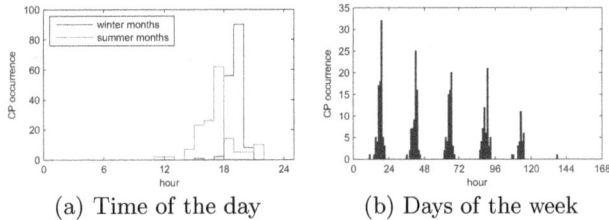

Figure 1: Occurrence of coincident peak. (a) Empirical frequency of occurrences on the time of day (b) Empirical frequency of occurrences over the week.

not meeting Environmental Protection Agency (EPA) emissions standards [5]. So, from an environmental perspective this form of response is far from ideal. Further, running a backup generator can be expensive. Alternatively, providing demand response via shifting workload can be more cost effective. A challenge with workload shifting is that we need to ensure that the Service Level Agreements (SLAs), e.g., completion deadlines, remain satisfied.

2. OVERVIEW OF RESULTS

In this abstract, we briefly discuss the main contributions of the work in [1]. First, we present **a detailed characterization study of coincident peak pricing** and provide insight about its properties. We characterize 26 years' coincident peak pricing data from Fort Collins Utilities. The data highlights a number of important observations. For example, the data set shows that the coincident peak occurrence has a strong diurnal pattern that differs considerably during different days of the week and across seasons, as shown in Figure 1. Further, the data highlights that coincident peak warnings are highly reliable – only twice did the coincident peak not occur during a warning hour.

Second, we develop **two online algorithms for avoiding the coincident peak and reducing the energy expenditure using workload shifting and local power generation.** The uncertainty of the occurrence of the coincident peak hour presents significant challenges for workload scheduling and local generation planning. For example, traditional workload scheduling can be done using workload and cost estimates a day in advance, but the coincident peak is not known until the end of the month. Similarly, warnings that the next hour could be a coincident peak may only arrive from the utility with, in many cases, 5 minutes notice. Given the uncertainty about the coincident peak hour, we consider two design goals when developing algorithms: good performance in the average case and in the worst case. We develop an algorithm for each goal. For the average case, we present a stochastic optimization based algorithm to minimizes the expected cost given the estimates of the likelihood of a coincident peak or warning during each hour of the day. For the worst case scenario, we propose a robust optimization based algorithm, which is computationally efficient, and guarantees that the cost is within a small constant of the optimal cost of an offline algorithm.

The third main contribution of our work is **a detailed study and comparison of the potential cost savings of algorithms via numerical simulations based on real world traces from production systems.** Our experimental results highlight a number of important observations. Most importantly, the results highlight that our proposed algorithms provide significant cost and emission reductions compared to industry practice and provide close to the minimal costs under real workloads. Further, our experimental results highlight that both local generation and workload shifting are crucial to ensuring minimal energy costs and emissions. Specifically, combining workload shifting with local generation can provide 35-40% reductions of energy

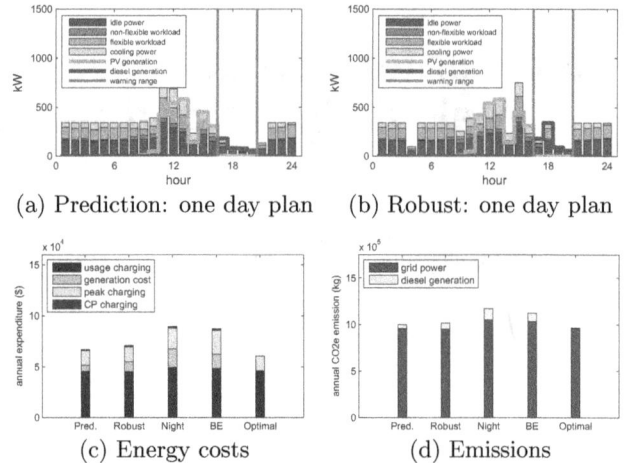

(a) Prediction: one day plan

(b) Robust: one day plan

(c) Energy costs

(d) Emissions

Figure 2: Comparison of energy costs and emissions for a data center with both local PV installations and local diesel generators. (a) and (b) show the plans computed by our algorithms.

costs, and 10-15% reductions of emissions. An example of these results is shown in Figure 2, where we compare energy costs and emissions of our algorithms (termed "*Prediction (Pred)*" and "*Robust*", respectively) with two baselines meant to mimic current industry standard planning: *Night* tries to run jobs during night if possible and otherwise run these jobs with a constant rate to finish them before their deadlines, while *Best Effort* finishes jobs in a first-come-first-serve manner as fast as possible. *Optimal* is the offline optimal plan given knowledge of when the coincident peak will occur. As shown in the figures, our algorithms provide about 20% savings compared to *Night* and *Best Effort* (up to 40% in other cases). Specifically, *Prediction* reshapes the flexible workload to prevent using the time slots that are likely to be warning periods or the coincident peak as shown in Figures 2(a), while *Robust* tries to make the grid power usage as flat as possible as shown in Figures 2(b). Both algorithms try to fully utilize PV generation. In contrast, *Night* and *Best Effort* do not consider the warnings, the coincident peak, or renewable generation. Therefore, they have significantly higher coincident peak charges and local generation costs. Our sensitivity analysis shows the costs and emissions of *Robust* are unaffected by the quality of the predictions; however, the costs and emissions of *Prediction* change dramatically.

Please refer to [1] for the full version.

Acknowledgements

This work was supported by NSF grants CNS 0846025, DoE grant DE-EE0002890, and HP Labs.

3. REFERENCES

[1] Z. Liu, A. Wierman, Y. Chen, B. Razon, and N. Chen, "Data center demand response: Avoiding the coincident peak via workload shifting and local generation [technical report],"

[2] National Institute of Standards and Technology, "NIST framework and roadmap for smart grid interoperability standards." NIST Special Publication 1108, 2010.

[3] Department of Energy, "The smart grid: An introduction."

[4] Federal Energy Regulatory Commission, "National assessment of demand response potential." 2009.

[5] NY Times, "Power, Pollution and the Internet."

[6] G. Ghatikar, V. Ganti, N. Matson, and M. Piette, "Demand response opportunities and enabling technologies for data centers: Findings from field studies," 2012.

[7] J. Koomey, "Growth in data center electricity use 2005 to 2010," *Oakland, CA: Analytics Press. August*, vol. 1, p. 2010, 2011.

Delivering Fairness and Priority Enforcement on Asymmetric Multicore Systems via OS Scheduling

Juan Carlos Sáez   Fernando Castro   Daniel Chaver   Manuel Prieto
Department of Computer Architecture. School of Computer Science
Complutense University of Madrid[*]
{jcsaezal,fcastror,dani02,mpmatias}@pdi.ucm.es

ABSTRACT

Symmetric-ISA (instruction set architecture) asymmetric-performance multicore processors (AMPs) were shown to deliver higher performance per watt and area than symmetric CMPs for applications with diverse architectural requirements. So, it is likely that future multicore processors will combine big power-hungry *fast* cores and small low-power *slow* ones. In this paper, we propose a novel thread scheduling algorithm that aims to improve the throughput-fairness trade-off on AMP systems. Our experimental evaluation on real hardware and using scheduler implementations on a general-purpose operating system, reveals that our proposal delivers a better throughput-fairness trade-off than previous schedulers for a wide variety of multi-application workloads, including single-threaded and multithreaded applications.

Categories and Subject Descriptors

D.4.1 [**Process Management**]: Scheduling; C.1.3 [**Processor Architectures**]: Other Architecture Styles—*Heterogeneous (hybrid) systems*

General Terms

Algorithms, Performance, Measurement

Keywords

Asymmetric Multicore, Operating Systems, Scheduling

1. INTRODUCTION

Asymmetric multicore processors (AMP) [3] were proposed as a more power-efficient alternative to conventional multicore processors that consist of identical cores. An AMP contains at least two core types, "fast" and "slow", which support the same instruction-set architecture, but differ in microarchitectural features, size, power consumption and performance. Early studies have demonstrated that having just two core types is sufficient to extract most of the benefits from AMPs [3] and simplifies their design. For that reason, in this work we target AMP systems with two core types.

---

[*]This research was funded by the Spanish government's research contracts TIN2012-32180 and the Ingenio 2010 Consolider ESP00C-07-20811.

Most existing proposals on scheduling for AMPs strive to maximize the system thoughput [5, 2]. Pursuing other important goals such as delivering fairness or priority enforcement on AMPs has drawn less attention from the research community. Schedulers such as RR [5] or A-DWRR [4] aim to provide fairness by alloting the same amount of heterogeneous CPU share to equal-priority applications. However, because applications in a multiprogram workload may derive different benefit from using the fast cores in an AMP, assigning the same heterogeneous CPU share to equal-priority application does not ensure an even slowdown (due to sharing the AMP) across applications. In addition, not taking into account the diversity in relative speedups may lead to degrading the system throughput significantly [5]. To address these shortcomings, we propose Prop-SP, a novel scheduling algorithm that supports priority enforcement on AMPs and attempts to even out the slowdown experienced by equal-priority applications due to sharing the system, while ensuring a high system throughput. Prop-SP is equipped with support to effectively accelerate some types of parallel applications on AMPs. We evaluated Prop-SP using real hardware and compared it against other scheduling schemes.

2. DESIGN

The Prop-SP scheduler assigns threads to fast and slow cores so as to preserve load balance in the AMP system, and migrates threads among fast and slow cores to ensure that they run on fast cores for a specific amount of time.

To enforce that threads receive a specific fast-core share, Prop-SP relies on a mechanism inspired by Xen's Credit Scheduler [1]. At a high level, this mechanism works as follows. Each thread has a fast-core credit counter associated with it. When a thread runs on a fast core it consumes credits. Threads that have fast-core credits left (i.e., their credit counter is greater than zero) are preferentially assigned to fast cores by the scheduler.

Every so often, the OS triggers a *credit assignment process* that allots fast-core credits to active applications (i.e., with runnable threads). Each application receives credits in proportion to its dynamic weight, which is defined as the product of its priority and its net speedup (speedup minus one). The application priority is set by the user. The speedup indicates the relative benefit that the application would derive if all fast cores in the AMP were devoted to running threads from this application, with respect to running all threads on slow cores. This speedup is estimated at runtime by Prop-SP without the user intervention. For single-threaded applications, determining the speedup entails determining the

Table 1: Metrics to assess throughput and fairness for a workload consisting of n applications running simultaneously under a given thread scheduler.

Metric	Definition
$CT_{fast,app}$	Completion time of application app when running alone in the system (with all the fast cores available)
$CT_{slow,app}$	Completion time of application app when it runs alone in the system but using slow cores only
$CT_{sched,app}$	Completion time of application app in the multiprogram workload running under a given scheduler.
$Slowdown_{app}$	$CT_{sched,app}/CT_{fast,app}$
Aggregate Speedup	$\sum_{i=1}^{n}\left(\frac{CT_{slow,i}}{CT_{sched,i}}-1\right)$
Unfairness	$\frac{MAX(Slowdown_1,...,Slowdown_n)}{MIN(Slowdown_1,...,Slowdown_n)}$

speedup factor (SF) of its single runnable thread: $\frac{IPS_{fast}}{IPS_{slow}}$, where IPS_{fast} and IPS_{slow} are the thread's instructions per second ratios achieved on fast and slow cores respectively. To this end we leverage the technique proposed in [5]. For multithreaded programs, several factors in addition to the SF must be taken into account to estimate the speedup, such as the amount of thread-level parallelism (TLP).

Credits awarded to the application are distributed among its runnable threads. For single-threaded programs, this boils down to increasing the fast-core credit counter of its single thread by the amount of credits awarded. For multithreaded programs, Prop-SP supports several credit distribution schemes to meet the needs of diverse applications.

3. RESULTS AND CONCLUSIONS

We assessed the effectiveness of two variants of Prop-SP (static and dynamic), which follow different approaches to determine a thread's SF. The *base* implementation of Prop-SP, referred to as *Prop-SP (dynamic)*, estimates SFs online using hardware counters (using the technique from [5]). *Prop-SP (static)*, on the other hand, asummes a constant SF value for each thread, measured prior to the execution. We compare both versions of Prop-SP against the RR (Round Robin) scheduler, which simply fair-shares fast cores among all applications in the workload, and HSP (High-SPeedup) [2, 5], which aims to maximize the system throughput by mapping to fast cores those applications that derive the greatest performance benefit from these cores.

All the evaluated algorithms have been implemented in the Solaris kernel and tested on real multicore hardware made asymmetric by reducing the processor frequency of a subset of cores in the platform. Figure 1 shows the results for various multi-application workloads consisting of both single-threaded and multithreaded applications running under the various schedulers. Overall, HSP, yields the best system throughput but fails to deliver fairness accross the board. RR, on the other hand, does rather a good job in terms of both fairness and throughput for workloads including single-threaded applications only. However, when multithreaded applications are present in the workload, it degrades the system throughput significantly. In contrast, Prop-SP is able to make efficient use of the AMPs and improve the throughput-fairness tradeoff for a wider range of workloads. Moreover, the potential inacuracies of the SF

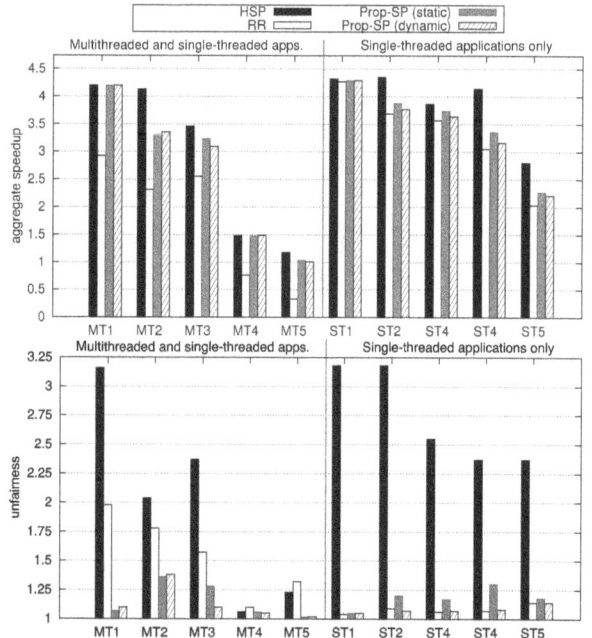

Figure 1: Results for various multi-application workloads running on an AMD-based emulated AMP system where fast cores run at 2.6Ghz and slow cores at 0.8Ghz. Both the aggregate speedup and unfairness metrics are defined in Table 1.

estimation model used by Prop-SP (dynamic), do not prevent this scheduler from reaping benefits similar to those of the static version. Overall, these benefits are especially pronounced for workloads including multithreaded programs.

We also experimented with scenarios where we gradually increase the priority of one or several *high-priority* (HP) applications in the workload. The results reveal that Prop-SP is able to effectively reduce the completion time of HP applications as the priority increases, while ensuring higher throughput and lower unfairness than RR.

Key elements for the success of Prop-SP are the credit-based mechanism enabling the scheduler to adjust the fast-core share alloted to the different programs, its reliance on estimation models to approximate per-thread speedup factors (SFs) online and the specific support to accelerate certain types of multithreaded programs.

4. REFERENCES

[1] L. Cherkasova, D. Gupta, and A. Vahdat. Comparison of the three CPU schedulers in Xen. *SIGMETRICS Perform. Eval. Rev.*, 35(2):42–51, Sept. 2007.

[2] D. Koufaty et al. Bias Scheduling in Heterogeneous Multi-core Architectures. In *Proc. of Eurosys '10*, 2010.

[3] R. Kumar et al. Single-ISA Heterogeneous Multi-Core Architectures: the Potential for Processor Power Reduction. In *Proc. of MICRO 36*, 2003.

[4] T. Li et al. Operating system support for overlapping-ISA heterogeneous multi-core architectures. In *HPCA'10*, pages 1–12, 2010.

[5] J. C. Saez et al. Leveraging core specialization via OS scheduling to improve performance on asymmetric multicore systems. *ACM Trans. Comput. Syst.*, 30(2):6:1–6:38, Apr. 2012.

Detecting User Dissatisfaction and Understanding the Underlying Reasons

Åke Arvidsson
Packet Technologies, Ericsson Research
SE-164 80 Stockholm, Sweden
Ake.Arvidsson@ericsson.com

Ying Zhang
Packet Technologies, Ericsson Research
200 Holger Way, San José, CA 95134, U.S.A.
Ying.Zhang@ericsson.com

Categories and Subject Descriptors

C.2.0 [**Computer Systems Organization**]: PERFORMANCE OF SYSTEMS

General Terms

Measurement

Keywords

Passive monitoring, QoE

1. INTRODUCTION

Today network operators face the challenges of accurately measuring Quality-of-Experience (QoE) for general web applications. QoE is a subjective metric relating to user expectation, satisfaction, and overall experience and despite the rich history in the multimedia community [1, 2, 3, 4] there is no scalable method to quantify QoE for general web applications. Traditional methods relies on users to indicate their satisfaction in surveys in a subjective manner. Such methods can be inaccurate as the results depend on the sampled test subjects and it does not scale.

A recent study proposes to infer user dissatisfaction related to web pages from the behaviour of early interruptions [5]. More specifically, unsatisfactory long times between requests and presentations could make impatient end-users push the STOP or RELOAD buttons in their web browsers thereby initiating end-user cancellations. Such cancellations would result in early closures of the HTTP sessions as well as the underlying TCP connections and may be interpreted as indicators of unsatisfactory QoE. However, naively using all early terminations as signs of bad QoE is not accurate as it may result in many false positives caused by, *e.g.,* user losing interest in the content or closing the browser accidentally. Thus, the first question we explore in this paper is, how to identify the set of terminations that reflects true user dissatisfaction? Once this set is narrowed down, we use it to answer questions like what the acceptable throughput and response time are for most users.

In this paper, we consider transaction-based web applications and develop a method to automatically search for early cancellations from passively collected traces. Our contribution in this paper is twofold. First, we propose a methodology to systematically examine the early cancellations and eliminate false positives. Our key idea is to identify *acceptable performance* by comparing normal transactions to cancelled ones and, since tolerance levels can deviate across users, to do this from user-specific profiles. We show that

the filtering method generates much more meaningful results than the naive approach. Second, we conduct comprehensive analysis of data collected in a wireline fibre network and a wireless cellular network. We present results of *acceptable* performance metrics such as throughput and response time in this paper.

2. METHODOLOGY

We will first introduce the data set, followed by our methods of identifying early termination from passively collected traffic traces, and finally describe the filtering methodology to reduce the false positives.

Data set. In this paper, we use three datasets of full-size packets. The first data set (*Wireline0*) is collected from a fibre access network in the Sweden. It is a two-day packet dump with 9.8M HTTP flows, 235K of which have client initiated RST sent. Both wireless data sets (*Wireless0* and *Wireless1*) were collected on a Gn interface between a GGSN and a SGSN in a cellular network. Both sets contain 354 hours of data collected at different locations. The first set contains 3.8M flows, among 783K of which contains reset packets. The second set is at the same scale of 3M flows. To guarantee user privacy, we were not given direct access to the data but our partner kindly ran our code and shared the resulting, anonymised metadata with us.

Identifying user early terminations. Our method to identify users' unsatisfactory experiences is to search for patterns from passively collected packet traces. The intuition is that when a user experiences bad performance, he or she will initiate the closure of the HTTP session and the communication pattern observed in the network will thus be different from the one during normal downloading cases. For example, when a client clicks "STOP" button on the browser before the download is completed, we observed that the client sends a TCP reset packet, *[RST,ACK]*, to close the TCP connection. It then keeps on replying with *[RST]* packet when receiving additional data packets from the web server. We have developed a tool that assembles web pages from packet traces and classify the outcomes by searching for such patterns, the details can be found in [5].

Filtering method. Although user-initiated cancellations are likely indicators of user dissatisfaction, it is clear that cancellations also may be related to other reasons but performance, *e.g.,* web navigation or loss of interest. One way to identify the reasons behind cancellations is to interview the end users but, since it cannot scale, we propose to heuristically classify cancellations as "performance related" or "for other reasons".

In more detail, we identify "acceptable performance" after which cancellations are said to be related to performance if their performance is worse than this threshold, but attributed to other reasons otherwise. Noting that tolerance may vary between different users and different content, we propose to determine "acceptance thresh-

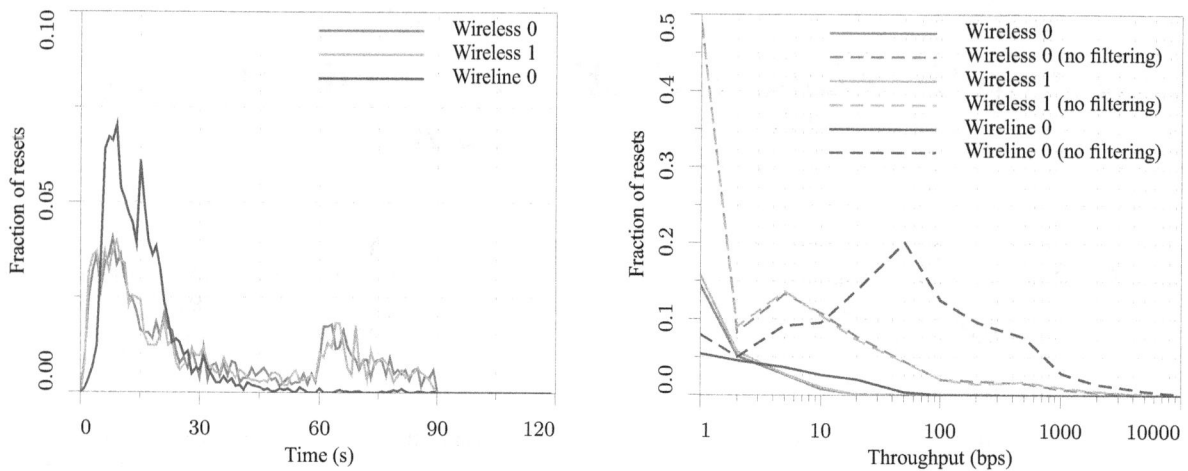

Figure 1: Occurrence of resets at different times (left) and rates (right). The dashed lines in the right graph refer to unfiltered results.

olds" *per user* (to account for different users) expressed *as percentiles* (to account for different content in a way which less sensitive to outliers).

The complete method may be described by the following steps:
1. Remove all requests for which it cannot be verified that they are related to web browsing. (We have used the criterion that the agent name should contain the word "Mozilla". This means that we capture, *e.g.,* Internet Explorer, Chrome and Firefox which correspond to about 46% and 83% of all pages in the wireless data sets and the wireline data set respectively.)
2. Build a list of all cancelled requests C and a list of all users (IP addresses) U with at least one cancelled request.
3. Build a list of all normal requests N the users (IP addresses) of which are found in U.
4. Remove all users in U the IP address of which is not seen in at least R_{min} normal requests. (We have used $R_{min} = 20$.) Then remove all requests in C and N related to users no longer seen in U.
5. For all users $u \in U$, compute the pth percentile of the response time, $\rho_u(p)$, and the πth percentile of the throughput, $\lambda_u(\pi)$, over all normal requests with the IP address of u. (We have used $p = 75$ and $\pi = 25$.)
6. Remove all requests in C the response time of which is below ρ_u or the throughput of which is above λ_u. Then remove all users in U the IP address of which is no longer seen in C and finally all requests in N related to users no longer seen in U.

3. RESULTS

We now present some results about what users accept in terms of response times and throughputs and how this is linked to the classical measure of QoE known as MOS.

Figure 1 shows at what times and rates resets occur. For **times** (left) we divide time into one second bins and show the number of resets per bin normalised by the number of resets in all bins per data set. It is seen that most resets occur within the first 20 seconds and that there are two peaks. The first, after a few seconds, is likely to be related to "impatient users", and the second one, after about one minute, is probably related to TCP time outs.

For **rates**, shown in the right in Figure 1, we divide rates in approximately logarithmic bins 1, 2 and 5 times 1, 10, 100 *etc.* and show the number of resets per bin normalised by the number of resets in all bins per data set. It is seen that most resets occur for low rates and that the number of resets decreases when the throughput

increases (solid lines). To demonstrate the effectiveness of the filtering method, we also plot the same metric using the naive method (dashed lines) and we note that there is no such strong correlation, *i.e.,* we have reset peaks at higher rates which presumably are related to, *e.g.,* navigation or correction rather than performance.

Nothing the difference between filtered and unfiltered data, it is concluded that filtering is necessary to obtain meaningful data. *It is also noted that the two accesses are remarkably similar although we note that resets in the wireline data set are more concentrated with respect to time (left diagram) and less concentrated with respect to rates (right diagram).*

4. CONCLUSION

We have presented a new method to identify a set of characteristics from traffic logs that are related to the user perceived experience. The method identifies such QoE indicators without active involvement of users and without active measurements injected into the network. To reduce the false positives of this approach, we developed a filtering method that identifies and compares to acceptable performance by building a profile for each user. We conducted a set of studies of the correlations between these indicators as well as their correlation with performance metrics.

5. REFERENCES

[1] ITU-T Recommendation, "P. 800. Methods for subjective determination of transmission quality." International Telecommunication Union, 1996.

[2] ITU-T Recommendation, "J. 144. Objective perceptual video quality measurement techniques for digital cable television in the presence of a full reference." International Telecommunication Union, 2001.

[3] ITU-T Recommendation, "P.862 Perceptual evaluation of speech quality (PESQ), an objective method for end-to-end speech quality assessment of narrow-band telephone networks and speech codecs." International Telecommunication Union, 2001.

[4] S. Voran, "The development of objective video quality measures that emulate human perception," in *Proc. IEEE GLOBECOM*, 1991.

[5] Å. Arvidsson, Y. Zhang, and N. Beheshti, "Detecting user dissatisfaction from passive monitoring," in *Proc. of EuroCon*, 2013.

Discriminant Malware Distance Learning on Structural Information for Automated Malware Classification

Deguang Kong
Dept. of Computer Science and Engineering
University of Texas at Arlington
doogkong@gmail.com

Guanhua Yan
Information Sciences Group (CCS-3)
Los Alamos National Laboratory
ghyan@lanl.gov

ABSTRACT

In this work, we explore techniques that can automatically classify malware variants into their corresponding families. Our framework extracts structural information from malware programs as attributed function call graphs, further learns discriminant malware distance metrics, finally adopts an ensemble of classifiers for automated malware classification. Experimental results show that our method is able to achieve high classification accuracy.

Categories and Subject Descriptors: I.2.6 [Artificial Intelligence], D.4.6 [Security and Protection]

General Terms: Algorithm, Security, Data Mining

Keywords: Malware categorization, Distance learning

1. INTRODUCTION

Malware are responsible for a large number of malicious activities in the cyber space, such as spamming, identity theft, and DDoS (Distributed Denial of Service) attacks. Behind the sheer number of malware instances, however, lies the fact that a large number of them came from the same origins. More than 75 percent of malware detected belong to as few as 25 families, based on the 2006 Microsoft Security Intelligence report [5]. Accurate prediction of the evolution trend of a malware family also enables us to deploy effective mitigation methods in advance and thus alleviate the damage caused by this malware family.

Therefore, there is an urgent need of developing methods that can automatically classify malware instances into their corresponding families accurately. The goal of this work is to develop a framework that automatically classifies malware instances according to their inherent rich structural information, such as their function call graphs and basic block graphs.

In this work, we present a new framework for automated malware classification using discriminant distance learning on structural information extracted from malware. This framework extracts the function call graph from each malware program, and collects various types of fine-grained features at the function level, such as what system calls are made and how many I/O read and write operations have been made in each function. For each type of features, our framework evaluates the similarity of two malware programs by iteratively applying the following two basic techniques: (1) *discriminant distance metric learning*, which projects the original feature space into a new one such that malware instances belonging to the same family are closely clustered while clusters formed by different malware families are separated with large margins; (2) *pairwise graph matching*, which aims to find the right pairwise

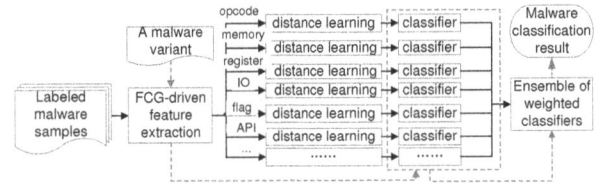

Figure 1: Overview of our automated malware classification framework (solid lines are used for the training process, and dashed line for the process of classifying a new malware variant)

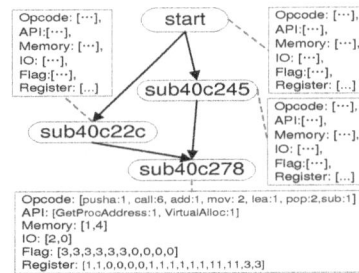

Figure 2: Illustration of an attributed FCG

function-level matching between the function call graphs of two malware instances in order to measure their structural similarity. The similarity score estimated between two malware instances for each type of features reflects the likelihood that they should be classified into the same malware family – if observed feature values of that type are used as our *evidence*. We further learn our *confidence* level in each type of evidence and henceforth build a classifier that predicts the family of a new malware instance by combining different types of evidences with their corresponding confidence levels.

2. OVERVIEW OF METHODOLOGY

The overview of our automated malware classification framework is depicted in Figure 1.

Step 1: FCG-driven feature extraction. To extract structural information from a malware program, we first disassemble the malware program, and build its function call graph. The function call graph is further used to drive the process of feature extraction: for every node (i.e., a function) in the graph, we extract various types of *attributes*, including what library APIs are made and how many I/O read and write operations have been made in this function. Information regarding each type of features is represented as a vector of numerical values. After Step 1, each labeled malware program is abstracted into an attributed function call graph (see Fig. 2).

Step 2: Discriminant malware distance learning. The next

Table 1: Different scenarios used in our experiments

Scenario	op-n	mem-n	reg-n	io-n	flag-n	api-n	ES-dis
Attribute	Opcode	Memory	Register	I/O	Flag	API	Ensemble
Distance learning	No	No	No	No	No	No	Yes

Table 2: Average F-1 measure in terms of percentage across all families. For SVM, we show the results when $\gamma = 0.3$, $\gamma = 0.7$, and also the average when γ is chosen from $[0.1, 0.3, \cdots, 1.9]$; for kNN, we show the results when $k = 6$, 10, and also the average when k is chosen from $[2, 4, ..., 16]$.

classifier	γ/k	op-n	mem-n	reg-n	io-n	flag-n	api-n	ES-dis
SVM	0.3	86.06	84.20	**86.14**	85.07	68.59	82.99	**93.88**
kNN	6	48.89	67.82	56.52	54.53	**85.33**	66.71	**91.23**
SVM	0.7	**88.61**	87.49	87.76	87.63	72.25	82.65	**98.73**
kNN	10	62.33	66.30	**87.79**	58.26	66.11	68.90	**95.31**
SVM	avg	84.54	84.51	83.57	**85.52**	68.39	84.72	**93.44**
kNN	avg	54.28	65.77	69.04	55.25	**73.52**	66.39	**90.54**

step concerns how to compute the distance between two malware distances represented as their attributed function call graphs. For each type of attribute, we project the original feature space onto a new one such that malware instances belonging to the same family are closely clustered while clusters formed by different malware families are separated with large margins. Moreover, we perform pairwise graph matching, which aims to find the right pairwise function-level matching between the attributed function call graphs of two malware instances for the purpose of measuring their structural similarity.

Step 3: Training individual classifiers. For each type of features, once we have computed the similarity between any two labeled malware instances, we train an individual classifier for it. Our framework is open to any classifier that, in order to classify a new sample, requires only information of a set of *anchor instances*, which are usually the subset of labeled samples in the original dataset. Such classifiers include the kNN classifier, for which the anchor instance set includes the k closest instances from the test instance, and the SVM classifier, whose support vector contains all the anchor instances.

Step 4: Building ensemble of weighted classifiers. For each type of features we have considered, the similarity measure between two malware instances reflects the likelihood that they belong to the same family. Given a new malware variant, for each type of features, we form its *evidence* as the distance it is from each of its anchor instances as well as the label information of each anchor instance. The *type* of an evidence is defined to be the type of *attribute* from which it is formed. To learn the confidence level associated with a type of evidence, we use an Adaboost-like approach, which gives an increasingly higher penalty to training samples that are wrongly classified. We henceforth build a classifier that predicts the family of a new malware instance by combining different types of evidences according to their corresponding confidence levels.

The output of the training phase of our automated malware classification framework is an ensemble of classifiers. Given a new unknown malware sample, we first construct its function call graph from the disassembly code, and for each function node in it, we extract different types of attribute. Next, for each type of attribute, we form its evidence that describes the distance between the new sample and the anchor instances as well as how each anchor instance is labeled. We then feed the evidence to the corresponding individual classifier. By combining all the evidences, the ensemble of weighted classifiers makes the final decision on which malware family it should be classified into.

3. EXPERIMENTS

We use a malware dataset from Offensive Computing [6], which contains 526,179 unique malware variants collected in the wild. The malware dataset contains both packed and unpacked instances, and in our evaluation, we only use unpacked ones, and disassemble them with IDA pro [1]. We obtain 11 families of malware: Bagle, Bifrose, Ldpinch, Swizzor, Zbot, Koobface, Lmir, Rbot, Sdbot, Vundo, and Zlob.

We use 80% of the malware samples from each family to train our model, and the remaining ones are used for testing the effec-

tiveness of our approach. This process is iterated for five times, and we report the averages as the classification performance.

Parameter setting: For the k-nearest neighbor classifier, we choose k between 6 and 10. For the SVM classifier, we use the Gaussian kernel: $k(\mathcal{G}_i, \mathcal{G}_j) = e^{-\gamma \frac{D_{i,j}^2}{t^2}}$, where γ is a tunable parameter, and t is the average distance of the k-nearest neighbors for each malware. We choose γ between 0.3 and 0.7, and t is computed using the three nearest neighbors. We compare the performances of the methods in different scenarios as shown in Table 1. Our method corresponds to the **ES-dis** scenario.

In Table 2, we show the average performance improvement across all malware families. Clearly, for both classifiers, the F_1 measure is significantly improved using our method (i.e., ES-dis). For instance, considering both the average cases, our method improves over the best individual method by 9.3% for the SVM classifier, and by 23.2% for the kNN classifier.

4. RELATED WORK

Since the seminal works done by Schultz *et al.* [8] and Kolter *et al.* [2], machine learning techniques have been used in a number of efforts to automatically distinguish malware from benign executable programs (e.g., [7, 3, 4]). In contrast to these earlier works on malware detection, this study focuses on malware classification by distinguishing instances from different families. In [9], Yan *et al.* compared the discriminative power of different types of malware features for automated malware classification.

5. CONCLUSIONS

We present a generic framework for automated malware classification. We develop methods to compute the similarity of two malware programs based on their attributed function call graphs, and use an ensemble of classifiers that learn from the pairwise malware distances and classify new malware instances automatically.

6. REFERENCES

[1] http://www.hex-rays.com/products/ida/index.shtml.
[2] J. Z. Kolter and M. A. Maloof. Learning to detect and classify malicious executables in the wild. *Journal of Machine Learning Research*, 7, 2006.
[3] D. Kong, Y. Jhi, T. Gong, S. Zhu, P. Liu, and H. Xi. Sas: Semantics aware signature generation for polymorphic worm detection. In *SecureComm*, pages 1–19, 2010.
[4] D. Kong, D. Tian, P. Liu, and D. Wu. Sa3: Automatic semantic aware attribution analysis of remote exploits. In *SecureComm*, pages 190–208, 2011.
[5] Microsoft security intelligence report, January-June 2006.
[6] http://www.offensivecomputing.net/. Accessed in March 2012.
[7] R. Perdisci, A. Lanzi, and W. Lee. Mcboost: Boosting scalability in malware collection and analysis using statistical classification of executables. In *ACSAC*, pages 301–310, 2008.
[8] M. G. Schultz, E. Eskin, E. Zadok, and S. J. Stolfo. Data mining methods for detection of new malicious executables. In *In Proceedings of the IEEE Symposium on Security and Privacy*, pages 38–49, 2001.
[9] G. Yan, N. Brown, and D. Kong. Exploring discriminatory features for automated malware classification. In *Proceedings of DIMVA'13*.

Elastic Paging

Enoch Peserico[*]
Univ. Padova, Dip. Ing. Informazione
via Gradenigo 6, Padova, Italy
enoch@dei.unipd.it

ABSTRACT

We study a generalization of the classic paging problem where memory capacity can vary over time – a property of many modern computing realities, from cloud computing to multi-core and energy-optimized processors. We show that good performance in the "classic" case provides no performance guarantees when memory capacity fluctuates: roughly speaking, moving from static to dynamic capacity can mean the difference between optimality within a factor 2 in space, time and energy, and suboptimality by an arbitrarily large factor. Surprisingly, several classic paging algorithms still perform remarkably well, maintaining that factor 2 optimality even if faced with adversarial capacity fluctuations – without taking those fluctuations into explicit account!

Categories and Subject Descriptors: C.4 [Computer Systems Organization]: Performance of Systems.

General Terms: Performance, Theory.

Keywords: Paging, Online, Competitive, Capacity, Adaptive, Energy, Multicore, Cloud.

1. INTRODUCTION

The problem of efficiently orchestrating the flow of information across the different layers of the memory hierarchy (cache, RAM, disk etc.) becomes ever more crucial as the gap between layers increases in terms of both capacity and access cost (time and/or energy). The most widely used model for this *paging problem* is that of a 2-layer system: a smaller *memory* layer with a capacity of k pages (data blocks), and a larger layer whose pages can only be accessed by first copying them into memory – an operation termed a *(page) fault*. Given a sequence of pages to access in order, a paging algorithm must choose which pages to maintain in memory so as to minimize the total number of faults.

The simple algorithm LFD (when space is needed, evict the page accessed furthest in the future) has long been known to be optimal [1]. However, paging is often studied as an *online* problem, i.e. an algorithm can decide evictions only on the basis of past requests. A common metric for the quality of an online paging algorithm ALG is ALG's $(h, k)-competitive ratio$ – informally, the maximum ratio over all possible request sequences between the faults incurred by ALG with

[*]Supported in part by Univ. Padova under Proj. AACSE.

memory k, and the faults incurred by an optimal offline (i.e. clairvoyant) algorithm with memory $h \leq k$. Many simple deterministic online paging algorithms like LRU or FIFO have an $(h, k)-competitive$ ratio equal to $\frac{k}{k-h+1}$, which is the best achievable [1]; thus, *they outperform even an optimal clairvoyant algorithm if given a memory system with twice the capacity and half the access cost, and they do so on every request sequence*. A large body of theoretical and experimental work ([1, 2, 6] provide excellent surveys) refines this factor 2, often sacrificing universality for finer resolution (e.g. benchmarking is inevitably tied to specific workloads).

2. ELASTIC PAGING

In the paging problem the amount of available memory is typically considered constant (even if possibly unknown) throughout a computation. This no longer reflects many important computing realities. In a cloud computing environment, the amount of physical memory available to a virtual machine varies over time depending on the virtual machine's load and on the number, load and relative class of service of other virtual machines on the same hardware. Even on a simple PC, most modern operating systems have and use the option of declaring some critical virtual pages temporarily "unswappable", reducing the amount of physical memory available to user processes. Capacity fluctuations also take place when considering the cache-RAM interface (in which case memory and pages represent, respectively, cache and cache lines): in many multi-core processor designs cache capacity is partitioned *dynamically* between different cores [9], and low-power chips can often dynamically disable underutilized portions of the cache to save energy [5].

Elastic paging is an extension of classic paging that models these realities allowing memory capacity to fluctuate between 1 and k pages (instead of being constantly equal to k). Then, the behaviour of a paging algorithm is determined not only by a page sequence, but also by a *capacity sequence* whose i^{th} value m_i is the capacity available on the ith page request. Like page requests, future capacities may or may not be known in advance, adding a second axis of "onlineness" to paging – e.g. LFD is *offline* in terms of page sequence but *online* in terms of capacity since it evicts pages without knowledge of future capacities.

One can easily extend the notion of $(h, k)-competitive$ ratio to elastic paging considering a *dynamic $(h, k)-competitive$ ratio* that compares for all page and capacity sequences the faults of an online algorithm with those of an optimal offline algorithm, the latter servicing the ith request with capacity $\lfloor \frac{h}{k} \cdot m_i \rfloor$ (when that of the online algorithm is m_i).

3. EVEN MINIMAL FLUCTUATIONS CAN HEAVILY DEGRADE PERFORMANCE

Good performance in the static case provides no performance guarantees whatsoever when memory capacity can fluctuate, even minimally. Consider the following paging algorithm LFRU, a hybrid of LFU (evict the least accessed page) and LRU (evict the least recently accessed page):

Initialize: PAGING ← LRU
At each page p requested:
If PAGING=LRU and p is last page of palindrome sequence with more faults in its 2nd half **then** PAGING ← LFU
Else If PAGING=LFU and p is last page of palindrome sequence with more faults in its 1st half **then** PAGING ← LFU

LFRU, while somewhat artificial, is not too different from many real-world paging designed for paging with static memory capacity (note that the behaviour of LFRU, like that of LRU and LFU, does not depend explicitly on capacity). In fact, pure LRU tends to be outperformed in practice by various LRU/LFU hybrids [6] which, informally, use LRU for managing heavily reused data and LRU to filter away streaming data that would otherwise "pollute" the memory.

LFRU turns out to have an optimal (h, k)−competitive ratio when memory capacity is fixed. At the same time, even if faced with capacity fluctuations of just a single page, and even if allowed the use of an arbitrarily large amount of memory, LFRU's fault rate can be arbitrarily larger than that of an offline algorithm running with just 3 pages of memory. In our technical report [7] we prove:

THEOREM 1. *LFRU has an (h, k)−competitive ratio equal to $\frac{k}{k-h+1}$ if memory capacity is constant, but has no finite dynamic (h, k)−competitive ratio for any $h \geq 3$ and any arbitrarily large k when capacity fluctuates by even 1 page.*

4. EVEN ADVERSARIAL FLUCTUATIONS CAN BE ADDRESSED EFFICIENTLY

In the light of theorem 1 it may be somewhat surprising many well-known "good" paging algorithms still perform remarkably well in the dynamic capacity setting – even though they do not take memory fluctuations into explicit account. In [7] we prove:

THEOREM 2. *LFD incurs the minimal number of faults on any request sequence, regardless of capacity fluctuations.*

THEOREM 3. *LRU, FIFO and CLOCK all have a dynamic (h, k)−competitive ratio equal to:*

$$\rho_{EL}(h, k) = \max_{k' \leq k, k' \in \mathcal{N}} \frac{k'}{k' - \lfloor h\frac{k'}{k} - \frac{h}{k} \rfloor}$$

which is optimal for deterministic algorithms, as well as for randomized ones if the request sequence can depend on past choices of the paging algorithm.

In [7] we analyse the complex expression of the optimal dynamic (h, k)-competitive ratio $\rho_{EL}(h, k)$ proving that, although it exceeds the static ratio $\frac{k}{k-h+1}$ for some "natural" values of h and k, it does so only by a very small factor never larger than $(1 + \frac{1}{k})$. In particular, $\rho_{EL}(\frac{k}{2}, k) < 2$, and thus some simple deterministic paging algorithms still

outperform even an optimal clairvoyant algorithm if given a memory system with twice the capacity and half the access cost; and they do so on every request sequence, even when faced with adversarial capacity fluctuations, even without taking those fluctuations into explicit account.

5. CONCLUSIONS

Even minimal capacity fluctuations can completely ruin the performance of paging algorithms that are optimal or near optimal with static capacity. This suggests the need of extreme caution when evaluating with classic methodologies paging algorithms meant for memory with dynamic capacity.

On the positive side, several simple classic paging algorithms still achieve optimal or nearly optimal performance even in the dynamic capacity framework. This is particularly surprising because none of these algorithms takes capacity fluctuations into explicit account: counterintuitively, while knowledge of future page requests provides an advantage, knowledge of future capacity does not. A practical corollary is that one can efficiently decouple the problem of allocating memory resources to different cores/processes/threads from the problem of managing allocated memory – greatly simplifying system design and analysis and providing a strong theoretical justification for the exokernel approach [3].

As in classic paging, it would certainly be important to refine the factor 2 beyond the resolution of the competitive ratio e.g. through experimental benchmarking. We are not aware of any benchmarks specifically designed to assess the impact of memory capacity fluctuations. A fundamental obstacle in their development seems to be the difficulty of characterizing "typical" fluctuation patterns encountered in practice. Also, it would be interesting to extend the "elastic" analysis to other problems where the amount of resources available for a task can realistically vary over time. Examples include call admission [4] (with variable circuit capacity) and the numerous variants of online scheduling [8] (with e.g. variable number or speed of servers). Which problems can be solved optimally or almost optimally without knowledge of the amount of resources available in the future (as in the case of paging with dynamic memory capacity)?

6. REFERENCES

[1] A. Borodin and R. El-Yaniv. *Online Computation and Competitive Analysis.* Cambridge University Press, 1998.
[2] R. Dorrigiv and A. López-Ortiz. A survey of performance measures for on-line algorithms. *SIGACT News*, 36(3):67–81, 2005.
[3] D. R. Engler, M. F. Kaashoek, and J. O'Toole. Exokernel: An operating system architecture for application-level resource management. In *Proc. SOSP*, 1995.
[4] J. A. Garay, I. S. Gopal, S. Kutten, Y. Mansour, and M. Yung. Efficient on-line call control algorithms. *Journal of Algorithms*, 23(1):180–194, 1997.
[5] H. Homayoun, M. Makhzan, and A. Veidenbaum. Multiple sleep mode leakage control for cache peripheral circuits in embedded processors. In *Proc. CASES*, 2008.
[6] D. Lee, J. Choi, J. hun Kim, S. H. Noh, S. L. Min, Y. Cho, and C. S. Kim. LRFU: A spectrum of policies that subsumes the least recently used and least frequently used policies. In *Proc. ACM SIGMETRICS*, 1999.
[7] E. Peserico. Paging with dynamic memory capacity. *CoRR*, abs/1304.6007, 2013.
[8] K. Pruhs. Competitive online scheduling for server systems. *SIGMETRICS Perform. Eval. Rev.*, 34(4):52–58, 2007.
[9] M. K. Qureshi and Y. N. Patt. Utility-based cache partitioning: A low-overhead, high-performance, runtime mechanism to partition shared caches. In *Proc. IEEE/ACM MICRO*, 2006.

Exact Convex Relaxation for Optimal Power Flow in Distribution Networks

Lingwen Gan, Na Li, and Steven H. Low
EAS, California Institute of Technology
Pasadena, CA, USA
lgan@caltech.edu, nali@caltech.edu,
slow@caltech.edu

Ufuk Topcu
ESE, University of Pennsylvania
philadelphia, PA, USA
utopcu@seas.upenn.edu

ABSTRACT

The optimal power flow (OPF) problem seeks to control the power generation/consumption to minimize the generation cost, and is becoming important for distribution networks. OPF is nonconvex and a second-order cone programming (SOCP) relaxation has been proposed to solve it. We prove that after a "small" modification to OPF, the SOCP relaxation is exact under a "mild" condition. Empirical studies demonstrate that the modification to OPF is "small" and that the "mild" condition holds for all test networks, including the IEEE 13-bus test network and practical networks with high penetration of distributed generation.

Categories and Subject Descriptors: J.2 [Physical Science and Engineering]: Engineering

Keywords: optimal power flow, second-order cone programming, exact convex relaxation

1. INTRODUCTION

The optimal power flow (OPF) problem seeks to control the power generation/consumption to minimize the generation cost. It is becoming increasingly important for distribution networks due to the advent of distributed generation and controllable loads such as electric vehicles.

OPF is nonconvex, and a second-order cone programming (SOCP) relaxation has also been proposed to solve it for tree networks [1]. If solution of the SOCP relaxation is feasible for OPF, then the solution is also optimal for OPF. In this case, the SOCP relaxation is called *exact*. Up to date, sufficient conditions that have been derived in literature for the exactness of the SOCP relaxation do not hold in practice, and whether the SOCP relaxation is exact can only be checked after solving it.

We study exactness of the SOCP relaxation in this paper. In particular, contributions of this paper are twofold.

First, we *modify OPF by imposing additional constraints on power injections*. Remarkably, only feasible points that are "close" to the voltage upper bounds are eliminated, and then the SOCP relaxation is exact under a "mild" condition C1. C1 can be checked prior to solving the SOCP relaxation, and holds for all test distribution networks considered in this paper, including the IEEE 13-bus test distribution network and practical distribution networks with high penetration of distributed generation. Empirical studies demonstrate that

SIGMETRICS'13, June 17-21, 2013, Pittsburgh, PA, USA.
ACM 978-1-4503-1900-3/13/06.

the modification to OPF is "small" for the same set of test networks.

Second, we prove that *the SOCP relaxation has at most a unique solution if it is exact.*

2. THE OPF PROBLEM

A distribution network is composed of buses and distribution lines connecting these buses, and has a tree topology.

There is a substation in the network, which has fixed voltage and flexible power injection for power balance. Index the substation bus by 0 and the other buses by $1, \ldots, n$. Let $N := \{0, \ldots, n\}$ denote the set of all buses and define $N^+ := N \backslash \{0\}$. Each line connects an ordered pair (i, j) of buses where bus j is in the middle of bus i and bus 0. Let E denote the set of all lines and abbreviate $(i, j) \in E$ by $i \to j$. If $i \to j$ or $j \to i$, denote $i \sim j$.

For each bus $i \in N$, let V_i denote its voltage and I_i denote its current injection. Specifically, the substation voltage, V_0, is given and fixed. Let $s_i = p_i + \mathbf{i}q_i$ denote the power injection of bus i. Specifically, s_0 is the power that the substation draws from the transmission network for power balance. Let $\mathcal{P}_i$ denote the path from bus i to bus 0.

For each line $i \sim j$, let $y_{ij} = g_{ij} - \mathbf{i}b_{ij}$ denote its admittance and define $z_{ij} = r_{ij} + \mathbf{i}x_{ij} := 1/y_{ij}$.

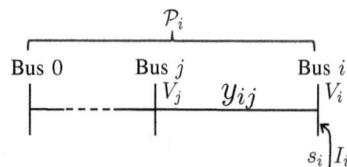

Figure 1: Some of the notations.

Some of the notations are summarized in Fig. 1. Further, a letter without subscript denotes a vector of the corresponding quantity, e.g., $V = (V_1, \ldots, V_n)$, $y = (y_{ij}, i \sim j)$. Note that subscript 0 is not included in nodal variables.

We can now formally state the OPF problem

$$\min \quad \sum_{i \in N} f_i(\mathbf{Re}(s_i)) \tag{1a}$$

$$\text{over} \quad s, V, s_0$$

$$\text{s.t.} \quad s_i = V_i \sum_{j:\, j \sim i} (V_i^* - V_j^*) y_{ij}^*, \qquad i \in N; \tag{1b}$$

$$\underline{s_i} \preceq s_i \preceq \overline{s_i}, \qquad i \in N^+; \tag{1c}$$

$$\underline{|V_i|} \leq |V_i| \leq \overline{|V_i|}, \qquad i \in N^+ \tag{1d}$$

where f_i is generation cost at bus i for $i \in N$ and V_0, y, $\bar{s}$, $\underline{s}$, $\overline{|V|}$, $\underline{|V|}$ are externally specified constants. We assume that f_0 is strictly increasing.

The objective function (1a) is the generation cost, equation (1b) is the physical law that power flow abides, equation (1c) is constraints on power injections, and equation (1d) is constraints on voltages. In practice, the control variable is s, after specifying which the other variables s_0, V are determined by physical laws in (1b).

The challenge in solving OPF comes from the nonconvex constraints (1b). To overcome this challenge, it is proposed to relax OPF to convex problems. To state the relaxation, first transform OPF to the following form for tree networks.

$$\min \quad \sum_{i \in N} f_i(\mathbf{Re}(s_i))$$

$$\text{over} \quad s, W, s_0$$

$$\text{s.t.} \quad s_i = \sum_{j:\, j \sim i} (W_{ii} - W_{ij}) y_{ij}^*, \quad i \in N; \quad (2a)$$

$$\underline{s}_i \preceq s_i \preceq \bar{s}_i, \qquad i \in N^+; \quad (2b)$$

$$\underline{|V_i|}^2 \leq W_{ii} \leq \overline{|V_i|}^2, \qquad i \in N^+; \quad (2c)$$

$$\mathbf{Rank}(W\{i,j\}) = 1, \qquad i \to j \quad (2d)$$

where $W := (W_{ij}, i \sim j \text{ or } i = j)$ and

$$W\{i,j\} := \begin{pmatrix} W_{ii} & W_{ij} \\ W_{ji} & W_{jj} \end{pmatrix}, \qquad i \sim j.$$

We can then relax OPF to a second-order-cone programming (SOCP) relaxation [1].

$$\min \quad \sum_{i \in N} f_i(\mathbf{Re}(s_i))$$

$$\text{over} \quad s, W, s_0$$

$$\text{s.t.} \quad (2a) - (2c);$$

$$W\{i,j\} \succeq 0, \qquad i \to j.$$

Definition 1 *The SOCP relaxation is exact if every of its solutions satisfies* (2d).

If the SOCP relaxation is exact, then a global optimum of OPF can be found by solving the convex SOCP relaxation.

3. A MODIFIED OPF PROBLEM

The SOCP relaxation for OPF is not always exact in practice. Hence, we propose a modified OPF problem, which will be shown to have an exact SOCP relaxation under a "mild" condition. The modified OPF problem OPF-m is

$$\min \quad \sum_{i \in N} f_i(\mathbf{Re}(s_i))$$

$$\text{over} \quad s, W, s_0$$

$$\text{s.t.} \quad (2a), (2b), (2d);$$

$$\underline{|V_i|}^2 \leq W_{ii}, \; W_{ii}^{\text{lin}}(s) \leq \overline{|V_i|}^2, \quad i \in N^+ \quad (3)$$

where $W_{ii}^{\text{lin}}(s) := W_{00} + 2 \sum_{(j,k) \in \mathcal{P}_i} \mathbf{Re}\left(z_{jk}^* S_{jk}^{\text{lin}}(s)\right)$ for $i \in N^+$.

The "mild" condition for the exactness of the SOCP relaxation for OPF-m is provided in Theorem 1. To state the theorem, define $P_{ij}^{\text{lin}}(p) := \sum_{k:\, i \in \mathcal{P}_k} p_k$, $Q_{ij}^{\text{lin}}(q) := \sum_{k:\, i \in \mathcal{P}_k} q_k$ for $i \to j$, and let $\bar{p} := \mathbf{Re}(\bar{s})$, $\bar{q} := \mathbf{Im}(\bar{s})$.

Theorem 1 *The SOCP relaxation for OPF-m is exact if*

$$a_j^1 r_{ij} > a_j^2 x_{ij}, \; a_j^3 r_{ij} < a_j^4 x_{ij}, \qquad i \to j, \quad (4)$$

where

$$a_i^1 := \prod_{(j,k) \in \mathcal{P}_i} \left(1 - \frac{2 r_{jk} \left[P_{jk}^{\text{lin}}(\bar{p})\right]^+}{\underline{|V_j|}^2}\right),$$

$$a_i^2 := \sum_{(j,k) \in \mathcal{P}_i} \frac{2 r_{jk} \left[Q_{jk}^{\text{lin}}(\bar{q})\right]^+}{\underline{|V_j|}^2},$$

$$a_i^3 := \sum_{(j,k) \in \mathcal{P}_i} \frac{2 x_{jk} \left[P_{jk}^{\text{lin}}(\bar{p})\right]^+}{\underline{|V_j|}^2},$$

$$a_i^4 := \prod_{(j,k) \in \mathcal{P}_i} \left(1 - \frac{2 x_{jk} \left[Q_{jk}^{\text{lin}}(\bar{q})\right]^+}{\underline{|V_j|}^2}\right)$$

for $i \in N^+$.

Condition (4) can be checked in priori since it does not depend on solutions of the SOCP relaxation. In fact, $\{a_j^k, j \in N, k = 1, 2, 3, 4\}$ are functions of $(r, x, \bar{p}, \bar{q}, \underline{|V|})$ that can be computed efficiently in $O(n)$ time.

Condition (4) requires $\bar{p}$ and $\bar{q}$ be "small". Fix $(r, x, \underline{|V|})$, then Condition (4) is a condition on $(\bar{p}, \bar{q})$. It can be verified that if $(\bar{p}, \bar{q}) \preceq (\bar{p}', \bar{q}')$, then

$$\text{(4) holds for } (\bar{p}', \bar{q}') \Rightarrow \text{(4) holds for } (\bar{p}, \bar{q}),$$

i.e., the smaller power injections, the more likely (4) holds. In particular, it can be verified that if $(\bar{p}, \bar{q}) \preceq (0, 0)$, i.e., there is no distributed generation, then (4) holds.

As will be shown in Section 4, Condition (4) holds for all test networks, even those with big $(\bar{p}, \bar{q})$. Hence, (4) should hold widely in practice.

If solution of the SOCP relaxation is unique, then any convex programming solver gives the same solution.

Theorem 2 *The SOCP relaxation has at most a unique solution if it is exact.*

4. CASE STUDIES

We have checked that 1) the feasible sets of OPF and OPF-m are close, and 2) C1 holds, for all test networks considered in this paper, including the IEEE 13-bus test network [2] and two practical networks with high penetration of distributed generation [3, 4].

5. CONCLUSION

We have proved that the SOCP relaxation for a modified OPF problem is exact under a prior checkable condition C1. Empirical studies demonstrate that the modification to OPF is "small" and that C1 holds for all test networks.

6. REFERENCES

[1] S. Sojoudi and J. Lavaei, "Physics of power networks makes hard optimization problems easy to solve," in *IEEE Power and Energy Society General Meeting*, 2012, pp. 1–8.

[2] IEEE distribution test feeders, available at http://ewh.ieee.org/soc/pes/dsacom/testfeeders/.

[3] M. Farivar, C. R. Clarke, S. H. Low, and K. M. Chandy, "Inverter var control for distribution systems with renewables," in *IEEE SmartGridComm*, 2011, pp. 457–462.

[4] M. Farivar, R. Neal, C. Clarke, and S. Low, "Optimal inverter var control in distribution systems with high pv penetration," in *arXiv:1112.5594*, 2011.

Exploiting the Past to Reduce Delay in CSMA Scheduling: A High-order Markov Chain Approach

Jaewook Kwak, Chul-Ho Lee, and Do Young Eun
Department of Electrical and Computer Engineering
North Carolina State University
Raleigh, NC 27695
jkwak@ncsu.edu, clee4@ncsu.edu, dyeun@ncsu.edu

ABSTRACT

Recently several CSMA algorithms based on the Glauber dynamics model have been proposed for multihop wireless scheduling, as viable solutions to achieve the throughput optimality, yet are simple to implement [1, 2, 4–6]. However, their delay performances still remain unsatisfactory, mainly due to the nature of the underlying Markov chains that imposes a fundamental constraint on how the link state can evolve over time. In this paper, we propose a new approach toward better queueing and delay performance, based on our observation that the algorithm needs not be Markovian, as long as it can be implemented in a distributed manner, achieving the same throughput optimality and better delay performance. Our approach hinges upon utilizing past state information observed by local link and then constructing a high-order Markov chain for the evolution of the feasible link schedules. Our proposed algorithm, named *delayed CSMA*, adds virtually no additional overhead onto the existing CSMA-based algorithms, achieves the throughput optimality under the usual choice of link weight as a function of queue length, and also provides much better delay performance by effectively resolving temporal link starvation problem. From our extensive simulations we observe that the delay under our algorithm can be often reduced by a factor of 20 over a wide range of scenarios, compared to the standard Glauber-dynamics-based CSMA algorithm.

Categories and Subject Descriptors

C.2.1 [**Network Architecture and Design**]: Distributed networks, Wireless communication

Keywords

CSMA scheduling, Glauber dynamics, high-order Markov chains, delay performance

1. NETWORK MODEL

We consider a wireless network with a *conflict graph* $\mathcal{G} = (\mathcal{N}, \mathcal{E})$ where $\mathcal{N}$ is the set of links (transmitter-receiver pair), and $\mathcal{E}$ is the set of edges which represents conflict relationship between links. An edge $(i, j) \in \mathcal{E}$ exists between two links i and j if simultaneous use of the two leads to failure of communications. We define a schedule by $\boldsymbol{\sigma} = (\sigma_v)_{v \in \mathcal{N}} \in$

$\{0, 1\}^{|\mathcal{N}|}$, which represents the set of transmitting links. A link v (or node v in the conflict graph $\mathcal{G}$) is active if it is included in the schedule, i.e., $\sigma_v = 1$, and is inactive if otherwise. A *feasible* schedule is a set of links that can be active at the same time slot according to the conflict relationship $\mathcal{E}$. Thus, a feasible schedule $\boldsymbol{\sigma}$ should satisfy the independent set constraint i.e., $\sigma_i + \sigma_j \leq 1$ for all $(i, j) \in \mathcal{E}$.

In our model, each link is associated with a queue fed by some exogenous traffic arrivals and serviced when the link is active. We consider that a packet arrives to the queue of link v at each time slot t according to a Bernoulli process $A_v(t)$, i.e., $A_v(t)$, $t = 1, 2, \ldots$ are *i.i.d.* with $\mathbb{E}\{A_v(t)\} = \eta_v$. Let $\boldsymbol{\eta} = (\eta_v)_{v \in \mathcal{N}}$ be the set of arrival rates to the queues in the network. Let $Q(t) = (Q_v(t))_{v \in \mathcal{N}}$ be the number of packets in the queue at time t. Then the queue dynamics is governed by the recursion: $Q_v(t) = [Q_v(t-1) + A_v(t) - \sigma_v(t)]^+$, $t \geq 1$.

2. MAIN ALGORITHM

The basic idea of throughput-optimal CSMA is to utilize the Glauber dynamics as a link scheduling algorithm. Let $W_v(t)$ denote a weight associated with node v. Our proposed algorithm with a parameter $T \in \mathbb{N}_+$ is described in Algorithm 1.

Algorithm 1 Delayed CSMA

1: Initialize: for all links $i \in \mathcal{N}$, $\sigma_i(t) = 0$, $t = 0, 1, \ldots, T{-}1$.
2: At each time $t \geq T$: links find an independent set, $\mathcal{D}(t)$ through a randomized procedure*, and
3: **for all** links $i \in \mathcal{D}(t)$ **do**
4:   **if** $\sum_{j \in N_i} \sigma_j(t - T) = 0$ **then**
5:     $\sigma_i(t) = 1$ with probability $\frac{\exp(W_i(t))}{1+\exp(W_i(t))}$
6:     $\sigma_i(t) = 0$ with probability $\frac{1}{1+\exp(W_i(t))}$
7:   **else**
8:     $\sigma_i(t) = 0$
9:   **end if**
10: **end for**
11: **for all** links $j \notin \mathcal{D}(t)$ **do**
12:   $\sigma_i(t) = \sigma_i(t - T)$
13: **end for**

Note that if $T = 1$, our algorithm reduces to the conventional CSMA-based scheduling algorithm. Our motivation

---

*For instance, each link attempts to access the channel with an access probability a_v, $v \in \mathcal{N}$, and link v is then selected with probability $a_v \prod_{j \in \{w:(v,w) \in \mathcal{E}\}} (1 - a_j)$. More practical implementation tailored to IEEE 802.11 can be found in [4].

(a) Conventional CSMA algorithm

(b) Proposed idea: delayed CSMA

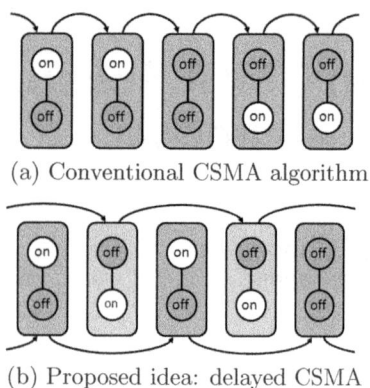

Figure 1: Comparison between the conventional CSMA and our proposed approach. A box indicates a schedule, and arrows indicate state transitions.

Figure 2: Impact of order parameter T: (a)Mean and CoV of 'off' duration. (b) Delay performance.

comes from the fact that the service process $\sigma_v(t)$ at link v under the standard CSMA policy is often heavily correlated over time. This is because once CSMA finds a schedule, it tends to stay in the same schedule or its similar set of schedules for a long time. The method we propose in this paper effectively resolves this problem. The main idea is as follows. Suppose we have two schedulers that respectively generate schedules independently, while preserving the feasibility constraint for each time slot. If we choose to use one scheduler at every odd time index, and the other one at every even time index (see Figure 1(b)), it is now possible to make a transition from 'active-inactive' directly to 'inactive-active' state, which would be impossible under the conventional CSMA (see Figure 1(a)). This alternate use of different schedulers produces more drastic change of states in consecutive time slots, thereby alleviating link starvation while maintaining the same long-term frequency of being active. Our idea is to generalize this concept by the use of multiple schedulers in a round-robin manner. In practice, this can be easily implemented in a distributed setting by having all links together update their schedules based on T-step-back state. For this purpose, each link only needs to remember its last T channel states. This way, the whole system behaves *as if* there are T separate schedulers (or chains) taking turns to generate next schedules.

3. THROUGHPUT OPTIMALITY

In our algorithm, we set $W_v(t)$ to be a function of the current queue length $Q_v(t)$ at time t, rather than T steps ago, such that the system can react more quickly by adjusting the parameter with the latest information. With the time-varying parameters, the state transition matrix becomes time-inhomogeneous, which we write as P_t, a function of $Q_v(t), v \in \mathcal{N}$ at time t. For each given such P_t, let π_t be its unique stationary distribution (in a row vector form), i.e., $\pi_t = \pi_t P_t$, and μ_t be the actual distribution of the link schedules $\boldsymbol{\sigma}(t)$ at time t under our algorithm with order parameter T. Then, we have $\mu_t = \mu_{t-T}P_{t-1}$. Similar to the steps via 'network adiabatic' theorem in [5,6], a key step involved toward the throughput optimality is to show $\mu_t \approx \pi_t$ for sufficiently large queue lengths under suitably chosen weight functions. Note that under our algorithm, the speed of convergence of μ_t is roughly T times slower, however since T is finite, we expect that μ_t is still able to catch

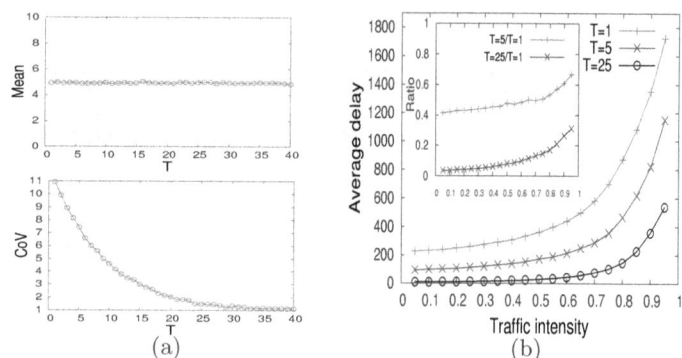

up the slowly varying target π_t in time. We verified that this is indeed the case, and see [3] for the detailed proof.

4. SIMULATION RESULTS

To evaluate the performance of the delayed CSMA algorithm, we have run simulations in a random network scenario with 25 nodes (The detailed simulation setup is given in [3]). To understand the benefits of having more drastic changes in the service process of a link under the delayed CSMA algorithm we look at the distribution of its 'off' duration U, the duration from an active slot to the next active slot. We measured its mean $\mathbb{E}\{U\}$ and the coefficient of variation (CoV) $\sqrt{\text{Var}\{U\}}/\mathbb{E}\{U\}$ as we increase the order parameter T. Figure 2(a) shows that the first-order statistics of the link state doesn't change with T, while its variability decreases for larger T, implying that our algorithm with larger T effectively removes link starvation. The Figure 2(b) shows the delay improvement over the conventional CSMA algorithm under different traffic intensity, where the inset figure displays the ratio of the delay under our algorithm with chosen T to that of standard CSMA. We note that the performance improvement is quite remarkable. For instance, with $T = 5$, the delay reduces by half, and with $T = 25$, it reduces by a factor of 20 compared to the conventional CSMA algorithm.

5. REFERENCES

[1] J. Ghaderi and R. Srikant. On the design of efficient csma algorithms for wireless networks. arXiv report http://arxiv.org/abs/1003.1364, arXiv, 2010.

[2] L. Jiang, M. Leconte, J. Ni, R. Srikant, and J. Walrand. Fast mixing of parallel glauber dynamics and low-delay csma scheduling. *IEEE Trans. on Information Theory*, 2012.

[3] J. Kwak, C.-H. Lee, and D. Y. Eun. Exploiting the past to reduce delay in csma scheduling: A high-order markov chain approach. arXiv report http://arxiv.org/abs/1302.3250, arXiv, 2013.

[4] J. Ni, B. Tan, and R. Srikant. Q-csma: Queue-length based CSMA/CA algorithms for achieving maximum throughput and low delay in wireless networks. *IEEE Trans. on Networking*.

[5] S. Rajagopalan, D. Shah, and J. Shin. Network adiabatic theorem: An efficient randomized protocol for contention resolution. In *ACM SIGMETRICS/Performance*, Seattle, WA, June 2009.

[6] D. Shah and J. Shin. Randomized scheduling algorithm for queueing networks. *Annals of Applied Probability*, 2012.

FaRNet: Fast Recognition of High Multi-Dimensional Network Traffic Patterns

Ignasi Paredes-Oliva
UPC BarcelonaTech
Barcelona, Spain
iparedes@ac.upc.edu

Pere Barlet-Ros
UPC BarcelonaTech
Barcelona, Spain
pbarlet@ac.upc.edu

Xenofontas
Dimitropoulos
ETH Zurich
Zurich, Switzerland
fontas@tik.ee.ethz.ch

ABSTRACT

Extracting knowledge from big network traffic data is a matter of foremost importance for multiple purposes ranging from trend analysis or network troubleshooting to capacity planning or traffic classification. An extremely useful approach to profile traffic is to extract and display to a network administrator the multi-dimensional hierarchical heavy hitters (HHHs) of a dataset. However, existing schemes for computing HHHs have several limitations: 1) they require significant computational overhead; 2) they do not scale to high dimensional data; and 3) they are not easily extensible. In this paper, we introduce a fundamentally new approach for extracting HHHs based on generalized frequent item-set mining (FIM), which allows to process traffic data much more efficiently and scales to much higher dimensional data than present schemes. Based on generalized FIM, we build and evaluate a traffic profiling system we call *FaRNet*. Our comparison with AutoFocus, which is the most related tool of similar nature, shows that *FaRNet* is up to three orders of magnitude faster.

Categories and Subject Descriptors: C.2.6 [Computer - Communication Networks]: Internetworking

Keywords: Network Operation and Management; Traffic Profiling; Data Mining

1. INTRODUCTION

In recent years, the Internet traffic mix has changed dramatically. Mobile applications, social networking, peer-to-peer applications and streaming services are only a few examples of the ever-growing list of applications that mold Internet traffic today. Furthermore, existing applications continuously change their behavior, while new applications, services and cyber-threats are emerging. In this rapidly changing network environment, it is critical to build traffic profiling tools that efficiently process big traffic data to extract knowledge about what is happening in a network.

AutoFocus [2], the state-of-the-art traffic profiling tool based on hierarchical heavy hitters, has some important limitations. First, its computational overhead grows exponentially with the number of dimensions. Because of this, it is restricted to 5-dimensional HHs (where the five dimensions correspond to the well-known 5-tuple) and it is very hard to extend it with additional traffic features.

We introduce a fundamentally new approach based on generalized frequent item-set mining (FIM) [3]. Generalized FIM scales much better to higher dimensional data than AutoFocus and supports attributes of hierarchical nature, like IP addresses or geolocation data. We exploit generalized FIM to design and implement a new system, called *FaRNet* (FAst Recognition of high multi-dimensional NETwork traffic patterns), for (near) real-time profiling of network traffic data. Our system is capable of analyzing multi-dimensional traffic records with both flat and hierarchical attributes.

2. FARNET

FaRNet receives three inputs: NetFlow data, *minimum support (s)* and data treatment. s is the threshold that determines if the size of a set of flows is big enough to be considered a frequent item-set. The next parameter indicates the type of mining: flat or hierarchical. While for the flat case the input data is considered to be completely plain, in the hierarchical scenario certain dimensions have associated hierarchies. For example, IPs consist of prefixes from length 8 to 32. *FaRNet* has a single output: frequent item-sets.

By default, *FaRNet* takes 10 dimensions from each input flow and builds transactions. Each transaction consists of the source and destination IP addresses, the source and destination port numbers, the protocol number, the inferred application that generated the flow, the source and destination ASes, and the geolocation of the IP addresses (continent, country, region and city). Note that although our current implementation of *FaRNet* is based on these features, any other hierarchical element could be trivially addded as the system scales well with the number of dimensions.

Depending on the selected type of mining, *FaRNet* will take different paths. For flat treatment, a FIM algorithm for flat data will be used. For hierarchical treatment, this paper presents an optimized FIM algorithm extended to deal with hierarchical traffic attributes. In particular, we first adapt, extend and optimize the implementations of different FIM algorithms (Apriori, Eclat, FP-growth, RElim and SaM) and then select the one performing the best.

The straightforward solution for allowing FIM to deal with the hierarchical nature of network traffic is expanding each element of a flow with its corresponding ancestor/s. For example, for an IP this means replacing it with all its possible prefixes from length 8 to 32, i.e., 25 items. For all 10 dimensions this accounts for 67 items per transaction.

Nonetheless, in most cases, extending e.g., all prefixes of an IP is not necessary because a fully defined 32-bit IP address is rarely frequent by itself. However, prefixes of inferior length have higher chances of being above s.

For simplicity, from here on, all the extensions and optimizations will refer only to IP addresses. However, note that all the proposals made are applicable to the other hierarchical features presented in this paper and, in general, to any other hierarchical element.

We first present *Progressive Expansion (PE)*, which will not always generate all 25 prefixes of an IP. A prefix of length k will only be explored if its corresponding $k-1$ prefix (parent prefix or ancestor) is frequent. Otherwise, the expansion for that IP will end at level $k-1$. This is because if a certain prefix is not frequent, all prefixes of superior length will not be frequent either (*downward-closure* property [3]). The frequency of a particular prefix is calculated by progressively counting the frequency of its shorter prefixes.

The main drawback of *PE* is that it needs to go through all transactions 25 times, which is very costly in terms of runtime. Note that the number of passes is due to the depth of the IP address hierarchy and, therefore, it would change depending on the hierarchical element we are dealing with (e.g., 4 for the geolocation). In order to improve this, we propose *Progressive Expansion k-by-k (PEK)*, which seeks to reduce this part of the process while avoiding the generation of useless prefixes. This is achieved by expanding k bits at each step instead of going one by one (*PE* is a particular case of *PEK* with $k = 1$). When using *PEK*, all transactions will be read $1 + 24/k$ times instead of 25.

First, *PEK* generates all prefixes of length $l = 8$ for all IPs of all the transactions and, uniquely for these that are frequent (i.e., these that at least have s flows), a binary tree is created (only the root node). Afterwards, for each prefix of length $l + k$ with a frequent ancestor (prefix of length l, tree level $l - 8$), its corresponding tree is expanded up to level $l + k - 8$. After going through all possible values of l ($8 \leq l \leq 32$), all frequencies in intermediate nodes (nodes between explored levels, i.e., among $l - 8$ and $l + k - 8$) are recursively computed. Finally, transactions are expanded only with those prefixes that are known to be frequent by going through the corresponding tree from the root to the leaves following a depth-first approach.

The following example illustrates how *PEK* would work for IP 192.168.10.5 and $k = 2$. The first step consists of generating the binary tree for its prefix of length 8, i.e., 192/8. Afterwards, if the root node is frequent, prefixes of length 10 are generated (2-bit expansion). Therefore, frequencies for prefixes 192.192/10, 192.128/10, 192.64/10 and 192.0/10 are calculated. Then, the computation for intermediate nodes (prefixes of length 9) is calculated by moving backwards in the binary tree. In this case, prefixes 192.192/10 and 192.128/10 have a common ancestor, i.e., 192.128/9. Thus, the frequency of the intermediate node 192.128/9 is the sum of frequencies of its two descendants, 192.192/10 and 192.128/10. Likewise, the frequency for 192.0/9 comes from prefixes 192.64/10 and 192.0/10.

3. PERFORMANCE EVALUATION

For the evaluation we used NetFlow traffic from 2011 from the European backbone network of GÉANT. The dataset used is 15 minutes long and has 0.51×10^6 flows, 5.46×10^6 packets and 5.55×10^9 bytes. Figure 1 shows how *FaRNet* and AutoFocus (AF) perform for different values of s. Note that only the first 10000 flows of the dataset are used for this

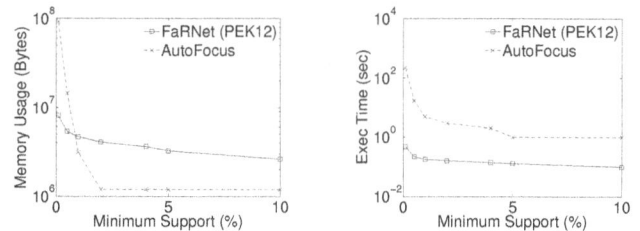

Figure 1: Memory usage (left) and execution time (right) comparison between *FaRNet* (*PEK12*) and AutoFocus for the first 10K flows of the dataset.

comparison. This is because the available implementation of AF [1] is not dimensioned to handle more flows (when it receives more than that amount, it does not count them accurately due to collisions). *FaRNet* uses *PEK* with k=12 (*PEK12*) on RElim algorithm, which holds the best tradeoff between memory consumption and execution time. In terms of runtime (right plot), *FaRNet* is clearly faster regardless of s. Moreover, as s decreases, AF's execution time increases exponentially, while *FaRNet* is able to handle it smoothly. Although for the highest s AF's runtime ($1s$) is relatively close to *FaRNet*'s ($0.10s$), for $s = 0.1\%$ AF is approximately three orders of magnitude slower ($223s$ vs $0.48s$).

As regards the memory consumption (left plot), AF is better than *FaRNet* for $s \geq 1\%$. However, for lower values of s, AF consumption rises rapidly and ends up consuming far more memory than *FaRNet* (88.77 MB vs 7.79 MB for $s = 0.1\%$). All in all, *FaRNet* shows to be quicker and more resilient to low s than AF, although it uses more memory for $s = 1\%$ and above. Nonetheless, note that the memory consumption of *FaRNet* is reasonably low in the worst case (below 10 MB).

4. CONCLUSIONS

We built *FaRNet*, a network traffic profiling system that offers better performance and flexibility and also scales to a much higher number of dimensions than AutoFocus. In order to validate the correctness of *FaRNet*, we compare it with AutoFocus by using a limited version of our system configured to produce the same output. Using traffic data from a large backbone network, we show that when mining only the 5-tuple, *FaRNet* is up to three orders of magnitude quicker than AutoFocus. As a consequence, *FaRNet* is able to process high volumes of multi-dimensional traffic data in (near) real-time, while AutoFocus was designed for offline analysis of a pre-defined set of 5 dimensions.

5. ACKNOWLEDGEMENTS

This work was supported by the Spanish Ministry of Education under contract TEC2011-27474.

6. REFERENCES

[1] AutoFocus. http://www.caida.org/tools/.
[2] C. Estan, S. Savage, and G. Varghese. Automatically inferring patterns of resource consumption in network traffic. In *Proc. of ACM SIGCOMM*, Aug. 2003.
[3] J. Han, H. Cheng, D. Xin, and X. Yan. Frequent pattern mining: current status and future directions. *Data Min. Knowl. Discov.*, 15(1):55–86, 2007.

Firming Solar Power

Yashar Ghiassi-Farrokhfal, S. Keshav,
Catherine Rosenberg
University of Waterloo

Florin Ciucu
T-Labs / TU Berlin

ABSTRACT

The high variability of solar power due to intrinsic diurnal variability, as well as additional stochastic variations due to cloud cover, have made it difficult for solar farms to participate in electricity markets that require pre-committed constant power generation. We study the use of battery storage to 'firm' solar power, that is, to remove variability so that such a pre-commitment can be made. Due to the high cost of storage, it is necessary to size the battery parsimoniously, choosing the minimum size to meet a certain reliability guarantee. Inspired by recent work that identifies an isomorphism between batteries and network buffers, we introduce a new model for solar power generation that models it as a stochastic traffic source. This permits us to use techniques from the stochastic network calculus to both size storage and to maximize the revenue that a solar farm owner can make from the day-ahead power market. Using a 10-year of recorded solar irradiance, we show that our approach attains 93% of the maximum revenue in a summer day that would have been achieved in daily market had the entire solar irradiance trace been known ahead of time.

Categories and Subject Descriptors

C.4 [**Performance of Systems**]: Modeling techniques

Keywords

solar power modelling, electricity market

1. INTRODUCTION

The intermittent nature of solar energy hinders its fast penetration in the day-ahead electricity market. Using storage to firm solar power is one of the most promising solutions. An important and complex problem in this area is maximizing revenue in the day-ahead market for a battery-equipped solar farm given the weather forecast and the battery size. This problem has been explored in the literature for wind power, but not solar power, which is different in that it exhibits stochastic fluctuations modulating a deterministic diurnal variation. Our work proposes a highly accurate technique for solar firming as illustrated by numerical examples.

Our key contributions are:

1. We provide a new stochastic model for solar output power which obviates the shortcomings of existing models. It lays the foundation of many analyses that require the stochastic characterization of the solar energy including storage sizing, and revenue maximization in the day-ahead market.

2. We use this model along with existing power loss formulations from the stochastic network calculus to provide solutions to the revenue maximization in the day-ahead market.

3. Using a large real data set consisting of the solar irradiance measurements gathered over 10 years, we numerically show that our analyses are quite accurate.

2. SOLAR POWER MODELLING

Solar power is measured by irradiance, which is the total power incident on a unit area, and is referred to as the global irradiance i_g. The output electricity power from a photovoltaic (PV) panel is $\alpha_{pv}I_g$[1], where α_{pv} is the product of PV area and PV panel efficiency in converting solar energy into electricity. Our aim is to characterize $\alpha_{pv}I_g$.

Fluctuations in i_g consist of two elements: (1) i_{det}: the deterministic variation in diurnal irradiance which mainly occurs due to the position of the sun in the sky (also called clear-sky irradiance) and (2) $i_{det}(t) - i_g(t)$: the high frequency fluctuations due to the effect of clouds which modulate the clear-sky irradiance.

Existing clear-sky irradiance models accurately capture variations in i_{det} as a function of location, date, and time. Hence, the fluctuation of $i_g(t)$ at a given time instant t is limited to $i_{det}(t) - i_g(t)$. Existing models, however, do not accurately capture short term fluctuations. To be more precise, the best known models (e.g., step changes [3, 4] and wavelet-based analysis [2]) require stationarity and for this reason they choose to model the clear-sky index ($\frac{i_g}{i_{det}}$) instead of $i_g(t) - i_{det}(t)$ assuming that clear sky index (CSI) is stationary which is not true in practice.

To characterize $\alpha_{pv}I_g$, we seek to find a statistical sample path lower envelope β^l with bounding function ε^l which satisfies the following for any time $t \geq 0$ and any $x \geq 0$

$$\mathbb{P}\left\{\sup_{s \leq t}\{\beta^l(t-s) - \alpha_{pv}I_g(s,t)\} > x\right\} \leq \varepsilon^l(x) . \quad (1)$$

Note that we do not require stationarity. We model the following stochastic process instead of CSI:

$$i_{aux}(t) = i_{det}(t) - i_g(t) + \text{offset} , \quad (2)$$

where offset is a constant chosen such that $i_{aux}(t)$ is always positive. One can simply set it to $\max_t(i_g(t) - i_{det}(t))$.

We model fluctuations in I_{aux} using an approach originally developed for teletraffic modelling by determining two functions $\mathcal{G}^u_{aux}$

---

[1]We use capital letters to denote cumulative processes, i.e., $I_g(t) = \sum_{\tau=1}^{t} i_g(\tau)$.

SIGMETRICS'13, June 17-21, 2013, Pittsburgh, PA, USA.
ACM 978-1-4503-1900-3/13/06.

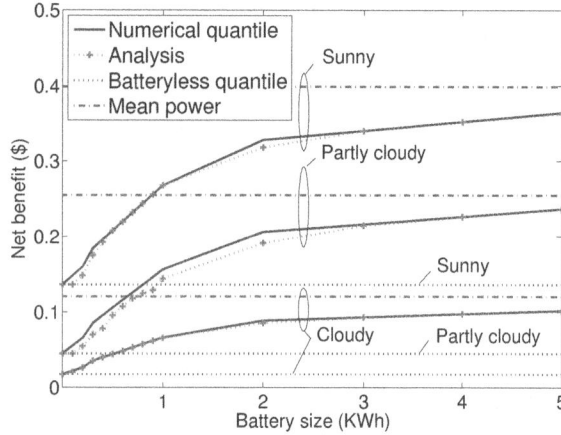

Figure 1: Day-ahead dispatch problem: net benefit as a function of the battery size in summer days in site C1 with $p = 58.51\$/MWh$, $c = 55.51\$/MWh$, $\alpha_{pv} = 1$, $T = 8$ hr, and $T_1 = 8$ am.

and ε^u such that

$$\mathbb{P}\left\{\underbrace{\sup_{s \leq t}\{I_{aux}(s,t) - \mathcal{G}^u_{aux}(t-s)\}}_{:= Y(t)} > x\right\} \leq \varepsilon^u(x) \quad (3)$$

for any $x \geq 0$ and $t \geq 0$. Note that ε^u can be chosen to be the complementary cumulative distribution function (CCDF) of Y. That is, $\varepsilon^u(x) = \int_x^\infty f_Y(y)dy$, where f_Y is the probability density function of Y.

Given $\mathcal{G}^u_{aux}$ and ε^u from Eq. (3) and combining it with Eq. (2), we are able to provide a sample path lower envelope β^l on $\alpha_{pv}I_g$ with bounding function ε^l in the sense of Eq. (1).

3. POWER LOSS CALCULATIONS

Using the above definitions and given a lower sample path envelope on the solar irradiance, we improve the power loss formulation from [5] using the following lemma.

LEMMA 1. *Suppose that an intermittent power source with process $\mathcal{S}$ is fed to a battery with size C and the battery is used to provide a constant output power $\overline{P}$. There is a statistical sample path lower envelope β^l on the intermittent energy source with bounding function ε_l in the sense of Eq. (1). Suppose that ε^{bl} is a constant which satisfies*

$$\forall \tau \geq 1: \quad \mathbb{P}\{\overline{P} > \mathcal{S}(\tau-1,\tau)\} \leq \varepsilon^{bl}. \quad (4)$$

If the initial state of deficit battery charge[2] is B_0^d, then the power loss at time t satisfies the following

$$\mathbb{P}\{l(t) > 0\} \leq \min\left(\varepsilon^{bl}, \varepsilon_l\left(C - B_0^d - \sup_{0 \leq \tau \leq t}(\overline{P}\tau - \beta^l(\tau))\right)\right). \quad (5)$$

4. ELECTRICITY MARKET

Suppose that a power supplier wants to trade the next day's available power in the electricity market for a time interval of size T, where the start time of the contract is T_1. Energy can be traded as

---

[2]defined as the amount of energy needed to fully charge the battery at a given time instant.

constant-power bids for time slots of size T_s (totalling $\frac{T}{T_s}$ contracts per day) and the supplier can propose a different constant power at each time slot. The supplier earns $\$c$ for each watt-hour it is scheduled for. During the day of operation, if the supplier cannot provide its scheduled power for a time interval of size larger than T_u, he is penalized $\$p$ for each watt-hour under-power. Thus, T_u is the time resolution (time unit) needed for the revenue maximization; note that there are $\frac{T_s}{T_u}$ time units in a time slot.

For a given battery size and lower bound sample path envelope on solar irradiance, we can compute the guaranteed output power $\overline{P}_{\varepsilon^*}(\tau)$ watt in τ'th time slot of the next day with loss of power less than $\varepsilon^*_{\overline{P}}(\tau)$ using Lemma 1. Denoting by P the actual available power, the revenue maximization is given by

$$\text{DA max revenue} \geq \max_{0 \leq \varepsilon^* \leq 1} \sum_{\tau=T_1}^{\frac{T+T_1}{T_s}} \left(c\overline{P}_{\varepsilon^*}(\tau)\right.$$
$$\left. - p\frac{T_s}{T_u}\varepsilon^*_{\overline{P}}(\tau)[\overline{P}_{\varepsilon^*}(\tau) - P(\tau)]_+\right)T_s. \quad (6)$$

5. EVALUATION

We use the the dataset from SGP-$C1$ permanent site of Atmospheric Radiation Measurement (ARM) program [1] for a large time interval of 10 years (from 2002 to 2011) to numerically evaluate the accuracy of our analysis; the results are shown in Fig. 1, illustrating that our analysis closely matches numerical simulations across a variety of weather conditions.

6. CONCLUSION

Our work provides an accurate approach, based on the stochastic network calculus, to compute probabilistic bounds on solar production. We believe that our solar power model captures solar generation variability over multiple time scales more accurately than the best-existing models. Using this approach, we pose and solve an optimization problem where we seek to maximize the expected revenue of a solar farm operator participating in a day-ahead market. Our framework can also be used to size a battery such that the overall revenue during battery life time is maximized. We have evaluated our analysis on ten year's traces of solar output and find that our analysis closely approximates the results found from an exact numerical evaluation.

This work assumes perfect batteries. In ongoing work, we are using teletraffic approaches to model battery imperfections.

7. REFERENCES

[1] http://www.archive.arm.gov.
[2] J. Kleissl and J. S. Stein. A wavelet-based variability model (wvm) for solar pv power plants. *IEEE Transactions on Sustainable Energy*, 99(8):1 – 9, 2013.
[3] M. Lave, J. Kleissl, and E. Arias-Castro. High-frequency irradiance fluctuations and geographic smoothing. *Solar Energy*, 86(8):2190 – 2199, 2012.
[4] A. Mills and R. Wiser. Implications of wide-area geographic diversity for short-term variability of solar power. Technical Report LBNL-3884E, Lawrence Berkeley National Laboratory, September 2010.
[5] K. Wang, F. Ciucu, C. Lin, and S. H. Low. A stochastic power network calculus for integrating renewable energy sources into the power grid. *IEEE Journal on Selected Areas in Communications*, 30(6):1037 – 1048, July 2012.

Greedy Name Lookup for Named Data Networking [*]

Yi Wang, Dongzhe Tai, Ting Zhang,
Jianyuan Lu, Boyang Xu, Huichen Dai, Bin Liu [†]
Dept. of Computer Science and Technology
Tsinghua University, Beijing, China

ABSTRACT

Different from the IP-based routers, Named Data Networking routers forward packets by content names, which consist of characters and have variable and unbounded length. This kind of complex name constitution plus the huge-sized name routing table makes wire speed name lookup an extremely challenging task. Greedy name lookup mechanism is proposed to speed up name lookup by dynamically adjusting the search path against the changes of the prefix table. Meanwhile, we elaborate a string-oriented perfect hash table to reduce memory consumption which stores the signature of the key in the entry instead of the key itself. Extensive experimental results on a commodity PC server with 3 million name prefix entries demonstrate that greedy name lookup mechanism achieves 57.14 million searches per second using only 72.95 MB memory.

Categories and Subject Descriptors

C.2.m [**Computer Communication Networks**]: Miscellaneous

General Terms

Algorithms, Design

Keywords

Named Data Networking, Name lookup, Perfect Hash Table, Greedy Strategy

1. INTRODUCTION

As a newly proposed Internet architecture, Named Data Networking [7] (NDN), an instance of the Content-Centric Networking [2] (CCN) paradigm, ignites widespread research interests in both academia and industry. Different from the current IP-based networking, NDN employs string name to identify content and is essentially a name-based networking. The name lookup in NDN for packet forwarding follows the longest prefix matching (LPM) rule [3, 5]. Compared to the IP lookup in a traditional IP-based router, name lookup in an NDN router is more challenging in achieving high-speed lookup, compressing the memory occupation and

---

[*]This work is supported by NSFC (61073171), Tsinghua University Initiative Scientific Research Program(20121080068), the Specialized Research Fund for the Doctoral Program of Higher Education of China(20100002110051).

[†]Corresponding Author: Bin Liu, liub@tsinghua.edu.cn.

Table 1: The distribution of 3M prefix table

Components	1	2	3	4	5	6	7	8	9
Names	224	2,129,835	391,377	21,664	1,598	76	17	2	1
Percentage (%)	0.01	83.70	15.38	0.85	0.06	0	0	0	0
Length (Byte)	3.41	16.47	18.88	21.95	28.66	35.05	40	36	55
Leaf Prefixes	31	2,125,845	390,244	21,538	1,594	76	17	2	1

supporting fast incremental update: 1) *Fast name lookup.* Unlike a fixed-length IP address, a name has variable and unbounded length, which makes name lookup an expensive time-consuming operation; 2) *Memory efficiency.* An NDN prefix table could be several orders of magnitude larger than the largest IP routing table today. Clearly, without elaborated compression, NDN prefix tables can by far exceed the capacity of today's commodity devices; 3) *High update rate.* In addition to network topology and routing policy changes, an NDN router has to handle frequent updates produced by content publishing and deletion, which makes Forwarding Information Base (FIB) update much more frequent than that of today's Internet.

As an NDN software prototype, the source project CCNx [1] is developed by PARC. In CCNx, the name lookup process first generates all possible prefixes from the searched name and sorts the candidate prefixes in a descending order according to their component number. Then, the program looks up the candidate prefixes in FIB one by one until matched or failure. The first found prefix is the longest prefix since there is no longer one in FIB. However, the name lookup performance is still too low to be satisfied [6].

The name lookup speed of CCNx is constrained by two factors: poor longest prefix search strategy and low hash table search performance. Therefore, in this paper, we present the greedy name lookup mechanism to improve the name lookup performance in NDN by breaking the two constraints in CCNx: 1) a greedy strategy described in Section 2 is employed to optimize the search path of name lookup; 2) a string-oriented perfect hash table is elaborated to boost the hash table search speed and compress memory space [4].

2. GREEDY NAME LOOKUP MECHANISM

Name lookup in NDN is a search process which finds the longest prefix corresponding to the name. The name lookup process in CCNx usually probes several hash tables before finding the right longest prefix. The experimental data on our collected prefix tables and traces indicate that CCNx takes 4.81 hash table searches to find the longest prefix in average. This is obviously too slow to meet the fast lookup speed.

The distributions of 3M prefix table enlighten us to optimize the name lookup process by rearranging the search order of candidate prefixes according to the prefixes distribution of the prefix table.

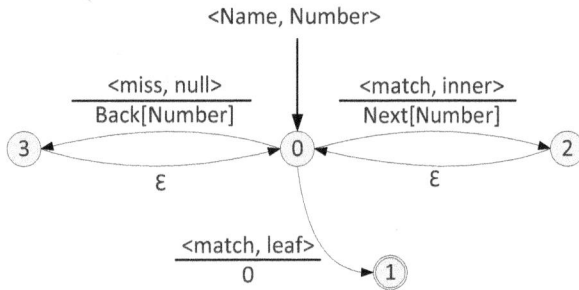

Figure 1: The state transition diagram of name lookup process.

Figure 2: The Next and Back arrays.

Table 1 demonstrates the prefixes distributions of 3M prefix table based on the component number of prefixes. Here, 2,129,835 prefixes consist of 2 components and 391,377 prefixes consist of 3 components, which are 83.70% and 15.38% of 3M prefix table, respectively. Meanwhile, 2,125,845 prefixes with 2 components are the longest prefixes (leaf prefixes[1]). Therefore, if we first search the prefix with 2 components of the name, the probability of returning the longest prefix is 83.54%.

For explaining the greedy name lookup mechanism clearly, the greedy name lookup process is presented in the form of state transition diagram demonstrated in Figure 1. There are 4 states, state-0 is the start state, state-1 is the end state, state-2 and state-3 are middle states. And the functions of the 4 states and the transitions between them are shown in the following:

- State-0 generates the prefix with $Number$ components from the input $Name$, and searches the prefix in the hash table. If the prefix is found, state-0 transits to state-1 when the prefix is a leaf prefix; or state-0 transits to state-2 when the prefix is an inner prefix[2]. If the prefix is missed, state-0 transits to state-3.
- State-1 stops the name lookup process and returns the result.
- State-2 gets the next prefix's component number $Number$ from the $Next$ array, and transits to state-0.
- State-3 gets the next prefix's component number $Number$ from the $Back$ array, and transits to state-0.

Here, we build $Next$ array and $Back$ array according to the distribution of the prefix table in advance. $Next$ array indicates the next component number when the prefix with current component number is found and the prefix is an inner prefix. Contrarily, $Back$ array indicates the next component number when the prefix with current component number is missed. Figure 2 illustrates the $Next$ array and $Back$ array of 3M prefix table. Since the prefixes with 2 components have the maximal number of leaf prefixes, the first input $Number$ in Figure 2 is 2. And $Next[2]$ is 3 as the number of leaf prefixes with 3 components is only the second to the number of leaf prefixes with 2 components. Besides, $Next[1]$ is 0 as the number of leaf prefixes with 2 components is greater than the number of leaf prefixes with 1 component, which means the prefixes with 2 components are always searched ahead of the prefixes with

---

[1] A leaf prefix is the longest prefix for which the name lookup process searches. Therefore, the search process stops and returns the result when finding a leaf prefix.

[2] A name prefix is an inner prefix, if and only if it is the prefix of another name prefix.

Table 2: The name lookup throughput of different methods.

Trace	Threads	Lookup Speed (MSPS)			
		CCNx	CCNx-PHT	Greedy-PHT	Greedy-SPHT
Average	1	0.205	0.692	1.369	3.961
Heavy	1	0.133	0.559	0.821	3.135
Average	24	3.444	11.296	29.476	57.138
Heavy	24	2.538	9.233	13.513	48.654

1 component and the process should be stopped. $Back$ array has the opposite characteristic. In $Back$ array, the longer prefixes with lower priority are set to 0, because the second only shorter prefix has been searched. Meanwhile, the $Next$ array and $Back$ array can be dynamically adjusted to the optimal search path of name lookup according to the changes of the prefix table.

3. EXPERIMENTAL EVALUATION

We implement and compare greedy name lookup mechanism with other 3 methods to expose its advantages. 1) CCNx is the baseline; 2) CCNx-PHT employs the basic string-oriented perfect hash table; 3) Greedy-PHT applies the greedy name lookup mechanism; and 4) Greedy-SPHT combines greedy name lookup mechanism with the improved string-oriented perfect hash table.

Throughput: Table 2 demonstrates the name lookup throughput of the 4 methods running on a commodity server. Running with one thread, CCNx achieves 0.205 MSPS and 0.133 MSPS on 3M prefix table under average workload and heavy workload, while CCNx-PHT realizes 0.692 MSPS and 0.559 MSPS, respectively. Greedy-PHT effectively improves the name lookup performance and speeds up to 1.369 MSPS and 0.821 MSPS, which is about 6.7 times speedup of CCNx and 1.98 times of CCNx-PHT. With negligible false positive, Greedy-SPHT achieves 3.961 MSPS and 3.135 MSPS. which is almost 19.3 times speedup of CCNx, 5.7 times speedup of CCNx-PHT and 2.9 times speedup of Greedy-PHT. Greedy-SPHT running with 24 parallel threads achieves 57.138 MSPS and 48.654 MSPS in average workload and heavy workload, respectively, which means 14.4 times speedup of Greedy-SPHT running with only one thread.

Memory: CCNx needs 119.20 MB on 3M prefix table. Compared with CCNx, CCNx-PHT needs extra 12% memory to construct FIB with basic string-oriented perfect hash table. For supporting greedy name lookup mechanism, Greedy-PHT stores additional information in FIB, so it consumes a little more memory than CCNx-PHT. However, Greedy-SPHT significantly reduces the memory consumption via storing the signature of the key instead of storing the key itself. Greedy-SPHT only costs 72.95 MB on 3M, which saves about 46.8%, 47.5% and 53.7% memory of CCNx, CCNx-PHT and Greedy-PHT, respectively.

4. REFERENCES

[1] CCNx project. http://www.ccnx.org/.
[2] V. Jacobson, D. K. Smetters, J. D. Thornton, M. F. Plass, N. H. Briggs, and R. L. Braynard. Networking Named Content. CoNEXT'09, pages 1–12. ACM, 2009.
[3] Y. Wang, K. He, H. Dai, W. Meng, J. Jiang, B. Liu, and Y. Chen. Scalable Name Lookup in NDN Using Effective Name Component Encoding. In *ICDCS'12*, 2012.
[4] Y. Wang and B. Liu. Greedy Name Lookup Technical Report. http://s-router.cs.tsinghua.edu.cn/~wangyi/GreedyNameLookupTechReport.pdf. 2013.
[5] Y. Wang, Y. Zu, T. Zhang, K. Peng, Q. Dong, B. Liu, W. Meng, H. Dai, X. Tian, Z. Xu, and D. Yang. Wire Speed Name lookup: A GPU-based Approach. In *NSDI'13*, 2013.
[6] H. Yuan, T. Song, and P. Crowley. Scalable NDN Forwarding: Concepts, Issues and Principles. In *ICCCN'12*, pages 1–9, 2012.
[7] L. Zhang, D. Estrin, V. Jacobson, and B. Zhang. Named Data Networking (NDN) Project. http://www.named-data.net/. 2010.

How does Energy Accounting Matter for Energy Management?

Mian Dong
Samsung Research America
mian.dong@samsung.com

Tian Lan
George Washington University
tlan@gwu.edu

Lin Zhong
Rice University
lzhong@rice.edu

Categories and Subject Descriptors: D.4.1 [Process Management]: Scheduling
General Terms: Management, Theory
Keywords: Energy accounting, energy management

1. INTRODUCTION

Energy accounting determines how much a software process contributes to the total system energy consumption. Given the system energy consumption E and the set of processes $\mathbb{N} = \{1, 2, \ldots, n\}$ that are active during time T, *energy accounting* is to determine the energy contribution by each process in $\mathbb{N}$. Energy accounting is the foundation for operating system (OS) based energy management that achieves certain trade-off between energy consumption and process utility by controlling how processes are scheduled, e.g., [4, 3].

In this paper, we provide the first investigation of the relation between energy accounting and energy management and answer the fundamental question about it for the first time: *how does energy accounting matter for energy management?* Toward answering the question, we formulate energy management as a utility optimization problem and show, surprisingly, that energy accounting does not matter for widely used budget based energy management (BEM) framework [4, 3]. In the BEM framework, OS first assigns each running process an energy budget and then charges each process from its budget based on energy accounting. A process will not be scheduled if it runs out of its budget. We further prove that this surprising result is due to the fact that BEM is sub-optimal and subsequently provide an optimal energy management (OEM) framework.

2. ENERGY MANAGEMENT AS UTILITY OPTIMIZATION

2.1 Theoretical Foundation

We first show energy management can be formulated as a utility optimization problem given the energy capacity by scheduling processes, i.e., by determining each process's run time.

Process Run Time: We consider n independent processes, denoted by $\mathbb{N} = \{1, 2, \ldots, n\}$, and a system that is capable of running up to m processes concurrently during a scheduler period, i.e., a set of processes $\mathbb{S}$ can be scheduled simultaneously only if $|\mathbb{S}| \leq m$. Suppose that during the time horizon of energy management, a coalition of concurrent processes $\mathbb{S}$ receive total run time $T_{\mathbb{S}}$. Note

that $T_{\mathbb{S}}$ does not have to be a single continuous time interval; it can be a collection of time intervals. Then, the run time received by an individual process i is given by

$$t_i = \sum_{\mathbb{S}: i \in \mathbb{S}, |\mathbb{S}| \leq m} T_{\mathbb{S}}. \qquad (1)$$

Here the summation is over all feasible process coalitions satisfying $|\mathbb{S}| \leq m$ and containing process i. We refer to $T_{\mathbb{S}}$ as the *scheduling decision* for coalition $\mathbb{S}$.

Energy Capacity: The total system energy consumption must be bounded by available energy capacity, C. The energy consumption of a set of processes $\mathbb{S}$ during a scheduling period T_0 is denoted by $E(\mathbb{S})$, and its average power $E(\mathbb{S})/T_0$. Since $T_{\mathbb{S}}$ is the total time that $\mathbb{S}$ is scheduled, our energy management is subject to the energy capacity constraint, i.e.,

$$\sum_{\mathbb{S}: |\mathbb{S}| \leq m} E(\mathbb{S}) \cdot T_{\mathbb{S}}/T_0 \leq C. \qquad (2)$$

Utility Function: In our optimization framework, each process is assigned a utility function $U_i(t_i)$, which measures the utility of process i receiving run time t_i. Such a utility optimization has been widely used in wireless communications and networking [2].

Problem Formulation: Energy management is to make scheduling decisions, i.e., $T_{\mathbb{S}}$, in order to maximize the aggregate utility of all processes, i.e., $\sum_{i=1}^{n} U_i(t_i)$, under energy capacity constraint C.

2.2 Budget based Energy Management (BEM)

We consider budget based energy management (BEM), a widely used energy management approach [4, 3], where each process receives an independent energy budget and disburses it according to a process-specific policy. BEM relies on energy accounting to split total energy consumption among individual processes. Let $\phi_i(E(\mathbb{S}))$ denote the energy consumption attributed to process i according to the energy accounting policy during a scheduling period in which $\mathbb{S}$ are scheduled to run and $i \in \mathbb{S}$. After this scheduling period, $\phi_i(E(\mathbb{S}))$ will be deducted from process i's energy budget B_i. When a process runs out of budget, it will not be scheduled any more.

We assume that each process is scheduled with a known probability p_i, until its budget runs out. To determine process run time, we suppose that processes reach zero energy budget in the following order: $\pi(1), \pi(2), \ldots, \pi(n)$, where $\pi(k)$ be the kth process that runs out of its budget (If multiple processes reach zero budget simultaneously, their ordering can be arbitrary). Then, the sequence of positive-budget processes $\mathbb{A}_k = \{\pi(k), \pi(k+1), \ldots, \pi(n)\}$ for $k = 1, \ldots, n$ form a contraction with $\mathbb{A}_{k+1} \subseteq \mathbb{A}_k$. We can partition the system execution into n distinct intervals, each of length T_k and containing a set of $|\mathbb{A}_k| = n - k + 1$ positive-budget processes.

Now we derive energy consumption and run time for BEM. We assume that the time scale of energy management is much larger than that of a scheduling period. That is, the energy budget for processes are determined for periods much longer than a scheduling period. The Law of Large Number applies and allows us to compute the approximated run time that each feasible subset of processes, $\mathbb{S} \subseteq \mathbb{A}_k$ and $|\mathbb{S}| \leq m$, receive during T_k:

$$T_{\mathbb{S},k} = T_k \cdot \text{Prob}\{\mathbb{S} \text{ is selected}\}$$
$$= \frac{T_k \Delta_{\mathbb{S},k}}{\sum_{\mathbb{S}:\mathbb{S}\subseteq\mathbb{A}_k,|\mathbb{S}|\leq m} \Delta_{\mathbb{S},k}} \quad (3)$$

where $\Delta_{\mathbb{S},k} = \prod_{i\in\mathbb{S}} p_i \prod_{j\in\mathbb{A}_k\setminus\mathbb{S}}(1-p_j)$ is the probability that only subset $\mathbb{S}$ is selected without constraint $|\mathbb{S}| \leq m$. Therefore, each process i receives aggregate run time from all feasible coalitions with $i \in \mathbb{S}$ as follows:

$$T_{i,k} = \sum_{\mathbb{S}:\mathbb{S}\subseteq\mathbb{A}_k,|\mathbb{S}|\leq m,i\in\mathbb{S}} T_{\mathbb{S},k} = T_k \frac{\sum_{\mathbb{S}:\mathbb{S}\subseteq\mathbb{A}_k,|\mathbb{S}|\leq m,i\in\mathbb{S}} \Delta_{\mathbb{S},k}}{\sum_{\mathbb{S}:\mathbb{S}\subseteq\mathbb{A}_k,|\mathbb{S}|\leq m} \Delta_{\mathbb{S},k}} \quad (4)$$

Similarly, process i is charged an energy cost by aggregating its attributions from all feasible coalitions $\mathbb{S}$ during T_k:

$$\Phi_i(\mathbb{A}_k, T_k) \triangleq \sum_{\mathbb{S}:\mathbb{S}\subseteq\mathbb{A}_k,|\mathbb{S}|\leq m} \phi_i(E(\mathbb{S})) \cdot T_{\mathbb{S},k}/T_0 \quad (5)$$

The objective of BEM is to maximize the aggregate utility by apportioning system energy budget among individual processes. We formulate it as the following optimization:

Problem BEM :

$$\text{maximize} \quad \sum_{i=1}^{n} U_i(t_i) \quad (6)$$

$$\text{subject to} \quad t_i = \sum_k T_{i,k}, \ \forall i, \quad (7)$$

$$\sum_k \Phi_i(\mathbb{A}_k, T_k) \leq B_i, \ \forall i \quad (8)$$

$$\mathbb{A}_k = \{\pi(k), \pi(k+1), \ldots, \pi(n)\}, \ \forall k \quad (9)$$

$$\sum_{i=1}^{n} B_i \leq C \quad (10)$$

$$\text{variables} \quad \pi, T_k, B_i. \quad (11)$$

where both $T_{i,k}$ and Φ_i are functions of T_k, as given in (4) and (5), respectively. The optimization is carried out over all ordering π of n processes. Note that π and T_k together determine process scheduling, i.e., $T_{\mathbb{S},k}$, $\forall k$ and $\forall \mathbb{S} \subseteq \mathbb{N}$, $|\mathbb{S}| \leq m$, as shown in (3).

Energy Accounting Policy does not Matter for BEM: Problem BEM formulated in (6-11) clearly relies on the choice of energy accounting policy $\phi_i(\cdot), \forall i$. However, in the following we prove a somehow counter-intuitive result, which shows that the optimal utility value and process tun time of Problem BEM is irrelevant of energy accounting policies.

THEOREM 1. *Problem BEM is independent of energy accounting, i.e., for an arbitrary energy accounting function that satisfies the Efficiency property, i.e., the energy contributions by all processes must add up to be the same as the total system energy consumption, there always exists a set of energy budget B_i, $\forall i$, which achieve the same optimal utility value.* [1]

The intuitive explanation of the proof is as follows. In particular, we show that for a feasible set of run time $t_i, \forall i$, there always exists a way to partition total energy C among individual budgets $B_i, \forall i$

---

[1] Proofs for Theorems (1-2) can be found in [1]

accordingly, no matter what energy accounting policy is used. Suppose one can achieve an optimal utility value with run time $t_i, \forall i$, using an ordering π and a specific energy accounting policy. Then the corresponding energy budget of each process should be calculated from (5) and (8). If one chooses to use another energy accounting policy and would like to achieve the same optimal utility value, the corresponding energy budget should be calculated in the same way, with the new energy accounting policy. The key idea is that as long as the Efficiency property holds, the sum of individual energy budget would remain unchanged and satisfy the total energy constraint $\sum_i B_i = C$.

2.3 Optimal Energy Management (OEM)

We consider an optimization which aims at maximizing aggregate process utilities under a sum energy constraint C. The Optimal Energy Management problem, denoted by Problem OEM, is formulated as follows:

Problem OEM :

$$\text{maximize} \quad \sum_{i=1}^{n} U_i(t_i) \quad (12)$$

$$\text{subject to} \quad t_i = \sum_{\mathbb{S}:i\in\mathbb{S},|\mathbb{S}|\leq m} T_{\mathbb{S}}, \ \forall i, \quad (13)$$

$$\sum_{\mathbb{S}} E(\mathbb{S}) \cdot T_{\mathbb{S}}/T_0 \leq C, \quad (14)$$

$$\text{variables} \quad T_{\mathbb{S}}. \quad (15)$$

The algorithm for solving Problem OEM and its complexity analysis can be found in [1]. While implementing the solution of Problem OEM in practice requires logging the run time of all feasible coalitions and results in higher overhead than that of BEM, it is guaranteed to outperform BEM in energy management.

THEOREM 2. *Problem OEM always dominates Problem BEM. Its optimal utility value is higher than or equal to that of Problem BEM.*

The intuitive explanation of the proof is as follows. Suppose there exists an optimal solution to Problem BEM. That is, to achieve the optimal BEM utility value, one divides total energy constraint C into individual budgets $B_i, \forall i$, schedules processes based on their budget and priority, and charges them accordingly until their energy budget reduces to zero. If all the scheduling decisions and run time (i.e. $\mathbb{S}$ and $T_{\mathbb{S}}$) are recorded during the entire process, one can apply them in Problem OEM and achieve the same process run time, resulting the same utility value. This is feasible because Problem OEM optimizes over all possible process coalitions and has a significant larger number of "control knobs" than Problem BEM does. Therefore, any optimal BEM utility is achievable in OEM. Optimal OEM utility must be higher than or equal to that of Problem BEM.

3. REFERENCES

[1] M. Dong. *Energy accounting and optimization of mobile systems*. PhD thesis, Rice University, Houston, Texas, 2013.

[2] T. Lan, D. Kao, M. Chiang, and A. Subharwal. An axiomatic theory of fairness for resource allocation. In *Proc. IEEE INFOCOM*, 2010.

[3] A. Roy, S. Rumble, R. Stutsman, P. Levis, D. Mazieres, and N. Zeldovich. Energy management in mobile devices with the Cinder operating system. In *Proc. ACM EuroSys*, 2011.

[4] H. Zeng, C. Ellis, A. Lebeck, and A. Vahdat. ECOSystem: Managing energy as a first class operating system resource. In *ACM SIGPLAN Notices*, volume 37, 2002.

Online Load Balancing Under Graph Constraints

Sharayu Moharir
Department of ECE
The University of Texas
Austin, Texas 78712
sharayu.moharir@gmail.com

Sujay Sanghavi
Department of ECE
The University of Texas
Austin, Texas 78712
sanghavi@mail.utexas.edu

Sanjay Shakkottai
Department of ECE
The University of Texas
Austin, Texas 78712
shakkott@mail.utexas.edu

ABSTRACT

In several data center settings, each arriving job may only be served by one of a subset of servers. Such a graph constraint can arise due to several reasons. One is locality of the data needed by a job; for example, in content farms (e.g. in Netflix or YouTube) a video request can only be served by a machine that possesses a copy. Motivated by this, we consider a setting where each job, on arrival, reveals a deadline and a subset of servers that can serve it. The job needs to be immediately allocated to one of these servers, and cannot be moved thereafter. Our objective is to maximize the fraction of jobs that are served before their deadlines.

For this online load balancing problem, we prove an upper bound of $1 - 1/e$ on the competitive ratio of non-preemptive online algorithms for systems with a large number of servers. We propose an algorithm - INSERT RANKING - which achieves this upper bound. The algorithm makes decisions in a correlated random way and it is inspired by the work of Karp, Vazirani and Vazirani on online matching for bipartite graphs. We also show that two more natural algorithm, based on independent randomness, are strictly suboptimal, with a competitive ratio of $1/2$.

Categories and Subject Descriptors

C.2.4 [**Computer-Communication Networks**]:
Distributed Systems

Keywords

Content Delivery Networks, Matchings

1. INTRODUCTION

This paper looks at the problem of load-balancing among servers in the setting where each job can only be served by a restricted subset of the servers. Such a constraint arises in several settings, including in content farms and spatially distributed cloud servers. In content farms like Netflix [5] and YouTube [6], videos are replicated only among a subset of the servers; thus a request for a specific video can be served only by the corresponding subset. As another example, web portals that provide a collection of services (e.g., Google providing Email, Maps, Video, Storage and News services) might not have all services replicated on every server. This naturally leads to an association between each request and a subset of servers, based on the request type. Further, the content requests typically have a short fuse, and requests need to be served in (near) real-time.

The above discussion motivates the problem in this paper: We consider online load balancing of jobs with deadlines on non-identical servers (i.e., jobs have "hard" server preferences). In other words, each job has a deadline and can be served by only a (job-specific) subset of the servers, and these preferences are revealed only when the job enters the multi-server queuing system.

Our objective is to design online algorithms which maximize the fraction of jobs that are served before their deadlines. In this work, the performance of an online algorithm is compared with the performance of a non-causal scheduler that has information of all future arrivals. We assume that the online algorithm has no knowledge of the statistics of the job arrival process. We characterize the performance of an online algorithm by its competitive ratio which is the ratio of the expected number of jobs served by the online algorithm to the number of jobs served by the optimal offline algorithm, minimized over all input sequences, i.e. we study the performance of the algorithm in the adversarial setting. The adversarial setting, providing worst-case guarantees, is more appropriate for this problem because stochastic models presuppose stationary statistics. These are hard to come by in a fast evolving setting (e.g. content farms like Youtube). Jobs on YouTube [6] are requests to view particular videos whose popularity is time varying. The statistics of the arrival process depend on the popularity of various videos and which videos are stored on which servers.

We visualize the system as a bipartite graph between servers and jobs, where an edge between a job and a server indicates that that particular job can be served by that particular server. The task of allocating jobs to servers is equivalent to the task of finding a generalized matching in the bipartite graph where a generalized matching is a matching where one server could be matched to multiple jobs but one job is matched to at most one server.

2. RELATED WORK

The problem of online matching in bipartite graphs has been studied in [2], where the authors introduced the idea of using correlated randomness for online matching. Various extensions to weighted graphs and the application of online weighted bipartite matching to ad-words has been studied. The problem of Online $b-$Matching has been studied in [1] and [3]. Closer to our setting, load balancing for a system without departures has been studied in [4].

SIGMETRICS'13, June 17-21, 2013, Pittsburgh, PA, USA.
ACM 978-1-4503-1900-3/13/06.

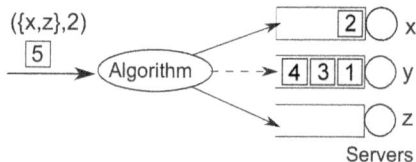

Figure 1: *System Model for Online Load Balancing: An illustration of a system with 3 servers. Job 5 has a server subset $\{S1, S3\}$ and a deadline of 2 time-slots and the scheduling algorithm needs to decide whether to send the job to server $S1$ or $S3$ or drop the job.*

3. SYSTEM MODEL

We consider a multi-server discrete time queueing system. We assume that jobs come into the system at the beginning of each slot. If there are multiple arrivals in a slot, they are ordered. Each job can only be served by a subset of the servers; *this subset is revealed only when a job arrives.* Each job takes 1 time slot, on any of the servers that can serve it. Furthermore, every job p has a *deadline d_p* associated with it; this is the maximum number of slots it can wait, after arrival. There exists a finite maximum $d_{max} < \infty$ such that $d_p \leq d_{max}$ for all p. See Figure 1 for an illustration of the system model.

Our task is to allocate jobs to servers so as to maximize the number served by their deadline. Any job, once allocated, cannot be revoked / moved to another choice. Thus, a job p will not be served if, at the time of its arrival, all the servers it can be allocated to already have more than d_p jobs in them. We consider algorithm design in the competitive ratio (aka worst-case / adversarial) setting, where the algorithm has no knowledge of any aspect of the arrivals – i.e. it does not know how many packets arrive at each time, and what the deadline and server-subset of each one is. We will allow for both deterministic and randomized algorithms.

We measure the performance of any online allocation algorithm in terms of its *competitive ratio ρ*, where

$$\rho(\text{alg}) = \inf_{t>0} \left(\min_{A \in A_t} \left(\frac{E[S_{alg}(A)]}{S_{opt}(A)} \right) \right).$$

where A_t is the set of all arrival processes such that there are no arrivals after time-slot t, $E[S_{alg}(A)]$ is the expected number of jobs served within their deadline by the (possibly randomized) algorithm and $S_{opt}(A)$ is the number of jobs served within their deadline by the offline optimal algorithm.

4. CONTRIBUTIONS

1. **Upper Bound:** We show an upper (i.e. outer) bound of $1 - 1/e$ on the competitive ratio of *any* randomized load balancing algorithm.

2. **Algorithm and its Performance:** Our main contribution is the INSERT RANKING algorithm. The INSERT RANKING algorithm is a probabilistic approximation to join-the-shortest-queue (i.e., join the least loaded allowed server). The important distinction, however, is the tie-breaking aspect. Specifically, the INSERT RANKING algorithm generates a random priority order among copies of the servers, and allocates a job to the smallest-index server copy with

respect to this priority order. Critically, this same priority order is used for tie-breaking decisions *for all jobs* that arrive within this time-slot. Thus, this results in *correlated tie-breaking* across users within a time-slot. At the end of each time-slot, INSERT RANKING updates this priority order in a manner such that the correlation is maintained across time-slots, and therefore resulting in correlated tie-breaking across time-slots. We show a lower bound (i.e. achievable) of $1 - 1/e$ on the competitive ratio of INSERT RANKING. This proves the optimality of INSERT RANKING.

3. **Other Algorithms:**
We analyze the performance of two intuitive randomized algorithms which do not use correlated tie-breaking. The first one is a join the shortest queue algorithm which breaks ties uniformly at random *independent* of past choices, and the second algorithm is biased towards joining shorter queues which also breaks ties in a random manner, independent of past choices. We show an upper (i.e. outer) bound of $1/2$ on the competitive ratio of both algorithms and show that INSERT RANKING strictly outperforms them, highlighting the importance of correlated randomization.

5. SUMMARY AND DISCUSSION

We study online load balancing under graph constraints in the adversarial setting. First, we design "bad" arrival patterns and use them to upper bound the performance any online load balancing algorithm. Next, we propose an algorithm called INSERT RANKING which uses correlated randomness for load balancing, and prove that it an optimal online load balancing algorithm. The main message of this paper is that correlated randomness is important, because we show that INSERT RANKING outperforms algorithms which make (the more natural) un-correlated/independent random choices for load balancing.

6. ACKNOWLEDGMENTS

We acknowledge the support of NSF grants 0954059 and 0964391.

7. REFERENCES

[1] B. Kalyanasundaram and K.R. Pruhs. An optimal deterministic algorithm for online b-matching. *Theoretical Computer Science*, 233:2000, 2000.

[2] R.M. Karp, U.V. Vazirani, and V.V. Vazirani. An optimal algorithm for on-line bipartite matching. In *Proceedings of the twenty-second annual ACM symposium on Theory of Computing*, Baltimore, Maryland, May 1990.

[3] A. Mehta, A. Saberi, U. Vazirani, and V. Vazirani. Adwords and generalized on-line matching. In *Proceedings of FOCS*, 2005.

[4] S. Moharir and S. Sanghavi. Online load balancing and correlated randomness. In *Annual Conference on Communication, Control and Computing (Allerton)*, 2012.

[5] www.netflix.com.

[6] www.youtube.com.

Parallel Scaling Properties from a Basic Block View

Melanie Kambadur
melanie@cs.columbia.edu

Kui Tang
kt2384@columbia.edu

Joshua Lopez
jl3497@columbia.edu

Martha A. Kim
martha@cs.columbia.edu

Department of Computer Science
Columbia University
New York, New York

ABSTRACT

As software scalability lags behind hardware parallelism, understanding scaling behavior is more important than ever. This paper demonstrates how to use Parallel Block Vector (PBV) profiles to measure the scaling properties of multi-threaded programs from a new perspective: the basic block's view. Through this lens, we guide users through quick and simple methods to produce high-resolution application scaling analyses. This method requires no manual program modification, new hardware, or lengthy simulations, and captures the impact of architecture, operating systems, threading models, and inputs. We apply these techniques to a set of parallel benchmarks, and, as an example, demonstrate that when it comes to scaling, functions in an application do not behave monolithically.

Categories and Subject Descriptors

D.2.8 [**Software Engineering**]: Metrics

Keywords

Parallel software; scaling; basic block vectors

1. INTRODUCTION

A host of factors determine an application's performance, including algorithmic and design choices, program inputs, source language, thread library selection, operating system configurations, and the hardware platform on which the program is run. Many tools and measurement methodologies are available to help identify parallel performance pathologies. The tools vary widely in the type and form of information they reveal and in their implementations, but they generally employ one of two broad strategies. The first strategy is to look for inefficiencies at important and commonly known sites such as memory access and locking points, or along critical paths. The second strategy is to profile per-thread hardware or OS resource usage over time looking for performance sub-optimalities, such as cache misses or low CPU utilization.

This work takes a third perspective, evaluating program scalability per region of code. This is accomplished through

This research was supported by the National Science Foundation (CNS-1117135).

fine-grained, application-wide profiling, where the only activity monitored is the total number of threads executing. This approach reveals how each basic block in a program scales as parallelism increases. Such "micro-scaling metrics" can be aggregated or cross-referenced with other sources of information (e.g. control or data flow graphs, or compiler debug information) to reveal the scaling properties of each line of code, function, algorithm, critical section, or data structure. The metrics can be simply and efficiently collected using techniques described in this paper, and require no software annotations, hardware support, or software simulation.

2. BASIC BLOCK VIEW OF SCALING

Background on Parallel Block Vectors. The parallel block vectors [1], or PBVs, on which the rest of this work is built, measure application-level parallelism each time a basic block is executed. As a parallel program runs, the number of active threads fluctuates, moving it through different *parallelism phases* that are defined by the number of threads working concurrently. PBV profiles capture the dynamic basic block composition of these phases. Figure 1 shows a simple, data-parallel example with five basic blocks: A, B, and C in `main` and D and E in `worker`. When the program is executed, the number of parallel threads will change over time. Of the four executions of block D in this example, two were during a three-thread phase and two during a five-thread phase.

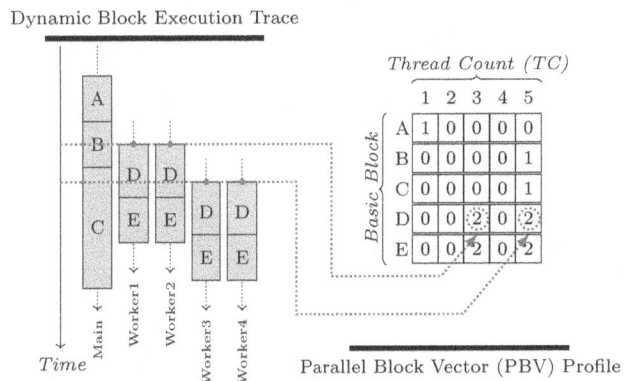

Figure 1: PBV profiles map basic blocks to dynamic execution counts per-parallelism phase.

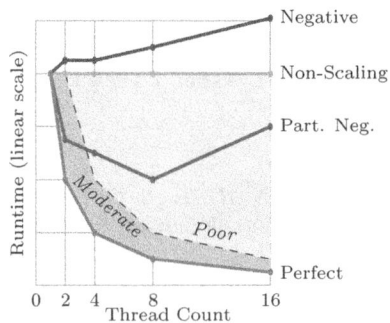

Figure 2: Qualitative basic block scaling categories

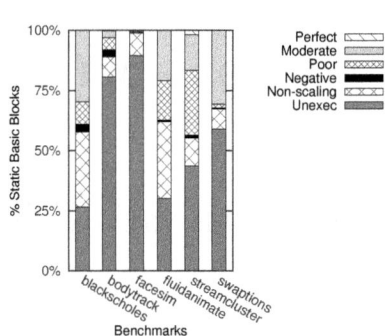

Figure 3: Static basic block breakdown by scaling behavior.

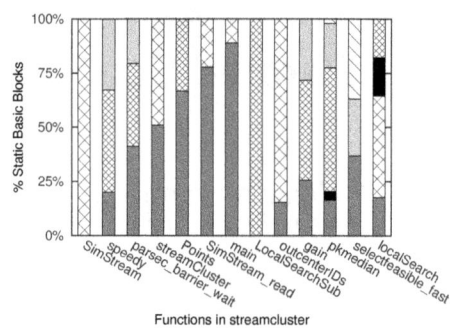

Figure 4: With respect to scaling behavior, functions are not monolithic.

Block-level Scaling. Block-level scaling metrics can be constructed from PBV profiles collected for a program at increasing available thread counts, thereby revealing how each basic block scales — or does not — to higher working thread counts.

Model of Runtime. Each basic block in a PBV profile can be traced back to the assembly code, enabling us to identify the instructions that compose the block and to model execution time. Using a simple model that counts the number of dynamic instructions executed by a particular region of the application divided by the number of working threads this model estimates the parallel runtime of each block. Across the Parsec benchmarks, our approximation has a correlation coefficient of 0.9502 (min = 0.803).

Scaling Classification. Using multiple PBVS collected at increasing thread counts and the model of program runtime, one can classify how *each basic block in the application scales*. Figure 2 suggests five useful classes:

- *Perfectly scaling* blocks' runtimes decrease linearly or superlinearly with the number of threads.
- *Moderately scaling* blocks come within 50% of perfect.
- *Non-scaling* blocks' runtimes do not change as threads increase.
- *Poorly scaling* blocks scale somewhat, but not enough to be considered moderate.
- *Negatively scaling* blocks have runtimes that increase as threads are added.
- If a block's runtime increases, but never exceeds the serial runtime, we call it *partly negatively scaling*.

3. EXPERIMENTS

Application-wide Block Scaling. To get a quick overall snapshot of a parallel program's scaling properties, a user can check how much of the program's source code falls into each of the qualitative micro-scaling categories. This view reveals whether scaling deficiencies are isolated to a small part of the code base or whether they are pervasive throughout a program. Figure 3 shows how the static basic blocks in Parsec benchmark applications are distributed amongst the six micro-scaling categories. Examining fluidanimate — the fourth bar from the left of the figure — we see that out of its 518 blocks, roughly 30% are unexecuted, 32% do not scale at all, 0.5% exhibit negative scaling, and 16.5% and

21% are poorly and moderately scaling, respectively. None of the blocks are perfectly scaling, which indicates that no part of the program consistently executes at the full number of available threads.

Per-Function Micro-scaling. Because basic blocks are so numerous and not typically exposed to the programmer, it is often preferable to group blocks into more congruous entities. Many tools profile in terms of functions, and while functions are natural for programmers to reason about, they might not be the most appropriate boundary for delineating scalability properties. In particular, functions are programmer constructs that, despite their name, do not always delineate actual functionality. Here, we classified the static blocks in each function according to their scaling properties. As an example, Figure 4 shows the distribution of blocks in streamcluster's functions. While several functions (e.g., SimStream, LocalSearchSub) are made up of homogeneous blocks (non- and poorly scaling, respectively), most are heterogeneous, comprising blocks from multiple scaling classes. pkmedian, for example, contains blocks from five out of the six categories. Similar patterns were visible in other applications, indicating that functions are not monolithic from a scaling perspective, and that it is important to have analyses that can capture and expose scaling nuances outside of function boundaries. Basic blocks, however, can be recomposed into *arbitrary regions of interest* including loops, critical sections, algorithms, sets of related functions, or even entire libraries so that a user can focus on relevant code regions to analyze.

4. CONCLUSION

Block-level scaling analyses give users a new way to approach multi-threaded performance analysis. This work demonstrates how to construct this perspective and shows how it might be leveraged to analyze the scaling behavior of large, complex applications.

5. REFERENCES

[1] M. Kambadur, K. Tang, and M. A. Kim. Harmony: Collection and analysis of parallel block vectors. In *ISCA*, June 2012. http://arcade.cs.columbia.edu/harmony.

Sharp Bounds in Stochastic Network Calculus

Florin Ciucu, Felix Poloczek
T-Labs / TU Berlin

Jens Schmitt
University of Kaiserslautern

ABSTRACT

The practicality of the stochastic network calculus (SNC) is often questioned on grounds of potential looseness of its performance bounds. In this paper it is uncovered that for bursty arrival processes (specifically Markov-Modulated On-Off (MMOO)), whose amenability to *per-flow* analysis is typically proclaimed as a highlight of SNC, the bounds can unfortunately indeed be very loose (e.g., by several orders of magnitude off). In response to this uncovered weakness of SNC, the (Standard) per-flow bounds are herein improved by deriving a general sample-path bound, using martingale based techniques, which accommodates FIFO, SP, and EDF scheduling disciplines. The obtained (Martingale) bounds capture an additional exponential decay factor of $\mathcal{O}\left(e^{-\alpha n}\right)$ in the number of flows n, and are remarkably accurate even in multiplexing scenarios with few flows.

Categories and Subject Descriptors

H.1.1 [**Systems and Information Theory**]: Information Theory; C.4 [**Performance of Systems**]: Modeling techniques

Keywords

Stochastic network calculus, scheduling

1. INTRODUCTION

The stochastic network calculus (SNC) is a relatively recent methodology to solve queueing problems (see Chang [2] and Jiang and Liu [7]). From a technical point of view, SNC is a combination between the deterministic network calculus conceived by Cruz [5] and the effective bandwidth theory. Because SNC solves queueing problems in terms of *bounds*, it is often regarded as an unconventional approach, especially by the queueing theory community.

Based on its ability to partially solve hard queueing problems (i.e., in terms of bounds), SNC is justifiably proclaimed as a valuable alternative to the classical queueing theory (see Ciucu and Schmitt [4]). At the same time, SNC is also justifiably questioned on the tightness of its bounds. While the asymptotic tightness generally holds (see Chang [2], p. 291, and Ciucu *et al.* [1]), doubts on the bounds' numerical tightness shed skepticism on the practical relevance of SNC. This skepticism is supported by the fact that SNC largely employs

the same probability methods as the effective bandwidth theory, which was argued to produce largely inaccurate results for non-Poisson arrival processes (see Choudhury *et al.* [3]). Moreover, although the importance of accompanying bounds by simulations has already been recognized in some early works (see Zhang *et al.* [11] for the analysis of GPS), the SNC literature is scarce in that respect.

In this paper we reveal what is perhaps 'feared' by SNC proponents and expected by others: the bounds are very loose for the class of MMOO processes. In addition to providing numerical evidence for this fact (the bounds can be off by arbitrary orders of magnitude), we also prove that the bounds are asymptotically loose in most multiplexing regimes. Concretely, we (analytically) prove that the Standard bounds are 'missing' an exponential decay factor of $\mathcal{O}\left(e^{-\alpha n}\right)$ in the number of flows n, where $\alpha > 0$; this missing factor has been indicated through numerical experiments in Choudhury *et al.* [3] in the context of effective bandwidth bounds (which scale identically as the SNC bounds).

While this paper convincingly uncovers a major weakness in the SNC literature, it also shows that the looseness of the bounds is generally not inherent in SNC but it is due to the 'temptatious' but 'poisonous' elementary tools from probability theory leveraged in its application. In this sense, we prove that by leveraging more advanced tools (i.e., martingale based techniques), the SNC bounds improve dramatically to the point that they almost match simulation results. Concretely, we show these improvements to hold for per-flow delay bounds in FIFO, SP, and EDF scheduling scenarios with MMOO flows. Based on these improvements we argue that the core analysis in SNC, being reminiscent from the deterministic network calculus, is not only asymptotically but also numerically tight.

The sharp bounds obtained in this paper are the first in the conventional stochastic network calculus literature (i.e., involving service processes) concerning bursty arrivals. Their significance, relative to existing sharp bounds in the effective bandwidth literature (e.g., Duffield [6] and Chang [2], pp. 339-343, using martingale inequalities, or Liu *et al.* [9] by extending an approach of Kingman involving integral inequalities [8]), is that they apply at the *per-flow* level for various scheduling disciplines; in turn, existing sharp bounds only apply at the *aggregate* level. Our sharp bounds thus generalize existing ones by accounting for scheduling.

A weakness of our results, from a purely *network calculus perspective*, is that they are restricted to a *specific* class of processes, i.e., MMOO; we point out that one of the conceptual promises of the SNC is to provide general bounds for much broader classes. While we thus deliberately sacrifice this conceptual generality, we also advocate a conceptual shift in running the SNC. Concretely, based on the results obtained in this paper, we believe that 1) SNC must be coupled with the mainstream queueing literature, in particular by "getting a firm grip on arrivals", and 2) the main two features of SNC (i.e., dealing with scheduling and multi-node) must be carefully leveraged in order to obtain sharp bounds.

2. MARTINGALE BOUNDS FOR MMOO

We consider a single queue whereby two cumulative arrival processes $A_1(t)$ and $A_2(t)$, each containing n_1 and n_2 MMOO processes, are served by a server with constant-rate $C = nc$, where $n = n_1 + n_2$. The time model is continuous. The following general result enables the per-flow analysis, in particular of the aggregate $A_1(t)$, for several scheduling algorithms (FIFO, SP, and EDF).

THEOREM 1. (MARTINGALE SAMPLE-PATH BOUND) *Consider the previous queueing system in which all $n_1 + n_2$ sub-flows are independent MMOO processes with transition rates μ and λ, and peak rate P, and starting in the steady-state. The aggregate arrival processes are $A_1(t)$ and $A_2(t)$, each being modulated by the (stationary) Markov processes $Z_1(t)$ and $Z_2(t)$ with n_1 and n_2 states, respectively. Assume that the utilization factor $\rho := \frac{pP}{c}$ satisfies $\rho < 1$ for stability, where $p := \frac{\mu}{\mu + \lambda}$ is the steady-state 'On' probability; assume also that $P > c$ to avoid a trivial scenario with zero delay. Then the following sample-path bound holds for all $0 \le u \le t$ and σ*

$$\mathbb{P}\left(\sup_{0 \le s < t - u} \{A_1(s, t-u) + A_2(s, t) - C(t-s)\} > \sigma \right)$$
$$\le K^n e^{-\gamma(C_1 u + \sigma)}, \tag{1}$$

where $C_1 = n_1 c$, $K = \rho \left(\frac{\rho - p}{1 - p} \right)^{\frac{p}{\rho} - 1}$, and $\gamma = \frac{(\lambda + \mu)(1 - \rho)}{P - c}$.

The theorem generalizes a result by Palmowski and Rolski [10], which is restricted to an *aggregate* analysis under FIFO. The key to our proof is the construction of a single martingale M_t, from two existing martingales, such that the per-flow analysis for the different scheduling algorithms becomes possible. The sample-path bound from Eq. (1) then follows from a standard technique based on the Optional Sampling theorem, applied to the martingale M_t.

Using existing service processes for $A_1(t)$ for each of the three scheduling algorithms, the sample path bound from Eq. (1) lends itself to bounds on the virtual delay process $W_1(t) := \inf \{d \ge 0 : A_1(t - d) \le D_1(t)\}$ of $A_1(t)$:

FIFO : $\mathbb{P}(W_1(t) > d) \le K^n e^{-\gamma C d}$

SP : $\mathbb{P}(W_1(t) > d) \le K^n e^{-\gamma C_1 d}$

EDF : $\mathbb{P}\left(W_1(t) > d \right) \le K^n e^{\gamma C_2 \min\{d_1^* - d_2^*, d\}} e^{-\gamma C d}$.

The EDF bound holds for $d_1^* \ge d_2^*$, where d_1^* and d_2^* are the relative deadlines associated to $A_1(t)$ and $A_2(t)$, respectively. The bound for $d_1^* < d_2^*$ is similar and is omitted here. The parameters K and γ are as in Theorem 1, and $C_2 = n_2 c$.

Figure 1 illustrates the Martingale delay bounds obtained using Theorem 1, in contrast to the Standard bounds obtained using existing SNC methods, and simulations. The

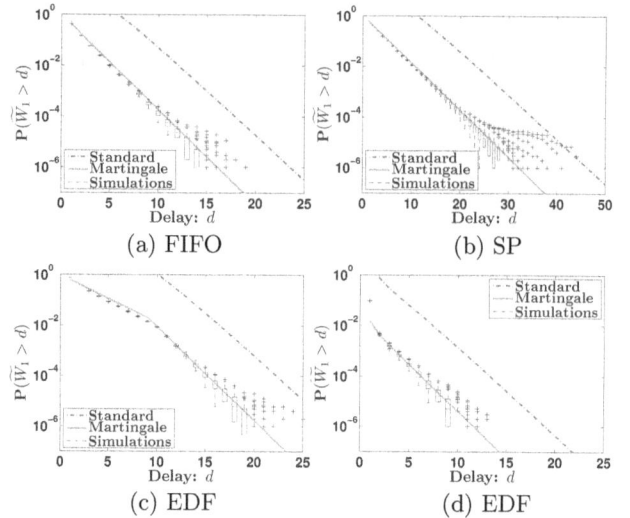

(a) FIFO	(b) SP
(c) EDF	(d) EDF

Figure 1: **Delay bounds** ($\lambda = 0.5$, $\mu = 0.1$, $P = 1$, $n_1 = n_2 = 10$, $\rho = 75\%$, $(d_1^* = 10$, $d_2^* = 1)$ **in (c) and** $d_1^* = 1$, $d_2^* = 10$ **in (d))**

figure convincingly shows that the Standard bounds are very loose whereas the new Martingale bounds are quite sharp[1].

3. REFERENCES

[1] A. Burchard, J. Liebeherr, and F. Ciucu. On superlinear scaling of network delays. *IEEE/ACM Transactions on Networking*, 19(4):1043–1056, Aug. 2011.

[2] C.-S. Chang. *Performance Guarantees in Communication Networks*. Springer Verlag, 2000.

[3] G. Choudhury, D. Lucantoni, and W. Whitt. Squeezing the most out of ATM. *IEEE Transactions on Communications*, 44(2):203–217, Feb. 1996.

[4] F. Ciucu and J. Schmitt. Perspectives on network calculus - No free lunch but still good value. In *ACM Sigcomm*, 2012.

[5] R. Cruz. A calculus for network delay, parts I and II. *IEEE Transactions on Information Theory*, 37(1):114–141, Jan. 1991.

[6] N. G. Duffield. Exponential bounds for queues with markovian arrivals. *Queueing Systems*, 17(3-4):413–430, Sept. 1994.

[7] Y. Jiang and Y. Liu. *Stochastic Network Calculus*. Springer, 2008.

[8] J. F. C. Kingman. Inequalities in the theory of queues. *Jour. Royal Slat. Soc. Series B*, 32(1):102–110, 1970.

[9] Z. Liu, P. Nain, and D. Towsley. Exponential bounds with applications to call admission. *Journal of the ACM*, 44(3):366–394, May 1997.

[10] Z. Palmowski and T. Rolski. A note on martingale inequalities for fluid models. *Statistics & Probability Letters*, 31(1):13–21, Dec. 1996.

[11] Z.-L. Zhang, D. Towsley, and J. Kurose. Statistical analysis of generalized processor sharing scheduling discipline. In *ACM Sigcomm*, pages 68–77, 1994.

---

[1]Outliers are depicted in the box-plots with the '+' symbol; on each box, the central mark is the median, and the edges of the box are the 25th and 75th percentiles.

Stable and Scalable Universal Swarms

Ji Zhu
University of Illinois
jizhu1@illinois.edu

Stratis Ioannidis and
Nidhi Hegde
Technicolor
stratis.ioannidis@technicolor.com,
nidhi.hegde@technicolor.com

Laurent Massoulié
MSR-Inria Joint Centre
laurent.massoulie@inria.fr

ABSTRACT

Hajek and Zhu recently showed that the BitTorrent protocol can become unstable when peers depart immediately after downloading all pieces of a file. In light of this result, Zhou *et al.* propose bundling swarms together, allowing peers to exchange pieces across different swarms, and claim that such "universal swarms" can increase BitTorrent's stability region. In this work, we formally characterize the stability region of universal swarms and show that they indeed exhibit excellent stability properties. In particular, bundling allows a single seed with limited upload capacity to serve an arbitrary number of disjoint swarms if the arrival rate of peers in each swarm is lower than the seed upload capacity. Our result also shows that the stability region is insensitive to peers' upload capacity, piece selection policies and number of swarms.

Categories and Subject Descriptors: C.2.1 [**Computer-Communication Networks**]: Network Architecture and Design - distributed networks

Keywords: Missing Piece Syndrome; P2P; Stability

1. INTRODUCTION

In BitTorrent [1], peers interested in downloading a single file from a distinguished user, termed the *seed*, form a so-called *swarm*. Peers in a swarm exchange file *pieces* with each other. Each peer thereby acts as both a client and a server, contributing to the aggregate upload capacity of the swarm. A question about a system like BitTorrent is what is its *stability region*: assuming the seed's upload capacity is U, what is the largest arrival rate of peers λ that can be supported without the swarm size growing to infinity? Intuitively, as every incoming peer increases the swarm's aggregate upload capacity, one would expect BitTorrent to support high arrival rates.

Determining the stability region of BitTorrent has been an open problem for more than ten years. It was resolved recently by Hajek and Zhu [2], who showed that the swarm remains stable if $\lambda < U$, and unstable if $\lambda > U$. This phenomenon is known as the *missing piece syndrome* [2, 6], and undermines BitTorrent's scalability: In light of this, a series of recent works have focused on extending the stability region of BitTorrent [9, 8, 7, 5, 3]. An approach proposed by Zhou *et al.* [8], is to bundle multiple autonomous swarms together into a *universal swarm*: peers again depart upon

retrieving the file they are interested in, but they store and exchange pieces with peers belonging to *different swarms*. Zhou *et al.* conjecture that a universal swarm exhibits an increased stability region compared to autonomous swarms.

In this paper, we make the following contributions: 1) we formally characterize the stability region of universal swarms, proving necessary and sufficient conditions under which such swarms remain stable; 2) we show that bundling swarms together significantly increases BitTorrent's stability region, making it scale in the number of bundled swarms. In fact, we show that the stability region under limited seed upload capacity *can be insensitive to the number of swarms*. In contrast to previous work (*e.g.*, [2, 9, 6, 8, 7, 4]), our stability result applies to a wider class of piece selection policies. As a consequence, our result has interesting implications for single swarms as well, characterizing their stability region for cases not considered before.

2. UNIVERSAL SWARM AND MAIN RESULT

We consider a BitTorrent-like multi-file-sharing system, consisting of multiple swarms. Suppose all files are divided into *pieces* of equal size. We denote by $\mathcal{F} = \{1, 2, \ldots, K\}$ the set of all pieces of all files. A distinguished peer, the seed, is always present and holds $\mathcal{F}$. Represent a *file* C to be a non-empty subset of $\mathcal{F}$: $\emptyset \neq C \subseteq \mathcal{F}$. We refer to the set of peers interested in downloading file C as *Swarm* C. Assume peers in Swarm C arrive according to a Poisson process with rate λ_C, independent across swarms. We do *not* require different swarms to be disjoint subsets of $\mathcal{F}$ so our model captures a scenario where arriving peers are interested in multiple files.

Each peer maintains a cache to store pieces it downloads. We assume peers arrive with empty caches, and each peer's cache is large enough to hold $\mathcal{F}$. Peers in Swarm C depart *immediately* upon retrieving all pieces in C. We partition peers into *types* according to (a) the swarm they belong to and (b) the set of pieces in their cache. Hence, a peer in Swarm C holding $S \subseteq \mathcal{F}$ is denoted to be of type $\langle C, S \rangle$. Assume the seed is of type $\langle \{\bot\}, \mathcal{F} \rangle$ for some piece $\bot \notin \mathcal{F}$. Denote $n_{\langle C, S \rangle}$ to be the number of type $\langle C, S \rangle$ peers and $\mathbf{n} = (n_{\langle C, S \rangle})$ to be the vector of numbers of peers in all types. The seed uploads pieces at instants of a Poisson process of rate U. At each of such instants, the seed contacts a peer selected uniformly at random among all peers across all swarms, and replicates a piece in $\mathcal{F}$ to this peer. Similarly, at instances that follow a Poisson process of rate $\mu > 0$, each peer contacts another peer (also selected uniformly among all peers) and replicates a piece from its cache.

The piece replicated when a source (either a peer or the

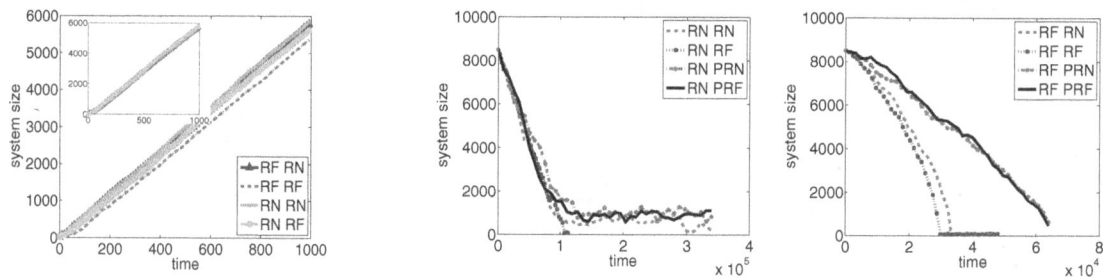

(a) Autonomous mode, static and dynamic (b) Universal mode, RN at seed. (c) Universal mode, RF at seed.
(inset) allocation.

Figure 1: System size VS time. ("RN RF" means RN at seed and RF at peers, other legends follow similarly.)

seed) contacts a receiver is determined by the source's piece selection policy. We consider a broad class of work-conserving piece selection policies satisfying: (a) no piece is replicated if the receiver owns all pieces in the source's cache, (b) exactly one piece in the source's cache absent from the receiver's cache is replicated with certain probability, and (c) the probability for a specific piece to be replicated when a source contacts a receiver is a function of the types of the source and the receiver, and the current state $\mathbf{n}$.

Suppose a type $\langle C, S \rangle$ source contacts a type $\langle C', S' \rangle$ receiver. Examples of work-conserving policies considered are:

Random Novel [RN]: If $S \setminus S' \neq \emptyset$, the source replicates a piece chosen uniformly from $S \setminus S'$.

Rarest First [RF]: Define the *availability* of a piece $i \in \mathcal{F}$ to be the number of peers holding it. The source replicates the piece in $S \setminus S'$ that has the least availability, with ties broken randomly.

Priority Rarest First [PRF]: The source prioritizes pieces within the swarm of the receiver: if $(S \setminus S') \cap C' \neq \emptyset$, it replicates the piece in $(S \setminus S') \cap C'$ that has the least availability; if $(S \setminus S') \cap C'$ is empty but $S \setminus S'$ is not, the source reverts to RF. **Priority Random Novel [PRN]** is defined similarly.

The system is a Markov process with state being $\mathbf{n}$. We say the system is *unstable* if it is transient and the number of peers converges to infinity with probability one; and we say it is *stable* if it is positive recurrent and it has a finite mean number of peers. The following is our main result:

THEOREM 1. *If the seed implements Random Novel and peers implement any of the work-conserving piece selection policies described above, the system is*

1) unstable if $\max_{i:i \in \mathcal{F}} \sum_{C:i \in C} \lambda_C > U$,

2) stable if $\max_{i:i \in \mathcal{F}} \sum_{C:i \in C} \lambda_C < U$.

The theorem states that the stability region is determined by the maximum swarm arrival rate instead of total arrival rate if swarms are disjoint, insensitive to peers' uploading rate μ, peers' piece selection policies, and number of swarms.

3. SIMULATION

In Figure 1, we simulate the system under different piece selection policies where $U = 3.1$ and there are 3 disjoint swarms each with arrival rate $\lambda = 3.0$. In Figures 1(b) and 1(c), the system works in the universal mode described

above. The simulation starts from a case where there are 8500 peers in the same swarm, each holding all pieces in $\mathcal{F}$ except one piece in the swarm. It shows that the system finally stabilizes, and it stabilizes faster when the seed applies RF instead of RN. Moreover, PRN or PRF leads to *slower* stabilization.

In Figure 1(a), the system works in autonomous mode: peers uniformly samples targets from their own swarm instead of across all swarms, and the seed statically allocates 1/3 of its upload rate to each swarm; in the inset of Figure 1(a), the seed allocating its rate dynamically, so that each swarm receives pieces from the seed at a rate proportional to its size. The simulation shows that the system size increases linearly, regardless of the piece selection policies.

4. ACKNOWLEDGMENTS

This work was supported by the National Science Foundation under Grant NSF CCF 10-16959, and was partially funded by the European Commission under the FIRE SCAMPI (FP7- IST-258414) project.

5. REFERENCES

[1] B. Cohen. Incentives build robustness in BitTorrent. In *Workshop on Economics of Peer-to-Peer Systems*, 2003.

[2] B. Hajek and J. Zhu. The missing piece syndrome in peer-to-peer communication. *Stochastic Systems*, 1(2):246–273, 2011.

[3] J. Han, T. Chung, S. Kim, T. T. Kwon, H.-c. Kim, and Y. Choi. How prevalent is content bundling in bittorrent. In *ACM SIGMETRICS*, 2011.

[4] L. Massoulié and M. Vojnović. Coupon replication systems. In *ACM SIGMETRICS*, 2005.

[5] D. S. Menasche, A. A. Rocha, B. Li, D. Towsley, and A. Venkataramani. Content availability and bundling in swarming systems. In *ACM CoNEXT*, 2009.

[6] I. Norros and H. Reitu. On the stability of two-chunk file sharing systems. *Queueing Systems*, 3, 2011.

[7] B. Oğuz, V. Anantharam, and I. Norros. Stable, distributed p2p protocols based on random peer sampling. In *IEEE Allerton*, pages 915–919, 2012.

[8] X. Zhou, S. Ioannidis, and L. Massoulié. On the stability and optimality of universal swarms. In *ACM SIGMETRICS*, 2011.

[9] J. Zhu and B. Hajek. Stability of a peer-to-peer communication system. *IEEE Transactions on Information Theory*, 2012.

Sustainability of Service Provisioning Systems under Attack

Georgios S. Paschos
MIT, USA
CERTH-ITI, Greece
gpasxos@mit.edu

Leandros Tassiulas
University of Thessaly, Greece
leandros@uth.gr

ABSTRACT

We propose a resource allocation model that captures the interaction between legitimate users of a distributed service provisioning system with malicious intruders attempting to disrupt its operation. The system consists of a bank of servers providing service to incoming requests. Malicious intruders generate fake traffic to the servers attempting to degrade service provisioning. Legitimate traffic may be balanced using available mechanisms in order to mitigate the damage from the attack. We characterize the guaranteed region, i.e. the set of legitimate traffic intensities that are sustainable given specific intensities of the fake traffic, under the assumption that the fake traffic is routed using static policies. This assumption will be relaxed, allowing arbitrary routing policies, in the full version of this work.

Categories and Subject Descriptors

H.1 [**Information Systems Applications**]: Models and Principles; Miscellaneous;

General Terms

Algorithms, Reliability, Theory

Keywords

Service provisioning system; guaranteed sustainability; stability

1. SYSTEM MODEL AND DEFINITIONS

Consider a set $\mathcal{N} \triangleq \{1, \ldots, N\}$ of parallel servers with constant service rates $\mu_n, n \in \mathcal{N}$. The servers are fed by a set of legitimate streams $\mathcal{L} \triangleq \{1, \ldots, |\mathcal{L}|\}$ of *traffic*, each stream $l \in \mathcal{L}$ associated with traffic intensity a_l and a set of reachable servers $\mathcal{S}_l \subseteq \mathcal{N}$. The traffic arriving from a stream l is *routed* to some of the servers in $\mathcal{S}_l$.

A malicious system launches a Degradation of Service attack (a type of Denial of Service attack) in order to disrupt the operation of the system. In particular, the malicious system has a set $\mathcal{M} \triangleq \{1, \ldots, |\mathcal{M}|\}$ of malicious traffic streams, where the stream $m \in \mathcal{M}$ generates fake traffic with intensity b_m and is capable of routing it towards a subset of servers $\mathcal{Q}_m \subseteq \mathcal{N}$. See Figure 1 for an example of the studied system in terms of a bipartite graph.

We assume the operation of two controllers with conflicting interests. Controller 1 splits legitimate traffic to al-

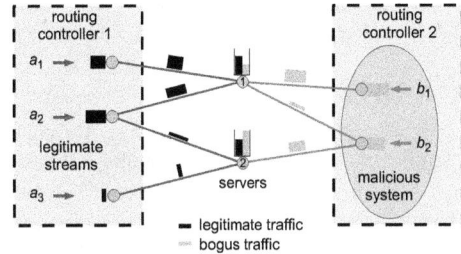

Figure 1: An example of the system for 2 servers, 3 legitimate streams and 2 malicious streams. Also, $\mathcal{S}_1 = \mathcal{Q}_1 = \{1\}$, $\mathcal{S}_2 = \mathcal{Q}_2 = \{1, 2\}$ and $\mathcal{S}_3 = \{2\}$.

lowable servers according to *routing coefficients* f_{ln}, $(l, n) \in \mathcal{L} \times \mathcal{N}$. We collect all policies that satisfy $\sum_{n \in \mathcal{N}} f_{ln} = a_l$ and $f_{ln} = 0$, if $n \notin \mathcal{S}_l$ in the *feasible* set Π_1. Controller 2 operates in a similar manner, choosing coefficients ϕ_{mn}, $(m, n) \in \mathcal{M} \times \mathcal{N}$ to satisfy $\sum_{n \in \mathcal{N}} \phi_{mn} = b_m$ and $\phi_{mn} = 0$, if $n \notin \mathcal{Q}_m$ for all m. Π_2 is the set of malicious policies.

The typical stability condition for a server reads: a server n is stable iff the aggregate arrival intensity is smaller or equal to its service rate; this is referred to as *rate stability*. From the practical viewpoint, though, the DEGoS attack is considered successful only if service to legitimate traffic fails. If some servers are unstable in the traditional sense but they are avoided by the legitimate traffic then the attack has failed to harm the system. Thus, we slightly change the definition of stability as follows:

DEFINITION 1. (*System Stability*) *A server* $n \in \mathcal{N}$ *is stable if*

$$\sum_{l \in \mathcal{L}} f_{ln} + \sum_{m \in \mathcal{M}} \phi_{mn} \leq \mu_n$$

or if $\sum_{l \in \mathcal{L}} f_{ln} = 0$. *The system is stable if all servers are stable.*

Let $\mathbf{a} \triangleq (a_1, \ldots, a_{|\mathcal{L}|})$ denote the vector of legitimate traffic intensities. We extend the standard notion of system stability region to include the impact of a malicious intruder with fake traffic intensities $\mathbf{b} \triangleq (b_1, \ldots, b_{|\mathcal{M}|})$ and policy ϕ.

DEFINITION 2. (*Sustainable region* $\Lambda_{\mathbf{b}}^{\phi}$) *The sustainable region* $\Lambda_{\mathbf{b}}^{\phi}$, *when the malicious adversary operates with a malicious policy* $\phi \in \Pi_2$ *and available fake traffic intensities* $\mathbf{b}$, *is the set of all* $\mathbf{a}$ *for which there exists a legitimate policy* $\mathbf{f} \in \Pi_1$ *such that the system is stable.*

Moreover, we define the notion of guaranteed sustainable (or simply "guaranteed") region as the set of legitimate traffic intensities $\mathbf{a}$ which are guaranteed to be sustainable regardless of the malicious policy used.

DEFINITION 3. (Guaranteed region $\Lambda_{\mathbf{b}}$) *The guaranteed region $\Lambda_{\mathbf{b}}$ of the system attacked by a malicious adversary with available traffic intensities $\mathbf{b}$, is the set of all $\mathbf{a}$ for which there exists a legitimate policy $\mathbf{f} \in \Pi_1$ such that the system remains stable **under any selection** $\phi \in \Pi_2$.*

The guaranteed region is parametrized by the fake traffic intensity, $\mathbf{b}$. For $\mathbf{b}$ large enough, $\Lambda_{\mathbf{b}}$ might contain only the zero element vector $\mathbf{0} \triangleq (0, 0, \ldots, 0)$, which implies that there is a malicious policy ϕ such that even arbitrarily small legitimate traffic intensities are not sustainable, regardless of the legitimate policy $\mathbf{f}$ used. In practical terms, we can think of such a situation as a DoS attack. *The DEGoS attack, on the other hand, corresponds to cases where the guaranteed region is not degenerated and legitimate traffic can still be sustained despite the attack, albeit in smaller intensities.*

2. MAIN RESULT

First, we fix a malicious policy ϕ and study the sustainable region of traffic intensities under this policy. Let $r_n(\phi) \triangleq \left(\mu_n - \sum_{m \in \mathcal{M}} \phi_{mn}\right)^+$ be the *available resource* of server n after the traffic arriving from malicious streams under ϕ is subtracted. We use $(.)^+ \triangleq \max\{., 0\}$. Using the stability definition, we conclude that the system is stable iff there exists a legitimate policy $\mathbf{f}$ such that

$$\sum_{l \in \mathcal{L}} f_{ln} \leq r_n(\phi), \text{ for all } n \in \mathcal{N}. \qquad (1)$$

In what follows, we will express the sustainable region $\Lambda_{\mathbf{b}}^{\phi}$ in terms of traffic intensities $\mathbf{a}, \mathbf{b}$ and service rates $\boldsymbol{\mu}$. For an arbitrary non-empty subset of the servers $\hat{\mathcal{N}} \subseteq \mathcal{N}$ consider the induced subsets $\hat{\mathcal{L}}, \hat{\mathcal{M}}$, where

- $\hat{\mathcal{L}} = \left\{ l \in \mathcal{L} : \mathcal{S}_l \subseteq \hat{\mathcal{N}} \right\}$ is the set of legitimate traffic streams that **must** direct all traffic to some of the servers in $\hat{\mathcal{N}}$ and

- $\hat{\mathcal{M}} = \left\{ m \in \mathcal{M} : \mathcal{Q}_m \cap \hat{\mathcal{N}} \neq \emptyset \right\}$ is the set of fake traffic streams that **can** direct fake traffic to some of the servers in $\hat{\mathcal{N}}$.

LEMMA 1 (CUT CONSTRAINTS). *The traffic intensities $\mathbf{a}$ are sustainable under ϕ if and only if*

$$\sum_{l \in \hat{\mathcal{L}}} a_l \leq \sum_{n \in \hat{\mathcal{N}}} r_n(\phi), \qquad \text{for all } \hat{\mathcal{N}} \subseteq \mathcal{N}.$$

2.1 Guaranteed region $\Lambda_{\mathbf{b}}$

Consider an auxiliary network $\mathcal{G}(\hat{\mathcal{N}}) = (\mathcal{V}, \mathcal{E})$. We define the set of nodes as $\mathcal{V} \triangleq \{s, t, u_i, v_j : i \in \hat{\mathcal{M}}, j \in \hat{\mathcal{N}}\}$, where s is the source node, t is the sink, nodes $u_i, i \in \hat{\mathcal{M}}$ correspond to members of $\hat{\mathcal{M}}$ and nodes $v_j, j \in \hat{\mathcal{N}}$ correspond to members of $\hat{\mathcal{N}}$. The set of links consists of three subsets $\mathcal{E} = \mathcal{E}_\mu \cup \mathcal{E}_Q \cup \mathcal{E}_b$, where each subset consists of directional links defined as follows

$$\mathcal{E}_b \triangleq \{(s, u_i) : i \in \hat{\mathcal{M}}\}, \mathcal{E}_\mu \triangleq \{(v_j, t) : j \in \hat{\mathcal{N}}\}$$
$$\mathcal{E}_Q \triangleq \{(u_i, v_j) : i \in \hat{\mathcal{M}}, j \in \mathcal{Q}_i\}.$$

A link (s, u_i) has capacity b_i, a link (v_i, t) has capacity μ_i, while all links in subset $\mathcal{E}_Q$ have infinite capacity. Let $M_{\max}(\hat{\mathcal{N}})$ denote the maximum s-t flow of network $\mathcal{G}(\hat{\mathcal{N}})$.

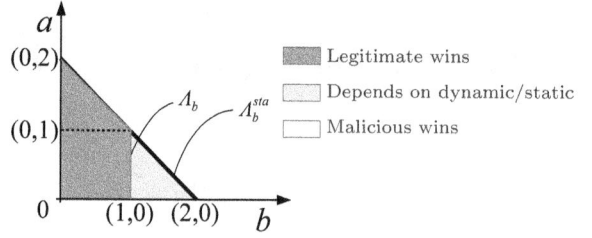

Figure 2: Regions of the studied example for the case of static policies (Λ_b^{sta}) and for the dynamic (Λ_b). The sensitivity of the guaranteed sustainability to dynamic malicious policies is visible.

DEFINITION 4 (CONDITIONS C.1). *The following inequality is satisfied*

$$\sum_{l \in \hat{\mathcal{L}}} a_l \leq \sum_{n \in \hat{\mathcal{N}}} \mu_n - M_{max}(\hat{\mathcal{N}}), \qquad \text{for all } \hat{\mathcal{N}} \subseteq \mathcal{N}. \qquad (2)$$

THEOREM 1. (Guaranteed region) *Conditions C.1 are necessary and sufficient to guarantee sustainability for the traffic intensity $\mathbf{a}$ under any ϕ.*

3. DISCUSSION OF THE DYNAMIC CASE

In the followup work we extend the study to the case of dynamic routing polices. In case controller 2 is static, *Join the Shortest Queue* turns out to be the optimal policy for the legitimate controller and it can be shown that the guaranteed region described here is achieved by this policy. If, however, the controller 2 is allowed to allocate bogus jobs in a dynamic fashion, the guaranteed region changes drastically. Below we demonstrate this in an example.

3.1 An example with two servers

Consider two servers with unit service rate fed by one legitimate stream with traffic a and one malicious with traffic b. Traffic can be routed to both servers. Using the results of the previous section, we conclude that $a + b \leq 2$ is a necessary and sufficient condition for guaranteed sustainability as long as the malicious intruder is constrained to static routing policies. We call this region Λ_b^{sta}, see Figure 2.

DEFINITION 5 (SWITCHING MALICIOUS POLICIES). *A switching malicious policy directs all fake traffic to one server during a time interval of length τ_i, alternating the server in each interval. During the ith interval, $i = 1, 2, \ldots$, the fake traffic is directed to server $1 + (i + 1 \mod 2)$. The duration of the ith interval is given by the sequence τ_i, $i = 1, 2, \ldots$.*

THEOREM 2 (REGION UNDER DYNAMIC POLICIES). *The guaranteed region for the example of two unit servers is*

$$\begin{aligned} a + b &\leq 2 &&\text{if } b \leq 1 \\ a &= 0 &&\text{if } b > 1. \end{aligned}$$

Examples of switching malicious policies that intuitively lead to the above result are: $\tau_i = i$ and $\tau_i = 2^i$.

4. ACKNOWLEDGMENTS

The work of G. Paschos is supported by the WiNC project of the Action:Supporting Postdoctoral Researchers, funded by national and Community funds (European Social Fund).

Temperature Aware Workload Management in Geo-distributed Datacenters

Hong Xu, Chen Feng, Baochun Li
Department of Electrical and Computer Engineering
University of Toronto
{henryxu, cfeng, bli}@eecg.toronto.edu

ABSTRACT

Datacenters consume an enormous amount of energy with significant financial and environmental costs. For geo-distributed datacenters, a workload management approach that routes user requests to locations with cheaper and cleaner electricity has been shown to be promising lately. We consider two key aspects that have not been explored in this approach. First, through empirical studies, we find that the energy efficiency of the cooling system depends directly on the ambient temperature, which exhibits a significant degree of geographical diversity. Temperature diversity can be used by workload management to reduce the overall cooling energy overhead. Second, energy consumption comes from not only interactive workloads driven by user requests, but also delay tolerant batch workloads that run at the back-end. The elastic nature of batch workloads can be exploited to further reduce the energy cost.

In this work, we propose to make workload management for geo-distributed datacenters *temperature aware*. We formulate the problem as a joint optimization of request routing for interactive workloads and capacity allocation for batch workloads. We develop a distributed algorithm based on an m-block *alternating direction method of multipliers* (ADMM) algorithm that extends the classical 2-block algorithm. We prove the convergence and rate of convergence results under general assumptions. Trace-driven simulations demonstrate that our approach is able to provide 5%–20% overall cost savings for geo-distributed datacenters.

Categories and Subject Descriptors

C.2.4 [**Computer-Communication Networks**]: Distributed Systems

Keywords

Geo-distributed datacenters; Energy; Request routing; Cooling efficiency; ADMM; Distributed optimization

1. INTRODUCTION

Geo-distributed datacenters operated by organizations such as Google and Amazon are the powerhouses behind many Internet-scale services. They are deployed across the globe to provide better latency and redundancy. These datacenters run hundreds of thousands of servers, consume megawatts of power with massive carbon footprint, and incur electricity bills of millions of dollars [2,6]. Recently, important progress has been made on a new *workload management* approach that focuses on the energy aspect of geo-distributed datacenters. It exploits the geographical diversity of electricity prices by optimizing the *request routing* algorithm to route user requests to locations with cheaper and cleaner electricity [2,5–7].

In this work, we consider two key aspects of geo-distributed datacenters that have not been explored in the existing literature.

First, cooling systems, which consume 30% to 50% of the total energy, are often modeled with a constant and location-independent energy efficiency factor in existing efforts. This tends to be an oversimplification in reality. Through our study of a state-of-the-art production cooling system, we find that temperature has direct and profound impact on cooling energy efficiency. This is especially true with *outside air cooling* technology, which has seen increasing adoption in mission-critical datacenters [8]. As shown in Table 1, the partial PUE (power usage effectiveness), defined as the sum of server power and cooling overhead divided by server power, varies significantly from 1.30 to 1.05 when temperature drops from 35 °C(90 °F) to -3.9 °C(25 °F). The reason is that when the ambient temperature is low, we can directly use the cold outside air to cool down servers without running the energy-gobbling mechanical chillers, which greatly improves the energy efficiency.

Outdoor ambient	Cooling mode	pPUE
35°C(90°F)	Mechanical	1.30
21.1°C(70°F)	Mechanical	1.21
15.6°C(60°F)	Mixed	1.17
10°C(50°F)	Outside air	1.1
-3.9°C(25°F)	Outside air	1.05

Table 1: Efficiency of Emerson's DSE^{TM} cooling system with an EconoPhase air-side economizer [8]. Return air is set at 29.4°C(85°F).

Through an extensive empirical analysis of daily and hourly climate data for 13 Google datacenters [8], we further find that temperature varies significantly across both time and location, which is intuitive to understand. The short-term volatilities are not well correlated across locations. These observations suggest that datacenters at different locations have distinct and time-varying cooling energy efficiency. This establishes a strong case for making workload management *temperature aware*, where such temperature diversity can be used along with price diversity in making request routing decisions to reduce the overall cooling energy overhead.

Second, energy consumption comes not only from interactive workloads driven by user requests, but also from delay tolerant batch workloads, such as indexing and data mining jobs, that run at the back-end. Existing efforts focus mainly on request routing for interactive workloads, which is only a part of the entire picture. Such a mixed nature of datacenter workloads provides more opportunities to utilize the cost diversity of energy. The key observation is that batch workloads are elastic to resource allocations, whereas interactive workloads are highly sensitive to latency and have more profound impact on revenue. Thus at times when one location is comparatively cost efficient, we can increase the capacity for interactive workloads by reducing the resources reserved for batch jobs. More requests can then be routed to and processed at this location, and the cost saving can be more substantial. We are thus motivated to advocate a holistic workload management approach, where *capacity allocation* between interactive and batch workloads is dynamically optimized with request routing.

2. CONTRIBUTIONS

Towards temperature aware workload management, we propose a general framework to capture the important trade-offs involved [8]. We model both energy cost and utility loss, which corresponds to performance-related revenue reduction. We develop an empirical cooling efficiency model based on the production system in Table 1 with both outside air and mechanical cooling capabilities. The problem is formulated as a joint optimization of request routing and capacity allocation. The technical challenge is then to develop a distributed algorithm to solve the large-scale optimization with tens of millions of variables for a production geo-distributed cloud. Dual decomposition with subgradient methods is often used to develop distributed optimization algorithms. However it requires delicate adjustment of step sizes that makes convergence difficult to achieve for large-scale problems. The method of multipliers achieves fast convergence, at the cost of introducing tight coupling among variables.

We rely on the *alternating direction method of multipliers* (ADMM), a simple yet powerful algorithm that blends the advantages of the two approaches. ADMM recently has found practical use in many large-scale distributed convex optimization problems [1]. It works for problems whose objective and variables can be divided into *two* disjoint parts. It alternatively optimizes part of the objective with one block of variables to iteratively reach the optimum. Our formulation has three blocks of variables, yet little is known about the convergence of m-block ($m \geq 3$) ADMM algorithms, with two exceptions [3,4] very recently. [3] establishes the convergence of m-block ADMM for strongly convex objective functions, but not linear convergence; [4] shows the linear convergence of m-block ADMM under the assumption that the relation matrix is full column rank, which is, however, not the case in our formation. This motivates us to refine the framework in [4] so that it can be applied to our setup. In particular, we show that by replacing the full-rank assumption with some mild assumptions on the objective functions, we are not only able to obtain the same convergence and rate of convergence results, but also to simplify the proof of [4] in [8]. The m-block ADMM algorithm is general and can be applied in other problem domains. For our case, we further develop a distributed algorithm, which is amenable to a parallel implementation in datacenters.

3. EVALUATION

We conduct extensive trace-driven simulations with Wikipedia request traffic traces, real-world electricity prices and historical temperature data at Google datacenter locations to realistically assess the potential of our approach [8]. We benchmark our ADMM algorithm against the state-of-the-art approach, which is a temperature agnostic strategy that separately considers capacity allocation and request routing of the workload management problem. It first allocates capacity to batch jobs by minimizing the back-end total cost

as the objective. The remaining capacity is used to solve the request routing optimization. Only the electricity price diversity is used, and cooling energy is calculated with a constant pPUE of 1.2 for the two cost minimization problems. Though naive, such an approach is widely used in current Internet-scale cloud services. It also allows for an implicit comparison with prior work [2,5–7]. We run the algorithms with our 24-hour traces at each day of January, May, and August 2011 [8]. The results are averaged over 31 runs.

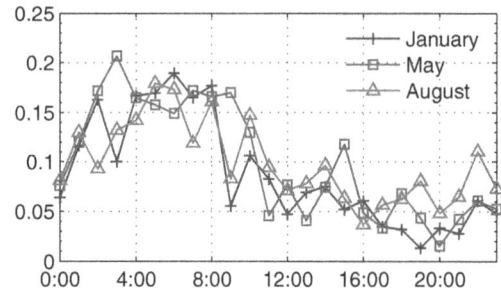

Figure 1: Overall cost savings of our approach compared to state-of-the-art workload management.

Figure 1 shows the average overall cost savings, including energy cost savings and utility loss reductions. We observe that the cost savings range from 5% to 20%. This shows that our approach is able to provide substantial cost savings for geo-distributed datacenters, using temperature-aware request routing and dynamic capacity allocation. The savings are also consistent and insensitive to seasonal changes. The reason is that our approach depends on: 1) the geographical diversity of temperature and cooling efficiency; 2) the mixed nature of datacenter workloads, both of which exist at all times of the year no matter which cooling method is used. Temperature aware workload management is thus expected to offer consistent and promising cost benefits.

4. REFERENCES

[1] S. Boyd, N. Parikh, E. Chu, B. Peleato, and J. Eckstein. Distributed optimization and statistical learning via the alternating direction method of multipliers. *Foundations and Trends in Machine Learning*, 3(1):1–122, 2010.

[2] P. X. Gao, A. R. Curtis, B. Wong, and S. Keshav. It's not easy being green. In *Proc. ACM SIGCOMM*, 2012.

[3] D. Han and X. Yuan. A note on the alternating direction method of multipliers. *J. Optim. Theory Appl.*, 155:227–238, 2012.

[4] M. Hong and Z.-Q. Luo. On the linear convergence of the alternating direction method of multipliers. http://arxiv.org/abs/1208.3922, August 2012.

[5] Z. Liu, M. Lin, A. Wierman, S. H. Low, and L. L. Andrew. Greening geographical load balancing. In *Proc. ACM Sigmetrics*, 2011.

[6] A. Qureshi, R. Weber, H. Balakrishnan, J. Guttag, and B. Maggs. Cutting the electricity bill for Internet-scale systems. In *Proc. ACM SIGCOMM*, 2009.

[7] L. Rao, X. Liu, L. Xie, and W. Liu. Minimizing electricity cost: Optimization of distributed Internet data centers in a multi-electricity-market environment. In *Proc. IEEE INFOCOM*, 2010.

[8] H. Xu, C. Feng, and B. Li. Temperature aware workload management in geo-distributed datacenters. Technical report, University of Toronto, http://iqua.ece.toronto.edu/~henryxu/share/geodc-preprint.pdf, 2013.

Tolerating Path Heterogeneity in Multipath TCP with Bounded Receive Buffers

Ming Li
Aalto University, Finland
ming.li@aalto.fi

Andrey Lukyanenko
Aalto University, Finland
andrey.lukyanenko@aalto.fi

Sasu Tarkoma
University of Helsinki, Finland
sasu.tarkoma@helsinki.fi

Yong Cui
Tsinghua Unversity, China
cuiyong@tsinghua.edu.cn

Antti Ylä-Jääski
Aalto University, Finland
antti.yla-jaaski@aalto.fi

Categories and Subject Descriptors

C.2.2 [**Computer-Comms Nets**]: Network Protocols

Keywords

TCP, MPTCP, systematic coding, flow control, NS-3

1. INTRODUCTION

Although delivering data over multiple paths has been discussed since the beginning of the Internet, the reordering issue associated with multipath transmission is still a challenge today. In the context of path heterogeneity, most existing multipath solutions assume that the receive buffer is infinite. Few of them really consider the fact that a large receive buffer may prevent multipath transmission from being used on busy servers and memory-scarce devices. In Multipath TCP (MPTCP) [1], for example, a large receive buffer (e.g., a few MB) could accommodate all the out-of-order data, whereas, if the receive buffer is bounded, the out-of-order data may overflow the buffer so that the flow control mechanism will be triggered, i.e., the next ACK will contain zero in the advertised window to stop transmission for a non-transient time period, significantly degrading the aggregate throughput.

In order to tolerate the path heterogeneity using bounded receive buffers, we propose a new multipath TCP protocol, namely SC-MPTCP, by integrating systematic coding [2] into MPTCP. SC-MPTCP makes use of redundant coded packets to counter against expensive retransmissions. The redundancy is provisioned into both proactive and reactive data. Specifically, SC-MPTCP estimates the aggregate retransmission ratio continuously to provide adaptive proactive redundancy and utilizes a pre-blocking warning mechanism to retrieve reactive redundancy from the sender particularly when the proactive redundancy is underestimated in dynamic networks.

2. SYSTEMATIC CODING

In coding theory, a systematic coding is any error-correcting code in which the input data is embedded in the encoded output. In contrast, in a non-systematic coding the output does not contain the input symbols. All existing cod-

SIGMETRICS'13, June 17–21, 2013, Pittsburgh, PA, USA.
ACM 978-1-4503-1900-3/13/06.

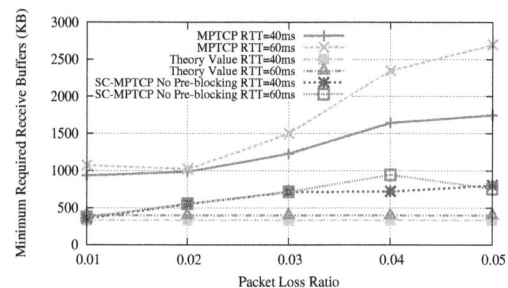

Figure 1: **Minimum required buffers to achieve maximum aggregate throughput**

ing solutions for multipath transmission, to the best of our knowledge, use non-systematic coding.

In SC-MPTCP, we divide the data stream into generations. In each generation, every original packet is encoded to itself and only the redundancy (proactive and reactive redundancy) is the linear combination of the original packets. The coded packets are generated by combining the packets from the same generation using random coefficients. In order to mitigate the buffer burden, we choose to send the redundancy at the beginning and transmit the uncoded packets later so that the in-order arriving original packets could be released immediately and only the redundancy is buffered. The generator matrix M for a generation is

$$M = \left[A_k | I_\theta \right], \qquad (1)$$

where θ denotes the generation size, I_θ is an identity matrix, k (the number of proactive redundant packets) is dynamically determined by the current path characteristics and A_k is the coefficient matrix.

In addition to reduce the buffer requirement, the use of systematic coding also improves the coding complexity. In non-systematic coding, the arithmetic complexity of generating $\theta + k$ coded packets is $O\left((\theta + k)^2\right)$ and the arithmetic complexity using Gaussian elimination to decode a generation of size θ is $O(\theta^3)$, whereas, in systematic coding, the computation complexity of generating k coded packets and decoding k coded packets are reduced to $O(\theta k)$ and $O(\theta k^2)$ respectively. In practice, k is usually one- or even two-order of magnitude smaller than θ. Thus, the computational overhead is significantly reduced.

Table 1: Subflow Parameters

Subflow	RTT	Bandwidth	Loss ratio
1	20ms	100Mbps	0.1%
2	40-60ms	100Mbps	1-5%

Table 2: Subflow Parameters

Subflow	RTT	Bandwidth	Loss ratio
1	20ms	100Mbps	0.1%
2	20ms	100Mbps	1-5%

3. EVALUATION

In our study, we have been interested in assessing the performance of SC-MPTCP in terms of minimum required receive buffer and aggregate goodput. The simulation platform we used is Network Simulator NS-3.11.

We first study the minimum required buffer to achieve the maximum aggregate throughput. The parameters are set according to Table 1. We use eq.(2) [1] to calculate the theory value as benchmark.

$$Buf = 2 \cdot \sum_{i=1}^{N} BW_i \cdot RTT_{max}, \qquad (2)$$

Fig. 1 shows the simulation results. We observe that the larger the path heterogeneity is, the more receive buffer is required. Under the same network conditions, SC-MPTCP without the pre-blocking warning mechanism requires much less receive buffer than MPTCP, but more than the benchmark. In the figure, we do not draw the curves of SC-MPTCP with the pre-blocking warning mechanism enabled, because, when we set the receive buffer according to eq.(2), SC-MPTCP always approaches the same aggregate throughput as MPTCP with a large receive buffer.

In ths simulation results presented next, we study the capability of SC-MPTCP to aggregate goodput from heterogeneous subflows. The parameters are set according to Table. 2. Fig. 2 presents the aggregate goodput with different packet loss ratios. We observe that, under the same network conditions, the goodput of MPTCP with a bounded receive buffer is even worse than that of a single-path TCP. SC-MPTCP with a bounded receive buffer could approach the same goodput as MPTCP with a large receive buffer, even if the path heterogeneity is large.

We now study the impact of the number of subflows on the aggregate goodput. In this simulation, we start from using two subflows. Each time we add one more subflow having a medium path quality. The parameters are set according to Table 3. Fig. 3 presents the simulation results. In this simulation we use the goodput achieved by MPTCP with large receive buffers (e.g., 8MB) as benchmark. The Y axis indicates the goodput percentage of it. As shown in the figure, MPTCP always achieves less than 20% of the maximum goodput. Its performance further degrades when the path

Table 3: Subflow Parameters

Subflow	RTT	Bandwidth	Loss ratio
1	20ms	100Mbps	0.1%
2	20ms	100Mbps	1-5%
3-4	20ms	100Mbps	0.5%

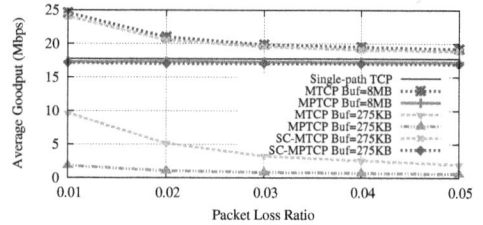

Figure 2: Average goodput with various path heterogeneity

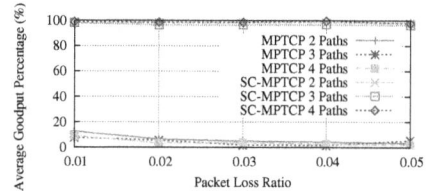

Figure 3: Average goodput percentage with multiple paths

heterogeneity grows. Furthermore, the curves of MPTCP using a different number of subflows almost overlap with each other. It implies that more subflows could help boost the aggregate goodput, but, if the receive buffer is bounded, the boost is limited, whereas SC-MPTCP always approaches the maximum goodput in all circumstances.

4. CONCLUSION

With bounded receive buffers, the aggregate throughput of multipath transmission degrades significantly in the presence of path heterogeneity. We propose to integrate linear Systematic Coding into MPTCP.

The simulation results show that in a heterogeneous network context, MPTCP requires large receive buffers to reach the maximum aggregate throughput. And the receive buffer requirement further increases when the path heterogeneity grows, whereas SC-MPTCP requires much smaller receive buffers to approach the maximum aggregate throughput. The results also demonstrate the effectiveness of a few key components of SC-MPTCP. For example, when the proactive redundancy is underestimated, a pre-blocking warning mechanism could retrieve the missing packets without incurring subflow flow control. In addition, we also demonstrate that the use of systematic coding could significantly reduce the computational overhead.

5. REFERENCES

[1] A. Ford, C. Raiciu, M. Handley, S. Barré, and J. Iyengar. Architectural guidelines for multipath TCP development. *RFC 6182, Mar. 2011.*

[2] S. Shamai, S. Verdú, and R. Zamir. *Information Theoretic Aspects of Systematic Coding.* CC pub. Technion, Israel Institute of Technology, 1997.

Understanding Architectural Characteristics of Multimedia Retrieval Workloads

Chen Dai
Parallel Process Institute
Fudan University
Shanghai, China
daichen@fudan.edu.cn

Chao Lv
Parallel Process Institute
Fudan University
Shanghai, China
lch@fudan.edu.cn

Jiaxin Li
Parallel Process Institute
Fudan University
Shanghai, China
lijiaxin@fudan.edu.cn

Weihua Zhang
Parallel Process Institute
Fudan University
Shanghai, China
zhangweihua@fudan.edu.cn

Binyu Zang
Parallel Process Institue
Fudan University
Shanghai, China
byzang@fudan.edu.cn

Categories and Subject Descriptors

H.3.4 [**Information Storage and Retrieval**]: Systems and Software—*performance evaluation*

Keywords

Multimedia retrieval, Computer architecture, Workload characterization

1. INTRODUCTION

Our society has entered into the *Big Data* era and multimedia data, such as images and videos, have become major data types. To extract useful information from them, multimedia retrieval applications are emerging, including video recommendation, travel guidance systems and content-based TV copyright identification. To guarantee retrieval accuracy, typical applications usually extract and utilize hundreds of features to represent an image or a video frame. Thus, in contrast to traditional text-based retrieval applications, multimedia retrieval applications are not only more data-intensive but also more computation-intensive, which lead to significant pressure on real-time processing. For example, SIFT [6] and SURF [1] are two most widely-used image or video retrieval algorithms. They can only achieve the process speed of a handful images or video frames per second on general-purpose processors. Furthermore, there are currently no systematic benchmark suites to understand the architectural characteristics of multimedia retrieval workloads, which are critical to design and implement optimizing architectures and systems for such workloads.

As a first attempt, we design and implement a multimedia retrieval benchmark suite (MMRBench) including state-of-art algorithms, different implementation versions, automation tools and a flexible system framework. Such a design enables the algorithms to be used individually or combined together to form an integrated system for evaluation. Furthermore, we study, both statistically and individually, the architectural characteristics of these algorithms, including the characteristics of core level, chip level and out of chip level. By comparing these algorithms with those in traditional multimedia benchmarks and traditional parallel benchmarks (i.e., ALPBench [5] and PARSEC [2]), we derived some key insights into the architectural characteristics and system evaluation of these multimedia retrieval algorithms.

2. BENCHMARK OVERVIEW

Multimedia retrieval applications generally consist of three stages: feature extraction, feature matching and spatial verification.

- **Feature Extraction:** Feature points are first extracted to represent an image or a video frame. Feature extraction algorithms can be divided into two classes: Global Feature Based Algorithms (GFBAs) and Local Feature Based Algorithms (LFBAs). We focus on LFBAs in this work because of its high precision.
- **Feature Matching:** The way to judge whether two images are similar is to check whether they have enough similar feature points. Due to the huge amount of image processing data, most multimedia retrieval applications apply approximate algorithms in their matching stages to avoid excessive computation.
- **Spatial Verification:** The matching results are usually polluted by false positive matching. To filter out these mismatched feature points, spatial verification algorithms are adopted to refine the matching results by checking the spatial relationship of the matched feature pairs from the above stage.

To choose the most representative ones, we conduct a survey and finally select eight multimedia retrieval algorithms. The chosen algorithms are shown in Table 1 (T:train/Q:query).

We also have implemented a multimedia retrieval evaluation framework which has features as follows:

- **Framework:** The framework includes the computation modules for all the stages in the workflow and the data transfer interfaces between them. Each algorithm module can be replaced with another one in the same stage. The intermediate result of an algorithm can be transformed into a format that can be processed by the next stage through the API interface.

SIGMETRICS'13, June 17-21, 2013, Pittsburgh, PA, USA.
ACM 978-1-4503-1900-3/13/06.

- **Input Sets:** In our current design, we assemble three input sets: small, standard and large. The small input set contains 48 images and the standard one contains about thousands of images. Large size input consists of twenty thousands of images.
- **Multiple Versions:** We provide three versions for each chosen algorithms: sequential version, multi-thread version and map-reduce version. The multi-thread version is implemented based on Linux POSIX library and map-reduce version is based on Apache Hadoop MapReduce framework.
- **Automation Tools:** Users may want to generate their own input data or prefer adjusting the parameters in algorithms. To ease their burden, we provide corresponding automation tools for generating input data and adjusting various parameters.

Table 1: Overview of the MMRBench.

Application	Function	Input
SIFT	Feature Extraction	Image/Video Frame
SURF	Feature Extraction	Image/Video Frame
MSER [7]	Feature Extraction	Image/Video Frame
HOG [3]	Feature Extraction	Image/Video Frame
KD-Tree(T/Q) [10]	Feature Matching	Feature Points
VOC-Tree(T/Q) [8]	Feature Matching	Feature Points
LSH(T/Q) [4]	Feature Matching	Feature Points
RANSAC [6]	Spatial Verification	Feature Points

3. CHARACTERISTICS ANALYSIS

To study the architectural characteristics of these algorithms, we use architecture-independent metrics and intensity metrics. The former metrics allow us to understand the inherent characteristics in programs. Such metrics guarantee the analysis being isolated from particular architectural features. We adopt the 29 metrics used in [9], which cover a wide range of program characteristics. The metrics include instruction mix, branch information, dependence distance and data/instruction locality information. For intensity metrics, we focus on computation intensity and memory intensity. For computation intensity, we deploy a metric that indicates how many instructions are committed over a byte of input data. It measures how much computational resources needed when processing unit size input. For memory intensity, we use the percentage of memory instructions over the total instructions. Since there are multiple architecture independent metrics, it is challenging to analyze the characteristics among different programs. Therefore, we deploy two statistical analysis methods, *Principle Component Analysis* and *Cluster Analysis* to reveal their characteristics more precisely. In evaluation, we compare chosen eight representative multimedia retrieval algorithms with conventional multimedia processing algorithms. Furthermore, we also analyze their architectural characteristics on core level, chip level and out-of-chip level. We summarize some insights to architecture design for multimedia retrieval applications.

Core Level Design: (1) Sophisticated branch prediction mechanism should be applied to deal with the high misprediction rate in these algorithms; (2) Many simple in-order cores may perform as well as fewer complex out-of-order cores, since half of multimedia retrieval algorithms exhibit poor ILP; (3) Larger cache line can improve performance greatly due to the applications' spatial locality; (4) Floating-point units can be replaced with fixed-point units to achieve high power efficiency and smaller die size without losing performance and accuracy.

Chip Level Design: Most of these algorithms show great computational intensity and memory intensity which requiring accelerating scheme and advanced memory hierarchy design to improve the performance. What's more, abundant thread-level parallelism exists in those algorithms at image-level, sub-block-level, feature-point-level and thread-level parallelism, which is a critical design point for optimization. Furthermore, load imbalance is also a critical problem. As shown with our case study, fine-grained feature-point level parallelism can be exploited for performance improvement, together with dynamic resource scheduling scheme or architectural support.

Out of Chip Level Design: With the explosion of multimedia data, high interconnection bandwidth is necessary to support communication between different stages in multimedia retrieval. As a result, large-scale data in data stores require a high-bandwidth I/O and interconnection design, a more sophisticated data layout and distribution strategy.

4. REFERENCES

[1] H. Bay, T. Tuytelaars, and L. V. Gool. SURF: Speeded up robust features. *European Conference on Computer Vision (ECCV)*, pages 404–417, 2006.

[2] C. Bienia and K. Li. PARSEC 2.0: A New Benchmark Suite for Chip-Multiprocessors. *Annual Workshop on Modeling, Benchmarking and Simulation (MoBS)*, June 2009.

[3] N. Dalal and B. Triggs. Histograms of Oriented Gradients for Human Detection. *IEEE Conference on Computer Vision and Pattern Recognition (CVPR)*, 2005.

[4] M. Datar and P. Indyk. Locality-sensitive hashing scheme based on p-stable distributions. *Annual Symposium on Computational Geometry (SoCG)*, 2004.

[5] M. lap Li, R. Sasanka, S. V. Adve, Y. kuang Chen, and E. Debes. The ALPBench benchmark suite for complex multimedia applications. *IEEE International Symposium on Workload Characterization (IISWC)*, 2005.

[6] D. G. Lowe. Distinctive Image Features from Scale-Invariant Keypoints. *International Journal of Computer Vision (IJCV)*, 60(2):91–110, 2004.

[7] J. Matas, O. Chum, M. Urban, and T. Pajdla. Robust wide baseline stereo from maximally stable extremal regions. *British Machine Vision Conference (BMVC)*, 2002.

[8] D. Nister and H. Stewenius. Scalable Recognition with a Vocabulary Tree. *IEEE Conference on Computer Vision and Pattern Recognition (CVPR)*, 2006.

[9] A. Phansalkar, A. Joshi, and L. K. John. Analysis of redundancy and application balance in the SPEC CPU2006 benchmark suite . *The 34th annual international symposium on Computer architecture*, pages 412–423, 2007.

[10] A. Vedaldi and B. Fulkerson. Vlfeat: an open and portable library of computer vision algorithms. *International Conference on Multimedia (MM)*, 2010.

Understanding Internet Video Viewing Behavior In the Wild

Athula Balachandran
Carnegie Mellon University
abalacha@cs.cmu.edu

Aditya Akella
University of Wisconisin Madison
akella@cs.wisconsin.edu

Vyas Sekar
Stony Brook University
vyas@cs.stonybrook.edu

Srinivasan Seshan
Carnegie Mellon University
srini@cs.cmu.edu

ABSTRACT

Over the past few years video viewership over the Internet has risen dramatically and market predictions suggest that video will account for more than 50% of the traffic over the Internet in the next few years. Unfortunately, there has been signs that the Content Delivery Network (CDN) infrastructure is being stressed with the increasing video viewership load. Our goal in this paper is to provide a first step towards a principled understanding of how the content delivery infrastructure must be designed and provisioned to handle the increasing workload by analyzing video viewing behaviors and patterns in the wild. We analyze various viewing behaviors using a dataset consisting of over 30 million video sessions spanning two months of viewership from two large Internet video providers. In these preliminary results, we observe viewing patterns that have significant impact on the design of the video delivery infrastructure.

Categories and Subject Descriptors

C.4 [**Performance of Systems**]: Performance Attributes

General Terms

Experimentation, Measurement, Performance

Keywords

Internet video, User behavior

1. INTRODUCTION

Video viewership over the Internet has increased dramatically over the past few years. Recent reports suggest that video constitutes 51% of the traffic on the Internet in 2011 and it is estimated to be as much as 56% in the next few years [2]. User expectations for quality of video streamed over the Internet has also increased placing more onus on various content providers (e.g., Hulu, Netflix) to efficiently distribute the content to its customers.

Content providers primarily rely on Content Distribution Networks(CDNs) that have presence across different geographical locations to increase their global availability with low costs and low latency. Unfortunately, there has been signs that the CDN infrastructure is being stressed with the increasing amount of video workload [8]. This raises the important question of how the delivery infrastructure should be designed, provisioned and managed to meet the growing demands for high quality video delivery.

The goal of this study is to take a first step towards this by trying to uncover and understand video access patterns in the wild that have implications for designing a video delivery system. In this work, we investigate various video access patterns using a large dataset consisting of client-side measurements provided by `conviva.com`. A longer-term goal is to characterize these viewing patterns and use them to analyze different infrastructure designs that have received significant industry traction recently [9, 5, 1, 10].

Our preliminary evaluation indicates several interesting video access patterns like time-of-day effects, regional interest in specific content and partial interest. In our ongoing work, we plan to understand these further by characterizing them and explore how these observations can be effectively used to tailor new delivery infrastructure designs.

2. DATA

For our study, we used data from two popular United States-based video content providers that appear consistently in the Top 500 sites in terms of overall popularity. The data was collected by `conviva.com` using their client-resident instrumentation library that runs in video players. The library listens to various events from the player as well as polls for additional statistics, and reports these to a data aggregation service that runs in the data center. The data was collected over two months and consists of information about more than 30 million video viewing sessions. The sessions can be classified based on the type of video that was viewed as:

(1) **Video on Demand (VOD):** VOD objects are between 35 minutes and 60 minutes long and consist of television series episodes, news shows and reality shows.

(2) **Live:** These objects are primarily sporting events that are broadcast while the event is happening.

We collect information about each session including: (1) clientID (a unique identifier assigned to the player and stored in the Flash cookie to be used by subsequent views), (2) geographical location (country, state and city of the user), (3) the Internet Service Provider of the user, (4) start time and duration of the session, (5) performance metrics (such as average bitrate of the video, estimated bandwidth at the client), and (6) other information such as name of the video and its actual duration.

3. RESULTS

Our preliminary analysis revealed several interesting video access patterns. Unsurprisingly, there is significant difference between VOD and live content in terms of user viewing behavior. Hence, we report the viewing patterns for VOD and live separately.

Some of the interesting observations in the case of VOD included:

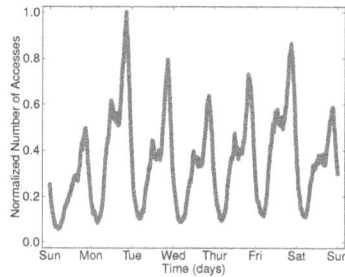

| (a) Diurnal pattern for VOD | (b) Longitudinal decay for VOD | (c) Partial User Interest for Live |

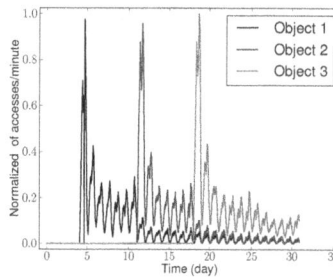

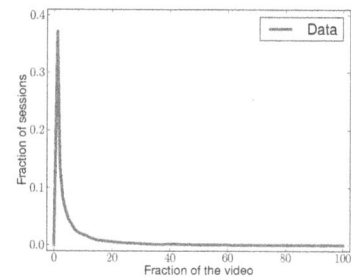

- **Time-of-day effects:** We observed strong diurnal patterns in the demand for VOD objects as shown in Figure 1a. Zooming into the data and observing accesses from different regions (e.g., US East Coast, US West Coast, US Mid-West) separately, we observed that the load typically peaks around 8pm local time for each region with a lull in the night (not shown due to lack of space). The strong predictable diurnal characteristcs points to high synchrony in viewing behavior. Similarly, the temporal shift in peak loads can be leveraged to handle peak loads in one region by using spare capacity from a different region.

- **Temporal decay in demand:** Figure 1b shows the temporal variation in demand for three sample video objects. We see that the peak demand for VOD objects typically occured on the day of release and then decayed in the subsequent days. We observed this pattern for other video objects as well. The strong diurnal patterns that are observed from this time series plot again points to high synchrony in viewing behavior on a per-object basis. Also, the temporal decay aspect has important implications to provisioning the infrastructure.

Live objects consisted of sporting events, some of which had regional sports teams. A few interesting observations in the case of live included:

- **Regional interest:** Typically, for VOD objects, we observed significant population-induced difference in load across different regions (eg., US East Coast, US West Coast, Mid-West). But for several live events that have regional biases like a local team playing a match, we obsered significantly skewed access rates from regions that exhibit low loads in the typical case. This is an important factor that has to be considered while provisioning the delivery infrastructure to handle unexpected high loads.

- **Partial Interest:** We also observed partial interest in the video objects. Users watched only part of the content during a session as shown in Figure 1c. We also observed that several users joined and quit multiple times during an event. Considering that our dataset consists of sporting events, we assume that this might be caused by users checking current score of the matches frequently.

4. RELATED WORK

There is a large body of related work that examines various aspects of video viewing behavior on the Internet. Our work is also similar in spirit. However considering the fact that Internet video has really taken off in the past few years, we revisit several of these behaviors. For example, there are several studies that have looked at content popularity in the context of content prefetching and caching [4, 7]. We build on these works by focusing on tem-

poral evolution of demand for VOD objects. Similarly there has been past work on user behavior including partial views [3, 6]. Our analysis reconfirms several of these observations. In our ongoing work we are looking at characterizing these behaviors more systematically and placing their implications in the context of delivery infrastructure design.

5. CONCLUSION AND FUTURE WORK

Internet video has really taken off in the past few years. Given this growth, we revisit the question of user access patterns in the wild. Our preliminary analysis reveals several patterns that have implications to designing and provisioning the infrastructure. In future work, we intend to analyze the data in greater detail to uncover other interesting video access patterns and characterize them. We also want to put these observations in the context of new delivery infrastructure designs (e.g., Federated CDNs and hybrid P2P-CDN architectures) and analyze them. The eventual goal is to understand how we can tailor and optimize these delivery infrastructure designs for the video viewing workloads.

Acknowledgements

The authors thank Conviva Inc. for making the video viewing data available for this study.

6. REFERENCES

[1] Akamai NetSession. http://www.akamai.com/client/.
[2] Cisco forecast. http://blogs.cisco.com/sp/comments/cisco_visual_networking_index_forecast_annual_update/.
[3] L. Plissonneau and E. Biersack. A Longitudinal View of HTTP Video Streaming Performance. In *Proc. MMSys*, 2012.
[4] M. Cha, H. Kwak, P. Rodriguez, Y.-Y. Ahn, and S. Moon. I Tube, You Tube, Everybody Tubes: Analyzing the World's Largest User Generated Content Video System. In *Proc. IMC*, 2007.
[5] D. Rayburn. Telcos and carriers forming new federated cdn group called ocx (operator carrier exchange). June 2011. StreamingMediaBlog.com.
[6] A. Finamore, M. Mellia, M. Munafo, R. Torres, and S. G. Rao. Youtube everywhere: Impact of device and infrastructure synergies on user experience. In *Proc. IMC*, 2011.
[7] H. Yu, D. Zheng, B. Y. Zhao, and W. Zheng. Understanding User Behavior in Large-Scale Video-on-Demand Systems. In *Proc. Eurosys*, 2006.
[8] X. Liu, F. Dobrian, H. Milner, J. Jiang, V. Sekar, I. Stoica, and H. Zhang. A Case for a Coordinated Internet-Scale Video Control Plane. In *Proc. SIGCOMM*, 2012.
[9] R. Powell. The federated cdn cometh. May 2011. TelecomRamblings.com.
[10] H. Yin, X. Liu, T. Zhan, V. Sekar, F. Qiu, C. Lin, H. Zhang, and B. Li. Design and Deployment of a Hybrid CDN-P2P System for Live Video Streaming: Experiences with LiveSky. In *Proc. ACM Multimedia*, 2008.

Understanding SMS Spam in a Large Cellular Network

Nan Jiang*
University of Minnesota, MN
njiang@cs.umn.edu

Yu Jin, Ann Skudlark
AT&T Labs, Florham Park, NJ
{yjin,aes}@research.att.com

Zhi-Li Zhang
University of Minnesota, MN
zhzhang@cs.umn.edu

ABSTRACT

In this paper, we conduct a comprehensive study of SMS spam in a large cellular network in the US. Using one year of user reported spam messages to the network carrier, we devise text clustering techniques to group associated spam messages in order to identify SMS spam campaigns and spam activities. Our analysis shows that spam campaigns can last for months and have a wide impact on the cellular network. Combining with SMS network records collected during the same time, we f nd that spam numbers within the same activity often exhibit strong similarity in terms of their sending patterns, tenure and geolocations. Our analysis sheds light on the intentions and strategies of SMS spammers and provides unique insights in developing better method for detecting SMS spam.

Categories and Subject Descriptors

C.2.0 [**Computer-Communication Networks**]: GeneralSecurity and protection (e.g., f rewalls)

Keywords

SMS Spam; Cellular Network; Detection; Clustering

1. INTRODUCTION

The explosion of mobile devices in the past decade has brought with it an onslaught of unwanted SMS (Short Message Service) spam [1]. These spam messages not only inf ict an annoying user experience, but also incur signif cant costs to both cellular carriers and customers alike.

To better understand and hence to devise effective tools for combating SMS spam, in this paper, we employ a novel data source – *user-generated spam reports* (*spam reports* in short) – to study SMS spam in a large cellular network. As a means to combat SMS spam, many cellular network carriers have adopted and deployed an SMS spam reporting mechanism for mobile users, whereby after receiving a spam message, a victim can report it via a text message forward. Mobile carriers can then investigate and confrm the reported spam and f nally restrict the offending spam phone numbers (referred to as *spam numbers* hereafter). Such user-generated spam reports not only contain the entire spam text, but they represent a more reliable and cleaner source of spam samples, as all the messages contained in spam reports have been vetted and classif ed by mobile users (using human intelligence).

*The work was supported in part by the NSF grants CNS-1017647 and CNS-1117536, the DTRA grant HDTRA1-09-1-0050.

Taking advantage of this SMS spam reporting mechanism, we collect one year of spam reports from a large cellular carrier in the US from June 2011 to May 2012 – which contains approximately 543K spam messages – and, together with anonymized SMS network records collected from the same network associated with the reported spam numbers (over 78K), carry out an extensive analysis of SMS spam. In particular, by grouping spam messages using text clustering tools, we identify many large and long-lasting spam campaigns. Meanwhile, we f nd that phone numbers initiating spam messages with similar text content tend to be correlated in space and time. Based on these f ndings, we innovate an algorithm that detects additional spam numbers which are temporally and spatially correlated with the confrmed numbers. Preliminary experiments on a one-month dataset demonstrate promising results, i.e., we can identify thousands of spam numbers ahead of user spam reports with less than 0.6% likely false alarms.

2. METHODOLOGY

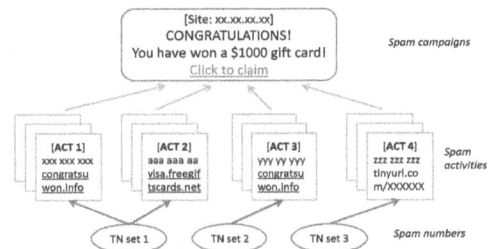

Figure 1: Entities in a typical SMS spam campaign.

We are primarily interested in SMS spam with potentially malicious intent. Spam messages generated by such malicious spammers often contain a URL, with the goal to entice users to visit a malicious website so as to, e.g., obtain users' personal information. Similar to prior studies of email spam campaigns [2], we def ne a *spam campaign* as a collection of SMS spam messages which advertise the same fraudulent website (as identif ed by its IP address). Within each SMS spam campaign, we refer to a group of spam messages with similar content as a *spam activity*. Fig. 1 shows four spam activities (labeled *Act 1, ..., Act 4*) to advertise the same fraudulent site. Activities 1 and 3 contain the same URL pointing to the fraudulent site, but with different spam content. Activities 2 and 4 contain different spam messages with different URLs; in particular, Activity 4 contains a shortened URL. The purpose of conducting different activities is plausibly to avoid content-based spam f ltering. In conducting Activities 1 and 2, the spammer employs the same set of spam numbers (TN 1, where TN stands for telephone numbers), whereas for Activities 3 and 4, s/he uses two different sets of spam numbers. The existence of multiple TN sets is often caused by cellular carriers restricting certain spam numbers, e.g., based on spam reports, hence spammers need to invest in a different set of spam numbers to continue the campaign.

Using the spam reports, we perform a two-level SMS spam analysis: we f rst group (reported) spam messages into *spam campaigns* by resolving and tracking the URLs contained in the spam messages; and within each SMS campaign, we apply a text clustering tool – CLUTO [3] – to group the spam messages into distinct *spam activities* based on content similarity. Finally, we identify 820 spam campaigns and 2,540 spam activities comprising these campaigns.

3. CHARACTERIZING SPAM CAMPAIGNS

In Table 1, we summarize the top 10 SMS spam campaigns found in our dataset (which cover nearly half of the spam reports).

Table 1: Top 10 spam campaigns in terms of # spam reports

ID	Campaign topic	#Reps	#Snbrs	#Acts	Dur
1	Walmart gift card	60304	6213	196	223
2	Free Apple product	11778	1840	21	321
3	Walmart/Bestbuy gift card	11124	736	37	116
4	Cash advance / cash loans	10941	2207	42	+365
5	Walmart/Starbucks gift card	9972	816	13	46
6	Free Apple product	8251	2257	111	360
7	Bestbuy gift card	7243	524	19	66
8	Cash loan services	7168	786	35	+363
9	Apple device test/keep	5403	303	7	110
10	Cash loan services	4275	618	16	+363

The second column in Table 1 shows the topics of the campaigns, which are all related to cash advance, gift card and free device for testing. Column 3 and 4 show the total number of spam reports and spam numbers associated with each campaign, respectively. Although some spam numbers involved in these campaigns were not reported by users, these campaigns still exhibit a large scale with spam numbers identif ed from the reports ranging from a few hundreds to more than 6K. Meanwhile, each campaign contains multiple spam activities, spam numbers within which initiate spam messages with very similar content. We shall further explore the correlation of these spam numbers in Section 4. More importantly, we observe (6th column) that these spam campaigns are long-lasting. We calculate the campaign duration as the time interval from the f rst observed report to the last. We note that "+" sign indicates the f rst report came in June 2011. Surprisingly, even the shortest campaign still lasts for more than one month and half of the campaigns have duration of approximately one year.

4. CORRELATION OF SPAM NUMBERS

We next investigate from various aspects the correlation of spam numbers within the same activity. We f rst explore whether spam numbers within each activity tend to send spam actively at the same time. We def ne the time similarity as the median pairwise overlapping time (in hours) with active spamming behaviors (i.e., more than 50 messages per hour), which is displayed in Fig. 2[a]. In most of the bins, the median values are above 20 hours, which implies a strong temporal correlation between these numbers.

Another spamming pattern we investigate is the spamming locations of spam numbers. We def ne the *location similarity* as the proportion of spam numbers within an activity with spamming locations being the most dominant one in that activity. Fig. 2[b] displays the distribution of the location similarity, which again appears to be very signif cant. The similarity reaches 0.8 when the activity size equals 5 and drops slightly as activity size further increases.

Moreover, we f nd spam numbers within the same activity also exhibit strong similarities in terms of the account ages, the spam-

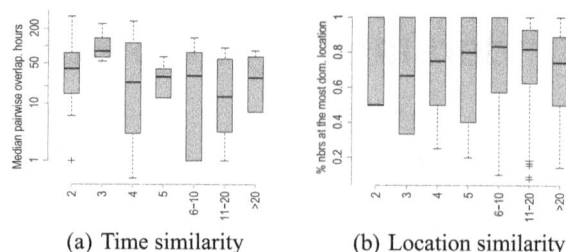

(a) Time similarity　　(b) Location similarity

Figure 2: Correlation of spam numbers.

ming devices associated and the strategies employed to select victims. We do not include these results due to space limit. We believe that the spam numbers in the same activities are likely employed by the same spammers. These spammers purchase bulk spamming devices and spam numbers and program them to initiate spam. The numbers thus exhibit strong spatial and temporal correlations.

Exploiting the correlation of spam numbers, once a spam number within an activity is reported, we can detect other spam numbers in the same activity that are temporally and spatially correlated with the conf rmed number. To test this idea, we implement a simple yet effective two-step detection algorithm. First, we monitor all SMS senders in the network and maintain a watchlist of phone numbers at different geolocations (node-B's) that have sent SMS messages to more than K recipients in each T interval [1]. Second, detection is triggered once a spam report arrives to conf rm a particular spam number in the watchlist, we then look for other numbers from the watchlist whose spamming locations (i.e., node-B's) are the same as the conf rmed one and report them as spam number candidates.

On one-month of SMS network records, the algorithm detects 5,121 spam number candidates, and 90.9% of them were reported later via spam reports. Fraud agents manually investigate the remaining ones and conf rm 465 also as spam numbers. In other words, the proposed algorithm is highly accurate, with only 3 (less than 0.06%) candidates not yet verif ed. Moreover, in more than 93% of the cases, the proposed algorithm detects spam numbers an hour ahead of spam reports. More than 72% and 40% of the detection results are 10 hours and 1 day before the spam reports.

5. CONCLUSION AND FUTURE WORK

We carried out extensive analysis of SMS spam using user reported spam messages collected from a large cellular network. We proposed a two-level text clustering method to identify spam campaigns and activities and studied interesting properties of representative SMS spam campaigns, which can last for months and have a wide impact the network. Assisted with SMS network records, we identif ed strong correlation of spam numbers used by the same spammer. Our future work involves designing and deploying effective spam detection algorithms based on our analysis results.

6. REFERENCES

[1] Mobile spam texts hit 4.5 billion. http://www.businessweek.com/news/2012-04-30/mobile-spam-texts-hit-4-dot-5-billion-raising-consumer-ire.

[2] A. Pathak, F. Qian, C. Hu, M. Mao, and S. Ranjan. Botnet spam campaigns can be long lasting: evidence, implications, and analysis. SIGMETRICS '09, 2009.

[3] Y. Zhao, G. Karypis, and U. Fayyad. Hierarchical clustering algorithms for document datasets. *Data Min. Knowl. Discov.*, 2005.

---

[1]The choices of K and T are proprietary to the carrier.

Web Performance Bottlenecks in Broadband Access Networks

Srikanth Sundaresan
Georgia Tech, Atlanta
srikanth@gatech.edu

Nazanin Magharei
Georgia Tech, Atlanta
nazanin@cc.gatech.edu

Nick Feamster
Georgia Tech, Atlanta
feamster@cc.gatech.edu

Renata Teixeira
CNRS and UPMC, Paris
renata.teixeira@lip6.fr

Sam Crawford
SamKnows, London
sam@samknows.com

ABSTRACT

We present the first large-scale analysis of Web performance bottlenecks as measured from broadband access networks, using data collected from extensive home router deployments. We analyze the limits of throughput on improving Web performance and identify the contribution of critical factors such as DNS lookups and TCP connection establishment to Web page load times. We find that, as broadband speeds continue to increase, other factors such as TCP connection setup time, server response time, and network latency are often dominant performance bottlenecks. Thus, realizing a "faster Web" requires not only higher download throughput, but also optimizations to reduce both client and server-side latency.

Categories and Subject Descriptors

C.2.3 [**Computer-Communication Networks**]: Network Operations—*Network Management*; C.2.3 [**Computer-Communication Networks**]: Network Operations—*Network Monitoring*

Keywords

Broadband Networks, Web performance, Bottlenecks

1. INTRODUCTION

Broadband speeds are getting faster: the OECD reports that speeds are increasing by about 15–20% every year; average advertised speeds are now about 16 Mbits/s in the U.S. and 37.5 Mbits/s across OECD areas [1]. As speeds continues to increase, one might expect the Web to get faster at home; yet, ISPs and application providers are increasingly finding that *latency* is becoming a critical performance bottleneck [2]. The Bing search engine experiences reduced revenue of 1.2% with just a 500-millisecond delay [3]. Forrester research found that most users expected online shopping sites to load in two seconds or fewer [2].

This paper presents initial results from a large-scale, longitudinal study of the effects of broadband access network performance on Web page load times. We find that throughput is the dominant bottleneck for access links with downstream throughput rates of less than 16 Mbits/s. In the case of the increasing number of access links with higher downstream throughput, latency has become the bottleneck for Web performance. This paper offers insight into the extent to which performance characteristics of the underlying network introduces bottlenecks in a Web download and this in turn

Metric	Type	Description
Page fetch time	Total	The time to set up TCP connections and retrieve all objects.
Page load time	Total	Page fetch time, plus the DNS time.
DNS lookup time	Per Domain	The DNS time for different domains.
Time to first byte	Per Object	The time from the initiation of the TCP connection to the arrival of the first byte of the requested object (including server processing time).
Object fetch time	Per Object	The time to download an object, exc. DNS time and time to first byte.

Table 1: *Performance metrics. For per-object metrics, the test measures the maximum, minimum, and average for each object.*

can help understand the limits of optimizations such as caching and prefetching in mitigating these bottlenecks.

2. MEASUREMENTS AND METHOD

Modern browsers and servers perform various optimizations to improve page load time. Independent of these optimizations, the effects of network parameters such as the access network throughput and latency on various components of Web page load time are worth understanding. Ideally, we would measure Web performance from each access link using a variety of browsers. However, logistically, and due to significant differences between browsers, this is not feasible. Therefore, we perform active measurements from routers in a large number of homes using a simple tool to characterize the network properties of Web performance in home networks. Understanding how network effects affect Web performance can better inform designers of both Web sites and browsers about bottlenecks and how to mitigate them.

Active measurements from the home router We measure Web performance by periodically requesting the home page of nine popular Web sites. We use measurements from 5,667 US participants in the SamKnows/Federal Communications Commission study from September 1–31, 2012 [4]. We include only ISPs with more than 100 users and users who have reported more than 100 measurements during the duration of the study.

Measuring Components of Page Load Time We call the process of downloading all objects for a Web site a *transaction*. Our tool measures the time for each component of a transaction, as shown in Table 1. It periodically fetches the home page of a Web site, determines the objects required to render the page, performs DNS lookups, and downloads all the objects. We thus separate the page load time into DNS time and the fetch time, and also tease out individual component times per object, including the DNS lookup time

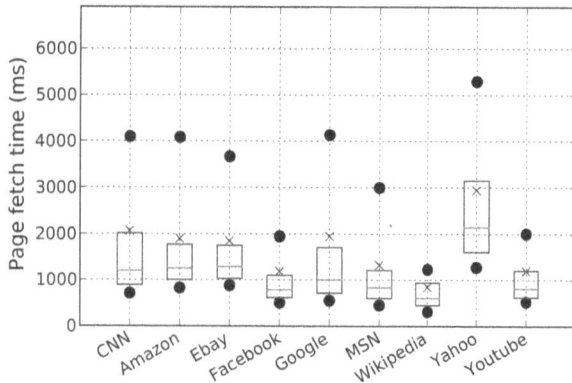

Figure 1: *Page fetch times for popular sites. We fetch the home page except for Google (http://www.google.com/mobile) and CNN (http://edition.cnn.com). Each box shows the inter-quartile range of the fetch times. The middle line is the median, the cross represents the average, and the dots the 10th and 90th percentile page fetch times.*

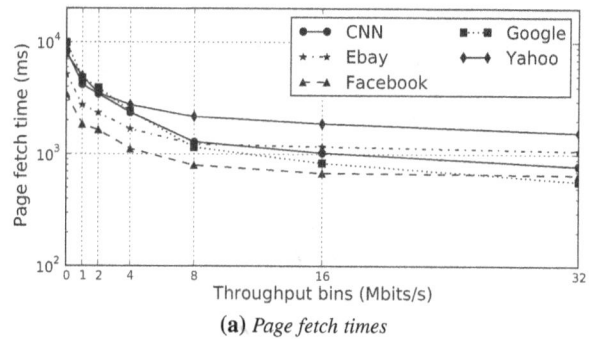

(a) *Page fetch times*

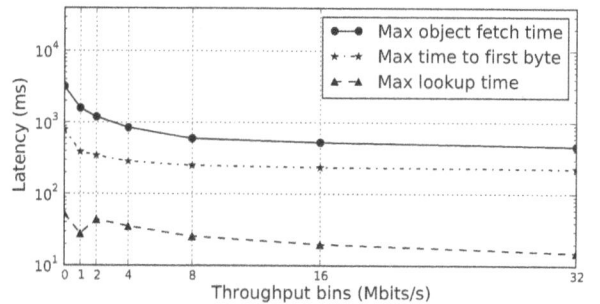

(b) *Components of page load time*

Figure 2: *Page fetch times decrease with downstream throughput, but only up to 16 Mbits/s. X-axis labels denote the start of each throughput bin (e.g., "0" is the set of users with downstream throughput up to 1 Mbits/s.)*

and the time to first byte. The tool uses persistent TCP connections if the server supports them and up to eight concurrent TCP connections to download objects. The tool does not attempt characterize page load times that a real Web browser might experience, but it reflects the same underlying network characteristics as the browser.

3. ACCESS-LINK BOTTLENECKS

We characterize page fetch times from clients in the deployment and evaluate the effect of throughput on page fetch times. Major takeaways are that page load time for even very popular sites are high, and that as downstream throughput exceeds 16 Mbits/s, page load times cease to improve; latency increasingly becomes a performance bottleneck for Web performance at higher throughputs.

Page Fetch Times of Popular Web Sites We study the page fetch times to nine popular Web sites. Figure 1 shows the fetch time for each site. We see that the fetch times can exceed one second for even popular sites. As expected, the fetch time varies both by site and the location of the access network. Some variability results from differences in page size and design; the largest four sites (CNN, Yahoo, Amazon, and Ebay) also have the largest fetch times (*e.g.*, the median fetch time for CNN is more than one second).

Effect of downstream Throughput We study how page fetch time and its components vary with downstream throughput. We group access links according to downstream throughput into bins that reflect common ranges of access plans: 0–1 Mbits/s, 1–2 Mbits/s, 2–4 Mbits/s, 4–8 Mbits/s, 8–16 Mbits/s, 16–32 Mbits/s, and 32–64 Mbits/s. Figure 2a shows how the median page fetch time decreases as throughput increases, up to 16 Mbits/s. Beyond that, page fetch times decrease only modestly. For example, the median time for CNN is 8.4 seconds for links with throughput 0–1 Mbits/s and 1.3 seconds when it is 8–16 Mbits/s. When throughput exceeds 32 Mbits/s, the page fetch time is 790 ms, only slightly better than for links with 8–16 Mbits/s. Figure 2b shows how the maximum object fetch time, maximum time to first byte, and DNS lookup time decrease as throughput increases. For each group with a particular downstream throughput range, we plot the median of each of these values. As downstream throughput increases to 32–64 Mbits/sec, the object fetch time decreases from 3.2 seconds to 530 ms; in contrast, the time to first byte decreases from 800 ms to 230 ms and DNS lookup time decreases from about 50 ms to

about 15 ms. Thus, as downstream throughput increases beyond 16 Mbits/sec, time to first byte and DNS lookup times become a significantly larger component of page fetch time.

4. CONCLUSION AND FUTURE WORK

We present the first large-scale, longitudinal study of Web performance bottlenecks in broadband access networks. We characterize performance from more than 5,000 broadband access networks to nine popular Web sites and identify factors that create Web performance bottlenecks. Our results show that as broadband access speeds continue to increase, latency becomes a performance bottleneck. Page load times stop improving as throughput rates increase beyond 16 Mbits/s, and latency components such as DNS and time to first byte become more important. Last-mile latency could become a significant overall contributor to both DNS lookup times and the time to first byte [4]. Therefore, *even when caches are close to users, implementing optimizations in the home to reduce the effects of last-mile latency can offer significant performance improvements*. We are currently investigating techniques to mitigate the impact of such overheads on Web performance.

5. REFERENCES

[1] *OECD Communications Outlook*. OECD Publishing, July 2011.
[2] S. Lohr. For Impatient Web Users, an Eye Blink Is Just Too Long to Wait. http://www.nytimes.com/2012/03/01/technology/impatient-web-users-flee-slow-loading-sites.html, Mar. 2012.
[3] S. Souders. Velocity and the bottom line. http://radar.oreilly.com/2009/07/velocity-making-your-site-fast.html, July 2009.
[4] S. Sundaresan, W. de Donato, N. Feamster, R. Teixeira, S. Crawford, and A. Pescapè. Broadband internet performance: A view from the gateway. In *Proc. ACM SIGCOMM*, Toronto, Ontario, Aug. 2011.

Tutorial on Geo-Replication in Data Center Applications

Marcos K. Aguilera
Microsoft Research Silicon Valley

ABSTRACT

Data center applications increasingly require a *geo-replicated* storage system, that is, a storage system replicated across many geographic locations. Geo-replication can reduce access latency, improve availability, and provide disaster tolerance. It turns out there are many techniques for geo-replication with different trade-offs. In this tutorial, we give an overview of these techniques, organized according to two orthogonal dimensions: level of synchrony (synchronous and asynchronous) and type of storage service (read-write, state machine, transactional). We explain the basic idea of these techniques, together with their applicability and trade-offs.

Categories and Subject Descriptors

C.2.4 [**Computer-Communication Networks**]: Distributed Systems—*Distributed applications*

General Terms

Algorithms, Reliability

Keywords

Geo-replication, geo-distribution, distributed systems, storage systems, replication, tutorial

The Fundamentals of Heavy-tails: Properties, Emergence, and Identification

Jayakrishnan Nair
California Institute of
Technology
Pasadena, CA, USA
ujk@caltech.edu

Adam Wierman
California Institute of
Technology
Pasadena, CA, USA
adamw@caltech.edu

Bert Zwart
Centrum voor Wiskunde en
Informatica
Amsterdam, The Netherlands
Bert.Zwart@cwi.nl

Categories and Subject Descriptors

G.3 [**Mathematics of computing**]: Probability and Statistics

Keywords

Heavy-tailed distributions

Tutorial overview

Heavy-tails are a continual source of excitement and confusion across disciplines as they are repeatedly "discovered" in new contexts. This is especially true within computer systems, where heavy-tails seemingly pop up everywhere – from degree distributions in the internet and social networks to file sizes and interarrival times of workloads. However, despite nearly a decade of work on heavy-tails they are still treated as mysterious, surprising, and even controversial.

The goal of this tutorial is to show that heavy-tailed distributions need not be mysterious and should not be surprising or controversial. In particular, we will demystify heavy-tailed distributions by showing how to reason formally about their counter-intuitive properties; we will highlight that their emergence should be *expected* (not surprising) by showing that a wide variety of general processes lead to heavy-tailed distributions; and we will highlight that most of the controversy surrounding heavy-tails is the result of bad statistics, and can be avoided by using the proper tools.

Intended audience

The tutorial is aimed at students, researchers, and practitioners interested in learning how to rigorously think about heavy-tailed distributions. The assumed background is only a basic understanding of probability and statistics.

References

The organizers of this tutorial are in the process of writing a book on the topic of heavy-tails, and this tutorial is meant to provide a brief overview of the material to be covered in the forthcoming book.

Speaker Biographies

Jayakrishnan Nair received his PhD from California Institute of Technology (Caltech) in 2012. His PhD thesis focused on scheduling for heavy-tailed and light-tailed workloads in queueing systems. He is currently a post-doctoral scholar at Caltech and will join CWI as a post-doctoral scholar in summer 2013. His research interests include modeling, performance evaluation, and design issues in queueing systems and communication networks. Jayakrishnan was a recipient of the best paper award at IFIP Performance, 2010.

Adam Wierman is a Professor in the Department of Computing and Mathematical Sciences at the California Institute of Technology, where he is a member of the Rigorous Systems Research Group (RSRG). He received his Ph.D., M.Sc. and B.Sc. in Computer Science from Carnegie Mellon University in 2007, 2004, and 2001, respectively. His research interests center around resource allocation and scheduling decisions in computer systems and services. More specifically, his work focuses both on developing analytic techniques in stochastic modeling, queueing theory, scheduling theory, and game theory, and applying these techniques to application domains such as energy-efficient computing, data centers, social networks, and electricity markets. He received the 2011 ACM SIGMETRICS Rising Star award, and has been co-recipient of best paper awards at ACM SIGMETRICS, IEEE INFOCOM, IFIP Performance, IEEE Green Computing Conference, and ACM GREENMETRICS.

Bert Zwart is currently a senior researcher at CWI, where he leads the Probability and Stochastic Networks group. He also holds a full professor position at VU University Amsterdam, is senior fellow at Eurandom, and holds an adjunct professor position at the H. Milton Stewart School of Industrial and Systems Engineering at Georgia Institute of Technology, where he was holding a Coca-Cola Chair until 2008. Bert Zwart is the 2008 recipient of the Erlang prize for outstanding contributions to applied probability by a researcher not older than 35 years old, and an IBM faculty award. His research is concerned with the application of analytic and probabilistic asymptotic methods to applied probability models in computer systems, communication networks, customer contact centers, and manufacturing systems. Dr. Zwart has published more than 70 refereed publications and is council member of the Applied Probability Society of INFORMS. Dr. Zwart has been area editor of Stochastic Models for Operations Research, the flagship journal of his profession, from 2009-2011. In addition, Dr. Zwart is editor-in-chief (with J.K. Lenstra and M. Trick) of the journal Surveys in Operations Research and Management Science, and serves on the editorial board of Mathematics of Operations Research, Mathematical Methods of Operations Research, Operations Research, Queueing Systems and Stochastic Systems.

Profiling and Analyzing the I/O Performance of NoSQL DBs

Jiri Schindler
NetApp
jiri.schindler@netapp.com

ABSTRACT

The advent of the so-called NoSQL databases has brought about a new model of using storage systems. While traditional relational database systems took advantage of features offered by centrally-managed, enterprise-class storage arrays, the new generation of database systems with weaker data consistency models is content with using and managing locally attached individual storage devices and providing data reliability and availability through high-level software features and protocols. This tutorial aims to review the architecture of selected NoSQL DBs to lay the foundations for understanding how these new DB systems behave. In particular, it focuses on how (in)efficiently these new systems use I/O and other resources to accomplish their work. The tutorial examines the behavior of several NoSQL DBs with an emphasis on Cassandra - a popular NoSQL DB system. It uses I/O traces and resource utilization profiles captured in private cloud deployments that use both dedicated directly attached storage as well as shared networked storage.

Categories and Subject Descriptors

H.4 [**Information Systems Applications**]: Miscellaneous

General Terms

Measurement, Performance

Keywords

Database systems, NoSQL, storage

1. INTRODUCTION

The performance of structured data management systems has always been determined to a large extent by the architecture and performance of the underlying storage system. The proliferation of the so-called NoSQL databases in the last few years as well as the adoption of Flash memory for latency-sensitive I/O operations has brought about a new model of using storage systems. Traditional relational database systems relied on high availability of centrally-managed, enterprise-class storage arrays and utilized their advanced features such as snapshots and transparent remote site replication. In contrast, the new generation of database systems with weaker data consistency models are content

with using locally attached individual storage devices and providing high availability through their own software features and protocols instead.

The majority of existing scale-out clustered NoSQL systems do not manage storage devices directly nor do they worry about RAID configuration alignment to stripe-unit boundaries etc. Instead, they rely on the OS and file system services to do so and use POSIX files as logical containers that can grow to store their data. Since most of these systems run on commodity nodes, The node-local disk file system (e.g., Linux ext3 or xfs) determines the performance and the set of features available to the database system.

These new data management systems are designed to support different workloads compared to traditional relational database systems (RDBMS) optimized for transactional processing with frequent updates. The workloads of these new systems are dominated by high-throughput append-style inserts rather than frequent updates of multiple values in a single transaction and read accesses in support of mostly point queries i.e., queries for a single value. As a result, the data access patterns these new systems generate can be quite different from traditional DBMSes. This work examines whether these new workloads and systems also exhibit different I/O behavior.

2. TRADITIONAL RDBMS

Traditional relational databases with well-defined schema and row-major orientation favor efficient record updates typical for online transactional processing. A single transaction may update few values in a handful of tables, which can result in dirtying many different pages including pages of system-maintained structures such as indexes and materialized views.

Databases use write-ahead logging to record to stable store the changes caused by the executed transactions. Periodically, the log is checkpointed by writing out to stable media dirty pages affected by recent updates. Thus, a checkpoint operation can amortize the cost of writing out a page across many update operations. However, it still results in inefficient random disk I/Os as the dirty pages are written out logically in-place to the data store.

Traditional RDBMSes were built for in-memory data access through page-based cache and optimized for hard disk drive I/O. Their architecture is not optimized for flash memory with efficient random I/O and sub-millisecond access latencies, although than can take advantage of these types of devices for fast logging of every committed transaction.

3. CLUSTERED NOSQL SYSTEMS

NoSQL DB systems run on a cluster of nodes, each running a separate OS instance. They were designed to use directly-attached storage for storing data on each node and to to replicate data across several nodes to prevent data loss when a node fails. Cluster services create a single system image, restore the data from the failed node, and redistribute it to balance load across the cluster.

There are three broad types of NoSQL DBs: key-value stores, document stores, and extensible large-scale columnar data stores. All three types have similar logical organization: a fixed key, typically generated by the system or derived from a user-provided key, followed by the value. In the most basic form, the value is a variable-length set of bytes opaque to the NoSQL DB system.

The internal data organization for NoSQL databases use a distributed hash table or variants of a partitioned B-tree that spread data across nodes. They perform random read I/Os as the system traverses the structure to locate the queried K/V pair(s). Some document stores also create secondary indexes on specific document elements for more efficient execution of range queries i.e., queries operating on a range of keys.

Generally, the I/O patterns of NoSQL DBs resemble those of traditional RDBMSes. They also use write-ahead logging even though they provide much weaker consistency compared to those of traditional RDBMS with ACID properties, Append-style log writes minimize the I/O cost by eliminating in-band B-tree update for systems that use it as their primary storage structure. Additionally, they perform a variant of a group commit, or more precisely, a periodic sync of the log to the disk. It is typically this relatively infrequent (ranging from 100ms up to 10s) sync of the log files that makes NoSQL DBs effective when handling high-throughput update or inserts. However, this comes at a cost of possible data loss in case of a multi-node failure.

NoSQL DB systems such as HBase and Cassandra vertically partition data into column families. They timestamp every value and store changes into an append-only log. Each column family is partitioned horizontally across different nodes with each node hosting partitions for all columns.

A single partition of a column family contains timestamped K/V pairs that include the name of the column for which the value was inserted and are appended at the tail-end of the file. The partition also includes an index, which sorts the pairs lexicographically and points to their current versions. Thus, the access patterns of the third type of NoSQL DBs are similar to those of document stores: Index scans are used to execute point queries. The system first locates the node responsible for the given key range and the node-local index locates the current version of the K/V pair. Table scans allow for serial I/O through the column segments; however, invalid K/V pairs must be skipped.

Since updates are appends to the data stores rather than in-place overwrites, old versions with stale data or deleted values in the column segments need to be periodically garbage-collected. The process called compaction is similar to whole-sale rewrite of a column in columnar RDMBSes as it moves live data from their original locations into a new segment, updates the index and deletes the old segment. Even though compaction is similar to checkpointing, the two activities are typically decoupled; compaction can proceed in the background on previously-written segments, while new data is being checkpointed from the log by writing it into a new segment and updating the index structure on the given column partition. Thus, unlike in traditional RDBMS, NoSQL systems also exhibit substantial amount of background I/O activity, which is mostly sequential. While the NoSQL DB distinguishes between foreground I/O, which includes write-ahead logging and read queries, and background activity such as compaction, the storage system is not aware of this distinction although it would leverage it to better schedule individual I/O requests.

4. ANALYZING I/O ACCESS PATTERNS

With the exception of HBase, which uses a distributed file system (HDFS), most NoSQL DBs use locally-attached storage and file systems for storing both data and logs. As stated before, the most critical I/Os for achieving high throughput of inserts and updates are sequential writes to the log. Most systems use memory-mapped access, whereby they treat the log as a memory region that is backed by a file. Individual writes are thus simple writes (typically of a few tens of bytes) followed by a periodic syncing of the file to the disk via the `msync()` system calls. Given the relatively large period between individual calls to `msync()` the small updates are turned into large I/Os with many pages flushed out.

Through profiling and tracing MongoDB and Cassandra NoSQL DBs, we discovered that the log write I/Os are not as sequential nor as big as one would expect. That is because file system fragmentation due to aging and the interactions between the virtual memory subsystem and the file system of the Linux kernel. When the virtual memory is under duress, it may not walk all pages and pick them up in an ascending order to make large I/O possible, subject to fragmentation. Using flash memory, where random I/O is nearly as effective as sequential I/O, for logging is useful irrespective of the faster I/O response time.

NoSQL DBs rely on the services and capabilities of the underlying storage systems. Since those are in most cases Linux local file systems they do not include features like snapshots or transparent backup to a remote location. However, as NoSQL DBs are increasingly deployed for business-critical applications, these features will become more important for providing continuous operation in the face of whole data center unavailability. Similarly, as many NoSQL DBs can benefit from fast access to local flash memory, it is likely we will see an adoption of architectures that provide automatic tiering and movement of data between local storage and networked storage systems. In short, we envision a gradual introduction of features in NoSQL DBs traditionally associated with centrally-managed storage systems.

5. SUMMARY

Even though NoSQL DB systems offer different programming styles and approaches to managing data, their I/O profile does not differ greatly from those of traditional RDBMSes. hey include logging writes dominated by small append-style I/O as well as checkpointing, and index scans that exhibit random I/O. NoSQL DBs for semi-structured data with columnar organization also exhibit large I/O for table scan reads or column compaction. What differs most is their approach to managing data. However, as their role in the enterprise shifts, so will the deployment model and the reliance on advanced data management features.

Author Index